ABSOLUTE JAVA™ 5th Edition

Walter Savitch

University of California, San Diego

Contributor

Kenrick Mock

University of Alaska Anchorage

International Edition contributions by
Piyali Sengupta

PEARSON

Boston   Columbus   Indianapolis   New York   San Francisco   Upper Saddle River
Amsterdam   Cape Town   Dubai   London   Madrid   Milan   Munich   Paris   Montréal   Toronto
Delhi   Mexico City   São Paulo   Sydney   Hong Kong   Seoul   Singapore   Taipei   Tokyo

Vice President and Editorial Director, ECS: Marcia Horton
Editor in Chief: Michael Hirsch
Executive Editor: Matt Goldstein
Editorial Assistant: Emma Snider
Vice President Marketing: Patrice Jones
Marketing Manager: Yez Alayan
Marketing Coordinator: Kathryn Ferranti
Vice President and Director of Production: Vince O'Brien
Managing Editor: Jeff Holcomb
Senior Production Project Manager: Marilyn Lloyd
Manufacturing Manager: Nick Skilitis
Publisher, International Edition: Angshuman Chakraborty
Acquisitions Editor, International Edition: Somnath Basu
Publishing Assistant, International Edition: Shokhi Shah
Print and Media Editor, International Edition:
   Ashwitha Jayakumar

Project Editor, International Edition: Jayashree Arunachalam
Publishing Administrator, International Edition: Hema Mehta
*Senior Manufacturing Controller, Production, International
   Edition:* Trudy Kimber
Operations Specialist: Lisa McDowell
Text Designer: Joyce Cosentino Wells
Cover Designer: Jodi Notowitz
Cover Image: Adelevin / iStockphoto.com
Media Editor: Dan Sandin
Text Permissions—assessment: Dana Weightman
Text Permissions—clearance: Jenn Kennett/Creative
   Compliance
Full-Service Vendor: GEX Publishing Services
Project Management: GEX Publishing Services
Cover Printer: Moore Langen

Pearson Education Limited
Edinburgh Gate
Harlow
Essex CM20 2JE
England

and Associated Companies throughout the world

Visit us on the World Wide Web at:
www.pearsoninternationaleditions.com

© Pearson Education Limited 2013

British Library Cataloguing-in-Publication Data
A catalogue record for this book is available from the British Library

10 9 8 7 6 5 4 3 2 1
14 13 12

Typeset in Adobe Garamond by GEX Publishing Services
Printed and bound by Courier Westford in The United States of America

The publisher's policy is to use paper manufactured from sustainable forests.

ISBN 10: 0-273-76479-9
ISBN 13: 978-0-273-76479-3

Preface

This book is designed to serve as a textbook and reference for programming in the Java language. Although it does include programming techniques, it is organized around the features of the Java language rather than any particular curriculum of programming techniques. The main audience I had in mind when writing this book was undergraduate students who have not had extensive programming experience with the Java language. As such, it would be a suitable Java text or reference for either a first programming course or a later computer science course that uses Java. This book is designed to accommodate a wide range of users. The introductory chapters are written at a level that is accessible to beginners, while the boxed sections of those chapters serve to quickly introduce more experienced programmers to basic Java syntax. Later chapters are still designed to be accessible, but are written at a level suitable for students who have progressed to these more advanced topics.

CHANGES IN THIS EDITION

This fifth edition presents the same programming philosophy as the fourth edition. For instructors, you can teach the same course, presenting the same topics in the same order with no changes in the material covered or the chapters assigned. The changes to this edition consist almost exclusively of supplementary material added to the chapters of the previous edition, namely:

- Updates have been made for language changes in Java 7, such as allowing strings in switch statements.
- Twenty-five new programming projects have been added. By request, some of these are longer and less prescriptive projects to give the student more practice designing programming solutions.
- 15 new video notes have been created for a total of 46 video notes. These videos cover specific topics and offer solutions to the programming projects; they have been added to the book's website. The solutions walk students through the process of problem solving and coding to reinforce key programming concepts. An icon appears in the margin of the book when a video is available regarding the corresponding topic in the text.
- Chapter 2 now describes how to use the Scanner class to read from a text file so data-based programming projects can be explored prior to detailed coverage of File I/O in Chapter 10.
- A brief introduction to the Random class has been added to Chapter 3.
- Chapter 9 on exception handling begins with a new introduction of try/catch for handling input mismatch exceptions before discussing how to throw custom exceptions.
- A recursive algorithm to search the file system has been added to Chapter 11.
- Material on race conditions and thread synchronization has been added to Chapter 19.
- Ten new self-test exercises have been added along with the new material.

NO NONSTANDARD SOFTWARE

Only classes in the standard Java libraries are used. No nonstandard software is used anywhere in the book.

JAVA COVERAGE

All programs have been tested with Java 7. Oracle is not proposing any changes to future versions of Java that would affect the approach in this book.

OBJECT-ORIENTED PROGRAMMING

This book gives extensive coverage of encapsulation, inheritance, and polymorphism as realized in the Java language. The chapters on Swing GUIs provide coverage of and extensive practice with event driven programming. A chapter on UML and patterns gives additional coverage of OOP-related material.

FLEXIBILITY IN TOPIC ORDERING

This book allows instructors wide latitude in reordering the material. This is important if a book is to serve as a reference. It is also in keeping with my philosophy of writing books that accommodate themselves to an instructor's style rather than tying the instructor to an author's personal preference of topic ordering. With this in mind, each chapter has a prerequisite section at the beginning; this section explains what material must be covered before doing each section of the chapter. Starred sections, which are explained next, further add to flexibility.

STARRED SECTIONS

Each chapter has a number of starred (★) sections, which can be considered optional. These sections contain material that beginners might find difficult and that can be omitted or delayed without hurting the continuity of the text. It is hoped that eventually the reader would return and cover this material. For more advanced students, the starred sections should not be viewed as optional.

ACCESSIBLE TO STUDENTS

It is not enough for a book to present the right topics in the right order. It is not even enough for it to be clear and correct when read by an instructor or other expert. The material needs to be presented in a way that is accessible to the person who does not yet know the content. Like my other textbooks that have proven to be very popular, this book was written to be friendly and accessible to the student.

SUMMARY BOXES

Each major point is summarized in a short boxed section. These boxed sections are spread throughout each chapter. They serve as summaries of the material, as a quick reference source, and as a way to quickly learn the Java syntax for features the reader knows about in general but for which he or she needs to know the Java particulars.

SELF-TEST EXERCISES

Each chapter contains numerous Self-Test Exercises at strategic points in the chapter. Complete answers for all the Self-Test Exercises are given at the end of each chapter.

VIDEO NOTES

VideoNote

VideoNotes are step-by-step videos that guide readers through the solution to an end-of-chapter problem or further illuminate a concept presented in the text. Icons in the text indicate where a VideoNote enhances a topic. Fully navigable problems allow for self-paced instruction. VideoNotes are located at www.pearsoninternationaleditions.com/savitch.

OTHER FEATURES

Pitfall sections, programming tip sections, and examples of complete programs with sample I/O are given throughout each chapter. Each chapter ends with a summary section and a collection of programming projects suitable to assign to students.

ONLINE PRACTICE AND ASSESSMENT WITH MyProgrammingLab

MyProgrammingLab helps students fully grasp the logic, semantics, and syntax of programming. Through practice exercises and immediate, personalized feedback, MyProgrammingLab improves the programming competence of beginning students who often struggle with the basic concepts and paradigms of popular high-level programming languages.

A self-study and homework tool, a MyProgrammingLab course consists of hundreds of small practice problems organized around the structure of this textbook. For students, the system automatically detects errors in the logic and syntax of their code submissions and offers targeted hints that enable students to figure out what went wrong—and why. For instructors, a comprehensive gradebook tracks correct and incorrect answers and stores the code inputted by students for review.

MyProgrammingLab is offered to users of this book in partnership with Turing's Craft, the makers of the CodeLab interactive programming exercise system. For a full demonstration, to see feedback from instructors and students, or to get started using MyProgrammingLab in your course, visit www.myprogramminglab.com.

SUPPORT MATERIAL

The following support materials are available to all users of this book at www.pearsoninternationaleditions.com/savitch:

- Source code from the book

The following resources are available to qualified instructors only at www.pearsoninternationaleditions.com/savitch. Please contact your local sales representative for access information:

- Instructor's Manual with Solutions
- PowerPoint® slides

ACKNOWLEDGMENTS

Numerous individuals have contributed invaluable help and support in making this book happen: My former editor, Susan Hartman at Addison-Wesley, first conceived of the idea for this book and worked with me on the first editions; My current editor, Matt Goldstein, provided support and inspiration for getting subsequent editions reviewed, revised, and out the door; Chelsea Kharakozova, Marilyn Lloyd, Yez Alayan, and the other fine people at Pearson also provided valuable assistance and encouragement. Thanks also to GEX Publishing Services for their expert work in producing the final typeset book.

The following reviewers provided corrections and suggestions for this book. Their contributions were a great help. I thank them all. In alphabetical order they are:

Jim Adams	Chandler-Gilbert Community College
Gerald W. Adkins	Georgia College & State University
Dr. Bay Arinze	Drexel University
Prof. Richard G. Baldwin	Austin Community College
Kevin Bierre	Rochester Institute of Technology
Jon Bjornstad	Gavilan College
Janet Brown-Sederberg	Massasoit Community College
Tom Brown	Texas A&M University, Commerce
Charlotte Busch	Texas A&M University, Corpus Christi
Stephen Chandler	NW Shoals Community College
KY Daisy Fan	Cornell University
Adrienne Decker	University of Buffalo
Brian Downs	Century College
Keith Frikken	Miami University
Ahmad Ghafarian	North Georgia College & State University
Arthur Geis	College of DuPage
Massoud Ghyam	University of Southern California
Susan G. Glenn	Gordon College
Nigel Gwee	Louisiana State University
Judy Hankins	Middle Tennessee State University
May Hou	Norfolk State University
Sterling Hough	NHTI
Chris Howard	DeVry University
Eliot Jacobson	University of California, Santa Barbara
Balaji Janamanchi	Texas Tech University
Suresh Kalathur	Boston University
Edwin Kay	Lehigh University

Dr. Clifford R. Kettemborough	IT Consultant and Professor
Frank Levey	Manatee Community College
Xia Lin	Drexel University
Mark M. Meysenburg	Doane College
Sridhar P. Nerur	The University of Texas at Arlington
Hoang M. Nguyen	Deanza College
Rick Ord	University of California, San Diego
Prof. Bryson R. Payne	North Georgia College & State University
David Primeaux	Virginia Commonwealth University
Neil Rhodes	University of California, San Diego
W. Brent Seales	University of Kentucky
Lili Shashaani	Duquesne University
Riyaz Sikora	The University of Texas at Arlington
Jeff Six	University of Delaware
Donald J Smith	Community College of Allegheny County
Tom Smith	Skidmore College
Xueqing (Clare) Tang	Governors State University
Ronald F. Taylor	Wright State University
Thomas VanDrunen	Wheaton College
Shon Vick	University of Maryland, Baltimore County
Natalie S. Wear	University of South Florida
Dale Welch	University of West Florida
David A. Wheeler	
Wook-Sung Yoo	Gannon University

Special thanks goes to Kenrick Mock (University of Alaska Anchorage) who executed the updating of this edition. He once again had the difficult job of satisfying me, the editor, and himself. I thank him for a truly excellent job.

Walter Savitch

The publishers would like to thank Victor Chakraborty for reviewing the content of the International Edition.

LOCATION OF VIDEONOTES IN THE TEXT

www.pearsoninternationaleditions.com/savitch

VideoNote

| Chapter 1 | Compiling a Java Program, page 42 |
| | Solution to Programming Project 1.7, page 88 |

Chapter 2	Pitfalls Involving `nextLine()`, page 115
	Solution to Programming Project 2.11, page 129
	Solution to Programming Project 2.12, page 130

Chapter 3	Nested Loop Example, page 177
	Debugging Walkthrough, page 184
	Solution to Programming Project 3.9, page 202
	Solution to Programming Project 3.13, page 203

Chapter 4	Information Hiding Example, page 239
	Example Using the `StringTokenizer` Class on a CSV File, page 279
	Solution to Programming Project 4.9, page 287

| Chapter 5 | Deep Copy vs. Shallow Copy Example, page 353 |
| | Solution to Programming Project 5.9, page 376 |

Chapter 6	Arrays of Objects, page 390
	Solution to Programming Project 6.8, page 454
	Solution to Programming Project 6.15, page 456

Chapter 7	Inheritance Walkthrough, page 464
	Solution to Programming Project 7.3, page 509
	Solution to Programming Project 7.5, page 511

Chapter 8	Late Binding Example, page 518
	Solution to Programming Project 8.1, page 550
	Solution to Programming Project 8.9, page 553

| Chapter 9 | Solution to Programming Project 9.1, page 606 |
| | Solution to Programming Project 9.7, page 608 |

Chapter 10	Reading a Text File, page 621
	Solution to Programming Project 10.1, page 675
	Solution to Programming Project 10.8, page 677

| Chapter 11 | Recursion and the Stack, page 692 |
| | Solution to Programming Project 11.3, page 716 |

| Chapter 12 | Solution to Programming Project 12.9, page 742 |

| Chapter 13 | Solution to Programming Project 13.1, page 786 |
| | Solution to Programming Project 13.11, page 789 |

| Chapter 14 | Solution to Programming Project 14.7, page 832 |

| Chapter 15 | Walkthrough of the Hash Table Class, page 900 |
| | Solution to Programming Project 15.1, page 925 |

Chapter 16	Solution to Programming Project 16.3, page 969
	Solution to Programming Project 16.5, page 970
Chapter 17	GUI Layout Using an IDE, page 1001
	Solution to Programming Project 17.1, page 1045
Chapter 18	Walkthrough of a Simple Drawing Program, page 1074
	Solution to Programming Project 18.7, page 1109
Chapter 19	Walkthrough of a Program with Race Conditions, page 1126
	Solution to Programming Project 19.3, page 1167
	Solution to Programming Project 19.11, page 1168
Chapter 20	No video notes (Chapter on website)

Brief Contents

Chapter 1   GETTING STARTED   33

Chapter 2   CONSOLE INPUT AND OUTPUT   89

Chapter 3   FLOW OF CONTROL   131

Chapter 4   DEFINING CLASSES I   205

Chapter 5   DEFINING CLASSES II   291

Chapter 6   ARRAYS   377

Chapter 7   INHERITANCE   459

Chapter 8   POLYMORPHISM AND ABSTRACT CLASSES   515

Chapter 9   EXCEPTION HANDLING   555

Chapter 10   FILE I/O   609

Chapter 11   RECURSION   679

Chapter 12   UML AND PATTERNS   721

Chapter 13   INTERFACES AND INNER CLASSES   743

Chapter 14   GENERICS AND THE `ArrayList` CLASS   791

Chapter 15   LINKED DATA STRUCTURES   833

Chapter 16   COLLECTIONS, MAPS AND ITERATORS   929

Chapter 17   SWING I   973

Chapter 18   SWING II   1049

Chapter 19   JAVA NEVER ENDS   1111

Chapter 20   APPLETS AND HTML   1169

Appendix 1   KEYWORDS   1171

Appendix 2   PRECEDENCE AND ASSOCIATIVITY RULES   1173

Appendix 3   ASCII CHARACTER SET   1175

Appendix 4   FORMAT SPECIFICATIONS FOR `printf`   1177

Appendix 5   SUMMARY OF CLASSES AND INTERFACES   1179

INDEX   1247

Contents

Chapter 1   Getting Started   33

1.1   INTRODUCTION TO JAVA   34
Origins of the Java Language ★   34
Objects and Methods   35
Applets ★   36
A Sample Java Application Program   37
Byte-Code and the Java Virtual Machine   40
Class Loader ★   42
Compiling a Java Program or Class   42
Running a Java Program   43
TIP: Error Messages   44

1.2   EXPRESSIONS AND ASSIGNMENT STATEMENTS   45
Identifiers   45
Variables   47
Assignment Statements   48
TIP: Initialize Variables   50
More Assignment Statements ★   51
Assignment Compatibility   52
Constants   53
Arithmetic Operators and Expressions   55
Parentheses and Precedence Rules ★   56
Integer and Floating-Point Division   58
PITFALL: Round-Off Errors in Floating-Point Numbers   59
PITFALL: Division with Whole Numbers   60
Type Casting   61
Increment and Decrement Operators   62

1.3   THE CLASS `String`   65
String Constants and Variables   65
Concatenation of Strings   66
Classes   67
String Methods   69
Escape Sequences   74
String Processing   75
The Unicode Character Set ★   75

1.4   **PROGRAM STYLE**   **78**
Naming Constants   78
Java Spelling Conventions   80
Comments   81
Indenting   82

Chapter Summary   83
Answers to Self-Test Exercises   84
Programming Projects   86

Chapter 2   **Console Input and Output**   **89**

2.1   **SCREEN OUTPUT**   **90**
`System.out.println`   90
TIP: Different Approaches to Formatting Output   93
Formatting Output with `printf`   93
TIP: Formatting Monetary Amounts with `printf`   97
TIP: Legacy Code   98
Money Formats Using `NumberFormat` ★   99
Importing Packages and Classes   102
The `DecimalFormat` Class ★   104

2.2   **CONSOLE INPUT USING THE `Scanner` CLASS**   **108**
The `Scanner` Class   108
PITFALL: Dealing with the Line Terminator, `'\n'`   115
The Empty String   116
TIP: Prompt for Input   116
TIP: Echo Input   116
EXAMPLE: Self-Service Checkout   118
Other Input Delimiters   119

2.3   **INTRODUCTION TO FILE INPUT**   **121**
The `Scanner` Class for Text File Input   121

Chapter Summary   124
Answers to Self-Test Exercises   124
Programming Projects   127

Chapter 3   **Flow of Control**   **131**

3.1   **BRANCHING MECHANISM**   **132**
`if-else` Statements   132
Omitting the `else`   133
Compound Statements   134
TIP: Placing of Braces   135
Nested Statements   136

Multiway `if-else` Statement   136
EXAMPLE: State Income Tax   137
The `switch` Statement   139
PITFALL: Forgetting a `break` in a `switch` Statement   143
The Conditional Operator ★   144

3.2   **BOOLEAN EXPRESSIONS   145**
Simple Boolean Expressions   145
PITFALL: Using = in Place of ==   146
PITFALL: Using == with Strings   147
Lexicographic and Alphabetical Order   148
Building Boolean Expressions   151
PITFALL: Strings of Inequalities   152
Evaluating Boolean Expressions   152
TIP: Naming Boolean Variables   155
Short-Circuit and Complete Evaluation   156
Precedence and Associativity Rules   157

3.3   **LOOPS   164**
`while` Statement and `do-while` Statement   164
Algorithms and Pseudocode   166
EXAMPLE: Averaging a List of Scores   169
The `for` Statement   170
The Comma in `for` Statements   173
TIP: Repeat N Times Loops   175
PITFALL: Extra Semicolon in a `for` Statement   175
PITFALL: Infinite Loops   176
Nested Loops   177
The `break` and `continue` Statements ★   180
The `exit` Statement   181

3.4   **DEBUGGING   182**
Loop Bugs   182
Tracing Variables   182
General Debugging Techniques   183
EXAMPLE: Debugging an Input Validation Loop   184
Preventive Coding   188
Assertion Checks ★   189

3.5   **RANDOM NUMBER GENERATION ★   191**
The `Random` Object   192
The `Math.random()` Method   193

Chapter Summary   194
Answers to Self-Test Exercises   194
Programming Projects   200

Chapter 4   **Defining Classes I   205**

4.1   CLASS DEFINITIONS   206
Instance Variables and Methods   209
More about Methods   212
TIP: Any Method Can Be Used as a `void` Method   216
Local Variables   218
Blocks   219
TIP: Declaring Variables in a `for` Statement   220
Parameters of a Primitive Type   220
PITFALL: Use of the Terms "Parameter" and "Argument"   227
Simple Cases with Class Parameters   229
The `this` Parameter   229
Methods That Return a Boolean Value   231
The Methods `equals` and `toString`   234
Recursive Methods   237
TIP: Testing Methods   237

4.2   INFORMATION HIDING AND ENCAPSULATION   239
`public` and `private` Modifiers   240
EXAMPLE: Yet Another Date Class   241
Accessor and Mutator Methods   242
TIP: A Class Has Access to Private Members of All Objects of the Class   247
TIP: Mutator Methods Can Return a Boolean Value ★   248
Preconditions and Postconditions   249

4.3   OVERLOADING   250
Rules for Overloading   250
PITFALL: Overloading and Automatic Type Conversion   254
PITFALL: You Cannot Overload Based on the Type Returned   256

4.4   CONSTRUCTORS   258
Constructor Definitions   258
TIP: You Can Invoke Another Method in a Constructor   266
TIP: A Constructor Has a `this` Parameter   266
TIP: Include a No-Argument Constructor   267
EXAMPLE: The Final Date Class   268
Default Variable Initializations   269
An Alternative Way to Initialize Instance Variables   269
EXAMPLE: A Pet Record Class   270
The `StringTokenizer` Class ★   274

Chapter Summary   279
Answers to Self-Test Exercises   280
Programming Projects   285

Chapter 5   Defining Classes II   291

5.1   **STATIC METHODS AND STATIC VARIABLES   293**
Static Methods   293
PITFALL: Invoking a Nonstatic Method Within a Static Method   295
TIP: You Can Put a `main` in Any Class   296
Static Variables   300
The `Math` Class   305
Wrapper Classes   309
Automatic Boxing and Unboxing   310
Static Methods in Wrapper Classes   312
PITFALL: A Wrapper Class Does Not Have a No-Argument Constructor   315

5.2   **REFERENCES AND CLASS PARAMETERS   316**
Variables and Memory   317
References   318
Class Parameters   323
PITFALL: Use of = and == with Variables of a Class Type   327
The Constant `null`   329
PITFALL: Null Pointer Exception   330
The `new` Operator and Anonymous Objects   330
EXAMPLE: Another Approach to Keyboard Input ★   331
TIP: Use Static Imports ★   333

5.3   **USING AND MISUSING REFERENCES   335**
EXAMPLE: A Person Class   336
PITFALL: `null` Can Be an Argument to a Method   341
Copy Constructors   345
PITFALL: Privacy Leaks   347
Mutable and Immutable Classes   351
TIP: Deep Copy versus Shallow Copy   353
TIP: Assume Your Coworkers Are Malicious   354

5.4   **PACKAGES AND `javadoc`   354**
Packages and `import` Statements   355
The Package `java.lang`   356
Package Names and Directories   356
PITFALL: Subdirectories Are Not Automatically Imported   359
The Default Package   359
PITFALL: Not Including the Current Directory in Your Class Path   360
Specifying a Class Path When You Compile ★   360
Name Clashes ★   361
Introduction to `javadoc` ★   362
Commenting Classes for `javadoc` ★   362
Running `javadoc` ★   364

20   Contents

Chapter Summary   366
Answers to Self-Test Exercises   367
Programming Projects   371

Chapter 6   Arrays   377

6.1   **INTRODUCTION TO ARRAYS**   378
Creating and Accessing Arrays   379
The `length` Instance Variable   382
TIP: Use `for` Loops with Arrays   384
PITFALL: Array Indices Always Start with Zero   384
PITFALL: Array Index Out of Bounds   384
Initializing Arrays   385
PITFALL: An Array of Characters Is Not a String   387

6.2   **ARRAYS AND REFERENCES**   388
Arrays Are Objects   388
PITFALL: Arrays with a Class Base Type   390
Array Parameters   390
PITFALL: Use of = and == with Arrays   392
Arguments for the Method `main` ★   397
Methods that Return an Array   399

6.3   **PROGRAMMING WITH ARRAYS**   400
Partially Filled Arrays   401
EXAMPLE: A Class for Partially Filled Arrays   404
TIP: Accessor Methods Need Not Simply Return Instance Variables   408
The "for-each" Loop ★   408
Methods with a Variable Number of Parameters ★   412
EXAMPLE: A String Processing Example ★   415
Privacy Leaks with Array Instance Variables   416
EXAMPLE: Sorting an Array   420
Enumerated Types ★   424
TIP: Enumerated Types in `switch` Statements ★   429

6.4   **MULTIDIMENSIONAL ARRAYS**   431
Multidimensional Array Basics   431
Using the `length` Instance Variable   434
Ragged Arrays ★   435
Multidimensional Array Parameters and Returned Values   435
EXAMPLE: A Grade Book Class   436

Chapter Summary   442
Answers to Self-Test Exercises   443
Programming Projects   450

Chapter 7   Inheritance   459

7.1   **INHERITANCE BASICS   460**
Derived Classes   461
Overriding a Method Definition   471
Changing the Return Type of an Overridden Method   471
Changing the Access Permission of an Overridden Method   472
PITFALL: Overriding versus Overloading   473
The `super` Constructor   474
The `this` Constructor   476
TIP: An Object of a Derived Class Has More than One Type   477
PITFALL: The Terms *Subclass* and *Superclass*   480
EXAMPLE: An Enhanced `StringTokenizer` Class ★   481

7.2   **ENCAPSULATION AND INHERITANCE   484**
PITFALL: Use of Private Instance Variables from the Base Class   485
PITFALL: Private Methods Are Effectively Not Inherited   486
Protected and Package Access   487
PITFALL: Forgetting about the Default Package   490
PITFALL: A Restriction on Protected Access ★   490

7.3   **PROGRAMMING WITH INHERITANCE   493**
TIP: Static Variables Are Inherited   493
TIP: "is a" versus "has a"   493
Access to a Redefined Base Method   493
PITFALL: You Cannot Use Multiple `supers`   495
The Class `Object`   496
The Right Way to Define `equals`   497
TIP: `getClass` versus `instanceof` ★   499

Chapter Summary   504
Answers to Self-Test Exercises   505
Programming Projects   508

Chapter 8   Polymorphism and Abstract Classes   515

8.1   **POLYMORPHISM   516**
Late Binding   517
The `final` Modifier   519
EXAMPLE: Sales Records   520
Late Binding with `toString`   527
PITFALL: No Late Binding for Static Methods   528
Downcasting and Upcasting   529
PITFALL: Downcasting   533

TIP: Checking to See Whether Downcasting Is Legitimate ★   533
A First Look at the `clone` Method   536
PITFALL: Sometimes the `clone` Method Return Type Is `Object`   537
PITFALL: Limitations of Copy Constructors ★   538

8.2   **ABSTRACT CLASSES   541**
Abstract Classes   542
PITFALL: You Cannot Create Instances of an Abstract Class   546
TIP: An Abstract Class Is a Type   547

Chapter Summary   548
Answers to Self-Test Exercises   548
Programming Projects   550

Chapter 9   Exception Handling   555

9.1   **EXCEPTION HANDLING BASICS   557**
`try-catch` Mechanism   557
Exception Handling with the `Scanner` Class   559
TIP: Exception Controlled Loops   560
Throwing Exceptions   562
EXAMPLE: A Toy Example of Exception Handling   564
Exception Classes   569
Exception Classes from Standard Packages   570
Defining Exception Classes   572
TIP: Preserve `getMessage`   576
TIP: An Exception Class Can Carry a Message of Any Type   578
Multiple `catch` Blocks   583
PITFALL: Catch the More Specific Exception First   585

9.2   **THROWING EXCEPTIONS IN METHODS   588**
Throwing an Exception in a Method   588
Declaring Exceptions in a `throws` Clause   590
Exceptions to the Catch or Declare Rule   593
`throws` Clause in Derived Classes   594
When to Use Exceptions   595
Event-Driven Programming ★   596

9.3   **MORE PROGRAMMING TECHNIQUES FOR EXCEPTION HANDLING   598**
PITFALL: Nested `try-catch` Blocks   598
The `finally` Block ★   598
Rethrowing an Exception ★   600
The `AssertionError` Class ★   600
`ArrayIndexOutOfBoundsException`   601

Chapter Summary   601
Answers to Self-Test Exercises   602
Programming Projects   606

Chapter 10   **File I/O   609**

10.1   **INTRODUCTION TO FILE I/O   610**
Streams   610
Text Files and Binary Files   611

10.2   **TEXT FILES   612**
Writing to a Text File   612
PITFALL: A `try` Block Is a Block   618
PITFALL: Overwriting an Output File   618
Appending to a Text File   619
TIP: `toString` Helps with Text File Output   620
Reading from a Text File   621
Reading a Text File Using `Scanner`   621
Testing for the End of a Text File with `Scanner`   624
Reading a Text File Using `BufferedReader`   631
TIP: Reading Numbers with `BufferedReader`   635
Testing for the End of a Text File with `BufferedReader`   635
Path Names   637
Nested Constructor Invocations   638
`System.in`, `System.out`, and `System.err`   639

10.3   **THE `File` CLASS   641**
Programming with the `File` Class   641

10.4   **BINARY FILES ★   645**
Writing Simple Data to a Binary File   646
UTF and `writeUTF`   650
Reading Simple Data from a Binary File   651
Checking for the End of a Binary File   656
PITFALL: Checking for the End of a File in the Wrong Way   657
Binary I/O of Objects   658
The `Serializable` Interface   659
PITFALL: Mixing Class Types in the Same File   662
Array Objects in Binary Files   662

10.5   **RANDOM ACCESS TO BINARY FILES ★   664**
Reading and Writing to the Same File   664
PITFALL: `RandomAccessFile` Need Not Start Empty   670

Chapter Summary   670
Answers to Self-Test Exercises   671
Programming Projects   675

Chapter 11   Recursion   679

11.1   RECURSIVE Void METHODS   681
EXAMPLE: Vertical Numbers   681
Tracing a Recursive Call   684
A Closer Look at Recursion   687
PITFALL: Infinite Recursion   689
Stacks for Recursion ★   690
PITFALL: Stack Overflow ★   692
Recursion versus Iteration   692

11.2   RECURSIVE METHODS THAT RETURN A VALUE   693
General Form for a Recursive Method That Returns a Value   694
EXAMPLE: Another Powers Method   694

11.3   THINKING RECURSIVELY   699
Recursive Design Techniques   699
Binary Search ★   700
Efficiency of Binary Search ★   706
EXAMPLE: Finding a File   708

Chapter Summary   711
Answers to Self-Test Exercises   711
Programming Projects   716

Chapter 12   UML and Patterns   721

12.1   UML   722
History of UML   723
UML Class Diagrams   723
Class Interactions   724
Inheritance Diagrams   724
More UML   726

12.2   PATTERNS ★   727
Adaptor Pattern ★   727
The Model-View-Controller Pattern ★   728
EXAMPLE: A Sorting Pattern   729
Restrictions on the Sorting Pattern   735
Efficiency of the Sorting Pattern ★   735

TIP: Pragmatics and Patterns   736
Pattern Formalism   736

Chapter Summary   737
Answers to Self-Test Exercises   737
Programming Projects   739

Chapter 13   Interfaces and Inner Classes   743

13.1   INTERFACES   745
Interfaces   745
Abstract Classes Implementing Interfaces   747
Derived Interfaces   747
PITFALL: Interface Semantics Are Not Enforced   749
The `Comparable` Interface   751
EXAMPLE: Using the `Comparable` Interface   752
Defined Constants in Interfaces   757
PITFALL: Inconsistent Interfaces   758
The `Serializable` Interface ★   761
The `Cloneable` Interface   761

13.2   SIMPLE USES OF INNER CLASSES   766
Helping Classes   766
TIP: Inner and Outer Classes Have Access to Each Other's Private Members   767
EXAMPLE: A Bank Account Class   767
The `.class` File for an Inner Class   771
PITFALL: Other Uses of Inner Classes   772

13.3   MORE ABOUT INNER CLASSES   772
Static Inner Classes   772
Public Inner Classes   773
TIP: Referring to a Method of the Outer Class   775
Nesting Inner Classes   777
Inner Classes and Inheritance   777
Anonymous Classes   778
TIP: Why Use Inner Classes?   780

Chapter Summary   781
Answers to Self-Test Exercises   781
Programming Projects   786

Chapter 14   Generics and the `ArrayList` Class   791

14.1   THE `ArrayList` CLASS   793
Using the `ArrayList` Class   794
TIP: Summary of Adding to an `ArrayList`   798

Methods in the Class `ArrayList`   799
The "for-each" Loop   802
EXAMPLE: Golf Scores   805
TIP: Use `trimToSize` to Save Memory   808
PITFALL: The `clone` Method Makes a Shallow Copy ★   808
The `Vector` Class   809
Parameterized Classes and Generics   810
PITFALL: Nonparameterized `ArrayList` and `Vector` Classes   810

14.2   **GENERICS   810**
Generic Basics   811
TIP: Compile with the `-Xlint` Option   813
EXAMPLE: A Generic Class for Ordered Pairs   813
PITFALL: A Generic Constructor Name Has No Type Parameter   816
PITFALL: You Cannot Plug in a Primitive Type for a Type Parameter   817
PITFALL: A Type Parameter Cannot Be Used Everywhere a Type Name
            Can Be Used   817
PITFALL: An Instantiation of a Generic Class Cannot be an
            Array Base Type   818
TIP: A Class Definition Can Have More Than One Type Parameter   819
PITFALL: A Generic Class Cannot Be an Exception Class   820
Bounds for Type Parameters   821
TIP: Generic Interfaces   824
Generic Methods ★   824
Inheritance with Generic Classes ★   826

Chapter Summary   828
Answers to Self-Test Exercises   828
Programming Projects   831

Chapter 15   **Linked Data Structures   833**

15.1   **JAVA LINKED LISTS   836**
EXAMPLE: A Simple Linked List Class   836
Working with Linked Lists   840
PITFALL: Privacy Leaks   845
Node Inner Classes   846
EXAMPLE: A Generic Linked List   849
PITFALL: Using `Node` Instead of `Node<T>`   854
The `equals` Method for Linked Lists   854

15.2   **COPY CONSTRUCTORS AND THE `clone` METHOD ★   856**
Simple Copy Constructors and `clone` Methods ★   856
Exceptions ★   857

PITFALL: The `clone` Method Is Protected in `object` ★   859
TIP: Use a Type Parameter Bound for a Better `clone` ★   860
EXAMPLE: A Linked List with a Deep Copy `clone` Method ★   864
TIP: Cloning Is an "All or Nothing" Affair   867

15.3   **ITERATORS   867**
Defining an Iterator Class   868
Adding and Deleting Nodes   873

15.4   **VARIATIONS ON A LINKED LIST   878**
Doubly Linked List   878
The Stack Data Structure   887
The Queue Data Structure   889
Running Times and Big-O Notation   892
Efficiency of Linked Lists   897

15.5   **HASH TABLES WITH CHAINING   898**
A Hash Function for Strings   899
Efficiency of Hash Tables   902

15.6   **SETS   903**
Fundamental Set Operations   904
Efficiency of Sets Using Linked Lists   909

15.7   **TREES   910**
Tree Properties   910
EXAMPLE: A Binary Search Tree Class ★   913
Efficiency of Binary Search Trees ★   918

Chapter Summary   919
Answers to Self-Test Exercises   920
Programming Projects   925

Chapter 16   Collections, Maps and Iterators   929

16.1   **COLLECTIONS   930**
Wildcards   932
The Collection Framework   932
PITFALL: Optional Operations   938
TIP: Dealing with All Those Exceptions   939
Concrete Collection Classes   940
Differences between `ArrayList<T>` and `Vector<T>`   950
Nonparameterized Version of the Collection Framework ★   950
PITFALL: Omitting the `<T>`   951

16.2 **MAPS 951**
Concrete Map Classes 954

16.3 **ITERATORS 958**
The Iterator Concept 958
The `Iterator<T>` Interface 958
TIP: For-Each Loops as Iterators 961
List Iterators 962
PITFALL: `next` Can Return a Reference 964
TIP: Defining Your Own Iterator Classes 966

Chapter Summary 967
Answers to Self-Test Exercises 967
Programming Projects 968

Chapter 17 Swing I 973

17.1 **EVENT-DRIVEN PROGRAMMING 975**
Events and Listeners 975

17.2 **BUTTONS, EVENTS, AND OTHER SWING BASICS 976**
EXAMPLE: A Simple Window 977
PITFALL: Forgetting to Program the Close-Window Button 982
Buttons 983
Action Listeners and Action Events 984
PITFALL: Changing the Heading for `actionPerformed` 986
TIP: Ending a Swing Program 986
EXAMPLE: A Better Version of Our First Swing GUI 987
Labels 990
Color 991
EXAMPLE: A GUI with a Label and Color 992

17.3 **CONTAINERS AND LAYOUT MANAGERS 994**
Border Layout Managers 995
Flow Layout Managers 998
Grid Layout Managers 999
Panels 1003
EXAMPLE: A Tricolor Built with Panels 1004
The `Container` Class 1008
TIP: Code a GUI's Look and Actions Separately 1011
The Model-View-Controller Pattern ★ 1012

17.4   **MENUS AND BUTTONS   1013**
EXAMPLE: A GUI with a Menu   1013
Menu Bars, Menus, and Menu Items   1013
Nested Menus ★   1018
The `AbstractButton` Class   1018
The `setActionCommand` Method   1021
Listeners as Inner Classes ★   1022

17.5   **TEXT FIELDS AND TEXT AREAS   1025**
Text Areas and Text Fields   1026
TIP: Labeling a Text Field   1032
TIP: Inputting and Outputting Numbers   1032
A Swing Calculator   1033

Chapter Summary   1038
Answers to Self-Test Exercises   1039
Programming Projects   1045

Chapter 18   Swing II   1049

18.1   **WINDOW LISTENERS   1050**
EXAMPLE: A Window Listener Inner Class   1052
The `dispose` Method   1055
PITFALL: Forgetting to Invoke `setDefaultCloseOperation`   1056
The `WindowAdapter` Class   1056

18.2   **ICONS AND SCROLL BARS   1058**
Icons   1058
Scroll Bars   1064
EXAMPLE: Components with Changing Visibility   1069

18.3   **THE `Graphics` CLASS   1073**
Coordinate System for Graphics Objects   1073
The Method `paint` and the Class `Graphics`   1074
Drawing Ovals   1079
Drawing Arcs   1079
Rounded Rectangles ★   1083
`paintComponent` for Panels   1084
Action Drawings and `repaint`   1084
Some More Details on Updating a GUI ★   1090

18.4   **COLORS   1090**
Specifying a Drawing Color   1091
Defining Colors   1092
PITFALL: Using `doubles` to Define a Color   1093
The `JColorChooser` Dialog Window   1094

18.5   **FONTS AND THE `drawString` METHOD   1097**
The `drawString` Method   1097
Fonts   1100

Chapter Summary   1103
Answers to Self-Test Exercises   1103
Programming Projects   1107

Chapter 19   Java Never Ends   1111

19.1   **MULTITHREADING   1112**
EXAMPLE: A Nonresponsive GUI   1113
`Thread.sleep`   1113
The `getGraphics` Method   1117
Fixing a Nonresponsive Program Using Threads   1118
EXAMPLE: A Multithreaded Program   1118
The Class `Thread`   1119
The `Runnable` Interface ★   1122
Race Conditions and Thread Synchronization ★   1125

19.2   **NETWORKING WITH STREAM SOCKETS   1130**
Sockets   1130
Sockets and Threading   1134

19.3   **JAVABEANS   1135**
The Component Model   1135
The JavaBeans Model   1136

19.4   **JAVA AND DATABASE CONNECTIONS   1137**
Relational Databases   1137
Java DB and JDBC   1137
SQL   1139

19.5   **WEB PROGRAMMING WITH JAVA SERVER PAGES   1150**
Applets, Servlets, and Java Server Pages   1150
Oracle GlassFish Enterprise Server   1152
HTML Forms—the Common Gateway Interface   1153
JSP Declarations, Expressions, Scriptlets, and Directives   1155

Chapter Summary   1164
Answers to Self-Test Exercises   1165
Programming Projects   1166

Chapter 20   **Applets and HTML**   (online at www.pearsoninternationaleditions.com/savitch)   **1169**

Appendix 1   **Keywords**   **1171**
Appendix 2   **Precedence and Associativity Rules**   **1173**
Appendix 3   **ASCII Character Set**   **1175**
Appendix 4   **Format Specifications for** `printf`   **1177**
Appendix 5   **Summary of Classes and Interfaces**   **1179**
             Index   **1247**

Getting Started 1

1.1 INTRODUCTION TO JAVA 34
Origins of the Java Language ★ 34
Objects and Methods 35
Applets ★ 36
A Sample Java Application Program 37
Byte-Code and the Java Virtual Machine 40
Class Loader ★ 42
Compiling a Java Program or Class 42
Running a Java Program 43

1.2 EXPRESSIONS AND ASSIGNMENT STATEMENTS 45
Identifiers 45
Variables 47
Assignment Statements 48
More Assignment Statements ★ 51
Assignment Compatibility 52
Constants 53
Arithmetic Operators and Expressions 55
Parentheses and Precedence Rules ★ 56
Integer and Floating-Point Division 58
Type Casting 61
Increment and Decrement Operators 62

1.3 THE CLASS String 65
String Constants and Variables 65
Concatenation of Strings 66
Classes 67
String Methods 69
Escape Sequences 74
String Processing 75
The Unicode Character Set ★ 75

1.4 PROGRAM STYLE 78
Naming Constants 78
Java Spelling Conventions 80
Comments 81
Indenting 82

Chapter Summary 83   **Answers to Self-Test Exercises** 84   **Programming Projects** 86

Getting Started

She starts—she moves—she seems to feel
The thrill of life along her keel.

HENRY WADSWORTH LONGFELLOW, *The Building of the Ship*

Introduction

This chapter introduces you to the Java language and gives you enough details to allow you to write simple programs involving expressions, assignments, and console output. The details about assignments and expressions are similar to that of most other high-level languages. Every language has its own way of handling strings and console output, so even the experienced programmer should look at that material. Even if you are already an experienced programmer in some language other than Java, you should read at least the subsection entitled "A Sample Java Application Program" in Section 1.1 and preferably all of Section 1.2. You should also read all of Section 1.3 (on strings) and at least skim Section 1.4 to find out about Java defined constants and comments.

Prerequisites

This book is self-contained and requires no preparation other than some simple high school algebra.

1.1   Introduction to Java

Eliminating the middle man is not necessarily a good idea.

Found in my old economics class notes.

In this section, we give you an overview of the Java programming language.

Origins of the Java Language ★

Java is well-known as a programming language for Internet applications. However, this book, and many other books and programmers, consider Java a general-purpose programming language that is suitable for most any application, whether it involves the Internet or not. The first version of Java was neither of these things, but it evolved into both.

In 1991, James Gosling led a team at Sun Microsystems that developed the first version of Java (which was not yet called *Java*). This first version of the language was designed for programming home appliances, such as washing machines and television sets. Although that may not be a very glamorous application area, it is no easy task to design such a language. Home appliances are controlled by a wide variety of computer processors (chips). The language that Gosling was designing needed to work on all these different processors. Moreover, a home appliance is typically an inexpensive item, so the manufacturer would be unwilling to invest large amounts of money into developing complicated compilers. (A *compiler* translates a program into a language the processor can understand.) To simplify the tasks of writing compilers (translation programs) for each class of appliances, the team used a two-step translation process.

intermediate language

The programs are first translated into an **intermediate language** that is the same for all appliances (or all computers), and then a small, easy-to-write—and hence, inexpensive—program translates this intermediate language into the machine language for a particular appliance or computer. This intermediate language is called **Java byte-code**, or simply, **byte-code**. Since there is only one intermediate language, the hardest step of the two-step translation from program to intermediate language to machine language is the same for all appliances (or all computers); hence, most of the cost of translating to multiple machine languages was saved. The language for programming appliances never caught on with appliance manufacturers, but the Java language into which it evolved has become a widely used programming language. Today, Java is owned by Oracle Corporation, which purchased Sun Microsystems in 2010.

byte-code

code

Why call it *byte-code*? The word **code** is commonly used to mean a program or part of a program. A byte is a small unit of storage (eight bits to be precise). Computer-readable information is typically organized into bytes. So the term *byte-code* suggests a program that is readable by a computer as opposed to a person.

In 1994, Patrick Naughton and Jonathan Payne at Sun Microsystems developed a Web browser that could run (Java) programs over the Internet, which has evolved into the browser known as HotJava. This was the start of Java's connection to the Internet. In the fall of 1995, Netscape Incorporated made its Web browser capable of running Java programs. Other companies followed suit and have developed software that accommodates Java programs.

Objects and Methods

OOP

Java is an **object-oriented programming (OOP)** language. What is OOP? The world around us is made up of objects, such as people, automobiles, buildings, streets, adding machines, papers, and so forth. Each of these objects has the ability to perform certain actions, and each of these actions has some effect on some of the other objects in the world. OOP is a programming methodology that views a program as similarly consisting of objects that interact with each other by means of actions.

object

method

class

Object-oriented programming has its own specialized terminology. The objects are called, appropriately enough, **objects**. The actions that an object can take are called **methods**. Objects of the same kind are said to have the same *type* or, more often, are said to be in the same **class**. For example, in an airport simulation program, all the

> **Why Is the Language Named "Java"?**
>
> The current custom is to name programming languages according to the whims of their designers. Java is no exception. There are conflicting explanations of the origin of the name "Java." Despite these differing stories, one thing is clear: The word "Java" does not refer to any property or serious history of the Java language. One believable story about where the name came from is that it was thought of when, after a fruitless meeting trying to come up with a new name for the language, the development team went out for coffee. Hence, the inspiration for the name "Java."

simulated airplanes might belong to the same class, probably called the `Airplane` class. All objects within a class have the same methods. Thus, in a simulation program, all airplanes have the same methods (or possible actions), such as taking off, flying to a specific location, landing, and so forth. However, all simulated airplanes are not identical. They can have different characteristics, which are indicated in the program by associating different data (that is, some different information) with each particular airplane object. For example, the data associated with an airplane object might be two numbers for its speed and altitude.

application program

If you have used some other programming language, it might help to explain Java terminology in terms of the vocabulary used in other languages. Things that are called *procedures*, *methods*, *functions*, or *subprograms* in other languages are all called *methods* in Java. In Java, all methods (and for that matter, any programming constructs whatsoever) are part of a *class*. As we will see, a Java **application program** is a class with a method named `main`; when you run the Java program, the run-time system automatically invokes the method named `main` (that is, it automatically initiates the `main` action). An application program is a "regular" Java program, and, as we are about to see, there is another kind of Java program known as an *applet*. Other Java terminology is pretty much the same as the terminology in most other programming languages and, in any case, will be explained when each concept is introduced.

Applets ★

applet

application

There are two kinds of Java programs, **applets** and **applications**. An application, or application program, is just a regular program. Although the name *applet* may sound like it has something to do with apples, it really means a *little Java application*, not a little apple. Applets and applications are almost identical. The difference is that applications are meant to be run on your computer like any other program, whereas an **applet** is meant to be run from a Web browser, and so can be sent to another location on the Internet and run there. Applets always use a windowing interface, but not all programs with a windowing interface are applets, as you will see in Chapters 16–18.

applet viewer

Although applets were designed to be run from a Web browser, they can also be run with a program known as an **applet viewer**. The applet viewer is really meant as a debugging aid and not as the final environment to allow users to run applets. Nonetheless, applets are now often run as stand-alone programs using an applet viewer.[1] We find this to be a somewhat unfortunate accident of history. Java has multiple libraries of software for designing windowing interfaces that run without a connection to a browser. We prefer to use these libraries, rather than applets, to write windowing programs that will not be run from a Web browser. In this book, we show you how to do windowing interfaces as applets and as programs with no connection to a Web browser. In fact, the two approaches have a large overlap of both techniques and the Java libraries that they use. Once you know how to design and write either applets or applications, it is easy to learn to write the other of these two kinds of programs.

An applet always has a windowing interface. An application program may have a windowing interface or use simple console I/O. So as not to detract from the code being studied, most of our example programs, particularly early in this book, use simple console I/O (that is, simple text I/O).

A Sample Java Application Program

Display 1.1 contains a simple Java program and the screen displays produced when it is run. A Java program is really a class definition (whatever that is) with a method named `main`. When the program is run, the method named `main` is invoked; that is, the action specified by `main` is carried out. The body of the method `main` is enclosed in braces, { }, so that when the program is run, the statements in the braces are executed. (If you are not even vaguely familiar with the words *class* and *method*, they will be explained. Read on.)

The following line says that this program is a class called `FirstProgram`:

```
public class FirstProgram
{
```

The next two lines, shown below, begin the definition of the `main` method:

```
public static void main(String[] args)
{
```

The details of exactly what a Java class is and what words such as `public`, `static`, `void`, and so forth mean will be explained in the next few chapters. Until then, think of these opening lines, repeated below, as being a rather wordy way of saying "Begin the program named `FirstProgram`."

```
public class FirstProgram
{
    public static void main(String[] args)
    {
```

---

[1]An applet viewer does indeed use a browser to run an applet, but the look and feel is that of a stand-alone program with no interaction with a browser.

Display 1.1   A Sample Java Program

```
1 public class FirstProgram          Name of class
2 {                                   (program)                    The main method
3     public static void main(String[] args)
4     {
5         System.out.println("Hello reader.");
6         System.out.println("Welcome to Java.");

7         System.out.println("Let's demonstrate a simple calculation.");
8         int answer;
9         answer = 2 + 2;
10        System.out.println("2 plus 2 is " + answer);
11    }
12 }
```

Sample Dialogue

```
Hello reader.
Welcome to Java.
Let's demonstrate a simple calculation.
2 plus 2 is 4
```

The next two lines, shown in what follows, are the first actions the program performs:

println

```
System.out.println("Hello reader.");
System.out.println("Welcome to Java.");
```

Each of these lines begins with System.out.println. Each one causes the quoted string given within the parentheses to be output to the screen. For example, consider

```
System.out.println("Hello reader.");
```

This causes the line

```
Hello reader.
```

to be written to the screen. The output produced by the next line that begins with System.out.println will go on the following line. Thus, these two lines cause the following output:

```
Hello reader.
Welcome to Java.
```

System.out.
println

These lines that begin with System.out.println are a way of saying "output what is shown in parentheses," and the details of why the instruction is written this way need not concern us yet. However, we can tell you a little about what is going on here.

As stated earlier, Java programs work by having things called *objects* perform actions. The actions performed by an object are called *methods*. System.out is an object used for sending output to the screen; println is the method (that is, the action) that this object performs. The action is to send what is in parentheses to the screen. When an object performs an action using a method, it is called **invoking** (or **calling**) the method. In a Java program, you write such a method invocation by writing the object followed by a **dot** (period), followed by the method name, and some parentheses that may or may not have something inside them. The thing (or things) inside the parentheses is called an **argument(s)**, which provides information needed by the method to carry out its action. In each of these two lines and the similar line that follows them, the method is println. The method println writes something to the screen, and the argument (a string in quotes) tells it what it should write.

Invoking a method is also sometimes called **sending a message** to the object. With this view, a message is sent to the object (by invoking a method) and in response, the object performs some action (namely the action taken by the method invoked). We seldom use the terminology *sending a message*, but it is standard terminology used by some programmers and authors.

Variable declarations in Java are similar to what they are in other programming languages. The following line from Display 1.1 declares the variable answer:

```
int answer;
```

The type int is one of the Java types for integers (whole numbers). So, this line says that answer is a variable that can hold a single integer (whole number).

The following line is the only real computing done by this first program:

```
answer = 2 + 2;
```

In Java, the equal sign is used as the **assignment operator**, which is an instruction to set the value of the variable on the left-hand side of the equal sign. In the preceding program line, the equal sign does not mean that answer *is equal to* 2 + 2. Instead, the equal sign is an instruction to the computer to *make* answer *equal to* 2 + 2.

The last program action is

```
System.out.println("2 plus 2 is " + answer);
```

This is an output statement of the same kind as we discussed earlier, but there is something new in it. Note that the string "2 plus 2 is " is followed by a plus sign and the variable answer. In this case, the plus sign is an operator to concatenate (connect) two strings. However, the variable answer is not a string. If one of the two operands to + is a string, Java will convert the other operand, such as the value of answer, to a string. In this program, answer has the value 4, so answer is converted to the string "4" and then concatenated to the string "2 plus 2 is ", so the output statement under discussion is equivalent to

```
System.out.println("2 plus 2 is 4");
```

invoking

dot

argument

sending a message

variable int

equal sign

assignment operator

The remainder of this first program consists of two closing braces. The first closing brace ends the definition of the method `main`. The last closing brace ends the definition of the class named `FirstProgram`.

MyProgrammingLab™

Self-Test Exercises

1. If the following statement were used in a Java program, it would cause something to be written to the screen. What would it cause to be written to the screen?

```
System.out.println("I am a Java fan.");
```

2. Give a statement or statements that can be used in a Java program to write the following to the screen:

```
I like Java.
You like tea.
```

3. Write a complete Java program that uses `System.out.println` to output the following to the screen when run:

```
Programming is great fun!
```

Note that you do not need to fully understand all the details of the program in order to write the program. You can simply follow the model of the program in Display 1.1.

Byte-Code and the Java Virtual Machine

high-level, low-level, and machine languages

Most modern programming languages are designed to be (relatively) easy for people to write and to understand. These languages are called **high-level languages**. The language that the computer can directly understand is called **machine language**. Machine language or any language similar to machine language is called a **low-level language**. A program written in a high-level language, such as Java, must be translated into a program in machine language before the program can be run. The program that does the translating (or at least most of the translating) is called a **compiler** and the translation process is called **compiling**.

compiler

Compiler

A **compiler** is a program that translates a high-level-language program, such as a Java program, into an equivalent low-level-language program.

One disadvantage of most programming languages is that the compiler translates the high-level-language program directly into the machine language for your computer. Since different computers have different machine languages, this means you need a different compiler for each type of computer. Java, however, uses a slightly different and much more versatile approach to compiling.

While some versions of Java do translate your program into machine language for your particular computer, the original Java compiler and most compilers today do not. Instead, the Java compiler translates your Java program into a language called **byte-code**. Byte-code is not the machine language for any particular computer; it is the machine language for a fictitious computer called the **Java Virtual Machine (JVM)**. The Java Virtual Machine is very similar to all typical computers. Thus, it is easy to translate a program written in byte-code into a program in the machine language for any particular computer. The term *JVM* is also used to refer to the software that implements the fictitious computer. There are two ways the JVM can do this translation: through an **interpreter** and through a **Just-In-Time (JIT)** compiler.

An interpreter combines the translation of the byte-code and the execution of the corresponding machine language instructions. The interpreter works by translating an instruction of byte-code into instructions expressed in your computer's machine language and then executing those instructions on your computer. It does this one byte-code instruction at a time. Thus, an interpreter translates and executes the instructions in the byte-code one after the other, rather than translating the entire byte-code program at once.

Modern implementations of the JVM use a JIT compiler, which uses a combination of interpretation and compilation. The JIT compiler reads the byte-code in chunks and compiles entire chunks to native machine language instructions as needed. The compiled machine language instructions are remembered—i.e., cached—for future use, so the chunk needs to be compiled only once. This model generally runs programs faster than the interpreted model, which always has to translate the next byte-code instruction to machine code instructions.

To run a Java program, first use the compiler to translate the Java program into byte-code. Then, use the JVM for your computer to translate byte-code instructions to machine language and to run the machine language instructions.

It sounds as though Java byte-code just adds an extra step in the process. Why not write compilers that translate directly from Java to the machine language for your particular computer? This is what is done for most other programming languages. However, Java byte-code makes your Java program very portable. After you compile your Java program into byte-code, you can use that byte-code on any computer. When you run your program on another type of computer, you do not need to recompile it. This means that you can send your byte-code over the Internet to another computer and have it easily run on that computer. This is one of the reasons Java is good for Internet applications. This model is also more secure. If a Java program behaves badly, it only does so within the context of the JVM instead of behaving badly directly on your native machine. Of course, every kind of computer must have its own program to implement the Java Virtual Machine.

Margin terms: byte-code, Java Virtual Machine (JVM), Interpreter, Just-In-Time (JIT)

Byte-Code

The Java compiler translates your Java program into a language called **byte-code**, which is the machine language for a fictitious computer. It is easy to translate this byte-code into the machine language of any particular computer. Each type of computer will have its own software to implement the Java Virtual Machine that translates and executes byte-code instructions.

run command

When compiling and running a Java program, you are usually not even aware of the fact that your program is translated into byte-code and not directly translated into machine language code. You normally give two commands: one to compile your program (into byte-code) and one to run your program. The **run command** executes the Java Virtual Machine on the byte-code.

When you use a compiler, the terminology can get a bit confusing, because both the input to the compiler program and the output from the compiler program are also programs. Everything in sight is some kind of program. To make sure it is clear which program we mean, we call the input program (which in our case will be a Java program) the **source program**, or **source code**, and call the translated low-level-language program that the compiler produces the **object program**, or **object code**. The word **code** just means a program or a part of a program.

source code

object code

code

Class Loader ★

A Java program is divided into smaller parts called *classes*, and normally each class definition is in a separate file and is compiled separately. In order to run your program, the byte-code for these various classes needs to be connected together. The connecting is done by a program known as the **class loader**. It is typically done automatically, so you normally need not be concerned with it. (In other programming languages, the program corresponding to the Java class loader is called a *linker*.)

VideoNote

Compiling a Java Program

Compiling a Java Program or Class

As we noted in the previous subsection, a Java program is divided into classes. Before you can run a Java program, you must compile these classes.

Before you can compile a Java program, each class definition used in the program (and written by you, the programmer) should be in a separate file. Moreover, the name of the file should be the same as the name of the class, except that the file name has .java added to the end. The program in Display 1.1 is a class called FirstProgram, so it should be in a file named FirstProgram.java. This program has only one class, but a more typical Java program would consist of several classes.

.java files

If you are using an IDE (Integrated Development Environment), there will be a simple command to compile your Java program from the editor. You will have to check your local documentation to see exactly what this command is, but it is bound to be very simple. (In the TextPad environment, the command is Compile Java on the Tools menu.)

If you want or need to compile your Java program or class with a one-line command given to the operating system, it is easy to do. We will describe the commands for the Java system distributed by Oracle (usually called "the SDK" or "the JDK") in the following paragraphs.

Suppose you want to compile a class named FirstProgram. It will be in a file named FirstProgram.java. To compile it, simply give the following command:

javac

```
javac FirstProgram.java
```

You should be in the same directory (folder) as the file `FirstProgram.java` when you give this `javac` command. To compile any Java class, whether it is a full program or not, the command is `javac` followed by the name of the file containing the class.

When you compile a Java class, the resulting byte-code for that class is placed in a file of the same name, except that the ending is changed from `.java` to `.class`. So, when you compile a class named `FirstProgram` in the file `FirstProgram.java`, the resulting byte-code is stored in a file named `FirstProgram.class`.

Running a Java Program

A Java program can consist of a number of different classes, each in a different file. When you run a Java application program, only run the class that you think of as the program; that is, the class that contains a `main` method. Look for the following line, which starts the `main` method:

```
public static void main(String[] args)
```

The critical words to look for are `public static void main`. The remaining portion of the line might be spelled slightly different in some cases.

If you are using an IDE, you will have a menu command that can be used to run a Java program. You will have to check your local documentation to see exactly what this command is. (In the TextPad environment, the command is Run Java Application on the Tools menu.)

If you want or need to run your Java program with a one-line command given to the operating system, then (in most cases) you can run a Java program by giving the command `java` followed by the name of the class containing the `main` method. For example, for the program in Display 1.1, you would give the following one-line command:

```
java FirstProgram
```

Note that when you run a program, you use the class name, such as `FirstProgram`, without any `.java` or `.class` ending.

When you run a Java program, you are actually running the Java byte-code interpreter on the compiled version of your program. When you run your program, the system will automatically load in any classes you need and run the byte-code interpreter on those classes as well.

We have been assuming that the Java compiler and related software are already set up for you. We are also assuming that all the files are in one directory. (Directories are also called *folders*.) If you need to set up the Java compiler and system software, consult the manuals that came with the software. If you wish to spread your class definitions across multiple directories, that is not difficult, but we will not concern ourselves with that detail until later.

Syntax and Semantics

The description of a programming language, or any other kind of language, can be thought of as having two parts, called the *syntax* and *semantics* of the language.

The **syntax** tells what arrangement of words and punctuation is legal in the language. The syntax is often called the language's *grammar rules*. For Java, the syntax describes what arrangements of words and punctuation are allowed in a class or program definition.

The **semantics** of a language describes the meaning of things written while following the syntax rules of the language. For a Java program, the syntax describes how you write a program and the semantics describes what happens when you run the program.

When writing a program in Java, you are always using both the syntax and the semantics of the Java language.

TIP: Error Messages

bug

debugging

syntax error

run-time error

logic error

A mistake in a program is called a **bug**. For this reason, the process of eliminating mistakes in your program is called **debugging**. There are three commonly recognized types of bugs or errors, which are known as *syntax errors*, *run-time errors*, and *logic errors*. Let's consider them in order.

A **syntax error** is a grammatical mistake in your program; that is, a mistake in the allowed arrangement of words and punctuations. If you violate one of these rules—for example, by omitting a required punctuation—it is a syntax error. The compiler will catch syntax errors and output an error message telling you that it has found the error, where it thinks the error is, and what it thinks the error is. If the compiler says you have a syntax error, you undoubtedly do. However, the compiler could be incorrect about where and what the error is.

An error that is not detected until your program is run is called a **run-time error**. If the computer detects a run-time error when your program is run, then it will output an error message. The error message may not be easy to understand, but at least it lets you know that something is wrong.

A mistake in the underlying algorithm for your program is called a **logic error**. If your program has only logic errors, it will compile and run without any error message. You have written a valid Java program, but you have not written a program that does what you want. The program runs and gives output, but the output is incorrect. For example, if you were to mistakenly use the multiplication sign in place of the addition sign, it would be a logic error. Logic errors are the hardest kind of error to locate, because the computer does not give you any error messages. ■

Self-Test Exercises

4. What is the purpose of a class loader?

5. What is the purpose of an interpreter?

6. What is byte-code?

7. What is the difference between syntax error and logic error?

8. Suppose you define a class named `NiceClass` in a file. What name should the file have?

9. Suppose you compile the class `NiceClass`. What will be the name of the file with the resulting byte-code?

1.2   Expressions and Assignment Statements

Once a person has understood the way variables are used in programming, he has understood the quintessence of programming.

E. W. DIJKSTRA, *Notes on Structured Programming*

Variables, expressions, and assignments in Java are similar to their counterparts in most other general purpose languages. In this section, we describe the details.

Identifiers

identifier

The name of a variable (or other item you might define in a program) is called an **identifier**. A Java identifier must not start with a digit and all the characters must be letters, digits, or the underscore (_) symbol. (The symbol $ is also allowed, but it is reserved for special purposes only, so you should not typically use $ in your Java identifiers.) For example, the following are all valid identifiers:

```
x x1 x_1 _abc ABC123z7 sum RATE count data2 bigBonus
```

All of the preceding names are legal and would be accepted by the compiler, but the first five are poor choices for identifiers, since they are not descriptive of the identifier's use. None of the following are legal identifiers and all would be rejected by the compiler:

```
12  3X  %change  data-1  myfirst.java  PROG.CLASS
```

The first two are not allowed because they start with a digit. The remaining four are not identifiers because they contain symbols other than letters, digits, and the underscore symbol.

case-sensitive Java is a **case-sensitive** language; that is, it distinguishes between upper- and lowercase letters in the spelling of identifiers. Hence, the following are three distinct identifiers and could be used to name three distinct variables:

```
rate RATE Rate
```

However, it is usually not a good idea to use two such variants in the same program, because that might be confusing. Although it is not required by Java, variables are usually spelled with their first letter in lowercase. The convention that has become universal in Java programming is to spell variable names with a mix of upper- and lowercase letters (and digits), to always start a variable name with a lowercase letter, and to indicate "word" boundaries with an uppercase letter, as illustrated by the following variable names:

```
topSpeed bankRate1 bankRate2 timeOfArrival
```

A Java identifier can theoretically be of any length, and the compiler will accept even unreasonably long identifiers.

Names (Identifiers)

The name of something in a Java program, such as a variable, class, method, or object name, must not start with a digit and may only contain letters, digits (0 through 9), and the underscore character (_). Upper- and lowercase letters are considered to be different characters. (The symbol $ is also allowed, but it is reserved for special purposes only, so you should not typically use $ in a Java name.)

Names in a program are called **identifiers**.

Although it is not required by the Java language, the common practice, and the one followed in this book, is to start the names of classes with uppercase letters and to start the names of variables, objects, and methods with lowercase letters. These names are usually spelled using only letters and digits.

---

keyword There is a special class of identifiers, called **keywords** or **reserved words**, that have a predefined meaning in Java and that you cannot use as names for variables or anything else. In the code displays of this book, keywords are shown in a different color, as illustrated by the keyword `public`. A complete list of keywords is given in Appendix 1.

Some predefined words, such as `System` and `println`, are not keywords. These predefined words are not part of the core Java language and you are allowed to redefine them. Although these words are not keywords, they are defined in libraries required by the Java language standard. Needless to say, using a predefined identifier for anything other than its standard meaning can be confusing and dangerous, and thus should be avoided. The safest and easiest practice is to treat all predefined identifiers as if they are keywords.

Variables

declare

Every variable in a Java program must be declared before it is used. When you **declare** a variable, you are telling the compiler—and, ultimately, the computer—what kind of data you will be storing in the variable. For example, the following are two declarations that might occur in a Java program:

```
int numberOfBeans;
double oneWeight, totalWeight;
```

The first declares the variable `numberOfBeans` so that it can hold a value of type `int`; that is, a whole number. The name `int` is an abbreviation for "integer." The type `int` is the default type for whole numbers. The second definition declares `oneWeight` and `totalWeight` to be variables of type `double`, which is the default type for numbers

floating-point number

with a decimal point (known as **floating-point numbers**). As illustrated here, when there is more than one variable in a declaration, the variables are separated by commas. Also, note that each declaration ends with a semicolon.

Every variable must be declared before it is used. A variable may be declared anyplace, so long as it is declared before it is used. Of course, variables should always be declared in a location that makes the program easier to read. Typically, variables are declared either just before they are used or at the start of a block (indicated by an opening brace {). Any legal identifier, other than a keyword, may be used for a variable name.

Variable Declarations

In Java, a variable must be declared before it is used. Variables are declared as described here.

SYNTAX

Type Variable_1, Variable_2,...;

EXAMPLES

```
int count, numberOfDragons, numberOfTrolls;
char answer;
double speed, distance;
```

Syntactic Variables

Remember that when you see something such as *Type*, *Variable_1*, or *Variable_2*, these words do not literally appear in your Java code. They are **syntactic variables**, which means they are replaced by something of the category that they describe. For example, *Type* can be replaced by `int`, `double`, `char`, or any other type name. *Variable_1* and *Variable_2* can each be replaced by any variable name.

primitive types

Java has basic types for characters, different kinds of integers, and different kinds of floating-point numbers (numbers with a decimal point), as well as a type for the values `true` and `false`. These basic types are known as **primitive types**. Display 1.2 shows all of Java's primitive types. The preferred type for integers is `int`. The type `char` is the type for single characters and can store common Unicode characters. The preferred type for floating-point numbers is `double`. The type `boolean` has the two values `true` and `false`. (Unlike some other programming languages, the Java values `true` and `false` are not integers and will not be automatically converted to integers.) Objects of the predefined class `String` represent strings of characters. `String` is not a primitive type, but is often considered a basic type along with the primitive types. The class `String` is discussed later in this chapter.

Assignment Statements

assignment statement

assignment operator

The most direct way to change the value of a variable is to use an **assignment statement**. In Java, the equal sign is used as the **assignment operator**. An assignment statement always consists of a variable on the left-hand side of the assignment operator (the equal sign) and an expression on the right-hand side. An assignment statement ends with a semicolon. The expression on the right-hand side of the equal sign may be a variable, a number, or a more complicated expression made up of variables, numbers,

Display 1.2   Primitive Types

TYPE NAME	KIND OF VALUE	MEMORY USED	SIZE RANGE
`boolean`	`true` or `false`	1 byte	Not applicable
`char`	Single character (Unicode)	2 bytes	Common Unicode characters
`byte`	Integer	1 byte	−128 to 127
`short`	Integer	2 bytes	−32768 to 32767
`int`	Integer	4 bytes	−2147483648 to 2147483647
`long`	Integer	8 bytes	−9223372036854775808 to 9223372036854775807
`float`	Floating-point number	4 bytes	$\pm 3.40282347 \times 10^{+38}$ to $\pm 1.40239846 \times 10^{-45}$
`double`	Floating-point number	8 bytes	$\pm 1.76769313486231570 \times 10^{+308}$ to $\pm 4.94065645841246544 \times 10^{-324}$

operators, and method invocations. An assignment statement instructs the computer to evaluate (that is, to compute the value of) the expression on the right-hand side of the equal sign and to set the value of the variable on the left-hand side equal to the value of that expression. The following are examples of Java assignment statements:

```
totalWeight = oneWeight * numberOfBeans;
temperature = 98.6;
count = count + 2;
```

The first assignment statement sets the value of `totalWeight` equal to the number in the variable `oneWeight` multiplied by the number in `numberOfBeans`. (Multiplication is expressed using the asterisk * in Java.) The second assignment statement sets the value of `temperature` to `98.6`. The third assignment statement increases the value of the variable `count` by 2.

Note that a variable may occur on both sides of the assignment operator (both sides of the equal sign). The assigned statement

```
count = count + 2;
```

sets the new value of `count` equal to the old value of `count` plus 2.

When used with variables of a class type, the assignment operator requires a bit more explanation, which we will give in Chapter 4.

Assignment Statements with Primitive Types

An assignment statement with a variable of a primitive type on the left-hand side of the equal sign causes the following actions: First, the expression on the right-hand side of the equal sign is evaluated, and then the variable on the left-hand side of the equal sign is set equal to this value.

SYNTAX

Variable = Expression;

EXAMPLE

```
distance = rate * time;
count = count + 2;
```

An assigned statement may be used as an expression that evaluates to a value. When used this way, the variable on the left-hand side of the equal sign is changed as we have described, and the new value of the variable is also the value of the assignment expression. For example,

```
number = 3;
```

both changes the value of `number` to 3 and evaluates to the value 3. This allows you to chain assignment statements. The following changes the values of both the variables, `number1` and `number2`, to 3:

```
number2 = (number1 = 3);
```

The assignment operator automatically is executed right to left if there are no parentheses, so this is normally written in the following equivalent way:

```
number2 = number1 = 3;
```

TIP: Initialize Variables

uninitialized variable

A variable that has been declared but that has not yet been given a value by some means, such as an assignment statement, is said to be **uninitialized**. In some instances, an uninitialized variable may be given some default value, but this is not true in all cases. Moreover, it makes your program clearer to explicitly give the variable a value, even if you are simply reassigning it the default value. (The exact details on default values have been known to change and should not be counted on.)[2]

One easy way to ensure that you do not have an uninitialized variable is to initialize it within the declaration. Simply combine the declaration and an assignment statement, as in the following examples:

```
int count = 0;
double speed = 65.5;
char grade = 'A';
int initialCount = 50, finalCount;
```

Note that you can initialize some variables and not initialize others in a declaration.

Sometimes the compiler may say that you have failed to initialize a variable. In most cases, this will indeed have occurred. Occasionally, the compiler is mistaken. However, the compiler will not compile your program until you convince it that the variable in question is initialized. To make the compiler happy, initialize the variable when it is declared, even if the variable will be given a different value before the variable is used for anything. In such cases, you cannot argue with the compiler. ■

---

[2]The official rules are that the variables we are now using, which we will later call *local variables*, are not automatically initialized. Later in this book, we will introduce variables called *static variables* and *instance variables*, which are automatically initialized. However, we urge you to never rely on automatic initialization.

Initializing a Variable in a Declaration

You can combine the declaration of a variable with an assignment statement that gives the variable a value.

SYNTAX

Type Variable_1 =, Variable_2 = Expression__2, ...;

Some of the variables may have no equal sign and no expression, as in the first example.

EXAMPLE

```
int numberReceived = 0, lastNumber, numberOfStations = 5;
double speed = 98.9, distance = speed * 10;
char initial = 'J';
```

More Assignment Statements ★

There is a shorthand notation that combines the assignment operator (=) and an arithmetic operator so that a given variable can have its value changed by adding, subtracting, multiplying, or dividing by a specified value. The general form is

Variable Op = Expression

which is equivalent to

Variable = Variable Op (Expression)

The *Expression* can be another variable, a constant, or a more complicated arithmetic expression. The *Op* can be any of +, -, *, /, or %, as well as some operators we have not yet discussed—the operator % has also not yet been discussed but is explained later in this chapter. (A full list of values for *Op* can be seen at the bottom of the precedence table in Appendix 2.) Below are examples:

EXAMPLE:	EQUIVALENT TO:
count += 2;	count = count + 2;
total -= discount;	total = total - discount;
bonus *= 2;	bonus = bonus * 2;
time /= rushFactor;	time = time / rushFactor;
change %= 100;	change = change % 100;
amount *= count1 + count2;	amount = amount * (count1 + count2);

MyProgrammingLab

Self-Test Exercises

10. Which of the following may be used as variable names in Java?

    ```
    m, employee#3, _employeeNum, 1stDayOfWeek, Nov2011,
    123Greetings, TaxRate, short
    ```

11. Are the variables `Total` and `total` the same? Why or why not?

12. What is wrong in the following declaration and assignment?

    ```
    int number = "10";
    ```

13. Give the declaration for two variables called `count` and `distance`. `count` is of type `int` and is initialized to zero. `distance` is of type `double` and is initialized to `1.5`.

14. Write a Java assignment statement that will set the value of the variable `speed` to the value of the variable `distance` divided by the variable `time`. All variables are of type `double`.

15. Write a Java assignment statement that will set the value of the variable `Name` to the value of the variables `firstName` and `surname` concatenated. The variables are of type `String`.

16. What is the output produced by the following lines of program code?

    ```
    char a, b;
    a = 'b';
    System.out.println(a);
    b = 'c';
    System.out.println(b);
    a = b;
    System.out.println(a);
    ```

Assignment Compatibility

As a general rule, you cannot store a value of one type in a variable of another type. For example, the compiler will object to the following:

```
int intVariable;
intVariable = 2.99;
```

The problem is a type mismatch. The constant `2.99` is of type `double` and the variable `intVariable` is of type `int`.

assigning int values to double variables

There are some special cases where it is permitted to assign a value of one type to a variable of another type. It is acceptable to assign a value of an integer type, such as `int`, to a variable of a floating-point type, such as the type `double`. For example, the following is both legal and acceptable style:

```
double doubleVariable;
doubleVariable = 2;
```

The preceding will set the value of the variable named `doubleVariable` equal to `2.0`.

Similarly, assignments of integer type variables to floating-point type variables are also allowed. For example, the following is permitted:

```
int intVariable;
intVariable = 42;
double doubleVariable;
doubleVariable = intVariable;
```

More generally, you can assign a value of any type in the following list to a variable of any type that appears further down in the list:

```
byte -> short -> int -> long -> float -> double
```

For example, you can assign a value of type `int` to a variable of type `long`, `float`, or `double` (or of course to a variable of type `int`), but you cannot assign a value of type `int` to a variable of type `byte` or `short`. Note that this is not an arbitrary ordering of the types. As you move down the list from left to right, the range of allowed values for the types becomes larger.

You can assign a value of type `char` to a variable of type `int` or to any of the numeric types that follow `int` in our list of types (but not to those that precede `int`). However, in most cases it is not wise to assign a character to an `int` variable, because the result could be confusing.[3]

If you want to assign a value of type `double` to a variable of type `int`, then you must change the type of the value by using a *type cast*, as explained in the subsection later in this chapter entitled "Type Casting."

integers and booleans In many languages other than Java, you can assign integers to variables of type `boolean` and assign `boolean` values to integer variables. You cannot do that in Java. In Java, the `boolean` values `true` and `false` are not integers nor will they be automatically converted to integers. (In fact, it is not even legal to do an explicit type cast from the type `boolean` to the type `int` or vice versa. Explicit type casts are discussed later in this chapter in the subsection "Type Casting.")

Constants

constants

literals

Constants or **literals** are names for one specific value. For example, `2` and `3.1459` are two constants. We prefer the name *constants* because it contrasts nicely with the word *variables*. Constants do not change value; variables can change their values.

---

[3]Readers who have used certain other languages, such as C or C++, may be surprised to learn that you cannot assign a value of type `char` to a variable of type `byte`. This is because Java uses the Unicode character set rather than the ASCII character set, and so Java reserves two bytes of memory for each value of type `char`, but naturally only reserves one byte of memory for values of type `byte`. This is one of the few cases where you might notice that Java uses the Unicode character set. Indeed, if you convert from an `int` to a `char` or vice versa, you can expect to get the usual correspondence of ASCII numbers and characters. It is also true that you cannot assign a value of type `char` to a variable of type `short`, even though they both use two bytes of memory.

Assignment Compatibilities

You can assign a value of any type on the following list to a variable of any type that appears further down on the list:

```
byte -> short -> int -> long -> float -> double
```

In particular, note that you can assign a value of any integer type to a variable of any floating-point type. You can also assign a value of type char to a variable of type int or of any type that followers int in the above list.

Integer constants are written in the way you are used to writing numbers. Constants of type int (or any other integer type) must not contain a decimal point. Constants of floating-point types (float and double) may be written in either of two forms. The simple form for floating-point constants is like the everyday way of writing decimal fractions. When written in this form, a floating-point constant must contain a decimal point. No number constant (neither integer nor floating point) in Java may contain a comma.

e notation   A more complicated notation for floating-point constants, such as constants of type double, is called **scientific notation** or **floating-point notation** and is particularly handy for writing very large numbers and very small fractions. For instance,

3.67×10^5, which is the same as 367000.0,

is best expressed in Java by the constant 3.67e5. The number

5.89×10^{-4}, which is the same as 0.000589,

is best expressed in Java by the constant 5.89e-4. The e stands for *exponent* and means "multiply by 10 to the power that follows." The e may be either upper- or lowercase.

Think of the number after the e as telling you the direction and number of digits to move the decimal point. For example, to change 3.49e4 to a numeral without an e, move the decimal point 4 places to the right to obtain 34900.0, which is another way of writing the same number. If the number after the e is negative, move the decimal point the indicated number of spaces to the left, inserting extra zeros if need be. So, 3.49e-2 is the same as 0.0349.

The number before the e may contain a decimal point, although that is not required. However, the exponent after the e definitely must *not* contain a decimal point.

Constants of type char are expressed by placing the character in single quotes, as illustrated in what follows:

```
char symbol = 'Z';
```

Note that the left and right single quote symbols are the same symbol.

What Is Doubled?

How did the floating-point type `double` get its name? Is there another type for floating-point numbers called "single" that is half as big? Something like that is true. There is a type that uses half as much storage, namely the type `float`. Many programming languages traditionally used two types for floating-point numbers. One type used less storage and was very imprecise (that is, it did not allow very many significant digits). The second type used *double* the amount of storage and so could be much more precise; it also allowed numbers that were larger (although programmers tend to care more about precision than about size). The kind of numbers that used twice as much storage were called *double precision* numbers; those that used less storage were called *single precision*. Following this tradition, the type that (more or less) corresponds to this double precision type in Java was named `double` in Java. The type that corresponds to single precision in Java was called `float`.

(Actually, the type name `double` was inherited from C++, but this explanation applies to why the type was named `double` in C++, and so ultimately it is the explanation of why the type is called `double` in Java.)

Constants for strings of characters are given in double quotes, as illustrated by the following line taken from Display 1.1:

```
System.out.println("Welcome to Java.");
```

quotes   Be sure to notice that string constants are placed inside of double quotes, while constants of type `char` are placed inside of single quotes. The two kinds of quotes mean different things. In particular, `'A'` and `"A"` mean different things. `'A'` is a value of type `char` and can be stored in a variable of type `char`. `"A"` is a string of characters. The fact that the string happens to contain only one character does *not* make the string `"A"` a value of type `char`. Also notice that, for both strings and characters, the left and right quotes are the same. We will have more to say about strings later in this chapter.

The type `boolean` has two constants, `true` and `false`. These two constants may be assigned to a variable of type `boolean` or used anyplace else an expression of type `boolean` is allowed. They must be spelled with all lowercase letters.

Arithmetic Operators and Expressions

As in most other languages, Java allows you to form expressions using variables, constants, and the arithmetic operators: + (addition), – (subtraction), * (multiplication), / (division), and % (modulo, remainder). These expressions can be used anyplace it is legal to use a value of the type produced by the expression.

mixing types   All of the arithmetic operators can be used with numbers of type `int`, numbers of type `double`, and even with one number of each type. However, the type of the value produced and the exact value of the result depend on the types of the numbers being combined. If both operands (that is, both numbers) are of type int, then the result of combining them with an arithmetic operator is of type int. If one, or both, of the operands is of type double, then the result is of type double. For example, if the variables baseAmount and increase are both of type int, then the number produced by the following expression is of type int:

```
baseAmount + increase
```

However, if one, or both, of the two variables is of type double, then the result is of type double. This is also true if you replace the operator + with any of the operators -, *, /, or %.

More generally, you can combine any of the arithmetic types in expressions. If all the types are integer types, the result will be the integer type. If at least one of the subexpressions is of a floating-point type, the result will be a floating-point type.

Knowing whether the value produced is of an integer type or a floating-point type is typically all that you need to know. However, if you need to know the exact type of the value produced by an arithmetic expression, it can be determined as follows: The type of the value produced is one of the types used in the expression. Of all the types used in the expression, it is, with rare exceptions, the last type (reading left to right) on the following list:

```
byte -> short -> int -> long -> float -> double
```

Here are the rare exceptions: Of all the types used in the expression, if the last type (reading left to right) is byte or short, then the type of the value produced is int. In other words, an expression never evaluates to either of the types byte or short. These exceptions have to do with an implementation detail that need not concern us, especially since we almost never use the types byte and short in this book.

Note that this sequence of types is the same sequence of types we saw when discussing assignment compatibility. As you go from left to right, the types increase in the range of values they allow.[4]

Parentheses and Precedence Rules ★

If you want to specify exactly what subexpressions are combined with each operator, you can fully parenthesize an expression. For example,

```
((base + (rate * hours))/(2 + rate))
```

If you omit some parentheses in an arithmetic expression, Java will, in effect, put in parentheses for you. When adding parentheses, Java follows rules called **precedence rules**

---

[4]Although we discourage the practice, you can use values and variables of type char in arithmetic expressions using operators such as +. If you do so, the char values and variables will contribute to the expression as if they were of type int.

that determine how the operators, such as + and *, are enclosed in parentheses. These precedence rules are similar to rules used in algebra. For example,

```
base + rate * hours
```

is evaluated by Java as if it were parenthesized as follows:

```
base + (rate * hours)
```

So, the multiplication will be done before the addition.

Except in some standard cases, such as a string of additions or a simple multiplication embedded inside an addition, it is usually best to include the parentheses, even if the intended groupings are the ones dictated by the precedence rules. The parentheses make the expression easier to read and less prone to programmer error.

A partial list of precedence rules is given in Display 1.3. A complete set of Java precedence rules is given in Appendix 2. Operators that are listed higher on the list are said to have **higher precedence**. When the computer is deciding which of two adjacent operations to group with parentheses, it groups the operation of higher precedence and its apparent arguments before the operation of lower precedence. Some operators have equal precedence, in which case the order of operations is determined by **associativity rules**. A brief summary of associativity rules is that binary operators of equal precedence are grouped in left-to-right order.[5] Unary operators of equal precedence are grouped in right-to-left order. So, for example,

```
base + rate + hours
```

is interpreted by Java to be the same as

```
(base + rate) + hours
```

And, for example,

```
+-+rate
```

is interpreted by Java to be the same as

```
+(-(+rate))
```

For now you can think of the explicit parentheses put in by the programmer and the implicit parentheses determined by precedence and associativity rules as determining the order in which operations are performed. For example, in

```
base + (rate * hours)
```

the multiplication is performed first and the addition is performed second.

---

[5]There is one exception to this rule. A string of assignment operators, such as n1 = n2 = n3;, is performed right to left, as we noted earlier in this chapter.

Display 1.3   **Precedence Rules**

Highest Precedence

First: the unary operators: `+`, `-`, `++`, `--`, and `!`

Second: the binary arithmetic operators: `*`, `/`, and `%`

Third: the binary arithmetic operators: `+` and `-`

Lowest Precedence

The actual situation is a bit more complicated than what we have described for evaluating expressions, but we will not encounter any of these complications in this chapter. A complete discussion of evaluating expressions using precedence and associativity rules will be given in Chapter 3.

Integer and Floating-Point Division

integer division

When used with one or both operands of type `double`, the division operator, `/`, behaves as you might expect. However, when used with two operands of type `int`, the division operator yields the integer part resulting from division. In other words, integer division discards the part after the decimal point. So, `10/3` is `3` (not `3.3333...`), `5/2` is `2` (not `2.5`), and `11/3` is `3` (not `3.6666...`). Notice that the number *is not rounded*; the part after the decimal point is discarded no matter how large it is.

the % operator

The operator `%` can be used with operands of type `int` to recover the information lost when you use `/` to do division with numbers of type `int`. When used with values of type `int`, the two operators `/` and `%` yield the two numbers produced when you perform the long division algorithm you learned in grade school. For example, `14` divided by `3` is `4` with a remainder of `2`. The `/` operation yields the number of times one number "goes into" another (often called the *quotient*). The `%` operation gives the remainder. For example, the statements

```
System.out.println("14 divided by 3 is " + (14 / 3));
System.out.println("with a remainder of " + (14 % 3));
```

yield the following output:

```
14 divided by 3 is 4
with a remainder of 2
```

The `%` operator can be used to count by 2s, 3s, or any other number. For example, if you want to do something to every other integer, you need to know if the integer is even or odd. Then, you can do it to every even integer (or alternatively every odd integer). An integer n is even if n `%` 2 is equal to 0 and the integer is odd if n `%` 2 is equal to 1. Similarly, to do something to every third integer, your program might step through all integers n but only do the action when n `%` 3 is equal to 0.

PITFALL: Round-Off Errors in Floating-Point Numbers

For all practical purposes, floating-point numbers are only approximate quantities. For example, in formal mathematics, the floating-point number `1.0/3.0` is equal to

```
0.3333333...
```

where the three dots indicate that the 3s go on forever. The computer stores numbers in a format somewhat like this decimal representation, but it has room for only a limited number of digits. If it can store only 10 digits after the decimal, then `1.0/3.0` is stored as

```
0.3333333333
```

with only 10 threes. Thus, `1.0/3.0` is stored as a number that is slightly smaller than one-third. In other words, the value stored as `1.0/3.0` is only approximately equal to one-third.

In reality, the computer stores numbers in binary notation, rather than in base 10 notation, but the principles and the consequences are the same. Some floating-point numbers lose accuracy when they are stored in the computer.

Floating-point numbers (such as numbers of type `double`) and integers (such as numbers of type `int`) are stored differently. Floating-point numbers are, in effect, stored as approximate quantities. Integers are stored as exact quantities. This difference sometimes can be subtle. For example, the numbers `42` and `42.0` are different in Java. The whole number `42` is of type `int` and is an exact quantity. The number `42.0` is of type `double` because it contains a fractional part (even though the fraction is `0`), and so `42.0` is stored with only limited accuracy.

As a result of this limited accuracy, arithmetic done on floating-point numbers only gives approximate results. Moreover, one can easily get results on floating-point numbers that are very far from the true result you would obtain if the numbers could have unlimited accuracy (unlimited number of digits after the decimal point). For example, if a banking program used numbers of type `double` to represent amounts of money and did not do sophisticated manipulations to preserve accuracy, it would quickly bring the bank to ruin since the computed amounts of money would frequently be very incorrect. Dealing with these inaccuracies in floating-point numbers is part of the field of Numerical Analysis, a topic we will not discuss in this book. But, there is an easy way to obtain accuracy when dealing with amounts of money: Use integers instead of floating-point numbers (perhaps one integer for the dollar amount and another integer for the cents amount). ■

Although the `%` operator is primarily used with integers, it can also be used with two floating-point numbers, such as two values of type `double`. However, we will not discuss nor use `%` with floating-point numbers.

PITFALL: Division with Whole Numbers

When you use the division operator / on two integers, the result is an integer. This can be a problem if you expect a fraction. Moreover, the problem can easily go unnoticed, resulting in a program that looks fine but is producing incorrect output without you even being aware of the problem. For example, suppose you are a landscape architect who charges $5,000 per mile to landscape a highway, and suppose you know the length in feet of the highway you are working on. The price you charge can easily be calculated by the following Java statement:

```
totalPrice = 5000 * (feet / 5280.0);
```

This works because there are 5,280 feet in a mile. If the stretch of highway you are landscaping is 15,000 feet long, this formula will tell you that the total price is

```
5000 * (15000 / 5280.0)
```

Your Java program obtains the final value as follows: `15000/5280.0` is computed as `2.84`. Then, the program multiplies `5000` by `2.84` to produce the value `14200.00`. With the aid of your Java program, you know that you should charge $14,200 for the project.

Now suppose the variable `feet` is of type `int`, and you forget to put in the decimal point and the zero, so that the assignment statement in your program reads as follows:

```
totalPrice = 5000 * (feet / 5280);
```

It still looks fine, but will cause serious problems. If you use this second form of the assignment statement, you are dividing two values of type `int`, so the result of the division `feet/5280` is `15000/5280`, which is the `int` value 2 (instead of the value `2.84`, which you think you are getting). So the value assigned to `totalPrice` is `5000*2`, or `10000.00`. If you forget the decimal point, you will charge $10,000. However, as we have already seen, the correct value is $14,200. A missing decimal point has cost you $4,200. Note that this will be true whether the type of `totalPrice` is `int` or `double`; the damage is done before the value is assigned to `totalPrice`. ∎

Self-Test Exercises

17. Convert each of the following mathematical formulas to a Java expression:

$$3x \qquad 3x + y \qquad \frac{x + y}{7} \qquad \frac{3x + y}{z + 2}$$

18. What is the output of the following program lines?

```
double number = (5/7) * 7;
System.out.println("(5/7) * 7 is equal to " + number);
```

Self-Test Exercises (continued)

19. What is the output produced by the following lines of program code?

```
int quotient, remainder;
quotient = 11 / (-4);
remainder = 11 % (-4);
System.out.println("quotient = " + quotient);
System.out.println("remainder = " + remainder);
```

20. What is the output produced by the following code?

```
int stored = 15, sold = 5;
stored -= sold;
System.out.println("Amount Stored " + stored);
```

21. Given the following fragment that purports to convert from degrees Celsius to degrees Fahrenheit, answer the following questions:

```
double celsius = 20;
double fahrenheit;
fahrenheit = (9 / 5) * celsius + 32.0;
```

a. What value is assigned to `fahrenheit`?

b. Explain what is actually happening, and what the programmer likely wanted.

c. Rewrite the code as the programmer intended.

Type Casting

A type cast takes a value of one type and produces a value of another type that is Java's best guess of an equivalent value. We will motivate type casts with a simple division example.

Consider the expression 9/2. In Java, this expression evaluates to 4, because when both operands are of an integer type, Java performs integer division. In some situations, you might want the answer to be the `double` value 4.5. You can get a result of 4.5 by using the "equivalent" floating-point value 2.0 in place of the integer value 2, as in the expression 9/2.0, which evaluates to 4.5. But, what if the 9 and the 2 are the values of variables of type `int` named n and m. Then, n/m yields 4. If you want floating-point division in this case, you must do a type cast from `int` to `double` (or another floating-point type), such as in the following:

```
double ans = n/(double)m;
```

The expression

```
(double)m
```

is a type cast. The expression takes an int (in this example, the value of m) and evaluates to an "equivalent" value of type double. So, if the value of m is 2, the expression (double)m evaluates to the double value 2.0.

Note that (double)m does not change the value of the variable m. If m has the value 2 before this expression is evaluated, then m still has the value 2 after the expression is evaluated.

You may use other type names in place of double to obtain a type cast to another type. We said this produces an "equivalent" value of the target type. The word "equivalent" is in quotes because there is no clear notion of equivalent that applies between any two types. In the case of a type cast from an integer type to a floating-point type, the effect is to add a decimal point and a zero. A type cast in the other direction, from a floating-point type to an integer type, simply deletes the decimal point and all digits after the decimal point. Note that when type casting from a floating-point type to an integer type, the number is truncated, not rounded: (int)2.9 is 2; it is not 3.

As we noted earlier, you can always assign a value of an integer type to a variable of a floating-point type, as in the following:

```
double d = 5;
```

In such cases Java performs an automatic type cast, converting the 5 to 5.0 and placing 5.0 in the variable d. You cannot store the 5 as the value of d without a type cast, but sometimes Java does the type cast for you. Such an automatic type cast is sometimes called a **type coercion**.

type coercion

By contrast, you cannot place a double value in an int variable without an explicit type cast. The following is illegal:

```
int i = 5.5; //Illegal
```

Instead, you must add an explicit type cast, like so:

```
int i = (int)5.5;
```

Increment and Decrement Operators

The **increment operator** ++ adds one to the value of a variable. The **decrement operator** -- subtracts one from the value of a variable. They are usually used with variables of type int, but they can be used with any numeric type. If n is a variable of a numeric type, then n++ increases the value of n by one and n-- decreases the value of n by one. So, n++ and n-- (when followed by a semicolon) are executable statements. For example, the statements

```
int n = 1, m = 7;
n++;
System.out.println("The value of n is changed to " + n);
m--;
System.out.println("The value of m is changed to " + m);
```

yield the following output:

```
The value of n is changed to 2
The value of m is changed to 6
```

An expression such as n++ also evaluates to a number as well as changing the value of the variable n, so n++ can be used in an arithmetic expression such as the following:

```
2*(n++)
```

The expression n++ changes the value of n by adding one to it, but it evaluates to the value n had *before* it was increased. For example, consider the following code:

```
int n = 2;
int valueProduced = 2*(n++);
System.out.println(valueProduced);
System.out.println(n);
```

This code produces the following output:

```
4
3
```

Notice the expression 2*(n++). When Java evaluates this expression, it uses the value that number has *before* it is incremented, not the value that it has after it is incremented. Thus, the value produced by the expression n++ is 2, even though the increment operator changes the value of n to 3. This may seem strange, but sometimes it is just what you want. And, as you are about to see, if you want an expression that behaves differently, you can have it.

The expression ++n also increments the value of the variable n by one, but it evaluates to the value n has after it is increased. For example, consider the following code:

```
int n = 2;
int valueProduced = 2*(++n);
System.out.println(valueProduced);
System.out.println(n);
```

This code is the same as the previous piece of code except that the ++ is before the variable, so this code will produce the following output:

```
6
3
```

v++ versus ++v   Notice that the two increment operators n++ and ++n have the exact same effect on a variable n: They both increase the value of n by one. But the two expressions evaluate to different values. Remember, if the ++ is *before* the variable, then the incrementing is done *before* the value is returned; if the ++ is *after* the variable, then the incrementing is done *after* the value is returned.

decrement operator

Everything we said about the increment operator applies to the decrement operator as well, except that the value of the variable is decreased by one rather than increased by one. For example, consider the following code:

```
int n = 8;
int valueProduced = n--;
System.out.println(valueProduced);
System.out.println(n);
```

This produces the following output:

```
8
7
```

On the other hand, the code

```
int n = 8;
int valueProduced = --n;
System.out.println(valueProduced);
System.out.println(n);
```

produces the following output:

```
7
7
```

Both n-- and --n change the value of n by subtracting one, but they evaluate to different values. n-- evaluates to the value n had before it was decremented; on the other hand, --n evaluates to the value n has after it is decremented.

You cannot apply the increment and decrement operators to anything other than a single variable. Expressions such as (x + y)++, --(x + y), 5++, and so forth are all illegal in Java.

The use of the increment and decrement operators can be confusing when used inside of more complicated expressions, and so, we prefer to not use increment or decrement operators inside of expressions, but to only use them as simple statements, such as the following:

```
n++;
```

Self-Test Exercises

22. What is the output produced by the following lines of program code?

```
int n = (int)3.9;
System.out.println("n == " + n);
```

Self-Test Exercises (continued)

23. What is the output produced by the following lines of program code?

```
int n = 5;
System.out.println(n++);
System.out.println(++n);
System.out.println(n--);
System.out.println(--n);
```

1.3   The Class `String`

Words, words, mere words, no matter from the heart.

WILLIAM SHAKESPEARE, *Troilus and Cressida*

`String`

There is no primitive type for strings in Java. However, there is a class called `String` that can be used to store and process strings of characters. This section introduces the class `String`.

String Constants and Variables

You have already seen constants of type `String`. The quoted string

```
"Hello reader."
```

which appears in the following statement from Display 1.1, is a string constant:

```
System.out.println("Hello reader.");
```

A quoted string is a value of type `String`, although it is normally called an *object* of type `String` rather than a value of type `String`. An object of type `String` is a sequence of characters treated as a single item. A variable of type `String` can name one of these string objects.

For example, the following declares `blessing` to be the name for a `String` variable:

```
String blessing;
```

The following assignment statement sets the value of `blessing` so that `blessing` serves as another name for the `String` object `"Live long and prosper."`:

```
blessing = "Live long and prosper.";
```

The declaration and assignment can be combined into a single statement, as follows:

```
String blessing = "Live long and prosper.";
```

You can write the object named by the `String` variable `blessing` to the screen as follows:

```
System.out.println(blessing);
```

which produces the screen output

```
Live long and prosper.
```

The `String` Class

The class `String` is a predefined class that is automatically made available to you when you are programming in Java. Objects of type `String` are strings of characters that are written within double quotes. For example, the following declares the variable `motto` to be of type `String` and makes `motto` a name for the `String` object `"We aim to please."`.

```
String motto = "We aim to please.";
```

Concatenation of Strings

+ operator

concatenation

When you use the **+ operator** on two strings, the result is the string obtained by connecting the two strings to get a longer string. This is called **concatenation**. So, when it is used with strings, the + is sometimes called the **concatenation operator**. For example, consider the following:

```
String noun = "Strings";
String sentence;
sentence = noun + "are cool.";
System.out.println(sentence);
```

This will set the variable `sentence` to `"Stringsare cool."` and will output the following to the screen:

```
Stringsare cool.
```

Note that no spaces are added when you concatenate two strings. If you want `sentence` set to `"Strings are cool."`, then you should change the assignment statement to add the extra space. For example, the following will add the desired space:

```
sentence = noun + " are cool.";
```

We added a space before the word `"are"`.

You can concatenate any number of `String`s using the + operator. Moreover, you can use the + operator to concatenate a `String` to almost any other type of item. The result is always a `String`. In most situations, Java will convert an item of any type to

> ## Using the + Sign with Strings
>
> If you connect two strings with the + operator, the result is the concatenation (pasting) of the two strings.
>
> **EXAMPLE**
>
> ```
> String name = "Chiana";
> String farewell = "Good bye " + name;
> System.out.println(farewell);
> ```
>
> This sets `farewell` to the string "Good bye Chiana". So, it outputs the following to the screen:
>
> ```
> Good bye Chiana
> ```
>
> Note that we added a space at the end of "Good bye ".

a string when you connect it to a string with the + operator. For numbers, it does the obvious thing. For example,

```
String solution = "The answer is " + 42;
```

will set the `String` variable `solution` to "The answer is 42". Java converts the integer constant 42 to the string "42" and then concatenates the two strings "The answer is " and "42" to obtain the longer string "The answer is 42".

Notice that a number or other value is converted to a string object only when it is connected to a string with a plus sign. If it is connected to another number with a plus sign, it is not converted to a string. For example,

```
System.out.println("100" + 42);
```

outputs

```
10042
```

but

```
System.out.println(100 + 42);
```

outputs

```
142
```

Classes

Classes are central to Java and you will soon be defining and using your own classes. The class `String` gives us an opportunity to introduce some of the notation and

class

object

method

terminology used for classes. A class is the name for a type whose values are objects. Objects are entities that store data and can take actions. For example, objects of the class `String` store data consisting of strings of characters, such as `"Hello"`. The actions that an object can take are called methods. Most of the methods for the class `String` return some value—that is, produce some value. For example, the method `length()` returns the number of characters in a `String` object. So, `"Hello".length()` returns the integer `5`, which can be stored in an `int` variable as follows:

```
int n = "Hello".length();
```

method call or method invocation

calling object

As indicated by the example `"Hello".length()`, a method is called into action by writing a name for the object followed by a dot followed by the method name with parentheses. When you call a method into action, you are (or your code is) said to invoke the method or call the method, and the object before the dot is known as the **calling object**.

Although you can call a method with a constant object, as in `"Hello".length()`, it is more common to use a variable as the calling object, as illustrated by the following:

```
String greeting = "Hello";
int n = greeting.length();
```

argument

Information needed for the method invocation is given in the parentheses. In some cases, such as the method `length`, no information is needed (other than the data in the calling object) and the parentheses are empty. In other cases, which we see soon, there is some information that must be provided inside the parentheses. The information in parentheses is known as an **argument** (or arguments).

sending a message

Invoking a method is also sometimes called **sending a message** to the object. With this view, a message is sent to the object (by invoking a method) and in response the object performs some action. For example, in response to the message

```
greeting.length()
```

the object `greeting` answers with the value `5`.

All objects within a class have the same methods, but each object can have different data. For example, the two `String` objects `"Hello"` and `"Good-Bye"` have different data—that is, different strings of characters. However, they have the same methods. Thus, because we know that the `String` object `"Hello"` has the method `length()`, we know that the `String` object `"Good-Bye"` must also have the method `length()`.

You now have seen two kinds of types in Java: primitive types and class types. The main difference you have seen between these two kinds of types is that classes have methods and primitive types do not. We will later see more differences between classes and primitive types. A smaller difference between primitive types and class types is that all the primitive types are spelled using only lowercase letters but, by convention, class types are spelled with their first letter in uppercase, as in `String`.

Classes, Objects, and Methods

A Java program works by having things called **objects** perform actions. The actions are known as **methods** and typically involve data contained in the object. All objects of the same kind are said to be of the same class. So, a **class** is a category of objects. When the object performs the action of a given method, it is called **invoking** the method (or **calling** the method). Information provided to the method in parentheses is called the **argument** (or arguments).

For example, in Display 1.1, `System.out` is an object, `println` is a method, and the following is an invocation of the method by this object using the argument `"Hello reader."`:

```
System.out.println("Hello reader.");
```

String Methods

The class `String` has a number of useful methods that can be used for string-processing applications. A sample of these `String` methods is presented in Display 1.4. Some of the notation and terminology used in Display 1.4 is described in the box entitled "Returned Value." A more complete list of String methods is given in Appendix 5.

Returned Value

An expression such as `numberOfGirls + numberOfBoys` produces a value. If `numberOfGirls` has the value 2 and `numberOfBoys` has the value 10, then the number produced is 12. The number 12 is the result of evaluating the expression.

Some method invocations are simple kinds of expression, and any such method invocation evaluates to some value. If a method invocation produces a value, we say that the method *returns* the value. For example, suppose your program executes

```
String greeting = "Hello!";
```

After that, if you evaluate `greeting.length()`, the value returned will be 6. So the following code outputs the integer 6:

```
String greeting = "Hello!";
System.out.println(greeting.length());
```

A method can return different values depending on what happens in your program. However, each method can return values of only one type. For example, the method `length` of the class `String` always returns an int value. In Display 1.4, the type given before the method name is the type of the values returned by that method. Since `length` always returns an int value, the entry for `length` begins

```
int length()
```

As with any method, a `String` method is called (invoked) by writing a `String` object, a dot, the name of the method, and finally a pair of parentheses that enclose any arguments to the method. Let's look at some examples.

length

As we've already noted, the method `length` can be used to find out the number of characters in a string. You can use a call to the method `length` anywhere that you can use a value of type `int`. For example, all of the following are legal Java statements:

```
String greeting = "Hello";
int count = greeting.length();
System.out.println("Length is " + greeting.length());
```

Display 1.4   Some Methods in the Class `string`   (part 1 of 4)

`int length()`

Returns the length of the calling object (which is a string) as a value of type `int`.

EXAMPLE

After program executes `String greeting = "Hello!";`
`greeting.length()` returns 6.

`boolean equals(Other_String)`

Returns `true` if the calling object string and the *Other_String* are equal. Otherwise, returns `false`.

EXAMPLE

After program executes `String greeting = "Hello";`
`greeting.equals("Hello")` returns `true`
`greeting.equals("Good-Bye")` returns `false`
`greeting.equals("hello")` returns `false`

Note that case matters. `"Hello"` and `"hello"` are not equal because one starts with an uppercase letter and the other starts with a lowercase letter.

`boolean equalsIgnoreCase(Other_String)`

Returns `true` if the calling object string and the *Other_String* are equal, considering upper- and lowercase versions of a letter to be the same. Otherwise, returns `false`.

EXAMPLE

After program executes `String name = "mary!";`
`greeting.equalsIgnoreCase("Mary!")` returns `true`

Display 1.4   **Some Methods in the Class String** (part 2 of 4)

`String toLowerCase( )`

Returns a string with the same characters as the calling object string, but with all letter characters converted to lowercase.

EXAMPLE

After program executes `String greeting = "Hi Mary!";`
`greeting.toLowerCase()` returns `"hi mary!"`.

`String toUpperCase( )`

Returns a string with the same characters as the calling object string, but with all letter characters converted to uppercase.

EXAMPLE

After program executes `String greeting = "Hi Mary!";`
`greeting.toUpperCase()` returns `"HI MARY!"`.

`String trim( )`

Returns a string with the same characters as the calling object string, but with leading and trailing white space removed. White space characters are the characters that print as white space on paper, such as the blank (space) character, the tab character, and the new-line character `'\n'`.

EXAMPLE

After program executes `String pause = " Hmm ";`
`pause.trim()` returns `"Hmm"`.

`char charAt(`*Position*`)`

Returns the character in the calling object string at the *Position*. Positions are counted 0, 1, 2, etc.

EXAMPLE

After program executes `String greeting = "Hello!";`
`greeting.charAt(0)` returns `'H'`, and
`greeting.charAt(1)` returns `'e'`.

`String substring(`*Start*`)`

Returns the substring of the calling object string starting from *Start* through to the end of the calling object. Positions are counted 0, 1, 2, etc. Be sure to notice that the character at position *Start* is included in the value returned.

EXAMPLE

After program executes `String sample = "AbcdefG";`
`sample.substring(2)` returns `"cdefG"`.

(continued)

Display 1.4   Some Methods in the Class `string`   (part 3 of 4)

`String substring(`*Start, End*`)`

Returns the substring of the calling object string starting from position *Start* through, but not including, position *End* of the calling object. Positions are counted 0, 1, 2, etc. Be sure to notice that the character at position *Start* is included in the value returned, but the character at position *End* is not included.

EXAMPLE

After program executes `String sample = "AbcdefG";`
`sample.substring(2, 5)` returns `"cde"`.

`int indexOf(`*A_String*`)`

Returns the index (position) of the first occurrence of the string *A_String* in the calling object string. Positions are counted 0, 1, 2, etc. Returns –1 if *A_String* is not found.

EXAMPLE

After program executes `String greeting = "Hi Mary!";`
`greeting.indexOf("Mary")` returns 3, and
`greeting.indexOf("Sally")` returns –1.

`int indexOf(`*A_String, Start*`)`

Returns the index (position) of the first occurrence of the string *A_String* in the calling object string that occurs at or after position *Start.* Positions are counted 0, 1, 2, etc. Returns –1 if *A_String* is not found.

EXAMPLE

After program executes `String name = "Mary, Mary quite contrary";`
`name.indexOf("Mary", 1)` returns 6.
The same value is returned if 1 is replaced by any number up to and including 6.
`name.indexOf("Mary", 0)` returns 0.
`name.indexOf("Mary", 8)` returns –1.

`int lastIndexOf(`*A_String*`)`

Returns the index (position) of the last occurrence of the string *A_String* in the calling object string. Positions are counted 0, 1, 2, etc. Returns –1, if *A_String* is not found.

EXAMPLE

After program executes `String name = "Mary, Mary, Mary quite so";`
`greeting.indexOf("Mary")` returns 0, and
`name.lastIndexOf("Mary")` returns 12.

Display 1.4   Some Methods in the Class **string** (part 4 of 4)

---

int compareTo(*A_String*)

Compares the calling object string and the string argument to see which comes first in the lexicographic ordering. Lexicographic order is the same as alphabetical order but with the characters ordered as in Appendix 3. Note that in Appendix 3, all the uppercase letters are in regular alphabetical order and all the lowercase letters are in alphabetical order, but all the uppercase letters precede all the lowercase letters. So, lexicographic ordering is the same as alphabetical ordering provided both strings are either all uppercase letters or both strings are all lowercase letters. If the calling string is first, it returns a negative value. If the two strings are equal, it returns zero. If the argument is first, it returns a positive number.

EXAMPLE

After program executes String entry = "adventure";
entry.compareTo("zoo") returns a negative number,
entry.compareTo("adventure") returns 0, and
entry.compareTo("above") returns a positive number.

---

int compareToIgnoreCase(*A_String*)

Compares the calling object string and the string argument to see which comes first in the lexicographic ordering, treating upper- and lowercase letters as being the same. (To be precise, all uppercase letters are treated as if they were their lowercase versions in doing the comparison.) Thus, if both strings consist entirely of letters, the comparison is for ordinary alphabetical order. If the calling string is first, it returns a negative value. If the two strings are equal ignoring case, it returns zero. If the argument is first, it returns a positive number.

EXAMPLE

After program executes String entry = "adventure";
entry.compareToIgnoreCase("Zoo") returns a negative number,
entry.compareToIgnoreCase("Adventure") returns 0, and
"Zoo".compareToIgnoreCase(entry) returns a positive number.

---

position

Some methods for the class String depend on counting **positions** in the string. Positions are counted starting with 0, not with 1. So, in the string "Surf time", 'S' is in position 0, 'u' is in position 1, and so forth. A position is usually referred to as an **index**. So, it would be preferable to say: 'S' is at index 0, 'u' is at index 1, and so on.

index

The method indexOf can be used to find the index of a substring of the calling objects. For example, consider

```
String phrase = "Java is fun.";
```

After this declaration, the invocation phrase.indexOf("is") will return 5 because the 'i' of "is" is at index 5. (Remember, the first index is 0, not 1.) This is illustrated in Display 1.5.

Display 1.5 String Indexes

The 12 characters in the string "Java is fun." have indexes 0 through 11.

*Notice that the blanks and the period
count as characters in the string.*

Escape Sequences

**backslash **

**escape
sequence**

A backslash, \\, preceding a character tells the compiler that the character following the \\ does not have its usual meaning. Such a sequence is called an **escape sequence** or an **escape character**. The sequence is typed in as two characters with no space between the symbols. Several escape sequences are defined in Java.

If you want to put a backslash, \\, or a quote symbol, ", into a string constant, you must escape the ability of the " to terminate a string constant by using \\", or the ability of the \\ to escape, by using \\\\. The \\\\ tells the compiler you mean a real backslash, \\, not an escape sequence, and \\" means a quote character, not the end of a string constant. A list of escape sequences is given in Display 1.6.

It is important to note that each escape sequence is a single character, even though it is spelled with two symbols. So, the string "Say \\"Hi\\"!" contains 9 characters ('S', 'a', 'y', the blank character, '\\"', 'H', 'i', '\\"', and '!'), not 11 characters.

Including a backslash in a quoted string is a little tricky. For example, the string "abc\\def" is likely to produce the error message "Invalid escape character." To include a backslash in a string, you need to use two backslashes. The string "abc\\\\ def", if output to the screen, would produce

```
abc\def
```

Display 1.6 Escape Sequences

```
\" Double quote.
\' Single quote.
\\ Backslash.
\n New line. Go to the beginning of the next line.
\r Carriage return. Go to the beginning of the current line.
\t Tab. White space up to the next tab stop.
```

The escape sequence \n indicates the start of a new line. For example, the statement

```
System.out.println("To be or\nNot to be.");
```

will write the following to the screen:

```
To be or
Not to be.
```

You do not need to use the escape sequence \' to include a single quote inside a quoted string. For example, "Time's up!" is a valid quoted string. However, you do need \' if you want to indicate the constant for the single-quote character, as in

```
char singleQuote = '\'';
```

String Processing

immutable object

In Java, an object of type string is an **immutable object**, meaning that the characters in the string object cannot be changed. This will eventually prove to be important to us, but at this stage of our exploration of Java, it is a misleading statement. To see that an object of type string cannot be changed, note that none of the methods in Display 1.4 changes the value of the string calling object. There are more string methods than those shown in Display 1.4, but none of them lets you write statements that say things such as "Change the fifth character in the calling object string to 'x'." This was done intentionally to make the implementation of the string class more efficient and for other reasons that we will discuss later in this book. There is another string class, called StringBuffer, that has methods for altering its string object. We will not discuss the class StringBuffer in this text, but a table explaining many of the methods of the class StringBuffer is included in Appendix 5.

Although there is no method that allows you to change the value of a string object, such as "Hello", you can still write programs that change the value of a string variable, which is probably all you want anyway. To perform the change, simply use an assignment statement, as in the following example:

```
String name = "Soprano";
name = "Anthony " + name;
```

The assignment statement in the second line changes the value of the name variable so that the string it names changes from "Soprano" to "Anthony Soprano". Display 1.7 contains a demonstration of some simple string processing.

The Unicode Character Set ★

ASCII

Until recently, most programming languages used the ASCII character set, which is given in Appendix 3. The **ASCII** character set is simply a list of all the characters normally used on an English-language keyboard plus a few special characters. In this list, each character has been assigned a number so that characters can be stored by storing the corresponding number. Java (and now many other programming languages) uses the Unicode character set. The **Unicode** character set includes the

Unicode

Display 1.7 Using the `string` Class

```
1   public class StringProcessingDemo
2   {
3       public static void main(String[] args)
4       {
5           String sentence = "I hate text processing!";
6           int position = sentence.indexOf("hate");
7           String ending =
8                   sentence.substring(position + "hate".length());
9
10          System.out.println("012345678901234456789012");
11          System.out.println(sentence);
12          System.out.println("The word \"hate\" starts at index "
13                                                  + position);
14          sentence = sentence.substring(0, position) + "adore"
15                                                  + ending;
16          System.out.println("The changed string is:");
17          System.out.println(sentence);
18      }
19  }
```

You could just use 4 *here, but if you had a* String *variable instead of* "hate"*, you would have to use* length *as shown.*

Sample Dialogue

```
012345678901234456789012
I hate text processing!
The word "hate" starts at index 2
The changed string is:
I adore text processing!
```

ASCII character set plus many of the characters used in languages with a different alphabet from English. This is not likely to be a big issue if you are using an English-language keyboard. Normally, you can just program as if Java were using the ASCII character set. The ASCII character set is a subset of the Unicode character set, and the subset you are likely to use. Thus, Appendix 3, which lists the ASCII character set, in fact lists the subset of the Unicode character set that we will use in this book. The advantage of the Unicode character set is that it makes it possible to easily handle languages other than English. For example, it is legal to spell a Java identifier using the letters of the Greek alphabet (although you may want a Greek-language keyboard and monitor to do this). The disadvantage of the Unicode character set is that it sometimes requires more computer memory to store each character than it would if Java used only the ASCII character set.

MyProgrammingLab™   **Self-Test Exercises**

24. What is the output produced by the following?

    ```
    String verbPhrase = "love";
    System.out.println("I " + verbPhrase + " cappuccino");
    ```

25. What is the output produced by the following?

    ```
    String text1 = "Have a Great Day", text2 = " Ahead";
    System.out.println(text1.substring(7) + text2);
    ```

26. What is the output produced by the following?

    ```
    String test = "Mississippi";
    System.out.println(test.length());
    System.out.println(test.charAt(1));
    ```

27. What is the output produced by the following?

    ```
    System.out.println("Beware! This \\n might be tricky.");
    ```

28. What is the output produced by the following?

    ```
    System.out.println("there's no trick.");
    ```

29. What is the output produced by the following?

    ```
    String phrase = "Common sense is not so common";
    phrase = phrase.substring(7).toUpperCase();
    System.out.println(phrase);
    ```

30. What is the output of the following two lines of Java code?

    ```
    System.out.println("2 + 2 = " + (2 + 2));
    System.out.println("2 + 2 = " + 2 + 2);
    ```

31. Suppose jimmy is an object of a class named Employee and suppose calculateBonus is a method for the class Employee that takes one argument that is an integer. How do you write an invocation of the method calculateBonus using jimmy as the calling object and using the argument 15? The method calculateBonus will calculate the bonus earned by Jimmy by working for 15 extra hours in the last month.

32. The following code is supposed to output the string in lowercase letters but it has an error. What is wrong?

    ```
    String test = "WHY ARE YOU SHOUTING?";
    test.toLowerCase();
    System.out.println(test);
    ```

1.4 Program Style

In matters of grave importance,
style, not sincerity, is the vital thing.

OSCAR WILDE, *The Importance of Being Earnest*

Java programming style is similar to that used in other languages. The goal is to make your code easy to read and easy to modify. This section gives some basic points on good programming style in general and some information on the conventions normally followed by Java programmers.

Naming Constants

There are two problems with numbers in a computer program. The first is that they carry no mnemonic value. For example, when the number 10 is encountered in a program, it gives no hint of its significance. If the program is a banking program, it might be the number of branch offices or the number of teller windows at the main office. To understand the program, you need to know the significance of each constant. The second problem is that when a program needs to have some numbers changed, the changing tends to introduce errors. Suppose that 10 occurs 12 times in a banking program. Four of the times it represents the number of branch offices, and eight of the times it represents the number of teller windows at the main office. When the bank opens a new branch and the program needs to be updated, there is a good chance that some of the 10s that should be changed to 11 will not be, or some that should not be changed will be. The way to avoid these problems is to name each number and use the name instead of the number within your program. For example, a banking program might have two constants with the names BRANCH_COUNT and WINDOW_COUNT. Both of these numbers might have a value of 10, but when the bank opens a new branch, all you need to do to update the program is to change the definition of BRANCH_COUNT.

One way to name a number is to initialize a variable to that number value, as in the following example:

```
int BRANCH_COUNT = 10;
int WINDOW_COUNT = 10;
```

There is, however, one problem with this method of naming number constants: You might inadvertently change the value of one of these variables. Java provides a way of marking an initialized variable so that it cannot be changed. The syntax is

```
public static final Type Variable = Constant;
```

For example, the names BRANCH_COUNT and WINDOW_COUNT can be given values that cannot be changed by your code as follows:

```
public static final int BRANCH_COUNT = 10;
public static final int WINDOW_COUNT = 10;
```

Constants defined this way must be placed outside of the main method and, when we start having more methods, outside of any other methods. This is illustrated in Display 1.8. When we start writing programs and classes with multiple methods, you will see that the defined constants can be used in all the methods of a class. However, if a constant is only going to be used inside a single method, then it can be defined inside the method without the keyword public.

Display 1.8   Comments and a Named Constant

```
1    /**
2     Program to show interest on a sample account balance.
3     Author: Jane Q. Programmer.
4     E-mail Address: janeq@somemachine.etc.etc.
5     Last Changed: September 21, 2004.
6    */
7    public class ShowInterest
8    {
9        public static final double INTEREST_RATE = 2.5;
10
11       public static void main(String[] args)
12       {
13           double balance = 100;
14           double interest; //as a percent
15
16           interest = balance * (INTEREST_RATE / 100.0);
17           System.out.println("On a balance of $" + balance);
18           System.out.println("you will earn interest of $"
19                                                 + interest);
20           System.out.println("All in just one short year.");
21       }
22
23   }
```

21   } *Although it would not be as clear,*
22 ←——————————————— *it is legal to place the definition of*
23   }   INTEREST_RATE *here instead.*

Sample Dialogue

```
On a balance of $100.0
you will earn interest of $2.5
All in just one short year.
```

We will fully explain the modifiers `public static final` later in this book, but we can now explain most of what they mean. The part

```
int BRANCH_COUNT = 10;
```

simply declares `BRANCH_COUNT` as a variable and initializes it to `10`. The words that precede this modify the variable `BRANCH_COUNT` in various ways. The word `public` says there are no restrictions on where you can use the name `BRANCH_COUNT`. The word static will have to wait until Chapter 5 for an explanation, but be sure to include it. The word `final` means that the value `10` is the *final* value assignment to `BRANCH_COUNT`, or, to phrase it another way, that the program is not allowed to change the value of `BRANCH_COUNT`.

Naming Constants

The syntax for defining a name for a constant outside of a method, such as a name for a number, is as follows:

SYNTAX

```
public static final Type Variable = Constant;
```

EXAMPLE

```
public static final int MAX_SPEED = 65;
public static final double MIN_SIZE = 0.5;
public static final String GREETING = "Hello friend!";
public static final char GOAL = 'A';
```

Although it is not required, it is the normal practice of programmers to spell named constants using all uppercase letters with the underscore symbol used to separate "words."

Java Spelling Conventions

In Java, as in all programming languages, identifiers for variables, methods, and other items should always be meaningful names that are suggestive of the identifiers' meanings. Although it is not required by the Java language, the common practice of Java programmers is to start the names of classes with uppercase letters and to start the names of variables, objects, and methods with lowercase letters. Defined constants are normally spelled with all uppercase letters and underscore symbols for "punctuation," as we did in the previous subsection, "Naming Constants."

For example, `String`, `FirstProgram`, and `JOptionPane` are classes, although we have not yet discussed the last one. The identifiers `println`, `balance`, and `readLine` should each be either a variable, an object, or a method.

Since blanks are not allowed in Java identifiers, "word" boundaries are indicated by an uppercase letter, as in `numberOfPods`. Since defined constants are spelled with all uppercase letters, the underscore symbol is used for "word" boundaries, as in `MAX_SPEED`.

The identifier `System.out` seems to violate this convention, since it names an object but yet begins with an uppercase letter. It does not violate the convention, but the explanation hinges on a topic we have not yet covered. `System` is the name of a class. Within the class named `System`, there is a definition of an object named `out`. So, the identifier `System.out` is used to indicate the object `out` (starting with a lowercase letter for an object) that is defined in the class `System` (starting with an uppercase letter for a class). This sort of dot notation will be explained later in the book.

There is one Java convention that people new to Java often find strange. Java programmers normally do not use abbreviations in identifiers, but rather spell things out in full. A Java programmer would not use `numStars`. He or she would use `numberOfStars`. A Java programmer would not use `FirstProg`. He or she would use `FirstProgram`. This can produce long identifiers and sometimes exceedingly long identifiers. For example, the names of two standard Java classes are `BufferedReader` and `ArrayIndexOutOfBoundsException`. The first will be used in the next chapter and the second will be used later in this book. These long names cause you to do more typing and program lines quickly become too long. However, there is a very good reason for using these long names: There is seldom any confusion on how the identifiers are spelled. With abbreviations, you often cannot recall how the identifier was abbreviated. Was it `BufReader` or `BuffReader` or `BufferedR` or `BR` or something else? Because all the words are spelled out, you know it must be `BufferedReader`. Once they get used to using these long names, most programmers learn to prefer them.

Comments

//comments

There are two ways to insert **comments** in a Java program. In Java, the symbols `//` are used to indicate the start of a comment. All of the text between the `//` and the end of the line is a comment. The compiler simply ignores anything that follows `//` on a line. If you want a comment that covers more than one line, place a `//` on each line of the comment. The symbols `//` are two slashes (without a space between them). Comments indicated with `//` are often called **line comments**.

line
comments

/*comments*/

There is another way to insert comments in a Java program. Anything between the symbol pair `/*` and the symbol pair `*/` is considered a comment and is ignored by the compiler. Unlike the `//` comments, which require an additional `//` on each line, the `/*` to `*/` comments can span several lines like so:

```
/*This is a multi-line comment.
Note that there is no comment symbol
of any kind on the second line.*/
```

block
comments

Comments of the `/* */` type are often called **block comments**. These block comments may be inserted anywhere in a program that a space or line break is allowed. However, they should not be inserted anywhere except where they do not distract from the layout of the program. Usually comments are only placed at the ends of lines or on separate lines by themselves.

Java comes with a program called `javadoc` that will automatically extract documentation from the classes you define. The workings of the `javadoc` program dictate when you normally use each kind of comment.

The `javadoc` program will extract a `/* */` comment in certain situations, but it will not extract a `//` comment. We will say more about `javadoc` and comments after we discuss defining classes. In the meantime, you may notice the following conventions in our code:

We use line comments (that is, the // kind) for comments meant only for the code writer or for a programmer who modifies the code and not for any other programmer who merely uses the code.

For comments that would become part of the documentation for users of our code, we use block comments (that is, the /* */ kind). The javadoc program allows you to indicate whether or not a block comment is eligible to be extracted for documentation. If the opening /* has an extra asterisk, as in /**, then the comment is eligible to be extracted. If there is only one asterisk, javadoc will not extract the comment. For this reason, our block comments invariably open with /**.

when to comment

It is difficult to say just how many comments a program should contain. The only correct answer is "just enough," which of course conveys little to the novice programmer. It will take some experience to get a feel for when it is best to include a comment. Whenever something is important and not obvious, it merits a comment. However, providing too many comments is as bad as providing too few. A program that has a comment on each line is so buried in comments that the structure of the program is hidden in a sea of obvious observations. Comments such as the following contribute nothing to understanding and should not appear in a program:

```
interest = balance * rate; //Computes the interest.
```

self-documenting

A well-written program is called **self-documenting**, which means that the structure of the program is clear from the choice of identifier names and the indenting pattern. A completely self-documenting program would need none of these // comments that are only for the programmer who reads or modifies the code. That may be an ideal that is not always realizable, but if your code is full of // comments and you follow our convention on when to use them, then either you simply have too many comments or your code is poorly designed.

A very simple example of the two kinds of comments is given in Display 1.8.

Indenting

We will say more about indenting as we introduce more Java. However, the general rule is easy to understand and follow. When one structure is nested inside another structure, the inside structure is indented one more level. For example, in our programs, the main method is indented one level, and the statements inside the main method are indented two levels. We prefer to use four spaces for each level of indenting because more than four spaces eats up too much line length. It is possible to get by with indenting only two or three spaces for each level so long as you are consistent. One space for a level of indenting is not enough to be clearly visible.

Self-Test Exercises

33. What is the purpose of the program `javadoc`?

34. What is the output produced by the following Java code?

```java
double income = 10000.0, tax = 0.0, rate;
rate = 5.0;    // income tax rate
tax = income * rate / 100.0;    // amount of tax to be paid
// income -= tax;
System.out.println("Net Income: " + income);
```

35. What is the normal spelling convention for named constants?

36. Write a line of Java code that will give the name TOTAL_MARKS to the int value 100. In other words, make TOTAL_MARKS a named constant for 100.

Chapter Summary

- Compiling a Java class or program produces *byte-code*, which is the machine language for a fictitious computer. When you run the byte-code, a program called an *interpreter* translates and executes the byte-code instructions on your computer one instruction at a time.

- A variable can be used to hold values, such as numbers. The type of the variable must match the type of the value stored in the variable. All variables must be declared before they are used.

- The equal sign, =, is used as the *assignment operator* in Java. An *assignment statement* is an instruction to change the value of a variable.

- Each variable should be initialized before the program uses its value.

- Parentheses in arithmetic expressions indicate which arguments are given to an operator. When parentheses are omitted, Java adds implicit parentheses using *precedence rules* and *associativity rules*.

- You can have variables and constants of type String. String is a class type, not a *primitive type*.

- You can use the plus sign to concatenate two strings.

- There are methods in the class String that can be used for string processing.

- Variables (and all other items in a program) should be given names that indicate how they are used.

- You should define names for number constants in a program and use these names rather than writing out the numbers within your program.

- Programs should be self-documenting to the extent possible. However, you should also insert comments to explain any unclear points.

Answers to Self-Test Exercises

1. `I am a Java fan.`

2. ```
   System.out.println("I like Java.");
   System.out.println("You like tea.");
   ```

3. ```
   public class ProgrammingIsFun
   {
       public static void main(String[] args)
       {
          System.out.println("Programming is great fun!");
       }
   }
   ```

4. A Java program is divided into smaller parts called *classes*, and normally each class definition is in a separate file and is compiled separately. A class loader is a program that connects the byte-codes for various classes in a program. It is equivalent to linker in other programming languages.

5. An *interpreter* is a program that runs Java byte-code instructions. It is also often called the *Java Virtual Machine*.

6. *Byte-code* is the machine language for the Java Virtual Machine. Java compiler translates the Java program to byte-code.

7. A *syntax error* is a grammatical mistake. It is detected by the compiler. A *logic error* is a mistake in the underlying algorithm in the program that is not detected by the compiler.

8. `NiceClass.java`

9. `NiceClass.class`

10. `m, _employeeNum, Nov2011, TaxRate`

11. No. Java is case-sensitive, so the variables `Total` and `total` are different in Java and could be used in a single program, though that would not be a good programming style.

12. The variable `number` is declared as an integer but assigned a value that is a `String` literal.

13. ```
    int count = 0;
    double distance = 1.5;
    ```

14. `speed = distance / time;`

15. `Name = firstName + surname;`

16. `b`
    `c`
    `c`
    ```

17. `3*x`
    `3*x + y`
    `(x + y)/7` Note that `x + y/7` is not correct.
    `(3*x + y)/(z + 2)`

18. `(5/7) * 7 is equal to 0.0`

    Since `5` and `7` are of type `int`, the `/` operator performs integer division, which discards the remainder, so the value of `5/7` is `0`, not `0.7143 . . . .` This makes the value of the entire expression `0 * 7`, which of course is `0`.

19. `quotient = -2`
    `remainder = 3`

20. `Amount Stored 10`

21. a. `52.0`

    b. `9/5` has `int` value `1`; because the numerator and denominator are both of type `int`, integer division is done; the fractional part is discarded. The programmer probably wanted floating-point division, which does not discard the part after the decimal point.

    c. `fahrenheit = (9.0/5) * celsius + 32.0;`
        or
        `fahrenheit = 1.8 * celsius + 32.0;`

22. `n = = 3`

23. `5`
    `7`
    `7`
    `5`

24. `I love cappuccino`

25. `Great Day Ahead`

26. `11`
    `i`

27. `Beware! This \n might be tricky.`

28. `there's no trick.`

29. `SENSE IS NOT SO COMMON`

30. The output is

    `2 + 2 = 4`
    `2 + 2 = 22`

    In the expression `"2 + 2 = " + (2 + 2)`, the integers `2` and `2` in `(2 + 2)` are added to obtain the integer `4`. When `4` is connected to the string `"2 + 2"` with a plus sign, the integer `4` is converted to the string `"4"` and the result is the string `"2 + 2 = 4"`. However `"2 + 2 = " + 2 + 2` is interpreted by Java to mean

    `("2 + 2 = " + 2) + 2`

The first integer 2 is changed to the string "2" because it is being combined with the string "2 + 2". The result is the string "2 + 2 = 2". The last integer 2 is combined with the string "2 + 2 = 2". So, the last 2 is converted to the string "2". So the final result is

```
"2 + 2 = 2" + "2"
```

which is "2 + 2 = 22".

31. `jimmy.calculateBonus(15);`

32. The method `toLowerCase` doesn't change the string `test`. To change it, we must set test equal to the string returned by `toLowerCase`:

```
test = test.toLowerCase();
```

33. The program `javadoc` comes with java and it is used for automatically extracting documentation from the classes in a file. If a block comment starts with an extra asterisk like `/**`, then the comment is eligible to be extracted. It extracts a `/* */` comment in certain situations, but does not extract a `//` comment.

34. `Net Income: 10000.0`

35. The normal spelling convention is to spell named constants using all uppercase letters with the underscore symbol used to separate words.

36. `public static final int TOTAL_MARKS = 100;`

MyProgrammingLab™   **Programming Projects**

Visit www.myprogramminglab.com to complete select exercises online and get instant feedback.

1. You want to put a fencing surrounding your garden. The various parameters you need to know for calculating the cost are:
   - Length of your garden: 40ft.
   - Width of your garden: 30ft.
   - Cost of fencing per foot: $1.75 per ft.

   Write a program that calculates the total cost of fencing your garden. The program should display all the parameters mentioned above and the total cost of fencing. For example, if length = 40 ft, width = 30 ft, and cost = $1.75 per foot, then it should display total cost as $245.0. Declare all the variables of type `double`.

2. Your math teacher loves to ask tricky questions and he wants fast answers. One day, he asks the class, "How many times can you subtract 23 from 917320550, and what will be the final remainder?" He mentions that you can't use a calculator, but he doesn't say that you can't use your computer. Impress him by writing a program to solve this problem and display the outcome.

3. Write a program that starts with the string variable `first` set to your first name and the string variable `last` set to your last name. Both names should be all lower-case. Your program should then create a new string that contains your full name in pig latin with the first letter capitalized for the first and last name. Use only the pig latin rule of moving the first letter to the end of the word and adding "ay." Output the pig latin name to the screen. Use the `substring` and `toUpperCase` methods to construct the new name.

   For example, given

   ```
   first = "walt";
   last = "savitch";
   ```

   the program should create a new string with the text "Altway Avitchsay" and print it.

4. A government research lab has concluded that an artificial sweetener commonly used in diet soda pop will cause death in laboratory mice. A friend of yours is desperate to lose weight but cannot give up soda pop. Your friend wants to know how much diet soda pop it is possible to drink without dying as a result. Write a program to supply the answer. The program has no input but does have defined constants for the following items: the amount of artificial sweetener needed to kill a mouse, the weight of the mouse, the starting weight of the dieter, and the desired weight of the dieter. To ensure the safety of your friend, be sure the program uses the weight at which the dieter will stop dieting, rather than the dieter's current weight, to calculate how much soda pop the dieter can safely drink. You may use any reasonable values for these defined constants. Assume that diet soda contains 1/10th of 1% artificial sweetener. Use another named constant for this fraction. You may want to express the percent as the `double` value `0.001`. (If your program turns out not to use a defined constant, you may remove that defined constant from your program.)

5. Write a program that starts with a line of text and then outputs that line of text with the first occurrence of `"hate"` changed to `"love"`. For example, a possible sample output might be

   ```
   The line of text to be changed is:
   I hate you.
   I have rephrased that line to read:
   I love you.
   ```

   You can assume that the word `"hate"` occurs in the input. If the word `"hate"` occurs more than once in the line, your program will replace only the first occurrence of `"hate"`. Since we will not discuss input until Chapter 2, use a defined constant for the string to be changed. To make your program work for another string, you should only need to change the definition of this defined constant.

6. Bicyclists can calculate their speed if the gear size and cadence is known. *Gear size* refers to the effective diameter of the wheel. Gear size multiplied by pi (3.14) gives the distance travelled with one turn of the pedals. *Cadence* refers to the number of pedal revolutions per minute (rpm). The speed in miles per hour is calculated by the following:

$$\text{Speed (mph)} =$$
$$\text{Gear Size (inches)} \times \pi \times \frac{1\,(\text{ft})}{12\,(\text{inches})} \times \frac{1\,(\text{mile})}{5280\,(\text{ft})} \times \text{Cadence (rpm)} \times \frac{60\,(\text{minutes})}{(\text{hour})}$$

This is a program that calculates the speed for a gear size of 100 inches and a cadence of 90 rpm. This would be considered a high cadence and a maximum gear size for a typical bicycle. In writing your program, don't forget that the expression 1/12 will result in 0, because both 1 and 12 are integers, and when the integer division is performed, the fractional part is discarded.

VideoNote
Solution to
Programming
Project 1.7

7. Write a program that outputs the number of hours, minutes, and seconds that corresponds to 50,391 total seconds. The output should be 13 hours, 59 minutes, and 51 seconds. Test your program with a different number of total seconds to ensure that it works for other cases.

8. The following program will compile and run, but it uses poor programming style. Modify the program so that it uses the spelling conventions, constant naming conventions, and formatting style recommended in this book.

```java
public class messy {
public static void main(String[] args)
{
double TIME; double PACE;
System.out.println("This program calculates your pace given a time
and distance traveled.");
TIME = 35.5; /* 35 minutes and 30 seconds */
PACE = TIME / distance;
System.out.println("Your pace is " + PACE + " miles per hour.");
}
public static final double distance = 6.21;
}
```

9. The world population is the total number of living humans on the planet. The United Nations estimated that the world population now exceeds 7 billion. Assuming the current population growth rate is 1.14%, write a program that displays the world population ten years from now. Assume the present world population is 7 billion and that after five years, the population growth rate would reduce by 1.1%. Based on these assumptions calculate the world population in the years 2016 and 2021, and the increase in population in these years.

Console Input and Output 2

2.1 SCREEN OUTPUT 90

System.out.println 90

Formatting Output with printf 93

Money Formats Using NumberFormat ★ 99

Importing Packages and Classes 102

The DecimalFormat Class ★ 104

2.2 CONSOLE INPUT USING THE Scanner CLASS 108

The Scanner Class 108

The Empty String 116

Example: Self-Service Checkout 118

Other Input Delimiters 119

2.3 INTRODUCTION TO FILE INPUT 121

The Scanner Class for Text File Input 121

Chapter Summary 124   Answers to Self-Test Exercises 124   Programming Projects 127

Don't imagine you know what a computer terminal is. A computer terminal is not some clunky old television with a typewriter in front of it. It is an interface where the mind and the body can connect with the universe and move bits of it about.

DOUGLAS ADAMS, *Mostly Harmless*
(the fifth volume in The Hitchhiker's Trilogy*)*

Introduction

console I/O

This chapter covers simple output to the screen and input from the keyboard, often called **console I/O**. We have already used console output, but this chapter covers it in more detail. In particular, this chapter shows you how to format numerical output so that you control such detail as the number of digits shown after the decimal point. This chapter also covers the Scanner class, which was introduced in version 5.0 of Java and can be used for console input.

Prerequisites

This chapter uses material from Chapter 1.

2.1   Screen Output

Let me tell the world.

WILLIAM SHAKESPEARE, *Henry IV*

In this section, we review System.out.println and present some material on formatting numeric output. As part of that material, we give a brief introduction to *packages* and *import statements*. Packages are Java libraries of classes. Import statements make classes from a package available to your program.

System.out.println

System.out
println

We have already been using System.out.println for screen output. In Display 1.7, we used statements such as the following to send output to the display screen:

```
System.out.println("The changed string is:");
System.out.println(sentence);
```

System.out is an object that is part of the Java language, and println is a method invoked by that object. It may seem strange to spell an object name with a dot in it, but that need not concern us for now.

When you use `System.out.println` for output, the data to be output is given as an argument in parentheses, and the statement ends with a semicolon. Things you can output are strings of text in double quotes, such as `"The changed string is:"`; `String` variables such as `sentence`; variables of other types such as variables of type `int`; numbers such as 5 or 7.3; and almost any other object or value. If you want to output more than one thing, simply place an addition sign between the things you want to output. For example,

```
System.out.println("Answer is = " + 42
                 + " Accuracy is = " + precision);
```

If the value of `precision` is 0.01, the output will be

```
Answer is = 42 Accuracy is = 0.01
```

Notice the space at the start of `" Accuracy is = "`. No space is added automatically.

The + operator used here is the concatenation operator that we discussed earlier. So the above output statement converts the number 42 to the string `"42"` and then forms the following string using concatenation:

```
"Answer is = 42 Accuracy is = 0.01"
```

`System.out.println` then outputs this longer string.

Every invocation of `println` ends a line of output. For example, consider the following statements:

```
System.out.println("A wet bird");
System.out.println("never flies at night.");
```

These two statements cause the following output to appear on the screen:

```
A wet bird
never flies at night.
```

print versus println

If you want the output from two or more output statements to place all their output on a single line, then use `print` instead of `println`. For example, consider the following statements:

```
System.out.print("A ");
System.out.print("wet ");
System.out.println("bird");
System.out.println("never flies at night.");
```

`println` Output

You can output one line to the screen using `System.out.println`. The items that are output can be quoted strings, variables, numbers, or almost any object you can define in Java. To output more than one item, place a plus sign between the items.

SYNTAX

```
System.out.println(Item_1 + Item_2 + ... + Last_Item);
```

EXAMPLE

```
System.out.println("Welcome to Java.");
System.out.println("Elapsed time = " + time + " seconds");
```

They produce the same output as our previous example:

```
A wet bird
never flies at night.
```

Notice that a new line is not started until you use `println`, rather than `print`. Also notice that the new line starts *after* outputting the items specified in the `println`. This is the only difference between `print` and `println`.

`println` versus `print`

The only difference between `System.out.println` and `System.out.print` is that with `println`, the *next* output goes on a *new line*, whereas with `print`, the next output is placed on the *same line*.

EXAMPLE

```
System.out.print("Tom ");
System.out.print("Dick ");
System.out.println("and ");
System.out.print("Harry ");
```

This produces the following output:

```
Tom Dick and
Harry
```

(The output would look the same whether the last line reads `print` or `println`.)

Another way to describe the difference between `print` and `println` is to note that

```
System.out.println(SomeThing);
```

is equivalent to

```
System.out.print(SomeThing + "\n");
```

Self-Test Exercises

1. What output is produced by the following lines?

```
String s = "I am going \n home";
System.out.println(s);
```

2. Write Java statements that will cause the following to be written to the screen:

```
Rain, rain, go away,
Little Johnny wants to play.
```

3. What is the difference between `System.out.println` and `System.out.print`?

4. What output is produced by the following lines?

```
String s = "Rosie! ";
s += s;
System.out.print(s + "Are you there?");
```

TIP: Different Approaches to Formatting Output

If you have a variable of type `double` that stores some amount of money, you would like your programs to output the amount in a nice format. However, if you just use `System.out.println`, you are likely to get output that looks like the following:

```
Your cost, including tax, is $19.98327634144
```

You would like the output to look like this:

```
    Your cost, including tax, is $19.98
```

To obtain this nicer form of output, you need some formatting tools.

In this chapter, we will present three approaches to formatting numeric (and other) output. We will discuss the method `printf` and the two formatting classes `NumberFormat` and `DecimalFormat`. The `printf` method is often the simplest way to format output. However, `printf` uses an older methodology and so some authorities prefer to use `NumberFormat`, `DecimalFormat`, or similar formatting classes because these classes use a programming methodology that is perhaps more in the spirit of modern (object-oriented) programming. We will let you (or your instructor if you are in a class) decide which methodology to use. After this chapter, this book seldom uses any of these formatting details. ∎

Formatting Output with `printf`

System.out. printf   Starting with version 5.0, Java includes a method named `printf` that can be used to give output in a specific format. This method is used the same way as the method print but allows you to add formatting instructions that specify such things as the number of digits to include after a decimal point. For example, consider the following:

```
double price = 19.8;
System.out.print("$");
System.out.printf("%6.2f", price);
System.out.println(" each");
```

This code outputs the following line:

```
$ 19.80 each
```

The line

```
System.out.printf("%6.2f", price);
```

outputs the string " 19.80" (one blank followed by 19.80), which is the value of the variable price written in the format %6.2f. In these simple examples, the first argument to printf is a string known as the **format specifier**, and the second argument is the number or other value to be output in that format. Let's explain this first sample format specifier.

field width   The format specifier %6.2f says to output a floating-point number in a **field** (number of spaces) of width 6 (room for six characters) and to show exactly two digits after the decimal point. So, 19.8 is expressed as "19.80" in a field of width 6. Because "19.80" has only five characters, a blank character is added to obtain the six-character string " 19.80". Any extra blank space is added to the front (left-hand end) of the value output. That explains the 6.2 in the format specifier %6.2f. The f means the output is a floating-point number, that is, a number with a decimal point. We will have more to say about the character % shortly, but among other things, it indicates that a format specification (in this case, 6.2f) follows.

Before we go on, let's note a few details about the method printf. Note that the first argument is a string that gives a format specifier. Also, note that printf, like print, does not advance the output to the next line. The method printf is like print, not like println, in this regard.

The first argument to printf can include text as well as a format specifier. For example, consider the following variant on our example:

```
double price = 19.8;
System.out.printf("$%6.2f each", price);
System.out.println();
```

This code also outputs the following line:

```
$ 19.80 each
```

The text before and after the format specifier %6.2f is output along with the formatted number. The character % signals the end of text to output and the start of the

format
specifier

conversion
character

format specifier. The end of a format specifier is indicated by a **conversion character** (f in our example).

Other possible format specifiers are described in Display 2.1. (A more complete list of specifiers is given in Appendix 4.) The conversion character specifies the type of value that is output in the specified format. Note that the first number specifies the total number of spaces used to output the value. If that number is larger than the number of spaces needed for the output, extra blanks are added to the beginning of the value output. If that number is smaller than the number of spaces needed for the output, enough extra space is added to allow the value to be output; no matter what field width is specified, printf uses enough space to fit in the entire value output. Both of the numbers in a format specifier such as %6.2f are optional. You may omit either or both numbers, in which case Java chooses an appropriate default value or values (for example, %6f and %.2f). Note that the dot goes with the second number. You can use a format specifier that is just a % followed by a conversion character, such as %f or %g, in which case Java decides on the format details for you. For example, the format specifier %f is equivalent to %.6f, meaning six spaces after the decimal point and no extra space around the output.

e and g

The e and g format specifiers are partially explained in Display 2.1. We still need to explain the meaning of the number after the decimal point in e and g format specifiers, such as %8.3e and %8.3g. The first number, 8 in the examples, is the total field width for the value output. The second number (the number after the decimal point) specifies the number of digits after the decimal point of the output. So the numbers, such as 8.3, have the same meaning in the f, e, and g formats.

Display 2.1 Format Specifiers for System.out.printf

CONVERSION CHARACTER	TYPE OF OUTPUT	EXAMPLES
d	Decimal (ordinary) integer	%5d %d
f	Fixed-point (everyday notation) floating point	%6.2f %f
e	E-notation floating point	%8.3e %e
g	General floating point (Java decides whether to use E-notation or not)	%8.3g %g
s	String	%12s %s
c	Character	%2c %c

The s and c formats, for strings and characters, may include one number that specifies the field width for outputting the value, such as %15s and %2c. If no number is given, the value is output with no leading or trailing blank space.

s and c

When the value output does not fill the field width specified, blanks are added in front of the value output. The output is then said to be **right justified**. If you add a hyphen after the %, any extra blank space is placed after the value output, and the output is said to be **left justified**. For example, the lines

right justified

left justified

```
double value = 12.123;
System.out.printf("Start%8.2fEnd", value);
System.out.println();
System.out.printf("Start%-8.2fEnd", value);
System.out.println();
```

produce the following output. The first line has three spaces before the 12.12 and the second has three spaces after the 12.12.

```
Start   12.12End
Start12.12   End
```

more arguments

So far we have used printf to output only one value. However, printf can output any number of values. The first argument always is a string known as the **format string**, which can be followed with any number of additional arguments, each of which is a value to output. The format string should include one format specifier, such as %6.2f or %s, for each value output, and they should be in the same order as the values to be output. For example,

format string

```
double price = 19.8;
String name = "magic apple";
System.out.printf("$%6.2f for each %s.", price, name);
System.out.println();
System.out.println("Wow");
```

This code outputs the following:

```
$ 19.80 for each magic apple.
Wow
```

Note that the format string may contain text as well as format specifiers, and this text is output along with the values of the other arguments to printf.

new lines

You can include line breaks in a format string. For example, the following two lines

```
System.out.printf("$%6.2f for each %s.", price, name);
System.out.println();
```

can be replaced by the single line below, which uses the escape sequence \n:

```
System.out.printf("$%6.2f for each %s.\n", price, name);
```

%n   Although it is legal to use the escape sequence \n to indicate a line break in a format string, it is preferable to use %n. Exactly what happens when a \n is output can be system dependent, whereas %n should always mean a simple new line on any system. So our last line of code would be a little more robust if rewritten using %n as follows:

```
System.out.printf("$%6.2f for each %s.%n", price, name);
```

Many of the details we have discussed about printf are illustrated in the program given in Display 2.2.

TIP: Formatting Monetary Amounts with printf

A good format specifier for outputting an amount of money stored as a value of type double (or other floating-point value) is %.2f. It says to include exactly two digits after the decimal point and to use the smallest field width that the value will fit into. For example,

```
double price = 19.99;
System.out.printf("The price is $%.2f each.", price);
```

produces the following output:

```
The price is $19.99 each.  ■
```

Display 2.2   **The printf Method** (part 1 of 2)

```
1  public class PrintfDemo
2  {
3      public static void main(String[] args)
4      {
5          String aString = "abc";

6          System.out.println("String output:");
7          System.out.println("START1234567890");
8          System.out.printf("START%sEND %n", aString);
9          System.out.printf("START%4sEND %n", aString);
10         System.out.printf("START%2sEND %n", aString);
11         System.out.println();

12         char oneCharacter = 'Z';

13         System.out.println("Character output:");
14         System.out.println("START1234567890");
15         System.out.printf("START%cEND %n", oneCharacter);
16         System.out.printf("START%4cEND %n", oneCharacter);
17         System.out.println();
```

(continued)

Display 2.2   The `printf` Method (part 2 of 2)

```
18          double d = 12345.123456789;

19          System.out.println("Floating-point output:");
20          System.out.println("START1234567890");
21          System.out.printf("START%fEND %n", d);
22          System.out.printf("START%.4fEND %n", d);
23          System.out.printf("START%.2fEND %n", d);
24          System.out.printf("START%12.4fEND %n", d);
25          System.out.printf("START%eEND %n", d);
26          System.out.printf("START%12.5eEND %n", d);
27      }
28  }
```

Sample Dialogue

```
String output:
START1234567890
STARTabcEND
START  abcEND
STARTabcEND
```

The value is always output. If the specified field width is too small, extra space is taken.

```
Character output:
START1234567890
STARTZEND
START  ZEND
```

```
Floating-point output:
START1234567890
START12345.123457END
START12345.1235END
START12345.12END
START  12345.1235END
START1.234512e+04END
START 1.23451e+04END
```

Note that the output is rounded, not truncated, when digits are discarded.

TIP: Legacy Code

legacy code

Some code is so expensive to replace, it is used even if it is "old fashioned" or otherwise less than ideal. This sort of code is called **legacy code**. One approach to legacy code is to translate it into a more modern language. The Java method `printf` is essentially the same as a function[1] in the C language that is also named `printf`. This was done intentionally so that it would be easier to translate C code into Java code. ■

[1] Methods are called *functions* in the C and C++ languages.

System.out.printf

`System.out.printf` is used for formatted screen output. `System.out.printf` can have any number of arguments. The first argument is always a format string for the remaining arguments. All the arguments except the first are values to be output to the screen, and these values are output in the formats specified by the format string. The format string can contain text as well as format specifiers, and this text is output along with the values.

MyProgrammingLab™

Self-Test Exercises

5. What output is produced by the following code?

```java
String s1 = "First Name ";
String s2 = "           ";
String s3 = "Last Name ";

String heading = s1 + s2 + s3;
System.out.println(heading);
System.out.printf("%-15s   %-10s %n", "John", "Smith");
System.out.printf("%-15s   %-10s %n", "Peter", "Haley");
```

6. What output is produced by the following code?

```java
double d = 123.9876543210;

System.out.println("Formatting Floating Point Number: \n");
System.out.printf(" %9.3f %n", d);
System.out.printf(" %9.3e %n", d);
System.out.printf(" %9.3g %n", d);
```

7. Write a Java statement to output the value in variable d of type `double` to the screen. The output should be in e-notation with three digits after the decimal point. The output should be in a field of width 15.

Money Formats Using `NumberFormat` ★

NumberFormat

Using the class `NumberFormat`, you can tell Java to use the appropriate format when outputting amounts of money. The technique is illustrated in Display 2.3. Let's look at the code in the `main` method that does the formatting. First consider the following:

```java
NumberFormat moneyFormatter =
            NumberFormat.getCurrencyInstance();
```

The method invocation `NumberFormat.getCurrencyInstance()` produces an object of the class `NumberFormat` and names the object `moneyFormatter`. You can use any

Display 2.3   **Currency Format** (part 1 of 2)

```
1   import java.text.NumberFormat;
2   import java.util.Locale;
3   public class CurrencyFormatDemo
4   {
5       public static void main(String[] args)
6       {
7           System.out.println("Without formatting:");

8           System.out.println(19.8);
9           System.out.println(19.81111);
10          System.out.println(19.89999);
11          System.out.println(19);
12          System.out.println();

13          System.out.println("Default location:");
14          NumberFormat moneyFormatter =
15                          NumberFormat.getCurrencyInstance();

16          System.out.println(moneyFormatter.format(19.8));
17          System.out.println(moneyFormatter.format(19.81111));
18          System.out.println(moneyFormatter.format(19.89999));
19          System.out.println(moneyFormatter.format(19));
20          System.out.println();

21          System.out.println("US as location:");
22          NumberFormat moneyFormatter2 =
23                          NumberFormat.getCurrencyInstance(Locale.US);

24          System.out.println(moneyFormatter2.format(19.8));
25          System.out.println(moneyFormatter2.format(19.81111));
26          System.out.println(moneyFormatter2.format(19.89999));
27          System.out.println(moneyFormatter2.format(19));
28      }

29  }
```

If you use only the default location, you do not need to import `Locale`*.*

Notice that this number is rounded to 19.90.

valid identifier (other than a keyword) in place of `moneyFormatter`. This object `moneyFormatter` has a method named `format` that takes a floating-point number as an argument and returns a `String` value representing that number in the local currency (the default currency). For example, the following invocation

```
moneyFormatter.format(19.8)
```

Display 2.3   **Currency Format** (part 2 of 2)

Sample Dialogue

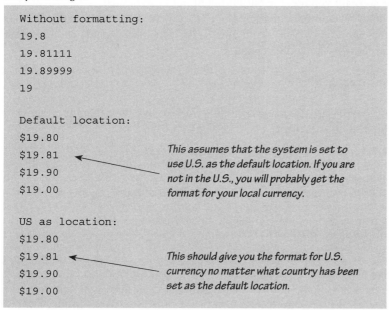

```
Without formatting:
19.8
19.81111
19.89999
19


Default location:
$19.80
$19.81  ←        This assumes that the system is set to
$19.90           use U.S. as the default location. If you are
$19.00           not in the U.S., you will probably get the
                 format for your local currency.

US as location:
$19.80
$19.81  ←        This should give you the format for U.S.
$19.90           currency no matter what country has been
$19.00           set as the default location.
```

returns the `String` value `"$19.80"`, assuming the default currency is the U.S. dollar. In Display 2.3, this method invocation occurs inside a `System.out.println` statement, but it is legal anyplace a `String` value is legal. For example, the following would be legal:

```
String moneyString = moneyFormatter.format(19.8);
```

In order to make the class `NumberFormat` available to your code, you must include the following near the start of the file with your program:

```
import java.text.NumberFormat;
```

This is illustrated in Display 2.3.

The method invocation `NumberFormat.getCurrencyInstance()` produces an object that formats numbers according to the default location. In Display 2.3, we are assuming the default location is the United States, and so the numbers are output as U.S. dollars. On other systems, the default should be set to the local currency. If you wish, you can specify the location, and hence the local currency, by giving an argument to `NumberFormat.getCurrencyInstance`. For example, in Display 2.3, we used the constant `Locale.US` to specify that the location is the United States. The relevant line from Display 2.3 is repeated in what follows:

```
NumberFormat moneyFormatter2 =
            NumberFormat.getCurrencyInstance(Locale.US);
```

Some constants for other countries (and hence other currencies) are given in Display 2.4. However, unless your screen is capable of displaying the currency symbol for the country whose constant you use, the output might not be as desired.

These location constants are objects of the class `Locale`. In order to make the class `Locale` and these constants available to your code, you must include the following near the start of the file with your program:

```
import java.util.Locale;
```

If you do not use any of these location constants and use only the default location, you do not need this `import` statement.

The notation `Locale.US` may seem a bit strange, but it follows a convention that is frequently used in Java code. The constant is named `US`, but we want specifically that constant named `US` that is defined in the class `Locale`. So we use `Locale.US`. The notation `Locale.US` means the constant `US` as defined in the class `Locale`.

Importing Packages and Classes

package

Libraries in Java are called **packages**. A package is simply a collection of classes that has been given a name and stored in such a way as to make it easily accessible to your Java programs. Java has a large number of standard packages that automatically come with Java. Two such packages are named `java.text` and `java.util`. In Display 2.3, we used the class `NumberFormat`, which is a member of the package `java.text`. In order to use `NumberFormat`, you must import the class, which we did as follows:

java.text

```
import java.text.NumberFormat;
```

Display 2.4   Locale Constants for Currencies of Different Countries

Locale.CANADA	Canada (for currency, the format is the same as U.S.)
Locale.CHINA	China
Locale.FRANCE	France
Locale.GERMANY	Germany
Locale.ITALY	Italy
Locale.JAPAN	Japan
Locale.KOREA	Korea
Locale.TAIWAN	Taiwan
Locale.UK	United Kingdom (English pound)
Locale.US	United States

Outputting Amounts of Money

Using the class `NumberFormat`, you can output an amount of money correctly formatted. The procedure to do so is described here.

Place the following near the start of the file containing your program:

```
import java.text.NumberFormat;
```

In your program code, create an object of the class `NumberFormat` as follows:

```
NumberFormat formatterObject =
                    NumberFormat.getCurrencyInstance();
```

When outputting numbers for amounts of money, change the number to a value of type `String` using the method `FormatterObject.format`, as illustrated in the following:

```
double moneyAmount = 9.99;
System.out.println(formatterObject.format(moneyAmount));
```

The string produced by invocations such as `formatterObject.format(moneyAmount)` adds the dollar sign and ensures that there are exactly two digits after the decimal point. (This is assuming the U.S. dollar is the default currency.)

The numbers formatted in this way may be of type `double`, `int`, or `long`. You may use any (nonkeyword) identifier in place of `formatterObject`. A complete example is given in Display 2.3.

The above always outputs the money amount in the default currency, which is typically the local currency. You can specify the country whose currency you want. See the text for details.

import statement

This kind of statement is called an **import statement**. In this example, the import statement tells Java to look in the package `java.text` to find the definition of the class `NumberFormat`.

If you want to import all the classes in the `java.text` package, use the following:

```
import java.text.*;
```

Then you can use any class in the `java.text` package.

You don't lose any efficiency in importing the entire package instead of importing only the classes you use. However, many programmers find that it is an aid to documentation if they import only the classes they use, which is what we will do in this book.

java.util

In Display 2.3, we also used the class `Locale`, which is in the `java.util` package. So we also included the following import statement:

```
import java.util.Locale;
```

java.lang

One package requires no import statement. The package java.lang contains classes that are fundamental to Java programming. These classes are so basic that the package is always imported automatically. Any class in java.lang does not need an import statement to make it available to your code. So, when we say that a class is in the package java.lang, you can simply use that class in your program without needing any import statement. For example, the class String is in the java.lang package, so you can use it without any import statement.

More material on packages is covered in Chapter 5.

MyProgrammingLab

Self-Test Exercises

8. What output is produced by the following code? (Assume a proper import statement has been given.)

```
NumberFormat exerciseFormatter =
                NumberFormat.getCurrencyInstance(Locale.US);
double d1 = 375.3243, d2 = 89.999;
System.out.println(exerciseFormatter.format(d1));
System.out.println(exerciseFormatter.format(d2));
```

9. Suppose the class Robot is a part of the standard Java libraries and is in the package named java.awt. What import statement do you need to make the class Robot available to your program or other class?

The DecimalFormat Class ★

System.out.println will let you output numbers but has no facilities to format the numbers. If you want to output a number in a specific format, such as having a specified number of digits after the decimal point, then you must convert the number to a string that shows the number in the desired format and then use System.out.println to output the string. Earlier in this chapter, we saw one way to accomplish this for amounts of money. The class DecimalFormat provides a versatile facility to format numbers in a variety of ways.

The class DecimalFormat is in the Java package named java.text. So you must add the following (or something similar) to the beginning of the file with your program or other class that uses the class DecimalFormat:

import

```
import java.text.DecimalFormat;
```

An object of the class DecimalFormat has a number of different methods that can be used to produce numeral strings in various formats. In this subsection, we discuss one of these methods, which is named format. The general approach to using the format method is discussed in the following pages.

patterns

Create an object of the class DecimalFormat, using a String *Pattern* as follows:

```
DecimalFormat Variable_Name = new DecimalFormat(Pattern);
```

For example,

```
DecimalFormat formattingObject = new DecimalFormat("000.000");
```

The method `format` of the class `DecimalFormat` can then be used to convert a floating-point number, such as one of type `double`, to a corresponding numeral `String` following the *Pattern* used to create the `DecimalFormat` object. Specifically, an invocation of `format` takes the form

Decimal_Format_Object.format(*Double_Expression*)

which returns a `String` value for a string representation of the value of *Double_Expression*. *Double_Expression* can be any expression, such as a variable or sum of variables, that evaluates to a value of type `double`.

For example, consider the following code:

```
DecimalFormat formattingObject = new DecimalFormat("000.0000");
String numeral = formattingObject.format(12.3456789);
System.out.println(numeral);
```

This produces the following output:

```
012.3457
```

Of course, you can use an invocation of `format`, such as `formattingObject.format (12.3456789)`, directly in `System.out.println`. So, the following code produces the same output:

```
System.out.println(formattingObject.format(12.3456789));
```

The format of the string produced is determined by the *Pattern* string that was used as the argument to the constructor that created the object of the class `DecimalFormat`. For example, the pattern `"000.0000"` means that there will be three digits before the decimal point and four digits after the decimal point. Note that the result is rounded when the number of digits is less than the number of digits available in the number being formatted. If the format pattern is not consistent with the value of the number, such as a pattern that asks for two digits before the decimal point for a number such as `123.456`, then the format rules are violated so that no digits are lost.

A pattern can specify the exact number of digits before and after the decimal, or it can specify minimum numbers of digits. The character `'0'` is used to represent a required digit, and the character `'#'` is used to indicate an optional digit. For example, the pattern `"#0.0##"` indicates one or two digits before the decimal point and one, two, or three digits after the decimal point. The optional digit `'#'` is shown if it is a nonzero digit and is not shown if it is a zero digit. The `'#'` optional digits should go where zero placeholders would appear in a numeral string; in other words, any `'#'` optional digits precede the zero digits `'0'` before the decimal point in the pattern, and any '#' optional digits follow the zero digits '0' after the decimal point in the pattern. Use "#0.0##"; do not use "0#.0##" or "#0.##0".

For example, consider the following code:

```
DecimalFormat formattingObject = new DecimalFormat("#0.0##");
System.out.println(formattingObject.format(12.3456789));
System.out.println(formattingObject.format(1.23456789));
```

This produces the following output:

```
12.346
1.235
```

percentages   The character '%' placed at the end of a pattern indicates that the number is to be expressed as a percentage. The '%' causes the number to be multiplied by 100 and appends a percent sign, '%'. Examples of this and other formatting patterns are given in Display 2.5.

E-notation   E-notation is specified by including an 'E' in the pattern string. For example, the pattern '00.###E0" approximates specifying two digits before the decimal point, three or fewer digits after the decimal point, and at least one digit after the 'E', as in 12.346E1. As you can see by the examples of E-notation in Display 2.5, the exact details of which E-notation string is produced can be a bit more involved than our explanation so far. Here are a couple more details:

The number of digits indicated after the 'E' is the minimum number of digits used for the exponent. As many more digits as are needed will be used.

mantissa   The **mantissa** is the decimal number before the 'E'. The minimum number of significant digits in the mantissa (that is, the sum of the number of digits before and after the decimal point) is the *minimum* of the number of digits indicated before the decimal point plus the *maximum* of the number of digits indicated after the decimal point. For example, 12345 formatted with "##0.##E0" is "12.3E3".

To get a feel for how E-notation patterns work, it would pay to play with a few cases. In any event, do not count on a very precisely specified number of significant digits.

`DecimalFormat` Class

Objects of the class `DecimalFormat` are used to produce strings of a specified format from numbers. As such, these objects can be used to format numeric output. The object is associated with a pattern when it is created using new. The object can then be used with the method `format` to create strings that satisfy the format. See Display 2.5 for examples of the `DecimalFormat` class in use.

Display 2.5   The **DecimalFormat** Class (part 1 of 2)

```
1   import java.text.DecimalFormat;

2   public class DecimalFormatDemo
3   {
4       public static void main(String[] args)
5       {
6           DecimalFormat pattern00dot000 = new DecimalFormat("00.000");
7           DecimalFormat pattern0dot00 = new DecimalFormat("0.00");

8           double d = 12.3456789;
9           System.out.println("Pattern 00.000");
10          System.out.println(pattern00dot000.format(d));
11          System.out.println("Pattern 0.00");
12          System.out.println(pattern0dot00.format(d));

13          double money = 19.8;
14          System.out.println("Pattern 0.00");
15          System.out.println("$" + pattern0dot00.format(money));
16
17          DecimalFormat percent = new DecimalFormat("0.00%");

18          System.out.println("Pattern 0.00%");
19          System.out.println(percent.format(0.308));

20          DecimalFormat eNotation1 =
21              new DecimalFormat("#0.###E0"); //1 or 2 digits before point
22          DecimalFormat eNotation2 =
23              new DecimalFormat("00.###E0"); //2 digits before point

24          System.out.println("Pattern #0.###E0");
25          System.out.println(eNotation1.format(123.456));
26          System.out.println("Pattern 00.###E0");
27          System.out.println(eNotation2.format(123.456));

28          double smallNumber = 0.0000123456;
29          System.out.println("Pattern #0.###E0");
30          System.out.println(eNotation1.format(smallNumber));
31          System.out.println("Pattern 00.###E0");
32          System.out.println(eNotation2.format(smallNumber));
33      }
34  }
```

(continued)

Display 2.5   The `DecimalFormat` Class (part 2 of 2)

Sample Dialogue

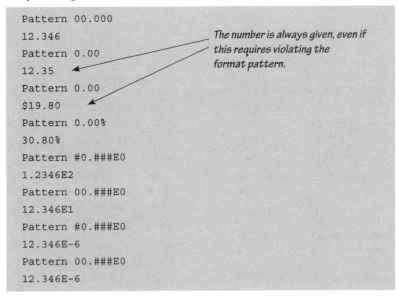

```
Pattern 00.000
12.346
Pattern 0.00
12.35
Pattern 0.00
$19.80
Pattern 0.00%
30.80%
Pattern #0.###E0
1.2346E2
Pattern 00.###E0
12.346E1
Pattern #0.###E0
12.346E-6
Pattern 00.###E0
12.346E-6
```

The number is always given, even if this requires violating the format pattern.

2.2   Console Input Using the `Scanner` Class

Let the world tell me.

FRANK SHAKESPEARE, *Franky I*

Starting with version 5.0, Java includes a class for doing simple keyboard input. In this section, we show you how to do keyboard input using this class, which is named `Scanner`.

The `Scanner` Class

Display 2.6 contains a simple program that uses the `Scanner` class to read two `int` values typed in on the keyboard. The numbers entered on the keyboard are shown in **bold**. Let's go over the `Scanner`-related details line by line. The following line, which should be placed near the start of the file, tells Java where to find the definition of the `Scanner` class:

import
       `import java.util.Scanner;`

    This line says the `Scanner` class is in the `java.util` package; `util` is short for *utility*, but in Java code, you always use the abbreviated spelling `util`. A package is simply a library of classes. This import statement makes the `Scanner` class available to your program.

Display 2.6   Keyboard Input Demonstration

```
1   import java.util.Scanner;              Makes the Scanner class available
                                           to your program.
2   public class ScannerDemo
3   {                                      Creates an object of the class
4       public static void main(String[] args)   Scanner and names the
5       {                                          object keyboard.
6           Scanner keyboard = new Scanner(System.in);

7           System.out.println("Enter the number of pods followed by");
8           System.out.println("the number of peas in a pod:");
9           int numberOfPods = keyboard.nextInt();          Each reads one int
10          int peasPerPod = keyboard.nextInt();            from the keyboard

11          int totalNumberOfPeas = numberOfPods*peasPerPod;

12          System.out.print(numberOfPods + " pods and ");
13          System.out.println(peasPerPod + " peas per pod.");
14          System.out.println("The total number of peas = "
15                                          + totalNumberOfPeas);
16      }
17  }
```

Sample Dialogue 1

```
Enter the number of pods followed by       The numbers that
the number of peas in a pod:               are input must be
22 10                                      separated by
                                           whitespace, such as
22 pods and 10 peas per pod.               one or more blanks.
The total number of peas = 220
```

Sample Dialogue 2

```
Enter the number of pods followed by
the number of peas in a pod:               A line break is also
22                                         considered whitespace and
                                           can be used to separate the
10                                         numbers typed in at the
22 pods and 10 peas per pod.               keyboard.
The total number of peas = 220
```

The following line creates an object of the class `Scanner` and names the object `keyboard`:

```
Scanner keyboard = new Scanner(System.in);
```

After this line appears, you can use methods of the `Scanner` class with the object `keyboard` to read data that the user types on the keyboard. For example, the method `nextInt` reads one `int` value typed on the keyboard. So, the following line from Display 2.6 reads one value of type `int` and makes that the value of the variable `numberOfPods`:

nextInt

```
int numberOfPods = keyboard.nextInt();
```

In Display 2.6, two such statements each read one `int` value that the user types in at the keyboard:

```
int numberOfPods = keyboard.nextInt();
int peasPerPod = keyboard.nextInt();
```

whitespace

The numbers typed in must be separated by **whitespace**, such as one or more spaces, a line break, or other whitespace. Whitespace is any string of characters, such as blank spaces, tabs, and line breaks, that prints as whitespace when written on (white) paper.

We often use the identifier `keyboard` for our `Scanner` object because the object is being used for keyboard input. However, you may use other names. If you instead want your object of the class `Scanner` to be named `scannerObject`, you would use the following:

```
Scanner scannerObject = new Scanner(System.in);
```

To read a single `int` value from the keyboard and save it in the `int` variable `n1`, you would then use the following:

```
n1 = scannerObject.nextInt();
```

This is illustrated in the program in Display 2.7.

The program in Display 2.7 also illustrates some of the other `Scanner` methods for reading values from the keyboard. The method `nextDouble` works in exactly the same way as `nextInt`, except that it reads a value of type `double`. The following example is from Display 2.7:

nextDouble

```
double d1, d2;
d1 = scannerObject.nextDouble();
d2 = scannerObject.nextDouble();
System.out.println("You entered " + d1 + " and " + d2);
```

Display 2.7   **Another Keyboard Input Demonstration** (part 1 of 2)

```
1 import java.util.Scanner;

2 public class ScannerDemo2
3 {
4     public static void main(String[] args)
5     {
6         int n1, n2;
7         Scanner scannerObject = new Scanner(System.in);

8         System.out.println("Enter two whole numbers");
9         System.out.println("separated by one or more spaces:");

10        n1 = scannerObject.nextInt();
11        n2 = scannerObject.nextInt();
12        System.out.println("You entered " + n1 + " and " + n2);

13        System.out.println("Next enter two numbers.");
14        System.out.println("Decimal points are allowed.");

15        double d1, d2;
16        d1 = scannerObject.nextDouble();
17        d2 = scannerObject.nextDouble();
18        System.out.println("You entered " + d1 + " and " + d2);

19        System.out.println("Next enter two words:");

20        String word1 = scannerObject.next();
21        String word2 = scannerObject.next();
22        System.out.println("You entered \"" +
23                               word1 + "\" and \"" + word2 + "\"");

24        String junk = scannerObject.nextLine(); //To get rid of '\n'

25        System.out.println("Next enter a line of text:");
26        String line = scannerObject.nextLine();
27        System.out.println("You entered: \"" + line + "\"");
28    }
29 }
```

Creates an object of the class Scanner *and names the object* scannerObject.

Reads one int *from the keyboard.*

Reads one double *from the keyboard.*

Reads one word from the keyboard.

(continued)

Display 2.7   Another Keyboard Input Demonstration (part 2 of 2)

Sample Dialogue

```
Enter two whole numbers
separated by one or more spaces:
  42    43
You entered 42 and 43
Next enter two numbers.
A decimal point is OK.
 9.99  57
You entered 9.99 and 57.0
Next enter two words:
jelly beans
You entered "jelly" and "beans"
Next enter a line of text:
Java flavored jelly beans are my favorite.
You entered "Java flavored jelly beans are my favorite."
```

The method `next` reads in a word, as illustrated by the following lines from Display 2.7:

```
String word1 = scannerObject.next();
String word2 = scannerObject.next();
```

If the input line is

jelly beans

then this will assign `w1` the string `"jelly"` and `w2` the string `"beans"`.

word   For the method `next`, a **word** is any string of nonwhitespace characters delimited by whitespace characters such as blanks or the beginning or ending of a line.

If you want to read in an entire line, you would use the method `nextLine`. For example,

```
String line = scannerObject.nextLine();
```

reads in one line of input and places the string that is read into the variable `line`.

The end of an input line is indicated by the escape sequence `'\n'`. This `'\n'` character is what you input when you press the Enter (Return) key on the keyboard. On the screen, it is indicated by the ending of one line and the beginning of the next line. When `nextLine` reads a line of text, it reads this `'\n'` character, so the next reading of input begins on the next line. However, the `'\n'` does not become part of the string value returned. So, in the previous code, the string named by the variable `line` does not end with the `'\n'` character.

These and other methods for reading in values from the keyboard are given in Display 2.8.

Display 2.8   **Methods of the Scanner Class** (part 1 of 2)

The Scanner class can be used to obtain input from files as well as from the keyboard. However, here we are assuming it is being used only for input from the keyboard.

To set things up for keyboard input, you need the following at the beginning of the file with the keyboard input code:

import java.util.Scanner;

You also need the following before the first keyboard input statement:

Scanner *Scanner_Object_Name* = new Scanner(System.in);

The *Scanner_Object_Name* can then be used with the following methods to read and return various types of data typed on the keyboard.

Values to be read should be separated by whitespace characters, such as blanks and/or new lines. When reading values, these whitespace characters are skipped. (It is possible to change the separators from whitespace to something else, but whitespace is the default and is what we will use.)

Scanner_Object_Name.nextInt()

Returns the next value of type int that is typed on the keyboard.

Scanner_Object_Name.nextLong()

Returns the next value of type long that is typed on the keyboard.

Scanner_Object_Name.nextByte()

Returns the next value of type byte that is typed on the keyboard.

Scanner_Object_Name.nextShort()

Returns the next value of type short that is typed on the keyboard.

Scanner_Object_Name.nextDouble()

Returns the next value of type double that is typed on the keyboard.

Scanner_Object_Name.nextFloat()

Returns the next value of type float that is typed on the keyboard.

Scanner_Object_Name.next()

Returns the String value consisting of the next keyboard characters up to, but not including, the first delimiter character. The default delimiters are whitespace characters.

(continued)

Display 2.8 Methods of the Scanner Class (part 2 of 2)

Scanner_Object_Name `.nextBoolean()`

Returns the next value of type `boolean` that is typed on the keyboard. The values of `true` and `false` are entered as the strings `"true"` and `"false"`. Any combination of upper- and/or lowercase letters is allowed in spelling `"true"` and `"false"`.

Scanner_Object_Name `.nextLine()`

Reads the rest of the current keyboard input line and returns the characters read as a value of type `String`. Note that the line terminator '\n' is read and discarded; it is not included in the string returned.

Scanner_Object_Name `.useDelimiter(`*New_Delimiter*`);`

Changes the delimiter for keyboard input with *Scanner_Object_Name*. The *New_Delimiter* is a value of type `String`. After this statement is executed, *New_Delimiter* is the only delimiter that separates words or numbers. See the subsection "Other Input Delimiters", later in this chapter, for details.

Keyboard Input Using the `Scanner` Class

You can use an object of the class `Scanner` to read input from the keyboard. To make the `Scanner` class available for use in your code, you should include the following at the start of the file that contains your program (or other code that does keyboard input):

```
import java.util.Scanner;
```

Before you do any keyboard input, you must create an object of the class `Scanner` as follows:

```
Scanner Object_Name = new Scanner(System.in);
```

where *Object_Name* is any (nonkeyword) Java identifier. For example,

```
Scanner keyboard = new Scanner(System.in);
```

The methods `nextInt`, `nextDouble`, and `next` read a value of type `int`, a value of type `double`, and a word, respectively. The method `nextLine` reads the remainder of the current input line including the terminating `'\n'`. However, the `'\n'` is not included in the string value returned. Other input methods are given in Display 2.8.

SYNTAX

```
Int_Variable = Object_Name.nextInt()
Double_Variable = Object_Name.nextDouble();
String_Variable = Object_Name.next();
String_Variable = Object_Name.nextLine();
```

EXAMPLE

```
int number;
number = keyboard.nextInt();
double cost;
cost = keyboard.nextDouble();
String word;
word = keyboard.next();
String line;
line = keyboard.nextLine();
```

PITFALL: Dealing with the Line Terminator, '\n'

The method nextLine of the class Scanner reads the *remainder* of a line of text *starting wherever the last keyboard reading left off.* For example, suppose you create an object of the class Scanner as follows:

```
Scanner keyboard = new Scanner(System.in);
```

Suppose you continue with the following code:

VideoNote
Pitfalls
Involving
nextLine()

```
int n = keyboard.nextInt();
String s1 = keyboard.nextLine();
String s2 = keyboard.nextLine();
```

Now, assume that the input typed on the keyboard is the following:

```
2 heads are
better than
1 head.
```

This sets the value of the variable n to 2, that of the variable s1 to "heads are", and that of the variable s2 to "better than".

So far there are no problems, but suppose the input were instead as follows:

```
2
heads are better than
1 head.
```

You might expect the value of n to be set to 2, the value of the variable s1 to "heads are better than", and that of the variable s2 to "1 head." But that is not what happens.

What actually happens is that the value of the variable n is set to 2, that of the variable s1 is set to the empty string, and that of the variable s2 to "heads are better than". The method nextInt reads the 2 but does not read the end-of-line character '\n'. So the first nextLine invocation reads the rest of the line that contains the 2.

(continued)

PITFALL: (continued)

There is nothing more on that line (except for '\n'), so nextLine returns the empty string. The second invocation of nextLine begins on the next line and reads "heads are better than".

When combining different methods for reading from the keyboard, you sometimes have to include an extra invocation of nextLine to get rid of the end of a line (to get rid of a '\n'). This is illustrated in Display 2.7. ■

The Empty String

empty string

A string can have any number of characters. For example, "Hello" has five characters. There is a string with zero characters, which is called the **empty string**. The empty string is written with a pair of double quotes, with nothing in between the quotes, like so: "". The empty string is encountered more often than you might think. If your code is executing the nextLine method to read a line of text, and the user types nothing on the line other than pressing the Enter (Return) key, then the nextLine method reads the empty string.

TIP: Prompt for Input

Always prompt the user when your program needs the user to input some data, as in the following example:

```
System.out.println("Enter the number of pods followed by");
System.out.println("the number of peas in a pod:"); ■
```

TIP: Echo Input

echo input

You should normally **echo input**. That is, you should write to the screen all input that your program receives from the keyboard. This way, the user can check that the input has been entered correctly. For example, the following two statements from the program in Display 2.9 echo the values that were read for the number of pods and the number of peas per pod:

```
System.out.print(numberOfPods + " pods and ");
System.out.println(peasPerPod + " peas per pod.");
```

It might seem that there is no need to echo input, because the user's input is automatically displayed on the screen as the user enters it. Why bother to write it to the screen a second time? The input might be incorrect even though it looks correct. For example, the user might type a comma instead of a decimal point or the letter O in place of a zero. Echoing the input can expose such problems. ■

Display 2.9 Self-Service Checkout Line

```
1 import java.util.Scanner;

2 public class SelfService
3 {
4     public static void main(String[] args)
5     {
6         Scanner keyboard = new Scanner(System.in);

7         System.out.println("Enter number of items purchased");
8         System.out.println("followed by the cost of one item.");
9         System.out.println("Do not use a dollar sign.");

10        int count = keyboard.nextInt();
11        double price = keyboard.nextDouble();
12        double total = count*price;

13        System.out.printf("%d items at $%.2f each.%n", count, price);
14        System.out.printf("Total amount due $%.2f.%n", total);

15        System.out.println("Please take your merchandise.");
16        System.out.printf("Place $%.2f in an envelope %n", total);
17        System.out.println("and slide it under the office door.");
18        System.out.println("Thank you for using the self-service line.");
19    }
20 }
```

The dot after `%.2f` is a period in the text, not part of the format specifier.

Sample Dialogue

```
Enter number of items purchased
followed by the cost of one item.
Do not use a dollar sign.
   10    19.99
10 items at $19.99 each.
Total amount due $199.90.
Please take your merchandise.
Place $199.90 in an envelope
and slide it under the office door.
Thank you for using the self-service line.
```

Self-Test Exercises

10. Which package do you need to import for using the `Scanner` class in your program?

11. Write a line of code that creates a `Scanner` object `inputObj`, reads a line of text from the keyboard using that object, and stores the text in a `String` variable `str`.

12. Write a line of code that uses the object `inputObj` from the previous exercise to read in an integer from the keyboard and store it in an `int` variable `number`.

13. Write a complete Java program that reads in a line of keyboard input containing two values of type `double` (separated by one or more spaces) and outputs the two numbers as well as the sum of the two numbers.

14. Write a complete Java program that reads in a line of text containing exactly three words (separated by any kind or amount of whitespace) and outputs the line with spacing corrected; that is, the output has no space before the first word and exactly one space between each pair of adjacent words.

15. Something could go wrong with the following code. Identify and fix the problem.

```
Scanner keyboard = new Scanner(System.in);
System.out.println("Enter your age.");
int age = keyboard.nextInt();
System.out.println("Enter your name.");
String name = keyboard.nextLine();
System.out.println(name + ",you are " + age + " years old.");
```

EXAMPLE: Self-Service Checkout

Display 2.9 contains a first draft of a program to use in the self-service line of a hardware store. It still needs some more details and even some more hardware for accepting payment. However, it does illustrate the use of the `Scanner` class for keyboard input and the `printf` method for formatted output.

Note that in `printf`, we used the format specifier `%.2f` for amounts of money. This specifies a floating-point number with exactly two digits after the decimal point, but gives no field width. Because no field width is given, the number output is placed in the fewest number of spaces that still allows the full value to be shown.

Other Input Delimiters

When using the `Scanner` class for keyboard input, you can change the delimiters that separate keyboard input to almost any combination of characters, but the details are a bit involved. In this book, we will describe only one simple kind of delimiter change. We will tell you how to change the delimiters from whitespace to one specific delimiter string.

For example, suppose you create a `Scanner` object as follows:

```
Scanner keyboard2 = new Scanner(System.in);
```

You can change the delimiter for the object `keyboard2` to `"##"` as follows:

```
keyboard2.useDelimiter("##");
```

After this invocation of the `useDelimiter` method, `"##"` will be the only input delimiter for the input object `keyboard2`. Note that whitespace will no longer be a delimiter for keyboard input done with `keyboard2`. For example, suppose the user enters the following keyboard input:

```
one two##three##
```

The following code would read the two strings `"one two"` and `"three"` and make them the values of the variables `word1` and `word2`:

```
String word1, word2;
word1 = keyboard2.next();
word2 = keyboard2.next();
```

This is illustrated in Display 2.10. Note that you can have two different objects of the class `Scanner` with different delimiters in the same program.

Note that no whitespace characters, not even line breaks, serve as an input delimiter for `keyboard2` once this change is made to `keyboard2`.

MyProgrammingLab™

Self-Test Exercises

16. Suppose your code creates an object of the class `Scanner` named `keyboard` (as described in this chapter). Write code to change the delimiter for `keyboard` to a comma followed by a blank.

17. Continue with the object `keyboard` from Self-Test Exercise 16. Consider the following input:

    ```
    one,two three, four, five
    ```

    What values will the following code assign to the variables `word1` and `word2`?

    ```
    String word1 = keyboard.next();
    String word2 = keyboard.next();
    ```

Display 2.10   Changing the Input Delimiter

```java
 1    import java.util.Scanner;

 2    public class DelimiterDemo
 3    {
 4        public static void main(String[] args)
 5        {
 6            Scanner keyboard1 = new Scanner(System.in);
 7            Scanner keyboard2 = new Scanner(System.in);
 8            keyboard2.useDelimiter("##");
 9            //Delimiter for keyboard1 is whitespace.
10            //Delimiter for keyboard2 is ##.

11            String word1, word2;
12            System.out.println("Enter a line of text:");
13            word1 = keyboard1.next();
14            word2 = keyboard1.next();
15            System.out.println("For keyboard1 the two words read are:");
16            System.out.println(word1);
17            System.out.println(word2);
18            String junk = keyboard1.nextLine(); //To get rid of rest of line.
19
20            System.out.println("Reenter the same line of text:");
21            word1 = keyboard2.next();
22            word2 = keyboard2.next();
23            System.out.println("For keyboard2 the two words read are:");
24            System.out.println(word1);
25            System.out.println(word2);
26        }
27    }
```

Sample Dialogue

```
Enter a line of text:
one two##three##
For keyboard1 the two words read are:
one
two##three##
Reenter the same line of text:
one two##three##
For keyboard2 the two words read are:
one two
three
```

2.3   Introduction to File Input

You shall see them on a beautiful quarto page, where a neat rivulet of text shall meander through a meadow of margin.

RICHARD BRINSLEY SHERIDAN, *The School for Scandal*

The Scanner class can also be used to read data from a text file. To do this, we must create a Scanner object and link it to the file on the disk. Once this is done, the program can read from the Scanner object in the same exact way that we read from the console, except the input will come from the file instead of typed from the keyboard. Details about reading and writing from files are not discussed until Chapter 10 and require an understanding of programming concepts we have not yet covered. However, we can provide just enough here so that your programs can read from text files. This will allow you to work on problems with real-world data that would otherwise be too much work to type into your program every time it is run.

The Scanner Class for Text File Input

To read from a text file, we need to import the classes FileInputStream and FileNotFoundException in addition to the Scanner class:

```
import java.io.FileInputStream;
import java.io.FileNotFoundException;
```

The FileInputStream class handles the connection between a Java program and a file on the disk. The FileNotFoundException class is used if a program attempts to open a file that doesn't exist.

To open the file, we create an object of type Scanner and then connect it with a FileInputStream object associated with the file. We have to handle the scenario where we try to open a file that doesn't exist. One way to do this is with a try/catch block. This is discussed more thoroughly in Chapter 9, but the basic format to open a file looks like this:

```
Scanner fileIn = null;  // initializes fileIn to empty
try
{
  // Attempt to open the file
  fileIn = new Scanner(new FileInputStream("PathToFile"));
}
catch (FileNotFoundException e)
{
  // If the file could not be found, this code is executed
  // and then the program exits
```

```
        System.out.println("File not found.");
        System.exit(0);
    }
    ...  Code continues here
```

This code will create a `Scanner` variable named `fileIn` and initialize it to an empty (`null`) object. Next, Java will run the code inside the `try` block. If the file is not found, then control jumps directly to the `catch` block. In our example, we print out an error message and make the program exit immediately with the statement `System.exit(0)`.

If the file is found, then the `catch` block is skipped entirely and the program continues to execute whatever code comes after the catch. At this point, we can use `fileIn` exactly the same way we used a `Scanner` object connected to the console, except input will be provided from the file, not the keyboard.

For example, we can use `fileIn.nextInt()` to read an integer from the file, `fileIn.nextDouble()` to read a double from the file, `fileIn.next()` to read a string token from the file, or `fileIn.nextLine()` to read an entire line from the text file. Java begins reading from the beginning of the file and proceeds toward the end as data is read.

Unlike reading from the console, we might want to know if we have reached the end of the file. We can use `fileIn.hasNextLine()` to determine if there is data to read. When we are done with the file, we can close it with `fileIn.close()`, which will release any resources that have been allocated by Java in association with the file.

A complete example is shown in Displays 2.11 and 2.12. Display 2.11 shows the contents of a text file named `player.txt`. This file can be created by any program that saves in the plain text format. As an example, let's say that the file contains information about the last player to play a game. The first line of the file contains the high score of the player, 100510, and the second line contains the name of the player, Gordon Freeman. The program in Display 2.12 reads in this information and displays it. It reads in the high score using `nextInt()` and then reads in the name using `nextLine()`. Note that we have to use an additional `nextLine()` after the `nextInt()` to deal with the newline character for the exact same reason discussed earlier in this chapter in the Pitfall in Section 2.2 titled Dealing with the Line Terminator, '\n'.

Display 2.11   Sample Text File, `player.txt`, to Store a Player's High Score and Name

```
100510
Gordon Freeman
```

Display 2.12   **Program to Read the Text File in Display 2.11**

```
1    import java.util.Scanner;
2    import java.io.FileInputStream;
3    import java.io.FileNotFoundException;
4
5    public class TextFileDemo
6    {
7      public static void main(String[] args)
8      {
9        Scanner fileIn = null;  // Initializes fileIn to empty
10       try
11       {
12         // Attempt to open the file
13         fileIn = new Scanner(
14             new FileInputStream("player.txt"));
15       }
16       catch (FileNotFoundException e)
17       {
18         // This block executed if the file is not found
19         // and then the program exits
20         System.out.println("File not found.");
21         System.exit(0);
22       }
23
24       // If the program gets here then
25       // the file was opened successfully
26       int highscore;
27       String name;
28
29       System.out.println("Text left to read? " +
30           fileIn.hasNextLine());
31       highscore = fileIn.nextInt();
32       fileIn.nextLine(); // Read newline left from nextInt()
33       name = fileIn.nextLine();
34
35       System.out.println("Name: " + name);
36       System.out.println("High score: " + highscore);
37       System.out.println("Text left to read? " +
38           fileIn.hasNextLine());
39       fileIn.close();
40     }
41   }
```

try and catch is explained in more detail in Chapter 9.

The file player.txt should be in the same directory as the Java program. You can also supply a full pathname to the file.

This line is explained earlier in this chapter in the Pitfall section "Dealing with the Line Terminator '\n'"

Sample Dialogue

```
Text left to read? true
Name: Gordon Freeman
High score: 100510
Text left to read? False
```

Self-Test Exercises

18. What would the program in Display 2.12 output if there is no file named `player.txt` in the same directory as the Java program?

19. What is missing from the following code, which attempts to open a file and read an integer?

```java
import java.util.Scanner;
import java.io.FileInputStream;
import java.io.FileNotFoundException;

public class ReadInteger
{
    public static void main(String[] args)
    {
        Scanner fileIn = new Scanner(
          new FileInputStream("datafile.txt"));
        int num = fileIn.nextInt();
        System.out.println(num);
    }
}
```

Chapter Summary

- You can use `System.out.println` for simple console output.
- You can use `System.out.printf` for formatted console output.
- You can use `NumberFormat.getCurrencyInstance()` to produce an object that can convert numbers to strings that show the number as a correctly formatted currency amount, for example, by adding a dollar sign and having exactly two digits after the decimal point.
- You can use the class `DecimalFormat` to output numbers using almost any format you desire.
- You can use an object of the class `Scanner` for reading keyboard input.
- You can use an object of the class `Scanner` for reading input from a text file.

Answers to Self-Test Exercises

1. `I am going home`

2. `System.out.println("Rain, rain, go away,");`
   `System.out.println("Little Johnny wants to play. ");`

3. `System.out.println` ends a line of input, so the next output goes on the next line. With `System.out.print`, the next output goes on the same line.

4. Rosie! Rosie! Are you there?

5. First Name   Last Name
   John   Smith
   Peter   Haley

6. 123.988
   1.240e+02
   124

7. System.out.printf("%15.3e", d);

8. $375.32
   $90.00

9. Either

   import java.awt.Robot;

   or

   import java.awt.*;

10. the java.util package.

11. Scanner inputObj = new Scanner(System.in);
           String str = inputObj.nextLine();

12. number = inputObj.nextInt();

13. import java.util.Scanner;

```java
public class self_ex13
{
    public static void main(String[] args)
    {
        Scanner keyboard = new Scanner(System.in);
        System.out.println("Enter two real numbers.");
        double d1 = keyboard.nextDouble();
        double d2 = keyboard.nextDouble();
        double sum = d1 + d2;
        System.out.println(d1 + " plus " + d2 + " is " + sum);
    }
}
```

14.
```java
import java.util.Scanner;

public class Exercise2
{
    public static void main(String[] args)
    {
        Scanner keyboard = new Scanner(System.in);

        System.out.println("Enter a line with three words:");
        String w1 = keyboard.next();
        String w2 = keyboard.next();
        String w3 = keyboard.next();

        System.out.println(w1 + " " + w2 + " " + w3);
    }
}
```

15. The newline character is left in the input buffer after the `nextInt()` call and should be removed prior to calling `nextLine()`. This can be fixed by adding another `nextLine()` call:

```java
Scanner keyboard = new Scanner(System.in);
System.out.println("Enter your age.");
int age = keyboard.nextInt();
keyboard.nextLine();
System.out.println("Enter your name.");
String name = keyboard.nextLine();
System.out.println(name+", you are "+age+" years old.");
```

16. `keyboard.useDelimiter(", ");`

17. `w1` is assigned `"one,two three"`; `w2` is assigned `"four"`.

18. The program will output `"File not found."` and exit.

19. The statement that attempts to open the file must be inside a try/catch block, as follows:

```java
try
{
    Scanner fileIn = new Scanner(
        new FileInputStream("datafile.txt"));
    int num = fileIn.nextInt();
    System.out.println(num);
}
catch (FileNotFoundException e)
{
    System.out.println("File not found.");
}
```

Alternately, the line `throws FileNotFoundException` could be added to the end of the definition of the main method, but this approach is not recommended because the exception will simply be handed off to the JVM and it will halt the program.

[MyProgrammingLab] **Programming Projects**

Visit www.myprogramminglab.com to complete select exercises online and get instant feedback.

1. The Babylonian algorithm to compute the square root of a positive number n is as follows:

    1. Make a `guess` at the answer (you can pick $n/2$ as your initial guess).
    2. Compute `r = n / guess`
    3. Set `guess = (guess +r)/ 2`
    4. Go back to step 2 for as many iterations as necessary. The more you repeat steps 2 and 3, the closer `guess` will become to the square root of n.

    Write a program that inputs a double for n, iterates through the Babylonian algorithm five times, and outputs the answer as a `double` to two decimal places. Your answer will be most accurate for small values of n.

2. Write a program which will calculate the total payable income tax for a person. It should ask for the gross income, standard deduction, personal exemption, and tax rate. Total payable tax should be charged on net income, which is obtained by deducting standard deduction and personal exemption from the gross income. The program should display a report like this:

Name:	"John Smith"
Gross Income:	$ 40000.00
Standard deduction:	$ 5700.00
Personal Exemption:	$ 3650.00
Net Income:	$ 30650.00
Tax Payable:	$ 4597.50

    Assume that the tax rate is 15 percent of the net income.

3. Write a program that reads in three integers typed on the keyboard and outputs their sum and average.

4. Write a program that reads in the radius of a circle and outputs the diameter, circumference and area of the circle. Use the constant value of 3.14159 for π.

5. Write a simple mortgage calculator. It will ask for the mortgage amount, mortgage term i.e., the number of years to pay the loan, and the interest rate. It should calculate the total payable interest and add it to the mortgage amount to get the gross amount. Then it should calculate the monthly payment amount by dividing the gross amount by the number of months. Finally, it should display the monthly payment.

    For example, if a user enters a mortgage amount of $165000, a mortgage term of 30 years, i.e., 360 months, and an interest rate of 7% per year, then the program should calculate the monthly payments as $1420.83.

6. (This is a better version of an exercise from Chapter 1.) A government research lab has concluded that an artificial sweetener commonly used in diet soda pop causes death in laboratory mice. A friend of yours is desperate to lose weight but cannot give up soda pop. Your friend wants to know how much diet soda pop it is possible to drink without dying as a result. Write a program to supply the answer. The input to the program is the amount of artificial sweetener needed to kill a mouse, the weight of the mouse, and the desired weight of the dieter. Assume that diet soda contains 1/10th of 1% artificial sweetener. Use a named constant for this fraction. You may want to express the percent as the `double` value `0.001`.

7. Write a program that determines the change to be dispensed from a vending machine. An item in the machine can cost between 25 cents and 1 dollar, in 5-cent increments (25, 30, 35, . . . 90, 95, or 100), and the machine accepts only a single dollar bill to pay for the item. For example, a possible sample dialog might be the following:

```
Enter price of item
(from 25 cents to a dollar, in 5-cent increments):
45

You bought an item for 45 cents and gave me a dollar,
so your change is
2 quarters,
0 dimes, and
1 nickels.
```

8. Write a program that reads in a line of text from a file and then outputs that line of text first in all uppercase letters and then in all lowercase letters.

9. (This is a better version of an exercise from Chapter 1.) Write a program that reads in a line of text and then outputs that line of text with the first occurrence of `"hate"` changed to `"love"`. For example, a possible sample dialog might be the following:

```
Enter a line of text.
I hate you.
I have rephrased that line to read:
I love you.
```

You can assume that the word `"hate"` occurs in the input. If the word `"hate"` occurs more than once in the line, your program should replace only the first occurrence of `"hate"`.

10. Write a program that inputs the name, quantity, and price of three items. The name may contain spaces. Output a bill with a tax rate of 6.25%. All prices should be output to two decimal places. The bill should be formatted in columns with 30 characters for the name, 10 characters for the quantity, 10 characters for the price, and 10 characters for the total. Sample input and output is shown as follows:

```
Input name of item 1:
lollipops
```

```
Input quantity of item 1:
10
Input price of item 1:
0.50
Input name of item 2:
diet soda
Input quantity of item 2:
3
Input price of item 2:
1.25

Input name of item 3:
chocolate bar
Input quantity of item 3:
20
Input price of item 3:
0.75

Your bill:

Item                 Quantity      Price        Total
lollipops            10            0.50         5.00
diet soda            3             1.25         3.75
chocolate bar        20            0.75         15.00

Subtotal                                        23.75
6.25% sales tax                                  1.48
Total                                           25.23
```

VideoNote
**Solution to
Programming
Project 2.11**

11. Write a program that calculates the total grade for three classroom exercises as a percentage. Use the `DecimalFormat` class to output the value as a percent. The scores should be summarized in a table. Input the assignment information in this order: name of assignment (may include spaces), points earned (integer), and total points possible (integer). The percentage is the sum of the total points earned divided by the total points possible. Sample input and output is shown as follows:

```
Name of exercise 1:
Group Project
Score received for exercise 1:
10
Total points possible for exercise 1:
10

Name of exercise 2:
Homework
Score received for exercise 2:
7
Total points possible for exercise 2:
12
```

```
Name of exercise 3:
Presentation
Score received for exercise 3:
5
Total points possible for exercise 3:
8

Exercise              Score              Total Possible
Group Project         10                 10
Homework              7                  12
Presentation          5                  8
Total                 22                 30

Your total is 22 out of 30, or 73.33%.
```

VideoNote
**Solution to
Programming
Project 2.12**

12. (This is a variant of an exercise from Chapter 1.) Create a text file that contains the text `"I hate programming!"` Write a program that reads in this line of text from the file and then the text with the first occurrence of `"hate"` changed to `"love"`. In this case, the program would output `"I love programming!"` Your program should work with any line of text that contains the word `"hate"`, not just the example given in this problem. If the word `"hate"` occurs more than once in the line, your program should replace only the first occurrence of `"hate"`.

13. (This is an extension of an exercise from Chapter 1.) A simple rule to estimate your ideal body weight is to allow 110 pounds for the first 5 feet of height and 5 pounds for each additional inch. Create the following text in a text file. It contains the names and heights in feet and inches of Tom Atto (6'3"), Eaton Wright (5'5"), and Cary Oki (5'11"):

```
Tom Atto
6
3
Eaton Wright
5
5
Cary Oki
5
11
```

Write a program that reads the data in the file and outputs the full name and ideal body weight for each person. In the next chapter, you will learn about loops, which allow for a more efficient way to solve this problem.

Flow of Control 3

3.1 BRANCHING MECHANISM 132
if-else Statements 132
Omitting the else 133
Compound Statements 134
Nested Statements 136
Multiway if-else Statement 136
Example: State Income Tax 137
The switch Statement 139
The Conditional Operator ★ 144

3.2 BOOLEAN EXPRESSIONS 145
Simple Boolean Expressions 145
Lexicographic and Alphabetical Order 148
Building Boolean Expressions 151
Evaluating Boolean Expressions 152
Short-Circuit and Complete Evaluation 156
Precedence and Associativity Rules 157

3.3 LOOPS 164
while Statement and do-while Statement 164
Algorithms and Pseudocode 166
Example: Averaging a List of Scores 169
The for Statement 170
The Comma in for Statements 173
Nested Loops 177
The break and continue Statements ★ 180
The exit Statement 181

3.4 DEBUGGING 182
Loop Bugs 182
Tracing Variables 182
General Debugging Techniques 183
Example: Debugging an Input Validation Loop 184
Preventive Coding 188
Assertion Checks ★ 189

3.5 RANDOM NUMBER GENERATION ★ 191
The Random Object 192
The Math.random() Method 193

Chapter Summary 194   **Answers to Self-Test Exercises** 194   **Programming Projects** 200

Flow of Control

If you think we're wax-works," he said, "you ought to pay, you know.
Wax-works weren't made to be looked at for nothing. Nohow!"
"Contrariwise," added the one marked "DEE," "if you think we're alive,
you ought to speak."

LEWIS CARROLL, *Through the Looking-Glass*

Introduction

As in most programming languages, Java handles flow of control with branching and looping statements. Java branching and looping statements are the same as in the C and C++ languages and are very similar to those in other programming languages. (However, the Boolean expressions that control Java branches and loops are a bit different in Java from what they are in C and C++.)

Most branching and looping statements are controlled by Boolean expressions. A Boolean expression is any expression that is either true or false. In Java, the primitive type `boolean` has only the two values, `true` and `false`, and Boolean expressions evaluate to one of these two values. Before we discuss Boolean expressions and the type `boolean`, we will introduce the Java branching statements using only Boolean expressions whose meaning is intuitively obvious. This will serve to motivate our discussion of Boolean expressions.

Prerequisites

This chapter uses material from Chapters 1 and 2.

3.1 Branching Mechanism

When you come to a fork in the road, take it.

Attributed to Yogi Berra

if-else Statements

An `if-else` statement chooses between two alternative statements based on the value of a Boolean expression. For example, suppose you want to design a program to compute a week's salary for an hourly employee. Assume the firm pays an overtime rate of one-and-one-half times the regular rate for all hours after the first 40 hours worked. When the employee works 40 or more hours, the pay is then equal to

```
rate*40 + 1.5*rate*(hours - 40)
```

However, if the employee works less than 40 hours, the correct pay formula is simply

```
rate*hours
```

The following `if-else` statement computes the correct pay for an employee whether the employee works less than 40 hours or works 40 or more hours:

```
if (hours > 40)
    grossPay = rate*40 + 1.5*rate*(hours - 40);
else
    grossPay = rate*hours;
```

The syntax for an `if-else` statement is given in the box entitled "`if-else` Statement." If the Boolean expression in parentheses (after the `if`) evaluates to `true`, then the statement before the `else` is executed. If the Boolean expression evaluates to `false`, then the statement after the `else` is executed.

Remember that when you use a Boolean expression in an `if-else` statement, the **parentheses**   Boolean expression must be enclosed in **parentheses**.

Notice that an `if-else` statement has smaller statements embedded in it. Most of the statement forms in Java allow you to make larger statements out of smaller ones by combining the smaller statements in certain ways.

Omitting the `else`

Sometimes you want one of the two alternatives in an `if-else` statement to do nothing at all. In Java, this can be accomplished by omitting the `else` part. These **if statement**   sorts of statements are referred to as **if statements** to distinguish them from `if-else` statements. For example, the first of the following two statements is an `if` statement:

```
if (sales > minimum)
    salary = salary + bonus;
System.out.println("salary = $" + salary);
```

If the value of `sales` is greater than the value of `minimum`, the assignment statement is executed and then the following `System.out.println` statement is executed. On the other hand, if the value of `sales` is less than or equal to `minimum`, then the embedded assignment statement is not executed, so the `if` statement causes no change (that is, no bonus is added to the base salary), and the program proceeds directly to the `System.out.println` statement.

Compound Statements

if-else
with multiple
statements

compound
statement

You will often want the branches of an if-else statement to execute more than one statement each. To accomplish this, enclose the statements for each branch between a pair of braces, { and }. A list of statements enclosed in a pair of braces is called a **compound statement**. A compound statement is treated as a single statement by Java and may be used anywhere that a single statement may be used. Thus, the "Multiple Statement Alternatives" version described in the box entitled "if-else Statement" is really just a special case of the "simple" case with one statement in each branch.

---

if-else Statement

The if-else statement chooses between two alternative actions based on the value of a Boolean_Expression; that is, an expression that is either true or false, such as balance < 0.

SYNTAX

```
if (Boolean_Expression)  ◄─────────  Be sure to note that the
    Yes_Statement                    Boolean_Expression must be
else                                 enclosed in parentheses.
    No_Statement
```

If *Boolean_Expression* is true, then *Yes_Statement* is executed. If *Boolean_Expression* is false, then *No_Statement* is executed.

EXAMPLE

```
if (time < limit)
    System.out.println("You made it.");
else
    System.out.println("You missed the deadline.");
```

Omitting the else Part

You may omit the else part to obtain what is often called an **if statement**.

SYNTAX

```
if (Boolean_Expression)
    Action_Statement
```

If *Boolean_Expression* is true, then *Action_Statement* is executed; otherwise, nothing happens and the program goes on to the next statement.

EXAMPLE

```
if (weight > ideal)
    calorieAllotment = calorieAllotment - 500;
```

Multiple Statement Alternatives

In an `if-else` statement, you can have one or both alternatives contain several statements. To accomplish this, group the statements using braces, as in the following example:

```java
if (myScore > yourScore)
{
     System.out.println("I win!");
     wager = wager + 100;
}
else
{
     System.out.println("I wish these were golf scores.");
     wager = 0;
}
```

TIP: Placing of Braces

There are two commonly used ways of indenting and placing braces in `if-else` statements. They are illustrated as follows:

```java
if (myScore > yourScore)
{
    System.out.println("I win!");
    wager = wager + 100;
}
else
{
    System.out.println("I wish these were golf scores.");
    wager = 0;
}
```

and

```java
if (myScore > yourScore) {
    System.out.println("I win!");
    wager = wager + 100;
} else {
    System.out.println("I wish these were golf scores.");
    wager = 0;
}
```

The only difference is the placement of braces. The first form is called the *Allman style,* named after programmer Eric Allman. We find the Allman style easier to read and so we prefer it in this book. The second form is called the *Kernighan & Ritchie* or *K&R style,* named after Dennis Ritchie (the designer of C) and Brian Kernighan (author of the first C tutorial). The K&R style saves lines, so some programmers prefer it or some minor variant of it.

Be sure to note the indenting pattern in these examples. ■

Nested Statements

As you have seen, `if-else` statements and `if` statements contain smaller statements within them. Thus far, we have used compound statements and simple statements, such as assignment statements, as these smaller substatements, but there are other possibilities. In fact, any statement at all can be used as a subpart of an `if-else` statement or other statement that has one or more statements within it.

indenting

When nesting statements, you normally indent each level of nested substatements, although there are some special situations (such as a multiway `if-else` statement) where this rule is not followed.

Self-Test Exercises

1. Write an `if-else` statement that outputs the word `"Even"` if the value of the variable num is an even number and outputs `"Odd"` if the value of num is an odd number. The variable num is of type `int`.

2. Suppose `inventory` and `sale` are variables of type `double` that have been given values. Write an `if-else` statement that outputs the number of items sold, decreases the value of `inventory` by the value of `sale`, and sets the value of `sale` to zero, provided that `inventory` is larger than `sale`. If, however, inventory is less than or equal to sale, the `if-else` statement should simply output the words `"Not enough Inventory-Place an Order"` without changing the value of any variables.

3. Suppose `season` is a variable of type `String`. Write an `if-else` statement that outputs the words `"Warm Clothing"` if the value of the variable `season` equals `'Winter'` or `'winter'`; otherwise outputs the words `"Normal Clothing"`.

4. Suppose `price` and `discount` are variables of type `double` that have been given values. Write an `if-else` statement that outputs the word `"Crazy"` if price is less than `discount`; otherwise, it should output `"OK"` and set the variable `netPrice` equal to price minus `discount`.

Multiway `if-else` Statement

multiway `if-else` statement

The **multiway `if-else` statement** is not really a different kind of Java statement. It is simply an ordinary `if-else` statement nested inside `if-else` statements, but it is thought of as a different kind of statement and is indented differently from other nested statements so as to reflect this thinking.

The syntax for a multiway `if-else` statement and a simple example are given in the box entitled "Multiway `if-else` Statement." Note that the Boolean expressions are aligned with one another, and their corresponding actions are also aligned with one another. This makes it easy to see the correspondence between Boolean expressions and actions. The Boolean expressions are evaluated in order until a `true` Boolean expression is found. At that point, the evaluation of Boolean expressions stops, and the action corresponding to the first `true` Boolean expression is executed. The final `else` is optional. If there is a final `else` and all the Boolean expressions are `false`, the final action is executed. If there is no final `else` and all the Boolean expressions are `false`, then no action is taken. An example of a multiway `if-else` statement is given in the following Programming Example.

Multiway `if-else` Statement

SYNTAX

```
if (Boolean_Expression_1)
     Statement_1
else if (Boolean_Expression_2)
     Statement_2
              .
              .
              .
else if (Boolean_Expression_n)
     Statement_n
else
     Statement_For_All_Other_Possibilities
```

EXAMPLE

```
if (numberOfPeople < 50)
   System.out.println("Less than 50 people");
else if (numberOfPeople < 100)
   System.out.println("At least 50 and less than 100 people");
else if (numberOfPeople < 200)
   System.out.println("At least 100 and less than 200 people");
else
   System.out.println("At least 200 people");
```

The Boolean expressions are checked in order until the first `true` Boolean expression is encountered, and then the corresponding statement is executed. If none of the Boolean expressions is `true`, then the *Statement_For_All_Other_Possibilities* is executed.

EXAMPLE: State Income Tax

Display 3.1 contains a program that uses a multiway `if-else` statement to compute state income tax. This state computes tax according to the following rate schedule:

1. No tax is paid on the first $15,000 of net income.

2. A tax of 5% is assessed on each dollar of net income from $15,001 to $30,000.

3. A tax of 10% is assessed on each dollar of net income over $30,000.

(continued)

EXAMPLE: (continued)

The program uses a multiway `if-else` statement with one action for each of the above three cases. The condition for the second case is actually more complicated than it needs to be. The computer will not get to the second condition unless it has already tried the first condition and found it to be `false`. Thus, you know that whenever the computer tries the second condition, it knows that `netIncome` is greater than `15000`. Hence, you can replace the line

```
else if ((netIncome > 15000) && (netIncome <= 30000))
```

with the following, and the program will perform exactly the same:

```
else if (netIncome <= 30000)
```

Self-Test Exercises

5. What output will be produced by the following code?

```
int marks = 70;
if (marks > 80)
    System.out.println("Great Achievement!");
else if (marks > 60)
    System.out.println("Good! You can do better!");
else
    System.out.println("You have scored less than 60\n Better
luck next time!");
```

6. What would be the output in Exercise 5 if the assignment were changed to the following?

```
int marks = 97;
```

7. What would be the output in Exercise 5 if the assignment were changed to the following?

```
int marks = -10;
```

8. Write a multiway `if-else` statement that classifies the value of an `int` variable n into one of the following categories and writes out an appropriate message:

```
n < 0 or 0 ≤ n < 100 or n ≥ 100
```

Hint: Remember that the Boolean expressions are checked in order.

Display 3.1   Tax Program

```
1   import java.util.Scanner;

2   public class IncomeTax
3   {
4       public static void main(String[] args)
5       {
6           Scanner keyboard = new Scanner(System.in);
7           double netIncome, tax, fivePercentTax, tenPercentTax;

8           System.out.println("Enter net income.\n"
9                           + "Do not include a dollar sign or any commas.");
10          netIncome = keyboard.nextDouble( );

11          if (netIncome <= 15000)
12              tax = 0;
13          else if ((netIncome > 15000) && (netIncome <= 30000))
14              //tax = 5% of amount over $15,000
15              tax = (0.05*(netIncome - 15000));
16          else //netIncome > $30,000
17          {
18              //fivePercentTax = 5% of income from $15,000 to $30,000.
19              fivePercentTax = 0.05*15000;
20              //tenPercentTax = 10% of income over $30,000.
21              tenPercentTax = 0.10*(netIncome - 30000);
22              tax = (fivePercentTax + tenPercentTax);
23          }

24          System.out.printf("Tax due = $%.2f", tax);
25      }
26  }
27
```

Sample Dialogue

```
Enter net income.
Do not include a dollar sign or any commas.
40000
Tax due = $1750.00
```

The switch Statement

switch
statement

The **switch statement** is the only other kind of Java statement that implements multiway branches. The syntax for a switch statement and a simple example are shown in the box entitled "The switch Statement."

When a `switch` statement is executed, one of a number of different branches is executed. The choice of which branch to execute is determined by a **controlling expression** given in parentheses after the keyword `switch`. Following this are a number of occurrences of the reserved word `case` followed by a constant and a colon. These constants are called

case labels. The controlling expression for a `switch` statement must be one of the types `char`, `int`, `short`, `byte`, or `String`.[1] The `String` data type is allowed only in Java 7 or higher. The case labels must all be of the same type as the controlling expression. No case label can occur more than once, because that would be an ambiguous instruction. There may also be a section labeled `default:`, which is usually last.

When the `switch` statement is executed, the controlling expression is evaluated and the computer looks at the case labels. If it finds a case label that equals the value of the controlling expression, it executes the code for that case label.

The `switch` statement ends when either a `break` statement is executed or the end of the `switch` statement is reached. A **break statement** consists of the keyword `break` followed by a semicolon. When the computer executes the statements after a case label, it continues until it reaches a `break` statement. When the computer encounters a `break` statement, the `switch` statement ends. If you omit the `break` statements, then after executing the code for one case, the computer will go on to execute the code for the next case.

Note that you can have two case labels for the same section of code, as in the following portion of a `switch` statement:

```
case 'A':
case 'a':
    System.out.println("Excellent. You need not take the final.");
    break;
```

Because the first case has no `break` statement (in fact, no statements at all), the effect is the same as having two labels for one case, but Java syntax requires one keyword case for each label, such as `'A'` and `'a'`.

If no case label has a constant that matches the value of the controlling expression,

then the statements following the **default** label are executed. You need not have a `default` section. If there is no `default` section and no match is found for the value of the controlling expression, then nothing happens when the `switch` statement is executed. However, it is safest to always have a `default` section. If you think your case labels list all possible outcomes, you can put an error message in the `default` section.

The default case need not be the last case in a `switch` statement, but making it the last case, as we have always done, makes the code clearer.

A sample `switch` statement is shown in Display 3.2. Notice that the case labels do not need to be listed in order and do not need to span a complete interval.

---

[1]As we will learn in Chapter 6, the type may also be an enumerated type.

The `switch` Statement

SYNTAX

```
switch (Controlling_Expression)
    {
        case Case_Label_1:
            Statement_Sequence_1
            break;
        case Case_Label_2:
                Statement_Sequence_2
            break;
                    .
                    .
                    .
        case Case_Label_n:
                Statement_Sequence_n
                break;
        default:
                Default_Statement_Sequence
                break;
    }
```

Each Case_Label is a constant of the same type as the Controlling_Expression. The Controlling_Expression must be of type `char`, `int`, `short`, `byte`, *or* `string`.

A break *may be omitted. If there is no* break, *execution just continues to the next case.*

The `default` *case is optional.*

EXAMPLE

```
int vehicleClass;
double toll;
        .
        .
        .
switch (vehicleClass)
{
    case 1:
        System.out.println("Passenger car.");
        toll = 0.50;
        break;
    case 2:
        System.out.println("Bus.");
        toll = 1.50;
        break;
    case 3:
        System.out.println("Truck.");
        toll = 2.00;
        break;
    default:
        System.out.println("Unknown vehicle class!");
        break;
}
```

Display 3.2 **A switch Statement** (part 1 of 2)

```
1   import java.util.Scanner;
2
3   public class SwitchDemo
4   {
5       public static void main(String[] args)
6       {
7           Scanner keyboard = new Scanner(System.in);
8
8           System.out.println("Enter number of ice cream flavors:");
9           int numberOfFlavors = keyboard.nextInt( );
10          switch (numberOfFlavors)
11          {
12              case 32:
13                  System.out.println("Nice selection.");
14                  break;
15              case 1:
16                  System.out.println("I bet it's vanilla.");
17                  break;
18              case 2:
19              case 3:
20              case 4:
21                  System.out.println(numberOfFlavors + "flavors");
22                  System.out.println("is acceptable.");
23                  break;
24              default:
25                  System.out.println("I didn't plan for");
26                  System.out.println(numberOfFlavors + " flavors.");
27                  break;
28          }
29      }
30  }
```

Controlling expression → (points to line 10)

Case labels → (points to line 12, 13)

break *statement* → (points to line 17)

Sample Dialogue 1

```
Enter number of ice cream flavors:
1
I bet it's vanilla.
```

Sample Dialogue 2

```
Enter number of ice cream flavors:
32
Nice selection.
```

Display 3.2 **A** `switch` **Statement** (part 2 of 2)

Sample Dialogue 3

```
Enter number of ice cream flavors:
3
3 flavors
is acceptable.
```

Sample Dialogue 4

```
Enter number of ice cream flavors:
9
I didn't plan for
9 flavors.
```

PITFALL: Forgetting a `break` in a `switch` Statement

If you forget a `break` in a `switch` statement, the compiler does not issue an error message. You will have written a syntactically correct `switch` statement, but it will not do what you intended it to do. Notice the annotation in the example in the box entitled "The `switch` Statement."

The last case in a `switch` statement does not need a `break`, but it is a good idea to include it nonetheless. That way, if a new case is added after the last case, you will not forget to add a `break` (because it is already there). This advice about `break` statements also applies to the default case when it is last. It is best to place the default case last, but that is not required by the Java language, so there is always a possibility of somebody adding a case after the default case. ∎

MyProgrammingLab™   ## Self-Test Exercises

9. What is the output produced by the following code?

```java
char account = 'S';
switch (account)
{
    case 'S':
    case 's':
        System.out.println("Savings Account.");
    case 'T':
    case 't':
        System.out.println("Term Deposit.");
        break;
    default:
        System.out.println("Something else.");
        break;
}
```

(continued)

Self-Test Exercises (continued)

10. What is the output produced by the following code?

```
int key = 1;
switch (key + 1)
{
    case 1:
        System.out.println("Apples");
        break;
    case 2:
        System.out.println("Oranges");
        break;
    case 3:
        System.out.println("Peaches");
    case 4:
        System.out.println("Plums");
        break;
    default:
        System.out.println("Fruitless");
}
```

11. What would be the output in Exercise 10 if the first line were changed to the following?

```
int key = 3;
```

12. What would be the output in Exercise 10 if the first line were changed to the following?

```
int key = 5;
```

The Conditional Operator ★

conditional operator

ternary operator

arithmetic if

You can embed a branch inside of an expression by using a ternary operator known as the **conditional operator** (also called the **ternary operator** or **arithmetic if**). Its use is reminiscent of an older programming style, and we do not advise using it. It is included here for the sake of completeness (and in case you disagree with our programming style).

The conditional operator is a notational variant on certain forms of the `if-else` statement. The following example illustrates the conditional operator. Consider the following `if-else` statement:

```
if (n1 > n2)
    max = n1;
else
    max = n2;
```

This can be expressed using the *conditional operator* as follows:

```
max = (n1 > n2) ? n1 : n2;
```

The expression on the right-hand side of the assignment statement is the conditional operator expression:

```
(n1 > n2) ? n1 : n2
```

The ? and : together form a ternary operator known as the conditional operator. A conditional operator expression starts with a Boolean expression followed by a ? and then followed by two expressions separated with a colon. If the Boolean expression is true, then the value of the first of the two expressions is returned as the value of the entire expression; otherwise, the value of the second of the two expressions is returned as the value of the entire expression.

3.2   Boolean Expressions

"Contrariwise," continued Tweedledee, *"if it was so, it might be; and if it were so, it would be; but as it isn't, it ain't. That's logic."*

LEWIS CARROLL, *Through the Looking-Glass*

Boolean expression

Now that we have motivated Boolean expressions by using them in if-else statements, we will discuss them and the type boolean in more detail. A **Boolean expression** is simply an expression that is either true or false. The name *Boolean* is derived from George Boole, a 19th-century English logician and mathematician whose work was related to these kinds of expressions.

Simple Boolean Expressions

We have already been using simple Boolean expressions in if-else statements. The simplest Boolean expressions are comparisons of two expressions, such as

```
time < limit
```

and

```
balance <= 0
```

A Boolean expression does not need to be enclosed in parentheses to qualify as a Boolean expression, although it does need to be enclosed in parentheses when it is used in an if-else statement.

Display 3.3 shows the various Java comparison operators you can use to compare two expressions.

PITFALL: Using = in Place of ==

Because the equal sign, =, is used for assignment in Java, something else is needed to indicate equality. In Java, equality is indicated with two equal signs with no space between them, as in

```
if (yourScore == myScore)
    System.out.println("A tie.");
```

Fortunately, if you do use = in place of ==, Java will probably give you a compiler error message. (The only case that does not give an error message is when the expression in parentheses happens to form a correct assignment to a `boolean` variable.) ∎

Display 3.3   Java Comparison Operators

MATH NOTATION	NAME	JAVA NOTATION	JAVA EXAMPLES
=	Equal to	==	`x + 7 == 2*y` `answer == 'y'`
≠	Not equal to	!=	`score != 0` `answer != 'y'`
>	Greater than	>	`time > limit`
≥	Greater than or equal to	>=	`age >= 21`
<	Less than	<	`pressure < max`
≤	Less than or equal to	<=	`time <=limit`

The Methods `equals` and `equalsIgnoreCase`

When testing strings for equality, do not use ==. Instead, use either `equals` or `equalsIgnoreCase`.

SYNTAX

String.`equals`(*Other_String*)
String.`equalsIgnoreCase`(*Other_String*)

EXAMPLE

```
String s1;
    .
    .
    .
```

```
if ( s1.equals("Hello") )
    System.out.println("The string is Hello.");
else
    System.out.println("The string is not Hello.");
```

PITFALL: Using == with Strings

Although == correctly tests two values of a primitive type, such as two numbers, to see whether they are equal, it has a different meaning when applied to objects, such as objects of the class String.[2] Recall that an object is something whose type is a class, such as a string. All strings are in the class String (that is, are of type String), so == applied to two strings does not test to see whether the strings are equal. Instead, it tests whether two strings refer to the same object. We will discuss references in Chapter 15. To test two strings (or any two objects) to see if they have equal values, you should use the method equals rather than ==. For example, suppose s1 and s2 are String variables that have been given values, and consider the statement

```
if (s1.equals(s2))
    System.out.println("They are equal strings.");
else
    System.out.println("They are not equal strings.");
```

If s1 and s2 name strings that contain the same characters in the same order, then the output will be

```
They are equal strings.
```

The notation may seem a bit awkward at first, because it is not symmetric between the two things being tested for equality. The two expressions

```
s1.equals(s2)
s2.equals(s1)
```

are equivalent.

The method equalsIgnoreCase behaves similarly to equals, except that with equalsIgnoreCase, the upper- and lowercase versions of the same letter are considered the same. For example, "Hello" and "hello" are not equal because their first characters, 'H' and 'h', are different characters. But they would be considered equal by the method equalsIgnoreCase. For example, the following will output Equal ignoring case.:

```
if ("Hello".equalsIgnoreCase("hello"))
    System.out.println("Equal ignoring case.");
```

(continued)

---

[2]When applied to two strings (or any two objects), == tests to see if they are stored in the same memory location, but we will not discuss that until Chapter 4. For now, we need only note that == does something other than test for the equality of two strings.

PITFALL: (continued)

Notice that it is perfectly legal to use a quoted string with a `String` method, as in the preceding use of `equalsIgnoreCase`. A quoted string is an object of type `String` and has all the methods that any other object of type `String` has.

For the kinds of applications we are looking at in this chapter, you could also use `==` to test for equality of objects of type `String`, and it would deliver the correct answer. However, there are situations in which `==` does not correctly test strings for equality, so you should get in the habit of using `equals` rather than `==` to test strings. ■

Lexicographic and Alphabetical Order

lexicographic ordering

The method `compareTo` tests two strings to determine their lexicographic order. **Lexicographic ordering** is similar to alphabetic ordering and is sometimes, but not always, the same as alphabetic ordering. The easiest way to think about lexicographic ordering is to think of it as being the same as alphabetic ordering *but with the alphabet ordered differently.* Specifically, in lexicographic ordering, the letters and other characters are ordered as in the ASCII ordering, which is shown in Appendix 3.

compareTo

If `s1` and `s2` are two variables of type `String` that have been given `String` values, then

```
s1.compareTo(s2)
```

returns a negative number if `s1` comes before `s2` in lexicographic ordering, returns zero if the two strings are equal, and returns a positive number if `s2` comes before `s1`. Thus,

```
s1.compareTo(s2) < 0
```

returns true if `s1` comes before `s2` in lexicographic order and returns false otherwise. For example, the following will produce correct output:

```
if (s1.compareTo(s2) < 0)
    System.out.println(
        s1 + " precedes " + s2 + " in lexicographic ordering");
else if (s1.compareTo(s2) < 0)
    System.out.println(
        s1 + " follows " + s2 + " in lexicographic ordering");
else //s1.compareTo(s2) == 0
    System.out.println(s1 + " equals " + s2);
```

If you look at the ordering of characters in Appendix 3, you will see that *all* uppercase letters come before *all* lowercase letters. For example, `'Z'` comes before `'a'` in lexicographic order. So when comparing two strings consisting of a mix of lower- and uppercase letters, lexicographic and alphabetic ordering are not the same. However, as shown in Appendix 3, all the lowercase letters are in alphabetic order. So for any two strings of all lowercase letters, lexicographic order is the same as ordinary alphabetic order. Similarly, in the ordering of Appendix 3, all the uppercase letters are in alphabetic order. So for any two strings of all uppercase letters, lexicographic order is the same as ordinary alphabetic order. Thus, if you treat all uppercase letters as if they were lowercase, then lexicographic ordering becomes the same as alphabetic ordering. This is exactly what the method `compareToIgnoreCase` does. Thus, the following produces correct output:

`compareTo`
`IgnoreCase`

```
if (s1.compareToIgnoreCase(s2) < 0)
    System.out.println(
        s1 + " precedes " + s2 + " in ALPHABETIC ordering");
else if (s1.compareToIgnoreCase(s2) > 0)
    System.out.println(
        s1 + " follows " + s2 + " in ALPHABETIC ordering");
else //s1.compareToIgnoreCase(s2) == 0
    System.out.println(s1 + " equals " + s2 + " IGNORING CASE");
```

The above code will compile and produce results no matter what characters are in the strings `s1` and `s2`. However, alphabetic order and the output make sense only if the two strings consist entirely of letters.

The program in Display 3.4 illustrates some of the string comparisons we have just discussed.

Self-Test Exercises

13. Suppose `n1` and `n2` are two `int` variables that have been given values. Write a Boolean expression that returns `true` if the value of `n1` is a multiple of the value of `n2`; otherwise, it should return `false`.

14. Suppose `sales` and `commission` are two `double` variables that have been given values. Write an `if-else` statement that sets the value of `commission` to `0.15` if the value of `sales` is greater than or equal to `10000`; otherwise it sets the value of `commission` to `0`.

15. Suppose `variable1` and `variable2` are two variables that have been given values. How do you test whether they are equal when the variables are of type `int`? How do you test whether they are equal when the variables are of type `String`?

16. Assume that `nextWord` is a `String` variable that has been given a `String` value consisting entirely of letters. Write some Java code that outputs the message `"First half of the alphabet"`, provided `nextWord` precedes `"N"` in alphabetic ordering. If `nextWord` does not precede `"N"` in alphabetic ordering, the code should output `"Second half of the alphabet"`. (Note that `"N"` uses double quotes to produce a `String` value, as opposed to using single quotes to produce a `char` value.)

Display 3.4   **Comparing Strings**

```
1  public class StringComparisonDemo
2  {
3      public static void main(String[] args)
4      {
5          String s1 = "Java isn't just for breakfast.";
6          String s2 = "JAVA isn't just for breakfast.";

7          if (s1.equals(s2))
8              System.out.println("The two lines are equal.");
9          else
10             System.out.println("The two lines are not equal.");
11         if (s2.equals(s1))
12             System.out.println("The two lines are equal.");
13         else
14             System.out.println("The two lines are not equal.");
15         if (s1.equalsIgnoreCase(s2))
16             System.out.println(
                   "But the lines are equal, ignoring case.");
17         else
18             System.out.println(
                   "Lines are not equal, even ignoring case.");

19         String s3 = "A cup of java is a joy forever.";
20         if (s3.compareToIgnoreCase(s1) < 0)
21         {
22             System.out.println("\"" + s3 + "\"");
23             System.out.println("precedes");
24             System.out.println("\"" + s1 + "\"");
25             System.out.println("in alphabetic ordering");
26         }
27         else
28             System.out.println("s3 does not precede s1.");
29     }
30 }
```

Sample Dialogue

```
The two lines are not equal.
The two lines are not equal.
But the lines are equal, ignoring case.
"A cup of java is a joy forever."
precedes
"Java isn't just for breakfast."
in alphabetic ordering
```

Building Boolean Expressions

&& means "and"

You can combine two Boolean expressions using the "and" operator, which is spelled && in Java. For example, the following Boolean expression is true provided number is greater than 2 and number is less than 7:

```
(number > 2) && (number < 7)
```

When two Boolean expressions are connected using &&, the entire expression is true, provided both of the smaller Boolean expressions are true; otherwise, the entire expression is false.

The "and" Operator &&

You can form a more elaborate Boolean expression by combining two simpler Boolean expressions using the "and" operator &&

SYNTAX (FOR A BOOLEAN EXPRESSION USING &&)

```
(Boolean_Exp_1) && (Boolean_Exp_2)
```

EXAMPLE (WITHIN AN if-else STATEMENT)

```
if ( (score > 0) && (score < 10) )
    System.out.println("score is between 0 and 10.");
else
    System.out.println("score is not between 0 and 10.");
```

If the value of score is greater than 0 and the value of score is also less than 10, then the first System.out.println statement is executed; otherwise, the second System.out.println statement is executed.

|| means "or"

You can also combine two Boolean expressions using the "or" operator, which is spelled || in Java. For example, the following is true provided count is less than 3 or count is greater than 12:

```
(count < 3) || (count > 12)
```

When two Boolean expressions are connected using ||, the entire expression is true, provided that one or both of the smaller Boolean expressions are true; otherwise, the entire expression is false.

You can negate any Boolean expression using the ! operator. If you want to negate a Boolean expression, place the expression in parentheses and place the ! operator in front of it. For example, ! (savings < debt) means "savings is not less than debt." The ! operator can usually be avoided. For example,

```
!(savings < debt)
```

is equivalent to savings >= debt. In some cases, you can safely omit the parentheses, but the parentheses never do any harm. The exact details on omitting parentheses are given later in this chapter in the subsection entitled "Precedence and Associativity Rules."

The "or" Operator ||

You can form a more elaborate Boolean expression by combining two simpler Boolean expressions using the "or" operator ||.

SYNTAX (FOR A BOOLEAN EXPRESSION USING ||)

(*Boolean_Exp_1*) || (*Boolean_Exp_2*)

EXAMPLE (WITHIN AN if-else STATEMENT)

```
if ((salary > expenses) || (savings > expenses))
    System.out.println("Solvent");
else
    System.out.println("Bankrupt");
```

If salary is greater than expenses or savings is greater than expenses (or both), then the first System.out.println statement is executed; otherwise, the second System.out.println statement is executed.

PITFALL: Strings of Inequalities

Do not use a string of inequalities such as min < result < max. If you do, your program will produce a compiler error message. Instead, you must use two inequalities connected with an &&, as follows:

(min < result) && (result < max) ■

Self-Test Exercises

17. Write an if-else statement that outputs the word "Passed" provided the value of the variable exam is greater than or equal to 60 and also the value of the variable programsDone is greater than or equal to 10. Otherwise, the if-else statement should output the word "Failed". The variables exam and programsDone are both of type int.

18. Write an if-else statement that outputs the word "Emergency" provided the value of the variable pressure is greater than 100 or the value of the variable temperature is greater than or equal to 212. Otherwise, the if-else statement should output the word "OK". The variables pressure and temperature are both of type int.

Evaluating Boolean Expressions

Boolean expressions are used to control branch and loop statements. However, a Boolean expression has an independent identity apart from any branch statement or loop statement you might use it in. A Boolean expression returns either true or false.

A variable of type `boolean` can store the values `true` and `false`. Thus, you can set a variable of type `boolean` equal to a Boolean expression. For example,

```
boolean madeIt = (time < limit) && (limit < max);
```

A Boolean expression can be evaluated in the same way that an arithmetic expression is evaluated. The only difference is that an arithmetic expression uses operations such as `+`, `*`, and `/` and produces a number as the final result, whereas a Boolean expression uses relational operations such as `==` and `<` and Boolean operations such as `&&`, `||`, and `!`, and produces one of the two values `true` and `false` as the final result.

First, let's review evaluating an arithmetic expression. The same technique will work in the same way to evaluate Boolean expressions. Consider the following arithmetic expression:

```
(number + 1) * (number + 3)
```

Assume that the variable `number` has the value 2. To evaluate this arithmetic expression, you evaluate the two sums to obtain the numbers 3 and 5, and then you combine these two numbers 3 and 5 using the `*` operator to obtain 15 as the final value. Notice that in performing this evaluation, you do not multiply the expressions (`number + 1`) and (`number + 3`). Instead, you multiply the values of these expressions. You use 3; you do not use (`number + 1`). You use 5; you do not use (`number + 3`).

The computer evaluates Boolean expressions the same way. Subexpressions are evaluated to obtain values, each of which is either `true` or `false`. In particular, `==`, `!=`, `<`, `<=`, and so forth operate on pairs of any primitive type to produce a Boolean value of `true` or `false`. These individual values of `true` or `false` are then combined according to the rules in the **truth tables** shown in Display 3.5. For example, consider the Boolean expression

truth tables

```
!( ( count < 3) || (count > 7) )
```

which might be the controlling expression for an `if-else` statement. Suppose the value of `count` is 8. In this case, (`count < 3`) evaluates to `false` and (`count > 7`) evaluates to `true`, so the preceding Boolean expression is equivalent to

```
!(false || true)
```

Consulting the tables for `||` (which is labeled "OR"), the computer sees that the expression inside the parentheses evaluates to `true`. Thus, the computer sees that the entire expression is equivalent to

```
!(true)
```

Consulting the tables again, the computer sees that `!(true)` evaluates to `false`, and so it concludes that `false` is the value of the original Boolean expression.

The `boolean` Values Are `true` and `false`

`true` and `false` are predefined constants of type `boolean`. (They must be written in lowercase.) In Java, a Boolean expression evaluates to the `boolean` value `true` when it is satisfied, and it evaluates to the `boolean` value `false` when it is not satisfied.

Display 3.5   **Truth Tables**

AND		
Exp_1	*Exp_2*	*Exp_1 && Exp_2*
true	true	true
true	false	false
false	true	false
false	false	false

NOT	
Exp	*!(Exp)*
true	false
false	true

OR		
Exp_1	*Exp_2*	*Exp_1 || Exp_2*
true	true	true
true	false	true
false	true	true
false	false	false

boolean variables in assignments   A boolean variable—that is, one of type boolean—can be given the value of a Boolean expression by using an assignment statement, in the same way that you use an assignment statement to set the value of an int variable or any other type of variable. For example, the following sets the value of the boolean variable isPositive to false:

```
int number = -5;
boolean isPositive;
isPositive = (number > 0);
```

If you prefer, you can combine the last two lines as follows:

```
boolean isPositive = (number > 0);
```

The parentheses are not needed, but they do make it a bit easier to read.

Once a boolean variable has a value, you can use the boolean variable just as you would use any other Boolean expression. For example, the following code

```
boolean isPositive = (number > 0);
if (isPositive)
    System.out.println("The number is positive.");
else
    System.out.println("The number is negative or zero.");
```

is equivalent to

```
if (number > 0)
    System.out.println("The number is positive.");
else
    System.out.println("The number is negative or zero.");
```

Of course, this is just a toy example. It is unlikely that anybody would use the first of the preceding two examples, but you might use something like it if the value of number, and therefore the value of the Boolean expression, might change. For example, the following code could (by some stretch of the imagination) be part of a program to evaluate lottery tickets:

```
boolean isPositive = (number > 0);
while (number > 0);
{
    System.out.println("Wow!");
    number = number - 1000;
}
if (isPositive)
    System.out.println("Your number is positive.");
else
    System.out.println("Sorry, number is not positive.");
System.out.println("Only positive numbers can win.");
```

---

true and false Are Not Numbers

Many programming languages traditionally use 1 and 0 for true and false. The latest versions of most languages have changed things so that now most languages have a type such as boolean with values for true and false. However, even in these newer language versions, values of type boolean are automatically converted to integers and vice versa when context requires it. In particular, C++ automatically makes such conversions.

In Java, the values true and false are not numbers, nor can they be type cast to any numeric type. Similarly, values of type int cannot be type cast to boolean values.

TIP: Naming Boolean Variables

Name a boolean variable with a statement that will be true when the value of the boolean variable is true, such as isPositive, pressureOK, and so forth. That way you can easily understand the meaning of the boolean variable when it is used in an if-else statement or other control statement. Avoid names that do not unambiguously describe the meaning of the variable's value. Do not use names such as numberSign, pressureStatus, and so forth. ■

Short-Circuit and Complete Evaluation

Java takes an occasional shortcut when evaluating a Boolean expression. Notice that in many cases, you need to evaluate only the first of two or more subexpressions in a Boolean expression. For example, consider the following:

```
(savings >= 0) && (dependents > 1)
```

If `savings` is negative, then `(savings >= 0)` is `false`, and, as you can see in the tables in Display 3.5, when one subexpression in an `&&` expression is `false`, then the whole expression is `false`, no matter whether the other expression is `true` or `false`. Thus, if we know that the first expression is `false`, there is no need to evaluate the second expression. A similar thing happens with `||` expressions. If the first of two expressions joined with the `||` operator is `true`, then you know the entire expression is `true`, whether the second expression is `true` or `false`. In some situations, the Java language can and does use these facts to save itself the trouble of evaluating the second subexpression in a logical expression connected with an `&&` or an `||`. Java first evaluates the leftmost of the two expressions joined by an `&&` or an `||`. If that gives it enough information to determine the final value of the expression (independent of the value of the second expression), then Java does not bother to evaluate the second expression. This method of evaluation is called **short-circuit evaluation** or **lazy evaluation**.

short-circuit evaluation

lazy evaluation

Now let's look at an example using `&&` that illustrates the advantage of short-circuit evaluation, and let's give the Boolean expression some context by placing it in an `if` statement:

```
if ( (kids != 0) && ((pieces/kids) >= 2) )
    System.out.println("Each child may have two pieces!");
```

If the value of `kids` is not zero, this statement involves no subtleties. However, suppose the value of `kids` is zero and consider how short-circuit evaluation handles this case. The expression `(kids != 0)` evaluates to `false`, so there would be no need to evaluate the second expression. Using short-circuit evaluation, Java says that the entire expression is `false`, without bothering to evaluate the second expression. This prevents a run-time error, since evaluating the second expression would involve dividing by zero.

complete evaluation

Java also allows you to ask for **complete evaluation**. In complete evaluation, when two expressions are joined by an "and" or an "or," both subexpressions are always evaluated, and then the truth tables are used to obtain the value of the final expression. To obtain complete evaluation in Java, you use `&` rather than `&&` for "and" and use `|` in place of `||` for "or."

In most situations, short-circuit evaluation and complete evaluation give the same result, but, as you have just seen, there are times when short-circuit evaluation can avoid a run-time error. There are also some situations in which complete evaluation is preferred, but we will not use those techniques in this book. We will always use `&&` and `||` to obtain short-circuit evaluation.

Precedence and Associativity Rules

precedence rules

associativity rules

Boolean expressions (and arithmetic expressions) need not be fully parenthesized. If you omit parentheses, Java follows **precedence rules** and **associativity rules** in place of the missing parentheses. One easy way to think of the process is to think of the computer adding parentheses according to these precedence and associativity rules. Some of the Java precedence and associativity rules are given in Display 3.6. (A complete set of precedence and associativity rules is given in Appendix 2.) The computer uses precedence rules to decide where to insert parentheses, but the precedence rules do not differentiate between two operators at the same precedence level, in which case the computer uses the associativity rules to "break the tie."

higher precedence

If one operator occurs higher on the list than another in the precedence table (Display 3.6), the higher one is said to have **higher precedence**. If one operator has higher precedence than another, the operator of higher precedence is grouped with its operands (its arguments) before the operator of lower precedence. For example, if the computer is faced with the expression

```
balance * rate + bonus
```

it notices that * has a higher precedence than +, so it first groups * and its operands, as follows:

```
(balance * rate) + bonus
```

Next, it groups + with its operands to obtain the fully parenthesized expression

```
((balance * rate) + bonus)
```

Sometimes two operators have the same precedence, in which case the parentheses are added using the associativity rules. To illustrate this, let's consider another example:

```
bonus + balance * rate / correctionFactor - penalty
```

The operators * and / have higher precedence than either + or -, so * and / are grouped first. But * and / have equal precedence, so the computer consults the associativity rule for * and /, which says they associate from left to right. This means that the *, which is the leftmost of * and /, is grouped first. So the computer interprets the expression as

```
bonus + (balance * rate) / correctionFactor - penalty
```

which in turn is interpreted as

```
bonus + ((balance * rate) / correctionFactor) - penalty
```

because / has higher precedence than either + or -.

This expression is still not fully parenthesized, however. The computer still must choose to group + first or - first. According to Display 3.6, + and - have equal precedence.

Display 3.6 **Precedence and Associativity Rules**

Highest Precedence

PRECEDENCE	ASSOCIATIVITY
From highest at top to lowest at bottom. Operators in the same group have equal precedence.	
Dot operator, array indexing, and method invocation., [ ], ( )	Left to right
++ (postfix, as in x++), -- (postfix)	Right to left
The unary operators: +, -, ++ (prefix, as in ++x), -- (prefix), and !	Right to left
Type casts (Type)	Right to left
The binary operators *, /, %	Left to right
The binary operators +, -	Left to right
The binary operators <, >, <=, >=	Left to right
The binary operators ==, ! =	Left to right
The binary operator &	Left to right
The binary operator		Left to right
The binary operator &&	Left to right
The binary operator			Left to right
The ternary operator (conditional operator) ?:	Right to left
The assignment operators =, *=, /=, %=, +=, -=, & =, |=	Right to left

Lowest Precedence

So the computer must use the associativity rules, which say that + and - are associated left to right. So, it interprets the expression as

```
(bonus + ((balance * rate) / correctionFactor)) - penalty
```

which in turn is interpreted as the following fully parenthesized expression:

```
((bonus + ((balance * rate) / correctionFactor)) - penalty)
```

As you can see from studying the table in Display 3.6, most binary operators associate from left to right. But the assignment operators associate from right to left. So the expression

```
number1 = number2 = number3
```

means

```
number1 = (number2 = number3)
```

which in turn is interpreted as the following fully parenthesized expression:

```
(number1 = (number2 = number3))
```

However, this fully parenthesized expression may not look like it means anything until we explain a bit more about the assignment operator.

Although we do not advocate using the assignment operator = as part of a complex expression, it is an operator that returns a value, just as + and * do. When an assignment operator = is used in an expression, it changes the value of the variable on the left-hand side of the assignment operator and also returns a value—namely, the new value of the variable on the left-hand side of the expression. So (number2 = number3) sets number2 equal to the value of number3 and returns the value of number3. Thus,

```
number1 = number2 = number3
```

which is equivalent to

```
(number1 = (number2 = number3))
```

sets both number2 and number1 equal to the value of number3. It is best to not use assignment statements inside of expressions, although simple chains of assignment operators such as the following are clear and acceptable:

```
number1 = number2 = number3;
```

Although we discourage using expressions that combine the assignment operator and other operators in complicated ways, let's try to parenthesize one just for practice. Consider the following:

```
number1 = number2 = number3 + 7 * factor
```

The operator of highest precedence is *, and the operator of next-highest precedence is +, so this expression is equivalent to

```
number1 = number2 = (number3 + (7 * factor))
```

which leaves only the assignment operators to group. They associate right to left, so the fully parenthesized equivalent version of our expression is

```
(number1 = (number2 = (number3 + (7 * factor))))
```

(Note that there is no case where two operators have equal precedence but one associates from left to right while the other associates from right to left. That must be true or else there would be cases with conflicting instructions for inserting parentheses.)

binding   The association of operands with operators is called **binding**. For example, when parentheses determine which two expressions (two operands) are being added by a particular + sign, that is called binding the two operands to the + sign. A fully parenthesized expression accomplishes binding for all the operators in an expression.

These examples should make it clear that it can be risky to depend too heavily on the precedence and associativity rules. It is best to include most parentheses and to omit parentheses only in situations where the intended meaning is very obvious, such as a simple combination of * and +, or a simple chain of &&'s or a simple chain of ||'s. The following examples have some omitted parentheses, but their meaning should be clear:

```
rate * time + lead
(time < limit) && (yourScore > theirScore) && (yourScore > 0)
(expenses < income) || (expenses < savings) || (creditRating > 0)
```

Notice that the precedence rules include both arithmetic operators such as + and * as well as Boolean operators such as && and ||. This is because many expressions combine arithmetic and Boolean operations, as in the following simple example:

```
(number + 1) > 2 || (number + 5) < -3
```

If you check the precedence rules given in Display 3.6, you will see that this expression is equivalent to

```
(((number + 1) > 2) || ((number + 5) < (-3)))
```

because > and < have higher precedence than ||. In fact, you could omit all the parentheses in the above expression and it would have the same meaning (but would be less clear).

It might seem that once an expression is fully parenthesized, the meaning of the expression is then determined. It would seem that to evaluate the expression, you (or the computer) simply evaluate the inner expressions before the outer ones. So, in

```
((number + 1) > 2) || ((number + 5) < (-3))
```

first the expressions (number + 1), (number + 5), and (-3) are evaluated (in any order), then the > and < are evaluated, and then the || is applied. That happens to work in this simple case. In this case, it does not matter which of (number + 1), (number + 5), and (-3) is evaluated first, but in certain other expressions it will be necessary to specify which subexpression is evaluated first. The rules for evaluating a fully parenthesized expression are (and indeed must be) more complicated than just evaluating inner expressions before outer expressions.

For an expression with no side effects, the rule of performing inner parenthesized expressions before outer ones is all you need. That rule will get you through most simple expressions, but for expressions with side effects, you need to learn the rest of the story, which is what we will do next.

side effects

The complications come from the fact that some expressions have *side effects*. When we say an expression has **side effects**, we mean that in addition to returning a value, the expression also changes something, such as the value of a variable. Expressions with the assignment operator have side effects; pay = bonus, for example, changes the value of pay. Increment and decrement operators have side effects; ++n changes the value of n. In expressions that include operators with side effects, you need more rules.

For example, consider

```
((result = (++n)) + (other = (2*(++n))))
```

The parentheses seem to say that you or the computer should first evaluate the two increment operators, ++n and ++n, but the parentheses do not say which of the two ++n's to do first. If n has the value 2 and we evaluate the leftmost ++n first, then the variable result is set to 3 and the variable other is set to 8 (and the entire expression evaluates to 11). But if we evaluate the rightmost ++n first, then other is set to 6 and result is set to 4 (and the entire expression evaluates to 10). We need a rule to determine the order of evaluation when we have a tie such as this. However, rather than simply adding a rule to break such ties, Java instead takes a completely different approach.

To evaluate an expression, Java uses the following three rules:

1. Java first does binding; that is, it first fully parenthesizes the expression using precedence and associativity rules, just as we have outlined.
2. Then it simply evaluates expressions left to right.
3. If an operator is waiting for its two (or one or three) operands to be evaluated, then that operator is evaluated as soon as its operands have been evaluated.

We will first do an example with no side effects and then an example of an expression with side effects. First, the simple example; consider the expression

```
6 + 7 * n - 12
```

and assume the value of n is 2. Using the precedence and associativity rules, we add parentheses one pair at a time as follows:

```
6 + (7 * n) - 12
```

then

```
(6 + (7 * n)) - 12
```

and finally the fully parenthesized version

```
((6 + (7 * n)) - 12)
```

Next, we evaluate subexpressions left to right. (6 evaluates to 6 and 7 evaluates to 7, but that is so obvious we will not make a big deal of it.) The variable n evaluates to 2. (Remember, we assumed the value of n was 2.) So, we can rewrite the expression as

```
((6 + (7 * 2)) - 12)
```

The * is the only operator that has both of its operands evaluated, so it evaluates to 14 to produce

```
((6 + 14) - 12)
```

Now + has both of its operands evaluated, so (6 + 14) evaluates to 20 to yield

```
(20 - 12)
```

which in turn evaluates to 8. So 8 is the value for the entire expression.

This may seem like more work than it should be, but remember, the computer is following an algorithm and proceeds step by step; it does not get inspired to make simplifying assumptions.

Next, let's consider an expression with side effects. In fact, let's consider the one we fully parenthesized earlier. Consider the following fully parenthesized expression and assume the value of n is 2:

```
((result = (++n)) + (other = (2*(++n))))
```

Subexpressions are evaluated left to right. So, result is evaluated first. When used with the assignment operator =, a variable simply evaluates to itself. So, result is evaluated and waiting. Next, ++n is evaluated, and it returns the value 3. The expression is now known to be equivalent to

```
((result = 3) + (other = (2*(++n))))
```

Now the assignment operator = has its two operands evaluated, so (result = 3) is evaluated. Evaluating (result = 3) sets the value of result equal to 3 and returns the value 3. Thus, the expression is now known to be equivalent to

```
(3 + (other = (2*(++n))))
```

(and the side effect of setting result equal to 3 has happened). Proceeding left to right, the next thing to evaluate is the variable other, which simply evaluates to itself, so you need not rewrite anything.

Proceeding left to right, the next subexpression that can be evaluated is n, which evaluates to 3. (Remember, n has already been incremented once, so n now has the value 3.) Then ++ has its only argument evaluated, so it is ready to be evaluated. The evaluation of (++n) has the side effect of setting n equal to 4 and evaluates to 4. So, the entire expression is equivalent to

```
(3 + (other = (2*4)))
```

The only subexpression that has its operands evaluated is (2*4), so it is evaluated to 8 to produce

```
(3 + (other = 8))
```

Now the assignment operator = has both of its operands evaluated, so it evaluates to 8 and has the side effect of setting `other` equal to 8. Thus, we know the value of the expression is

```
(3 + 8)
```

which evaluates to 11. So, the entire expression evaluates to 11 (and has the side effects of setting `result` equal to 3, setting n equal to 4, and setting other equal to 8). These rules also allow for method invocations in expressions. For example, in

```
(++n > 0) && (s.length( ) > n)
```

the variable n is incremented before n is compared to s. length( ). When we start defining and using more methods, you will see less-contrived examples of expressions that include method invocations.

All of these rules for evaluating expressions are summarized in the box entitled "Rules for Evaluating Expressions."

Rules for Evaluating Expressions

Expressions are evaluated as follows:

1. Binding: Determine the equivalent fully parenthesized expression using the precedence and associativity rules.
2. Proceeding left to right, evaluate whatever subexpressions you can evaluate. (These subexpressions will be operands or method arguments. For example, in simple cases they may be numeric constants or variables.)
3. Evaluate each outer operation (and method invocation) as soon as all of its operands (all its arguments) have been evaluated.

MyProgrammingLab

Self-Test Exercises

19. Determine the value, true or false, of each of the following Boolean expressions, assuming that the value of the variable count is 0 and the value of the variable limit is 10. (Give your answer as one of the values true or false.)

    a. `(count == 0) && (limit < 20)`

    b. `count == 0 && limit < 20`

    c. `(limit > 20) || (count < 5)`

(continued)

Self-Test Exercises (continued)

    d. `!(count == 12)`

    e. `(count == 1) && (x < y)`

    f. `(count < 10) || (x < y)`

    g. `!( ((count < 10) || (x < y)) && (count >= 0) )`

    h. `((limit/count) > 7) || (limit < 20)`

    i. `(limit < 20) || ((limit/count) > 7)`

    j. `((limit/count) > 7) && (limit < 0)`

    k. `(limit < 0) && ((limit/count) > 7)`

20. Does the following sequence produce a division by zero?

    ```
    int j = -1;
    if ((j > 0) && (1/(j+1) > 10))
        System.out.println(i);
    ```

21. Convert the following expression to an equivalent fully parenthesized expression:

    ```
    bonus + day * rate / correctionFactor * newGuy - penalty
    ```

3.3 Loops

"Few tasks are more like the torture of Sisyphus than housework, with its endless repetition: the clean becomes soiled, the soiled is made clean, over and over, day after day."

SIMONE DE BEAUVOIR

Looping mechanisms in Java are similar to those in other high-level languages. The three Java loop statements are the `while` statement, the `do-while` statement, and the `for` statement. The same terminology is used with Java as with other languages. The code that is repeated in a loop is called the **body of the loop**. Each repetition of the loop body is called an **iteration** of the loop.

body of the loop

iteration

`while` Statement and `do-while` Statement

while and do-while compared

The syntax for the `while` statement and its variant, the `do-while` statement, is given later in this chapter in the box entitled "Syntax for `while` and `do-while` Statements." In both cases, the multistatement body is a special case of the loop with a single-statement body. The multistatement body is a single compound statement. Examples of `while` and `do-while` statements are given in Display 3.7.

The important difference between the while and do-while loops involves when the controlling Boolean expression is checked. With a while statement, the Boolean expression is checked *before* the loop body is executed. If the Boolean expression evaluates to false, then the body is not executed at all. With a do-while statement, the body of

---

Display 3.7   Demonstration of while Loops and do-while Loops (part 1 of 2)

```
1 public class WhileDemo
2 {
3     public static void main(String[] args)
4     {
5         int countDown;

6         System.out.println("First while loop:");
7         countDown = 3;
8         while (countDown > 0)
9         {
10            System.out.println("Hello");
11            countDown = countDown - 1;
12        }

13        System.out.println("Second while loop:");
14        countDown = 0;
15        while (countDown > 0)
16        {
17            System.out.println("Hello");
18            countDown = countDown - 1;
19        }

20        System.out.println("First do-while loop:");
21        countDown = 3;
22        do
23        {
24            System.out.println("Hello");
25            countDown = countDown - 1;
26        } while (countDown > 0);

27        System.out.println("Second do-while loop:");
28        countDown = 0;
29        do
30        {
31            System.out.println("Hello");
32            countDown = countDown - 1;
33        } while (countDown > 0);
34    }
35 }
```

(continued)

Display 3.7 Demonstration of `while` Loops and `do-while` Loops (part 2 of 2)

Sample Dialogue

```
First while loop:
Hello
Hello
Hello
Second while loop:
First do-while loop:
Hello
Hello
Hello
Second do-while loop:
Hello
```

A `while` *loop can iterate its body zero times.*

A `do-while` *loop always iterates its body at least one time.*

the loop is executed first and the Boolean expression is checked *after* the loop body is executed. Thus, the `do-while` statement always executes the loop body at least once. After this start-up, the `while` loop and the `do-while` loop behave the same way. After each iteration of the loop body, the Boolean expression is again checked, and if it is `true`, the loop is iterated again. If it has changed from `true` to `false`, then the loop statement ends.

executing the body zero times

The first thing that happens when a `while` loop is executed is that the controlling Boolean expression is evaluated. If the Boolean expression evaluates to `false` at that point, the body of the loop is never executed. It might seem pointless to execute the body of a loop zero times, but that is sometimes the desired action. For example, a `while` loop is often used to sum a list of numbers, but the list could be empty. To be more specific, a checkbook-balancing program might use a `while` loop to sum the values of all the checks you have written in a month, but you might take a month's vacation and write no checks at all. In that case, there are zero numbers to sum, so the loop is iterated zero times.

Algorithms and Pseudocode

Dealing with the syntax rules of a programming language is not the hard part of solving a problem with a computer program. The hard part is coming up with the underlying method of solution. This method of solution is called an algorithm. An **algorithm** is a set of precise instructions that leads to a solution. Some approximately equivalent words to *algorithm* are *recipe*, *method*, *directions*, *procedure*, and *routine*.

algorithm

An algorithm is normally written in a mixture of a programming language (in our case, Java) and English (or other human language). This mixture of programming language and human language is known as **pseudocode**. Using pseudocode frees you from worrying about fine details of Java syntax so that you can concentrate on the method of solution. Underlying the program in Display 3.8 is an algorithm that can be expressed as the following pseudocode:

pseudocode

Syntax for `while` and `do-while` Statements

A `while` STATEMENT WITH A SINGLE-STATEMENT BODY

```
while (Boolean_Expression)
     Statement
```

A `while` STATEMENT WITH A MULTISTATEMENT BODY

```
while (Boolean_Expression)
{
     Statement_1
     Statement_2
          .
          .
          .
     Statement_Last
}
```

A `do-while` STATEMENT WITH A SINGLE-STATEMENT BODY

```
do
     Statement
while (Boolean Expression);
```

A `do-while` STATEMENT WITH A MULTISTATEMENT BODY

Do not forget the final semicolon.

```
do
{
     Statement_1
     Statement_2
          .
          .
          .
     Statement_Last
} while (Boolean_Expression);
```

```
Give the user instructions.
count = 0;
sum = 0;
Read a number and store it in a variable named next.
while (next >= 0)
{
    sum = sum + next;
    count++;
    Read a number and store it in next.
}
The average is sum/count provided count is not zero.
Output the results.
```

Display 3.8   Averaging a List of Scores

```
1   import java.util.Scanner;
2   public class Averager
3   {
4       public static void main(String[] args)
5       {
6           Scanner keyboard = new Scanner(System.in);
7           System.out.println("Enter a list of nonnegative scores.");
8           System.out.println("Mark the end with a negative number.");
9           System.out.println("I will compute their average.");

10          double next, sum = 0;
11          int count = 0;

12          next = keyboard.nextDouble( );
13          while (next >= 0)
14          {
15              sum = sum + next;
16              count++;
17              next = keyboard.nextDouble( );
18          }

19          if (count == 0)
20              System.out.println("No scores entered.");
21          else
22          {
23              double average = sum/count;
24              System.out.println(count + " scores read.");
25              System.out.println("The average is " + average);
26          }
27      }
28  }
```

Sample Dialogue

```
Enter a list of nonnegative scores.
Mark the end with a negative number.
I will compute their average.
87.5 0 89 99.9 -1
4 scores read.
The average is 69.1.
```

Note that when using pseudocode, we do not necessarily declare variables or worry about the fine syntax details of Java. The only rule is that the pseudocode must be precise and clear enough for a good programmer to convert the pseudocode to syntactically correct Java code.

As you will see, significant programs are written not as a single algorithm, but as a set of interacting algorithms; however, each of these algorithms is normally designed in pseudocode unless the algorithm is exceedingly simple.

EXAMPLE: Averaging a List of Scores

Display 3.8 shows a program that reads in a list of scores and computes their average. It illustrates a number of techniques that are commonly used with loops.

sentinel values

The scores are all nonnegative. This allows the program to use a negative number as an end marker. Note that the negative number is not one of the numbers being averaged in. This sort of end marker is known as a **sentinel value**. A sentinel value need not be a negative number, but it must be some value that cannot occur as a "real" input value. For example, if the input list were a list of even integers, then you could use an odd integer as a sentinel value.

To get the loop to end properly, we want the Boolean expression

```
next >= 0
```

checked before adding in the number read. This way we avoid adding in the sentinel value. So, we want the loop body to end with

```
next = keyboard.nextDouble( );
```

To make things work out, this in turn requires that we also place this line before the loop. A loop often needs some preliminary statements to set things up before the loop is executed.

Self-Test Exercises

MyProgrammingLab™

22. What is the output produced by the following?

```
int n = 5;
while (n > 1)
{
    System.out.println(n);
    n = n - 3;
}
```

23. What output would be produced in Exercise 22 if the > sign were replaced with < ?

(continued)

Self-Test Exercises (continued)

24. What is the output produced by the following?

```
int n = 5;
do
{
    System.out.println(n);
    n --;
} while (n > 1);
```

25. What output would be produced in Exercise 24 if the > sign were replaced with < ?

26. What is the output produced by the following?

```
int n = 10;
while (n > 0)
{
    System.out.println(n);
    n = n - 3;
}
```

27. What is the most important difference between a `while` statement and a `do-while` statement?

The `for` Statement

for statement

The third and final loop statement in Java is the **`for` statement**. The `for` statement is most commonly used to step through some integer variable in equal increments. The `for` statement is, however, a completely general looping mechanism that can do anything that a `while` loop can do.

For example, the following `for` statement sums the integers 1 through 10:

```
sum = 0;
for (n = 1; n <= 10; n++)
    sum = sum + n;
```

A `for` statement begins with the keyword `for` followed by three expressions in parentheses that tell the computer what to do with the controlling variable(s). The beginning of a `for` statement looks like the following:

```
for (Initialization; Boolean_Expression; Update)
```

The first expression tells how the variable, variables, or other things are initialized, the second expression gives a Boolean expression that is used to check for when the loop should end, and the last expression tells how the loop control variable or variables are updated after each iteration of the loop body. The loop body is a single statement (typically a compound statement) that follows the heading we just described.

The three expressions at the start of a `for` statement are separated by two, and only two, semicolons. Do not succumb to the temptation to place a semicolon after the third expression. (The technical explanation is that these three things are expressions, not statements, and so do not require a semicolon at the end.)

A `for` statement often uses a single `int` variable to control loop iteration and loop ending. However, the three expressions at the start of a `for` statement may be any Java expressions and therefore may involve more (or even fewer) than one variable, and the variables can be of any type.

The semantics of the `for` statement are given in Display 3.9. The syntax for a `for` statement is given in Display 3.10. Display 3.10 also explains how the `for` statement can be viewed as a notational variant of the `while` loop.

The `for` Statement

SYNTAX

```
for (Initialization; Boolean_Expression; Update)
        Body
```

The *Body* may be any Java statement—either a simple statement or, more likely, a compound statement consisting of a list of statements enclosed in braces, {}. Notice that the three things in parentheses are separated by two, not three, semicolons.

You are allowed to use any Java expression for the *Initializing* and the *Update* expressions. Therefore, you may use more, or fewer, than one variable in the expressions; moreover, the variables may be of any type.

EXAMPLE

```
int next, sum = 0;
for (next = 0; next <= 10; next++)
{
    sum = sum + next;
    System.out.println("sum up to " + next + " is " + sum);
}
```

A variable can be declared in the heading of a `for` statement at the same time that it is initialized. For example,

```
for (int n = 1; n < 10; n++)
    System.out.println(n);
```

There are some subtleties to worry about when you declare a variable in the heading of a `for` statement. These subtleties are discussed in Chapter 4 in the Programming Tip subsection entitled "Declaring Variables in a `for` Statement." It might be wise to avoid such subtle declarations within a `for` statement until you reach Chapter 4, but we mention it here for reference value.

Display 3.9 Semantics of the `for` Statement

for (*Initialization*; *Boolean_Expression*; *Update*)
    Body

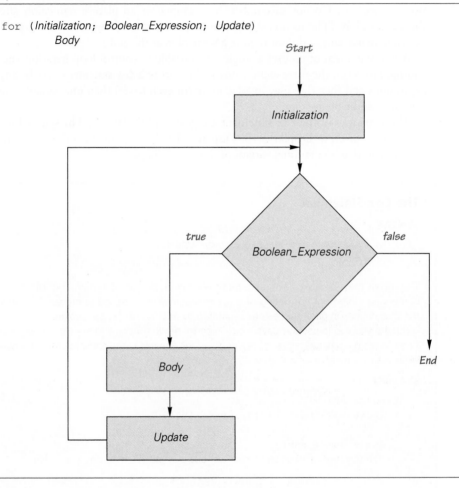

Display 3.10 **`for` Statement Syntax and Alternate Semantics** (part 1 of 2)

`for` Statement Syntax

for (*Initialization*; *Boolean_Expression*; *Update*)
    Body

EXAMPLE

```
for (number = 100; number >= 0; number--)
    System.out.println(number + " bottles of beer on the shelf.");
```

Display 3.10   `for` Statement Syntax and Alternate Semantics (part 2 of 2)

Equivalent `while` Loop Syntax

Initialization;

```
while (Boolean_Expression)
{
      Body;
      Update;
}
```

EQUIVALENT EXAMPLE

```
number = 100;
while (number >= 0)
{
     System.out.println(number + " bottles of beer on the shelf.");
     number--;
}
```

Sample Dialogue

```
100 bottles of beer on the shelf.
99 bottles of beer on the shelf.
               .
               .
               .
0 bottles of beer on the shelf.
```

The Comma in `for` Statements

A `for` loop can contain multiple initialization actions. Simply separate the actions with commas, as in the following:

```
for (term = 1, sum = 0; term <= 10; term++)
    sum = sum + term;
```

This `for` loop has two initializing actions. The variable `term` is initialized to 1, and the variable `sum` is also initialized to 0. Note that you use a comma, not a semicolon, to separate the initialization actions.

You can also use commas to place multiple update actions in a `for` loop. This can lead to a situation in which the `for` loop has an empty body but still does something useful. For example, the previous `for` loop can be rewritten to the following equivalent version:

```
for (term = 1, sum = 0; term <= 10; sum = sum + term, term++)
    //Empty body;
```

This, in effect, makes the loop body part of the update action. We find that it makes for a more readable style if you use the update action only for variables that control the loop, as in the previous version of this `for` loop. We do not advocate using `for` loops with no body, but if you do so, annotate it with a comment such as we did in the preceding `for` loop. As indicated in the upcoming Pitfall, "Extra Semicolon in a `for` Statement," a `for` loop with no body can also occur as the result of a programmer error.

The comma used in a `for` statement, as we just illustrated, is quite limited in how it can be used. You can use it with assignment statements and with incremented and decremented variables (such as `term++` or `term--`), but not with just any arbitrary statements. In particular, both declaring variables and using the comma in `for` statements can be troublesome. For example, the following is illegal:

```
for (int term = 1, double sum = 0; term <= 10; term++)
    sum = sum + term;
```

Even the following is illegal:

```
double sum;
for (int term = 1, sum = 0; term <= 10; term++)
    sum = sum + term;
```

Java will interpret

```
int term = 1, sum = 0;
```

as declaring both `term` and `sum` to be `int` variables and complain that `sum` is already declared.

If you do not declare `sum` anyplace else (and it is acceptable to make `sum` an `int` variable instead of a `double` variable), then the following, although we discourage it, is legal:

```
for (int term = 1, sum = 0; term <= 10; term++)
    sum = sum + term;
```

The first part in parentheses (up to the semicolon) declares both `term` and `sum` to be `int` variables and initializes both of them.

It is best to simply avoid these possibly confusing examples. When using the comma in a `for` statement, it is safest to simply declare all variables outside the `for` statement. If you declare all variables outside the `for` loop, the rules are no longer complicated.

A `for` loop can have only one Boolean expression to test for ending the `for` loop. However, you can perform multiple tests by connecting the tests using `&&` or `||` operators to form one larger Boolean expression.

(C, C++, and some other programming languages have a general-purpose comma operator. Readers who have programmed in one of these languages need to be warned that, in Java, there is no comma operator. In Java, the comma is a separator, not an operator, and its use is very restricted compared with the comma operator in C and C++.)

TIP: Repeat *N* Times Loops

The simplest way to produce a loop that repeats the loop body a predetermined number of times is with a `for` statement. For example, the following is a loop that repeats its loop body three times:

```
for (int count = 1; count <= 3; count++)
    System.out.println("Hip, Hip, Hurray");
```

The body of a `for` statement need not make any reference to a loop control variable, such as the variable `count`. ■

PITFALL: Extra Semicolon in a `for` Statement

You normally do not place a semicolon after the closing parenthesis at the beginning of a `for` loop. To see what can happen, consider the following `for` loop:

```
for (int count = 1; count <= 10; count++);          ← Problem
    System.out.println("Hello");                       semicolon.
```

If you did not notice the extra semicolon, you might expect this `for` loop to write `Hello` to the screen 10 times. If you do notice the semicolon, you might expect the compiler to issue an error message. Neither of those things happens. If you embed this `for` loop in a complete program, the compiler will not complain. If you run the program, only one `Hello` will be output instead of 10 Hellos. What is happening? To answer that question, we need a little background.

One way to create a statement in Java is to put a semicolon after something. If you put a semicolon after `number++`, you change the expression

```
number++
```

into the statement

```
number++;
```

empty statement

null statement

If you place a semicolon after nothing, you still create a statement. Thus, the semicolon by itself is a statement, which is called the **empty statement** or the **null statement**. The empty statement performs no action, but still is a statement. Therefore, the following is a complete and legitimate `for` loop, whose body is the empty statement:

```
for (int count = 1; count <= 10; count++);
```

(continued)

PITFALL: (continued)

This `for` loop is indeed iterated 10 times, but since the body is the empty statement, nothing happens when the body is iterated. This loop does nothing, and it does nothing 10 times! After completing this `for` loop, the computer goes on to execute the following, which writes `Hello` to the screen one time:

```
System.out.println("Hello");
```

This same sort of problem can arise with a `while` loop. Be careful to not place a semicolon after the closing parenthesis that encloses the Boolean expression at the start of a `while` loop. A `do-while` loop has just the opposite problem. You must remember to always end a `do-while` loop with a semicolon. ■

PITFALL: Infinite Loops

A `while` loop, `do-while` loop, or `for` loop does not terminate as long as the controlling Boolean expression evaluates to `true`. This Boolean expression normally contains a variable that will be changed by the loop body, and usually the value of this variable eventually is changed in a way that makes the Boolean expression false and therefore terminates the loop. However, if you make a mistake and write your program so that the Boolean expression is always true, then the loop will run forever.

infinite loop   A loop that runs forever is called an **infinite loop**.

Unfortunately, examples of infinite loops are not hard to come by. First, let's describe a loop that *does* terminate. The following Java code writes out the positive even numbers less than 12. That is, it outputs the numbers 2, 4, 6, 8, and 10, one per line, and then the loop ends.

```
number = 2;
while (number != 12)
{
    System.out.println(number);
    number = number + 2;
}
```

The value of `number` is increased by 2 on each loop iteration until it reaches 12. At that point, the Boolean expression after the word `while` is no longer true, so the loop ends.

Now suppose you want to write out the odd numbers less than 12, rather than the even numbers. You might mistakenly think that all you need to do is change the initializing statement to

```
number = 1;
```

But this mistake will create an infinite loop. Because the value of `number` goes from 11 to 13, the value of `number` is never equal to 12, so the loop never terminates.

PITFALL: (continued)

This sort of problem is common when loops are terminated by checking a numeric quantity using `==` or `!=`. When dealing with numbers, it is always safer to test for passing a value. For example, the following will work fine as the first line of our `while` loop:

```
while (number < 12)
```

With this change, `number` can be initialized to any number and the loop will still terminate.

There is one subtlety about infinite loops that you need to keep in mind. A loop might terminate for some input values but be an infinite loop for other values. Just because you tested your loop for some program input values and found that the loop ended does not mean that it will not be an infinite loop for some other input values.

A program that is in an infinite loop might run forever unless some external force stops it, so it is a good idea to learn how to force a program to terminate. The method for forcing a program to stop varies from operating system to operating system. The keystrokes Control-C will terminate a program on many operating systems. (To type Control-C, hold down the Control key while pressing the C key.)

In simple programs, an infinite loop is almost always an error. However, some programs are intentionally written to run forever, such as the main outer loop in an airline reservation program that just keeps asking for more reservations until you shut down the computer (or otherwise terminate the program in an atypical way). ■

Nested Loops

nested loops

VideoNote
Nested Loop Example

It is perfectly legal to nest one loop statement inside another loop statement. For example, the following nests one `for` loop inside another `for` loop:

```
int rowNum, columnNum;
for (rowNum = 1; rowNum <= 3; rowNum++)
{
    for (columnNum = 1; columnNum <= 2; columnNum++)
        System.out.print(" row " + rowNum + " column " + columnNum);
    System.out.println( );
}
```

This produces the following output:

```
row 1 column 1 row 1 column 2
row 2 column 1 row 2 column 2
row 3 column 1 row 3 column 2
```

For each iteration of the outer loop, the inner loop is iterated from beginning to end and then one `println` statement is executed to end the line.

(It is best to avoid nested loops by placing the inner loop inside a method definition and placing a method invocation inside the outer loop. Method definitions are covered in Chapters 4 and 5.)

Self-Test Exercises

28. What is the output of the following?

```
for (int count = 1; count < 10; count += 2)
    System.out.print((3 * count) + " ");
```

29. What is the output of the following?

```
int i, j;
for (i = 100, j = 10; i >= j; i -= 10, j += 10 )
    System.out.println(i + " ");
```

30. What is the output of the following?

```
for (String s = "Newzealand"; s.length() >= 1; s =
s.substring(2) )
    System.out.print(s + " ");
```

31. Rewrite the following `for` statement as a `while` loop (and possibly some additional statements):

```
int n;
for (n = 100; n > 10; n -= 20)
    System.out.println("Hello " + n);
```

32. What is the output of the following loop? Identify the connection between the value of n and the value of the variable `log`.

```
int n = 1024;
int log = 0;
for (int i = 1; i < n; i = i * 2)
    log++;
System.out.println(n + " " + log);
```

33. What is the output of the following loop? Comment on the code. (This is not the same as the previous exercise.)

```
int n = 1024;
int log = 0;
for (int i = 1; i < n; i = i * 2);
    log++;
System.out.println(n + " " + log);
```

34. Predict the output of the following nested loops:

```
int n, m;
    for (n = 0; n < 3; n++)
    {
        for (m = 0; m < 3; m++)
            System.out.println("* ");
        System.out.println(" ");
    }
```

Self-Test Exercises (continued)

35. For each of the following situations, tell which type of loop (`while`, `do-while`, or `for`) would work best:

    a. Summing a series, such as `1/2 + 1/3 + 1/4 + 1/5 + . . . 1/10`.

    b. Reading in the list of exam scores for one student.

    c. Reading in the number of days of sick leave taken by employees in a department.

36. What is the output of the following?

```java
int number = 10;
while (number > 0)
{
    System.out.println(number);
    number = number + 3;
}
```

37. What is the output of the following?

```java
int n, limit = 10;
for (n = 1; n < limit; n++)
{
    System.out.println("n == " + n);
    System.out.println("limit == " + limit);
    limit = n + 2;
}
```

38. What is the output produced by the following?

```java
int number = 10;
while (number > 0)
{
    number = number - 2;
    if (number == 4)
        break;
    System.out.println(number);
}
System.out.println("The end.");
```

39. What is the output produced by the following?

```java
int number = 10;
while (number > 0)
{
    number = number - 2;
    if (number == 4)
        continue;
    System.out.println(number);
}
System.out.println("The end.");
```

The `break` and `continue` Statements ★

In previous subsections, we described the basic flow of control for the `while`, `do-while`, and `for` loops. This is how the loops should normally be used and they are usually are. However, you can alter the flow of control in two additional ways: You can insert either a `break` statement or insert a `continue` statement. The `break` statement ends the loop. The `continue` statement ends the current iteration of the loop body. The `break` and `continue` statements can be used with any of the Java loop statements.

break statement

We described the `break` statement earlier in this chapter when we discussed the `switch` statement. The **break statement** consists of the keyword `break` followed by a semicolon. When executed, the `break` statement ends the nearest enclosing `switch` or loop statement.

continue statement

The **continue statement** consists of the keyword `continue` followed by a semicolon. When executed, the `continue` statement ends the current loop body iteration of the nearest enclosing loop statement.

One point that you should note when using the `continue` statement in a `for` loop is that the `continue` statement transfers control to the update expression. Thus, any loop control variable will be updated immediately after the `continue` statement is executed.

Note that a `break` statement completely ends the loop. In contrast, a `continue` statement merely ends one loop iteration, and the next iteration (if any) continues the loop.

You never absolutely need a `break` or `continue` statement. Any code that uses a `break` or `continue` statement can be rewritten to do the same thing without a `break` or `continue` statement. The `continue` statement can be particularly tricky and can make your code hard to read. It may be best to avoid the `continue` statement completely or at least use it only on very rare occasions. The use of the `break` and `continue` statements in loops is controversial, with many experts saying they should never be used. You will need to make your own decision on whether you will use either or both of these statements.

You can nest one loop statement inside another loop statement. When doing so, remember that any `break` or `continue` statement applies to the innermost loop statement containing the `break` or `continue` statement. If there is a `switch` statement inside a loop, any `break` statement applies to the innermost loop or `switch` statement.

There is a type of `break` statement that, when used in nested loops, can end any containing loop, not just the innermost loop. If you label an enclosing loop statement with an *Identifier*, then the following version of the `break` statement will exit the labeled loop, even if it is not the innermost enclosing loop:

```
break Identifier;
```

label

To **label** a loop statement, simply precede it with an *Identifier* and a colon. The following is an outline of some sample code that uses a labeled `break` statement:

```
outerLoop:
do
```

```
    {
        ...
        while (next >= 0)
        {
          next = keyboard.nextInt ( );
          if (next < -100)
              break outerLoop;
          ...
        }
        ...
        answer = ...
    } while (answer.equalsIgnoreCase("yes"));
```

The identifier outerLoop labels the outer loop, which is a do loop. If the number read into the variable next is negative but not less than −100, then the inner while loop ends normally. If, however, the number read is less than −100, then the labeled break statement is executed, and that ends the enclosing do loop.

You can actually label any statement, not just loop statements and switch statements. A labeled break will always end the enclosing statement with the matching label, no matter what kind of statement is labeled.

The labeled break can be handy when you have a switch statement in the body of a loop and you want a break statement that ends the loop rather than just ending the switch statement.

The exit Statement

The break statement ends a loop (or switch statement) but does not end the program. The following statement immediately ends the program:

```
System.exit(0);
```

System is a predefined Java class that is automatically provided by Java, and exit is a method in the class System. The method exit ends the program as soon as it is invoked. In the programs that we will write, the integer argument 0 can be any integer, but by tradition we use 0, because 0 is used to indicate a normal ending of the program.

The following is a bit of code that uses the exit statement:

```
System.out.println("Enter a negative number:");
int negNumber = keyboard.nextInt ( );
if (negNumber >= 0)
{
    System.out.println(negNumber + " is not a negative number.");
    System.out.println("Program aborting.");
    System.exit(0);
}
```

There are more examples of the use of System.exit in Chapter 4.

3.4 Debugging

A man who has committed a mistake and doesn't correct it is committing another mistake.

CONFUCIUS

Loop Bugs

There is a pattern to the kinds of mistakes you are most likely to make when programming with loops. Moreover, there are some standard techniques you can use to locate and fix bugs in your loops.

The two most common kinds of loop errors are unintended infinite loops and *off-by-one* errors. We have already discussed infinite loops, but we still need to consider off-by-one errors.

off-by-one error

If your loop has an **off-by-one error**, that means the loop repeats the loop body one too many or one too few times. These sorts of errors can result from carelessness in designing a controlling Boolean expression. For example, if you use less-than when you should use less-than-or-equal, this can easily make your loop iterate the body the wrong number of times.

Use of == to test for equality in the controlling Boolean expression of a loop can often lead to an off-by-one error or an infinite loop. This sort of equality testing can work satisfactorily for integers and characters, but is not reliable for floating-point numbers. This is because the floating-point numbers are approximate quantities, and == tests for exact equality. The result of such a test is unpredictable. When comparing floating-point numbers, always use something involving less-than or greater-than, such as <=; do not use == or !=. Using == or != to test floating-point numbers can produce an off-by-one error or an unintended infinite loop or even some other type of error. Even when using integer variables, it is best to avoid using == and != and to instead use something involving less-than or greater-than.

Off-by-one errors can easily go unnoticed. If a loop is iterated one too many times or one too few times, the results might still look reasonable but be off by enough to cause trouble later on. Always make a specific check for off-by-one errors by comparing your loop results to results you know to be true by some other means, such as a pencil-and-paper calculation.

Tracing Variables

tracing variables

One good way to discover errors in a loop or any kind of code is to trace some key variables. **Tracing variables** means watching the variables change value while the program is running. Most programs do not output each variable's value every time the variable changes, but being able to see all of these variable changes can help you to debug your program.

Many IDEs (Integrated Development Environments) have a built-in utility that lets you easily trace variables without making any changes to your program. These debugging systems vary from one IDE to another. If you have such a debugging facility, it is worth learning how to use it.

If you do not want to use such a debugging facility, you can trace variables by inserting some temporary output statements in your program. For example, the following code compiles but still contains an error:

```
int n = 10;
int sum = 10;
while (n > 1)
{
    sum = sum + n;
    n--;
}
System.out.println("The sum of the integers 1 to 10 is " + sum);
```

To find out what is wrong, you can trace the variables n and sum by inserting output statements as follows:

```
int n = 10;
int sum = 10;
while (n > 1)
{
    System.out.println("At the beginning of the loop: n = " + n);
    //trace
    System.out.println("At the beginning of the loop: sum = " + sum);
    //trace
    sum = sum + n;
    n--;
    System.out.println("At the end of the loop: n = " + n); //trace
    System.out.println("At the end of the loop: sum = " + sum);
    //trace
}
System.out.println("The sum of the integers 1 to 10 is " + sum);
```

The first four lines of the execution are as follows:

```
At the beginning of the loop: n = 10
At the beginning of the loop: sum = 10
At the end of the loop: n = 9
At the end of the loop: sum = 20
```

We can immediately see that something is wrong. The variable sum has been set to 20. Since it was initialized to 10, it is set to 10 + 10, which is incorrect if we want to sum the numbers from 1 to 10. There are several ways to correct the problem. One solution is given as the answer to Self-Test Exercise 40.

General Debugging Techniques

Tracing errors can sometimes be a difficult and time-consuming task. It is not uncommon to spend more time debugging a piece of code than it took to write the code in the first place. If you are having difficulties finding the source of your errors, then there are some general debugging techniques to consider.

Examine the system as a whole and do not assume that the bug occurs in one particular place. If the program is giving incorrect output values, then you should examine the source code, different test cases using a range of input and output values, and the logic behind the algorithm itself. For example, consider the tax program in Display 3.1. If the wrong tax is displayed, you might spend a lot of time trying to find an error in the code that calculates the tax. However, the error might simply be that the input values were different from those you were expecting, leading to an apparently incorrect program output. For example, in German the decimal point and comma are reversed from the English usage. Thus, an income of 25,000.50 becomes 25.000,50. A German programmer might make this type of error if the code was written assuming input in the English format. Although this scenario might seem like a stretch, consider the $125 million Mars Climate Orbiter launched by NASA in 1998. In 1999, it was lost approaching the planet because one team used metric units while another used English units to control the spacecraft's thrusters.

Determining the precise cause and location of a bug is one of the first steps in fixing the error. Examine the input and output behavior for different test cases to try to localize the error. A related technique is to trace variables to show what code the program is executing and what values are contained in key variables. You might also focus on code that has recently changed or code that has had errors before. Finally, you can also try removing code. If you comment out blocks of code and the error still remains, then the culprit is in the uncommented code. The process can be repeated until the location of the error can be pinpointed. The /* and */ notation is particularly useful to comment out large blocks of code. After the error has been fixed, it is easy to remove the comments and reactivate the code.

The first mistakes you should look for are common errors that are easy to make. These are described throughout this textbook in the Pitfall sections. Examples of common errors include off-by-one errors, comparing floating-point types with ==, adding extra semicolons that terminate a loop early, or using == to compare strings for equality.

Some novice programmers may become frustrated if they cannot find the bug and may resort to guessing. This technique involves changing the code without really understanding the effect of the change but hoping that it will fix the error. Avoid such slipshod hackery at all costs! Sometimes this method will work for the first few simple programs that you write. However, it will almost certainly fail for larger programs and will most likely introduce new errors to the program. Make sure that you understand the logical impact a change to the code will make before committing the modification.

Finally, if allowed by your instructor, you could show the program to someone else. A fresh set of eyes can sometimes quickly pinpoint an error that you have been missing. Taking a break and returning to the problem a few hours later or the next day can also sometimes help in discovering an error.

EXAMPLE: Debugging an Input Validation Loop

VideoNote
Debugging
Walkthrough

Let's illustrate both good and bad debugging techniques with an example. Suppose our program is presenting a menu where the user can select 'A' or 'B'. The purpose of the following code is to validate user input from the keyboard and to make the user type a choice again if something other than 'A' or 'B' is entered. To be more user-friendly, the program should allow users to make their selections in either upper- or lowercase.

EXAMPLE: (continued)

```
String s = "";
char c = ' ';
Scanner keyboard = new Scanner(System.in);

do
{
  System.out.println("Enter 'A' for option A " +
    "or 'B' for option B.");
  s = keyboard.next( );
  s.toLowerCase( );
  c = s.substring(0,1);
}
while ((c != 'a') || (c != 'b'));
```

This program generates a syntax error when compiled:

```
c = s.substring(0,1); : incompatible types
found : java.lang.String
required: char
```

The intent was to extract the first character from the string entered by the user and check to see whether it is 'a' or 'b'. The substring(0,1) call returns a String containing the first character of s, but c is of type char and the types need to match on both sides of the assignment. If we employ the "guessing" debugging technique, then we might make the types match by changing the data type of c to String. Such a change will "fix" this error, but it will cause new errors because the rest of the code treats c like a char. As a result, we have added even more errors! Before making any change, consider the larger context and what the effect of the change will be. In this case, the simplest and best fix is to use

```
c = s.charAt(0)
```

to retrieve the first character from s instead of retrieving a substring.

At this point, we have corrected the syntax error and our program will compile, but it will still not run correctly. A sample execution is shown as follows:

```
Enter 'A' for option A or 'B' for option B.
C
Enter 'A' for option A or 'B' for option B.
B
Enter 'A' for option A or 'B' for option B.
A
Enter 'A' for option A or 'B' for option B.
(Control-C)
```

The program is stuck in an infinite loop even when we type in a valid choice. The only way to stop it is to break out of the program (in the sample output this is done by hitting Control-C, but you may have to use a different method depending on your computing environment).

(continued)

EXAMPLE: (continued)

At this point, we could employ tracing to try to locate the source of the error. Here is the code with output statements inserted:

```
do
{
    System.out.println("Enter 'A' for option A " +
        "or 'B' for option B.");
    s = keyboard.next( );
    System.out.println("String s = " + s);
    s.toLowerCase( );
    System.out.println("Lowercase s = " + s);
    c = s.charAt(0);
    System.out.println("c = " + c);
}
while ((c != 'a') || (c != 'b'));
```

Sample output is as follows:

```
Enter 'A' for option A or 'B' for option B.
A
String s = A
Lowercase s = A
c = A
Enter 'A' for option A or 'B' for option B.
```

The println statements make it clear what is wrong—the string s does not change to lowercase. A review of the toLowerCase( ) documentation reveals that this method does not change the calling string, but instead returns a new string converted to lowercase. The calling string remains unchanged. To fix the error, we can assign the lowercase string back to the original string with

```
s = s.toLowerCase( );
```

However, we are not done yet. Even after fixing the lowercase error, the program is still stuck in an infinite loop, even when we enter 'A' or 'B'. A novice programmer might "patch" the program like so to exit the loop:

```
do
{
    System.out.println("Enter 'A' for option A " +
        "or 'B' for option B.");
    s = keyboard.next( );
    s = s.toLowerCase( );
    c = s.charAt(0);
    if ( c == 'a')
        break;
    if (c == 'b')
        break;
}
```

EXAMPLE: (continued)

```
while ((c != 'a') || (c != 'b'));
```

This forces the loop to exit if `'a'` or `'b'` is entered, and it will make the program work. Unfortunately, the result is a coding atrocity that should be avoided at all costs. This "quick fix" does not address the root cause of the error—only the symptoms. Moreover, such patches usually will not work for new cases. This particular fix also results in inconsistent code because the expression `((c! = 'a') || (c! = 'b'))` becomes meaningless when we already handle the `'a'` and `'b'` with the `if` and `break` statements.

To really find the bug, we can turn again to tracing, this time focusing on the Boolean values that control the `do-while` loop:

```
do
{
    System.out.println("Enter 'A' for option A " +
      "or 'B' for option B.");
    s = keyboard.next( );
    s = s.toLowerCase( );
    c = s.charAt(0);
    System.out.println("c != 'a' is " + (c!= 'a'));
    System.out.println("c != 'b' is " + (c!= 'b'));
    System.out.println("(c != 'a') || (c != 'b')) is "
            + ((c != 'a') || (c != 'b')));
}
while ((c != 'a') || (c != 'b'));
```

The sample output is now as follows:

```
Enter 'A' for option A or 'B' for option B.
A
c != 'a' is false
c != 'b' is true
(c != 'a') || (c != 'b')) is true
```

Since c equals `'a'`, the statement `(c != 'a')` evaluates to `false` and the statement `(c !='b')` evaluates to `true`. When combined, `(false || true)` is `true`, which makes the loop repeat. In spoken English, it sounds like "c not equal to `'a'`" or "c not equal to `'b'`" is a correct condition to repeat the loop. After all, if the character typed in is not `'a'` or the character typed in is not `'b'`, then the user should be prompted to try again. Logically however, if `(c != 'a')` is `false` (i.e., the character is `'a'`), then `(c != 'b')` must be true. A character cannot make both expressions `false`, so the final Boolean condition will always be `true`. The solution is to replace the "or" with an "and" so that the loop repeats only if `(c != 'a') && (c != 'b'))`. This makes the loop repeat as long as the input character is not `'a'` and it is not `'b'`.

(continued)

EXAMPLE: (continued)

An even better solution is to declare a `boolean` variable to control the `do-while` loop. Inside the body of the loop, we can set this variable to `false` when the loop should exit. This technique has the benefit of making the code logic easier to follow, especially if we pick a meaningful name for the variable. In the following example, it is easy to see that the loop repeats if `invalidKey` is `true`:

```
boolean invalidKey;
do
{
    System.out.println("Enter 'A' for option A " +
      "or 'B' for option B.");
    s = keyboard.next( );
    s = s.toLowerCase( );
    c = s.charAt(0);
    if (c == 'a')
     invalidKey = false;
    else if (c == 'b')
     invalidKey = false;
    else
     invalidKey = true;
}
while (invalidKey);
```

Preventive Coding

The best way to make debugging easier is to make no mistakes in the first place. Although this is unrealistic for programs of any complexity, there are some techniques we can use to eliminate or reduce the number of bugs in a program.

incremental
development

Incremental development is the technique of writing a small amount of code and testing it before moving on and writing more code. The test may require some new code, or a "test harness," that will not be part of your final program but exercises your code in some way to see if it is working. This technique makes debugging easier because if the test fails, then the error is likely in the small section of the new code that was just written.

When an error is made, be sure to learn from your mistake so you do not make it again in the future. Did the mistake occur because of sloppy programming? Was there some aspect of the program's design that you did not understand or left off before writing the code? Was there something you could have done to find the error more quickly or prevent it from happening at all? Are there other errors in your program similar to the one you just fixed? A critical review of your coding and debugging techniques should become a learning experience so you do not repeat your mistakes.

Finally, show your code to other programmers. Another developer might be able to immediately spot an error in your code and eliminate a lengthy debugging process.

code review

Many software development organizations have a formal process called **code review** that involves the inspection of code by other programmers. Such reviews have the additional benefit that programmers end up sharing coding techniques and learning best practices in the process of reviewing each other's code. A related technique is called **pair programming**, in which two programmers work together at the same computer. The programmers take turns, one typing while the other watches and looks for errors and thinks about the task at hand.

pair programming

Assertion Checks ★

assertion

An **assertion** is a sentence that says (asserts) something about the state of your program. An assertion must be a sentence that is either true or false and should be true if there are no mistakes in your program. You can place assertions in your code by making them comments. For example, all the comments in the following code are assertions:

```
int n = 0;
int sum = 0;
//n == 0 and sum == 0
while (n < 100)
{
    n++;
    sum = sum + n;
    //sum == 1 + 2 + 3 + ... + n
}
//sum == 1 + 2 + 3 + ... + 100
```

Note that each of these assertions can be either true or false, depending on the values of n and sum, and they all should be true if the program is performing correctly.

Java has a special statement to check whether an assertion is true. An assertion check statement has the following form:

assert

```
assert Boolean_Expression;
```

If you run your program in the proper way, the assertion check behaves as follows: If the *Boolean_Expression* evaluates to true, nothing happens, but if the *Boolean_Expression* evaluates to false, the program ends and outputs an error message saying that an assertion failed.

For example, the previously displayed code can be written as follows, with the first comment replaced by an assertion check:

```
int n = 0;
int sum = 0;
assert (n == 0) && (sum == 0);
while (n < 100)
{
    n++;
    sum = sum + n;
    //sum == 1 + 2 + 3 + ... + n
}
//sum == 1 + 2 + 3 + ... + 100
```

Note that we translated only one of the three comments into an assertion check. Not all assertion comments lend themselves to becoming assertion checks. For example, there is no simple way to convert the other two comments into Boolean expressions. Doing so would not be impossible, but you would need to use code that would itself be more complicated than what you would be checking.

assertion
check

Assertion Checking

An **assertion check** is a Java statement consisting of the keyword `assert` followed by a Boolean expression and a semicolon. If assertion checking is turned on and the Boolean expression in the assertion check evaluates to `false` when the assertion check is executed, the program will end and output a suitable error message. If assertion checking is not turned on, the assertion check is treated as a comment.

SYNTAX

```
assert Boolean_Expression;
```

EXAMPLE

```
assert (n == 0) && (sum == 0);
```

You can turn assertion checking on and off. When debugging code, you can turn assertion checking on so that a failed assertion will produce an error message. Once your code is debugged, you can turn assertion checking off and your code will run more efficiently.

A program or other class containing assertions is compiled in the usual way. After all classes used in a program are compiled, you can run the program with assertion checking either turned on or turned off.

If you compile your classes from the command line, you would compile a class with assertion in the usual way:

```
javac YourProgram.java
```

You can then run your program with assertion checking turned on or off. The normal way of running a program has assertion checking turned off. To run your program with assertion checking turned on, use the following command:

```
java -enableassertions YourProgram
```

If you are using an IDE, check the documentation for your IDE to see how to handle assertion checking. If you do not find an entry for "assertion checking," which is likely, check to see how you set run options. (With TextPad, you can set things up for assertion checking as follows: On the Configure menu, choose Preferences, and then choose the

Run Java Application command and set the "Prompt for parameters" option for it.[3] After you set this preference, when you run a program, a window will appear in which you can enter options for the `java run` command—for example, `-enableassertions`.)

Self-Test Exercises

40. Fix the bug in the code in the earlier subsection "Tracing Variables."

41. Add some suitable output statements to the following code so that all variables are traced:

```
int n, sum = 0;
for (n = 1; n < 10; n++)
    sum = sum + n;
System.out.println("1 + 2 + ...+ 9 + 10 == " + sum);
```

42. What is the bug in the following code? What do you call this kind of loop bug?

```
int n, sum = 0;
for (n = 1; n < 10; n++)
    sum = sum + n;
System.out.println("1 + 2 + ...+ 9 + 10 == " + sum);
```

43. Write an assertion check that checks to see that the value of the variable `time` is less than or equal to the value of the variable `limit`. Both variables are of type `int`.

3.5   Random Number Generation ★

The generation of random numbers is too important to be left to chance.

ROBERT COVEYOU

random numbers

pseudorandom

Games and simulation programs often require the computer to generate random numbers. For example, a card game might need a way to randomly shuffle the cards in the deck or to roll a pair of dice. In this section, we briefly discuss two ways to generate random numbers in Java. Although we generally use the term **random**, Java really generates **pseudorandom** numbers. That is, Java can generate a sequence of numbers that looks random but this sequence of numbers is initialized by a "seed" value. If the same seed value is used to initialize the random number generator, then the exact same sequence of numbers will be generated.

---

[3]If you are running applets, you also need to select the "Prompt for parameters" option for the Run Java Applet command on the Tools submenu.

The `Random` Object

Java includes an object called `Random` that can be used to generate many different types of random numbers. In this section, we discuss only how to generate random integers and doubles from a uniform distribution (this is when every number that could possibly be generated has an equally likely chance to appear) but the `Random` class supports other distributions.

To use the `Random` class, we first have to import it just like we imported the `Scanner` class:

```
import java.util.Random;
```

Next, we have to create an object of type `Random` that can generate the random numbers for us. This follows the same pattern as creating a `Scanner` object to read from the keyboard.

```
Random randomGenerator = new Random();
```

Similarly, just as you created only one `Scanner` object to read in all of your keyboard inputs, in general you should create only one `Random` object to generate all of your random numbers. In particular, older versions of Java used the computer's clock to seed the random number generator. This meant that two `Random` objects created within the same millisecond would generate the same sequence of numbers. Newer versions of Java do not have this limitation, but normally only one instance of a `Random` object is needed.

To generate a random integer in the range of all possible integers, use

```
int r = randomGenerator.nextInt();
```

To generate a random integer in the range from 0 to n-1, use

```
int r = randomGenerator.nextInt(n);
```

If you want a random number in a different range, then you can scale the number by adding an offset. For example, to generate a random number that is 4, 5, or 6, use

```
int r = randomGenerator.nextInt(3) + 4;
```

This generates a number that is 0, 1, or 2 and then adds 4 to get a number that is 4, 5, or 6.

To generate a random `double`, use

```
double r = randomGenerator.nextDouble();
```

This returns a number that is greater than or equal to 0.0 but less than 1.0. Display 3.11 demonstrates flipping a virtual coin five times by generating five random numbers that are either 0 or 1, where 0 corresponds to tails and 1 corresponds to heads.

Display 3.11   **Comparing Strings**

```
 1 import java.util.Random;
 2 public class CoinFlipDemo
 3 {
 4     public static void main(String[] args)
 5     {
 6         Random randomGenerator = new Random();
 7         int counter = 1;
 8
 9         while (counter <= 5)
10         {
11             System.out.print("Flip number " + counter + ": ");
12             int coinFlip = randomGenerator.nextInt(2);
13             if (coinFlip == 1)
14                 System.out.println("Heads");
15             else
16                 System.out.println("Tails");
17             counter++;
18         }
19     }
20 }
```

Sample Dialogue (output will vary)

```
Flip number 1: Heads
Flip number 2: Tails
Flip number 3: Heads
Flip number 4: Heads
Flip number 5: Tails
```

The `Math.random()` Method

Java also includes a method to generate random doubles without requiring the user to create an instance of the `Random` class. The method `Math.random()` returns a random double that is greater than or equal to 0.0 but less than 1.0. In fact, when this method is called for the first time, Java internally creates an instance of the `Random` class and invokes the `nextDouble()` method. This can be convenient if you do not want to create your own `Random` object.

Often the range between 0.0 and 1.0 is not what is desired, so it becomes necessary to scale the range by multiplying and translating the value by addition. Commonly, an `int` is desired, which requires a typecast. For example, if you need an `int` in the range from 1 to 6, the following code could be used:

```
int num = (int)(Math.random() * 6) + 1;
```

MyProgrammingLab™

Self-Test Exercises

44. What numbers could be generated by `randomGenerator.nextInt(5) + 10;` where `randomGenerator` is an object of type `Random`?

45. What numbers could be generated by `randomGenerator.nextDouble() * 3 + 1;` where `randomGenerator` is an object of type `Random`?

46. Use the method `Math.random()` to generate a random `double` that is greater than or equal to 10.0 but less than 20.0.

Chapter Summary

- The Java branching statements are the `if-else` statement and the `switch` *statement*.

- A `switch` statement is a multiway branching statement. You can also form multiway branching statements by nesting `if-else` statements to form a multiway `if-else` statement.

- *Boolean expressions* are evaluated similar to the way arithmetic expressions are evaluated. The value of a Boolean expression can be saved in a variable of type `boolean`.

- The Java loop statements are the `while`, `do-while`, and `for` statements.

- A `do-while` statement always iterates its loop body at least one time. Both a `while` statement and a `for` *statement* might iterate its loop body zero times.

- A `for` loop can be used to obtain the equivalent of the instruction "repeat the loop body *n* times."

- Tracing variables is a good method for debugging loops.

- An *assertion* check can be added to your Java code so that if the assertion is false, your program halts with an error message.

- The object `Random` can be used to generate *pseudorandom* integers or doubles.

Answers to Self-Test Exercises

```java
1. if (num % 2 == 0)
       System.out.println("Even")
   else
       System.out.println("Odd");
```

2.
```java
if (inventory > sale)
{
    System.out.println("Amount Sold: " + sale);
    inventory = inventory - sale;
    sale = 0;
}
else
{
    System.out.println("Not enough Inventory - Place an Order");
}
```

3.
```java
if (season.equalsIgnoreCase("winter"))
    System.out.println("Warm Clothing");
else
    System.out.println("Normal Clothing");
```

4.
```java
if (price < discount)
{
    System.out.println("Crazy");
}
else
{
    System.out.println("OK");
    netPrice = price - discount;
}
```

5. Good! You can do better!

6. Great Achievement!

7. You have scored less than 60
         Better luck next time!

8.
```java
if (n < 0)
    System.out.println(n + " is less than zero.");
else if(n < 100)
    System.out.println(
            n + " is between 0 and 99 (inclusive).");
else
    System.out.println(n + " is 100 or larger.");
```

9. Savings Account.
         Term Deposit.

10. Oranges

11. Plums

12. Fruitless

13. n1 % n2 == 0

14.
```java
if (sales >= 10000)
    commission = 0.15;
else
    commission = 0.0;
```

15. When the variables are of type `int`, you test for equality using `==`, as follows:

    ```
    variable1 == variable2
    ```

    When the variables are of type `String`, you test for equality using the method `equals`, as follows:

    ```
    variable1.equals(variable2)
    ```

    In some cases, you might want to use `equalsIgnoreCase` instead of `equals`.

16. ```
    if (nextWord.compareToIgnoreCase("N") < 0)
        System.out.println("First half of the alphabet");
    else
        System.out.println("Second half of the alphabet");
    ```

17. ```
    if ( (exam >= 60) && (programsDone >= 10) )
        System.out.println("Passed");
    else
        System.out.println("Failed");
    ```

18. ```
    if ( (pressure > 100) || (temperature >= 212) )
        System.out.println("Emergency");
    else
        System.out.println("OK");
    ```

19. a. `true`.

    b. `true`. Note that expressions a and b mean exactly the same thing. Because the operators `==` and `<` have higher precedence than `&&`, you do not need to include the parentheses. The parentheses do, however, make it easier to read. Most people find the expression in option a easier to read than the expression in option b, even though they mean the same thing.

    c. `true`.

    d. `true`.

    e. `false`. Because the value of the first subexpression, `(count == 1)`, is `false`, you know that the entire expression is `false` without bothering to evaluate the second subexpression. Thus, it does not matter what the values of `x` and `y` are. This is called *short-circuit evaluation*, which is what Java does.

    f. `true`. Since the value of the first subexpression, `(count < 10)`, is `true`, you know that the entire expression is `true` without bothering to evaluate the second subexpression. Thus, it does not matter what the values of `x` and `y` are. This is called *short-circuit evaluation*, which is what Java does.

    g. `false`. Notice that the expression in g includes the expression in option f as a subexpression. This subexpression is evaluated using short-circuit evaluation as we described for option f. The entire expression in g is equivalent to

    ```
    !( (true || (x < y)) && true )
    ```

    which in turn is equivalent to `!( true && true )`, and that is equivalent to `!(true)`, which is equivalent to the final value of `false`.
    ```

h. This expression produces an error when it is evaluated because the first subexpression, `((limit/count) > 7)`, involves a division by zero.

i. `true`. Since the value of the first subexpression, `(limit < 20)`, is true, you know that the entire expression is `true` without bothering to evaluate the second subexpression. Thus, the second subexpression, `((limit/count) > 7)`, is never evaluated, so the fact that it involves a division by zero is never noticed by the computer. This is *short-circuit evaluation*, which is what Java does.

j. This expression produces an error when it is evaluated because the first subexpression, `((limit/count) > 7)`, involves a division by zero.

k. `false`. Since the value of the first subexpression, `(limit < 0)`, is `false`, you know that the entire expression is `false` without bothering to evaluate the second subexpression. Thus, the second subexpression, `((limit/count) > 7)`, is never evaluated, so the fact that it involves a division by zero is never noticed by the computer. This is *short-circuit evaluation*, which is what Java does.

20. No. Since (`j > 0`) is `false` and Java uses short-circuit evaluation for `&&`, the expression (`1/(j+1) > 10`) is never evaluated.

21. `((bonus + (((day * rate) / correctionFactor) * newGuy)) - penalty)`

22. `5`
    `2`

23. There will be no output. Because `n < 0` is false, the loop body is executed zero times.

24. `5`
    `4`
    `3`
    `2`

25. `5`

    A `do-while` loop always executes its body at least one time.

26. It will be an infinite loop.

27. With a `do-while` statement, the loop body is always executed at least once. With a `while` statement, there can be conditions under which the loop body is not executed at all.

28. `3 9 15 21 27`

29. `100 90 80 70 60`

30. `Newzealand    wzealand    ealand    land    nd`

31.
```
n = 100;
while (n > 10)
{
    System.out.println("Hello " + n);
    n = n - 20;
}
```

32. The output is `1024 10`. The second number is the log to the base 2 of the first number. (If the first number is not a power of 2, then only an approximation to the log base 2 is produced.)

33. The output is `1024 1`. The semicolon after the first line of the `for` loop is probably a pitfall error.

34.
```
* * *
* * *
* * *
```

35. a. A `for` loop

    b. and c. Both require a `while` loop because the input list might be empty. (A `for` loop also might work, but a `do-while` loop definitely would not work.)

36. This is an infinite loop. The first few lines of output are
```
10
12
16
19
21
```

37. This is an infinite loop. The first few lines of output are
```
n == 1
limit == 10;
n == 2
limit == 3
n == 3
limit == 4
n == 4
limit == 5
```

38.
```
8
6
The end.
```

39.
```
8
6
2
0
The end.
```

40. If you look at the trace, you will see that after one iteration, the value of `sum` is 20. But the value should be 10 + 9, or 19. This should lead you to think that the variable `n` is not decremented at the correct time. Indeed, the bug is that the two statements

    ```
    sum = sum + n;
    n-- ;
    ```

    should be reversed to

    ```
    n-- ;
    sum = sum + n;
    ```

41. ```
    int n, sum = 0;
    for (n = 1; n < 10; n++)
    {
        System.out.println("n == " + n + " sum == " + sum);
            //Above line is a trace.
        sum = sum + n;
    }
    System.out.println("After loop");//trace
    System.out.println("n == " + n + " sum == " + sum);//trace
    System.out.println("1 + 2 + ...+ 9 + 10 == " + sum);
    ```

    If you study the output of this trace, you will see that 10 is never added in. This is a bug in the loop.

42. This is the code you traced in the previous exercise. If you study the output of this trace, you will see that 10 is never added in. This is an off-by-one error.

43. `assert (time <= limit);`

44. 10, 11, 12, 13 or 14

45. A double that is greater than or equal to 1 but less than 4.

46. `double d = Math.random() * 10 + 10;`
    ```

Programming Projects

Visit www.myprogramminglab.com to complete select exercises online and get instant feedback.

1. (This is a version of Programming Project 2.1 from Chapter 2.) The Babylonian algorithm to compute the square root of a positive number n is as follows:

   1. Make a guess at the answer (you can pick n/2 as your initial guess).
   2. Compute r = n / guess.
   3. Set guess = (guess +r) / 2.
   4. Go back to step 2 until the last two guess values are within 1% of each other.

   Write a program that inputs a double for n, iterates through the Babylonian algorithm until the guess is within 1% of the previous guess, and outputs the answer as a double to two decimal places. Your answer should be accurate even for large values of n.

2. In the game of craps, a pass line bet proceeds as follows: Two six-sided dice are rolled; the first roll of the dice in a craps round is called the "come out roll." A come out roll of 7 or 11 automatically wins, and a come out roll of 2, 3, or 12 automatically loses. If 4, 5, 6, 8, 9, or 10 is rolled on the come out roll, that number becomes "the point." The player keeps rolling the dice until either 7 or the point is rolled. If the point is rolled first, then the player wins the bet. If a 7 is rolled first, then the player loses.

   Write a program that simulates a game of craps using these rules without human input. Instead of asking for a wager, the program should calculate whether the player would win or lose. The program should simulate rolling the two dice and calculate the sum. Add a loop so that the program plays 10,000 games. Add counters that count how many times the player wins, and how many times the player loses. At the end of the 10,000 games, compute the probability of winning [i.e., Wins / (Wins + Losses)] and output this value. Over the long run, who is going to win the most games, you or the house?

3. One way to estimate the adult height of a child is to use the following formula, which uses the height of the parents:

   $$H_{\text{male\_child}} = ((H_{\text{mother}} \times 13/12) + H_{\text{father}})/2$$
   $$H_{\text{female\_child}} = ((H_{\text{father}} \times 12/13) + H_{\text{mother}})/2$$

   All heights are in inches. Write a program that takes as input the gender of the child, the height of the mother in inches, and the height of the father in inches, and outputs the estimated adult height of the child in inches. The program should allow the user to enter a new set of values and output the predicted height until the user decides to exit. The user should be able to input the heights in feet and inches, and the program should output the estimated height of the child in feet and inches. Use the int data type to store the heights.

4. You have used the value of π as 3.14159 in previous examples. The value of π can be calculated from the infinite series:

$$\pi = 4 - \tfrac{4}{3} + \tfrac{4}{5} - \tfrac{4}{7} + \tfrac{4}{9} - \tfrac{4}{11} + \ldots$$

Write a program that prints the approximate value of π after 10000 terms of this series. You program should also display a table that shows the value of π after terms that are multiples of 100, i.e., it should show π values at 100, 200, 300, ..., 10000 terms.

5. You have just purchased a stereo system that cost $1,000 on the following credit plan: no down payment, an interest rate of 18% per year (and hence 1.5% per month), and monthly payments of $50. The monthly payment of $50 is used to pay the interest, and whatever is left is used to pay part of the remaining debt. Hence, the first month you pay 1.5% of $1,000 in interest. That is $15 in interest. So, the remaining $35 is deducted from your debt, which leaves you with a debt of $965.00. The next month, you pay interest of 1.5% of $965.00, which is $14.48. Hence, you can deduct $35.52 (which is $50 – $14.48) from the amount you owe. Write a program that tells you how many months it will take you to pay off the loan, as well as the total amount of interest paid over the life of the loan. Use a loop to calculate the amount of interest and the size of the debt after each month. (Your final program need not output the monthly amount of interest paid and remaining debt, but you may want to write a preliminary version of the program that does output these values.) Use a variable to count the number of loop iterations and hence, the number of months until the debt is zero. You may want to use other variables as well. The last payment may be less than $50 if the debt is small, but do not forget the interest. If you owe $50, your monthly payment of $50 will not pay off your debt, although it will come close. One month's interest on $50 is only 75 cents.

6. The Fibonacci numbers F_n are defined as follows: F_0 is 1, F_1 is 1, and

$$F_{i+2} \;=\; F_i \;+\; F_{i+1}$$

$i = 0, 1, 2, \ldots$. In other words, each number is the sum of the previous two numbers. The first few Fibonacci numbers are 1, 1, 2, 3, 5, and 8. One place where these numbers occur is as certain population growth rates. If a population has no deaths, then the series shows the size of the population after each time period. It takes an organism two time periods to mature to reproducing age, and then the organism reproduces once every time period. The formula applies most straightforwardly to asexual reproduction at a rate of one offspring per time period. In any event, the green crud population grows at this rate and has a time period of five days. Hence, if a green crud population starts out as 10 pounds of crud, then in 5 days, there is still 10 pounds of crud; in 10 days, there is 20 pounds of crud; in 15 days, 30 pounds; in 20 days, 50 pounds; and so forth. Write a program that takes both the initial size of a green crud population (in pounds) and a number of days as input and outputs the number of pounds of green crud after that many days. Assume that the population size is the same for four days and then increases every fifth day. Your program should allow the user to repeat this calculation as often as desired.

7. The value e^x can be approximated by the following sum:

$$1 + x + x^2/2! + x^3/3! + \ldots + x^n/n!$$

Write a program that takes a value x as input and outputs this sum for n taken to be each of the values 1 to 10, 50, and 100. Your program should repeat the calculation for new values of x until the user says she or he is through. The expression $n!$ is called the *factorial* of n and is defined as

$$n! = 1*2*3*\ldots*n$$

Use variables of type double to store the factorials (or arrange your calculation to avoid any direct calculation of factorials); otherwise, you are likely to produce integer overflow, that is, integers larger than Java allows.

8. In cryptarithmetic puzzles, mathematical equations are written using letters. Each letter can be a digit from 0 to 9, but no two letters can be the same. Here is a sample problem:

SEND + MORE = MONEY

A solution to the puzzle is S = 9, R = 8, O = 0, M = 1, Y = 2, E = 5, N = 6, D = 7. Write a program that finds a solution to the cryptarithmetic puzzle of the following:

TOO + TOO + TOO + TOO = GOOD

The simplest technique is to use a nested loop for each unique letter (in this case T, O, G, D). The loops would systematically assign the digits from 0 to 9 to each letter. For example, it might first try T = 0, O = 0, G = 0, D = 0, then T = 0, O = 0, G = 0, D = 1, then T = 0, O = 0, G = 0, D = 2, etc., up to T = 9, O = 9, G = 9, D = 9. In the loop body, test that each variable is unique and that the equation is satisfied. Output the values for the letters that satisfy the equation.

VideoNote
Solution to Programming Project 3.9

9. Write a program that calculates the total grade for N classroom exercises as a percentage. Use the DecimalFormat class to output the value as a percent. The user should input the value for N followed by each of the N scores and totals. Calculate the overall percentage (sum of the total points earned divided by the total points possible) and output it using the DecimalFormat class. Sample input and output is shown below.

```
How many exercises to input?
3

Score received for exercise 1:
10
Total points possible for exercise 1:
10

Score received for exercise 2:
7
Total points possible for exercise 2:
12

Score received for exercise 3:
5
```

```
Total points possible for exercise 3:
8

Your total is 22 out of 30, or 73.33%.
```

10. The game of Pig is a simple two-player dice game in which the first player to reach 100 or more points wins. Players take turns. On each turn, a player rolls a six-sided die:

    - If the player rolls a 1, then the player gets no new points and it becomes the other player's turn.
    - If the player rolls 2 through 6, then he or she can either
      - ROLL AGAIN or
      - HOLD. At this point, the sum of all rolls is added to the player's score and it becomes the other player's turn.

    Write a program that plays the game of Pig, where one player is a human and the other is the computer. When it is the human's turn, the program should show the score of both players and the previous roll. Allow the human to input "r" to roll again or "h" to hold.

    The computer program should play according to the following rule:

    - Keep rolling when it is the computer's turn until it has accumulated 20 or more points, then hold. If the computer wins or rolls a 1, then the turn ends immediately.

    Allow the human to roll first.

11. Write a program that produces a bar chart showing the sales figures for ten departmental stores. Each bar in the bar graph is displayed as a row of asterisks. The program should read in the sales figures (rounded to the nearest 1,000) for the stores from a file. For each store it should display the sale and a bar consisting of one asterisk for each $1000 of sales. The data can be found in the sales.txt file.

12. You are working for a company that keeps its employee details in simple text files. You are upgrading the software. Write a program that reads the names and identification numbers of the employees from a file. Your program should also handle an arbitrary number of entries in the file. Your program must check to see if there is still data left to read (i.e., whether it has reached the end of the file). The appropriate methods to read from a file are described in Section 2.3.

VideoNote
Solution to
Programming
Project 3.13

13. The file words.txt on the book's website contains 87,314 words from the English language. Write a program that reads through this file and finds the longest word that is a palindrome.

14. The file words.txt on the book's website contains 87,314 words from the English language. Write a program that reads through this file and finds the word that has the most consecutive vowels. For example, the word "bedouin" has three consecutive vowels.

15. This problem is based on a "Nifty Assignment" by Steve Wolfman (http://nifty. stanford.edu/2006/wolfman-pretid). Consider lists of numbers from real-life data sources; for example, a list containing the number of students enrolled in different course sections, the number of comments posted for different Facebook status updates, the number of books in different library holdings, the number of votes per precinct, etc. It might seem like the leading digit of each number in the list could be 1–9 with an equally likely probability. However, Benford's Law states that the leading digit is 1 about 30% of the time and drops with larger digits. The leading digit is 9 only about 5% of the time.

Write a program that tests Benford's Law. Collect a list of at least 100 numbers from some real-life data source and enter them into a text file. Your program should loop through the list of numbers and count how many times 1 is the first digit, 2 is the first digit, etc. For each digit, output the percentage it appears as the first digit.

Defining Classes I 4

4.1 CLASS DEFINITIONS 206
Instance Variables and Methods 209
More about Methods 212
Local Variables 218
Blocks 219
Parameters of a Primitive Type 220
Simple Cases with Class Parameters 229
The this Parameter 229
Methods That Return a Boolean Value 231
The Methods equals and toString 234
Recursive Methods 237

**4.2 INFORMATION HIDING AND
ENCAPSULATION** 239
public and private Modifiers 240
Example: Yet Another Date Class 241
Accessor and Mutator Methods 242
Preconditions and Postconditions 249

4.3 OVERLOADING 250
Rules for Overloading 250

4.4 CONSTRUCTORS 258
Constructor Definitions 258
Example: The Final Date Class 268
Default Variable Initializations 269
An Alternative Way to Initialize
Instance Variables 269
Example: A Pet Record Class 270
The StringTokenizer Class ★ 274

Chapter Summary 279   **Answers to Self-Test Exercises** 280   **Programming Projects** 285

The loftier the building,
the deeper must the
foundation be laid.

THOMAS KEMPIS

Introduction

Classes are the single most important language feature that facilitates object-oriented programming (OOP), the dominant programming methodology in use today. You have already been using predefined classes. `String` and `Scanner` are two of the classes we have used. An object is a value of a class type and is referred to as an *instance of the class*. An object differs from a value of a primitive type in that it has methods (actions) as well as data. For example, `"Hello"` is an object of the class `String`. It has the characters in the string as its data and also has a number of methods, such as `length`. You already know how to use classes, objects, and methods. This chapter tells you how to define classes and their methods.

Prerequisites

This chapter uses material from Chapters 1, 2, and 3. This chapter requires a basic understanding of the Java programming language, including the ability to write simple programs using expressions, assignments, and console I/O. You should be able to output numbers, as well as have an understanding of how the `Scanner` class can be used in console I/O. You should also know how to manage the flow of control using branching and looping statements, as well as understand how to use Boolean expressions.

4.1   Class Definitions

"The Time has come," the Walrus said,
"to talk of many things:
of shoes and ships and sealing wax
of cabbages and kings."

LEWIS CARROLL, *Through the Looking-Glass*

A Java program consists of objects from various classes interacting with one another. Before we go into the details of how you define classes, let's review some of the terminology used with classes. Among other things, a class is a type and you can declare variables of a class type. A value of a class type is called an **object**. An object has both data and actions. The actions are called **methods**. Each object can have different data,

object

method

instance

but all objects of a class have the same types of data and all objects in a class have the same methods. An object is usually referred to as an object of the class or as an **instance of the class** rather than as a value of the class, but it is a value of the class type. To make this abstract discussion come alive, we need a sample definition.

A Class Is a Type

If A is a class, then the phrases "bla is of type A," "bla is an instance of the class A," and "bla is an object of the class A" all mean the same thing.

Display 4.1 contains a definition for a class named `DateFirstTry` and a program that demonstrates using the class. Objects of this class represent dates such as December 31, 2012 and July 4, 1776. This class is unrealistically simple, but it will serve to introduce you to the syntax for a class definition. Each object of this class has three pieces of data: a string for the month name, an integer for the day of the month, and another integer for the year. The objects have only one method, which is named `writeOutput`. Both the data items and the methods are sometimes called

member

field

instance variable

members of the object, because they belong to the object. The data items are also sometimes called **fields**. We will call the data items **instance variables** and use the term *method* instead of *member*.

The following three lines from the start of the class definition define three instance variables (three data members):

```
public String month;
public int day;
public int year; //a four digit number.
```

The word `public` simply means that there are no restrictions on how these instance variables are used. Each of these lines declares one instance variable name. You can think of an object of the class as a complex item with instance variables inside of it. So, an instance variable can be thought of as a smaller variable inside each object of the class. In this case, the instance variables are called `month`, `day`, and `year`.

An object of a class is typically named by a variable of the class type. For example, the program `DateFirstTryDemo` in Display 4.1 declares the two variables `date1` and `date2` to be of type `DateFirstTry`, as follows:

```
DateFirstTry date1, date2;
```

This gives us variables of the class `DateFirstTry`, but so far there are no objects of the class. Objects are class values that are named by the variables. To obtain an object, you

new

must use the `new` operator to create a "new" object. For example, the following creates an object of the class `DateFirstTry` and names it with the variable `date1`:

```
date1 = new DateFirstTry();
```

Display 4.1   A Simple Class

```
1    public class DateFirstTry              This class definition goes in a file named
2    {                                      DateFirstTry.java.
3        public String month;
4        public int day;   ◄───────────────────────── Later in this chapter, we will
5        public int year; //a four digit number.       see that these three public
                                                        modifiers should be replaced
6        public void writeOutput()                      with private.
7        {
8            System.out.println(month + " " + day + ", " + year);
9        }
10   }
```

```
1    public class DateFirstTryDemo        This class definition (program) goes in a file named
2    {                                    DateFirstTryDemo.java.
3        public static void main(String[] args)
4        {
5            DateFirstTry date1, date2;
6            date1 = new DateFirstTry();
7            date2 = new DateFirstTry();
8            date1.month = "December";
9            date1.day = 31;
10           date1.year = 2012;
11           System.out.println("date1:");
12           date1.writeOutput();

13           date2.month = "July";
14           date2.day = 4;
15           date2.year = 1776;
16           System.out.println("date2:");
17           date2.writeOutput();
18       }
19   }
```

Sample Dialogue

```
date1:
December 31, 2012
date2:
July 4, 1776
```

We will discuss this kind of statement in more detail later in this chapter when we discuss something called a *constructor*. For now simply note that

```
Class_Variable = new Class_Name( );
```

creates a new object of the specified class and associates it with the class variable.[1] Because the class variable now names an object of the class, we will often refer to the class variable as an object of the class. (This is really the same usage as when we refer to an int variable n as "the integer n," even though the integer is, strictly speaking, not n but the value of n.)

Unlike what we did in Display 4.1, the declaration of a class variable and the creation of the object are more typically combined into one statement, as follows:

```
DateFirstTry date1 = new DateFirstTry();
```

The new Operator

The new operator is used to create an object of a class and associate the object with a variable that names it.

SYNTAX

Class_Variable = new *Class_Name*( );

EXAMPLE

```
DateFirstTry date;
date = new DateFirstTry();
```

which is usually written in the following equivalent form:

```
DateFirstTry date = new DateFirstTry();
```

Instance Variables and Methods

We will illustrate the details about instance variables using the class and program in Display 4.1. Each object of the class DateFirstTry has three instance variables, which can be named by giving the object name followed by a dot and the name of the instance variable. For example, the object date1 in the program DateFirstTryDemo has the following three instance variables:

```
date1.month
date1.day
date1.year
```

Similarly, if you replace date1 with date2, you obtain the three instance variables for the object date2. Note that date1 and date2 together have a total of six instance variables. The instance variables date1.month and date2.month, for example, are two different (instance) variables.

---

[1] For many, the word "new" suggests a memory allocation. As we will see, the new operator does indeed produce a memory allocation.

The instance variables in Display 4.1 can be used just like any other variables. For example, `date1.month` can be used just like any other variable of type `String`. The instance variables `date1.day` and `date1.year` can be used just like any other variables of type `int`. Thus, although the following is not in the spirit of the class definition, it is legal and would compile:

```
date1.month = "Hello friend.";
```

More likely assignments to instance variables are given in the program `DateFirstTryDemo`.

The class `DateFirstTry` has only one method, which is named `writeOutput`. We reproduce the definition of the method here:

```
public void writeOutput ()◄─────────── Heading                          ╱ Body
{
    System.out.println(month + " " + day + ", " + year);◄─────
}
```

All method definitions belong to some class, and all method definitions are given inside the definition of the class to which they belong. A method definition is divided into two parts, a **heading** and a **method body**, as illustrated by the annotation on the method definition. The word `void` means this is a method for performing an action as opposed to producing a value. We will say more about method definitions later in this chapter (including some indication of why the word `void` was chosen to indicate an action). You have already been using methods from predefined classes. The way you invoke a method from a class definition you write is the same as the way you do it for a predefined class. For example, the following from the program `DateFirstTryDemo` is an invocation of the method `writeOutput` with `date1` as the calling object:

heading

method body

```
date1.writeOutput();
```

This invocation is equivalent to execution of the method body. So, this invocation is equivalent to

```
System.out.println(month + " " + day + ", " + year);
```

However, we need to say more about exactly how this is equivalent. If you simply replace the method invocation with this `System.out.println` statement, you will get a compiler error message. Note that within the definition for the method `writeOutput`, the names of the instance variables are used without any calling object. This is because the method will be invoked with different calling objects at different times. When an instance variable is used in a method definition, it is understood to be the instance variable of the calling object. So in the program `DateFirstTryDemo`,

```
date1.writeOutput();
```

Class Definition

The following shows the form of a class definition that is most commonly used; however, it is legal to intermix the method definitions and the instance variable declarations.

SYNTAX

```
public class Class_Name
{
      Instance_Variable_Declaration_1
      Instance_Variable_Declaration_2
           . . .
      Instance_Variable_Declaration_Last

      Method_Definition_1
      Method_Definition_2
           . . .
      Method_Definition_Last
}
```

EXAMPLES

See Displays 4.1 and 4.2.

---

is equivalent to

```
System.out.println(date1.month + " " + date1.day
                                 + ", " + date1.year);
```

Similarly,

```
date2.writeOutput();
```

is equivalent to

```
System.out.println(date2.month + " " + date2.day
                                 + ", " + date2.year);
```

File Names and Locations

Remember that a file must be named the same as the class it contains with an added `.java` at the end. For example, a class named `MyClass` must be in a file named `MyClass.java`.

We will eventually see other ways to arrange files, but at this point, your program and all the classes it uses should be in the same directory (same folder).

Self-Test Exercises

1. Write a method called `makeItChristmas` that could be added to the class `DateFirstTry` in Display 4.1. The method `makeItChristmas` has no parameters and sets the `month` instance variable to `"December"` and the `day` instance variable to `25`. It does not change the `year` instance variable.

2. Write a method called `greetingsOnChristmas` that could be added to the class `DateFirstTry` in Display 4.1. The method `greetingsOnChristmas` has no parameters and outputs the string `"Merry Christmas!"` provided the `month` instance variable has the value `"December"` and the `day` instance variable has the value `25`. Otherwise, it outputs the string `"Not Christmas Day."`

More about Methods

As we noted for predefined methods, methods of the classes you define are of two kinds: methods that return (compute) some value and methods that perform an action other than returning a value. For example, the method `println` of the object `System.out` is an example of a method that performs an action other than returning a value; in this case, the action is to write something to the screen. The method `nextInt` of the class `Scanner`, introduced in Chapter 2, is a method that returns a value; in this case, the value returned is a number typed in by the user. A method that performs some action other than returning a value is called a `void` method. This same distinction between `void` methods and methods that return a value applies to methods in the classes you define. The two kinds of methods require slight differences in how they are defined.

Both kinds of methods have a method heading and a method body, which are similar but not identical for the two kinds of methods. The method heading for a `void` method is of the form

```
public void Method_Name(Parameter_List)
```

The method heading for a method that returns a value is

```
public Type_Returned Method_Name (Parameter_List)
```

Later in the chapter, we will see that `public` may sometimes be replaced by a more restricted modifier and that it is possible to add additional modifiers, but these templates will do right now. For now, our examples will have an empty *Parameter_List*.

If a method returns a value, then it can return different values in different situations, but all values returned must be of the same type, which is specified as the type returned. For example, if a method has the heading

```
public double myMethod()
```

then the method always returns a value of type `double`, and the heading

```
public String yourMethod()
```

indicates a method that always returns a value of type `String`.

The following is a `void` method heading:

```
public void ourMethod()
```

Notice that when the method returns no value at all, we use the keyword `void` in place of a type. If you think of `void` as meaning "no returned type," the word `void` begins to make sense.

invocation

An **invocation** of a method that returns a value can be used as an expression anyplace that a value of the *Type_Returned* can be used. For example, suppose `anObject` is an object of a class with methods having our sample heading; in this case, the following are legal:

```
double d = anObject.myMethod();
String aStringVariable = anObject.yourMethod();
```

A `void` method does not return a value, but simply performs an action, so an invocation of a `void` method is a statement. A `void` method is invoked as in the following example:

```
anObject.ourMethod();
```

Note the ending semicolon.

So far, we have avoided the topic of parameter lists by only giving examples with empty parameter lists, but note that parentheses are required even for an empty parameter list. Parameter lists are discussed later in this chapter.

body

The **body** of a `void` method definition is simply a list of declarations and statements enclosed in a pair of braces, { }. For example, the following is a complete `void` method definition:

```
public void ourMethod()
{
    System.out.println("Hello");
    System.out.println("from our method.");
}
```

The body of a method that returns a value is the same as the body of a `void` method but with one additional requirement. The body of a method that returns a value must contain at least one `return` statement. A **return statement** is of the form

return statement

```
return Expression;
```

where *Expression* can be any expression that evaluates to something of the *Type_Returned* that is listed in the method heading. For example, the following is a complete definition of a method that returns a value:

```java
public String yourMethod()
{
    Scanner keyboard = new Scanner(System.in);
    System.out.println("Enter a line of text");
    String result = keyboard.nextLine();
    return result + " was entered.";
}
```

Notice that a method that returns a value can do other things besides returning a value, but style rules dictate that whatever else it does should be related to the value returned.

A `return` statement always ends a method invocation. Once the `return` statement is executed, the method ends, and any remaining statements in the method definition are not executed.

return in a void method

If you want to end a `void` method before it runs out of statements, you can use a return statement without any expression, as follows:

```java
return;
```

A `void` method need not have any `return` statements, but you can place a `return` statement in a `void` method if there are situations that require the method to end before all the code is executed.

Method Definitions

There are two kinds of methods: methods that return a value and methods, known as `void` methods, that perform some action other than returning a value.

Definition of a Method That Returns a Value

SYNTAX

```java
public Type_Returned Method_Name(Parameter_List)
{
    <List of statements, at least one of which
            must contain a return statement.>
}
```

If there are no *Parameters*, then the parentheses are empty.

EXAMPLE

```
public int getDay()
{
    return day;
}
```

void Method Definition

SYNTAX

```
public void Method_Name(Parameter_List)
{
    <List of statements>
}
```

If there are no *Parameters*, then the parentheses are empty.

EXAMPLE

```
public void writeOutput( )
{
    System.out.println(month + " " + day + ", " + year);
}
```

All method definitions are inside of some class definition. See Display 4.2 to see these example method definitions in the context of a class.

When an instance variable name is used in a method definition, it refers to an instance variable of the calling object.

return Statements

The definition of a method that returns a value must have one or more return statements. A return statement specifies the value returned by the method and ends the method invocation.

SYNTAX

```
return Expression;
```

EXAMPLE

```
public int getYear( )
{
    return year;
}
```

A void method definition need not have a return statement. However, a return statement can be used in a void method to cause the method to immediately end. The form for a return statement in a void method is

```
return;
```

Although it may seem that we have lost sight of the fact, all these method definitions must be inside of some class definition. Java does not have any stand-alone methods that are not in any class. Display 4.2 rewrites the class given in Display 4.1 but this time we have added a more diverse set of methods. Display 4.3 contains a sample program that illustrates how the methods of the class in Display 4.2 are used.

TIP: Any Method Can Be Used as a `void` Method

A method that returns a value can also perform some action besides returning a value. If you want that action, but do not need the returned value, you can invoke the method as if it were a `void` method and the returned value will simply be discarded. For example, the following contains two invocations of the method `nextLine()`, which returns a value of type `String`. Both are legal.

```
Scanner keyboard = new Scanner(System.in);
       . . .
String inputString = keyboard.nextLine();
       . . .
System.out.println("Press Enter to continue with program.");
keyboard.nextLine(); //Reads a line and discards it. ■
```

Display 4.2   A Class with More Methods (part 1 of 2)

```
1   import java.util.Scanner;

2   public class DateSecondTry
3   {
4       private String month;
5       private int day;
6       private int year; //a four digit number.

7       public void writeOutput()
8       {
9           System.out.println(month + " " + day + ", " + year);
10      }

11      public void readInput()
12      {
13          Scanner keyboard = new Scanner(System.in);
14          System.out.println("Enter month, day, and year.");
15          System.out.println("Do not use a comma.");
16          month = keyboard.next();
17          day = keyboard.nextInt();
18          year = keyboard.nextInt();
19      }
```

The significance of the modifier `private` *is discussed in the subsection "public and `private` Modifiers" in Section 4.2 a bit later in this chapter.*

Display 4.2   **A Class with More Methods** (part 2 of 2)

```
20        public int getDay()
21        {
22            return day;
23        }
24        public int getYear()
25        {
26            return year;
27        }

28        public int getMonth()
29        {
30            if (month.equalsIgnoreCase("January"))
31                return 1;
32            else if (month.equalsIgnoreCase("February"))
33                return 2;
34            else if (month.equalsIgnoreCase("March"))
35                return 3;
36            else if (month.equalsIgnoreCase("April"))
37                return 4;
38            else if (month.equalsIgnoreCase("May"))
39                return 5;
40            else if (month.equals("June"))
41                return 6;
42            else if (month.equalsIgnoreCase("July"))
43                return 7;
44            else if (month.equalsIgnoreCase("August"))
45                return 8;
46            else if (month.equalsIgnoreCase("September"))
47                return 9;
48            else if (month.equalsIgnoreCase("October"))
49                return 10;
50            else if (month.equalsIgnoreCase("November"))
51                return 11;
52            else if (month.equalsIgnoreCase("December"))
53                return 12;
54            else
55            {
56                System.out.println("Fatal Error");
57                System.exit(0);
58                return 0; //Needed to keep the compiler happy
59            }
60        }
61  }
```

MyProgrammingLab™

Self-Test Exercises

3. Write a method called `getNextYear` that could be added to the class `DateSecondTry` in Display 4.2. The method `getNextYear` returns an `int` value equal to the value of the `year` instance variable plus one.

Display 4.3   Using the Class in Display 4.2

```
1   public class DemoOfDateSecondTry
2   {
3       public static void main(String[] args)
4       {
5           DateSecondTry date = new DateSecondTry();
6           date.readInput();

7           int dayNumber = date.getDay();
8           System.out.println("That is the " + dayNumber
9                                 + "th day of the month.");
10      }
11  }
```

An invocation of a void *method is a statement.*

An invocation of a method that returns a value is an expression that can be used anyplace that a value of the type returned by the method can be used.

Sample Dialogue

```
Enter month, day, and year.
Do not use a comma.
July 4 1776
That is the 4th day of the month.
```

Local Variables

local variable

Look at the definition of the method `readInput()` given in Display 4.2. That method definition includes the declaration of a variable called `keyboard`. A variable declared within a method is called a **local variable**. It is called *local* because its meaning is local to—that is, confined to—the method definition. If you have two methods and each of them declares a variable of the same name—for example, if both were named `keyboard`—they would be two different variables that just happen to have the same name. Any change that is made to the variable named `keyboard` within one method would have no effect upon the variable named `keyboard` in the other method.

As we noted in Chapter 1, the `main` part of a program is itself a method. All variables declared in `main` are variables local to the method `main`. If a variable declared in `main` happens to have the same name as a variable declared in some other method, they are two different variables that just happen to have the same name. Thus, all the variables we have seen so far are either local variables or instance variables. There is only one more kind of variable in Java, which is known as a *static variable*. Static variables will be discussed in Chapter 5.

Local Variable

A variable declared within a method definition is called a **local variable**. If two methods each have a local variable of the same name, they are two different variables that just happen to have the same name.

Global Variables

Thus far, we have discussed two kinds of variables: instance variables, whose meaning is confined to an object of a class, and local variables, whose meaning is confined to a method definition. Some other programming languages have another kind of variable called a **global variable**, whose meaning is confined only to the program. Java does not have these global variables.

Blocks

block

compound statement

The terms **block** and **compound statement** mean the same thing—namely, a set of Java statements enclosed in braces, {}. However, programmers tend to use the two terms in different contexts. When you declare a variable within a compound statement, the compound statement is usually called a *block*.

Blocks

A **block** is another name for a compound statement—that is, a list of statements enclosed in braces. However, programmers tend to use the two terms in different contexts. When you declare a variable within a compound statement, the compound statement is usually called a *block*. The variables declared in a block are local to the block, so these variables disappear when the execution of the block is completed. However, even though the variables are local to the block, their names cannot be used for anything else within the same method definition.

If you declare a variable within a block, that variable is local to the block. This means that when the block ends, all variables declared within the block disappear. In many programming languages, you can even use that variable's name to name some other variable outside the block. However, *in Java, you cannot have two variables with the same name inside a single method definition.* Local variables within blocks can sometimes create problems in Java. It is sometimes easier to declare the variables outside the block. If you declare a variable outside a block, you can use it both inside and outside the block, and it will have the same meaning in both locations.

TIP: Declaring Variables in a `for` Statement

You can declare a variable (or variables) within the initialization portion of a `for` statement, as in the following:

```
int sum = 0;
for (int n = 1; n < 10; n++)
    sum = sum + n;
```

If you declare n in this way, the variable n will be *local to the* `for` *loop*. This means that n cannot be used outside the `for` loop. For example, the following use of n in the `System.out.println` statement is illegal:

```
for (int n = 1; n < 10; n++)
    sum = sum + n;
System.out.println(n); //Illegal
```

Declaring variables inside a `for` loop can sometimes be more of a nuisance than a helpful feature. We tend to avoid declaring variables inside a `for` loop except for very simple cases that have no potential for confusion. ■

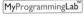

Self-Test Exercises

4. Write a method called `happyGreeting` that could be added to the class `DateSecondTry` in Display 4.2. The method `happyGreeting` writes the string `"Happy Days!"` to the screen a number of times equal to the value of the instance variable `day`. For example, if the value of `day` is 3, then it should write the following to the screen:

```
Happy Days!
Happy Days!
Happy Days!
```

Use a local variable.

Parameters of a Primitive Type

parameter

All the method definitions we have seen thus far had no parameters, which was indicated by an empty set of parentheses in the method heading. A **parameter** is like a blank that is filled in with a particular value when the method is invoked. (What we are calling *parameters* are also called *formal parameters*.) The value that is plugged in for

argument   the parameter is called an **argument**.[2] We have already used arguments with predefined methods. For example, the string `"Hello"` is the argument to the method `println` in the following method invocation:

```
System.out.println("Hello");
```

Display 4.4 contains the definition of a method named `setDate` that has the three parameters `newMonth`, `newDay`, and `newYear`. It also contains the definition of a method named `monthString` that has one parameter of type `int`.

Arguments are given in parentheses at the end of the method invocation. For example, in the following call from Display 4.4, the integers `6` and `17` and the variable `year` are the arguments plugged in for `newMonth`, `newDay`, and `newYear`, respectively:

```
date.setDate(6, 17, year);
```

When you have a method invocation such as the preceding, the argument (such as `6`) is plugged in for the corresponding formal parameter (such as `newMonth`) *everywhere that the parameter occurs in the method definition*. After all the arguments have been plugged in for their corresponding parameters, the code in the body of the method definition is executed.

The following invocation of the method `monthString` occurs within the definition of the method `setDate` in Display 4.4:

```
month = monthString(newMonth);
```

The argument is `newMonth`, which is plugged in for the parameter `monthNumber` in the definition of the method `monthString`.

Note that each of the formal parameters must be preceded by a type name, even if there is more than one parameter of the same type. Corresponding arguments must match the type of their corresponding formal parameter, although in some simple cases, an automatic type cast might be performed by Java. For example, if you plug in an argument of type `int` for a parameter of type `double`, Java automatically type casts the `int` value to a value of type `double`. The following list shows the type casts that Java automatically performs for you. An argument in a method invocation that is of any of these types is automatically type cast to any of the types that appear to its right, if that is needed to match a formal parameter.[3]

```
byte -> short -> int -> long -> float -> double
```

---

[2] Some programmers use the term *actual parameters* for what we are calling *arguments*.

[3] An argument of type `char` is also converted to a matching number type, if the formal parameter is of type `int` or any type to the right of `int` in our list of types.

Display 4.4   Methods with Parameters (part 1 of 2)

```
1    import java.util.Scanner;

2    public class DateThirdTry
3    {
4        private String month;
5        private int day;
6        private int year; //a four digit number.

7        public void setDate(int newMonth, int newDay, int newYear)
8        {
9            month = monthString(newMonth);
10           day = newDay;
11           year = newYear;
12       }

13       public String monthString(int monthNumber)
14       {
15           switch (monthNumber)
16           {
17           case 1:
18               return "January";
19           case 2:
20               return "February";
21           case 3:
22               return "March";
23           case 4:
24               return "April";
25           case 5:
26               return "May";
27           case 6:
28               return "June";
29           case 7:
30               return "July";
31           case 8:
32               return "August";
33           case 9:
34               return "September";
35           case 10:
36               return "October";
37           case 11:
38               return "November";
39           case 12:
40               return "December";
```

The significance of the modifier `private` *is discussed later in the subsection "*`public` *and* `private` *Modifiers" in Section 4.2.*

The method `setDate` *has an* `int` *parameter for the month, even though the month instance variable is of type* `String`. *The method* `setDate` *converts the month* `int` *value to a string with a call to the method* `monthString`.

This is the file `DateThirdTry.java`.

Display 4.4   Methods with Parameters (part 2 of 2)

```
41              default:
42                  System.out.println("Fatal Error");
43                  System.exit(0);
44                  return "Error"; //to keep the compiler happy
45              }
46          }
```
         <The rest of the method definitions are identical to the ones given in Display 4.2>.
```
47 }
```
                                            This is the file `DateThirdTry.java.`

```
1   public class DateThirdTryDemo
2   {                                        This is the file
3       public static void main(String[]args)    DateThirdTryDemo.java.
4       {
5           DateThirdTry date = new DateThirdTry();
6           int year = 1882;            The variable year is NOT plugged in for the
7           date.setDate(6, 17, year);  parameter newYear in the definition of the
8           date.writeOutput();         method setDate. Only the value of year,
9       }                               namely 1882, is plugged in for the parameter
10  }                                   newYear.
```

Sample Dialogue

```
June 17, 1882
```

Note that this is exactly the same as the automatic type casting we discussed in Chapter 1 for storing values of one type in a variable of another type. The more general rule is that you can use a value of any of the listed types anywhere that Java expects a value of a type further down on the list.

Note that the correspondence of the parameters and arguments is determined by their order in the lists in parentheses. In a method invocation, there must be exactly the same number of arguments in parentheses as there are formal parameters in the method definition heading. The first argument in the method invocation is plugged in for the first parameter in the method definition heading, the second argument in the method invocation is plugged in for the second parameter in the heading of the method definition, and so forth. This is diagrammed in Display 4.5.

Display 4.5 Correspondence between Formal Parameters and Arguments

```
Public class DateThirdTry
{
    private String month;
    private int day;
    private int year; //a four digit number.
    public void setDate(int newMonth, int newDay, int newYear)
    {
        month = monthString(newMonth);
        day = newDay;
        year = newYear;
    }
    . . .
```

This is in the file
`DateThirdTry.java.`

Only the value of `year`,
*Namely 1882, is plugged
in for the parameter*
`newYear`.

```
public class DateThirdTryDemo
{
    public static void main(String[] args)
    {
        DateThirdTry date = new DateThirdTry();
        int year = 1882;
        date.setDate(6, 17, year);
        date.writeOutput();
    }
}
```

This is in the file
`DateThirdTryDemo.java.`
*This is the file for a program that
uses the class* `DateThirdTry`.

*The arrows show which argument is
plugged in for which formal
parameter.*

Parameters of a Primitive Type

Parameters are given in parentheses after the method name in the heading of a method definition. A parameter of a primitive type, such as `int`, `double`, or `char`, is a local variable. When the method is invoked, the parameter is initialized to the value of the corresponding argument in the method invocation. This mechanism is known as the **call-by-value** parameter mechanism. The argument in a method invocation can be a literal constant, such as 2 or `'A'`; a variable; or any expression that yields a value of the appropriate type. This is the only kind of parameter that Java has for parameters of a primitive type. (Parameters of a class type are discussed in Chapter 5.)

> ### `main` Is a `void` Method
>
> The `main` part of a program is a `void` method, as indicated by its heading:
>
> ```
> public static void main(String[] args)
> ```
>
> The word `static` will be explained in Chapter 5. The identifier `args` is a parameter of type `String[]`, which is the type for an array of strings. Arrays are discussed in Chapter 6, and you need not be concerned about them until then. In the examples in this book, we never use the parameter `args`. Because `args` is a parameter, you may replace it with any other nonkeyword identifier and your program will have the same meaning. Aside from possibly changing the name of the parameter `args`, the heading of the `main` method must be exactly as shown above. Although we will not be using the parameter `args`, we will tell you how to use it in Chapter 6.
>
> A program in Java is just a class that has a `main` method. When you give a command to run a Java program, the run-time system invokes the method `main`.

call-by-value

It is important to note that only the value of the argument is used in this substitution process. If an argument in a method invocation is a variable (such as `year` in Display 4.4), it is the value of the variable that is plugged in for its corresponding parameter; it is not the variable name that is plugged in. For example, in Display 4.4, the value of the variable `year` (that is, `1882`) is plugged in for the parameter `newYear`. The variable `year` is not plugged into the body of the method `setDate`. Because only the value of the argument is used, this method of plugging in arguments for formal parameters is known as the **call-by-value** mechanism. In Java, this is the only method of substitution that is used with parameters of a primitive type, such as `int`, `double`, and `char`. As you will eventually see, this is, strictly speaking, also the only method of substitution that is used with parameters of a class type. However, there are other differences that make parameters of a class type appear to use a different substitution mechanism. For now, we are concerned only with parameters and arguments of primitive types, such as `int`, `double`, and `char`. (Although the type `String` is a class type, you will not go wrong if you consider it to behave like a primitive type when an argument of type `String` is plugged in for its corresponding parameter. However, for most class types, you need to think a bit differently about how arguments are plugged in for parameters. We discuss parameters of a class type in Chapter 5.)

parameters as local variables

In most cases, you can think of a parameter as a kind of blank, or placeholder, that is filled in by the value of its corresponding argument in the method invocation. However, parameters are more than just blanks; a parameter is actually a local variable. When the method is invoked, the value of an argument is computed, and the corresponding parameter, which is a local variable, is initialized to this value. Occasionally, it is useful to use a parameter as a local variable. An example of a parameter used as a local variable is given in Display 4.6. In that display, notice the parameter `minutesWorked` in the method `computeFee`. The value of `minutesWorked` is changed within the body of the method definition. This is allowed because a parameter is a local variable.

Display 4.6 A Formal Parameter Used as a Local Variable (part 1 of 2)

```
1   import java.util.Scanner;                          This is the file Bill.java.

2   public class Bill
3   {
4       public static final double RATE = 150.00; //Dollars per quarter hour

5       private int hours;
6       private int minutes;
7       private double fee;

8       public void inputTimeWorked()
9       {
10          System.out.println("Enter number of full hours worked");
11          System.out.println("followed by number of minutes:");
12          Scanner keyboard = new Scanner(System.in);   computeFee uses the
13          hours = keyboard.nextInt();                  parameter minutesWorked
14          minutes = keyboard.nextInt();                as a local variable.
15      }

16      private double computeFee(int hoursWorked, int minutesWorked)
17      {
18          minutesWorked = hoursWorked * 60 + minutesWorked;  ◄
19          int quarterHours = minutesWorked/15;
20              //Any remaining fraction of a quarter hour is not
                //charged for.
21          return quarterHours * RATE;
22      }
                                                  Although minutes is plugged in
                                                  for minutesWorked and
23      public void updateFee()                   minutesWorked is changed, the
24      {                                         value of minutes is not changed.
25          fee = computeFee(hours, minutes);
26      }

27      public void outputBill()
28      {
29          System.out.println("Time worked: ");
30          System.out.println(hours + " hours and " + minutes +
31                              " minutes");
32          System.out.println("Rate: $" + RATE + " per quarter hour.");
33          System.out.println("Amount due: $" + fee);
34      }
35  }
```

Display 4.6   A Formal Parameter Used as a Local Variable (part 2 of 2)

```
 1  public class BillingDialog
 2  {                                                   This is the file
 3      public static void main(String[] args)          BillingDialog.java.
 4      {
 5          System.out.println("Welcome to the law offices of");
 6          System.out.println("Dewey, Cheatham, and Howe.");
 7          Bill yourBill = new Bill();
 8          yourBill.inputTimeWorked();
 9          yourBill.updateFee();
10          yourBill.outputBill();
11          System.out.println("We have placed a lien on your house.");
12          System.out.println("It has been our pleasure to serve you.");
13      }
14  }
```

Sample Dialogue

```
Welcome to the law offices of
Dewey, Cheatham, and Howe.
Enter number of full hours worked
followed by number of minutes:
3 48
Time worked:
2 hours and 48 minutes
Rate: $150.0 per quarter hour.
Amount due: $2250.0
We have placed a lien on your house.
It has been our pleasure to serve you.
```

PITFALL: Use of the Terms "Parameter" and "Argument"

The use of the terms *parameter* and *argument* that we follow in this book is consistent with common usage, but people also often use the terms *parameter* and *argument* interchangeably. When you see these terms, you must determine their exact meaning from context. Many people use the term *parameter* for both what we call *parameters* and what we call *arguments*. Other people use the term *argument* both for what we call *parameters* and what we call *arguments*. Do not expect consistency in how people use these two terms.

formal parameters

The term **formal parameter** is often used for what we describe as a *parameter*. We will sometimes use this term for emphasis. The term **actual parameter** is often used for what we call an *argument*. We do not use this term in this book, but you will encounter it in other books. ■

actual parameter

Self-Test Exercises

5. Write a method called `fractionDone` that could be added to the class `DateThirdTry` in Display 4.4. The method `fractionDone` has a parameter `targetDay` of type `int` (for a day of the month) and returns a value of type `double`. The value returned is the value of the `day` instance variable divided by the `int` parameter `targetDay`. (So it returns the fraction of the time passed so far this month where the goal is reaching the `targetDay`.) Use floating-point division, not integer division. To get floating-point division, copy the value of the `day` instance variable into a local variable of type `double` and use this local variable in place of the day instance variable in the division. (You may assume the parameter `targetDay` is a valid day of the month that is greater than the value of the `day` instance variable.)

6. Write a method called `calculateDays` that could be added to the class `DateThirdTry` in Display 4.4. The method `calculateDays` has one parameter of type `int` named `monthNo`. It calculates and returns the total number of days in the month given by the `int` parameter `monthNo`. It assumes the year is not a leap year.

7. Suppose we redefine the method `setDate` in Display 4.4 to the following:

```
public void setDate(int newMonth, int newDay, int newYear)
{
    month = monthString(newMonth);
    day = newDay;
    year = newYear;
    System.out.println("Date changed to "
                    + newMonth + " " + newDay + ", " + newYear);
}
```

Indicate all instances of `newMonth` that have their value changed to `6` in the following invocation (also from Display 4.4):

```
date.setDate(6, 17, year);
```

8. Is the following a legal method definition that could be added to the class `DateThirdTry` in Display 4.4?

```
public void multiWriteOutput(int count)
{
    while (count > 0)
    {
        writeOutput();
        count--;
    }
}
```

9. Consider the definition of the method `monthString` in Display 4.4. What would happen if you put `break` statements in each case in the `switch` statement?

Simple Cases with Class Parameters

Methods can have parameters of a class type. Parameters of a class type are more subtle and more powerful than parameters of a primitive type. We will discuss parameters of class types in detail in Chapter 5. In the meantime, we will occasionally use a class type parameter in very simple situations. For these cases, you do not need to know any details about class type parameters except that, in some sense or other, the class argument is plugged in for the class parameter.

The `this` Parameter

As we noted earlier, if `today` is of type `DateSecondTry` (see Display 4.2), then

```
today.writeOutput();
```

is equivalent to

```
System.out.println(today.month + " " + today.day
                                    + ", " + today.year);
```

This is because, although the definition of `writeOutput` reads

```
public void writeOutput()
{
    System.out.println(month + " " + day + ", " + year);
}
```

it really means

```
public void writeOutput()
{
    System.out.println(<the calling object>.month + " "
        + <the calling object>.day + ", " + <the calling object>.year);
}
```

The instance variables are understood to have `<the calling object>.` in front of them. Sometimes it is handy, and on rare occasions even necessary, to have an explicit name for the calling object. Inside a Java method definition, you can use the keyword `this` as a name for the calling object. So, the following is a valid Java method definition that is equivalent to the one we are discussing:

```
public void writeOutput()
{
    System.out.println(this.month + " " + this.day
                                    + ", " + this.year);
}
```

The definition of `writeOutput` in Display 4.2 could be replaced by this completely equivalent version. Moreover, this version is in some sense the true version. The version without the this and a dot in front of each instance variable is just an abbreviation for this version. However, the abbreviation of omitting the this is used frequently.

this parameter

The keyword this is known as the **this parameter**. The this parameter is a kind of hidden parameter. It does not appear on the parameter list of a method, but is still a parameter. When a method is invoked, the calling object is automatically plugged in for this.

The this Parameter

Within a method definition, you can use the keyword this as a name for the calling object. If an instance variable or another method in the class is used without any calling object, then this is understood to be the calling object.

There is one common situation that requires the use of the this parameter. You often want to have the parameters in a method such as setDate be the same as the instance variables. A first, although incorrect, try at doing this is the following rewriting of the method setDate from Display 4.4:

```
public void setDate(int month, int day, int year) //Not correct
{
    month = monthString(month);
    day = day;
    year = year;
}
```

This rewritten version does not do what we want. When you declare a local variable in a method definition, then within the method definition, that name always refers to the local variable. A parameter is a local variable, so this rule applies to parameters. Consider the following assignment statement in our rewritten method definition:

```
day = day;
```

mask a variable

Both the identifiers day refer to the parameter day. The identifier day does not refer to the instance variable day. All occurrences of the identifier day refer to the parameter day. This is often described by saying the parameter day **masks** or hides the instance variable day. Similar remarks apply to the parameters month and year.

This rewritten method definition of the method setDate will produce a compiler error message because the following attempts to assign a String value to the int variable (the parameter) month:

```
month = monthString(month);
```

However, in many situations, this sort of rewriting will produce a method definition that will compile but that will not do what it is supposed to do.

To correctly rewrite the method `setDate`, we need some way to say "the instance variable `month`" as opposed to the parameter `month`. The way to say "the instance variable `month`" is `this.month`. Similar remarks apply to the other two parameters. So, the correct rewriting of the method `setDate` is as follows:

```
public void setDate(int month, int day, int year)
{
    this.month = monthString(month);
    this.day = day;
    this.year = year;
}
```

This version is completely equivalent to the version in Display 4.4.

Self-Test Exercises

10. The method `writeOutput` in Display 4.2 uses the instance variables `month`, `day`, and `year`, but gives no object name for these instance variables. Every instance variable must belong to some object. To what object or objects do these instance variables in the definition of `writeOutput` belong?

11. Rewrite the definitions of the methods `getDay` and `getYear` in Display 4.2 using the `this` parameter.

12. Rewrite the method `getMonth` in Display 4.2 using the `this` parameter.

Methods That Return a Boolean Value

There is nothing special about methods that return a value of type `boolean`. The type `boolean` is a primitive type, just like the types `int` and `double`. A method that returns a value of type `boolean` must have a `return` statement of the form

```
return Boolean_Expression;
```

So, an invocation of a method that returns a value of type `boolean` returns either `true` or `false`. It thus makes sense to use an invocation of such a method to control an `if-else` statement, to control a `while` loop, or to control anyplace else that a Boolean expression is allowed. Although there is nothing new here, people who have not used `boolean` valued methods before sometimes find them to be uncomfortable. So we will go through one small example.

The following is a method definition that could be added to the class `DateThirdTry` in Display 4.4:

```
public boolean isBetween(int lowYear, int highYear)
{
    return ( (year > lowYear) && (year < highYear) );
}
```

Consider the following lines of code:

```
DateThirdTry date = new DateThirdTry();
date.setDate(1, 2, 3001);
if (date.isBetween(2000, 4000))
    System.out.println(
            "The date is between the years 2000 and 4000");
else
    System.out.println(
            "The date is not between the years 2000 and 4000");
```

The expression `date.isBetween(2000, 4000)` is an invocation of a method that returns a `boolean` value—that is, returns one of the two values `true` and `false`. So, it makes perfectly good sense to use it as the controlling Boolean expression in an `if-else` statement. The expression `year` in the definition of `isBetween` really means `this.year`, and `this` stands for the calling object. In `date.isBetween(2000, 4000)` the calling object is `date`. So, this returns the value

```
(date.year > lowYear) && (date.year < highYear)
```

But, `2000` and `4000` are plugged in for the parameters `lowYear` and `highYear`, respectively. So, this expression is equivalent to

```
(date.year > 2000) && (date.year < 4000)
```

Thus, the `if-else` statement is equivalent to[4]

```
if ((date.year > 2000) && (date.year < 4000))
    System.out.println(
                "The date is between the years 2000 and 4000.");
else
    System.out.println(
                "The date is not between the years 2000 and 4000.");
```

Thus, the output produced is

```
The date is between the years 2000 and 4000.
```

Another example of a `boolean` valued method, which we will, in fact, add to our date class, follows:

```
public boolean precedes(DateFourthTry otherDate)
{
    return ( (year < otherDate.year) ||
```

_____

[4] Later in this chapter, we will see that because `year` is marked `private`, it is not legal to write `date.year` in a program, but the meaning of such an expression is clear even if you cannot include it in a program.

```
        (year == otherDate.year && getMonth() < otherDate.getMonth())
        ||
        (year == otherDate.year && month.equals(otherDate.month)
                                    && day < otherDate.day) );
    }
```

The version of our date class with this method is given in Display 4.7. The other new methods in that class will be discussed shortly in the subsection entitled "The Methods equals and toString." Right now, let's discuss this new method named precedes.

An invocation of the method precedes has the following form, where date1 and date2 are two objects of our date class:

```
    date1.precedes(date2)
```

This is a Boolean expression that returns true if date1 comes before date2. Because it is a Boolean expression, it can be used anyplace a Boolean expression is allowed, such as to control an if-else or while statement. For example,

```
    if (date1.precedes(date2))
        System.out.println("date1 comes before date2.");

    else
        System.out.println("date2 comes before or is equal to date1.");
```

Display 4.7   **A Class with Methods equals and toString** (part 1 of 2)

```
1   import java.util.Scanner;

2   public class DateFourthTry
3   {
4       private String month;
5       private int day;
6       private int year; //a four digit number.

7       public String toString()
8       {
9           return (month + " " + day + ", " + year);
10      }

11      public void writeOutput()
12      {
13          System.out.println(month + " " + day + ", " + year);
14      }
```
This is the method **equals** *in the class* **DateFourthTry.**

This is the method **equals** *in the class* **String.**

```
15      public boolean equals(DateFourthTry otherDate)
16      {
17          return ( (month.equals(otherDate.month))
18                  && (day == otherDate.day) && (year == otherDate.year) );
19      }
```

(continued)

Display 4.7   A Class with Methods `equals` and `toString` (part 2 of 2)

```
20      public boolean precedes(DateFourthTry otherDate)
21      {
22          return ( (year < otherDate.year) ||
                (year == otherDate.year && getMonth() <
                    otherDate.getMonth()) ||
24              (year == otherDate.year && month.equals(otherDate.month)
25                                      && day < otherDate.day) );
26      }
```

<The rest of the method definitions are identical to the ones in `DateThirdTry` *in Display 4.4.>*

```
27  }
```

The `return` statement in the definition of the method `precedes` may look intimidating, but it is really straightforward. It says that `date1.precedes(date2)` returns `true`, provided one of the following three conditions is satisfied:

```
date1.year < date2.year
date1.year equals date2.year and date1.month comes before
date2.month date1 and date2 have the same year and month and
                date1.day < date2.day.
```

If you give it a bit of thought, you will realize that `date1` precedes `date2` in time precisely when one of these three conditions is satisfied.

The Methods `equals` and `toString`

Java expects certain methods to be in all, or almost all, classes. This is because some of the standard Java libraries have software that assumes such methods are defined. Two of these methods are `equals` and `toString`. Therefore, you should include such methods and be certain to spell their names exactly as we have done. Use `equals`, not `same` or `areEqual`. Do not even use `equal` without the `s`. Similar remarks apply to the `toString` method. After we have developed more material, we will explain this in more detail. In particular, we will then explain how to give a better method definition for `equals`. For now, just get in the habit of including these methods.

equals   The method `equals` is a `boolean` valued method to compare two objects of the class to see if they satisfy the intuitive notion of "being equal." So, the heading should be

```
public boolean equals(Class_Name Parameter_Name)
```

Display 4.7 contains definitions of the methods `equals` and `toString` that we might add to our date class, which is now named `DateFourthTry`. The heading of that `equals` method is

```
public boolean equals(DateFourthTry otherDate)
```

When you use the method `equals` to compare two objects of the class `DateFourthTry`, one object is the calling object and the other object is the argument, like so:

        date1.equals(date2)

or equivalently,

        date2.equals(date1)

Because the method `equals` returns a value of type `boolean`, you can use an invocation of `equals` as the Boolean expression in an `if-else` statement, as shown in Display 4.8. Similarly, you can also use it anyplace else that a Boolean expression is allowed.

There is no absolute notion of "equality" that you must follow in your definition of `equals`. You can define the method `equals` any way you wish, but to be useful, it should reflect some notion of "equality" that is useful for the software you are

Display 4.8   Using the Methods `equals` and `toString`

```
1   public class EqualsAndToStringDemo
2   {
3       public static void main(String[] args)
4       {
5           DateFourthTry date1 = new DateFourthTry(),
6                         date2 = new DateFourthTry();
7           date1.setDate(6, 17, 1882);
8           date2.setDate(6, 17, 1882);

9           if (date1.equals(date2))
10              System.out.println(date1 + " equals " + date2);
11          else
12              System.out.println(date1 + " does not equal " + date2);

13          date1.setDate(7, 28, 1750);

14          if (date1.precedes(date2))
15              System.out.println(date1 + " comes before " + date2);
16          else
17              System.out.println(date2 + " comes before or is equal to "
18                                  + date1);
19      }
20  }
```

These are equivalent to `date1.toString()`.

These are equivalent to `date2.toString()`.

Sample Dialogue

```
June 17, 1882 equals June 17, 1882
July 28, 1750 comes before June 17, 1882
```

designing. A common way to define `equals` for simple classes of the kind we are looking at now is to say `equals` returns `true` if each instance variable of one object equals the corresponding instance variable of the other object. This is how we defined `equals` in Display 4.7.

If the definition of `equals` in Display 4.7 seems less than clear, it may help to rewrite it as follows using the `this` parameter:

```
public boolean equals(DateFourthTry otherDate)
{
    return ( ((this.month).equals(otherDate.month))
      && (this.day == otherDate.day) && (this.year ==
      otherDate.year) );
}
```

So, if `date1` and `date2` are objects of the class `DateFourthTry`, then `date1.equals(date2)` returns `true` provided the three instance variables in `date1` have values that are equal to the three instance variables in `date2`.

Also, note that the method in the definition of `equals` that is used to compare months is not the `equals` for the class `DateFourthTry` but the `equals` for the class `String`. You know this because the calling object, which is `this.month`, is of type `String`.

Remember that we use the `equals` method of the class `String` because `==` does not work correctly for comparing `String` values. This was discussed in the Pitfall section of Chapter 3 entitled "Using `==` with Strings.")

In Chapter 7, you will see that there are reasons to make the definition of the `equals` method a bit more involved. But the spirit of what an `equals` method should be is very much like what we are now doing, and it is the best we can do with what we know so far.

toString   The method `toString` should be defined so that it returns a `String` value that represents the data in the object. One nice thing about the method `toString` is that it makes it easy to output an object to the screen. If `date` is of type `DateFourthTry`, then you can output the date to the screen as follows:

```
System.out.println(date.toString());
```

println used with objects   In fact, `System.out.println` was written so that it automatically invokes `toString()` if you do not include it. So, the object `date` can also be output by the following simpler and equivalent statement:

```
System.out.println(date);
```

This means that the method `writeOutput` in Display 4.7 is superfluous and could safely be omitted from the class definition.

If you look at Display 4.8, you will see that `toString` is also called automatically when the object is connected to some other string with a `+`, as in

```
System.out.println(date1 + " equals " + date2);
```

+ used with objects

In this case, it is really the plus operator that causes the automatic invocation of toString(). So, the following is also legal:

```
String s = date1 + " equals " + date2;
```

The preceding is equivalent to

```
String s = date1.toString() + " equals " + date2.toString();
```

Recursive Methods

recursive method

Java does allow **recursive method** definitions. Recursive methods are covered in Chapter 11. If you do not know what recursive methods are, do not be concerned until you reach that chapter. If you want to read about these methods early, you can read Sections 11.1 and 11.2 of Chapter 11 after you complete Chapter 5.

The Methods equals and toString

Usually, your class definitions should contain an equals method and a toString method. An equals method compares the calling object to another object and should return true when the two objects are intuitively equal. When comparing objects of a class type, you normally use the method equals not ==.

The toString method should return a string representation of the data in the calling object. If a class has a toString method, you can use an object of the class as an argument to the methods System.out.println and System.out.print.

See Display 4.7 for an example of a class with equals and toString methods.

TIP: Testing Methods

driver program

Each method should be tested in a program in which it is the only untested program. If you test methods this way, then when you find an error, you will know which method contains the error. A program that does nothing but test a method is called a **driver program**.

bottom-up testing

If one method contains an invocation of another method in the same class, this can complicate the testing task. One way to test a method is to first test all the methods invoked by that method and then test the method itself. This is called **bottom-up testing**.

(continued)

TIP: (continued)

It is sometimes impossible or inconvenient to test a method without using some other method that has not yet been written or has not yet been tested. In this case, you can use a simplified version of the missing or untested method. These simplified methods are called **stubs**. These stubs will not necessarily perform the correct calculation, but they will deliver values that suffice for testing, and they are simple enough that you can have confidence in their performance. For example, the following is a possible stub:

stub

```
/**
 Computes the probability of rain based on temperature, barometric
 pressure, and relative humidity. Returns the probability as a
 fraction between 0 and 1.
*/
public double rainChance(double temperature,
                                 double pressure,double humidity)
{
    return 0.5; //Not correct but good enough for a stub.
}
```

The Fundamental Rule for Testing Methods

Every method should be tested in a program in which every other method in the testing program has already been fully tested and debugged.

Self-Test Exercises

13. In the definition of `precedes` in Display 4.7, we used

    `month.equals(otherDate.month)`

    to test whether two months are equal; but we used

    `getMonth() < otherDate.getMonth()`

    to test whether one month comes before another. Why did we use `month` in one case and `getMonth` in another case?

14. What is the fundamental rule for testing methods?

4.2   Information Hiding and Encapsulation

We all know—the Times *knows—but we pretend we don't.*

VIRGINIA WOOLF, *Monday or Tuesday*

information hiding

Information hiding means that you separate the description of how to use a class from the implementation details, such as how the class methods are defined. You do this so that a programmer who uses the class does not need to know the implementation details of the class definition. The programmer who uses the class can consider the implementation details as hidden, since he or she does not need to look at them. Information hiding is a way of avoiding information overloading. It keeps the information needed by a programmer using the class within reasonable bounds.

abstraction

Another term for information hiding is **abstraction**. The use of the term *abstraction* for information hiding makes sense if you think about it a bit. When you abstract something, you are discarding some of the details.

encapsulation

Encapsulation means grouping software into a unit in such a way that it is easy to use because there is a well-defined simple interface. So, encapsulation and information hiding are two sides of the same coin.

Java has a way of officially hiding details of a class definition. To hide details, mark them as `private`, a concept we discuss next.

VideoNote
Information Hiding Example

Encapsulation

Encapsulation means that the data and the actions are combined into a single item (in our case, a class object) and that the details of the implementation are hidden. The terms *information hiding* and *encapsulation* deal with the same general principle: If a class is well designed, a programmer who uses a class need not know all the details of the implementation of the class but need only know a much simpler description of how to use the class.

API

The term **API** stands for *application programming interface*. The API for a class is a description of how to use the class. If your class is well designed, using the encapsulation techniques we discuss in this book, then a programmer who uses your class need only read the API and need not look at the details of your code for the class definition.

ADT

The term **ADT** is short for *abstract data type*. An ADT is a data type that is written using good information hiding techniques.

`public` and `private` Modifiers

Compare the instance variables in Displays 4.1 and 4.2. In Display 4.1, each instance variable is prefaced with the modifier `public`. In Display 4.2, each instance variable is prefaced with the modifier `private`. The modifier `public` means that there are no restrictions on where the instance variable can be used. The modifier `private` means that the instance variable cannot be accessed by name outside of the class definition.

For example, the following would produce a compiler error message if used in a program:

```
DateSecondTry date = new DateSecondTry();
date.month = "January";
date.day = 1;
date.year = 2006;
```

In fact, any one of the three assignments would be enough to trigger a compiler error. This is because, as shown in Display 4.2, each of the instance variables `month`, `day`, and `year` is labeled `private`.

If, on the other hand, we had used the class `DateFirstTry` from Display 4.1 instead of the class `DateSecondTry` in the preceding code, the code would be legal and would compile and run with no error messages. This is because, in the definition of `DateFirstTry` (Display 4.1), each of the instance variables `month`, `day`, and `year` is labeled `public`.

It is considered good programming practice to make all instance variables private. As we will explain a little later in this chapter, this is intended to simplify the task of any programmer using the class. But before we say anything about how, on balance, this simplifies the job of a programmer who uses the class, let's see how it complicates the job of a programmer who uses the class.

Once you label an instance variable as `private`, there is then no way to change its value (nor to reference the instance variable in any other way) except by using one of the methods belonging to the class. Note that even when an instance variable is private, you can still access it through methods of the class. For the class `DateSecondTry`, you can change the values of the instance variables with the method `readInput`, and you can obtain the values of the instance variables with the methods whose names start with `get`. So, the qualifier `private` does not make it impossible to access the instance variables. It just makes it illegal to use their names, which can be a minor nuisance.

The modifiers `public` and `private` before a method definition have a similar meaning. If the method is labeled `public`, there are no restrictions on its usage. If the method is labeled `private`, the method can only be used in the definition of another method of the same class.

Any instance variable can be labeled either `public` or `private`. Any method can be `public` or `private`. However, normal good programming practices require that *all* instance variables be private and that typically, most methods be public. Normally, a method is private only if it is being used solely as a helping method in the definition of other methods.

EXAMPLE: Yet Another Date Class

Display 4.9 contains another, much improved, definition of a class for a date. Note that all instance variables are private and that two methods are private. We made the methods `dateOK` and `monthString` private because they are just helping methods used in the definitions of other methods. A user of the class `DateFifthTry` would not (in fact, cannot) use either of the methods `dateOK` or `monthString`. This is all hidden information that need not concern a programmer using the class. The method `monthString` was public in previous versions of our date classes because we had not yet discussed the `private` modifier. It is now marked `private` because it is just a helping method.

Note that the class `DateFifthTry` uses the method `dateOK` to make sure that any changes to instance variables make sense. Because the methods of the class `DateFifthTry` use the method `dateOK` to check for impossible dates, you cannot use any methods, such as `readInput` or `setDate`, to set the instance variables so that they represent an impossible date such as January 63, 2005. If you try to do so, your program would end with an error message. (To make our definition of the method `dateOK` simple, we did not check for certain impossible dates, such as February 31, but it would be easy to exclude these dates as well.)

The methods `dateOK` and `equals` each return a value of type `boolean`. That means they return a value that is either `true` or `false` and so can be used as the Boolean expression in an `if-else` statement, `while` statement, or other loop statement. This is illustrated by the following, which is taken from the definition of the method `setDate` in Display 4.9:

```
if (dateOK(month, day, year))
{
    this.month = monthString(month);
    this.day = day;
    this.year = year;
}
else
{
    System.out.println("Fatal Error");
    System.exit(0);
}
```

Note that, although all the instance variables are private, a programmer using the class can still change or access the value of an instance variable using the methods that start with `set` or `get`. This is discussed more fully in the next subsection, "Accessor and Mutator Methods."

(continued)

EXAMPLE: (continued)

Note that there is a difference between what we might call the *inside view* and the *outside view* of the class DateFifthTry. A date such as July 4, 1776, is represented inside the class object as the string value "July" and the two int values 4 and 1776. But if a programmer using the same class object asks for the date using getMonth, getDay, and getYear, he or she will get the three int values 7, 4, and 1776. From inside the class, a month is a string value, but from outside the class, a month is an integer. The description of the data in a class object need not be a simple direct description of the instance variables. (To further emphasize the fact that the month has an inside view as a string but an outside view as a number, we have written the method readInput for the class DateFifthTry so that the user enters the month as an integer rather than a string.)

Note that the method definitions in a class need not be given in any particular order. In particular, it is perfectly acceptable to give the definition the method dateOK after the definitions of methods that use dateOK. Indeed, any ordering of the method definitions is acceptable. Use whatever order seems to make the class easiest to read. (Those who come to Java from certain other programming languages should note that there is no kind of forward reference needed when a method is used before it is defined.)

Self-Test Exercises

15. Following the style guidelines given in this book, when should an instance variable be marked private?

16. Following the style guidelines given in this book, when should a method be marked private?

Accessor and Mutator Methods

You should always make all instance variables in a class private. However, you may sometimes need to do something with the data in a class object. The special-purpose methods, such as toString, equals, and any input methods, will allow you to do many things with the data in an object. But sooner or later you will want to do something with the data for which there are no special-purpose methods. How can you do anything new with the data in an object? The answer is that you can do anything that you might reasonably want (and that the class design specifications consider to be legitimate), provided you equip your classes with suitable *accessor* and *mutator* methods. These are methods that allow you to access and change the data in an object, **accessor** usually in a very general way. **Accessor methods** allow you to obtain the data. In **methods** Display 4.9, the methods getMonth, getDay, and getYear are accessor methods. The accessor methods need not literally return the values of each instance variable, but they must return something equivalent to those values. For example, the method `getMonth` returns the number of the month, even though the month is stored in a `String` instance variable. Although it is not required by the Java language, it is a generally accepted good programming practice to spell the names of accessor methods starting with `get`.

mutator methods

Mutator methods allow you to change the data in a class object. In Display 4.9, the methods whose names begin with the word `set` are mutator methods. It is a generally accepted good programming practice to use names that begin with the word `set` for mutator methods. Your class definitions will typically provide a complete set of public accessor methods and at least some public mutator methods. There are, however, important classes, such as the class `String`, that have no public mutator methods.

At first glance, it may seem as if accessor and mutator methods defeat the purpose of making instance variables private, but if you look carefully at the mutator methods in Display 4.9, you will see that the mutator and accessor methods are not equivalent to making the instance variables public. Notice the mutator methods, that is, the ones that begin with `set`. They all test for an illegal date and end the program with an error message if there is an attempt to set the instance variables to any illegal values. If the variables were public, you could set the data to values that do not make sense for a date, such as January 42, 1930. With mutator methods, you can control and filter changes to the data. (As it is, you can still set the data to values that do not represent a real date, such as February 31, but as we already noted, it would be easy to exclude these dates as well. We did not exclude these dates to keep the example simple. See Self-Test Exercise 19 for a more complete date check method.)

Display 4.9   Yet Another Date Class (part 1 of 4)

```
1   import java.util.Scanner;

2   public class DateFifthTry
3   {
4       private String month;
5       private int day;
6       private int year; //a four digit number.

7       public void writeOutput()
8       {
9           System.out.println(month + " " + day + ", " + year);
10      }

11      public void readInput()
12      {
```

Note that this version of `readInput` has the user enter the month as an integer rather than as a string. In this class, a month is an integer to the user, but is a string inside the class.

(continued)

Display 4.9 Yet Another Date Class (part 2 of 4)

```
13      boolean tryAgain = true;
14      Scanner keyboard = new Scanner(System.in);
15      while (tryAgain)
16      {
17          System.out.println("Enter month, day, and year");
18          System.out.println("as three integers:");
19          System.out.println("do not use commas or other punctuations.");
20          int monthInput = keyboard.nextInt();
21          int dayInput = keyboard.nextInt();
22          int yearInput = keyboard.nextInt();
23          if (dateOK(monthInput, dayInput, yearInput))
24          {
25              setDate(monthInput, dayInput, yearInput);
26              tryAgain = false;
27          }
28          else
29              System.out.println("Illegal date. Reenter input.");
30      }
31  }

32      public void setDate(int month, int day, int year)
33      {
34          if (dateOK(month, day, year))
35          {
36              this.month = monthString(month);
37              this.day = day;
38              this.year = year;
39          }
40          else
41          {
42              System.out.println("Fatal Error");
43              System.exit(0);
44          }
45      }

46      public void setMonth(int monthNumber)
47      {
48          if ((monthNumber <= 0) || (monthNumber > 12))
49          {
50              System.out.println("Fatal Error");
51              System.exit(0);
52          }
53          else
54              month = monthString(monthNumber);
55      }
```

Note that this version of readInput *checks to see that the input is reasonable.*

Display 4.9   **Yet Another Date Class** (part 3 of 4)

```
56      public void setDay(int day)
57      {
58          if ((day <= 0) || (day > 31))
59          {
60              System.out.println("Fatal Error");
61              System.exit(0);
62          }
63          else
64              this.day = day;
65      }

66      public void setYear(int year)
67      {
68          if ( (year < 1000) || (year > 9999) )
69          {
70              System.out.println("Fatal Error");
71              System.exit(0);
72          }
73          else
74              this.year = year;
75      }

76      public boolean equals(DateFifthTry otherDate)
77      {
78          return ( (month.equalsIgnoreCase(otherDate.month))
79                  && (day == otherDate.day) && (year ==
                    otherDate.year) );
80      }
```

Within the definition of DateFifthTry*, you can directly access private instance
variables of any object of type* DateFifthTry*.*

```
81      public boolean precedes(DateFifthTry otherDate)
82      {
83          return ( (year < otherDate.year) ||
84              (year == otherDate.year && getMonth() <
                otherDate.getMonth()) ||
85              (year == otherDate.year && month.equals(otherDate.month)
86                                  && day < otherDate.day) );
87      }
```

Within the definition of DateFifthTry*, you can directly access private instance
variables of any object of type* DateFifthTry*.*

<*The definitions of the following methods are the same as in Displays 4.2 and 4.7:*
        getMonth, getDay, getYear, *and* toString. >

```
88      private boolean dateOK(int monthInt, int dayInt, int yearInt)
89      {
```

(continued)

Display 4.9 **Yet Another Date Class** (part 4 of 4)

```
90              return (  (monthInt >= 1) && (monthInt <= 12) &&
91                        (dayInt >= 1) && (dayInt <= 31) &&
92                        (yearInt >= 1000) && (yearInt <= 9999) );
93          }

94      private String monthString(int monthNumber)
95      {
96          switch (monthNumber)
97          {
98          case 1:
99              return "January";
100         case 2:
101             return "February";
102         case 3:
103             return "March";
104         case 4:
105             return "April";
106         case 5:
107             return "May";
108         case 6:
109             return "June";
110         case 7:
111             return "July";
112         case 8:
113             return "August";
114         case 9:
115             return "September";
116         case 10:
117             return "October";
118         case 11:
119             return "November";
120         case 12:
121             return "December";
122         default:
123             System.out.println("Fatal Error");
124             System.exit(0);
125             return "Error"; //to keep the compiler happy
126         }
127     }
128 }
```

The way that a well-designed class definition uses private instance variables and public accessor and mutator methods to implement the principle of encapsulation is diagrammed in Display 4.10.

Display 4.10   Encapsulation

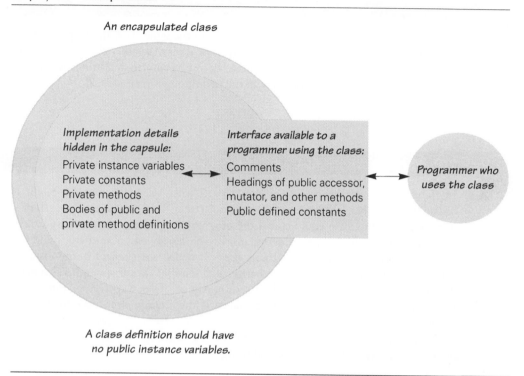

An encapsulated class

Implementation details hidden in the capsule:
Private instance variables
Private constants
Private methods
Bodies of public and private method definitions

Interface available to a programmer using the class:
Comments
Headings of public accessor, mutator, and other methods
Public defined constants

Programmer who uses the class

A class definition should have no public instance variables.

TIP: A Class Has Access to Private Members of All Objects of the Class

Consider the definition of the method `equals` for the class `DateFifthTry`, given in Display 4.9 and repeated as follows:

```
public boolean equals(DateFifthTry otherDate)
{
    return ( (month.equalsIgnoreCase(otherDate.month))
            && (day == otherDate.day) &&
            (year == otherDate.year) );
}
```

You might object that `otherDate.month`, `otherDate.day`, and `otherDate.year` are illegal because `month`, `day`, and `year` are private instance variables of some object other than the calling object. Normally, that objection would be correct. However, the object `otherDate` is of the same type as the class being defined, so this is legal. In the definition of a class, you can access private members of any object of the class, not just private members of the calling object.

(continued)

TIP: (continued)

Similar remarks apply to the method `precedes` in the same class. In one place in the definition of `precedes`, we used `otherDate.getMonth()` rather than `otherDate.month` only because we wanted the month as an integer instead of a string. We did, in fact, use `otherDate.month` elsewhere in the definition of `precedes`. ■

TIP: Mutator Methods Can Return a Boolean Value ★

In the definition of the class `DateFifthTry` (Display 4.9), the mutator methods tested to see if the new values for instance variables were sensible values. If they were not, the mutator method ended the program and issued an error message. An alternative approach is to have the mutator do the test, but to never have it end the program. Instead, it returns a `boolean` value. It makes the changes to the instance variables and returns `true` if the changes are sensible. If the attempted changes are not sensible, the mutator method returns `false`. That way a programmer can program in an alternative action to be taken if the attempted changes to instance variables do not make sense.

For example, an alternative definition of the method `setMonth` of the class `DateFifthTry` (Display 4.9) is the following:

```java
public boolean setMonth(int monthNumber)
{
    if ((monthNumber <= 0) || (monthNumber > 12))
        return false;
    else
    {
        month = monthString(monthNumber);
        return true;
    }
}
```

A sample use of this `boolean` valued version of `setMonth` could be the following:

```java
DateFifthTry date = new DateFifthTry();
...
System.out.println("Enter month as a number:");
int number = keyboard.nextInt();
while (!date.setMonth(number))
{
    System.out.println("Not a legal month number. Try again.");
    System.out.println("Enter month as a number:");
    number = keyboard.nextInt();
}
```

■

Preconditions and Postconditions

precondition

postcondition

One good way to write a method comment is to break it down into two kinds of information, called the *precondition* and the *postcondition*. The **precondition** states what is assumed to be true when the method is called. The method should not be used and cannot be expected to perform correctly unless the precondition holds. The **postcondition** describes the effect of the method call; that is, the postcondition tells what will be true after the method is executed in a situation in which the precondition holds. For a method that returns a value, the postcondition describes the value returned by the method.

The following is an example of a method heading from Display 4.9 with a precondition and postcondition added:

```
/**
 Precondition: All instance variables of the calling object have
 values.
 Postcondition: The data in the calling object has been written to
 the screen.
*/
public void writeOutput()
```

You do not need to know the definition of the method `writeOutput` to use this method. All that you need to know to use this method is given by the precondition and postcondition. (The importance of this is more dramatic when the definition of the method is longer than that of `writeOutput`.)

When the only postcondition is a description of the value returned, programmers usually omit the word `Postcondition`, as in the following example:

```
/**
 Precondition: All instance variables of the calling object have
 values.
 Returns a string describing the data in the calling object.
*/
public String toString()
```

Some programmers choose not to use the words *precondition* and *postcondition* in their method comments. However, whether you use the words or not, you should always think in terms of precondition and postcondition when designing a method and when deciding what to include in the method comment.

MyProgrammingLab™

Self-Test Exercises

17. List all the accessor methods in the class `DateFifthTry` in Display 4.9.

18. List all the mutator methods in the class `DateFifthTry` in Display 4.9.

(continued)

Self-Test Exercises (continued)

19. Write a better version of the method `dateOK` with three `int` parameters (Display 4.9). This version should check for the correct number of days in each month and should not just allow 31 days in any month. It will help to define another helping method named `leapYear`, which takes an `int` argument for a year and returns `true` if the year is a leap year. February has 29 days in leap years and only 28 days in other years. Use the following rule for determining if the year is a leap year: A year is a leap year if it is divisible by 4 but is not divisible by 100, or if it is divisible by 400.

4.3 Overloading

A good name is better than precious ointment.

Ecclesiastes 7:1

Two (or more) different classes can have methods with the same name. For example, many classes have a method named `toString`. It is easy to see why this is acceptable. The type of the calling object allows Java to decide which definition of the method `toString` to use. It uses the definition of `toString` given in the definition of the class for the calling object. You may be more surprised to learn that two or more methods *in the same class* can have the same method name. This is called **overloading** and is the topic of this section.

overloading

Rules for Overloading

In Display 4.11, we have added two methods named `setDate` to our date class so that there is a total of three methods named `setDate`. This is an example of overloading the method name `setDate`. On the following three lines, we display the headings of these three methods:

```
public void setDate(int month, int day,int year)
public void setDate(String month, int day,int year)
public void setDate(int year)
```

Notice that each method has a different parameter list. The first two differ in the type of their first parameter. The last one differs from the other two by having a different number of parameters.

Method signature

The name of a method and the list of parameter types in the heading of the method definition is called the **method signature**. The signatures for these three method definitions are

```
setDate(int, int, int)
setDate(String, int, int)
setDate(int)
```

Display 4.11   Overloading Method Names (part 1 of 2)

```
1    import java.util.Scanner;

2    public class DateSixthTry
3    {
4        private String month;
5        private int day;
6        private int year; //a four digit number.

7        public void setDate(int monthInt, int day, int year)
8        {
9            if (dateOK(monthInt, day, year))
10           {
11               this.month = monthString(monthInt);
12               this.day = day;
13               this.year = year;
14           }
15           else
16           {
17               System.out.println("Fatal Error");
18               System.exit(0);
19           }
20       }

21       public void setDate(String monthString, int day, int year)
22       {
23           if (dateOK(monthString, day, year))
24           {
25               this.month = monthString;
26               this.day = day;
27               this.year = year;
28           }
29           else
30           {
31               System.out.println("Fatal Error");
32               System.exit(0);
33           }
34       }

35       public void setDate(int year)
36       {
37           setDate(1, 1, year);
38       }
```

There are three different methods named setDate.

Two different methods named setDate.

(continued)

Display 4.11   Overloading Method Names (part 2 of 2)

```
39      private boolean dateOK(int monthInt, int dayInt, int yearInt)
40      {
41          return ( (monthInt >= 1) && (monthInt <= 12) &&
42                   (dayInt >= 1) && (dayInt <= 31) &&
43                   (yearInt >= 1000) && (yearInt <= 9999) );
44      }

45      private boolean dateOK(String monthString, int dayInt, int yearInt)
46      {
47          return ( monthOK(monthString) &&
48                   (dayInt >= 1) && (dayInt <= 31) &&
49                   (yearInt >= 1000) && (yearInt <= 9999) );
50      }

51      private boolean monthOK(String month)
52      {
53          return (month.equals("January") || month.equals("February") ||
54                  month.equals("March") || month.equals("April") ||
55                  month.equals("May") || month.equals("June") ||
56                  month.equals("July") || month.equals("August") ||
57                  month.equals("September") || month.equals("October") ||
58                  month.equals("November") || month.equals("December") );
59      }

60      public void readInput()
61      {
62          boolean tryAgain = true;
63          Scanner keyboard = new Scanner(System.in);
64          while (tryAgain)
65          {
66              System.out.println("Enter month, day, and year.");
67                System.out.println("Do not use a comma.");
68              String monthInput = keyboard.next();
69              int dayInput = keyboard.nextInt();
70              int yearInput = keyboard.nextInt();
71              if (dateOK(monthInput, dayInput, yearInput) )
72              {
73                  setDate(monthInput, dayInput, yearInput);
74                  tryAgain = false;
75              }
76              else
77                  System.out.println("Illegal date. Reenter input.");
78          }
79      }
```

Two different methods named dateOK.

<The rest of the methods are the same as in Display 4.9, except that
the parameter to *equals* and *precedes* is, of course, of type *DateSixthTry*.>

```
80      }
```

When you overload a method name, each of the method definitions in the class must have a different signature.

Signature

The **signature** of a method consists of the method name and the list of types for parameters that are listed in the heading of the method name.

EXAMPLE

If a method has the heading

```
public int computeSomething(int n1, double x1,
                                     double x2, String name);
```

then the signature is

```
computeSomething(int, double, double, String)
```

Note that the return type is not part of the method signature.

In Display 4.11, we also overloaded the method name `dateOK` so that there are two different methods named `dateOK`. The two signatures for the two methods named `dateOK` are

```
dateOK(int, int, int)
dateOK(String, int, int)
```

Display 4.12 gives a simple example of a program using the overloaded method name `setDate`. Note that for each invocation of a method named `setDate`, only one of the definitions of `setDate` has a signature that matches the types of the arguments.

Overloading

Within one class, you can have two (or more) definitions of a single method name. This is called **overloading** the method name. When you overload a method name, any two definitions of the method name must have different signatures; that is, any two definitions of the method name either must have different numbers of parameters or some parameter position must be of differing types in the two definitions.

PITFALL: Overloading and Automatic Type Conversion

Automatic type conversion of arguments (such as converting an `int` to a `double` when the parameter is of type `double`) and overloading can sometimes interact in unfortunate ways. So, you need to know how these two things interact.

For example, consider the following method that might be added to the class `DateSixthTry` in Display 4.11:

```
public void increase(double factor)
{
    year = (int)(year + factor*year);
}
```

If you add this method to the class `DateSixthTry`, then the following presents no problems, where `date` is an object of type `DateSixthTry` that has been set to some date:

```
date.increase(2);
```

The `int` value of 2 is type cast to the `double` value `2.0`, and the value of `date.year` is changed as follows:

```
date.year = (int)(date.year + 2.0*date.year);
```

(Because `year` is private in the class `DateSixthTry`, you cannot write this in a program that uses the class `DateSixthTry`, but the meaning of this expression is clear.)

So far, so good. But now suppose we also add the following method definition to the class `DateSixthTry`:

```
public void increase(int term)
{
    year = year + term;
}
```

This is a valid overloading because the two methods named `increase` take parameters of different types. With both of these methods named `increase` added to the class, the following now behaves differently:

```
date.increase(2);
```

If Java can find an exact match of types, it uses the method definition with an exact match before it tries to do any automatic type casts. So now the displayed invocation of `date.increase` is equivalent to

```
date.year = date.year + 2;
```

However, if you meant to use an argument of `2.0` for `date.increase` and instead used 2, counting on an automatic type cast, then this is not what you want. It is best to avoid overloading where there is a potential for interacting dangerously with automatic type casting, as in the examples discussed in this Pitfall section.

PITFALL: (continued)

In some cases of overloading, a single method invocation can be resolved in two different ways, depending on how overloading and type conversion interact. Such ambiguous method invocations are not allowed in Java and will produce an error message. For example, you can overload a method named doSomething by giving two definitions that have the following two method headings in a SampleClass:

```
public class SampleClass
{
    public void doSomething(double n1, int n2)
        .
        .
        .

    public void doSomething(int n1, double n2)
        .
        .
        .
```

Such overloading is legal, but there is a problem. Suppose aSampleObject is an object of type SampleClass. An invocation such as the following will produce an error message, because Java cannot decide which overloaded definition of doSomething to use:

```
aSampleObject.doSomething(5, 10);
```

Java cannot decide whether it should convert the int value 5 to a double value and use the first definition of doSomething, or whether it should convert the int value 10 to a double value and use the second definition. In this situation, the Java compiler issues an error message indicating that the method invocation is ambiguous.

The following two method invocations are allowed:

```
aSampleObject.doSomething(5.0, 10);
aSampleObject.doSomething(5, 10.0);
```

However, such situations, while legal, are confusing and should be avoided. ■

Display 4.12   **Using an Overloaded Method Name** (part 1 of 2)

```
1  public class OverloadingDemo
2  {
3      public static void main(String[] args)
4      {
5          DateSixthTry date1 = new DateSixthTry(),
6                       date2 = new DateSixthTry(),
7                       date3 = new DateSixthTry();
```

(continued)

Display 4.12   Using an Overloaded Method Name (part 2 of 2)

```
 8          date1.setDate(1, 2, 2008);
 9          date2.setDate("February", 2, 2008);
10          date3.setDate(2008);

11          System.out.println(date1);
12          System.out.println(date2);
13          System.out.println(date3);
14      }
15  }
```

Sample Dialogue

```
January 2, 2008
February 2, 2008
January 1, 2008
```

Overloading and Automatic Type Conversion

Java always looks for a method signature that exactly matches the method invocation before it tries to use automatic type conversion. If Java can find a definition of a method that exactly matches the types of the arguments, it uses that definition. Only after it fails to find an exact match does Java try automatic type conversions to find a method definition that matches the (type cast) types of the method invocation.

PITFALL: You Cannot Overload Based on the Type Returned

Note that the signature of a method lists only the method name and the types of the parameters and does not include the type returned. When you overload a method name, any two methods must have different signatures. The type returned has nothing to do with the signature of a method. For example, a class could not have two method definitions with the following headings:

```
public class SampleClass2
{
    public int computeSomething(int n)
        .
        .
        .

    public double computeSomething(int n)
        .
        .
        .
```

PITFALL: (continued)

If you think about it, there is no way that Java could allow this sort of overloading. Suppose anObject is an object of the class SampleClass2. Then in the following assignment, Java could not decide which of the above two method definitions to use:

```
double answer = anObject.computeSomething(10);
```

Either a value of type int or a value of type double can legally be assigned to the variable answer. So, either method definition could be used. Because of such problems, Java says it is illegal to have both of these method headings in the same class. ■

You Cannot Overload Operators in Java

Many programming languages, such as C++, allow you to overload an operator, such as +, so that the operator can be used with objects of some class you define, as well as be used for such things as numbers. You cannot do this in Java. If you want to have an "addition" in your class, you must use a method name, such as add, and ordinary method syntax; you cannot define operators, such as the + operator, to work with objects of a class you define.

Self-Test Exercises

20. What is the signature of each of the following method headings?

```
public void showDetails(String name)
public double calculateTax(double income, double taxrate)
public boolean leapYear(int year)
public int amount(int balance, int duration, double interest)
public double amount(int balance, int duration, double interest)
```

21. Consider the class DateSixthTry in Display 4.11. Would it be legal to add two method definitions with the following two method headings to the class DateSixthTry?

```
public DateSixthEntry getADate(int aMonth, int aDay, int aYear )
public DateSixthEntry getADate(String aMonth, int aDay, int aYear )
```

22. Consider the class DateSixthTry in Display 4.11. Would it be legal to add two method definitions with the following two method headings to the class DateSixthTry?

```
public DateSixthEntry getADate(int aMonth, int aDay, int aYear )
private DateSixthEntry getADate(int aMonth, int aDay, int aYear )
```

(continued)

Self-Test Exercises (continued)

23. Consider the class DateSixthTry in Display 4.11. Would it be legal to add two method definitions with the following two method headings to the class DateSixthTry?

```
public int getMonth()
public String getMonth()
```

4.4   Constructors

Well begun is half done.

Proverb

constructor

You often want to initialize the instance variables for an object when you create the object. As you will see later in this book, there are other initializing actions you might also want to take, but initializing instance variables is the most common sort of initialization. A **constructor** is a special variety of method that is designed to perform such initialization. In this section, we tell you how to define and use constructors.

Constructor Definitions

Although you may not have realized it, you have already been using constructors every time you used the new operator to create an object, as in the following example:

```
DateSixthTry date1 = new DateSixthTry();
```

The expression new DateSixthTry() is an invocation of a constructor. A constructor is a special variety of method that, among other things, must have the same name as the class. So, the first occurrence of DateSixthTry in the previous code is a class name, and the second occurrence of DateSixthTry is the name of a constructor. If you add no constructor definitions to your class, then Java automatically creates a constructor that takes no arguments. We have been using this automatically provided constructor up until now. The automatically provided constructor creates the object but does little else. It is preferable to define your own constructors so that you can have the constructor initialize instance variables, or do whatever other initialization actions you want.

In Display 4.13, we have rewritten our date class one last time by adding five constructors. Since this is our final date class, we have included all method definitions in the display so you can see the entire class definition. (We have omitted writeOutput because it would be superfluous, as noted in the earlier subsection entitled "The Methods equals and toString.")

Display 4.13   **A Class with Constructors** (part 1 of 5)

```
1    import java.util.Scanner;                          This is our final definition of a class
                                                        whose objects are dates.
2    public class Date
3    {
4        private String month;
5        private int day;
6        private int year; //a four digit number.

7        public Date()
8        {
9            month = "January";                          No-argument constructor.
10           day = 1;
11           year = 1000;
12       }

13       public Date(int monthInt, int day, int year)
14       {
15           setDate(monthInt, day, year);               You can invoke another
16       }                                               method inside a
                                                         constructor definition.
17       public Date(String monthString, int day, int year)
18       {
19           setDate(monthString, day, year);
20       }

21       public Date(int year)
22       {
23           setDate(1, 1, year);                        A constructor usually initializes all
24       }                                               instance variables, even if there is not a
                                                         corresponding parameter.
25       public Date(Date aDate)
26       {
27           if (aDate == null) //Not a real date.           We will have more to
28           {                                               say about this
29               System.out.println("Fatal Error.");         constructor in
30               System.exit(0);                             Chapter 5. Although you
31           }                                               have had enough
                                                             material to use this
32           month = aDate.month;                            constructor, you need
33           day = aDate.day;                                not worry about it
34           year = aDate.year;                              until Section 5.3 of
35       }                                                   Chapter 5.
```

(continued)

Display 4.13   A Class with Constructors (part 2 of 5)

```
36        public void setDate(int monthInt, int day, int year)
37        {
38            if (dateOK(monthInt, day, year))
39            {
40                this.month = monthString(monthInt);
41                this.day = day;
42                this.year = year;
43            }
44            else
45            {
46                System.out.println("Fatal Error");
47                System.exit(0);
48            }
49        }

50        public void setDate(String monthString, int day, int year)
51        {
52            if (dateOK(monthString, day, year))
53            {
54                this.month = monthString;
55                this.day = day;
56                this.year = year;
57            }
58            else
59            {
60                System.out.println("Fatal Error");
61                System.exit(0);
62            }
63        }

64        public void setDate(int year)
65        {
66            setDate(1, 1, year);
67        }

68        public void setYear(int year)
69        {
70            if ( (year < 1000) || (year > 9999) )
71            {
72                System.out.println("Fatal Error");
73                System.exit(0);
74            }
75            else
76                this.year = year;
77        }
```

The mutator methods, whose names begin with **set**, *are used to reset the data in an object after the object has been created using* **new** *and a constructor.*

Display 4.13   **A Class with Constructors** (part 3 of 5)

```
78       public void setMonth(int monthNumber)
79       {
80           if ((monthNumber <= 0) || (monthNumber > 12))
81           {
82               System.out.println("Fatal Error");
83               System.exit(0);
84           }
85           else
86               month = monthString(monthNumber);
87       }

88       public void setDay(int day)
89       {
90           if ((day <= 0) || (day > 31))
91           {
92               System.out.println("Fatal Error");
93               System.exit(0);
94           }
95           else
96               this.day = day;
97       }

98       public int getMonth()
99       {
100          if (month.equals("January"))
101              return 1;
102          else if (month.equals("February"))
103              return 2;
104          else if (month.equals("March"))
105              return 3;
                 . . .
```

   <The omitted cases are obvious, but if need be, you can see all the cases in Display 4.2.>

```
                 . . .
106          else if (month.equals("November"))
107              return 11;
108          else if (month.equals("December"))
109              return 12;
110          else
111          {
112              System.out.println("Fatal Error");
113              System.exit(0);
114              return 0; //Needed to keep the compiler happy
115          }
116      }
```

(continued)

Display 4.13 **A Class with Constructors** (part 4 of 5)

```
117        public int getDay()
118        {
119            return day;
120        }
121        public int getYear()
122        {
123            return year;
124        }

125        public String toString()
126        {
127            return (month + " " + day + ", " + year);
128        }

129        public boolean equals(Date otherDate)
130        {
131            return ( (month.equals(otherDate.month))
132                    && (day == otherDate.day) && (year ==
                        otherDate.year) );
133        }

134        public Boolean precedes(Date otherDate)
135        {
136            return ( (year < otherDate.year) ||
137               (year == otherDate.year && getMonth() <
                   otherDate.getMonth()) ||
138               (year == otherDate.year && month.equals(otherDate.month)
139                                     && day < otherDate.day) );
140        }

141        public void readInput()
142        {
143            boolean tryAgain = true;
144            Scanner keyboard = new Scanner(System.in);
145            while (tryAgain)
146            {
147                System.out.println("Enter month, day, and year.");
148                System.out.println("Do not use a comma.");
149                String monthInput = keyboard.next();
150                int dayInput = keyboard.nextInt();
151                int yearInput = keyboard.nextInt();
152                if (dateOK(monthInput, dayInput, yearInput) )
153                {
154                    setDate(monthInput, dayInput, yearInput);
155                    tryAgain = false;
156                }
```

We have omitted the method writeOutput *because it would be superfluous, as noted in the subsection entitled "The Methods* equals *and* toString.*"*

The method equals *of the class* String.

Display 4.13   **A Class with Constructors** (part 5 of 5)

```
157              else
158                  System.out.println("Illegal date. Reenter input.");
159          }
160      }

161      private boolean dateOK(int monthInt, int dayInt, int yearInt)
162      {
163          return ( (monthInt >= 1) && (monthInt <= 12) &&
164                  (dayInt >= 1) && (dayInt <= 31) &&
165                  (yearInt >= 1000) && (yearInt <= 9999) );
166      }

167      private boolean dateOK(String monthString, int dayInt, int
                                        yearInt)
168      {
169          return ( monthOK(monthString) &&
170                  (dayInt >= 1) && (dayInt <= 31) &&
171                  (yearInt >= 1000) && (yearInt <= 9999) );
172      }

173      private boolean monthOK(String month)
174      {
175          return (month.equals("January") || month.equals("February") ||
176                  month.equals("March") || month.equals("April") ||
177                  month.equals("May") || month.equals("June") ||
178                  month.equals("July") || month.equals("August") ||
179                  month.equals("September") ||
                        month.equals("October") ||
180                  month.equals("November") ||
                        month.equals("December") );
181      }

182      private String monthString(int monthNumber)
183      {
184          switch (monthNumber)                    The private methods need not be
185          {                                       last, but that's as good a place
186          case 1:                                 as any.
187              return "January";
                    . . .
```

<The omitted cases are obvious, but if need be, you can see all the cases in Display 4.9.>

```
                    . . .
188          default:
189              System.out.println("Fatal Error");
190              System.exit(0);
191              return "Error"; //to keep the compiler happy
192          }
193      }
194 }
```

In Display 4.13, we have used overloading to create five constructors for the class Date. It is normal to have more than one constructor. Because every constructor must have the same name as the class, all the constructors in a class must have the same name. So, when you define multiple constructors, you must use overloading.

Note that when you define a constructor, you do not give any return type for the constructor; you do not even use void in place of a return type. Also notice that constructors are normally public.

All the constructor definitions in Display 4.13 initialize all the instance variables, even if there is no parameter corresponding to that instance variable. This is normal.

In a constructor definition, you can do pretty much anything that you can do in any ordinary method definition, but normally you perform only initialization tasks such as initialization of instance variables.

constructor arguments

When you create a new object with the operator new, you must always include the name of a constructor after the operator new. This is the way you invoke a constructor. As with any method invocation, you list any arguments in parentheses after the constructor name (which is the same as the class name). For example, suppose you want to use new to create a new object of the class Date defined in Display 4.13. You might do so as follows:

```
Date birthday = new Date("December", 16, 1770);
```

This is a call to the constructor for the class Date that takes three arguments: one of type String and two of type int. This creates a new object to represent the date December 16, 1770, and sets the variable birthday so that it names this new object. Another example is the following:

```
Date newYearsDay = new Date(3000);
```

This creates a new object to represent the date January 1, 3000, and sets the variable newYearsDay so that it names this new object.

Constructor

A **constructor** is a variety of method that is called when an object of the class is created using new. Constructors are used to initialize objects. A constructor must have the same name as the class to which it belongs. Arguments for a constructor are given in parentheses after the class name, as in the following examples.

EXAMPLES

```
Date birthday = new Date("December", 16, 1770),
    theDate = new Date(2008);
```

A constructor is defined very much like any ordinary method except that it does not have a type returned and does not even include a void in the constructor heading. See Display 4.13 for examples of constructor definitions.

resetting object values   A constructor is called when you create a new object, such as with the operator new. An attempt to call a constructor in any other way, such as the following, is illegal:

```
birthday.Date("January", 27, 1756); //Illegal!
```

Because you cannot call a constructor for an object after it is created, you need some other way to change the values of the instance variables of an object. That is the purpose of the setDate methods and other methods that begin with set in Display 4.13. If birthday already names an object that was created with new, you can change the values of the instance variables as follows:

```
birthday.setDate("January", 27, 1756);
```

Although it is not required, such methods that reset instance variables normally are given names that start with set.

Although you cannot use a constructor to reset the instance variables of an already created object, you can do something that looks very similar. The following is legal:

```
Date birthday = new Date("December", 16, 1770);
            .
            .
            .
birthday = new Date("January", 27, 1756);
```

However, the second invocation of the constructor does not simply change the values of instance variables for the object. Instead, it discards the old object and allocates storage for a new object before setting the instance variables. So, for efficiency (and occasionally for other reasons we have not yet discussed), it is preferable to use a method such as setDate to change the data in the instance variables of an already created object.

Display 4.14 contains a demonstration program for the constructors defined in Display 4.13.

Display 4.14   Use of Constructors (part 1 of 2)

```
1   public class ConstructorsDemo
2   {
3       public static void main(String[] args)
4       {
5           Date date1 = new Date("December", 16, 1770),
6                date2 = new Date(1, 27, 1756),
7                date3 = new Date(1882),
8                date4 = new Date();
9           System.out.println("Whose birthday is " + date1 + "?");
10          System.out.println("Whose birthday is " + date2 + "?");
11          System.out.println("Whose birthday is " + date3 + "?");
12          System.out.println("The default date is " + date4 + ".");
13      }
14  }
```

(continued)

Display 4.14   Use of Constructors (part 2 of 2)

Sample Dialogue

```
Whose birthday is December 16, 1770?
Whose birthday is January 27, 1756?
Whose birthday is January 1, 1882?
The default date is January 1, 1000.
```

Is a Constructor Really a Method?

There are differing opinions on whether or not a constructor should be called a *method*. Most authorities call a constructor a method but emphasize that it is a special kind of method with many properties not shared with other kinds of methods. Some authorities say a constructor is a method-like entity but not, strictly speaking, a method. All authorities agree about what a constructor is; the only disagreement is over whether or not it should be referred to as *a method*. Thus, this is not a major issue. However, whenever you hear a phrase such as "all methods," you should make sure you know whether it does or does not include constructors. To avoid confusion, we try to use the phrase "constructors and methods" when we want to include constructors.

TIP: You Can Invoke Another Method in a Constructor

It is perfectly legal to invoke another method within the definition of a constructor. For example, several of the constructors in Display 4.13 invoke a mutator method to set the values of the instance variables. This is legal because the first action taken by a constructor is to automatically create an object with instance variables. You do not write any code to create this object. Java creates it automatically when the constructor is invoked. Any method invocation in the body of the constructor definition has this object as its calling object.

You can even include an invocation of one constructor within the definition of another constructor. However, we will not discuss the syntax for doing that in this chapter. It will be covered in Chapter 7. ∎

TIP: A Constructor Has a `this` Parameter

Just like the ordinary methods we discussed before we introduced constructors, every constructor has a `this` parameter. The `this` parameter can be used explicitly, but it is more often understood to be present although not written down. Whenever an instance variable of the class is used in a constructor (without an object name and a dot before it), it is understood to have an implicit `this` and dot before it. Similarly, whenever

TIP: (continued)

a method is used in a constructor and the method has no explicit calling object, the method is understood to have `this` and a dot before it; that is, it is understood to have `this` as its calling object.

As noted in the previous Programming Tip, the first action taken by a constructor is to automatically create an object with instance variables. This object is automatically plugged in for the `this` parameter. So, within the definition of a constructor, the `this` parameter refers to the object created by the constructor. ∎

TIP: Include a No-Argument Constructor

**no-argument
costructor**

A constructor that takes no arguments is called a **no-argument constructor** or **no-arg constructor**. If you define a class and include absolutely no constructors of any kind, then a no-argument constructor is automatically created. This no-argument constructor does not do much, but it does give you an object of the class type. So, if the definition of the class `MyClass` contains absolutely no constructor definitions, then the following is legal:

```
MyClass myObject = new MyClass();
```

If your class definition includes one or more constructors of any kind, then no constructor is generated automatically. So, for example, suppose you define a class called `YourClass`. If you include one or more constructors that each take one or more arguments, but you do not include a no-argument constructor in your class definition, then there is not a no-argument constructor and the following is illegal:

```
YourClass yourObject = new YourClass();
```

The problem with the above declaration is that it asks the compiler to invoke the no-argument constructor, but there is not a no-argument constructor present.

To avoid problems, you should normally include a no-argument constructor in any class you define. If you do not want the no-argument constructor to initialize any instance variables, you can simply give it an empty body when you implement it. The following constructor definition is perfectly legal. It does nothing but create an object (and, as we will see later in this chapter, set the instance variables equal to default values):

```
public MyClass()
{/*Do nothing.*/}
```

(continued)

default constructor

TIP: (continued)

A no-argument constructor is also known as a **default constructor**. However, the term *default constructor* is misleading because, as we have explained, a no-argument constructor is not always provided by default. There is now a movement to replace *default constructor* with the term *no-argument constructor*, but you will frequently encounter the former term. ■

No-Argument Constructor

A constructor with no parameters is called a **no-argument constructor**. If your class definition contains absolutely no constructor definitions, then Java will automatically create a no-argument constructor. If your class definition contains one or more constructor definitions, then Java does not automatically generate any constructor; in this case, what you define is what you get. Most of the classes you define should include a definition of a no-argument constructor.

EXAMPLE: The Final Date Class

The final version of our class for a date is given in Display 4.13. We will be using this class Date again in Chapter 5.

MyProgrammingLab™   ### Self-Test Exercises

24. If a class is named `Automobile`, what names are allowed as names for constructors in the class `Automobile`?

25. Suppose you have defined a class like the following for use in a program:

```java
public class Citizen
{
    private String name;
    private int age;
    private String SSN;
    public Citizen (String n, int a, String s)
    {
        <Details not shown.>
    }
    public Citizen ()
    {
```

Self-Test Exercises (continued)

```
                     <Details not shown.>
        }
        public void getRegistered()
        {
            <Details not shown.>
        }
}
```

Which of the following are legal in a program that uses this class?

```
Citizen Smith = new Citizen  (42, "John Smith", "987-65-4320");
Citizen Carey = new YourClass(35.5, "William Carey");
Citizen c = new Citizen();
c.getRegistered();
Citizen Robin;
Robin.getRegistered();
Alex.Citizen(29, "Alex Adams");
```

26. What is a constructor? What is a default constructor? Can you invoke other class methods from a constructor?

Default Variable Initializations

Local variables are not automatically initialized in Java, so you must explicitly initialize a local variable before using it. Instance variables, on the other hand, are automatically initialized. Instance variables of type boolean are automatically initialized to false. Instance variables of other primitive types are automatically initialized to the zero of their type. Instance variables of a class type are automatically initialized to null, which is a kind of placeholder for an object that will be filled in later. We will discuss null in Chapter 5. Although instance variables are automatically initialized, we prefer to always explicitly initialize them in a constructor, even if the initializing value is the same as the default initialization. That makes the code clearer.

An Alternative Way to Initialize Instance Variables

Instance variables are normally initialized in constructors, which is where we prefer to initialize them. However, there is an alternative. You can initialize instance variables when you declare them in a class definition, as illustrated by the following:

```
public class Date
{
    private String month = "January";
    private int day = 1;
    private int year = 1000;
```

If you initialize instance variables in this way, you may or may not want to define constructors. But if you do define any constructors, it is usually best to define a no-argument constructor even if the body of the no-argument constructor is empty.

EXAMPLE: A Pet Record Class

Display 4.15 contains another example of a class definition. In this case, the objects of the class represent pet records consisting of the pet's name, age, and weight. Notice the similarities and differences between the constructors and the mutator methods (the ones whose names begin with `set`). They both set instance variables, but they are used differently. The constructors are used to create and initialize new objects of the class. However, after the object is created using a constructor and `new`, any changes to the object are performed by the mutator methods such as `set` or `setAge`. This is illustrated by the program in Display 4.16.

It would be possible to use constructors in place of the mutators, such as the method `set`. For example, the program in Display 4.16 would produce the same dialogue if you replace the line

```
usersPet.set(name, age, weight);
```

with

```
usersPet = new Pet(name, age, weight);
```

Even so, this use of constructors is a bad idea.

The following mutator method invocation simply changes the values of the instance variables of the object named by `usersPet`:

```
usersPet.set(name, age, weight);
```

However, the following use of a constructor creates a completely new object, which is a much less efficient process than just changing the values of some instance variables:

```
usersPet = new Pet(name, age, weight);
```

Display 4.15   A Class for Pet Records (part 1 of 4)

```
1   /**
2   Class for basic pet records: name, age, and weight.
3   */
4   public class Pet
5   {
6       private String name;
7       private int age; //in years
8       private double weight; //in pounds
9
```

Display 4.15   **A Class for Pet Records** (part 2 of 4)

```
10     public String toString()
11     {
12         return ("Name: " + name + " Age: " + age + " years"
13                         + "\nWeight: " + weight + " pounds");
14     }
15
16     public Pet(String initialName,int initialAge,
17                                         double initialWeight)
18     {
19         name = initialName;
20         if ((initialAge < 0) || (initialWeight < 0))
21         {
22             System.out.println("Error: Negative age or weight.");
23             System.exit(0);
24         }
25         else
26         {
27             age = initialAge;
28             weight = initialWeight;
29         }
30     }
31
32     public void set(String newName,int newAge,double newWeight)
33     {
34         name = newName;
35         if ((newAge < 0) || (newWeight < 0))
36         {
37             System.out.println("Error: Negative age or weight.");
38             System.exit(0);
39         }
40         else
41         {
42             age = newAge;
43             weight = newWeight;
44         }
45     }
46     public Pet(String initialName)
47     {
48         name = initialName;
49         age = 0;
50         weight = 0;
51     }
52
53     public void setName(String newName)
54     {
55         name = newName;
56     }
57
```

Constructors are only called when you create an object, such as with new. *To change an already existing object, you use one or more methods such as these* set *methods.*

Constructors normally set all instance variables, even if there is not a full set of parameters.

Age and weight are unchanged.

(continued)

Display 4.15   A Class for Pet Records (part 3 of 4)

```
58      public Pet(int initialAge)
59      {
60          name = "No name yet.";
61          weight = 0;
62          if (initialAge < 0)
63          {
64              System.out.println("Error: Negative age.");
65              System.exit(0);
66          }
67          else
68              age = initialAge;
69      }
70
71      public void setAge(int newAge)
72      {
73          if (newAge < 0)
74          {
75              System.out.println("Error: Negative age.");
76              System.exit(0);
77          }                              Name and weight are unchanged.
78          else
79              age = newAge;   ◄
80      }
81
82
83
84
85
86      public Pet(double initialWeight)
87      {
88          name = "No name yet";
89          age = 0;
90          if (initialWeight < 0)
91          {
92              System.out.println("Error: Negative weight.");
93              System.exit(0);
94          }
95          else
96              weight = initialWeight;
97      }
98      public void setWeight(double newWeight)
99      {
```

Display 4.15   **A Class for Pet Records** (part 4 of 4)

```
100            if (newWeight < 0)
101            {
102                System.out.println("Error: Negative weight.");
103                System.exit(0);
104            }
105            else                          Name and age are unchanged.
106                weight = newWeight;  ◄——
107        }
108    public Pet()
109    {
110        name = "No name yet.";
111        age = 0;
112        weight = 0;
113    }

114    public String getName()
115    {
116        return name;
117    }

118    public int getAge()
119    {
120        return age;
121    }

122    public double getWeight()
123    {
124        return weight;
125    }
126 }
```

Display 4.16   **Using Constructors and Set Methods** (part 1 of 2)

```
1    import java.util.Scanner;
2    public class PetDemo
3    {
4        public static void main(String[] args)
5        {
```

(continued)

Display 4.16   Using Constructors and Set Methods (part 2 of 2)

```
6        Pet usersPet = new Pet("Jane Doe");
7        System.out.println("My records on your pet are incomplete.");
8        System.out.println("Here is what they currently say:");
9        System.out.println(usersPet);

10       Scanner keyboard = new Scanner(System.in);
11       System.out.println("Please enter the pet's name:");
12       String name = keyboard.nextLine();
13       System.out.println("Please enter the pet's age:");
14       int age = keyboard.nextInt();
15       System.out.println("Please enter the pet's weight:");
16       double weight = keyboard.nextDouble();
17       usersPet.set(name, age, weight);
18       System.out.println("My records now say:");
19       System.out.println(usersPet);
20   }
21 }
```

This is equivalent to
`System.out.println(usersPet.toString());`

Sample Dialogue

```
My records on your pet are incomplete.
Here is what they currently say:
Name: Jane Doe Age: 0 years
Weight: 0.0 pounds
Please enter the pet's name:
Fang Junior
Please enter the pet's age:
5
Please enter the pet's weight:
87.5
My records now say:
Name: Fang Junior Age: 5 years
Weight: 87.5 pounds
```

The StringTokenizer Class ✳

The StringTokenizer class is used to recover the words in a multiword string. It is often used when reading input. However, when we covered input in Chapter 2, we could not cover the StringTokenizer class because use of the StringTokenizer class normally involves knowledge of loops and constructors, two topics that we had not yet covered. We now have covered enough material to explain the StringTokenizer class.

One approach to reading keyboard input is to read an entire line of input into a variable of type String—for example, with the method nextLine of the Scanner class—and then to use the StringTokenizer class to decompose the string in the variable into words.

The class StringTokenizer is in the standard Java package (library) java.util. To tell Java where to find the class StringTokenizer, any class or program that uses the class StringTokenizer must contain the following (or something similar) at the start of the file:

import

```
import java.util.StringTokenizer;
```

Perhaps the most common use of the StringTokenizer class is to decompose a line of input. However, the StringTokenizer class can be used to decompose any string. The following example illustrates a typical way that the class StringTokenizer is used:

```
StringTokenizer wordFactory =
    new StringTokenizer("A single word can be critical.");
while(wordFactory.hasMoreTokens())
{
    System.out.println(wordFactory.nextToken());
}
```

This will produce the following output:

```
A
single
word
can
be
critical.
```

The constructor invocation

```
new StringTokenizer("A single word can be critical.")
```

produces a new object of the class StringTokenizer. The assignment statement

```
StringTokenizer wordFactory =
    new StringTokenizer("A single word can be critical.");
```

gives this StringTokenizer object the name wordFactory. You may use any string in place of "A single word can be critical." and any variable name in place of wordFactory. The StringTokenizer object created in this way can be used to produce the individual words in the string used as the argument to the

tokens

StringTokenizer constructor. These individual words are called **tokens**.

`nextToken`

The method `nextToken` returns the first token (word) when it is invoked for the first time, returns the second token when it is invoked the second time, and so forth. If your code invokes `nextToken` after it has returned all the tokens in its string, then your program will halt and issue an error message.

`hasMore`
`Tokens`

The method `hasMoreTokens` is a method that returns a value of type `boolean`; that is, it returns either `true` or `false`. Thus, an invocation of `hasMoreTokens`, such as the following

```
wordFactory.hasMoreTokens()
```

is a Boolean expression, and so it can be used to control a `while` loop. The method `hasMoreTokens` returns `true` as long as `nextToken` has not yet returned all the tokens in the string, and it returns `false` after the method `nextToken` has returned all the tokens in the string.

choosing
delimeters

When the constructor for `StringTokenizer` is used with a single argument, as in the preceding example, the tokens are substrings of nonwhitespace characters, and the whitespace characters are used as the separators for the tokens. Any string of one or more whitespace characters is considered a separator. Thus, in the preceding example, the last token produced by the method `nextToken` is `"critical."` including the period. This is because the period is not a whitespace character and so is not a separator.

You can specify your own set of separator characters. When you create your own set of separator characters, you give a second argument to the constructor for `StringTokenizer`. The second argument is a string consisting of all the separator characters. Thus, if you want your separators to consist of the blank, the new-line character, the period, and the comma, you could proceed as in the following example:

```
StringTokenizer wordfactory2 =
    new StringTokenizer("Give me the word, my friend.", " \n.,");
while(wordfactory2.hasMoreTokens())
{
    System.out.println(wordfactory2.nextToken());
}
```

This will produce the output

```
Give
me
the
word
my
friend
```

Notice that the period and comma are not part of the tokens produced, because they are now token separators. Also note that the string of token separators is the second argument to the constructor.

Some of the methods for the class `StringTokenizer` are summarized in Display 4.17. A sample use of `StringTokenizer` is given in Display 4.18.

Display 4.17   Some Methods in the Class `StringTokenizer`

The class `StringTokenizer` is in the `java.util` package.

`public StringTokenizer(String theString)`

Constructor for a tokenizer that will use whitespace characters as separators when finding tokens in `theString`.

`public StringTokenizer(String theString, String delimiters)`

Constructor for a tokenizer that will use the characters in the string `delimiters` as separators when finding tokens in `theString`.

`public boolean hasMoreTokens()`

Tests whether there are more tokens available from this tokenizer's string. When used in conjunction with `nextToken`, it returns true as long as `nextToken` has not yet returned all the tokens in the string; returns `false` otherwise.

`public String nextToken()`

Returns the next token from this tokenizer's string. (Throws `NoSuchElementException` if there are no more tokens to return.)[5]

`public String nextToken(String delimiters)`

First changes the delimiter characters to those in the string `delimiters`. Then returns the next token from this tokenizer's string. After the invocation is completed, the delimiter characters are those in the string `delimiters`. (Throws `NoSuchElementException` if there are no more tokens to return. Throws `NullPointer-Exception` if `delimiters` is null.)[5]

`public int countTokens()`

Returns the number of tokens remaining to be returned by `nextToken`.

---

[5]Exceptions are covered in Chapter 9. You can ignore any reference to `NoSuchElementException` until you reach Chapter 9. We include it here for reference value only.

Display 4.18   Use of the `StringTokenizer` Class

```
1   import java.util.Scanner;
2   import java.util.StringTokenizer;
```

```
1   public class StringTokenizerDemo
2   {
3       public static void main(String[] args)
4           {
5               Scanner keyboard = new Scanner(System.in);

6               System.out.println("Enter your last name");
7               System.out.println("followed by your first and middle names.");
8               System.out.println("If you have no middle name,");
9               System.out.println("enter \"None\".");
10              String inputLine = keyboard.nextLine();

11              String delimiters = ", "; //Comma and blank space
12              StringTokenizer nameFactory =
13                  new StringTokenizer(inputLine, delimiters);

14              String lastName = nameFactory.nextToken();
15              String firstName = nameFactory.nextToken();
16              String middleName = nameFactory.nextToken();
17              if (middleName.equalsIgnoreCase("None"))
18                  middleName = ""; //Empty string
19              System.out.println("Hello " + firstName
20                                      + " " + middleName + " " + lastName);
21          }
22  }
```

Sample Dialogue

```
Enter your last name
followed by your first and middle names.
If you have no middle name,                  Note that the comma is
enter None.                                  not read because it is a
Savitch, Walter None    ◄━━━━━━━━━━━          delimiter.
Hello Walter Savitch
```

Self-Test Exercises

27. What would be the last line in the dialog in Display 4.18 if the user entered the following input line instead of the one shown in Display 4.18? (The comma is omitted.)

   ```
   Savitch Walter None
   ```

VideoNote
Example Using the String Tokenizer Class on a CSV File

28. What would be the last line in the dialog in Display 4.18 if the user entered the following input line instead of the one shown in Display 4.18?

   ```
   Tom, Dick, and Harry
   ```

Chapter Summary

- Objects have both instance variables and methods. A class is a type whose values are objects. All objects in a class have the same methods and the same types of instance variables.

- There are two main kinds of methods: methods that return a value and `void` methods. (Some specialized methods, such as constructors, are neither `void` methods nor methods that return a value.)

- When defining a method, the `this` parameter is a name used for the calling object.

- Normally, your classes should have both an `equals` method and a `toString` method.

- If an instance variable or method is marked `private`, then it cannot be directly referenced anyplace except in the definition of a method of the same class.

- Outside of the class in which it is defined, a private instance variable can be accessed via accessor methods and changed via mutator methods.

- A variable declared in a method is said to be a *local variable*. The meaning of a local variable is confined to the method in which it is declared. The local variable goes away when a method invocation ends. The name of a local variable can be reused for something else outside of the method in which it is declared.

- A parameter is like a blank in a method definition that is filled in with an argument when the method is invoked. A parameter is actually a local variable that is initialized to the value of the corresponding argument. This is known as the *call-by-value* parameter-passing mechanism.

- If a variable is used as an argument to a method, then only the value of the variable, not the variable itself, is plugged in to the corresponding parameter.

- *Encapsulation* means that the data and the actions are combined into a single item (in our case, a class object) and that the *details of the implementation are hidden*. Making all instance variables private is part of the encapsulation process.

- A class can have two (or more) different definitions for the same method name, provided the two definitions have different numbers of parameters or some parameters of differing types. This is called *overloading* the method name.

- A constructor is a variety of method that is called when you create an object of the class using new. A constructor is intended to be used to perform initialization tasks such as initializing instance variables. A constructor must have the same name as the class to which it belongs.

- A constructor with no parameters is called a *no-argument constructor*. If your class definition includes no constructor definitions at all, then Java automatically provides a no-argument constructor. If your class definition contains any constructor definitions at all, then no additional constructors are provided by Java. Your class definitions should usually include a no-argument constructor.

Answers to Self-Test Exercises

1.
```java
public void makeItChristmas ()
{
    month = "December";
    day = 25;
}
```

2.
```java
public void greetingsOnChristmas ()
{
    if ( (month.equalsIgnorewCase("December")) && (day == 25) )
        System.out.println("Merry Christmas!");
    else
        System.out.println("Not Christmas Day.");
}
```

3.
```java
public int getNextYear( )
{
    int nextYear = year + 1;
    return nextYear;
}
```

4.
```java
public void happyGreeting( )
{
    int count;
    for (count = 1; count <= day; count++)
        System.out.println("Happy Days!");
}
```

5.
```java
public double fractionDone (int targetDay)
{
    double doubleDay = day;
    return doubleDay/targetDay;
}
```

6.
```java
public void calculateDays (int monthNo)
{
    if(monthNo == 2)
    return 28;
    else if ((monthNo == 4)|| (monthNo == 6)|| (monthNo == 9)||
    (monthNo == 11))
    return 30;
    else
    return 31;
}
```

7. The instances of newMonth that have their values changed to 6 are indicated in color as follows:

```java
public void setDate(int newMonth, int newDay, int newYear)
{
    month = monthString(newMonth);
    day = newDay;
    year = newYear;
    System.out.println("Date changed to "
            + newMonth + " " + newDay + ", " + newYear);
}
```

The point being emphasized here is that all instances of newMonth have their values changed to 6. Technically speaking, the parameter newMonth is a local variable. So, there is only one local variable named newMonth whose value is changed to 6, but the net effect, in this case, is the same as replacing all occurrences of newMonth with 6.

8. Yes, it is legal. The point being emphasized here is that the parameter count is a local variable and so can have its value changed, in this case by the decrement operator.

9. Each case has a return statement. A return statement always ends the method invocation, and hence ends the execution of the switch statement. So a break statement would be redundant.

10. They are assumed to be instance variables of the calling object.

11.
```java
public int getDay()
{
    return this.day;
}
public int getYear()
{
    return this.year;
}
```

12.
```java
public int getMonth()
{
    if (this.month.equals("January"))
        return 1;
    else if (this.month.equals("February"))
        return 2;
    else if (this.month.equals("March"))
        return 3;
    else if (this.month.equals("April"))
        return 4;
    else if (this.month.equals("May"))
        return 5;
    else if (this.month.equals("June"))
        return 6;
    else if (this.month.equals("July"))
        return 7;
    else if (this.month.equals("August"))
        return 8;
    else if (this.month.equals("September"))
        return 9;
    else if (this.month.equals("October"))
        return 10;
    else if (this.month.equals("November"))
        return 11;
    else if (this.month.equals("December"))
        return 12;
    else
    {
        System.out.println("Fatal Error");
        System.exit(0);
        return 0; //Needed to keep the compiler happy
    }
}
```

13. The instance variable `month` contains a string, so we used `month` with `equals`. It would have been just as good to use

```java
getMonth() == otherDate.getMonth()
```

We used `getMonth()` with the less-than sign because it is of type `int` and so works with the less-than sign. The instance variable `month` is of type `String` and does not work with the less-than sign.

14. Every method should be tested in a program in which every other method in the testing program has already been fully tested and debugged.

15. All instance variables should be marked `private`.

16. Normally, a method is private only if it is being used solely as a helping method in the definition of other methods.

17. `getMonth`, `getDay`, and `getYear`.

18. `setDate`, `setMonth`, `setDay`, and `setYear`.

19.
```java
private boolean dateOK(int monthInt, int dayInt, int yearInt)
{
    if ((yearInt < 1000) || (yearInt > 999))
        return false;

    switch (monthInt)
    {
    case 1:
        return (dayInt >= 1) && (dayInt <= 31);
    case 2:
        if (leapYear(yearInt))
            return (dayInt >= 1) && (dayInt <= 29);
        else
            return (dayInt >= 1) && (dayInt <= 28);
    case 3:
        return (dayInt >= 1) && (dayInt <= 31);
    case 4:
        return (dayInt >= 1) && (dayInt <= 30);
    case 5:
        return (dayInt >= 1) && (dayInt <= 31);
    case 6:
        return (dayInt >= 1) && (dayInt <= 30);
    case 7:
        return (dayInt >= 1) && (dayInt <= 31);
    case 8:
        return (dayInt >= 1) && (dayInt <= 31);
    case 9:
        return (dayInt >= 1) && (dayInt <= 30);
    case 10:
        return (dayInt >= 1) && (dayInt <= 31);
    case 11:
        return (dayInt >= 1) && (dayInt <= 30);
    case 12:
        return (dayInt >= 1) && (dayInt <= 31);
    default:
        return false;
    }
}
```

```
/**
Returns true if yearInt is a leap year.
*/
private boolean leapYear(int yearInt)
{
     return ((yearInt % 4 == 0) && (yearInt % 100 != 0))
             || (yearInt % 400 == 0);
}
```

20. `showDetails(String)`
    `calculateTax(double, double)`
    `leapYear(int)`
    `amount(int, int, double)`
    `amount(int, int, double)`

21. Yes, it is legal because they have different signatures. This is a valid example of over-loading. Notice the method is returning a `DateSixthEntry` data type. This is also very much possible because creating a class is basically creating a user-defined data type.

22. No, it would be illegal because they have the same signature.

23. No, it would be illegal. You cannot overload on the basis of the type of the returned value.

24. If a class is named `Automobile`, then all constructors must be named `Automobile`.

25. `Citizen Smith = new Citizen (42, "John Smith", "987-65-4320");`
    `// Legal`
    `Citizen Carey = new YourClass(35.5, "William Carey");`
    `//Not legal`
    `Citizen c = new Citizen();`   `//Legal`
    `c.getRegistered();`   `//Legal`
    `Citizen Robin;`   `//Legal`
    `Robin.getRegistered();`   `//Not legal`
    `Alex.Citizen(29, "Alex Adams");`   `//Not legal`

26. A constructor is a variety of method that is called when an object of the class is created using `new`. Constructors are used to initialize objects. A default constructor is a constructor with no parameters, though the term is misleading. It is perfectly legal to invoke another method within the definition of a constructor.

27. The last line would be the same. Because the blank space is a delimiter, a blank space is enough to separate the tokens.

28. `Hello Dick and Tom`

    The other token in the input line is just not used.

MyProgrammingLab™ **Programming Projects**

Visit www.myprogramminglab.com to complete select exercises online and get instant feedback.

1. Write a program that outputs the lyrics for "Ninety-nine Bottles of Beer on the Wall." Your program should print the number of bottles in English, not as a number. For example,

   Ninety-nine bottles of beer on the wall,

   Ninety-nine bottles of beer,

   Take one down, pass it around,

   Ninety-eight bottles of beer on the wall.

   ...

   One bottle of beer on the wall,

   One bottle of beer,

   Take one down, pass it around,

   Zero bottles of beer on the wall.

   Your program should not use ninety-nine output statements!

   Design your program with a class named BeerSong whose constructor takes an integer parameter that is the number of bottles of beer initially on the wall. If the parameter is less than zero, set the number of bottles to zero. Similarly, if the parameter is greater than 99, set the number of beer bottles to 99. Then make a public method called printSong that outputs all stanzas from the number of bottles of beer down to zero. Add any additional private methods you find helpful.

2. Define a class called Complex. This class is used to represent a complex number of the form $a + bi$. Include mutator methods that allow the user to set the real and the complex part. Your class should have a reasonable set of accessor and mutator methods, an equals method, and a toString method, whether or not your program uses them. Also include two methods that take another complex number as parameter and return the results of addition and subtraction of the complex numbers. Embed your class in a test program.

3. Define an Automobile class for a secondhand car dealer. It will be used to track a car's make, model, color, license number, mileage, and fuel efficiency. The class should have instance variables to track various parameters along with the fuel efficiency of the vehicle in miles per gallon. Include a mutator method to reset the mileage to zero miles, a mutator method to set the fuel efficiency, a mutator method that accepts miles driven for a trip and adds it to the automobile's total, and an accessor method that returns the number of gallons of gasoline that the vehicle has consumed since its odometer was last reset.

   Use your class with a test program that creates several trips with different fuel efficiencies. You should decide which variables should be public, if any.

4. Define a class called `Sophomore` that could be used to store an entry for the second year students of your college. The class should have instance variables to store the student's name, a few lines of text introducing the student, and his/her date of birth using the `Date class` from Chapter 4. Add a constructor that allows the user of the class to set all instance variables. Also add a method `showDetails` that outputs all of the instance variables, and another method called `getSummary` that returns the first 10 words from the text of the introduction (or the entire introduction if it is less than 10 words). Test your class from your main method.

5. Define a `Circle` class that calculates and displays the diameter, perimeter and the area of any circle. It should have two member variables of `double` type – `radius` and `pi`. The class should have a default constructor that sets `radius` to `0.0`. It should also have a parameterized constructor that takes the radius of the circle. Include the mutator and accessor methods needed. Write a method for displaying the diameter, circumference, and area of the circle. Also, include a `toString` method and an `equals` method. Write a program (or programs) to test all the methods in your class definition.

6. Write a grading program for a class with the following grading policies:

   a. There are three quizzes, each graded on the basis of 10 points.

   b. There is one midterm exam, graded on the basis of 100 points.

   c. There is one final exam, graded on the basis of 100 points.

   The final exam counts for 40% of the grade. The midterm counts for 35% of the grade. The three quizzes together count for a total of 25% of the grade. (Do not forget to convert the quiz scores to percentages before they are averaged in.)

   Any grade of 90 or more is an A, any grade of 80 or more (but less than 90) is a B, any grade of 70 or more (but less than 80) is a C, any grade of 60 or more (but less than 70) is a D, and any grade below 60 is an F. The program should read in the student's scores and output the student's record, which consists of three quiz scores and two exam scores, as well as the student's overall numeric score for the entire course and final letter grade.

   Define and use a class for the student record. The class should have instance variables for the quizzes, midterm, final, overall numeric score for the course, and final letter grade. The overall numeric score is a number in the range 0 to 100, which represents the weighted average of the student's work. The class should have methods to compute the overall numeric grade and the final letter grade. These last methods should be `void` methods that set the appropriate instance variables. Your class should have a reasonable set of accessor and mutator methods, an `equals` method, and a `toString` method, whether or not your program uses them. You may add other methods if you wish.

7. Write a `Temperature` class that has two instance variables: a temperature value (a floating-point number) and a character for the scale, either `C` for Celsius or `F` for Fahrenheit. The class should have four constructor methods: one for each instance

variable (assume zero degrees if no value is specified and Celsius if no scale is specified), one with two parameters for the two instance variables, and a no-argument constructor (set to zero degrees Celsius). Include the following: (1) two accessor methods to return the temperature—one to return the degrees Celsius, the other to return the degrees Fahrenheit—use the following formulas to write the two methods, and round to the nearest tenth of a degree:

DegreesC = 5(degreesF − 32)/9
DegreesF = (9(degreesC)/5) + 32;

(2) three mutator methods: one to set the value, one to set the scale (F or C), and one to set both; (3) three comparison methods: an equals method to test whether two temperatures are equal, one method to test whether one temperature is greater than another, and one method to test whether one temperature is less than another (note that a Celsius temperature can be equal to a Fahrenheit temperature as indicated by the above formulas); and (4) a suitable toString method. Then write a driver program (or programs) that tests all the methods. Be sure to use each of the constructors, to include at least one true and one false case for each of the comparison methods, and to test at least the following temperature equalities: 0.0 degrees C = 32.0 degrees F, –40.0 degrees C = –40.0 degrees F, and 100.0 degrees C = 212.0 degrees F.

8. Redefine the class Date in Display 4.13 so that the instance variable for the month is of type int instead of type String. None of the method headings should change in any way. In particular, no String type parameters should change to int type parameters. You must redefine the methods to make things work out. Any program that uses the Date class from Display 4.13 should be able to use your Date class without any changes in the program. In particular, the program in Display 4.14 should work the same whether the Date class is defined as in Display 4.13 or is defined as you do it for this project. Write a test program (or programs) that tests each method in your class definition.

VideoNote
Solution to
Programming
Project 4.9

9. Define a class whose objects are records on animal species. The class should have instance variables for the species name, population, and growth rate. The growth rate is a percentage that can be positive or negative and can exceed 100%. Include a suitable collection of constructors, mutator methods, and accessor methods. Include a toString method and an equals method. Include a boolean valued method named endangered that returns true when the growth rate is negative and returns false otherwise. Write a test program (or programs) that tests each method in your class definition.

10. Your vet's office is using the Pet class defined in Display 4.15 and would like to include a way to calculate the dosage amount for drugs that are commonly administered for dogs and cats. Make the following modifications to the class:

- Add an instance variable that indicates if the type of the pet is a dog or a cat.
- Modify the constructor and the set method to include the type of pet (i.e., dog or cat).

- Add a method named `acepromazine( )` that returns as a `double` the dosage in ml for the sedative acepromazine.

- Add a method named `carprofen( )` that returns as a `double` the dosage in ml for the pain killer carprofen.

The dosage calculation is

$$\text{Dosage}(\text{ml}) = \frac{\text{Weight}}{2.2} \times \frac{\text{mg per kg}}{\text{mg per ml}}$$

Weight is in pounds.

- For acepromazine, use mg per ml = 10, and mg per kg = 0.03 for dogs and 0.002 for cats.

- For carprofen, use mg per ml = 12, and mg per kg = 0.5 for dogs and 0.25 for cats.

Modify the main method in Display 4.16 to include tests of the new methods.

11. Create a class named `Pizza` that stores information about a single pizza. It should contain the following:

    - Private instance variables to store the size of the pizza (either small, medium, or large), the number of cheese toppings, the number of pepperoni toppings, and the number of ham toppings.

    - Constructor(s) that set all of the instance variables.

    - Public methods to get and set the instance variables.

    - A public method named `calcCost( )` that returns a `double` that is the cost of the pizza.

      Pizza cost is determined by:

      Small: $10 + $2 per topping
      Medium: $12 + $2 per topping
      Large: $14 + $2 per topping

    - A public method named `getDescription( )` that returns a String containing the pizza size, quantity of each topping, and the pizza cost as calculated by `calcCost( )`.

    Write test code to create several pizzas and output their descriptions. For example, a large pizza with one cheese, one pepperoni and two ham toppings should cost a total of $22.

12. This programming project extends Programming Project 4.11. Create a `PizzaOrder` class that allows up to three pizzas to be saved in an order. Each pizza saved should be a `Pizza` object as described in Programming Project 4.11. In addition to appropriate instance variables and constructors, add the following methods:

    - `public void setNumPizzas(int numPizzas)` —sets the number of pizzas in the order. `numPizzas` must be between 1 and 3.

- `public void setPizza1(Pizza pizza1)`—sets the first pizza in the order.
- `public void setPizza2(Pizza pizza2)`—sets the second pizza in the order.
- `public void setPizza3(Pizza pizza3)`—sets the third pizza in the order.
- `public double calcTotal()`—returns the total cost of the order.

Write a `main` method to test the class. The `setPizza2` and `setPizza3` methods will be used only if there are two or three pizzas in the order, respectively. Sample code illustrating the methods is shown below. Note that first three lines are incomplete. You must complete them as part of the Programming Project.

```
Pizza pizza1 = // Code to create a large pizza, 1 cheese, 1 ham
Pizza pizza2 = // Code to create a medium pizza, 2 cheese, 2 pepperoni
PizzaOrder order = // Code to create an order
order.setNumPizzas(2); // 2 pizzas in the order
order.setPizza1(pizza1); // Set first pizza
order.setPizza2(pizza2); // Set second pizza
double total = order.calcTotal(); // Should be 18+20 = 38
```

13. Your Community Supported Agriculture (CSA) farm delivers a box of fresh fruits and vegetables to your house once a week. For this Programming Project, define the class `BoxOfProduce` that contains exactly three bundles of fruits or vegetables. You can represent the fruits or vegetables as three instance variables of type `String`. Add an appropriate constructor, accessor, and mutator methods. Also write a `toString()` method that returns as a String the complete contents of the box.

Next, write a main method that creates a `BoxOfProduce` with three items randomly selected from this list:

```
Broccoli
Tomato
Kiwi
Kale
Tomatillo
```

This list should be stored in a text file that is read in by your program. For now you can assume that the list contains exactly five types of fruits or vegetables.

Do not worry if your program randomly selects duplicate produce for the three items. Next, the main method should display the contents of the box and allow the user to substitute any one of the five possible fruits or vegetables for any of the fruits or vegetables selected for the box. After the user is done with substitutions, output the final contents of the box to be delivered. If you create additional methods to select the random items and to select valid substitutions, then your main method will be simpler to write.

14. A comma-separated values (CSV) file is a simple text format used to store a list of records. A comma is used as a delimiter to separate the fields for each record. This format is commonly used to transfer data between a spreadsheet or database. In this Programming Project, consider a store that sells five products abbreviated as A, B, C, D, and E. Customers can rate each product from 1–5, where 1 is poor and 5 is excellent. The ratings are stored in a CSV file where each row contains the customer's rating for each product. Here is a sample file with three customer ratings:

```
A,B,C,D,E
3,0,5,1,2
1,1,4,2,1
0,0,5,1,3
```

In this file format, the first line gives the products. The digit 0 indicates that a customer did not rate a product. In this case, the first customer rated A as 3, C as 5, D as 1, and E as 2. Product B was not rated. The third customer rated C as 5, D as 1, and E as 3. The third customer did not rate A or B.

Create a text file in this format with sample ratings. Then, write a program that reads in this text file and extracts each rating using the StringTokenizer class. Finally, the program should output the average rating for each product. Customers that did not rate a product should not be considered when computing the average rating for that product. Your program can assume there will always be exactly five products but it should work with an arbitrary number of customer ratings.

Defining Classes II 5

5.1 STATIC METHODS AND STATIC VARIABLES   293

Static Methods   293
Static Variables   300
The Math Class   305
Wrapper Classes   309
Automatic Boxing and Unboxing   310
Static Methods in Wrapper Classes   312

5.2 REFERENCES AND CLASS PARAMETERS   316

Variables and Memory   317
References   318
Class Parameters   323
The Constant null   329
The new Operator and Anonymous Objects   330
Example: Another Approach to
    Keyboard Input ★   331

5.3 USING AND MISUSING REFERENCES   335

Example: A Person Class   336
Copy Constructors   345
Mutable and Immutable Classes   351

5.4 PACKAGES AND javadoc   354

Packages and import Statements   355
The Package java.lang   356
Package Names and Directories   356
The Default Package   359
Specifying a Class Path When You Compile ★   360
Name Clashes ★   361
Introduction to javadoc ★   362
Commenting Classes for javadoc ★   362
Running javadoc ★   364

Chapter Summary   366   Answers to Self-Test Exercises   367   Programming Projects   371

5 Defining Classes II

After a certain high level of technical skill is achieved, science and art tend to coalesce in esthetics, plasticity, and form. The greatest scientists are always artists as well.

ALBERT EINSTEIN, Quoted in Alice Calaprice, *The Quotable Einstein*

Introduction

This chapter is a continuation of Chapter 4. It covers the rest of the core material on defining classes. We start by discussing *static methods* and *static variables*, which are methods and variables that belong to the class as a whole and not to particular objects. We then go on to discuss how class type variables name objects of their class and how class type parameters are handled in Java.

This chapter also discusses *packages*, which are Java's way of grouping classes into libraries. We end this chapter with a discussion of javadoc, a program that automatically extracts documentation from classes and packages.

Prerequisites

This chapter uses material from Chapters 1 through 4.

Sections 5.3 and 5.4 are independent of each other and may be covered in any order. Section 5.3 covers some subtle points about references, and Section 5.4 covers packages and javadoc. The material on javadoc is not used in the rest of this book. The other material in Sections 5.3 and 5.4 is not heavily used in the next few chapters and can be digested as needed if the material seems difficult on first reading.

The material on packages in Section 5.4 assumes that you know about directories (which are called folders in some operating systems), that you know about path names for directories (folders), and that you know about PATH (environment) variables. These are not Java topics. They are part of your operating system, and the details depend on your particular operating system. If you can find out how to set the PATH variable on your operating system, then you will know enough about these topics to understand the material on packages in Section 5.4.

5.1   Static Methods and Static Variables

All for one, one for all, that is our device.

ALEXANDRE DUMAS, *The Three Musketeers*

Static Methods

static methods

Some methods do not require a calling object. Methods to perform simple numeric calculations are good examples. For example, a method to compute the maximum of two integers has no obvious candidate for a calling object. In Java, you can define a method so that it requires no calling object. Such methods are known as **static methods**. You define a static method in the same way as any other method, but you add the keyword static to the method definition heading, as in the following example:

```
public static int maximum(int n1, int n2)
{
    if (n1 > n2)
        return n1;
    else
        return n2;
}
```

Although a static method requires no calling object, it still belongs to some class, and its definition is given inside the class definition. When you invoke a static method, you normally use the class name in place of a calling object. So if the above definition of the method maximum were in a class named SomeClass, then the following is a sample invocation of maximum:

```
int budget = SomeClass.maximum(yourMoney, myMoney);
```

where yourMoney and myMoney are variables of type int that contain some values.

A sample of some static method definitions, as well as a program that uses the methods, are given in Display 5.1.

We have already been using one static method. The method exit in the class System is a static method. To end a program immediately, we have used the following invocation of the static method exit:

```
System.exit(0);
```

Note that with a static method, the class name serves the same purpose as a calling object. (It would be legal to create an object of the class System and use it to invoke the method exit, but that is confusing style; we usually use the class name when invoking a static method.)

Display 5.1   Static Methods (part 1 of 2)

```
1   /**
2   Class with static methods for circles and spheres.
3   */
4   public class RoundStuff
5   {
6       public static final double PI = 3.14159;
7
8       /**
9        Return the area of a circle of the given radius.
10       */
11      public static double area(double radius)
12      {
13          return (PI*radius*radius);
14      }                                          This is the file
15                                                 RoundStuff.java.
16      /**
17       Return the volume of a sphere of the given radius.
18       */
19       public static double volume(double radius)
20       {
21           return ((4.0/3.0)*PI*radius*radius*radius);
22       }
23  }
```

```
1   import java.util.Scanner;
                                                This is the file
2   public class RoundStuffDemo              RoundStuffDemo.java.
3   {
4       public static void main(String[] args)
5       {
6           Scanner keyboard = new Scanner(System.in);
7           System.out.println("Enter radius:");
8           double radius = keyboard.nextDouble();

9           System.out.println("A circle of radius"
10                                  + radius + "inches");
11          System.out.println("has an area of " +
12              RoundStuff.area(radius) + " square inches.");
13          System.out.println("A sphere of radius"
14                                  + radius + "inches");
15          System.out.println("has an volume of " +
16              RoundStuff.volume(radius) + "cubic inches.");
17      }
18  }
```

Display 5.1   **Static Methods** (part 2 of 2)

Sample Dialogue

```
Enter radius:
2
A circle of radius 2.0 inches
has an area of 12.56636 square inches.
A sphere of radius 2.0 inches
has a volume of 33.51029333333333 cubic inches.
```

Within the definition of a static method, you cannot do anything that refers to a calling object, such as accessing an instance variable. This makes perfectly good sense, because a static method can be invoked without using any calling object and so can be invoked when there are no instance variables. (Remember instance variables belong to the calling object.) The best way to think about this restriction is in terms of the `this` parameter. In a static method, you cannot use the `this` parameter, either explicitly or implicitly. For example, the name of an instance variable by itself has an implicit `this` and a dot before it. So you cannot use an instance variable in the definition of a static method.

Static Methods

A **static method** is one that can be used without a calling object. With a static method, you normally use the class name in place of a calling object.

When you define a static method, you place the keyword `static` in the heading of the definition.

Since it does not need a calling object, a static method cannot refer to an instance variable of the class, nor can it invoke a nonstatic method of the class (unless it creates a new object of the class and uses that object as the calling object). Another way to phrase it is that, in the definition of a static method, you cannot use an instance variable or method that has an implicit or explicit `this` for a calling object.

PITFALL: Invoking a Nonstatic Method Within a Static Method

If `myMethod()` is a nonstatic (that is, ordinary) method in a class, then within the definition of any method of this class, an invocation of the form

```
myMethod();
```

means

```
this.myMethod();
```

(continued)

PITFALL: (continued)

and so it is illegal within the definition of a static method. (A static method has no `this`.)

However, it is legal to invoke a static method within the definition of another static method.

There is one way that you can invoke a nonstatic method within a static method: if you create an object of the class and use that object (rather than `this`) as the calling object. For example, suppose `myMethod()` is a nonstatic method in the class `MyClass`. Then, as we already discussed, the following is illegal within the definition of a static method in the class `MyClass`:

```
myMethod();
```

However, the following is perfectly legal in a static method or any method definition:

```
MyClass anObject = new MyClass();
anObject.myMethod();
```

The method `main` is a static method, and you will often see code similar to this in the `main` method of a class. This point is discussed in the Tip "You Can Put a `main` in Any Class." ■

TIP: You Can Put a `main` in Any Class

So far, whenever we have used a class in the `main` part of a program, that `main` method was by itself in a different class definition within another file. However, sometimes it makes sense to have a `main` method within a regular class definition. The class can then be used for two purposes: It can be used to create objects in other classes, or it can be run as a program. For example, you can combine the class definition `RoundStuff` and the program `RoundStuffDemo` (both in Display 5.1) by placing the `main` method inside the definition of the class `RoundStuff`, to obtain the class definition shown in Display 5.2.

Another example of a class with a `main` added is given in Display 5.3. Note that in addition to the static method `main`, the class has another static method named `toCelsius`. The class has both static and nonstatic methods. Note that the static method `toCelsius` can be invoked without the class name or a calling object because it is in another static method (namely `main`) in the same class. However, the nonstatic method `toString` requires an explicit calling object (`temperatureObject`). Java requires that a program's `main` method be static. Thus, within a `main` method, you cannot invoke a nonstatic method of the same class (such as `toString`) unless you create an object of the class and use it as a calling object for the nonstatic method.

You do not want to place just any `main` method in a class definition that is to be used as a regular class to create objects. One handy trick is to place a small diagnostic program in a `main` method that is inside of your class definition. ■

Display 5.2   Class Definition with a `main` Added

```
1   import java.util.Scanner;

2   /**
3   Class with static methods for circles and spheres.
4   */
5   public class RoundStuff2
6   {
7       public static final double PI = 3.14159;

8       /**
9        Return the area of a circle of the given radius.
10       */
11      public static double area(double radius)
12      {
13          return (PI*radius*radius);
14      }

15

16      /**
17      Return the volume of a sphere of the given radius.
18      */
19      public static double volume(double radius)
20      {
21              return ((4.0/3.0)*PI*radius*radius*radius);
22      }

23      public static void main(String[] args)
24      {
25          Scanner keyboard = new Scanner(System.in);
26          System.out.println("Enter radius:");
27          double radius = keyboard.nextDouble();

28

29          System.out.println("A circle of radius "
30                                          + radius + "inches");
31          System.out.println("has an area of " +
32              RoundStuff.area(radius) + " square inches.");
33          System.out.println("A sphere of radius "
34                                          + radius + "inches");
35          System.out.println("has an volume of " +
36              RoundStuff.volume(radius) + " cubic inches.");
37      }
38  }
```

The dialogue is the same as in Display 5.1.

Display 5.3 **Another Class with a `main` Added** (part 1 of 2)

```
 1   import java.util.Scanner;

 2   /**
 3    Class for a temperature (expressed in degrees Celsius).
 4   */
 5   public class Temperature
 6   {
 7       private double degrees; //Celsius

 8       public Temperature()
 9       {
10           degrees = 0;
11       }

12       public Temperature (double initialDegrees)
13       {
14           degrees = initialDegrees;
15       }

16       public void setDegrees (double newDegrees)
17       {
18           degrees = newDegrees;
19       }

20       public double getDegrees()
21       {
22           return degrees;
23       }

24       public String toString()
25       {
26           return (degrees + "C");
27       }
28
29       public boolean equals(Temperature otherTemperature)
30       {
31           return (degrees == otherTemperature.degrees);
32       }
33       /**
34        Returns number of Celsius degrees equal to
35        degreesF Fahrenheit degrees.
36       */
```

Note that this class has a `main` method and both static and nonstatic methods.

Display 5.3   **Another Class with a `main` Added** (part 2 of 2)

```
37       public static double toCelsius(double degreesF)
38       {
39
40           return 5*(degreesF - 32)/9;
41       }
42       public static void main(String[] args)
43       {
44           double degreesF, degreesC;
45
46           Scanner keyboard = new Scanner(System.in);
47           System.out.println("Enter degrees Fahrenheit:");
48           degreesF = keyboard.nextDouble();
49
50           degreesC = toCelsius(degreesF);
51
52           Temperature temperatureObject = new Temperature(degreesC);
53           System.out.println("Equivalent Celsius temperature is"
54                              + temperatureObject.toString());
55       }
56  }
```

Because this is in the definition of the class `Temperature`, *this is equivalent to* `Temperature.toCelsius(degreesF)`.

Because `main` *is a static method,* `toString` *must have a specified calling object such as* `temperatureObject`.

Sample Dialogue

```
Enter degrees Fahrenheit:
212
Equivalent Celsius temperature is 100.0 C
```

MyProgrammingLab™   ## Self-Test Exercises

1. Is the following legal? The class `RoundStuff` is defined in Display 5.1.

```
RoundStuff roundObject = new RoundStuff();
System.out.println("A circle of radius 5.5 has area"
                   + roundObject.area(5.5);
```

2. Can a non-static method refer to a static variable?

3. If a class contains only static methods, would you need a constructor for the class?

4. How do you call a non-static method from within a static method?

5. Can you invoke a static method within a nonstatic method?

6. Can you reference an instance variable within a static method? Why or why not?

Static Variables

static variable   A class can have static variables as well as static methods. A **static variable** is a variable that belongs to the class as a whole and not just to one object. Each object has its own copies of the instance variables. However, with a static variable, there is only one copy of the variable, and all the objects can use this one variable. Thus, a static variable can be used by objects to communicate between the objects. One object can change the static variable, and another object can read that change. To make a variable static, you declare it like an instance variable but add the modifier `static` as follows:

```
private static int turn;
```

Or if you wish to initialize the static variable, which is typical, you might declare it as follows instead:

```
private static int turn = 0;
```

default initialization   If you do not initialize a static variable, it is automatically initialized to a default value: Static variables of type `boolean` are automatically initialized to `false`. Static variables of other primitive types are automatically initialized to the zero of their type. Static variables of a class type are automatically initialized to `null`, which is a kind of placeholder for an object that we will discuss later in this chapter. However, we prefer to explicitly initialize static variables, either as just shown or in a constructor.

Display 5.4 shows an example of a class with a static variable along with a demonstration program. Notice that the two objects, `lover1` and `lover2`, access the same static variable `turn`.

As we already noted, you cannot directly access an instance variable within the definition of a static method. However, it is perfectly legal to access a static variable within a static method, because a static variable belongs to the class as a whole. This is illustrated by the method `getTurn` in Display 5.4. When we write `turn` in the definition of the static method `getTurn`, it does not mean `this.turn`; it means `TurnTaker.turn`. If the static variable `turn` were marked `public` instead of `private`, it would even be legal to use `TurnTaker.turn` outside of the definition of the class `TurnTaker`.

Defined constants that we have already been using, such as the following, are a special kind of static variable:

```
public static final double PI = 3.14159;
```

The modifier `final` in this example means that the static variable `PI` cannot be changed. Such defined constants are normally public and can be used outside the class. This defined constant appears in the class `RoundStuff` in Display 5.1. To use this constant outside of the class `RoundStuff`, you write the constant in the form `RoundStuff.PI`.

Good programming style dictates that static variables should normally be marked `private` unless they are marked `final`, that is, unless they are defined constants. The reason is the same as the reason for making instance variables `private`.

Display 5.4   **A Static Variable** (part 1 of 2)

```
1   public class TurnTaker
2   {
3       private static int turn = 0;

4       private int myTurn;
5       private String name;

6       public TurnTaker(String theName, int theTurn)
7       {
8           name = theName;
9           if (theTurn >= 0)
10              myTurn = theTurn;
11          else
12          {
13              System.out.println("Fatal Error.");
14              System.exit(0);
15          }
16      }

17      public TurnTaker()                      This is the file
18      {                                       TurnTaker.java.
19          name = "No name yet";
20          myTurn = 0; //Indicating no turn.
21      }

22      public String getName()
23      {
24          return name;
25      }

26      public static int getTurn()
27      {                                       You cannot access an instance
28          turn++;  ◄─────────────────────     variable in a static method, but you
29          return turn;                        can access a static variable in a
30      }                                       static method.

31      public boolean isMyTurn()
32      {
33          return (turn == myTurn);
34      }
35  }
```

(continued)

Display 5.4   **A Static Variable** (part 2 of 2)

```
36   public class StaticDemo
37   {                                              This is the file
38       public static void main(String[] args)    StaticDemo.java.
39       {
40           TurnTaker lover1 = new TurnTaker("Romeo", 1);
41           TurnTaker lover2 = new TurnTaker("Juliet", 3);
42           for (int i = 1; i < 5; i++)
43           {
44               System.out.println("Turn = " + TurnTaker.getTurn());
45               if (lover1.isMyTurn())
46                   System.out.println("Love from" + lover1.getName());
47               if (lover2.isMyTurn())
48                   System.out.println("Love from" + lover2.getName());
49           }
50       }
51   }
```

Sample Dialogue

```
Turn = 1
Love from Romeo
Turn = 2
Turn = 3
Love from Juliet
Turn = 4
```

Another example of a static variable is given in Display 5.5. The static variable numberOfInvocations is used to keep track of how many invocations have been made by all objects of the class StaticDemo. The program counts all invocations of the methods defined in Display 5.4, except for the method main.

Display 5.5   **A Static Variable** (part 1 of 2)

```
1   public class InvocationCounter
2   {
3       private static int numberOfInvocations = 0;

4       public void demoMethod()
5       {
6           numberOfInvocations++;                          object1 and object2 use
7           //In a real example, more code would go here.   the same static variable
8   }                                                       numberOfInvocations.
```

Display 5.5   **A Static Variable** (part 2 of 2)

```
 9      public void outPutCount()
10      {
11          numberOfInvocations++;
12          System.out.println("Number of invocations so far = "
13                                            + numberOfInvocations);
14      }

15      public static int numberSoFar()
16      {
17          numberOfInvocations++;
18          return numberOfInvocations;
19      }

20      public static void main(String[] args)
21      {
22          int i;
23          InvocationCounter object1 = new InvocationCounter();
24          for (i= 1; i <= 5 ; i++)         Outputs 6 for five invocations of
25          object1.demoMethod();         — demoMethod and one invocation of
26          object1.outPutCount();◄          outputCount.
27
28          InvocationCounter object2 = new InvocationCounter();
29          for (i= 1; i <= 5 ; i++)
30          {
31              object2.demoMethod();
32              object2.outPutCount();
33          }

34          System.out.println("Totalnumber of invocations = "
35                                  + numberSoFar());
36      }
37  }
```

Sample Dialogue

```
Number of invocations so far = 6
Number of invocations so far = 8
Number of invocations so far = 10
Number of invocations so far = 12
Number of invocations so far = 14
Number of invocations so far = 16
Total number of invocations = 17
```

Static Variables

A **static variable** belongs to the class as a whole. All objects of the class can read and change the static variable. Static variables should normally be private, unless they happen to be defined constants.

SYNTAX

```
private static Type Variable_Name;
private static Type Variable_Name = Initial_Value;
public static final Type Variable_Name = Constant_Value;
```

EXAMPLES

```
private static String lastUser;
private static int turn = 0;
public static final double PI = 3.14159;
```

MyProgrammingLab™   **Self-Test Exercises**

7. How could static variables be used for communication between the objects?

8. What is wrong in the declaration:

   ```
   private int static counter = 0;
   ```

9. What would happen if a *static variable* is not initialized? Are the static variables of class types initialized automatically?

10. Static variables should normally be private. In which cases should these variables be declared as `public`?

11. When we defined the class `Date` in Display 4.11 in Chapter 4, we had not yet discussed static methods, so we did not mark any of the methods `static`. However, some of the methods could have been marked `static` (and should have been marked `static`, if only we had known what that meant). Which of the methods can be marked `static`? (If you omit the modifier `static` when it is appropriate, then the method cannot be invoked with the class name; it must be invoked with a calling object.)

12. Following the style guidelines given in this book, when should a static variable be marked `private`?

13. What do static methods and static variables have in common? After all, they are both called *static*, so it sounds like they have something in common.

The Math Class

Math methods   The class Math provides a number of standard mathematical methods. The class Math is provided automatically and requires no import statement. Some of the methods in the class Math are described in Display 5.6. A more complete list of methods is given in Appendix 5. All of these methods are static, which means that you normally use the class name Math in place of a calling object.

Display 5.6   Some Methods in the Class **Math** (part 1 of 2)

The Math class is in the java.lang package, so it requires no import statement.

```
public static double pow(double base, double exponent)
```

Returns base to the power exponent.

EXAMPLE

Math.pow(2.0,3.0) returns 8.0.

```
public static double abs(double argument)
public static float abs(float argument)
public static long abs(long argument)
public static int abs(int argument)
```

Returns the absolute value of the argument. (The method name abs is overloaded to produce four similar methods.)

EXAMPLE

Math.abs(-6) and Math.abs(6) both return 6. Math.abs(-5.5) and Math.abs(5.5) both return 5.5.

```
public static double min(double n1, double n2)
public static float min(float n1, float n2)
public static long min(long n1, long n2)
public static int min(int n1, int n2)
```

Returns the minimum of the arguments n1 and n2. (The method name min is overloaded to produce four similar methods.)

EXAMPLE

Math.min(3, 2) returns 2.

```
public static double max(double n1, double n2)
public static float max(float n1, float n2)
public static long max(long n1, long n2)
public static int max(int n1, int n2)
```

Returns the maximum of the arguments n1 and n2. (The method name max is overloaded to produce four similar methods.)

EXAMPLE

Math.max(3, 2) returns 3.

(continued)

Display 5.6   Some Methods in the Class `Math` (part 2 of 2)

```
public static long round(double argument)
public static int round(float argument)
```

Rounds its `argument`.

EXAMPLE

`Math.round(3.2)` returns `3`; `Math.round(3.6)` returns `4`.

```
public static double ceil(double argument)
```

Returns the smallest whole number greater than or equal to the `argument`.

EXAMPLE

`Math.ceil(3.2)` and `Math.ceil(3.9)` both return `4.0`.

```
public static double floor(double argument)
```

Returns the largest whole number less than or equal to the `argument`.

EXAMPLE

`Math.floor(3.2)` and `Math.floor(3.9)` both return `3.0`.

```
public static double sqrt(double argument)
```

Returns the square root of its argument.

EXAMPLE

`Math.sqrt(4)` returns `2.0`.

```
public static double random()
```

Returns a random number greater than or equal to 0.0 and less than 1.0.

EXAMPLE

`Math.random()` returns 0.5505562535943004 (sample number; returns a pseudo-random number that is less than 1 and greater than or equal to 0).

The class `Math` has three similar methods named `round`, `floor`, and `ceil`. Some of these return a value of type `double`, but they all return a value that is intuitively a whole number that is close to the value of their arguments. The method `round` rounds a number to the nearest whole number, and (if the argument is a `double`) it returns that whole number as a value of type `long`. If you want that whole number as a value of type `int`, you must use a type cast as in the following:

```
double exact = 7.56;
int roundedValue = (int)Math.round(exact);
```

You cannot assign a `long` value to a variable of type `int`, even if it is a value such as 8, which could just as well have been an `int`. A value such as 8 can be of type either `int` or `long` (or even of type `short` or `byte`) depending on how it was created.

floor and ceil   The methods `floor` and `ceil` are similar to, but not identical to, `round`. Neither one rounds, although they both yield a whole number that is close to their argument. They both return a whole number as a value of type `double` (not of type `int` or `long`). The method `floor` returns the nearest whole number that is less than or equal to its argument. So `Math.floor(5.9)` returns `5.0`, not `6.0`. `Math.floor(5.2)` also returns `5.0`.

The method `ceil` returns the nearest whole number that is greater than or equal to its argument. The word `ceil` is short for "ceiling." `Math.ceil(5.1)` returns `6.0`, not `5.0`. `Math.ceil(5.9)` also returns `6.0`.

If you want to store the value returned by either `floor` or `ceil` in a variable of type `int`, you must use a type cast as in the following example:

```
double exact = 7.56;
int lowEstimate = (int)Math.floor(exact);
int highEstimate = (int)Math.ceil(exact);
```

`Math.floor(exact)` returns the `double` value `7.0`, and the variable `lowEstimate` receives the `int` value `7`. `Math.ceil(exact)` returns the `double` value `8.0`, and the variable `highEstimate` receives the `int` value `8`.

Because values of type `double` are effectively approximate values, a safer way to compute the floor or ceiling as an `int` value is the following:

```
double exact = 7.56;
int lowEstimate = (int)Math.round(Math.floor(exact));
int highEstimate = (int)Math.round(Math.ceil(exact));
```

This way, if `Math.floor(exact)` returns slightly less than `7.0`, the final result will still be `7` and not `6`, and if `Math.ceil(exact)` returns slightly less than `8.0`, the final result will still be `8` and not `7`.

Math constants   The class `Math` also has the two predefined constants `E` and `PI`. The constant `PI` (often written π in mathematical formulas) is used in calculations involving circles, spheres, and other geometric figures based on circles. `PI` is approximately `3.14159`. The constant `E` is the base of the natural logarithm system (often written *e* in mathematical formulas) and is approximately `2.72`. (We do not use the predefined constant `E` in this text.) The constants `PI` and `E` are defined constants, as described in Chapter 1. For example, the following computes the area of a circle, given its radius:

```
area = Math.PI * radius * radius;
```

Notice that because the constants `PI` and `E` are defined in the class `Math`, they must have the class name `Math` and a dot before them. For example, in Display 5.7, we have redone the program in Display 5.2, but this time we used the constant `Math.PI` instead of including our own definition of `PI`.

Display 5.7   Using `Math.PI`

```
1   import java.util.Scanner;

2   /**
3    Class with static methods for circles and spheres.
4   */
5   public class RoundStuff3
6   {

7        /**
8         Return the area of a circle of the given radius.
9        */
10       public static double area(double radius)
11       {
12            return (Math.PI*radius*radius);
13       }

14

15       /**
16        Return the volume of a sphere of the given radius.
17       */
18       public static double volume(double radius)
19       {
20            return ((4.0/3.0)*Math.PI*radius*radius*radius);
21       }

22       public static void main(String[] args)
23       {
24            Scanner keyboard = new Scanner(System.in);
25            System.out.println("Enter radius:");
26            double radius = keyboard.nextDouble();

27
28            System.out.println("A circle of radius"
29                                           + radius + "inches");
30            System.out.println("has an area of" +
31                 RoundStuff.area(radius) + "square inches.");
32            System.out.println("A sphere of radius"
33                                           + radius + "inches");
34            System.out.println("has a volume of " +
35                 RoundStuff.volume(radius) + "cubic inches.");
36       }
37   }
38
39
```

The dialogue is the same as in Display 5.1.

Finally, the class Math also includes a method to generate random numbers. The method random returns a pseudo-random number that is greater than or equal to 0.0 and less than 1.0. A pseudo-random number is a number that appears random, but is really generated by a deterministic function. See Chapter 3 for additional discussion about random number generation.

MyProgrammingLab

Self-Test Exercises

14. What values are returned by each of the following?

    ```
    Math.round(7.3), Math.round(7.9),
    Math.floor(7.3), Math.floor(7.9),
    Math.ceil(7.3), and Math.ceil(7.9).
    ```

15. Suppose answer is a variable of type double. Write an assignment statement to assign Math.round(answer) to the int variable roundedAnswer.

16. Suppose n is of type int and m is of type long. What is the type of the value returned by Math.min(n, m)? Is it int or long?

Wrapper Classes

wrapper class

Java treats the primitive types, such as int and double, differently from the class types, such as the class String and the programmer-defined classes. For example, later in this chapter you will see that an argument to a method is treated differently depending on whether the argument is of a primitive or class type. At times, you may find yourself in a situation where you want to use a value of a primitive type but you want or need the value to be an object of a class type. **Wrapper classes** provide a class type corresponding to each of the primitive types so that you can have an object of a class type that behaves somewhat like its corresponding value of a primitive type.

integer class

To convert a value of a primitive type to an "equivalent" value of a class type, you create an object of the corresponding wrapper class using the primitive type value as an argument to the wrapper class constructor. The wrapper class for the primitive type int is the predefined class Integer. If you want to convert an int value, such as 42, to an object of type Integer, you can do so as follows:

```
Integer integerObject = new Integer(42);
```

The variable integerObject now names an object of the class Integer that corresponds to the int value 42. (The object integerObject does, in fact, have the int value 42 stored in an instance variable of the object integerObject.) This process of going from a value of a primitive type to an object of its wrapper class is sometimes called **boxing**, and as you will see in the next subsection, you can let Java automatically do all the work of boxing for you.

boxing

To go in the reverse direction, from an object of type Integer to the corresponding int value, you can do the following:

```
int i = integerObject.intValue();
```

unboxing

The method `intValue()` recovers the corresponding `int` value from an object of type `Integer`. This process of going from an object of a wrapper class to the corresponding value of a primitive type is sometimes called **unboxing**, and as you will see in the next subsection, you can let Java automatically do all the work of unboxing for you.

other wrapper classes

The wrapper classes for the primitive types `byte`, `short`, `long`, `float`, `double`, and `char` are `Byte`, `Short`, `Long`, `Float`, `Double`, and `Character`, respectively. The methods for converting from the wrapper class object to the corresponding primitive type are `intValue` for the class `Integer`, as we have already seen, `byteValue` for the class `Byte`, `shortValue` for the class `Short`, `longValue` for the class `Long`, `floatValue` for the class `Float`, `doubleValue` for the class `Double`, and `charValue` for the class `Character`.

Wrapper Classes

Every primitive type has a corresponding wrapper class. A **wrapper class** allows you to have a class object that corresponds to a value of a primitive type. Wrapper classes also contain a number of useful predefined constants and static methods.

Automatic Boxing and Unboxing

Converting from a value of a primitive type, such as `int`, to a corresponding object of its associated wrapper class, such as `Integer`, is called **boxing**. You can think of the object as a "box" that contains the value of the primitive type. In fact, the wrapper object does contain the value of the primitive type as the value of a private instance variable. The following are examples of boxing:

```
Integer numberOfSamuri = new Integer(47);
Double price = new Double(499.99);
Character grade = new Character('A');
```

automatic boxing

Starting with version 5.0, Java will automatically do this boxing, so the previous three assignments can be written in the following equivalent, but simpler, forms:

```
Integer numberOfSamuri = 47;
Double price = 499.99;
Character grade = 'A';
```

This is an automatic type cast. What is actually done by Java is what we showed in the forms using the `new`, but it is handy to be able to write the assignments in the simpler form.

automatic
unboxing

The reverse conversion from an object of a wrapper class to a value of its associated primitive type is called **unboxing**. Unboxing is also done automatically in Java (starting in version 5.0). The following are examples of automatic unboxing:

```
Integer numberOfSamuri = new Integer(47);
int n = numberOfSamuri;
Double price = new Double(499.99);
double d = price;
Character grade = new Character('A');
char c = grade;
```

Java automatically applies the appropriate accessor method (intValue, doubleValue, or charValue in these cases) to obtain the value of the primitive type that is assigned to the variable. So the previous examples of automatic unboxing are equivalent to the following code, which is what you had to write in older versions of Java that did not do automatic unboxing:

```
Integer numberOfSamuri = new Integer(47);
int n = numberOfSamuri.intValue();
Double price = new Double(499.99);
double d = price.doubleValue();
Character grade = new Character('A');
char c = grade.charValue();
```

Our previous examples involved either only automatic boxing or only automatic unboxing. That was done to simplify the discussion by allowing you to see each of automatic boxing and automatic unboxing in isolation. However, code can often involve a combination of automatic boxing and unboxing. For example, consider the following code, which uses both automatic boxing and automatic unboxing:

```
Double price = 19.90;
price = price + 5.12;
```

This code is equivalent to the following, which is what you had to write in older versions of Java that did not do automatic boxing and unboxing:

```
Double price = new  Double(19.90);
price = new Double(price.doubleValue() + 5.12);
```

Automatic boxing and unboxing applies to parameters as well as to the simple assignment statements we just discussed. You can plug in a value of a primitive type, such as a value of type int, for a parameter of the associated wrapper class, such as Integer. Similarly, you can plug a wrapper class argument, such as an argument of type Integer, for a parameter of the associated primitive type, such as int.

Self-Test Exercises

17. Which of the following are legal?

```
Double d1 = new Double(78.59);
double d2 = 78.59 ;
d1 = d2;
d2 = d1;
```

If any are illegal, explain how to write a valid Java statement that does what the illegal statement is trying to do.

18. In the following, is the value of the variable `marks` after the assignment statement an object of the class `Integer` or a value of the primitive type `int`?

```
Integer marks = 60;
```

19. In the following, is the value of the variable `taxRate` after the assignment statement an object of the class `Float` or a value of the primitive type `float`?

```
float taxRate = new Float(5.0);
```

Static Methods in Wrapper Classes

The material on wrapper classes that we have seen thus far explains why they are called *wrapper classes*. However, possibly more importantly, the wrapper classes contain a number of useful constants and static methods. So, wrapper classes have two distinct personalities: one is their ability to produce class objects corresponding to values of primitive types, and the other is as a repository of useful constants and methods. It was not necessary to combine these two personalities into one kind of class. Java could have had two sets of classes, one for each personality, but the designers of the Java libraries chose to have only one set of classes for both personalities.

largest and smallest values

You can use the associated wrapper class to find the value of the **largest and smallest values** of any of the primitive number types. For example, the largest and smallest values of type `int` are

```
Integer.MAX_VALUE and Integer.MIN_VALUE
```

The largest and smallest values of type `double` are

```
Double.MAX_VALUE and Double.MIN_VALUE
```

parseDouble

Wrapper classes have static methods that can be used to convert back and forth between string representations of numbers and the corresponding number of type `int`, `double`, `long`, or `float`. For example, the static method `parseDouble` of the wrapper class `Double` converts a string to a value of type `double`. So, the code

```
Double.parseDouble("199.98")
```

returns the `double` value `199.98`. If there is any possibility that the string named by `theString` has extra leading or trailing blanks, you should instead use

```
Double.parseDouble(theString.trim())
```

The method `trim` is a method in the class `String` that trims off leading and trailing whitespace, such as blanks.

If the string is not a correctly formed numeral, then the invocation of `Double.parseDouble` will cause your program to end. The use of `trim` helps somewhat in avoiding this problem.

parseInt   Similarly, the static methods `Integer.parseInt`, `Long.parseLong`, and `Float.parseFloat` convert from string representations to numbers of the corresponding primitive types `int`, `long`, and `float`, respectively.

Each of the numeric wrapper classes also has a static method called `toString` that converts in the other direction, from a numeric value to a string representation of the numeric value. For example,

```
Double.toString(123.99)
```

returns the string value `"123.99"`.

Character   `Character`, the wrapper class for the primitive type `char`, contains a number of static methods that are useful for string processing. Some of these methods are shown in Display 5.8. A simple example of using the static method `toUpperCase` of the class `Character` is given in Display 5.9. As is typical, this program combines the string-processing methods of the class `String` with the character-processing methods in the class `Character`.

There is also a wrapper class `Boolean` corresponding to the primitive type `boolean`. **Boolean**   It has names for two constants of type `Boolean`: `Boolean.TRUE` and `Boolean.FALSE`, which are the `Boolean` objects corresponding to the values `true` and `false` of the primitive type `boolean`.

Display 5.8   Some Methods in the Class Character (part 1 of 2)

The class `Character` is in the `java.lang` package, so it requires no `import` statement.

`public static char toUpperCase(char argument)`

Returns the uppercase version of its argument. If the argument is not a letter, it is returned unchanged.

EXAMPLE

`Character.toUpperCase('a')` and `Character.toUpperCase('A')` both return `'A'`.

`public static char toLowerCase(char argument)`

Returns the lowercase version of its argument. If the argument is not a letter, it is returned unchanged.

EXAMPLE

`Character.toLowerCase('a')` and `Character.toLowerCase('A')` both return `'a'`.

(continued)

Display 5.8   **Some Methods in the Class Character** (part 2 of 2)

```
public static boolean isUpperCase(char argument)
```

Returns `true` if its argument is an uppercase letter; otherwise returns `false`.

EXAMPLE

`Character.isUpperCase('a')` returns `true`. `Character.isUpperCase('a')` and `Character.isUpperCase('%')` both return `false`.

```
public static boolean isLowerCase(char argument)
```

Returns `true` if its argument is a lowercase letter; otherwise returns `false`.

EXAMPLE

`Character.isLowerCase('a')` returns true. `Character.isLowerCase('A')` and `Character.isLowerCase('%')` both return `false`.

```
public static boolean isWhitespace(char argument)
```

Returns `true` if its argument is a whitespace character; otherwise returns `false`. Whitespace characters are those that print as white space, such as the space character (blank character), the tab character (`'\t'`), and the line break character (`'\n'`).

EXAMPLE

`Character.isWhitespace(' ')` returns `true`.
`Character.isWhitespace('A')` returns `false`.

```
public static boolean isLetter(char argument)
```

Returns `true` if its argument is a letter; otherwise returns `false`.

EXAMPLE

`Character.isLetter('A')` returns `true`. `Character.isLetter('%')` and `Character.isLetter ('5')` both return `false`.

```
public static boolean isDigit(char argument)
```

Returns `true` if its argument is a digit; otherwise returns `false`.

EXAMPLE

`Character.isDigit('5')` returns true. `Character.isDigit('A')` and `Character.isDigit('%')` both return `false`.

```
public static boolean isLetterOrDigit(char argument)
```

Returns `true` if its argument is a letter or a digit; otherwise returns `false`.

EXAMPLE

`Character.isLetterOrDigit('A')` and `Character.isLetterOrDigit('5')` both return true. `Character.isLetterOrDigit('&')` returns `false`.

PITFALL: A Wrapper Class Does Not Have a No-Argument Constructor

Normally, it is good programming practice to define a no-argument constructor for any class you define. However, on rare occasions, a no-argument constructor simply does not make sense. The wrapper classes discussed in the previous subsection do not have a no-argument constructor, which is reasonable if you think about it. To use the static methods in a wrapper class, you need no calling object and hence need no constructor at all. The other function of a wrapper class is to provide a class object corresponding to a value of a primitive type. For example,

```
new Integer(42)
```

creates an object of the class `Integer` that corresponds to the `int` value `42`. There is no no-argument constructor for the class `Integer`, because it makes no sense to have an object of the class `Integer` unless it corresponds to an `int` value, and if it does correspond to an `int` value, that `int` value is naturally an argument to the constructor. ∎

Display 5.9   String Processing with a Method from the Class `Character`   (part 1 of 2)

```
1   import java.util.Scanner;

2   /**
3   Illustrate the use of a static method from the class Character.
4   */
5
6   public class StringProcessor
7   {
8       public static void main (String[] args)
9       {
10          System.out.println("Enter a one line sentence:");
11          Scanner keyboard = new Scanner(System.in);
12          String sentence = keyboard.nextLine();
13
14          sentence = sentence.toLowerCase();
15          char firstCharacter = sentence.charAt(0);
16          sentence = Character.toUpperCase(firstCharacter)
17                        + sentence.substring(1);
18
19          System.out.println("The revised sentence is:");
20          System.out.println(sentence);
21      }
22   }
```

(continued)

Display 5.9   String Processing with a Method from the Class `Character` (part 2 of 2)

Sample Dialogue

```
Enter a one line sentence:
is you is OR is you ain't my BABY?
The revised sentence is:
Is you is or is you ain't my baby?
```

MyProgrammingLab™ **Self-Test Exercises**

20. What is the output produced by the following code?

```java
Character characterObject1 = new Character('a');
Character characterObject2 = new Character('A');
if (characterObject1.equals(characterObject2))
    System.out.println("Objects are equal.");
else
    System.out.println("Objects are Not equal.");
```

21. Suppose `average` is a variable of type `float` that has a value. Write a Java expression that returns a string that is the normal way of writing the value in `average`.

22. Suppose `stringForm` is a variable of type `String` that names a `String` that is the normal way of writing some `double`, such as `"41.99"`. Write a Java expression that returns the `double` value named by `stringForm`.

23. Suppose `tempReading` is a variable of type `String` that has the value `"29.73"`. Write the Java statements that return the `double` value from `tempReading`.

24. Write Java code to output the largest and smallest values of type `long` allowed in Java.

25. How do you create an object of the class `Character` that corresponds to '*'?

26. Does the class `Character` have a no-argument constructor?

5.2   References and Class Parameters

Do not mistake the pointing finger for the moon.

ZEN SAYING

Variables of a class type and variables of a primitive type behave quite differently in Java. Variables of a primitive type name their values in a straightforward way. For example, if n is an `int` variable, then n can contain a value of type `int`, such as 42. If v is a variable of a class type, then v does not directly contain an object of its class. Instead, v names an object by containing the memory address of where the object is located in memory. In this section, we discuss how a variable of a class type names objects, and we also discuss the related topic of how method parameters of a class type behave in Java.

Variables and Memory

secondary and main memory

A computer has two forms of memory called *secondary memory* and *main memory*. The **secondary memory** is used to hold files for more or less permanent storage. The **main memory** is used by the computer when it is running a program. Values stored in a program's variables are kept in this main memory. It will help our understanding of class type variables to learn a few details about how program variables are represented in main memory. For now, assume that each variable in a program is of some primitive type, such as int, double, or char. Once you understand how variables of a primitive type are stored in memory, it will be easier to describe how variables of a class type behave.

byte

address

Main memory consists of a long list of numbered locations called **bytes**, each containing eight bits; that is, eight 0/1 digits. The number that identifies a byte is called its **address**. A data item, such as a number or a letter, can be stored in one of these bytes, and the address of the byte is then used to find the data item when it is needed.

memory location

Most data types have values that require more than one byte of storage. When a data type requires more than one byte of storage, several adjacent bytes are used to hold the data item. In this case, the entire chunk of memory that holds the data item is still called a **memory location**. The address of the first of the bytes that make up this memory location is used as the address for this larger memory location. Thus, as a practical matter, you can think of the computer's main memory as a long list of memory locations of *varying sizes*. The size of each of these locations is expressed in bytes, and the address of the first byte is used as the address (name) of that memory location. Display 5.10 shows a picture of a hypothetical computer's main memory. Each primitive type variable in a program is assigned one of these memory locations, and the value of the variable is stored in this memory location.

variables of a primitive type

Bytes and Addresses

Main memory is divided into numbered locations called **bytes**. The number associated with a byte is called its **address**. A group of consecutive bytes is used as the location for the value of a variable. The address of the first byte in the group is used as the address of this larger memory location.

Why Eight Bits?

A **byte** is a memory location that can hold 8 bits. What is so special about 8? Why not 10 bits? There are two reasons why 8 is special. First, 8 is a power of 2 (8 is 2^3). Since computers use bits, which have only two possible values, powers of 2 are more convenient than powers of 10. Second, it turns out that 7 bits are required to code a single character of the ASCII character set. So 8 bits (1 byte) is the smallest power of 2 that will hold a single ASCII character.

Display 5.10   Variables in Memory

References

In order to have a simple example to help explain *references*, we will use the class ToyClass defined in Display 5.11.

Variables of a class type name objects of their class differently than how variables of primitive types, such as int or char, store their values. Every variable, whether of a primitive type or a class type, is implemented as a location in the computer memory. For a variable of a primitive type, the value of the variable is stored in the memory location assigned to the variable. However, a variable of a class type stores only the memory address of where an object is located. The object named by the variable is stored in some other location in memory, and the variable contains only the memory

Display 5.11   **A Simple Class**

```java
1   public class ToyClass
2   {
3       private String name;
4       private int number;

5       public ToyClass(String initialName, int initialNumber)
6       {
7           name = initialName;
8           number = initialNumber;
9       }

10      public ToyClass()
11      {
12          name = "No name yet.";
13          number = 0;
14      }

15      public void set(String newName, int newNumber)
16      {
17          name = newName;
18          number = newNumber;
19      }

20      public String toString()
21      {
22          return (name + " " + number);
23      }

24      public static void changer(ToyClass aParameter)
25      {
26          aParameter.name = "Hot Shot";
27          aParameter.number = 42;
28      }

29      public boolean equals(ToyClass otherObject)
30      {
31          return ((name.equals(otherObject.name))
32                  && (number = otherObject.number) );
33      }
34  }
```

references   address of where the object is stored. This memory address is called a **reference** (to the object).[1] This is diagrammed in Display 5.12.

Variables of a primitive type and variables of a class type are different for a reason. A value of a primitive type, such as the type int, always requires the same amount of memory to store one value. There is a maximum value of type int, so values of type int have a limit on their size. However, an object of a class type, such as an object of the class String, might be of any size. The memory location for a variable of type String is of a fixed size, so it cannot store an arbitrarily long string. It can, however, store the address of any string because there is a limit to the size of an address.

Because variables of a class type contain a reference (memory address), two variables may contain the same reference, and in such a situation, both variables name the same object. Any change to the object named by one of these variables will produce a change to the object named by the other variable, because they are the same object. For example, consider the following code. (The class ToyClass is defined in Display 5.11, but the meaning of the code should be obvious and you should not need to look up the definition.)

```
ToyClass variable1 = new ToyClass("Joe", 42);
ToyClass variable2;
variable2 = variable1; //Now both variables name the same object.
variable2.set("Josephine", 1);
System.out.println(variable1); //Invokes variable1's toString
                                //method
```

The output is

```
Josephine 1
```

The object named by variable1 has been changed without ever using the name variable1. This is diagrammed in Display 5.13.

Variables of a Class Type Hold References

A variable of a primitive type stores a value of that type. However, a variable of a class type does not store an object of that class. A variable of a class type stores the reference (memory address) of where the object is located in the computer's memory. This causes some operations, such as = and ==, to behave quite differently for variables of a class type than they do for variables of a primitive type.

Reference Types

A type whose variables contain references are called **reference types**. In Java, class types are reference types, but primitive types are not reference types.

---

[1] Readers familiar with languages that use pointers will recognize a reference as another name for a pointer. However, Java does not use the term *pointer*, but instead uses the term *reference*. Moreover, these references are handled automatically. There are no programmer-accessible pointer (reference) operations for dereferencing or other pointer operations. The details are all handled automatically in Java.

Display 5.12   Class Type Variables Store a Reference

```
public class ToyClass
{
        private String name;
        private int number;
```
*The complete definition of the class
ToyClass is given in Display 5.11.*

```
ToyClass sampleVariable;
```
*Creates the variable sampleVariable in
memory but assigns it no value.*

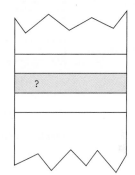

sampleVariable

```
sampleVariable =
        new ToyClass("Josephine Student", 42);
```
*Creates an object, places the object someplace in memory, and then
places the address of the object in the variable sampleVariable. We
do not know what the address of the object is, but let's assume it is
2056. The exact number does not matter.*

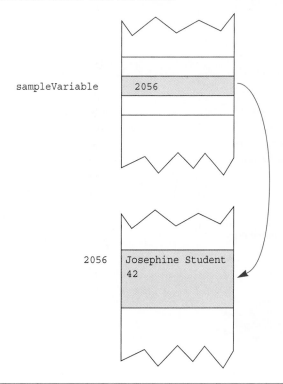

*For emphasis, we made the
arrow point to the memory
location referenced.*

Display 5.13 Assignment Operator with Class Type Variables (part 1 of 2)

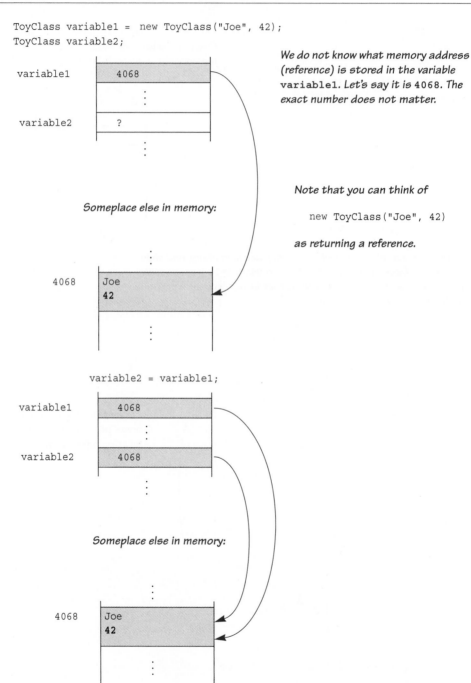

```
ToyClass variable1 = new ToyClass("Joe", 42);
ToyClass variable2;
```

variable1   4068

variable2   ?

We do not know what memory address (reference) is stored in the variable variable1. *Let's say it is* 4068. *The exact number does not matter.*

Someplace else in memory:

Note that you can think of

```
new ToyClass("Joe", 42)
```

as returning a reference.

4068   Joe
              42

```
variable2 = variable1;
```

variable1   4068

variable2   4068

Someplace else in memory:

4068   Joe
              42

Display 5.13   Assignment Operator with Class Type Variables (part 2 of 2)

```
variable2.set("Josephine", 1);
```

Note that when you use the assignment operator with variables of a class type, you are assigning a reference (memory address), so the result of the following is to make `variable1` and `variable2` two names for the same object:

assignment with variables of a class type

```
variable2 = variable1;
```

A variable of a class type stores a memory address, and a memory address is a number. However, a variable of a class type cannot be used like a variable of a number type, such as `int` or `double`. This is intentional. The important property of a memory address is that it identifies a memory location. The fact that the implementors used numbers, rather than letters or strings or something else, to name memory locations is an accidental property. Java prevents you from using this accidental property to stop you from doing things such as obtaining access to restricted memory or otherwise screwing up the computer.

Class Parameters

Strictly speaking, all parameters in Java are call-by-value parameters. This means that when an argument is plugged in for a parameter (of any type), the argument is evaluated and the value obtained is used to initialize the value of the parameter. (Recall that a parameter is really a local variable.) However, in the case of a parameter of a class type, the value plugged in is a reference (memory address), which makes class parameters behave quite differently from parameters of a primitive type.

Recall that the following makes variable1 and variable2 two names for the same object:

```
ToyClass variable1 = new ToyClass("Joe", 42);
ToyClass variable2;
variable2 = variable1;
```

So, any change made to variable2 is, in fact, made to variable1. The same thing happens with parameters of a class type. The parameter is a local variable that is set equal to the value of its argument. But if its argument is a variable of a class type, this copies a reference into the parameter. So, the parameter becomes another name for the argument, and any change made to the object named by the parameter is made to the object named by the argument, because they are the same object. Thus, a method can change the instance variables of an object given as an argument. A simple program to illustrate this is given in Display 5.14. Display 5.15 contains a diagram of the computer's memory as the program in Display 5.14 is executed.

Many programming languages have a parameter passing mechanism known as *call-by-reference*. If you are familiar with call-by-reference parameters, we should note that the Java parameter passing mechanism is similar to, but is not exactly the same as, call-by-reference.

Display 5.14   **Parameters of a Class Type**

ToyClass *is defined in Display 5.11.*

```
1  public class ClassParameterDemo
2  {
3      public static void main(String[] args)
4      {
5          ToyClass anObject = new ToyClass("Mr. Cellophane", 0);
6          System.out.println(anObject);
7          System.out.println(
8                  "Now we call changer with anObject as argument.");
9          ToyClass.changer(anObject);
10         System.out.println(anObject);
11     }
12 }
```

Notice that the method changer *changed the instance variables in the object* anObject.

Sample Dialogue

```
Mr. Cellophane 0
Now we call changer with anObject as argument.
Hot Shot 42
```

Differences Between Primitive and Class-Type Parameters

A method cannot change the value of a variable of a primitive type that is an argument to the method. On the other hand, a method can change the values of the instance variables of an argument of a class type. This is illustrated in Display 5.16.

Display 5.15   Memory Picture for Display 5.14 (part 1 of 2)

We do not know what memory address (reference) is stored in the variable anObject. *Let's say it is 3078. The exact number does not matter.*

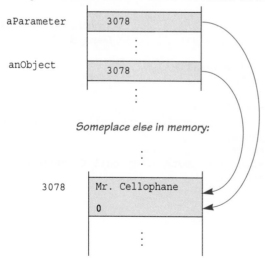

(continued)

Display 5.15   Memory Picture for Display 5.14 (part 2 of 2)

```
ToyClass.changer(anObject); is executed
and so the following are executed:
  aParameter.name = "Hot Shot";
  aParameter.number = 42;
As a result, anObject is changed.
```

aParameter   3078

anObject   3078

Someplace else in memory:

3078   Hot Shot
            42

Display 5.16   Comparing Parameters of a Class Type and a Primitive Type (part 1 of 2)

```
1  public class ParametersDemo
2  {
3      public static void main(String[] args)
4      {
5          ToyClass2 object1 = new ToyClass2(),
6                    object2 = new ToyClass2();
7          object1.set("Scorpius",1);
8          object2.set("John Crichton", 2);
9          System.out.println("Value of object2 before call to method:");
10         System.out.println(object2);
11         object1.makeEqual(object2);
12         System.out.println("Value of object2 after call to method:");
13         System.out.println(object2);
14
```

ToyClass2 is defined in Display 5.17.

Display 5.16   Comparing Parameters of a Class Type and a Primitive Type (part 2 of 2)

```
15          int aNumber = 42;
16          System.out.println("Value of aNumber before call to method:"
17                          + aNumber);
18          object1.tryToMakeEqual(aNumber);
19          System.out.println("Value of aNumber after call to method:"
20                          + aNumber);
21      }
22  }
```

Sample Dialogue

```
Value of object2 before call to method:
John Crichton 2  ◄──────────────            An argument of a class type
Value of object2 after call to method:       can change.
Scorpius 1  ◄──────────
Value of aNumber before call to method: 42  ◄──────   An argument of a primitive
Value of aNumber after call to method: 42  ◄──────    type cannot change.
```

PITFALL: Use of = and == with Variables of a Class Type

You have already seen that the assignment operator used with variables of a class type produces two variables that name the same object, which is very different from how assignment behaves with variables of a primitive type.

== with variables of a class type

The test for equality using == with variables of a class type also behaves in what may seem like a peculiar way. The operator == does not check that the objects have the same values for their instance variables. It merely checks for equality of memory addresses, so two objects in two different locations in memory would test as being "not equal" when compared using ==, even if their instance variables contain equivalent data. For example, consider the following code. (The class ToyClass2 is defined in Display 5.17.)

```
ToyClass2 variable1 = new ToyClass2("Chiana", 3),
          variable2 = new ToyClass2("Chiana", 3);
if (variable1 == variable2)
    System.out.println("Equal using ==");
else
    System.out.println("Not equal using ==");
```

This code will produce the output

```
Not equal using ==
```

(continued)

PITFALL: (continued)

Even though these two variables name objects that are intuitively equal, they are stored in two different locations in the computer's memory. This is why you usually use an `equals` method to compare objects of a class type. The variables `variable1` and `variable2` would be considered "equal" if compared using the `equals` method as defined for the class `ToyClass2` (Display 5.17). ■

Display 5.17   A Toy Class to Use in Display 5.16

```
1   public class ToyClass2
2   {
3       private String name;
4       private int number;

5       public void set(String newName, int newNumber)
6       {
7           name = newName;
8           number = newNumber;
9       }

10      public String toString()
11      {
12          return (name + " " + number);
13      }

14      public void makeEqual(ToyClass2 anObject)
15      {
16          anObject.name = this .name;
17          anObject.number = this .number;
18      }

19      public void tryToMakeEqual(int aNumber)
20      {
21          aNumber = this .number;
22      }

23      public boolean equals(ToyClass2 otherObject)
24      {
25          return ( (name.equals(otherObject.name))
26                  && (number == otherObject.number) );
27      }
```

Read the text for a discussion of the problem with this method.

<Other methods can be the same as in Display 5.11, although no other methods are needed or used in the current discussion.>

```
28  }
```

Self-Test Exercises

27. What is a reference type? Are class types reference types? Are primitive types (such as `int`) reference types?

28. When comparing two objects of a class type to see if they are "equal" or not, should you use `==` or the method `equals`?

29. When comparing two objects of a primitive type (such as `int`) to see if they are "equal" or not, should you use `==` or the method `equals`?

30. Can a method with an argument of a class type change the values of the instance variables in the object named by the argument? For example, if the argument is of type `ToyClass` defined in Display 5.11, can the method change the `name` of its argument?

31. Suppose a method has a parameter of type `int` and the method is given an `int` variable as an argument. Could the method have been defined so that it changes the value of the variable given as an argument?

The Constant `null`

null

The constant `null` is a special constant that may be assigned to a variable of any class type. It is used to indicate that the variable has no "real value." If the compiler insists that you initialize a variable of a class type and there is no suitable object with which to initialize it, you can use the value `null`, as in the following example:

```
YourClass yourObject = null;
```

It is also common to use `null` in constructors to initialize instance variables of a class type when there is no obvious object to use. We will eventually see other uses for the constant `null`.

Note that `null` is not an object. It is like a reference (memory address) that does not refer to any object (does not name any memory location). So if you want to test whether a class variable contains `null`, you use `==` or `!=`; you do not use an `equals` method. For example, the following correctly tests for `null`:

```
if (yourObject == null)
    System.out.println("No real object here.");
```

`null`

`null` is a special constant that can be used to give a value to any variable of any class type. The constant `null` is not an object but a sort of placeholder for a reference to an object. Because it is like a reference (memory address), use `==` and `!=` rather than the method `equals` when you test to see whether a variable contains `null`.

PITFALL: Null Pointer Exception

If the compiler asks you to initialize a class variable, you can always initialize the variable to `null`. However, `null` is not an object, so you cannot invoke a method using a variable that is initialized to `null`. If you try, you will get an error message that says "Null Pointer Exception." For example, the following code would produce a "Null Pointer Exception" if it were included in a program:

```
ToyClass2 aVariable = null;
String representation = aVariable.toString();
```

The problem is that you are trying to invoke the method `toString()` using `null` as a calling object. But `null` is not an object; it is just a placeholder. So `null` has no methods. Because you are using `null` incorrectly, the error message reads "Null Pointer Exception." You get this error message any time a class variable has not been assigned a (reference to an) object, even if you have not assigned `null` to the variable. Any time you get a "Null Pointer Exception," look for an uninitialized class variable.

The way to correct the problem is to use `new` to create a class object, as follows:

```
ToyClass2 aVariable = new ToyClass2("Chiana", 3);
String representation = aVariable.toString();
```
■

The `new` Operator and Anonymous Objects

Consider an expression such as the following, where `ToyClass` is defined in Display 5.11:

```
ToyClass variable1 = new ToyClass("Joe", 42);
```

As illustrated in Display 5.13, the portion `new ToyClass("Joe", 42)` is an invocation of a constructor. You can think of the constructor as returning a reference to the location in memory of the object created by the constructor. If you take this view, the equal sign in this line of code is just an ordinary assignment operator.

There are times when you create an object using `new` and use the object as an argument to a method, but then never again use the object. In such cases, you need not give the object a variable name. You can instead use the expression with the `new` operator and the constructor directly as the argument. For example, suppose you want to test to see whether the object in `variable1` (in the earlier line of code) is equal to an object with the same number and with the name spelled in all uppercase letters. You can do so as follows:

```
if (variable1.equals(new ToyClass("JOE", 42)))
    System.out.println("Equal");
else
    System.out.println("Not equal");
```

This is equivalent to the following:

```
ToyClass temp = new ToyClass("JOE", 42);
if (variable1.equals(temp))
    System.out.println("Equal");
else
    System.out.println("Not equal");
```

In the second version, the object is created, and its reference is placed in the variable temp. Then temp is plugged in for the parameter in the equals method. But all the parameter passing mechanism does is to take the reference stored in temp and plug it into the parameter for equals. The first version simplifies the process. It creates the reference to the object and directly plugs it into the parameter in equals. It bypasses the variable temp but ends up plugging in the same reference as the argument to equals.

When not assigned to a variable, an expression such as

```
new ToyClass("JOE", 42)
```

anonymous object

is known as an **anonymous object**. It evaluates a reference to an object of the class. It is called *anonymous* because the object is not assigned a variable to serve as its name. We will eventually encounter situations where the use of such anonymous objects is common.

Anonymous Objects

An expression with a new operator and a constructor creates a new object and returns a reference to the object. If this reference is not assigned to a variable, but instead the expression with new and the constructor is used as an argument to some method, then the object produced is called an **anonymous object**.

EXAMPLE
```
if (variable1.equals(new ToyClass("JOE", 42)))
    System.out.println("Equal");
else
    System.out.println("Not equal");
```

The expression new ToyClass("JOE", 42) (or more exactly, the object it creates) is an example of an anonymous object.

EXAMPLE: Another Approach to Keyboard Input ★

This example uses the class StringTokenizer, which was covered in a starred section of Chapter 4. If you have not yet studied the StringTokenizer class, you may omit this example until you have done so.

The program in Display 5.18 is an example of the use of both the StringTokenizer class and the method Double.parseDouble to read multiple values of type double entered on a single line and separated with something other than whitespace.

(continued)

EXAMPLE: (continued)

The entire line is read as a single long string using the method nextLine of the Scanner class. The long string is decomposed into tokens using the class StingTokenizer. The tokens are the numbers that were input, but they are in the form of string values, not values of type double. Finally, the tokens are converted to values of type double using the method Double.parseDouble.

Note that the String variables are initialized to null. If you omit the nulls, the compiler will complain that the variables string1 and string2 might not be initialized before they are used. The compiler is incorrect but it does no good to argue with it. Including null as initial values for the variables string1 and string2 will keep the compiler happy and allow you to run the program.

Display 5.18   Use of the Method Double.parseDouble (part 1 of 2)

```
1    import java.util.Scanner;
2    import java.util.StringTokenizer;

3    public class InputExample
4    {
5        public static void main(String[] args)
6        {
7            Scanner keyboard = new Scanner(System.in);

8            System.out.println("Enter two numbers on a line.");
9            System.out.println("Place a comma between the numbers.");
10           System.out.println("Extra blank space is OK.");
11           String inputLine = keyboard.nextLine();

12           String delimiters = ", "; //Comma and blank space
13           StringTokenizer numberFactory =
14               new StringTokenizer(inputLine, delimiters);

15           String string1 = null;
16           String string2 = null;
17           if (numberFactory.countTokens() >= 2)
18           {
19               string1 = numberFactory.nextToken();
20               string2 = numberFactory.nextToken();
21           }
22           else
23           {
24               System.out.println("Fatal Error.");
25               System.exit(0);
26           }
```

Display 5.18   Use of the Method `Double.parseDouble` (part 2 of 2)

```
27          double number1 = Double.parseDouble(string1);
28          double number2 = Double.parseDouble(string2);

29          System.out.print("You input ");
30          System.out.println(number1 + " and " + number2);
31      }
32  }
```

Sample Dialogue

```
Enter two numbers on a line.
Place a comma between the numbers.
Extra blank space is OK.
    41.98, 42
You input is 41.98 and 42.0
```

 MyProgrammingLab™

Self-Test Exercises

32. What is wrong with a program that starts as follows? The class `ToyClass` is defined in Display 5.11.

    ```
    ToyClass anObject = null ;
    anObject.set("Josephine", 42);
    ```

33. What is the type of the constant `null`?

34. Suppose `aVariable` is a variable of a class type. Which of the following correctly tests to see whether `aVariable` contains `null`?

    ```
    aVariable.equals(null)
    aVariable == null
    ```

35. Is the following legal in Java? The class `ToyClass` is defined in Display 5.11.

    ```
    System.out.println(new ToyClass("Mr. Cellophane", 0));
    ```

TIP: Use Static Imports ★

You have already seen `import` statements, such as the following from Display 5.9:

```
import java.util.Scanner;
```

**static `import`
statement**

There is another form of `import` statement which, while not essential, can be a convenience. These are called **static `import` statements** and are best explained with an example.

(continued)

TIP: (continued)

It would be convenient to be able to write static method invocations in the following simple form:

```
toUpperCase(firstCharacter)
```

instead of having to write the following longer version (taken from Display 5.9):

```
Character.toUpperCase(firstCharacter)
```

If you add the following static `import` statement to the start of your program, you can then write the invocation of `toUpperCase` in the desired shorter way:

```
import static java.lang.Character.toUpperCase;
```

The class `Character` is in the Java package `java.lang`. Note that you need to give the package name as well as the class name, just as you did with ordinary `import` statements, such as the above `import` statement for the class `Scanner` in the `java.util` package.

The package `java.lang` is imported automatically. So you can, for example, use the method `Character.toUpperCase` without any `import` statement of any kind. But note that there is nothing special about the package `java.lang` when it comes to static import statements. If you want to use the abbreviated form `toUpperCase`, you must give a static `import` statement.

If you use the following form of the static `import` statement, then your code can use the name of any static method in the class `Character` without the preface of `Character` and a dot.

```
import static java.lang.Character.*;
```

For example, consider the program in Display 5.9. If you replace

```
import java.util.Scanner;
```

with either

```
import java.util.Scanner;
import static java.lang.Character.toUpperCase;
```

or

```
import java.util.Scanner;
import static java.lang.Character.*;
```

then you can change the statement

```
sentence = Character.toUpperCase(firstCharacter)
                                   + sentence.substring(1);
```

to

TIP: (continued)

```
sentence = toUpperCase(firstCharacter)
                    + sentence.substring(1);
```

One word of warning: This works for static methods only. This does not in any way apply to ordinary nonstatic methods.

extra code on website

The program `StaticImportDemo.java` on the accompanying website redoes the program in Display 5.9 using a static `import` statement in this way.

You can, of course, do this with `Character` replaced by any other class, and then you can use static methods in that class without the need to preface the method name with the class name and a dot.

static `import` of constants

You can use static `import` statements for constants as well as methods. If you want to use `PI` instead of `Math.PI` in the program in Display 5.7, just include one of the following `import` statements at the beginning of the program file:

```
import static java.lang.Math.PI;
```

or

```
import static java.lang.Math.*;
```

extra code on website

The program `StaticImportDemo2.java` on the accompanying website redoes the program in Display 5.7 using a static `import` statement in this way. ■

5.3   Using and Misusing References

Loose lips sink ships.

MILITARY SLOGAN

Just as a military campaign requires constant vigilance to ensure that its plans are kept secret, so your programming requires constant vigilance to ensure that private instance variables remain truly private. As we will see, adding the `private` modifier before instance variable declarations is not always all that you need to do. There can be privacy leaks in a poorly designed class just as there can be privacy leaks in a military campaign.

The material in this section is important but more subtle and harder to digest than the material we have seen before now. If you want, you may postpone reading this section until you have had more practice defining and using classes. You do not need the material in this section to understand Section 5.4.

EXAMPLE: A Person Class

It is common to have instance variables of a class type. The class `Person` defined in Display 5.19 has two instance variables of type `Date`. So, the class `Person` has instance variables of a class type. (The class `Date` was defined in Chapter 4, Display 4.11. We have reproduced the relevant portions of the date class definition in Display 5.20.) In fact, all the instance variables for the class `Person` are of class types. An object of the class `Person` has the basic data about people that is found in such places as on tombstones and in author listings in library catalogues. It describes a person by giving the person's name, date of birth, and date of death. If the person is still alive, then the value `null` is used as the date of death. (So `null` is good.) A simple program illustrating the class `Person` is given in Display 5.21. We will discuss a few details about the class `Person` here, but most of the various methods in the class `Person` will be discussed as we cover the corresponding topic in the following subsections.

Normally, a class definition should include a no-argument constructor. However, there are cases where a no-argument constructor makes little sense. For example, the wrapper classes such as `Integer` and `Double` do not have no-argument constructors, as we explained in the Pitfall subsection "A Wrapper Class Does Not Have a No-Argument Constructor," which appeared earlier in this chapter. The class `Person` also does not have a no-argument constructor for a reason. A person may have no date of death, but a person always has a date of birth. A no-argument constructor should initialize all instance variables, but there is no suitable value to initialize the instance variable `born` unless it is provided as an argument to the constructor. In particular, it makes no sense to initialize the instance variable `born` to `null`; that would indicate that the person was never born. It makes little sense to have a person who was never born, so it makes little sense to have a no-argument constructor for the class `Person`. Note that because we defined some constructors for the class `Person` but did not define a no-argument constructor, it follows that the class `Person` does not have a no-argument constructor.

Since we are assuming that an object of the class `Person` always has a birth date (which is not `null`), the following should always be true of an object of the class `Person`:

An object of the class `Person` has a date of birth (which is not `null`), and if the object has a date of death, then the date of death is equal to or later than the date of birth.

If you check the definition of the class `Person`, you will see that this statement is always true. It is true of every object created by a constructor, and all the other methods preserve the truth of this statement. In fact, the private method `consistent` was designed to provide a check for this property. A statement, such as the above, that is always true for every object of the class is called a **class invariant**.

Note that the definition of `equals` for the class `Person` includes an invocation of `equals` for the class `String` and an invocation of the method `equals` for the class `Date`. Java determines which `equals` method is being invoked from the type of its calling object. Because the instance variable `name` is of type `String`, the invocation `name.equals(...)` is an invocation of the method `equals` for the class `String`. Because the instance variable `born` is of type `Date`, the invocation `born.equals(...)` is an invocation of the method `equals` for the class `Date`.

Similarly, the definition of the method `toString` for the class `Person` includes invocations of the method `toString` for the class `Date`.

Display 5.19   **A Person Class** (part 1 of 5)

```
1   /**
2   Class for a person with a name and dates for birth and death.
3   Class invariant: A Person always has a date of birth, and if the Person
4   has a date of death, then the date of death is equal to or later than the
5   date of birth.
6   */
7   public class Person
8   {
9       private String name;
10      private Date born;
11      private Date died; //null indicates still alive.

12      public Person(String initialName, Date birthDate, Date deathDate)
13      {
14          if (consistent(birthDate, deathDate))
15          {
16              name = initialName;
17              born = new Date(birthDate);
18              if (deathDate == null)
19                  died = null;
20              else
21                  died = new Date(deathDate);
22          }
23          else
24          {
25              System.out.println("Inconsistent dates.Aborting.");
26              System.exit(0);
27          }
28      }

29      public Person(Person original)
30      {
31          if (original == null )
32          {
33              System.out.println("Fatal error.");
34              System.exit(0);
35          }

36          name = original.name;
37          born = new Date(original.born);

38          if (original.died == null)
39              died = null;
40          else
41              died = new Date(original.died);
42      }
```

*The class **Date** was defined in Display 4.11 and many of the details are repeated in Display 5.20.*

*We will discuss **Date** and the significance of these constructor invocations later in this chapter in the subsection entitled "Copy Constructors."*

— *Copy constructor.*

(continued)

Display 5.19   **A Person Class** (part 2 of 5)

```
43      public void set(String newName, Date birthDate, Date deathDate)
        <Definition of this method is Self Test Exercise 4.1>

44      public String toString()
45      {
46          String diedString;
47          if (died == null)
48              diedString = ""; //Empty string
49          else
50              diedString = died.toString();

51          return (name + ", " + born + "-" + diedString);
52      }

53      public boolean equals(Person otherPerson)
54      {
55          if (otherPerson == null)
56              return false;
57          else
58              return (name.equals(otherPerson.name)
59                      && born.equals(otherPerson.born)
60                      && datesMatch(died, otherPerson.died) );
61      }

62      /**
63      To match, date1 and date2 must either be the same date or must both be null.
64      */
65      private static boolean datesMatch(Date date1, Date date2)
66      {
67          if (date1 == null)
68              return (date2 == null);
69          else if (date2 == null) //&& date1 != null
70              return false ;
71          else //both dates are not null.
72              return (date1.equals(date2));
73      }

74      /**
75       Precondition: newDate is a consistent date of birth.
76       Postcondition: Date of birth of the calling object is newDate.
77      */
78      public void setBirthDate(Date newDate)
79      {
80          if (consistent(newDate, died))
81              born = new Date(newDate);
82          else
```

This is the **toString** *method of the class* **Date**.

This is equivalent to **born.toString( )**.

This is the **equals** *method for the class* **String**.

This is the **equals** *method for the class* **Date**.

Display 5.19   **A Person Class** (part 3 of 5)

```
83             {
84                  System.out.println("Inconsistent dates. Aborting.");
85                  System.exit(0);
86             }
87         }

88     /**
89      Precondition: newDate is a consistent date of death.
90      Postcondition: Date of death of the calling object is newDate.
91     */
92     public void setDeathDate(Date newDate)
93         {
94
95         if (!consistent(born, newDate))
96             {
97                  System.out.println("Inconsistent dates. Aborting.");
98                  System.exit(0);
99             }
100
101        if (newDate == null)
102             died = null ;
103        else
104             died = new Date(newDate);
105        }

106    public void setName(String newName)
107        {
108        name = newName;
109        }

110    /**
111     Precondition: The date of birth has been set, and changing the year
112     part of the date of birth will give a consistent date of birth.
113     Postcondition: The year of birth is (changed to) newYear.
114    */
115    public void setBirthYear(int newYear)
116        {
117        if (born == null) //Precondition is violated.
118            {
119                 System.out.println("Fatal Error. Aborting.");
120                 System.exit(0);
121            }
122        born.setYear(newYear);
123        if (!consistent(born, died))
124            {
125                 System.out.println("Inconsistent dates. Aborting.");
126                 System.exit(0);
127            }
128        }
```

The date of death can be **null**. *However, there is no corresponding code in* **setBirthDate** *because the method* consistent *ensures that the date of* **birth** *is never* **null**.

(continued)

Display 5.19 **A Person Class** (part 4 of 5)

```
129     /**
130      Precondition: The date of death has been set, and changing the year
131      part of the date of death will give a consistent date of death.
132      Postcondition: The year of death is (changed to) newYear.
133     */
134     public void setDeathYear(int newYear)
135     {
136         if (died == null) //Precondition is violated
137         {
138             System.out.println("Fatal Error. Aborting.");
139             System.exit(0);
140         }
141         died.setYear(newYear);
142         if (!consistent(born, died))
143         {
144             System.out.println("Inconsistent dates. Aborting.");
145             System.exit(0);
146         }
147     }

148     public String getName()
149     {
150         return name;
151     }

152     public Date getBirthDate()
153     {
154         return new Date(born);
155     }

156     public Date getDeathDate()
157     {
158         if (died == null)
159             return null;
160         else
161             return new Date(died);
162     }

163     /**
164      To be consistent, birthDate must not be null. If there is no date of
165      death (deathDate == null), that is consistent with any birthDate.
166      Otherwise, the birthDate must come before or be equal to the
         deathDate.
167     */
```

Display 5.19   **A Person Class** (part 5 of 5)

```
168     private static boolean consistent(Date birthDate, Date deathDate)
169     {
170         if (birthDate == null)
171             return false;
172         else if (deathDate == null)
173             return true;
174         else
175             return (birthDate.precedes(deathDate)
176                         || birthDate.equals(deathDate));
177     }
178 }
```

Class Invariant

A statement that is always true for every object of the class is called a **class invariant**. A class invariant can help to define a class in a consistent and organized way.

PITFALL: `null` Can Be an Argument to a Method

If a method has a parameter of a class type, then `null` can be used as the corresponding argument when the method is invoked. Sometimes using `null` as an argument can be the result of an error, but it can sometimes be an intentional argument. For example, the class `Person` (Display 5.19) uses `null` for a date of death to indicate that the person is still alive. So `null` is sometimes a perfectly normal argument for methods such as `consistent`. Method definitions should account for `null` as a possible argument and not assume the method always receives a true object to plug in for a class parameter.

Notice the definition of the method `equals` for the class `Person`. A test for equality has the form

```
object1.equals(object2)
```

The calling object `object1` must be a true object of the class `Person`; a calling object cannot be `null`. However, the argument `object2` can be either a true object or `null`. If the argument is `null`, then `equals` should return `false`, because a true object cannot reasonably be considered to be equal to `null`. In fact, the Java documentation specifies that when the argument to an `equals` method is `null`, the `equals` method should return `false`. Notice that our definition does return `false` when the argument is `null`. ∎

Display 5.20 **The Class Date (Partial Definition)** (part 1 of 2)

```
1   public class Date
2   {
3       private String month;
4       private int day;
5       private int year; //A four digit number.

6       public Date(String monthString, int day, int year)
7       {
8           setDate (monthString, day, year);
9       }

10      public Date(Date aDate)
11      {
12          if (aDate == null) //Not a real date.
13          {
14              System.out.println("Fatal Error.");
15              System.exit(0);
16          }

17          month = aDate.month;
18          day = aDate.day;
19          year = aDate.year;
20      }

21      public void setDate(String monthString, int day, int year)
22      {
23          if (dateOK(monthString, day, year))
24          {
25              this.month = monthString;
26              this.day = day;
27              this.year = year;
28          }
29          else
30          {
31              System.out.println("Fatal Error");
32              System.exit(0);
33          }
34      }
35      public void setYear(int year)
36      {
37          if ( (year < 1000) || (year > 9999) )
38          {
```

This is not a complete definition of the class Date. The complete definition of the class Date is in Display 4.11, but this has the details that are important to what we are discussing in this chapter.

Copy constructor.

The method dateOK checks that the date is a legitimate date, such as not having more than 31 days.

Display 5.20   **The Class** Date **(Partial Definition) (part 2 of 2)**

```
39                System.out.println("Fatal Error");
40                System.exit(0);
41          }
42        else
43                this.year = year;
44      }
45      public String toString()
46              ...
47      public boolean equals(Date otherDate)
48              ....
49      /**
50        Returns true if the calling object date is before otherDate (in time).
51      */
52      public boolean precedes(Date otherDate)
53              ...
54      private boolean dateOK(String monthString, int dayInt, int yearInt)
55              ...

56  }
```

The complete definition of equals *is given later in this chapter in the answer to Self-Test Exercise 37, and is a better version than the one given in Chapter 4.*

These methods have the obvious meanings. If you need to see a full definition, see Display 4.11 in Chapter 4 and Self-Test Exercise 37 later in this chapter.

Self-Test Exercises

36. What is the difference between the following two pieces of code? The first piece appears in Display 5.21.

```
Person adams =
            new Person("John Adams",
                    new Date("February", 15, 1947), null);
//Second piece is below:

Date theDate = new Date("February", 15, 1947);
Person adams = new Person("John Adams", theDate, null);
```

37. When we defined the class Date in Chapter 4 (Display 4.11), we had not yet discussed null. So, the definition of equals given there did not account for the possibility that the argument could be null. Rewrite the definition of equals for the class Date to account for the possibility that the argument might be null.

Display 5.21   Demonstrating the Class `Person`

```
1   public class PersonDemo
2   {
3       public static void main(String[]args)
4       {
5           Person bach =
6               new Person("Johann Sebastian Bach",
7                   new Date("March", 21, 1685), new Date("July", 28, 1750));
8           Person stravinsky =
9               new Person("Igor Stravinsky",
10                  new Date("June", 17, 1882), new Date("April", 6, 1971));
11          Person adams =
12              new Person("John Adams",
13                  new Date("February", 15, 1947), null );

14          System.out.println("A Short List of Composers:");
15          System.out.println(bach);
16          System.out.println(stravinsky);
17          System.out.println(adams);

18          Person bachTwin = new Person(bach);
19          System.out.println("Comparing bach and bachTwin:");
20          if (bachTwin == bach)
21              System.out.println("Same reference for both.");
22          else
23              System.out.println("Distinct copies.");

24          if (bachTwin.equals(bach))
25              System.out.println("Same data.");
26          else
27              System.out.println("Not same data.");
28      }
29  }
```

Sample Dialogue

```
A Short List of Composers:
Johann Sebastian Bach, March 21, 1685-July 28, 1750
Igor Stravinsky, June 17, 1882-April 6, 1971
John Adams, February 15, 1947-
Comparing bach and bachTwin:
Distinct copies.
Same data.
```

Copy Constructors

copy
constructor

A **copy constructor** is a constructor with a single argument of the same type as the class. The copy constructor should create an object that is a separate, independent object but with the instance variables set so that it is an exact copy of the argument object.

For example, Display 5.20 reproduces the copy constructor for the class Date defined in Display 4.11. The copy constructor, or any other constructor, creates a new object of the class Date. This happens automatically and is not shown in the code for the copy constructor. The code for the copy constructor then goes on to set the instance variables to the values equal to those of its one parameter, aDate. But the new date created is a separate object even though it represents the same date. Consider the following code:

```
Date date1 = new Date("January", 1, 2006);
Date date2 = new Date(date1);
```

After this code is executed, both date1 and date2 represent the date January 1, 2006, but they are two different objects. So, if we change one of these objects, it will not change the other. For example, consider

```
date2.setDate("July", 4, 1776);
System.out.println(date1);
```

The output produced is

```
January 1, 2006
```

When we changed date2, we did not change date1. This may not be a difficult or even subtle point, but it is critically important to much of what we discuss in this section of the chapter. (See Self-Test Exercise 39 in this chapter to see the copy constructor contrasted with the assignment operator.)

Now let's consider the copy constructor for the class Person (Display 5.19), which is a bit more complicated. It is reproduced in what follows:

```
public Person(Person original)
{
    if (original == null)
    {
        System.out.println("Fatal error.");
        System.exit(0);
    }
    name = original.name;
    born = new Date(original.born);
    if (original.died == null)
        died = null;
    else
        died = new Date(original.died);
}
```

We want the object created to be an independent copy of `original`. That would not happen if we had used the following instead:

```
public Person(Person original) //Unsafe
{
    if (original == null )
    {
        System.out.println("Fatal error.");
        System.exit(0);
    }
    name = original.name;
    born = original.born; //Not good.
    died = original.died; //Not good.
}
```

Although this alternate definition looks innocent enough and may work fine in many situations, it does have serious problems.

Assume we had used the unsafe version of the copy constructor instead of the one in Display 5.19. The "Not good." code simply copies references from `original.born` and `original.died` to the corresponding arguments of the object being created by the constructor. So, the object created is not an independent copy of the `original` object. For example, consider the code

```
Person original =
        new Person("Natalie Dressed",
        new Date("April", 1, 1984), null);
Person copy = new Person(original);
copy.setBirthYear(1800);
System.out.println(original);
```

The output would be

```
Natalie Dressed, April 1, 1800-
```

When we changed the birth year in the object `copy`, we also changed the birth year in the object `original`. This is because we are using our unsafe version of the copy constructor. Both `original.born` and `copy.born` contain the same reference to the same `Date` object.

This all happens because we used the unsafe version of the copy constructor. Fortunately, here we use a safer version of the copy constructor that sets the `born` instance variables as follows:

```
born = new Date(original.born);
```

which is equivalent to

```
this.born = new Date(original.born);
```

This version, which we did use, makes the instance variable `this.born` an independent `Date` object that represents the same date as `original.born`. So if you change a date in the `Person` object created by the copy constructor, you will not change that date in the `original Person` object.

Note that if a class, such as `Person`, has instance variables of a class type, such as the instance variables `born` and `died`, then to define a correct copy constructor for the class `Person`, you must already have copy constructors for the class `Date` of the instance variables. The easiest way to ensure this for all your classes is to always include a copy constructor in every class you define.

Copy Constructor

A **copy constructor** is a constructor with one parameter of the same type as the class. A copy constructor should be designed so the object it creates is intuitively an exact copy of its parameter, but a completely independent copy. See Displays 5.19 and 5.20 for examples of copy constructors.

---

clone

The Java documentation says to use a method named `clone` instead of a copy constructor, and, as you will see later in this book, there are situations where the copy constructor will not work as desired and you need the `clone` method. However, we do not yet have enough background to delve into this method.(It is discussed later in this book in Chapters 8 and 13.) Despite the Java documentation, many excellent programmers prefer to sometimes use copy constructors. In this book, we will use both copy constructors and the clone method.

PITFALL: Privacy Leaks

leaking accessor methods

Consider the accessor method `getBirthDate` for the class `Person` (Display 5.19), which we reproduce in what follows:

```java
public Date getBirthDate()
{
    return new Date(born);
}
```

Do not make the mistake of defining the accessor method as follows:

```java
public Date getBirthDate() //Unsafe
{
    return born; //Not good
}
```

(continued)

Assume we had used the unsafe version of getBirthDate instead of the one in Display 5.19. It would then be possible for a program that uses the class Person to change the private instance variable born to any date whatsoever and bypass the checks in constructor and mutator methods of the class Person. For example, consider the following code, which might appear in some program that uses the class Person:

```
Person citizen = new Person(
"Joe Citizen", new Date("January", 1, 1900), new Date("January", 1,
    1990));
Date dateName = citizen.getBirthDate();
dateName.setDate("April", 1, 3000);
```

This code changes the date of birth so it is after the date of death (an impossibility in the universe as we know it). This citizen was not born until after he or she died! This sort of situation is known as a **privacy leak**, because it allows a programmer to circumvent the private modifier before an instance variable such as born, and to change the private instance variable to anything whatsoever.

privacy leak

The following code would be illegal in our program:

```
citizen.born.setDate("April", 1, 3000); //Illegal
```

This is illegal because born is a private instance variable. However, with the unsafe version of getBirthDate (and we are now assuming that we did use the unsafe version), the variable dateName contains the same reference as citizen.born and so the following is legal and equivalent to the illegal statement:

```
dateName.setDate("April", 1, 3000); //Legal and equivalent to
    //illegal statement.
```

It is as if you have a friend named Robert who is also known as Bob. Some bully wants to beat up Robert, so you say "You cannot beat up Robert." The bully says "OK, I will not beat up Robert, but I will beat up Bob." Bob and Robert are two names for the same person. So, if you protect Robert but do not protect Bob, you have really accomplished nothing.

This is all if we used the unsafe version of getBirthDate, which simply returns the reference in the private instance variable born. Fortunately, here we use a safer version of getBirthDate, which has the following return statement:

```
return new Date(born);
```

This `return` statement does not return the reference in the private instance variable `born`. Instead, it uses the copy constructor to return a reference to a new object that is an exact copy of the object named by `born`. If the copy is changed, that has no effect on the date whose reference is in the instance variable `born`. Thus, a privacy leak is avoided.

leaking mutator methods

Note that returning a reference is not the only possible source of privacy leaks. A privacy leak can also arise from an incorrectly defined constructor or mutator method. Notice the definition for the method `setBirthDate` in Display 5.19 and reproduced as follows:

```
public void setBirthDate(Date newDate)
{
    if (consistent(newDate, died))
        born = new Date(newDate);
    else
    {
        System.out.println("Inconsistent dates. Aborting.");
        System.exit(0);
    }
}
```

Note that the instance variable `born` is set to a copy of the parameter `newDate`. Suppose that instead of

```
born = new Date(newDate);
```

we simply use

```
born = newDate;
```

And suppose we use the following code in some program:

```
Person personObject = new Person(
    "Josephine", new Date("January", 1, 2000), null);
Date dateName = new Date("February", 2, 2002);
personObject.setBirthDate(dateName);
```

where `personObject` names an object of the class `Person`. The following will change the year part of the `Date` object named by the `born` instance variable of the object `personObject` and will do so without going through the checks in the mutator methods for `Person`:

```
dateName.setYear(1000);
```

(continued)

PITFALL: (continued)

Because `dateName` contains the same reference as the private instance variable born of the object `personObject`, changing the year part of `dateName` changes the year part of the private instance variable born of `personObject`. Not only does this bypass the consistency checks in the mutator method `setBirthDate`, but it also is a likely source of an inadvertent change to the `born` instance variable.

If we define `setBirthDate` as we did in Display 5.19 and as shown in the following, this problem does not happen. (If you do not see this, go through the code step by step and trace what happens.)

```
public void setBirthDate(Date newDate)
{
    if (consistent(newDate, died))
        born = new Date(newDate);
    . . .
```

clone

One final word of warning: Using copy constructors in this manner is not the officially sanctioned way to make copies of an object in Java. The authorized way to is to define a method named `clone`. We will discuss `clone` methods in Chapters 8 and 13. In Chapter 8, we show you that, in some situations, there are advantages to using a `clone` method instead of a copy constructor. In Chapter 13, we describe the official way to define the `clone` method. For what we will be doing until then, a copy constructor will be a very adequate way of creating copies of an object.

MyProgrammingLab™ ## Self Test Exercises

38. What is a copy constructor?

39. What output is produced by the following code?

```
Date date1 = new Date("January", 1, 2006);
Date date2;
date2 = date1;
date2.setDate("July", 4, 1776);
System.out.println(date1);
```

What output is produced by the following code? Only the third line is different from the previous case.

```
Date date1 = new Date("January", 1, 2006);
Date date2;
date2 = new Date(date1);
date2.setDate("July", 4, 1776);
System.out.println(date1);
```

Self Test Exercises

40. What output is produced by the following code?

```
Person original =
                new Person("Natalie Dressed",
                              new Date("April", 1, 1984), null);
Person copy = new Person(original);
copy.setBirthDate(new Date("April", 1, 1800));
System.out.println(original)
```

Mutable and Immutable Classes

Contrast the accessor methods getName and getBirthDate of the class Person (Display 5.19). We reproduce the two methods in what follows:

```
public String getName()
{
    return name;
}
```

```
public Date getBirthDate()
{
    return new Date(born);
}
```

Notice that the method getBirthDate does not simply return the reference in the instance variable born, but instead uses the copy constructor to return a reference to a copy of the birth date object. We already explained why we do this. If we return the reference in the instance variable born, then we can place this reference in a variable of type Date, and that variable could serve as another name for the private instance variable born, which would allow us to violate the privacy of the instance variable born by changing it using a mutator method of the class Date. This is exactly what we discussed in the previous subsection. So why not do something similar in the method getName?

The method getName simply returns the reference in the private instance variable name. So, if we do the following in a program, then the variable nameAlias will be another name for the String object of the private instance variable name:

```
Person citizen = new Person(
"Joe Citizen", new Date("January", 1, 1900), new Date("January",
1, 1990));
String nameAlias = citizen.getName();
```

It looks as though we could use a mutator method from the class String to change the name referenced by nameAlias and so violate the privacy of the instance variable name. Is something wrong? Do we have to rewrite the method getName to use the copy constructor for the class String? No, everything is fine. We cannot use a mutator method with nameAlias because the class String has no mutator methods! The class String contains no methods that change any of the data in a String object.

At first, it may seem as though you can change the data in an object of the class String. What about the string processing we have seen, such as the following?

```
String greeting = "Hello";
greeting = greeting + "friend.";
```

Have we not changed the data in the String object from "Hello" to "Hello friend."? No, we have not. The expression greeting + "friend." does not change the object "Hello"; it creates a new object, so the assignment statement

```
greeting = greeting + "friend.";
```

replaces the reference to "Hello" with a reference to the different String object "Hello friend." The object "Hello" is unchanged. To see that this is true, consider the following code:

```
String greeting = "Hello";
String helloVariable = greeting;
greeting = greeting + "friend.";
System.out.println(helloVariable);
```

This produces the output "Hello". If the object "Hello" had been changed, the output would have been "Hello friend."

immutable

A class that contains no methods (other than constructors) that change any of the data in an object of the class is called an **immutable class**, and objects of the class are called **immutable objects**. The class String is an immutable class. It is perfectly safe to return a reference to an immutable object, because the object cannot be changed in any undesirable way; in fact, it cannot be changed in any way whatsoever.

mutable

A class that contains public mutator methods or other public methods, such as input methods, that can change the data in an object of the class is called a **mutable class**, and objects of the class are called **mutable objects**. The class Date is an example of a mutable class; many, perhaps most, of the classes you define will be mutable classes. As we noted in the Pitfall entitled "Privacy Leaks" (but using other words): You should never write a method that returns a mutable object, but should instead use a copy constructor (or other means) to return a reference to a completely independent copy of the mutable object.

TIP: Deep Copy versus Shallow Copy

In the previous two subsections, we contrasted the following two ways of defining the method `getBirthDate` (Display 5.19):

```
public Date getBirthDate()
{
    return new Date(born);
}
public Date getBirthDate() //Unsafe
{
    return born; //Not good
}
```

VideoNote
**Deep Copy
vs. Shallow
Copy Example**

As we noted, the first definition is the better one (and the one used in Display 5.19). The first definition returns what is known as a *deep copy* of the object born. The second definition returns what is known as a *shallow copy* of the object `born`.

deep copy

A **deep copy** of an object is a copy that, with one exception, has no references in common with the original. The one exception is that references to immutable objects are allowed to be shared (because immutable objects cannot change in any way and so cannot be changed in any undesirable way). For example, the first definition of `getBirthDate` returns a deep copy of the date stored by the instance variable `born`. So, if you change the object returned by `getBirthDate`, this does not change the `Date` object named by the instance variable `born`. The reason is that we defined the copy constructor for the class `Date` to create a deep copy (Display 5.20). Normally, copy constructors and accessor methods should return a deep copy.

shallow copy

Any copy that is not a deep copy is called a **shallow copy**. For example, the second definition of `getBirthDate` returns a shallow copy of the date stored by the instance variable `born`.

We will have more to say about deep and shallow copies in later chapters. ∎

Never Return a Reference to a Mutable Private Object

A class that contains mutator methods or other methods, such as input methods, that can change the data in an object of the class is called a **mutable class**, and objects of the class are called **mutable objects**. When defining accessor methods (or almost any methods), your method should not return a reference to a mutable object. Instead, use a copy constructor (or other means) to return a reference to a completely independent copy of the mutable object.

TIP: Assume Your Coworkers Are Malicious

Our discussion of privacy leaks in the previous subsections was concerned with the effect of somebody trying to defeat the privacy of an instance variable. You might object that your coworkers are nice people and would not knowingly sabotage your software. That is probably true, and we do not mean to accuse your coworkers of malicious intent. However, the same action that can be performed intentionally by a malicious enemy can also be performed inadvertently by your friends or even by you yourself. The best way to guard against such honest mistakes is to pretend that you are defending against a malicious enemy. ■

MyProgrammingLab™

Self-Test Exercises

41. What do you understand by mutable class and mutable objects? Give one example of a mutable class.

42. What is the difference between a deep copy and a shallow copy?

43. Your methods should not return a reference to a mutable object; instead you may use a copy constructor. What should be special in the copy constructor?

5.4 Packages and `javadoc`

> *... he furnished me,*
> *From mine own library with volumes that*
> *I prize above my dukedom.*

> WILLIAM SHAKESPEARE, *The Tempest*

In this section, we cover packages, which are Java libraries, and then cover the `javadoc` program, which automatically extracts documentation from packages and classes. Although these are important topics, they are not used in the rest of this book. You can study this section at any time you wish; you need not cover this section before studying any other topic in this book.

This section does not use any of the material in Section 5.3, and so can be covered before Section 5.3.

This section assumes that you know about directories (which are called folders in some operating systems), that you know about path names for directories (folders), and that you know about PATH (environment) variables. These are not Java topics. They are part of your operating system, and the details depend on your particular operating system. If you can find out how to set the PATH variable on your operating system, you will know enough about these topics to understand this section.

Packages and `import` Statements

package

import statement

A **package** is Java's way of forming a library of classes. You can make a package from a group of classes and then use the package of classes in any other class or program you write without the need to move the classes to the directory (folder) in which you are working. All you need to do is include an **`import` statement** that names the package. We have already used `import` statements with some predefined standard Java packages. For example, the following, which we have used before, makes available the class `Scanner` of the package `java.util`:

```
import java.util.Scanner;
```

You can make all the classes in the package available by using the following instead:

```
Import java.util.*;
```

There is no overhead cost for importing the entire package as opposed to just a few classes.

The `import` statements should be at the beginning of the file. Only blank lines, comments, and `package` statements may precede the list of `import` statements. We discuss `package` statements next.

`import` Statement

You can use a class from a package in any program or class definition by placing an **`import` statement** that names the package and the class from the package at the start of the file containing the program (or class definition). The program (or class definition) need not be in the same directory as the classes in the package.

SYNTAX

```
import Package_Name.Class;
```

EXAMPLE

```
import java.util.Scanner;
```

You can import all the classes in a package by using an asterisk in place of the class's name.

SYNTAX

```
import Package_Name.*;
```

EXAMPLE

```
import java.util.*;
```

To make a package, group all the classes together into a single directory (folder) and add the following `package` statement to the beginning of each class file:

```
package Package_Name;
```

This `package` statement should be at the beginning of the file. Only blank lines and comments may precede the `package` statement. If there are both `import` statements and `package` statements, any `package` statements come before the `import` statements. Aside from the addition of the `package` statement, class files are just as we have already described them. (It is technically only the `.class` files that must be in the package directory.)

The Package `java.lang`

The package `java.lang` contains classes that are fundamental to Java programming. These classes are so basic that the package is always imported automatically. Any class in `java.lang` does not need an `import` statement to make it available to your code. For example, the classes `Math` and `String` and the wrapper classes introduced earlier in this chapter are all in the package `java.lang`.

Package

A **package** is a collection of classes that have been grouped together into a directory and given a package name. The classes in the package are each placed in a separate file, and the file is given the same name as the class, just as we have been doing all along. Each file in the package must have the following at the beginning of the file. Only comments and blank lines may precede this package statement.

SYNTAX

```
package Package_Name;
```

EXAMPLES

```
package utilities.numericstuff;
package java.util;
```

Package Names and Directories

A package name is not an arbitrary identifier. It is a form of path name to the directory containing the classes in the package.

In order to find the directory for a package, Java needs two things: the name of the package and the value of your *CLASSPATH variable*.

You should already be familiar with the environment variable of your operating system that is known as the *PATH variable*. The **CLASSPATH variable** is a similar environment variable used to help locate Java packages. The value of your CLASSPATH

CLASSPATH variable

variable tells Java where to begin its search for a package. It is not a Java variable. It is an environment variable that is part of your operating system. The value of your CLASSPATH variable is a list of directories. The exact syntax for this list varies from one operating system to another, but it should be the same syntax as that used for the (ordinary) PATH variable. When Java is looking for a package, it begins its search in the directories listed in the CLASSPATH variable.

The name of a package specifies the relative path name for the directory that contains the package classes. It is a relative path name because it assumes that you start in one of the directories listed in the value of your CLASSPATH variable. For example, suppose the following is a directory listed in your CLASSPATH variable (your operating system might use / instead of \):

```
\libraries\newlibraries
```

And suppose your package classes are in the directory

```
\libraries\newlibraries\utilities\numericstuff
```

In this case, the package *should* be named

```
utilities.numericstuff
```

and all the classes in the file must start with the package statement

```
package utilities.numericstuff;
```

The dot in the package name means essentially the same thing as the \ or /, whichever symbol your operating system uses for directory paths. The package name tells you (and Java) what subdirectories to go through to find the package classes, starting from a directory on the class path. This is depicted in Display 5.22. (If there happen to be two directories in the CLASSPATH variable that can be used, then of all the ones that can be used, Java always uses the first one listed in the CLASSPATH variable.)

Any class that uses the class in this `utilities.numericstuff` package must contain either the `import` statement

```
import utilities.numericstuff.*;
```

or an `import` statement for each class in the package that is used.

The way you set the value of your CLASSPATH variable depends on your operating system, but we can give you some suggestions that may work. The CLASSPATH variable is usually spelled as one word with all uppercase letters, as in CLASSPATH. You will probably have a plain old PATH variable that tells the operating system where to find the code for commands such as `javac` and other commands that you can give as single-line commands. If you can find out how to set the PATH variable, you should be able to set the CLASSPATH variable in the same way.

Display 5.22   **A Package Name**

If you are on a UNIX system, you are likely to be able to set the CLASSPATH with some command similar to the following:

```
set CLASSPATH=/libraries/newlibraries;/otherstuff/specialjava;.
export CLASSPATH
```

If this does not work, you might try omitting the word set or replacing set with setenv. You might also try placing the list of directories in quotes. There are many versions of UNIX, all with their own minor variations. You may need to consult a local expert or check the documentation for your operating system.

If you are using a Windows machine, you can set the CLASSPATH variable by setting or creating an environment variable named `CLASSPATH` using the Control Panel.

In this book, we are assuming that class path directories are separated by a semicolon. That is common, but some operating systems use some other separator, such as a colon. Check your documentation if a semicolon does not work as a separator.

Package Names and the CLASSPATH Variable

A package name must be a path name for the directory that contains the classes in the package, but the package name uses dots in place of \ or / (whichever your operating system uses). When naming the package, use a relative path name that starts from any directory listed in the value of the CLASSPATH (environment) variable.

EXAMPLES

```
utilities.numericstuff
java.util
```

PITFALL: Subdirectories Are Not Automatically Imported

Suppose you have two packages, `utilities.numericstuff` and `utilities.numericstuff.statistical`. In this case, you know that `utilities.numericstuff.statistical` is in a subdirectory (subfolder) of the directory (folder) containing `utilities.numericstuff`. This leads some programmers to assume that the following import statement imports both packages:

```
import utilities.numericstuff.*;
```

This is not true. When you import an entire package, you do not import subdirectory packages.

To import all classes in both of these packages, you need

```
import utilities.numericstuff.*;
```

```
import utilities.numericstuff.statistical.*;
```

The Default Package

default package

All the classes in your current directory (that do not belong to some other package) belong to an unnamed package called the **default package**. As long as the current directory is on your CLASSPATH, all the classes in the default package are automatically available to your code. This is why we always assume that all the classes we defined are in the same directory. That way, we need not clutter our discussion with concern about import statements.

PITFALL: Not Including the Current Directory in Your Class Path

current directory

Your CLASSPATH variable allows you to list more than one directory. Most operating systems use the dot to indicate the current directory. The **current directory** is not any one specific directory; it is the directory in which you are currently "located." If you do not know what your current directory is, then it is probably the directory that contains the class you are writing. For example, the following value for a CLASSPATH variable lists two ordinary directories and the current directory:

```
\libraries\newlibraries;\otherstuff\specialjava;.
```

Whenever you set or change the CLASSPATH variable, be sure to include the current directory as one of the alternatives. With the above displayed CLASSPATH value, if the package is not found by starting in either of the previous two directories, Java will look in the subdirectories of the current directory. If you want Java to check the current directory before the other directories on the CLASSPATH variable, list the current directory (the dot) first, as follows:

```
.;\libraries\newlibraries;\otherstuff\specialjava
```

When looking for a package, Java tries the directories in the class path in order and uses the first one that works.

Omitting the current directory from the CLASSPATH variable can interfere with running Java programs, regardless of whether or not the programs use packages. If the current directory is omitted, then Java may not even be able to find the `.class` file for the program itself, so you may not be able to run any programs at all. Thus, if you do set the CLASSPATH variable, it is critical that you include the current directory in the CLASSPATH. No such problems will occur if you have not set the CLASSPATH variable at all; it arises only if you decide to set the CLASSPATH variable.

If you are having problems setting the CLASSPATH variable, one interim solution is to delete the CLASSPATH variable completely and to keep all the class files for one program in the same directory. This will allow you to still do some work while you seek advice on setting the CLASSPATH variable. ■

Specifying a Class Path When You Compile ★

You can specify a class path when you compile a class. To do so, add `-classpath` followed by the class path as illustrated in the following:

```
javac -classpath .;C:\lib\numeric;C:\otherstuff YourClass.java
```

In a UNIX environment, replace the semicolons with colons. This will compile `YourClass.java`, overriding any CLASSPATH setting, and use the class path given after `-classpath`. Note that the directories are separated by semicolons. If you want classes in the current directory to be available to your class, then be sure the class path includes the current directory, which is indicated by a dot.

When you run the class compiled as just shown, you should again use the `-classpath` option as follows:

```
java -classpath .;C:\libraries\numeric;C:\otherstuff YourClass
```

It is important to include the current directory on the class path when you run the program. If your program is in the default package, it will not be found unless you include the current directory. It is best to get in the habit of always including the current directory in all class paths.

Because the class path specified in compiling and running your classes is input to a program (`javac` or `java`) that is part of the Java environment and is not a command to the operating system, you can use either / or \ in the class path, no matter which of these two your operating system uses.

Name Clashes ★

name clash

In addition to being a way of organizing libraries, packages also provide a way to deal with *name clashes*. A **name clash** is a situation in which two classes have the same name. If different programmers writing different packages used the same name for a class, the ambiguity can be resolved by using the package name.

Suppose a package named `sallyspack` contains a class called `HighClass`, and another package named `joespack` also contains a class named `HighClass`. You can use both classes named `HighClass` in the same program by using the more complete names `sallyspack.HighClass` and `joespack.HighClass`. For example,

```
sallyspack.HighClass object1 = new sallyspack.HighClass();
joespack.HighClass object2 = new joespack.HighClass();
```

fully qualified class name

These names that include the package name, such as `sallyspack.HighClass` and `joespack.HighClass`, are called **fully qualified class names**.

If you use fully qualified class names, you do not need to import the class, since this longer class name includes the package name.

Self-Test Exercises

44. Suppose you want to use the class `CoolClass` in the package `mypackages.library1` in a program you write. What do you need to do to make this class available to your program? What do you need to do to make all the classes in the package available to your program?

45. What do you need to do to make a class a member of the package named `mypackages.library1`?

46. Can a package have any name you want, or are there restrictions on what you can use for a package name? Explain any restrictions.

Introduction to `javadoc` ★

The principles of encapsulation using information hiding say that you should separate the *interface* of a class (the instructions on how to use the class) from the *implementation* (the detailed code that tells the computer how the class does its work). In some other programming languages, such as C++, you normally define a class in two files. One file contains something like the interface or API that tells a programmer all that he or she needs to know to use the class. The other file contains the implementation details that are needed for the class code to run. This system is an obvious way to separate interface from implementation, but it is not what Java does.

Java does not divide a class definition into two files. Instead, Java has the interface and implementation of a class mixed together into a single file. If this were the end of the story, Java would not do a good job of encapsulation using information hiding. However, Java has a very good way of separating the interface from the implementation
`javadoc` of a class. Java comes with a program named `javadoc` that automatically extracts the interface from a class definition. If your class definition is correctly commented, a programmer using your class need only look at this API (documentation) produced by `javadoc`. The documentation produced by `javadoc` is identical in format to the documentation for the standard Java library classes.

The result of running `javadoc` on a class is to produce an HTML file with the API (interface) documentation for the class. *HTML* is the basic language used to produce documents to view with a Web browser, so the documentation produced by `javadoc` is viewed on a Web browser. A brief introduction to HTML is given in Chapter 20. However, you need not know any HTML to run `javadoc` or to read the documentation it produces.

`javadoc` can be used to obtain documentation for a single class. However, it is primarily intended to obtain documentation for an entire package.

We will first discuss how you should comment your classes so that you can get the most value out of `javadoc`. We will then describe how you run the `javadoc` program.

Commenting Classes for `javadoc` ★

To get a more useful `javadoc` document, you must write your comments in a particular way. All the classes in this book have been commented for use with `javadoc`. However, to save space, the comments in this book are briefer than what would be ideal for `javadoc`.

The `javadoc` program extracts the heading for your class (or classes) as well as the headings for all public methods, public instance variables, public static variables, and certain comments. No method bodies and no private items are extracted when `javadoc` is run in the normal default mode.

For `javadoc` (in default mode) to extract a comment, the comment must satisfy two conditions:

1. The comment must *immediately precede* a public class definition, a public method definition, or other public item.
2. The comment must be a block comment (that is, the /* and */ style of comment), and the opening /* must contain an extra *. So the comment must be marked by /** at the beginning and */ at the end.

Unless you explicitly set an extra option to `javadoc`, line comments (that is, // style comments) are not extracted, and comments preceding any private items also are not extracted.

The comment that precedes a public method definition can include any general information that you would like. There is also special syntax for inserting descriptions of parameters, any value returned, and any exceptions that might be thrown. We have not yet discussed exceptions. That is done in Chapter 9, but we include mention of them here so this section will serve as a more complete reference on `javadoc`. You need not worry about exceptions or the details about "throws" discussed here until you reach Chapter 9.

@ tag

The special information about parameters and so forth are preceded by the @ symbol and are called **@ tags**. The following is an example of a method comment for use with `javadoc`:

```
/**
 Tests for equality of two objects of type Person. To be equal,
 the two objects must have the same name, same birth date, and
 same death date.

 @param otherPerson The person being compared to the calling
 object.
 @return Returns true if the calling object equals otherPerson.
*/
public boolean equals(Person otherPerson)
```

(The method `equals` is from the class `Person` defined in Display 5.19. If you need more context, look at that display.)

Note that the @ tags all come after any general comment and that each @ tag is on a line by itself. The following are some of the @ tags allowed:

```
@param Parameter_Name Parameter_Description
@return Description_Of_Value_Returned
@throws Exception_Type Explanation
@deprecated
@see Package_Name.Class_Name
@author Author
@version Version_Information
```

The @ tags should appear in the above order—first @param, then @return, then @throws, and so forth. If there are multiple parameters, they should each have their own @param and appear on a separate line. The parameters and their @param description should be listed in their left-to-right order in the parameter list. If there are multiple authors, they should each have their own @author and appear on a separate line. The author and version information is not extracted unless suitable option flags have been set, as described in the next subsection.

deprecated

If @deprecated is included in a method comment, then the documentation notes that the method is *deprecated*. A **deprecated** method is one that is being phased out. To allow for backward compatibility, the method still works, but it should not be used in new code.

If an @ tag is included for an item, javadoc extracts the explanation for that item and includes it in the documentation. You should always include a more or less complete set of @ tags in the comment for each of your methods. In this book, we omit the @ tags to save space, but we encourage you to always include them. The comments that are not part of an @ tag appear as a general comment for the method, along with the method heading.

You can also insert HTML commands in your comments so that you gain more control over javadoc, but that is not necessary and may not even be desirable. HTML commands can clutter the comments, making them harder to read when you look at the source code.

Running javadoc ★

To run javadoc on a package, all you need to do is give the following command:

```
javadoc -d Documentation_Directory Package_Name
```

It would be normal to run this command from the directory containing the classes in the package, but it can be run from any directory, provided you have correctly set the CLASSPATH environment variable. The *Documentation_Directory* is the name of the directory in which you want javadoc to place the HTML documents that it produces. For example, the following might be used to obtain documentation on the package mylibraries.numericstuff:

```
javadoc -d documentation/mypackages mylibraries.numericstuff
```

The HTML documents produced will be in the subdirectory documentation/mypackages of where this command is run. If you prefer, you may use a complete path name in place of the relative path name documentation/mypackages. If you omit the -d and *Documentation_Directory*, javadoc will create suitable directories for the documentation.

You can link to standard Java documents so that your HTML documents include live links to standard classes and methods. The syntax is as follows:

```
javadoc -link Link_To_Standard_Docs -d Documentation_Directory
Package_Name
```

Link_To_Standard_Docs is either a path to a local version of the Java documentation or the URL of the Oracle Web site with standard Java documentation. As of this writing, that URL is

```
http://download.oracle.com/javase/7/docs/api/
```

You need not run `javadoc` on an entire package. You can run `javadoc` on a single class file. For example, the following should be run from the directory containing `Date.java` and will produce documentation for the class `Date`:

```
javadoc Date.java
```

You can run `javadoc` on all classes in a directory with

```
javadoc *.java
```

You can add the `-d` and/or `-link` options to any of these commands. For example,

```
javadoc -link http://download.oracle.com/javase/7/docs/api/ -d
mydocs *.java
```

These and other options for `javadoc` are summarized in Display 5.23.

When running `javadoc`, you typically get more directories and many more HTML files than you might expect. To get a better understanding of `javadoc`, you should try running it in various settings and observe the files it produces.

Display 5.23 Options for `java.doc`

OPTIONS	DESCRIPTION
`-link`	Provides a link to another set of documentation. Normally, this is used with either a path name to a local version of the Java documentation or the URL of the Oracle Web site with standard Java documentation.
`-d`	Specifies a directory to hold the documentation generated. *Documentation_Directory* may be a relative or absolute path name.
`-author`	Includes author information (from `@author` tags). This information is omitted unless this option is set.
`-version`	Includes version information (from `@version` tags). This information is omitted unless this option is set.
`-classpath`	Overrides the CLASSPATH environment variable and makes the CLASSPATH for the execution of this invocation of `javadoc`. It does not permanently change the CLASSPATH variable.
`-private`	Includes private members as well as public members in the documentation.

MyProgrammingLab™

Self-Test Exercises

47. When run in default mode, does `javadoc` ever extract the body of a method definition? When run in default mode, does `javadoc` ever extract anything marked private in a class definition?

48. When run in default mode, what comments does `javadoc` extract and what comments does it not extract?

Chapter Summary

- A *static method* is one that does not require a calling object, but can use the class name in place of the calling object.

- A *static variable* is similar to an instance variable except that there is only one copy of the static variable that is used by all objects of the class.

- A *wrapper class* allows you to have a class object that corresponds to a value of a primitive type. Wrapper classes also contain a number of useful predefined constants and static methods.

- A variable of a class type stores the reference (memory address) of where the object is located in the computer's memory. This causes some operations, such as = and ==, to behave quite differently for variables of a class type than they do for variables of a primitive type.

- When you use the assignment operator with two variables of a class type, the two variables become two names for the same object.

- A method cannot change the value of a variable of a primitive type that is an argument to the method. On the other hand, a method can change the values of the instance variables of an argument of a class type. This is because with class parameters, it is a reference that is plugged in to the parameter.

- `null` is a special constant that can be used to give a value to any variable of any class type.

- An expression with a `new` operator and a constructor can be used as an argument to a method. Such an argument is called an *anonymous object*.

- A *copy constructor* is a constructor with one parameter of the same type as the class. A copy constructor should be designed so the object it creates is intuitively an exact copy of its parameter, but is a completely independent copy—that is, a *deep copy*.

- A class that contains mutator methods or any methods that can change the data in an object of the class is called a *mutable class*, and objects of the class are called *mutable objects*. When defining accessor methods (or almost any methods), your method should not return a reference to a mutable object. Instead, use a copy constructor (or other means) to return a reference to a deep copy of the mutable object.

- *Packages* are Java's version of class libraries.

- Java comes with a program named `javadoc` that automatically extracts the interface from all the classes in a package or from a single class definition.

Answers to Self-Test Exercises

1. Yes, it is legal, although it would be preferable style to use the class name `RoundStuff` in place of `roundObject`.

2. Yes.

3. No, all methods in the class are static, so there is no need to create objects as in Display 5.1; there is no constructor for the class `RoundStuff`.

4. A non-static method could be called from within a static method by creating an object of the class within the static method and using this object for calling the non-static method.

5. You can invoke a static method within a nonstatic method.

6. You cannot reference an instance variable within a static method, because a static method can be used without a calling object and hence without any instance variables.

7. With a static variable there is only one copy of the variable in memory, and all the objects can use this one variable. If one object changes the static variable, another object can read that change. Thus, a static variable can be used by objects to communicate between the objects.

8. The *static* modifier should be right after the access specifier `private`. So the right declaration is:

   ```
   private static int counter = 0;
   ```

9. If a static variable is not initialized in a program, it is automatically initialized to the default value. Static variables of class type are initialized to null.

10. When these variables define constants.

11. All methods with the following names could and should be marked `static`: `dateOK`, `monthOK`, and `monthString`.

12. All static variables should be marked `private` with the exception of one case: If the static variable is used as a named constant (that is, if it is marked `final`), then it can be marked either `public` or `private` depending on the particular situation.

13. They can both be named by using the class name and a dot, rather than an object name and a dot.

14. `7, 8`

    `7.0, 7.0`

    `8.0, 8.0`

15. `roundedAnswer = (int)Math.round(answer);`

16. `long`. Because one argument is of type long, the int argument is automatically type cast to `long`.

17. They are all legal.

18. An object of the class `Integer`; the assignment is equivalent to

    `Integer marks = new Integer(60);`

19. A value of the primitive type `float`; the assignment is equivalent to

    `float taxRate = (new Float(5.0)).floatValue();`

20. `Objects are Not equal.`

21. `Float.toString(average)`

22. `Double.parseDouble(stringForm)`

23. `double temp = Double.parseDouble(tempReading.trim())`

24. `System.out.println("Largest long is" + Long.MAX_VALUE +`
    `                "Smallest long is" + Long.MIN_VALUE);`

25. `Character star = new Character('*');`

26. No, none of the wrapper classes discussed in this chapter have no-argument constructors.

27. A *reference type* is a type whose variables contain references, that is, memory addresses. Class types are reference types. Primitive types are not reference types.

28. When comparing two objects of a class type, you should use the method `equals`.

29. When comparing two objects of a primitive type, you should you use `==`.

30. Yes, a method with an argument of a class type can change the values of the instance variables in the object named by the argument.

31. No, a method cannot change the value of an `int` variable given as an argument to the method.

32. The variable `anObject` names no object, so the invocation of the `set` method is an error. One way to fix things is as follows:

    `ToyClass anObject = new ToyClass();`
    `anObject.set("Josephine", 42);`

33. The constant `null` can be assigned to a variable of any class type. It does not really have a type, but you can think of its type as being the type of a memory address. You can also think of `null` as being of every class type.

34. `aVariable == null`

35. It is unlikely but it is legal. This is an example of an anonymous object, as described in the text.

extra code on website

36. The only difference is that the object of type `Date` is given the name `theDate` in the second version. It makes no difference to the object `adams`.

37. The following definition of `equals` is used in the file `Date.java` in the Chapter 5 directory of the source code on the website:

```java
public boolean equals(Date otherDate)
{
    if (otherDate == null)
        return false;
    else
        return ( (month.equals(otherDate.month)) &&
            (day == otherDate.day) && (year == otherDate.year) );
}
```

38. A copy constructor is a constructor with one parameter of the same type as the class. A copy constructor should be designed so that the object it creates is intuitively an exact copy of its parameter, but a completely independent copy, that is, a deep copy.

39. The first piece of code produces the output

```
July 4, 1776
```

The second piece of code produces the output

```
January 1, 2006
```

40. `Natalie Dressed, April 1, 1984-`

41. A class that contains no methods (other than constructors) that change any of the data in an object of the class is called an immutable class, and objects of the class are called immutable objects. The class `String` is an immutable class.

42. A deep copy of an object is a copy that, with one exception, has no references in common with the original. The one exception is that references to immutable objects are allowed to be shared. For example:

```java
public Date getBirthDate() // safe
{
    return new Date(born);
}
```

Any copy that is not a deep copy is called a shallow copy. For example:

```java
public Date getBirthDate() //Unsafe
{
    return born;
}
```

43. The copy constructor or other accessor methods should return a reference to a completely independent copy of the mutable object.

44. To make the class available to your program, you need to insert the following at the start of the file containing your class:

```
import mypackages.library1.CoolClass;
```

To make all the classes in the package available to your program, insert the following instead:

```
import mypackages.library1.*;
```

45. To make a class a member of the package named `mypackages.library1`, you must insert the following at the start of the file with the class definition and place the file in the directory corresponding to the package (as described in the text):

```
package mypackages.library1;
```

(Only the `.class` file is required to be in the directory corresponding to the package, but it may be cleaner and easier to place both the `.java` file and the `.class` file there.)

46. A package name must be a path name for the directory that contains the classes in the package, but the package name uses dots in place of \ or / (whichever your operating system uses). When naming the package, you use a relative path name that starts from any directory named in the value of the CLASSPATH (environment) variable.

47. `javadoc` never extracts the body of a method definition, nor (when run in default mode) does `javadoc` ever extract anything marked `private` in a class definition.

48. When run in default mode, `javadoc` extracts only comments that satisfy the following two conditions:

    1. The comment must immediately precede a public class definition, a public method definition, or other public item.

    2. The comment must use the `/*` and `*/` style, and the opening `/*` must contain an extra `*`. So the comment must be marked by `/**` at the beginning and `*/` at the end. In particular, `javadoc` does not extract any `//` style comments.

MyProgrammingLab™ **Programming Projects**

Visit www.myprogramminglab.com to complete select exercises online and get instant feedback.

1. You operate several hot dog stands distributed throughout town. Define a class named `HotDogStand` that has an instance variable for the hot dog stand's ID number and an instance variable for how many hot dogs the stand has sold that day. Create a constructor that allows a user of the class to initialize both values.

   Also create a method named `justSold` that increments by one the number of hot dogs the stand has sold. The idea is that this method will be invoked each time the stand sells a hot dog so that you can track the total number of hot dogs sold by the stand. Add another method that returns the number of hot dogs sold.

   Finally, add a static variable that tracks the total number of hot dogs sold by all hot dog stands and a static method that returns the value in this variable.

   Write a main method to test your class with at least three hot dog stands that each sell a variety of hot dogs.

2. Define a class called `Fraction`. This class is used to represent a ratio of two integers. Include mutator methods that allow the user to set the numerator and the denominator. Also include a method that displays the fraction on the screen as a ratio (e.g., 5/9). This method does not need to reduce the fraction to lowest terms.

   Include an additional method, `equals`, that takes as input another `Fraction` and returns `true` if the two fractions are identical and `false` if they are not. This method should treat the fractions reduced to lowest terms; that is, if one fraction is 20/60 and the other is 1/3, then the method should return `true`.

   Embed your class in a test program that allows the user to create a fraction. Then the program should loop repeatedly until the user decides to quit. Inside the body of the loop, the program should allow the user to enter a target fraction into an anonymous object and learn whether the fractions are identical.

3. In the land of Puzzlevania, Aaron, Bob, and Charlie had an argument over which one of them was the greatest puzzler of all time. To end the argument once and for all, they agreed on a duel to the death. Aaron was a poor shooter and only hit his target with a probability of 1/3. Bob was a bit better and hit his target with a probability of 1/2. Charlie was an expert marksman and never missed. A hit means a kill and the person hit drops out of the duel.

   To compensate for the inequities in their marksmanship skills, the three decided that they would fire in turns, starting with Aaron, followed by Bob, and then by Charlie. The cycle would repeat until there was one man standing, and that man would be the Greatest Puzzler of All Time.

   An obvious and reasonable strategy is for each man to shoot at the most accurate shooter still alive, on the grounds that this shooter is the deadliest and has the best chance of hitting back.

Write a program to simulate the duel using this strategy. Your program should use random numbers and the probabilities given in the problem to determine whether a shooter hits the target. Create a class named `Duelist` that contains the dueler's name and shooting accuracy, a Boolean indicating whether the dueler is still alive, and a method `ShootAtTarget(Duelist target)` that sets the target to dead if the dueler hits his target (using a random number and the shooting accuracy) and does nothing otherwise.

Once you can simulate a single duel, add a loop to your program that simulates 10,000 duels. Count the number of times that each contestant wins and print the probability of winning for each contestant (e.g., for Aaron your program might output "Aaron won 3,595/10,000 duels or 35.95%").

An alternate strategy is for Aaron to intentionally miss on his first shot. Modify the program to accommodate this new strategy and output the probability of winning for each contestant. Which strategy is better for Aaron: to intentionally miss on the first shot or to try and hit the best shooter? Who has the best chance of winning, the best shooter or the worst shooter?

4. You are interested in keeping track of the team members and competition information for your school's annual entries in computer science programming competitions. Each team consists of exactly four team members. Every year your team competes in two competitions. As an initial start for your database, create a class named `Team` that has the following instance variables:

```
// Name for the team
String teamName;
// Names for each team members.
String name1, name2, name3, name4;
// Info on each competition
Competition competition1, competition2;
```

Note that there is a much better way to represent the team members and competitions using arrays; this is covered in a subsequent chapter. The class should also have a method that outputs all the names of all team members and the competition information to the console.

The `Competition` class contains variables to track the following:

String: Name of the competition, Name of the winning team, Name of the runner-up

Integer: Year of the competition

Implement the `Team` and `Competition` classes with appropriate constructor, accessor, and mutator methods. In entering data for past competitions, you note that an entry is usually very similar to the previous year's entry. To help with the data entry, create a deep copy constructor for the `Team` class. Test your copy constructor by creating a copy of an existing team object, changing the competition information for the copy, and outputting the data for the original and the copy. The original object should be unchanged if your deep copy constructor is working properly.

5. Part One: Define a class named `Money` whose objects represent amounts of U.S. money. The class should have two instance variables of type `int` for the dollars and cents in the amount of money. Include a constructor with two parameters of type `int` for the dollars and cents, one with one constructor of type `int` for an amount of dollars with zero cents, and a no-argument constructor. Include the methods `add` and `minus` for addition and subtraction of amounts of money. These methods should be static methods, should each have two parameters of type `Money`, and return a value of type `Money`. Include a reasonable set of accessor and mutator methods as well as the methods `equals` and `toString`. Write a test program for your class.

   Part Two: Add a second version of the methods for addition and subtraction. These methods should have the same names as the static version but should use a calling object and a single argument. For example, this version of the `add` method (for addition) has a calling object and one argument. So `m1.add(m2)` returns the result of adding the `Money` objects `m1` and `m2`. Note that your class should have all these methods; for example, there should be two methods named `add`.

   Alternate Part Two: Add a second version of the methods for addition and subtraction. These methods should have the same names as the static version but should use a calling object and a single argument. The methods should be `void` methods. The result should be given as the changed value of the calling object. For example, this version of the `add` method (for addition) has a calling object and one argument. Therefore,

   ```
   m1.add(m2);
   ```

   changes the values of the instance variables of `m1` so they represent the result of adding `m2` to the original version of `m1`. Note that your class should have all these methods; for example, there should be two methods named `add`.

   (If you want to do both Part Two and Alternate Part Two, they must be two classes. You cannot include the methods from both Part Two and Alternate Part Two in a single class. Do you know why?)

6. Part One: Define a class for rational numbers. A rational number is a number that can be represented as the quotient of two integers. For example, 1/2, 3/4, 64/2, and so forth are all rational numbers. (By 1/2 and so forth, we mean the everyday meaning of the fraction, not the integer division this expression would produce in a Java program.) Represent rational numbers as two values of type `int`, one for the numerator and one for the denominator. Your class should have two instance variables of type `int`. Call the class `Rational`. Include a constructor with two arguments that can be used to set the instance variables of an object to any values. Also include a constructor that has only a single parameter of type `int`; call this single parameter `wholeNumber` and define the constructor so that the object will be initialized to the rational number `wholeNumber/1`. Also include a no-argument constructor that initializes an object to 0 (that is, to 0/1). Note that the numerator,

the denominator, or both may contain a minus sign. Define methods for addition, subtraction, multiplication, and division of objects of your class `Rational`. These methods should be static methods that each have two parameters of type `Rational` and return a value of type `Rational`. For example, `Rational.add(r1, r2)` will return the result of adding the two rational numbers (two objects of the class `Rational`, `r1` and `r2`). Define accessor and mutator methods as well as the methods `equals` and `toString`. You should include a method to normalize the sign of the rational number so that the denominator is positive and the numerator is either positive or negative. For example, after normalization, $4/-8$ would be represented the same as $-4/8$. Also write a test program to test your class.

Hints: Two rational numbers a/b and c/d are equal if $a*d$ equals $c*b$.

Part Two: Add a second version of the methods for addition, subtraction, multiplication, and division. These methods should have the same names as the static version but should use a calling object and a single argument. For example, this version of the `add` method (for addition) has a calling object and one argument. So `r1.add(r2)` returns the result of adding the rationals `r1` and `r2`. Note that your class should have all these methods; for example, there should be two methods named `add`.

Alternate Part Two: Add a second version of the methods for addition, subtraction, multiplication, and division. These methods should have the same names as the static version but should use a calling object and a single argument. The methods should be `void` methods. The result is given as the changed value of the calling object. For example, this version of the `add` method (for addition) has a calling object and one argument. Therefore,

```
r1.add(r2);
```

changes the values of the instance variables of `r1` so they represent the result of adding `r2` to the original version of `r1`. Note that your class should have all these methods; for example, there should be two methods named `add`.

(If you want to do both Part Two and Alternate Part Two, they must be two classes. You cannot include the methods from both Part Two and Alternate Part Two in a single class. Do you know why?)

7. Part One: Define a class for complex numbers. A complex number is a number of the form

```
a + b*i
```

For our purposes, a and b are numbers of type `double`, and i is a number that represents the quantity $\sqrt{-1}$. Represent a complex number as two values of type `double`. Name the instance variables `real` and `imaginary`. (The instance variable for the number that is multiplied by i is the one called `imaginary`.) Call the class `Complex`. Include a constructor with two parameters of type `double` that can be used to set the instance variables of an object to any values. Also include a constructor that has only a single parameter of type `double`; call this parameter `realPart` and define the constructor so that the object will be initialized to realPart + 0*i. Also include a no-argument constructor that initializes an object to 0 (that is, to 0 + 0*i). Define accessor and mutator methods as well as the methods equals and toString. Define static methods for addition, subtraction, and multiplication of objects of your class Complex. These methods should be static and should each have two parameters of type Complex and return a value of type Complex. For example, Complex.add(c1, c2) will return the result of adding the two complex numbers (two objects of the class Complex) c1 and c2. Also write a test program to test your class.

Hints: To add or subtract two complex numbers, you add or subtract the two instance variables of type double. The product of two complex numbers is given by the following formula:

```
(a + b *i)*(c + d *i) = (a *c - b *d) + (a *d + b *c)*i
```

Part Two: Add a second version of the methods for addition, subtraction, and multiplication. These methods should have the same names as the static version but should use a calling object and a single argument. For example, this version of the add method (for addition) has a calling object and one argument. So c1.add(c2) returns the result of adding the complex numbers c1 and c2. Note that your class should have all these methods; for example, there should be two methods named add.

Alternate Part Two: Add a second version of the methods for addition, subtraction, and multiplication. These methods should have the same names as the static version but should use a calling object and a single argument. The methods will be void methods. The result is given as the changed value of the calling object. For example, this version of the add method (for addition) has a calling object and one argument. Therefore,

```
c1.add(c2);
```

changes the values of the instance variables of c1 so they represent the result of adding c2 to the original version of c1. Note that your class should have all these methods; for example, there should be two methods named add.

(If you want to do both Part Two and Alternate Part Two, they must be two classes. You cannot include the methods from both Part Two and Alternate Part Two in a single class. Do you know why?)

8. Programming Project 4.12 asked you to create a PizzaOrder class that stores an order consisting of up to three pizzas. Extend this class with the following methods and constructor:

- public int getNumPizzas()—returns the number of pizzas in the order.
- public Pizza getPizza1()—returns the first pizza in the order or null if pizza1 is not set.
- public Pizza getPizza2()—returns the second pizza in the order or null if pizza2 is not set.
- public Pizza getPizza3()—returns the third pizza in the order or null if pizza3 is not set.

- A copy constructor that takes another `PizzaOrder` object and makes an independent copy of its pizzas. This might be useful if using an old order as a starting point for a new order.

Write a main method to test the new methods. Changing the pizzas in the new order should not change the pizzas in the original order. For example,

```
Pizza pizza1 = // Code to create a large pizza, 1 cheese, 1 ham
Pizza pizza2 = // Code to create a medium pizza, 2 cheese,
               // 2 pepperoni
PizzaOrder order1 = // Code to create an order
order1.setNumPizzas(2); // 2 pizzas in the order
order1.setPizza1(pizza1); // Set first pizza
order1.setPizza2(pizza2); // Set second pizza
double total = order1.calcTotal(); // Should be 18+20 = 38
PizzaOrder order2 = new PizzaOrder(order1); // Use copy
                        // constructor
order2.getPizza1().setNumCheeseToppings(3); // Change toppings
double total = order2.calcTotal(); // Should be 22 + 20 = 42
double origTotal = order1.calcTotal(); // Should still be 38
```

Note that the first three lines of code are incomplete. You must complete them as part of the Programming Project.

VideoNote
Solution to Programming Project 5.9

9. Use `javadoc` to generate HTML documentation for the code in Display 5.19. Use the `@author` and `@version` tag for the description of the entire class. Add a comment for every public method or constructor using the `@param` and `@return` tags when appropriate.

10. First, complete Programming Project 4.13 from Chapter 4.

Modify the main method with a loop so that an arbitrary number of `BoxOfProduce` objects are created and substitutions are allowed for each box. Add a menu so the user can decide when to stop creating boxes.

You would like to throw in a free recipe flyer for salsa verde if the box contains tomatillos. However, there are only five recipe flyers. Add a static variable to the `BoxOfProduce` class that counts the number of recipe flyers remaining and initialize it to 5. Also add an instance variable that indicates whether or not the box contains a recipe flyer and modify the `toString()` method to also output "salsa verde recipe" if the box contains a recipe flyer. Finally, add logic inside the class so that if the box contains at least one order of tomatillos then it automatically gets a recipe flyer until all of the recipe flyers are gone. Note that a box should only get one recipe flyer even if there are multiple orders of tomatillos.

Test your class by creating boxes with tomatillos from your menu until all of the flyers are gone.

Arrays 6

6.1 INTRODUCTION TO ARRAYS 378
Creating and Accessing Arrays 379
The `length` Instance Variable 382
Initializing Arrays 385

6.2 ARRAYS AND REFERENCES 388
Arrays Are Objects 388
Array Parameters 390
Arguments for the Method `main` ★ 397
Methods that Return an Array 399

6.3 PROGRAMMING WITH ARRAYS 400
Partially Filled Arrays 401
Example: A Class for Partially Filled Arrays 404
The "for-each" Loop ★ 408
Methods with a Variable Number
   of Parameters ★ 412
Example: A String Processing Example ★ 415
Privacy Leaks with Array Instance Variables 416
Example: Sorting an Array 420
Enumerated Types ★ 424

6.4 MULTIDIMENSIONAL ARRAYS 431
Multidimensional Array Basics 431
Using the `length` Instance Variable 434
Ragged Arrays ★ 435
Multidimensional Array Parameters and Returned
   Values 435
Example: A Grade Book Class 436

Chapter Summary 442   **Answers to Self-Test Exercises** 443   **Programming Projects** 450

6 Arrays

Memory is necessary for all the operations of reason.

BLAISE PASCAL, *Pensées*

Introduction

An *array* is a data structure used to process a collection of data that is all of the same type, such as a list of numbers of type `double` or a list of strings. In this chapter, we introduce you to the basics of defining and using arrays in Java.

Prerequisites

Section 6.1 requires understanding of only Chapters 1 through 3 and Section 4.1 of Chapter 4. Indeed, much less than all of Section 4.1 is needed. All you really need from Section 4.1 is to have some idea of what an object is and what an instance variable is.

The remaining sections require Chapters 1 through 5 with the exception that an understanding of Section 5.4 on packages and `javadoc` is not required.

6.1 Introduction to Arrays

It is a capital mistake to theorize before one has data.

SIR ARTHUR CONAN DOYLE, *Scandal in Bohemia* (SHERLOCK HOLMES)

Suppose we wish to write a program that reads in five test scores and performs some manipulations on these scores. For instance, the program might compute the highest test score and then output the amount by which each score falls short of the highest. The highest score is not known until all five scores are read in. Hence, all five scores must be retained in storage so that after the highest score is computed, each score can be compared to it. To retain the five scores, we will need something equivalent to five variables of type `int`. We could use five individual variables of type `int`, but keeping track of five variables is hard, and we may later want to change our program to handle 100 scores; certainly, keeping track of 100 variables is impractical. An array **array** is the perfect solution. An **array** behaves like a list of variables with a uniform naming mechanism that can be declared in a single line of simple code. For example, the names for the five individual variables we need might be `score[0]`, `score[1]`, `score[2]`, `score[3]`, and `score[4]`. The part that does not change—in this case, `score`—is the name of the array. The part that can change is the integer in the square brackets `[]`.

Creating and Accessing Arrays

In Java, an array is a special kind of object, but it is often more useful to think of it as a collection of variables all of the same type. For example, an array that behaves like a collection of five variables of type double can be created as follows:

```
double[] score = new double[5];
```

This is like declaring the following to be five variables of type double:

```
score[0], score[1], score[2], score[3], score[4]
```

indexed variable

subscripted variable

element

index, subscript

length, size

The individual variables that make up the array are referred to in a variety of different ways. We will call them **indexed variables**, though they are also sometimes called **subscripted variables** or **elements** of the array. The number in square brackets is called an **index** or a **subscript**. In Java, *indices are numbered starting with* 0, *not any number*. The number of indexed variables in an array is called the **length** or **size** of the array. When an array is created, the length of the array is given in square brackets after the array name. The indexed variables are then numbered (also using square brackets) starting with 0 and ending with the integer that is *one less than the length of the array*.

The following example:

```
double[] score = new double[5];
```

is really shorthand for the following two statements:

```
double[] score;
score = new double[5];
```

The first statement declares the variable score to be of the array type double[]. The second statement creates an array with five indexed variables of type double and makes the variable score a name for the array. You may use any expression that evaluates to a nonnegative int value in place of the 5 in square brackets. In particular, you can fill a variable with a value read from the keyboard and use the variable in place of the 5. In this way, the size of the array can be determined when the program is run.

base type

An array can have indexed variables of any type, as long as they are all of the same type. This type is called the **base type** of the array. In our example, the base type of the array score is double. To declare an array with base type int, simply use the type name int instead of double when the array is declared and created. The base type of an array can be any type. In particular, it can be a class type.

Each of the five indexed variables of our example array score can be used just like any other variable of type double. For example, all of the following are allowed in Java:

```
score[3] = 32;
score[0] = score[3] + 10;
System.out.println(score[0]);
```

The five indexed variables of our sample array score are more than just five plain old variables of type double. That number in square brackets is part of the indexed variable's name. So, your program can compute the name of one of these variables.

Declaring and Creating an Array

Declare an array name and create an array in almost the same way that you create and name objects of classes. There is only a slight difference in the syntax.

SYNTAX

Base_Type[] *Array_Name* = new *Base_Type*[*Length*];

The *Length* may be given as any expression that evaluates to a nonnegative integer. In particular, *Length* can be an int variable.

EXAMPLES

```
char[] line = new char[80];
double[] reading = new double[300];
Person[] specimen = new Person[100];
```

Person is a class.

Instead of writing an integer constant in the square brackets, you can use any expression that evaluates to an integer that is at least 0 and at most 4. So, the following is allowed:

```
System.out.println(score[index] + " is at position " + index);
```

where index is a variable of type int that has been given one of the values 0, 1, 2, 3, or 4.

When we refer to these indexed variables grouped together into one collective item, we will call them an *array*. So, we can refer to the array named score (without using any square brackets).

The program in Display 6.1 shows an example of using our sample array score as five indexed variables, all of type double.

Note that the program can compute the name of an indexed variable by using a variable as the index, as in the following for loop:

```
for (index = 0; index < 5; index++)
    System.out.println(score[index] + " differs from max by "
                            + (max - score[index]));
```

square brackets [ ]   Do not confuse the three ways to use the **square brackets** [] with an array name. First, the square brackets can be used to create a type name, such as the double[] in the following:

```
double[] score;
```

Second, the square brackets can be used with an integer value as part of the special syntax Java uses to create a new array, as in

```
score = new double[5];
```

Display 6.1   **An Array Used in a Program** (part 1 of 2)

```
1   import java.util.Scanner;

2   public class ArrayOfScores
3   {
4       /**
5        Reads in 5 scores and shows how much each
6        score differs from the highest score.
7       */
8       public static void main(String[] args)
9       {
10          Scanner keyboard = new Scanner(System.in);
11          double[] score = new double[5];
12          int index;
13          double max;

14          System.out.println("Enter 5 scores:");
15          score[0] = keyboard.nextDouble();
16          max = score[0];
17          for (index = 1; index < 5; index++)
18          {
19              score[index] = keyboard.nextDouble();
20              if (score[index] > max)
21                  max = score[index];
22          //max is the largest of the values score[0],..., score[index].
23          }

24          System.out.println("The highest score is " + max);
25          System.out.println("The scores are:");
26          for (index = 0; index < 5; index++)
27              System.out.println(score[index] + " differs from max by "
28                                      + (max - score[index]));
29      }
30  }
```

Sample Dialogue

```
Enter 5 scores:
80  99.9  75  100  85.5
The highest score is 100
The scores are:
80.0 differs from max by 20
99.9 differs from max by 0.1
75.0 differs from max by 25
100.0 differs from max by 0.0
85.5 differs from max by 14.5
```

Due to imprecision in floating-point arithmetic, this value probably will only be a close approximation to 0.1.

(continued)

Display 6.1 An Array Used in a Program (part 2 of 2)

A Common Way to Visualize an Array:

The third use of square brackets is to name an indexed variable of the array, such as `score[0]` or `score[3]`, as illustrated by the following line:

```
max = score[0];
```

As we mentioned previously, the integer inside the square brackets can be any expression that evaluates to a suitable integer, as illustrated by the following:

```
int next = 1;
score[next + 3] = 100;
System.out.println(
            "Score at position 4 is " + score[next + 3]);
```

Note that, in the preceding code, `score[next + 3]` and `score[4]` are the same indexed variable, because `next + 3` evaluates to 4.

The `length` Instance Variable

In Java, an array is considered to be an object, and, like other objects, it might have instance variables. As it turns out, an array has only one public instance variable, which is named `length`. This instance variable is automatically set to the size of the array when the array is created. For example, if you create an array as follows,

```
double[] score = new double[5];
```

then `score.length` has a value of 5.

The `length` instance variable can be used to make your program clearer by replacing an unnamed constant (such as 5), whose meaning may not be obvious, with a meaningful name such as `score.length`. In Display 6.2, we rewrote the program in Display 6.1 using the `length` instance variable.

Display 6.2   The `length` Instance Variable

```
1    import java.util.Scanner;

2    public class ArrayOfScores2
3    {
4        /**
5         Reads in 5 scores and shows how much each
6         Score differs from the highest score.
7        */
8        public static void main(String[] args)
9        {
10           Scanner keyboard = new Scanner(System.in);
11           double[] score = new double[5];
12           int index;
13           double max;

14           System.out.println("Enter " + score.length + " scores:");
15           score[0] = keyboard.nextDouble();
16           max = score[0];
17           for (index = 1; index < score.length; index++)
18           {
19               score[index] = keyboard.nextDouble();
20               if (score[index] > max)
21                   max = score[index];
22           //max is the largest of the values score[0],..., score[index].
23           }

24           System.out.println("The highest score is " + max);
25           System.out.println("The scores are:");
26           for (index = 0; index < score.length; index++)
27               System.out.println(score[index] + " differs from max by "
28                                               + (max - score[index]));
29       }
30   }
```

*The sample dialogue is the
same as in Display 6.1.*

The `length` instance variable cannot be changed by your program (other than by creating a new array with another use of new).[1] For example, the following is illegal:

```
score.length = 10; //Illegal
```

---

[1]The technical details are as follows: The instance variable `length` is created when the array is created and is declared to be `public final int`.

TIP: Use `for` Loops with Arrays

The second `for` loop in Display 6.2 illustrates a common way to step through an entire array using a `for` loop:

```
for (index = 0; index < score.length; index++)
    System.out.println(score[index] + " differs from max by "
                                   + (max - score[index]));
```

The `for` loop is ideally suited for performing array manipulations. ■

PITFALL: Array Indices Always Start with Zero

The indices of an array always start with 0 and end with the integer that is one less than the size of the array. ■

PITFALL: Array Index Out of Bounds

The most common programming error made when using arrays is attempting to use a nonexistent array index. For example, consider the following:

```
int[] a = new int[6];
```

illegal array index

out of bounds

When using the array `a`, every index expression must evaluate to one of the integers 0 through 5. For example, if your program contains the indexed variable `a[i]`, the `i` must evaluate to one of the six integers 0, 1, 2, 3, 4, or 5. If `i` evaluates to anything else, that is an error. When an index expression evaluates to some value other than those allowed by the array declaration, the index is said to be **out of bounds**. If your program attempts to use an array index that is out of bounds, then your program will end with an error message.[2] Note that this is a run-time error message, not a compiler error message.

Array indices get out of bounds most commonly at the first or last iteration of a loop that processes the array. So, it pays to carefully check all array processing loops to be certain that they begin and end with legal array indices. ■

---

[2]Technically speaking, an `ArrayIndexOutOfBounds` Exception is thrown. We will discuss exceptions in Chapter 9. Until you learn about handling exceptions, they will simply appear as error conditions to you.

Initializing Arrays

An array can be initialized when it is declared. When initializing the array, the values for the various indexed variables are enclosed in braces and separated with commas. The expression with the braces is placed on the right-hand side of an assignment operator. For example,

```
int[] age = {2, 12, 1};
```

The array length (size) is automatically set to the number of values in the braces. So, this initializing declaration is equivalent to the following statements:

```
int[] age = new int[3];
age[0] = 2;
age[1] = 12;
age[2] = 1;
```

You can also initialize array elements using a for loop. For example,

```
double[] reading = new double[100];
int index;
for (index = 0; index < reading.length; index++)
    reading[index] = 42.0;
```

automatic initialization   If you do not initialize the elements of an array, they will automatically be initialized to a default value for the base type. The default values are the usual ones. For numeric types, the default value is the zero of the type. For base type char, the default value is the nonprintable zeroth character (char)0, not the space character. For the type boolean, the default value is false. For class types, the default value is null. For example, if you do not initialize an array of doubles, each element of the array will be initialized to 0.0.

Self-Test Exercises

1. In the array declaration

```
Double[] reading = new Double[100];
```

what is

a. the array name?

b. the base type?

c. the length of the array?

d. the range of values an index accessing this array can have?

e. Is it legal to write reading[100] = 79.45; ?

(continued)

Self-Test Exercises (continued)

2. Predict the output:

```
Double a[] = new Double[5];

int i;
for(i = 0; i < 5; i++)
    a[i] = 2.0 * i;
System.out.println(a[i-1]);
```

What would be the output if we change the index in the last line to
`System.out.println(a[i])`?

3. What is the output of the following code?

```
char[] letter = {'a', 'b', 'c'};
for (int index = 0; index < letter.length; index++)
        System.out.print(letter[index] + ", ");
```

4. What is the output of the following code?

```
String[] rhymes = {"Humpty Dumpty", "Twinkle Twinkle",
"Itsy Bitsy"};
    for (int index = 0; index < rhymes.length; index++)
        System.out.println("I love "  + rhymes[index]);
```

5. What is the output of the following code?

```
double[] a = {1.5, 2.5, 3.5};
    for (int i = 0; i < a.length; i++)
    {
        a[i] /= 5;
    System.out.print(a[i] + ", ");
    }
```

6. Suppose we expect the elements of the array a to be ordered so that

```
a[0] ≤ a[1] ≤ a[2] ≤ ...
```

However, to be safe we want our program to test the array and issue a warning
in case it turns out that some elements are out of order. The following code is
supposed to output such a warning, but it contains a bug. What is the bug?

```
double[] a = new double[10];
    <Some code to fill the array a goes here.>
for (int index = 0; index < a.length; index++)
    if (a[index] > a[index + 1])
        System.out.println("Array elements " + index +
            " and " + (index + 1) + " are out of order.");
```

PITFALL: An Array of Characters Is Not a String

An array of characters, such as the array a created below, is conceptually a list of characters; therefore, it is conceptually like a string:

```
char[] a = {'A', ' ', 'B', 'i', 'g', ' ', 'H', 'i', '!'};
```

However, an array of characters, such as a, is not an object of the class String. In particular, the following is illegal in Java:

```
String s = a;
```

Similarly, you cannot normally use an array of characters, such as a, as an argument for a parameter of type String.

It is, however, easy to convert an array of characters to an object of type String. The class String has a constructor that has a single parameter of type char[]. So, you can obtain a String value corresponding to an array of characters, such as a, as follows:

```
String s = new String(a);
```

The object s will have the same sequence of characters as the array a. The object s is an independent copy; any changes made to a will have no effect on s. Note that this always uses the entire array a.

There is also a String constructor that allows you to specify a subrange of an array of characters a. For example,

```
String s2 = new String(a, 2, 3);
```

produces a String object with 3 characters from the array a starting at index 2. So, if a is as above, then

```
System.out.println(s2);
```

outputs

```
Big
```

Although an array of characters is not an object of the class String, it does have some things in common with String objects. For example, you can output an array of characters using println, as follows,

```
System.out.println(a);
```

which produces the output

```
A Big Hi!
```

provided a is as given previously. ∎

6.2 Arrays and References

A little more than kin, and less than kind.

WILLIAM SHAKESPEARE, *Hamlet*

Just like a variable of one of the class types you have seen, a variable of an array type holds a reference. In this section, we explore the consequences of this fact, including a discussion of array parameters. We will see that arrays are objects and that array types can be considered class types, but somewhat different kinds of class types than what you are used to. Arrays and the kinds of classes we have seen before this chapter are *a little more than kin, and less than kind.*

Arrays Are Objects

There are two ways to view an array: as a collection of indexed variables and as a single item whose value is a collection of values of the base type. In Section 6.1, we discussed using arrays as a collection of indexed variables. We will now discuss arrays from the second point of view.

An array can be viewed as a single item whose value is a collection of values of the base type. An array variable (as opposed to an array indexed variable) names the array as a single item. For example, the following declares a variable of an array type:

```
double[] a;
```

This variable a can and will contain a single value. The expression

```
new double[10]
```

creates an array object and stores the object in memory. The following assignment statement places a reference to (the memory address of) this array object in the variable a:

```
a = new double[10];
```

Typically, we combine all this into a single statement as follows:

```
double[] a = new double[10];
```

Notice that this is almost exactly the same as the way that we view objects of a class type. In Java, an array is considered an object. Whenever Java documentation says that something applies to objects, it means that it applies to arrays as well as objects of the class types we have seen up to now. You will eventually see examples of methods that can take arguments that may be objects of any kind. These methods will accept array objects as arguments as well as objects of an ordinary class type. Arrays are somewhat peculiar in how they relate to classes. Some authorities say array types are not classes and some say they are. But, all authorities agree that the arrays themselves are objects. Given that arrays are objects, it seems that one should view array types as classes, and we will do so. However, although an array type `double[]` is a class, the syntax for creating an array object is a bit different. To create an array, use the following syntax:

```
double[] a = new double[10];
```

You can view the expression `new double[10]` as an invocation of a constructor that uses a nonstandard syntax. (The nonstandard syntax was used to be consistent with the syntax used for arrays in older programming languages.)

As we have already seen, every array has an instance variable named `length`, which is a good example of viewing an array as an object. As with any other class type, array variables contain memory addresses, or, as they are usually called in Java, *references*. So, array types are reference types.[3]

Since an array is an object, you might be tempted to think of the indexed variables of an array, such as `a[0]`, `a[1]`, and so forth, as being instance variables of the object. This is actually a pretty good analogy, but it is not literally true. Indexed variables are not instance variables of the array. Indexed variables are a special kind of variable peculiar to arrays. The only instance variable in an array is the `length` instance variable.

An array object is a collection of items of the base type. Viewed as such, an array is an object that can be assigned with the assignment operator and plugged in for a parameter of an array type. Because an array type is a reference type, the behaviors of arrays with respect to assignment `=`, `==`, and parameter passing mechanisms are the same as what we have already described for classes. In the next few subsections, we discuss these details about arrays.

Arrays Are Objects

In Java, arrays are considered to be objects, and, although there is some disagreement on this point, you can safely view an array type as a class type.

Array Types Reference Types

A variable of an array type holds the address of where the array object is stored in memory. This memory address is called a **reference** to the array object.

---

[3]In many programming languages, such as C++, arrays are also reference types just as they are in Java. So, this detail about arrays is not peculiar to Java.

PITFALL: Arrays with a Class Base Type

The base type of an array can be of any type, including a class type. For example, suppose Date is a class and consider the following:

```
Date[] holidayList = new Date[20];
```

VideoNote
Arrays of
Objects

This creates the 20 indexed variables (holidayList[0], holidayList[1], ..., holidayList[19]). It is important to note that this creates 20 *indexed variables* of type Date. This does not create 20 *objects* of type Date. (The index variables are automatically initialized to null, not to an object of the class Date.) Like any other variable of type Date, the indexed variables require an invocation of a constructor using new to create an object. One way to complete the initialization of the array holidayList is as follows:

```
Date[] holidayList = new Date[20];
for (int i = 0; i < holidayList.length; i++)
    holidayList[i] = new Date( );
```

If you omit the for loop (and do not do something else more or less equivalent), then when you run your code, you will undoubtedly get an error message indicating a "null pointer exception." If you do not use new to create an object, an indexed variable like holidayList[i] is just a variable that names no object and hence cannot be used as the calling object for any method. Whenever you are using an array with a class base type and you get an error message referring to a "Null Pointer Exception," it is likely that your indexed variables do not name any objects and you need to add something such as the above for loop. ■

Array Parameters

You can use both array indexed variables and entire arrays as arguments to methods, although they are different types of parameters. We first discuss array indexed variables as arguments to methods.

indexed
variable
arguments

An indexed variable can be an argument to a method in exactly the same way that any variable of the array base type can be an argument. For example, suppose a program contains the following declarations:

```
double n = 0;
double[] a = new double[10];
int i;
```

If myMethod takes one argument of type double, then the following is legal:

```
myMethod(n);
```

Since an indexed variable of the array a is also a variable of type `double`, just like n, the following is equally legal:

```
myMethod(a[3]);
```

There is one subtlety that does apply to indexed variables used as arguments. For example, consider the following method call:

```
myMethod(a[i]);
```

If the value of i is 3, then the argument is a[3]. On the other hand, if the value of i is 0, then this call is equivalent to the following:

```
myMethod(a[0]);
```

The indexed expression is evaluated to determine exactly which indexed variable is given as the argument.

Array Indexed Variables as Arguments

An array indexed variable can be used as an argument anyplace that a variable of the array's base type can be used. For example, suppose you have the following:

```
double[] a = new double[10];
```

Indexed variables such as a[3] and a[index] can then be used as arguments to any method that accepts a `double` as an argument.

---

entire array parameters

You can also define a method that has a formal parameter for an entire array so that when the method is called, the argument that is plugged in for this formal parameter is an entire array. Whenever you need to specify an array type, the type name has the form *Base_Type*[], so this is how you specify a parameter type for an entire array. For example, the method `doubleArrayElements`, given in what follows, will accept any array of `double` as its single argument:

```
public class SampleClass
{
    public static void doubleArrayElements(double[] a)
    {
        int i;
        for (i = 0; i < a.length; i++)
            a[i] = a[i]*2;
    }
    < The rest of the class definition goes here.>
}
```

To illustrate this, suppose you have the following in some method definition,

```
double[] a = new double[10];
double[] b = new double[30];
```

and suppose that the elements of the arrays a and b have been given values. Both of the following are then legal method invocations:

```
SampleClass.doubleArrayElements(a);
SampleClass.doubleArrayElements(b);
```

Note that no square brackets are used when you give an entire array as an argument to a method.

An array type is a reference type just as a class type is, so, as with a class type argument, a method can change the data in an array argument. To phrase it more precisely, a method can change the values stored in the indexed variables of an array argument. This is illustrated by the preceding method doubleArrayElements.

An array type parameter does not specify the length of the array argument that may be plugged in for the parameter. An array knows its length and stores it in the length instance variable. The same array parameter can be replaced with array arguments of different lengths. Note that the preceding method doubleArrayElements can take an array of any length as an argument.

length of array arguments

PITFALL: Use of = and == with Arrays

assignment with arrays

Array types are reference types; that is, an array variable contains the memory address of the array it names. The assignment operator copies this memory address. For example, consider the following code:

```
double[] a = new double[10];
double[] b = new double[10];
int i;
for (i = 0; i < a.length; i++)
    a[i] = i;
b = a;
System.out.println("a[2] = " + a[2] + " b[2] = " + b[2]);
a[2] = 42;
System.out.println("a[2] = " + a[2] + " b[2] = " + b[2]);
```

This will produce the following output:

```
a[2] = 2.0 b[2] = 2.0
a[2] = 42.0 b[2] = 42.0
```

PITFALL: (continued)

The assignment statement b = a; copies the memory address from a to b so that the array variable b contains the same memory address as the array variable a. After the assignment statement, a and b are two different names for the same array. Thus, when we change the value of a[2], we are also changing the value of b[2].

Unless you want two array variables to be two names for the same array (and on rare occasions, you do want this), you should not use the assignment operator with arrays. If you want the arrays a and b in the preceding code to be different arrays with the same values in each index position, then instead of the assignment statement

```
b = a;
```

you need to use something such as the following:

```
int i;
for (i = 0; (i < a.length) && (i < b.length); i++)
    b[i] = a[i];
```

Note that the above code will not make b an exact copy of a, unless a and b have the same length.

==
with arrays

The equality operator == does not test two arrays to see if they contain the same values. It tests two arrays to see if they are stored in the same location in the computer's memory. For example, consider the following code:

```
int[]  c = new int[10];
int[]  d = new int[10];
int i;
for (i = 0; i < c.length; i++)
    c[i] = i;
for (i = 0; i < d.length; i++)
    d[i] = i;

if (c == d)
    System.out.println("c and d are equal by ==.");
else
    System.out.println("c and d are not equal by ==.");
```

This produces the output

```
c and d are not equal by ==
```

(continued)

PITFALL: (continued)

even though c and d contain the same integers in the same indexed variables. A comparison using == will say they are not equal because == checks only the contents of the array variables c and d, which are memory addresses, and c and d contain different memory addresses.

If you want to test two arrays to see if they contain the same elements, then you can define an equalArrays method for the arrays, just as you defined an equals method for a class. Display 6.3 contains one possible definition of equalArrays for arrays in a small demonstration class. ■

Self-Test Exercises

7. Consider the following class definition:

```
public class Addnumber
{
    public static void add(int a)
    {
        <Some code goes in here.>
    }
<The rest of the definition is irrelevant to this question.>
```

Which of the following are acceptable method calls?

```
int[] a = {23, 67, 89, 34, 56, 78};
int number = a.length;
Addnumber.add(number);
Addnumber.add(a[2]);
Addnumber.add (a[3]);
Addnumber.add(a[number]);
Addnumber.add(a);
```

8. Write a method definition for a static void method called decrement, which has a formal parameter for an array of integers and an integer which is to be subtracted from each number in the array. (The definition will go in some class, but you need only give the method definition.)

9. Write a method named outOfOrder that takes as a parameter an array of double and returns a value of type int. This method will test the array for being out of order, meaning that the array violates the condition:

```
a[0] <= a[1] <= a[2] <= ...
```

Self-Test Exercises (continued)

The method returns -1 if the elements are not out of order; otherwise, it returns the index of the first element of the array that is out of order. For example, consider the following declaration:

```
double[] a = {1.2, 2.1, 3.3, 2.5, 4.5,
                7.9, 5.4, 8.7, 9.9, 1.0};
```

In the array above, a[2] and a[3] are the first pair out of order, and a[3] is the first element out of order, so the method returns 3. If the array is sorted, the method returns -1.

10. The following method definition will compile, but does not work as you might hope. What is wrong with it?

```
public static void doubleSize(int[] a)
{
    a = new int[a.length * 2];
}
```

Array Parameters and Array Arguments

An argument to a method may be an entire array. Array arguments are like objects of a class, in that the method can change the data in an array argument; that is, a method can change the values stored in the indexed variables of an array argument. A method with an array parameter is defined and invoked as illustrated by the following examples. Note that the array parameter specifies the base type of the array, but not the length of the array.

EXAMPLE (OF ARRAY PARAMETERS)

```
public class AClass
{
    public static void listChars(char[] a)
    {
        int i;
        for (i = 0; i < a.length; i++)
            System.out.println(a[i] + " ");
    }
    public static void zeroAll(int[] anArray)
    {
        int i;
        for (i = 0; i < anArray.length; i++)
            anArray[i] = 0;
    }
    ...
}
```

EXAMPLE (OF ARRAY ARGUMENTS)

```
char[] c = new char[10];
int[] a = new int[10];
int[] b = new int[20];
```

Note that arrays a and b have different lengths. Also note that no square brackets are used with array arguments.

```
        <Some code to fill the arrays goes here.>

AClass.listChars(c);
AClass.zeroAll(a);
AClass.zeroAll(b);
```

Display 6.3   **Testing Arrays for Equality** (part 1 of 2)

```
1    public class DifferentEquals
2    {
3        /**
4         A demonstration to see how == and an equalArrays method are different.
5        */
6        public static void main(String[] args)
7        {
8            int[]  c = new int[10];
9            int[]  d = new int[10];


10           int i;
11           for (i = 0; i < c.length; i++)
12               c[i] = i;
13           for (i = 0; i < d.length; i++)
14               d[i] = i;
15           if  (c == d)
16               System.out.println("c and d are equal by ==.");
17           else
18               System.out.println("c and d are not equal by ==.");

19           System.out.println("== only tests memory addresses.");

20           if (equalArrays(c, d))
21               System.out.println(
22                       "c and d are equal by the equalArrays method.");
23           else
24               System.out.println(
25                       "c and d are not equal by the equalArrays method.");
```

The arrays c and d contain the same integers in each index position.

Display 6.3   Testing Arrays for Equality (part 1 of 2)

```
26              System.out.println(
27                  "An equalArrays method is usually a more useful test.");
28          }

29      public static boolean equalArrays(int[] a, int[] b)
30      {
31          if (a.length != b.length)
32              return false;
33          else
34          {
35              int i = 0;
36              while (i < a.length)
37              {
38                  if (a[i] != b[i])
39                      return false;
40                  i++;
41              }
42          }

43          return true;
44      }

45  }
```

Sample Dialogue

```
c and d are not equal by ==.
== only tests memory addresses.
c and d are equal by the equalArrays method.
An equalArrays method is usually a more useful test.
```

Arguments for the Method main ★

The heading for the main method of a program looks as if it has a parameter for an array of base type of String:

```
public static void main(String[] args)
```

The identifier args is in fact a parameter of type String[]. Because args is a parameter, it could be replaced by any other nonkeyword identifier. The identifier args is traditional, but it is perfectly legal to use some other identifier.

We have never given main an array argument, or any other kind of argument, when we ran any of our programs. So, what did Java use as an argument to plug in for args? If no argument is given when you run your program, then a default empty array of strings is automatically provided as a default argument to `main` when you run your program.

It is possible to run a Java program in a way that provides an argument to plug in for this array of `String` parameters. You do not provide it as an array. You provide any number of string arguments when you run the program, and those string arguments will automatically be made elements of the array argument that is plugged in for `args` (or whatever name you use for the parameter to `main`). This is normally done by running the program from the command line of the operating system, like so:

```
java YourProgram Do Be Do
```

This will set `args[0]` to `"Do"`, `args[1]` to `"Be"`, `args[2]` to `"Do"`, and `args.length` to 3. These three indexed variables can be used in the method `main`, as in the following sample program:

```
public class YourProgram
{
    public static void main(String[] args)
    {
        System.out.println(args[1] + " " + args[0]
                                        + " " + args[1]);
    }
}
```

If the above program is run from the command line as follows,

```
java YourProgram Do Be Do
```

the output produced by the program will be

```
Be Do Be
```

Be sure to note that the argument to `main` is an array of *strings*. If you want numbers, you must convert the string representations of the numbers to values of a number type or types.

The Method `main` Has an Array Parameter

The heading for the `main` method of a program is as follows:

```
public static void main(String[] args)
```

The identifier `args` is a parameter for an array of base type `String`. The details are explained in the text.

Methods that Return an Array

In Java, a method may return an array. You specify the return type for a method that returns an array in the same way that you specify a type for an array parameter. For example, the following is an example of a method that returns an array:

```java
public static char[] upperCaseVersion(char[] a)
{
    char[] temp = new char[a.length];
    char i;
    for (i = 0; i < a.length; i++)
        temp[i] = Character.toUpperCase(a[i]);
    return temp;
}
```

Returning an Array

A method can return an array. The details are basically the same as for a method that returns an object of a class type.

SYNTAX (FOR A TYPICAL WAY OF RETURNING AN ARRAY)

```java
public static Base_Type [] Method_Name(Parameter_List)
{
    Base_Type[] temp = new Base_Type[Array_Size]
    <Some code to fill temp goes here.>
    return temp;
}
```

The method need not be static and need not be public. You do not necessarily need to use a local array variable such as temp.

EXAMPLE (ASSUMED TO BE IN A CLASS DEFINITION)

```java
public static int [] incrementedArray(int[] a, int increment)
{
    int[] temp = new int[a.length];
    int i;
    for (i = 0; i < a.length; i++)
        temp[i] = a[i] + increment;
    return temp;
}
```

Array Type Names

Whenever you need an array type name, whether for the type of an array variable declaration, the type of an array parameter, or the type for a method that returns an array, you specify the type name in the same way.

SYNTAX

Base_Type[]

EXAMPLES

```
double[] a = new double[10];
int[] giveIntArray(char[] arrayParameter)
{ ... }
```

MyProgrammingLab™

Self-Test Exercises

11. Give the definition of a method called `multiplyArray` that has two parameters – an array of base type `double` and an integer `multiplier`. The method returns another array of base type `double` that has the same length and in which each element has been multiplied by the given number. Make it a static method. To test it, you can add it to any class or, better yet, write a class with a test program in the method `main`.

12. What is wrong with the following method definition? It is an alternate definition of the method by the same name defined in the previous subsection. It will compile.

```
public static char[] upperCaseVersion(char[] a)
{
    char i;
    for (i = 0; i < a.length; i++)
        a[i] = Character.toUpperCase(a[i]);
    return a;
}
```

6.3 Programming with Arrays

Never trust to general impressions, my boy,
but concentrate yourself upon details.

SIR ARTHUR CONAN DOYLE,
A Case of Identity (SHERLOCK HOLMES)

In this section, we discuss partially filled arrays as well as how to use arrays as class instance variables.

Partially Filled Arrays

Often the exact size needed for an array is not known when a program is written or the size may vary from one run of the program to another. One common and easy way to handle this situation is to declare the array to be of the largest size the program could possibly need. The program is then free to use as much or as little of the array as needed.

partially filled array

Partially filled arrays require some care. The program must keep track of how much of the array is used and must not reference any indexed variable that has not been given a meaningful value. The program in Display 6.4 illustrates this point. It reads in a list of golf scores and shows how much each score differs from the average. This program will work for lists as short as 1 score, as long as 10 scores, and of any length in between. The scores are stored in the array `score`, which has 10 indexed variables, but the program uses only as much of the array as it needs. The variable `numberUsed` keeps track of how many elements are stored in the array. The elements (that is, the scores) are stored in positions `score[0]` through `score[numberUsed − 1]`. The details are very similar to what they would be if `numberUsed` were `score.length` and the entire array were used. Note that the variable `numberUsed` usually must be an argument to any method that manipulates the partially filled array. For example, the methods `showDifference` and `computeAverage` use the argument `numberUsed` to ensure that only meaningful array indices are used.

Display 6.4   **Partially Filled Array** (part 1 of 3)

```
1    import java.util.Scanner;

2    public class GolfScores
3    {
4        public static final int MAX_NUMBER_SCORES = 10;

5        /**
6         Shows differences between each of a list of golf scores and their
         average.
7        */
8        public static void main(String[] args)
9        {
10           double[] score = new double[MAX_NUMBER_SCORES];
11           int numberUsed = 0;

12           System.out.println("This program reads golf scores and shows");
13           System.out.println("how much each differs from the average.");
14           System.out.println("Enter golf scores:");
15           numberUsed = fillArray(score);
16           showDifference(score, numberUsed);
17       }
```

Contrary to normal practice, this allows fractional scores, such as 71.5. However, this makes it a better example for our purposes. (Anyway, when I play golf, losing a ball is only half a stroke penalty. Try it sometime.)

(continued)

Display 6.4   Partially Filled Array (part 2 of 3)

```
18      /**
19       Reads values into the array a. Returns the number of values placed
         in the array a.
20       */
21      public static int fillArray(double[] a)
22      {
23          System.out.println("Enter up to " + a.length
24                                  + " nonnegative numbers.");
25          System.out.println("Mark the end of the list with a negative
            number.");
26          Scanner keyboard = new Scanner(System.in);
27
28          double next;
29          int index = 0;
30          next = keyboard.nextDouble();
31          while ((next >= 0) && (index < a.length))
32          {
33              a[index] = next;
34              index++;
35              next = keyboard.nextDouble();
36              //index is the number of array indexed variables used so far.
37          }
38          //index is the total number of array indexed variables used.
39          if (next >= 0)
40              System.out.println("Could only read in "
41                                  + a.length + " input values.");
42
43          return index;
44      }
```

The value of index is the number of values stored in the array.

```
44      /**
45       Precondition: numberUsed <= a.length.
46                     a[0] through a[numberUsed-1] have values.
47       Returns the average of numbers a[0] through a[numberUsed-1].
48       */
49      public static double computeAverage(double[] a, int numberUsed)
50      {
51          double total = 0;
52          for (int index = 0; index < numberUsed; index++)
53              total = total + a[index];
54          if (numberUsed > 0)
55          {
56              return (total/numberUsed);
57          }
58          else
59          {
60              System.out.println("ERROR: Trying to average 0 numbers.");
61              System.out.println("computeAverage returns 0.");
62              return 0;
63          }
64      }
```

Display 6.4   **Partially Filled Array** (part 3 of 3)

```
65       /**
66        Precondition: numberUsed <= a.length.
67                        The first numberUsed indexed variables of a have values.
68        Postcondition: Gives screen output showing how much each of the first
69        numberUsed elements of the array a differ from their average.
70       */
71       public static void showDifference(double[] a, int numberUsed)
72       {
73           double average = computeAverage(a, numberUsed);
74           System.out.println("Average of the " + numberUsed
75                                           + " scores = " + average);
76           System.out.println("The scores are:");
77           for (int index = 0; index < numberUsed; index++)
78               System.out.println(a[index] + " differs from average by "
79                                           + (a[index] - average));
80       }
81   }
```

Sample Dialogue

```
This program reads golf scores and shows
how much each differs from the average.
Enter golf scores:
Enter up to 10 nonnegative numbers.
Mark the end of the list with a negative number.
69  74  68  -1
Average of the 3 scores = 70.3333
The scores are:
69.0 differs from average by -1.33333
74.0 differs from average by 3.66667
68.0 differs from average by -2.33333
```

Self-Test Exercises

13. Complete the definition of the following method that could be added to the class GolfScores in Display 6.4:

```
/**
 Precondition: numberUsed <= argumentArray.length;
 the first numberUsed indexed variables of argumentArray
 have values.
 Returns an array of length numberUsed whose ith element
 is argumentArray[i] - adjustment.
*/
public static double[] differenceArray(
  double[] argumentArray, int numberUsed, double adjustment)
```

(continued)

Self-Test Exercises (continued)

14. Rewrite the class GolfScores from Display 6.4 using the method differenceArray from Self-Test Exercise 13.

15. Rewrite the class GolfScores from Display 6.4 making the array of scores a static variable. Also, make the int variable numberUsed a static variable. Start with Display 6.4, not with the answer to Self-Test Exercise 14. *Hint:* All, or at least most, methods will have no parameters.

EXAMPLE: A Class for Partially Filled Arrays

If you are going to use some array in a disciplined way, such as using the array as a partially filled array, then it is often best to create a class that has the array as an instance variable and to have the constructors and methods of the class provide the needed operations as methods. For example, in Display 6.5, we wrote a class for a partially filled array of doubles. In Display 6.6, we wrote the program in Display 6.4 using this class.

In Display 6.6, we wrote the code to be exactly analogous to that of Display 6.4 so that you could see how one program mirrors the other. However, this resulted in occasionally recomputing a value several times. For example, the method computeAverage contains the following expression three times:

```
a.getNumberOfElements( )
```

Because the PartiallyFilledArray a is not changed in this method, these each return the same value. Some programmers advocate computing this value once only and saving the value in a variable. These programmers would use something such as the following for the definition of computeAverage rather than what we used in Display 6.6. The variable numberOfElementsIna is used to save a value so it need not be recomputed.

```
public static double computeAverage(PartiallyFilledArray a)
{
    double total = 0;
    double numberOfElementsIna = a.getNumberOfElements();
    for (int index = 0; index < numberOfElementsIna; index++)
        total = total + a.getElement(index);
    if (numberOfElementsIna > 0)
    {
        return (total/numberOfElementsIna);
    }
    else
    {
```

EXAMPLE: (continued)

```
System.out.println(
                "ERROR: Trying to average 0 numbers.");
System.out.println("computeAverage returns 0.");
return 0;
        }
    }
```

This is not likely to produce a noticeable difference in the efficiency of the program
in Display 6.6, but if the number of elements in the PartiallyFilledArray were
large so that the for loop would be executed many times, it might make a difference
in a situation where efficiency is critical.

Display 6.5 **Partially Filled Array Class** (part 1 of 4)

```
1   /**
2    Class for a partially filled array of doubles. The class enforces the
3    following invariant: All elements are at the beginning of the array in
4    locations 0, 1, 2, and so forth up to a highest index with no gaps.
5   */
6   public class PartiallyFilledArray
7   {
8       private int maxNumberElements; //Same as a.length
9       private double[] a;
10      private int numberUsed; //Number of indices currently in use

11      /**
12       Sets the maximum number of allowable elements to 10.
13      */
14      PartiallyFilledArray()
15      {
16          maxNumberElements = 10;
17          a = new double[maxNumberElements];
18          numberUsed = 0;
19      }

20      /**
21       Precondition arraySize > 0.
22      */
23      PartiallyFilledArray(int arraySize)
24      {
25          if (arraySize <= 0)
26          {
27              System.out.println("Error Array size zero or negative.");
28              System.exit(0);
29          }
```

(continued)

Display 6.5   **Partially Filled Array Class** (part 2 of 4)

```
30              maxNumberElements = arraySize;
31              a = new double[maxNumberElements];
32              numberUsed = 0;
33          }
34      PartiallyFilledArray(PartiallyFilledArray original)
35          {
36              if (original == null)
37              {
38                  System.out.println("Fatal Error: aborting program.");
39                  System.exit(0);
40              }
41              maxNumberElements =
42                      original.maxNumberElements;
43              numberUsed = original.numberUsed;
44              a = new double[maxNumberElements];
45              for (int i = 0; i < numberUsed; i++)
46                  a[i] = original.a[i];
47          }
```

Note that the instance variable a *is a copy of* original.a. *The following would not be correct:* a = original.a;. *This point is discussed later in this chapter in the subsection entitled "Privacy Leaks with Array Instance variables."*

```
48      /**
49       Adds newElement to the first unused array position.
50      */
51      public void add(double newElement)
52          {
53              if (numberUsed >= a.length)
54              {
55                  System.out.println("Error: Adding to a full array.");
56                  System.exit(0);
57              }
58              else
59              {
60                  a[numberUsed] = newElement;
61                  numberUsed++;
62              }
63          }

64      public double getElement(int index)
65          {
66              if (index < 0 || index >= numberUsed)
67              {
68                  System.out.println("Error:Illegal or unused index.");
69                  System.exit(0);
70              }
71              return a[index];
72          }
```

Display 6.5 **Partially Filled Array Class** (part 3 of 4)

```
73      /**
74       index must be an index in use or the first unused index.
75      */
76      public void resetElement(int index, double newValue)
77      {
78          if (index < 0 || index >= maxNumberElements)
79          {
80              System.out.println("Error:Illegal index.");
81              System.exit(0);
82          }
83          else if (index > numberUsed)
84          {
85              System.out.println(
86                          "Error: Changing an index that is too large.");
87              System.exit(0);
88          }
89          else
90              a[index] = newValue;
91      }

92      public void deleteLast()
93      {
94          if (empty())
95          {
96              System.out.println("Error:Deleting from an empty array.");
97              System.exit(0);
98          }
99          else
100             numberUsed--;
101     }
102     /**
103      Deletes the element in position index. Moves down all elements with
104       indices higher than the deleted element.
105     */
106     public void delete(int index)
107     {
108         if (index < 0 || index >= numberUsed)
109         {
110             System.out.println("Error:Illegal or unused index.");
111             System.exit(0);
112         }

113         for (int i = index; i < numberUsed; i++)
114             a[i] = a[i + 1];
115         numberUsed--;
116     }
```

(continued)

Display 6.5 **Partially Filled Array Class** (part 4 of 4)

```
117     public boolean empty()
118     {
119         return (numberUsed == 0);
120     }

121     public boolean full()
122     {
123         return (numberUsed == maxNumberElements);
124     }

125     public int getMaxCapacity()
126     {
127         return maxNumberElements;
128     }
129
130     public int getNumberOfElements()
131     {
132         return numberUsed;
133     }
134 }
```

TIP: Accessor Methods Need Not Simply Return Instance Variables

Note that in the class `PartiallyFilledArray` in Display 6.5, there is no accessor method that returns a copy of the entire instance variable a. The reason this was not done is that, when the class is used as intended, a user of the class `PartiallyFilledArray` would have no need for the entire array a. That is an implementation detail. The other methods that start with `get` allow a programmer using the class to obtain all the data that he or she needs. ∎

The "for-each" Loop ★

As you have already seen, you can use a `for` loop to cycle through all the elements in an array. For example,

```
double[] a = new double[10];
<Some code to fill the array a>
for (int i = 0; i < a.length; i++)
    System.out.println(a[i]);
```

The standard Java libraries contain definitions of a number of so-called *collection classes*. A collection class is a class whose objects store a collection of values. You cannot cycle

Display 6.6   Display 6.4 Redone Using the Class `PartiallyFilledArray` (part 1 of 2)

```
1   import java.util.Scanner;                    Sample dialog is the same as in Display 6.4.

2   /**
3    Demonstrates Using the class PartiallyFilledArray,
4    */
5   public class GolfScoresVersion2
6   {

7       public static final int MAX_NUMBER_SCORES = 10;

8       /**
9        Shows the differences between each of a list of golf scores and
         their average.
10       */
11      public static void main(String[] args)
12      {
13          PartiallyFilledArray score =
14                          new PartiallyFilledArray(MAX_NUMBER_SCORES);

15          System.out.println("This program reads golf scores and shows");
16          System.out.println("how much each differs from the average.");

17          System.out.println("Enter golf scores:");
18          fillArray(score);
19          showDifference(score);
20      }
21      /**
22       Reads values into the PartiallyFilledArray a.
23       */
24      public static void fillArray(PartiallyFilledArray a)
25      {
26          System.out.println("Enter up to " + a.getMaxCapacity()
27                          + " nonnegative numbers, one per line.");
28          System.out.println("Mark the end of the list with a negative
            number");
29          Scanner keyboard = new Scanner(System.in);
31
32          double next = keyboard.nextDouble();
31          while ((next >= 0) && (!a.full()))
33          {
34              a.add(next);
35              next = keyboard.nextDouble();
36          }
37          if (next >= 0)
38              System.out.println("Could only read in "
39                          + a.getMaxCapacity() + " input values.");
40      }
```

(continued)

Display 6.6   **Display 6.4 Redone Using the Class `PartiallyFilledArray`** (part 2 of 2)

```
41        /**
42         Returns the average of numbers in the PartiallyFilledArray a.
43         */
44        public static double computeAverage(PartiallyFilledArray a)
45        {
46            double total = 0;
47            for (int index = 0; index < a.getNumberOfElements(); index++)
48                total = total + a.getElement(index);

49            if (a.getNumberOfElements() > 0)
50            {
51                return (total/a.getNumberOfElements());
52            }
53            else
54            {
55                System.out.println("ERROR: Trying to average 0 numbers.");
56                System.out.println("computeAverage returns 0.");
57                return 0;
58            }
59        }

60        /**
61         Gives screen output showing how much each of the
62         elements in the PartiallyFilledArray a differ from the average.
63         */
64        public static void showDifference(PartiallyFilledArray a)
65        {
66            double average = computeAverage(a);
67            System.out.println("Average of the " + a.getNumberOfElements()
68                                  + " scores = " + average);
69            System.out.println("The scores are:");
70            for (int index = 0; index < a.getNumberOfElements(); index++)
71                System.out.println(a.getElement(index)
72                                  + "differs from average by"
73                                  + (a.getElement(index) - average));
73        }

74    }
```

through all the elements of a collection object with this kind of `for` loop, because these collection classes normally do not have indices associated with their elements, as an array does.[4] However, starting with version 5.0, Java has added a new kind of `for` loop that can cycle through all the elements in a collection even though there are no indices

---

[4]You can construct a similar for loop using something called an *iterator* in place of the array index but we will not go into that until later in this book.

for-each loop

for the elements (as there are with an array). This new kind of `for` loop is called a **for-each loop** or **enhanced for loop**. We will discuss these for-each loops in detail when we cover collections (Chapter 16). However, these new for-each loops can be used with arrays as well as with objects of these collection classes. In this subsection, we tell you how to use for-each loops with arrays in case you want to get started using them. However, we do not use the for-each loop in this book until we discuss collection classes in Chapter 16.

The following code ends with a for-each loop that is equivalent to the regular `for` loop that we gave at the start of this subsection:

```
double[] a = new double[10];
<Some code to fill the array a>
for (double element : a)
    System.out.println(element);
```

You can read the line beginning with `for` as "for each `element` in `a`, do the following." Note that the variable, `element`, has the same type as the elements in the array. The variable, like `element`, must be declared in the for-each loop as we have done. If you attempt to declare `element` before the for-each loop, you will get a compiler error message.

The general syntax for a for-each loop statement used with an array is

```
for (Array_Base_Type Variable : Array_Name)
    Statement
```

Be sure to notice that you use a colon (not a semicolon) after the *Variable*. You may use any legal variable name for the *Variable*; you do not have to use `element`. Although it is not required, the *Statement* typically contains the *Variable*. When the for-each loop is executed, the *Statement* is executed once for each element of the array. More specifically, for each `element` of the array, the *Variable* is set to the array element and then the *Statement* is executed.

The for-each loop can make your code a lot cleaner and a lot less error prone. If you are not using the indexed variable in a `for` loop for anything other than as a way to cycle through all the array elements, then a for-each loop is preferable. For example,

```
for (double element : a)
    sum += element;
```

is preferable to

```
for (int i = 0; i < a.length; i++)
    sum += a[i];
```

The two loops do the same thing, but the second one mentions an index `i` that is not used for anything other than enumerating the array elements. Also, the syntax for the for-each loop is simpler than that of the regular `for` loop.

On the other hand, you should leave the following `for` loop as is and not attempt to convert it to a for-each loop:

```
for (int i = 0; i < a.length; i++)
    a[i]= 2*i;
```

Because this `for` loop uses the index `i` in the body of the `for` loop and uses it in an essential way, it does not make sense to convert this `for` loop to a for-each loop.

For-Each Loop for Arrays

SYNTAX

```
for (Array_Base_Type Variable : Array_Name)
    Statement
```

EXAMPLES

```
for (double element : a)
    sum += element;
```

The array a has base type `double`. This for-each loop sets each element of the array a to `0.0`.

A good way to read the first line of the example is "For each `element` in a, do the following."

Methods with a Variable Number of Parameters ★

Because of overloading, you can have a method named `max` that returns the largest of two `int` values and have another method named `max` that takes three `int` arguments and returns the largest of the three. If you decide you need a method that returns the largest of four `int` values, you can define a version of the method `max` that takes four arguments. However, with this approach, there is no way to cover all cases of computing the maximum of some number of `int` values. Covering all cases in this way would require an infinite number of definitions for the method name `max`, and no programmer has enough time to write an infinite number of definitions. What we would like is a single method definition for a method named `max` that can take any number of `int` arguments. Starting with version 5.0, Java lets you define methods that take any number of arguments. For example, the following is the definition of a method named `max` that takes any number of `int` arguments and returns the largest of its arguments:

```
public static int max(int... arg)
{
    if (arg.length == 0)
    {
        System.out.println("Fatal Error: "+
            "maximum of zero values.");
        System.exit(0);
    }
```

```
        int largest = arg[0];
        for (int i = 1; i < arg.length; i++)
            if (arg[i] > largest)
                largest = arg[i];
        return largest;
    }
```

This method max works by taking its int arguments and placing them in an array named arg whose base type is int. For example, suppose this definition of the method max is in a class named UtilityClass, and consider the following method call:

```
    int highestScore = UtilityClass.max(3, 2, 5, 1);
```

The array arg is automatically declared and initialized as follows:

```
    int[] arg = {3, 2, 5, 1};
```

So, arg[0] == 3, arg[1] == 2, arg[2] == 5, and arg[3] == 1. After this, the code in the body of the method definition is executed. Display 6.7 shows a sample program that uses this method max.

Note that a method (such as max) that takes any number of arguments is basically a method that takes an array as an argument, except that the job of placing values in the

---

Display 6.7   Method with a Variable Number of Parameters (part 1 of 2)

```
 1   public class UtilityClass
 2   {
 3       /**
 4        Returns the largest of any number of int values.
 5        */
 6       public static int max(int... arg)
 7       {
 8           if (arg.length == 0)
 9           {
10               System.out.println("Fatal Error: maximum of zero values.");
11               System.exit(0);
12           }
13           int largest = arg[0];
14           for (int i = 1; i < arg.length; i++)
15               if (arg[i] > largest)
16                   largest = arg[i];
17           return largest;                         This is the file UtilityClass.java
18       }
19   }
20
```

(continued)

Display 6.7   Method with a Variable Number of Parameters (part 2 of 2)

```
1    import java.util.Scanner;                    This is the file
                                                  VariableParameterDemo.java
2    public class VariableParameterDemo
3    {

4        public static void main(String[] args)
5        {
6            System.out.println("Enter scores for Tom, Dick, and Harriet:");
7            Scanner keyboard = new Scanner(System.in);
8            int tomsScore = keyboard.nextInt();
9            int dicksScore = keyboard.nextInt();
10           int harrietsScore = keyboard.nextInt();

11           int highestScore = UtilityClass.max(tomsScore, dicksScore,
                                              harrietsScore);

12           System.out.println("Highest score = " + highestScore);
13       }
14   }
```

Sample Dialogue

```
Enter scores for Tom, Dick, and Harriet:
55   100   99
Highest score = 100
```

array is done automatically for the programmer. The values for the array are given as arguments, and Java automatically creates an array and places the arguments in the array.

vararg specification

ellipsis

A parameter specification that specifies any number of parameters, such as int... arg, is called a **vararg specification**. (It would make more sense to call it a *varparameter* specification, but the word *vararg* is too well entrenched, so we will go along with common usage.) The three dots in a vararg specification are called an **ellipsis**. Note that the ellipsis is part of the Java syntax and not an abbreviation used in this book. You type in the three dots.

You can have only one variable parameter specification, such as int... arg, in a method definition. However, you may also have any number of ordinary parameters, in which case the vararg specification must be the last item on the parameter list. This is illustrated in Display 6.8, which we discuss in the next subsection.

In Chapter 2, you saw one example of a method that accepts a variable number of arguments, namely the method System.out.printf. However, we could not tell you how to define such methods yourself until we covered the basics about arrays.

Method with a Variable Number of Parameters

A method with a variable number of parameters has a vararg specification as the last item on its parameter list. A vararg specification has the following form:

Type... Array_Name

Some examples of vararg specifications are

```
int... arg
double... a
String... unwanted
```

Displays 6.7 and 6.8 show two of these vararg specifications in complete method definitions.

In any invocation of a method with a vararg specification, you handle arguments corresponding to regular parameters in the usual way. Following the arguments for regular parameters, you can have any number of arguments of the type given in the vararg specification. These arguments are automatically placed in an array, and the array can be used in the method definition. A full description of the details is given in this chapter.

MyProgrammingLab™

Self-Test Exercises

16. Write a method min for the UtilityClass in Display 6.7, which will return the smallest of any number of int values. Use a for-each loop in place of the regular for loop.

17. What would be the dialogue in Display 6.8 if we omit the following line from the program?

```
sentence = Utility2.censor(sentence, " ,"); //Deletes extra commas
```

EXAMPLE: A String Processing Example ★

This example uses material from the earlier starred subsection "Methods with a Variable Number of Parameters." If you have not read that subsection, you should skip this example.

Display 6.8 contains a utility class with the string processing method named censor and an example of a program that uses that method. The method censor takes a single String parameter followed by any number of additional parameters of type String. The first parameter will be a sentence or other string that may contain substrings you want to delete. The method returns its first parameter with all occurrences of the remaining string parameters removed.

(continued)

EXAMPLE: (continued)

Note that the method censor has one regular parameter followed by a specification for any number of additional string parameters. In this case, all parameters are of type String. However, that first regular parameter (or parameters) in a method heading can be of any type (or types); they need not match the type of the vararg specification. We just happen to want the type String here.

Because the first parameter is of type String and the vararg specification in this case says the remaining arguments are of type String, you might wonder why we did not omit the first String parameter sentence, have only a vararg specification, and then use unwanted[0] to serve the same role as sentence. If we did so, then the method censor could be called with no arguments at all. A vararg specification allows any number of arguments, including the possibility of zero arguments. However, we want to insist that the method censor have at least one argument, and the parameter sentence ensures that censor will always have at least one argument.

Privacy Leaks with Array Instance Variables

In Chapter 5, we explained why it is a compromise of privacy for a class to have an accessor (or other method) that returns a reference to a private mutable object. As we noted there, an accessor method should instead return a reference to a *deep copy* of the private object. (See the Pitfall subsection of Chapter 5 entitled "Privacy Leaks.") At the time, we had in mind returning the contents of a private instance variable of a class type. However, the lesson applies equally well to private instance variables of an array type.

For example, suppose that you decide that you want an accessor method for the array instance variable in the class PartiallyFilledArray in Display 6.5. You might be tempted to define the accessor method as follows:

```
public double[] getInsideArray( ) // Problematic version
{
    return a;
}
```

As indicated in the comment, this definition has a problem, which is this accessor method allows a programmer to change the array object named by the private instance variable a in ways that bypass the checks built into the mutator methods of the class PartiallyFilledArray. To see why this is true, *suppose we added this definition of the method* getInsideArray *to the class* PartiallyFilledArray, and then consider the following code:

```
PartiallyFilledArray leakyArray =
                new PartiallyFilledArray(10);
double[] arrayName = leakyArray.getInsideArray( );
```

The variable arrayName and the private instance variable a now contain the same reference, so both arrayName and the private instance variable a name the same array. Using arrayName as a name for the array named by the private instance variable a, we

Display 6.8   String Processing Method with a Variable Number of Parameters (part 1 of 2)

```
1   public class Utility2
2   {
3       /**
4        Returns the first argument with all occurrences of other arguments
             deleted;
5        */
6       public static String censor(String sentence, String... unwanted)
7       {
8           for (int i = 0; i < unwanted.length; i++)
9               sentence = deleteOne(sentence, unwanted[i]);
10          return sentence;
11      }
12      /**
13       Returns sentence with all occurrences of oneUnwanted removed.
14       */
15      private static String deleteOne(String sentence, String oneUnwanted)
16      {
17          String ending;
18          int position = sentence.indexOf(oneUnwanted);
19          while (position >= 0) //While word was found in sentence
20          {
21              ending = sentence.substring(position + oneUnwanted.length());
22              sentence = sentence.substring(0, position) + ending;
23              position = sentence.indexOf(oneUnwanted);
24          }
25          return sentence;
26      }
27  }
```

Both methods use the parameter sentence as a local variable. If this puzzles you, review the material on parameters in Chapters 4 and 5, particularly Display 4.5 in Chapter 4.

If you have trouble following this string processing, review the subsection entitled "String Processing" in Chapter 1.

This is the file `Utility2.java.`

```
1   import java.util.Scanner;
2   public class StringProcessingDemo
3   {
4       public static void main(String[] args)
5       {
6           System.out.println("What did you eat for dinner?");
7           Scanner keyboard = new Scanner(System.in);
8           String sentence = keyboard.nextLine();
9           sentence = Utility2.censor(sentence,
10                              "candy", "french fries", "salt", "beer");
11          sentence = Utility2.censor(sentence, " ,"); //Deletes extra commas
12          System.out.println("You would be healthier if you could answer:");
13          System.out.println(sentence);
14      }
15  }
```

This is the file `StringProcessingDemo.java.`

(continued)

Display 6.8 String Processing Method with a Variable Number of Parameters (part 2 of 2)

Sample Dialogue

```
What did you eat for dinner?
I ate salt cod, broccoli, french fries, salt peanuts, and apples.
You would be healthier if you could answer:
I ate cod, broccoli, peanuts, and apples.
```

can now fill the indexed variables of a in any order and need not fill the array starting at the first element. This violates the spirit of the private modifier for the array instance variable a. For this reason, the accessor method getInsideArray should return a deep copy of the array named by the private instance variable a. A safe definition of getInsideArray is the following:

```
public double[] getInsideArray( ) // Good version
{
    //Recall that maxNumberElements == a.length.
    double[] temp = new double[maxNumberElements];
    for (int i = 0; i < maxNumberElements; i++)
        temp[i] = a[i];
    return temp;
}
```

If a private instance variable is an array type that has a class as its base type, then you need to be sure to make copies of the class objects in the array when you make a copy of the array. This is illustrated by the toy class in Display 6.9.

Display 6.9 also includes a copy constructor. As illustrated in that display, the copy constructor should make a completely independent copy of the array instance variable (that is, a deep copy) in the same way that the accessor method does. This same point is also illustrated by the copy constructor in Display 6.5.

Display 6.9 Accessor Method for an Array Instance Variable (part 1 of 2)

```
1  /**
2   Demonstrates the correct way to define an accessor
3   method to a private array of class objects.
4  */
5  public class ToyExample
6  {
7      private Date[] a;
```

The class Date is defined in Display 4.11, but you do not need to know the details of the definition to understand the point of this example.

Display 6.9   Accessor Method for an Array Instance Variable (part 2 of 2)

```
8       public ToyExample(int arraySize)
9       {
10          a = new Date[arraySize];
11          for (int i = 0; i < arraySize; i++)
12              a[i] = new Date();
13      }

14      public ToyExample(ToyExample object)    ← Copy constructor for ToyExample.
15      {
16          int lengthOfArrays = object.a.length;
17          this.a = new Date[lengthOfArrays];
18          for (int i = 0; i < lengthOfArrays; i++)    ← Copy constructor for Date.
19              this.a[i] = new Date(object.a[i]);
20      }

21      public Date[] getDateArray()    ← Accessor method.
22      {
23          Date[] temp = new Date[a.length];
24          for (int i = 0; i < a.length; i++)
25              temp[i] = new Date(a[i]);
26          return temp;
27      }
```
                                              Copy constructor for Date.

<There presumably are other methods that are not shown,
                    but they are irrelevant to the point at hand.>

```
28  }
```

MyProgrammingLab   ## Self-Test Exercises

18. Define a method named removeAll that can be added to the class
    PartiallyFilledArray. This method has no parameters. When invoked, the
    method removeAll deletes all the elements in its calling object.

19. Define a method named increaseCapacity that can be added to the
    class PartiallyFilledArray in Display 6.5. The method has one
    int parameter named newCapacity that increases the capacity of the
    PartiallyFilledArray so that it can hold up to newCapacity numbers. If
    newCapacity is less than or equal to maxNumberOfElements, then the method
    does nothing. If newCapacity is greater than maxNumberOfElements, then
    maxNumberElements is set equal to newCapacity and a new array of length
    newCapacity is created for the array instance variable a. The old values of the
    array instance variable are copied to the newly created array.

EXAMPLE: Sorting an Array

In this example, we define a method called `sort` that will sort a partially filled array of numbers so that they are ordered from smallest to largest.

The procedure `sort` has one array parameter, `a`. The array `a` will be partially filled, so there is an additional formal parameter called `numberUsed`, which tells how many array positions are used. Thus, the heading for the method `sort` will be

```
public static void sort(double[] a, int numberUsed)
```

The method `sort` rearranges the elements in array `a` so that after the method call is completed, the elements are sorted as follows:

```
a[0] ≤ a[1] ≤ a[2] ≤ ... ≤ a[numberUsed - 1]
```

The algorithm we use to do the sorting is called **selection sort**. It is one of the easiest of the sorting algorithms to understand.

One way to design an algorithm is to rely on the definition of the problem. In this case, the problem is to sort an array `a` from smallest to largest. That means rearranging the values so that `a[0]` is the smallest, `a[1]` the next smallest, and so forth. That definition yields an outline for the selection sort algorithm:

```
for (int index = 0; index < numberUsed; index++)
    Place the indexth smallest element in a[index]
```

There are many ways to realize this general approach. The details could be developed by using two arrays and copying the elements from one array to the other in sorted order, but using one array should be both adequate and economical. Therefore, the method `sort` uses only the one array containing the values to be sorted. The method `sort` rearranges the values in the array `a` by interchanging pairs of values. Let us go through a concrete example so that you can see how the algorithm works.

Consider the array shown in Display 6.10. The selection sort algorithm will place the smallest value in `a[0]`. The smallest value is the value in `a[4]`. So the algorithm interchanges the values of `a[0]` and `a[4]`. The algorithm then looks for the next smallest element. The value in `a[0]` is now the smallest element, so the next smallest element is the smallest of the remaining elements `a[1]`, `a[2]`, `a[3]`,..., `a[9]`. In the example in Display 6.10, the next smallest element is in `a[6]`, so the algorithm interchanges the values of `a[1]` and `a[6]`. This positioning of the second smallest element is illustrated in the fourth and fifth array pictures in Display 6.10. The algorithm then positions the third smallest element, and so forth. As the sorting proceeds, the beginning array elements are set equal to the correct sorted values. The sorted portion of the array grows by adding elements one after the other from the elements in the unsorted end of the array. Notice that the algorithm need not do anything with the value in the last indexed variable, `a[9]`, because once the other elements are positioned correctly, `a[9]` must also have the correct value. After all, the correct value for `a[9]` is the smallest value left to be moved, and the only value left to be moved is the value that is already in `a[9]`.

EXAMPLE: (continued)

The definition of the method sort, included in a class, is given in Display 6.11. sort uses the method indexOfSmallest to find the index of the smallest element in the unsorted end of the array, and then it does an interchange to move this next smallest element down into the sorted part of the array.

The method interchange, shown in Display 6.11, is used to interchange the values of indexed variables. For example, the following call will interchange the values of a[0] and a[4]:

```
interchange(0, 4, a);
```

A sample use of the sort method is given in Display 6.12.

Display 6.10   Selection Sort

a[0]	a[1]	a[2]	a[3]	a[4]	a[5]	a[6]	a[7]	a[8]	a[9]
8	6	11	17	3	15	5	19	28	12

Unsorted array (pointing to a[6])

8	6	11	17	3	15	5	19	28	12

3	6	11	17	8	15	5	19	28	12

3	6	11	17	8	15	5	19	28	12

3	5	11	17	8	15	6	19	28	12

.
.
.

3	5	6	8	11	12	15	17	19	28

MyProgrammingLab™

Self-Test Exercises

20. How would you need to change the method sort in Display 6.11 so that it can sort an array of values of type double into decreasing order, instead of increasing order?

21. If an array of int values has a value that occurs twice (such as b[0] == 42 and b[7] == 42) and you sort the array using the method SelectionSort.sort, will there be one or two copies of the repeated value after the array is sorted?

Display 6.11   Selection Sort Class (part 1 of 2)

```
1   public class SelectionSort
2   {
3       /**
4        Precondition: numberUsed <= a.length;
5                    The first numberUsed indexed variables have values.
6        Action: Sorts a so that a[0] <= a[1] <= ... <= a[numberUsed - 1].
7        */
8       public static void sort(double[] a, int numberUsed)
9       {
10          int index, indexOfNextSmallest;
11          for (index = 0; index < numberUsed - 1; index++)
12          {//Place the correct value in a[index]:
13              indexOfNextSmallest = indexOfSmallest(index, a, numberUsed);
14              interchange(index,indexOfNextSmallest, a);
15              //a[0] <= a[1] <= ...<= a[index] and these are the smallest
16              //of the original array elements. The remaining positions
17              //contain the rest of the original array elements.
18          }
19      }
20      /**
21       Returns the index of the smallest value among
22       a[startIndex], a[startIndex+1], ... a[numberUsed - 1]
23       */
24      private static int indexOfSmallest(int startIndex,
25                                          double[] a, int numberUsed)
26      {
27          double min = a[startIndex];
28          int indexOfMin = startIndex;
29          int index;
30          for (index = startIndex + 1; index < numberUsed; index++)
31              if (a[index] < min)
32              {
33                  min = a[index];
34                  indexOfMin = index;
35                  //min is smallest of a[startIndex] through a[index]
36              }
37          return indexOfMin;
38      }
```

Display 6.11   **Selection Sort Class** (part 2 of 2)

```
39      /**
40       Precondition: i and j are legal indices for the array a.
41       Postcondition: Values of a[i] and a[j] have been interchanged.
42      */
43      private static void interchange(int i, int j, double[] a)
44      {
45          double temp;
46          temp = a[i];
47          a[i] = a[j];
48          a[j] = temp; //original value of a[i]
49      }
50  }
```

Display 6.12   **Demonstration of the SelectionSort Class**

```
1   public class SelectionSortDemo
2   {
3       public static void main(String[] args)
4       {
5           double[] b = {7.7, 5.5, 11, 3, 16, 4.4, 20, 14, 13, 42};

6           System.out.println("Array contents before sorting:");
7           int i;
8           for (i = 0; i < b.length; i++)
9               System.out.print(b[i] + " ");
10          System.out.println();

11
12          SelectionSort.sort(b, b.length);

13          System.out.println("Sorted array values:");
14          for (i = 0; i < b.length; i++)
15              System.out.print(b[i] + " ");
16          System.out.println();
17      }
18  }
```

Sample Dialogue

```
Array contents before sorting:
7.7 5.5 11.0 3.0 16.0 4.4 20.0 14.0 13.0 42.0
Sorted array values:
3.0 4.4 5.5 7.7 11.0 13.0 14.0 16.0 20.0 42.0
```

Enumerated Types ★

Sometimes you need a simple type consisting of a short list of named values. For example, the values might be clothing sizes, the days of the week, or some other brief list. Starting with version 5.0, Java allows you to have such an **enumerated type**. For example, the following is an enumerated type for the days of a five-day work week:

enumerated type

```
enum WorkDay {MONDAY, TUESDAY, WEDNESDAY, THURSDAY, FRIDAY};
```

A value of an enumerated type is a kind of named constant and so, by convention, is spelled with all uppercase letters. So, we used, for example, MONDAY, not Monday, in the above definition of the enumerated type WorkDay. Using Monday would have been legal, but poor style.

As with any other type, you can have variables of an enumerated type; for example,

```
WorkDay meetingDay, availableDay;
```

A variable of an enumerated type can have a value that must be either one of the values listed in the definition of the type or else the special value null, which serves as a placeholder indicating that the variable has no "real" value. For example, you can set the value of a variable of an enumerated type with an assignment statement, as follows:

```
meetingDay = WorkDay.THURSDAY;
```

Note that when you write the value of an enumerated type, you need to preface the name of the value, such as THURSDAY, with the name of the type. For example, you use WorkDay.THURSDAY, not THURSDAY.

As with any other type, you can combine the declaration of a variable with the assignment of a value to the variable, as in

```
WorkDay meetingDay = WorkDay.THURSDAY;
```

A program that demonstrates the syntax for using enumerated types is given in Display 6.13. Be sure to notice that we placed the definition of the enumerated type outside of the main method in the same place that you would give named constants.

Display 6.13   An Enumerated Type (part 1 of 2)

```
1  public class EnumDemo
2  {
3      enum WorkDay {MONDAY, TUESDAY, WEDNESDAY, THURSDAY, FRIDAY};

4      public static void main(String[] args)
5      {
6          WorkDay startDay = WorkDay.MONDAY;
7          WorkDay endDay = WorkDay.FRIDAY;
```

Display 6.13   **An Enumerated Type** (part 2 of 2)

```
8              System.out.println("Work starts on " + startDay);
9              System.out.println("Work ends on " + endDay);
10      }
11  }
```

Sample Dialogue

```
Work starts on MONDAY
Work ends on FRIDAY
```

Enumerated Type

An **enumerated type** is a type for which you give all the values of the type in a typically short list. A value of an enumerated type is a kind of named constant and so, by convention, is spelled with all uppercase letters.

SYNTAX

enum *Type_Name* {*FIRST_VALUE*, *SECOND_VALUE*, ..., *LAST_VALUE*};

Starting with version 5.0, enum is a keyword in Java.

EXAMPLE

enum Flavor {VANILLA, CHOCOLATE, STRAWBERRY};

The definition of an enumerated type is normally placed outside of all methods in the same place that you give named constants. The location for an enumerated type definition is illustrated in Display 6.13. (The definition can be placed in other locations, but we will not need to place them anywhere else.)

You can output the value of a variable of an enumerated type using `println`. For example,

```
System.out.println(WorkDay.THURSDAY);
```

will produce the following screen output:

```
THURSDAY
```

Note that the type name `WorkDay` is not output. Other examples of outputting an enumerated type value are given in Display 6.13.

The values of an enumerated type, such as `WorkDay.THURSDAY`, are not `String` values. In fact, you should not care what kind of values they are. How they are implemented is not relevant to being able to use the values of an enumerated type. All you really need to know is that, for example, `WorkDay.THURSDAY` and `WorkDay.FRIDAY` are different values and will test as being different if you compare them with `==`.

Although values of an enumerated type are not `String` values, they are used for tasks that could be done by `String` values; however, enumerated types work better than `String` values for some tasks. You could use a `String` variable in place of a variable of an enumerated type. For example, you could use

```
String meetingDay = "THURSDAY";
```

instead of

```
WorkDay meetingDay = WorkDay.THURSDAY;
```

However, using a `String` variable allows for the possibility of setting the variable equal to a nonsense value, such as `"SUNDAY"` or `"GaGa"` for a work day, and to do so without the computer issuing any warning statement. With an enumerated type, you know the only possible values for a variable of that type are the values given in the enumerated type definition; if you try to give the variable a different value, you will get an error message.

An enumerated type is actually a class, and its values are objects of the class. Some methods that are automatically provided with every enumerated type are given in Display 6.14.

Display 6.14   **Some Methods Included with Every Enumerated Type** (part 1 of 2)

```
public boolean equals(Any_Value_Of_An_Enumerated_Type)
```

Returns `true` if its argument is the same value as the calling value. While it is perfectly legal to use `equals`, it is easier and more common to use `==`.

EXAMPLE

For enumerated types, `(Value1.equals(Value2))` is equivalent to `(Value1 == Value2)`.

```
public String toString( )
```

Returns the calling value as a string. This is often invoked automatically. For example, this method is invoked automatically when you output a value of the enumerated type using `System.out.println` or when you concatenate a value of the enumerated type to a string. See Display 6.15 for an example of this automatic invocation.

EXAMPLE

`WorkDay.MONDAY.toString( )` returns `"MONDAY"`. The enumerated type `WorkDay` is defined in Display 6.13.

Display 6.14   Some Methods Included with Every Enumerated Type (part 2 of 2)

```
public int ordinal( )
```

Returns the position of the calling value in the list of enumerated type values. The first position is 0.

EXAMPLE

`WorkDay.MONDAY.ordinal( )` returns 0, `WorkDay.TUESDAY.ordinal( )` returns 1, and so forth. The enumerated type `WorkDay` is defined in Display 6.13.

```
public int compareTo(Any_Value_Of_The_Enumerated_Type)
```

Returns a negative value if the calling object precedes the argument in the list of values, returns 0 if the calling object equals the argument, and returns a positive value if the argument precedes the calling object.

EXAMPLE

`WorkDay.TUESDAY.compareTo(WorkDay.THURSDAY)` returns a negative value. The type `WorkDay` is defined in Display 6.13.

```
public EnumeratedType [] values( )
```

Returns an array whose elements are the values of the enumerated type in the order in which they are listed in the definition of the enumerated type.

EXAMPLE

See Display 6.15.

```
public static EnumeratedType valueOf(String name)
```

Returns the enumerated type value with the specified name. The string name must be an exact match.

EXAMPLE

`WorkDay.valueOf("THURSDAY")` returns `WorkDay.THURSDAY`. The type `WorkDay` is defined in Display 6.13.

When comparing two variables (or constants) of an enumerated type, you can use the `equals` method, but it is more common to instead use the `==` operator. For example,

```
if (meetingDay == availableDay)
    System.out.println("Meeting will be on schedule.");
if (meetingDay == WorkDay.THURSDAY)
    System.out.println("Long weekend!");
```

With enumerated types, the `equals` method and the `==` operator are equivalent, but the `==` operator has nicer syntax.

To get the full potential from an enumerated type, you need some way to cycle through all its values. The static method `values( )` provides you with that ability. This method returns an array whose elements are the values of the enumerated type, and is provided automatically for every enumerated type. Display 6.15 gives a simple example of using the method `values( )` to cycle through all the values in an enumerated type. (This is one situation where it is much cleaner to use a for-each loop instead of an ordinary `for` loop. If you have read the starred section on the for-each loop, be sure to do Self-Test Exercise 22, which redoes Display 6.15 using a for-each loop.)

The `values` Method

Every enumerated type has a static method named `values( )`, which returns an array whose elements are the values of the enumerated type in the order in which they are listed in the definition of the enumerated type. The base type for the array returned is the enumerated type. See Display 6.15 for an example.

Display 6.15   The Method `values` (part 1 of 2)

```
1    import java.util.Scanner;
2
3    public class EnumValuesDemo
4    {
5        enum WorkDay {MONDAY, TUESDAY, WEDNESDAY, THURSDAY, FRIDAY};

6        public static void main(String[] args)
7        {
8            WorkDay[] day = WorkDay.values();

9            Scanner keyboard = new Scanner(System.in);
10           double hours = 0, sum = 0;                This is equivalent to day[i].toString().

11           for (int i = 0; i < day.length; i++)
12           {
13               System.out.println("Enter hours worked for " + day[i]);
14               hours = keyboard.nextDouble();
15                sum = sum + hours;
16           }

17           System.out.println("Total hours work = " + sum);
18       }
19   }
```

Display 6.15   **The Method values (part 2 of 2)**

Sample Dialogue

```
Enter hours worked for MONDAY
8
Enter hours worked for TUESDAY
8
Enter hours worked for WEDNESDAY
8
Enter hours worked for THURSDAY
8
Enter hours worked for FRIDAY
7.5
Total hours worked = 39.5
```

TIP: Enumerated Types in `switch` Statements ★

You can use an enumerated type to control a `switch` statement. In other words, the type of the controlling expression in a `switch` statement can be an enumerated type. This is illustrated in Display 6.16. Note that the case labels must be unqualified names; use `VANILLA`, not `Flavor.VANILLA`.

This program uses the static method `valueOf` to convert an input string to a value of the enumerated type. For example,

```
Flavor.valueOf("STRAWBERRY")
```

returns `Flavor.STRAWBERRY`. Note that the program changes the input to all uppercase letters before giving it as an argument to the method `valueOf`. The method `valueOf` requires an exact match. An invocation of `Flavor.valueOf("Vanilla")` will end your program with an error message;[5] you must use `"VANILLA"` to match the exact spelling (including upper- versus lowercase) of the value in `Flavor`.

At this point, you may wonder what the difference is between `STRAWBERRY` and `Flavor.STRAWBERRY` and how to tell which one to use in a given situation. The value of the enumerated type is `STRAWBERRY`. We write `Flavor.STRAWBERRY` to say we mean `STRAWBERRY` as defined in `Flavor`, as opposed to `STRAWBERRY` as defined in some other type, such as

```
enum Berry {STRAWBERRY. BLUEBERRY, RASPBERRY};
```

(continued)

---

[5]After you cover exceptions in Chapter 9, you will be able to cope with answers such as `PISTACHIO` that do not correspond to any value of type `Flavor` . An invocation of `Flavor.valueOf("PISTACHIO")` will throw an *IlllegalArgumentException*, something explained in Chapter 9. Until then, your program will simply give an error message when `valueOf` cannot cope with its argument.

TIP: (continued)

A single program with both type definitions (`Flavor` and `Berry`) could use both `Flavor.STRAWBERRY` and `Berry.STRAWBERRY`.

So, when can you use `STRAWBERRY` instead of `Flavor.STRAWBERRY`? The approximate answer is when there is enough context for the compiler to know `STRAWBERRY` means `STRAWBERRY` as defined in the type `Flavor`. For example, in a `switch` statement, if the type of the controlling expression is `Flavor`, then `STRAWBERRY` can only mean `Flavor.STRAWBERRY`. This rule will help in remembering when to use `STRAWBERRY` and when to use `Flavor.STRAWBERRY`. But, sometimes you may simply have to check a reference or try the two possibilities out and see which one (or ones) the compiler accepts. ∎

Display 6.16   Enumerated Type in a `switch` Statement (part 1 of 2)

```
 1   import java.util.Scanner;
 2
 3   public class EnumSwitchDemo
 4   {
 5       enum Flavor {VANILLA, CHOCOLATE, STRAWBERRY};
 6       public static void main(String[] args)
 7       {
 8           Flavor favorite = null;
 9           Scanner keyboard = new Scanner(System.in);
10           System.out.println("What is your favorite flavor?");
11           String answer = keyboard.next();
12           answer = answer.toUpperCase();
13           favorite = Flavor.valueOf(answer);
14           switch (favorite)
15           {
16               case VANILLA:
17                   System.out.println("Classic");
18                   break;
19               case CHOCOLATE:
20                   System.out.println("Rich");
21                   break;
22               default:
23                   System.out.println("I bet you said STRAWBERRY.");
24                   break;
25           }
26       }
27   }
```

The case labels must have just the name of the value without the type name and dot.

Display 6.15   **The Method values** (part 2 of 2)

Sample Dialogue

```
Enter hours worked for MONDAY
8
Enter hours worked for TUESDAY
8
Enter hours worked for WEDNESDAY
8
Enter hours worked for THURSDAY
8
Enter hours worked for FRIDAY
7.5
Total hours worked = 39.5
```

TIP: Enumerated Types in `switch` Statements ★

You can use an enumerated type to control a `switch` statement. In other words, the type of the controlling expression in a `switch` statement can be an enumerated type. This is illustrated in Display 6.16. Note that the case labels must be unqualified names; use `VANILLA`, not `Flavor.VANILLA`.

This program uses the static method `valueOf` to convert an input string to a value of the enumerated type. For example,

```
Flavor.valueOf("STRAWBERRY")
```

returns `Flavor.STRAWBERRY`. Note that the program changes the input to all uppercase letters before giving it as an argument to the method `valueOf`. The method `valueOf` requires an exact match. An invocation of `Flavor.valueOf("Vanilla")` will end your program with an error message;[5] you must use `"VANILLA"` to match the exact spelling (including upper- versus lowercase) of the value in `Flavor`.

At this point, you may wonder what the difference is between `STRAWBERRY` and `Flavor.STRAWBERRY` and how to tell which one to use in a given situation. The value of the enumerated type is `STRAWBERRY`. We write `Flavor.STRAWBERRY` to say we mean `STRAWBERRY` as defined in `Flavor`, as opposed to `STRAWBERRY` as defined in some other type, such as

```
enum Berry {STRAWBERRY. BLUEBERRY, RASPBERRY};
```

(continued)

---

[5]After you cover exceptions in Chapter 9, you will be able to cope with answers such as `PISTACHIO` that do not correspond to any value of type `Flavor`. An invocation of `Flavor.valueOf("PISTACHIO")` will throw an *IlllegalArgumentException*, something explained in Chapter 9. Until then, your program will simply give an error message when `valueOf` cannot cope with its argument.

TIP: (continued)

A single program with both type definitions (Flavor and Berry) could use both Flavor.STRAWBERRY and Berry.STRAWBERRY.

So, when can you use STRAWBERRY instead of Flavor.STRAWBERRY? The approximate answer is when there is enough context for the compiler to know STRAWBERRY means STRAWBERRY as defined in the type Flavor. For example, in a switch statement, if the type of the controlling expression is Flavor, then STRAWBERRY can only mean Flavor.STRAWBERRY. This rule will help in remembering when to use STRAWBERRY and when to use Flavor.STRAWBERRY. But, sometimes you may simply have to check a reference or try the two possibilities out and see which one (or ones) the compiler accepts. ∎

Display 6.16 Enumerated Type in a `switch` Statement (part 1 of 2)

```
1   import java.util.Scanner;
2
3   public class EnumSwitchDemo
4   {
5       enum Flavor {VANILLA, CHOCOLATE, STRAWBERRY};
6
7       public static void main(String[] args)
8       {
9           Flavor favorite = null;
10          Scanner keyboard = new Scanner(System.in);

11          System.out.println("What is your favorite flavor?");
12          String answer = keyboard.next();
13          answer = answer.toUpperCase();
14          favorite = Flavor.valueOf(answer);

15          switch (favorite)
16          {
17              case VANILLA:
18                  System.out.println("Classic");
19                  break;
20              case CHOCOLATE:
21                  System.out.println("Rich");
22                  break;
23              default:
24                  System.out.println("I bet you said STRAWBERRY.");
25                  break;
26          }
27      }
28  }
```

The case labels must have just the name of the value without the type name and dot.

Display 6.16   Enumerated Type in a `switch` Statement (part 2 of 2)

Sample Dialogue

```
What is your favorite flavor?
Vanilla
Classic
```

Sample Dialogue

```
What is your favorite flavor?
STRAWBERRY
I bet you said STRAWBERRY.
```

Sample Dialogue

```
What is your favorite flavor?
PISTACHIO          ◄──────    This input causes the program to
                              end and issue an error message.
```

MyProgrammingLab™ ## Self-Test Exercise

22. Rewrite the program in Display 6.15 using a for-each loop.

6.4   Multidimensional Arrays

Two indices are better than one.

ANONYMOUS

Java allows you to declare arrays with more than one index. In this section, we describe these multidimensional arrays.

Multidimensional Array Basics

array declarations

It is sometimes useful to have an array with more than one index, and this is allowed in Java. The following creates an array of characters called `page`. The array `page` has two indices, the first index ranging from 0 to 29 and the second from 0 to 99.

```
char[][] page = new char[30][100];
```

This is equivalent to the following two steps:

```
char[][] page;
page = new char[30][100];
```

indexed
variables

The **indexed variables** for this array each have two indices. For example, `page[0]`
`[0]`, `page[15][32]`, and `page[29][99]` are three of the indexed variables for this
array. Note that each index must be enclosed in its own set of square brackets. As was
true of the one-dimensional arrays we have already seen, each indexed variable for a
multidimensional array is a variable of the base type—in this case, the type `char`.

An array may have any number of indices, but perhaps the most common number is
two. A two-dimensional array can be visualized as a two-dimensional display with the
first index giving the row and the second index giving the column. For example, the
array indexed variables of the two-dimensional array a, declared and created as

```
char[][] a = new char[5][12];
```

can be visualized as follows:

```
a[0][0], a[0][1], a[0][2], ..., a[0][11]
a[1][0], a[1][1], a[1][2], ..., a[1][11]
a[2][0], a[2][1], a[2][2], ..., a[2][11]
a[3][0], a[3][1], a[3][2], ..., a[3][11]
a[4][0], a[4][1], a[4][2], ..., a[4][11]
```

You might use the array a to store all the characters on a (very small) page of text that has
5 lines (numbered 0 through 4) and 12 characters on each line (numbered 0 through 11).

Declaring and Creating a Multidimensional Array

You declare a multidimensional array variable and create a multidimensional array object in
basically the same way that you create and name a one-dimensional array. You simply use
as many square brackets as there are indices.

SYNTAX

Base_Type [] ... [] *Variable_Name* = new *Base_Type* [*Length_l*]...[*Length_n*];

EXAMPLES

```
char[][] a = new char[5][12];
char[][] page = new char[30][100];
double[][] table = new double[100][10];
int[][][] figure = new int[10][20][30];
Person[][] entry = new Person[10][10];
```

Person is a class.

---

a multi-
dimensional
array is an
array of
arrays

In Java, a two-dimensional array, such as a, is actually an array of arrays. The
above array a is actually a one-dimensional array of size 5, whose base type is a one-
dimensional array of characters of size 12. This is diagrammed in Display 6.17. As
shown in that display, the array variable a contains a reference to a one-dimensional
array of length 5 with a base type of `char[]`; that is, the base type of a is the type for an
entire one-dimensional array of characters. Each indexed variable `a[0]`, `a[1]`, and so
forth contains a reference to a one-dimensional array of characters.

Display 6.17 Two-Dimensional Array as an Array of Arrays

```
char[][] a = new char[5][12];
```

A three-dimensional array is an array of arrays of arrays, and so forth for higher dimensions.

Normally, the fact that a two-dimensional array is an array of arrays need not concern you, and you can usually act as if the array a is actually an array with two indices (rather than an array of arrays, which is harder to keep track of). There are, however, some situations where a two-dimensional array looks very much like an array of arrays. For example, you will see that when using the instance variable `length`, you must think of a two-dimensional array as an array of arrays.

Using the `length` Instance Variable

Suppose you want to fill all the elements in the following two-dimensional array with `'Z'`:

```
char[][] page = new char[30][100];
```

You can use a nested `for` loop such as the following:

```
int row, column;
for (row = 0; row < page.length; row++)
    for (column = 0; column < page[row].length; column++)
        page[row][column] = 'Z';
```

Let's analyze this nested `for` loop in a bit more detail. The array `page` is actually a one-dimensional array of length `30`, and each of the 30 indexed variables `page[0]` through `page[29]` is a one-dimensional array with base type `char` and with a length of `100`. That is why the first `for` loop is terminated using `page.length`. For a two-dimensional array such as `page`, the value of `length` is the number of first indices or, equivalently, the number of rows—in this case, `30`. Now let's consider the inside `for` loop.

The 0th row in the two-dimensional array `page` is the one-dimensional array `page[0]`, and it has `page[0].length` entries. More generally, `page[row]` is a one-dimensional array of `chars`, and it has `page[row].length` entries. This is why the inner for loop is terminated using `page[row].length`. Of course, in this case, `page[0].length`, `page[1].length`, and so forth through to `page[29].length` are all equal and all equal to `100`. (If you read the optional section entitled "Ragged Arrays," which follows this section, you will see that these need not all be equal.)

Self-Test Exercise

23. What is the output produced by the following code?

```
int[][] myArray = new int[4][4];
int index1, index2;
for (index1 = 0; index1 < myArray.length; index1++)
    for (index2 = 0;
            index2 < myArray[index1].length; index2++)
        myArray[index1][index2] = index2;
for (index1 = 0; index1 < myArray.length; index1++)
{
    for (index2 = 0;
            index2 < myArray[index1].length; index2++)
        System.out.print(myArray[index1][index2] + " ");
    System.out.println();
}
```

Ragged Arrays ★

ragged arrays

Most programmers typically create a two-dimensional array with the same number of entries for each row. However, it is possible for different rows to have a different numbers of columns. These sorts of arrays are called **ragged arrays**.

To help explain the details, let's start with an ordinary, nonragged two-dimensional array, created as follows:

```
double[][] a = new double[3][5];
```

This is equivalent to the following:

```
double[][] a;
a = new double[3][];
a[0] = new double[5];
a[1] = new double[5];
a[2] = new double[5];
```

The line

```
a = new double[3][];
```

makes a the name of an array with room for three entries, each of which can be an array of doubles that can be of any length. The next three lines each create an array of doubles of length 5 to be named by a[0], a[1], and a[2]. The net result is a two-dimensional array of base type double with three rows and five columns.

If you want, you can make each of a[0], a[1], and a[2] a different length. The following code makes a ragged array b in which each row has a different length:

```
double[][] b;
b = new double[3][];
b[0] = new double[5];
b[1] = new double[10];
b[2] = new double[4];
```

There are situations in which you can profitably use ragged arrays, but most applications do not require them. However, if you understand ragged arrays, you will have a better understanding of how all multidimensional arrays work in Java.

Multidimensional Array Parameters and Returned Values

array arguments

Methods may have multidimensional array parameters and may have a multidimensional array type as the type for the value returned. The situation is similar to that of the one-dimensional case, except that you use more square brackets when specifying the type name. For example, the following method will display a two-dimensional array in the usual way as rows and columns:[6]

```
public static void showMatrix(int[][] a)
{
    int row, column;
    for (row = 0; row < a.length; row++)
    {
        for (column = 0; column < a[row].length; column++)
            System.out.print(a[row][column] + " ");
        System.out.println();
    }
}
```

returning an array

If you want to return a multidimensional array, you use the same kind of type specification as you use for a multidimensional array parameter. For example, the following method returns a two-dimensional array with base type `double`:

```
/**
 Precondition: Each dimension of a is at least the value of size.
 The array returned is the same as the size-by-size upper upper-
 left corner of the array a.
*/
public static double[][] corner(double[][] a, int size)
{
    double[][] temp = new double[size][size];
    int row, column;
    for (row = 0; row < size; row++)
        for (column = 0; column < size; column++)
            temp[row][column] = a[row][column];
    return temp;
}
```

EXAMPLE: A Grade Book Class

Display 6.18 contains a class for grade records in a class whose only recorded scores are quiz scores. An object of this class has three array instance variables. One is a two-dimensional array named `grade` that records the grade of each student on each quiz. For example, the score that student number 4 received on quiz number 1 is recorded in `grade[3][0]`. Because the student numbers and quiz numbers start with 1 and the array indices start with 0, we subtract one from the student number or quiz number to obtain the corresponding array index.

---

[6]It is worth noting that this method works fine for ragged arrays.

EXAMPLE: (continued)

All the raw data is in the array grade, but two other arrays hold computed data. The array studentAverage is used to record the average quiz score for each of the students. For example, the program sets studentAverage[0] equal to the average of the quiz scores received by student 1, studentAverage[1] equal to the average of the quiz scores received by student 2, and so forth. The array quizAverage is used to record the average score for each quiz. For example, the program sets quizAverage[0] equal to the average of all the student scores for quiz 1, quizAverage[1] records the average score for quiz 2, and so forth. Display 6.19 illustrates the relationship between the arrays grade, studentAverage, and quizAverage. In that display, we have shown some sample data for the array grade. The data in grade, in turn, determines the values that are stored in studentAverage and in quizAverage. Display 6.19 also shows these computed values for studentAverage and quizAverage. The two arrays studentAverage and quizAverage are created and filled by the constructor that creates the GradeBook object. (The constructors do this by calling private helping methods.)

The no-argument constructor for the class GradeBook obtains the data for the array instance variable grade via a dialog with the user. Although this is not my favorite way to define a no-argument constructor, some programmers like it and you should see an example of it. Another alternative would be to have a no-argument constructor that essentially does nothing and then have an input method that sets all the instance variables, including creating the array objects.

A very simple demonstration program along with the dialog it produces is given in Display 6.20.

Display 6.18   A Grade Book Class (part 1 of 4)

```
1   import java.util.Scanner;

2   public class GradeBook
3   {

4       private int numberOfStudents; // Same as studentAverage.length.
5       private int numberOfQuizzes; // Same as quizAverage.length.

6       private int[][] grade; //numberOfStudents rows and numberOfQuizzes
                                //columns.
7       private double[] studentAverage;
8       private double[] quizAverage;

9       public GradeBook(int[][] a)
10      {
11          if (a.length == 0 || a[0].length == 0)
12          {
13              System.out.println("Empty grade records. Aborting.");
14              System.exit(0);
15          }
```

(continued)

Display 6.18   A Grade Book Class (part 2 of 4)

```
16          numberOfStudents = a.length;
17          numberOfQuizzes = a[0].length;
18          fillGrade(a);
19          fillStudentAverage();
20          fillQuizAverage();
21      }

22      public GradeBook(GradeBook book)
23      {
24          numberOfStudents = book.numberOfStudents;
25          numberOfQuizzes = book.numberOfQuizzes;
26          fillGrade(book.grade);
27          fillStudentAverage();
28          fillQuizAverage();
29      }

30      public GradeBook()
31      {
32          Scanner keyboard = new Scanner(System.in);

33          System.out.println("Enter number of students:");
34          numberOfStudents = keyboard.nextInt();

35          System.out.println("Enter number of quizzes:");
36          numberOfQuizzes = keyboard.nextInt();

37          grade = new int[numberOfStudents][numberOfQuizzes];
38          for (int studentNumber = 1;
39                      studentNumber <= numberOfStudents; studentNumber++)
40            for (int quizNumber = 1;
41                        quizNumber <= numberOfQuizzes; quizNumber++)
42            {
43                System.out.println("Enter score for student number "
44                                            + studentNumber);
45                System.out.println("on quiz number " + quizNumber);
46                grade[studentNumber - 1][quizNumber - 1] =
47                                            keyboard.nextInt();
48            }

49          fillStudentAverage();
50          fillQuizAverage();
51      }

52      private void fillGrade(int[][] a)
53      {
54          grade = new int[numberOfStudents][numberOfQuizzes];
55          for (int studentNumber = 1;
56                      studentNumber <= numberOfStudents; studentNumber++)
57          {
```

This class should have more accessor and mutator methods, but we have omitted them to save space. See Self-Test Exercises 24 through 27.

Display 6.18   **A Grade Book Class** (part 3 of 4)

```
58              for (int quizNumber = 1;
59                         quizNumber <= numberOfQuizzes; quizNumber++)
60                 grade[studentNumber][quizNumber] =
61                                      a[studentNumber][quizNumber];
62          }
63      }

64      /**
65        Fills the array studentAverage using the data from the array grade.
66      */
67      private void fillStudentAverage()
68      {
69          studentAverage = new double[numberOfStudents];

70          for (int studentNumber = 1;
71                         studentNumber<=numberOfStudents; studentNumber++)
72          {//Process one studentNumber:
73            double sum = 0;
74            for (int quizNumber = 1;
75                         quizNumber <= numberOfQuizzes; quizNumber++)
76              sum = sum + grade[studentNumber - 1][quizNumber - 1];
77            //sum contains the sum of the quiz scores for student number
78            //studentNumber.
78            studentAverage[studentNumber - 1] = sum/numberOfQuizzes;
79            //Average for student studentNumber is
              //studentAverage[studentNumber - 1]
80          }
81      }
82      /**
83        Fills the array quizAverage using the data from the array grade.
84      */
85      private void fillQuizAverage()
86      {
87          quizAverage = new double[numberOfQuizzes];

88          for (int quizNumber = 1; quizNumber <= numberOfQuizzes; quizNumber++)
89          {//Process one quiz (for all students):
90            double sum = 0;
91            for (int studentNumber = 1;
92                         studentNumber <= numberOfStudents;
                           studentNumber++)
93              sum = sum + grade[studentNumber - 1][quizNumber - 1];
94            //sum contains the sum of all student scores on quiz number
              //quizNumber.
95            quizAverage[quizNumber - 1] = sum/numberOfStudents;
96            //Average for quiz quizNumber is the value of
              //quizAverage[quizNumber - 1]
97          }
98      }
```

(continued)

Display 6.18 **A Grade Book Class** (part 4 of 4)

```
99      public void display()
100     {
101         for (int studentNumber = 1;
102                     studentNumber <= numberOfStudents; studentNumber++)

103         {//Display for one studentNumber:
104             System.out.print("Student " + studentNumber + " Quizzes: ");
105             for (int quizNumber = 1;
106                         quizNumber <= numberOfQuizzes; quizNumber++)
107               System.out.print(grade[studentNumber - 1][quizNumber - 1] +
                    " ");
108             System.out.println(" Ave = " +
                            studentAverage[studentNumber - 1] );
109         }

110         System.out.println("Quiz averages: ");
111         for (int quizNumber = 1; quizNumber <= numberOfQuizzes;
                            quizNumber++)
112           System.out.print("Quiz " + quizNumber
113                         + " Ave = " + quizAverage[quizNumber - 1] +
                    " ");
114         System.out.println();
115     }
116
```

Display 6.19 The Two-Dimensional Array grade

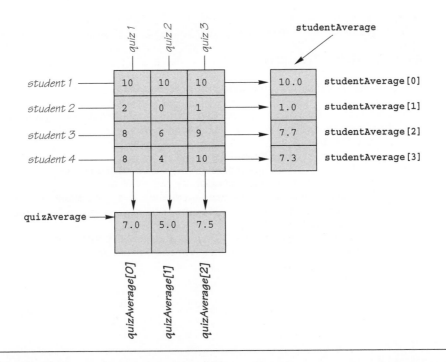

Display 6.20   Demonstration of the Class GradeBook

```
1  public class GradeBookDemo
2  {
3      public static void main(String[] args)
4      {
5          GradeBook book = new GradeBook();
6          book.display();
7      }
8  }
```

Sample Dialogue

```
Enter number of students:
4
Enter number of quizzes:
3
Enter score for student number 1
on quiz number 1
10
Enter score for student number 1
on quiz number 2
10

    <The rest of the input dialog is omitted to save space.>

Student 1 Quizzes: 10 10 10 Ave = 10.0
Student 2 Quizzes: 2 0 1 Ave = 1.0
Student 3 Quizzes: 8 6 9 Ave = 7.66666666667
Student 4 Quizzes: 8 4 10 Ave = 7.33333333333
Quiz averages:
Quiz 1 Ave = 7.0 Quiz 2 Ave = 5.0 Quiz 3 Ave = 7.5
```

MyProgrammingLab™

Self-Test Exercises

24. Write a method definition for a method with the following heading. The
method is to be added to the class GradeBook in Display 6.18.

```
/**
 Returns the grade that student numbered studentNumber received
 on quiz number quizNumber.
*/
public int getGrade(int studentNumber, int quizNumber)
```

(continued)

Self-Test Exercises (continued)

25. Write a method definition for a method with the following heading. The method is to be added to the class `GradeBook` in Display 6.18.

```
/**
 Changes the grade for student number studentNumber on quiz
 number quizNumber to newGrade.
*/
public void changeGrade(int studentNumber,
                   int quizNumber, int newGrade))
```

26. Write a method definition for a method with the following heading. The method is to be added to the class `GradeBook` in Display 6.18.

```
/**
 Returns an array with the average quiz score for each student.
*/
public double[] getStudentAverages( )
```

27. Write a method definition for a method with the following heading. The method is to be added to the class `GradeBook` in Display 6.18.

```
/**
 Returns an array with the average score for each quiz.
*/
public double[] getQuizAverages( )
```

Chapter Summary

- An *array* can be used to store and manipulate a collection of data that is all of the same type.

- The *indexed variables* of an array can be used just like any other variables of the *base type* of the array.

- Arrays are objects that are created with new just like the class objects we discussed before this chapter (although there is a slight difference in the syntax used).

- A for loop is a good way to step through the elements of an array and perform some program action on each indexed variable.

- The most common programming error made when using arrays is to attempt to access a nonexistent array index. Always check the first and last iterations of a loop that manipulates an array to make sure it does not use an index that is illegally small or illegally large.

- The indexed variables of an array can be used as an argument to be plugged in for a parameter of the array's base type.

- A method can have parameters of an array type. When the method is invoked, an entire array is plugged in for the array parameter.

- A method may return an array as the value returned by the method.

- When using a *partially filled array*, your program needs an additional variable of type int to keep track of how much of the array is being used.

- An instance variable of a class can be of an array type.

- If you need an array with more than one index, you can use a multidimensional array, which is actually an array of arrays.

Answers to Self-Test Exercises

1. a. `reading`
   b. `Double`
   c. `100`
   d. `0 through 99 inclusive`
   e. `No, the index would be out of bounds`

2. `8.0`. It would compile but won't run, and would throw an exception: `ArrayIndexOutOfBounds`.

3. `97, 98, 99,`

4. `I love Humpty Dumpty`

   `I love Twinkle Twinkle`

   `I love Itsy Bitsy`

5. `0.3, 0.5, 0.7,`

6. The last value of `index` is `a.length − 1`, which is the last index of the array. However, when `index` has the value `a.length − 1`, `a[index + 1]` has an index that is out of bounds because `index + 1` is one more than the largest array index. The `for` loop ending condition should instead be `index < a.length − 1`.

7. ```
Addnumber.add(number); //Legal.
Addnumber.add(a[2]); //Legal.
Addnumber.add(a[3]); //Illegal. Index out of bounds.
Addnumber.add(a[number]); //Illegal. Index out of bounds.
Addnumber.add(a); //Illegal.
```

8. ```
public static void decrement(int[] a, int n)
{
    for (int i = 0; i < a.length; i++)
        a[i] = a[i] - n;
}
```

9. ```
public static int outOfOrder(double[]a)
{
    for (int index = 0; index < a.length - 1; index++)
    if (a[index] > a[index + 1])
        return (index + 1);
    return - 1;
}
```

10. This method is legal but pointless. When invoked, it has no effect on its argument. The parameter a is a local variable that contains a reference. The reference does indeed get changed so it refers to an array of double the size of the argument, but that reference goes away when the method ends. A method can change the values of the indexed variables of its argument, but it cannot change the reference in the array variable used as an argument.

11. ```
public static double[] multiplyArray(double[] a, int b)
{
    double[] temp = new double[a.length];
    for (int i = 0; i < a.length; i++)
        temp[i] = a[i] * b;
    return temp;

}
```

12. The method will compile and run. The array returned has the correct values for its elements. However, the method will change the values of its array argument. If you want to change the values in the array argument, a void method would make more sense. If you want to return an array, you should probably return a new array (as in the version in the previous subsection), not return a changed version of the argument array.

13. ```
/**
 Precondition: numberUsed <= argumentArray.length;
 the first numberUsed indexed variables of argumentArray
 have values.
 Returns an array of length numberUsed whose ith element
 is argumentArray[i] - adjustment.
*/
```
```

```
public static double[] differenceArray(
 double[] argumentArray, int numberUsed, double adjustment)
{
    double[] temp = new double[numberUsed];
    for (int i = 0; i < numberUsed; i++)
        temp[i] = argumentArray[i] - adjustment;
    return temp;
}
```

14. The only changes are to add the method `differenceArray` and to rewrite the method `showDifference` as follows (the complete class definition is in the file `GolfScoresExercise.java` on the accompanying website):

extra code on website

```
public static void showDifference(double[] a,
                                            int numberUsed)
{
    double average = computeAverage(a, numberUsed);
    System.out.println("Average of the " + numberUsed
                            + " scores = " + average);
    double[] difference =
                differenceArray(a, numberUsed, average);
    System.out.println("The scores are:");
    for (int index = 0; index < numberUsed; index++)
        System.out.println(a[index] +
                    " differs from average by "
                            + difference[index]);
}
```

15. The main differences are to remove parameters, replace the array name `a` by `score`, and make the method `fillArray` a `void` method. This code is in the file `GolfScoresStaticExercise.java` on the accompanying website.

extra code on website

```
import java.util.Scanner;

public class GolfScoresStaticExercise
{
    public static final int MAX_NUMBER_SCORES = 10;
    private static double[] score =
                        new double[MAX_NUMBER_SCORES];
    private static int numberUsed = 0;

    /**
     Shows differences between each of a list of golf scores
     and their average.
    */
    public static void main(String[] args)
    {
```

```java
        System.out.println(
                    "This program reads golf scores and shows");
        System.out.println(
                    "how much each differs from the average.");

        System.out.println("Enter golf scores:");
        fillArray( );
        showDifference( );
    }


    /**
     Reads values into the array score.
    */
    public static void fillArray( )
    {
        System.out.println("Enter up to " + score.length
                        + " nonnegative numbers:");
        System.out.println(
            "Mark the end of the list with a negative number.");
        Scanner keyboard = new Scanner(System.in);

        double next;
        int index = 0;
        next = keyboard.nextDouble( );
        while ((next >= 0) && (index < score.length))
        {
            score[index] = next;
            index++;
            next = keyboard.nextDouble( );
            //index is the number of
            //array indexed variables used so far.
        }
        //index is the total number of array indexed variables used.

        if (next >= 0)
            System.out.println("Could only read in "
                            + score.length + " input values.");

        numberUsed = index;
    }


    /**
     Precondition: numberUsed <= score.length.
                    score[0] through score[numberUsed-1] have values.
     Returns the average of numbers ascore[0] through
     score[numberUsed-1].
    */
```

```java
public static double computeAverage( )
{
    double total = 0;
    for (int index = 0; index < numberUsed; index++)
        total = total + score[index];
    if (numberUsed > 0)
    {
        return (total/numberUsed);
    }
    else
    {
        System.out.println(
                "ERROR: Trying to average 0 numbers.");
        System.out.println("computeAverage returns 0.");
        return 0;
    }
}


/**
 Precondition: numberUsed <= score.length.
 The first numberUsed indexed variables of score have values.
 Postcondition: Gives screen output showing how much each of the
 first numberUsed elements of the array a differ from the average.
*/
public static void showDifference( )
{
    double average = computeAverage( );
    System.out.println("Average of the " + numberUsed
                                + " scores = " + average);
    System.out.println("The scores are:");
    for (int index = 0; index < numberUsed; index++)
    System.out.println(score[index] +
                        " differs from average by "
                        + (score[index] - average));
}
}
```

16.
```java
public static int min(int... arg)
{
    if (arg.length == 0)
    {
        System.out.println("Fatal Error: minimum of zero
                        values.");
        System.exit(0);
    }
```

```
        int smallest = Integer.MAX_VALUE;
        for (int element : arg)
            if (element < smallest)
                smallest = element;
        return smallest;
    }
```

17. The last line would change to the following:

    ```
    I ate cod, broccoli, , peanuts, and apples.
    ```

18.
    ```
    public void removeAll( )
    {
        numberUsed = 0;
    }
    ```

19.
    ```
    public void increaseCapacity(int newCapacity)
    {
        if (newCapacity > numberUsed)
        {
            maxNumberElements = newCapacity;
            double[] temp = new double[newCapacity];
            for (int i = 0; i < a.length; i++)
                temp[i] = a[i];
            a = temp;
        }//else do nothing.
    }
    ```

20. All you need to do to make your code work for sorting into decreasing order is to replace the with in the following line of the definition of `indexOfSmallest`:

    ```
    if (a[index] < min)
    ```

    However, to make your code easy to read, you should also rename the method `indexOfSmallest` to `indexOfLargest`, rename the variable `min` to `max`, and rename the variable `indexOfMin` to `indexOfMax`. You should rewrite some of the comments to reflect these changes as well.

extra code
on website

21. If an array has a value that occurs more than once and you sort the array using the method `SelectionSort.sort`, then there will be as many copies of the repeated value after the array is sorted as there originally were in the array.

22. We give two slightly different versions. Both versions are on the accompanying website.

    ```
    import java.util.Scanner;

    public class ForEachEnumDemo
    {
        enum WorkDay {MONDAY, TUESDAY, WEDNESDAY, THURSDAY,FRIDAY};

        public static void main(String[] args)
        {
            WorkDay[] day = WorkDay.values( );
    ```

```
        Scanner keyboard = new Scanner(System.in);
        double hours = 0, sum = 0;

        for (WorkDay oneDay : day)
        {
            System.out.println("Enter hours worked for " +
            oneDay);
            hours = keyboard.nextDouble();
            sum = sum + hours;
        }

        System.out.println("Total hours work = " + sum);
    }
}

import java.util.Scanner;

public class ForEachEnumDemo2
{
    enum WorkDay {MONDAY, TUESDAY, WEDNESDAY, THURSDAY, FRIDAY};
    public static void main(String[] args)
    {
        Scanner keyboard = new Scanner(System.in);
        double hours = 0, sum = 0;

        for (WorkDay oneDay : WorkDay.values())
        {
            System.out.println("Enter hours worked for " + oneDay);
            hours = keyboard.nextDouble();
            sum = sum + hours;
        }

        System.out.println("Total hours work = " + sum);
    }
}
```

23. 0 1 2 3
    0 1 2 3
    0 1 2 3
    0 1 2 3

24. If the array indices are out of bounds, then Java will halt the program with an error message, so no other checks on the parameters are needed.

```
/**
 Returns the grade that student number studentNumber received on
 quiz number quizNumber.
*/
public int getGrade(int studentNumber, int quizNumber)
{
    return grade[studentNumber][quizNumber];
}
```

25. If the array indices are out of bounds, then Java will halt the program with an error message, so no other checks on the parameters are needed.

```
/**
Changes the grade for student number studentNumber on quiz number
quizNumber to newGrade.
*/
public void changeGrade(int studentNumber,
                    int quizNumber, int newGrade)
{
    grade[studentNumber][quizNumber] = newGrade;
}
```

26.
```
/**
 Returns an array with the average quiz score for each student.
*/
public double[] getStudentAverages( )
{
    int arraySize = studentAverage.length;
    double[] temp = new double[arraySize];
    for (int i = 0; i < arraySize; i++)
        temp[i] = studentAverage[i];
    return temp;
}
```

27.
```
/**
 Returns an array with the average score for each quiz.
*/
public double[] getQuizAverages( )
{
    int arraySize = quizAverage.length;
    double[] temp = new double[arraySize];
    for (int i = 0; i < arraySize; i++)
        temp[i] = quizAverage[i];
    return temp;
}
```

MyProgrammingLab™ ## Programming Projects

Visit www.myprogramminglab.com to complete select exercises online and get instant feedback.

1. A multinational company has five departmental stores. The company keeps sales information for all four quarters. Write a program that asks for the quarterly sales figures for the five stores. The program should display: the sales figure for each store in each quarter, the total sales for each store, the average sales for each store,

the total sales for each quarter, and the average sales per quarter. The program should also highlight the store with the highest sales for each quarter. The figures should be stored in a two-dimensional array.

2. A common memory matching game played by young children is to start with a deck of cards that contain identical pairs. For example, given six cards in the deck, two might be labeled 1, two labeled 2, and two labeled 3. The cards are shuffled and placed face down on the table. A player then selects two cards that are face down, turns them face up, and if the cards match, they are left face up. If the two cards do not match, they are returned to their original face down position. The game continues until all cards are face up.

Write a program that plays the memory matching game. Use 16 cards that are laid out in a 4 × 4 square and are labeled with pairs of numbers from 1 to 8. Your program should allow the player to specify the cards that he or she would like to select through a coordinate system.

For example, in the following layout,

```
     1   2   3   4
   ┌─────────────────
1  │ 8   *   *   *
2  │ *   *   *   *
3  │ *   8   *   *
4  │ *   *   *   *
```

all of the face down cards are indicated by *. The pairs of 8 that are face up are at coordinates (1,1) and (2,3). To hide the cards that have been temporarily placed face up, output a large number of newlines to force the old board off the screen.

Hint: Use a 2D array for the arrangement of cards and another 2D array that indicates if a card is face up or face down. Or, a more elegant solution is to create a single 2D array where each element is an object that stores both the card's value and face. Write a function that "shuffles" the cards in the array by repeatedly selecting two cards at random and swapping them.

3. Write a program that reads in the average monthly rainfall for a city for each month of the year and then reads in the actual monthly rainfall for each of the previous 12 months. The program should then print out a nicely formatted table showing the rainfall for each of the previous 12 months as well as how much above or below average the rainfall was for each month. The average monthly rainfall is given for the months January, February, and so forth, in order. To obtain the actual rainfall for the previous 12 months, the program should first ask what the current month is and then ask for the rainfall figures for the previous 12 months. The output should correctly label the months. There are a variety of ways to deal with the month names. One straightforward method is to code the months as integers and then do a conversion to a string for the month name before doing the output. A large

switch statement is acceptable in an output method. The month input can be handled in any manner you wish so long as it is relatively easy and pleasant for the user. Include a loop that allows the user to repeat this entire calculation until the user requests that the program end.

4. Write a static method called `deleteRepeats` that has a partially filled array of characters as a formal parameter and that deletes all repeated letters from the array. Because a partially filled array requires two arguments, the method should actually have two formal parameters: an array parameter and a formal parameter of type `int` that gives the number of array positions used. When a letter is deleted, the remaining letters are moved one position to fill in the gap. This creates empty positions at the end of the array so that less of the array is used. Because the formal parameter is a partially filled array, a second formal parameter of type `int` should tell how many array positions are filled. This second formal parameter cannot be changed by a Java method, so have the method return the new value for this parameter. For example, consider the following code:

```
char a[10];
a[0] = 'a';
a[1] = 'b';
a[2] = 'a';
a[3] = 'c';
int size = 4;
size = deleteRepeats(a, size);
```

After this code is executed, the value of `a[0]` is `'a'`, the value of `a[1]` is `'b'`, the value of `a[2]` is `'c'`, and the value of `size` is `3`. (The value of `a[3]` is no longer of any concern, because the partially filled array no longer uses this indexed variable.) You may assume that the partially filled array contains only lowercase letters. Write a suitable test program for your method.

5. The standard deviation of a list of numbers is a measure of how much the numbers deviate from the average. If the standard deviation is small, the numbers are clustered close to the average. If the standard deviation is large, the numbers are scattered far from the average. The standard deviation of a list of numbers n_1, n_2, n_3, and so forth is defined as the square root of the average of the following numbers:

$$(n_1 - a)^2, \quad (n_2 - a)^2, \quad (n_3 - a)^2, \quad \text{and so forth.}$$

The number a is the average of the numbers n_1, n_2, n_3, and so forth.

Define a static method that takes a partially filled array of numbers as its argument and returns the standard deviation of the numbers in the partially filled array. Because a partially filled array requires two arguments, the method should actually have two formal parameters, an array parameter and a formal parameter of type `int` that gives the number of array positions used. The numbers in the array should be of type `double`. Write a suitable test program for your method.

6. Write a program that reads numbers from the keyboard into an array of type int[]. You may assume that there will be 50 or fewer entries in the array. Your program allows any number of numbers to be entered, up to 50. The output is to be a two-column list. The first column is a list of the distinct array elements; the second column is the count of the number of occurrences of each element. The list should be sorted on entries in the first column, largest to smallest.

For the array

```
-12 3 -12 4 1 1 -12 1 -1 1 2 3 4 2 3 -12
```

the output should be

```
N     Count

4     2

3     3

2     2

1     4

-1    1

-12   4
```

7. An array can be used to store large integers one digit at a time.

For example, the integer 1234 could be stored in the array a by setting a[0] to 1, a[1] to 2, a[2] to 3, and a[3] to 4. However, for this exercise you might find it more useful to store the digits backward; that is, place 4 in a[0], 3 in a[1], 2 in a[2], and 1 in a[3]. In this exercise, write a program that reads in 2 positive integers that are 20 or fewer digits in length and then outputs the sum of the 2 numbers. Your program will read the digits as values of type char so that the number 1234 is read as the four characters '1', '2', '3', and '4'. After they are read into the program, the characters are changed to values of type int. The digits should be read into a partially filled array; you might find it useful to reverse the order of the elements in the array after the array is filled with data from the keyboard. (Whether or not you reverse the order of the elements in the array is up to you. It can be done either way, and each way has its advantages and disadvantages.) Your program should perform the addition by implementing the usual paper-and-pencil addition algorithm. The result of the addition should be stored in an array of size 20, and the result should then be written to the screen. If the result of the addition is an integer with more than the maximum number of digits (that is, more than 20 digits), then your program should issue a message saying that it has encountered "integer overflow." You should be able to change the maximum length of the integers by changing only one named constant. Include a loop that allows the user to continue to do more additions until the user says the program should end.

VideoNote

Solution to
Programming
Project 6.8

8. Design a class called `BubbleSort` that is similar to the class `SelectionSort` given in Display 6.11. The class `BubbleSort` will be used in the same way as the class `SelectionSort`, but it will use the bubble sort algorithm.

   The bubble sort algorithm checks all adjacent pairs of elements in the array from the beginning to the end and interchanges any two elements that are out of order. This process is repeated until the array is sorted. The algorithm is as follows:

   Bubble Sort Algorithm to Sort an Array a

   Repeat the following until the array a is sorted:

   ```
   for (index = 0; index < a.length - 1; index++)
       if (a[index] > a[index + 1])
           Interchange the values of a[index] and a[index + 1].
   ```

   The bubble sort algorithm is good for sorting an array that is "almost sorted." It is not competitive with other sorting methods for most other situations.

9. Enhance the definition of the class `PartiallyFilledArray` (Display 6.5) in the following way: When the user attempts to add one additional element and there is no room in the array instance variable a, the user is allowed to add the element. The object creates a second array that is twice the size of the array a, copies values from the array a to the user's new array, makes this array (or more precisely its reference) the new value of a, and then adds the element to this new larger array a. Hence, this new class should have no limit (other than the physical size of the computer) to how many numbers it can hold. The instance variable `maxNumberOfElements` remains and the method `getMaxCapacity` is unchanged, but these now refer to the currently allocated memory and not to an absolute upper bound. Write a suitable test program.

10. Write a program that will allow two users to play tic-tac-toe. The program should ask for moves alternately from player X and player O. The program displays the game positions as follows:

    ```
    1   2   3
    4   5   6
    7   8   9
    ```

    The players enter their moves by entering the position number they wish to mark. After each move, the program displays the changed board. A sample board configuration is

    ```
    X   X   O
    4   5   6
    O   8   9
    ```

11. Write a program to assign passengers seats in an airplane. Assume a small airplane with seat numberings as follows:

```
1  A  B  C  D
2  A  B  C  D
3  A  B  C  D
4  A  B  C  D
5  A  B  C  D
6  A  B  C  D
7  A  B  C  D
```

The program should display the seat pattern, with an 'X' marking the seats already assigned. For example, after seats 1A, 2B, and 4C are taken, the display should look like the following:

```
1  X  B  C  D
2  A  X  C  D
3  A  B  C  D
4  A  B  X  D
5  A  B  C  D
6  A  B  C  D
7  A  B  C  D
```

After displaying the seats available, the program should prompt for the seat desired, the user can type in a seat, and then the display of available seats should be updated. This continues until all seats are filled or until the user signals that the program should end. If the user types in a seat that is already assigned, the program should say that that seat is occupied and ask for another choice.

12. Write a program that plays a simple trivia game. The game should have five questions. Each question has a corresponding answer and point value between 1 and 3 based on the difficulty of the question. Implement the game using three arrays. An array of type String should be used for the questions. Another array of type String should be used to store the answers. An array of type int should be used for the point values. All three arrays should be declared to be of size 5.

The index into the three arrays can be used to tie the question, answer, and point value together. For example, the item at index 0 for each array would correspond to question 1, answer 1, and the point value for question 1. The item at index 1 for each array would correspond to question 2, answer 2, and the point value for question 2, and so forth. Manually hardcode the five questions, answers, and point values into your program using trivia of your choice.

Your program should ask the player each question one at a time and allow the player to enter an answer. If the player's answer matches the actual answer, the player wins the number of points for that question. If the player's answer is incorrect, the player wins no points for the question. Your program should show the correct answer if the player is incorrect. After the player has answered all five questions, the game is over, and your program should display the player's total score.

13. Modify Programming Project 12 to use a single array instead of three arrays. This can be accomplished by creating a `Trivia` object that encapsulates the question, answer, and point value for a particular trivia question. Next, create a single array of five `Trivia` objects instead of three separate arrays for the question, answer, and point values. This change will make your game more scalable if there were ever additional properties to add to a `Trivia` object (you would not need to add another array for each property). Although the program has internally changed to a single array of objects, the execution of the program should be identical to before.

14. Traditional password entry schemes are susceptible to "shoulder surfing" in which an attacker watches an unsuspecting user enter his or her password or PIN number and uses it later to gain access to the account. One way to combat this problem is with a randomized challenge-response system. In these systems, the user enters different information every time based on a secret in response to a randomly generated challenge. Consider the following scheme in which the password consists of a five-digit PIN number (00000 to 99999). Each digit is assigned a random number that is 1, 2, or 3. The user enters the random numbers that correspond to their PIN instead of their actual PIN numbers.

    For example, consider an actual PIN number of 12345. To authenticate it, the user would be presented with a screen such as the following:

    ```
    PIN: 0 1 2 3 4 5 6 7 8 9
    NUM: 3 2 3 1 1 3 2 2 1 3
    ```

    The user would enter 23113 instead of 12345. This does not divulge the password even if an attacker intercepts the entry because 23113 could correspond to other PIN numbers, such as 69440 or 70439. The next time the user logs in, a different sequence of random numbers would be generated, such as the following:

    ```
    PIN: 0 1 2 3 4 5 6 7 8 9
    NUM: 1 1 2 3 1 2 2 3 3 3
    ```

    Your program should simulate the authentication process. Store an actual PIN number in your program. The program should use an array to assign random numbers to the digits from 0 to 9. Output the random digits to the screen, input the response from the user, and output whether or not the user's response correctly matches the PIN number.

VideoNote

Solution to Programming Project 6.15

15. Programming Project 4.12 asked you to create a `PizzaOrder` class that stores an order consisting of up to three pizzas. Modify the class to store the pizzas using an array. This will allow the class to include an arbitrary number of pizzas in the order instead of a maximum of three. The `setNumPizzas` method can be used to create an array of the appropriate size. The array structure allows you to eliminate the methods `setPizza1`, `setPizza2`, and `setPizza3` and replace them with a single method, `setPizza(int index, Pizza newPizza)`. Include appropriate tests to determine if the new `PizzaOrder` class is working correctly.

16. Programming Project 3.15 asked you to explore Benford's Law. An easier way to write the program is to use an array to store the digit counts. That is, count[0] might store the number of times 0 is the first digit (if that is possible in your data set), count[1] might store the number of times 1 is the first digit, and so forth. Redo Programming Project 3.15 using arrays.

    Write a program that tests Benford's Law. Collect a list of at least 100 numbers from some real-life data source and enter them into a text file. Your program should use an array to store the digit counts. That is, count[0] might store the number of times 0 is the first digit (if that is possible in your data set), count[1] might store the number of times 1 is the first digit, and so forth. For each digit, output the percentage it appears as the first digit.

17. Programming Project 4.14 asked you to read in a CSV file of product ratings. The file was limited to exactly five products. Redo Programming Project 4.14, except calculate the name of each product and how many products are in the file based on the header line. Then read the CSV file and translate the data into a 2D array that stores all of the ratings. Finally, output the average rating for each product.

18. Programming Project 4.13 asked you to create a BoxOfProduce class representing a box of produce to deliver from a CSA farm. The box contained exactly three items. Modify the class so it uses an array of type String to represent the items in the box. You can still start with three random items to place in the box, but your menu should be modified to allow the user to add additional items and still substitute one item for another. You will likely need to modify the constructor of the BoxOfProduce class and also add new methods.

19. Some word games require the player to find words that can be formed using the letters of another word. For example, given the word *SWIMMING*, other words that can be formed using the letters include *SWIM, WIN, WING, SING, MIMING*, etc. Write a program that lets the user enter a word and then output all the words contained in the file words.txt that can be formed from the letters of the entered word. One algorithm to do this is to compare the letter histograms for each word. Create an array that counts up the number of each letter in the entered word (e.g., one S, one W, two I, two M, etc.) and then creates a similar array for the current word read from the file. The two arrays can be compared to see if the word from the file could be created out of the letters from the entered word.

Inheritance 7

7.1 INHERITANCE BASICS 460

Derived Classes 461

Overriding a Method Definition 471

Changing the Return Type of an Overridden
Method 471

Changing the Access Permission of an Overridden
Method 472

The super Constructor 474

The this Constructor 476

Example: An Enhanced StringTokenizer
Class ★ 481

**7.2 ENCAPSULATION AND
INHERITANCE** 484

Protected and Package Access 487

**7.3 PROGRAMMING WITH
INHERITANCE** 493

Access to a Redefined Base Method 493

The Class Object 496

The Right Way to Define equals 497

7 Inheritance

Like mother, like daughter.

COMMON SAYING

Introduction

Object-oriented programming (OOP) is a popular and powerful programming philosophy. One of the main techniques of OOP is known as *inheritance*. **Inheritance** means that a very general form of a class can be defined and compiled. Later, more specialized versions of that class may be defined by starting with the already defined class and adding more specialized instance variables and methods. The specialized classes are said to *inherit* the methods and instance variables of the previously defined general class. In this chapter, we cover inheritance in general and more specifically how it is realized in Java.

Prerequisites

This chapter does not use any material on arrays from Chapter 6. It does require Chapters 1 through 5 with the exception that most of the chapter does not require Section 5.4 on packages and `javadoc`. In this chapter, the subsection "Protected and Package Access" is the only section that requires any knowledge from Section 5.4, and it requires only the material on packages, and not the material on `javadoc`. If you omit the subsection "Protected and Package Access," you will not suffer any loss of continuity in reading this chapter.

7.1   Inheritance Basics

> *If there is anything that we wish to change in the child, we should*
> *first examine it and see whether it is not something that could better*
> *be changed in ourselves.*
>
> CARL GUSTAV JUNG, *the integration of the personality*

Inheritance is the process by which a new class—known as a *derived class*—is created from another class, called the *base class*. A derived class automatically has all the instance variables and all the methods that the base class has, and can have additional methods and/or additional instance variables.

Derived Classes

Suppose we are designing a record-keeping program that has records for salaried employees and hourly employees. There is a natural hierarchy for grouping these classes. These are all classes of people who share the property of being employees.

Employees who are paid an hourly wage are one subset of employees. Another subset consists of salaried employees who are paid a fixed wage each month. Although the program may not need any type corresponding to the set of all employees, thinking in terms of the more general concept of employees can be useful. For example, all employees have a name and a hire date (when they started working for the company), and the methods for setting and changing names and hire dates will be the same for salaried and hourly employees. The classes for hourly employees and salaried employees may be further subdivided as diagrammed in Display 7.1.

Within Java, you can define a class called Employee that includes all employees (salaried or hourly), and then use this class to define classes for hourly employees and salaried employees. You can then, in turn, use classes such as HourlyEmployee to define classes such as PartTimeHourlyEmployee, and so forth.

Display 7.2 shows our definition for the class Employee. This class is a pretty ordinary class. What is interesting about this class is how we use it to create a class for hourly employees and a class for salaried employees. It is legal to create an object of the class Employee, but our reason for defining the class Employee is so that we can define derived classes for different kinds of employees.

Display 7.1   A Class Hierarchy

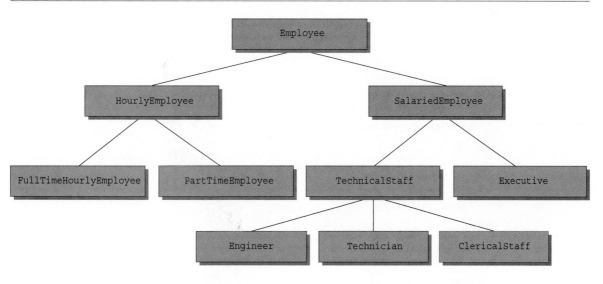

Display 7.2   **The Base Class Employee** (part 1 of 2)

```
1   /**
2   Class Invariant: All objects have a name string and hire date.
3   A name string of "No name" indicates no real name specified yet.
4   A hire date of January 1, 1000 indicates no real hire date specified yet.
5   */
6   public class Employee
7   {
8       private String name;                    The class Date is defined in
9       private Date hireDate;                   Display 4.13.
10      public Employee()
11      {
12          name = "No name";
13          hireDate = new Date("January", 1, 1000); //Just a placeholder.
14      }

15      /**
16      Precondition: Neither theName nor theDate is null.
17      */
18      public Employee(String theName, Date theDate)
19      {
20          if (theName == null || theDate == null)
21          {
22              System.out.println("Fatal Error creating employee.");
23              System.exit(0);
24          }
25          name = theName;
26          hireDate = new Date(theDate);
27      }

28      public Employee(Employee originalObject)
29      {
30          name = originalObject.name;
31          hireDate = new Date(originalObject.hireDate);
32      }

33      public String getName()
34      {
35          return name;
36      }

37      public Date getHireDate()
38      {
39          return new Date(hireDate);
40      }
```

Display 7.2   **The Base Class Employee** (part 2 of 2)

```java
41        /**
42         Precondition newName is not null.
43        */
44        public void setName(String newName)
45        {
46            if (newName == null)
47            {
48                System.out.println("Fatal Error setting employee name.");
49                System.exit(0);
50            }
51            else
52                name = newName;
53        }

54        /**
55        Precondition newDate is not null.
56        */
57        public void setHireDate(Date newDate)
58        {
59            if (newDate == null)
60            {
61                System.out.println("Fatal Error setting employee hire " +
                   "date.");
62                System.exit(0);
63            }
64            else
65                hireDate = new Date(newDate);
66        }


67        public String toString()
68        {
69            return (name + " " + hireDate.toString());
70        }

71        public boolean equals(Employee otherEmployee)
72        {
73            return (name.equals(otherEmployee.name)
74                        && hireDate.equals(otherEmployee.hireDate));
75        }
76    }
```

derived class

base class

Display 7.3 contains the definition of a class for hourly employees. An hourly employee is an employee, so we define the class `HourlyEmployee` to be a *derived* class of the class `Employee`. A **derived class** is a class defined by adding instance variables and methods to an existing class. The existing class that the derived class is built upon is called the **base class**. In our example, `Employee` is the base class and `HourlyEmployee` is the derived class. As you can see in Display 7.3, the way we indicate that `HourlyEmployee` is a derived class of `Employee` is by including the phrase `extends Employee` on the first line of the class definition, like so:

extends

```
public class HourlyEmployee extends Employee
```

subclass and superclass

A derived class is also called a **subclass**, in which case the base class is usually called a **superclass**. However, we prefer to use the terms *derived class* and *base class*.

When you define a derived class, you give only the added instance variables and the added methods. For example, the class `HourlyEmployee` has all the instance variables and all the methods of the class `Employee`, but you do not mention them in the definition of `HourlyEmployee`. Every object of the class `HourlyEmployee` has instance variables called `name` and `hireDate`, but you do not specify the instance variable `name` or the instance variable `hireDate` in the definition of the class `HourlyEmployee`. The class `HourlyEmployee` (or any other derived class) is said to **inherit** the instance variables and methods of the base class that it extends. For this reason, the topic of derived classes is called **inheritance**.

inheritance

Just as it inherits the instance variables of the class `Employee`, the class `HourlyEmployee` inherits all the methods from the class `Employee`. So, the class `HourlyEmployee` inherits the methods `getName`, `getHireDate`, `setName`, and `setHireDate`, from the class `Employee`.

For example, suppose you create a new object of the class `HourlyEmployee` as follows:

```
HourlyEmployee joe = new HourlyEmployee();
```

Then, the name of the object `joe` can be changed using the method `setName`, which the class `HourlyEmployee` inherited from the class `Employee`. The inherited method `setName` is used just like any other method; for example,

```
joe.setName("Josephine");
```

VideoNote
Inheritance Walkthrough

A small demonstration of this is given in Display 7.4.

Display 7.5 contains the definition of the class `SalariedEmployee`, which is also derived from the class `Employee`. The class `SalariedEmployee` inherits all the instance variables and methods of the class `Employee`. Inheritance allows you to reuse code, such as the code in the class `Employee`, without needing to literally copy the code into the definitions of the derived classes, such as `HourlyEmployee` and `SalariedEmployee`.

Display 7.3   **The Derived Class** `HourlyEmployee` (part 1 of 3)

```
1    /**
2    Class Invariant: All objects have a name string, hire date, nonnegative
3    wage rate, and nonnegative number of hours worked. A name string of
4    "No name" indicates no real name specified yet. A hire date of
5    January 1, 1000 indicates no real hire date specified yet.
6    */
7    public class HourlyEmployee extends Employee
8    {
9        private double wageRate;
10       private double hours; //for the month

11       public HourlyEmployee()
12       {
13           super();
14           wageRate = 0;
15           hours = 0;
16       }

17       /**
18        Precondition: Neither theName nor theDate is null;
19        theWageRate and theHours are nonnegative.
20        */
21       public HourlyEmployee(String theName, Date theDate,
22                        double theWageRate, double theHours)
23       {
24           super(theName, theDate);
25           if ((theWageRate >= 0) && (theHours >= 0))
26           {
27               wageRate = theWageRate;
28               hours = theHours;
29           }
30           else
31           {
32               System.out.println(
33                   "Fatal Error: creating an illegal hourly employee.");
34               System.exit(0);
35           }
36       }

37       public HourlyEmployee(HourlyEmployee originalObject)
38       {
39           super(originalObject);
```

It will take the rest of Section 7.1 to explain this class definition.

If this line is omitted, Java will still invoke the no-argument constructor for the base class.

An object of the class `HourlyEmployee` is also an instance of the class `Employee`.

(continued)

Display 7.3   **The Derived Class `HourlyEmployee`** (part 2 of 3)

```
40              wageRate = originalObject.wageRate;
41              hours = originalObject.hours;
42          }
43      public double getRate()
44      {
45              return wageRate;
46      }
47      public double getHours()
48      {
49              return hours;
50      }

51      /**
52       Returns the pay for the month.
53       */
54      public double getPay()
55      {
56              return wageRate*hours;
57      }

58      /**
59       Precondition: hoursWorked is nonnegative.
60       */
61      public void setHours(double hoursWorked)
62      {
63              if (hoursWorked >= 0)
64                  hours = hoursWorked;
65              else
66              {
67                  System.out.println("Fatal Error: Negative hours worked.");
68                  System.exit(0);
69              }
70      }

71      /**
72       precondition: newWageRate is nonnegative.
73       */
74      public void setRate(double newWageRate)
75      {
76              if (newWageRate >= 0)
77                  wageRate = newWageRate;
78              else
79              {
80                  System.out.println("Fatal Error: Negative wage rate.");
81                  System.exit(0);
```

Display 7.3   **The Derived Class** `HourlyEmployee` (part 3 of 3)

```
82              }
83          }
```

The method `toString` *is overridden so it is different in the derived class* `HourlyEmployee` *than it is in the base class* `Employee`.

```
84      public String toString()
85      {
86          return (getName() + " " + getHireDate().toString()
87                  + "\n$" + wageRate + " per hour for " + hours + " hours");
88      }

89      public boolean equals(HourlyEmployee other)
90      {
91          return (getName().equals(other.getName())
92                  && getHireDate().equals(other.getHireDate())
93                  && wageRate == other.wageRate
94                  && hours == other.hours);
95      }
96  }
```

We will show you a better way to define `equals` *in the subsection "The Right Way to Define* equals.*"*

Derived Class (Subclass)

Define a **derived class** by starting with another already defined class and adding (or changing) methods, instance variables, and static variables. The class you start with is called the **base class**. The derived class inherits all the public methods, all the public and private instance variables, and all the public and private static variables from the base class, and it can add more instance variables, more static variables, and more methods. So, of the things we have seen thus far, the only members not inherited are private methods. (As discussed in the subsection "Overriding a Method Definition," the derived class definition can also change the definition of an inherited method.) A derived class is also called a **subclass**, in which case the base class is usually called a **superclass**.

SYNTAX

```
public class Derived_Class_Name extends  Base_Class_Name
{

        Declarations_of_Added_Static_Variables
        Declarations_of_Added_Instance_Variables
        Definitions_of_Added__And_Overridden_Methods

}
```

EXAMPLE

See Displays 7.3 and 7.5.

Display 7.4   **Inheritance Demonstration**

```
1   public class InheritanceDemo                    The methods getName and setName are
2   {                                               inherited from the base class Employee.
3       public static void main(String[] args)
4       {
5           HourlyEmployee joe = new HourlyEmployee("Joe Worker",
6                                   new Date("January", 1, 2004),
                                        50.50, 160);

7           System.out.println("joe's longer name is " +
                joe.getName());

8           System.out.println("Changing joe's name to Josephine.");
9           joe.setName("Josephine");

10          System.out.println("joe's record is as follows:");
11          System.out.println(joe);
12      }
13  }
```

Sample Dialogue

```
joe's longer name is Joe Worker
Changing joe's name to Josephine.
joe's record is as follows:
Josephine January 1, 2004
$50.5 per hour for 160 hours
```

Inherited Members

A derived class automatically has all the instance variables, all the static variables, and all the public methods of the base class. These members from the base class are said to be **inherited**. These inherited methods and inherited instance and static variables are, with one exception, not mentioned in the definition of the derived class, but they are automatically members of the derived class. The one exception is as follows: As explained in the subsection "Overriding a Method Definition," you can give a definition for an inherited method in the definition of the derived class; this will redefine the meaning of the method for the derived class.

Display 7.5   **The Derived Class** `SalariedEmployee` (part 1 of 2)

```
1   /**
2    Class Invariant: All objects have a name string, hire date,
3    and nonnegative salary. A name string of "No name" indicates
4    no real name specified yet. A hire date of January 1, 1000 indicates
5    no real hire date specified yet.
6   */
7   public class SalariedEmployee extends Employee
8   {
9       private double salary; //annual
```

It will take the rest of Section 7.1 to fully explain this class definition.

```
10      public SalariedEmployee()
11      {
12          super();
13          salary = 0;
14      }
```

If this line is omitted, Java will still invoke the no-argument constructor for the base class.

```
15      /**
16       Precondition: Neither theName nor theDate are null;
17       theSalary is nonnegative.
18      */
19      public SalariedEmployee(String theName, Date theDate, double theSalary)
20      {
21          super(theName, theDate);
22          if (theSalary >= 0)
23              salary = theSalary;
24          else
25          {
26              System.out.println("Fatal Error: Negative salary.");
27              System.exit(0);
28          }
29      }

30      public SalariedEmployee(SalariedEmployee originalObject)
31      {
32          super(originalObject);
33          salary = originalObject.salary;
34      }
```

An object of the class `SalariedEmployee` is also an object of the class `Employee`.

```
35      public double getSalary()
36      {
37          return salary;
38      }
```

(continued)

Display 7.5 The Derived Class `SalariedEmployee` (part 2 of 2)

```
39      /**
40       Returns the pay for the month.
41      */
42      public double getPay()
43      {
44          return salary/12;
45      }

46      /**
47       Precondition: newSalary is nonnegative.
48      */
49      public void setSalary(double newSalary)
50      {
51          if (newSalary >= 0)
52              salary = newSalary;
53          else
54          {
55              System.out.println("Fatal Error: Negative salary.");
56              System.exit(0);
57          }
58      }

59      public String toString()
60      {
61          return (getName() + " " + getHireDate().toString()
62                              + "\n$" + salary + " per year");
63      }

64      public boolean equals(SalariedEmployee other)
65      {
66          return (getName().equals(other.getName())
67                  && getHireDate().equals(other.getHireDate())
68                  && salary == other.salary);
69      }
70  }
```

We will show you a better way to define `equals` *in the subsection "The Right Way to Define equals."*

parent class

child class

ancestor class

descendent class

Parent and Child Classes

A base class is often called the **parent class**. A derived class is then called a **child class**. This analogy is often carried one step further. A class that is a parent of a parent of a parent of another class (or some other number of "parent of" iterations) is often called an **ancestor class**. If class A is an ancestor of class B, then class B is often called a **descendent** of class A.

Overriding a Method Definition

overriding

The definition of an inherited method can be changed in the definition of a derived class so that it has a meaning in the derived class that is different from what it is in the base class. This is called **overriding** the definition of the inherited method. For example, the methods `toString` and `equals` are overridden (redefined) in the definition of the derived class `HourlyEmployee`. They are also overridden in the class `SalariedEmployee`. To override a method definition, simply give the new definition of the method in the class definition, just as you would with a method that is added in the derived class.

Overriding a Method Definition

A derived class inherits methods that belong to the base class. However, if a derived class requires a different definition for an inherited method, the method may be redefined in the derived class. This is called **overriding** the method definition.

The `final` Modifier

If you add the modifier `final` to the definition of a method, it indicates that the method may not be redefined in a derived class. If you add the modifier `final` to the definition of a class, it indicates that the class may not be used as a base class to derive other classes. We will say more about the `final` modifier in Chapter 8.

Changing the Return Type of an Overridden Method

covariant return type

In a derived class, you can override (change) the definition of a method from the base class. As a general rule, when overriding a method definition, you may *not* change the type returned by the method, and you may not change a `void` method to a method that returns a value, nor a method that returns a value to a `void` method. The one exception to this rule is if the returned type is a class type, then you may change the returned type to that of any descendent class of the returned type. For example, if a function returns the type `Employee` (Display 7.2), when you override the function definition in a derived class, you may change the returned type to `HourlyEmployee` (Display 7.3), `SalariedEmployee` (Display 7.5), or any other descendent class of the class `Employee`. This sort of changed return type is known as a **covariant return type** and is new in Java version 5.0; it was not allowed in earlier versions of Java. Earlier versions of Java allowed absolutely no changes to the returned type. We will give complete examples of changing the returned type of an overridden method in Chapter 8. Here we will just outline an example.

For example, suppose one class definition includes the following details:

```
public class BaseClass
{
    . . .
    public Employee getSomeone(int someKey)
    . . .
```

In this case, the following details would be allowed in a derived class:

```
public class DerivedClass extends BaseClass
{
    . . .
    public HourlyEmployee getSomeone(int someKey)
    . . .
```

When the method definition for `getSomeone` is overridden in `DerivedClass`, the returned type is changed from `Employee` to `HourlyEmployee`.

It is worth noting that when you change the returned type of an overridden method in this way, such as from `Employee` to `HourlyEmployee`, you are not really changing the returned type so much as placing additional restrictions on it. Every `HourlyEmployee` is an `Employee` with some additional properties that, while they are properties of every `HourlyEmployee`, are not properties of every `Employee`. Any code that was written for a method of the base class and that assumed the value returned by the method is `Employee` will be legal for an overridden version of the method that returns an `HourlyEmployee`. This is true because every `HourlyEmployee` is an `Employee`.

Changing the Access Permission of an Overridden Method

You can change the access permission of an overridden method from `private` in the base class to `public` in the derived class (or in any other way that makes access permissions more permissive). For example, if the following is a method heading in a base case,

```
private void doSomething()
```

then you can use the following heading when overriding the method definition in a derived class:

```
public void doSomething()
```

Note that you cannot change permissions to make them more restricted in the derived class. You can change `private` to `public`, but you cannot change `public` to `private`.

This makes sense, because you want code written for the base class method to work for the derived class method. You can use a public method anyplace that you can use a private method, but it is not true that you can use a private method anyplace that you can use a public method.

PITFALL: Overriding versus Overloading

Do not confuse *overriding* (that is, redefining) a method definition in a derived class with *overloading* a method name. When you override a method definition, the new method definition given in the derived class has the exact same number and types of parameters. On the other hand, if the method in the derived class were to have a different number of parameters or a parameter of a different type from the method in the base class, then the derived class would have both methods. That would be overloading. For example, suppose we add the following method to the definition of the class `HourlyEmployee` (Display 7.3):

```java
public void setName(String firstName, String lastName)
{
    if ( (firstName == null) || (lastName == null) )
    {
        System.out.println("Fatal Error setting employee name.");
        System.exit(0);
    }
    else
        name = firstName + " " + lastName;
}
```

The class `HourlyEmployee` would then have this two-argument method `setName`, and it would also inherit the following one-argument method `setName` from the base class `Employee`:

```java
public void setName(String newName)
{
    if (newName == null)
    {
        System.out.println("Fatal Error setting employee name.");
        System.exit(0);
    }
    else
        name = newName;
}
```

The class `HourlyEmployee` would have two methods named `setName`. This would be *overloading* the method name `setName`.

(continued)

PITFALL: (continued)

On the other hand, both the class `Employee` and the class `HourlyEmployee` define a method with the following method heading:

```
public String toString()
```

In this case, the class `HourlyEmployee` has only one method named `toString()`, but the definition of the method `toString()` in the class `HourlyEmployee` is different from the definition of `toString()` in the class `Employee`; the method `toString()` has been *overridden* (that is, redefined).

If you get overriding and overloading confused, you do have one consolation. They are both legal. ■

The `super` Constructor

You can invoke a constructor of the base class within the definition of a derived class constructor. A constructor for a derived class uses a constructor from the base class in a special way. A constructor for the base class normally initializes all the data inherited from the base class. So a constructor for a derived class begins with an invocation of a constructor for the base class. The details are described next.

There is a special syntax for invoking the base class constructor that is illustrated by the constructor definitions for the class `HourlyEmployee` given in Display 7.3. In what follows, we have reproduced the beginning of one of the constructor definitions for the class `HourlyEmployee` taken from that display:

```
public HourlyEmployee(String theName, Date theDate,
                      double theWageRate, double theHours)
{
    super (theName, theDate);
    if ((theWageRate >= 0) && (theHours >= 0))
    {
        wageRate = theWageRate;
        hours = theHours;
    }
    else
    . . .
```

The line

super

```
    super (theName, theDate);
```

is a call to a constructor for the base class, which in this case is a call to a constructor for the class `Employee`.

Self-Test Exercises

1. Suppose the class named `SavingsAccount` is a derived class of a class called `Account`. Suppose the class `Account` has instance variables named `accountNo`, `balance`, and `interestRate`. Will an object of the class `SavingsAccount` also have instance variables named `accountNo`, `balance`, and `interestRate`?

2. Suppose the class named `SavingsAccount` is a derived class of a class called `Account`, and suppose the class `Account` has public methods named `deposit` and `withdraw`. Will an object of the class `SavingsAccount` have methods named `deposit` and `withdraw`? If so, do these methods have to perform the exact same actions in the class `SavingsAccount` as in the class `Account`?

3. Suppose the class named `SavingsAccount` is a derived class of a class called `Account`, and suppose the class `Account` has a method with the following heading and no other methods named `getInterest()`, as follows:

```
public double getInterest()
```

And suppose the definition of the class `SavingsAccount` has a method definition with the following heading and no other method definitions for methods named `getInterest`, as follows:

```
public double getInterest(double rate)
```

How many methods named `getInterest` will the class `SavingsAccount` have and what are their headings?

4. The class `HourlyEmployee` (Display 7.3) has methods named `getName` and `getRate` (among others). Why does the definition of the class `HourlyEmployee` contain a definition of the method `getRate` but no definition of the method `getName`?

There are some restrictions on how you can use the base class constructor call `super`. You cannot use an instance variable as an argument to `super`. Also, the call to the base class constructor (`super`) must always be the first action taken in a constructor definition. You cannot use it later in the definition of a constructor.

Notice that you use the keyword `super` to call the constructor of the base class. You do not use the name of the constructor; you do *not* use

```
Employee(theName, theDate); //ILLEGAL
```

If a constructor definition for a derived class does not include an invocation of a constructor for the base class, then the no-argument constructor of the base class is invoked automatically as the first action of the derived class constructor. So, the following definition of the no-argument constructor for the class `HourlyEmployee` (with `super` omitted) is equivalent to the version we gave in Display 7.3:

```
public HourlyEmployee()
{
    wageRate = 0;
    hours = 0;
}
```

A derived class object has all the instance variables of the base class. These inherited instance variables should be initialized, and the base class constructor is the most convenient place to initialize these inherited instance variables. That is why you should always include a call to one of the base class constructors when you define a constructor for a derived class. As already noted, if you do not include a call to a base class constructor (using `super`), then the no-argument constructor of the base class is called automatically. (If there is no no-argument constructor for the base class, that is an error condition.)

Call to a Base Class Constructor

Within the definition of a constructor for a class, you can use `super` as a name for a constructor of the base class. Any invocation of `super` must be the first action taken by the constructor.

EXAMPLE

```
public SalariedEmployee(SalariedEmployee originalObject)
{
    super(originalObject); //Invocation of base class
                           //constructor.
    salary = originalObject.salary;
}
```

The `this` Constructor

this

When defining a constructor, it is sometimes convenient to be able to call one of the other constructors in the same class. You can use the keyword `this` as a method name to invoke a constructor in the same class. This use of `this` is similar to the use of `super`, but with `this`, the call is to a constructor of the same class, not to a constructor for the base class. For example, consider the following alternate, and equivalent, definition of the no-argument constructor for the class `HourlyEmployee` (from Display 7.3):

```
public HourlyEmployee()
{
    this("No name", new Date("January", 1, 1000), 0, 0);
}
```

The line with `this` is an invocation of the constructor with the following heading:

```
public HourlyEmployee(String theName, Date theDate,
                      double theWageRate, double theHours)
```

The restrictions on how you can use the base class constructor call `super` also apply to the `this` constructor. You cannot use an instance variable as an argument to `this`. Also, any call to the constructor `this` must always be the first action taken in a constructor definition. Thus, a constructor definition cannot contain both an invocation of `super` and an invocation of `this`. If you want to include both a call to `super` and a call to `this`, use a call with `this`, and have the constructor that is called with `this` have `super` as its first action.

Call to Another Constructor in the Same Class

Within the definition of a constructor for a class, you can use `this` as a name for another constructor in the same class. Any invocation of `this` must be the first action taken by the constructor.

EXAMPLE

```
public HourlyEmployee()
{
    this("No name", new Date("January", 1, 1000), 0,0);
}
```

TIP: An Object of a Derived Class Has More than One Type

An object of a derived class has the type of the derived class. It also has the type of the base class, and more generally, it has the type of every one of its ancestor classes. For example, consider the following copy constructor definition from the class `HourlyEmployee` (Display 7.3):

```
public HourlyEmployee(HourlyEmployee originalObject)
{
    super(originalObject);
    wageRate = originalObject.wageRate;
    hours = originalObject.hours;
}
```

(continued)

TIP: (continued)

The line

```
super(originalObject);
```

is an invocation of a constructor for the base class `Employee`. The class `Employee` has no constructor with a parameter of type `HourlyEmployee`, but `originalObject` is of type `HourlyEmployee`. Fortunately, every object of type `HourlyEmployee` is also of type `Employee`. So, this invocation of `super` is an invocation of the copy constructor for the class `Employee`.

The fact that every object is not only of its own type but is also of the type of its ancestor classes simply reflects what happens in the everyday world. An hourly employee is an employee as well as an hourly employee. This sometimes is referred to as the **"is a" relationship**: For example, an `HourlyEmployee` is an `Employee`.

"is a" relationship

Display 7.6 contains a program demonstrating that an `HourlyEmployee` and a `SalariedEmployee` are also `Employee` objects. The method `showEmployee` requires an argument of type `Employee`. The objects `joe` and `sam` are of type `Employee` because they are instances of classes derived from the class `Employee` and so are suitable arguments for `showEmployee`. ■

An Object of a Derived Class Has More than One Type

An object of a derived class has the type of the derived class, and it also has the type of the base class. More generally, a derived class has the type of every one of its ancestor classes. So, you can assign an object of a derived class to a variable of any ancestor type (but not the other way around). You can plug in a derived class object for a parameter of any of its ancestor types. More generally, you can use a derived class object anyplace you can use an object of any of its ancestor types.

Display 7.6   An Object Belongs to Multiple Classes

```
1    public class IsADemo
2    {
3        public static void main(String[] args)
4        {
5            SalariedEmployee joe = new SalariedEmployee("Josephine",
6                                new Date("January", 1, 2004), 100000);
7            HourlyEmployee sam = new HourlyEmployee("Sam",
8                                new Date("February", 1, 2003), 50.50, 40);

9            System.out.println("joe's longer name is " + joe.getName());
10           System.out.println("showEmployee(joe) invoked:");
11           showEmployee(joe);              A SalariedEmployee
                                             is an Employee.
12           System.out.println("showEmployee(sam) invoked:");
13           showEmployee(sam);        An HourlyEmployee is an Employee.

14       }

15       public static void showEmployee(Employee employeeObject)
16       {
17               System.out.println(employeeObject.getName());
18               System.out.println(employeeObject.getHireDate());
19       }
20   }
```

Sample Dialogue

```
joe's longer name is Josephine
showEmployee(joe) invoked:
Josephine
January 1, 2004
showEmployee(sam) invoked:
Sam
February 1, 2003
```

PITFALL: The Terms *Subclass* and *Superclass*

subclass and superclass

Many programmers and authors use the term *subclass* for a derived class and use *superclass* for its base class (or any of its ancestor classes). This is logical. For example, the collection of all hourly employees in the world is a subclass of all employees. Similarly, the collection of all objects of type `HourlyEmployee` is a subcollection of the collection of all objects of the class `Employee`. As you add more instance variables and methods, you restrict the number of objects that can satisfy the class definition. Despite this logic, people often reverse the terms *subclass* and *superclass*. Remember that these terms refer to the collections of objects of the derived class and the base class and not to the number of instance variables or methods. A derived class is a *subclass* (not a *superclass*) of its base class. Another way to remember which is a superclass is to recall that the `super` constructor invocation is an invocation of the base class and so the base class is the *superclass*. ∎

Self-Test Exercises

5. Is the following program legal? The relevant classes are defined in Displays 7.2, 7.3, and 7.5.

```java
public class EmployeeDemo
{
    public static void main(String[] args)
    {
        HourlyEmployee joe =
            new HourlyEmployee("Joe Young",
                new Date("February", 1, 2004), 10.50, 40);
        SalariedEmployee boss =
            new SalariedEmployee("Mr. Big Shot",
                new Date("January", 1, 1999), 100000);
        System.out.println(yearOfJoining(joe));
        System.out.println(yearOfJoining(boss));
    }
    public int yearOfJoining(Employee object)
    {
        System.out.println(object.hiredate.getYear());
    }
}
```

6. Give a definition for a class `TitledEmployee` that is a derived class of the base class `SalariedEmployee` given in Display 7.5. The class `TitledEmployee` has one additional instance variable of type `String` called `title`. It also has two additional methods: `getTitle`, which takes no arguments and returns a `String`, and `setTitle`, which is a `void` method that takes one argument of type `String`. It also overrides (redefines) the method definition for `getName`, so that the string returned includes the title as well as the name of the employee.

EXAMPLE: An Enhanced `StringTokenizer` Class ★

Inheritance allows you to reuse all the code written for a base class in a derived class, and it lets you reuse it without copying it or even seeing the code in the base class. This means that, among other things, if one of the standard Java library classes does not have all the methods you want it to have, you can, in most cases, define a derived class that has the desired additional methods. In this subsection, we give a simple example of this process. This example requires that you have already covered the basics about arrays given in Section 6.1 of Chapter 6. It also requires you to have read the starred section on the `StringTokenizer` class in Chapter 4. If you have not covered this material, you will have to skip this example until you cover it.

The `StringTokenizer` class allows you to generate all the tokens in a string one time, but sometimes you want to cycle through the tokens a second or third time. There are lots of ways to accomplish this. For example, you can use the `StringTokenizer` constructor two (or more) times to create two (or more) `StringTokenizer` objects. However, it would be cleaner and more efficient if you could do it with just one `StringTokenizer` object. Display 7.7 shows a derived class of the `StringTokenizer` class that allows you to cycle through the tokens in a string any number of times. This class is called `EnhancedStringTokenizer`. The class `EnhancedStringTokenizer` behaves exactly the same as the `StringTokenizer` class, except that the class `EnhancedStringTokenizer` has one additional method named `tokensSoFar`. This method has no parameters and returns an array of strings containing all the tokens that have so far been returned by the methods named `nextToken`. After an object of the class `EnhancedStringTokenizer` has gone through all the tokens with the methods `nextToken`, it can invoke the method `tokensSoFar` to produce an array containing all the tokens. This array can be used to cycle through the tokens any number of additional times. A simple example of this is given in the program in Display 7.8.

The class `EnhancedStringTokenizer` has methods, such as `countTokens`, that it inherits unchanged from the class `StringTokenizer`. The class `EnhancedString Tokenizer` also has two methods—namely, the two methods named `nextToken`—whose definitions are overridden. From the outside, the methods named `nextToken` of the class `EnhancedStringTokenizer` behave exactly the same as the methods named `nextToken` in the class `StringTokenizer`. However, each of the two methods named `nextToken` of the class `EnhancedStringTokenizer` also save the tokens in an array instance variable, `a`, so that an array of tokens can be returned by the method `tokensSoFar`. The method `tokensSoFar` is the only completely new method in the derived class `EnhancedStringTokenizer`.

(continued)

EXAMPLE: (continued)

Notice that the definitions of the methods named `nextToken` in the class `EnhancedStringTokenizer` each include an invocation of `super.nextToken`, which is the version of the corresponding method `nextToken` in the base class `StringTokenizer`. Each overridden version of the method `nextToken` uses the method `super.nextToken` to produce the token it returns, but before returning the token, it stores the token in the array instance variable a. The instance variable `count` contains a count of the number of tokens stored in the array instance variable a.[1]

Display 7.7   Enhanced `StringTokenizer` (part 1 of 2)

```
1    import java.util.StringTokenizer;
2
3    public class EnhancedStringTokenizer extends StringTokenizer
4    {
5        private String[] a;
6        private int count;
7
8        public EnhancedStringTokenizer(String theString)
9        {
10            super(theString);
11            a = new String[countTokens()];
12            count = 0;
13        }
14
15        public EnhancedStringTokenizer(String theString, String delimiters)
16        {
17            super(theString, delimiters);
18            a = new String[countTokens()];
19            count = 0;
20        }
21
22        /**
23         Returns the same value as the same method in the StringTokenizer
24         class, but it also stores data for the method tokensSoFar to use.
25        */
26        public String nextToken()
27        {
```

*The method **countTokens** is inherited and is not overridden.*

*This method **nextToken** has its definition overridden.*

---

[1]The class `StringTokenizer` also has a method named `nextElement` with a return type of `Object`. This method should also be overridden. We have not yet even mentioned this method because we have not yet discussed the class `Object`. For now, you can simply pretend `StringTokenizer` has no such method `nextElement`. We will discuss this point in Self-Test Exercise 23 later in this chapter after we introduce the class `Object`.

Display 7.7   Enhanced `StringTokenizer` (part 2 of 2)

```
25          String token = super.nextToken();
26          a[count] = token;
27          count++;
28           token;
29      }
```

super.nextTokens is the version of nextToken defined in the base class StringTokenizer. This is explained more fully in Section 7.3.

```
30      /**
31       Returns the same value as the same method in the StringTokenizer
32       class, and changes the delimiter set in the same way as does the
33       same method in the StringTokenizer class, but it also stores data
         for the method tokensSoFar to use.
34      */
35      public String nextToken(String delimiters)
36      {
37          String token = super.nextToken(delimiters);
38          a[count] = token;
39          count++;
40          return token;
41      }
42      /**
43       Returns an array of all tokens produced so far. Array returned
44       has length equal to the number of tokens produced so far.
45      */
46      public String[] tokensSoFar()
47      {
48          String[] arrayToReturn = new String[count];
49          for (int i = 0; i < count; i++)
50              arrayToReturn[i] = a[i];
51          return arrayToReturn;
52      }
53  }
```

This method nextToken also has its definition overridden.

super.nextTokens is the version of nextToken defined in the base class StringTokenizer.

tokensSoFar is a new method.

Display 7.8   Use of the `EnhancedStringTokenizer` Class (part 1 of 2)

```
1  import java.util.Scanner;

2  public class EnhancedStringTokenizerDemo
3  {
4      public static void main(String[] args)
5      {
6          Scanner keyboard = new Scanner(System.in);

7          System.out.println("Enter a sentence:");
8          String sentence = keyboard.nextLine();
```

(continued)

Display 7.8 Use of the `EnhancedStringTokenizer` Class (part 2 of 2)

```
 9          EnhancedStringTokenizer wordFactory =
10              new EnhancedStringTokenizer(sentence);
11          System.out.println("Your sentence with extra blanks deleted:");
12          while (wordFactory.hasMoreTokens())
13              System.out.print(wordFactory.nextToken() + " ");
14          System.out.println();
15      //All tokens have been dispensed.

16          System.out.println("Sentence with each word on a separate line:");
17          String[] token = wordFactory.tokensSoFar();
18          for (int i = 0; i < token.length; i++)
19              System.out.println(token[i]);
20      }
21  }
```

Sample Dialogue

```
Enter a sentence:
    I    love    you,    madly.
Your sentence with extra blanks deleted:
I love you, madly.
Sentence with each word on a separate line:
I
love
you,
madly.
```

7.2   Encapsulation and Inheritance

Ignorance is bliss.

PROVERB

This section is a continuation of Section 7.1 and uses the same example classes we used there. In this section, we consider how the information-hiding facilities of Java, primarily the `private` modifier, interact with inheritance.

PITFALL: Use of Private Instance Variables from the Base Class

An object of the class HourlyEmployee (Display 7.3) inherits, among other things, an instance variable called name from the class Employee (Display 7.2). For example, the following would set the value of the instance variable name of the HourlyEmployee object joe to "Josephine":

```
joe.setName("Josephine");
```

But you must be a bit careful about how you manipulate inherited instance variables such as name. The instance variable name of the class HourlyEmployee was inherited from the class Employee, but the instance variable name is a private instance variable in the definition of the class Employee. That means that name can only be accessed by name within the definition of a method in the class Employee. An instance variable (or method) that is private in a base class is not accessible *by name* in the definition of a method in *any other class, not even in a method definition of a derived class.*

For example, notice the following method definition taken from the definition of the class HourlyEmployee in Display 7.3:

```
public String toString()
{
    return (getName() + " " + getHireDate().toString()
        + "\n$" + wageRate + " per hour for " + hours + " hours");
}
```

You might wonder why we needed to use the methods getName and getHireDate. You might be tempted to rewrite the method definition as follows:

```
public String toString() //Illegal version
{
    return (name + " " + hireDate.toString()
        + "\n$" + wageRate + " per hour for " + hours + " hours");
}
```

As the comment indicates, this will not work. The instance variables name and hireDate are private instance variables in the class Employee, and although a derived class such as HourlyEmployee inherits these instance variables, it cannot access them directly. You must instead use some public methods to access the instance variable name or hireDate, as we did in Display 7.3.

In the definition of a derived class, you cannot mention a private inherited instance variable by name. You must instead use public accessor and mutator methods (such as getName and setName) that were defined in the base class.

The fact that a private instance variable of a base class cannot be accessed in the definition of a method of a derived class often seems wrong to people. After all, if you are an hourly employee and you want to change your name, nobody says, "Sorry, name is a private instance variable of the class Employee." If you are an hourly employee, you

(continued)

PITFALL: (continued)

are also an employee. In Java, this is also true; an object of the class `HourlyEmployee` is also an object of the class `Employee`. However, the laws on the use of private instance variables and methods must be as we described, or else they would be compromised. If private instance variables of a class were accessible in method definitions of a derived class, then anytime you want to access a private instance variable, you could simply create a derived class and access it in a method of that class, which would mean that all private instance variables would be accessible to anybody who wants to put in a little extra effort. This scenario illustrates the problem, but the big problem is unintentional errors, not intentional subversion. If private instance variables of a class were accessible in method definitions of a derived class, then the instance variables might be changed by mistake or in inappropriate ways. (Remember, accessor and mutator methods can guard against inappropriate changes to instance variables.)

We will discuss one possible way to get around this restriction on private instance variables of the base class in the upcoming subsection entitled "Protected and Package Access." ■

Self-Test Exercises

7. Would the following be legal for the definition of a method to add to the class `Employee` (Display 7.2)? (Remember, the question is whether it is legal, not whether it is sensible.)

```
public void crazyMethod()
{
    Employee object = new Employee("Joe",
                                new Date("January", 1, 2005));
    System.out.println("Hello " + object.name);
}
```

Would it be legal to add this `crazyMethod` to the class `HourlyEmployee`?

8. Suppose you change the modifier before the instance variable `name` from `private` to `public` in the class `Employee`. Would it then be legal to add the method `crazyMethod` (from Self-Test Exercise 7) to the class `HourlyEmployee`?

PITFALL: Private Methods Are Effectively Not Inherited

As we noted in the Pitfall section, "Use of Private Instance Variables from the Base Class," an instance variable (or method) that is private in a base class is not directly accessible outside of the definition of the base class, *not even in a method definition for a derived class*. The private methods of the base class are just like private variables in terms of not being directly available. But in the case of methods, the restriction

PITFALL: (continued)

is more dramatic. A private variable can be accessed indirectly via an accessor or mutator method. A private method is simply not available. It is just as if the private method were not inherited. (In one sense, private methods in the base class may be indirectly available in the derived class. If a private method is used in the definition of a public method of the base class, then that public method can be invoked in the derived class, or any other class, so the private method can be indirectly invoked.)

This should not be a problem. Private methods should just be used as helping methods, so their use should be limited to the class in which they are defined. If you want a method to be used as a helping method in a number of inherited classes, then it is not *just* a helping method, and you should make the method public. ◼

Protected and Package Access

As you have seen, you cannot access (by name) a private instance variable or private method of the base class within the definition of a derived class. There are two classifications of instance variables and methods that allow them to be accessed by name in a derived class. The two classifications are *protected access*, which always gives access, and *package access*, which gives access if the derived class is in the same package as the base class.

If a method or instance variable is modified by `protected` (rather than `public` or `private`), then it can be accessed by name inside its own class definition, it can be accessed by name inside any class derived from it, and it can also be accessed by name in the definition of any class in the same package (even if the class in the same package is not derived from it). However, the `protected` method or instance variable cannot be accessed by name in any other classes. Thus, if an instance variable is marked `protected` in the class `Parent` and the class `Child` is derived from the class `Parent`, then the instance variable can be accessed by name inside any method definition in the class `Child`. However, in a class that is not in the same package as `Parent` and is not derived from `Parent`, it is as if the `protected` instance variable were `private`.

For example, consider the class `HourlyEmployee` that was derived from the base class `Employee`. We were required to use accessor and mutator methods to manipulate the inherited instance variables in the definition of `HourlyEmployee`. Consider the definition of the `toString` method of the class `HourlyEmployee`, which we repeat here:

```
public String toString()
{
    return (getName() + " " + getHireDate().toString()
        + "\n$" + wageRate + " per hour for " + hours + " hours");
}
```

If the private instance variables `name` and `hireDate` had been marked `protected` in the class `Employee`, the definition of `toString` in the derived class `HourlyEmployee` could be simplified to the following:

```
public String toString() //Legal if instance variables in
                         // Employee are marked protected
{
    return (name + " " + hireDate.toString()
        + "\n$" + wageRate + " per hour for " + hours + " hours");
}
```

The `protected` Modifier

If a method or instance variable is modified by `protected` (rather than `public` or `private`), then it can be accessed by name inside its own class definition, by name inside any class derived from it, and by name in the definition of any class in the same package.

The `protected` modifier provides very weak protection compared to the `private` modifier, because it allows direct access to any programmer who is willing to go through the bother of defining a suitable derived class. Many programming authorities discourage the use of the `protected` modifier. Instance variables should normally not be marked `protected`. On rare occasions, you may want to have a method marked `protected`. If you want an access intermediate between `public` and `private`, then the access described in the next paragraph is often a preferable alternative to `protected`.

You may have noticed that if you forget to place one of the modifiers `public`, `private`, or `protected` before an instance variable or method definition, then your class definition will still compile. If you do not place any of these modifiers before an instance variable or method definition, then the instance variable or method can be accessed by name inside the definition of any class in the same package, but not outside of the package. This is called **package access**, **default access**, or **friendly access**. Use package access in situations where you have a package of cooperating classes that act as a single encapsulated unit. Note that package access is more restricted than `protected`, and that package access gives more control to the programmer defining the classes. If you control the package directory (folder), then you control who is allowed package access.

The diagram in Display 7.9 may help you to understand who has access to members with public, private, protected, and package access. The diagram tells who can directly access, by name, variables that have public, private, protected, and package access. The same access rules apply to methods that have public, private, protected, and package access.

Display 7.9   Access Modifiers

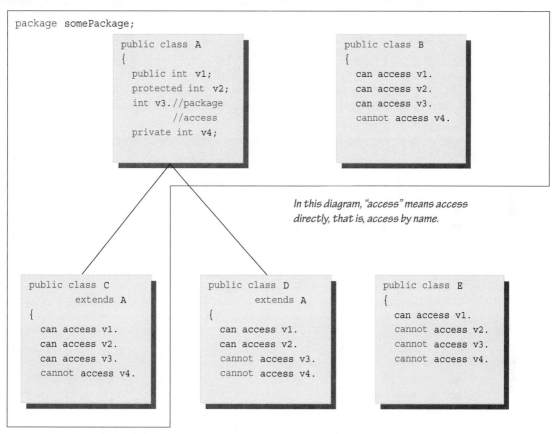

```
package somePackage;
```

```
public class A
{
    public int v1;
    protected int v2;
    int v3.//package
           //access
    private int v4;
}
```

```
public class B
{
    can access v1.
    can access v2.
    can access v3.
    cannot access v4.
}
```

In this diagram, "access" means access directly, that is, access by name.

```
public class C
        extends A
{
    can access v1.
    can access v2.
    can access v3.
    cannot access v4.
}
```

```
public class D
        extends A
{
    can access v1.
    can access v2.
    cannot access v3.
    cannot access v4.
}
```

```
public class E
{
    can access v1.
    cannot access v2.
    cannot access v3.
    cannot access v4.
}
```

A line from one class to another means the lower class is a derived class of the higher class.

If the instance variables are replaced by methods, the same access rules apply.

Package Access

If you do not place any of the modifiers `public`, `private`, or `protected` before an instance variable or method definition, then the instance variable or method is said to have **package access**. Package access is also known as **default access** and as **friendly access**. If an instance variable or method has package access, it can be accessed by name inside the definition of any class in the same package, but not outside of the package.

PITFALL: Forgetting about the Default Package

When considering package access, do not forget the default package. Recall that all the classes in your current directory (that do not belong to some other package) belong to an unnamed package called the *default package*. So, if a class in your current directory is not in any other package, then it is in the default package. If an instance variable or method has package access, then that instance variable or method can be accessed by name in the definition of any other class in the default package. ■

PITFALL: A Restriction on Protected Access ★

The situation described in this pitfall does not occur often, but when it does, it can be very puzzling if you do not understand what is going on.

Suppose class D is derived from class B, the instance variable n has protected access in class B, and the classes D and B are in different packages, so the class definitions begin as follows:

```
package one;

public class B
{
    protected int n;
    . . .
}

package two;

import one.B;

public class D extends B
{
    . . .
}
```

Then the following is a legitimate method that can appear in the definition of class D:

```
public void demo()
{
    n = 42; //n is inherited from B.
}
```

PITFALL: (continued)

The following is also a legitimate method definition for the derived class D:

```
public void demo2()
{
    D object = new D();
    object.n = 42; //n is inherited from B.
}
```

However, the following is not allowed as a method of D:

```
public void demo3()
{
    B object = new B();
    object.n = 42;//Error
}
```

The compiler will give an error message saying that n is protected in B.

Similar remarks apply to protected methods.

A class can access its own classes' inherited variables and methods that are marked protected in the base class, but cannot directly access any such instance variables or methods of an object of the base class (or of any other derived class of the base class). In the above example, n is an instance variable of the base class B and an instance variable of the derived class D. D can access n whenever n is used as an instance variable of D, but D cannot access n when n is used as an instance variable of B.

If the classes B and D are in the same package, you will not get the error message because, in Java, protected access implies package access. In particular, if the classes B and D are both in the default package, you will not get the error message. ■

Self-Test Exercises

9. Suppose you do not put any modifier before the instance variable name from in the class Employee (Display 7.2). Would it then be legal to add the method crazyMethod (from Self-Test Exercise 7) to the class HourlyEmployee (Display 7.3)?

10. Why is protected access discouraged by many programming authorities?

(continued)

Self-Test Exercises (continued)

11. Suppose class D is derived from class B. The method `display()` has protected access in class B, and the classes D and B are in different packages, so the class definitions begin as follows:

```
package one;
public class B
{
int n;
    protected void display()
    {
        System.out.println(n);
    }

package two;
import one.B;
public class D extends B
{
    . . .
}
```

Is the following a legitimate method that can appear in the definition of the class D?

```
public void demo()
{
    display(); //display() is inherited from B.
}
```

12. Suppose B and D are as described in Self-Test Exercise 11. Is the following a legitimate method that can appear in the definition of the class D?

```
public void demo2()
{
    D object = new D();
    System.out.println(object.n);
}
```

13. Suppose B and D are as described in Self-Test Exercise 11. Is the following a legitimate method that can appear in the definition of the class D?

```
public void demo3()
{
    B object = new B();
    object.display();
}
```

7.3   Programming with Inheritance

The devil is in the details.

COMMON SAYING

In the previous section, we described the basic idea and details of derived classes. In this section, we continue that discussion and go on to cover some more subtle points about derived classes. In the process, we also discuss the class `Object`, which is an ancestor class of all Java classes, and we describe a better way to define an `equals` method.

TIP: Static Variables Are Inherited

Static variables in a base class are inherited by any derived classes. The modifiers `public`, `private`, and `protected`, and package access have the same meaning for static variables as they do for instance variables. ■

TIP: "is a" versus "has a"

"is a" relationship

"has a" relationship

composition

Early in this chapter, we defined a derived class called `HourlyEmployee` using the class `Employee` as the base class. In such a case, an object of the derived class `HourlyEmployee` is also an instance of the class `Employee`, or, stated more simply, an `HourlyEmployee` *is an* `Employee`. This is an example of the **"is a" relationship** between classes. It is one way to make a more complex class out of a simpler class.

Another way to make a more complex class out of a simpler class is known as the **"has a" relationship**. For example, the class `Employee` defined earlier has an instance variable of the class type `Date`. We express this relationship by saying an `Employee` "has a" `Date`. Using the "has a" relationship to build a class (such as building the class `Employee` by using `Date` as an instance variable) is often called **composition**.

Because the class `HourlyEmployee` inherits the instance variable of type `Date` from the class `Employee`, it is also correct to say an `HourlyEmployee` "has a" `Date`. Thus, an `HourlyEmployee` *is an* `Employee` and *has a* `Date`. ■

Access to a Redefined Base Method

super relationship

Suppose you redefine a method so that it has a different definition in the derived class from what it has in the base class. The definition that was given in the base class is not completely lost to the derived class objects. However, if you want to invoke the version of the method given in the base class with an object in the derived class, you need some way to say, "use the definition of this method as given in the base class (even though I am an object of the derived class)." The way you say this is to use the keyword `super` as if it were a calling object.

For example, the method `toString` of the class `HourlyEmployee` (Display 7.3) is defined as follows:

```
public String toString() //in the derived class HourlyEmployee
{
    return (getName() + " " + getHireDate().toString()
        + "\n$" + wageRate + " per hour for " + hours + " hours");
}
```

This overrides the following definition of `toString()` that was given in the definition of the base class `Employee`:

```
public String toString() //in the base class Employee
{
    return (name + " " + hireDate.toString());
}
```

We can use the version of the method `toString()` defined in the base class `Employee` to simplify the definition of the method `toString()` in the derived class `HourlyEmployee`. The following is an equivalent way to define `toString()` in the derived class `HourlyEmployee`:

```
public String toString() //in the derived class HourlyEmployee
{
    return (super.toString()
        + "\n$" + wageRate + " per hour for " + hours + " hours");
}
```

The expression `super.toString()` is an invocation of the method `toString()` using the definition of `toString()` given in the base class `Employee`.

You can only use `super` in this way within the definition of a method in a derived class. Outside of the definition of the derived class, you cannot invoke an overridden method of the base class using an object of the derived class.

Invoking the Old Version of an Overridden Method?

Within the definition of a method of a derived class, you can invoke the base class version of an overridden method of the base class by prefacing the method name with `super` and a dot. Outside of the derived class definition, there is no way to invoke the base class version of an overridden method using an object of the derived class.

EXAMPLE

```
public String toString()
{
    return (super.toString()
        + "\n$" + wageRate + " per hour for " + hours + " hours");
}
```

PITFALL: You Cannot Use Multiple supers

As we already noted, within the definition of a method of a derived class, you can call an overridden method of the base class by prefacing the method name with `super` and a dot. However, you cannot repeat the use of `super` to invoke a method from some ancestor class other than a direct parent. For example, suppose that the class `Employee` were derived from the class `Person`, and the class `HourlyEmployee` is derived from the class `Employee`. You might think that you can invoke a method of the class `Person` within the definition of the class `HourlyEmployee`, by using `super.super`, as in

```
super.super.toString() //ILLEGAL!
```

However, as the comment indicates, it is illegal to have such multiple `supers` in Java. ■

Self-Test Exercises

14. Redefine the `toString` method of the class `SalariedEmployee` (Display 7.5) so that it uses `super.toString()`. This new definition of `toString` will be equivalent to the one given in Display 7.5.

15. Redefine the `equals` method for the class `HourlyEmployee` (Display 7.3) using `super.equals` to invoke the `equals` method of the base class `Employee`.

16. Is the following program legal? The relevant classes are defined in Displays 7.2 and 7.3.

```java
public class EmployeeDemo
{
    public static void main(String[] args)
    {
        HourlyEmployee joe =
            new HourlyEmployee("Joe Young",
                    new Date("Feb", 1, 2004), 10.50, 40);
        String nameNDate = joe.super.toString();
        System.out.println(nameNDate);
    }
}
```

(continued)

Self-Test Exercises (continued)

17. Suppose you add the following defined constant to the class Employee (Display 7.2):

    ```
    public static final int STANDARD_HOURS = 160; //per month
    ```

    Would it then be legal to add the following method to the class HourlyEmployee (Display 7.3)?

    ```
    public void setHoursToStandard()
    {
        hours = STANDARD_HOURS;
    }
    ```

The Class Object

object class

Java has a class that is an ancestor of every class. In Java, every class is a derived class of a derived class of . . . (for some number of iterations of "a derived class of") of the class Object. So, every object of every class is of type Object, as well as being of the type of its class (and also of the types of all its ancestor classes). Even classes that you define yourself are descendent classes of the class Object. If you do not make your class a derived class of some class, then Java will automatically make it a derived class of the class Object.

The class Object allows you to write Java code for methods with a parameter of type Object that can be replaced by an object of any class whatsoever. You will eventually encounter library methods that accept an argument of type Object and hence can be used with an argument that is an object of absolutely any class.

The Class Object

In Java, every class is a descendent of the class Object. So, every object of every class is of type Object, as well as being of the type of its class.

The class Object is in the package java.lang, which is always imported automatically. So, you do not need any import statement to make the class Object available to your code.

The class Object does have some methods that every Java class inherits. For example, every object inherits the methods equals and toString from some ancestor class, which either is the class Object or a class that itself inherited the methods ultimately from the class Object. However, the inherited methods equals and toString will not work correctly for (almost) any class you define. You need to override the inherited method definitions with new, more appropriate definitions.

toString

It is important to include definitions of the methods toString and equals in the classes you define, because some Java library classes assume your class has such methods. There are no subtleties involved in defining (actually redefining or overriding) the method toString. We have seen good examples of the method toString in many of our class definitions. The definition of the overridden method equals does have some subtleties; we discuss them in the next subsection.

equals

clone   Another method inherited from the class `Object` is the method `clone`, which is intended to return a copy of the calling object. We discuss the method `clone` in Chapters 8 and 13.

The Right Way to Define `equals`

Earlier we said that the class `Object` has an `equals` method, and that when you define a class with an `equals` method, you should override the definition of the method `equals` given in the class `Object`. However, we did not, strictly speaking, follow our own advice. The heading for the method `equals` in our definition of the class `Employee` (Display 7.2) is as follows:

```
public boolean equals(Employee otherEmployee)
```

On the other hand, the heading for the method `equals` in the class `Object` is as follows:

```
public boolean equals(Object otherObject)
```

The two `equals` methods have different parameter types, so we have not overridden the definition of `equals` We have merely overloaded the method `equals`. The class `Employee` has both of these methods named `equals`.

In most situations, this will not matter. However, there are situations in which it does. Some library methods assume your class's definition of `equals` has the following heading, the same as in the class `Object`:

```
public boolean equals(Object otherObject)
```

We need to change the type of the parameter for the `equals` method in the class `Employee` from type `Employee` to type `Object`. A first try might produce the following:

```
public boolean equals(Object otherObject)
{
    Employee otherEmployee = (Employee)otherObject;
    return (name.equals(otherEmployee.name)
            && hireDate.equals(otherEmployee.hireDate));
}
```

We needed to type cast the parameter `otherObject` from type `Object` to type `Employee`. If we omit the type cast and simply proceed with `otherObject`, the compiler will give an error message when it sees the following:

```
otherObject.name
```

The class `Object` does not have an instance variable named `name`.

This first try at an improved `equals` method does override the definition of `equals` given in the class `Object` and will work well in many cases. However, it still has a shortcoming.

Our definition of `equals` now allows an argument that can be any kind of object whatsoever. What happens if the method `equals` is used with an argument that is not an `Employee`? A run-time error will occur when the type cast to `Employee` is executed.

We need to make our definition work for any kind of object. If the object is not an `Employee`, we simply return `false`. The calling object is an `Employee`, so if the argument is not an `Employee`, they should not be considered equal. But how can we tell whether the parameter is or is not of type `Employee`?

Every object inherits the method `getClass()` from the class `Object`. The method `getClass()` is marked `final` in the class `Object`, so it cannot be overridden. For any object o, `o.getClass()` returns a representation of the class used to create o. For example, after the following is executed,

```
o = new Employee();
```

`o.getClass()` returns a representation `Employee`.

We will not describe the details of this representation except to say that two such representations should be compared with `==` or `!=` if you want to know if two representations are the same. Thus,

```
if (object1.getClass() == object2.getClass())
    System.out.println("Same class.");
else
    System.out.println("Not the same class.");
```

will output `"Same class."` if `object1` and `object2` were created with the same class when they were created using `new`, and output `"Not the same class."` otherwise.

Our final version of the method `equals` is shown in Display 7.10. Note that we have also taken care of one more possible case. The predefined constant `null` can be plugged in for a parameter of type `Object`. The Java documentation says that an `equals` method should return `false` when comparing an object and the value `null`. So that is what we have done.

extra code on website

On the accompanying website, the subdirectory `improvedEquals` (of the directory for this chapter) has a definition of the class `Employee` that includes this definition of `equals`.

Display 7.10   A Better `equals` Method for the Class `Employee`

```
1   public boolean equals(Object otherObject)
2   {
3       if (otherObject == null)
4           return false;
5       else if (getClass() != otherObject.getClass())
6           return false;
7       else
8       {
9           Employee otherEmployee = (Employee)otherObject;
10          return (name.equals(otherEmployee.name)
11              && hireDate.equals(otherEmployee.hireDate));
12      }
13  }
```

Many authors suggest that in the definition of `equals` for a class such as `Employee`, given in Display 7.10, you should not use

```
else if (getClass() != otherObject.getClass())
    return false;
```

but should instead use

```
else if (!(otherObject instanceof Employee))
    return false;
```

instanceof

What is the difference and which should you use? At first glance, it seems like you should use `instanceof` in the definition of `equals`. The `instanceof` operator checks to see if an object is of the type given as its second argument. The syntax is

Object `instanceof` *Class_Name*

which returns `true` if *Object* is of type *Class_Name*; otherwise it returns `false`. So, the following will return `true` if `otherObject` is of type `Employee`:

```
(otherObject instanceof Employee)
```

Suppose that (contrary to what we really did) we instead used `instanceof` in our definition of `equals` for the class `Employee` and also used `instanceof` in our definition for the class `HourlyEmployee`, so that the definition of `equals` for `HourlyEmployee` is as follows:

```
public boolean equals(Object otherObject)
//This is NOT the right way to define equals.
{
    if (otherObject == null)
        return false;
    else if (!(otherObject instanceof HourlyEmployee))
        return false;
    else
    {
        HourlyEmployee otherHourlyEmployee =
                            (HourlyEmployee)otherObject;
        return (super.equals(otherHourlyEmployee)
            && (wageRate == otherHourlyEmployee.wageRate)
            && (hours == otherHourlyEmployee.hours));
    }
}
```

(continued)

TIP: (continued)

Assuming that the `equals` method for both `Employee` and `HourlyEmployee` are defined using `instanceof` (as previously mentioned), consider the following situation:

```
Employee e =
        new Employee("Joe Worker", new Date("January", 1, 2004));
HourlyEmployee hourlyE = new HourlyEmployee("Joe Worker",
                    new Date("January", 1, 2004), 50.50, 160);
```

Then, with the definition of `equals` that uses `instanceof`, we get that

```
e.equals(hourlyE)
```

returns `true`, because `hourlyE` is an `Employee` with the same name and hire date as e. So far, it sounds reasonable.

However, since we are assuming that we also used `instanceof` in the definition of `equals` for the class `HourlyEmployee`, we also get that

```
hourlyE.equals(e)
```

returns `false` because e `instanceof  HourlyEmployee` returns `false`. (e is an `Employee` but e is not an `HourlyEmployee`.)

So, if we define `equals` in both classes using `instanceof`, then e equals `hourlyE`, but `hourlyE` does not equal e. That is no way for `equals` to behave.

Since `instanceof` does not yield a suitable definition of `equals`, you should instead use `getClass()` as we did in Display 7.10. If we use `getClass()` in a similar way in the definition of `equals` for the class `HourlyEmployee` (see Self-Test Exercise 19), then

```
e.equals(hourlyE)
```

and

```
hourlyE.equals(e)
```

both return `false`. ■

`instanceof` and `getClass()` ★

Both the `instanceof` operator and the `getClass()` method can be used to check the class of an object. The `instanceof` operator simply tests an object for type. The `getClass()` method, used in a test with `==` or `!=`, tests if two objects were created with the same class. The details follow.

THE `instanceof` OPERATOR

The `instanceof` operator checks if an object is of the type given as its second argument. The syntax is

Object `instanceof` *Class_Name*

which returns `true` if *Object* is of type *Class_Name*; otherwise it returns `false`. So, the following will return `true` if `otherObject` is of type `Employee`:

```
(otherObject instanceof Employee)
```

Note that this means it returns `true` if `otherObject` is of the type of any descendent class of `Employee`, because in that case `otherObject` is also of type `Employee`.

THE `getClass()` METHOD

Every object inherits the method `getClass()` from the class `Object`. The method `getClass()` is marked `final` in the class `Object`, so it cannot be overridden. For any object of any class,

```
object.getClass()
```

returns a representation of the class that was used with `new` to create `object`. Any two such representations can be compared with `==` or `!=` to determine whether or not they represent the same class. Thus,

```
if (object1.getClass() == object2.getClass())
    System.out.println("Same class.");
else
    System.out.println("Not the same class.");
```

will output `Same class` if `object1` and `object2` were created with the same class when they were created using `new`, and output `Not same class` otherwise.

(continued)

EXAMPLE

Suppose that `HourlyEmployee` is a derived class of `Employee` and that `employeeObject` and `hourlyEmployeeObject` are created as follows:

```
Employee employeeObject = new Employee();
HourlyEmployee hourlyEmployeeObject = new HourlyEmployee();
```

Then,

```
employeeObject.getClass() == hourlyEmployeeObject.getClass()
```

returns `false`.

```
employeeObject instanceof Employee
```

returns `true`.

```
hourlyEmployeeObject instanceof Employee
```

returns `true`.

```
employeeObject instanceof HourlyEmployee
```

returns `false`.

```
hourlyEmployeeObject instanceof HourlyEmployee
```

returns `true`.

MyProgrammingLab™

Self-Test Exercises

18. Redefine the method `equals` given in Display 7.10 using `instanceof` instead of `getClass()`. Give the complete definition. Remember, we do not want you to define `equals` this way in your class definitions; this is just an exercise.

19. Redefine the `equals` method of the class `HourlyEmployee` (Display 7.3) so that it has a parameter of type `Object` and follows the other guidelines we gave for an `equals` method. Assume the definition of the method `equals` for the class `Employee` has been changed to be as in Display 7.10. (Remember, you should use `getClass()`, not `instanceof`.)

Self-Test Exercises (continued)

20. Redefine the `equals` method of the class `SalariedEmployee` (Display 7.5) so that it has a parameter of type `Object` and follows the other guidelines we gave for an `equals` method. Assume the definition of the method `equals` for the class `Employee` has been changed to be as in Display 7.10. (Remember, you should use `getClass()`, not `instanceof`.)

21. Redefine the `equals` method of the class `Date`(Display 4.13) so that it has a parameter of type `Object` and follows the other guidelines we gave for an `equals` method. (Remember, you should use `getClass()`, not `instanceof`.)

22. What is the output produced by the following program? (The classes `Employee` and `HourlyEmployee` were defined in this chapter.)

```
public class Test
{
    public static void main(String[] args)
    {
        Employee object1 = new Employee();
        Employee object2 = new HourlyEmployee();

        if (object1.getClass( ) == object2.getClass( ))
            System.out.println("Same class.");
        else
            System.out.println("Not the same class.");
    }
}
```

23. (This exercise requires that you have covered the starred subsection "An Enhanced `StringTokenizer` Class *," earlier in this chapter.)

    Although we did not discuss it when we covered the class `StringTokenizer`, the class `StringTokenizer` has a method with the following heading:

    ```
    public Object nextElement()
    ```

    The method `nextElement()` returns the same string as the method `nextToken()`, but `nextElement()` returns it as something of type `Object`, as opposed to type `String`. Give a suitable definition of `nextElement` to add to the definition of `EnhancedStringTokenizer`. This definition will override the definition of `nextElement` in the class `StringTokenizer`. (*Hint*: the definition is just like the definition of `nextToken` except for fixing the type of the string returned.)

Chapter Summary

- *Inheritance* provides a tool for code reuse by deriving one class from another. The *derived class* automatically inherits the features of the old (base) class and may add features as well.

- A derived class object inherits the instance variables, static variables, and public methods of the *base class*, and may add additional instance variables, static variables, and methods.

- An object of a derived class has the type of the derived class, and it also has the type of the base class, and more generally, has the type of every one of its *ancestor classes*.

- If an instance variable is marked `private` in a base class, then it cannot be accessed by name in a derived class.

- Private methods are effectively not inherited.

- A method may be redefined in a derived class so that it performs differently from how it performs in the base class. This is called *overriding* the method definition. The definition for an overridden method is given in the class definition of the derived class, in the same way as the definitions of any added methods.

- A constructor of a base class can be used in the definition of a constructor for a derived class. The keyword `super` is used as the name for a constructor of the base class.

- A constructor definition can use the keyword `this`, as if it were a method name, to invoke a constructor of the same class.

- If a constructor does not contain an invocation of either `super` or `this`, then Java automatically inserts an invocation of `super()` as the first action in the body of the constructor definition.

- A `protected` instance variable or method in the base class can be accessed by name in the definition of a method of a derived class and in the definition of any method in the same package.

- If an instance variable or method has none of the modifiers `public`, `private`, or `protected`, then it is said to have *package access*. An instance variable or method with package access can be accessed by name in the definition of any method in the same package.

- The class `Object` is an ancestor class of every class in Java.

- The `equals` method for a class should have `Object` as the type of its one parameter.

Answers to Self-Test Exercises

1. Yes, it will have the instance variables. A derived class has all the instance variables that the base class has and can add more instance variables besides.

2. Yes, it will have the methods. A derived class has all the public methods that the base class has and can also add more methods. If the derived class does not override (redefine) a method definition, then it performs exactly the same action in the derived class as it does in the base class. However, the base class can contain an overriding definition of (a new definition of) a method and the new definition will replace the old definition (provided it has the same number and types of parameters).

3. The class `SavingsAccount` will have two methods named `getInterest` and they will have the following two headings. This is an example of overloading.

```
public double getInterest()
public double getInterest(double rate)
```

4. The method `getName` is inherited from the class `Employee` and so needs no definition. The method `getRate` is a new method added in the class `HourlyEmployee` and so needs to be defined.

5. No, it is not legal because the method `yearOfJoining` cannot access the private variable `hiredate` of the instance variable object.

6.
```java
public class TitledEmployee extends SalariedEmployee
{
    private String title;

    public TitledEmployee()
    {
        super ("no name", newDate("January," 1, 1000), 0);
        title = "No title";
    }

    public TitledEmployee(String theName, String theTitle,
                          Date theDate, double theSalary)
    {
        super (theName, theDate, theSalary);
        title = theTitle;
    }

    public String getTitle()
    {
        return title;
    }
}
```

```
    public void setTitle(String theTitle)
    {
        title = theTitle;
    }

    public String getName()
    {
        return (title + super.getName());
    }
}
```

7. It would be legal to add `crazyMethod` to the class `Employee`. It would not be legal to add `crazyMethod` to the class `HourlyEmployee` because, although the class `HourlyEmployee` has an instance variable `name`, `name` is private in the base class `Employee` and so cannot be accessed by name in `HourlyEmployee`.

8. Yes, it would be legal as long as `name` is marked `public` in the base class `Employee`.

9. It would be legal if and only if `HourlyEmployee` is in the same package.

10. The protected modifier provides very weak protection compared to the private modifier; in fact, package access is more restricted than protected, it gives more control to the programmer defining the classes.

11. Yes, it is legitimate.

12. No, it is not legitimate, as n has package access and the Class D is outside the package, so no method in D can access n directly.

13. No, it is not legitimate. The compiler will give an error message saying `display()` is protected in B.

14.
```
public String toString()
{
        return (super.toString()
                        + "\n$" + salary + " per year");
}
```

15.
```
public boolean equals(HourlyEmployee other)
{
    return (super.equals(other)
                && wageRate == other.wageRate
                && hours == other.hours);
}
```

A better definition of `equals` for the class `HourlyEmployee` is given in Display 7.10.

16. It is not legal. You cannot use `super` in this way. `super.toString()` as used here refers to `toString()` in the class `Employee` and can only be used in definitions of classes derived from `Employee`. Moreover, you cannot have a calling object, such as `joe`, before `super`, so this is even illegal if you add `extends Employee` to the first line of the class definition.

17. Yes, all static variables are inherited. Because a defined constant is a form of static variable, it is inherited. So, the class `HourlyEmployee` inherits the constant `STANDARD_HOURS` from the class `Employee`.

18.
```
public boolean equals(Object otherObject)
//This is NOT the right way to define equals.
{
    if (otherObject == null)
        return false;
    else if (!(otherObject instanceof Employee))
        return false;
    else
    {
        Employee otherEmployee = (Employee)otherObject;
        return (name.equals(otherEmployee.name)
            && hireDate.equals(otherEmployee.hireDate));
    }
}
```

extra code on website

19. A version of the `HourlyEmployee` class with this definition of `equals` is in the subdirectory `improvedEquals` of the `ch07` directory on the accompanying website.

```
public boolean equals(Object otherObject)
{
    if (otherObject == null)
        return false;
    else if (getClass() != otherObject.getClass())
        return false;
    else
    {
        HourlyEmployee otherHourlyEmployee =
                            (HourlyEmployee)otherObject;
        return (super.equals(otherHourlyEmployee)
            && (wageRate == otherHourlyEmployee.wageRate)
            && (hours == otherHourlyEmployee.hours));
    }
}
```

extra code on website

20. A version of the `SalariedEmployee` class with this definition of `equals` is in the subdirectory `improvedEquals` of the `ch07` directory on the accompanying website.

```
public boolean equals(Object otherObject)
{
    if (otherObject == null)
        return false;
    else if (getClass() != otherObject.getClass())
        return false;
    else
    {
```

```
                    SalariedEmployee otherSalariedEmployee =
                                     (SalariedEmployee)otherObject;
                return (super.equals(otherSalariedEmployee)
                    && (salary == otherSalariedEmployee.salary));
            }
        }
```

extra code
on website

21. A version of the Date class with this definition of equals is in the subdirectory improvedEquals of the ch07 directory on the accompanying website.

```
public boolean equals(Object otherObject)
{
    if (otherObject == null)
      return false;
    else if (getClass() != otherObject.getClass())
       return false;
    else
    {
        Date otherDate =
                    (Date)otherObject;
        return ( month.equals(otherDate.month)
              && (day == otherDate.day)
              && (year == otherDate.year) );
    }
}
```

22. Not the same class.

extra code
on website

23. The following is included in the definition of EnhancedStringTokenizer on the accompanying website.

```
public Object nextElement()
{
    String token = super.nextToken();
    a[count] = token;
    count++;
    return (Object)token;
}
```

MyProgrammingLab™   **Programming Projects**

Visit www.myprogramminglab.com to complete select exercises online and get instant feedback.

1. Define a class named Sale that contains an instance variable of type double that stores the amount of the sale and appropriate accessor and mutator methods. Also create a method named saleDetails that outputs an English sentence to describe the amount of the sale.

Next, define a class named `CashSale` that is derived from `Sale`. This class should redefine the `saleDetails` method to indicate that the payment was made in cash. Include appropriate constructor(s).

Define a class named `CreditCardSale` that is derived from `Sale`. This class should contain instance variables for the name on the card, expiration date, and credit card number. Include appropriate constructor(s). Finally, redefine the `saleDetails` method to include all credit card information in the printout.

Create a `main` method that creates at least two `CashSale` and two `CreditCardSale` objects with different values and calls `saleDetails` for each.

2. Define a class named `Document` that contains an instance variable of type `String` named `text` that stores any textual content for the document. Create a method named `toString` that returns the `text` field and also include a method to set this value.

Next, define a class for `Email` that is derived from `Document` and includes instance variables for the `sender`, `recipient`, and `title` of an email message. Implement appropriate accessor and mutator methods. The body of the email message should be stored in the inherited variable `text`. Redefine the `toString` method to concatenate all text fields.

Similarly, define a class for `File` that is derived from `Document` and includes a instance variable for the `pathname`. The textual contents of the file should be stored in the inherited variable `text`. Redefine the `toString` method to concatenate all text fields.

Finally, create several sample objects of type `Email` and `File` in your `main` method. Test your objects by passing them to the following subroutine that returns true if the object contains the specified keyword in the text property.

```
public static boolean ContainsKeyword(Document docObject,
                                              String keyword)
{
        if (docObject.toString().indexOf(keyword,0) >= 0)
           return true;
        return false;
}
```

VideoNote
Solution to
Programming
Project 7.3

3. The following is some code designed by J. Hacker for a video game. There is an `Alien` class to represent a monster and an `AlienPack` class that represents a band of aliens and how much damage they can inflict:

```
class Alien
{
        public static final int SNAKE_ALIEN = 0;
        public static final int OGRE_ALIEN = 1;
        public static final int MARSHMALLOW_MAN_ALIEN = 2;

        public int type; // Stores one of the three above types
        public int health; // 0=dead, 100=full strength
        public String name;
```

```java
        public Alien (int type, int health, String name)
        {
            this.type = type;
            this.health = health;
            this.name = name;
        }
}
public class AlienPack
{
        private Alien[] aliens;

        public AlienPack (int numAliens)
        {
            aliens = new Alien[numAliens];
        }
        public void addAlien(Alien newAlien, int index)
        {
            aliens[index] = newAlien;
        }
        public Alien[] getAliens()
        {
            return aliens;
        }
}
public int calculateDamage()
{
        int damage = 0;
        for (int i=0; i < aliens.length; i++)
        {
            if (aliens[i].type==Alien.SNAKE_ALIEN)
            {
                damage +=10;// Snake does 10 damage
            }
            else if (aliens[i].type==Alien.OGRE_ALIEN)
            {
                damage +=6;// Ogre does 6 damage
            }
             else if (aliens[i].type==
            Alien.MARSHMALLOW_MAN_ALIEN)
            {
                damage +=1;
            // Marshmallow Man does 1 damage
            }
        }
        return damage;
    }
}
```

The code is not very object oriented and does not support information hiding in the Alien class. Rewrite the code so that inheritance is used to represent the different types of aliens instead of the "type" parameter. This should result in deletion of the "type" parameter. Also rewrite the Alien class to hide the instance variables and create a getDamage method for each derived class that returns the amount of damage the alien inflicts. Finally, rewrite the calculateDamage method to use getDamage and write a main method that tests the code.

4. Define a class called Pensioner, which is a derived class of the class SalariedEmployee in Display 7.5. You are to supply the following additional instance variables and methods:

   - An instance variable of type String that contains the last position held by the pensioner (such as "Director" or "Vice President").
   - An instance variable of type String that contains the area of responsibility the pensioner had worked in (such as "Production", "Accounting", or "Personnel").
   - An instance variable of type String that contains the name of the successor who took responsibility and his place when this employee retired.
   - Suitable constructors, and suitable accessor and mutator methods.
   - A method for reading in the pensioner's data from the keyboard.

   Override the definitions for the methods equals and toString so they are appropriate to the class Pensioner.

   Also, write a suitable test program.

VideoNote
Solution to
Programming
Project 7.5

5. Give the definition of a class named Doctor whose objects are records for a clinic's doctors. This class will be a derived class of the class SalariedEmployee given in Display 7.5. A Doctor record has the doctor's specialty (such as "Pediatrician", "Obstetrician", "General Practitioner", and so forth; so use the type String) and office visit fee (use type double). Be sure your class has a reasonable complement of constructors, accessor, and mutator methods, and suitably defined equals and toString methods. Write a program to test all your methods.

6. Create a class called Vehicle that has the manufacturer's name (type String), number of cylinders in the engine (type int), and owner (type Person given next). Then, create a class called Truck that is derived from Vehicle and has the following additional properties: the load capacity in tons (type double since it may contain a fractional part) and towing capacity in pounds (type int). Be sure your class has a reasonable complement of constructors, accessor and mutator methods, and suitably defined equals and toString methods. Write a program to test all your methods.

   The definition of the class Person follows. Completing the definitions of the methods is part of this programming project.

```
public class Person
{
    private String name;
```

```
        public Person()
        {...}
        public Person(String theName)
        {...}
        public Person(Person theObject)
        {...}
        public String getName()
        {...}
        public void setName(String theName)
        {...}
        public String toString()
        {...}
        public boolean equals(Object other)
        {...}
    }
```

7. Give the definition of two classes, Patient and Billing, whose objects are records for a clinic. Patient will be derived from the class Person given in Programming Project 7.6. A Patient record has the patient's name (inherited from the class Person) and primary physician of type Doctor defined in Programming Project 7.5 A Billing object will contain a Patient object, a Doctor object, and an amount due of type double. Be sure your classes have a reasonable complement of constructors, accessor, and mutator methods, and suitably defined equals and toString methods. First write a driver program to test all your methods, then write a test program that creates at least two patients, at least two doctors, and at least two Billing records, and then prints out the total income from the Billing records.

8. Programming Project 4.10 required adding an instance variable to the Pet class defined in Display 4.15 to indicate if the pet is a dog or cat. A better organization is to define Pet as a superclass of the Dog and Cat classes. This organization eliminates the need for an instance variable to indicate the type of the pet. Do or redo Programming Project 4.10 with inheritance. The acepromazine() and carprofen() methods should be defined in the Pet class to simply return 0. Override both methods in the Dog and Cat classes to calculate the correct dosage. Write a main method with appropriate tests to exercise the changes.

9. Programming Project 6.18 asked you to use an array of Strings to store the fruits and vegetables shipped in a `BoxOfProduce` object for a CSA farm.

Modify your solution further by creating a `Produce` class. This class should have an instance variable of type `String` for the name, appropriate constructors, and a public `toString()` method. Then create a `Fruit` and a `Vegetable` class that are derived from `Produce`. These classes should have constructors that take the name as a `String` and invoke the appropriate constructor from the base class to set the name.

Next, modify the text file of produce so it indicates whether each item is a fruit or a vegetable. Here is one possible organization, although you can use others:

```
Broccoli,Vegetable
Tomato,Fruit
Kiwi,Fruit
Kale,Vegetable
Tomatillo,Fruit
```

Finally, modify the `BoxOfProduce` class so it creates an array of type `Produce` instead of type `String`. The class should read the produce from the text file and create instances of either `Fruit` or `Vegetable`, with the appropriate name, in the array. After a box is finished, loop through the contents of the array and output how many fruit and how many vegetables are in the box. The rest of the program should behave the same as the solution to Programming Project 6.18.

Polymorphism and Abstract Classes 8

8.1 POLYMORPHISM 516
Late Binding 517
The final Modifier 519
Example: Sales Records 520
Late Binding with toString 527

Downcasting and Upcasting 529
A First Look at the clone Method 536

8.2 ABSTRACT CLASSES 541
Abstract Classes 542

Chapter Summary 548   **Answers to Self-Test Exercises 548**   **Programming Projects 550**

8 Polymorphism and Abstract Classes

Don't make any commitments until you have to.

ANONYMOUS

Introduction

The three main programming mechanisms that constitute object-oriented programming (OOP) are encapsulation, inheritance, and polymorphism. We have already covered the first two. In this chapter, we discuss polymorphism. *Polymorphism* refers to the ability to associate many meanings to one method name by means of a special mechanism known as *late binding* or *dynamic binding*.

This chapter also covers *abstract classes*, which are classes in which some methods are not fully defined. Abstract classes are designed to be used only as base classes for defining new classes. You cannot create instances of (objects of) an abstract class; you can only create instances of its descendent classes.

Both polymorphism and abstract classes deal with code in which a method is used before it is defined. Although this may sound paradoxical, it all works out smoothly in Java.

Prerequisites

This chapter requires Chapters 1 through 5 and Chapter 7, with the exception that Section 5.4 on packages and `javadoc` is not required. This chapter does not use any material on arrays from Chapter 6.

Sections 8.1 on polymorphism and 8.2 on abstract classes are independent of each other, and you may cover Section 8.2 before Section 8.1 if you wish.

8.1　Polymorphism

I did it my way.

FRANK SINATRA

Inheritance allows you to define a base class and to define software for the base class. That software can then be used not only for objects of the base class but also for objects of any class derived from the base class. *Polymorphism* allows you to make changes in the method definition for the derived classes and to have those changes apply to the software written *in the base class*. This all happens automatically in Java, but it is important to understand the process. To understand polymorphism, we need a concrete example. The next subsection begins with such an example.

Late Binding

Suppose you are designing software for a graphics package that has classes for several kinds of figures, such as rectangles, circles, ovals, and so forth. Each figure might be an object of a different class. For example, the `Rectangle` class might have instance variables for a height, width, and center point, while the `Circle` class might have instance variables for a center point and a radius. In a well-designed programming project, all of these classes would be descendents of a single parent class called, for example, `Figure`. Now, suppose you want a method to draw a figure on the screen. To draw a circle, you need different instructions from those you need to draw a rectangle. So, each class needs to have a different method to draw its kind of figure. However, because the methods belong to the classes, they can all be called `draw`. If `r` is a `Rectangle` object and `c` is a `Circle` object, then `r.draw()` and `c.draw()` can be methods implemented with different code. All this is not new, but next we are going to expand on this.

Now, the parent class `Figure` may have methods that apply to all figures. For example, it might have a method called `center` that moves a figure to the center of the screen by erasing it and then redrawing it in the center of the screen. The method `center` of the class `Figure` might use the method `draw` to redraw the figure in the center of the screen. When you think of using the inherited method `center` with figures of the classes `Rectangle` and `Circle`, you begin to see that there are complications here.

To make the point clear and more dramatic, let's suppose the class `Figure` is already written and in use and at some later time you add a class for a brand-new kind of figure—say, the class `Triangle`. Now `Triangle` can be a derived class of the class `Figure`, so the method `center` will be inherited from the class `Figure` and thus should apply to (and perform correctly for!) all `Triangle`s. But there is a complication. The method `center` uses `draw`, and the method `draw` is different for each type of figure. But, the method `center` is defined in the class `Figure`, which means the method `center` was compiled before we wrote the code for the method `draw` of the class `Triangle`. When we invoke the method `center` with an object of the class `Triangle`, we want the code for the method `center` to use a method that was not even defined when we compiled the method `center`—namely, the method `draw` for the class `Triangle`. Can this be made to happen in Java? Yes, it can, and moreover, it happens automatically. You need not do anything special when you define either the base class `Figure` or the derived class `Triangle`.

The situation we discussed for the method `center` in the derived class `Triangle` works out as we want because Java uses a mechanism known as **late binding** or **dynamic binding**. Let's see how late binding works in this case involving figure classes.

Binding refers to the process of associating a method definition with a method invocation. If the method definition is associated with the method invocation when the code is compiled, that is called **early binding**. If the method invocation is associated with the method invocation when the method is invoked (at run time), that is called **late binding** or **dynamic binding**. Java uses late binding for all methods except for a few cases discussed later in this chapter. Let's see how late binding works in the case of our method `center`.

late binding

dynamic binding

binding

early binding

Recall that the method `center` was defined in the class `Figure` and that the definition of the method `center` included an invocation of the method `draw`. If, contrary to fact, Java used early binding, then when the code for the method `center` compiles, the invocation of the method `draw` would be bound to the currently available definition of `draw`, which is the one given in the definition of `Figure`. If early binding were used, the method `center` would behave exactly the same for all derived classes of the class `Figure` as it does for objects created using the class `Figure`. But, fortunately, Java uses late binding, so when `center` is invoked by an object of the class `Triangle`, the invocation of `draw` (inside the method `center`) is not bound to a definition of `draw` until the invocation actually takes place. At this point in time, the run-time system knows the calling object is an instance of the class `Triangle` and so uses the definition of `draw` given in the definition of the class `Triangle` (even if the invocation of `draw` is inside the definition of the method `center`). So, the method `center` behaves differently for an object of the class `Triangle` than it would for an object that is just a plain old `Figure`. With late binding, as in Java, things automatically work out the way you normally want them to.

Note that in order for late binding to work, each object must somehow know which definition of each method applies to that object. So, when an object is created in a system using late binding, the description of the object must include (either directly or indirectly) a description of where the appropriate definition of each method is located. This additional overhead is the penalty you pay for the convenience of late binding.

VideoNote
**Late Binding
Example**

Late Binding

With **late binding**, the definition of a method is not bound to an invocation of the method until run time—in fact, not until the time at which the particular invocation takes place. Java uses late binding (for all methods except those discussed in the Pitfall section entitled "No Late Binding for Static Methods").

polymorphism

The terms **polymorphism** and *late binding* are essentially just different words for the same concept. The term *polymorphism* refers to the processes of assigning multiple meanings to the same method name using late binding.

Polymorphism

Polymorphism refers to the ability to associate many meanings to one method name by means of the late binding mechanism. Thus, polymorphism and late binding are really the same topic.

The `final` Modifier

final

You can mark a method to indicate that it cannot be overridden with a new definition in a derived class. Do this by adding the `final` modifier to the method heading, as in the following sample heading:

```
public final void someMethod()
{
        .
        .
        .
```

An entire class can be declared final, in which case you cannot use it as a base class to derive any other class from it. The syntax for declaring a class to be final is illustrated in what follows:

```
public final class SomeClass
{
        .
        .
        .
```

If a method is marked as `final`, it means the compiler can use early binding with that particular method, which enables the compiler to be more efficient. However, the added efficiency is normally not great, and we suggest not using the `final` modifier solely for reasons of efficiency. (Also, it can sometimes aid security to mark certain methods as `final`.)

You can view the `final` modifier as a way of turning off late binding for a method (or an entire class). Of course, it does more than just turn off late binding—it turns off the ability to redefine the method in any descendent class.

The `final` Modifier

If you add the modifier `final` to the definition of a method, it indicates that the method may not be redefined in a derived class. If you add the modifier `final` to the definition of a class, it indicates that the class may not be used as a base class to derive other classes.

EXAMPLE: Sales Records

Suppose you are designing a record-keeping program for an automobile parts store. You want to make the program versatile, but you are not sure you can account for all possible situations. For example, you want to keep track of sales, but you cannot anticipate all types of sales. At first, there will only be regular sales to retail customers who go to the store to buy one particular part. However, later you may want to add sales with discounts or mail order sales with a shipping charge. All of these sales will be for an item with a basic price and ultimately will produce some bill. For a simple sale, the bill is just the basic price, but if you later add discounts, then some kinds of bills will also depend on the size of the discount. Now your program needs to compute daily gross sales, which intuitively should just be the sum of all the individual sales bills. You may also want to calculate the largest and smallest sales of the day or the average sale for the day. All of these can be calculated from the individual bills, but many of the methods for computing the bills will not be added until later, when you decide what types of sales you will be dealing with. Because Java uses late binding, you can write a program to total all bills, even though you will not determine the code for some of the bills until later. (For simplicity in this first example, we assume that each sale is for just one item, although we could—but will not here—account for sales of multiple items.)

Display 8.1 contains the definition for a class named `Sale`. All types of sales will be derived classes of the class `Sale`. The class `Sale` corresponds to simple sales of a single item with no added discounts and no added charges. Note that the methods `lessThan` and `equalDeals` both include invocations of the method `bill`. We can later define derived classes of the class `Sale` and define their versions of the method `bill`, and the definitions of the methods `lessThan` and `equalDeals` (which we gave with the class `Sale`) will use the version of the method `bill` that corresponds to the object of the derived class.

For example, Display 8.2 shows the derived class `DiscountSale`. Notice that this class requires a different definition for its version of the method `bill`. Now the methods `lessThan` and `equalDeals`, which use the method `bill`, are inherited from the base class `Sale`. But, when the methods `lessThan` and `equalDeals` are used with an object of the class `DiscountSale`, they will use the version of the method definition for `bill` that was given with the class `DiscountSale`. This is indeed a pretty fancy trick for Java to pull off. Consider the method call `d1.lessThan(d2)` for objects `d1` and `d2` of the class `DiscountSale`. The definition of the method `lessThan` (even for an object of the class `DiscountSale`) is given in the definition of the base class `Sale`, which was compiled before we ever even thought of the class `DiscountSale`. Yet, in the method call `d1.lessThan(d2)`, the line that calls the method `bill` knows enough to use the definition of the method `bill` given for the class `DiscountSale`. This all works out because Java uses late binding.

Display 8.3 gives a sample program that illustrates how the late binding of the method bill and the methods that use bill work in a complete program.

Display 8.1   The Base Class `Sale` (part 1 of 3)

```
1  /**
2  Class for a simple sale of one item with no tax, discount, or other
   adjustments.
3  Class invariant: The price is always nonnegative; the name is a nonempty
   string.
4  */
5  public class Sale
6  {
7      private String name; //A nonempty string
8      private double price; //nonnegative

9      public Sale()
10     {
11         name = "No name yet";
12         price = 0;
13     }

14     /**
15      Precondition: theName is a nonempty string; thePrice is nonnegative.
16     */
17     public Sale(String theName, double thePrice)
18     {
19         setName(theName);
20         setPrice(thePrice);
21     }

22     public Sale(Sale originalObject)
23     {
24       if (originalObject == null)
25       {
26           System.out.println("Error: null Sale object.");
27           System.exit(0);
28       }
29       //else
30       name = originalObject.name;
31       price = originalObject.price;
32     }

33     public static void announcement()
34     {
35         System.out.println("This is the Sale class.");
36     }

37     public double getPrice()
38     {
39         return price;
40     }
```

(continued)

Display 8.1   **The Base Class `Sale`** (part 2 of 3)

```
41      /**
42       Precondition: newPrice is nonnegative.
43       */
44      public void setPrice(double newPrice)
45      {
46          if (newPrice >= 0)
47              price = newPrice;
48          else
49          {
50              System.out.println("Error: Negative price.");
51              System.exit(0);
52          }
53      }

54      public String getName()
55      {
56          return name;
57      }

58      /**
59       Precondition: newName is a nonempty string.
60       */
61      public void setName(String newName)
62      {
63          if (newName != null && newName != "")
64              name = newName;
65          else
66          {
67              System.out.println("Error: Improper name value.");
68              System.exit(0);
69          }
70      }

71      public String toString()
72      {
73          return (name + " Price and total cost = $" + price);
74      }

75      public double bill()
76      {
77          return price;
78      }
```

Display 8.1   The Base Class `Sale` (part 3 of 3)

```
 79      /*
 80       Returns true if the names are the same and the bill for the calling
 81       object is equal to the bill for otherSale; otherwise returns false.
 82       Also returns false if otherObject is null.
 83      */
 84      public boolean equalDeals(Sale otherSale)
 85      {
 86          if (otherSale == null)
 87              return false;
 88          else
 89              return (name.equals(otherSale.name)
 90                  && bill() == otherSale.bill());
 91      }

 92      /*
 93       Returns true if the bill for the calling object is less
 94       than the bill for otherSale; otherwise returns false.
 95      */
 96      public boolean lessThan (Sale otherSale)
 97      {
 98          if (otherSale == null)
 99          {
100              System.out.println("Error: null Sale object.");
101              System.exit(0);
102          }
103          //else
104          return (bill() < otherSale.bill());
105      }

106      public boolean equals(Object otherObject)
107      {
108          if (otherObject == null)
109              return false;
110          else if (getClass() != otherObject.getClass())
111              return false;
112          else
113          {
114            Sale otherSale = (Sale)otherObject;
115            return (name.equals(otherSale.name)
116               && (price == otherSale.price));
117          }
118      }
119 }
```

When invoked, these methods will use the definition of the method `bill` that is appropriate for each of the objects.

Display 8.2 **The Derived Class** `DiscountSale` (part 1 of 2)

```
1   /**
2    Class for a sale of one item with discount expressed as a percent of
3    the price, but no other adjustments.
4    Class invariant: The price is always nonnegative; the name is a
5    nonempty string; the discount is always nonnegative.
6   */

7   public class DiscountSale extends Sale
8   {
9       private double discount; //A percent of the price. Cannot be
                                  //negative.

10      public DiscountSale()
11      {
12          super();                                    The meaning would be unchanged if
13          discount = 0;                               this line were omitted.
14      }

15      /**
16       Precondition: theName is a nonempty string; thePrice is
         nonnegative; theDiscount is expressed as a percent of the price
17       and is nonnegative.
18      */
19      public DiscountSale(String theName,
20                                      double thePrice, double theDiscount)
21      {
22          super (theName, thePrice);
23          setDiscount(theDiscount);
24      }

25      public DiscountSale(DiscountSale originalObject)
26      {
27          super (originalObject);
28          discount = originalObject.discount;
29      }

30      public static void announcement()
31      {
32          System.out.println("This is the DiscountSale class.");
33      }

34      public double bill()
35      {
36          double fraction = discount/100;
37          return (1 - fraction)*getPrice();
38      }
```

Display 8.2   **The Derived Class DiscountSale** (part 2 of 2)

```
39        public double getDiscount()
40        {
41            return discount;
42        }

43        /**
44         Precondition: Discount is nonnegative.
45        */
46        public void setDiscount(double newDiscount)
47        {
48            if (newDiscount >= 0)
49                discount = newDiscount;
50            else
51            {
52                System.out.println("Error: Negative discount.");
53                System.exit(0);
54            }
55        }

56        public String toString()
57        {
58            return (getName() + " Price = $" + getPrice()
59                    + " Discount = " + discount + "%\n"
60                    + " Total cost = $" + bill());
61        }

62        public boolean equals(Object otherObject)
```
          The rest of the definition of **equals** *is located in Self-Test Exercise 4.*

```
63    }
```

Display 8.3   Late Binding Demonstration

```
1   /**
2    Demonstrates late binding.
3   */
4   public class LateBindingDemo
5   {
6       public static void main(String[] args)
7       {
8           Sale simple = new Sale("floor mat", 10.00);
                //One item at $10.00.
9           DiscountSale discount = new DiscountSale("floor mat", 11.00,
10              10); //One item at $11.00 with a 10% discount.
11          System.out.println(simple);
12          System.out.println(discount);

13          if (discount.lessThan(simple))
14              System.out.println("Discounted item is cheaper.");
15          else
16              System.out.println("Discounted item is not cheaper.");

17          Sale regularPrice = new Sale("cup holder", 9.90);
                //One item at $9.90.
18          DiscountSale specialPrice = new DiscountSale("cup holder",
                11.00,10);
19              //One item at $11.00 with a 10% discount.
20          System.out.println(regularPrice);
21          System.out.println(specialPrice);

22          if (specialPrice.equalDeals(regularPrice))
23              System.out.println("Deals are equal.");
24          else
25              System.out.println("Deals are not equal.");
26      }
27  }
```

The method lessThan *uses different definitions for* discount.bill() *and* simple.bill().

The method equalDeals *uses different definitions for* specialPrice.bill() *and* regularPrice.bill().

The equalDeals *method says that two items are equal provided they have the same name and the same bill (same total cost). It does not matter how the bill (the total cost) is calculated.*

Sample Dialogue

```
floor mat Price and total cost = $10.0
floor mat Price = $11.0 Discount = 10.0%
   Total cost = $9.9
Discounted item is cheaper.
cup holder Price and total cost = $9.9
cup holder Price = $11.0 Discount = 10.0%
   Total cost = $9.9
Deals are equal
```

Self-Test Exercises

1. Explain the difference between *late binding* and `early binding`.

2. What would happen if you add the final modifier to a method definition? If the final modifier is added to a class definition, would it affect your program?

3. Would it be legal to add the following method definition to the class `DiscountSale`?

```
public static boolean isAGoodBuy(DiscountSale dSale)
{
    return (dSale.getDiscount() > 20);
}
```

What would happen if the formal parameter `isAGoodBuy` method is of `Sale` type?

4. Complete the definition of the method `equals` for the class `DiscountSale` (Display 8.2).

Late Binding with `toString`

In the subsection "The Methods `equals` and `toString`" in Chapter 4, we noted that if you include an appropriate `toString` method in the definition of a class, then you can output an object of the class using `System.out.println`. For example, the following works because `Sale` has a suitable `toString` method:

```
Sale aSale = new Sale("tire gauge", 9.95);
System.out.println(aSale);
```

This produces the following screen output:

```
tire gauge Price and total cost = $9.95
```

This happens because Java uses late binding. We explain this here.

The method invocation `System.out.println(aSale)` is an invocation of the method `println` with the calling object `System.out`. One definition of the method `println` has a single argument of type `Object`. The definition is equivalent to the following:

```
public void println(Object theObject)
{
    System.out.println(theObject.toString());
}
```

(The invocation of the method `println` inside the braces is a different, overloaded definition of the method `println`. That invocation inside the braces uses a method `println` that has a parameter of type `String`, not a parameter of type `Object`.)

This definition of println was given before the class Sale was defined. Yet in the invocation

```
System.out.println(aSale);
```

with an argument aSale of type Sale (and hence also of type Object), it is the definition of toString in the class Sale that is used, not the definition of toString in the class Object. Late binding is what makes this work.

PITFALL: No Late Binding for Static Methods

Java does not use late binding with private methods, methods marked final, or static methods. With private methods and final methods, this is not an issue because dynamic binding would serve no purpose anyway. However, with static methods it can make a difference when the static method is invoked using a calling object. Such cases arise more often than you might think.

static binding When Java (or any language) does not use late binding, it uses **static binding**. With static binding, the decision of which definition of a method to use with a calling object is made at compile time based on the type of the variable naming the object.

Display 8.4 illustrates the effect of static binding on a static method with a calling object. Note that the static method announcement() in the class Sale has its definition overridden in the derived class DiscountSale. However, when an object of type DiscountSale is named by a variable of type Sale, it is the definition announcement() in the class Sale that is used, not the definition of announcement in the class DiscountSale.

"So, what's the big deal?" you may ask. A static method is normally called with a class name and not a calling object. It may look that way, but there are cases where a static method has a calling object in an inconspicuous way. If you invoke a static method within the definition of a nonstatic method but without any class name or calling object, then the calling object is an implicit this, which is a calling object. For example, suppose you add the following method to the class Sale:

```
public void showAdvertisement()
{
    announcement();
    System.out.println(toString( ));
}
```

Suppose further that the method showAdvertisement is not overridden in the class DiscountSale, then the method showAdvertisement is inherited unchanged from Sale.

Now consider the following code:

```
Sale s = new Sale("floor mat", 10.00);
DiscountSale discount = new DiscountSale("floor mat", 11.00,10);
s.showAdertisement();
discount.showAdertisement();
```

You might expect the following output:

```
This is the Sale class.
floor mat Price and total cost = $10.0
This is the DiscountSale class.
floor mat Price = $11.0 Discount = 10.0%
Total cost = $9.9
```

However, because the definition used for the static method `announcement`, inside of `showAdvertisement`, is determined at compile time (based on the type of the variable holding the calling object), the output actually is the following, where the change is shown in blue:

```
This is the Sale class.
floor mat Price and total cost = $10.0
This is the Sale class.
floor mat Price = $11.0 Discount = 10.0%
Total cost = $9.9
```

Java uses late binding with the nonstatic method `toString` but static binding with the static method `announcement`. ■

Downcasting and Upcasting

The following is perfectly legal (given the class definitions in Displays 8.1 and 8.2):

```
Sale saleVariable;
DiscountSale discountVariable =
                  new DiscountSale("paint", 15, 10);
saleVariable = discountVariable;
System.out.println(saleVariable.toString());
```

An object of a derived class (in this case, the derived class `DiscountSale`) also has the type of its base class (in this case, `Sale`) and so can be assigned to a variable of the base class type. Now let's consider the invocation of the method `toString()` on the last line of the preceding code.

Display 8.4   No Late Binding with Static Methods ★

```
1   /**
2    Demonstrates that static methods use static binding.
3    */
4   public class StaticMethodsDemo
5   {
6       public static void main(String[] args)
7       {
8           Sale.announcement();
9           DiscountSale.announcement();
10          System.out.println(
11              "That showed that you can override a static method " +
                "definition.");

12          Sale s = new Sale();
13          DiscountSale discount = new DiscountSale();
14          s.announcement();
15          discount.announcement();
16          System.out.println("No surprises so far, but wait.");

17          Sale discount2 = discount;
18          System.out.println(
19              "discount2 is a DiscountSale object in a Sale variable.");
20          System.out.println("Which definition of announcement() will " +
                "it use?");
21          discount2.announcement();
22          System.out.println(
23              "It used the Sale version of announcement()!");
24      }
25  }
```

Java uses static binding with static methods so the choice of which definition of a static method to use is determined by the type of the variable, not by the object.

discount and discount2 name the same object, but one is a variable of type Sale and one is a variable of type DiscountSale.

Sample Dialogue

```
This is the Sale class.
This is the DiscountSale class.
That showed that you can override a static method definition.
This is the Sale class.
This is the DiscountSale class.
No surprises so far, but wait.
discount2 is a DiscountSale object in a Sale variable.
Which definition of announcement() will it use?
This is the Sale class.    ◄
It used the Sale version of announcement()!
```

If Java had used late binding with static methods, then this would have been the other announcement.

Because Java uses late binding, the invocation

```
saleVariable.toString()
```

uses the definition of the method `toString` given in the class `DiscountSale`. So the output is

```
paint Price = $15.0 Discount = 10.0%
    Total cost = $13.5
```

Because of late binding, the meaning of the method `toString` is determined by the object, not by the type of the variable `saleVariable`.

You may well respond, "Who cares? Why would I ever want to assign an object of type `DiscountSale` to a variable of type `Sale`?"[1] You make such assignments more often than you might think, but you tend to not notice them because they happen behind the scenes. Recall that a parameter is really a local variable, so every time you use an argument of type `DiscountSale` for a parameter of type `Sale`, you are assigning an object of type `DiscountSale` to a variable of type `Sale`. For example, consider the following invocation taken from the definition of the copy constructor for `DiscountSale` (Display 8.2):

```
super(originalObject);
```

In this invocation, `originalObject` is of type `DiscountSale`, but `super` is the copy constructor for the base class `Sale`. Therefore, `super` has a parameter of type `Sale`, which is a local variable of type `Sale` that is set equal to the argument `originalObject` of type `DiscountSale`.

Note that the type of the variable naming an object determines which method names can be used in an invocation with that calling object. (Self-Test Exercise 3 may help you to understand this point.) However, the object itself always determines the meaning of a method invocation performed by an object; this is what we mean by *late binding*.

An Object Knows the Definitions of Its Methods

The type of a class variable determines which method names can be used with the variable, but the object named by the variable determines which definition of the method name is used. A special case of this rule is the following: The type of a class parameter determines which method names can be used with the parameter, but the argument determines which definition of the method name is used.

---

[1]It is actually the references to the object that are assigned, not the objects themselves, but that subtlety is not relevant to what we are discussing here, and the language is already complicated enough.

upcasting

Assigning an object of a derived class to a variable of a base class (or any ancestor class) is often called **upcasting** because it is like a type cast to the type of the base class. In the normal way of writing inheritance diagrams, base classes are drawn above derived classes.[2]

downcasting

When you do a type cast from a base case to a derived class (or from any ancestor class to any descendent class), it is called a **downcast**. Upcasting is pretty straightforward; there are no funny cases to worry about, and in Java things always work out the way you want them to. Downcasting is more troublesome. First of all, downcasting does not always make sense. For example, the downcast

```
Sale saleVariable = new Sale("paint", 15);
DiscountSale discountVariable;
discountVariable = (DiscountSale)saleVariable;//Error
```

does not make sense because the object named by `saleVariable` has no instance variable named `discount` and so cannot be an object of type `DiscountSale`. Every `DiscountSale` is a `Sale`, but not every `Sale` is a `DiscountSale`, as indicated by this example. It is your responsibility to use downcasting only in situations where it makes sense.

It is instructive to note that

```
discountVariable = (DiscountSale)saleVariable;
```

produces a run-time error but will compile with no error. However, the following, which is also illegal, produces a compile-time error:

```
discountVariable = saleVariable;
```

Java catches these downcasting errors as soon as it can, which may be at compile time or at run time, depending on the case.

Although downcasting can be dangerous, it is sometimes necessary. For example, we inevitably use downcasting when we define an `equals` method for a class. For example, note the following line from the definition of `equals` in the class `Sale` (Display 8.1):

```
Sale otherSale = (Sale)otherObject;
```

This is a downcast from the type `Object` to the type `Sale`. Without this downcast, the instance variables `name` and `price` in the `return` statement, reproduced as follows, would be illegal, because the class `Object` has no such instance variables:

```
return (name.equals(otherSale.name)
        && (price == otherSale.price));
```

---

[2] We prefer to think of an object of the derived class as actually having the type of its base class as well as its own type. So this is not, strictly speaking, a type cast, but it does no harm to follow standard usage and call it a type cast in this case.

PITFALL: Downcasting

It is the responsibility of the programmer to use downcasting only in situations where it makes sense. The compiler makes no checks to see if downcasting is reasonable. However, if you use downcasting in a situation in which it does not make sense, you will usually get a run-time error message. ■

TIP: Checking to See Whether Downcasting Is Legitimate ★

You can use the `instanceof` operator to test whether or not downcasting is sensible. Downcasting to a specific type is reasonable if the object being cast is an instance of that type, which is exactly what the `instanceof` operator tests for.

instanceof
The `instanceof` operator checks whether an object is of the type given as its second argument. The syntax is

```
Object instanceof Class_Name
```

which returns `true` if `Object` is of type `Class_Name`; otherwise it returns `false`. So, the following will return `true` if `someObject` is of type `DiscountSale`:

```
someObject instanceof DiscountSale
```

Note that because every object of every descendent class of `DiscountSale` is also of type `DiscountSale`, this expression will return `true` if `someObject` is an instance of any descendent class of `DiscountSale`.

So, if you want to type cast to `DiscountSale`, then you can make the casts safer as follows:

```
DiscountSale ds = new DiscountSale();
if (someObject instanceof DiscountSale)
{
    ds = (DiscountSale)someObject;
    System.out.println("ds was changed to " + someObject);
}
else
    System.out.println("ds was not changed.");
```

`someObject` might be, for example, a variable of type `Sale` or of type `Object`. ■

Self-Test Exercises

5. Consider the following code, which is identical to the code discussed earlier in the opening of the subsection, "Downcasting and Upcasting," except that we added the type cast shown in color:

```
Sale saleVariable;
DiscountSale discountVariable =
            new DiscountSale("paint", 15, 10);
saleVariable = (Sale)discountVariable;
System.out.println(saleVariable.toString());
```

We saw that without the type cast, the definition of the toString method used is the one given in the definition of the class DiscountSale. With this added type cast, will the definition of the toString method used still be the one given in DiscountSale or will it be the one given in the definition of Sale?

6. Would it be legal to add the following method definition to the class DiscountSale?

What about adding it to the class Sale?

```
public static void increasePrice(Sale object, double increment)
{
    object.price += increment;
            System.out.println("New Price = " + price);
}
```

7. ★ What output is produced by the following code?

```
Sale someObject = new DiscountSale("map", 5, 0);
DiscountSale ds = new DiscountSale();
if (someObject instanceof DiscountSale)
{
    ds = (DiscountSale)someObject;
    System.out.println("ds was changed to " + someObject);
}
else
    System.out.println("ds was not changed.");
```

Self-Test Exercises (continued)

8. ★ What output is produced by the following code?

```
Sale someObject = new Sale("map", 5);
DiscountSale ds = new DiscountSale();
if (someObject instanceof DiscountSale)
{
    ds = (DiscountSale)someObject;
    System.out.println("ds was changed to " + someObject);
}
else
    System.out.println("ds was not changed.");
```

9. ★ Suppose we removed the qualifier static from the method announcement()
   in both Sale (Display 8.1) and DiscountSale (Display 8.2). What would
   be the output produced by the following code (which is similar to the end of
   Display 8.4)?

```
Sale s = new Sale( );
DiscountSale discount = new DiscountSale( );
s.announcement( );
discount.announcement( );
System.out.println("No surprises so far, but wait.");

Sale discount2 = discount;
System.out.println(
    "discount2 is a DiscountSale object in a Sale variable.");
System.out.println(
      "Which definition of announcement( ) will it use?");
discount2.announcement( );
System.out.println(
        "Did it use the Sale version of announcement()?");
```

A First Look at the `clone` Method

clone

Every object inherits a method named `clone` from the class `Object`. The method `clone` has no parameters and is supposed to return a copy of the calling object. However, the inherited version of `clone` was not designed to be used as is. Instead, you are expected to override the definition of `clone` with a version appropriate for the class you are defining. The officially sanctioned way to define the method `clone` turns out to be a bit complicated and requires material we do not cover until Chapter 13, so we will describe how to do so in that chapter. In this section, we will describe a simple way to define `clone` that will work in most situations and will allow us to discuss how polymorphism interacts with the `clone` method. If you are in a hurry to see the officially sanctioned way to define `clone`, you can read Chapter 13 immediately after this section (Section 8.1) with no loss of continuity in your reading.

The method `clone` has no parameters and should return a copy of the calling object. The returned object should have identical data to that of the calling object, but it normally should be a different object (an identical twin or "a clone"). You usually want the `clone` method to return the same kind of copy as what we have been defining for copy constructors, which is what is known as a *deep copy*. (You many want to review the subsection entitled "Copy Constructors" in Chapter 5.)

A `clone` method serves very much the same purpose as a copy constructor but, as you will see in the Pitfall titled "Limitations of Copy Constructors" there are situations where a `clone` method works as you want, whereas a copy constructor does not perform as desired.

As with other methods inherited from the class `Object`, the method `clone` needs to be redefined (overridden) before it performs properly. The heading for the method `clone` in the class `Object` is as follows:

```
protected Object clone()
```

If a class has a copy constructor, you can define the `clone` method for that class by using the copy constructor to create the copy returned by the `clone` method. For example, consider the class `Sale` defined in Display 8.1. The following definition of the `clone` method can be added to the definition of `Sale` given in Display 8.1:

```
public Sale clone()
{
    return new Sale(this);
}
```

Using a copy constructor is not the officially sanctioned way to define a `clone` method, and in fact, the Java documentation says you should not define it this way. However, it does work correctly, and some authorities say it is acceptable. In Chapter 13, we will discuss the official way of defining the method `clone` when we introduce the `Cloneable` interface.

Note that, as we defined the method `clone` for the class `Sale`, the method `clone` has `Sale` as its return type and is given `public` rather than `protected` access. Despite these changes in the method heading, this definition overrides the method `clone` inherited from the class `Object`. As we noted in Chapter 7, a change to a more permissive access, such as from `protected` to `public`, is always allowed when overriding a method definition. Changing the return type from `Object` to `Sale` is allowed because `Sale` (and every other class, for that matter) is a descendent class of the class `Object`. This is an example of a covariant return type, as discussed in the subsection of Chapter 7 entitled "Changing the Return Type of an Overridden Method."

The `clone` method for the `DiscountSale` class can be defined similarly:

```
public DiscountSale clone()
{
    return new DiscountSale(this);
}
```

extra code on website

The definitions of the classes `Sale` and `DiscountSale` on the website that accompanies this book each include the method `clone` defined as we just described.

PITFALL: Sometimes the `clone` Method Return Type Is `Object`

Prior to version 5.0, Java did not allow covariant return types, and so did not allow any changes whatsoever in the return type of an overridden method. In those earlier versions of Java, the `clone` method for all classes had `Object` as its return type. This is because the `clone` method for a class overrides the `clone` method of the class `Object`, and the `clone` method of the class `Object` has a return type of `Object`. If you encounter a `clone` method for a class that was designed and coded before version 5.0 of Java, the `clone` method will have a return type of `Object`. When using such older `clone` methods, you will need to use a type cast on the value returned by `clone`.

For example, suppose the class `OldClass` was defined before Java 5.0. If `original` is an object of the class `OldClass`, then the following will produce a compiler error message:

```
OldClass copy = original.clone();
```

The problem is that `original.clone()` returns a value of type `Object`, while the variable `copy` is of type `OldClass`. To correct the situation, you must add a type cast as follows:

```
OldClass copy = (OldClass)original.clone();
```

(continued)

PITFALL: (continued)

You may encounter this problem even with classes defined after Java version 5.0. In Java version 5.0 and later, it is perfectly legal to use Object as a return type for a clone method (even if that is not the preferred return type). When in doubt, it causes no harm to include the type cast. For example, the following is legal for the clone method of the class Sale defined in the previous section:

```
Sale copySale = originalSale.clone();
```

However, adding the following type cast produces no problems:

```
Sale copySale = (Sale)originalSale.clone();
```

When in doubt about the clone method of a class, include the type cast. ■

PITFALL: Limitations of Copy Constructors ★

Copy constructors work well in most simple cases. However, there are situations where they do not—indeed, cannot—do their job. That is why Java favors using the method clone in place of using a copy constructor. Here is a simple example of where the copy constructor does not do its job, but the clone method does.

For this discussion, assume that the classes Sale and DiscountSale each have a clone method added. The definitions of these clone methods are given in the previous subsection.

Suppose you have a method with the following heading (the methods Sale and DiscountSale were defined in Displays 8.1 and 8.2):

```
/**
 Supposedly returns a safe copy of a. That is, if b is the array
 returned, then b[i] is supposedly an independent copy of a[i].
*/
public static Sale[] badCopy(Sale[] a)
{
    Sale[] b = new Sale[a.length];
    for (int i = 0; i < a.length; i++)
        b[i] = new Sale(a[i]);//Problem here!
    return b;
}
```

Now if your array a contains objects from derived classes of Sale, such as objects of type DiscountSale, then badCopy(a) will not return a true copy of a. Every element of the array badCopy(a) will be a plain old Sale, because the Sale copy constructor produces only plain old Sale objects; no element in badCopy(a) will be an instance of the class DiscountSale.

PITFALL: (continued)

If we instead use the method `clone`, things work out as they should; the following is the correct way to define our copy method:

```
public static Sale[] goodCopy(Sale[] a)
{
    Sale[] b = new Sale[a.length];
    for (int i = 0; i < a.length; i++)
        b[i] = a[i].clone();
    return b;
}
```

Because of late binding (polymorphism), `a[i].clone()` always means the correct version of the `clone` method. If `a[i]` is an object created with a constructor of the class `DiscountSale`, `a[i].clone()` will invoke the definition of `clone()` given in the definition of the class `DiscountSale`. If `a[i]` is an object created with a constructor of the class `Sale`, `a[i].clone()` will invoke the definition of `clone()` given in the definition of the class `Sale`. This is illustrated in Display 8.5.

This may seem like a sleight of hand. After all, in the classes `Sale` and `DiscountSale`, we defined the method `clone` in terms of copy constructors. We reproduce the definitions of `clone` from the class `Sale` and `DiscountSale` as follows:

```
//For Sale class
public Sale clone()
{
    return new Sale(this);
}
//For DiscountSale class
public DiscountSale clone()
{
    return new DiscountSale(this);
}
```

So, why is using the method `clone` any different than using a copy constructor? The difference is simply that the method creating the copy of an element `a[i]` has the same name `clone` in all the classes, and polymorphism works with method names. The copy constructors named `Sale` and `DiscountSale` have different names, and polymorphism has nothing to do with methods of different names.

We will have more to say about the clone method in Chapter 13 when we discuss the `Cloneable` interface. ■

Display 8.5 Copy Constructor Versus `clone` Method (part 1 of 2)

```
1   /**
2    Demonstrates where the clone method works,
3    but copy constructors do not.
4   */
5   public class CopyingDemo
6   {
7       public static void main(String[] args)
8       {
9           Sale[] a = new Sale[2];
10          a[0] = new Sale("atomic coffee mug", 130.00);
11          a[1] = new DiscountSale("invisible paint", 5.00, 10);
12          int i;

13          Sale[] b = badCopy(a);

14          System.out.println("With copy constructors:");
15          for (i = 0; i < a.length; i++)
16          {
17              System.out.println("a[" + i + "] = " + a[i]);
18              System.out.println("b[" + i + "] = " + b[i]);
19              System.out.println();
20          }
21          System.out.println();

22          b = goodCopy(a);

23          System.out.println("With clone method:");
24          for (i = 0; i < a.length; i++)
25          {
26              System.out.println("a[" + i + "] = " + a[i]);
27              System.out.println("b[" + i + "] = " + b[i]);
28              System.out.println();
29          }

30      }

31      /**
32       Supposedly returns a safe copy of a. That is, if b is the
33       array returned, then b[i] is supposedly an independent copy of a[i].
34      */

35      public static Sale[] badCopy(Sale[] a)
36      {
37          Sale[] b = new Sale[a.length];
38          for (int i = 0; i < a.length; i++)
39              b[i] = new Sale(a[i]);//Problem here!
40          return b;
41      }
42
```

This program assumes that a `clone` *method has been added to the class* `Sale` *and to the class* `DiscountSale`*.*

Display 8.5   Copy Constructor Versus `clone` Method (part 2 of 2)

```
43        /**
44         Returns a safe copy of a. That is, if b is the
45         array returned, then b[i] is an independent copy of a[i].
46        */
47        public static Sale[] goodCopy(Sale[] a)
48        {
49            Sale[] b = new Sale[a.length];
50            for (int i = 0; i < a.length; i++)
51                b[i] = a[i].clone( );
52            return b;
53        }
54    }
```

Sample Dialogue

```
With copy constructors:
a[0] = atomic coffee mug Price and total cost = $130.0
b[0] = atomic coffee mug Price and total cost = $130.0

a[1] = invisible paint Price = $5.0 Discount 10.0%        The copy constructor
    Total cost = $4.5                                      lost the discount.
b[1] = invisible paint Price and total cost = $5.0 ←

With clone method:
a[0] = atomic coffee mug Price and total cost = $130.0
b[0] = atomic coffee mug Price and total cost = $130.0

a[1] = invisible paint Price = $5.0 Discount 10.0%        The clone method did
    Total cost = $4.5                                      not lose the discount.
b[1] = invisible paint Price = $5.0 Discount 10.0%
    Total cost = $4.5
```

8.2   Abstract Classes

It is for us, the living, rather to be dedicated here to the unfinished work which they who fought here have thus far so nobly advanced.

ABRAHAM LINCOLN, *Gettysburg address*

An abstract class is a class that has some methods without complete definitions. You cannot create an object using an abstract class constructor, but you can use an abstract class as a base class to define a derived class.

Abstract Classes

In Chapter 7, we defined a class named `Employee` and two of its derived classes, `HourlyEmployee` and `SalariedEmployee`. Display 8.6 repeats the details of these class definitions, which we will use in this discussion.

Suppose that when we define the class `Employee`, we know that we are going to frequently compare employees to see if they have the same pay. We might add the following method to the class `Employee`:

```java
public boolean samePay(Employee other)
{
    return (this.getPay() == other.getPay());
}
```

There is, however, one problem with adding the method `samePay` to the class `Employee`: The method `samePay` includes an invocation of the method `getPay`, and the class `Employee` has no `getPay` method. Moreover, there is no reasonable definition we might give for a `getPay` method so that we could add it to the class `Employee`. The only instance variables in the class `Employee` give an employee's name and hire date, but give no information about pay. To see how we should proceed, let's compare objects of the class `Employee` to employees in the real world.

Every real-world employee does have some pay because every real-world employee is either an hourly employee or a salaried employee, and the two derived classes `HourlyEmployee` and `SalariedEmployee` each have a `getPay` method. The problem is that we do not know how to define the `getPay` method until we know if the employee is an hourly or salaried. We would like to postpone the definition of the `getPay` method and give it only in each derived class of the `Employee` class. We would like to simply add a note to the `Employee` class that says: "There will be a method `getPay` for each `Employee` but we do not yet know how it is defined." Java lets us do exactly what we want. The official Java equivalent of our promissory note about the method `getPay` is to make `getPay` an **abstract method**. An abstract method has a heading just like an ordinary method, but no method body. The syntax rules of Java require the modifier `abstract` and require a semicolon in place of the missing method body, as illustrated by the following:

abstract method

```java
public abstract double getPay();
```

Display 8.6 **Employee** Class and Its Derived Classes (part 1 of 2)

These show the details needed for the current discussion. You should not need to review the entire class definitions from Chapter 7. Complete definitions of all these classes are given in the subdirectory for this chapter on the website that comes with this text.

```
1  public class Employee
2  {
3      private String name;
4      private Date hireDate;

5      public Employee()
```

The class Date is defined in Display 4.13, but the details are not important to the current discussion. There is no need to review the definition of the class Date.

The body of the constructor is given in Display 7.2 should initialize the instance variables, but the details are not needed for this discussion.

```
6      public boolean equals(Object otherObject)
```

The body of the method equals is the same as in Display 7.10, but the details of the definition are not important to the current discussion.

All other constructor and other method definitions are exactly the same as in Display 7.2.

The class Employee has no method named getPay.

```
7  }
```

```
1  public class SalariedEmployee extends Employee
2  {
3      private double salary; //annual

4      /**
5       Returns the pay for the month.
6      */
7      public double getPay()
8      {
9          return salary / 12;
10     }

11     public boolean equals(Object otherObject)
```

The rest of the definition of equals is the same as in the answer to Self-Test Exercise 20 of Chapter 7, but the details of the definition are not important to the current discussion.

All constructor and other method definitions are exactly the same as in Display 7.5.

```
12 }
```

(continued)

Display 8.6   **Employee** Class and Its Derived Classes (part 2 of 2)

```
1   public class HourlyEmployee extends Employee
2   {
3       private double wageRate;
4       private double hours; //for the month

5       /**
6        Returns the pay for the month.
7        */
8       public double getPay()
9       {
10          return wageRate * hours;
11      }

12      public boolean equals(Object otherObject)
13      {
14          if (otherObject == null)
15              return false;
16          else if (getClass() != otherObject.getClass( ))
17              return false;
18          else
19          {
20              HourlyEmployee otherHourlyEmployee =
21                                  (HourlyEmployee)otherObject;
22              return (super.equals(otherHourlyEmployee)
23                  && (wageRate == otherHourlyEmployee.wageRate)
24                  && (hours == otherHourlyEmployee.hours));
25          }
26      }
```

All constructor and other method definitions are exactly the same as in Display 7.3.

```
27  }
```

If we add this abstract method getPay to the class Employee, then we are free to add the method samePay to the class Employee.

An abstract method can be thought of as the interface part of a method with the implementation details omitted. Because a private method is normally only a helping method and so not part of the interface for a programmer using the class, it follows that it does not make sense to have a private abstract method. Java enforces this reasoning. In Java, an abstract method cannot be private. Normally an abstract method is public but protected, and package (default) access is allowed.

abstract cannot be private

An abstract method serves a purpose, even though it is not given a full definition. It serves as a placeholder for a method that must be defined in all (nonabstract) derived classes. Note that in Display 8.7, the method samePay includes invocations of the method getPay. If the abstract method getPay were omitted, this invocation of getPay would be illegal.

Abstract Method

An **abstract method** serves as a placeholder for a method that will be fully defined in a descendent class. An abstract method has a complete method heading with the addition of the modifier `abstract`. It has no method body but does end with a semicolon in place of a method body. An abstract method cannot be private.

EXAMPLES

```
public abstract double getPay();
public abstract void doSomething(int count);
```

abstract class   A class that has at least one abstract method is called an **abstract class** and, in Java, must have the modifier `abstract` added to the class heading. The redefined, now abstract, class `Employee` is shown in Display 8.7.

An abstract class can have any number of abstract methods. In addition, it can have, and typically does have, other regular (fully defined) methods. If a derived class of an abstract class does not give full definitions to all the abstract methods, or if the derived class adds an abstract method, then the derived class is also an abstract class and must include the modifier `abstract` in its heading.

In contrast with the term *abstract class*, a class with no abstract methods is called a **concrete class**.

concrete class

Display 8.7   `Employee` Class as an Abstract Class (part 1 of 2)

```
 1  /**
 2   Class Invariant: All objects have a name string and hire date.
 3   A name string of "No name" indicates no real name specified yet.
 4   A hire date of January 1, 1000 indicates no real hire date specified
     yet.
 5  */
 6  public abstract class Employee
 7  {
 8      private String name;
 9      private Date hireDate;

10      public abstract double getPay();

11      public Employee()
12      {
13          name = "No name";
14          hireDate = new Date("January", 1, 1000);
                    //Just a placeholder.
15      }

16      public boolean samePay(Employee other)
17      {
18          if (other == null)
```

The class `Date` *is defined in Display 4.13, but the details are not relevant to the current discussion of abstract methods and classes. There is no need to review the definition of the class* `Date`.

(continued)

Display 8.7 **Employee** Class as an Abstract Class (part 2 of 2)

```
19              {
20                  System.out.println("Error: null Employee object.");
21                  System.exit(0);
22              }
23              //else
24              return (this.getPay() == other.getPay());
25          }
```

All other constructor and other method definitions are exactly the same as in Display 7.2.
In particular, they are not abstract methods.

```
26      }
```

Abstract Class

An **abstract class** is a class with one or more abstract methods. An abstract class must have the modifier abstract included in the class heading, as illustrated by the example.

EXAMPLE

```
public abstract class Employee
{
    private String name;
    private Date hireDate;

    public abstract double getPay();
        ...
```

PITFALL: You Cannot Create Instances of an Abstract Class

You cannot use an abstract class constructor to create an object of the abstract class. You can only create objects of the derived classes of the abstract class. For example, with the class Employee defined as in Display 8.7, the following would be illegal:

```
Employee joe = new Employee(); //Illegal because
                    //Employee is an abstract class.
```

But, this is no problem. The object joe could not correspond to any real-world employee. Any real-world employee is either hourly or a salaried. In the real world, one cannot be just an employee. One must be either an hourly employee or a salaried employee. Still, it is useful to discuss employees in general. In particular, we can compare employees to see if they have the same pay, even though the way of calculating the pay might be different for the two employees. ∎

TIP: An Abstract Class Is a Type

You cannot create an object of an abstract class (unless it is actually an object of some concrete descendent class). Nonetheless, it makes perfectly good sense to have a parameter of an abstract class type such as `Employee` (as defined in Display 8.7). Then, an object of any of the descendent classes of `Employee` can be plugged in for the parameter. It even makes sense to have a variable of an abstract class type such as `Employee`, although it can only name objects of its concrete descendent classes. ∎

An Abstract Class Is a Type

You can have a parameter of an abstract class type such as the abstract class `Employee` defined in Display 8.7. Then, an object of any of the concrete descendent classes of `Employee` can be plugged in for the parameter. You can also have variables of an abstract class type such as `Employee`, although it can only name objects of its concrete descendent classes.

MyProgrammingLab™ **Self-Test Exercises**

10. Can a method definition include an invocation of an abstract method?

11. What is the purpose of an abstract method?

12. What is an abstract class?

13. Is it legal to have a parameter of an abstract class type?

14. The abstract class `Employee` (Display 8.7) uses the method definitions from Display 7.2. After we did Display 7.2, we later gave the following improved version of `equals`:

```java
public boolean equals(Object otherObject)
{
    if (otherObject == null)
        return false;
    else if (getClass() != otherObject.getClass())
        return false;
    else
    {
        Employee otherEmployee =
                      (Employee)otherObject;
        return(name.equals(otherEmployee.name)
          && hireDate.equals(otherEmployee.hireDate));
    }
}
```

Would it be legal to replace the version of `equals` for the abstract class `Employee` with this improved version?

(continued)

Self-Test Exercises (continued)

15. The abstract class `Employee` given in Display 8.7 has a constructor (in fact, it has more than one, although only one is shown in Display 8.7). But using a constructor to create an instance of an abstract class, as in the following, is illegal:

```
Employee joe = new Employee(); //Illegal
```

So why bother to have any constructors in an abstract class? Aren't they useless?

Chapter Summary

- *Late binding* (also called *dynamic binding*) means that the decision of which version of a method is appropriate is decided at run time. Java uses late binding.

- *Polymorphism* means using the process of late binding to allow different objects to use different method actions for the same method name. *Polymorphism* is essentially another word for *late binding*.

- You can assign an object of a derived class to a variable of its base class (or any ancestor class), but you cannot do the reverse.

- If you add the modifier `final` to the definition of a method, it indicates that the method may not be redefined in a derived class. If you add the modifier `final` to the definition of a class, it indicates that the class may not be used as a base class to derive other classes.

- An *abstract method* serves as a placeholder for a method that will be fully defined in a descendent class.

- An *abstract class* is a class with one or more abstract methods.

- An abstract class is designed to be used as a base class to derive other classes. You cannot create an object of an abstract class type (unless it is an object of some concrete descendent class).

- An abstract class is a type. You can have variables whose type is an abstract class and you can have parameters whose type is an abstract type.

Answers to Self-Test Exercises

1. *Late binding* or dynamic binding happens when a method invocation is associated with the method definition only when the method is invoked (i.e., at run time). When the method call is bound to the method definition at compile time, it is called *early binding*.

2. If the final modifier is added to a method definition, it cannot be overridden with a new definition in a derived class. Similarly an entire class can be declared final, in which case it cannot be used as a base class to derive any other class from it. Thus the program loses on extensibility.

3. Yes it is legal. However, it would not be legal if the formal parameter is of `Sale` type because the class `Sale` has no method named `getDiscount` and so the invocation of the method `getDiscount` using an object of type `Sale` is not allowed.

4.
```
public boolean equals(Object otherObject)
{
    if (otherObject == null)
        return false;
    else if (getClass() != otherObject.getClass())
        return false;
    else
    {
        DiscountSale otherDiscountSale =
                        (DiscountSale)otherObject;
        return (super.equals(otherDiscountSale)
            && discount == otherDiscountSale.discount);
    }
}
```

5. The definition of `toString` always depends on the object and not on any type cast. So, the definition used is the same as without the added type cast; that is, the definition of `toString` that is used is the one given in `DiscountSale`.

6. It will not be legal to add the method in the class `DiscountSale` because price is private variable of `Sale` and cannot be accessed directly from `DiscountSale`. However, the lines associated with the price variable could be changed to

```
double p = object.getPrice() + increment;
object.setPrice(p);
System.out.println("New Price = " + object.getPrice());
```

Yes, it could be added to the class `Sale`.

7.
```
ds was changed to map Price $ 5.0 discount 0.0%
Total cost $5.0
```

8. `ds` was not changed.

9. The output would be the following (the main change from Display 8.4 is shown in blue):

```
This is the Sale class.
This is the DiscountSale class.
No surprises so far, but wait.
discount2 is a DiscountSale object in a Sale variable.
Which definition of announcement() will it use?
This is the DiscountSale class.
Did it use the Sale version of announcement()?
```

10. Yes. See Display 8.7.

11. An abstract method has a heading just like an ordinary method, but no method body. So it acts as the interface part of a method with the implementation details omitted.

12. A class that has at least one abstract method is called an abstract class and you cannot create an instance of such a class. It must have the modifier abstract added to the class heading.

13. Yes, it is absolutely legal to have a parameter of an abstract class type. Then, an object of any of the descendent classes of the abstract class can be plugged in for the parameter.

14. Yes, it would be legal to replace the version of equals for the abstract class Employee with this improved version. In fact, the version of Employee on the accompanying website does use the improved version of equals.

15. No, you can still use constructors to hold code that might be useful in derived classes. The constructors in the derived classes can—in fact, must—include invocations of constructors in the base (abstract) class. (Recall the use of super as a name for the base class constructor.)

Programming Projects

Visit www.myprogramminglab.com to complete select exercises online and get instant feedback.

VideoNote
Solution to Programming Project 8.1

1. In Programming Project 7.3 from Chapter 7, the Alien class was rewritten to use inheritance. The rewritten Alien class should be made abstract because there will never be a need to create an instance of it, only its derived classes. Change this to an abstract class and also make the getDamage method an abstract method. Test the class from your main method to ensure that it still operates as expected.

2. Create a class named Movie that can be used with your video rental business. The Movie class should track the Motion Picture Association of America (MPAA) rating (e.g., Rated G, PG-13, R), ID Number, and movie title with appropriate accessor and mutator methods. Also create an equals() method that overrides Object's equals() method, where two movies are equal if their ID number is identical. Next, create three additional classes named Action, Comedy, and Drama that are derived from Movie. Finally, create an overridden method named calcLateFees that takes as input the number of days a movie is late and returns the late fee for that movie. The default late fee is $2/day. Action movies have a late fee of $3/day, comedies are $2.50/day, and dramas are $2/day. Test your classes from a main method.

3. Extend the previous problem with a Rental class. This class should store a Movie that is rented, an integer representing the ID of the customer that rented the movie, and an integer indicating how many days late the movie is. Add a method

that calculates the late fees for the rental. In your `main` method, create an array of type `Rental` filled with sample data of all types of movies. Then, create a method named `lateFeesOwed` that iterates through the array and returns the total amount of late fees that are outstanding.

4. The goal for this programming project is to create a simple 2D predator–prey simulation. In this simulation, the prey is ants, and the predators are doodlebugs. These critters live in a world composed of a 20 × 20 grid of cells. Only one critter may occupy a cell at a time. The grid is enclosed, so a critter is not allowed to move off the edges of the grid. Time is simulated in time steps. Each critter performs some action every time step.

The ants behave according to the following model:

- Move. Every time step, randomly try to move up, down, left, or right. If the cell in the selected direction is occupied or would move the ant off the grid, then the ant stays in the current cell.

- Breed. If an ant survives for three time steps, then at the end of the third time step (i.e., after moving), the ant will breed. This is simulated by creating a new ant in an adjacent (up, down, left, or right) cell that is empty. If there is no empty cell available, no breeding occurs. Once an offspring is produced, the ant cannot produce an offspring until three more time steps have elapsed.

The doodlebugs behave according to the following model:

- Move. Every time step, if there is an adjacent cell (up, down, left, or right) occupied by an ant, then the doodlebug will move to that cell and eat the ant. Otherwise, the doodlebug moves according to the same rules as the ant. Note that a doodlebug cannot eat other doodlebugs.

- Breed. If a doodlebug survives for eight time steps, then at the end of the time step, it will spawn off a new doodlebug in the same manner as the ant.

- Starve. If a doodlebug has not eaten an ant within the last three time steps, then at the end of the third time step, it will starve and die. The doodlebug should then be removed from the grid of cells.

During one turn, all the doodlebugs should move before the ants.

Write a program to implement this simulation and draw the world using ASCII characters of "o" for an ant and "X" for a doodlebug. Create a class named `Organism` that encapsulates basic data common to both ants and doodlebugs.

This class should have an overridden method named `move` that is defined in the derived classes of `Ant` and `Doodlebug`. You may need additional data structures to keep track of which critters have moved.

Initialize the world with 5 doodlebugs and 100 ants. After each time step, prompt the user to press Enter to move to the next time step. You should see a cyclical pattern between the population of predators and prey, although random perturbations may lead to the elimination of one or both species.

5. Consider a graphics system that has classes for various figures—say, rectangles, boxes, triangles, circles, and so on. For example, a rectangle might have data

members' height, width, and center point, while a box and circle might have only a center point and an edge length or radius, respectively. In a well-designed system, these would be derived from a common class, Figure. You are to implement such a system.

The class Figure is the base class. You should add only Rectangle and Triangle classes derived from Figure. Each class has stubs for methods erase and draw. Each of these methods outputs a message telling the name of the class and what method has been called. Because these are just stubs, they do nothing more than output this message. The method center calls the erase and draw methods to erase and redraw the figure at the center. Because you have only stubs for erase and draw, center will not do any "centering" but will call the methods erase and draw, which will allow you to see which versions of draw and center it calls. Also, add an output message in the method center that announces that center is being called. The methods should take no arguments. Also, define a demonstration program for your classes.

For a real example, you would have to replace the definition of each of these methods with code to do the actual drawing. You will be asked to do this in Programming Project 8.6.

6. Flesh out Programming Project 8.5. Give new definitions for the various constructors and methods center, draw, and erase of the class Figure; draw and erase of the class Triangle; and draw and erase of the class Rectangle. Use character graphics; that is, the various draw methods will place regular keyboard characters on the screen in the desired shape. Use the character '*' for all the character graphics. That way, the draw methods actually draw figures on the screen by placing the character '*' at suitable locations on the screen. For the erase methods, you can simply clear the screen (by outputting blank lines or by doing something more sophisticated). There are a lot of details in this project and you will have to decide on some of them on your own.

7. Define a class named MultiItemSale that represents a sale of multiple items of type Sale given in Display 8.1 (or of the types of any of its descendent classes). The class MultiItemSale will have an instance variable whose type is Sale[], which will be used as a partially filled array. There will also be another instance variable of type int that keeps track of how much of this array is currently used. The exact details on methods and other instance variables, if any, are up to you. Use this class in a program that obtains information for items of type Sale and of type DiscountSale (Display 8.2) and that computes the total bill for the list of items sold.

8. Programming Project 7.8 required rewriting the solution to Programming Project 4.10 with inheritance. Redo or do Programming Project 7.8, but instead define the Pet class as an abstract class. The acepromazine() and carprofen() methods should be defined as abstract methods.

In your main method, define an array of type Pet and add two instances of cats and two instances of dogs to the array. Iterate through the array and output how much carprofen and acepromazine each pet would require.

VideoNote
**Solution to
Programming
Project 8.9**

9. The following is a short snippet of code that simulates rolling a 6-sided dice 100 times. There is an equal chance of rolling any digit from 1 to 6.

```java
public static void printDiceRolls(Random randGenerator)
{
    for (int i = 0; i < 100; i++)
    {
        System.out.println(randGenerator.nextInt(6) + 1);
    }
}

public static void main(String[] args)
{
    Random randGenerator = new Random();
    printDiceRolls(randGenerator);
}
```

Create your own class, `LoadedDice`, that is derived from `Random`. The constructor for `LoadedDice` needs to only invoke `Random`'s constructor. Override the `public int nextInt(int num)` method so that with a 50% chance, your new method always returns the largest number possible (i.e., num − 1), and with a 50% chance, it returns what `Random`'s `nextInt` method would return.

Test your class by replacing the main method with the following:

```java
LoadedDice myDice = new LoadedDice();
printDiceRolls(myDice);
```

You do not need to change the `printDiceRolls` method even though it takes a parameter of type `Random`. Polymorphism tells Java to invoke `LoadedDice`'s `nextInt()` method instead of `Random`'s `nextInt()` method.

Exception Handling 9

9.1 EXCEPTION HANDLING BASICS 557

try-catch Mechanism 557
Exception Handling with the Scanner Class 559
Throwing Exceptions 562
Example: A Toy Example of Exception Handling 564
Exception Classes 569
Exception Classes from Standard Packages 570
Defining Exception Classes 572
Multiple catch Blocks 583

9.2 THROWING EXCEPTIONS IN METHODS 588

Throwing an Exception in a Method 588
Declaring Exceptions in a throws Clause 590

Exceptions to the Catch or Declare Rule 593
throws Clause in Derived Classes 594
When to Use Exceptions 595
Event-Driven Programming ★ 596

9.3 MORE PROGRAMMING TECHNIQUES FOR EXCEPTION HANDLING 598

The finally Block ★ 598
Rethrowing an Exception ★ 600
The AssertionError Class ★ 600
ArrayIndexOutOfBoundsException 601

Chapter Summary 601   **Answers to Self-Test Exercises** 602   **Programming Projects** 606

9 Exception Handling

It's the exception that proves the rule.

COMMON SAYING

Introduction

One way to divide the task of designing and coding a method is to code two main cases separately: the case where nothing unusual happens and the case where exceptional things happen. Once you have the program working for the case where things always go smoothly, you can then code the second case where notable things can happen. In Java, there is a way to mirror this approach in your code. Write your code more or less as if nothing very unusual happens. After that, use the Java exception handling facilities to add code for those unusual cases.

The most important use of exceptions is to deal with methods that have some special case that is handled differently depending on how the method is used. For example, if there is a division by zero in the method, then it may turn out that for some invocations of the method, the program should end, but for other invocations of the method, something else should happen. Such a method can be defined to throw an exception if the special case occurs; that exception will permit the special case to be handled outside of the method. This allows the special case to be handled differently for different invocations of the method.

throw exception
handle exception
In Java, exception handling proceeds as follows: Either some library software or your code provides a mechanism that signals when something unusual happens. This is called **throwing an exception**. At another place in your program, you place the code that deals with the exceptional case. This is called **handling the exception**. This method of programming makes for cleaner code. Of course, we still need to explain the details of how you do this in Java.

Prerequisites

Almost this entire chapter uses only material from Chapters 1 through 5 and Chapter 7. The only exception is the subsection "`ArrayIndexOutOfBoundsException`," which also uses material from Chapter 6. However, that subsection may be omitted if you have not yet covered Chapter 6. Chapter 8 is not needed for this chapter.

9.1   Exception Handling Basics

Well the program works for most cases. I didn't know it had to work for that case.

COMPUTER SCIENCE STUDENT, *appealing a grade*

Exception handling is meant to be used sparingly and in some situations that are more involved than what is reasonable to include in an introductory example. So, in some cases, we will teach you the exception handling details of Java by means of simple examples that would not normally use exception handling. This makes a lot of sense for learning about the exception handling details of Java, but do not forget that these examples are toy examples and, in practice, you would not use exception handling for anything this simple.

`try-catch` Mechanism

The basic way of handling exceptions in Java consists of the `try-throw-catch` trio. At this point, we will start with only `try` and `catch`. The general setup consists of a `try` block followed by one or more `catch` blocks. First let's describe what a try block is. A **try block** has the following syntax:

try block

```
try
{
    Some_Code_That_May_Throw_An_Exception
}
```

This `try` block contains the code for the basic algorithm that tells what to do when everything goes smoothly. It is called a `try` block because it "tries" to execute the case where all goes well.

Now, an exception can be "thrown" as a way of indicating that something unusual happened. For example, if our code tries to divide by zero, then an `ArithmeticException` object is thrown. In most of this chapter, our own code will throw the exception, but initially we will have existing Java classes do the throwing.

As the name suggests, when something is "thrown," something goes from one place to another place. In Java, what goes from one place to another is the flow of control as well as the exception object that is thrown. When an exception is thrown, the code in the surrounding `try` block stops executing and (normally) another portion of code, known as a **catch block**, begins execution. The `catch` block has a parameter, and the exception object thrown is plugged in for this `catch` block parameter. This executing of the `catch` block is called **catching the exception** or **handling the exception**. When an exception is thrown, it should ultimately be handled by (caught by) some `catch` block. The appropriate `catch` block immediately follows the `try` block; for example,

catch block

handling an exception

```
catch(Exception e)
{
    String message = e.getMessage();
    System.out.println(message);
    System.exit(0);
}
```

This `catch` block looks very much like a method definition that has a parameter of a type `Exception`. By using the type `Exception`, this `catch` block will catch any possible exception that is thrown. We will see at the end of this section that we can also restrict the `catch` block to specific exception classes. The `catch` block is not a method definition, but in some ways, it is like a method. It is a separate piece of code that is executed when your code throws an exception. The `catch` block in the previous example will print out a message about the exception that was thrown.

So, when an exception is thrown, it is similar to a method call, but instead of calling a method, it calls the `catch` block and says to execute the code in the `catch` block.

exception handler

A `catch` block is often referred to as an **exception handler**.

Let's focus on the identifier e in the following line from a `catch` block:

```
catch(Exception e)
```

`catch` block parameter

That identifier e in the `catch` block heading is called the `catch` **block parameter**. Each `catch` block can have at most one `catch` block parameter. The `catch` block parameter does two things:

- The `catch` block parameter is preceded by an exception class name that specifies what type of thrown exception object the `catch` block can catch. If the class name is `Exception`, then the block can catch any exception.

- The `catch` block parameter gives you a name for the thrown object that is caught, so you can write code in the `catch` block that does things with the thrown object that is caught.

Although the identifier e is often used for the `catch` block parameter, this is not required. You may use any nonkeyword identifier for the `catch` block parameter just as you can for a method parameter.

`catch` Block Parameter

The `catch` block parameter is an identifier in the heading of a `catch` block that serves as a placeholder for an exception that might be thrown. When a suitable exception is thrown in the preceding `try` block, that exception is plugged in for the `catch` block parameter. The identifier e is often used for `catch` block parameters, but this is not required. You can use any legal (nonkeyword) identifier for a `catch` block parameter.

SYNTAX

```
catch(Exception_Class_Name Catch_Block_Parameter)
{
      Code to be performed if an exception of the named exception class is thrown in
      the try block.
}
```

You may use any legal identifier for the *Catch_Block_Parameter*.

EXAMPLE

In the following, e is the catch block parameter.

```
catch(Exception e)
{
    System.out.println(e.getMessage());
    System.out.println("Aborting program.");
    System.exit(0);
}
```

Let's consider two possible cases of what can happen when a try block is executed: (1) no exception is thrown in the try block, and (2) an exception is thrown in the try block and caught in the catch block. (Later in the Tip, "What Happens if an Exception Is Never Caught?," we will describe a third case where the catch block does not catch the exception.)

- If no exception is thrown, the code in the try block is executed to the end of the try block, the catch block is skipped, and execution continues with the code placed after the catch block.

- If an exception is thrown in the try block, the rest of the code in the try block is skipped and (in simple cases) control is transferred to a following catch block. The thrown object is plugged in for the catch block parameter, and the code in the catch block is executed. And then (provided the catch block code does not end the program or do something else to end the catch block code prematurely), the code that follows that catch block is executed.

Exception Handling with the `Scanner` Class

As a concrete example, consider a program that reads an int value from the keyboard using the nextInt method of the Scanner class. You have probably noticed that the program will end with an error message if the user enters something other than a well-formed int value. That is true as far as it goes, but the full detail is that if the user enters something other than a well-formed int value, an exception of type InputMismatchException will be thrown. If the exception is not caught, your program ends with an error message. However, you can catch the exception, and in the catch block, give code for some alternative action, such as asking the user to reenter the input. You are not required to account for an InputMismatchException by catching it in a catch block or declaring it in a throws clause (this is because InputMismatchException is a descendent class of RuntimeException). However, you are allowed to catch an InputMismatchException in a catch block, which can sometimes be useful.

InputMismatchException is in the standard Java package java.util, so if your program mentions InputMismatchException, then it needs an import statement, such as the following:

```
import java.util.InputMismatchException;
```

Display 9.1 contains an example of how you might usefully catch an InputMismatchException. This program gets an input int value from the keyboard and then does nothing with it other than echo the input value. However, you can use code such as this to require robust input for any program that uses keyboard input. The Tip "Exception Control Loops" explains the general technique we used for the loop in Display 9.1.

TIP: Exception Controlled Loops

Sometimes when an exception is thrown, such as an InputMismatchException for an ill-formed input, you want your code to simply repeat some code so that the user can get things right on a second or subsequent try. One way to set up your code to repeat a loop every time a particular exception is thrown is as follows:

```
boolean done = false;

while (!done)
{
    try
    {
        Code that may throw an exception in the class Exception_Class.
        done = true; //Will end the loop.
        <Possibly more code.>
    }
    catch(Exception_Class e)
    {
        <Some code.>
    }
}
```

Note that if an exception is thrown in the first piece of code in the try block, then the try block ends before the line that sets done to true is executed, so the loop body is repeated. If no exception is thrown, then done is set to true and the loop body is not repeated.

Display 9.1 contains an example of such a loop. Minor variations on this outline can accommodate a range of different situations for which you want to repeat code on throwing an exception. ■

Display 9.1   An Exception Controlled Loop

```java
1   import java.util.Scanner;
2   import java.util.InputMismatchException;

3   public class InputMismatchExceptionDemo
4   {
5       public static void main(String[] args)
6       {
7           Scanner keyboard = new Scanner(System.in);
8           int number = 0; //to keep compiler happy
9           boolean done = false;

10          while (! done)
11          {
12              try
13              {
14                  System.out.println("Enter a whole number:");
15                  number = keyboard.nextInt();
16                  done = true;
17              }
18              catch(InputMismatchException e)
19              {
20                  keyboard.nextLine();
21                  System.out.println("Not a correctly written whole
                        number.");
22                  System.out.println("Try again.");
23              }
24          }

25          System.out.println("You entered " + number);
26      }
27  }
```

If nextInt *throws an exception, the* try *block ends and the* Boolean *variable* done *is not set to* true.

Sample Dialogue

```
Enter a whole number:
forty two
Not a correctly written whole number.
Try again.
Enter a whole number:
Fortytwo
Not a correctly written whole number.
Try again.
Enter a whole number:
42
You entered 42
```

Self-Test Exercises

1. What is the purpose of the line: `keyboard.nextLine();` within the catch block in Display 9.1? Would it change the program output if we omit this line?

2. Give the definition for the following method. Use the techniques given in Display 9.1.

```
/**
 Precondition: keyboard is an object of the class Scanner that
 has been set up for keyboard input (as we have been doing
 right along). Returns: An int value entered at the keyboard.
 If the user enters an incorrectly formed input, she or he
 is prompted to reenter the value,
 */
public static int getInt(Scanner keyboard)
```

Throwing Exceptions

In the previous example, an exception was thrown by the `nextInt()` method if a noninteger was entered. We did not write the method that threw the exception; we were responsible only for catching and handling any exceptions. For many programs, this pattern is all that is necessary.

However, it is also possible for your own code to throw the exception. To do this, use a `throw` statement inside the `try` block in the format

```
throw new Exception(String_describing _the_exception);
```

The following is an example of a `try` block with `throw` statements included (copied from Display 9.3, which computes pairs of men and women for a dance studio):

```
try
{
    if (men == 0 && women == 0)
        throw new Exception("Lesson is canceled. No students.");
    else if (men == 0)
        throw new Exception("Lesson is canceled. No men.");
    else if (women == 0)
        throw new Exception("Lesson is canceled. No women.");
    // women >= 0 && men >= 0
    if (women >= men)
        System.out.println("Each man must dance with " +
                                    women/(double)men + "women.");
    else
        System.out.println("Each woman must dance with " +
                                    men/(double)women + " men.");

}
```

throw statement

This `try` block contains the following three `throw` statements:

```
throw new Exception("Lesson is canceled. No students.");
throw new Exception("Lesson is canceled. No men.");
throw new Exception("Lesson is canceled. No women.");
```

throwing an exception

The value thrown is an argument to the `throw` operator and is always an object of some exception class. The execution of a `throw` statement is called *throwing an exception*.

---

throw Statement

SYNTAX

```
throw new Exception_Class_Name (Possibly_Some_Arguments);
```

When the `throw` statement is executed, the execution of the surrounding `try` block is stopped and (normally) control is transferred to a `catch` block. The code in the `catch` block is executed next. See the box entitled `"try-throw-catch"` later in this chapter for more details.

EXAMPLE

```
throw new Exception("Division by zero.");
```

The getMessage Method

Every exception has a `String` instance variable that contains some message, which typically identifies the reason for the exception. For example, if the exception is thrown as follows,

```
throw new Exception(String_Argument);
```

then the string given as an argument to the constructor `Exception` is used as the value of this `String` instance variable. If the object is called `e`, then the method call `e.getMessage()` returns this string.

EXAMPLE

Suppose the following `throw` statement is executed in a `try` block:

```
throw new Exception("Input must be positive.");
```

And suppose the following is a `catch` block immediately following the `try` block:

```
catch (Exception e)
{
    System.out.println(e.getMessage());
    System.out.println("Program aborted.");
    System.exit(0);
}
```

In this case, the method call `e.getMessage()` returns the string `"Input must be positive."`

EXAMPLE: A Toy Example of Exception Handling

Display 9.2 contains a simple program that might, by some stretch of the imagination, be used at a dance studio. This program does not use exception handling, and you would not normally use exception handling for anything this simple. The setting for use of the program is a dance lesson. The program simply checks to see if there are more men than women or more women than men and then announces how many partners each man or woman will have. The exceptional case is when there are no men or no women or both. In that exceptional case, the dance lesson is canceled.

In Display 9.3, we rewrote the program using exception handling. The nonexceptional cases go inside the `try` block, and the `try` block checks for the exceptional cases. The exceptional cases are not handled in the `try` block, but if detected, they are signaled by throwing an exception. The following three lines taken from inside the multiway `if-else` statement are the code for throwing the exception:

```
throw new Exception("Lesson is canceled. No students.");
throw new Exception("Lesson is canceled. No men.");
throw new Exception("Lesson is canceled. No women.");
```

If the program does not encounter an exceptional case, then none of these statements that throw an exception is executed. In that case, we need not even know what happens when an exception is thrown. If no exception is thrown, then the code in the section labeled "`catch` block" is skipped and the program proceeds to the last statement, which happens to output `"Begin the lesson."` Now, let's see what happens in an exceptional case.

If the number of men or the number of women is zero (or both), that is an exceptional case in this program and results in an exception being **thrown**. To make things concrete, let's say that the number of men is zero, but the number of women is not zero. In that case, the following statement is executed, which is how Java throws an exception:

```
throw new Exception("Lesson is canceled. No men.");
```

Let's analyze this statement. The following is the invocation of a constructor for the class `Exception`, which is the standard Java package `java.lang`.

```
new Exception("Lesson is canceled. No men.");
```

The created `Exception` object is not assigned to a variable, but rather is used as an (anonymous) argument to the `throw` operator. (Anonymous arguments were discussed in Chapter 5.) The keyword `throw` is an operator with syntax similar to the

EXAMPLE: (continued)

unary + or unary – operators. To make it look more like an operator, you can write it with parentheses around the argument, as follows:

```
throw (new Exception("Lesson is canceled. No men."));
```

Although it is perfectly legal and sensible to include these extra parentheses, nobody includes them.

To understand this process of throwing, you need to know two things: What is this `Exception` class? And what does the `throw` operator do with the `Exception` object? The class `Exception` is another class from the standard Java package `java.lang`. As you have already seen, the class `Exception` has a constructor that takes a single `String` argument. The `Exception` object created stores this `String` argument (in a private instance variable). As you will see, this `String` argument can later be retrieved from the `Exception` object.

The `throw` operator causes a change in the flow of control and delivers the `Exception` object to a suitable place, as we are about to explain. When the `throw` operator is executed, the `try` block ends immediately and control passes to the following `catch` block. (If it helps, you can draw an analogy between the execution of the `throw` operator in a `try` block and the execution of a `break` statement in a loop or `switch` statement.) When control is transferred to the `catch` block, the `Exception` object that is thrown is plugged in for the `catch` block parameter `e`. So, the expression `e.getMessage()` returns the string "Lesson is canceled. No men." The method `getMessage()` of the class `Exception` is an accessor method that retrieves the `String` in the private instance variable of the `Exception` object—that is, the `String` used as an argument to the `Exception` constructor.

To see if you get the basic idea of how this exception throwing mechanism works, study the Sample Dialogues in Displays 9.2 and 9.3. The next few sections explain this mechanism in more detail.

Display 9.2   Handling a Special Case without Exception Handling (part 1 of 3)

```
1    import java.util.Scanner;

2    public class DanceLesson
3    {
4        public static void main(String[] args)
5        {
6            Scanner keyboard = new Scanner(System.in);

7
8            System.out.println("Enter number of male dancers:");
9            int men = keyboard.nextInt();

10           System.out.println("Enter number of female dancers: ");
11           int women = keyboard.nextInt();
```

(continued)

Display 9.2 Handling a Special Case without Exception Handling (part 2 of 3)

```
12          if (men == 0 && women == 0)
13          {
14              System.out.println("Lesson is canceled. No students.");
15              System.exit(0);
16          }
17          else if (men == 0)
18          {
19              System.out.println("Lesson is canceled. No men.");
20              System.exit(0);
21          }
22          else if (women == 0)
23          {
24              System.out.println("Lesson is canceled. No women.");
25              System.exit(0);
26          }

27          // women >= 0 && men >= 0
28          if (women >= men)
29              System.out.println("Each man must dance with " +
30                                      women/(double)men + " women.");
31          else
32              System.out.println("Each woman must dance with " +
33                                      men/(double)women + " men.");
34          System.out.println("Begin the lesson.");
35      }
36  }
```

Sample Dialogue 1

```
Enter number of male dancers:
4
Enter number of female dancers:
6
Each man must dance with 1.5 women.
Begin the lesson.
```

Sample Dialogue 2

```
Enter number of male dancers:
0
Enter number of female dancers:
0
Lesson is canceled. No students.
```

Display 9.2 Handling a Special Case without Exception Handling (part 3 of 3)

Sample Dialogue 3

```
Enter number of male dancers:
0
Enter number of female dancers:
5
Lesson is canceled. No men.
```

Sample Dialogue 4

```
Enter number of male dancers:
4
Enter number of female dancers:
0
Lesson is canceled. No women.
```

Display 9.3 Same Thing Using Exception Handling (part 1 of 3)

```
1   import java.util.Scanner;

2   public class DanceLesson2
3   {
4       public static void main(String[] args)
5       {
6           Scanner keyboard = new Scanner(System.in);

7           System.out.println("Enter number of male dancers:");
8           int men = keyboard.nextInt();
9           System.out.println("Enter number of female dancers:");
10          int women = keyboard.nextInt();
```

This is just a toy example to learn Java syntax. Do not take it as an example of good typical use of exception handling.

(continued)

Display 9.3 **Same Thing Using Exception Handling** (part 2 of 3)

```
11          try
12          {
13              if (men == 0 && women == 0)
14                  throw new Exception("Lesson is canceled. No students.");
15              else if (men == 0)
16                  throw new Exception("Lesson is canceled. No men.");
17              else if (women == 0)
18                  throw new Exception("Lesson is canceled. No women.");

19              // women >= 0 && men >= 0
20              if (women >= men)
21                  System.out.println("Each man must dance with " +
22                                          women/(double)men + " women.");
23              else
24                  System.out.println("Each woman must dance with " +
25                                          men/(double)women + " men.");
26          }
27          catch(Exception e)
28          {
29              String message = e.getMessage();
30              System.out.println(message);
31              System.exit(0);
32          }

33          System.out.println("Begin the lesson.");
34      }

35  }
```

try block — lines 11–26
catch block — lines 27–32

Sample Dialogue 1

```
Enter number of male dancers:
4
Enter number of female dancers:
6
Each man must dance with 1.5 women.
Begin the lesson.
```

Sample Dialogue 2

```
Enter number of male dancers:
0
Enter number of female dancers:
0
Lesson is canceled. No students.
```

Note that this dialogue and the dialogues that follow do not say "Begin the lesson".

Display 9.3   **Same Thing Using Exception Handling** (part 3 of 3)

Sample Dialogue 3

```
Enter number of male dancers:
0
Enter number of female dancers:
5
Lesson is canceled. No men.
```

Sample Dialogue 4

```
Enter number of male dancers:
4
Enter number of female dancers:
0
Lesson is canceled. No women.
```

Exception Classes

There are more exception classes than just the single class `Exception`. There are more exception classes in the standard Java libraries and you can define your own. All the exception classes in the Java libraries have—and the exception classes you define should have—the following properties:

- There is a constructor that takes a single argument of type `String`.
- The class has an accessor method `getMessage()` that can recover the string given as an argument to the constructor when the exception object was created.

`try-throw-catch`

When used together, the `try`, `throw`, and `catch` statements are the basic mechanism for throwing and catching exceptions. The `throw` statement throws the exception. The `catch` block catches the exception. The `throw` statement is normally included in a `try` block. When the exception is thrown, the `try` block ends and then the code in the `catch` block is executed. After the `catch` block is completed, the code after the `catch` block(s) is executed (provided the `catch` block has not ended the program or performed some other special action).

If no exception is thrown in the `try` block, then after the `try` block is completed, program execution continues with the code after the `catch` block(s). (In other words, if no exception is thrown, the `catch` block(s) are ignored.)

(continued)

SYNTAX

```
try
{
     Some_Statements
    <Either a throw statement or
                a method invocation that might throw an exception
                or other statement that might throw an exception.>
     Some_More_Statements
}
catch (Exception_Class_Name Catch_Block_Parameter)
{
     <Code to be performed if an exception of the named exception
                               class is thrown in the try block.>
}
```

You may use any legal identifier for the *Catch_Block_Parameter*, a common choice is e.
The code in the catch block may refer to the *Catch_Block_Parameter*. If there is an explicit
throw statement, it is usually embedded in an if statement or an if-else statement.
There may be any number of throw statements and/or any number of method invocations
that may throw exceptions. Each catch block can list only one exception, but there can be
more than one catch block.

EXAMPLE

See Display 9.3.

Exception Classes from Standard Packages

Numerous predefined exception classes are included in the standard packages that come
with Java. The names of predefined exceptions are designed to be self-explanatory.
Some sample predefined exceptions are

```
IOException
NoSuchMethodException
FileNotFoundException
```

Exception   The predefined exception class Exception is the root class for all exceptions. Every
exception class is a descendent of the class Exception (that is, it is derived directly
from the class Exception or from a class that is derived from the class Exception,
or it arises from some longer chain of derivations ultimately starting with the class
Exception). You can use the class Exception itself, just as we did in Display 9.3, but
you are even more likely to use it to define a derived class of the class Exception. The
class Exception is in the java.lang package and so requires no import statement.

The Class `Exception`

Every exception class is a descendent class of the class `Exception`. You can use the class `Exception` itself in a class or program, but you are even more likely to use it to define a derived class of the class `Exception`. The class `Exception` is in the `java.lang` package and so requires no import statement.

Self-Test Exercises

3. What output is produced by the following code?

```
int temperature = 45;
try
{
    System.out.println("Testing temperature for the self service
    water boiler.");
    if (temperature > 60)
        throw new Exception("Over Max limit.");
    else if (temperature < 20)
        throw new Exception("Below 20.");
    else
        System.out.println("Normal temperature.");
    System.out.println("Testing Completed.");
}
catch(Exception tmpException)
{
    System.out.println(tmpException.getMessage());
}
System.out.println("Resuming Work.");
```

4. Suppose that in Self-Test Exercise 3, the line

```
int temperature = 45;
```

is changed to

```
int temperature = 12;
```

How would this affect the output?

5. In the code given in Self-Text Exercise 3, what are the `throw` statements?

6. What happens when a `throw` statement is executed? This is a general question. Explain what happens in general, not simply what happens in the code in Exercise 1 or some other sample code.

7. In the code given in Self-Test Exercise 3, what is the `try` block?

(continued)

Self-Test Exercises (continued)

8. In the code given in Self-Text Exercise 3, what is the catch block?

9. In the code given in Self-Test Exercise 3, what is the catch block parameter?

10. Is the following legal?

```
Exception exceptionObject = new Exception();
```

11. Is the following legal?

```
Exception exceptionObject = new Exception("Oops!");
catch exceptionObject;
```

Defining Exception Classes

A throw statement can throw an exception object of any exception class. A common thing to do is to define an exception class whose objects can carry the precise kinds of information you want thrown to the catch block. An even more important reason for defining a specialized exception class is so that you can have a different type to identify each possible kind of exceptional situation.

Every exception class you define must be a derived class of some already defined exception class. An exception class can be a derived class of any exception class in the standard Java libraries or of any exception class that you have already successfully defined. Our examples will be derived classes of the class Exception.

constructors   When defining an exception class, the constructors are the most important members. Often there are no other members, other than those inherited from the base class. For example, in Display 9.4, we have defined an exception class called DivisionByZeroException whose only members are a no-argument constructor and a constructor with one String parameter. In most cases, these two constructors are all the exception class definition contains. However, the class does inherit all the methods of the class Exception.[1] In particular, the class DivisionByZeroException inherits the method getMessage, which returns a string message. In the no-argument constructor, this string message is set with the following, which is the first line in the no-argument constructor definition:

```
super("Division by Zero!");
```

This is a call to a constructor of the base class Exception. As we have already noted, when you pass a string to the constructor for the class Exception, it sets the value

---

[1]Some programmers would prefer to derive the DivisionByZeroException class from the predefined class ArithmeticException, but that would make it a kind of exception that you are not required to catch in your code, so you would lose the help of the compiler in keeping track of uncaught exceptions. For more details, see the subsection "Exceptions to the Catch or Declare Rule" later in this chapter. If this footnote does not make sense to you, you can safely ignore it.

of a `String` instance variable that can later be recovered with a call to `getMessage`. The method `getMessage` is an ordinary accessor method of the class `Exception`. The class `DivisionByZeroException` inherits this `String` instance variable as well as the accessor method `getMessage`.

For example, in Display 9.5, we give a sample program that uses this exception class. The exception is thrown using the no-argument constructor, as follows:

```
throw new DivisionByZeroException();
```

Display 9.4   A Programmer-Defined Exception Class

```
1   public class DivisionByZeroException extends Exception
2   {
3       public DivisionByZeroException()
4       {
5           super("Division by Zero!");
6       }

7       public DivisionByZeroException(String message)
8       {
9           super(message);
10      }
11  }
```

You can do more in an exception constructor, but this form is common.

super is an invocation of the constructor for the base class Exception.

Display 9.5   Using a Programmer-Defined Exception Class (part 1 of 3)

```
1   import java.util.Scanner;

2   public class DivisionDemoFirstVersion
3   {

4       public static void main(String[] args)
5       {
6           try
7           {
8               Scanner keyboard = new Scanner(System.in);

9               System.out.println("Enter numerator:");
10              int numerator = keyboard.nextInt();
11              System.out.println("Enter denominator:");
12              int denominator = keyboard.nextInt();
```

We will present an improved version of this program later in this chapter in Display 9.10.

(continued)

Display 9.5   Using a Programmer-Defined Exception Class (part 2 of 3)

```
13              if (denominator == 0)
14                  throw new DivisionByZeroException();

15              double quotient = numerator/(double)denominator;
16              System.out.println(numerator + "/"
17                                  + denominator
18                                  + " = " + quotient);
19          }
20      catch (DivisionByZeroException e)
21      {
22          System.out.println(e.getMessage());
23          secondChance();
24      }

25      System.out.println("End of program.");
26  }

27  public static void secondChance()
28  {
29      Scanner keyboard = new Scanner(System.in);
30      System.out.println("Try again:");
31      System.out.println("Enter numerator:");
32      int numerator = keyboard.nextInt();
33      System.out.println("Enter denominator:");
34      System.out.println("Be sure the denominator is not zero.");
35      int denominator = keyboard.nextInt();
36
37      if (denominator == 0)
38      {
39          System.out.println("I cannot do division by zero.");
40          System.out.println("Aborting program.");
41          System.exit(0);
42      }

43      double quotient = ((double)numerator)/denominator;
44      System.out.println(numerator + "/"
45                          + denominator
46                          + " = " + quotient);
47      }
48  }
```

Sometimes it is better to handle an exceptional case without throwing an exception.

Display 9.5   **Using a Programmer-Defined Exception Class** (part 3 of 3)

Sample Dialogue 1

```
Enter numerator:
11
Enter denominator:
5
11/5 = 2.2
End of program.
```

Sample Dialogue 2

```
Enter numerator:
11
Enter denominator:
0
Division by Zero!
Try again.
Enter numerator:
11
Enter denominator:
Be sure the denominator is not zero.
5
11/5 = 2.2
End of program.
```

Sample Dialogue 3

```
Enter numerator:
11
Enter denominator:
0
Division by Zero!
Try again.
Enter numerator:
11
Enter denominator:
Be sure the denominator is not zero.
0
I cannot do division by zero.
Aborting program.
```

This exception is caught in the `catch` block shown in Display 9.5. Consider the following line from that `catch` block:

```
System.out.println(e.getMessage());
```

This line produces the following output to the screen in Sample Dialogues 2 and 3 (in Display 9.5):

```
Division by Zero!
```

The definition of the class `DivisionByZeroException` in Display 9.4 has a second constructor with one parameter of type `String`. This constructor allows you to choose any message you like when you throw an exception. If the `throw` statement in Display 9.5 had instead used the string argument

```
throw new DivisionByZeroException(
                    "Oops. Shouldn't divide by zero.");
```

then in Sample Dialogues 2 and 3, the statement

```
System.out.println(e.getMessage());
```

would have produced the following output to the screen:

```
Oops. Shouldn't divide by zero.
```

Notice that in Display 9.5, the `try` block is the normal part of the program. If all goes routinely, that is the only code that will be executed, and the dialogue will be like the one shown in Sample Dialogue 1. In the exceptional case, when the user enters a zero for a denominator, the exception is thrown and then is caught in the `catch` block. The `catch` block outputs the message of the exception and then calls the method `secondChance`. The method `secondChance` gives the user a second chance to enter the input correctly and then carries out the calculation. If the user tries a second time to divide by zero, the method ends the program. The method `secondChance` is there only for this exceptional case. So, we have separated the code for the exceptional case of a division by zero into a separate method, where it will not clutter the code for the normal case.

TIP: Preserve `getMessage`

For all predefined exception classes, `getMessage` will return the string that is passed as an argument to the constructor (or will return a default string if no argument is used with the constructor). For example, if the exception is thrown as follows,

```
throw new Exception("Wow, this is exceptional!");
```

then "Wow, this is exceptional!" is used as the value of the `String` instance variable of the object created. If the object is called `e`, the method invocation `e.getMessage()` returns "Wow, this is exceptional!" You want to preserve this behavior in the exception classes you define.

TIP: (continued)

For example, suppose you are defining an exception class named `NegativeNumber Exception`. Be sure to include a constructor with a string parameter that begins with a call to `super`, as illustrated by the following constructor:

```
public NegativeNumberException(String message)
{
    super (message);
}
```

The call to `super` is a call to a constructor of the base class. If the base class constructor handles the message correctly, then so will a class defined in this way.

You should also include a no-argument constructor in each exception class. This no-argument constructor should set a default value to be retrieved by `getMessage`. The constructor should begin with a call to `super`, as illustrated by the following constructor:

```
public NegativeNumberException()
{
    super("Negative Number Exception!");
}
```

If `getMessage` works as we described for the base class, then this sort of no-argument constructor will work correctly for the new exception class being defined. A full defini-tion of the class `NegativeNumberException` is given in Display 9.9. ∎

Exception Object Characteristics

The two most important things about an exception object are its type (the exception class) and a message that it carries in an instance variable of type `String`. This string can be recovered with the accessor method `getMessage`. This string allows your code to send a message along with an exception object, so that the `catch` block can use the message.

Programmer-Defined Exception Classes

You may define your own exception classes, but every such class must be a derived class of an already existing exception class (either from one of the standard Java libraries or programmer defined).

GUIDELINES

- If you have no compelling reason to use any other class as the base class, use the class `Exception` as the base class.

- You should define two (or more) constructors, as described later in this list.

(continued)

- Your exception class inherits the method `getMessage`. Normally, you do not need to add any other methods, but it is legal to do so.

- You should start each constructor definition with a call to the constructor of the base class, such as the following:

  ```
  super("Sample Exception thrown!");
  ```

- You should include a no-argument constructor, in which case the call to `super` should have a string argument that indicates what kind of exception it is. This string can then be recovered by using the `getMessage` method.

- You should also include a constructor that takes a single string argument. In this case, the string should be an argument in a call to `super`. That way, the string can be recovered with a call to `getMessage`.

EXAMPLE

```java
public class SampleException extends Exception
{
    public SampleException()
    {
        super("Sample Exception thrown!");
    }

    public SampleException(String message)
    {
        super(message);
    }
}
```

extra code on website

The class `SampleException` is on the website that comes with this text.

TIP: An Exception Class Can Carry a Message of Any Type

It is possible to define your exception classes so they have constructors that take arguments of other types that are stored in instance variables. In such cases, you would define accessor methods for the value stored in the instance variable. For example, if that is desired, you can have an exception class that carries an `int` as a message. In that case, you would need a new accessor method name, perhaps `getBadNumber()`. An example of one such exception class is given in Display 9.6. Display 9.7 is a demonstration of how to use the accessor method `getBadNumber()`. This is just a toy program, but it does illustrate the details of how an exception object can carry a numeric message. ■

Display 9.6   An Exception Class with an `int` Message (part 1 of 2)

```java
1  public class BadNumberException extends Exception
2  {
3      private int badNumber;
4      public BadNumberException(int number)
5      {
```

Display 9.6   An Exception Class with an `int` Message (part 2 of 2)

```
 6            super ("BadNumberException");
 7            badNumber = number;
 8        }

 9      public BadNumberException()
10      {
11            super ("BadNumberException");
12      }

13      public BadNumberException(String message)
14      {
15            super (message);
16      }

17      public int getBadNumber()
18      {
19            return badNumber;
20      }
21  }
```

Display 9.7   Demonstration of How to Use `BadNumberException` (part 1 of 2)

```
 1   import java.util.Scanner;

 2   public class BadNumberExceptionDemo

 3   {
 4       public static void main(String[] args)
 5       {
 6           try
 7           {
 8               Scanner keyboard = new Scanner(System.in);

 9               System.out.println("Enter one of the numbers 42 and 24:");
10               int inputNumber = keyboard.nextInt();

11               if ((inputNumber != 42) && (inputNumber != 24))
12                   throw new BadNumberException(inputNumber);

13               System.out.println("Thank you for entering " + inputNumber);
14           }
15           catch(BadNumberException e)
16           {
17               System.out.println(e.getBadNumber() +
18                                           " is not what I asked for.");
19           }
20           System.out.println("End of program.");
21       }
22   }
23
```

(continued)

Display 9.7   Demonstration of How to Use `BadNumberException` (part 2 of 2)

Sample Dialogue 1

```
Enter one of the numbers 42 and 24:
42
Thank you for entering 42
End of program.
```

Sample Dialogue 2

```
Enter one of the numbers 42 and 24:
44
44 is not what I asked for.
End of program.
```

MyProgrammingLab

Self-Test Exercises

12. Define an exception class called `PowerFailureException`. The class should have a constructor with no parameters. If an exception is thrown with this zero-argument constructor, `getMessage` should return `"Power Failure!"` The class should also have a constructor with a single parameter of type `String`. If an exception is thrown with this constructor, then `getMessage` returns the value that was used as an argument to the constructor.

13. Define an exception class called `TooMuchStuffException`. The class should have a constructor with no parameters. If an exception is thrown with this zero-argument constructor, `getMessage` should return `"Too much stuff!"` The class should also have a constructor with a single parameter of type `String`. If an exception is thrown with this constructor, then `getMessage` returns the value that was used as an argument to the constructor.

14. Suppose the exception class `ExerciseException` is defined as follows:

```java
public class ExerciseException extends Exception
{
    public ExerciseException()
    {
        super("Exercise Exception thrown!");
        System.out.println("Exception thrown.");
    }

    public ExerciseException(String message)
    {
        super(message);
        System.out.println(
          "ExerciseException invoked with an argument.");
    }
}
```

Self-Test Exercises (continued)

What output would be produced by the following code (which is just an exercise and not likely to occur in a program)?

```
ExerciseException e =
                new ExerciseException("Do Be Do");
System.out.println(e.getMessage());
```

**extra code
on website**

The class `ExerciseException` is on the website that comes with this text.

15. Suppose the exception class `TestException` is defined as follows:

```
public class TestException extends Exception
{
    public TestException()
    {
        super("Test Exception thrown!");
        System.out.println(
                "Test exception thrown!!");
    }

    public TestException(String message)
    {
        super(message);
        System.out.println(
         "Test exception thrown with an argument!");
    }

    public void testMethod()
    {
        System.out.println("Message is " + getMessage());
    }
}
```

What output would be produced by the following code (which is just an exercise and not likely to occur in a program)?

```
TestException exceptionObject = new TestException();
System.out.println(exceptionObject.getMessage());
exceptionObject.testMethod();
```

**extra code
on website**

The class `TestException` is on the website that comes with this text.

16. Suppose the exception class `MyException` is defined as follows:

```
public class MyException extends Exception
{
    public MyException()
    {
        super("My Exception thrown!");
    }
```

(continued)

Self-Test Exercises (continued)

```
public MyException(String message)
{
    super("MyException: " + message);
}
}
```

What output would be produced by the following code (which is just an exercise and not likely to occur in a program)?

```
int number;
try
{
    System.out.println("try block entered:");
    number = 42;
    if (number > 0)
        throw new MyException("Hi Mom!");
    System.out.println("Leaving try block.");
}
catch(MyException exceptionObject)
{
    System.out.println(exceptionObject.getMessage());
}
System.out.println("End of example.");
```

extra code on website

The class `MyException` is on the website that comes with this text.

17. Suppose that in Self-Test Exercise 16, the `catch` block were changed to the following. (The type `MyException` is replaced with `Exception`.) How would this affect the output?

```
catch(Exception exceptionObject)
{
    System.out.println(exceptionObject.getMessage());
}
```

18. Suppose that in Self-Test Exercise 16, the line

```
number = 42;
```

were changed to

```
number = -58;
```

How would this affect the output?

Self-Test Exercises (continued)

19. Although an exception class normally carries only a string message, you can define exception classes to carry a message of any type. For example, objects of the following type can also carry a `double` "message" (as well as a string message):

```java
public class DoubleException extends Exception
{
    private double doubleMessage;

    public DoubleException()
    {
        super("DoubleException thrown!");
    }

    public DoubleException(String message)
    {
        super(message);
    }

    public DoubleException(double number)
    {
        super("DoubleException thrown!");
        doubleMessage = number;
    }

    public double getNumber()
    {
        return doubleMessage;
    }
}
```

What output would be produced by the following code (which is just an exercise and not likely to occur in a program)?

```java
DoubleException e =
            new DoubleException(41.9);

System.out.println(e.getNumber());
System.out.println(e.getMessage());
```

extra code on website   The class `DoubleException` is on the website that comes with this text.

20. There is an exception class named `IOException` that is defined in the standard Java libraries. Can you define an exception class as a derived class of the predefined class `IOException`, or must a defined exception class be derived from the class `Exception`?

Multiple `catch` Blocks

A `try` block can potentially throw any number of exception values, and they can be of differing types. In any one execution of the `try` block, at most one exception will be thrown (since a `throw` statement ends the execution of the `try` block), but different types of exception values can be thrown on different occasions when the `try` block is executed. Each `catch` block can only catch values of the exception class type given in the `catch` block heading. However, you can catch exception values of differing types by placing more than one `catch` block after a `try` block. For example, the program in Display 9.8 has two `catch` blocks after its `try` block. The class `NegativeNumberException`, which is used in that program, is given in Display 9.9.

Display 9.8   Catching Multiple Exceptions (part 1 of 2)

```
1    import java.util.Scanner;

2    public class MoreCatchBlocksDemo
3    {
4        public static void main(String[] args)
5        {
6            Scanner keyboard = new Scanner(System.in);

7
8            try
9            {
10               System.out.println("How many pencils do you have?");
11               int pencils = keyboard.nextInt();

12               if (pencils < 0)
13                   throw new NegativeNumberException("pencils");

14               System.out.println("How many erasers do you have?");
15               int erasers = keyboard.nextInt();
16               double pencilsPerEraser;

17               if (erasers < 0)
18                   throw new NegativeNumberException("erasers");
19               else if (erasers != 0)
20                   pencilsPerEraser = pencils/(double)erasers;
21               else
22                   throw new DivisionByZeroException();

23               System.out.println("Each eraser must last through "
24                   + pencilsPerEraser + " pencils.");
25           }
26           catch(NegativeNumberException e)
27           {
28               System.out.println("Cannot have a negative number of "
29                   + e.getMessage());
30           }
31           catch(DivisionByZeroException e)
32           {
33               System.out.println("Do not make any mistakes.");
```

Display 9.8   Catching Multiple Exceptions (part 2 of 2)

```
34              }

35              System.out.println("End of program.");
36          }
37  }
```

Sample Dialogue 1

```
How many pencils do you have?
5
How many erasers do you have?
2
Each eraser must last through 2.5 pencils
End of program.
```

Sample Dialogue 2

```
How many pencils do you have?
-2
Cannot have a negative number of pencils
End of program.
```

Sample Dialogue 3

```
How many pencils do you have?
5
How many erasers do you have?
0
Do not make any mistakes.
End of program.
```

PITFALL: Catch the More Specific Exception First

When catching multiple exceptions, the order of the catch blocks can be important. When an exception is thrown in a try block, the catch blocks are examined in order, and the first one that matches the type of the exception thrown is the one that is executed. Thus, the following ordering of catch blocks would not be good:

```
catch (Exception e)
{
    .
    .
    .
}
```

(continued)

PITFALL: (continued)

```
catch(NegativeNumberException e)
{
        .                           The second catch block can
        .                           never be reached.
        .
}
```

With this ordering, the `catch` block for `NegativeNumberException` would never be used, because all exceptions are caught by the first `catch` block. Fortunately, the compiler will warn you about this. The correct ordering is to reverse the `catch` blocks so that the more specific exception comes before its parent exception class, as shown in the following:

```
catch(NegativeNumberException e)
{
        .

        .

        .
}

catch(Exception e)
{
        .

        .

        .
}
```

Display 9.9   The Class `NegativeNumberException`

```
 1  public class NegativeNumberException extends Exception
 2  {
 3      public NegativeNumberException()
 4      {
 5          super("Negative Number Exception!");
 6      }
 7      public NegativeNumberException(String message)
 8      {
 9          super(message);
10      }
11  }
```

Self-Test Exercises

21. What output will be produced by the following code? (The definition of the class `NegativeNumberException` is given in Display 9.9.)

```java
int n;
try
{
    n = 42;
    if (n > 0)
        throw new Exception();
    else if (n < 0)
        throw new NegativeNumberException();
    else
        System.out.println("Caught a zero!");
}
catch(Exception e)
{
    System.out.println("Positive number.");
}
catch(NegativeNumberException e)
{
    System.out.println("Negative number.");
}
System.out.println("End of exercise.");
```

22. Suppose that in Self-Test Exercise 21 the line

    ```java
    n = 42;
    ```

    is changed to

    ```java
    n = -42;
    ```

    How would this affect the output?

23. Suppose that in Self-Test Exercise 21 the line

    ```java
    n = 42;
    ```

    is changed to

    ```java
    n = 0;
    ```

    How would this affect the output?

9.2 Throwing Exceptions in Methods

The buck stops here.

HARRY S TRUMAN (sign on Truman's desk while he was president)

So far, our examples of exception handling have been toy examples. We have not yet shown any examples of a program that makes good and realistic use of exception handling. However, now you know enough about exception handling to discuss more realistic uses of it. This section explains the single most important exception handling technique, namely throwing an exception in a method and catching it outside the method.

Throwing an Exception in a Method

Sometimes it makes sense to throw an exception in a method but not catch it in the method. For example, you might have a method with code that throws an exception if there is an attempt to divide by zero, but you may not want to catch the exception in that method. Perhaps some programs that use that method should simply end if the exception is thrown, and other programs that use the method should do something else. So, you would not know what to do with the exception if you caught it inside the method. In such cases, it makes sense to not catch the exception in the method definition, but instead to have any program (or other code) that uses the method place the method invocation in a `try` block and catch the exception in a `catch` block that follows that `try` block.

Look at the program in Display 9.10. It has a `try` block, but there is no `throw` statement visible in the `try` block. The statement that does the throwing in that program is

```
if (bottom == 0)
    throw new DivisionByZeroException();
```

This statement is not visible in the `try` block. However, it is in the `try` block in terms of program execution, because it is in the definition of the method `safeDivide`, and there is an invocation of `safeDivide` in the `try` block.

The meaning of `throws DivisionByZero` in the heading of `safeDivide` is discussed in the next subsection.

Display 9.10   **Use of a throws Clause** (part 1 of 2)

```
1   import java.util.Scanner;

2   public class DivisionDemoSecondVersion
3   {
4       public static void main(String[] args)
5       {
6           Scanner keyboard = new Scanner(System.in);

7           try
8           {
9               System.out.println("Enter numerator:");
10              int numerator = keyboard.nextInt();
11              System.out.println("Enter denominator:");
12              int denominator = keyboard.nextInt();
13              double quotient = safeDivide(numerator, denominator);
14              System.out.println(numerator + "/"
15                                          + denominator
16                                          + " = " + quotient);
17          }
18          catch (DivisionByZeroException e)
19          {
20              System.out.println(e.getMessage());
21              secondChance();
22          }

23
24          System.out.println("End of program.");
25      }
26


27      public static double safeDivide(int top, int bottom)
28                              throws DivisionByZeroException
29      {
30          if (bottom == 0)
31              throw new DivisionByZeroException();

32          return top/(double)bottom;
33      }
```

(continued)

Display 9.10   Use of a `throws` Clause (part 2 of 2)

```
34       public static void secondChance()
35       {
36           Scanner keyboard = new Scanner(System.in);
37
38           try
39           {
40               System.out.println("Enter numerator:");
41               int numerator = keyboard.nextInt();
42               System.out.println("Enter denominator:");
43               int denominator = keyboard.nextInt();
44               double quotient = safeDivide(numerator, denominator);
45               System.out.println(numerator + "/"
46                                           + denominator
47                                           + " = " + quotient);
48           }
49           catch(DivisionByZeroException e)
50           {
51               System.out.println("I cannot do division by zero.");
52               System.out.println("Aborting program.");
53               System.exit(0);
54           }
55       }
56   }
```

The input/output dialogues are identical to those for the program in Display 9.5.

Declaring Exceptions in a `throws` Clause

throws clause

declaring an exception

If a method does not catch an exception, then (in most cases) it must at least warn programmers that any invocation of the method might possibly throw an exception. This warning is called a *throws clause*, and including an exception class in a `throws` clause is called **declaring the exception**. For example, a method that might possibly throw a `DivisionByZeroException` and that does not catch the exception would have a heading similar to the following:

```
public void sampleMethod() throws DivisionByZeroException
```

throws clause

The part `throws DivisionByZeroException` is a **throws clause** stating that an invocation of the method `sampleMethod` might throw a `DivisionByZeroException`.

If there is more than one possible exception that can be thrown in the method definition, then the exception types are separated by commas, as illustrated in what follows:

```
public void sampleMethod()
             throws DivisionByZeroException, SomeOtherException
```

Most "ordinary" exceptions that might be thrown when a method is invoked must be accounted for in one of two ways:

- The possible exception can be caught in a `catch` block within the method definition.
- The possible exception can be declared at the start of the method definition by placing the exception class name in a `throws` clause (and letting whoever uses the method worry about how to handle the exception).

Catch or Declare Rule

This is often called the **Catch or Declare Rule**. In any one method, you can mix the two alternatives, catching some exceptions and declaring others in a `throws` clause.

You already know about the first technique, handling exceptions in a `catch` block. The second technique is a form of shifting responsibility ("passing the buck"). For example, suppose `yourMethod` has a `throws` clause as follows:

```
public void yourMethod()throws DivisionByZeroException
```

In this case, `yourMethod` is absolved of the responsibility of catching any exceptions of type `DivisionByZeroException` that might occur when `yourMethod` is executed. If, however, there is another method (`myMethod`) that includes an invocation of `yourMethod`, then `myMethod` must handle the exception. When you add a `throws` clause to `yourMethod`, you are saying to `myMethod`, "If you invoke `yourMethod`, you must handle any `DivisionByZeroException` that is thrown." In effect, `yourMethod` has passed the responsibility for any exceptions of type `DivisionByZeroException` from itself to any method that calls it.

Of course, if `yourMethod` passes responsibility to `myMethod` by including `DivisionByZeroException` in a `throws` clause, then `myMethod` may also pass the responsibility to whoever calls it by including the same `throws` clause in its definition. But in a well-written program, every exception that is thrown should eventually be caught by a `catch` block in some method that does not just declare the exception class in a `throws` clause.

---

throws Clause

If you define a method that might throw exceptions of some particular class, then normally either your method definition must include a `catch` block that will catch the exception or you must declare (that is, list) the exception class within a `throws` clause, as described in what follows.

SYNTAX (COVERS MOST COMMON CASES)

```
public Type_Or_void Method(Parameter_List)throws List_Of_Exceptions
Body_Of_Method
```

EXAMPLE

```
public void yourMethod(int n) throws MyException, YourException
{
        .
        .
        .
}
```

When an exception is thrown in a method but not caught in that method, that immediately ends the method invocation.

Be sure to note that the `throws` clause for a method is for exceptions that "get outside" the method. If they do not get outside the method, they do not belong in the `throws` clause. If they get outside the method, they belong in the `throws` clause no matter where they originate. If an exception is thrown in a `try` block that is inside a method definition and is caught in a `catch` block inside the method definition, then its exception class need not be listed in the `throws` clause. If a method definition includes an invocation of another method and that other method can throw an exception that is not caught, then the exception class of that exception should be placed in the `throws` clause.

Throwing an Exception Can End a Method

If a method throws an exception, and the exception is not caught inside the method, then the method invocation ends immediately after the exception is thrown.

In Display 9.10, we have rewritten the program from Display 9.5 so that the exception is thrown in the method `safeDivide`. The method `main` includes a call to the method `safeDivide` and puts the call in a `try` block. Because the method `safeDivide` can throw a `DivisionByZeroException` that is not caught in the method `safeDivide`, we need to declare this in a `throws` clause at the start of the definition of `safeDivide`. If we set up our program in this way, the case in which nothing goes wrong is completely isolated and easy to read. It is not even cluttered by `try` blocks and `catch` blocks.

Catch or Declare Rule

Most "ordinary" exceptions that might be thrown when a method is invoked must be accounted for in one of two ways:

- The possible exception can be caught in a `catch` block within the method definition.
- The possible exception can be declared at the start of the method definition by placing the exception class name in a `throws` clause (and letting whoever uses the method worry about how to handle the exception).

This is known as the **Catch or Declare Rule**. In any one method, you can mix the two alternatives, catching some exceptions and declaring others in a `throws` clause.

If you use a class that is subject to the Catch or Declare Rule and you do not follow the rule, you will get a compiler error message. The box entitled "Checked and Unchecked Exceptions" explains exactly which exception classes are subject to the Catch or Declare Rule.

The next subsection, entitled "Exceptions to the Catch or Declare Rule," explains exactly which exception classes are subject to the Catch or Declare Rule. However, the compiler will ensure that you follow the Catch or Declare Rule when it is required. So if you do not know whether a class is subject to the Catch or Declare Rule, you can rely on the compiler to tell you. If you use a class that is subject to the Catch or Declare Rule and you do not follow the rule, you will get a compiler error message.

Exceptions to the Catch or Declare Rule

As we already noted, in most "ordinary" cases, an exception must either be caught in a catch block or declared in a throws clause. This is the Catch or Declare Rule, but there are exceptions to this rule. There are some classes whose exceptions you do not need to account for in this way (although you can catch them in a catch block if you want to). These are typically exceptions that result from errors of some sort. They usually indicate that your code should be fixed, not that you need to add a catch block. They are often thrown by methods in standard library classes, but it would be legal to throw one of these exceptions in the code you write.

Exceptions that are descendents of the class RuntimeException do not need to be accounted for in a catch block or throws clause. Another category of classes called Error classes behave like exception classes in that they can be thrown and caught in a catch block. However, you are not required to account for Error objects in a catch block or throws clause. The situation is diagrammed as a class hierarchy in Display 9.11. All the classes shown in blue follow the Catch or Declare Rule, which says that if their objects are thrown, then they must either be caught in a catch block or declared in a throws clause. All the classes shown in yellow are exempt from the Catch or Declare Rule.

Display 9.11   Hierarchy of Throwable Objects

All descendents of the class Throwable can be thrown and caught in a catch block.

Throwable

Exception

Error

These are checked exceptions, which means they are subject to the Catch or Declare Rule.

RuntimeException

Exceptions that must either be caught in a catch block or declared in a throws clause.

Errors, all of which do not need to be accounted for in a catch block or throws clause.

Exceptions that do not need to be accounted for in a catch block or throws clause.

What Happens if an Exception Is Never Caught?

If every method up to and including the `main` method simply includes a `throws` clause for a particular class of exceptions, then it may turn out that an exception of that class is thrown but never caught. In such cases, when an exception is thrown but never caught, then for the kinds of programs we have seen so far, the program ends with an error message giving the name of the exception class. (In Chapter 17 we will discuss programs with windowing interfaces that are known as *GUI programs.* For GUI programs, if an exception is thrown but never caught, then nothing happens, but if your code does not somehow account for the thrown exception, then the user may be left in an unexplained situation.)

In a well-written program, every exception that is thrown should eventually be caught by a `catch` block in some method.

---

checked and
unchecked
exceptions

Exception classes that follow the Catch or Declare Rule are often called **checked exceptions**. Exceptions that are exempt from the Catch or Declare Rule are often called **unchecked exceptions**.

Checked and Unchecked Exceptions

Exceptions that are subject to the Catch or Declare Rule are called **checked exceptions** because the compiler *checks* to see if they are accounted for with a `catch` block or `throws` clause. Exceptions that are *not* subject to the Catch or Declare Rule are called **unchecked exceptions.** The classes `Throwable`, `Exception`, and all descendents of the class `Exception` are checked exceptions. All other exceptions are unchecked exceptions. The class `Error` and all its descendent classes are called **error classes** and are *not* subject to the Catch or Declare Rule. Although they are technically not exceptions, you can safely consider these error classes to be unchecked exceptions. (Strictly speaking, the class `Throwable` is neither an exception nor an error class, but it is seldom used and can be treated as a checked exception if it is used.)

You need not worry too much about which exceptions you do and do not need to declare in a `throws` clause. If you fail to account for some exception that Java requires you to account for, the compiler will tell you about it, and you can then either catch it or declare it in a `throws` clause.

`throws` Clause in Derived Classes

When you override a method definition in a derived class, it should have the same exception classes listed in its `throws` clause that it had in the base class, or it should have a `throws` clause whose exceptions are a subset of those in the base class `throws` clause. Put another way, when you override a method definition, you cannot add any exceptions to the `throws` clause (but you can delete some exceptions if you want; you also can replace an exception class by any descendent exception class). This makes sense, because an object of the derived class might be used anyplace an object of the base class can be used, so an overridden method must fit into any code written for an object of the base class.

When to Use Exceptions

So far, most of our examples of exception handling have been unrealistically simple. A better guideline for how you should use exceptions is to separate throwing an exception and catching the exception into separate methods. In most cases, you should include any `throw` statement within a method definition, list the exception class in a `throws` clause for that method, and place the `try` and `catch` blocks in *a different method*. In outline form, the technique is as follows:

```
public void yourMethod() throws YourException
{
        . . .
    throw new YourException(<Maybe an argument.>);
        . . .
}
```

Then, when `yourMethod` is used by some `otherMethod`, the `otherMethod` must account for the exception. For example,

```
public void otherMethod()
{
        . . .
    try
    {
            . . .
        yourMethod();
            . . .
    }
    catch(YourException e)
    {
        <Handle exception.>
    }
        . . .
}
```

Even this kind of use of a `throw` statement should be reserved for cases where it is unavoidable. *If you can easily handle a problem in some other way, do not throw an exception. Reserve* `throw` *statements for situations in which the way the exceptional condition is handled depends on how and where the method is used.* If the way that the exceptional condition is handled depends on how and where the method is invoked, then the best thing to do is to let the programmer who invokes the method handle the exception. In all other situations, it is preferable to avoid throwing exceptions. Let's outline a sample scenario of this kind of situation.

Suppose you are writing a library of methods to deal with patient monitoring systems for hospitals. One method might compute the patient's average daily temperature by accessing the patient's record in some file and dividing the sum of the temperatures by the number of times the temperature was taken. Now suppose these methods are used for creating different systems to be used in different situations. What should happen if the patient's temperature was never taken and so the averaging would involve a division by zero? In an intensive care unit, this would indicate something is very wrong. So for this system, when this potential division by zero would occur, an emergency message should be sent out. However, for a system that is to be used in a less urgent setting, such as outpatient care or even in some noncritical wards, it might have no significance, and so a simple note in the patient's record would suffice. In this scenario, the method for doing the averaging of the temperatures should throw an exception when this division by zero occurs, list the exception in the `throws` clause, and let each system handle the exception case in the way that is appropriate to that system.

When to Throw an Exception

Exceptions should be reserved for situations where a method has an exceptional case and individual invocations of the method would handle the exceptional case differently. In this situation, you would throw an exception in the method definition and not catch the exception in the method, but list it in the `throws` clause for the method. This way the programmers who invoke the method can handle the exception differently in different situations.

Event-Driven Programming ★

event-driven programming

firing an event

Exception handling is our first example of a programming methodology known as **event-driven programming**. With event-driven programming, objects are defined so that they send **events**, which are themselves objects, to other objects that handle the events. Sending the event is called **firing the event**. In exception handing, the event objects are the exception objects. They are fired (thrown) by an object when the object invokes a method that throws the exception. An exception event is sent to a `catch` block, where it is handled. Of course, a `catch` block is not exactly an object, but the idea is the same. Also, our programs have mixed event-driven programming (exception handling) with more traditional programming techniques. When we study how you construct windowing systems using the Swing libraries (Chapter 17), you will see examples of programming where the dominant technique is event-driven programming.

MyProgrammingLab™   ## Self-Test Exercises

24. What is the output produced by the following program?

```
public class Exercise
{
    public static void main(String[] args)
    {
        try
            try
```

Self-Test Exercises (continued)

```
   {
      System.out.println("Trying");
      sampleMethod(98.6);
      System.out.println("Trying after call.");
   }
   catch(Exception e)
   {
      System.out.println("Catching.");
   }

   System.out.println("End program.");
}

public static void sampleMethod(double test)
                                    throws Exception
{
   System.out.println("Starting sampleMethod.");
   if (test < 100)
         throw new Exception();
}
}
```

**extra code
on website**

The class `Exercise` is on the website that comes with this text.

25. Suppose that in Self-Test Exercise 22, the line

    ```
    sampleMethod(98.6);
    ```

    in the `try` block is changed to

    ```
    sampleMethod(212);
    ```

    How would this affect the output?

26. Correct the following method definition by adding a suitable `throws` clause:

    ```
    public static void doStuff(int n)
    {
        if (n < 0)
            throw new Exception("Negative number.");
    }
    ```

27. What should be the ideal scenario when you should use a `throws` clause instead of catching the exception inside the method?

28. Suppose there is an invocation of method A inside of method B, and an invocation of method B inside of method C. When method C is invoked, this leads to an invocation of method B, and that in turn leads to an invocation of method A. Now, suppose that method A throws an exception but does not catch it within A. Where might the exception be caught? In B? In C? Outside of C?

9.3 More Programming Techniques for Exception Handling

Only use this in exceptional circumstances.

WARREN PEACE, *The Lieutenant's Tool*

In this section, we present a number of the finer points about programming with exception handling in Java.

PITFALL: Nested `try-catch` Blocks

You can place a try block and its following catch blocks inside a larger try block or inside a larger catch block. On rare occasions this may be useful, but it is almost always better to place the inner try catch blocks inside a method definition and place an invocation of the method in the outer try or catch block (or maybe just eliminate one or more try blocks completely).

If you place a try block and its following catch blocks inside a larger catch block, you will need to use different names for the catch block parameters in the inner and outer blocks. This has to do with how Java handles nested blocks of any kind. Remember, try blocks and catch blocks are blocks.

If you place a try block and its following catch blocks inside a larger try block, and an exception is thrown in the inner try block but is not caught in the inner catch blocks, then the exception is thrown to the outer try block for processing and might be caught in one of its catch blocks. ■

The `finally` Block ★

The finally block contains code to be executed whether or not an exception is thrown in a try block. The finally block, if used, is placed after a try block and its following catch blocks. The general syntax is as follows:

```
try
{
    ...
}
catch(ExceptionClass1 e)
{
    ...
}
.
.
.
```

```
catch(ExceptionClassLast e)
{
    ...
}
finally
{
    < Code to be executed whether or not an exception is thrown or caught.>
}
```

Now, suppose that the `try-catch-finally` blocks are inside a method definition. (After all, every set of `try-catch-finally` blocks is inside of some method, even if it is only the method `main`.) There are three possibilities when the code in the `try-catch-finally` blocks is run:

- The `try` block runs to the end and no exception is thrown. In this case, the `finally` block is executed after the `try` block.
- An exception is thrown in the `try` block and is caught in one of the `catch` blocks positioned after the `try` block. In this case, the `finally` block is executed after the `catch` block is executed.
- An exception is thrown in the `try` block and there is no matching `catch` block in the method to catch the exception. In this case, the method invocation ends and the exception object is thrown to the enclosing method. However, the `finally` block is executed before the method ends. Note that you cannot account for this last case simply by placing code after the `catch` blocks.

MyProgrammingLab

Self-Test Exercises

29. What is the purpose of a `finally` block?

30. What do you understand by nested `try-catch` block?

31. What is the output produced by the following program? What would the output be if the argument to `exerciseMethod` were -42 instead of 42? (The class `NegativeNumberException` is defined in Display 9.8, but you need not review that definition to do this exercise.)

```
public class FinallyDemo
{
    public static void main(String[] args)
    {
        try
        {
            exerciseMethod(42);
        }
```

(continued)

Self-Test Exercises (continued)

```
        catch(Exception e)
        {
            System.out.println("Caught in main.");
        }
    }
    public static void exerciseMethod(int n) throws Exception
    {
        try
        {
            if (n > 0)
                throw new Exception();
            else if (n < 0)
                throw new NegativeNumberException();
            else
                System.out.println("No Exception.");
            System.out.println("Still in sampleMethod.");
        }
        catch(NegativeNumberException e)
        {
            System.out.println("Caught in sampleMethod.");
        }
        finally
        {
            System.out.println("In finally block.");
        }
        System.out.println("After finally block.");
    }
}
```

**extra code
on website**

The class `FinallyDemo` is on the website that comes with this text.

Rethrowing an Exception ★

A `catch` block can contain code that throws an exception. In rare cases, you may find it useful to catch an exception and then, depending on the string produced by `getMessage` or depending on something else, decide to throw the same or a different exception for handling further up the chain of exception handling blocks.

The `AssertionError` Class ★

When we discussed the `assert` operator and assertion checking in Chapter 3, we said that if your program contains an assertion check and the assertion check fails, your program will end with an error message. This statement is more or less true, but it is incomplete. What happens is that an object of the class `AssertionError` is thrown. If it is not caught in a `catch` block, your program ends with an error message. However, if you wish, you can catch it in a `catch` block, although that is not a very common thing to do. The `AssertionError` class is in the `java.lang` package and so requires no import statement.

As the name suggests, the class `AssertionError` is derived from the class `Error`, so you are not required to either catch it in a `catch` block or declare it in a `throws` clause.

ArrayIndexOutOfBoundsException

Read Section 6.1 of Chapter 6, which covers array basics, before reading this short subsection. If you have not yet covered some of Chapter 6, omit this section and return to it at a later time.

If your program attempts to use an array index that is out of bounds, an `ArrayIndexOutOfBoundsException` is thrown and your program ends, unless the exception is caught in a `catch` block. `ArrayIndexOutOfBoundsException` is a descendent of the class `RuntimeException` and so need not be caught or accounted for in a `throws` clause. This sort of exception normally indicates that there is something wrong with your code and means that you need to fix your code, not catch an exception. Thus, an `ArrayIndexOutOfBoundsException` normally functions more like a run-time error message than a regular exception.

`ArrayIndexOutOfBoundsException` is in the standard Java package `java.lang` and so requires no import statement should you decide to use it by name.

Chapter Summary

- Exception handling allows you to design and code the normal case for your program separately from the code that handles exceptional situations.

- An exception can be thrown in a *try block*. Alternatively, an exception can be thrown in a method definition that does not include a `try` block (or does not include a `catch` block to catch that type of exception). In this case, an invocation of the method can be placed in a `try` block.

- An exception is caught in a *catch block*.

- A `try` block must be followed by at least one `catch` block and can be followed by more than one `catch` block. If there are multiple `catch` blocks, always list the `catch` block for a more specific exception class before the `catch` block for a more general exception class.

- The best use of exceptions is to throw an exception in a method (but not catch it in the method)—but to do this only when the way the exception is handled will vary from one invocation of the method to another. There is seldom any other situation that can profitably benefit from throwing an exception.

- If an exception is thrown in a method but not caught in that method, then if the exception is not a descendent of the class `RuntimeException` (and is not a descendent of the class `Error`), the exception type must be listed in the `throws` clause for that method.

Answers to Self-Test Exercises

1. The code snippet `keyboard.nextLine();` catches the new line entered by the user. Considering that the user enters a wrong input, then after the first input, the program will go into an infinite loop after reading the first item input.

2. The following is the method definition embedded in a test program. This program would give the same dialogue as the one in Display 9.1. The program is included on the website that accompanies this book.

extra code on website

```java
import java.util.Scanner;
import java.util.InputMismatchException;
public class getIntDemo
{
    /**
    Precondition: keyboard is an object of the class Scanner that
    has been set up for keyboard input (as we have been doing right
    along).
    Returns: An int value entered at the keyboard.
    If the user enters an incorrectly formed input, she or he
    is prompted to reenter the value,
    */
    public static int getInt(Scanner keyboard)
    {
        int number = 0; //to keep compiler happy
        boolean done = false;

        while (! done)
        {
          try
          {
              System.out.println("Enter a whole number:");
              number = keyboard.nextInt();
              done = true;
          }
          catch(InputMismatchException e)
          {
              keyboard.nextLine();
              System.out.println(
                    "Not a correctly written whole number.");
              System.out.println("Try again.");
          }
        }
        return number;
    }
```

```
        public static void main(String[] args)
        {
            Scanner keyboardArg = new Scanner(System.in);
            int number = getInt(keyboardArg);
            System.out.println("You entered " + number);
        }
    }
```

3. Testing temperature for the self service water boiler.
   Normal temperature.
   Resuming Work.

4. Testing temperature for the self service water boiler.
   Below 20.
   Resuming Work.

5. There are two throw statements:

```
throw new Exception("Over Max limit.");
throw new Exception("Below 20.");
```

6. When a throw statement is executed, it is the end of the enclosing try block. No other statements in the try block are executed, and control passes to the following catch block(s). When we say that control passes to the following catch block, we mean that the exception object that is thrown is plugged in for the catch block parameter and the code in the catch block is executed.

7.
```
try
{
    System.out.println("Testing temperature for the self service
    water boiler.");
    if (temperature > 60)
        throw new Exception("Over Max limit.");
    else if (temperature < 20)
        throw new Exception("Below 20.");
    else
        System.out.println("Normal temperature.");
    System.out.println("Testing Completed.");
}
```

8.
```
catch(Exception tmpException)
{
    System.out.println(tmpException.getMessage());
}
```

9. tmpException

10. Yes, it is legal.

11. No, it is not legal.

12.
```
public class PowerFailureException extends Exception
{
    public PowerFailureException()
    {
        super("Power Failure!");
    }
    public PowerFailureException(String message)
    {
        super(message);
    }
}
```

13.
```
public class TooMuchStuffException extends Exception
{
    public TooMuchStuffException()
    {
        super("Too much stuff!");
    }
    public TooMuchStuffException(String message)
    {
        super(message);
    }
}
```

14. `ExerciseException invoked with an argument.`

    `Do Be Do`

15. `Test exception thrown!!`

    `Test Exception thrown!`
    `Message is Test Exception thrown!`

16. `try block entered:`

    `MyException: Hi Mom!`
    `End of example.`

17. The output would be the same.

18. The output would then be

    `try block entered:`
    `Leaving try block.`
    `End of example.`

19. `41.9`

    `DoubleException thrown!`

20. Yes, you can define an exception class as a derived class of the class

    `IOException.`

21. `Positive number.`

    `End of exercise.`

22. The output would still be:

    ```
    Positive number.
    End of exercise.
    ```

    as all exceptions will be caught by the first `catch` block.

23. The output would then be:

    ```
    Caught a zero!
    End of exercise.
    ```

24. `Trying`

    ```
    Starting sampleMethod.
    Catching.
    End program.
    ```

25. The output would then be

    ```
    Trying
    Starting sampleMethod.
    Trying after call.
    End program.
    ```

26.
    ```
    public static void doStuff(int n)throws Exception
    {
        if (n < 0)
            throw new Exception("Negative number.");
    }
    ```

27. In some situations, a method has an exceptional case and different invocations of the method would handle the exceptional case differently. In such situations, you should throw an exception in the method definition, not catch the exception in the method, but list the exception in the throws clause for the method, so other programmers who invoke the method can handle the exception differently in different situations.

28. It might be caught in method B. If it is not caught in method B, it might be caught in method C. If it is not caught in method C, it might be caught outside of method C.

29. The `finally` block contains code to be executed whether or not an exception is thrown in a `try` block. The `finally` block, if used, is placed after a `try` block and its following `catch` blocks.

30. When a `try` block and its following `catch` blocks are placed inside a larger `try` block or inside a larger `catch` block, it is called nested `try-catch` block.

31.
    ```
    In finally block.
    Caught in main.
    ```
    If the argument to `sampleMethod` is -42 instead of 42, the output would be
    ```
    Caught in sampleMethod.
    In finally block.
    After finally block.
    ```

Programming Projects

Visit www.myprogramminglab.com to complete select exercises online and get instant feedback.

VideoNote
Solution to Programming Project 9.1

1. Write a program that calculates the average of *N* integers. The program should prompt the user to enter the value for *N* and then afterward must enter all *N* numbers. If the user enters a nonpositive value for *N*, then an exception should be thrown (and caught) with the message "*N* must be positive." If there is any exception as the user is entering the *N* numbers, an error message should be displayed, and the user prompted to enter the number again.

2. Here is a snippet of code that inputs two integers and divides them:

```
Scanner scan = new Scanner(System.in);
int n1, n2;
double r;

n1 = scan.nextInt();
n2 = scan.nextInt();
r = (double) n1 / n2;
```

Place this code into a try-catch block with multiple catches so that different error messages are printed if we attempt to divide by zero or if the user enters textual data instead of integers (java.util.InputMismatchException). If either of these conditions occurs, then the program should loop back and let the user enter new data.

3. Modify the previous exercise so that the snippet of code is placed inside a method. The method should be named ReturnRatio, read the input from the keyboard, and throw different exceptions if there is a division by zero or an input mismatch between text and an integer. Create your own exception class for the case of division by zero. Invoke ReturnRatio from your main method and catch the exceptions in main. The main method should invoke the ReturnRatio method again if any exception occurs.

4. (This is a version of an exercise from Chapter 5.) Programming Project 5.2 from Chapter 5 asked you to create a class named Fraction. This class is used to represent a ratio of two integers. It should include mutator functions that allow the user to set the numerator and the denominator along with a method that displays the fraction on the screen as a ratio (e.g., 5/9). Modify the class so that it throws the exception DenominatorIsZeroException if the denominator is set to zero. Do not forget to account for the constructors! You will have to create the DenominatorIsZeroException class and it should be derived from Exception.

Write a main method that tests the new Fraction class, attempts to set the denominator to zero, and catches the DenominatorIsZeroException exception.

5. Write a program that converts dates from numerical month/day/year format to normal "month day, year" format (for example, 12/25/2000 corresponds to December 25, 2000). You will define three exception classes, one called MonthException, another called DayException, and a third called YearException. If the user enters

anything other than a legal month number (integers from 1 to 12), your program will throw and catch a MonthException and ask the user to reenter the month. Similarly, if the user enters anything other than a valid day number (integers from 1 to either 28, 29, 30, or 31, depending on the month and year), then your program will throw and catch a DayException and ask the user to reenter the day. If the user enters a year that is not in the range 1000 to 3000 (inclusive), then your program will throw and catch a YearException and ask the user to reenter the year. (There is nothing very special about the numbers 1000 and 3000 other than giving a good range of likely dates.) See Self-Test Exercise 19 in Chapter 4 for details on leap years.

6. Write a program that can serve as a simple calculator. This calculator keeps track of a single number (of type double) that is called result and that starts out as 0.0. Each cycle allows the user to repeatedly add, subtract, multiply, or divide by a second number. The result of one of these operations becomes the new value of result. The calculation ends when the user enters the letter R for "result" (either in upper- or lowercase). The user is allowed to do another calculation from the beginning as often as desired.

The input format is shown in the following sample dialogue. If the user enters any operator symbol other than +, -, *, or /, then an UnknownOperatorException is thrown and the user is asked to reenter that line of input. Defining the class UnknownOperatorException is part of this project.

```
Calculator is on.
result = 0.0
+5
result + 5.0 = 5.0
new result = 5.0
* 2.2
result * 2.2 = 11.0
updated result = 11.0
% 10
% is an unknown operation.
Reenter, your last line:
* 0.1
result * 0.1 = 1.1
updated result = 1.1
r
Final result = 1.1
Again? (y/n)
yes
result = 0.0
+10
result + 10.0 = 10.0
new result = 10.0
/2
result / 2.0 = 5.0
```

```
updated result = 5.0
r
Final result = 5.0
Again? (y/n)
N
End of Program
```

7. A method that returns a special error code is usually better accomplished throwing an exception instead. The following class maintains an account balance.

```
class Account
{
    private double balance;
    public Account()
    {
        balance = 0;
    }
    public Account(double initialDeposit)
    {
        balance = initialDeposit;
    }
    public double getBalance()
    {
        return balance;
    }
    // returns new balance or -1 if error
    public double deposit(double amount)
    {
        if (amount > 0)
            balance += amount;
        else
            return -1;// Code indicating error
        return balance;
    }
    // returns new balance or -1 if invalid amount
    public double withdraw(double amount)
    {
        if ((amount > balance) || (amount < 0))
            return -1;
        else
            balance -= amount;
        return balance;
    }
}
```

Rewrite the class so that it throws appropriate exceptions instead of returning -1 as an error code. Write test code that attempts to withdraw and deposit invalid amounts and catches the exceptions that are thrown.

File I/O 10

10.1 INTRODUCTION TO FILE I/O 610
Streams 610
Text Files and Binary Files 611

10.2 TEXT FILES 612
Writing to a Text File 612
Appending to a Text File 619
Reading from a Text File 621
Reading a Text File Using `Scanner` 621
Testing for the End of a Text File with
  `Scanner` 624
Reading a Text File Using `BufferedReader` 631
Testing for the End of a Text File with
  `BufferedReader` 635
Path Names 637
Nested Constructor Invocations 638
`System.in`, `System.out`, and `System.err` 639

10.3 THE `File` CLASS 641
Programming with the `File` Class 641

10.4 BINARY FILES ★ 645
Writing Simple Data to a Binary File 646
UTF and `writeUTF` 650
Reading Simple Data from a Binary File 651
Checking for the End of a Binary File 656
Binary I/O of Objects 658
The `Serializable` Interface 659
Array Objects in Binary Files 662

**10.5 RANDOM ACCESS TO
      BINARY FILES** ★ 664
Reading and Writing to the Same File 664

Chapter Summary 670   **Answers to Self-Test Exercises 671**   **Programming Projects 675**

As a leaf is carried by a stream, whether the stream ends in a lake or in the sea, so too is the output of your program carried by a stream, not knowing if the stream goes to the screen or to a file.

WASHROOM WALL OF A COMPUTER SCIENCE DEPARTMENT (1995)

Introduction

In this chapter, we explain how you can write your programs to take input from a file and send output to a file. This chapter covers the most common ways of doing file I/O in Java. However, it is not an exhaustive study of Java I/O classes. The Java I/O class library contains bewilderingly many classes and an exhaustive treatment of all of them would be a book by itself.

Prerequisites

You need only some of Chapter 9 on exception handling to read this chapter. You do not need Chapters 6, 7, or 8 on arrays, inheritance, and polymorphism, except in the final subsection, which covers writing and reading of arrays to binary files. If you have not yet covered some basic material on one-dimensional arrays, you can, of course, simply omit this last subsection.

You may postpone all or part of this chapter if you wish. Nothing in the rest of this book requires any of this chapter.

10.1 Introduction to File I/O

Good Heavens! For more than forty years I have been speaking prose without knowing it.

MOLIÈRE, *LE Bourgeois Gentilhomme*

In this section, we go over some basic concepts about file I/O before we go into any Java details.

Streams

stream

input stream

output stream

A **stream** is an object that allows for the flow of data between your program and some I/O device or some file. If the flow is into your program, the stream is called an **input stream**. If the flow is out of your program, the stream is called an **output stream**. If the input stream flows from the keyboard, then your program will take input from the keyboard. If the input stream flows from a file, then your program will take its input from that file. Similarly, an output stream can go to the screen or to a file.

Although you may not realize it, you have already been using streams in your programs when you have output something to the screen. `System.out` (used in `System.out.println`) is an output stream connected to the screen. `System.in` is an input stream connected to the keyboard. You used `System.in` in expressions such as the following:

`System.out`

`System.in`

```
Scanner keyboard = new Scanner(System.in);
```

These two streams are automatically available to your program. You can define other streams that come from or go to files. Once you have defined them, you can use them in your program in ways that are similar to how you use `System.out` and `System.in`.

Streams

A **stream** is a flow of data. If the data flows *into your program*, then the stream is called an **input stream**. If the data flows *out of your program*, the stream is called an **output stream**.

Streams are used for both console I/O, which you have been using already, and file I/O.

Text Files and Binary Files

Text files are files that appear to contain sequences of characters when viewed in a text editor or read by a program. For example, the files that contain your Java programs are text files. **Text files** are sometimes also called **ASCII files** because they contain data encoded using a scheme known as ASCII coding. Files whose contents must be handled as sequences of binary digits are called **binary files**.

text file

ASCII file

binary file

Although it is not technically correct, you can safely think of a text file as containing a sequence of characters, and think of a binary file as containing a sequence of binary digits. Another way to distinguish between binary files and text files is to note that text files are designed to be read by human beings, whereas binary files are designed to be read only by programs.

One advantage of text files is that they are usually the same on all computers, so you can move your text files from one computer to another with few or no problems. The implementation of binary files usually differs from one computer to another, so your binary data files ordinarily must be read only on the same type of computer, and with the same programming language, as the computer that created that file.

The benefit of binary files is that they are more efficient to process than text files. Unlike other programming languages, Java also gives its binary files some of the advantages of text files. In particular, Java binary files are platform independent; that is, with Java, you can move your binary files from one type of computer to another and your Java programs will still be able to read the binary files. This combines the portability of text files with the efficiency of binary files.

The one big asset of text files is that you can read and write to them using a text editor. With binary files, all the reading and writing must normally be done by a program.

> **Text Files versus Binary Files**
>
> Files that you write and read using an editor are called **text files**. **Binary files** represent data in a way that is not convenient to read with a text editor, but that can be written to and read from a program very efficiently.

Self-Test Exercises

1. What is a stream? What do you understand by input and output stream?

2. What is the difference between a binary file and a text file?

10.2 Text Files

Polonius: What do you read, my lord?
Hamlet: Words, words, words.

WILLIAM SHAKESPEARE, *Hamlet*

In this section, we describe the most common ways to do text file I/O in Java.

Writing to a Text File

PrintWriter

The class `PrintWriter` is the preferred stream class for writing to a text file. An object of the class `PrintWriter` has the methods `print` and `println`, which are like the methods `System.out.print` and `System.out.println` that you can use for screen output. However, with an object of the class `PrintWriter`, the output goes to a text file. Display 10.1 contains a simple program that uses `PrintWriter` to send output to a text file. Let's look at the details of that program.

java.io

All the file I/O–related classes we introduce in this chapter are in the package `java.io`, so all our program files begin with import statements similar to the ones in Display 10.1.

The program in Display 10.1 creates a text file named `stuff.txt` that a person can read using an editor, or that another Java program can read. The program creates an object of the class `PrintWriter` as follows:

```
outputStream =
        new PrintWriter(new FileOutputStream("stuff.txt"));
```

opening a file

The variable `outputStream` is of type `PrintWriter` and is declared outside the `try` block. The preceding two lines of code connect the stream named `outputStream` to the file named `stuff.txt`. This is called **opening the file**. When you connect a file to a stream in this way, your program always starts with an empty file. If the file `stuff.txt` already exists, the old contents of stuff.txt will be lost. If the file stuff.txt does not exist, then a new, empty file named stuff.txt will be created.

We want to associate the output stream outputStream with the file named stuff.txt. However, the class PrintWriter has no constructor that takes a file name as its argument. So we use the class FileOutputStream to create a stream that can be used as an argument to a PrintWriter constructor. The expression

FileOutput Stream

```
new FileOutputStream("stuff.txt")
```

takes a file name as an argument and creates an anonymous object of the class FileOutputStream, which is then used as an argument to a constructor for the class PrintWriter as follows:

```
new PrintWriter(new FileOutputStream("stuff.txt"))
```

file name

This produces an object of the class PrintWriter that is connected to the file stuff.txt. Note that the name of the file, in this case, stuff.txt, is given as a String value and so is given in quotes.

reading the file name

If you want to read the file name from the keyboard, you could read the name to a variable of type String and use the String variable as the argument to the FileOutputStream constructor.

FileNot Found Exception

When you open a text file in the way just discussed, a FileNotFoundException can be thrown, and any such possible exception should be caught in a catch block. (Actually, it is the FileOutputStream constructor that might throw the FileNotFoundException, but the net effect is the same.)

Notice that the try block in Display 10.1 encloses only the opening of the file. That is the only place that an exception might be thrown. Also note that the variable outputStream is declared outside of the try block—this is so that this variable can be used outside of the try block. Remember, anything declared in a block (even in a try block) is local to the block.

Display 10.1   **Sending Output to a Text File** (part 1 of 2)

```
1  import java.io.PrintWriter;
2  import java.io.FileOutputStream;
3  import java.io.FileNotFoundException;

4  public class TextFileOutputDemo
5  {
6      public static void main(String[] args)
7      {
8          PrintWriter outputStream = null;
9          try
10         {
11             outputStream =
12                 new PrintWriter(new FileOutputStream("stuff.txt"));
13         }
14         catch (FileNotFoundException e)
```

(continued)

Display 10.1   Sending Output to a Text File (part 2 of 2)

```
15              {
16                      System.out.println("Error opening the file stuff.txt.");
17                      System.exit(0);
18              }

19              System.out.println("Writing to file.");

20              outputStream.println("The quick brown fox");
21              outputStream.println("jumps over the lazy dog.");

22              outputStream.close();

23              System.out.println("End of program.");
24      }
25  }
```

Sample Dialogue

```
Writing to file.
End of program.
```

FILE stuff.txt (after the program is run.)

```
The quick brown fox
jumps over the lazy dog.
```

*You can read this file
using a text editor.*

Opening a Text File for Writing Output

You create a stream of the class PrintWriter and connect it to a text file for writing as follows.

SYNTAX

```
PrintWriter Output_Stream_Name;
Output_Stream_Name =
        new PrintWriter(new FileOutputStream(File_Name));
```

EXAMPLE

```
PrintWriter outputStream = null;
outputStream =
        new PrintWriter(new FileOutputStream("stuff.txt"));
```

After this, you can use the methods println and print to write to the file.

When used in this way, the FileOutputStream constructor, and thus the PrintWriter constructor invocation, can throw a FileNotFoundException, which is a kind of IOException.

File Names

The rules for how you spell file names depend on your operating system, not on Java. When you give a file name to a Java constructor for a stream, you are not giving the constructor a Java identifier. You are giving the constructor a string corresponding to the file name. A suffix, such as `.txt` in `stuff.txt`, has no special meaning to a Java program. We are using the suffix `.txt` to indicate a text file, but that is just a common convention. You can use any file names that are allowed by your operating system.

A File Has Two Names

Every input file and every output file used by your program has two names: (1) the real file name that is used by the operating system and (2) the name of the stream that is connected to the file.

The stream name serves as a temporary name for the file and is the name that is primarily used within your program. After you connect the file to the stream, your program always refers to the file by using the stream name.

We said that when you open a text file for writing output to the file, the constructor might throw a `FileNotFoundException`. But in this situation you want to create a new file for output, so why would you care that the file was not found? The answer is simply that the exception is poorly named. A `FileNotFoundException` does not mean that the file was not found. In this case, it actually means that the file could not be created. A `FileNotFoundException` is thrown if it is impossible to create the file—for example, because the file name is already used for a directory (folder) name.

IOException

When dealing with file I/O, there are many situations in which your code might throw an exception of some class, such as `FileNotFoundException`. Many of these various exception classes are descended classes of the class `IOException`. The class `IOException` is the root class for various exception classes having to do with input and output.

A `FileNotFoundException` is a kind of `IOException`, so a `catch` block for an `IOException` would also work and would look more sensible. However, it is best to catch the most specific exception that you can, because that can give more information.

`println`   As illustrated in Display 10.1, the method `println` of the class `PrintWriter` works the same for writing to a text file as the method `System.out.println` works `print`   for writing to the screen. The class `PrintWriter` also has the methods `print` and

printf   printf, which behave just like System.out.print and System.out.printf except that the output goes to a text file. Display 10.2 describes some of the methods in the class PrintWriter.

Display 10.2   Some Methods of the Class PrintWriter (part 1 of 2)

PrintWriter and FileOutputStream are in the java.io package.

    public PrintWriter(OutputStream streamObject)

This is the only constructor you are likely to need. There is no constructor that accepts a file name as an argument. If you want to create a stream using a file name, use

    new PrintWriter(new FileOutputStream(*File_Name*))

When the constructor is used in this way, a blank file is created. If there already is a file named *File_Name*, then the old contents of the file are lost. If you want instead to append new text to the end of the old file contents, use

    new PrintWriter(new FileOutputStream(*File_Name*, true))

(For an explanation of the argument true, read the later subsection "Appending to a Text File.")

When used in either of these ways, the FileOutputStream constructor, and so the PrintWriter constructor invocation, can throw a FileNotFoundException, which is a kind of IOException.

If you want to create a stream using an object of the class File, you can use a File object in place of the *File_Name*. (The File class will be covered later in Section 10.3. We discuss it here so that you will have a more complete reference in this display, but you can ignore the reference to the class File until after you have read that section.)

    public void println(*Argument*)

The *Argument* can be a string, character, integer, floating-point number, boolean value, or any combination of these, connected with + signs. The *Argument* can also be any object, although it will not work as desired unless the object has a properly defined toString() method. The *Argument* is output to the file connected to the stream. After the *Argument* has been output, the line ends, and so the next output is sent to the next line.

    public void print(*Argument*)

This is the same as println, except that this method does not end the line, so the next output will be on the same line.

    public PrintWriter printf(*Argument*)

This is the same as System.out.printf, except that this method sends output to a text file rather than to the screen. It returns the calling object. However, we have always used printf as a void method.

Display 10.2   Some Methods of the Class `PrintWriter` (part 2 of 2)

```
public void close()
```

Closes the stream's connection to a file. The following method calls `flush` before closing the file:

```
public void flush()
```

Flushes the output stream. This forces an actual physical write to the file of any data that has been buffered and not yet physically written to the file. Normally, you should not need to invoke `flush`.

When your program is finished writing to a file, it should **close** the stream connected to that file. In Display 10.1, the stream connected to the file `stuff.txt` is closed with the statement

```
outputStream.close();
```

The class `PrintWriter`, and every other class for file output or file input streams, has a method named `close`. When this method is invoked, the system releases any resources used to connect the stream to the file and does any other housekeeping that is needed. If your program does not close a file before the program ends, Java will close it for you when the program ends, but it is safest to close the file with an explicit call to `close`.

buffered

buffer

Output streams connected to files are often **buffered**, which means that, rather than physically writing every instance of output data as soon as possible, the data is saved in a temporary location, known as a **buffer**; when enough data is accumulated in this temporary location, it is physically written to the file. This can add to efficiency, since physical writes to a file can be slow. The method `flush` causes a physical write to the file of any buffered data. The method `close` includes an invocation of the method `flush`.

Closing a File

When your program is finished writing to a file or reading from a file, it should close the stream connected to that file by invoking the method named `close`.

SYNTAX

```
Stream_Object.close();
```

EXAMPLE

```
outputStream.close();
inputStream.close();
```

It may seem like there is no reason to use the method `close` to close a file. If your program ends normally but without closing a file, the system will automatically close it for you. So why should you bother to close files with an explicit call to the method `close`? There are at least two reasons. First, if your program ends abnormally, then

Java may not be able to close the file for you. This could damage the file. In particular, if it is an output file, any buffered output will not have been physically written to the file. So, the file will be incomplete. The sooner you close a file, the less likely it is that this will happen. Second, if your program writes to a file and later reads from the same file, it must close the file after it is through writing to the file and then reopen the file for reading. (Java does have a class that allows a file to be opened for both reading and writing, which we will discuss later in Section 10.5.)

PITFALL: A `try` Block Is a Block

Notice that in Display 10.1, we declare the variable `outputStream` outside of the `try` block. If you were to move that declaration inside the `try` block, you would get a compiler error message. Let's see why.

Suppose you replace

```
PrintWriter outputStream = null;
try
{
    outputStream =
        new PrintWriter(new FileOutputStream("stuff.txt"));
}
```

in Display 10.1 with the following:

```
try
{
    PrintWriter outputStream =
        new PrintWriter(new FileOutputStream("stuff.txt"));
}
```

This replacement looks innocent enough, but it makes the variable `outputStream` a local variable for the `try` block, which would mean that you could not use `outputStream` outside of the `try` block. If you make this change and `try` to compile the changed program, you will get an error message saying that `outputStream`, when used outside the `try` block, is an undefined identifier. ■

PITFALL: Overwriting an Output File

When you connect a stream to a text file for writing to the text file, as illustrated by what follows, you always produce an empty file:

```
outputStream =
        new PrintWriter(new FileOutputStream("stuff.txt"));
```

If there is no file named `stuff.txt`, this will create an empty file named `stuff.txt`. If a file named `stuff.txt` already exists, then this will eliminate that file and create a new, empty file named `stuff.txt`. So if there is a file named `stuff.txt` before this file opening, then all the data in that file will be lost. The later section

PITFALL: (continued)

"The File Class" tells you how to test to see whether a file already exists so that you can avoid accidentally overwriting a file. The following subsection, "Appending to a Text File," shows you how to add data to a text file without losing the data that is already in the file. ∎

Appending to a Text File

When you open a text file for writing in the way we did it in Display 10.1, and a file with the given name already exists, the old contents are lost. However, sometimes you instead want to add the program output to the end of the file. This is called **appending to a file**. If you want to append program output to the file stuff.txt, connect the file to the stream outputStream in the following manner:

appending

```
outputStream =
    new PrintWriter(new FileOutputStream("stuff.txt", true ));
```

If the file stuff.txt does not already exist, Java will create an empty file of that name and append the output to the end of this empty file. So if there is no file named stuff.txt, the effect of opening the file is the same as in Display 10.1. However, if the file stuff.txt already exists, then the old contents will remain, and the program's output will be placed after the old contents of the file.

When appending to a text file in this way, you would still use the same try and catch blocks as in Display 10.1.

That second argument of true deserves a bit of explanation. Why did the designers use true to signal appending? Why not something such as the string "append"? The reason is that this version of the constructor for the class FileOutputStream was designed to also allow you to use a Boolean variable (or expression) to decide whether you append to an existing file or create a new file. For example, the following might be used:

```
System.out.println(
            "Enter A for append or N for a new file:");
char answer;
<Use your favorite way to read a single character into the variable answer.>
boolean append = (answer == 'A' || answer == 'a');
outputStream = new PrintWriter(
    new FileOutputStream("stuff.txt", append));
```

From this point on, your program writes to the file in exactly the same way that the program in Display 10.1 does. If the user answers with upper- or lowercase A, then any input will be added after the old file contents. If the user answers with upper- or lowercase N (or with anything other than an A), then any old contents of the file are lost.

TIP: toString Helps with Text File Output

In Chapter 4, we noted that if a class has a suitable toString() method and anObject is an object of that class, then anObject can be used as an argument to System.out.println, which will produce sensible output.[1] The same thing applies to the methods println and print of the class PrintWriter. Both println and print of the class PrintWriter can take any object as an argument and will produce reasonable output so long as the object has a sensible toString() method. ∎

Opening a Text File for Appending

To create an object of the class **PrintWriter** and connect it to a text file for appending to the end of the text already in the file, proceed as follows.

SYNTAX

```
Output_Stream_Name =
    new PrintWriter(
        new FileOutputStream(File_Name, True_Boolean_Expression));
```

EXAMPLE

```
PrintWriter outputStream;
outputStream =
    new PrintWriter(new FileOutputStream("stuff.txt", true));
```

After this statement, you can use the methods println and print to write to the file, and the new text will be written after the old text in the file.

(If you want to create a stream using an object of the class File, you can use a File object in place of the *File_Name*. The File class is discussed later in the section entitled "The File Class.")

When used in this way, the FileOutputStream constructor, and so the PrintWriter constructor invocation, can throw a FileNotFoundException, which is a kind of IOException.

MyProgrammingLab™

Self-Test Exercises

3. What kind of exception might be thrown by the following, and what would it indicate if this exception is thrown?

```
PrintWriter outputStream =
    new PrintWriter(new FileOutputStream("stuff.txt"));
```

---

[1]There is a more detailed discussion of this in Chapter 8, but you need not read Chapter 8 to use this fact.

Self-Test Exercises (continued)

4. What is wrong in the following code snippet?

```
PrintWriter outputStream = new
PrintWriter("EmployeeData.doc");
        outputStrem.println("Employee Details: \n");
```

5. Write some code that will create a stream named `outStream` that is a member of the class `PrintWriter`, and that connects this stream to a text file named `sam` so that your program can send output to the file. Do this so that the file `sam` always starts out empty. So, if there already is a file named `sam`, the old contents of `sam` are lost.

6. As in Self-Test Exercise 5, write some code that will create a stream named `outStream` that is a member of the class `PrintWriter`, and that connects this stream to a text file named `sam` so that your program can send output to the file. This time, however, do it in such a way that, if the file `sam` already exists, the old contents of `sam` will not be lost and the program output will be written after the old contents of the file.

7. The class `Person` was defined in Display 5.19 of Chapter 5. Suppose `mary` is an object of the class `Person`, which has a `toString` method defined, and suppose `outputStream` is connected to a text file as in Display 10.1. Will the following send sensible output to the file connected to `outputStream`?

```
outputStream.println(mary);
```

Reading from a Text File

VideoNote
Reading a Text File

The two most common stream classes used for reading from a text file are the `Scanner` class and the `BufferedReader` class. We will discuss both of these approaches to reading from a text file. The `Scanner` class offers a richer group of methods for reading from a text file and is our preferred class to use when reading from a text file. However, the `BufferedReader` class is also widely used and is a reasonable choice. You, or your instructor, will need to decide which class you will use.

Reading a Text File Using `Scanner`

The same `Scanner` class that we used for reading from the keyboard can also be used for reading from a text file. To do so, replace the argument `System.in` (in the `Scanner` constructor) with a suitable stream that is connected to the text file. This is a good illustration of the notion of a *stream*. The class `Scanner` does not care if its stream argument comes from the keyboard or from a text file.

The use of `Scanner` for reading from a text file is illustrated in Display 10.3, which contains a program that reads three numbers and a line of text from a text file named `morestuff.txt` and writes them back to the screen. The file `morestuff.txt` is a text file that a person could have created with a text editor or that a Java program could have created using `PrintWriter`.

opening a file

The program opens the `Scanner` stream and connects it to the text file `morestuff.txt` as follows:

```
Scanner inputStream = null;
  . . .
inputStream = new Scanner(new FileInputStream("stuff.txt"));
```

The class `Scanner`, like the class `PrintWriter`, has no constructor that takes a file name as its argument, so we need to use another class—in this case, the class `FileInputStream`—to convert the file name to an object that can be a suitable argument to the `Scanner` constructor.

Note that the methods `nextInt` and `nextLine` read from the text files in exactly the same way as they read from the keyboard. The other `Scanner` methods for reading input (given in Display 2.6 and repeated in Display 10.6) also behave the same when reading from a text file as they do when used to read from the keyboard.

Opening a Text File for Reading with `Scanner`

Create a stream of the class `Scanner` and connect it to a text file for reading as follows:

SYNTAX

```
Scanner Stream_Object =
            new Scanner(new FileInputStream(File_Name));
```

EXAMPLE

```
Scanner inputStream =
        new Scanner(new FileInputStream("morestuff.txt"));
```

After this statement, you can use the methods `nextInt`, `nextDouble`, `nextLine`, and so forth to read from the named text files just as you have used these methods to read from the keyboard.

When used in this way, the `FileInputStream` constructor, and hence the `Scanner` constructor invocation, can throw a `FileNotFoundException`, which is a kind of `IOException`.

`FileNotFoundException`

If your program attempts to open a file for reading and there is no such file, then a `FileNotFoundException` is thrown. As you saw earlier in this chapter, a `FileNotFoundException` is also thrown in some other situations. A `FileNotFoundException` is a kind of `IOException`.

Display 10.3   **Reading Input from a Text File Using `Scanner`** (part 1 of 2)

```java
1  import java.util.Scanner;
2  import java.io.FileInputStream;
3  import java.io.FileNotFoundException;
4
5  public class TextFileScannerDemo
6  {
7      public static void main(String[] args)
8      {
9          System.out.println("I will read three numbers and a line");
10         System.out.println("of text from the file morestuff.txt.");
11
12         Scanner inputStream = null;
13
14         try
15         {
16             inputStream =
17                 new Scanner(new FileInputStream("morestuff.txt"));
18         }
19         catch (FileNotFoundException e)
20         {
21             System.out.println("File morestuff.txt was not found");
22             System.out.println("or could not be opened.");
23             System.exit(0);
24         }
25         int n1 = inputStream.nextInt( );
26         int n2 = inputStream.nextInt( );
27         int n3 = inputStream.nextInt( );
28
29         inputStream.nextLine(); //To go to the next line
30
31         String line = inputStream.nextLine();
32
33         System.out.println("The three numbers read from the file are:");
34         System.out.println(n1 + ", " + n2 + ", and " + n3);
35
36         System.out.println("The line read from the file is:");
37         System.out.println(line);
38
39         inputStream.close( );
40     }
41 }
```

FILE `morestuff.txt`

*This file could have been made with a
text editor or by another Java program.*

```
1 2
3 4
Eat my shorts.
```

(continued)

Display 10.3 Reading Input from a Text File Using `Scanner` (part 2 of 2)

Screen Output

```
I will read three numbers and a line
of text from the file morestuff.txt.
The three numbers read from the file are:
1, 2, and 3
The line read from the file is:
Eat my shorts.
```

Testing for the End of a Text File with `Scanner`

When using the class `Scanner`, if your program tries to read beyond the end of the file with any of the input methods, such as `nextInt` or `nextLine`, then the method throws an exception. If all goes well and there are no problems, such as using `nextInt` when the input is not a correctly formed `int`, then the exception thrown will be `NoSuchElementException`. This throwing of a `NoSuchElementException` can be used to signal the end of input. However, there is a more robust way of testing for the end of input from a text file. Each of the input methods (such as `nextInt` and `nextLine`) has a corresponding method (such `hasNextInt` and `hasNextLine`) that checks to see if there is any more well-formed input of the appropriate type. The nice thing about these methods is that they report when there is not a suitable next token for any reason; they do not check only for the end of a file. For example, `hasNextInt` returns `false` if there is no more file input of any kind or if the next token is not a well-formed `int` value. It returns `true` if there is a well-formed `int` as the next token.

A sample program that illustrates the use of `hasNextLine` to test for the end of input is given in Display 10.4. A sample program that illustrates the use of `hasNextInt` to test for the end of input is given in Display 10.5. A summary of some of the methods in the `Scanner` class is given in Display 10.6.

Checking for the End of a Text File with `Scanner`

You can check for the end of input with methods such as `hasNextInt`, `hasNextLine`, and so forth.

Display 10.4   Checking for the End of a Text File with `hasNextLine` (part 1 of 2)

```
1   import java.util.Scanner;
2   import java.io.FileInputStream;
3   import java.io.FileNotFoundException;
4   import java.io.PrintWriter;
5   import java.io.FileOutputStream;
6
7   public class HasNextLineDemo
8   {
9       public static void main(String[] args)
10      {
11          Scanner inputStream = null;
12          PrintWriter outputStream = null;

13          try
14          {
15           inputStream =
16               new Scanner(new FileInputStream("original.txt"));
17           outputStream = new PrintWriter(
18                       new FileOutputStream("numbered.txt"));
19          }
20          catch(FileNotFoundException e)
21          {
22             System.out.println("Problem opening files.");
23             System.exit(0);
24          }

25          String line = null;
26          int count = 0;
27          while (inputStream.hasNextLine( ))
28          {
29              line = inputStream.nextLine( );
30              count++;
31              outputStream.println(count + " " + line);
32          }

33          inputStream.close( );
34          outputStream.close( );
35      }
36  }
```

```
File original.txt

Little Miss Muffet
sat on a tuffet
eating her curves away.
Along came a spider
who sat down beside her
and said "Will you marry me?"
```

(continued)

Display 10.4 Checking for the End of a Text File with `hasNextLine` (part 2 of 2)

```
File numbered.txt (after the program is run)

    1 Little Miss Muffet
    2 sat on a tuffet
    3 eating her curves away.
    4 Along came a spider
    5 who sat down beside her
    6 and said "Will you marry me?"
```

Display 10.5 Checking for the End of a Text File with `hasNextInt`

```
1    import java.util.Scanner;
2    import java.io.FileInputStream;
3    import java.io.FileNotFoundException;

4    public class HasNextIntDemo
5    {
6        public static void main(String[] args)
7        {
8            Scanner inputStream = null;

9            try
10           {
11               inputStream =
12                   new Scanner(new FileInputStream("data.txt"));
13           }
14           catch (FileNotFoundException e)
15           {
16               System.out.println("File data.txt was not found");
17               System.out.println("or could not be opened.");
18               System.exit(0);
19           }

20           int next, sum = 0;
21           while (inputStream.hasNextInt( ))
22           {
23               next = inputStream.nextInt( );
24               sum = sum + next;
25           }

26           inputStream.close( );

27           System.out.println("The sum of the numbers is " + sum);
28       }
29   }
```

```
File data.txt

    1 2
    3 4 hi 5
```

Reading ends when either the end of the file is reached or a token that is not an int is reached. So, the 5 is never read.

Screen Output

```
The sum of the numbers is 10
```

Display 10.6   Methods in the Class `Scanner` (part 1 of 4)

`Scanner` is in the `java.util` package.

```
public Scanner(InputStream streamObject)
```

There is no constructor that accepts a file name as an argument. If you want to create a stream using a file name, you can use

```
new Scanner(new FileInputStream(File_Name))
```

When used in this way, the `FileInputStream` constructor, and thus the `Scanner` constructor invocation, can throw a `FileNotFoundException`, which is a kind of `IOException`.

To create a stream connected to the keyboard, use

```
new Scanner(System.in)
```

```
public Scanner(File fileObject)
```

The `File` class will be covered in the section entitled "The `File` Class," later in this chapter. We discuss it here so that you will have a more complete reference in this display, but you can ignore this entry until after you have read that section.

If you want to create a stream using a file name, you can use

```
new Scanner(new File(File_Name))
```

```
public int nextInt()
```

Returns the next token as an `int`, provided the next token is a well-formed string representation of an `int`.

Throws a `NoSuchElementException` if there are no more tokens.

Throws an `InputMismatchException` if the next token is not a well-formed string representation of an `int`.

Throws an `IllegalStateException` if the `Scanner` stream is closed.

```
public boolean hasNextInt()
```

Returns `true` if the next token is a well-formed string representation of an `int`; otherwise returns `false`.

Throws an `IllegalStateException` if the `Scanner` stream is closed.

```
public long nextLong()
```

Returns the next token as a `long`, provided the next token is a well-formed string representation of a `long`.

Throws a `NoSuchElementException` if there are no more tokens.

Throws an `InputMismatchException` if the next token is not a well-formed string representation of a `long`.

Throws an `IllegalStateException` if the `Scanner` stream is closed.

(continued)

Display 10.6   **Methods in the Class `Scanner`** (part 2 of 4)

`public boolean hasNextLong()`

Returns `true` if the next token is a well-formed string representation of a `long`; otherwise returns `false`.

Throws an `IllegalStateException` if the `Scanner` stream is closed.

`public byte nextByte()`

Returns the next token as a `byte`, provided the next token is a well-formed string representation of a `byte`.

Throws a `NoSuchElementException` if there are no more tokens.

Throws an `InputMismatchException` if the next token is not a well-formed string representation of a `byte`.

Throws an `IllegalStateException` if the `Scanner` stream is closed.

`public boolean hasNextByte()`

Returns `true` if the next token is a well-formed string representation of a `byte`; otherwise returns `false`.

Throws an `IllegalStateException` if the `Scanner` stream is closed.

`public short nextShort()`

Returns the next token as a `short`, provided the next token is a well-formed string representation of a `short`.

Throws a `NoSuchElementException` if there are no more tokens.

Throws an `InputMismatchException` if the next token is not a well-formed string representation of a `short`.

Throws an `IllegalStateException` if the `Scanner` stream is closed.

`public boolean hasNextShort()`

Returns `true` if the next token is a well-formed string representation of a `short`; otherwise returns `false`.

Throws an `IllegalStateException` if the `Scanner` stream is closed.

`public double nextDouble()`

Returns the next token as a `double`, provided the next token is a well-formed string representation of a `double`.

Throws a `NoSuchElementException` if there are no more tokens.

Throws an `InputMismatchException` if the next token is not a well-formed string representation of a `double`.

Throws an `IllegalStateException` if the `Scanner` stream is closed.

Display 10.6   Methods in the Class `Scanner` (part 3 of 4)

```
public boolean hasNextDouble()
```

Returns `true` if the next token is a well-formed string representation of a `double`; otherwise returns `false`.

Throws an `IllegalStateException` if the `Scanner` stream is closed.

```
public float nextFloat()
```

Returns the next token as a `float`, provided the next token is a well-formed string representation of a `float`.

Throws a `NoSuchElementException` if there are no more tokens.

Throws an `InputMismatchException` if the next token is not a well-formed string representation of a `float`.

Throws an `IllegalStateException` if the `Scanner` stream is closed.

```
public boolean hasNextFloat()
```

Returns `true` if the next token is a well-formed string representation of a `float`; otherwise returns `false`.

Throws an `IllegalStateException` if the `Scanner` stream is closed.

```
public String next()
```

Returns the next token.

Throws a `NoSuchElementException` if there are no more tokens.

Throws an `IllegalStateException` if the `Scanner` stream is closed.

```
public boolean hasNext()
```

Returns `true` if there is another token. May wait for a next token to enter the stream.

Throws an `IllegalStateException` if the `Scanner` stream is closed.

```
public boolean nextBoolean()
```

Returns the next token as a `boolean` value, provided the next token is a well-formed string representation of a `boolean`.

Throws a `NoSuchElementException` if there are no more tokens.

Throws an `InputMismatchException` if the next token is not a well-formed string representation of a `boolean` value.

Throws an `IllegalStateException` if the `Scanner` stream is closed.

```
public boolean hasNextBoolean()
```

Returns `true` if the next token is a well-formed string representation of a `boolean` value; otherwise returns `false`.

Throws an `IllegalStateException` if the `Scanner` stream is closed.

(continued)

Display 10.6 Methods in the Class `Scanner` (part 4 of 4)

```
public String nextLine()
```

Returns the rest of the current input line. Note that the line terminator `'\n'` is read and discarded; it is not included in the string returned.

Throws a `NoSuchElementException` if there are no more lines.

Throws an `IllegalStateException` if the Scanner stream is closed.

```
public boolean hasNextLine()
```

Returns `true` if there is a next line. May wait for a next line to enter the stream.

Throws an `IllegalStateException` if the `Scanner` stream is closed.

```
public Scanner useDelimiter(String newDelimiter);
```

Changes the delimiter for input so that `newDelimiter` will be the only delimiter that separates words or numbers. See the subsection "Other Input Delimiters" in Chapter 2 for the details. (You can use this method to set the delimiters to a more complex pattern than just a single string, but we are not covering that.)

Returns the calling object, but we have always used it as a `void` method.

Unchecked Exceptions

The exception classes `NoSuchElementException`, `InputMismatchException`, and `IllegalStateException` are all unchecked exceptions, which means that an exception of any of these classes is not required to be caught or declared in a `throws` clause.

Self-Test Exercises

8. Write some code that will create a stream named `fileIn` that is a member of the class `Scanner`. It should connect the stream to a text file named `sally` so that your program can read input from the text file `sally`.

9. Might the method `nextLine` in the class `Scanner` throw an exception? If so, what type of exception?

10. How does the method `nextLine` treat a `'\n'` character found at the end of the line?

Self-Test Exercises (continued)

11. Would it be accurate if you directly write the code snippet,

```
Scanner inputStream =
        new Scanner(new FileInputStream("morestuff.txt"));
```

without using the try block?

Reading a Text File Using BufferedReader

Buffered Reader

Until the Scanner class was introduced with version 5.0 of Java, the class BufferedReader was the preferred stream class to use for reading from a text file. It is still a commonly used class for reading from a text file. The use of BufferedReader is illustrated in Display 10.7, which contains a program that reads two lines from a text file named morestuff2.txt and writes them back to the screen. The file morestuff2.txt is a text file that a person could have created with a text editor or that a Java program could have created using PrintWriter.

opening a file

The program opens the text file morestuff2.txt as follows:

```
BufferedReader inputStream =
        new BufferedReader(new FileReader("morestuff2.txt"));
```

The class BufferedReader, like the classes PrintWriter and Scanner, has no constructor that takes a file name as its argument, so we need to use another class—in this case, the class FileReader—to convert the file name to an object that can be an argument to BufferedReader.

readLine

An object of the class BufferedReader that is connected to a text file, as in Display 10.7, has a method named readLine that is like the method nextLine of the Scanner class. This use of readLine to read from a text file is illustrated in Display 10.7.

Display 10.8 describes some of the methods in the class BufferedReader. Notice that there are only two methods for reading from a text file, readLine and read. We have already discussed readLine.

Display 10.7   Reading Input from a Text File Using **BufferedReader** (part 1 of 2)

```
1    import java.io.BufferedReader;
2    import java.io.FileReader;
3    import java.io.FileNotFoundException;
4    import java.io.IOException;

5    public class TextFileInputDemo
6    {
7        public static void main(String[] args)
8        {
```

(continued)

Display 10.7   **Reading Input from a Text File Using `BufferedReader`** (part 2 of 2)

```
 9              try
10              {
11                      BufferedReader inputStream =
12                         new BufferedReader(new FileReader("morestuff2.txt"));

13                      String line = inputStream.readLine();
14                      System.out.println(
15                                  "The first line read from the file is:");
16                      System.out.println(line);

18                      line = inputStream.readLine();
19                      System.out.println(
20                                  "The second line read from the file is:");
21                      System.out.println(line);
22                      inputStream.close();
23              }
24          catch(FileNotFoundException e)
25              {
26                      System.out.println("File morestuff2.txt was not found");
27                      System.out.println("or could not be opened.");
28              }
29          catch(IOException e)
30              {
31                      System.out.println("Error reading from morestuff2.txt.");
32              }
33          }
34      }
```

FILE `morestuff2.txt`

1 2 3
Jack jump over
the candle stick.

*This file could have been made with a
text editor or by another Java program.*

Screen Output

```
The first line read from the file is:
1 2 3
The second line read from the file is:
Jack jump over
```

Opening a Text File for Reading with `BufferedReader`

Create a stream of the class `BufferedReader` and connect it to a text file for reading as follows:

SYNTAX

```
BufferedReader Stream_Object =
              new BufferedReader(new FileReader(File_Name));
```

EXAMPLE

```
BufferedReader inputStream =
        new BufferedReader(new FileReader("morestuff2.txt"));
```

After this statement, you can use the methods `readLine` and `read` to read from the file.

When used in this way, the `FileReader` constructor, and hence the `BufferedReader` constructor invocation, can throw a `FileNotFoundException`, which is a kind of `IOException`.

Display 10.8   **Some Methods of the Class `BufferedReader`** (part 1 of 2)

`BufferedReader` and `FileReader` are in the `java.io` package.

   `public BufferedReader(Reader readerObject)`

This is the only constructor you are likely to need. There is no constructor that accepts a file name as an argument. If you want to create a stream using a file name, use

   `new BufferedReader(new FileReader(File_Name))`

When used in this way, the `FileReader` constructor, and thus the `BufferedReader` constructor invocation, can throw a `FileNotFoundException`, which is a kind of `IOException`.

The `File` class will be covered later in the section entitled "The `File` Class." We discuss it here so that you will have a more complete reference in this display, but you can ignore the following reference to the class `File` until after you have read that section.

If you want to create a stream using an object of the class `File`, use

   `new BufferedReader(new FileReader(File_Object))`

When used in this way, the `FileReader` constructor, and thus the `BufferedReader` constructor invocation, can throw a `FileNotFoundException`, which is a kind of `IOException`.

   `public String readLine()throws IOException`

Reads a line of input from the input stream and returns that line. If the read goes beyond the end of the file, `null` is returned. (Note that an `EOFException` is not thrown at the end of a file. The end of a file is signaled by returning `null`.)

(continued)

Display 10.8   Some Methods of the Class `BufferedReader` (part 2 of 2)

```
public int read()throws IOException
```
Reads a single character from the input stream and returns that character as an `int` value. If the read goes beyond the end of the file, then `-1` is returned. Note that the value is returned as an `int`. To obtain a `char`, you must perform a type cast on the value returned. The end of a file is signaled by returning `-1`. (All of the "real" characters return a positive integer.)

```
public long skip(long n) throws IOException
```
Skips n characters.

```
public void close()throws IOException
```
Closes the stream's connection to a file.

read method

The method `read` reads a single character. But note that `read` returns a value of type `int` that corresponds to the character read; it does not return the character itself. Thus, to get the character, you must use a type cast, as in

```
char next = (char)(inputStream.read());
```

If `inputStream` is in the class `BufferedReader` and is connected to a text file, this will set `next` equal to the first character in the file that has not yet been read.

Notice that the program in Display 10.7 catches two kinds of exceptions, `FileNotFoundException` and `IOException`. An attempt to open the file may throw a `FileNotFoundException`, and any of the invocations of `inputStream.readLine()` may throw an `IOException`. Because `FileNotFoundException` is a kind of `IOException`, you could use only the `catch` block for `IOException`. However, if you were to do this, then you would get less information if an exception were thrown. If you use only one `catch` block and an exception is thrown, you will not know if the problem occurred when opening the file or when reading from the file after it was opened.

MyProgrammingLab™   ## Self-Test Exercises

12. Write some code that will create a stream named `fileIn` that is a member of the class `BufferedReader` and that connects the stream to a text file named `joe` so that your program can read input from the text file `joe`.

13. What is the type of a value returned by the method `readLine` in the class `BufferedReader`? What is the type of a value returned by the method `read` in the class `BufferedReader`?

14. How do the methods `read` and `readLine` in the class `BufferedReader` signal the end of file?

15. One difference between the `try` blocks in Display 10.1 and Display 10.7 is that the `try` block in Display 10.1 encloses only the opening of the file, while the `try` block in Display 10.7 encloses most of the action in the program. Why is the `try` block in Display 10.7 larger than the one in Display 10.1?

16. Might the following throw an exception that needs to be caught or declared in a `throws` clause?

```
BufferedReader inputStream =
    new BufferedReader(new FileReader("morestuff2.txt"));
```

(The stream `inputStream` would be used to read from the text file `morestuff2.txt`.)

TIP: Reading Numbers with `BufferedReader`

Unlike the `Scanner` class, the class `BufferedReader` has no methods to read a number from a text file. You must write your code to read the number as a string and convert the string to a value of a numeric type, such as `int` or `double`. To read a single number on a line by itself, read it using the method `readLine`, and then use `Integer.parseInt`, `Double.parseDouble`, or some similar method to convert the string read to a number. If there are multiple numbers on a single line, read the line using `readLine` and then use the `StringTokenizer` class to decompose the string into tokens. Next, use `Integer.parseInt` or a similar method to convert each token to a number.

   `Integer.parseInt`, `Double.parseDouble`, and similar methods that convert strings to numbers are explained in Chapter 5 in the subsection entitled "Wrapper Classes." The `StringTokenizer` class is discussed in Chapter 4 in the starred subsection entitled "The `StringTokenizer` Class". ■

Testing for the End of a Text File with `BufferedReader`

When using the class `BufferedReader`, if your program tries to read beyond the end of the file with either of the methods `readLine` or `read`, then the method returns a special value to signal that the end of the file has been reached. When `readLine` tries to read beyond the end of a file, it returns the value `null`. Thus, your program can test for the end of the file by testing to see if `readLine` returns `null`. This technique is illustrated in Display 10.9. When the method `read` tries to read beyond the end of a file, it returns the value `-1`. Because the `int` value corresponding to each ordinary character is positive, this can be used to test for the end of a file.

Checking for the End of a Text File with `BufferedReader`

The method `readLine` of the class `BufferedReader` returns `null` when it tries to read beyond the end of a text file. The method `read` of the class `BufferedReader` returns `-1` when it tries to read beyond the end of a text file.

Display 10.9   Checking for the End of a Text File with `BufferedReader` (part 1 of 2)

```
 1   import java.io.BufferedReader;
 2   import java.io.FileReader;
 3   import java.io.PrintWriter;
 4   import java.io.FileOutputStream;
 5   import java.io.FileNotFoundException;
 6   import java.io.IOException;

 7   /**
 8    Makes numbered.txt the same as original.txt, but with each line numbered.
 9   */
10   public class TextEOFDemo
11   {
12       public static void main(String[] args)
13       {
14           try
15           {
16               BufferedReader inputStream =
17                       new BufferedReader(new FileReader("original.txt"));
18               PrintWriter outputStream =
19                       new PrintWriter(new FileOutputStream("numbered.txt"));

20               int count = 0;
21               String line = inputStream.readLine();
22               while (line != null)
23               {
24                   count++;
25                   outputStream.println(count + " " + line);
26                   line = inputStream.readLine();
27               }
28               inputStream.close();
29               outputStream.close();
30           }
31           catch(FileNotFoundException e)
32           {
33               System.out.println("Problem opening files.");
34           }
35           catch(IOException e)
36           {
37               System.out.println("Error reading from original.txt.");
38           }
39       }
40   }
```

Display 10.9   Checking for the End of a Text File with `BufferedReader` (part 2 of 2)

FILE `original.txt`

```
Little Miss Muffet
sat on a tuffet
eating her curves away.
Along came a spider
who sat down beside her
and said "Will you marry me?"
```

FILE `numbered.txt` (after the program is run)

```
1 Little Miss Muffet
2 sat on a tuffet
3 eating her curves away.
4 Along came a spider
5 who sat down beside her
6 and said "Will you marry me?"
```

If your version of `numbered.txt` *has numbered blank lines after line 6, that means you had blank lines at the end of* `original.txt`.

Self-Test Exercises

17. How do you read a `double` value from a text file using the class `BufferedReader`?

18. How do you read multiple numbers from a text file using the class `BufferedReader`?

19. What is the type of the value returned by the method `read` in the class `BufferedReader`?

20. The method `read` in the class `BufferedReader` reads a single character from the file. Is it accurate to write

    ```
    char next = inputStream.read();
    ```
    if `inputStream` is in the class `BufferedReader`, and connected to a text file?

21. Does the program in Display 10.9 work correctly if `original.txt` is an empty file?

Path Names

When giving a file name as an argument to a constructor for opening a file in any of the ways we have discussed, you may use a simple file name, in which case it is assumed that the file is in the same directory (folder) as the one in which the program is run. You can also use a full or relative path name.

path names   A **path name** not only gives the name of the file, but also tells what directory (folder) the file is in. A **full path name**, as the name suggests, gives a complete path name, starting from the root directory. A **relative path name** gives the path to the file, starting with the directory that your program is in. The way that you specify path names depends on your particular operating system.

A typical UNIX path name is

```
/user/sallyz/data/data.txt
```

To create a `BufferedReader` input stream connected to this file, use

```
BufferedReader inputStream =
        new BufferedReader(
            new FileReader("/user/sallyz/data/data.txt"));
```

Windows uses \ instead of / in path names. A typical Windows path name is

```
C:\dataFiles\goodData\data.txt
```

To create a `BufferedReader` input stream connected to this file, use

```
BufferedReader inputStream =
    new BufferedReader(
        new FileReader("C:\\dataFiles\\goodData\\data.txt"));
```

using \,
\\, or /

Note that you need to use \\ in place of \, since otherwise Java will interpret a backslash paired with a character, such as \d, as an escape character. Although you must worry about using a backslash (\) in a quoted string, this problem does not occur with path names read in from the keyboard.

One way to avoid these escape character problems altogether is to always use UNIX conventions when writing path names. A Java program will accept a path name written in either Windows or UNIX format, even if it is run on a computer with an operating system that does not match the syntax. Thus, an alternate way to create a `BufferedReader` input stream connected to the Windows file

```
C:\dataFiles\goodData\data.txt
```

is the following:

```
BufferedReader inputStream =
    new BufferedReader(
        new FileReader("C:/dataFiles/goodData/data.txt"));
```

Nested Constructor Invocations

Expressions with two constructors, such as the following, are common when dealing with Java's library of I/O classes:

```
new BufferedReader(new FileReader("original.txt"))
```

This is a manifestation of the general approach to how Java I/O libraries work. Each I/O class serves one or a small number of functions. To obtain full functionality, you normally need to combine two (or more) class constructors. For example, in the previous code, the object `new FileReader("original.txt")` establishes a connection with the file `original.txt` but provides only very primitive methods for input. The constructor for `BufferedReader` takes this file reader object and adds a richer collection of input methods. In these cases, the inner object, such as `new FileReader("original.txt")`, is transformed into an instance variable of the outer object, such as `BufferedReader`.

Self-Test Exercises

22. Of the classes `PrintWriter`, `Scanner`, `BufferedReader`, `FileReader`, and `FileOutputStream`, which have a constructor that accepts a file name as an argument so that the stream created by the constructor invocation is connected to the named file?

23. Is the following legal?

```
FileReader readerObject =
            new FileReader("myFile.txt");
BufferedReader inputStream =
            new BufferedReader(readerObject);
```

`System.in`, `System.out`, and `System.err`

The streams `System.in`, `System.out`, and `System.err` are three streams that are automatically available to your Java code. You have already been using `System.in` and `System.out`. `System.err` is just like `System.out`, except that it has a different name. For example, both of the following statements will send the string `"Hello"` to the screen so the screen receives two lines, each containing `"Hello"`:

```
System.out.println("Hello");
System.err.println("Hello");
```

The output stream `System.out` is intended to be used for normal output from code that is not in trouble. `System.err` is meant to be used for error messages.

redirecting output   Having two different standard output streams can be handy when you redirect output. For example, you can redirect the regular output to one file and redirect the error messages to a different file. Java allows you to redirect any of these three standard streams to or from a file (or other I/O device). This is done with the static methods `setIn`, `setOut`, and `setErr` of the class `System`.

For example, suppose your code connects the output stream `errStream` (of a type to be specified later) to a text file. You can then redirect the stream `System.err` to this text file as follows:

```
System.setErr(errStream);
```

If the following appears later in your code,

```
System.out.println("Hello from System.out.");
System.err.println("Hello from System.err.");
```

then `"Hello from System.out."` will be written to the screen, but `"Hello from System.err."` will be written to the file connected to the output stream `errStream`. A simple program illustrating this is given in Display 10.10.

Note that the arguments to the redirecting methods must be of the types shown in the following headings, and that these are classes we do not discuss in this book:

```
public static void setIn(InputStream inStream)
public static void setOut(PrintStream outStream)
public static void setErr(PrintStream outStream)
```

None of the input or output streams we constructed in our previous programs are of a type suitable to be an argument to any of these redirection methods. Space constraints keep us from giving any more details on the stream classes that are suitable for producing arguments for these redirection methods. However, you can use Display 10.10 as a model to allow you to redirect either System.err or System.out to a text file of your choice.

MyProgrammingLab™   ## Self-Test Exercises

24. Suppose you want the program in Display 10.10 to send an error message to the screen and regular (System.out) output to the file errormessages.txt. (This is the reverse of what the program in Display 10.10 does.) How would you change the program in Display 10.10?

25. Suppose you want the program in Display 10.10 to send all output (both System.out and System.err) to the file errormessages.txt. How would you change the program in Display 10.10?

Display 10.10   Redirecting Error Messages (part 1 of 2)

```
1   import java.io.PrintStream;
2   import java.io.FileOutputStream;
3   import java.io.FileNotFoundException;

4   public class RedirectionDemo
5   {
6       public static void main(String[] args)
7       {                                              Note the
8           PrintStream errStream = null;              stream
9           try                                        classes
10          {                                          used.
11              errStream =
12                  new PrintStream(
13                      new FileOutputStream("errormessages.txt"));
14          }
15          catch(FileNotFoundException e)
16          {
17              System.out.println(
18                      "Error opening file with FileOutputStream.");
19              System.exit(0);
20          }
```

Display 10.10   **Redirecting Error Messages** (part 2 of 2)

```
21          System.setErr(errStream);

22          System.err.println("Hello from System.err.");
23          System.out.println("Hello from System.out.");
24          System.err.println("Hello again from System.err.");

25          errStream.close();
26      }
27 }
```

None of `System.in`, `System.out`, *or* `System.err` *needs to be closed, but the streams you create should be explicitly closed.*

FILE `errormessages.txt`

```
Hello from System.err.
Hello again from System.err.
```

Screen Output

```
Hello from System.out.
```

10.3 The `File` Class

The scars of others should teach us caution.

SAINT JEROME

In this section, we describe the class `File`, which is not really an I/O stream class but is often used in conjunction with file I/O. The class `File` is so important to file I/O programming that it was even placed in the `java.io` package.

Programming with the `File` Class

The `File` class contains methods that allow you to check various properties of a file, such as whether there is a file with a specified name, whether the file can be written to, and so forth. Display 10.11 gives a sample program that uses the class `File` with text files. (The class `File` works the same with binary files as it does with text files.)

abstract name   Note that the `File` class constructor takes a name, known as the **abstract name**, as an (string) argument. So the `File` class really checks properties of names. For example, the method `exists` tests whether there is a file with the abstract name. Moreover, the abstract name may be a potential directory (folder) name. For example, the method `isDirectory` tests whether the abstract name is the name of a directory (folder). The abstract name may be either a relative path name (which includes the case of a simple file name) or a full path name.

Display 10.12 lists some of the methods in the class `File`.

The `File` Class

The `File` class is like a wrapper class for file names. The constructor for the class `File` takes a string as an argument and produces an object that can be thought of as the file with that name. You can use the `File` object and methods of the class `File` to answer questions, such as the following: Does the file exist? Does your program have permission to read the file? Does your program have permission to write to the file? Display 10.14 has a summary of some of the methods for the class `File`.

EXAMPLE

```
File fileObject = new File("data.txt");
if ( ! fileObject.canRead())
    System.out.println("File data.txt is not readable.");
```

Display 10.11   Using the `File` Class (part 1 of 2)

```
1   import java.util.Scanner;
2   import java.io.File;
3   import java.io.PrintWriter;
4   import java.io.FileOutputStream;
5   import java.io.FileNotFoundException;
6   public class FileClassDemo
7   {
8       public static void main(String[] args)
9       {
10          Scanner keyboard = new Scanner(System.in);
11          String line = null;
12          String fileName = null;

13          System.out.println("I will store a line of text for you.");
14          System.out.println("Enter the line of text:");
15          line = keyboard.nextLine();
16          System.out.println("Enter a file name to hold the line:");
17          fileName = keyboard.nextLine();
18          File fileObject = new File(fileName);

20          while (fileObject.exists())
21          {
22              System.out.println("There already is a file named "
23                                          + fileName);
24              System.out.println("Enter a different file name:");
25              fileName = keyboard.nextLine();
26              fileObject = new File(fileName);
27          }
```

```
28          PrintWriter outputStream = null;   If you wish, you can use fileObject
29          try                                instead of fileName as the argument to
30          {                                  FileOutputStream.
31              outputStream =
32                  new PrintWriter(new FileOutputStream(fileName));
33          }
34          catch(FileNotFoundException e)
35          {
36              System.out.println("Error opening the file " + fileName);
37              System.exit(0);
38          }

39          System.out.println("Writing \"" + line + "\"");
40          System.out.println("to the file" + fileName);
41          outputStream.println(line);

42          outputStream.close();
43          System.out.println("Writing completed.");
44      }
45  }
```

Sample Dialogue

The dialogue assumes that there already is a file named myLine.txt but that there is no file named mySaying.txt.

```
I will store a line of text for you.
Enter the line of text:
May the hair on your toes grow long and curly.
Enter a file name to hold the line:
myLine.txt
There already is a file named myLine.txt
Enter a different file name:
mySaying.txt
Writing "May the hair on your toes grow long and curly."
to the file mySaying.txt
Writing completed.
```

Display 10.12   Some Methods in the Class File (part 1 of 3)

File is in the java.io package.

`public File(String File_Name)`

A constructor. *File_Name* can be either a full or a relative path name (which includes the case of a simple file name). *File_Name* is referred to as the **abstract path name**.

`public boolean exists()`

Tests whether there is a file with the abstract path name.

(continued)

Display 10.12 Some Methods in the Class `File` (part 2 of 3)

---

    public boolean canRead()

Tests whether the program can read from the file. Returns `true` if the file named by the abstract path name exists and is readable by the program; otherwise returns `false`.

    public boolean setReadOnly()

Sets the file represented by the abstract path name to be read only. Returns `true` if successful; otherwise returns `false`.

    public boolean canWrite()

Tests whether the program can write to the file. Returns `true` if the file named by the abstract path name exists and is writable by the program; otherwise returns `false`.

    public boolean delete()

Tries to delete the file or directory named by the abstract path name. A directory must be empty to be removed. Returns `true` if it was able to delete the file or directory. Returns `false` if it was unable to delete the file or directory.

    public boolean createNewFile()throws IOException

Creates a new empty file named by the abstract path name, provided that a file of that name does not already exist. Returns `true` if successful, and returns `false` otherwise.

    public String getName()

Returns the last name in the abstract path name (that is, the simple file name). Returns the empty string if the abstract path name is the empty string.

    public String getPath()

Returns the abstract path name as a `String` value.

    public boolean renameTo(File *New_Name*)

Renames the file represented by the abstract path name to *New_Name*. Returns `true` if successful; otherwise returns `false`. *New_Name* can be a relative or absolute path name. This may require moving the file. Whether or not the file can be moved is system dependent.

    public boolean isFile()

Returns `true` if a file exists that is named by the abstract path name and the file is a normal file; otherwise returns `false`. The meaning of *normal* is system dependent. Any file created by a Java program is guaranteed to be normal.

    public boolean isDirectory()

Returns `true` if a directory (folder) exists that is named by the abstract path name; otherwise returns `false`.

    public boolean mkdir()

Makes a directory named by the abstract path name. Will not create parent directories. See `mkdirs`, which follows. Returns `true` if successful; otherwise returns `false`.

Display 10.12   **Some Methods in the Class `File`** (part 3 of 3)

```
public boolean mkdirs()
```

Makes a directory named by the abstract path name. Will create any necessary but nonexistent parent directories. Returns `true` if successful; otherwise returns `false`. Note that if it fails, then some of the parent directories may have been created.

```
public long length()
```

Returns the length in bytes of the file named by the abstract path name. If the file does not exist or the abstract path name designates a directory, then the value returned is not specified and may be anything.

MyProgrammingLab™

Self-Test Exercises

26. Write a complete (although simple) Java program that tests whether or not the directory (folder) containing the program also contains a file named `Sally.txt`. The program has no input, and the only output tells whether or not there is a file named `Sally.txt`.

27. Write a complete Java program that asks the user for a file name, tests whether the file exists, and, if the file exists, asks the user whether or not it should be deleted. It then either deletes or does not delete the file as the user requests.

10.4 Binary Files ★

A little more than kin, and less than kind.

WILLIAM SHAKESPEARE, *Hamlet*

Binary files store data in the same format that is used in the computer's memory to store the values of variables. For example, a value of type `int` is stored as the same sequence of bytes (same sequence of zeros and ones) whether it is stored in an `int` variable in memory or in a binary file. So, no conversion of any kind needs to be performed when you store or retrieve a value in a binary file. This is why binary files can be handled more efficiently than text files.

Java binary files are unlike binary files in other programming languages in that they are portable. A binary file created by a Java program can be moved from one computer to another and still be read by a Java program—but only by a Java program. They cannot normally be read with a text editor or with a program written in any programming language other than Java.

The preferred stream classes for processing binary files are `ObjectInputStream` and `ObjectOutputStream`. Each has methods to read or write data one byte at a time. These streams can also automatically convert numbers and characters to bytes that can be stored in a binary file. They allow your program to be written as if the data placed in the file, or read from the file, is not just bytes but also strings or items of any of Java's primitive data types, such as int, char, and double, or even objects of classes you define. If you do not need to access your files using an editor, then the easiest and most efficient way to read data from and write data to files is to use binary files in the way we describe here.

We conclude this section with a discussion of how you can use ObjectOutputStream and ObjectInputStream to write and later read objects of any class you define. This will let you store objects of the classes you define in binary files and later read them back, all with the same convenience and efficiency that you get when storing strings and primitive type data in binary files.

Writing Simple Data to a Binary File

The class ObjectOutputStream is the preferred stream class for writing to a binary file.[2] An object of the class ObjectOutputStream has methods to write strings and values of any of the primitive types to a binary file. Display 10.13 shows a sample program that writes values of type int to a binary file. Display 10.14 describes the methods used for writing data of other types to a binary file.

Display 10.13   Writing to a Binary File (part 1 of 2)

```
1   import java.io.ObjectOutputStream;
2   import java.io.FileOutputStream;
3   import java.io.IOException;

4   public class BinaryOutputDemo
5   {
6       public static void main(String[] args)
7       {
8           try
9           {
10              ObjectOutputStream outputStream =
11                  new ObjectOutputStream(
                        new FileOutputStream("numbers.dat"));

12              int i;
13              for (i = 0; i < 5; i++)
14                  outputStream.writeInt(i);

15              System.out.println("Numbers written to the file numbers.dat.");
16              outputStream.close();
17          }
```

---

[2] DataOutputStream is also widely used and behaves exactly as we describe for ObjectOutputStream in this section. However, the techniques given in the subsections "Binary I/O of Objects" and "Array Objects in Binary Files" work only for ObjectOutputStream; they do not work for DataOutputStream.

Display 10.13   **Writing to a Binary File** (part 2 of 2)

```
18          catch (IOException e)
19          {
20              System.out.println("Problem with file output.");
21          }
22      }
23  }
```

FILE REPRESENTATION (after program is run)

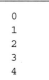

| 0 |
| 1 |
| 2 |
| 3 |
| 4 |

This is a binary file. It really contains representations of each number as bytes—that is, zeros and ones—and is read as bytes. You cannot read this file with your text editor.

Display 10.14   **Some Methods in the Class `ObjectOutputStream`** (part 1 of 2)

`ObjectOutputStream` and `FileOutputStream` are in the `java.io` package.

`public ObjectOutputStream(OutputStream streamObject)`

There is no constructor that takes a file name as an argument. If you want to create a stream using a file name, use

`new ObjectOutputStream(new FileOutputStream(File_Name))`

This creates a blank file. If there already is a file named *File_Name*, then the old contents of the file are lost.

If you want to create a stream using an object of the class `File`, use

`new ObjectOutputStream(new FileOutputStream(File_Object))`

The constructor for `FileOutputStream` may throw a `FileNotFoundException`, which is a kind of `IOException`. If the `FileOutputStream` constructor succeeds, then the constructor for `ObjectOutputStream` may throw a different `IOException`.

`public void writeInt(int n) throws IOException`

Writes the `int` value n to the output stream.

`public void writeShort(short n) throws IOException`

Writes the `short` value n to the output stream.

`public void writeLong(long n) throws IOException`

Writes the `long` value n to the output stream.

`public void writeDouble(double x) throws IOException`

Writes the `double` value x to the output stream.

(continued)

Display 10.14 Some Methods in the Class `ObjectOutputStream` (part 2 of 2)

```
public void writeFloat(float x) throws IOException
```

Writes the `float` value `x` to the output stream.

```
public void writeChar(int n) throws IOException
```

Writes the `char` value `n` to the output stream. Note that it expects its argument to be an `int` value. However, if you simply use the `char` value, then Java will automatically type cast it to an `int` value. The following are equivalent:

```
outputStream.writeChar((int)'A');
```

and

```
outputStream.writeChar('A');
```

```
public void writeUTF(String aString) throws IOException
```

Writes the `String` value `aString` to the output stream. `UTF` refers to a particular method of encoding the string. To read the string back from the file, you should use the method `readUTF` of the class `ObjectInputStream`.

```
public void writeObject(Object anObject) throws IOException
```

Writes its argument to the output stream. The object argument should be an object of a serializable class, a concept discussed later in the section titled "The `Serializable` Interface." Throws various `IOExceptions`.

```
public void close() throws IOException
```

Closes the stream's connection to a file. This method calls `flush` before closing the file.

```
public void flush() throws IOException
```

Flushes the output stream. This forces an actual physical write to the file of any data that has been buffered and not yet physically written to the file. Normally, you should not need to invoke `flush`.

Notice that almost all the code in the sample program in Display 10.13 is in a `try` block. Any part of the code that does binary file I/O in the ways we are describing can throw an `IOException`.

The output stream for writing to the binary file `numbers.dat` is created and named with the following:

```
ObjectOutputStream outputStream =
  new ObjectOutputStream(new
  FileOutputStream("numbers.dat"));
```

opening a file   As with text files, this is called **opening the file**. If the file `numbers.dat` does not already exist, this statement will create an empty file named `numbers.dat`. If the file `numbers.dat` already exists, this statement will erase the contents of the file so that the file starts out empty. The situation is basically the same as what you learned for text files, except that we are using a different class.

As is typical of Java I/O classes, the constructor for the class `ObjectOutputStream` takes another I/O class object as an argument—in this case, an anonymous argument of the class `FileOutputStream`.

Opening a Binary File for Output

You create a stream of the class `ObjectOutputStream` and connect it to a binary file as follows:

SYNTAX

```
ObjectOutputStream Output_Stream_Name =
    new ObjectOutputStream(new FileOutputStream(File_Name));
```

The constructor for `FileOutputStream` may throw a `FileNotFoundException`, which is a kind of `IOException`. If the `FileOutputStream` constructor succeeds, then the constructor for `ObjectOutputStream` may throw a different `IOException`. A single catch block for `IOException` would cover all cases.

EXAMPLES

```
ObjectOutputStream myOutputStream =
            new ObjectOutputStream(new
            FileOutputStream("mydata.dat"));
```

After opening the file, you can use the methods of the class `ObjectOutputStream` (Display 10.14) to write to the file.

The class `ObjectOutputStream` does not have a method named `println`, as we had with text file output and screen output. However, as shown in Display 10.13, an object of the class `ObjectOutputStream` does have a method named `writeInt` that can write a single `int` value to a file, and it also has the other output methods described in Display 10.14.

writeInt

In Display 10.13, we made it look as though the numbers in the file `numbers.dat` were written one per line in a human-readable form. That is not what happens, however. There are no lines or other separators between the numbers. Instead, the numbers are written in the file one immediately after the other, and they are encoded as a sequence of bytes in the same way that the numbers would be encoded in the computer's main memory. These coded `int` values cannot be read using your editor. Realistically, they can be read only by another Java program.

You can use a stream from the class `ObjectOutputStream` to output values of any primitive type and also to write data of the type `String`. Each primitive data type has a corresponding write method in the class `ObjectOutputStream`. We have already mentioned the write methods for outputting `int` values. The methods for the other primitive types are completely analogous to `writeInt`. For example, the following would write a `double` value, a `boolean` value, and a `char` value to the binary file connected to the `ObjectOutputStream` object `outputStream`:

```
outputStream.writeDouble(9.99);
outputStream.writeBoolean(false);
outputStream.writeChar((int)'A');
```

writeChar   The method `writeChar` has one possibly surprising property: It expects its argument to be of type `int`. So if you start with a value of type `char`, the `char` value can be type cast to an `int` before it is given to the method `writeChar`. For example, to output the contents of a `char` variable named `symbol`, you can use

```
outputStream.writeChar((int)symbol);
```

In actual fact, you do not need to write in the type cast to an `int`, because Java automatically performs a type cast from a `char` value to an `int` value for you. So, the following is equivalent to the previous invocation of `writeChar`:

```
outputStream.writeChar(symbol);
```

writeUTF
for strings   To output a value of type `String`, use the method `writeUTF`. For example, if `outputStream` is a stream of type `ObjectOutputStream`, the following will write the string `"Hello friend."` to the file connected to that stream:

```
outputStream.writeUTF("Hello friend.");
```

You may write output of different types to the same file. So, you may write a combination of, for example, `int`, `double`, and `String` values. However, mixing types in a file does require special care to make it possible to read them back out of the file. To read them back, you need to know the order in which the various types appear in the file, because, as you will see, a program that reads from the file will use a different method to read data of each different type.

closing a
binary file   Note that, as illustrated in Display 10.13 and as you will see shortly, you close a binary output or input stream in the same way that you close a stream connected to a text file.

UTF and `writeUTF`

Recall that Java uses the Unicode character set, which is a set of characters that includes many characters used in languages whose character sets are different from English. Readers of this book are undoubtedly using editors and operating systems that use the ASCII character set, which is the character set normally used for English and for our Java programs. The ASCII character set is a subset of the Unicode character set, so the Unicode character set has a lot of characters you probably do not need. There is a standard way of encoding all the Unicode characters, but for English-speaking countries, it is not a very efficient coding scheme. The UTF coding scheme is an alternative scheme that still codes all Unicode characters, but that favors the ASCII character set. The UTF coding method gives short, efficient codes for the ASCII characters. The price is that it gives long, inefficient codes to the other Unicode characters. However, because you probably do not use the other Unicode characters, this is a very favorable trade-off. The method `writeUTF` uses the UTF coding method to write strings to a binary file.

The method `writeInt` writes integers into a file using the same number of bytes—that is, the same number of zeros and ones—to store any integer. Similarly, the method `writeLong` uses the same number of bytes to store each value of type `long`. (But the methods `writeInt` and `writeLong` use a different number of bytes from each other.) The situation is the same for all the other write methods that write primitive types to binary files. However, the method writeUTF uses differing numbers of bytes to store different strings in a file. Longer strings require more bytes than shorter strings. This can present a problem to Java, because there are no separators between data items in a binary file. The way that Java manages to make this work is by writing some extra information at the start of each string. This extra information tells how many bytes are used to write the string, so readUTF knows how many bytes to read and convert. (The method readUTF will be discussed a little later in this chapter, but, as you may have already guessed, it reads a String value that was written using the UTF coding method.)

The situation with writeUTF is even a little more complicated than what we discussed in the previous paragraph. Notice that we said that the information at the start of the string code in the file tells how many *bytes* to read, *not how many characters are in the string.* These two figures are not the same. With the UTF way of encoding, different characters are encoded in different numbers of bytes. However, all the ASCII characters are stored in just one byte, and you are undoubtedly using only ASCII characters, so this difference is more theoretical than real to you now.

Reading Simple Data from a Binary File

The stream class ObjectInputStream is used to read from a file that has been written to using ObjectOutputStream. Display 10.15 gives some of the most commonly used methods for this class. If you compare that table with the methods for ObjectOutputStream given in Display 10.14, you will see that each output method in ObjectOutputStream has a corresponding input method in ObjectInputStream. For example, if you write an integer to a file using the method writeInt of ObjectOutputStream, then you can read that integer back with the method readInt of ObjectInputStream. If you write a number to a file using the method writeDouble of ObjectOutputStream, then you can read that number back with the method readDouble of ObjectInputStream, and so forth. Display 10.16 gives an example of using readInt in this way.

Self-Test Exercises

28. How do you open the binary file bindata.dat so that it is connected to an output stream of type ObjectOutputStream that is named outputThisWay?

29. Give two statements that will write the values of the two double variables v1 and v2 to the file bindata.dat. Use the stream outputThisWay that you created as the answer to Self-Test Exercise 28.

30. Give a statement that will write the string value "Hello" to the file bindata.dat. Use the stream outputThisWay that you created as the answer to Self-Test Exercise 28.

31. Give a statement that will close the stream outputThisWay created as the answer to Self-Test Exercise 28.

The input stream for reading from the binary file `numbers.dat` is opened as follows:

```
ObjectInputStream inputStream =
          new ObjectInputStream(new
          FileInputStream("numbers.dat"));
```

Note that this is identical to how we opened a file using `ObjectOutputStream` in Display 10.13, except that here we have used the classes `ObjectInputStream` and `FileInputStream` instead of `ObjectOutputStream` and `FileOutputStream`.

Opening a Binary File for Reading

Create a stream of the class `ObjectInputStream` and connect it to a binary file as follows:

SYNTAX

```
ObjectInputStream Input_Stream_Name =
          new ObjectInputStream(new FileInputStream(File_Name));
```

The constructor for `FileInputStream` may throw a `FileNotFoundException`, which is a kind of `IOException`. If the `FileInputStream` constructor succeeds, then the constructor for `ObjectInputStream` may throw a different `IOException`.

EXAMPLES

```
ObjectInputStream inputFile =
          new ObjectInputStream(new
          FileInputStream("somefile.dat"));
```

After this, you can use the methods in Display 10.15 to read from the file.

Display 10.15   Some Methods in the Class `ObjectInputStream`   (part 1 of 3)

The classes `ObjectInputStream` and `FileInputStream` are in the `java.io` package.

```
public ObjectInputStream(InputStream streamObject)
```

There is no constructor that takes a file name as an argument. If you want to create a stream using a file name, use

```
new ObjectInputStream(new FileInputStream(File_Name))
```

Alternatively, you can use an object of the class `File` in place of the *File_Name*, as follows:

```
new ObjectInputStream(new FileInputStream(File_Object))
```

The constructor for `FileInputStream` may throw a `FileNotFoundException`, which is a kind of `IOException`. If the `FileInputStream` constructor succeeds, then the constructor for `ObjectInputStream` may throw a different `IOException`.

Display 10.15   Some Methods in the Class `ObjectInputStream` (part 2 of 3)

```
public int readInt()throws IOException
```

Reads an `int` value from the input stream and returns that `int` value. If `readInt` tries to read a value from the file and that value was not written using the method `writeInt` of the class `ObjectOutputStream` (or written in some equivalent way), then problems will occur. If an attempt is made to read beyond the end of the file, an `EOFException` is thrown.

```
public int readShort()throws IOException
```

Reads a `short` value from the input stream and returns that `short` value. If `readShort` tries to read a value from the file and that value was not written using the method `writeShort` of the class `ObjectOutputStream` (or written in some equivalent way), then problems will occur. If an attempt is made to read beyond the end of the file, an `EOFException` is thrown.

```
public long readLong()throws IOException
```

Reads a `long` value from the input stream and returns that `long` value. If `readLong` tries to read a value from the file and that value was not written using the method `writeLong` of the class `ObjectOutputStream` (or written in some equivalent way), then problems will occur. If an attempt is made to read beyond the end of the file, an `EOFException` is thrown.

```
public double readDouble()throws IOException
```

Reads a `double` value from the input stream and returns that `double` value. If `readDouble` tries to read a value from the file and that value was not written using the method `writeDouble` of the class `ObjectOutputStream` (or written in some equivalent way), then problems will occur. If an attempt is made to read beyond the end of the file, an `EOFException` is thrown.

```
public float readFloat()throws IOException
```

Reads a `float` value from the input stream and returns that `float` value. If `readFloat` tries to read a value from the file and that value was not written using the method `writeFloat` of the class `ObjectOutputStream` (or written in some equivalent way), then problems will occur. If an attempt is made to read beyond the end of the file, an `EOFException` is thrown.

```
public char readChar()throws IOException
```

Reads a `char` value from the input stream and returns that `char` value. If `readChar` tries to read a value from the file and that value was not written using the method `writeChar` of the class `ObjectOutputStream` (or written in some equivalent way), then problems will occur. If an attempt is made to read beyond the end of the file, an `EOFException` is thrown.

```
public boolean readBoolean()throws IOException
```

Reads a `boolean` value from the input stream and returns that `boolean` value. If `readBoolean` tries to read a value from the file and that value was not written using the method `writeBoolean` of the class `ObjectOutputStream` (or written in some equivalent way), then problems will occur. If an attempt is made to read beyond the end of the file, an `EOFException` is thrown.

(continued)

Display 10.15   Some Methods in the Class `ObjectInputStream` (part 3 of 3)

```
public String readUTF() throws IOException
```

Reads a `String` value from the input stream and returns that `String` value. If `readUTF` tries to read a value from the file and that value was not written using the method `writeUTF` of the class `ObjectOutputStream` (or written in some equivalent way), then problems will occur. If an attempt is made to read beyond the end of the file, an `EOFException` is thrown.

```
Object readObject() throws ClassNotFoundException, IOException
```

Reads an object from the input stream. The object read should have been written using `writeObject` of the class `ObjectOutputStream`. Throws a `ClassNotFoundException` if a serialized object cannot be found. If an attempt is made to read beyond the end of the file, an `EOFException` is thrown. May throw various other `IOExceptions`.

```
public int skipBytes(int n) throws IOException
```

Skips `n` bytes.

```
public void close() throws IOException
```

Closes the stream's connection to a file.

---

reading multiple types   `ObjectInputStream` allows you to read input values of different types from the same file. So, you may read a combination of, for example, `int` values, `double` values, and `String` values. However, if the next data item in the file is not of the type expected by the reading method, the result is likely to be a mess. For example, if your program writes an integer using `writeInt`, then any program that reads that integer should read it using `readInt`. If you instead use `readLong` or `readDouble`, your program will misbehave.

closing a binary file   Note that, as illustrated in Display 10.16, you close a binary input stream in the same way that you close all the other I/O streams we have seen.

MyProgrammingLab™

Self-Test Exercises

32. Write code to open the binary file named `someStuff` and connect it to an `ObjectInputStream` object named `inputThing` so it is ready for reading.

33. Give a statement that will read a number of type `double` from the file `someStuff` and place the value in a variable named `number`. Use the stream `inputThing` that you created in Self-Test Exercise 32. (Assume the first thing written to the file was written using the method `writeDouble` of the class `ObjectOutputStream` and assume `number` is of type `double`.)

34. Give a statement that will close the stream `inputThing` created in Self-Test Exercise 32.

35. Can one program write a number to a file using `writeInt` and then have another program read that number using `readLong`? Can a program read that number using `readDouble`?

36. Can you use `readUTF` to read a string from a text file?

Display 10.16   Reading from a Binary File

```
1   import java.io.ObjectInputStream;
2   import java.io.FileInputStream;
3   import java.io.IOException;
4   import java.io.FileNotFoundException;

5   public class BinaryInputDemo
6   {
7     public static void main(String[] args)
8     {
9         try
10        {
11            ObjectInputStream inputStream =
12              new ObjectInputStream(new FileInputStream("numbers.dat"));

13            System.out.println("Reading the file numbers.dat.");
14            int n1 = inputStream.readInt();
15            int n2 = inputStream.readInt();

16            System.out.println("Numbers read from file:");
17            System.out.println(n1);
18            System.out.println(n2);
19            inputStream.close();
20        }
21        catch(FileNotFoundException e)
22        {
23            System.out.println("Cannot find file numbers.dat.");
24        }
25        catch(IOException e)
26        {
27            System.out.println("Problems with input from numbers.dat.");
28        }
29        System.out.println("End of program.");
30    }
31  }
```

Sample Dialogue

```
Reading the file numbers.dat.
Numbers read from file:            Assumes the program in
0                                  Display 10.13 was run to
1                                  create the file numbers.dat.
End of program.
```

Checking for the End of a Binary File

EOF-
Exception

All of the `ObjectInputStream` methods that read from a binary file will throw an `EOFException` when they try to read beyond the end of a file. So, your code can test for the end of a binary file by catching an `EOFException` as illustrated in Display 10.17.

In Display 10.17, the reading is placed in an "infinite loop" through the use of `true` as the Boolean expression in the `while` loop. The loop is not really infinite, because when the end of the file is reached, an exception is thrown, and that ends the entire `try` block and passes control to the `catch` block.

EOFException

If your program is reading from a binary file using any of the methods listed in Display 10.15 for the class `ObjectInputStream`, and your program attempts to read beyond the end of the file, then an `EOFException` is thrown. This can be used to end a loop that reads all the data in a file.

The class `EOFException` is a derived class of the class `IOException`. So, every exception of type `EOFException` is also of type `IOException`.

Display 10.17   Using **EOFException** (part 1 of 2)

```
1    import java.io.ObjectInputStream;
2    import java.io.FileInputStream;
3    import java.io.EOFException;
4    import java.io.IOException;
5    import java.io.FileNotFoundException;

6    public class EOFDemo
7    {
8        public static void main(String[] args)
9        {
10           try
11           {
12               ObjectInputStream inputStream =
13                 new ObjectInputStream(new FileInputStream("numbers.dat"));
14               int number;
15               System.out.println("Reading numbers in numbers.dat");
16               try
17               {
18                   while (true)
19                   {
20                       number = inputStream.readInt( );
21                       System.out.println(number);
22                   }
23               }
```

Display 10.17   Using `EOFException` (part 2 of 2)

```
24                catch(EOFException e)
25                {
26                    System.out.println("No more numbers in the file.");
27                }
28                inputStream.close();
29            }
30            catch(FileNotFoundException e)
31            {
32                System.out.println("Cannot find file numbers.dat.");
33            }
34            catch(IOException e)
35            {
36                System.out.println("Problem with input from file
                    numbers.dat.");
37            }
38        }
39    }
```

Sample Dialogue

```
Reading numbers in numbers.dat
0                                    Assumes the program in
1                                    Display 10.13 was run to
2                                    create the file numbers.dat.
3
4
No more numbers in the file.
```

PITFALL: Checking for the End of a File in the Wrong Way

Different file-reading methods check for the end of a file in different ways. If you test for the end of a file in the wrong way, one of two things will probably happen: Your program will either go into an unintended infinite loop, or it will terminate abnormally.

For the classes discussed in this book , the following rules apply: If your program is reading from a binary file, then an `EOFException` will be thrown when the reading goes beyond the end of the file. If your program is reading from a text file, then no `EOFException` will be thrown when reading goes beyond the end of the file. ■

Self-Test Exercises

37. When opening a binary file for output in the ways discussed in this chapter, might an exception be thrown? What kind of exception? When opening a binary file for input in the ways discussed in this chapter, might an exception be thrown? What kind of exception?

38. Suppose a binary file contains three numbers written to the file with the method writeDouble of the class ObjectOutputStream. Suppose further that your program reads all three numbers with three invocations of the method readDouble of the class ObjectInputStream. When will an EOFException be thrown? Right after reading the third number? When your program tries to read a fourth number? Some other time?

39. The following appears in the program in Display 10.17:

```
try
{
    while (true)
    {
        number = inputStream.readInt();
        System.out.println(number);
    }
}
catch(EOFException e)
{
    System.out.println("No more numbers in the file.");
}
```

Why isn't this an infinite loop?

Binary I/O of Objects

You can output objects of classes you define as easily as you output int values using writeInt, and you can later read the objects back into your program as easily as you read int values with the method readInt. For you to be able to do this, the class of objects that your code is writing and reading must implement the Serializable interface.

Serializable interface

We will discuss interfaces in general in Chapter 13. However, the Serializable interface is particularly easy to use and requires no knowledge of interfaces. All you need to do to make a class implement the Serializable interface is add the two words implements Serializable to the heading of the class definition, as in the following example:

```
public class Person implements Serializable
{
```

The Serializable interface is in the same java.io package that contains all the I/O classes we have discussed in this chapter. For example, in Display 10.18, we define a toy class named SomeClass that implements the Serializable interface. We will explain the effect of the `Serializable` interface a bit later in this chapter, but first let's see how you do binary file I/O with a serializable class, such as this class `SomeClass` in Display 10.18.

Display 10.19 illustrates how class objects can be written to and read from a binary file. To write an object of a class such as `SomeClass` to a binary file, simply use the method `writeObject` of the class `ObjectOutputStream`. You use `writeObject` in the same way that you use the other methods of the class `ObjectOutputStream`, such as `writeInt`, but you use an object as the argument.

writeObject

If an object is written to a file with `writeObject`, then it can be read back out of the file with `readObject` of the stream class `ObjectInputStream`, as also illustrated in Display 10.19. The method `readObject` returns its value as an object of type `Object`. If you want to use the values retuned by `readObject` as an object of a class such as `SomeClass`, you must do a type cast, as shown in Display 10.19.

readObject

The `Serializable` Interface

serializable

A class that implements the `Serializable` interface is said to be a **serializable** class. To use objects of a class with `writeObject` and `readObject`, that class must be serializable. But to make the class serializable, we change nothing in the class. All we do is add the phrase `implements Serializable`. This phrase tells the run-time system that it is OK to treat objects of the class in a particular way when doing file I/O. If a class is

Display 10.18   A Serializable Class

```
1   import java.io.Serializable;

2   public class SomeClass implements Serializable
3   {
4       private int number;
5       private char letter;

6       public SomeClass()
7       {
8           number = 0;
9           letter = 'A';
10      }

11      public SomeClass(int theNumber, char theLetter)
12      {
13          number = theNumber;
14          letter = theLetter;
15      }
16      public String toString()
17      {
18          return "Number = " + number
19                          + " Letter = " + letter;
20      }
21  }
```

Display 10.19   **Binary File I/O of Objects** (part 1 of 2)

```
1   import java.io.ObjectOutputStream;
2   import java.io.FileOutputStream;
3   import java.io.ObjectInputStream;
4   import java.io.FileInputStream;
5   import java.io.IOException;
6   import java.io.FileNotFoundException;

7   /**
8    Demonstrates binary file I/O of serializable class objects.
9   */
10  public class ObjectIODemo
11  {
12      public static void main(String[] args)
13      {
14          try
15          {
16              ObjectOutputStream outputStream =
17                  new ObjectOutputStream(new FileOutputStream("datafile"));

18              SomeClass oneObject = new SomeClass(1, 'A');
19              SomeClass anotherObject = new SomeClass(42, 'Z');

20              outputStream.writeObject(oneObject);
21              outputStream.writeObject(anotherObject);

22              outputStream.close();

23              System.out.println("Data sent to file.");
24          }
25          catch(IOException e)
26          {
27              System.out.println("Problem with file output.");
28          }

29          System.out.println(
30                  "Now let's reopen the file and display the data.");
31          try
32          {
33              ObjectInputStream inputStream =
34                  new ObjectInputStream(new FileInputStream("datafile"));
```
Notice the type casts.
```
35              SomeClass readOne = (SomeClass)inputStream.readObject( );
36              SomeClass readTwo = (SomeClass)inputStream.readObject( );

37              System.out.println("The following were read from the file:");
38              System.out.println(readOne);
39              System.out.println(readTwo);
40          }
41          catch(FileNotFoundException e)
42          {
43              System.out.println("Cannot find datafile.");
44          }
```

Display 10.19   Binary File I/O of Objects (part 2 of 2)

```
45              catch(ClassNotFoundException e)
46              {
47                  System.out.println("Problems with file input.");
48              }
49              catch(IOException e)
50              {
51                  System.out.println("Problems with file input.");
52              }
53                  System.out.println("End of program.");
54          }
55  }
```

Sample Dialogue

```
Data sent to file.
Now let's reopen the file and display the data.
The following were read from the file:
Number = 1 Letter = A
Number = 42 Letter = Z
End of program.
```

serializable, Java assigns a serial number to each object of the class that it writes to a stream of type `ObjectOutputStream`. If the same object is written to the stream more than once, then after the first time, Java writes only the serial number for the object and not a full description of the object's data. This makes file I/O more efficient and makes the files smaller. When read back out with a stream of type `ObjectInputStream`, duplicate serial numbers are returned as references to the same object. Note that this means that if two variables contain references to the same object and you write the objects to the file and later read them from the file, then the two objects that are read will again be references to the same object. So nothing in the structure of your object data is lost when you write the objects to the file and later read them back.

class instance variables
When a serializable class has instance variables of a class type, then the classes for the instance variables must also be serializable, and so on for all levels of **class instance variables** within classes. So, a class is not serializable unless the classes for all instance variables are also serializable.

Why aren't all classes made serializable? For security reasons. The serial number system makes it easier for programmers to get access to the object data written to secondary storage. Also, for some classes, it may not make sense to write objects to secondary storage, because they would be meaningless when read out again later. For example, if the object contains system-dependent data, the data may be meaningless when later read out.

PITFALL: Mixing Class Types in the Same File

The best way to write and read objects using `ObjectOutputStream` and `ObjectInputStream` is to store only data of one class type in any one file. If you store objects of multiple class types or even objects of only one class type mixed in with primitive type data, it has been our experience that the system can get confused and you could lose data. ∎

Array Objects in Binary Files

An array is an object and hence a suitable argument for `writeObject`. An entire array can be saved to a binary file using `writeObject` and later read using `readObject`. When doing so, if the array has a base type that is a class, then the class must be serializable. This means that if you store all your data for one serializable class in a single array, then you can output all your data to a binary file with one invocation of `writeObject`.

This way of storing an array in a binary file is illustrated in Display 10.20. Note that the base class type, `SomeClass`, is serializable. Also, notice the type cast that uses the array type `SomeClass[]`. Because `readObject` returns its value as an object of type `Object`, it must be type cast to the correct array type.

MyProgrammingLab™ ### Self-Test Exercises

40. How do you make a class implement the `Serializable` interface?

41. What import statement do you need to be able to use the `Serializable` interface?

42. What is the return type for the method `readObject` of the class `ObjectInputStream`?

43. Is an array of type `Object`?

Display 10.20   File I/O of an Array Object (part 1 of 3)

```
1   import java.io.ObjectOutputStream;
2   import java.io.FileOutputStream;
3   import java.io.ObjectInputStream;
4   import java.io.FileInputStream;
5   import java.io.IOException;
6   import java.io.FileNotFoundException;

7   public class ArrayIODemo
8   {

9       public static void main(String[] args)
```

Display 10.20   File I/O of an Array Object (part 2 of 3)

```
10        {
11            SomeClass[] a = new SomeClass[2];
12            a[0] = new SomeClass(1, 'A');
13            a[1] = new SomeClass(2, 'B');

14            try
15            {
16                ObjectOutputStream outputStream =
17                        newObjectOutputStream(newFileOutputStream("arrayfile"));
18                outputStream.writeObject(a);
19                outputStream.close( );
20            }
21            catch(IOException e)
22            {
23                System.out.println("Error writing to file.");
24                System.exit(0);
25            }

26             System.out.println(
27                        "Array written to file arrayfile.");

28            System.out.println(
29                 "Now let's reopen the file and display the array.");

30            SomeClass[] b = null ;

31            try
32            {
33                ObjectInputStream inputStream =
34                        new ObjectInputStream(new FileInputStream("arrayfile"));
35                b = (SomeClass[])inputStream.readObject();
36                inputStream.close();
37            }
38            catch(FileNotFoundException e)
39            {                                            Notice the type cast.
40               System.out.println("Cannot find file arrayfile.");
41                System.exit(0);
42            }
43            catch(ClassNotFoundException e)
44            {
45                System.out.println("Problems with file input.");
46                System.exit(0);
47            }
48            catch(IOException e)
49            {
50                System.out.println("Problems with file input.");
51                System.exit(0);
52            }
53            System.out.println(
54                 "The following array elements were read from the file:");
55            int i;
```

(continued)

Display 10.20   File I/O of an Array Object (part 3 of 3)

```
56              for (i = 0; i < b.length; i++)
57                  System.out.println(b[i]);
58          System.out.println("End of program.");
59      }
60  }
```

Sample Dialogue

```
Array written to file arrayfile.
Now let's reopen the file and display the array.
The following array elements were read from the file:
Number = 1 Letter = A
Number = 2 Letter = B
End of program.
```

10.5 Random Access to Binary Files ★

Anytime, anywhere.

Common response to a challenge for a confrontation

The streams for sequential access to files, which we discussed in the previous sections of this chapter, are the ones most often used for file access in Java. However, some applications that require very rapid access to records in very large databases require some sort of random access to particular parts of a file. Such applications might best be done with specialized database software. But perhaps you are given the job of writing such a package in Java, or perhaps you are just curious about how such things are done in Java. Java does provide for random access to files so that your program can both read from and write to random locations in a file. In this section, we will describe simple uses of random access to files.

Reading and Writing to the Same File

If you want random access to both read and write to a file in Java, use the stream class RandomAccessFile, which is in the java.io package like all other file I/O classes.

    A random access file consists of a sequence of numbered bytes. There is a kind of marker called the **file pointer** that is always positioned at one of these bytes. All reads and writes take place starting at the location of the file pointer. You can move the file pointer to a new location with the method seek.

    Although a random access file is byte oriented, there are methods to allow for reading or writing values of the primitive types and of string values to a random access file. In fact, these are the same methods as those we already used for sequential access files, as previously discussed. A RandomAccessFile stream has methods writeInt, writeDouble, writeUTF, and so forth, as well as methods readInt, readDouble,

file pointer

Display 10.21   Some Methods of the Class `RandomAccessFile` (part 1 of 3)

The class `RandomAccessFile` is in the `java.io` package.

```
public RandomAccessFile(String fileName, String mode)

public RandomAccessFile(File fileObject, String mode)
```

Opens the file, does not delete data already in the file, but does position the file pointer at the first (zeroth) location.

The mode must be one of the following:

"`r`" Open for reading only.
"`rw`" Open for reading and writing.
"`rws`" Same as "`rw`", and also requires that every update to the file's content or metadata be written synchronously to the underlying storage device.
"`rwd`" Same as "`rw`", and also requires that every update to the file's content be written synchronously to the underlying storage device.
"`rws`" and "`rwd`" are not covered in this book text.

```
public long getFilePointer() throws IOException
```

Returns the current location of the file pointer. Locations are numbered starting with 0.

```
public void seek(long location) throws IOException
```

Moves the file pointer to the specified `location`.

```
public long length() throws IOException
```

Returns the length of the file.

```
public void setLength(long newLength) throws IOException
```

Sets the length of this file.

If the present length of the file as returned by the `length` method is greater than the `newLength` argument, then the file will be truncated. In this case, if the file pointer location as returned by the `getFilePointer` method is greater than `newLength`, then after this method returns, the file pointer location will be equal to `newLength`.

If the present `length` of the file as returned by the `length` method is smaller than `newLength`, then the file will be extended. In this case, the contents of the extended portion of the file are not defined.

```
public void close() throws IOException
```

Closes the stream's connection to a file.

```
public void write(int b) throws IOException
```

Writes the specified byte to the file.

```
public void write(byte [] a) throws IOException
```

Writes `a.length` bytes from the specified byte array to the file.

(continued)

Display 10.21   Some Methods of the Class `RandomAccessFile` (part 2 of 3)

---

    public final void writeByte(byte b) throws IOException

Writes the byte b to the file.

    public final void writeShort(short n) throws IOException

Writes the short n to the file.

    public final void writeInt(int n) throws IOException

Writes the int n to the file.

    public final void writeLong(long n) throws IOException

Writes the long n to the file.

    public final void writeDouble(double d) throws IOException

Writes the double d to the file.

    public final void writeFloat(float f) throws IOException

Writes the float f to the file.

    public final void writeChar(char c) throws IOException

Writes the char c to the file.

    public final void writeBoolean(boolean b) throws IOException

Writes the boolean b to the file.

    public final void writeUTF(String s) throws IOException

Writes the String s to the file.

    public int read() throws IOException

Reads a byte of data from the file and returns it as an integer in the range 0 to 255.

    public int read(byte [] a) throws IOException

Reads a.length bytes of data from the file into the array of bytes a. Returns the number of bytes read or -1 if the end of the file is encountered.

    public final byte readByte() throws IOException

Reads a byte value from the file and returns that value. If an attempt is made to read beyond the end of the file, an EOFException is thrown.

    public final short readShort() throws IOException

Reads a short value from the file and returns that value. If an attempt is made to read beyond the end of the file, an EOFException is thrown.

Display 10.21   Some Methods of the Class `RandomAccessFile` (part 3 of 3)

```
public final int readInt) throws IOException
```

Reads an `int` value from the file and returns that value. If an attempt is made to read beyond the end of the file, an `EOFException` is thrown.

```
public final long readLong() throws IOException
```

Reads a `long` value from the file and returns that value. If an attempt is made to read beyond the end of the file, an `EOFException` is thrown.

```
public final double readDouble() throws IOException
```

Reads a `double` value from the file and returns that value. If an attempt is made to read beyond the end of the file, an `EOFException` is thrown.

```
public final float readFloat() throws IOException
```

Reads a `float` value from the file and returns that value. If an attempt is made to read beyond the end of the file, an `EOFException` is thrown.

```
public final char readChar() throws IOException
```

Reads a `char` value from the file and returns that value. If an attempt is made to read beyond the end of the file, an `EOFException` is thrown.

```
public final boolean readBoolean() throws IOException
```

Reads a `boolean` value from the file and returns that value. If an attempt is made to read beyond the end of the file, an `EOFException` is thrown.

```
public final String readUTF() throws IOException
```

Reads a `String` value from the file and returns that value. If an attempt is made to read beyond the end of the file, an `EOFException` is thrown.

---

opening a file

`readUTF`, and so on. However, the class `RandomAccessFile` does not have the methods `writeObject` or `readObject`. The most important methods of the class `RandomAccessFile` are given in Display 10.21. A demonstration program for random access files is given in Display 10.22.

The constructor for `RandomAccessFile` takes either a string name for the file or an object of the class `File` as its first argument. The second argument must be one of the four strings `"rw"`, `"r"`, and two modes we do not discuss in this book, `"rws"` and `"rwd"`. The string `"rw"` means your code can both read and write to the file after it is open. The string `"r"` means your code can read from the file but cannot write to the file.

If the file already exists, then when it is opened, the length is not reset to `0`, but the file pointer will be positioned at the start of the file, which is what you would expect at least for `"r"`. If the length of the file is not what you want, you can change it with the method `setLength`. In particular, you can use `setLength` to empty the file.

Display 10.22   **Random Access to a File (part 1 of 2)**

```
1   import java.io.RandomAccessFile;
2   import java.io.IOException;
3   import java.io.FileNotFoundException;

4   public class RandomAccessDemo
5   {
6     public static void main(String[] args)
7     {
8         try
9         {
10            RandomAccessFile ioStream =
11              new RandomAccessFile("bytedata", "rw");

12            System.out.println("Writing 3  bytes to the file bytedata.");
13            ioStream.writeByte(1);
14            ioStream.writeByte(2);
15            ioStream.writeByte(3);
16            System.out.println("The length of the file is now = "
17                              + ioStream.length());
18            System.out.println("The file pointer location is "
19                              + ioStream.getFilePointer());

20            System.out.println("Moving the file pointer to location 1.");
21            ioStream.seek(1);
22            byte oneByte = ioStream.readByte();
23            System.out.println("The value at location 1 is " + oneByte);
24            oneByte = ioStream.readByte();
25            System.out.println("The value at the next location is "
26                              + oneByte);

27            System.out.println("Now we move the file pointer back to");
28            System.out.println("location 1, and change the byte.");
29            ioStream.seek(1);
30            ioStream.writeByte(9);
31            ioStream.seek(1);
32            oneByte = ioStream.readByte();
33            System.out.println("The value at location 1 is now "
34                              + oneByte);

34            System.out.println("Now we go to the end of the file");
35            System.out.println("and write a double.");
36            ioStream.seek(ioStream.length());
37            ioStream.writeDouble(41.99);
38            System.out.println("The length of the file is now = "
39                              + ioStream.length());
```

Display 10.22   **Random Access to a File** (part 2 of 2)

```
40              System.out.println("Returning to location 3,");
41              System.out.println("where we wrote the double.");
42              ioStream.seek(3);
43              double oneDouble = ioStream.readDouble();
44              System.out.println("The double value at location 3  is "
45                                       + oneDouble);

46              ioStream.close();
47          }
48          catch(FileNotFoundException e)
49          {
50              System.out.println("Problem opening file.");
51          }
52          catch(IOException e)
53          {
54              System.out.println("Problems with file I/O.");
55          }
56          System.out.println("End of program.");
57      }
58  }
```

The location of **readDouble**
must be a location where
writeDouble *wrote to the file.*

The dialog assumes the file **bytedata**
did not exist before the program was run.

Sample Dialogue

```
Writing 3 bytes to the file bytedata.
The length of the file is now = 3
The file pointer location is 3
Moving the file pointer to location 1.
The value at location 1 is 2
The value at the next location is 3
Now we move the file pointer back to
location 1, and change the byte.
The value at location 1 is now 9
Now we go to the end of the file
and write a double.
The length of the file is now = 11
Returning to location 3,
where we wrote the double.
The double value at location 3 is 41.99
End of program.
```

*Byte locations are numbered
starting with zero.*

Three 1-byte values and 1 **double**
*value that uses 8 bytes =
11 bytes total.*

PITFALL: RandomAccessFile Need Not Start Empty

If a file already exists, then when it is opened with RandomAccessFile, the length is not reset to 0, but the file pointer will be positioned at the start of the file. So, old data in the file is not lost and the file pointer is set for the most likely position for reading, not the most likely position for writing.

MyProgrammingLab™

Self-Test Exercises

44. If you run the program in Display 10.22 a second time, will the output be the same?

45. How can you modify the program in Display 10.22 so the file always starts out empty?

Chapter Summary

- Files that are considered to be strings of characters and that look like characters to your program and your editor are called *text files*. Files whose contents must be handled as strings of binary digits are called *binary files*.

- You can use the class PrintWriter to write to a text file and can use the class Scanner or BufferedReader to read from a text file.

- The class File can be used to check whether there is a file with a given name. It can also check whether your program is allowed to read the file and/or allowed to write to the file.

- Your program can use the class ObjectOutputStream to write to a binary file and can use the class ObjectInputStream to read from a binary file.

- Your program can use the method writeObject of the class ObjectOutputStream to write class objects to a binary file. The objects can be read back with the method readObject of the class ObjectInputStream.

- To use the method writeObject of the class ObjectOutputStream or the method readObject of the class ObjectInputStream, the class whose objects are written to a file must implement the Serializable interface.

- The way that you test for the end of a file depends on whether your program is reading from a text file or a binary file.

- You can use the class RandomAccessFile to create a stream that gives random access to the bytes in a file.

Answers to Self-Test Exercises

1. A stream is an object that allows for the flow of data between a program and some I/O device or some file. If the flow is into the program, the stream is called an input stream. If the flow is out of the program, the stream is called an output stream.

2. A binary file contains data that is processed as binary data. A text file allows your program and editor to view the file as if it contained a sequence of characters. A text file can be viewed with an editor, whereas a binary file cannot.

3. A `FileNotFoundException` would be thrown if the file cannot be opened because, for example, there is already a directory (folder) named `stuff.txt`. Note that if the file does not exist but can be created, then no exception is thrown. If you answered `IOException`, you are not wrong, because a `FileNotFoundException` is an `IOException`. However, the better answer is the more specific exception class—namely, `FileNotFoundException`.

4. The class `PrintWriter` does not have a constructor that accepts a string (for a file name) as an argument, so the first line of code is not legal. The correct code would be:

```
PrintWriter outputStream =
    new PrintWriter(new FileOutputStream("EmployeeData.doc"));
    outputStrem.println("Employee Details: \n");
```

5.
```
PrintWriter outputStream =
    new PrintWriter(new FileOutputStream("sam");
```

6.
```
PrintWriter outStream =
    new PrintWriter(new FileOutputStream("sam", true ));
```

7. Yes, it will send suitable output to the text file because the class `Person` has a well-defined `toString()` method.

8.
```
Scanner fileIn =
        new Scanner(new FileInputStream("sally"));
```

9. It throws a `NoSuchElementException` if there are no more lines, and throws an `IllegalStateException` if the `Scanner` stream is closed.

10. Line terminator `'\n'` is read and discarded; it is not included in the string returned.

11. Your program may generate an error, because, the `FileInputStream` constructor, and thus the `Scanner` constructor invocation, can throw a `FileNotFoundException`, and this exception needs to be caught or declared in a `throws` clause.

12.
```
BufferedReader fileIn =
                new BufferedReader(new FileReader("joe"));
```

13. The method `readLine` returns a value of type `String`. The method `read` reads a single *character*, but it returns it as a value of type `int`. To get the value to be of type `char`, you need to do a type cast.

14. The `read` method returns `-1` and the `readLine` method returns null.

15. The `try` block in Display 10.7 is larger so that it includes the invocations of the method `readLine`, which might throw an `IOException`. The method `println` in Display 10.1 does not throw any exceptions that must be caught. '

16. Yes.

17. You may read the `double` value as a string and then convert the string to a double with `Double.parseDouble` (or in some other way).

18. If there are multiple numbers on a single line, you can read the line using `readLine` method and then use the `StringTokenizer` class to decompose the string into tokens. Then you will have to use `Integer.parseInt` or `Double.parseDouble` or a similar method to convert each token to a number.

19. The method `read` reads a single *character*, but it returns it as a value of type `int`. To get the value to be of type `char`, you need to do a type cast.

20. The method `read` reads a single character but it returns a value of type `int` that corresponds to the character `read`; it does not return the character itself. Thus, to get the character, you must use a type cast, as in

```
char next = (char)(inputStream.read())
```

21. Yes, if `original.txt` is an empty file, then the file `numbered.txt` produced by the program will also be empty.

22. Only the classes `FileReader` and `FileOutputStream` have a constructor that accepts a file name as an argument. (Although we have not discussed it, the class `Scanner` has a constructor that takes a `String` argument, but the argument is not a file name.)

23. Yes, it is legal.

24. Replace

```
System.setErr(errStream);
```

with

```
System.setOut(errStream);
```

25. Add

```
System.setOut(errStream);
```

to get

```
System.setErr(errStream);
System.setOut(errStream);
```

26.
```
import java.io.File;
public class FileExercise
{
    public static void main(String[] args)
    {
```

```java
        File fileObject = new File("Sally.txt");

    if (fileObject.exists())
        System.out.println(
            "There is a file named Sally.txt.");

    else
        System.out.println(
            "There is no file named Sally.txt.");

    }

}
```

27.
```java
import java.io.IOException;
import java.io.File;
import java.util.Scanner;

public class FileExercise2
{
    public static void main(String[] args)
    {
        Scanner keyboard = new Scanner(System.in);
        String fileName = null;
        File fileObject = null;

        try
        {
            System.out.print("Enter a file name and I will");
            System.out.println(" tell you if it exists.");
            fileName = keyboard.next();
            fileObject = new File(fileName);

            if (fileObject.exists())
            {
                System.out.println("There is a file named"
                                            + fileName);
                System.out.println("Delete the file? (y/n)");
                char answer = (char)System.in.read();

                if ((answer == 'y') || (answer == 'Y'))
                {
                    if (fileObject.delete())
                        System.out.println("File deleted.");
                    else
                        System.out.println(
                                    "Cannot delete file.");
                }
            }
            else
                System.out.println(
                            "No file named " + fileName);
```

```
            }
            catch(IOException e)
            {
                System.out.println(
                            "Error reading from keyboard.");
            }
        }
    }
```

28. ```
    ObjectOutputStream outputThisWay =
                new ObjectOutputStream(
                    new FileOutputStream("bindata.dat"));
    ```

29. ```
    outputThisWay.writeDouble(v1);
    outputThisWay.writeDouble(v2);
    ```

30. ```
    outputThisWay.writeUTF("Hello");
    ```

31. ```
    outputThisWay.close();
    ```

32. ```
    ObjectInputStream inputThing =
                new ObjectInputStream(
                    new FileInputStream("someStuff"));
    ```

33. ```
    number = inputThing.readDouble();
    ```

34. ```
    inputThing.close();
    ```

35. If a number is written to a file with `writeInt`, it should be read only with `readInt`. If you use `readLong` or `readDouble` to read the number, something will go wrong.

36. You should not use `readUTF` to read a string from a text file. You should use `readUTF` only to read a string from a binary file. Moreover, the string should have been written to that file using `writeUTF`.

37. When opening a binary file for either output or input in the ways discussed in this chapter, a `FileNotFoundException` might be thrown and other `IOExceptions` may be thrown.

38. An `EOFException` is thrown when your program tries to read the (nonexisting) fourth number.

39. It is not an infinite loop because when the end of the file is reached, an exception will be thrown, and that will end the entire `try` block.

40. You add the two words `implements Serializable` to the beginning of the class definition. You also must do this for the classes for the instance variables and so on for all levels of class instance variables within classes.

41. `import java.io.Serializable;` or `import java.io.*;`

42. The return type is `Object`, which means the returned value usually needs to be type cast.
    ```

43. Yes. That is why it is a legitimate argument for `writeObject`.

44. No. Each time the program is run, the file will get longer.

45. Add the following near the start of `main`:

    ```
    ioStream.setLength(0);
    ```

Programming Projects

Visit www.myprogramminglab.com to complete select exercises online and get instant feedback.

PROJECTS INVOLVING ONLY TEXT FILES

VideoNote
Solution to Programming Project 10.1

1. The text files `boynames.txt` and `girlnames.txt`, which are included in the source code for this book text, contain a list of the 1,000 most popular boy and girl names in the United States for the year 2003 as compiled by the Social Security Administration.

    These are blank-delimited files, where the most popular name is listed first, the second most popular name is listed second, and so on, to the 1,000th most popular name, which is listed last. Each line consists of the first name followed by a blank space and then the number of registered births using that name in the year. For example, the `girlnames.txt` file begins with

    > Emily 25494
    >
    > Emma 22532
    >
    > Madison 19986

    This indicates that Emily was the most popular name with 25,494 registered namings, Emma was the second most popular with 22,532, and Madison was the third most popular with 19,986.

    Write a program that reads both the girl and boy files into memory using arrays. Then, allow the user to input a name. The program should search through both arrays. If there is a match, then it should output the popularity ranking and the number of namings. The program should also indicate if there is no match.

    For example, if the user enters the name "Justice," then the program should output

    ```
    Justice is ranked 456 in popularity among girls with 655 namings.
    Justice is ranked 401 in popularity among boys with 653 namings.
    ```

    If the user enters the name "Walter," then the program should output

    ```
    Walter is not ranked among the top 1000 girl names.
    Walter is ranked 356 in popularity among boys with 775 namings.
    ```

2. You have a text file named `marks.txt` that stores the marks obtained by the students of a particular grade. It is a text file of strings representing numbers of type int and each line stores one number. Write a program that will read the marks from the file and display the highest and lowest marks on screen.

3. Write a program that takes its input from a text file of strings representing numbers of type `double` and outputs the average of the numbers in the file to the screen. The file contains nothing but strings representing numbers of type `double`, one per line.

4. You have collected yearly rainfall data for a few years in your locality for an irrigation design project. It is stored in a text file named `rainfall.txt` that stores the yearly rainfall data as strings representing numbers of type `double` indicating rainfall in mm for each year. Write a program that outputs the average rainfall (mm) from the data collected. It should also display a bar chart displaying a star (*) for every 100 mm of rainfall.

5. Write a program to edit text files for extra blanks. The program will replace any string of two or more blanks with a single blank. Your program should work as follows: Create a temporary file. Copy from the file to the temporary file but do not copy extra blanks. Copy the contents of the temporary file back into the original file. Use a method (or methods) in the class `File` to remove the temporary file. You will also want to use the class `File` for other things in your program. The temporary file should have a name that is different from all existing files so that the existing files are not affected (except for the file being edited). Your program will ask the user for the name of the file to be edited. However, it will not ask the user for the name of the temporary file but instead will generate the name within the program. You can generate the name any way that is clear and efficient. One possible way to generate the temporary file is to start with an unlikely name, such as `"TempX"`, and to append a character, such as `'X'`, until a name is found that does not name an existing file.

6. Write a program that takes its input from a text file of strings representing numbers of type double. Each line in the file contains three numbers representing the coefficients a, b and c of a quadratic equation of the form: $ax^2 + bx + c = 0$.

   The roots of such an equation can be found using the formula:

   $$x = \frac{-b \pm \sqrt{b^2 - 4ac}}{2a}$$

   Your program should read each line and check if the roots are real, imaginary or equal and display the roots or appropriate messages accordingly.

7. Write a class that keeps track of the top five high scores that could be used for a video game. Internally, the class should store the top scores in a data structure of your choice (the most straightforward way is to use arrays). Each entry consists of a name and a score. The data stored in memory should be synchronized with a text file for persistent storage. For example, here are the contents of a sample file where Ronaldo has the highest score and Pele has the third highest score:

```
Ronaldo
10400
Didier
9800
Pele
9750
Kaka
8400
Cristiano
8000
```

The constructor should test if the file exists. If it does not exist, then the file should be created with blank names for each of the players and a score of 0. If the file does exist, then the data from the file should be read into the class's instance variables. Along with appropriate constructors, accessors, and mutators, add the following methods:

- `void playerScore(String name, int score)`: Whenever a game is over, this method is called with the player's name and final score. If the name is one of the top five, then it should be added to the list and the lowest score should be dropped out. If the score is not in the top five, then nothing happens.

- `String[] getTopNames()`: Returns an array of the names of the top players, with the top player first, the second best player second, etc.

- `int[] getTopScores()`: Returns an array of the scores of the top players, with the highest score first, the second highest score second, etc.

Test your program with several calls to `playerScore` and print out the list of top names and scores to ensure that the correct values are stored. When the program is restarted, it should remember the top scores from the last session.

PROJECTS INVOLVING BINARY FILES

VideoNote
Solution to
Programming
Project 10.8

8. Write a program that will search a binary file of numbers of type `int` and write the largest and the smallest numbers to the screen. The file contains nothing but numbers of type `int` written to the file with `writeInt`.

9. Write a program that takes its input from a binary file of numbers of type `double` and outputs the average of the numbers in the file to the screen. The file contains nothing but numbers of type `double` written to the file with `writeDouble`.

10. Write a program that takes its input from a binary file of numbers of type `double`. The file contains nothing but numbers of type `double` written to the file with `writeDouble`. The program outputs to the screen the average and standard deviation of the numbers in the file. The standard deviation of a list of numbers n_1, n_2, n_3, and so forth is defined as the square root of the average of the following numbers:

$$(n_1 - a)^2, (n_2 - a)^2, (n_3 - a)^2, \text{and so forth.}$$

The number a is the average of the numbers n_1, n_2, n_3, and so forth. *Hint:* Write your program so that it first reads the entire file and computes the average of all the numbers, then closes the file, and then reopens the file and computes the standard deviation. You will find it helpful to first do Programming Project 10.8 and then modify that program in order to obtain the program for this project.

11. Change the definition of the class `Person` in Display 5.19 to be serializable. Note that this requires that you also change the class `Date`. Then write a program to maintain a binary file of records of people (records of type `Person`). Allow commands to delete a record specified by the person's name, to add a record, to retrieve and display a record, and to obtain all records of people within a specified

age range. To obtain the age of a person, you need the current date. Your program will ask the user for the current date when the program begins. You can do this with random access files, but do not use random access files for this exercise. Use a file or files that record records with the method `writeObject` of the class `ObjectOutputStream`.

12. Programming Projects 6.12 and 6.13 asked you to write a program to play a simple trivia game consisting of five questions. The questions, answers, and point values were hardcoded into array(s). This programming project involves moving the trivia questions into one or more binary files instead, and then loading the trivia questions into memory when the program starts.

First, write a program that allows an administrator to manage the questions for the trivia game. When the program is run, it should check to see if a data file exists. If the data file exists, then the trivia questions should be loaded from the data file into array(s) in memory. If the data file does not exist, start the program with no trivia questions in memory. The program should then present a menu that allows the administrator to list all trivia items (question, answer, and value) in the database, add a new trivia item, or delete an existing trivia item. Upon exiting the program, the trivia data in memory should be stored to one or more binary files using the `writeObject` method.

Second, modify either solution to Programming Projects 6.12 or 6.13 to read in the trivia data from the binary file created by the administrator's program. Note that the game is no longer limited to five questions, since an arbitrary number of trivia items may be created by the administrator's program and stored in the binary file(s).

Recursion 11

11.1 RECURSIVE void **METHODS**   681
Example: Vertical Numbers   681
Tracing a Recursive Call   684
A Closer Look at Recursion   687
Stacks for Recursion ★   690
Recursion versus Iteration   692

**11.2 RECURSIVE METHODS THAT
RETURN A VALUE**   693
General Form for a Recursive Method That
Returns a Value 694
Example: Another Powers Method   694

11.3 THINKING RECURSIVELY   699
Recursive Design Techniques   699
Binary Search ★   700
Efficiency of Binary Search ★   706
Example: Finding a File   708

Chapter Summary 711   **Answers to Self-Test Exercises** 711   **Programming Projects** 716

11 Recursion

After a lecture on cosmology and the structure of the solar system,
William James was accosted by a little old lady.

"Your theory that the sun is the center of the solar system, and the earth is
a ball which rotates around it has a very convincing ring to it, Mr. James,
but it's wrong. I've got a better theory," said the little old lady.

"And what is that, madam?" inquired James politely.

"That we live on a crust of earth which is on the back of a giant turtle."

Not wishing to demolish this absurd little theory by bringing to bear the
masses of scientific evidence he had at his command, James decided
to gently dissuade his opponent by making her see some of the
inadequacies of her position.

"If your theory is correct, madam," he asked, "what does this turtle stand on?"

"You're a very clever man, Mr. James, and that's a very good question"
replied the little old lady, "but I have an answer to it. And it is this:
the first turtle stands on the back of a second, far larger, turtle, who
stands directly under him."

"But what does this second turtle stand on?" persisted James patiently.

To this the little old lady crowed triumphantly. "It's no use, Mr. James—
it's turtles all the way down."

J. R. ROSS, *Constraints on Variables in Syntax*

Introduction

recursive method

A method definition that includes a call to itself is said to be **recursive**. Like most modern programming languages, Java allows methods to be recursive; if used with a little care, this can be a useful programming technique. In this chapter, we introduce the basic techniques needed for defining successful recursive methods. There is nothing in this chapter that is truly unique to Java. If you are already familiar with recursion, you can safely skip this chapter. No new Java elements are introduced here.

Prerequisites

Except for the subsections on binary search and searching for a file, this chapter uses material only from Chapters 1–5. The subsection entitled "Binary Search" also uses the basic material on one-dimensional arrays from Chapter 6 and the Example entitled "Finding a File" uses material from the `File` class in Chapter 10.

You may postpone all or part of this chapter if you wish. Nothing in the rest of this book requires any of this chapter.

11.1   Recursive `void` Methods

I remembered too that night which is at the middle of the Thousand and One Nights when Scheherazade (through a magical oversight of the copyist) begins to relate word for word the story of the Thousand and One Nights, establishing the risk of coming once again to the night when she must repeat it, and thus to infinity.

JORGE LUIS BORGES, *The Garden of Forking Paths*

When you are writing a method to solve a task, one basic design technique is to break the task into subtasks. Sometimes it turns out that at least one of the subtasks is a smaller example of the same task. For example, if the task is to search a list for a particular value, you might divide this into the subtask of searching the first half of the list and the subtask of searching the second half of the list. The subtasks of searching the halves of the list are "smaller" versions of the original task. Whenever one subtask is a smaller version of the original task to be accomplished, you can solve the original task by using a recursive method. We begin with a simple example to illustrate this technique. (For simplicity, our examples are static methods; however, recursive methods need not be static.)

Recursion

In Java, a method definition may contain an invocation of the method being defined. In such cases, the method is said to be **recursive**.

EXAMPLE: Vertical Numbers

Display 11.1 contains a demonstration program for a recursive method named `writeVertical`, which takes one (nonnegative) `int` argument and writes that `int` to the screen with the digits going down the screen one per line. For example, the invocation

    writeVertical(1234);

would produce the output

    1
    2
    3
    4

(continued)

Display 11.1   A Recursive void Method

```
1   public class RecursionDemo1
2   {
3       public static void main(String[] args)
4       {
5           System.out.println("writeVertical(3):");
6           writeVertical(3);

7           System.out.println("writeVertical(12):");
8           writeVertical(12);

9           System.out.println("writeVertical(123):");
10          writeVertical(123);
11      }

12      public static void writeVertical(int n)
13      {
14          if (n < 10)
15          {
16              System.out.println(n);
17          }
18          else //n is two or more digits long:
19          {
20              writeVertical(n / 10);
21              System.out.println(n % 10);
22          }
23      }
24  }
```

Sample Dialogue

```
writeVertical(3):
3
writeVertical(12):
1
2
writeVertical(123):
1
2
3
```

EXAMPLE: (continued)

The task to be performed by `writeVertical` may be broken down into the following two subtasks:

Simple Case: If n < 10, then write the number n to the screen.

After all, if the number is only one digit long, the task is trivial.

Recursive Case: If n >= 10, then do two subtasks:

1. Output all the digits except the last digit.

2. Output the last digit.

For example, if the argument were 1234, the first part would output

```
1
2
3
```

and the second part would output 4. This decomposition of tasks into subtasks can be used to derive the method definition.

Subtask 1 is a smaller version of the original task, so we can implement this subtask with a recursive call. Subtask 2 is just the simple case we listed previously. Thus, an outline of our algorithm for the method `writeVertical` with parameter n is given by the following pseudocode:

```
if (n < 10)
{
    System.out.println(n);
}
else //n is two or more digits long:
{
    writeVertical (the number n with the last digit removed) ;
    System.out.println (the last digit of n) ;
}
```

Recursive subtask

If you observe the following identities, it is easy to convert this pseudocode to a complete Java method definition:

```
n / 10 is the number n with the last digit removed.
n % 10 is the last digit of n.
```

For example, 1234 / 10 evaluates to 123 and 1234 % 10 evaluates to 4.

(continued)

EXAMPLE: (continued)

The following is the complete code for the method:

```java
public static void writeVertical(int n)
{
    if (n < 10)
    {
        System.out.println(n);
    }
    else //n is two or more digits long:
    {
        writeVertical(n / 10);
        System.out.println(n % 10);
    }
}
```

Tracing a Recursive Call

Let's see exactly what happens when the following method call is made (as in Display 11.1):

```java
writeVertical(123);
```

When this method call is executed, the computer proceeds just as it would with any method call. The argument 123 is substituted for the parameter n, and the body of the method is executed. After the substitution of 123 for n, the code to be executed is equivalent to

```java
if (123 < 10)
{
    System.out.println(123);
}
else //n is two or more digits long:
{                                         Computation will stop here
    writeVertical(123 / 10);  ◄────────── until the recursive call
    System.out.println(123 % 10);         returns.
}
```

Because 123 is not less than 10, the else part is executed. However, the else part begins with the method call

```java
writeVertical(n / 10);
```

which (because n is equal to 123) is the call

```
writeVertical(123 / 10);
```

which is equivalent to

```
writeVertical(12);
```

When execution reaches this recursive call, the current method computation is placed in suspended animation and this recursive call is executed. When this recursive call is finished, the execution of the suspended computation will return to this point and the suspended computation will continue from this point.

The recursive call

```
writeVertical(12);
```

is handled just like any other method call. The argument 12 is substituted for the parameter n, and the body of the method is executed. After substituting 12 for n, there are two computations, one suspended and one active, as follows:

```
if (123 < 10)
{
    System|  if (12 < 10)
}        {
else //n i       System.out.println(12);
{            }
    writeV  else //n is two or more digits long:
    System  {
}                writeVertical(12 / 10);  ←——  Computation will stop here
}                System.out.println(12 % 10);       until the recursive call
             }                                       returns.
```

Because 12 is not less than 10, the else part is executed. However, as you already saw, the else part begins with a recursive call. The argument for the recursive call is n/10, which in this case is equivalent to 12/10. So, this second computation of the method writeVertical is suspended, and the following recursive call is executed:

```
writeVertical(12 / 10);
```

which is equivalent to

```
writeVertical(1);
```

At this point, there are two suspended computations waiting to resume, and the computer begins to execute this new recursive call, which is handled just like all the previous recursive calls. The argument 1 is substituted for the parameter n, and the body of the method is executed. At this point, the computation looks like the following:

```
if (123 < 10)
{
                if (12 < 10)
}               {
else
{                                   if (1 < 10)
                    }               {
                else                                                    No recursive
                {                           System.out.println(1);      call this time.
                    }               }
                                    else //n is two or more digits long:
}                                   {
                    }                       writeVertical(1 / 10);
                                            System.out.println(1 % 10);

                                    }
```

When the body of the method is executed this time, something different happens.

output the digit 1
Because 1 is less than 10, the Boolean expression in the if-else statement is true, so the statement before the else is executed. That statement is simply an output statement that writes the argument 1 to the screen, so the call writeVertical(1) writes 1 to the screen and ends without any recursive call.

When the call writeVertical(1) ends, the suspended computation that is waiting for it to end resumes where that suspended computation left off, as shown by the following:

```
if (123 < 10)
{
                if (12 < 10)
}               {
else                    System.out.println(12);
{                   }
                else //n is two or more digits long:
                {
}                       writeVertical(12 / 10);    ◄──────  Computation resumes
                        System.out.println(12 % 10);   here.

                }
```

output the
digit 2

When this suspended computation resumes, it executes an output statement that outputs the value 12 % 10, which is 2. That ends that computation, but there is yet another suspended computation waiting to resume. When this last suspended computation resumes, the situation is

```
if (123 < 10)
{
    System.out.println(123);
}
else //n is two or more digits long:
{
    writeVertical(123 / 10);          Computation resumes
    System.out.println(123 % 10);     here.
}
```

output the
digit 3

When this last suspended computation resumes, it outputs the value 123 % 10, which is 3, and the execution of the original method call ends. And, sure enough, the digits 1, 2, and 3 have been written to the screen one per line, in that order.

A Closer Look at Recursion

The definition of the method writeVertical uses recursion. Yet, we did nothing new or different in evaluating the method call writeVertical(123). We treated it just like any of the method calls we saw in previous chapters. We simply substituted the argument 123 for the parameter n and then executed the code in the body of the method definition. When we reached the recursive call

```
writeVertical(123 / 10)
```

we simply repeated this process one more time.

how
recursion
works

The computer keeps track of recursive calls in the following way. When a method is called, the computer plugs in the arguments for the parameter(s) and begins to execute the code. If it should encounter a recursive call, then it temporarily stops its computation, because it must know the result of the recursive call before it can proceed. It saves all the information it needs to continue the computation later on, and proceeds to evaluate the recursive call. When the recursive call is completed, the computer returns to finish the outer computation.

how
recursion
ends

The Java language places no restrictions on how recursive calls are used in method definitions. However, in order for a recursive method definition to be useful, it must be designed so that any call of the method must ultimately terminate with some piece of code that does not depend on recursion. The method may call itself, and that recursive call may call the method again. The process may be repeated any number of times. However, the process will not terminate unless eventually one of the recursive calls does not depend on recursion to return a value. The general outline of a successful recursive method definition is as follows:

- One or more cases in which the method accomplishes its task by using recursive call(s) to accomplish one or more smaller versions of the task.

base case

stopping case

- One or more cases in which the method accomplishes its task without the use of any recursive calls. These cases without any recursive calls are called **base cases** or **stopping cases**.

Often an `if-else` statement determines which of the cases will be executed. A typical scenario is for the original method call to execute a case that includes a recursive call. That recursive call may in turn execute a case that requires another recursive call. For some number of times, each recursive call produces another recursive call, but eventually one of the stopping cases should apply. *Every call of the method must eventually lead to a stopping case, or else the method call will never end because of an infinite chain of recursive calls.* (In practice, a call that includes an infinite chain of recursive calls will usually terminate abnormally rather than actually running forever.)

The most common way to ensure that a stopping case is eventually reached is to write the method so that some (positive) numeric quantity is decreased on each recursive call and to provide a stopping case for some "small" value. This is how we designed the method `writeVertical` in Display 11.1. When the method `writeVertical` is called, that call produces a recursive call with a smaller argument. This continues with each recursive call producing another recursive call until the argument is less than `10`. When the argument is less than `10`, the method call ends without producing any more recursive calls and the process works its way back to the original call and the process ends.

General Form of a Recursive Method Definition

The general outline of a successful recursive method definition is as follows:

- One or more cases that include one or more recursive calls to the method being defined. These recursive calls should solve "smaller" versions of the task performed by the method being defined.

- One or more cases that include no recursive calls. These cases without any recursive calls are called **base cases** or **stopping cases**.

PITFALL: Infinite Recursion

In the example of the method writeVertical discussed in the previous subsections, the series of recursive calls eventually reached a call of the method that did not involve recursion (that is, a stopping case was reached). If, on the other hand, every recursive call produces another recursive call, then a call to the method will, in theory, run forever. This is called **infinite recursion**. In practice, such a method will typically run until the computer runs out of resources and the program terminates abnormally.

Examples of infinite recursion are not hard to come by. The following is a syntactically correct Java method definition, which might result from an attempt to define an alternative version of the method writeVertical:

```java
public static void newWriteVertical(int n)
{
        newWriteVertical(n / 10);
        System.out.println(n % 10);
}
```

If you embed this definition in a program that calls this method, the program will compile with no error messages and you can run the program. Moreover, the definition even has a certain reasonableness to it. It says that to output the argument to newWriteVertical, first output all but the last digit and then output the last digit. However, when called, this method will produce an infinite sequence of recursive calls. If you call newWriteVertical(12), that execution will stop to execute the recursive call newWriteVertical(12/10), which is equivalent to newWriteVertical(1). The execution of that recursive call will, in turn, stop to execute the recursive call

```java
newWriteVertical(1 / 10);
```

which is equivalent to

```java
newWriteVertical(0);
```

This, in turn, will stop to execute the recursive call newWriteVertical(0 / 10); which is also equivalent to

```java
newWriteVertical(0);
```

This will produce another recursive call to again execute the same recursive method call newWriteVertical(0); and so on, forever. Because the definition of newWriteVertical has no stopping case, the process will proceed forever (or until the computer runs out of resources). ■

Self-Test Exercises

1. What is the output of the following program?

```
public class self_ex1
{
    public static void main(String[] args)
    {
        drawStar(5);
    }
    public static void drawStar(int n)
    {
        if (n > 0)
        {
            for (int x = 0; x < n; x++)
            System.out.print("*");
            System.out.println();
              drawStar(n - 1);
        }
    }
}
```

2. Write a recursive void method that has one parameter that is an integer and that writes to the screen the number of asterisks '*' given by the argument. The output should be all on one line. You can assume the argument is positive.

3. Write a recursive void method that has one parameter, which is a string type variable. When called, the method writes its argument to the screen backward. That is, if the argument is 'regional', it outputs the following to the screen:

```
lanoiger
```

4. Write a recursive void method that takes a single (positive) int argument n and writes the integers 1, 2, ..., n to the screen.

5. Write a recursive void method that takes a single (positive) int argument n and writes integers n, n-1, ..., 3, 2, 1 to the screen. *Hint:* The solution for Self-Test Exercise 4 and this exercise vary by an exchange of as little as two lines.

Stacks for Recursion ★

stack

To keep track of recursion, and a number of other things, most computer systems use a structure called a *stack*. A **stack** is a very specialized kind of memory structure that is analogous to a stack of paper. In this analogy, there is an inexhaustible supply of extra blank sheets of paper. To place some information in the stack, it is written on one of these sheets of paper and placed on top of the stack of papers. To place more information in the stack, a clean sheet of paper is taken, the information is written on it, and this new sheet of paper is placed on top of the stack. In this straightforward way, more and more information may be placed on the stack.

Getting information out of the stack is also accomplished by a very simple procedure. The top sheet of paper can be read, and when it is no longer needed, it is thrown away. There is one complication: Only the top sheet of paper is accessible. In order to read, say, the third sheet from the top, the top two sheets must be thrown away. Because the **last-in/** last sheet that is put on the stack is the first sheet taken off the stack, a stack is often **first-out** called a **last-in/first-out** memory structure, abbreviated as **LIFO**.

Using a stack, the computer can easily keep track of recursion. Whenever a method is called, a new sheet of paper is taken. The method definition is copied onto this sheet of paper, and the arguments are plugged for the method parameters. Then the computer starts to execute the body of the method definition. When it encounters a recursive call, it stops the computation it is doing on that sheet in order to compute the value returned by the recursive call. But, before computing the recursive call, it saves enough information so that, when it does finally determine the value returned by the recursive call, it can continue the stopped computation. This saved information is written on a sheet of paper and placed on the stack. A new sheet of paper is used for the recursive call. The computer writes a second copy of the method definition on this new sheet of paper, plugs in the arguments for the method parameters, and starts to execute the recursive call. When it gets to a recursive call within the recursively called copy, it repeats the process of saving information on the stack and using a new sheet of paper for the new recursive call. This process is illustrated in the earlier subsection entitled "Tracing a Recursive Call." Even though we did not call it a stack at the time, the illustrations of computations placed one on top of the other illustrate the actions of the stack.

This process continues until some recursive call to the method completes its computation without producing any more recursive calls. When this happens, the computer turns its attention to the top sheet of paper on the stack. This sheet contains the partially completed computation that is waiting for the recursive computation that just ended. So, it is possible to proceed with that suspended computation. When that suspended computation ends, the computer discards that sheet of paper and the suspended computation that is below it on the stack becomes the computation on top of the stack. The computer turns its attention to the suspended computation that is now on the top of the stack, and so forth. The process continues until the computation on the bottom sheet is completed. Depending on how many recursive calls are made and how the method definition is written, the stack may grow and shrink in any fashion. Notice that the sheets in the stack can only be accessed in a last-in/first-out fashion—but, this is exactly what is needed to keep track of recursive calls. Each suspended version is waiting for the completion of the version directly above it on the stack.

stack frame Of course, computers do not have stacks of paper. This is just an analogy. The computer uses portions of memory rather than pieces of paper. The contents of one **activation** of these portions of memory ("sheets of paper") is called a **stack frame** or **activation** **record** **record**. These stack frames are handled in the last-in/first-out manner we just discussed.

(These stack frames do not contain a complete copy of the method definition, but merely reference a single copy of the method definition. However, a stack frame contains enough information to allow the computer to act as if the stack frame contains a complete copy of the method definition.)

VideoNote
Recursion and the Stack

Stack ★

A **stack** is a last-in/first-out memory structure. The first item referenced or removed from a stack is always the last item entered into the stack. Stacks are used by computers to keep track of recursion (and for other purposes).

PITFALL: Stack Overflow ★

There is always some limit to the size of the stack. If there is a long chain in which a method makes a recursive call to itself, and that call results in another recursive call, and that call produces yet another recursive call, and so forth, then each recursive call in this chain will cause another suspended computation to be placed on the stack. If this chain is too long, then the stack will attempt to grow beyond its limit. This is an error condition known as a **stack overflow**. If you receive an error message that says *stack overflow*, it is likely that some method call has produced an excessively long chain of recursive calls. One common cause of stack overflow is infinite recursion. If a method is recursing infinitely, then it will eventually try to make the stack exceed any stack size limit. ■

Recursion versus Iteration

Recursion is not absolutely necessary. In fact, some programming languages do not allow it. Any task that can be accomplished using recursion can also be done in some other way without using recursion. For example, Display 11.2 contains a nonrecursive version of the method given in Display 11.1. The nonrecursive version of a method typically uses a loop (or loops) of some sort in place of recursion. For this reason, the
iterative version nonrecursive version is usually referred to as an **iterative version**. If the definition of the method writeVertical given in Display 11.1 is replaced by the version given in Display 11.2, then the output will be the same. As is true in this case, a recursive version of a method can sometimes be much simpler than an iterative version. The full
extra code on website program with the iterative version of the method is given in the file IterativeDemo1 on the accompanying website.

A recursively written method will usually run slower and use more storage than an equivalent iterative version. The computer must do extra work manipulating the stack to keep track of the recursion. However, because the system does all this for you automatically, using recursion can sometimes make your job as a programmer easier, and can sometimes produce code that is easier to understand. Additionally, there are some cases in which the compiler or JVM can convert a recursive algorithm into an iterative version for you.

Display 11.2   Iterative Version of the Method in Display 11.1

```
1   public static void writeVertical(int n)
2   {
3       int nsTens = 1;
4       int leftEndPiece = n;
5       while (leftEndPiece > 9)
6       {
7           leftEndPiece = leftEndPiece / 10;
8           nsTens = nsTens * 10;
9       }
10      //nsTens is a power of 10 that has the same number
11      //of digits as n. For example, if n is 2345, then
12      //nsTens is 1000.

13      for (int powerOf10 = nsTens;
14              powerOf10 > 0; powerOf10 = powerOf10 / 10)
15      {
16          System.out.println(n / powerOf10);
17          n = n % powerOf10;
18      }
19  }
```

Self-Test Exercises

6. If your program produces an error message that says *stack overflow*, what is a likely source of the error?

7. Write an iterative version of the method `drawStar` defined in Self-Test Exercise 1.

8. Write an iterative version of the method defined in Self-Test Exercise 2.

9. Write an iterative version of the method defined in Self-Test Exercise 3.

10. Trace the recursive solution you made to Self-Test Exercise 4.

11. Trace the recursive solution you made to Self-Test Exercise 5.

11.2   Recursive Methods That Return a Value

To iterate is human, to recurse divine.

ANONYMOUS

General Form for a Recursive Method That Returns a Value

The recursive methods you have seen thus far are all `void` methods, but recursion is not limited to these methods. A recursive method can return a value of any type. The technique for designing recursive methods that return a value is basically the same as what you learned for `void` methods. An outline for a successful recursive method definition that returns a value is as follows:

- One or more cases in which the value returned is computed in terms of calls to the same method (that is, using recursive calls). As is the case with `void` methods, the arguments for the recursive calls should intuitively be "smaller."

- One or more cases in which the value returned is computed without the use of any recursive calls. These cases without any recursive calls are called **base cases** or **stopping cases** (just as they were with `void` methods).

This technique is illustrated in the next Programming Example.

EXAMPLE: Another Powers Method

In Chapter 5, we introduced the static method `pow` of the class `Math`, that computes powers. For example, `Math.pow(2.0,3.0)` returns $2.0^{3.0}$, so the following sets the variable `result` equal to `8.0`:

```
double result = Math.pow(2.0, 3.0);
```

The method `pow` takes two arguments of type `double` and returns a value of type `double`. Display 11.3 contains a recursive definition for a static method that is similar to `pow`, but that works with the type `int` rather than `double`. This new method is called `power`. For example, the following will set the value of `result2` equal to 8, because 2^3 is 8:

```
int result2 = power(2, 3);
```

Outside the defining class, this would be written as

```
int result2 = RecursionDemo2.power(2, 3);
```

Our main reason for defining the method `power` is to have a simple example of a recursive method, but there are situations in which the method `power` would be preferable to the method `pow`. The method `pow` returns a value of type `double`, which is only an approximate quantity. The method `power` returns a value of type `int`, which is an exact quantity. In some situations, you might need the additional accuracy provided by the method `power`.

The definition of the method `power` is based on the following formula:

```
xⁿ is equal to xⁿ⁻¹ * x
```

EXAMPLE: (continued)

Translating this formula into Java says that the value returned by `power(x, n)` should be the same as the value of the expression

```
power(x, n - 1)*x
```

The definition of the method `power` given in Display 11.3 does return this value for `power(x, n)`, provided $n > 0$.

The case where n is equal to 0 is the stopping case. If n is 0, then `power(x, n)` simply returns 1 (because x^0 is 1).

Let's see what happens when the method `power` is called with some sample values. First, consider the simple expression:

```
power(2, 0)
```

When the method is called, the value of x is set equal to 2, the value of n is set equal to 0, and the code in the body of the method definition is executed. Because the value of n is a legal value, the `if-else` statement is executed. Because this value of n is not greater than 0, the `return` statement after the `else` is used, so the method call returns 1. Thus, the following would set the value of `result3` equal to 1:

```
int result3 = power(2, 0);
```

Now let's look at an example that involves a recursive call. Consider the expression

```
power(2, 1)
```

When the method is called, the value of x is set equal to 2, the value of n is set equal to 1, and the code in the body of the method definition is executed. Because this value of n is greater than 0, the following `return` statement is used to determine the value returned:

```
return ( power(x, n - 1)*x );
```

which in this case is equivalent to

```
return ( power(2, 0)*2 );
```

At this point, the computation of `power(2, 1)` is suspended, a copy of this suspended computation is placed on the stack, and the computer then starts a new method call to compute the value of `power(2, 0)`. As you have already seen, the value of `power(2, 0)` is 1. After determining the value of `power(2, 0)`, the computer replaces the expression

(continued)

EXAMPLE: (continued)

power(2, 0) with its value of 1 and resumes the suspended computation. The resumed computation determines the final value for power(2, 1) from the above return statement as

```
Power(2, 0)*2 is 1*2 which is 2
```

so the final value returned for power(2, 1) is 2. So, the following would set the value of result4 equal to 2:

```
int result4 = power(2, 1);
```

Larger numbers for the second argument will produce longer chains of recursive calls. For example, consider the statement

```
System.out.println(power(2, 3));
```

The value of power(2, 3) is calculated as follows:

```
power(2, 3) is power(2, 2)*2
    power(2, 2) is power(2, 1)*2
        power(2, 1) is power(2, 0)*2
            power(2, 0) is 1 (stopping case)
```

When the computer reaches the stopping case, power(2, 0), there are three suspended computations. After calculating the value returned for the stopping case, it resumes the most recently suspended computations to determine the value of power(2, 1). After that, the computer completes each of the other suspended computations, using each value computed as a value to plug into another suspended computation, until it reaches and completes the computation for the original call power(2, 3). The details of the entire computation are illustrated in Display 11.4.

Display 11.3   The Recursive Method **power** (part 1 of 2)

```
1   public class RecursionDemo2
2   {
3       public static void main(String[] args)
4       {
5           for (int n = 0; n < 4; n++)
6               System.out.println("3 to the power " + n
7                   + " is " + power(3, n));
8       }

9       public static int power(int x, int n)
10      {
```

Display 11.3   The Recursive Method `power` (part 2 of 2)

```
11              if (n < 0)
12              {
13                  System.out.println("Illegal argument to power.");
14                  System.exit(0);
15              }
16              if (n > 0)
17                  return ( power(x, n - 1)*x );
18              else // n == 0
19                  return (1);
20          }
21  }
```

Sample Dialogue

```
3 to the power 0 is 1
3 to the power 1 is 3
3 to the power 2 is 9
3 to the power 3 is 27
```

Display 11.4   Evaluating the Recursive Method Call `power(2,3)`

SEQUENCE OF RECURSIVE CALLS:

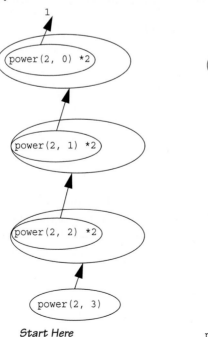

Start Here

HOW THE FINAL VALUE IS COMPUTED:

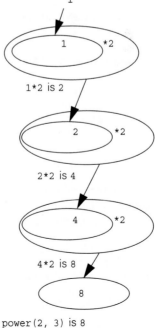

power(2, 3) is 8

Self-Test Exercises

12. What is the output of the following program? What does the program calculate?

```java
public class Exercise12
{
    public static void main(String[] args)
      {
        System.out.println(mystery(5));
      }

    public static int mystery(int n)
    {
        if (n <= 1)
            return 1;
        else
            return ( mystery(n - 1) + n*n);
    }
}
```

13. What is the output of the following program? What well-known mathematical method is rose?

```java
public class Exercise13
{
    public static void main(String[] args)
    {
        System.out.println(rose(4));
    }

    public static int rose(int n)
    {
        if (n <= 0)
            return 1;
        else
            return ( rose(n - 1) * n );
    }
}
```

14. Redefine the method power (Display 11.3) so that it also works for negative exponents. To do this, you also have to change the type of the value returned to double. The method heading for the redefined version of power is as follows:

```java
/**
 Precondition: If n < 0, then x is not 0.
 Returns x to the power n.
*/
public static double power(int x, int n)
```

Hint: x^{-n} is equal to $1/(x^n)$.

11.3   Thinking Recursively

There are two kinds of people in the world, those who divide the world into two kinds of people and those who do not.

ANONYMOUS

Recursive Design Techniques

When defining and using recursive methods, you do not want to be continually aware of the stack and the suspended computations. The power of recursion comes from the fact that you can ignore that detail and let the computer do the bookkeeping for you. Consider the example of the method power in Display 11.3. The way to think of the definition of power is as follows:

```
power(x, n) returns power(x, n - 1)*x
```

Because x^n is equal to $x^{n-1}*x$, this is the correct value to return, provided that the computation will always reach a stopping case and will correctly compute the stopping case. So, after checking that the recursive part of the definition is correct, all you need to check is that the chain of recursive calls will always reach a stopping case and that the stopping case will always return the correct value. In other words, all that you need to do is check that the following three properties are satisfied:

criteria for methods that return a value

1. There is no infinite recursion. (A recursive call may lead to another recursive call, which may lead to another, and so forth, but every such chain of recursive calls eventually reaches a stopping case.)

2. Each stopping case returns the correct value for that case.

3. For the cases that involve recursion: *if* all recursive calls return the correct value, *then* the final value returned by the method is the correct value.

For example, consider the method power in Display 11.3:

1. **There is no infinite recursion**: The second argument to power(x, n) is decreased by one in each recursive call, so any chain of recursive calls must eventually reach the case power(x, 0), which is the stopping case. Thus, there is no infinite recursion.

2. **Each stopping case returns the correct value for that case**: The only stopping case is power(x, 0). A call of the form power(x, 0) always returns 1, and the correct value for x^0 is 1. So, the stopping case returns the correct value.

3. **For the cases that involve recursion, *if* all recursive calls return the correct value, *then* the final value returned by the method is the correct value**: The only case that involves recursion is when n > 1. When n > 1, power(x, n) returns

```
power(x, n - 1)*x.
```

To see that this is the correct value to return, note that, *if* power(x, n - 1) returns the correct value, *then* power(x, n - 1) returns x^{n-1} and so power(x, n) returns

x^{n-1} * x, which is x^n

This is the correct value for power(x, n).

That is all you need to check to be sure that the definition of power is correct. (The previous technique is known as *mathematical induction*, a concept that you may have heard about in a mathematics class. However, you do not need to be familiar with the term *mathematical induction* to use this technique.)

We gave you three criteria to use in checking the correctness of a recursive method that returns a value. Basically, the same rules can be applied to a recursive void method. If you show that your recursive void method definition satisfies the following three criteria, then you will know that your void method performs correctly:

criteria for void methods

1. There is no infinite recursion.
2. Each stopping case performs the correct action for that case.
3. For each of the cases that involve recursion, *if* all recursive calls perform their actions correctly, *then* the entire case performs correctly.

Binary Search ★

In this subsection, we will develop a recursive method that searches an array to find out whether it contains a specified value. For example, the array may contain a list of the numbers for credit cards that are no longer valid. A store clerk needs to search the list to see if a customer's card is valid or invalid.

The indices of the array a are the integers 0 through finalIndex. To make the task of searching the array easier, we will assume that the array is sorted. Hence, we know the following:

```
a[0]  ≤  a[1]  ≤  a[2]  ≤  …  ≤  a[finalIndex]
```

In fact, the binary search algorithm we will use requires that the array be sorted like this.

When searching an array, you are likely to want to know both whether the value is in the array and, if it is, where it is in the array. For example, if you are searching for a credit card number, then the array index may serve as a record number. Another array indexed by these same indices may hold a phone number or other information to use for reporting the suspicious card. Hence, if the sought-after value is in the array, we will have our method return an index of where the sought-after value is located. If the value is not in the array, our method will return -1. (The array may contain repeats, which is why we say "an index" and not "the index.")

Now let us proceed to produce an algorithm to solve this task. It will help to visualize the problem in very concrete terms. Suppose the list of numbers is so long that it takes a book to list them all. This is in fact how invalid credit card numbers are distributed to stores that do not have access to computers. If you are a clerk and are handed a credit card, you must check to see if it is on the list and hence invalid. How would you proceed? Open the book to the middle and see if the number is there. If it is not and it is smaller than the middle number, then work backward toward the beginning of the book. If the number is larger than the middle number, you work your way toward the end of the book. This idea produces our first draft of an algorithm:

algorithm
first version

```
mid = approximate midpoint between 0 and finalIndex;
if (key == a[mid])
    return mid;
else if (key < a[mid])
    search a[0] through a[mid - 1];
else if (key > a[mid])
    search a[mid + 1] through a[finalIndex];
```

Because the searchings of the shorter lists are smaller versions of the very task we are designing the algorithm to perform, this algorithm naturally lends itself to the use of recursion. The smaller lists can be searched with recursive calls to the algorithm itself.

Our pseudocode is a bit too imprecise to be easily translated into Java code. The problem has to do with the recursive calls. There are two recursive calls shown:

```
search a[0] through a[mid - 1];
             and
search a[mid + 1] through a[finalIndex];
```

more
parameters

To implement these recursive calls, we need two more parameters. A recursive call specifies that a subrange of the array is to be searched. In one case, it is the elements indexed by 0 through mid − 1. In the other case, it is the elements indexed by mid + 1 through finalIndex. The two extra parameters will specify the first and last indices of the search, so we will call them first and last. Using these parameters for the lowest and highest indices, instead of 0 and finalIndex, we can express the pseudocode more precisely as follows:

algorithm
first
refinement

```
To search a[first] through a[last] do the following:
mid = approximate midpoint between first and last;
if (key == a[mid])
    return mid;
else if (key < a[mid])
    return the result of searching a[first] through a[mid - 1];
else if (key > a[mid])
    return the result of searching a[mid + 1] through a[last];
```

To search the entire array, the algorithm would be executed with first set equal to 0 and last set equal to finalIndex. The recursive calls will use other values for first and last. For example, the first recursive call would set first equal to 0 and last equal to the calculated value mid − 1.

stopping case

As with any recursive algorithm, we must ensure that our algorithm ends rather than producing infinite recursion. If the sought-after number is found on the list, then there is no recursive call and the process terminates, but we need some way to detect when the number is not on the list. On each recursive call, the value of `first` is increased or the value of `last` is decreased. If they ever pass each other and `first` actually becomes larger than `last`, then we will know that there are no more indices left to check and that the number `key` is not in the array. If we add this test to our pseudocode, we obtain a complete solution, as shown in Display 11.5.

algorithm final version

Now we can routinely translate the pseudocode into Java code. The result is shown in Display 11.6. The method `search` is an implementation of the recursive algorithm given in Display 11.5. A diagram of how the method performs on a sample array is given in Display 11.7. Display 11.8 illustrates how the method `search` is used.

Notice that the method `search` solves a more general problem than the original task. Our goal was to design a method to search an entire array. Yet the method will let us search any interval of the array by specifying the indices `first` and `last`. This is common when designing recursive methods. Frequently, it is necessary to solve a more general problem in order to be able to express the recursive algorithm. In this case, we want only the answer in the case where `first` and `last` are set equal to 0 and `finalIndex`. However, the recursive calls will set them to values other than 0 and `finalIndex`.

Display 11.5 Pseudocode for Binary Search ★

ALGORITHM TO SEARCH `a[first]` THROUGH `a[last]`

```
/**
 Precondition:
 a[first]<= a[first + 1] <= a[first + 2] <= … <= a[last]
*/
```

TO LOCATE THE VALUE KEY

```
if (first > last) //A stopping case
    return -1;
else
{
    mid = approximate midpoint between first and last;
    if (key == a[mid]) //A stopping case
        return mid;
    else if key < a[mid] //A case with recursion
        return the result of searching a[first] through a[mid - 1];
    else if key > a[mid] //A case with recursion
        return the result of searching a[mid + 1] through a[last];
}
```

Display 11.6   Recursive Method for Binary Search ★

```
1   public class BinarySearch
2   {
3       /**
4        Searches the array a for key. If key is not in the array segment,
5        then -1 is returned. Otherwise returns an index in the segment such
         that key == a[index].
6        Precondition: a[first] <= a[first + 1]<= … <= a[last]
7       */
8       public static int search(int[] a, int first, int last, int key)
9       {
10          int result = 0; //to keep the compiler happy.

11          if (first > last)
12              result = -1;
13          else
14          {
15              int mid = (first + last)/2;

16              if (key == a[mid])
17                  result = mid;
18              else if (key < a[mid])
19                  result = search(a, first, mid - 1, key);
20              else if (key > a[mid])
21                  result = search(a, mid + 1, last, key);
22          }
23          return result;
24      }
25  }
```

In the earlier subsection entitled "Tracing a Recursive Call," we gave three criteria that you should check to ensure that a recursive void method definition is correct. Let's check these three things for the method search given in Display 11.6:

1. **There is no infinite recursion**: On each recursive call, the value of first is increased or the value of last is decreased. If the chain of recursive calls does not end in some other way, then eventually the method will be called with first larger than last, which is a stopping case.

2. **Each stopping case performs the correct action for that case**: There are two stopping cases, when first > last and when key == a[mid]. Let's consider each case.

   If first > last, there are no array elements between a[first] and a[last], so key is not in this segment of the array. (Nothing is in this segment of the array!) So, if first > last, the method search correctly returns -1, indicating that key is not in the specified range of the array.

   If key == a[mid], the algorithm correctly sets location equal to mid. Thus, both stopping cases are correct.

Display 11.7 Execution of the Method `search` ★

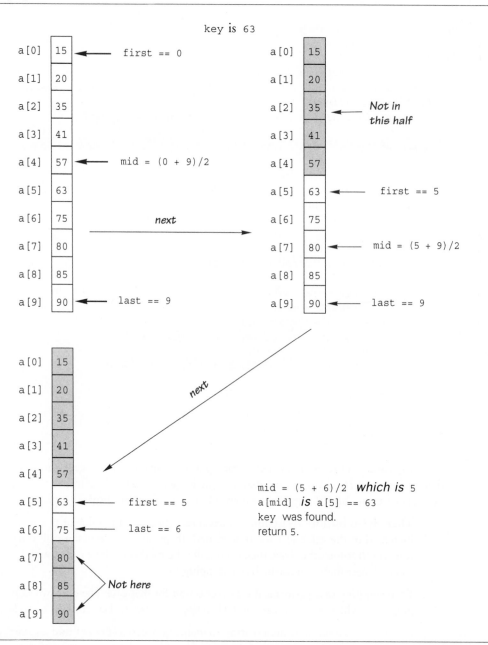

key is 63

a[0] 15 ← first == 0

a[4] 57 ← mid = (0 + 9)/2

a[9] 90 ← last == 9

next →

a[0] 15

a[2] 35 ← Not in this half

a[5] 63 ← first == 5

a[7] 80 ← mid = (5 + 9)/2

a[9] 90 ← last == 9

next

a[5] 63 ← first == 5

a[6] 75 ← last == 6

a[7] 80
a[8] 85 } Not here
a[9] 90

mid = (5 + 6)/2 *which is* 5
a[mid] *is* a[5] == 63
key was found.
return 5.

Display 11.8   Using the `search` Method ★

```
1    public class BinarySearchDemo
2    {
3        public static void main(String[] args)
4        {
5            int[] a = {-2, 0, 2, 4, 6, 8, 10, 12, 14, 16};
6            int finalIndex = 9;

7            System.out.println("Array contains:");
8            for (int i = 0; i < a.length; i++)
9                System.out.print(a[i] + " ");
10           System.out.println();
11           System.out.println();

12           int result;
13           for (int key = -3; key < 5; key++)
14           {
15               result = BinarySearch.search(a, 0, finalIndex, key);
16               if (result >= 0)
17                   System.out.println(key + " is at index " + result);
18               else
19                   System.out.println(key + " is not in the array.");
20           }
21       }
22   }
```

Sample Dialogue

```
Array contains:
-2 0 2 4 6 8 10 12 14 16

-3 is not in the array.
-2 is at index 0
-1 is not in the array.
0 is at index 1
1 is not in the array.
2 is at index 2
3 is not in the array.
4 is at index 3
```

3. **For each of the cases that involve recursion,** *if* **all recursive calls perform their actions correctly,** *then* **the entire case performs correctly**: There are two cases in which there are recursive calls, when `key < a[mid]` and when `key > a[mid]`. We need to check each of these two cases.

First, suppose `key < a[mid]`. In this case, because the array is sorted, we know that if `key` is anywhere in the array, then `key` is one of the elements `a[first]` through `a[mid - 1]`. Thus, the method need only search these elements, which is exactly what the recursive call

```
search(a, first, mid - 1, key)
```

does. So if the recursive call is correct, then the entire action is correct.

Next, suppose `key > a[mid]`. In this case, because the array is sorted, we know that if `key` is anywhere in the array, then `key` is one of the elements `a[mid + 1]` through `a[last]`. Thus, the method need only search these elements, which is exactly what the recursive call

```
search(a, mid + 1, last, key)
```

does. So if the recursive call is correct, then the entire action is correct. Thus, in both cases, the method performs the correct action (assuming that the recursive calls perform the correct action).

The method `search` passes all three of our tests, so it is a good recursive method definition.

Efficiency of Binary Search ★

The binary search algorithm is extremely fast compared to an algorithm that simply tries all array elements in order. In the binary search, you eliminate about half the array from consideration right at the start. You then eliminate a quarter, then an eighth of the array, and so forth. These savings add up to a dramatically fast algorithm. For an array of 100 elements, the binary search will never need to compare more than 7 array elements to the key. A serial search could compare as many as 100 array elements to the key, and on the average will compare about 50 array elements to the key. Moreover, the larger the array is, the more dramatic the savings will be. On an array with 1,000 elements, the binary search will only need to compare about 10 array elements to the key value, as compared to an average of 500 for the serial search algorithm.[1]

iterative version

An iterative version of the method `search` is given in Display 11.9. On some systems, the iterative version will run more efficiently than the recursive version. The algorithm for the iterative version was derived by mirroring the recursive version. In the iterative version, the local variables `first` and `last` mirror the roles of the parameters in the recursive version, which are also named `first` and `last`. As this example

---

[1]The binary search algorithm has worst-case running time that is logarithmic—that is, $O(\log n)$. The serial search algorithm is linear—that is, $O(n)$. If the terms used in this footnote are not familiar to you, you can safely ignore it.

Display 11.9   Iterative Version of Binary Search ★

```java
1   /**
2     Searches the array a for key. If key is not in the array segment, then
3     -1 is returned. Otherwise returns an index in the segment such that key
      == a[index].
4     Precondition: a [lowEnd] <= a[lowEnd + 1]<= … <= a[highEnd]
5   */
6   public static int search(int[] a, int lowEnd, int highEnd, int key)
7   {
8       int first = lowEnd;
9       int last = highEnd;
10      int mid;

11      boolean found = false; //so far
12      int result = 0; //to keep compiler happy

13      while ( (first <= last) && !(found) )
14      {
15          mid = (first + last)/2;

16          if (key == a[mid])
17          {
18              found = true;
19              result = mid;
20          }
21          else if (key < a[mid])
22          {
23              last = mid - 1;
24          }
25          else if (key > a[mid])
26          {
27              first = mid + 1;
28          }
29      }

30      if (first > last)
31          result = -1;
32      return result;
33  }
```

illustrates, it often makes sense to derive a recursive algorithm even if you expect to later convert it to an iterative algorithm. You can see the iterative method from Display 11.9 embedded in a full demonstration in the files `IterativeBinarySearch.java` and `IterativeBinarySearchDemo.java` on the accompanying website.

tail
recursion

Most modern compilers will convert certain simple recursive method definitions to iterative ones before running the program. A method that uses **tail recursion** has the property that it does nothing after the recursive call except return the method's value. In this case, a tail recursive method can be easily converted to an equivalent iterative solution. This operation may be performed by the compiler or by the JVM.

MyProgrammingLab™

Self-Test Exercise

15. The program calculates the sum of n natural number. Write a recursive method definition for the following method:

```
/**
 Precondition: n >= 1
 Returns the sum of n natural numbers.
*/
public static int sum(int n)
```

For example, sum(20) returns 210 because 1 + 2 + 3 + 4 ... + 20 = 210

EXAMPLE: Finding a File

The next program is an example where a recursive solution is much easier to write and understand than an iterative solution. Consider the problem of finding a file buried somewhere in your file system. For example, using the Windows file system, let's say that you have the following file and directory structure on your hard drive:

Display 11.10   Sample File System Structure

```
C:\
   JavaPrograms\
      Recursion\
         FindFile.java
         BinarySearch.java
      Homework\
         Homework1.java
         Homework2.java
      Test.java
   Papers\
      TermPaper.odt
      Workfile.docx
   Letter.txt
```

We would like to find the location of a file given its name. For example, given `TermPaper.odt`, we would like to know that it is located in `C:\Papers`. Given `FindFile.java`, we would like to know that it is located in `C:\JavaPrograms\Recursion`. The general solution is to start at some root directory, such as `C:\`, and to go through all the items in that directory. If an item is a file, check if it matches the target. If an item is a directory, then make a recursive call to restart the search using that directory as the new root directory.

Pseudocode of our recursive solution follows:

```
searchForFile(currentPath, targetFile)
    if currentPath is not a directory
            return error
    for every item i in currentPath
        if i is a directory
            r = searchForFile(i, targetFile)
            if r is a successful match
                return r
        if i is a file
            if i matches targetFile
                    return path to file i
    return target not found
```

To implement our algorithm, we need a way to determine if a path is a directory or a file, and we need to find a way to get all of the items within a directory. Java's `File` object will do all of this for us. To use it, we must import `java.io.File`. Here is the relevant constructor and methods:

CONSTRUCTORS AND METHODS	DESCRIPTION
`File(String pathname)`	The constructor takes a pathname and creates a `File` object corresponding to the file or directory with that pathname.
`String getAbsolutePath()`	Returns the pathname of the `File` object, e.g., `C:\Papers\TermPaper.odt`.
`String getName()`	Returns the name of the `File` object, e.g., `TermPaper.odt`.
`boolean isDirectory()`	Returns `true` if the `File` object is a directory.
`File[] listFiles()`	If the `File` object is a directory then this returns an array of `File` objects corresponding to all the items within the directory.

Using the `File` object, we can implement the recursive algorithm to find a file. The implementation in Display 11.11 returns an empty string if the target file is not found. If the initial root folder supplied is not a directory, then an error message is returned. The sample results assume the program runs using the directory structure given in Display 11.10.

Display 11.11   Program to Recursively Find a File

```
1   import java.io.File;
2   public class FindFile
3   {
4     public static String searchForFile(File dir, String target)
5     {
6       String result = "";
7       // If dir is not a directory, return
8       if (!dir.isDirectory())
9           return "Path is not a directory.";
10
11      // Check each item in the directory
12      for (File folderItem : dir.listFiles())
13      {
14          // Recurse if it's a directory
15          if (folderItem.isDirectory())
16          {
17              result = searchForFile(folderItem,target);
18              // Return the result if it is not empty
19              if (!result.equals(""))
20                  return result;
21          }
22          // If it's a file, check for a match
23          else
24          {
25              if (folderItem.getName().equals(target))
26                  return folderItem.getAbsolutePath();
27          }
28      }
29      // If we got here, nothing was found
30      return "";
31    }
32
33    public static void main(String[] args)
34    {
35      // The root folder to search
36      File rootFolder = new File("C:\\");
37      String result = searchForFile(rootFolder, "FindFile.java");
38      if (!result.equals(""))
39              System.out.println(result);
40      else
41              System.out.println("File not found.");
42    }
43  }
```

Sample Dialogue Using Directory Structure of Display 11.10

```
C:\JavaPrograms\Recursion\FindFile.java
```

Self-Test Exercises

16. How might you write a nonrecursive version of the program in Display 11.11? You do not have to write actual code, just think of what approach you might use.

17. The program in Display 11.11 could make thousands of recursive calls if you have a lot of subdirectories on your hard drive. Why is it unlikely that you will encounter a stack overflow error?

18. What is the stopping case in Display 11.11?

Chapter Summary

- If a problem can be reduced to smaller instances of the same problem, then a recursive solution is likely to be easy to find and implement.

- A recursive algorithm for a method definition normally contains two kinds of cases: one or more cases that include at least one recursive call and one or more stopping cases in which the problem is solved without any recursive calls.

- When writing a recursive method definition, always check to see that the method will not produce infinite recursion.

- When you define a recursive method, use the three criteria given in the subsection "Recursive Design Techniques" to check that the method is correct.

- When you design a recursive method to solve a task, it is often necessary to solve a more general problem than the given task. This may be required to allow for the proper recursive calls, because the smaller problems may not be exactly the same problem as the given task. For example, in the binary search problem, the task was to search an entire array, but the recursive solution is an algorithm to search any portion of the array (either all of it or a part of it).

Answers to Self-Test Exercises

1. ```
   *****
   ****
   ***
   **
   *
   ```

2. ```java
   public static void stars(int n)
   {
       System.out.print('*');
       if (n > 1)
           stars(n - 1);
   }
   ```

The following answer to Self-Test Exercise 3 is also correct, but is more complicated.

3.
```
public static void reverse(String s)
{
    if (s.length() == 1)
    {
        System.out.println(s);
    }
    else
    {
    int l = s.length() -1;
    System.out.print(s.charAt(l));
    reverse(s.substring(0, l));
    }
}
```

4.
```
public static void writeUp(int n)
{
    if (n >= 1)
    {
        writeUp(n - 1);
        System.out.print(n + " "); //write while the
                            //recursion unwinds
    }
}
```

5.
```
public static void writeDown(int n)
{
    if (n >= 1)
    {
        System.out.print(n + " "); //write while the
                            //recursion winds
        writeDown(n - 1);
    }
}
```

6. An error message that says *stack overflow* is telling you that the computer has attempted to place more stack frames on the stack than are allowed on your system. A likely cause of this error message is infinite recursion.

7.
```java
public static void drawStar(int n)
        {
            for (int (i = n; i > 0; i--)
                {
            for(int j = 0; j < i; j++)
            System.out.print("*");
            System.out.println();
                }
        }
```

8.
```java
public static void stars(int n)
    {
        for (int count = 1; count <= n; count++)
            System.out.print('*');
    }
```

9.
```java
public static void reverse(String s)
        {
            int l = s.length() -1;
            for(int i = l; i >= 0; i--)
            System.out.print(s.charAt(i));
        }
```

10. The trace for Self-Test Exercise 4: If n = 3, the code to be executed is

```java
if (3 >= 1)
{
    writeUp(2);
    System.out.print(3 + " ");
}
```

The execution is suspended before the System.out.println. On the next recursion, n = 2; the code to be executed is

```java
if (2 >= 1)
{
    writeUp(1);
    System.out.print(2 + " ");
}
```

The execution is suspended before the System.out.println. On the next recursion, n = 1 and the code to be executed is

```java
if (1 >= 1)
{
    writeUp(0);
    System.out.print(1 + " ");
}
```

The execution is suspended before the `System.out.println`. On the final recursion, `n = 0` and the code to be executed is

```
if (0 >= 1) // condition false, body skipped
{
    // skipped
}
```

The suspended computations are completed from the most recent to the least recent. The output is `1 2 3`.

11. The trace for Self-Test Exercise 5: If `n = 3`, the code to be executed is

```
if (3 >= 1)
{
    System.out.print(3 + " ");
    writeDown(2);
}
```

Next recursion, `n = 2`, the code to be executed is

```
if (2 >= 1)
{
    System.out.print(2 + " ");
    writeDown(1)
}
```

Next recursion, `n = 1`, the code to be executed is

```
if (1 >= 1)
{
    System.out.print(1 + " ");
    writeDown(0)
}
```

Final recursion, `n = 0`, and the `if` statement does nothing, ending the recursive calls:

```
if (0 >= 1) // condition false
{
    // this clause is skipped
}
```

The output is `3 2 1`.

12. `55`.

13. The output is `24`. The method `rose` is the factorial method, usually written as *n!* and defined as follows:

n! is equal to $n*(n - 1)*(n - 2)*...*1$

14.
```
public static double power(int x, int n)
{
    if (n < 0 && x == 0)
    {
        System.out.println(
                "Illegal argument to power.");
        System.exit(0);
    }

    if (n < 0)
        return ( 1/power(x, - n));
    else if (n > 0)
        return ( power(x, n - 1)*x );
    else // n == 0
        return (1.0);
}
```

15.
```
public static int sum(int num)
{
        if (num <= 0)
    return 0;
    else
    return sum(num - 1) + num;
    }
```

16. One approach is to keep a list of all directories that have been encountered. The list could be implemented with an array. Initially, this list would be set to the root directory. While there is at least one directory on the list, repeat the following:
    - Remove a directory from the list.
        ○ Find all files within the directory. If one of these files matches the target, return the pathname to the file.
        ○ Find all subdirectories within the directory. Add each subdirectory to the list.

    This approach is a little more complicated than the recursive version because we have to manage the list. In the recursive version, the list is essentially managed for us through the series of recursive calls.

17. A stack overflow in the context of recursion occurs when there is a long chain of recursive calls. In the FindFile program, one link of this chain is created when a subdirectory is in another directory. To create a stack overflow, we would need to have a folder in a folder, which is in a folder, which is in a folder, etc. How many folders must be linked in this way to cause a stack overflow will vary from one system to another, but you can expect hundreds would be necessary, an unlikely scenario in a typical file system. Although there could be thousands of recursive calls when searching for a file, there will likely be many short chains instead of single long chains. This allows recursive calls to exit and prevent a stack overflow.

18. Recursion stops if the file passed in is not a directory, if there are no subdirectories in the directory, or after all subdirectories have been recursively called. If a match is found, then recursion also stops.

MyProgrammingLab™ **Programming Projects**

Visit www.myprogramminglab.com to complete select exercises online and get instant feedback.

1. By definition, a palindrome is a word, phrase, number, or other sequence of units that can be read the same way in either direction, with general allowances for adjustments to punctuation and word dividers. Examples of palindromes are *civic, madam,* and *kayak.* Write a Boolean recursive function that determines if a string argument is a palindrome. The function should return true if the argument reads the same forward and backward. Write a driver program that asks the user for a string and uses the function for checking whether the entered string is a palindrome or not.

2. There are *n* people in a room, where *n* is an integer greater than or equal to 1. Each person shakes hands once with every other person. What is the total number, *h(n)*, of handshakes? Write a recursive function to solve this problem. To get you started, if there are only one or two people in the room, then

```
handshake(1) = 0
handshake(2) = 1
```

If a third person enters the room, he or she must shake hands with each of the two people already there. This is two handshakes in addition to the number of handshakes that would be made in a room of two people, or a total of three handshakes.

If a fourth person enters the room, he or she must shake hands with each of the three people already present. This is three handshakes in addition to the number of handshakes that would be made in a room of three people, or six handshakes.

If you can generalize this to *n* handshakes, then it should help you write the recursive solution.

3. Consider a frame of bowling pins shown below, where each * represents a pin:

```
        *

      *   *

    *   *   *

  *   *   *   *

*   *   *   *   *
```

VideoNote
Solution to Programming Project 11.3

There are 5 rows and a total of 15 pins.

If we had only the top 4 rows, then there would be a total of 10 pins.

If we had only the top three rows, then there would be a total of six pins.

If we had only the top two rows, then there would be a total of three pins.

If we had only the top row, then there would be a total of one pin.

Write a recursive function that takes as input the number of rows n and outputs the total number of pins that would exist in a pyramid with n rows. Your program should allow for values of n that are larger than 5.

4. The game of "Jump It" consists of a board with n positive integers in a row except for the first column, which always contains zero. These numbers represent the cost to enter each column. Here is a sample game board where n is 6:

0	3	80	6	59	10

The object of the game is to move from the first column to the last column in the lowest total cost. The number in each column represents the cost to enter that column. Always start the game in the first column and have two types of moves. You can either move to the adjacent column or jump over the adjacent column to land two columns over. The cost of a game is the sum of the costs of the visited columns.

In the board shown above, there are several ways to get to the end. Starting in the first column, our cost so far is 0. We could jump to 80, then jump to 57, then move to 10 for a total cost of $80 + 57 + 10 = 147$. However, a cheaper path would be to move to 3, jump to 6, then jump to 10, for a total cost of $3 + 6 + 10 = 19$.

Write a recursive solution to this problem that computes the cheapest cost of the game and outputs this value for an arbitrarily large game board represented as an array. Your program does not have to output the actual sequence of jumps, only the cheapest cost of this sequence. After making sure that your solution works on small arrays, test your solution on boards of larger and larger values of n to get a feel for how efficient and scalable your solution is.

5. Write a recursive method definition for a static method that has one parameter n of type `int` and that returns the nth Fibonacci number. The Fibonacci numbers are F_0 is 1, F_1 is 1, F_2 is 2, F_3 is 3, F_4 is 5, and in general

$$F_{i+2} = F_i + F_{i+1} \text{ for } i = 0, 1, 2, \ldots$$

Place the method in a class that has a `main` that tests the method.

6. The formula for computing the number of ways of choosing r different things from a set of n things is the following:

$$C(n, r) = n!/(r! * (n - r)!)$$

The factorial method $n!$ is defined by

$$n! = n*(n - 1)*(n - 2)*\ldots*1$$

Discover a recursive version of the formula for $C(n, r)$ and write a recursive method that computes the value of the formula. Place the method in a class that has a `main` that tests the method.

7. *Towers of Hanoi.* There is a story about Buddhist monks who are playing this puzzle with 64 stone disks. The story claims that when the monks finish moving the disks from one post to a second via the third post, time will end.

A stack of n disks of decreasing size (from bottom to top) is placed on one of three posts. The task is to move the disks one at a time from the first post to the second. To do this, any disk can be moved from any post to any other post, subject to the rule that you can never place a larger disk over a smaller disk. The (spare) third post is provided to make the solution possible. Your task is to write a recursive static method that gives instructions for a solution to this problem. We do not want to bother with graphics, so you should output a sequence of instructions that will solve the problem. The number of disks is a parameter to the method.

Hint: If you could move up n-1 of the disks from the first post to the third post using the second post as a spare, the last disk could be moved from the first post to the second post. Then, by using the same technique (whatever that may be), you can move the n-1 disks from the third post to the second post, using the first disk as a spare. There! You have the puzzle solved. You have only to decide what the nonrecursive case is, what the recursive case is, and when to output instructions to move the disks.

8. Write a recursive method named `contains` with the following header:

   `public static boolean contains(String haystack, String needle)`

   The method should return `true` if `needle` is contained within `haystack` and `false` if `needle` is not in `haystack`. For example,

   `contains("Java programming", "ogr")` should return `true`

   `contains("Java programming", "grammy")` should return `false`

   You are not allowed to use the `substring` method to find a match.

9. The program to recursively find a file in Display 11.11 stops searching when the first match is found. Modify the program so that if there are multiple files with the same name in different directories, then all matching files are found and output. The simplest way to do this is to output all matches in the recursive method with a print statement. For a more challenging version, modify the method to return an array of Strings containing the pathnames of all matching files. It can return `null` or an empty array if there are no matches. Feel free to create additional helper classes if needed (e.g., to manage the number of items in the array of Strings). In Chapter 14, we will introduce ArrayLists, which make it easier to create an array-like structure with an arbitrary number of entries.

10. Given the definition of a 2D array such as the following,

```
String[][] data = {
    {"A", "B"},
    {"1", "2"},
    {"XX","YY","ZZ"}
};
```

write a recursive program that outputs all combinations of each subarray in order. In the previous example, the desired output (although it does not have to be in this order) is

```
A 1 XX
A 1 YY
A 1 ZZ
A 2 XX
A 2 YY
A 2 ZZ
B 1 XX
B 1 YY
B 1 ZZ
B 2 XX
B 2 YY
B 2 ZZ
```

Your program should work with arbitrarily sized arrays in either dimension. For example, the following data

```
String[][] data = {
    {"A"},
    {"1"},
    {"2"},
    {"XX","YY"}
};
```

should output:

```
A 1 2 YY
A 1 2 YY
```

UML and Patterns

12.1 UML   722
History of UML   723
UML Class Diagrams   723
Class Interactions   724
Inheritance Diagrams   724
More UML   726

12.2 PATTERNS   727
Adaptor Pattern ★   727
The Model-View-Controller Pattern ★   728
Example: A Sorting Pattern   729
Restrictions on the Sorting Pattern   735
Efficiency of the Sorting Pattern ★   735
Pattern Formalism   736

Chapter Summary   737   **Answers to Self-Test Exercises   737**   **Programming Projects   739**

12 UML and Patterns

Einstein argued that there must be simplified explanations of nature, because God is not capricious or arbitrary. No such faith comforts the software engineer. Much of the complexity that he must master is arbitrary complexity.

F. BROOKS, "No Silver Bullet: Essence and Accidents of Software Engineering," *IEEE Computer*, April 1987

Introduction

UML and patterns are two software design tools that apply no matter what programming language you are using, as long as the language provides for classes and related facilities for object-oriented programming (OOP). This chapter presents a very brief introduction to these two topics. It contains no new details about the Java language.

UML is a graphical language that is used for designing and documenting software created within the OOP framework.

A pattern in programming is very similar to a pattern in any other context. It is a kind of template or outline of a software task that can be realized as different code in different, but similar, applications.

Prerequisites

Section 12.1 on UML and Section 12.2 on patterns can be read in either order. Nothing in the rest of this book requires any of this chapter. Section 12.1 on UML uses material from Chapters 1–5 and Chapter 7 on inheritance. Section 12.2 on patterns uses material from Chapters 1–7 and Chapter 11.

12.1 UML

One picture is worth a thousand words.

Chinese proverb

Most people do not think in Java or in any other programming language. As a result, computer scientists have always sought to produce more human-oriented ways of representing programs. One widely used representation is pseudocode, which is a mixture of a programming language, such as Java, and a natural language, such as English. To think about a programming problem without needing to worry about the syntax details of a language such as Java, you can simply relax the syntax rules and write in pseudocode. Pseudocode has become a standard tool used by programmers, but it is a linear and algebraic representation of programming. Computer scientists have long sought to give software design a graphical representation. To this end, a number of graphical representation systems for program design have been proposed, used, and ultimately found to be wanting. Terms such as *flowchart, structure diagram*, and many more names of graphical program representations are today recognized only by those of the older generation. Today's candidate for a graphical representation formalism is the **Unified Modeling Language** (**UML**). UML was designed to reflect and be used with the OOP philosophy. It is too early to say whether or not UML will stand the test of time, but it is off to a good start. A number of companies have adopted the UML formalism to use in their software design projects.

UML

History of UML

UML developed along with OOP. As the OOP philosophy became more and more commonly used, different groups worked out their own graphical or other representations for OOP design. In 1996, Grady Booch, Ivar Jacobson, and James Rumbaugh released an early version of UML. UML was intended to bring together the various different graphical representation methods to produce a standardized graphical representation language for object-oriented design and documentation. Since that time, UML has been developed and revised in response to feedback from the OOP community. Today the UML standard is maintained and certified by the Object Management Group (OMG), a nonprofit organization that promotes the use of object-oriented techniques.

UML Class Diagrams

class diagram

Classes are central to OOP, and the **class diagram** is the easiest of the UML graphical representations to understand and use. Display 12.1 shows the class diagram for a class to represent a square. The diagram consists of a box divided into three sections. (The colors are optional and not standardized.) The top section has the class name, Square. The next section has the data specification for the class. In this example, there are three pieces of data (three instance variables), a value of type double giving the length of a side, and two more values of type double giving the x and y coordinates of the center of the square. The third section gives the actions (class methods). The notation for method entries is not identical to that of a Java method heading, but it contains the same information. A minus sign indicates a private member. So, for the class Square, all data is private. A plus sign indicates a public member. A sharp (#) indicates a protected member. A tilde (~) indicates package access. So, for the class Square, the class diagram shows two public methods and one protected method. A class diagram need not give a complete description of the class. When you do not need all the members in a class for the analysis at hand, you do not list all the members in the class diagram. Missing members are indicated with an ellipsis (three dots).

Display 12.1   A UML Class Diagram

```
┌─────────────────────────────────────────────────┐
│                    Square                        │
├─────────────────────────────────────────────────┤
│ – side: double                                   │
│ – xCoordinate: double                            │
│ – yCoordinate: double                            │
├─────────────────────────────────────────────────┤
│ + resize(double newSide): void                   │
│ + move(double newX, double newY): void           │
│ # erase(): void                                  │
│ . . .                                            │
└─────────────────────────────────────────────────┘
```

Class Interactions

Class diagrams by themselves are of little value, because they simply repeat the class interface, possibly with ellipses. To understand a design, you need to indicate how objects of the various classes interact. UML has various ways to indicate class interactions; for example, various sorts of annotated arrows indicate the information flow from one class object to another. UML also has annotations for class groupings into packages, annotations for inheritance, and annotations for other interactions. Moreover, UML is extensible. If what you want and need is not in UML, you can add it. Of course, this all takes place inside a prescribed framework so that different software developers can understand each other's UML. One of the most fundamental of class interactions is inheritance, which is discussed in the next subsection.

Inheritance Diagrams

inheritance diagram

arrows

Display 12.2 shows a possible **inheritance diagram** used in a university's record-keeping software for some of its classes. Note that the class diagrams are incomplete. You normally show only as much of the class diagram as you need for the design task at hand. Note that the arrow heads point up from a derived class to its base class. In UML an unfilled arrowhead is used to indicate an inheritance relationship between two classes.

The arrows also help in locating method definitions. If you are looking for a method definition for some class, the arrows show the path you (or the computer) should follow. If you are looking for the definition of a method used by an object of the class Undergraduate, first look in the definition of the class Undergraduate; if it is not there, look in the definition of Student; if it is not there, look in the definition of the class Person.

Display 12.2   **A Class Hierarchy in UML Notation**

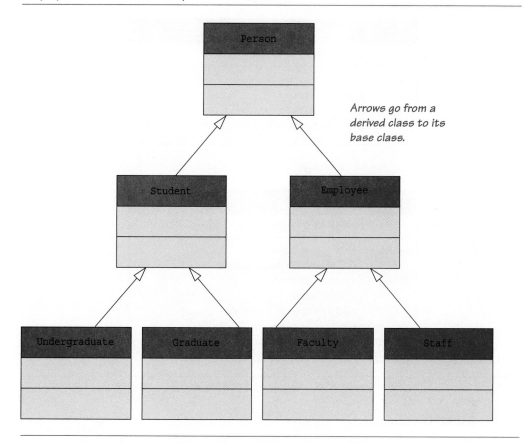

Display 12.3 shows some possible additional details of the inheritance hierarchy for the two classes `Person` and one of its derived classes, `Student`. Suppose `s` is an object of the class `Student`. The diagram in Display 12.3 tells you that you can find the definition of

```
s.toString();
```

and

```
s.set("Joe Student", 4242);
```

in the class `Student`, but the definition of

```
s.setName("Josephine Student");
```

is found in the definition of the class `Person`.

Display 12.3   Some Details of a UML Class Hierarchy

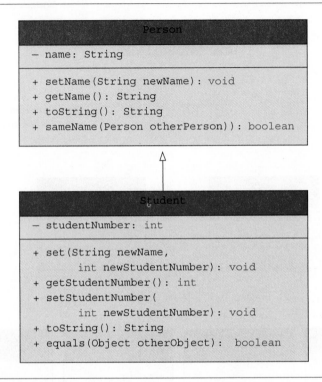

More UML

This is just a hint of what UML is all about. If you are interested in learning more, consult one of the many available references on UML.

Self-Test Exercises

1. Draw a class diagram for a class whose objects represent circles. Use Display 12.1 as a model.

2. Suppose aStudent is an object of the class Student. Based on the inheritance diagram in Display 12.3, where will you find the definition of the method sameName used in the following invocation, which compares aStudent and another object named someStudent? Explain your answer.

```
Student someStudent =
            new Student("Joe Student", 7777);
if (aStudent.sameName(someStudent))
    System.out.println("wow");
```

Self-Test Exercises (continued)

3. Suppose aStudent is an object of the class Student. Based on the inheritance diagram in Display 12.3, where will you find the definition of the method used in the following invocation? Explain your answer.

```
aStudent.setNumber(4242);
```

12.2   Patterns ★

I bid him look into the lives of men as though into a mirror, and from others to take an example for himself.

TERENCE (Publius Terentius Afer) 190–159 B.C., *Adelphoe*

pattern

Container-Iterator

container

iterator

Patterns are design outlines that apply across a variety of software applications. To be useful, the pattern must apply across a variety of situations. To be substantive, the pattern must make some assumptions about the domain of applications to which it applies. For example, one well-known pattern is the **Container-Iterator** pattern. A **container** is a class (or other construct) whose objects hold multiple pieces of data. One example of a container is an array. Other examples, which will be discussed later in this book, are vectors and linked lists. Any class or other construct designed to hold multiple values can be viewed as a container. For example, a String value can be viewed as a container that contains the characters in the string. Any construct that allows you to cycle through all the items in a container is an **iterator**. For example, an array index is an iterator for an array. It can cycle through the array as follows:

```
for (int i; i < a.length; i++)
    Do something with a[i]
```

The index variable i is the iterator. The Container-Iterator pattern describes how an iterator is used on a container.

In this brief chapter, we can give you only a taste of what patterns are all about. In this section, we will discuss a few sample patterns to let you see what patterns look like. There are many more known and used patterns and many more yet to be explicated. This is a new and still developing field of software engineering.

Adaptor Pattern ★

Adaptor

The **Adaptor** or **Adapter** pattern transforms one class into a different class without changing the underlying class but merely by adding a new interface. (The new interface replaces the old interface of the underlying class.) For example, in Chapter 11, we mentioned the stack data structure, which is used to, among other things, keep track of recursion. One way to create a stack data structure is to start with an array and add the stack interface. The Adaptor pattern says to start with a container, such as an array, and add an interface, such as the stack interface.

The Model-View-Controller Pattern ★

Model-View-
Controller

The **Model-View-Controller** pattern is a way of separating the I/O task of an application from the rest of the application. The Model part of the pattern performs the heart of the application. The View part is the output part; it displays a picture of the Model's state. The Controller is the input part; it relays commands from the user to the Model. Normally, each of the three interacting parts is realized as an object with responsibilities for its own tasks. The Model-View-Controller pattern is an example of a divide-and-conquer strategy. One big task is divided into three smaller tasks with well-defined responsibilities. Display 12.4 gives a diagram of the Model-View-Controller pattern. Note that the arrowheads are open. In UML, an open arrowhead indicates an association where one object has a reference to another object of the type connected by the arrow.

As a very simple example, the Model might be a container class, such as an array. The View might display one element of the array. The Controller gives commands to display the element at a specified index. The Model (the array) notifies the View to display a new element whenever the array contents change or a different index location is given.

Any application can be made to fit the Model-View-Controller pattern, but it is particularly well suited to GUI (Graphical User Interface) design projects where the View can indeed be a visualization of the state of the Model. (A GUI interface is simply a windowing interface of the form you find in most modern software applications, as opposed to the simple text I/O we have used so far in this book.) For example, the Model might be an object to represent your list of computer desktop object names. The View could then be a GUI object that produces a screen display of your desktop icons. The Controller relays commands to the Model (which is a desktop object) to add or delete names. The Model object notifies the View object when the screen needs to be updated.

Display 12.4   Model-View-Controller Pattern

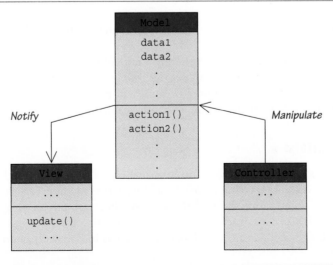

We have presented the Model-View-Controller pattern as if the user is the Controller, primarily to simplify the examples. The Controller need not be under the direct control of the user, but could be some other kind of software or hardware component.

EXAMPLE: A Sorting Pattern

The most efficient sorting algorithms all seem to follow a similar pattern. Expressed recursively, they divide the list of elements to be sorted into two smaller lists, recursively sort the two smaller lists, and then recombine the two sorted lists to obtain the final sorted list. In Display 12.5, this pattern is expressed as pseudocode (in fact, almost correct Java code) for a method to sort an array into increasing order using the < operator.

Our sorting pattern uses a divide-and-conquer strategy. It divides the entire collection of elements to be sorted into two smaller collections, sorts the smaller collections by recursive calls, and then combines the two sorted collections to obtain the final sorted array. The following is the heart of our sorting pattern:

```
int splitPoint = split(a, begin, end);
sort(a, begin, splitPoint);
sort(a, splitPoint + 1, end);
join(a, begin, splitPoint, end);
```

Although the pattern does impose some minimum requirements on the methods split and join, it does not say exactly how the methods split and join are defined. Different definitions of split and join will yield different sorting algorithms.

The method split rearranges the elements in the interval a[begin] through a[end] and divides the rearranged interval at a split point, splitPoint. The two smaller intervals a[begin] through a[splitPoint] and [splitPoint + 1] through a[end] are then sorted by a recursive call to the method sort. Note that the split method both rearranges the elements in the array interval a[begin] through a[end] and returns the index splitPoint that divides the interval. After the two smaller intervals are sorted, the method join then combines the two sorted intervals to obtain the final sorted version of the entire larger interval.

The pattern says nothing about how the method split rearranges and divides the interval a[begin] through a[end]. In a simple case, split might simply choose a value splitPoint between begin and end and divide the interval into the points before splitPoint and the points after splitPoint, with no rearranging. Display 12.6 realizes the sorting pattern by defining split this way. On the other hand, the method split could do something more elaborate such as move all the "small" elements to the front of the array and all the "large" elements toward the end of the array. This would be a step on the way to fully sorting the values. We will also see an example in Display 12.8 that realizes the sorting pattern in this second way.

(continued)

Display 12.5   Divide-and-Conquer Sorting Pattern

```
1   /**
2    Precondition: Interval a[begin] through a[end] of a have elements.
3    Postcondition: The values in the interval have
4    been rearranged so that a[begin] <=a[begin+1] <= . . . <= a[end].
5   */
6   public static void sort(Type [] a, int begin, int end)
7   {
8       if ((end - begin) >= 1)
9       {
10          int splitPoint = split(a, begin, end);
11          sort(a, begin, splitPoint);
12          sort(a, splitPoint + 1, end);
13          join(a, begin, splitPoint, end);
14      }//else sorting one (or fewer) elements so do nothing.
15  }
```

To get a correct Java method definition, Type must be replaced with a suitable type name.

Different definitions for the methods split and join will give different realizations of this pattern.

EXAMPLE: (continued)

The simplest realization of this sorting pattern is the **merge sort** realization given in Display 12.6. In this realization, the array base type, *Type*, is specialized to the type double. The merge sort is an example where the definition of split is very simple. It just divides the array into two intervals with no rearranging of elements. The join method is more complicated. After the two subintervals are sorted, the method join merges the two sorted subintervals, copying elements from the array to a temporary array. The merging starts by comparing the smallest elements in each smaller sorted interval. The smaller of these two elements is the smallest of all the elements in either subinterval, so it is moved to the first position in the temporary array. The process is then repeated with the remaining elements in the two smaller sorted intervals to find the next smallest element, and so forth. A demonstration of using the merge sort version of sort is given in Display 12.7.

There is a trade-off between the complexity of the methods split and join. You can make either of them simple at the expense of making the other more complicated. For merge sort, split was simple and join was complicated. We next give a realization where split is complicated and join is simple.

Display 12.8 gives the **quick sort** realization of our sorting pattern for the type double.

In the quick sort realization, the definition of split is quite sophisticated. An arbitrary value in the array is chosen; this value is called the **splitting value**. In our realization, we chose a[begin] as the splitting value, but any value will do equally well. The elements in the array are rearranged so that all those elements that are less than or equal to the splitting value are at the front of the array, all the values that are greater

Display 12.6   Merge Sort Realization of Sorting Pattern (part 1 of 2)

```
1   /**
2      Class that realizes the divide-and-conquer sorting pattern and
3      uses the merge sort algorithm.
4   */
5   public class MergeSort
6   {
7          /**
8           Precondition: Interval a[begin] through a[end] of a have elements.
9           Postcondition: The values in the interval have
10          been rearranged so that a[begin] < = a[begin+1] < = . . . < =
             a[end].
11         */
12         public static void sort(double [] a, int begin, int end)
13         {                                   The method sort is identical to the version in
14             if ((end — begin) >= 1)         the pattern (Display 12.5) except that Type is
15             {                               replaced with double.
16                 int splitPoint = split(a, begin, end);
17                 sort(a, begin, splitPoint);
18                 sort(a, splitPoint + 1, end);
19                 join(a, begin, splitPoint, end);
20             }//else sorting one (or fewer) elements so do nothing.
21         }

22         private static int split(double [] a, int begin, int end)
23         {
24             return ((begin + end)/2);
25         }

26         private static void join(double [] a, int begin, int splitPoint,
             int end)
27         {
28             double[] temp;
29             int intervalSize = (end - begin + 1);
30             temp = new double [intervalSize];
31             int nextLeft = begin; //index for first chunk
32             int nextRight = splitPoint + 1; //index for second chunk
33             int i = 0; //index for temp

34             //Merge till one side is exhausted:
35             while ((nextLeft <= splitPoint) && (nextRight <= end))
36             {
37                 if (a[nextLeft] < a[nextRight])
38                 {
39                     temp[i] = a[nextLeft];
40                     i++; nextLeft++;
41                 }
```

(continued)

Display 12.6   Merge Sort Realization of Sorting Pattern (part 2 of 2)

```
42                else
43                {
44                    temp[i] = a[nextRight];
45                    i++; nextRight++;
46                }
47            }

48            while (nextLeft <= splitPoint)
             //Copy rest of left chunk, if any.
49            {
50                temp[i] = a[nextLeft];
51                i++; nextLeft++;
52            }
53            while (nextRight <= end) //Copy rest of right chunk, if any.
54            {
55                temp[i] = a[nextRight];
56                i++; nextRight++;
57            }

58            for (i = 0; i < intervalSize; i++)
59                a[begin + i] = temp[i];
60        }

61    }
```

EXAMPLE: (continued)

than the splitting value are at the other end of the array, and the splitting value is placed so that it divides the entire array into these smaller and larger elements. Note that the smaller elements are not sorted and the larger elements are not sorted, but all the elements before the splitting value are smaller than any of the elements after the splitting value. The smaller elements are sorted by a recursive call, the larger elements are sorted by another recursive call, and then these two sorted segments are combined with the join method. In this case, the join method is as simple as it could be. It does nothing. Because the sorted smaller elements all precede the sorted larger elements, the entire array is sorted.

A demonstration program for the quick sort method sort in Display 12.8 is given in the file QuickSortDemo.java on the accompanying website.

(Both the merge sort and the quick sort realizations can be done without the use of a second temporary array, temp. However, that detail would only distract from the message of this example. In a real application, you may or may not, depending on details, want to consider the possibility of doing a sort realization without the use of the temporary array.)

Display 12.7   Using the `MergeSort` Class

```
1   public class MergeSortDemo
2   {
3       public static void main(String[] args)
4       {
5           double[]b = {7.7, 5.5, 11, 3, 16, 4.4, 20, 14, 13, 42};

6           System.out.println("Array contents before sorting:");
7           int i;
8           for (i = 0; i < b.length; i++)
9               System.out.print(b[i] + " ");
10          System.out.println();

11          MergeSort.sort(b, 0, b.length-1);
12          System.out.println("Sorted array values:");
13          for (i = 0; i < b.length; i++)
14              System.out.print(b[i] + " ");
15          System.out.println();
16      }
17  }
```

Sample Dialogue

```
Array contents before sorting:
7.7 5.5 11.0 3.0 16.0 4.4 20.0 14.0 13.0 42.0
Sorted array values:
3.0 4.4 5.5 7.7 11.0 13.0 14.0 16.0 20.0 42.0
```

Display 12.8   Quick Sort Realization of Sorting Pattern (part 1 of 3)

```
1   /**
2    Class that realizes the divide-and-conquer sorting pattern and
3    uses the quick sort algorithm.
4   */
5   public class QuickSort
6   {
7       /**
8        Precondition: Interval a[begin] through a[end] of a have elements.
9        Postcondition: The values in the interval have
10       been rearranged so that a[begin] <= a[begin+1] <= . . . <=
         a[end].
```

(continued)

Display 12.8   Quick Sort Realization of Sorting Pattern (part 2 of 3)

```
11        */
12      public static void sort(double[] a, int begin, int end)
13      {                                   The method sort is identical to the version in the
14          if ((end - begin) >= 1)         pattern (Display 12.5) except that Type is replaced
15          {                               with double.
16              int splitPoint = split(a, begin, end);
17              sort(a, begin, splitPoint);
18              sort(a, splitPoint + 1, end);
19              join(a, begin, splitPoint, end);
20          }//else sorting one (or fewer) elements so do nothing.
21      }

22      private static int split(double [] a, int begin, int end)
23      {
24          double[] temp;
25          int size = (end - begin + 1);
26          temp = new double [size];

27          double splitValue = a[begin];
28          int up = 0;
29          int down = size - 1;

30          //Note that a[begin] = splitValue is skipped.
31          for (int i = begin + 1; i < = end; i++)
32          {
33              if (a[i] <= splitValue)
34              {
35                  temp[up] = a[i];
36                  up++;
37              }
38              else
39              {
40                  temp[down] = a[i];
41                  down--;
42              }
43          }

44          //0 < = up = down < size

45          temp[up] = a[begin]; //Positions the split value

46          //temp[i] <= splitValue for i < up
47          // temp[up] = splitValue
48          // temp[i] > splitValue for i > up

49          for (int i = 0; i < size; i++)
```

Display 12.8   Quick Sort Realization of Sorting Pattern (part 3 of 3)

```
50              a[begin + i] = temp[i];
51          return (begin + up);
52      }

53      private static void join(double [] a, int begin,
54                               int splitPoint, int end)
55      {
56          //Nothing to do.
57      }

58  }
```

Restrictions on the Sorting Pattern

The sorting pattern, like all patterns, has some restrictions on where it applies. As we formulated the sorting pattern, it applies only to types for which the < operator is defined. Also, it applies only to sorting into increasing order; it does not apply to sorting into decreasing order. However, this is a result of our simplifying details to make the presentation clearer. You can make the pattern more general by replacing the < operator with a boolean valued method called compare that has two arguments of the base type of the array, which returns true or false depending on whether the first "comes before" the second. Then, the only restriction is that the compare method must have a reasonable definition.[1] This sort of generalization is discussed in Chapter 13 in the subsection entitled "The Comparable Interface."

Efficiency of the Sorting Pattern ★

Essentially any sorting algorithm can be realized using this sorting pattern. However, the most efficient implementations are those for which the split method divides the array into two substantial size chunks, such as half-and-half, or one-fourth and three-fourths. A realization of split that divides the array into one or a very few elements and the rest of the array will not be very efficient.

For example, the merge sort realization of split divides the array into two roughly equal parts, and merge sort is indeed very efficient. It can be shown (although we will not do so here) that merge sort has a worst-case running time that is the best possible "up to an order of magnitude."

---

[1]The technical requirement is that the compare method be a *total ordering*, a concept discussed in Chapter 13. Essentially, all common orderings that you might want to sort by are total orderings.

The Comparable interface has a method compareTo, which is slightly different from compare. However, the method we described as compare can easily be defined using the method compareTo as a helping method.

The quick sort realization of `split` divides the array into two portions that might be almost equal or might be very different in size depending on the choice of a splitting value. Since in extremely unfortunate cases the split might be very uneven, the worst-case running time for quick sort is not as fast as that of merge sort. However, in practice, quick sort turns out to be a very good sorting algorithm and usually preferable to merge sort.

Selection sort, which we discussed in Chapter 6, divides the array into two pieces, one with a single element and one with the rest of the array interval. (See Self-Test Exercise 4.) Because of this uneven division, selection sort has a poor running time, although it does have the virtue of simplicity.

TIP: Pragmatics and Patterns

You should not feel compelled to follow all the fine details of a pattern. Patterns are guides, not requirements. For example, we did the quick sort implementation by exactly following the pattern. We did this to have a clean example. In practice, we would have taken some liberties. Notice that, with quick sort, the `join` method does nothing. In practice, we would simply eliminate the calls to `join`. These calls incur overhead and accomplish nothing. Other optimizations can also be done once the general pattern of the algorithm is clear. ■

Pattern Formalism

There is a well-developed body of techniques for using patterns. We will not go into the details here. The UML discussed in Section 12.1 is one formalism used to express patterns. The place within the software design process of patterns and any specific formalisms for patterns is not yet clear. However, it is evident that the basic idea of patterns, as well as certain pattern names, such as *Model-View-Controller*, have become standard and useful tools for software design.

MyProgrammingLab™

Self-Test Exercises

4. Give an implementation of the divide-and-conquer sorting pattern (Display 12.5) that will realize the selection sort algorithm (Display 6.11) for an array with base type `double`.

5. Which of the following would give the fastest run time when an array is sorted using the quick sort algorithm: a fully sorted array, an array of random values, or an array sorted from largest to smallest (that is, sorted backward)? Assume all arrays are of the same size and have the same base type.

Chapter Summary

- The *Unified Modeling Language (UML)* is a graphical representation language for object-oriented software design.

- *Patterns* are design principles that apply across a variety of software applications.

- The patterns discussed in this chapter are the *Container-Iterator, Adaptor, Model-View-Controller,* and *Divide-and-Conquer Sorting* patterns.

- UML is one formalism that can and is used to express patterns.

Answers to Self-Test Exercises

1. There are many correct answers. The following is one:

Circle
— radius: double
— centerX: double
— centerY: double
+ resize(double newRadius): void
+ move(double newX, double newY): void
# erase(): void
. . .

2. The method sameName is not listed in the class diagram for Student. So, you follow the arrow to the class diagram for Person. The method sameName with a single parameter of type Person is in the class diagram for Person. Because you know a Student is a Person, you know that this definition works for the method sameName with a single parameter of type Student. So, the definition used for the method sameName is in the class definition of Person.

3. You start at the class diagram for Student. The method setStudentNumber with a single parameter of type int is in the class diagram for Student, so you need look no further. The definition used for the method setStudentNumber is in the class definition of Student.

extra code on website

4. The code for this is also on the website that comes with this book. This code is in the file SelectionSort.java. A demonstration program is in the file SelectionSortDemo.java.

```java
public class SelectionSort
{
    public static void sort(double [] a,
                                       int begin, int end)
    {
        if ((end - begin) >= 1)
        {
            int splitPoint = split(a, begin, end);
            sort(a, begin, splitPoint);
            sort(a, splitPoint + 1, end);
            join(a, begin, splitPoint, end);
        }//else sorting one (or fewer) elements
         //so do nothing.
    }

    private static int split(double [] a,
                                int begin , int end)
    {
        int index = indexOfSmallest(begin, a, end);
        interchange(begin,index, a);

         return begin;
    }

    private static void join(double [] a, int begin,
                                int splitPoint, int end)
    {
      //Nothing to do.
    }

    private static int indexOfSmallest(int startIndex,
                                double [] a, int endIndex)
    {
        double min = a[startIndex];
        int indexOfMin = startIndex;
        int index;
        for (index = startIndex + 1;
                           index < endIndex; index++)
            if (a[index] < min)
            {
                min = a[index];
                indexOfMin = index;
                //min is smallest of a[startIndex]
                //through a[index]
            }
        return indexOfMin;
    }
```

```
        private static void interchange(int i,int j, double [] a)
        {
                double temp;
                temp = a[i];
                a[i] = a[j];
                a[j] = temp; //original value of a[i]
        }
}
```

5. An array of random values would have the fastest run time, because it would divide the array segments into approximately equal subarrays most of the time. The other two cases would give approximately the same running time and would be significantly slower, because the algorithms would always divide an array segment into very unequal size pieces, one piece with only one element and one piece with the rest of the elements. It is ironic but true that our version of the quick sort algorithms has its worst behavior on an already sorted array. There are variations on the quick sort algorithms that perform well on a sorted array. For example, choosing the middle element as the splitting value will give good performance on an already sorted array. But, whatever splitting value you choose, there will always be a few cases with slow running time.

MyProgrammingLab **Programming Projects**

Visit www.myprogramminglab.com to complete select exercises online and get instant feedback.

1. The UML diagram below describes a class named `Movie`. Implement this class in Java and test it from a `main` method that creates several `Movie` objects. The `printDescription()` method should output all member variables for the class.

Movie
− title: String
− minutes: int
− year: int
price: double
+ Movie(in String title, in int year, in double price)
+ getTitle( ): String
+ setTitle(in String newTitle)
+ printDescription( )

The word "in" means the parameter is used to deliver data to the method.

2. The following UML diagram shows the relationship between a class called `PizzaOrder` and a class called `Pizza`:

The word "in" means the parameter is used to deliver data to the method.

The `Pizza` class contains information about a specific `pizza`. The variables of pepperoni, sausage, and mushrooms are booleans that indicate whether or not these toppings are present on the pizza. The size variable is a character of value `'s'`, `'m'`, or `'l'` to indicate small, medium, or large. There is also a `Pizza` constructor that initializes all of these values. The `getSize()` method returns the size of the pizza and the `getNumToppings()` method returns a number from 0–3 depending on what toppings are present (e.g., if the pizza has pepperoni and mushrooms, it would be 2).

The `PizzaOrder` class contains an array of `Pizza`'s. There is a method to add a new pizza to the array (which increments `numPizzas`) and also a method to calculate the cost of the entire order. A small pizza costs $8, a medium pizza is $10, and a large pizza costs $12. Each topping adds $1 to the pizza.

The arrow connecting `PizzaOrder` to `Pizza` indicates that the `PizzaOrder` class has a reference to the `Pizza` class, but not vice versa. The solid diamond on the `PizzaOrder` class is a UML construct that indicates that the `PizzaOrder` class has a collection of the `Pizza` class. There may be many (*) `Pizza`'s for a single (one) `PizzaOrder`.

Given this information, write Java code that implements the `Pizza` and `PizzaOrder` classes. Also, write a test main function that creates a pizza order, adds several `pizzas` to it, and outputs the cost of the order.

3. The UML diagram below shows the relationship between four classes. Implement the classes in a test program that creates instances of `CreditCard`, `Cash`, and `Check`. Output the string description of each. Note that the italicized *Payment* class indicates that this is an abstract class. The word "in" means the parameter is used to deliver data to the method.

4. Use the Model-View-Controller pattern to implement a simple timer-based counter. The counter should start at a user-specified initial value and increment by one every second until it reaches a user-specified final value. A UML diagram depicting the three classes for the pattern is shown below. The word "in" means the parameter is used to deliver data to the method.

The CounterView class should simply take an input counter value and print it on the console screen.

The CounterModel class should have a variable that represents the counter's value. The Increment method increments the counter by one and calls CounterView's Display method.

The CounterController class takes a start and end value that is specified by the user. CounterModel is then initialized with the start value. When the Start method is invoked, it calls CounterModel's increment method once per second until endValue − startValue seconds have elapsed.

You will need to implement additional variables or methods in addition to those shown above in order to create the linkages between classes.

You can use the method call Thread.sleep(1000) to make the CounterController wait for one second. The call must be placed inside a try/catch block.

Test your program with a main method that counts several different ranges of values.

5. It is possible to purchase "geek" watches that output the time of day in binary. To illustrate the flexibility of the Model-View-Controller pattern, modify the view class (CounterView) of the previous problem so that the display outputs the counter's value in binary.

Test your new program by counting values in binary. You should not have to change the model or controller classes.

6. Recode the QuickSort class implementation by adding two efficiency improvements to the method sort: (1) Eliminate the calls to join, because it accomplishes nothing. (2) Add code for the special case of an array of exactly two elements and make the general case apply to arrays of three or more elements.

7. Redo the QuickSort class so that it chooses the splitting point as follows: The splitting point is the middle (in size) of the first element, the last element, and an element at approximately the middle of the array. This will make a very uneven split less likely.

8. Redo the QuickSort class to have the modifications given for Programming Projects 12.6 and 12.7.

VideoNote
Solution to Programming Project 12.9

9. Use the sorting pattern to implement insertion sort. In insertion sort, the split method always returns the value (end − 1). This results in splitting the array into two pieces, one with a single value at the end of the array, and the other with everything else. The join method does more work. A precondition for entry into join is that the elements from a[begin] to a[end-1] will be in sorted order. The method should insert a[end] into the correct spot from a[begin] to a[end] such that sorted order is maintained. For example, if array a contains {2, 4, 6, 8, 5} where begin = 0 and end = 4 then a[end] = 5 and the method should insert the value 5 between the 4 and 6, resulting in {2, 4, 5, 6, 8}. This entails copying the 6 and 8 one element to the right, and then copying the value 5 to index 2.

Interfaces and Inner Classes 13

13.1 INTERFACES 745

Interfaces 745
Abstract Classes Implementing Interfaces 747
Derived Interfaces 747
The Comparable Interface 751
Example: Using the Comparable Interface 752
Defined Constants in Interfaces 757
The Serializable Interface ★ 761
The Cloneable Interface 761

13.2 SIMPLE USES OF INNER CLASSES 766

Helping Classes 766
Example: A Bank Account Class 767
The .class File for an Inner Class 771

13.3 MORE ABOUT INNER CLASSES 772

Static Inner Classes 772
Public Inner Classes 773
Nesting Inner Classes 777
Inner Classes and Inheritance 777
Anonymous Classes 778

Chapter Summary 781   Answers to Self-Test Exercises 781   Programming Projects 786

13 Interfaces and Inner Classes

Art, it seems to me, should simplify. That, indeed, is very nearly the whole of the higher artistic process; finding what conventions of form and what details one can do without and yet preserve the spirit of the whole....

WILLA SIBERT CATHER, *On the Art of Fiction*

Introduction

A Java *interface* specifies a set of methods that any class that implements the interface must have. An interface is itself a type, which allows you to define methods with parameters of an interface type and then have the code apply to all classes that implement the interface. One way to view an interface is as an extreme form of an abstract class. However, as you will see, an interface allows you to do more than an abstract class allows you to do. Interfaces are Java's way of approximating multiple inheritance. You cannot have multiple base classes in Java, but interfaces allow you to approximate the power of multiple base classes.

The second major topic of this chapter is *inner classes*. An inner class is simply a class defined within another class. Because inner classes are local to the class that contains them, they can help make a class self-contained by allowing you to make helping classes inner classes.

Prerequisites

Section 13.1 on interfaces and Section 13.2 on simple uses of inner classes are independent of each other and can be covered in any order. Section 13.3 on more subtle details of inner classes requires both Sections 13.1 and 13.2.

Section 13.1 on interfaces requires Chapters 1 through 9. No material from Chapters 10 through 12 is used anywhere in this chapter.

Section 13.2 on simple uses of inner classes requires Chapters 1 through 5. It does not use any material from Chapters 6 through 12.

Section 13.3 on more advanced inner class material requires both Sections 13.1 and 13.2 (and of course their prerequisites). The material in Section 13.3 is not used elsewhere in this book.

13.1 Interfaces

Autonomy of Syntax

A linguistic concept attributed to Noam Chomsky

In this section, we describe *interfaces*. An interface is a type that groups together a number of different classes that all include method definitions for a common set of method headings.

Interfaces

interface

An **interface** is something like the extreme case of an abstract class. *An interface is not a class. It is, however, a type that can be satisfied by any class that implements the interface.* An interface is a property of a class that says what methods it must have.

An interface specifies the headings for methods that must be defined in any class that implements the interface. For example, Display 13.1 shows an interface named `Ordered`. Note that an interface contains only method headings. It contains no instance variables nor any complete method definitions. (Although, as we will see, it can contain defined constants.)

implementing an interface

To **implement an interface**, a concrete class (that is, a class other than an abstract class) must do two things:

1. It must include the phrase

```
implements Interface_Name
```

at the start of the class definition. To implement more than one interface, you list all the interface names, separated by commas, as in

```
implements SomeInterface, AnotherInterface
```

Display 13.1 **The `Ordered` Interface**

```
1  public interface Ordered
2  {
3      public boolean precedes(Object other);

4      /**
5       For objects of the class o1 and o2,
6       o1.follows(o2) == o2.preceded(o1).
7      */
8      public boolean follows(Object other);
9  }
```

Do not forget the semicolons at the end of the method headings.

Neither the compiler nor the run-time system will do anything to ensure that this comment is satisfied. It is only advisory to the programmer implementing the interface.

2. The class must implement *all* the method headings listed in the definitions of the interfaces.

For example, to implement the `Ordered` interface, a class definition must contain the phrase `implements Ordered` at the start of the class definition, as shown in the following:

```
public class OrderedHourlyEmployee
            extends HourlyEmployee implements Ordered
    {
```

The class must also implement the two methods `precedes` and `follows`. The full definition of `OrderedHourlyEmployee` is given in Display 13.2.

Display 13.2   Implementation of an Interface

```
 1  public class OrderedHourlyEmployee
 2          extends HourlyEmployee implements Ordered
 3  {
 4      public boolean precedes(Object other)
 5      {
 6          if (other == null)
 7              return false;
 8          else if (!(other instanceof OrderedHourlyEmployee))
 9              return false;
10          else
11          {
12              OrderedHourlyEmployee otherOrderedHourlyEmployee =
13                          (OrderedHourlyEmployee)other;
14              return (getPay() < otherOrderedHourlyEmployee.getPay());
15          }
16      }
17
18      public boolean follows(Object other)
19      {
20          if (other == null)
21              return false;
22          else if (!(other instanceof OrderedHourlyEmployee))
23              return false;
24          else
25          {
26              OrderedHourlyEmployee otherOrderedHourlyEmployee =
27                          (OrderedHourlyEmployee)other;
28              return (otherOrderedHourlyEmployee.precedes(this));
29          }
30      }
    }
```

Although `getClass` works better than `instanceof` for defining `equals`, `instanceof` works better in this case. However, either will do for the points being made here.

An interface and all of its method headings are normally declared to be public. They cannot be given private, protected, or package access. (The modifier `public` may be omitted, but all the methods will still be treated as if they are public.) When a class implements an interface, it must make all the methods in the interface public.

An interface is a type. This allows you to write a method with a parameter of an interface type, such as a parameter of type `Ordered`, and that parameter will accept as an argument any class you later define that implements the interface.

An interface serves a function similar to a base class, but it is important to note that it is not a base class. (In fact, it is not a class of any kind.) Some programming languages (such as C++) allow one class to be a derived class of two or more different base classes. This is not allowed in Java. In Java, a derived class can have only one base class. However, in addition to any base class that a Java class may have, it can also implement any number of interfaces. This allows Java programs to approximate the power of multiple base classes without the complications that can arise with multiple base classes.

You might want to say the argument to `precedes` in the `Ordered` interface (Display 13.2) is the same as the class doing the implementation (for example, `OrderedHourlyEmployee`). There is no way to say this in Java, so we normally make such parameters of type `Object`. It would be legal to make the argument to `precedes` of type `Ordered`, but that is not normally preferable to using `Object` as the parameter type. If you make the argument of type `Ordered`, you would still have to handle the case of `null` and the case of an argument that (while `Ordered`) is not of type `OrderedHourlyEmployee`.

An interface definition is stored in a `.java` file and compiled just as a class definition is compiled.

Abstract Classes Implementing Interfaces

As you saw in the previous subsection, a concrete class (that is, a regular class) must give definitions for all the method headings given in an interface in order to implement the interface. However, you can define an abstract class that implements an interface but gives only definitions for some of the method headings given in the interface. The method headings given in the interface that are not given definitions are made into abstract methods. A simple example is given in Display 13.3.

Derived Interfaces

extending an interface

You can derive an interface from a base interface. This is often called **extending** the interface. The details are similar to deriving a class. An example is given in Display 13.4.

Display 13.3   An Abstract Class Implementing an Interface ★

```
1   public abstract class MyAbstractClass implements Ordered
2   {
3       private int number;
4       private char grade;
5
6       public boolean precedes(Object other)
7       {
8           if (other == null)
9               return false;
10          else if (!(other instanceof HourlyEmployee))
11              return false;
12          else
13          {
14              MyAbstractClass otherOfMyAbstractClass =
15                                      (MyAbstractClass)other;
16              return (this.number < otherOfMyAbstractClass.number);
17          }
18      }
19
19      public abstract boolean follows(Object other);
20  }
```

Display 13.4   Extending an Interface

```
1   public interface ShowablyOrdered extends Ordered
2   {
3       /**
4        Outputs an object of the class that precedes the calling object.
5        */
6       public void showOneWhoPrecedes();
7   }
```

*Neither the compiler nor the run-time system
will do anything to ensure that this comment is
satisfied.*

A (concrete) class that implements the ShowablyOrdered interface must have a
definition for the method showOneWhoPrecedes and also have definitions for the
methods precedes and follows given in the Ordered interface.

Interfaces

An interface is a type that specifies method headings (and, as we will see, possibly defined constants as well). The syntax for defining an interface is similar to the syntax of defining a class, except that the word `interface` is used in place of `class` and the method headings without any method body (but followed by a semicolon) are given only.

Note that an interface has no instance variables and no method definitions.

A class can implement any number of interfaces. To implement an interface, the class must include

    implements *Interface_Name*

at the end of the class heading and must supply definitions for the method headings given in the interface. If the class does not supply definitions for all the method headings given in the interface, then the class must be an abstract class and the method headings without definitions must be abstract methods.

EXAMPLE

See Displays 13.1, 13.2, and 13.3.

Self-Test Exercises

1. Can you have a variable of an interface type? Can you have a parameter of an interface type?

2. Can an abstract class ever implement an interface?

3. Can a derived class have two base classes? Can it implement two interfaces?

4. Can an interface implement another interface?

PITFALL: Interface Semantics Are Not Enforced

As far as the Java compiler is concerned, an interface has syntax but no semantics. For example, the definition of the `Ordered` interface (Display 13.1) says the following in a comment:

```
/**
 For objects of the class o1 and o2,
 o1.follows(o2) == o2.preceded(o1).
*/
```

You might have assumed that this is true even if there were no comment in the interface. After all, in the real world, if I precede you, then you follow me. However, that is giving your intuitive interpretation to the word "`precedes`".

(continued)

PITFALL: (continued)

As far as the compiler and run-time systems are concerned, the `Ordered` interface merely says that the methods `precedes` and `follows` each take one argument of type `Object` and return a `boolean` value. The interface does not really require that the `boolean` value be computed in any particular way. For example, the compiler would be satisfied if both `precedes` and `follows` always return `true` or if they always return `false`. It would even allow the methods to use a random number generator to generate a random choice between `true` and `false`.

It would be nice if we could safely give an interface some simple semantics, such as saying that `o1.follows(o2)` means the same as `o2.preceded(o1)`. However, if Java did allow that, there would be problems with having a class implement two interfaces or even with having a class derived from one base class and implementing an interface. Either of these situations could produce two semantic conditions, both of which must be implemented for the same method, and the two semantics may not be consistent. For example, suppose that (contrary to fact) you could require that `o1.follows(o2)` means the same as `o2.preceded(o1)`. You could also define another interface with an inconsistent semantics, such as saying that `precedes` always returns `true` and that `follows` always returns `false`. As long as a class can have two objects, there is no way a class could implement both of these semantics. Interfaces in Java are very well behaved, the price of which is that you cannot count on Java to enforce any semantics in an interface.

If you want to require semantics for an interface, you can add it to the documentation, as illustrated by the comments in Displays 13.1 and 13.4, but always remember that these are just comments; they are not enforced by either the compiler or the run-time system, so you cannot necessarily rely on such semantics being followed. However, we live in an imperfect world, and sometimes you will find that you must specify a semantics for an interface; do so in the interface's documentation. It then becomes the responsibility of the programmers implementing the interface to follow the semantics.

Having made our point about interface semantics not being enforced by the compiler or run-time system, we want to nevertheless urge you to follow the specified semantics for an interface. Software written for classes that implement an interface will assume that any class that implements the interface does satisfy the specified semantics. So, if you define a class that implements an interface but does not satisfy the semantics for the interface, then software written for classes that implement that interface will probably not work correctly for your class. ■

Interface Semantics Are Not Enforced

When you define a class that implements an interface, the compiler and run-time system will let you define the body of an interface method any way you want, provided you keep the method heading as it is given in the interface. However, you should follow the specified semantics for an interface whenever you define a class that implements that interface; otherwise, software written for that interface may not work for your class.

The `Comparable` **Interface**

This subsection requires material on arrays from Chapter 6. If you have not yet covered Chapter 6, you can skip this section and the following Programming Example without any loss of continuity. But if you have read Chapter 6, you should not consider this section to be optional.

In Chapter 6 (Display 6.11), we introduced a method for sorting a partially filled array of base type `double` into increasing order. It is very easy to transform the code into a method to sort into decreasing order instead of increasing order. (See Self-Test Exercise 20 of Chapter 6 and its answer if this is not clear to you.) It is also easy to modify the code to obtain methods for sorting integers instead of `doubles` or sorting strings into alphabetical order. Although these changes are easy, they seem to be—and in fact are—a useless nuisance. All these sorting methods are essentially the same. The only differences are the types of the values being sorted and the definition of the ordering. It would seem that we should be able to give a single sorting method that covers all these cases. The `Comparable` interface lets us do this.

The `Comparable` interface is in the `java.lang` package and so is automatically available to your program. The `Comparable` interface has only the following method heading that must be implemented for a class to implement the `Comparable` interface:

```
public int compareTo(Object other);
```

The `Comparable` interface has semantics, and it is the programmer's responsibility to follow the semantics when implementing the `Comparable` interface. The semantics says that `compareTo` returns

`compareTo`

a negative number if the calling object "comes before" the parameter `other`,

a zero if the calling object "equals" the parameter `other`,

and a positive number if the calling object "comes after" the parameter `other`.[1]

Almost any reasonable notions of "comes before" should be acceptable. In particular, all of the standard less-than relations on numbers and lexicographic ordering on strings are suitable ordering for `compareTo`. (The relationship "comes after" is just the reverse of "comes before.") If you need to consider other ordering, the precise rule is that the ordering must be a total ordering, which means the following rules must be satisfied:

(Irreflexive) For no object o does o come before o.

(Trichotomy) For any two objects o1 and o2, one, and only one, of the following holds true: o1 comes before o2, o1 comes after o2, or o1 equals o2.

(Transitivity) If o1 comes before o2 and o2 comes before o3, then o1 comes before o3.

The "equals" of the `compareTo` method semantics should coincide with the `equals` methods if possible, but this is not absolutely required by the semantics.

---

[1]Because the parameter to `CompareTo` is of type `Object`, an argument to `CompareTo` might not be an object of the class being defined. If the parameter `other` is not of the same type as the class being defined, then the semantics specifies that a `ClassCastException` should be thrown.

The `Comparable` Interface

The `Comparable` interface is in the `java.lang` package and so is automatically available to your program. The `Comparable` interface has only the following method heading that must be given a definition for a class to implement the `Comparable` interface:

```
public int compareTo(Object other);
```

The method `compareTo` should return

a negative number if the calling object "comes before" the parameter `other`,
a zero if the calling object "equals" the parameter `other`,
and a positive number if the calling object "comes after" the parameter `other`.

The "comes before" ordering that underlies `compareTo` should be a total ordering. Most normal ordering, such as less-than ordering on numbers and lexicographic ordering on strings, is total ordering.

If you define a class that implements the `Comparable` interface but that does not satisfy these conditions, then code written for `Comparable` objects will not work properly. It is the responsibility of you, the programmer, to ensure that the semantics is satisfied. Neither the compiler nor the run-time system enforces any semantics on the `Comparable` interface.

If you have read this subsection, you should also read the following Programming Example.

EXAMPLE: Using the `Comparable` Interface

Display 13.5 shows a class with a method that can sort any partially filled array whose base type implements the `Comparable` interface (including implementing the semantics we discussed in the previous subsection). To obtain the code in Display 13.5, we started with the sorting code in Display 6.11 and mechanically replaced all occurrences of the array type `double[]` with the type `Comparable[]`. We replaced all Boolean expressions of the form

Expression_1 < *Expression_2*

with

Expression_1.`compareTo`(*Expression_2*) < 0

We also changed the comments a bit to make them consistent with the `compareTo` notation. The changes are highlighted in Display 13.5. Only four small changes to the code were needed.

(continued on page 754)

Display 13.5   **Sorting Method for Array of Comparable** (part 1 of 2)

```
1   public class GeneralizedSelectionSort
2   {
3       /**
4        Precondition: numberUsed <= a.length;
5                    The first numberUsed indexed variables have values.
6        Action: Sorts a so that a[0], a[1], ... , a[numberUsed - 1] are in
7        increasing order by the compareTo method.
8        */
9       public static void sort(Comparable[] a, int numberUsed)
10      {
11          int index, indexOfNextSmallest;
12          for (index = 0; index < numberUsed - 1; index++)
13          {   //Place the correct value in a[index]:
14              indexOfNextSmallest = indexOfSmallest(index, a,
                                      numberUsed);
15              interchange(index,indexOfNextSmallest, a);
16              //a[0], a[1],..., a[index] are correctly ordered and
                //these are
17              //the smallest of the original array elements. The remaining
18              //positions contain the rest of the original array elements.
19          }
20      }

21      /**
22       Returns the index of the smallest value among
23       a[startIndex], a[startIndex+1], ... a[numberUsed - 1]
24       */
25      private static int indexOfSmallest(int startIndex,
26                                      Comparable [] a, int numberUsed)
27      {
28          Comparable min = a[startIndex];
29          int indexOfMin = startIndex;
30          int index;
31          for (index = startIndex + 1; index < numberUsed; index++)
32            if (a[index].compareTo(min) < 0)//if a[index] is less than min
33            {
34              min = a[index];
35              indexOfMin = index;
36              //min is smallest of a[startIndex] through a[index]
37            }
38          return indexOfMin;
39      }
```

(continued)

Display 13.5   Sorting Method for Array of `Comparable` (part 2 of 2)

```
40      /**
41       Precondition: i and j are legal indices for the array a.
42       Postcondition: Values of a[i] and a[j] have been interchanged.
43       */
44      private static void interchange(int i, int j, Comparable[] a)
45      {
46          Comparable temp;
47          temp = a[i];
48          a[i] = a[j];
49          a[j] = temp; //original value of a[i]
50      }
51  }
```

EXAMPLE: (continued)

Display 13.6 shows a demonstration of using the sorting method given in Display 13.5. To understand why the demonstration works, you need to be aware of the fact that both of the classes `Double` and `String` implement the `Comparable` interface.

If you were to check the full documentation for the class `Double`, you would see that `Double` implements the `Comparable` interface and so has a `compareTo` method. Moreover, for objects `o1` and `o2` of `Double`,

```
o1.compareTo(o2) < 0 //o1 "comes before" o2
```

means the same thing as

```
o1.doubleValue() < o2.doubleValue()
```

So, the implementation of the `Comparable` interface for the class `Double` is really just the ordinary less-than relationship on the `double` values corresponding to the `Double` objects.

Similarly, if you were to check the full documentation for the class `String`, you would see that `String` implements the `Comparable` interface and so has a `compareTo` method. Moreover, the implementation of the `compareTo` method for the class `String` is really just the ordinary lexicographic relationship on the strings.

This Programming Example uses the standard library classes `Double` and `String` for the base type of the array. You can do the same thing with arrays whose base class is a class you defined, so long as the class implements the `Comparable` interface (including the standard semantics, which we discussed earlier in the Pitfall "Interface Semantics Are Not Enforced").

This Programming Example does point out one restriction on interfaces. They can apply only to classes. A primitive type cannot implement an interface. So, in Display 13.6, we could not sort an array with base type `double` using the sorting method for an array of `Comparable`. We had to settle for sorting an array with base type `Double`. This is a good example of using a wrapper class with its "wrapper class personality."

Display 13.6   **Sorting Arrays of `Comparable`** (part 1 of 2)

```
1    /**
2     Demonstrates sorting arrays for classes that
3     implement the Comparable interface.
4    */
5    public class ComparableDemo              The classes Double and String do
6    {                                         implement the Comparable interface.
7        public static void main(String[] args)
8        {
9            Double[] d = new Double[10];
10           for (int i = 0; i < d.length; i++)
11               d[i] = new Double(d.length - i);

12           System.out.println("Before sorting:");
13           int i;
14           for (i = 0; i < d.length; i++)
15               System.out.print(d[i].doubleValue() + ", ");
16           System.out.println();

17           GeneralizedSelectionSort.sort(d, d.length);

18           System.out.println("After sorting:");
19           for (i = 0; i < d.length; i++)
20               system.out.print(d[i].doubleValue() + ", ");
21           System.out.println();

22           String[] a = new String[10];
23           a[0] = "dog";
24           a[1] = "cat";
25           a[2] = "cornish game hen";
26           int numberUsed = 3;

27           System.out.println("Before sorting:");
28           for (i = 0; i < numberUsed; i++)
29               System.out.print(a[i] + ", ");
30           System.out.println();
31
32           GeneralizedSelectionSort.sort(a, numberUsed);

33           System.out.println("After sorting:");
34           for (i = 0; i < numberUsed; i++)
35               System.out.print(a[i] + ", ");
36           System.out.println();
37       }
38   }
```

(continued)

Display 13.6 Sorting Arrays of `Comparable` (part 2 of 2)

Sample Dialogue

```
Before Sorting
10.0, 9.0, 8.0, 7.0, 6.0, 5.0, 4.0, 3.0, 2.0, 1.0,
After sorting:
1.0, 2.0, 3.0, 4.0, 5.0, 6.0, 7.0, 8.0, 9.0, 10.0,
Before sorting;
dog, cat, cornish game hen,
After sorting:
cat, cornish game hen, dog,
```

MyProgrammingLab™

Self-Test Exercises

These exercises are for the material on the `Comparable` interface.

5. The method `interchange` in Display 13.5 makes no use of the fact that its second argument is an array with base type `Comparable`. Suppose we change the parameter type `Comparable[]` to `Object[]` and change the type of the variable `temp` to `Object`. Would the program in Display 13.6 produce the same dialogue?

6. Is the following a suitable implementation of the `Comparable` interface?

```java
public class Double2 implements Comparable
{
    private double value;
    public Double2(double theValue)
    {
        value = theValue;
    }
    public int compareTo(Object other)
    {
        return −1;
    }
    public double doubleValue()
    {
        return value;
    }
}
```

You can think of the underlying "comes before" relationship as saying that for any objects `d1` and `d2`, `d1` comes before `d2`.

Self-Test Exercises (continued)

7. Suppose you have a class `Circle` that represents circles which all have centers at the same point. (To make it concrete, you can take the circles to be in the usual *x,y* plain and to all have their centers at the origin.) Suppose there is a `boolean` valued method `inside` of the class `Circle` such that, for circles `c1` and `c2`,

```
c1.inside(c2)
```

returns `true` if `c1` is completely inside of `c2` (and `c2` is not the same as `c1`). Is the following a total ordering?

c1 comes before c2 if c1 is inside of c2
(that is, if `c1.inside(c2)` returns `true`).

You could represent objects of the class `Circle` by a single value of type `double` that gives the radius of the circle, but the answer does not depend on such details.

Defined Constants in Interfaces

The designers of Java often used the interface mechanism to take care of a number of miscellaneous details that do not really fit the spirit of what an interface is supposed to be. One example of this is the use of an interface as a way to name a group of defined constants.

An interface can contain defined constants as well as method headings, or instead of method headings. When a method implements the interface, it automatically gets the defined constants. For example, the following interface defines constants for months:

```java
public interface MonthNumbers
{
    public static final int JANUARY = 1,
        FEBRUARY = 2, MARCH = 3, APRIL = 4, MAY = 5,
        JUNE = 6, JULY = 7, AUGUST = 8, SEPTEMBER = 9,
        OCTOBER = 10, NOVEMBER = 11, DECEMBER = 12;
}
```

Any class that implements the `MonthNumbers` interface will automatically have the 12 constants defined in the `MonthNumbers` interface. For example, consider the following toy class:

```java
public class DemoMonthNumbers implements MonthNumbers
{
    public static void main(String[] args)
    {
        System.out.println(
            "The number for January is " + JANUARY);
    }
}
```

Note that the constant JANUARY is used in the class DemoMonthNumbers but is not defined there. The class DemoMonthNumbers automatically gets the month constants because it implements the MonthNumbers interface.

no instance variables

An interface cannot have instance variables, although it can use the syntax for instance variables as a way to define constants. Any variables defined in an interface must be public, static, and final, so Java allows you to omit those modifiers. The following is an equivalent definition of the interface MonthNumbers:

```
public interface MonthNumbers
{
    int JANUARY = 1,
        FEBRUARY = 2, MARCH = 3, APRIL = 4, MAY = 5,
        JUNE = 6, JULY = 7, AUGUST = 8, SEPTEMBER = 9,
        OCTOBER = 10, NOVEMBER = 11, DECEMBER = 12;
}
```

Thus, an interface can be used to give a name for a group of defined constants, so that you can easily add the needed constants to any class by implementing the interface. This is really a different use for interfaces than what we have seen before, which was to use interfaces to specify method headings. It is legal to mix these two uses by including both defined constants and method headings in a single interface.

PITFALL: Inconsistent Interfaces

Java allows a class to have only one base class but also allows the class to implement any number of interfaces. The reason that a class can have only one base class is that if Java allowed two base classes, the two base classes could provide different and inconsistent definitions of a single method heading. Because interfaces have no method bodies at all, this problem cannot arise when a class implements two interfaces. The ideal that the designers of Java apparently hoped to realize was that any two interfaces will always be consistent. However, this ideal was not fully realized. Although it is a rare phenomenon, two interfaces can be inconsistent. In fact, there is more than one kind of inconsistency that can be exhibited. If you write a class definition that implements two inconsistent interfaces, that is an error and the class definition is illegal. Let's see how two interfaces can be inconsistent.

inconsistent constants

The most obvious way that two interfaces can be inconsistent is by defining two constants with the same name but with different values. For example,

```
public interface Interface1
{
    int ANSWER = 42;
}

public interface Interface2
{
    int ANSWER = 0;
}
```

PITFALL: (continued)

Suppose a class definition begins with

```
public class MyClass
    implements Interface1, Interface2
{ ...
```

Clearly this has to be, and is, illegal. The defined constant ANSWER cannot be simultaneously 42 and 0.[2]

inconsistent method headings

Even two method headings can be inconsistent. For example, consider the following two interfaces:

```
public interface InterfaceA
{
    public int getStuff();
}
public interface InterfaceB
{
    public String getStuff();
}
```

Suppose a class definition begins with

```
public class YourClass
                implements InterfaceA, InterfaceB
{ ...
```

Clearly this has to be, and is, illegal. The method getStuff in the class YourClass cannot be simultaneously a method that returns an int and a method that returns a value of type String. (Remember that you cannot overload a method based on the type returned; so, overloading cannot be used to get around this problem.) ∎

MyProgrammingLab™   **Self-Test Exercises**

8. Will the following program compile? If it does compile, will it run? Interface1 and Interface2 were defined in the previous subsection.

```
public class MyClass
                implements Interface1, Interface2
{
    public static void main(String[] args)
    {
        System.out.println(ANSWER);
    }
}
```

(continued)

---

[2]If the class never uses the constant ANSWER, then there is no inconsistency and the class will compile and run with no error messages.

Self-Test Exercises (continued)

9. Will the following program compile? If it does compile, will it run?
   `Interface1` and `Interface2` were defined in the previous subsection.

   ```
   public class MyClass
                   implements Interface1, Interface2
   {
       public static void main(String[] args)
       {
           System.out.println("Hello");
       }
   }
   ```

10. Will the following program compile? If it does compile, will it run?
    `InterfaceA` and `InterfaceB` were defined in the previous subsection.

    ```
    public class YourClass
                    implements InterfaceA, InterfaceB
    {
        public String getStuff()
        {
            return "one";
        }
    }
    ```

11. Will the following two interfaces and the following program class compile? If
    they compile, will the program run with no error messages?

    ```
    public interface InterfaceA
    {
        public int getStuff();
    }
    public interface InterfaceOtherB
    {
        public String getStuff(String someStuff);
    }
    public class OurClass
                    implements InterfaceA, InterfaceOtherB
    {
        private int intStuff = 42;

        public static void main(String[] args)
        {
            OurClass object = new OurClass();
            System.out.println(object.getStuff()
                            + object.getStuff("Hello"));
        }
    ```

Self-Test Exercises (continued)

```
        public int getStuff()
        {
            return intStuff;
        }
        public String getStuff(String someStuff)
        {
            return someStuff;
        }
    }
```

The `Serializable` Interface ★

As we have already noted, the designers of Java often used the interface mechanism to take care of miscellaneous details that do not really fit the spirit of what an interface is supposed to be. An extreme example of this is the `Serializable` interface. The `Serializable` interface has no method headings and no defined constants. As a traditional interface, it is pointless. However, Java uses it as a type tag that means the programmer gives permission to the system to implement file I/O in a particular way. If you want to know what that way of implementing file I/O is, see Chapter 10, in which the `Serializable` interface is discussed in detail.

The `Cloneable` Interface

The `Cloneable` interface is another example where Java uses the interface mechanism for something other than its traditional role. The `Cloneable` interface has no method headings that must be implemented (and has no defined constants). However, it is used to say something about how the method `clone`, which is inherited from the class `Object`, should be used and how it should be redefined.

So, what is the purpose of the `Cloneable` interface? When you define a class to implement the `Cloneable` interface, you are agreeing to redefine the `clone` method (inherited from `Object`) in a particular way. The primary motivation for this appears to be security issues. Cloning can potentially copy private data if not done correctly. Also, some software may depend on your redefining the `clone` method in a certain way. Programmers have strong and differing views on how to handle cloning and the `Cloneable` interface. What follows is the official Java line on how to do it.

The method `Object.clone()` does a bit-by-bit copy of the object's data in storage. If the data is all primitive type data or data of immutable class types (such as `String`), then this works fine and has no unintended side effects. However, if the data in the object includes instance variables whose type is a mutable class, then this would cause what we refer to as *privacy leaks*. (See the Pitfall section entitled "Privacy Leaks" in Chapter 5.) To avoid these privacy leaks when you define the `clone` method in a derived class, you should invoke the `clone` method of the base class `Object` (or whatever the base class is) and then reset the values of any new instance variables whose types are mutable class types. Reset these instance variables to copies of the instance variables in the calling object. There are also issues of exception handling to deal with. An example may be clearer than an abstract discussion.

Let's start with the simple case. Suppose your class has no instance variables of a mutable class type, or to phrase it differently, suppose your class has instance variables all of whose types are either a primitive type or an immutable class type, like `String`. And to make it even simpler, suppose your class has no specified base class, so the base class is `Object`. If you want to implement the `Cloneable` interface, you should define the `clone` method as in Display 13.7.

The `try-catch` blocks are required because the inherited method `clone` can throw the exception `CloneNotSupportedException` if the class does not correctly implement the `Cloneable` interface. Of course, in this case the exception will never be thrown, but the compiler will still insist on the `try-catch` blocks.

Now let's suppose your class has one instance variable of a mutable class type named `DataClass`. Then, the definition of the `clone` method should be as in Display 13.8. First, a bit-by-bit copy of the object is made by the invocation of `super.clone()`. The dangerous part of copy is the reference to the mutable object in the instance variable

Display 13.7   Implementation of the Method clone (Simple case)

```
1   public class YourCloneableClass implements Cloneable
2   {                                  Works correctly if each instance variable is of
3            .                         a primitive type or of an immutable type like
4            .                         String.
5            .
6       public Object clone()
7       {
8          try
9          {
10             return super.clone();//Invocation of clone
11                                  //in the base class Object
12          }
13          catch (CloneNotSupportedException e)
14          {//This should not happen.
15              return null; //To keep the compiler happy.
16          }
17      }
18           .
19           .
20           .
21  }
```

Display 13.8   Implementation of the Method clone (Harder Case)

```
1   public class YourCloneableClass2  implements Cloneable
2   {
3       private DataClass someVariable;
4           .
5           .                           DataClass is a mutable class. Any other
6           .                           instance variables are each of a primitive
7       public Object clone()           type or of an immutable type like String.
8       {
9           try
10          {
11              YourCloneableClass2 copy =
12                          (YourCloneableClass2)super.clone();
13              copy.someVariable = (DataClass)someVariable.clone();
14              return copy;
15          }
16          catch(CloneNotSupportedException e)
17          {//This should not happen.
18              return null; //To keep the compiler happy.
19          }
20      }
21          .                    If the clone method return type is DataClass rather
22          .                    than Object, then this type cast is not needed.
23          .
24  }
```

The class DataClass must also properly implement
the Cloneable interface including defining the clone
method as we are describing.

someVariable. So, the reference is replaced by a reference to a copy of the object named by someVariable. This is done with the following line:[3]

```
copy.someVariable = (DataClass)someVariable.clone();
```

The object named by copy is now safe and so can be returned by the clone method.

If there are more instance variables that have a mutable class type, then you repeat what we did for someVariable for each of the mutable instance variables.

This requires that the class type DataClass has a correctly working clone method that is marked public, but that will be true if the class type DataClass implements the Cloneable interface in the way we are now describing. That is, DataClass should implement the Cloneable interface following the model of Displays 13.7 or 13.8,

[3]Depending on how the clone method was defined in the class DataClass, the type cast may or may not be needed, but causes no harm in any case.

whichever is appropriate; similarly, all classes for instance variables in DataClass should follow the model of Displays 13.7 or 13.8, and so forth for classes for instance variables inside of classes all the way down. You want every class in sight and every class used in every class in sight to follow the model of Displays 13.7 or 13.8.

The same basic technique applies if your class is derived from some class other than Object, except that, in this case, there normally is no required exception handling. To implement the Cloneable interface in a derived class with a base class other than Object, the details are as follows: The base class must properly implement the Cloneable interface, and the derived class must take care of any mutable class instance variable added in the definition of the derived class. These new mutable class instance variables are handled by the technique shown in Display 13.8 for the instance variable someVariable. As long as the base class properly implements the Cloneable interface, including defining the clone method as we are describing, then the derived class's clone method need not worry about any inherited instance variables. Also, usually, you do not need to have try and catch blocks for CloneNotSupportedException because the base class clone method, super.clone(), normally catches all its CloneNotSupportedExceptions, so super.clone() will never throw a CloneNotSupportedException. (See Self-Test Exercise 15 for an example.)

Self-Test Exercises

12. Modify the following class definition so it correctly implements the Cloneable interface (all the instance variables are shown):

```
public class StockItem
{
    private int number;
    private String name;
    public void setNumber(int newNumber)
    {
        number = newNumber;
    }
        . . .
}
```

13. Modify the following class definition so it correctly implements the Cloneable interface (all the new instance variables are shown):

```
public class PricedItem extends StockItem
{
    private double price;

        . . .
}
```

14. Modify the following class definition so it correctly implements the `Cloneable` interface (all the new instance variables are shown):

```
public class PricedItem extends StockItem
{
    private double price;

        . . .

}
```

15. Modify the following class definition so it correctly implements the `Cloneable` interface (all the instance variables are shown):

```
public class Record
{
    private StockItem item1;
    private StockItem item2;
    private String description;

        . . .

}
```

16. Modify the following class definition so it correctly implements the `Cloneable` interface (all the new instance variables are shown):

```
public class BigRecord extends Record
{
    private StockItem item3;

        . . .

}
```

17. Modify the definition of the class `Date` (Display 4.13) so it implements the `Cloneable` interface. Be sure to define the method `clone` in the style of Display 13.7.

18. Modify the definition of the class `Employee` (Display 7.2) so it implements the `Cloneable` interface. Be sure to define the method `clone` in the style of Display 13.8.

19. Modify the definition of the class `HourlyEmployee` (Display 7.3) so it implements the `Cloneable` interface. Be sure to define the method `clone` in the style of Display 13.8.

13.2 Simple Uses of Inner Classes

The ruling ideas of each age have ever been the ideas of its ruling class.

KARL MARX and FRIEDRICH ENGELS, *The Communist Manifesto*

Inner classes are classes defined within other classes. In this section, we will describe one of the most useful applications of inner classes, namely, inner classes used as helping classes.

Helping Classes

inner class

Defining an **inner class** is straightforward; simply include the definition of the inner class within another class, as follows:

```
public class OuterClass
{
    private class InnerClass
    {
        Declarations_of_InnerClass_Instance_Variables
        Definitions_of_InnerClass_Methods
    }
    Declarations_of_OuterClass_Instance_Variables
    Definitions_of_OuterClass_Methods
}
```

outer class

As this outline suggests, the class that includes the inner class is called an **outer class**. The definition of the inner class (or classes) need not be the first item(s) of the outer class, but it is good to place it either first or last so that it is easy to find. The inner class need not be private, but that is the only case we will consider in this section. We will consider other modifiers besides `private` in Section 13.3.

An inner class definition is a member of the outer class in the same way that the instance variables of the outer class and the methods of the outer class are members of the outer class. Thus, an inner class definition is local to the outer class definition. So you may reuse the name of the inner class for something else outside the definition of the outer class. If the inner class is private, as ours will always be in this section, then the inner class cannot be accessed by name outside the definition of the outer class.

There are two big advantages to inner classes. First, because they are defined within a class, they can be used to make the outer class self-contained or more self-contained than it would otherwise be. The second advantage is that the inner and outer classes' methods have access to each other's private methods and private instance variables.

TIP: Inner and Outer Classes Have Access to Each Other's Private Members

Within the definition of a method of an inner class, it is legal to reference a private instance variable of the outer class and to invoke a private method of the outer class. To facilitate this, Java follows this convention: If a method is invoked in an inner class and the inner class has no such method, then it is assumed to be an invocation of the method by that name in the outer class. (If the outer class also has no method by that name, that is, of course, an error.) Similarly, an inner class can use the name of an instance variable of the outer class.

The reverse situation, invoking a method of the inner class from the outer class, is not so simple. To invoke a (nonstatic) method of the inner class from within a method of the outer class, you need an object of the inner class to use as a calling object, as we do in Display 13.9.

As long as you are within the definition of the inner or outer classes, the modifiers `public` and `private` (used within the inner or outer classes) are equivalent.

These sorts of invocations and variable references that cross between inner and outer classes can get confusing. So, it is best to confine such invocations and variable references to cases that are clear and straightforward. It is easy to tie your code in knots if you get carried away with this sort of thing. ■

Access Privileges between Inner and Outer Classes

Inner and outer classes have access to each other's private members.

EXAMPLE: A Bank Account Class

Display 13.9 contains a simplified bank account program with an inner class for amounts of money. The bank account class uses values of type `String` to obtain or return amounts of money, such as the amount of a deposit or the answer to a query for the account balance. However, inside the class it stores amounts of money as values of type `Money`, which is an inner class. Values of type `Money` are not stored as `Strings`, which would be difficult to do arithmetic on, nor are they stored as values of type `double`, which would allow round-off errors that would not be acceptable in banking transactions. Instead, the class `Money` stores amounts of money as two integers, one for the dollars and one for the cents. In a real banking program, the class `Money` might have a larger collection of methods, such as methods to do addition, subtraction, and compute percentages, but in this simple example we included only the method for adding an amount of money to the calling object. The outer class `BankAccount` would also have more methods in a real class, but here we included only methods to deposit an amount of money to the account and to obtain the account balance. Display 13.10 contains a simple demonstration program using the class `BankAccount`.

(continued)

EXAMPLE: (continued)

The class Money is a private inner class of the class BankAccount. So, the class Money cannot be used outside of the class BankAccount. (Public inner classes are discussed in Section 13.3 and have some subtleties involved in their use.) Because the class Money is local to the class BankAccount, the name Money can be used for the name of another class outside of the class BankAccount. (This would be true even if Money were a public inner class.)

We have made the instance variables in the class Money private following our usual conventions for class members. When we discuss public inner classes, this will be important. However, for use within the outer class (and a private inner class cannot be used anyplace else), there is no difference between public and private or other member modifiers. All instance variables and all methods of the inner class are public to the outer class no matter whether they are marked public or private or anything else. Notice the method closeAccount of the outer class. It uses the private instance variables dollars and cents of the inner class.

This is still very much a toy example, but we will have occasion to make serious use of private inner classes when we discuss linked lists in Chapter 15 and when we study Swing GUIs starting in Chapter 17.

Display 13.9   Class with an Inner Class (part 1 of 2)

```
1   public class BankAccount
2   {
3       private class Money            ← The modifier private in this line
4       {                                should not be changed to public.
5           private long dollars;        However, the modifiers public and
6           private int cents;           private inside the inner class Money
                                         can be changed to anything else and
7           public Money(String stringAmount)   it would have no effect on the class
8           {                            BankAccount.
9               abortOnNull(stringAmount);
10              int length = stringAmount.length();
11              dollars = Long.parseLong(
12                      stringAmount.substring(0, length - 3));
13              cents = Integer.parseInt(
14                      stringAmount.substring(length - 2, length));
15          }
16
17          public String getAmount()
18          {
19              if (cents > 9)
```

Display 13.9   Class with an Inner Class (part 2 of 2)

```
19                    return (dollars + "." + cents);
20               else
21                    return (dollars + ".0" + cents);
22          }

23     public void addIn(Money secondAmount)
24     {
25          abortOnNull(secondAmount);
26          int newCents = (cents + secondAmount.cents)%100;
27          long carry = (cents + secondAmount.cents)/100;
28          cents = newCents;
29          dollars = dollars + secondAmount.dollars + carry;
30     }
31     private void abortOnNull(Object o)
32     {
33          if (o == null)
34          {
35               System.out.println("Unexpected null argument.");
36               System.exit(0);
37          }
38     }
39 }
40     private Money balance;

41     public BankAccount()
42     {
43          balance = new Money("0.00");
44     }

45     public String getBalance()
46     {
47          return balance.getAmount();
48     }

49     public void makeDeposit(String depositAmount)
50     {
51          balance.addIn(new Money(depositAmount));
52     }

53     public void closeAccount()
54     {
55          balance.dollars = 0;
56          balance.cents = 0;
57     }
58 }
```

The definition of the inner class ends here, but the definition of the outer class continues in this display.

To invoke a nonstatic method of the inner class outside of the inner class, you need to create an object of the inner class.

This invocation of the inner class method getAmount() would be allowed even if the method getAmount() were marked as private.

Notice that the outer class has access to the private instance variables of the inner class.

This class would normally have more methods, but we have only included the methods we need to illustrate the points covered here.

Display 13.10   Demonstration Program for the Class **BankAccount**

```
1    public class BankAccount
2    {
3        public static void main(String[] args)
4        {
5            System.out.println("Creating a new account.");
6            BankAccount account = new BankAccount( );
7            System.out.println("Account balance now = $"
8                                              + account.getBalance( ));

9            System.out.println("Depositing $100.00");
10           account.makeDeposit("100.00");
11           System.out.println("Account balance now = $"
12                                             + account.getBalance( ));
13           System.out.println("Depositing $99.99");
14           account.makeDeposit("99.99");
15           System.out.println("Account balance now = $"
16                                             + account.getBalance( ));
17           System.out.println("Depositing $0.01");
18           account.makeDeposit("0.01");
19           System.out.println("Account balance now = $"
20                                             + account.getBalance( ));
21           System.out.println("Closing account.");
22           account.closeAccount( );
23           System.out.println("Account balance now = $"
24                                             + account.getBalance( ));
25       }
26   }
```

Sample Dialogue

```
Creating a new account.
Account balance now = $0.00
Depositing $100.00
Account balance now = $100.00
Depositing $99.99
Account balance now = $199.99
Depositing $0.01
Account balance now = $200.00
Closing account.
Account balance now = $0.00
```

Helping Inner Classes

You may define a class within another class. The inside class is called an **inner class**. A common and simple use of an inner class is to use it as a helping class for the outer class, in which case the inner class should be marked `private`.

Self-Test Exercises

20. Would the following invocation of `getAmount` in the method `getBalance` of the outer class `BankAccount` still be legal if we change the method `getAmount` of the inner class `Money` from `public` to `private`?

```
public String getBalance()
{
    return balance.getAmount();
}
```

21. Because it does not matter if we make the members of a private inner class public or private, can we simply omit the `public` or `private` modifiers from the instance variables and methods of a private inner class?

22. Would it be legal to add the following method to the inner class `Money` in Display 13.9? Remember, the question is would it be legal, not would it be sensible.

```
public void doubleBalance()
{
    balance.addIn(balance);
}
```

23. Would it be legal to add the following method to the inner class `Money` in Display 13.9? Remember, the question is would it be legal, not would it be sensible.

```
public void doubleBalance2()
{
    makeDeposit(balance.getAmount());
}
```

The `.class` File for an Inner Class

When you compile any class in Java, it produces a `.class` file. When you compile a class with an inner class, this compiles both the outer class and the inner class and produces two `.class` files. For example, when you compile the class `BankAccount` in Display 13.9, this produces the following two `.class` files:

`BankAccount.class` and `BankAccount$Money.class`

If `BankAccount` had two inner classes, then three `.class` files would be produced.

PITFALL: Other Uses of Inner Classes

In this section, we have shown you how to use an inner class in only one way, namely to create and use objects of the inner class from within the outer class method definitions. There are other ways to use inner classes, but they can involve subtleties. If you intend to use inner classes in any of these other ways, you should consult Section 13.3. ■

13.3 More about Inner Classes

Something deeply hidden had to be behind things.

ALBERT EINSTEIN, Note quoted in *New York Times Magazine* (August 2, 1964)

In this section, we cover some of the more subtle details about using inner classes. It might be best to treat this section as a reference section and look up the relevant cases as you need them. None of the material in this section is used in the rest of this book.

Static Inner Classes

A normal (nonstatic) inner class, which is the kind of inner class we have discussed so far, has a connection between each of its objects and the object of the outer class that created the inner class object. Among other things, this allows an inner class definition to reference an instance variable or invoke a method of the outer class. If you do not **static** need this connection, you can make your inner class **static** by adding the `static` modifier to your inner class definition, as illustrated by the following sample beginning of a class definition:

```
public class OuterClass
{
    private static class InnerClass
    {
```

A static inner class can have nonstatic instance variables and methods, but an object of a static inner class has no connection to an object of the outer class.

You may encounter situations where you need an inner class to be static. For example, if you create an object of the inner class within a static method of the outer class, then the inner class must be static. This follows from the fact that a nonstatic inner class object must arise from an outer class object.

Also, if you want your inner class to itself have static members, then the inner class must be static.

Because a static inner class has no connection to an object of the outer class, you cannot reference an instance variable or invoke a nonstatic method of the outer class within the static inner class.

To invoke a static method of a static inner class within the outer class, simply preface the method name with the name of the inner class and a dot. Similarly, to name a static variable of a static inner class within the outer class, just preface the static variable name with the name of the inner class and a dot.

Static Inner Class

A **static** inner class is one that is not associated with an object of the outer class. It is indicated by including the modifier static in its class heading.

MyProgrammingLab™

Self-Test Exercises

24. Can you have a static method in a nonstatic inner class?

25. Can you have a nonstatic method in a static inner class?

Public Inner Classes

public inner class

If an inner class is marked with the public modifier instead of the private modifier, then it can be used in all the ways we discussed so far, but it can also be used outside of the outer class.

The way that you create an object of the inner class outside of the outer class is a bit different for static and nonstatic inner classes. We consider the case of a nonstatic inner class first. When creating an object of a nonstatic inner class, you need to keep in mind that every object of the nonstatic inner class is associated with some object of the outer class. To put it another way, to create an object of the inner class, you must start with an object of the outer class. This has to be true, because an object of the inner class may invoke a method of the outer class or reference an instance variable of the outer class, and you cannot have an instance variable of the outer class unless you have an object of the outer class.

For example, if you change the class Money in Display 13.9 from private to public, so that the class definition begins

```
public class BankAccount
{
    public class Money
```

then you can use an object of the nonstatic inner class Money outside of the class BankAccount as illustrated by the following:

```
BankAccount account = new BankAccount();
BankAccount.Money amount =
                account.new Money("41.99");
System.out.println(amount.getAmount());
```

This code produces the output

```
41.99
```

Note that the object amount of the inner class Money is created starting with an object, account, of the outer class BankAccount, as follows:

```
BankAccount.Money amount =
                  account.new Money("41.99");
```

Also, note that the syntax of the second line is *not*

```
new account.Money("41.99"); //Incorrect syntax
```

Within the definition of the inner class Money, an object of the inner class can invoke a method of the outer class. However, this is not true outside of the inner class. Outside of the inner class, an object of the inner class can only invoke methods of the inner class. So, we could *not* have continued the previous sample code (which is outside the class BankAccount and so outside the inner class Money) with the following:

```
System.out.println(amount.getBalance()); //Illegal
```

The meaning of amount.getBalance() is clear, but it is still not allowed. If you want something equivalent to amount.getBalance(), you should use the corresponding object of the class BankAccount; in this case, you would use account. getBalance(). (Recall that account is the BankAccount object used to create the inner class object amount.)

Now let's consider the case of a static inner class. You can create objects of a public *static* inner class and do so outside of the inner class—in fact, even outside of the outer class. To do so outside of the outer class, the situation is similar to, but not exactly the same as, what we outlined for nonstatic inner classes. Consider the following outline:

```
public class OuterClass
{
    public static class InnerClass
    {
        public void nonstaticMethod()
        { ... }

        public static void staticMethod()
        {...}

        Other_Members_of_InnerClass
    }

    Other_Members_of_OuterClass
}
```

You can create an object of the inner class outside of the outer class as in the following example:

```
OuterClass.InnerClass innerObject =
                new OuterClass.InnerClass();
```

Note that the syntax is *not*

```
OuterClass.new InnerClass();
```

This may seem like an apparent inconsistency with the syntax for creating the object of a nonstatic inner class. It may help to keep in mind that for a static inner class, `OuterClass.InnerClass` is a well-specified class name and all the information for the object is in that class name. To remember the syntax for a nonstatic inner class, remember that for that case, the object of the outer class modifies how the `new` operator works to create an object of the inner class.

Once you have created an object of the inner class, the object can invoke a nonstatic method in the usual way. For example,

```
innerObject.nonstaticMethod();
```

You can also use the object of the inner class to invoke a static method in the same way. For example,

```
innerObject.staticMethod();
```

However, it is more common, and clearer, to use class names when invoking a static method. For example,

```
OuterClass.InnerClass.staticMethod();
```

TIP: Referring to a Method of the Outer Class

As we have already noted, if a method is invoked in an inner class and the inner class has no such method, then it is assumed to be an invocation of the method by that name in the outer class. For example, we could add a method `showBalance` to the inner class `Money` in Display 13.9, as outlined in what follows:

```
public class BankAccount
{
    private class Money
    {
        private long dollars;
        private int cents;

        public void showBalance()
        {
            System.out.println(getBalance());
        }
        . . .
    }//End of Money
```

(continued)

TIP: (continued)

```
                public String getBalance()
                {...}
                    ...
}       //End of BankAccount
```

This invocation of getBalance is within the definition of the inner class Money. But the inner class Money has no method named getBalance, so it is presumed to be the method getBalance of the outer class BankAccount.

But suppose the inner class did have a method named getBalance; then this invocation of getBalance would be an invocation of the method getBalance defined in the inner class.

If both the inner and outer classes have a method named getBalance, then you can specify that you mean the method of the outer class as follows:

```
public void showBalance()
{
    System.out.println(
                    BankAccount.this.getBalance());
}
```

The syntax

Outer_Class_Name.this.*Method_Name*

always refers to a method of the outer class. In the example, BankAccount.this means the this of BankAccount, as opposed to the this of the inner class Money. ∎

Self-Test Exercises

26. Consider the following class definition:

```
public class OuterClass
{
    public static class InnerClass
    {
        public static void someMethod()
        {
            System.out.println("From inside.");
        }
    }
    Other_Members_of_OuterClass
}
```

Write an invocation of the static method someMethod that you could use in some class you define.

27. Consider the following class definition:

```
public class Outs
{
    private int outerInt = 100;

    public class Ins
    {
        private int innerInt = 25;
        public void specialMethod()
        {
            System.out.println(outerInt);
            System.out.println(innerInt);
        }
    }
    Other_Members_of_OuterClass
}
```

Write an invocation of the method `specialMethod` with an object of the class `Ins`. Part of this exercise is to create the object of the class `Ins`. This should be code that you could use in some class you define.

Nesting Inner Classes

It is legal to nest inner classes within inner classes. The rules are the same as what we have already discussed except that names can get longer. For example, if A has a public inner class B, and B has a public inner class C, then the following is valid code:

```
A aObject = new A();
A.B bObject =
                aObject.new B();
A.B.C cObject =
                bObject.new C();
```

Inner Classes and Inheritance

Suppose `OuterClass` has an inner class named `InnerClass`. If you derive `DerivedClass` from `OuterClass`, then `DerivedClass` automatically has `InnerClass` as an inner class just as if it were defined within `DerivedClass`.

Just as with any other kind of class in Java, you can make an inner class a derived class of some other class. You can also make the outer class a derived class of a different (or the same) base class.

It is not possible to override the definition of an inner class when you define a derived class of the outer class.

It is also possible to use an inner class as a base class to derive classes, but we will not go into those details in this book; there are some subtleties to worry about.

Anonymous Classes

If you wish to create an object but have no need to name the object's class, then you can embed the class definition inside the expression with the `new` operator. These sorts of class definitions are called **anonymous classes** because they have no class name. An expression with an anonymous class definition is, like everything in Java, inside of some class definition. Thus, an anonymous class is an inner class. Before we go into the details of the syntax for anonymous classes, let's say a little about where one might use them.

The most straightforward way to create an object is the following:

```
YourClass anObject = new YourClass();
```

If `new YourClass()` is replaced by some expression that defines the class but does not give the class any name, then there is no name `YourClass` to use to declare the variable `anObject`. So, it does not make sense to use an anonymous class in this situation. However, it can make sense in the following scenario:

```
SomeOtherType anObject = new YourClass();
```

Here `SomeOtherType` must be a type such that an object of the class `YourClass` is also an object of `SomeOtherType`. In this case, you can replace `new YourClass()` with an expression including an anonymous class instead of `YourClass`. The type `SomeOtherType` is usually a Java interface.

Here is an example of an anonymous class. Suppose you define the following interface:

```
public interface NumberCarrier
{
    public void setNumber(int value);
    public int getNumber();
}
```

Then the following creates an object using an anonymous class definition:

```
NumberCarrier anObject = new NumberCarrier()
                {
                    private int number;
                    public void setNumber(int value)
                    {
                        number = value;
                    }
                    public int getNumber()
                    {
                        return number;
                    }
                };
```

The part in the braces is the same as the part inside the main braces of a class definition. The closing brace is followed by a semicolon, unlike a class definition. (This is because the entire expression will be used as a Java statement.) The beginning part, repeated as follows, may seem strange:

```
new NumberCarrier()
```

The `new` is sensible enough but what is the point of `NumberCarrier()`? It looks like this is an invocation of a constructor for `NumberCarrier`. But, `NumberCarrier` is an interface and has no constructors. The meaning of `new NumberCarrier()` is simply

```
implements NumberCarrier
```

So what is being said is that the anonymous class implements the `NumberCarrier` interface and is defined as shown between the main braces.

Display 13.11 shows a simple demonstration with two anonymous class definitions. For completeness, we have also repeated the definition of the `NumberCarrier` interface in this display.

Display 13.11   Anonymous Classes (part 1 of 2)

```
 1  public class AnonymousClassDemo
 2  {
 3      public static void main(String[] args)
 4      {
 5          NumberCarrier anObject =
 6                  new NumberCarrier()
 7                  {
 8                      private int number;
 9                      public void setNumber(int value)
10                      {
11                          number = value;
12                      }
13                      public int getNumber()
14                      {
15                          return number;
16                      }
17                  };
18          NumberCarrier anotherObject =
19                  new NumberCarrier()
20                  {
21                      private int number;
22                      public void setNumber(int value)
23                      {
24                          number = 2*value;
25                      }
```

This is just a toy example to demonstrate the Java syntax for anonymous classes.

(continued)

Display 13.11   **Anonymous Classes** (part 2 of 2)

```
26                          public int getNumber()
27                          {
28                              return number;
29                          }
30                      };

31          anObject.setNumber(42);
32          anotherObject.setNumber(42);
33          showNumber(anObject);
34          showNumber(anotherObject);
35          System.out.println("End of program.");
36      }

37      public static void showNumber(NumberCarrier o)
38      {
39          System.out.println(o.getNumber());
40      }
```
                                          This is the file `AnonymousClassDemo.java`.
```
41  }
```

Sample Dialogue

```
42
84
End of program.
```

```
1  public interface NumberCarrier    This is the file NumberCarrier.java.
2  {
3      public void setNumber(int value);
4      public int getNumber();
5  }
```

TIP: Why Use Inner Classes?

Most simple situations do not need inner classes. However, there are situations for which inner classes are a good solution. For example, suppose you want to have a class with two base classes. This is not allowed in Java. However, you can have an outer class derived from one base class with an inner class derived from the other base class. Because the inner and outer classes have access to each other's instance variables and methods, this can often serve as if it were a class with two base classes.

As another example, if you need only one object of a class and the class definition is very short, many programmers like to use an anonymous class (but I must admit I am not one of them).

When we study *linked lists* in Chapter 15, you will see cases where using an inner class as a helping class makes the linked list class self-contained in a very natural way. We will also use inner classes when defining Graphical User Interfaces (GUIs) starting in Chapter 17. But until you learn what linked lists and GUIs are, these are not likely to be compelling examples. ∎

Self-Test Exercise

28. Suppose we replace

    ```
    NumberCarrier anObject
    ```

    with

    ```
    Object anObject
    ```

    in Display 13.11. What would be the first statement in the program to cause an error message? Would it be a compiler error message or a run-time error message?

Chapter Summary

- An *interface* is a property of a class that says what methods a class that implements the interface must have.

- An interface is defined the same way as a class is defined except that the keyword `interface` is used in place of the keyword `class` and method bodies are replaced by semicolons.

- An interface may not have any instance variables, with one exception: An interface may have defined constants. If you use the syntax for an instance variable in an inner class, the variable is automatically a constant, not a real instance variable.

- An *inner class* is a class defined within another class.

- One simple use of an inner class is as a helping class to be used in the definition of the outer class methods and/or instance variables.

- A *static* inner class is one that is not associated with an object of the *outer class*. It must include the modifier `static` in its class heading.

- To create an object of a nonstatic inner class outside the definition of the outer class, you must first create an object of the outer class and use it to create an object of the inner class.

Answers to Self-Test Exercises

1. Yes to both. An interface is a type and can be used like any other type.
2. Yes. Any of the interface methods that it does not fully define must be made abstract methods.
3. A derived class can have only one base class, but it can implement any number of interfaces.

4. No, but the way to accomplish the same thing is to have one interface extend the other.

These exercises are for the material on the `Comparable` interface.

5. Yes, the dialogue would be the same. The change from the parameter type `Comparable[]` to `Object[]` in the method `interchange` is in fact a good idea.

6. No. This will compile without any error messages. However, the less-than ordering does not satisfy the semantics of the `Comparable` interface. For example, the trichotomy law does not hold.

7. Yes. The three required conditions are true for objects of the class `Circle`:
   (Irreflexive) By definition, no circle is inside itself.

   (Trichotomy) For any two circles `c1` and `c2` with centers at the origin, one, and only one, of the following holds true: `c1` is inside of `c2`, `c2` is inside of `c1`, or `c1` equals `c2`.

   (Transitivity) If `c1` is inside of `c2` and `c2` is inside of `c3`, then `c1` is inside of `c3`.

8. The class will produce a compiler error message saying that there is an inconsistency in the definitions of `ANSWER`.

9. The class will compile and run with no error messages. Because the named constant `ANSWER` is never used, there is no inconsistency.

10. The class will produce a compiler error message saying that you have not implemented the heading for `getStuff` in `InterfaceA`.

11. They will all compile and the program will run. The two definitions of `getStuff` have different numbers of parameters, so this is overloading. There is no inconsistency.

12.
```java
public class StockItem implements Cloneable
{
    private int number;
    private String name;
    public void setNumber(int newNumber)
    {
        number = newNumber;
    }

        . . .

    public Object clone()
    {
        try
        {
            return super.clone();
        }
        catch (CloneNotSupportedException e)
        {//This should not happen.
            return null; //To keep compiler happy.
        }
    }
}
```

13. Note that you do not catch a `CloneNotSupportedException` because any
    such thrown exception in `super.clone` is caught inside the base class method
    `super.clone`.

```java
public class PricedItem extends StockItem
                          implements Cloneable
{
    private double price;
        ...
    public Object clone()
    {
        return super.clone();
    }
}
```

14.
```java
public class Record implements Cloneable
{
    private StockItem item1;
    private StockItem item2;
    private String description;

        ...

    public Object clone()
    {
        try
        {
            Record copy =
                    (Record)super.clone();
            copy.item1 =
                    (StockItem)item1.clone();
            copy.item2 =
                    (StockItem)item2.clone();
            return copy;
        }
        catch (CloneNotSupportedException e)
        {//This should not happen.
            return null; //To keep compiler happy.
        }
    }
}
```

15. Note that you do not catch a `CloneNotSupportedException` because any such thrown exception in `super.clone` is caught inside the base class method `super.clone`.

```java
public class BigRecord extends Record
                       implements Cloneable
{
    private StockItem item3;

        . . .
    public Object clone()
    {
        BigRecord copy =
                (BigRecord)super.clone();
        copy.item3 =
                (StockItem)item3.clone();
        return copy;
    }
}
```

extra code on website

16. The heading of the class definition changes to what is shown in the following and the method `clone` shown there is added. The version of `Date` for this chapter on the accompanying website includes this definition of `clone`.

```java
public class Date implements Cloneable
{
    private String month;
    private int day;
    private int year;

        . . .
    public Object clone()
    {
        try
        {
            return super.clone();//Invocation of
                    //clone in the base class Object
        }
        catch(CloneNotSupportedException e)
        {//This should not happen.
            return null; //To keep compiler happy.
        }
    }
}
```

extra code on website

17. The heading of the class definition changes to what is shown in the following and the method `clone` shown there is added. The version of `Employee` for this chapter on the accompanying website includes this definition of `clone`.

```
public class Employee implements Cloneable
{
    private String name;
    private Date hireDate;

        . . .
    public Object clone()
    {
        try
        {
        Employee copy =
                (Employee)super.clone();
        copy.hireDate =
            (Date)hireDate.clone();
        return copy;
        }
    catch (CloneNotSupportedException e)
    {//This should not happen.
        return null; //To keep compiler happy.
    }
    }
}
```

18. The heading of the class definition changes to what is shown in the following and the method `clone` shown there is added. Note that you do not catch a `CloneNotSupportedException` because any such thrown exception in `super.` `clone` is caught inside the base class method `super.clone`. The version of `HourlyEmployee` for this chapter on the accompanying website includes this definition of `clone`.

extra code on website

```
public class HourlyEmployee extends Employee
                            implements Cloneable
{
    private double wageRate;
    private double hours;

        . . .
    public Object clone()
    {
        HourlyEmployee copy =
                (HourlyEmployee)super.clone();
        return copy;
    }
}
```

19. It would still be legal. An outer class has access to all the private members of an inner class.

20. Yes, they can be omitted, but the reason is that it indicates package access, and in a private inner class, all privacy modifiers, including package access, are equivalent to public. (Note that the situation for public inner classes will be different.)

21. Yes, it is legal to add the method `doubleBalance` to the inner class `Money` because an inner class has access to the instance variables, such as `balance` of the outer class. To test this out, add the following as a method of the outer class:

```
public void test()
{
    balance.doubleBalance();
}
```

22. It would be legal. The method `makeDeposit` is assumed to be the method `makeDeposit` of the outer class. The calling object `balance` is assumed to be the instance variable of the outer class. These sorts of tricks can lead to confusing code. So, use them sparingly. This is just an exercise.

23. No, a nonstatic inner class cannot have any static methods.

24. Yes, you can have a nonstatic method in a static inner class.

25. `OuterClass.InnerClass.someMethod();`

26.
```
Outs outerObject = new Outs();
Outs.Ins innerObject =
                outerObject.new Ins();
innerObject.specialMethod();
```

27. You would get your first error on the following statement and it would be a complier error:

```
anObject.setNumber(42);
```

With the change described in the exercise, `anObject` is of type `Object` and `Object` has no method named `setNumber`.

Programming Projects

Visit www.myprogramminglab.com to complete select exercises online and get instant feedback.

VideoNote
Solution to Programming Project 13.1

1. Modify the recursive implementation of binary search from Chapter 11 so that the search method works on any array of type `Comparable[]`. Test the implementation with arrays of different types to see if it works.

2. Listed below is the skeleton for a class named `CityPopulation` to be used by the census authority. Each item of the `CityPopulation` class has two instance variables name and population:

```
class CityPopulation
{
private String name;
 private long population;
}
```

Flesh out the class with appropriate accessors, constructors, and mutators. The census authority should be able to assign a value to the variable population to each city that comes under their supervision. Next, modify the class so that it implements the Comparable interface. The compareTo() method should compare the value of the variable population; e.g., a city with a lower population should precede a city with a higher population. Test your class by creating an array of sample CityPopulation's and sort them using a sorting method that takes as input an array of type Comparable.

3. Listed next is a code skeleton for an interface called Enumeration and a class called NameCollection. Enumeration provides an interface to sequentially iterate through some type of collection. In this case, the collection will be the class NameCollection that simply stores a collection of names using an array of strings.

```
interface Enumeration
{
 // Returns true if another element in the collection exists
 public boolean hasNext();

 // Returns the next element in the collection as an Object
 public Object getNext();
}

/**
 * NameCollection implements a collection of names using
 * a simple array.
 */
class NameCollection
{
  String[] names;

 /**
  * The list of names is initialized from outside
  * and passed in as an array of strings
  */
 NameCollection(String[] names)
 {
  this.names = names;
 }

 /**
  * getEnumeration should return an instance of a class that
    implements
  * the Enumeration interface where hasNext() and getNext()
  * correspond to data stored within the names array.
  */
 Enumeration getEnumeration ()
 {
  // Complete code here using an inner class
 }
}
```

Complete the method `getEnumeration()` so that it returns an anonymous inner class that corresponds to the `Enumeration` interface for the names array in `NamesCollection`. Then write a `main` method that creates a `NamesCollection` object with a sample array of strings, retrieves the `Enumeration` for this class via `getEnumeration()`, and then iterates through the enumeration outputting each name using the `getNext()` method.

4. In Display 13.5, we described a sorting method to sort an array of type `Comparable[]`. In Display 12.6, we described a sorting method that used the merge sort algorithm to sort an array of type `double[]` into increasing order. Redo the method in Display 12.6 so it applies to an array of type `Comparable[]`. Also, do a suitable test program.

5. In Display 13.5, we described a sorting method to sort an array of type `Comparable[]`. In Display 12.8, we described a sorting method that used the quick sort algorithm to sort an array of type `double[]` into increasing order. Redo the method in Display 12.8 so it applies to an array of type `Comparable[]`. Also, do a suitable test program.

6. Redo the class `Person` in Display 5.19 so that it implements the `Cloneable` interface. This may require that you also redo the class `Date` so it implements the `Cloneable` interface. Also, do a suitable test program.

7. Redo the class `Person` in Display 5.19 so that the class `Date` is a private inner class of the class `Person`. Also, do a suitable test program. (You need not start from the version produced in Programming Project 13.6. You can ignore Programming Project 13.6 when you do this project.)

8. This is a combination of Programming Projects 13.6 and 13.7. Redo the class `Person` in Display 5.19 so that the class `Date` is a private inner class of the class `Person`, and so that the class `Person` implements the `Cloneable` interface. Also, do a suitable test program.

9. Redo the class `Employee` and the class `HourlyEmployee` in Displays 7.2 and 7.3 so that the class `Date` is an inner class of the class `Employee` and an inherited inner class of the class `HourlyEmployee`. Also, do a suitable test program.

10. Define an interface named `Shape` with a single method named `area` that calculates the area of the geometric shape:

```
public double area();
```

Next, define a class named `Circle` that implements `Shape`. The `Circle` class should have an instance variable for the radius, a constructor that sets the radius, accessor/mutator methods for the radius, and an implementation of the `area` method. Also define a class named `Rectangle` that implements `Shape`. The `Rectangle` class should have instance variables for the height and width, a constructor that sets the height and width, accessor and mutator methods for the height and width, and an implementation of the `area` method.

The following test code should then output the area of the Circle and Rectangle objects:

```
public static void main(String[] args)
{
    Circle c = new Circle(4); // Radius of 4
    Rectangle r = new Rectangle(4,3); // Height = 4, Width = 3
    ShowArea(c);
    ShowArea(r);
}

public static void ShowArea(Shape s)
{
    double area = s.area();
    System.out.println("The area of the shape is " + area);
}
```

VideoNote

Solution to Programming Project 13.11

11. Create a Student class that has instance variables for the student's last name and ID number, along with appropriate constructors, accessors, and mutators. Make the Student class implement the Comparable interface. Define the compareTo method to order Student objects based on the student ID number. In the main method, create an array of at least five Student objects, sort them using Arrays.sort, and output the students. They should be listed by ascending student number. Next, modify the compareTo method so it orders Student objects based on the lexicographic ordering of their last name. Without modification to the main method, the program should now output the students ordered by name.

Generics and the ArrayList Class 14

14.1 THE ArrayList CLASS 793
Using the ArrayList Class 794
Methods in the Class ArrayList 799
The "for-each" Loop 802
Example: Golf Scores 805
The Vector Class 809
Parameterized Classes and Generics 810

14.2 GENERICS 810
Generic Basics 811
Example: A Generic Class for Ordered Pairs 813
Bounds for Type Parameters 821
Generic Methods ★ 824
Inheritance with Generic Classes ★ 826

Chapter Summary 828   **Answers to Self-Test Exercises 828**   **Programming Projects 831**

14 Generics and the `ArrayList` Class

Hamlet: Do you see yonder cloud that's almost in shape of a camel?

Polonius: By the mass, and 'tis like a camel, indeed.

Hamlet: Me think it is like a weasel.

Polonius: It is backed like a weasel.

Hamlet: Or like a whale.

Polonius: Very like a whale.

WILLIAM SHAKESPEARE, *Hamlet*

Introduction

generics

Beginning with version 5.0, Java allows class and method definitions that include parameters for types. Such definitions are called **generics**. Generic programming with a type parameter allows you to write code that applies to any class. For example, you can define a class for a list of items of type `T`, where `T` is a type parameter. You can then use this class with the class `String` plugged in for `T` to automatically get a class for a list of `String` objects. Similarly, you can plug in the class `Double` for `T` to obtain a class for a list of `Double`s, and you can do a comparable thing for any other class. The class `ArrayList` in the standard Java libraries is, in fact, just such a class for a list of items of type `T`, where `T` is a type parameter. We will first show you how to use classes with a type parameter by using the `ArrayList` class as an example. We will then tell you how you can define other classes with a type parameter.

Prerequisites

Section 14.1 covering the `ArrayList` class requires only Chapters 1 through 6 and Chapter 9. It can reasonably be read without first reading Chapter 9 if you ignore all references to "exceptions."

Section 14.2 on generics requires Chapters 1 through 7 and Chapter 9. (There is one very short Tip section entitled "Generic Interfaces" that requires Section 13.1 on interfaces, but that Tip section can easily be skipped if you have not yet read Section 13.1.) You need not read Section 14.1 before Section 14.2, but you are encouraged to do so; Section 14.1 can serve as a motivation for Section 14.2.

14.1 The `ArrayList` Class

"Well, I'll eat it," said Alice, "and if it makes me grow larger, I can reach the key; and if it makes me grow smaller, I can creep under the door; so either way I'll get into the garden. . . ."

LEWIS CARROLL, *Alice's Adventures In Wonderland*

`ArrayList`   `ArrayList` is a class in the standard Java libraries. You can think of an `ArrayList` object as an array that can grow (and shrink) in length while your program is running. In Java, you can read in the length of an array when the program is running, but once your program creates an array of that length, it cannot change the length of the array. For example, suppose you write a program to record customer orders for a mail-order house, and suppose you store all the orders for one customer in an array of objects of some class called `Item`. You could ask the user how many items she or he will order, store the number in a variable called `numberOfItems`, and then create the array `item` with the following statement:

```
Item[] item = new Item[numberOfItems];
```

But suppose the customer enters `numberOfItems` and then decides to order another item? There is no way to increase the size of the array `item`. There are ways around this problem with arrays, but they are all rather complicated. `ArrayList`s serve the same purpose as arrays, except that an `ArrayList` can change length while the program is running. So an `ArrayList` could handle the customer's extra order without any problems.

The class `ArrayList` is implemented using an array as a private instance variable. When this hidden array is full, a new larger hidden array is created and the data is transferred to this new array. However, you need not concern yourself with this implementation detail. All you need to know is how to use the `ArrayList` class, and we are about to tell you that.

If `ArrayList`s are like arrays but have the nice added feature of being able to change length, then why don't we just always use `ArrayList`s instead of arrays? It often seems that every silver lining has a cloud, and this is true of `ArrayList`s as well. There are three main disadvantages of `ArrayList`s: (1) They are less efficient than arrays; (2) they do not have the square bracket notation, and so using an `ArrayList` is sometimes notationally more awkward than using ordinary arrays; and (3) the base type of an `ArrayList` must be class type (or other reference type); it cannot be a primitive type, such as `int`, `double`, or `char`. For example, if you want an `ArrayList` of `int` values, you must simulate this structure with an `ArrayList` of `Integer` values, where `Integer` is the wrapper class whose objects simulate `int` values. Automatic boxing and unboxing (as discussed in Chapter 5) make (3) less of a problem, because an `ArrayList` with base type, for example, `Integer` can, in effect, store values of type `int`.

Using the `ArrayList` Class

**import
statement**

`ArrayList`s are used in much the same way as arrays, but there are some important differences. First, the definition of the class `ArrayList` is not provided automatically. The definition is in the package `java.util`, and any code that uses the class `ArrayList` must contain the following, normally at the start of the file:

```
import java.util.ArrayList;
```

An `ArrayList` is created and named in the same way as objects of any class, except that you specify the base type using a new notation. For example,

```
ArrayList<String> list = new ArrayList<String>(20);
```

capacity

This statement makes `list` the name of an `ArrayList` that stores objects of the class `String` and that has an *initial* **capacity** of 20 items. When we say that an `ArrayList` has a certain capacity, we mean that it has been allocated memory for that many items, but if it needs to hold more items, the system will automatically allocate more memory. By carefully choosing the initial capacity of an `ArrayList`, you can often make your code more efficient, but this capacity has no effect on how many items the `ArrayList` can hold. If you choose your capacity to be large enough, then the system will not need to reallocate memory too often, and as a result, your program should run faster. On the other hand, if you make your capacity too large, you will waste storage space. However, no matter what capacity you choose, you can still do anything you want with the `ArrayList`.

Java 7 supports a slightly shorter but equivalent way to define the `ArrayList`. In this format, the base type in the call to the constructor is not needed. For example,

```
ArrayList<String> list = new ArrayList<>(20);
```

This feature is called **type inference** and is briefly discussed in Section 14.2.

base type

The type `String` in the previous `ArrayList` example is the **base type** of the `ArrayList` class. An `ArrayList`—that is, an object of the `ArrayList` class—stores objects of its base type. You can use any reference type as the base type of an `ArrayList` class. In particular, you can use any class or interface type. However, you cannot use a primitive type, such as `int` or `double`, as the base type of an `ArrayList` class. This is an example of a type parameter. The `ArrayList` class is defined as having a type parameter for the type of the elements in the list. Create a concrete class by specifying, in angular brackets, a class type to be substituted for this type parameter. For example, the following code, which we saw earlier in this section, substitutes the type `String` for the type parameter to create the class `ArrayList<String>` and an object of this class named `list`:

```
ArrayList<String> list = new ArrayList<String>(20);
```

`ArrayList` objects can be used like arrays, but they do not have the array square-bracket notation. If you use

```
a[index] = "Hi Mom!";
```

set

for an array of strings `a`, then the analogous statement for a suitable `ArrayList` named `list` is

```
list.set(index, "Hi Mom!");
```

Creating and Naming an `ArrayList` Object

An object of the class `ArrayList` is created and named in the same way as any other object, except that you specify the base type of the `ArrayList`.

SYNTAX

```
ArrayList<Base_Type> Object_Name = new ArrayList<Base_Type>();
ArrayList<Base_Type> Object_Name =
                        new ArrayList<Base_Type>(Initial_Capacity);
```

The *Base_Type* must be a reference type, usually a class type; it cannot be a primitive type such as `int` or `double`. When a number is given as an argument to the constructor, that number determines the initial capacity of the `ArrayList`.

EXAMPLES

```
ArrayList<String> list = new ArrayList<String>();
ArrayList<Double> list2 = new ArrayList<Double>(30);
```

If you would use

```
String temp = a[index];
```

for an array of strings a, then the analogous statement for a suitable `ArrayList` named list would be

```
String temp = list.get(index);
```

Accessing at an Index

If list is an `ArrayList`, its elements can be accessed as follows:

EXAMPLES

```
ArrayList<String> list = new ArrayList<String>();
int index;
   . . .

list.set(index, "Here"); //Sets the element
                         //at index to "Here".
String temp = list.get(index); //The expression
                               //list.get(index)
                               //returns the element
                               //at position index.
ArrayList<Integer> list2 = new ArrayList<Integer>();
  . . .
list2.set(42, index); //Sets the element at index to
                //new Integer(42). This example relies on
                // automatic boxing.
```

(continued)

```
int temp2 = list2.get(index); //The expression
                    //v.get(index) returns the
                    //element at position index.
                    // This example
                    //relies on automatic unboxing.
```
The `index` must be greater than or equal to `0` and less than the current size of the
`ArrayList list`.

**Creating and
Using an
`ArrayList`**

The two methods `set` and `get` give `ArrayLists` approximately the same
functionality that square brackets give to arrays. However, you need to be aware of one
important point: The method invocation

```
list.set(index, "Hi Mom!");
```

is *not* always completely analogous to

```
a[index] = "Hi Mom!";
```

The method `set` can replace any existing element, but you cannot use `set` to put
an element at just any index, as you could with an array. The method `set` is used to
change the value of elements, not to set them for the first time. To set an element for

add

the first time, you usually use the method `add`. The basic form of the method `add` adds
elements at index position `0`, position `1`, position `2`, and so forth in that order. This
means that `ArrayLists` must always be filled in this order. But your code can then go
back and change any individual element, just as it can in an array.

For example, suppose `list` is an `ArrayList` with base type `String`, which has not
yet had any elements added to it; that is, `list` is empty. The following statements will
add the strings `"One"`, `"Two"`, and `"Three"` to positions `0`, `1`, and `2`:

```
list.add("One");
list.add("Two");
list.add("Three");
```

The method name `add` is overloaded. There is also a two-argument method named
`add` that allows you to add an element at any currently used index position or at the
first unused position. When inserting into an `ArrayList` with this version of `add`,
elements at the specified index and higher (if any) are moved up one position to make
room for the new element. For example,

```
list.add(0, "Zero");
```

adds the string `"Zero"` at position `0` and moves elements originally at positions `0`, `1`, `2`,
and so forth up one position to positions `1`, `2`, `3`, and so forth.

Suppose list starts out empty and your code executes our four add invocations, which we repeat below:

```
list.add("One");
list.add("Two");
list.add("Three");
list.add(0, "Zero");
```

After these four invocations of list.add, the list would contain the strings "Zero", "One", "Two", and "Three" in positions 0, 1, 2, and 3, respectively.

Note that the two-argument version of add cannot add an element at just any position. It can only insert an element at some already used position or at the first unused position. The elements in an ArrayList always occupy a contiguous set of positions starting at 0; that is, they are always at positions 0, 1, 2, and so forth up to some last position. This is just like a partially filled array (as discussed in Chapter 6), but unlike a partially filled array, you do not need to do anything to keep track of how many elements are on the list. The method size automatically takes care of this for any ArrayList.

The add Methods

Elements can be added to an ArrayList by using the methods named add. The elements are added to index position 0, then 1, then 2, and so forth so there are no gaps in the indices of elements.

The most straightforward method to use for adding to an ArrayList is the method named add that has only one parameter.

EXAMPLES

```
list.add("Salud");
list.add("Dinero");
list.add("Java");
```

The object list is an ArrayList with base type String.

A second method named add allows you to add an element at any currently used index position or at the first unused position. When inserting into an ArrayList with this version of add, elements at the specified index and higher (if any) are moved up one position to make room for the new element.

```
list.add(1, "Amor");
```

If list starts out empty and all four statements in the two sets of examples are executed, then list would contain the following strings in the order given: "Salud", "Amor", "Dinero", and "Java".

---

size   You can find out how many indices already have elements by using the method size. If list is an ArrayList, list.size() returns the **size** of the ArrayList, which is the number of elements stored in it. The indices of these elements go from 0 to one less than list.size().

The `size` Method

The method `size` returns the number of elements in an `ArrayList`.

EXAMPLE

```
for (int index = 0; index < list.size(); index++)
    System.out.println(list.get(index));
```

`list` is an `ArrayList` object.

TIP: Summary of Adding to an `ArrayList`

add

To place an element in an `ArrayList` position (at an `ArrayList` index) for the first time, you usually use the method `add`. The simplest method named `add` has a single parameter for the element to be added and adds elements at index positions 0, 1, 2, and so forth, in that order.

You can add an element at an already occupied list position by using the two-parameter version of `add`. When inserting into an `ArrayList` with this version of `add`, elements at the specified index and higher are moved up one position to make room for the new element. For example, suppose `list` is an `ArrayList` object with base type `String` that has three elements already on its list. Consider the following method invocation:

```
list.add(1, "Amor");
```

Before, there were elements at index positions 0, 1, and 2. When this invocation of `add` is executed, the element `"Amor"` is inserted at index 1, and the elements at index positions 1 and 2 are moved to positions 2 and 3.

You can also use the two-argument version of `add` to add an element at the first unused position. If `list` has elements at index positions 0, 1, 2, and 3, then the following is legal:

```
list.add(4, "Mucho Amor");
```

Your code can then go back and change any individual element, using `set`. However, `set` can reset only the element at an index that already has an element.

The method `size` can be used to determine how many elements are stored in an `ArrayList`. ■

Self-Test Exercises

1. Suppose `list` is an object of the class `ArrayList<String>`. How do you add the string `"Hello"` to the `ArrayList` `list`?

2. Suppose `instruction` is an object of the class `ArrayList<String>` that contains the string `"Stop"` at index position 5. How do you change the string at index position 5 to `"Go"` (without changing any of the elements at other positions)?

3. Suppose `instruction` is an object of the class `ArrayList<String>` that contains strings at index positions 0 through 10. How do you insert the string `"Go"` at index position 5 so that no strings are removed from the list `instruction`?

Self-Test Exercises (continued)

4. Can you use the method `set` to place an element in an `ArrayList` at any index you want?

5. In the `ArrayList` list from Self-Test Exercise 3, how do you change the string at index position 2 to `"mangoes"` without changing any of the elements at other positions?

6. Using the `ArrayList` list from Self-Test Exercise 3, what is the output of the following code?

   ```
   System.out.println(list.size());
   ```

7. If you create an `ArrayList` with the following statement, can the `ArrayList` contain more than 20 elements?

   ```
   ArrayList<Double> myList = new ArrayList<Double>(20);
   ```

Methods in the Class `ArrayList`

With arrays, the square brackets and the instance variable `length` are the only tools automatically provided for you, the programmer. If you want to use arrays for other things, you must write code to manipulate the arrays. `ArrayLists`, on the other hand, come with a selection of powerful methods that can do many of the things for which you would need to write code in order to do with arrays. For example, the class `ArrayList` has a version of the method `add` that inserts a new element between two elements in the `ArrayList`. Most of these methods are described in Display 14.1.

Display 14.1 Some Methods in the Class `ArrayList` (part 1 of 3)

CONSTRUCTORS

```
public ArrayList<Base_Type>(int initialCapacity)
```
Creates an empty `ArrayList` with the specified *Base_Type* and initial capacity.

```
public ArrayList<Base_Type>()
```
Creates an empty `ArrayList` with the specified *Base_Type* and an initial capacity of 10.

ARRAYLIKE METHODS

```
public Base_Type set(int index, Base_Type newElement)
```
Sets the element at the specified `index` to `newElement`. Returns the element previously at that position, but the method is often used as if it were a `void` method. If you draw an analogy between the `ArrayList` and an array a, this statement is analogous to setting a`[index]` to the value `newElement`. The index must be a value greater than or equal to 0 and less than the current size of the `ArrayList`. Throws an `IndexOutOfBoundsException` if the index is not in this range.

(continued)

Display 14.1 Some Methods in the Class `ArrayList` (part 2 of 3)

public *Base_Type* get(int index)

Returns the element at the specified index. This statement is analogous to returning a[index] for an array a. The index must be a value greater than or equal to 0 and less than the current size of the `ArrayList`. Throws `IndexOutOfBoundsException` if the index is not in this range.

METHODS TO ADD ELEMENTS

public boolean add(*Base_Type* newElement)

Adds the specified element to the end of the calling `ArrayList` and increases the `ArrayList`'s size by one. The capacity of the `ArrayList` is increased if that is required. Returns true if the add is successful. (The return type is boolean, but the method is typically used as if it were a void method.)

public void add(int index, *Base_Type* newElement)

Inserts newElement as an element in the calling `ArrayList` at the specified index. Each element in the `ArrayList` with an index greater or equal to index is shifted upward to have an index that is one greater than the value it had previously. The index must be a value greater than or equal to 0 and less than or equal to the current size of the `ArrayList`. Throws `IndexOutOfBoundsException` if the index is not in this range. Note that you can use this method to add an element after the last element. The capacity of the `ArrayList` is increased if that is required.

METHODS TO REMOVE ELEMENTS

public *Base_Type* remove(int index)

Deletes and returns the element at the specified index. Each element in the `ArrayList` with an index greater than index is decreased to have an index that is one less than the value it had previously. The index must be a value greater than or equal to 0 and less than the current size of the `ArrayList`. Throws `IndexOutOfBoundsException` if the index is not in this range. Often used as if it were a void method.

protected void removeRange(int fromIndex, int toIndex)

Deletes all the elements with indices *i* such that fromIndex $\leq$ *i* < toIndex. Elements with indices greater than or equal to toIndex are decreased appropriately.

public boolean remove(Object theElement)

Removes one occurrence of theElement from the calling `ArrayList`. If theElement is found in the `ArrayList`, then each element in the `ArrayList` with an index greater than the removed element's index is decreased to have an index that is one less than the value it had previously. Returns true if theElement was found (and removed). Returns false if theElement was not found in the calling `ArrayList`.

public void clear()

Removes all elements from the calling `ArrayList` and sets the `ArrayList`'s size to zero.

SEARCH METHODS

public boolean contains(Object target)

Returns true if the calling `ArrayList` contains target; otherwise, returns false. Uses the method equals of the object target to test for equality with any element in the calling `ArrayList`.

Display 14.1   Some Methods in the Class `ArrayList` (part 3 of 3)

`public int indexOf(Object target)`

Returns the index of the first element that is equal to `target`. Uses the method `equals` of the object `target` to test for equality. Returns −1 if `target` is not found.

`public int lastIndexOf(Object target)`

Returns the index of the last element that is equal to `target`. Uses the method `equals` of the object `target` to test for equality. Returns −1 if `target` is not found.

MEMORY MANAGEMENT (SIZE AND CAPACITY)

`public boolean isEmpty()`

Returns `true` if the calling `ArrayList` is empty (that is, has size 0); otherwise, returns `false`.

`public int size()`

Returns the number of elements in the calling `ArrayList`.

`public void ensureCapacity(int newCapacity)`

Increases the capacity of the calling `ArrayList`, if necessary, in order to ensure that the `ArrayList` can hold at least `newCapacity` elements. Using `ensureCapacity` can sometimes increase efficiency, but its use is not needed for any other reason.

`public void trimToSize()`

Trims the capacity of the calling `ArrayList` to the `ArrayList`'s current size. This method is used to save storage space.

MAKE A COPY

`public Object[] toArray()`

Returns an array containing all the elements on the list. Preserves the order of the elements.

`public Type[] toArray(Type[] a)`

Returns an array containing all the elements on the list. Preserves the order of the elements. *Type* can be any class types. If the list will fit in a, the elements are copied to a and a is returned. Any elements of a not needed for list elements are set to `null`. If the list will not fit in a, a new array is created.

(As we will discuss in Section 14.2, the correct Java syntax for this method heading is

`public <Type> Type[] toArray(Type[] a)`

However, at this point we have not yet explained this kind of type parameter syntax.)

`public Object clone()`

Returns a shallow copy of the calling `ArrayList`. *Warning:* The clone is not an independent copy. Subsequent changes to the clone may affect the calling object and vice versa. (See Chapter 5 for a discussion of shallow copy.)

EQUALITY

`public boolean equals(Object other)`

If `other` is another `ArrayList` (of any base type), then `equals` returns `true` if, and only if, both `ArrayLists` are of the same size and contain the same list of elements in the same order. (In fact, if `other` is any kind of *list*, then `equals` returns `true` if, and only if, both the calling `ArrayList` and `other` are of the same size and contain the same list of elements in the same order. Lists are discussed in Chapter 16.)

> ## Why Are Some Parameters of Type *Base_Type* and Others of Type `Object`?
>
> Look at the table of methods in Display 14.1. In some cases, when a parameter is naturally an object of the base type, the parameter type is the base type, but in other cases, it is the type `Object`.
>
> For example, look at the `add` methods and the second `remove` method in the table. The `add` methods have a parameter of the base type; the `remove` method has a parameter of type `Object`. Why the difference in parameter types? The class `ArrayList` implements a number of interfaces and inherits methods from various ancestor classes. These interfaces and ancestor classes specify that certain parameters have type `Object`.
>
> For example, in Chapter 7, we explained that the parameter for the `equals` method is always of type `Object` because the method heading is inherited from the class `Object`. In other cases, the designers of the `ArrayList` class were free to specify the parameter types for the method.

The "for-each" Loop

In Chapter 16, we will cover a family of classes known as *collections*. The `ArrayList` classes are our first examples of collection classes. Starting with version 5.0, Java has added a new kind of `for` loop that can cycle through all the elements in a collection and can, in particular, cycle through all the elements in an `ArrayList`. This new kind of `for` loop is called a **for-each loop** or **enhanced for loop**. A for-each loop can also be used to cycle through all the elements in an array. The for-each loop was introduced for use with arrays in a starred section of Chapter 6, but you need not go back and read that subsection. The presentation of for-each loops here is complete.

for-each loop

For example, the following code ends with a for-each loop that outputs all the elements in the `ArrayList` named `mylist`:

```
ArrayList<String> myList = new ArrayList<String>(20);
<Some code to fill myList>
for (String element : myList)
    System.out.println(element);
```

You can read the line beginning with `for` as "for each `element` in `myList`, do the following." Note that the variable, `element`, has the same type as the elements in the `ArrayList`. The variable (in this case, `element`), must be declared in the for-each loop as we have done. If you attempt to declare `element` before the for-each loop, you will get a compiler error message.

The general syntax for a for-each loop statement is

```
for (Base_Type Variable : Collection_Object)
        Statement
```

Be sure to notice that you use a colon (not a semicolon) after the *Variable*. You may use any legal variable name for the *Variable*; you do not have to use `element`. The only

*Collection_Object*s we have seen so far are arrays and ArrayList objects. Although it is not required, the *Statement* typically contains the *Variable*. When the for-each loop is executed, the *Statement* is executed once for each element of the *Collection_Object*. More specifically, for each element of the *Collection_Object*, the *Variable* is set to the collection element and then the *Statement* is executed.

The program in Display 14.2 includes an example of a for-each loop as well as examples of some of the other ArrayList details we have presented.

For-each Loop for **ArrayList** Objects

SYNTAX

```
for (Array_Base_Type Variable : ArrayList_Object) Statement
```

EXAMPLE

```
for (Integer element : numberList)
              element = 42;
```

numberList is an ArrayList with base type Integer. This for-each loop changes the value of each element of numberList to 42. (This example uses automatic boxing. So, 42 really means new Integer(42).)

A good way to read the first line of the example is "For each element in numberList, do the following."

Display 14.2   A for-each Loop Used with an **ArrayList** (part 1 of 2)

```
 1   import java.util.ArrayList;
 2   import java.util.Scanner;

 3   public class ArrayListDemo
 4   {
 5       public static void main(String[] args)
 6       {
 7           ArrayList<String> toDoList = new ArrayList<String>(20);
 8           System.out.println(
 9                      "Enter list entries, when prompted.");
10           boolean done = false;
11           String next = null;
12           String answer;
13           Scanner keyboard = new Scanner(System.in);

14           while (! done)
15           {
16               System.out.println("Input an entry:");
17               next = keyboard.nextLine();
18               toDoList.add(next);
```

(continued)

Display 14.2   A for-each Loop Used with an **`ArrayList`** (part 2 of 2)

```
19              System.out.print("More items for the list? ");
20              answer = keyboard.nextLine();
21              if (!(answer.equalsIgnoreCase("yes")))
22                  done = true;
23          }

24          System.out.println("The list contains:");
25          for (String entry : toDoList)
26              System.out.println(entry);
27      }
28  }
```

Sample Dialogue

```
Enter list entries, when prompted.
Input an entry:
Practice Dancing.
More items for the list? yes
Input an entry:
Buy tickets.
More items for the list? yes
Input an entry:
Pack clothes.
More items for the list? no
The list contains:
Practice Dancing.
Buy tickets.
Pack clothes.
```

MyProgrammingLab™   ## Self-Test Exercises

8. Suppose `numberList` is an object of the class `ArrayList<Double>`. Give code that will output all the elements in `numberList` to the screen.

9. Write a class for sorting strings into lexicographic order that follows the outline of the class `SelectionSort` in Display 6.11 of Chapter 6. Your definition, however, will use an `ArrayList` of the class `ArrayList<String>`, rather than an array of elements of type `double`. For words, lexicographic order reduces to alphabetic order if all the words are in either all lowercase or all uppercase letters. You can compare two strings to see which is lexicographically first by using the `String` method `compareTo`. For strings `s1` and `s2`, `s1.compareTo(s2)` returns a negative number if `s1` is lexicographically before `s2`, returns `0` if `s1` equals `s2`, and returns a positive number if `s1` is lexicographically after `s2`. Call

Self-Test Exercises (continued)

your class StringSelectionSort. A test program you can use to test your class follows. (The program is included with the source code provided on the website that accompanies this book.)

```java
Import java.util.ArrayList;

public class StringSelectionSortDemo
{
    public static void main(String[] args)
    {
        ArrayList<String> b = new ArrayList<String>();
        b.add("time");
        b.add("tide");
        b.add("clouds");
        b.add("rain");
        System.out.println("ArrayList values before sorting:");
        for (String e : b)
            System.out.print(e + " ");
        System.out.println();
        StringSelectionSort.sort(b);
        System.out.println("ArrayList values after sorting:");
        for (String e : b)
            System.out.print(e + " ");
        System.out.println();
    }
}
```

EXAMPLE: Golf Scores

The program in Display 14.3 reads in a list of golf scores and then outputs the average of the scores and how much each differs from the average. The scores are read and stored in an ArrayList so that they will be available later in the program to be output along with how much each differs from the average. This is the kind of thing that is well suited to being done with an ordinary array. However, it is much easier and cleaner to use an ArrayList as we did in Display 14.3.

Our program deals with a list of values of type double. But we use an ArrayList with base type Double to store these values. We did not use an ArrayList with base type double because there is no such thing. The base type for an ArrayList must be a class type (or other reference type). However, thanks to Java's automatic boxing, we can program as if an object of type ArrayList<Double> can store values of type double.

The ArrayList automatically keeps track of how many elements are stored in the ArrayList. If we had used an ordinary partially filled array in our program instead of an ArrayList, we would need an extra int variable to keep track of how much of the array is used. When we use an ArrayList, we are spared all the overhead associated

(continued)

EXAMPLE: (continued)

with partially filled arrays. Those details are taken care of for us automatically. The code for those details is in the definition of the `ArrayList` class, but there is no need to look at that code. That code is all implementation detail that we need not worry about when using an `ArrayList`.

Notice the use of for-each loops in our program. The cleanest and easiest way to cycle through all the elements in an `ArrayList` is to use a for-each loop.

It is instructive to compare the program in Display 14.3, which uses an `ArrayList`, with the program in Display 6.4, which does the same thing but uses an ordinary array. The version that uses an `ArrayList` is much cleaner and even much shorter than the one that uses an ordinary array. This is because an `ArrayList` does so many things for you automatically that you would have to explicitly code for if you used an ordinary array. This is a good example of information hiding and code reuse. The programmers who defined the `ArrayList` class did a lot of programming for you so that your programming task is simpler than it would otherwise be.

Display 14.3 Golf Score Program (part 1 of 3)

```
1   import java.util.ArrayList;
2   import java.util.Scanner;

3   public class GolfScores
4   {
5       /**
6        Shows differences between each of a list of golf scores and their
          average.
7       */
8       public static void main(String[] args)
9       {
10          ArrayList<Double> score = new ArrayList<Double>();

11          System.out.println("This program reads golf scores and shows");
12          System.out.println("how much each differs from the average.");

13          System.out.println("Enter golf scores:");
14          fillArrayList(score);
15          showDifference(score);
16      }

17      /**                                    Parameters of type ArrayList<Double>()
18       Reads values into the array a.        are handled just like any other class parameter.
19      */
20      public static void fillArrayList(ArrayList<Double> a)
```

Display 14.3   **Golf Score Program** (part 2 of 3)

```
21      {
22          System.out.println("Enter a list of nonnegative numbers.");
23          System.out.println(
                    "Mark the end of the list with a negative number.");
24          Scanner keyboard = new Scanner(System.in);

25          double next;
26          int index = 0;
27          next = keyboard.nextDouble();
28          while (next >= 0)
29          {
30              a.add(next);
31              next = keyboard.nextDouble();
32          }
33      }
34      /**
35       Returns the average of numbers in a.
36      */
37      public static double computeAverage(ArrayList<Double> a)
38      {
39          double total = 0;
40          for (Double element : a)
41              total = total + element;
42          int numberOfScores = a.size();
43          if (numberOfScores > 0)
44          {
45              return (total/numberOfScores);
46          }
47          else
48          {
49              System.out.println("ERROR: Trying to average 0 numbers.");
50              System.out.println("computeAverage returns 0.");
51              return 0;
52          }
53      }

54      /**
55       Gives screen output showing how much each of the elements
56       in a differ from their average.
57      */
58      public static void showDifference(ArrayList<Double> a)
59      {
60          double average = computeAverage(a);
61          System.out.println("Average of the " + a.size()
62                              + " scores = " + average);
63          System.out.println("The scores are:");
64          for (Double element : a)
65              System.out.println(element + " differs from average by "
66                                  + (element - average));
67      }
68  }
```

Because of automatic boxing, we can treat values of type double *as if their type were* Double.

A for-each loop is the nicest way to cycle through all the elements in an ArrayList.

(continued)

Display 14.3   Golf Score Program (part 3 of 3)

Sample Dialogue

```
This program reads golf scores and shows
how much each differs from the average.
Enter golf scores:
Enter a list of nonnegative numbers.
Mark the end of the list with a negative number.
69   74   68   −1
Average of the 3 scores = 70.3333
The scores are:
69.0 differs from average by −1.33333
74.0 differs from average by 3.66667
68.0 differs from average by −2.33333
```

TIP: Use `trimToSize` to Save Memory

`trimToSize`

`ArrayLists` automatically increase their capacity when your program needs them to have additional capacity. However, the capacity may increase beyond what your program requires. Also, when your program needs less capacity in an `ArrayList`, the `ArrayList` does not automatically shrink. If your `ArrayList` has a large amount of excess capacity, you can save memory by using the method `trimToSize` to shrink the capacity of an `ArrayList`. If `list` is an `ArrayList`, an invocation of `list.trimToSize()` will shrink the capacity of the `ArrayList` `list` down to the size of `list`, so that there is no unused capacity in `list`. Normally, you should use `trimToSize` only when you know that the `ArrayList` will not need its extra capacity later. ∎

PITFALL: The `clone` Method Makes a Shallow Copy ★

There are situations in which you would like to make an independent copy of an `ArrayList` object; that is, you would like to make a deep copy of the `ArrayList` object. (Deep copying and shallow copying were discussed in Chapter 5; you may want to review that material.) For example, if you define a class with a private instance variable of an `ArrayList` type, then you would like an accessor method to return a deep copy of the `ArrayList` stored in the private instance variable. The reason you want a deep copy is the same as the reason that you want a deep copy of an array instance variables. This was discussed in Chapter 6 in the subsection entitled "Privacy Leaks with Array Instance Variables." It would be a good idea to review that subsection before going on with reading this subsection.

As we have often observed, the assignment operator merely copies a reference so that you have another name for the object being copied. So, you do not have an independent

PITFALL: (continued)

copy. You have what is known as a *shallow copy*. For example, assume that `Pet` is a class with the usual kinds of accessor methods and consider the following code:

```
ArrayList<Pet> petList1 = new ArrayList<Pet>();
<Some code to set the instance variables of elements of petList1.>
ArrayList<Pet> petList2 = petList1;
```

`petList2` and `petList1` are just two names for the same `ArrayList` object. Making a change to `petList1` or to an element of `petList1` will also change `petList2` because they are the same list.

If you want an independent copy (deep copy) of `petList1`, you might think the following would give you your independent copy:

```
ArrayList<Pet> petList2 = petList1.clone();
```

Unfortunately, the `clone` method also makes a shallow copy. There is no built-in method to give you a deep copy (independent copy) of an `ArrayList`.

When you need a deep copy of an `ArrayList`, you will have to resort to some ad hoc tricks. If you have a way to make a deep copy of objects of the base type, then you can create a deep copy of each element in the `ArrayList` and place them into a new `ArrayList` object. This is the exact same approach as the one we discussed for making a deep copy of an ordinary array in the subsection of Chapter 6 entitled "Privacy Leaks with Array Instance Variables." The situation with respect to deep copying of an `ArrayList` is exactly the same as the situation with respect to deep copying of an ordinary array. Although the details of this subsection may seem subtle and difficult, they are not new. You have already faced the exact same problem with ordinary arrays. ∎

Self-Test Exercises

10. Can you have an `ArrayList` of ints?

11. The following for-each loop was used in the method `showDifference` in Display 14.3. Rewrite it as an ordinary `for` loop. This should help you to see how much cleaner it is to use a for-each loop.

```
for (Double element : a)
    System.out.println(element + " differs from average by "
                                    + (element - average));
```

The `Vector` Class

`Vector` The Java standard libraries have a class named `Vector` that behaves almost exactly the same as the class `ArrayList`. In fact, everything we have said about the class `ArrayList` holds true for the `Vector` class. Although in almost all situations, you could use either the class `ArrayList` or the class `Vector`, a clear preference seems to be developing among programmers for the class `ArrayList`. There are some differences between the classes `Vector` and `ArrayList`, but the differences involve material we have not covered. If you encounter the class `Vector` in somebody's code, chances are the class `Vector` could be replaced by the class `ArrayList`, which would require at most cosmetic changes in the code.[1]

Parameterized Classes and Generics

parameterized class

The class `ArrayList` is a **parameterized class**. It has a parameter, which we have been denoting *Base_Type*, that can be replaced by any reference type to obtain a class for `ArrayList`s with the specified base type. `ArrayList` is just a class that somebody defined (and placed in the standard Java library package `java.util`), so you should also be able to define these kinds of classes. Starting with version 5.0, Java allows class definitions with parameters for types. These classes that have type parameters

generics

are called parameterized class or **generic definitions** or, more simply, **generics**. You already know how to use classes with a type parameter, because we have been using the parameterized class `ArrayList`. In Section 14.2, we will show you how to write your own parameterized classes.

PITFALL: Nonparameterized `ArrayList` and `Vector` Classes

The `ArrayList` and `Vector` classes we discussed in this section have a type parameter for the base type. There are also `ArrayList` and `Vector` classes with no parameter for the base type. (They have base type `Object`.) These `ArrayList` and `Vector` classes without type parameters are left over from earlier versions of Java. When checking details in the Java documentation, be sure you get the documentation for the `ArrayList` and `Vector` classes that have a type parameter. Using notation we introduce in Section 14.2, the versions with type parameters are usually written as `ArrayList<E>` and `Vector<E>` or as `ArrayList<T>` and `Vector<T>` in the Java documentation. ■

14.2 Generics

You can have this dish prepared with any type of meat or fish.

Entry on a restaurant menu

Starting with version 5.0, Java allows class definitions that contain a parameter (or parameters) for a type (or types). In this section, we teach you how to write class definitions that contain a type parameter.

---

[1] The biggest difference between the `Vector` and `ArrayList` classes is that `Vector`s are *synchronized* whereas `ArrayList`s are not. However, synchronization is a topic that we do not cover and is not relevant to the kinds of programming we are doing.

Generic Basics

Classes and methods can have a type parameter. The type parameter may then have any reference type, and hence any class type, plugged in for the type parameter. This plugging in produces a specific class type or method. For example, Display 14.4 shows a very simple class definition with a **type parameter** T. You may use any nonkeyword identifier for the type parameter; you need not use T. However, by convention, type parameters start with an uppercase letter, and there is some tradition of using a single letter for a type parameter. Starting with an uppercase letter makes sense because typically a class type is plugged in for the type parameter. The tradition of using a single letter is not so compelling.

A class definition with a type parameter is stored in a file and compiled just like any other class. For example, the parameterized class shown in Display 14.4 would be stored in a file named `Sample.java`. Once the parameterized class is compiled, it can be used like any other class, except that when used in your code, you must specify a class type to be plugged in for the type parameter. For example, the class `Sample` from Display 14.4 could be used as follows:

```
Sample<String> object1 = new Sample<String>();
object1.setData("Hello");
System.out.println(object1.getData());
Sample<Pet> object2 = new Sample<Pet>();
Pet p = new Pet();
<Some code to set the data for the object p>
object2.setData(p);
```

The class `Pet` can be as defined in Chapter 4, but the details do not matter; it could be any class.

A class, such as `Sample<String>`, that you obtain from a generic class by plugging in a type for the type parameter is said to **instantiate** the generic class. So, we would say "`Sample<String>` instantiates the generic class `Sample`."

Notice the angular bracket notation for the type parameter and also for the class type that is plugged in for the type parameter.

type parameter (margin note)

instantiate (margin note)

Display 14.4   A Class Definition with a Type Parameter

```
1  public class Sample<T>
2  {
3      private T data;

4      public void setData(T newData)
5      {
6          data = newData;                    T is a parameter for a type.
7      }

8      public T getData()
9      {
10         return data;
11     }
12 }
```

Class Definition with a Type Parameter

You can define classes with a parameter for a type. Such a class is called a **generic class** or a **parameterized class**. The type parameter is included in angular brackets after the class name in the class definition heading. You may use any nonkeyword identifier for the type parameter, but by convention, the type parameter starts with an uppercase letter. The type parameter may be used like any other type in the definition of the class. (There are some restrictions on where the type parameter can be used. These are discussed later in the Pitfall section entitled "A Type Parameter Cannot Be Used Everywhere a Type Name Can Be Used.") For an example, see Display 14.4.

A generic class is used like any other class, except that you specify a reference type, typically a class type, to be plugged in for the type parameter. This class type (or other reference type) is given in angular brackets after the name of the generic class, as shown in the following example:

EXAMPLE

```
Sample<String> object1 = new Sample<String>();
object1.setData("Hello");
```

`Sample<String>` is said to **instantiate** the generic class `Sample`.

Type Inference in Java 7

Starting with version 7, Java supports a feature called **type inference**. In type inference, Java is able to infer the base type in the call to the constructor based on the base type used in the variable declaration. That is, the following

```
ClassName<Base_Type> Object_Name = new ClassName<Base_Type>();
```

can equivalently be written in Java 7 as:

```
ClassName<Base_Type> Object_Name = new ClassName<>();
```

The new format saves a little bit of typing and is also somewhat cleaner to read. However, programmers have been using the earlier format for many years, so you are likely to see it in existing code. For greater compatibility, the examples in this book do not use the new syntax supported in JDK 7.

EXAMPLES

```
ArrayList<String> list = new ArrayList<>();
ArrayList<Double> list2 = new ArrayList<>(30);
```

TIP: Compile with the `-Xlint` Option

There are many pitfalls that you can encounter when using type parameters. If you compile with the `-Xlint` option, you will receive more informative diagnostics of any problems or potential problems in your code. For example, the class `Sample` in Display 14.4 should be compiled as follows:

```
javac -Xlint Sample.java
```

If you are using an IDE to compile your programs, check your documentation to see how to set compiler options. (For the TextPad environment, you can set compiler options in the `Preferences` box under the `Configure` menu.)

When compiling with the `-Xlint` option, you will get more warnings than you would otherwise get. A warning is not an error, and if the compiler gives only warnings and no error message, then the class has compiled and can be used. However, in most cases, be sure you understand the warning and feel confident that it does not indicate a problem, or else change your code to eliminate the warning. One warning that you may get on some programs in this text is "no definition of `serialVersionUID`." Discussion of this warning is beyond the scope of this book, but you can safely ignore the warning. ■

EXAMPLE: A Generic Class for Ordered Pairs

In Display 14.5, we have given a parameterized class for ordered pairs of values.

Notice that the constructor heading does not include the type parameter `T`. This is counter to many people's intuition, but that is the way it is done. A constructor can use the type parameter, such as `T`, as the type for a parameter for the constructor, but the constructor heading does not include the type parameter in angular brackets, such as `<T>`.

By using this parameterized class with the type `String` plugged in for the type parameter `T`, as shown next, you get a class whose objects are pairs of `String` values:

```
Pair<String> secretPair =
        new Pair<String>("Happy", "Day");
```

By using this parameterized class with the type `Integer` plugged in for the type parameter `T`, as shown next, you get a class whose objects are pairs of `Integer` objects:

```
Pair<Integer> rollOfDice =
        new Pair<Integer>(new Integer(2), new Integer(3));
```

If `Pet` is some class you defined, you can plug in `Pet` for the type parameter `T`, as shown next, to get a class whose objects are pairs of objects of type `Pet`:

```
Pet male = new Pet();
Pet female = new Pet();
<Some code to set the data for the objects male and female.>
Pair<Pet> breedingPair =
        new Pair<Pet>(male, female);
```

Display 14.6 contains a simple example of using our generic class `Pair`.

Display 14.5 **A Generic Ordered Pair Class** (part 1 of 2)

```
1   public class Pair<T>
2   {
3       private T first;
4       private T second;

5       public Pair()
6       {
7           first = null;
8           second = null;
9       }

10      public Pair(T firstItem, T secondItem)
11      {
12          first = firstItem;
13          second = secondItem;
14      }

15      public void setFirst(T newFirst)
16      {
17          first = newFirst;
18      }

19      public void setSecond(T newSecond)
20      {
21          second = newSecond;
22      }

23      public T getFirst()
24      {
25          return first;
26      }

27      public T getSecond()
28      {
29          return second;
30      }

31      public String toString()
32      {
33          return ( "first: " + first.toString() + "\n"
34                      + "second: " + second.toString() );
35      }
36
```

Constructor headings do not include the type parameter in angular brackets.

Display 14.5   A Generic Ordered Pair Class (part 2 of 2)

```
37      public boolean equals(Object otherObject)
38      {
39          if (otherObject = = null)
40              return false;
41          else if (getClass() != otherObject.getClass())
42              return false;
43          else
44          {
45              Pair<T> otherPair = (Pair<T>)otherObject;
46              return (first.equals(otherPair.first)
47                  && second.equals(otherPair.second));
48          }
49      }
50  }
```

Terminology

The terms *generic class* and *parameterized class* mean the same thing, namely a class with one or more type parameters.

Display 14.6   Using Our Ordered Pair Class (part 1 of 2)

```
1   import java.util.Scanner;

2   public class GenericPairDemo
3   {
4       public static void main(String[] args)
5       {
6           Pair<String> secretPair =
7               new Pair<String>("Happy", "Day");

9           Scanner keyboard = new Scanner(System.in);
10          System.out.println("Enter two words:");
11          String word1 = keyboard.next();
12          String word2 = keyboard.next();
13          Pair<String> inputPair =
14              new Pair<String>(word1, word2);
15          if (inputPair.equals(secretPair))
16          {
17              System.out.println("You guessed the secret words");
18              System.out.println("in the correct order!");
```

(continued)

Display 14.6   **Using Our Ordered Pair Class** (part 2 of 2)

```
19              }
20          else
21          {
22                  System.out.println("You guessed incorrectly.");
23                  System.out.println("You guessed");
24                  System.out.println(inputPair);
25                  System.out.println("The secret words are");
26                  System.out.println(secretPair);
27          }
28      }
29  }
```

Sample Dialogue

```
Enter two words:
two words
You guessed incorrectly.
You guessed
first: two
second: words
The secret words are
first: Happy
second: Day
```

PITFALL: A Generic Constructor Name Has No Type Parameter

The class name in a parameterized class definition has a type parameter attached, such as `Pair<T>` in Display 14.5. This can mislead you into thinking you need to use the type parameter in the heading of the constructor definition, but you do not repeat the type parameter specification `<T>` in the heading of the constructor definition. For example, use

```
public Pair()
```

Do not use

```
public Pair<T>()
```

A constructor can use the type parameter, such as `T`, as the type for a parameter for the constructor, as in the following, but the constructor heading does not include the type parameter in angular brackets, such as `<T>`:

```
public Pair(T firstItem, T secondItem)
```

For a complete example, see Display 14.5.

Sometimes it seems that people stay up late at night thinking of ways to make things confusing. As we just noted, in the definition of a parameterized class, a constructor has no type parameter in angular brackets. So, you see the following in Display 14.5:

```
public Pair(T firstItem, T secondItem)
```

But as shown in Display 14.6, when you instantiate a generic class by specifying a type for the type parameter, you do specify the type in angular brackets when writing the constructor name, as in the following from Display 14.6:

```
Pair<String> secretPair =
            new Pair<String>("Happy", "Day");
```

However, this second case is not hard to remember. If you leave out the `<String>`, Java would not know which `Pair` class you meant. If you leave out the `<String>`, the compiler could not tell if you meant `Pair<String>`, `Pair<Double>`, or some other `Pair` class. ■

PITFALL: You Cannot Plug in a Primitive Type for a Type Parameter

The type plugged in for a type parameter must be a reference type. It cannot be a primitive type such as `int`, `double`, or `char`. However, now that Java has automatic boxing, this is not a big restriction in practice. For example, if you want `Pair<int>`, you cannot have it, but you can have `Pair<Integer>`, and thanks to automatic boxing, you can use `Pair<Integer>` with `int` values. This is illustrated by the program in Display 14.7.

The most typical type to plug in for a type parameter is a class type. However, you can plug in any reference type. So, in particular, you can plug in an array type for a type parameter. ■

PITFALL: A Type Parameter Cannot Be Used Everywhere a Type Name Can Be Used

Within the definition of a parameterized class definition, there are places where an ordinary class name would be allowed but a type parameter is not allowed. In particular, you cannot use the type parameter in simple expressions using `new` to create a new object. For example, the following are all illegal within the definition of a parameterized class definition with type parameter `T`:

```
T object = new T(); //The first T is legal,
                    //the second one is illegal.
T[] a = new T[10]; //The first T is legal,
                   //the second one is illegal.
```

This restriction is not as arbitrary as it might at first appear. In the first case, `T` is not being used as a type name; it is being used as a constructor name. In the second case, `T` is being used as something like a constructor, although it is not officially a constructor. ■

PITFALL: An Instantiation of a Generic Class Cannot be an Array Base Type

Arrays such as the following are illegal (the generic class `Pair` is the one defined in Display 14.5):

```
Pair<String>[] a = new Pair<String>[10]; //Illegal
```

This is a reasonable thing to want to do, but it is not allowed because of technical details having to do with how Java implements generic classes. The full explanation for this restriction is beyond the scope of this book. ■

Display 14.7   Using Our Ordered Pair Class and Automatic Boxing (part 1 of 2)

```java
1   import java.util.Scanner;

2   public class GenericPairDemo2
3   {
4       public static void main(String[] args)
5       {
6           Pair<Integer> secretPair =
7               new Pair<Integer>(42, 24);

9           Scanner keyboard = new Scanner(System.in);
10          System.out.println("Enter two numbers:");
11          int n1 = keyboard.nextInt();
12          int n2 = keyboard.nextInt();
13          Pair<Integer> inputPair =
14              new Pair<Integer>(n1, n2);
15          if (inputPair.equals(secretPair))
16          {
17              System.out.println("You guessed the secret numbers");
18              System.out.println("in the correct order!");
19          }
20          else
21          {
22              System.out.println("You guessed incorrectly.");
23              System.out.println("You guessed");
24              System.out.println(inputPair);
25              System.out.println("The secret numbers are");
26              System.out.println(secretPair);
27          }
28      }
29  }
```

Automatic boxing allows you to use an int argument for an Integer parameter.

Display 14.7   Using Our Ordered Pair Class and Automatic Boxing (part 2 of 2)

Sample Dialogue

```
Enter two numbers:
42 24
You guessed the secret numbers
in the correct order!
```

TIP: A Class Definition Can Have More Than One Type Parameter

A generic class definition can have any number of type parameters. The multiple type parameters are listed in angular brackets just as in the single type parameter case, but are separated by commas. For example, in Display 14.8, we have rewritten the class Pair so the first and second items of a pair can be of different types. In Display 14.9, we give a simple example of using our generic class with two type parameters. ∎

Display 14.8   Multiple Type Parameters (part 1 of 2)

```java
1   public class TwoTypePair<T1, T2>
2   {
3       private T1 first;
4       private T2 second;

5       public TwoTypePair()
6       {
7           first = null;
8           second = null;
9       }

10      public TwoTypePair(T1 firstItem, T2 secondItem)
11      {
12          first = firstItem;
13          second = secondItem;
14      }

15      public void setFirst(T1 newFirst)
16      {
17          first = newFirst;
18      }
19      public void setSecond(T2 newSecond)
20      {
21          second = newSecond;
22      }
23      public T1 getFirst()
```

(continued)

Display 14.8 Multiple Type Parameters (part 2 of 2)

```
24        {
25            return first;
26        }

27        public T2 getSecond()
28        {
29            return second;
30        }

31        public String toString()
32        {
33            return ( "first: " + first.toString() + "\n"
34                    + "second: " + second.toString() );
35        }
36
37        public boolean equals(Object otherObject)
38        {
39            if (otherObject = = null)
40                return false;
41            else if (getClass() != otherObject.getClass())
42                return false;
43            else
44            {
45                TwoTypePair<T1, T2> otherPair =
46                            (TwoTypePair<T1, T2>)otherObject;
47                return (first.equals(otherPair.first)
48                    && second.equals(otherPair.second));
49            }
50        }
51 }
```

The first `equals` *is the* `equals` *of the type* `T1`.
The second `equals` *is the* `equals` *of the type* `T2`.

PITFALL: A Generic Class Cannot Be an Exception Class

If you begin an exception class definition as follows, you will get a compiler error message:

```
public class MyException<T> extends Exception //Illegal
```

It is still illegal if you replace `Exception` with `Error`, `Throwable`, or any descendent class of `Throwable`. You cannot create a generic class whose objects are throwable. ∎

Display 14.9   Using a Generic Class with Two Type Parameters

```
1   import java.util.Scanner;

2   public class TwoTypePairDemo
3   {
4       public static void main(String[] args)
5       {
6           TwoTypePair<String, Integer> rating =
7               new TwoTypePair<String, Integer>("The Car Guys", 8);

8           Scanner keyboard = new Scanner(System.in);
9           System.out.println(
10                  "Our current rating for " + rating.getFirst());
11          System.out.println(" is " + rating.getSecond());

12          System.out.println("How would you rate them?");
13          int score = keyboard.nextInt();
14          rating.setSecond(score);
15          System.out.println(
16                  "Our new rating for " + rating.getFirst());
17          System.out.println(" is " + rating.getSecond());
18      }
19  }
```

Sample Dialogue

```
Our current rating for The Car Guys
is 8
How would you rate them?
10
Our new rating for The Car Guys
is 10
```

Bounds for Type Parameters

Sometimes it does not make sense to plug in just any reference type for the type parameter in a generic class definition. For example, consider the generic class `Pair` defined in Display 14.5. Suppose we want to add a method that returns the maximum of the two elements in an ordered pair. We could add the following method definition to the class `Pair` in Display 14.5:

max
```
public T max()
{
    if (first.compareTo(second) <= 0)
        return first;
    else
        return second;
}
```

compareTo   Recall that the method compareTo is required to be a member of any class that implements the Comparable interface. The Comparable interface is a standard Java interface that was discussed in Chapter 13. Recall that the Comparable interface has only the following method heading that must be implemented:

```
public int compareTo(Object other);
```

When defining a class that implements the Comparable interface, the programmer is expected to define compareTo so that it returns

a negative number if the calling object "comes before" the parameter other,

a zero if the calling object "equals" the parameter other,

and a positive number if the calling object "comes after" the parameter other.

This all works fine, except for one problem: This makes sense only if the type plugged in for the type parameter T satisfies the Comparable interface, but Java allows you to plug in any type for the type parameter T.

You can have Java enforce this restriction on the possible types that can be plugged in for T. To ensure that only classes that implement the Comparable interface are plugged in for T, begin the class definition as follows:

```
public class Pair<T extends Comparable>
```

extends   The part extends Comparable is called a **bound** on the type parameter T. If you attempt to plug in a type for T that does not implement the Comparable interface, you

bound   will get a compiler error message. Note that you use the keyword extends, not the keyword implements as you would naturally expect.

Note that the bound extends Comparable is not just an optional little nicety. If you omit it, you will get an error message from the compiler saying it does not know about the method compareTo.

This version of the generic class Pair with the method max is summarized in Display 14.10. On the accompanying website, this version of Pair is in a subdirectory named Bounded Pair.

A bound on a type may be a class name (rather than an interface name) in which case only descendent classes of the bounding class may be plugged in for the type parameters. For example, the following says that only descendent classes of the class Employee may be plugged in for T, where Employee is some class:

```
public class SameGenericClass<T extends Employee>
```

Display 14.10   A Bounded Type Parameter

```
 1   public class Pair<T extends Comparable>
 2   {
 3       private T first;
 4       private T second;

 5       public T max()
 6       {
 7           if (first.compareTo(second) <= 0)
 8               return first;
 9           else
10               return second;
11       }
```

<All the constructors and methods given in Display 14.5
                are also included as part of this generic class definition>

```
12   }
```

This explains why the keyword extends is used in the bounds expression rather than implements.

multiple bounds
You can have multiple interfaces and possibly one class in a bounds expression. Just separate the entries with the ampersand sign, &, as in the following example:

```
public class AnotherGenericClass<T extends Employee & Comparable>
```

If you have more than one type parameter, the syntax follows the following example:

```
public class YetAnotherGeneric
    <T1 extends Employee & Comparable, T2 extends Comparable>
```

You can list any number of interfaces in a bounds expression, but you may list only one class in a bounds expression. Moreover, if you do list a class and some interfaces, the class must be first in the list.

Type Parameter Bounds

You can specify that the class plugged in for a type parameter must be a descendent class of a specified class, must implement specified interfaces, or both.

(continued)

TIP: Generic Interfaces

An interface can have one or more type parameters. The details and notation are the same as they are for classes with type parameters. ■

Generic Methods ★

(This is a starred subsection because it is needed only for Chapter 16, which covers the Java collection classes. If you choose to read Chapter 16, you will need to read this subsection first.)

When you define a generic class, you can use the type parameter in the definitions of the methods for that generic class. You also can define a generic method that has its own type parameter that is not the type parameter of any class. This generic method can be a member of an ordinary (nongeneric) class or a member of some generic class with some other type parameter. For example,

```
public class Utility
{
    ...
    public static <T> T getMidpoint(T[] a)
    {
        return a[a.length/2];
    }
    public static <T> T getFirst(T[] a)
    {
        return a[0];
    }
    ...
}
```

In this case, the class (`Utility`) has no type parameters, but the methods `getMidpoint` and `getFirst` each have a type parameter. Note that the type parameter in angular brackets, `<T>`, is placed after all the modifiers—in this case, `public static`—and before the returned type.

When you invoke one of these generic methods, preface the method name with the type to be plugged in, given in angular brackets, as in the following examples:

```
String midString = Utility.<String>getMidpoint(b);

double firstNumber = Utility.<Double>getFirst(c);
```

Note that the dot is before the type in angular brackets; the type is part of the method name, not part of the class name. Also note that the methods `getMidpoint` and `getFirst` use different types plugged in for their type parameter. The type parameter is local to the method, not to the class. (The argument `b` is an array with base type `String`. The argument `c` is an array with base type `Double`.)

You can also define such generic methods inside of generic classes, as in the following example:

```
public class Sample<T>
{
    private T data;

    public Sample(T forData)
    {
        data = forData;
    }
    public <ViewerType> void showTo(ViewerType viewer)
    {
        System.out.println("Hello " + viewer);
        System.out.println("Data is " + data);
    }
    ...
}
```

Note that `T` and `ViewerType` are different type parameters. `T` is a type parameter for the entire class, but `ViewerType` is a type parameter only for the method `showTo`. What follows is a sample use of these generic methods:

```
Sample<Integer> object = new Sample<Integer>(42);
object.<String>showTo("Friend");
```

This produces the output

```
Hello Friend
Data is 42
```

Inheritance with Generic Classes ★

You can define a generic class to be a derived class of an ordinary class or a derived class of another generic class. Display 14.11 contains the definition of a generic class called `UnorderedPair`, which is a derived class of the generic class `Pair` (which we gave in Display 14.5). The class `UnorderedPair` overrides the definition of `equals` that it inherits from `Pair`. To a programmer using the class, `UnorderedPair` is just like the class `Pair` with one exception. In `UnorderedPair`, the two components do not have to be in the same order for two pairs to be equal. Less formally, in the `Pair<String>` world, `"beer"` and `"peanuts"` is not the same as `"peanuts"` and `"beer"`. In the `UnorderedPair<String>` world, they are the same. This is illustrated by the demonstration program in Display 14.12.

Just as you would expect, an object of type `UnorderedPair<String>` is also of type `Pair<String>`. As we have seen so far, inheritance with generic classes is straightforward in most cases. However, there are some situations with subtle pitfalls. We discuss those next.

Display 14.11   **A Derived Generic Class** (part 1 of 2)

```
 1   public class UnorderedPair<T> extends Pair<T>
 2   {
 3       public UnorderedPair()
 4       {
 5           setFirst(null);
 6           setSecond(null);
 7       }

 8       public UnorderedPair(T firstItem, T secondItem)
 9       {
10           setFirst(firstItem);
11           setSecond(secondItem);
12       }

13       public boolean equals(Object otherObject)
14       {
15           if (otherObject = = null)
16               return false;
17           else if (getClass() != otherObject.getClass())
18               return false;
19           else
20           {
21               UnorderedPair<T> otherPair =
22                               (UnorderedPair<T>)otherObject;
23               return (getFirst().equals(otherPair.getFirst())
24                   && getSecond().equals(otherPair.getSecond()))
25                       ||
```

Display 14.11   **A Derived Generic Class** (part 2 of 2)

```
26                        (getFirst().equals(otherPair.getSecond())
27                    && getSecond().equals(otherPair.getFirst())));
28            }
29        }
30 }
```

Suppose `HourlyEmployee` is a derived class of the class `Employee`. You might think that an object of type `Pair<HourlyEmployee>` is also of type `Pair<Employee>`. You might think that, but you would be wrong. If `G` is a generic class, there is no relationship between `G<A>` and `G<B>`, no matter what the relationship is between the classes `A` and `B`.

Display 14.12   **Using** `UnorderedPair`

```
1   public class UnorderedPairDemo
2   {
3       public static void main(String[] args)
4       {
5           UnorderedPair<String> p1 =
6               new UnorderedPair<String>("peanuts", "beer");
7           UnorderedPair<String> p2 =
8               new UnorderedPair<String>("beer", "peanuts");
9           if (p1.equals(p2))
10          {
11              System.out.println(p1.getFirst() + " and " +
12                          p1.getSecond() + " is the same as");
13              System.out.println(p2.getFirst() + " and "
14                          + p2.getSecond());
15          }
16      }
17  }
```

Sample Dialogue[2]

```
peanuts and beer is the same as
beer and peanuts
```

___

[2]A note to the grammar police: I intentionally used "is" instead of "are." If you read and understand the text, you will realize that "peanuts and beer" is a single item. Starting the sentence with a lowercase letter and the absence of a period are also intentional.

Self-Test Exercises

12. (This question refers to the starred section "Generic Methods." You should skip this question if you have not yet read that subsection.) Define a generic method named getMidindex, which is like getMidpoint, but returns the index of the array midpoint as opposed to the element at the midpoint.

13. (This question refers to the starred section "Inheritance with Generic Classes." You should skip this question if you have not yet read that subsection.) Is an array of type UnorderedPair<String>[] also of type Pair<String>[]?

Chapter Summary

- ArrayList is a *parameterized class* that is like an array that can grow (and shrink) while the program is running.

- An ArrayList has a number of methods that allow you to use it as a kind of automated partially filled array.

- You can cycle through all the elements in an ArrayList using a *for-each loop*.

- You can define classes with one or more type parameters. Such classes are known as *generic classes*.

Answers to Self-Test Exercises

1. list.add("Hello");
2. instruction.set(5, "Go");
3. melon
4. No. The index for set must be greater than or equal to 0 and less than the size of the ArrayList. Thus, you can replace any existing element, but you cannot place the element at any higher index. This situation is unlike that of an array. If an array is partially filled to index 10, you can add an element at index 20, as long as the array is that large. With an ArrayList, you cannot add an element beyond the last-used index.
5. list.set(2, "mangoes");

6. 4

7. Yes. The `ArrayList` can contain more than 20 elements. The number 20 used as an argument to the constructor merely gives the initial memory allocation for the `ArrayList`. More memory is automatically allocated when it is needed.

8. ```
for (Double element : numberList)
    System.out.println(element);
```

9. ```
import java.util.ArrayList;
/**
 Class for sorting an ArrayList of Strings lexicographically
 (approximately alphabetically).
*/
public class StringSelectionSort
{
    /**
     Sorts the ArrayList a so that a.get(0), a.get(1),...,
     a.get(a.size() - 1) are in lexicographic order.
    */
    public static void sort(ArrayList<String> a)
    {
        int index, indexOfNextSmallest;
        for (index = 0; index < a.size() 1; index++)
        {//Place the correct value in position index:
            indexOfNextSmallest =
                            indexOfSmallest(index, a);
            interchange(index, indexOfNextSmallest, a);
            //a.get(0), a.get(1),...,a.get(index)
            //are sorted. The rest of the
            //elements are in the remaining positions.
        }
    }
    /**
     Precondition: i and j are legal indices for the ArrayList a.
     Postcondition: The values of a.get(i) and
     a.get(j) have been interchanged.
    */
    private static void interchange(
                            int i, int j, ArrayList<String> a)
```

```
    {
        String temp;
        temp = a.get(i);
        a.set(i, a.get(j));
        a.set(j, temp);
    }
    /**
     Returns the index of the lexicographically first value among
     a.get(startIndex), a.get(startIndex+1),...,a.get(a.size()
     - 1)
    */
    private static int indexOfSmallest(
        int startIndex, ArrayList<String> a)
    {
        String min = a.get(startIndex);
        int indexOfMin = startIndex;
        int index;
        for (index = startIndex + 1; index < a.size(); index++)
        if ((a.get(index)).compareTo(min) < 0)
        {
            min = a.get(index);
            indexOfMin = index;
        }
        return indexOfMin;
    }
}
```

10. No, the base type of an `ArrayList` cannot be a primitive type, such as `int`, `double`, or `char`. You can, however, have an `ArrayList` with base type `Integer` that can be used to store integers.

11. Notice that the following, while correct, is not as easy to understand as the for-each loop.

```
for (int i; i < a.size(); i++)
    System.out.println(a.get(i) + " differs from average by "
                                    + (a.get(i) average));
```

12.
```
public static <T> int getMidindex(T[] a)
{
    return a.length/2;
}
```

13. This is a trick question. As we explained in the text, you cannot have an array of type `UnorderedPair<String>[]` or of type `Pair<String>[]`.

Programming Projects

Visit www.myprogramminglab.com to complete select exercises online and get instant feedback.

1. In the sport of diving, seven judges award a score between 0 and 10, where each score may be a floating-point value. The highest and lowest scores are thrown out and the remaining scores are added together. The sum is then multiplied by the degree of difficulty for that dive. The degree of difficulty ranges from 1.2 to 3.8 points. The total is then multiplied by 0.6 to determine the diver's score.

   Write a computer program that inputs a degree of difficulty and seven judges' scores and outputs the overall score for that dive. The program should use an ArrayList of type Double to store the scores.

2. Write a program that uses an ArrayList of parameter type Contact to store a database of contacts. The Contact class should store the contact's first and last name, phone number, and email address. Add appropriate accessor and mutator methods. Your database program should present a menu that allows the user to add a contact, display all contacts, search for a specific contact and display it, or search for a specific contact and give the user the option to delete it. The searches should find any contact where any instance variable contains a target search string. For example, if "elmore" is the search target, then any contact where the first name, last name, phone number, or email address contains "elmore" should be returned for display or deletion. Use the "for-each" loop to iterate through the ArrayList.

3. Many Global Positioning Satellite (GPS) units can record waypoints. The waypoint marks the coordinates of a location on a map along with a timestamp. Consider a GPS unit that stores waypoints in terms of an (X, Y) coordinate on a map together with a timestamp t that records the number of seconds that have elapsed since the unit was turned on. Write a program that allows the user to enter as many waypoints as desired, storing each waypoint in an ArrayList, where each waypoint is represented by a class that you design. Each waypoint represents a successive sample point during a hike along some route. The coordinates should be input as doubles, and the timestamp as an integer. Have your program compute the total distance traveled and the average speed in miles per hour. Use the map scaling factor of 1 = 0.1 miles. For example, if the only two waypoints are (X=1,Y=1,T=0) and (X=2,Y=1,T=3600), then the hiker traveled a distance of 0.1 miles in 3,600 seconds, or 0.1 miles per hour.

4. Write a generic class, MyMathClass, with a type parameter T where T is a numeric object type (e.g., Integer, Double, or any class that extends java.lang.Number). Add a method named standardDeviation that takes an ArrayList of type T and returns as a double the standard deviation of the values in the ArrayList. Use the doubleValue() method in the Number class to retrieve the value of each number as a double. Refer to Programming Project 6.5 for a definition of computing the standard deviation. Test your method with suitable data. Your program should generate a compile-time error if your standard deviation method is invoked on an ArrayList that is defined for nonnumeric elements (e.g., Strings).

5. Create a generic class with a type parameter that simulates drawing an item at random out of a box. This class could be used for simulating a random drawing. For example, the box might contain `String`s representing names written on a slip of paper, or the box might contain `Integer`s representing a random drawing for a lottery based on numeric lottery picks. Create an `add` method that allows the user of the class to add an object of the specified type along with an `isEmpty` method that determines whether or not the box is empty. Finally, your class should have a `drawItem` method that randomly selects an object from the box and returns it. If the user attempts to drawn an item out of an empty box, return `null`. Write a `main` method that tests your class.

6. Implement a priority queue capable of holding objects of an arbitrary type, `T`, by defining a `PriorityQueue` class that implements the queue with an `ArrayList`. A priority queue is a type of list where every item added to the queue also has an associated priority. Define priority in your application so that those items with the largest numerical value have the highest priority. Your class should support the following methods:

   • `Add(item, priority)`—Adds a new item to the queue with the associated priority.

   • `Remove()`—Returns the item with the highest priority and removes it from the queue. If the user attempts to remove from an empty queue, return `null`.

   For example, if q is a priority queue defined to take `String`s

   ```
   q.add("X", 10);
   q.add("Y", 1);
   q.add("Z", 3);

   System.out.println(q.remove()); // Returns X
   System.out.println(q.remove()); // Returns Z
   System.out.println(q.remove()); // Returns Y
   ```

   Test your queue on data with priorities in various orders (e.g., ascending, descending, mixed). You can implement the priority queue by performing a linear search through the `ArrayList`. In future courses, you may study a data structure called a *heap* that is a more efficient way to implement a priority queue.

7. Programming Project 6.13 implemented a simple trivia game using an array of `Trivia` objects. Redo this project but use an `ArrayList` of `Trivia` objects instead of an array. The run-time behavior should remain identical to before.

VideoNote
Solution to
Programming
Project 14.7

8. In Programming Project 11.9, you were asked to implement a recursive algorithm to find all files that matched a target file name. Redo this Programming Project where the recursive method returns an `ArrayList` of `String` objects. Each string should store the pathname to the matching file. Return `null` if no matching files are found.

Linked Data Structures 15

15.1 JAVA LINKED LISTS 836
Example: A Simple Linked List Class 836
Working with Linked Lists 840
Node Inner Classes 846
Example: A Generic Linked List 849
The `equals` Method for Linked Lists 854

15.2 COPY CONSTRUCTORS AND THE `Clone` METHOD ★ 856
Simple Copy Constructors and `clone` Methods ★ 856
Exceptions ★ 857
Example: A Linked List with a Deep Copy `clone` Method ★ 864

15.3 ITERATORS 867
Defining an Iterator Class 868
Adding and Deleting Nodes 873

15.4 VARIATIONS ON A LINKED LIST 878
Doubly Linked List 878
The Stack Data Structure 887
The Queue Data Structure 889
Running Times and Big-O Notation 892
Efficiency of Linked Lists 897

15.5 HASH TABLES WITH CHAINING 898
A Hash Function for Strings 899
Efficiency of Hash Tables 902

15.6 SETS 903
Fundamental Set Operations 904
Efficiency of Sets Using Linked Lists 909

15.7 TREES 910
Tree Properties 910
Example: A Binary Search Tree Class ★ 913
Efficiency of Binary Search Trees ★ 918

Chapter Summary 919　　　**Answers to Self-Test Exercises** 920　　　**Programming Projects** 925

15 Linked Data Structures

If somebody there chanced to be
Who loved me in a manner true
My heart would point him out to me
And I would point him out to you.

GILBERT AND SULLIVAN, *Ruddigore*

Introduction

node and link

A linked data structure consists of capsules of data, known as **nodes**, which are connected via what are known as **links**. These links can be viewed as arrows and thought of as one-way passages from one node to another. The simplest kind of linked data structure consists of a single chain of nodes, each connected to the next by a link; this is known as a **linked list**. A sample linked list can be depicted as shown in Display 15.1. In Display 15.1, the nodes are represented by boxes that can each hold two kinds of data, a string and an integer, as in a shopping list. The links are depicted as arrows, which reflect the fact that your code must traverse the linked list in one direction without backing up. So there is a first node, a second node, and so on up to the last node. The first node is called the **head node**.

linked list

head node

That information is all very vague but provides the general picture of what is going on in a linked list. It becomes concrete when you realize a linked list in some programming language. In Java, the nodes are realized as objects of a node class. The data in a node is stored via instance variables. The links are realized as references. Recall that a reference is simply a memory address. A reference is what is stored in a variable of a class type. So the link is realized as an instance variable of the type of the node class itself. In Java, a node in a linked list is connected to the next node by having an instance variable of the node type contain a reference (that is, a memory address) of where in memory the next node is stored.

Java comes with a `LinkedList` library class as part of the `java.util` package. It makes sense to use this library class, because it is well designed and well tested, and will save you a lot of work. However, using the library class will not teach you how to implement linked data structures in Java. To do that, you need to see an implementation of a simple linked data structure, such as a linked list. So to let you see how this sort of thing is done in Java, we will construct our own simplified example of a linked list.

After discussing linked lists, we then go on to discuss more elaborate linked data structures, including sets, hash tables, and trees.

Display 15.1   Nodes and Links in a Linked List

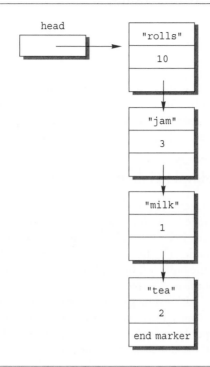

Prerequisites

If you prefer, you may skip this chapter and go directly to Chapter 16 on collection classes or to Chapter 17 to begin your study of windowing interfaces using the Swing library. You have a good deal of flexibility in how you order the later chapters of this book.

This chapter requires material from Chapters 1 through 5, Chapter 14, and simple uses of inner classes (Section 13.2 of Chapter 13). Section 15.7 on trees additionally requires Chapter 11 on recursion.

Sections 15.2 through 15.7 do not depend on each other in any essential way. In particular, you may omit Section 15.2 on cloning and still read the following sections. Sections 15.2 through 15.7 do not depend in any essential way on the material on generic linked lists in subsections of Section 15.1.

15.1 Java Linked Lists

A chain is only as strong as its weakest link.

PROVERB

A linked list is a linked data structure consisting of a single chain of nodes, each connected to the next by a link. This is the simplest kind of linked data structure, but it is nevertheless widely used. In this section, we give examples of linked lists and develop techniques for defining and working with linked lists in Java.

EXAMPLE: A Simple Linked List Class

Display 15.1 is a diagram of a linked list. In the display, the nodes are the boxes. In your Java code, a node is an object of some node class, such as the class `Node1` given in Display 15.2. Each node has a place (or places) for some data and a place to hold a link to another node. The links are shown as arrows that point to the node they "link" to. In Java, the links will be implemented as references to a node stored in an instance variable of the `node` type.

The `Node1` class is defined by specifying, among other things, an instance variable of type `Node1` that is named `link`. This allows each node to store a reference to another node of the same type. There is a kind of circularity in such definitions, but this circularity is allowed in Java. (One way to see that this definition is not logically inconsistent is to note that we can draw pictures, or even build physical models, of our linked nodes.)

The first node, or start node, in a linked list is called the *head node*. If you start at the head node, you can traverse the entire linked list, visiting each node exactly once. As you will see shortly, in Java your code must intuitively "follow the link arrows." In Display 15.1, the box labeled `head` is not itself the head node; it is not even a node. The box labeled `head` is a variable of type `Node1` that contains a reference to the first node in the linked list—that is, a reference to the head node. The function of the variable `head` is that it allows your code to find that first or head node. The variable `head` is declared in the obvious way:

```
Node1 head;
```

In Java, a linked list is an object that in some sense contains all the nodes of the linked list. Display 15.3 contains a definition of a linked list class for a linked list such as the one in Display 15.1. Notice that a linked list object does not directly contain all the nodes in the linked list. It contains only the instance variable `head` that contains a reference to the first or head node. However, every node can be reached from this first or head node. The `link` instance variable of the first and every `Node1` of the linked list contains a reference to the next `Node1` in the linked list. Thus, the arrows shown in the diagram in Display 15.1 are realized as references in Java. Each node object of a linked list contains (in its `link` instance variable) a reference to another object of the class `Node1`, and this other object contains a reference to another object of the class `Node1`, and so on until the end of the linked list. Thus, a linked list object, indirectly at least, contains all the nodes in the linked list.

Display 15.2   A Node Class

```java
public class Node1
{
    private String item;
    private int count;
    private Node1 link;

    public Node1( )
    {
        link = null;
        item = null;
        count = 0;
    }
    public Node1(String newItem, int newCount, Node1 linkValue)
    {
        setData(newItem, newCount);
        link = linkValue;
    }

    public void setData(String newItem, int newCount)
    {
        item = newItem;
        count = newCount;
    }
    public void setLink(Node1 newLink)
    {
        link = newLink;
    }

    public String getItem( )
    {
        return item;
    }

    public int getCount( )
    {
        return count;
    }

    public Node1 getLink( )
    {
        return link;
    }
}
```

A node contains a reference to another node. That reference is the link to the next node.

We will define a number of node classes so we numbered the names as in Node1.

We will give a better definition of a node class later in this chapter.

Display 15.3   A Linked List Class (part 1 of 2)

```
1   public class LinkedList1
2   {
3       private Node1 head;                     We will define a letter linked list class later in
4                                               this chapter.
5       public LinkedList1( )
6       {
7           head = null;
8       }

9       /**
10       Adds a node at the start of the list with the specified data.
11       The added node will be the first node in the list.
12       */
13       public void addToStart(String itemName, int itemCount)
14       {
15           head = new Node1(itemName, itemCount, head);
16       }

17       /**
18       Removes the head node and returns true if the list contains at
19       least one node. Returns false if the list is empty.
20       */
21       public boolean deleteHeadNode( )
22       {
23           if (head != null)
24           {
25               head = head.getLink( );
26               return true;
27           }
28           else
29               return false;
30       }

31       /**
32       Returns the number of nodes in the list.
33       */
34       public int size( )
35       {
36           int count = 0;
37           Node1 position = head;
38
```

Display 15.3   **A Linked List Class** (part 2 of 2)

```
39              while (position != null)
40              {
41                  count++;
42                  position = position.getLink( );
43              }
44              return count;
45          }

46          public boolean contains(String item)
47          {
48              return (find(item) != null);
49          }

50          /**
51           Finds the first node containing the target item, and returns a
52           reference to that node. If target is not in the list, null is
               returned.
53           */
54          private Node1 find(String target)
55          {
56              Node1 position = head;
57              String itemAtPosition;
58              while (position != null)
59              {
60                  itemAtPosition = position.getItem( );
61                  if (itemAtPosition.equals(target))
62                      return position;
63                  position = position.getLink( );
64              }
65              return null; //target was not found
66          }
67          public void outputList( )
68          {
69              Node1 position = head;
70              while (position != null)
71              {
72                  System.out.println(position.getItem( ) + " "
73                                       + position.getCount( ));
74                  position = position.getLink( );
75              }
76          }
77  }
```

This last node is indicated by the `link` *field being equal to* `null`.

This is the way you traverse an entire linked list.

Working with Linked Lists

When dealing with a linked list, your code needs to be able to "get to" that first or head node, and you need some way to detect when the last node is reached. To get your code to the first node, use a variable of type `Node1` that always contains a reference to the first node. In Display 15.3, the variable with a reference to the first node is named `head`. From that first or head node, your code can follow the links through the linked list. But how does your code know when it is at the last node in a linked list?

In Java, indicate the end of a linked list by setting the `link` instance variable of the last node in the linked list to `null`, as shown in Display 15.4. That way your code can test whether or not a node is the last node in a linked list by testing whether its link instance variable contains `null`. Remember that you check for a link being "equal" to `null` by using `==`, and not using any equals method.

Also use `null` to indicate an empty linked list. The `head` instance variable contains a reference to the first node in the linked list, or it contains `null` if the linked list is **empty list**   empty (that is, if the linked list contains no nodes). The only constructor sets this `head` instance variable to `null`, indicating that a newly created linked list is empty.

Display 15.4   Traversing a Linked List

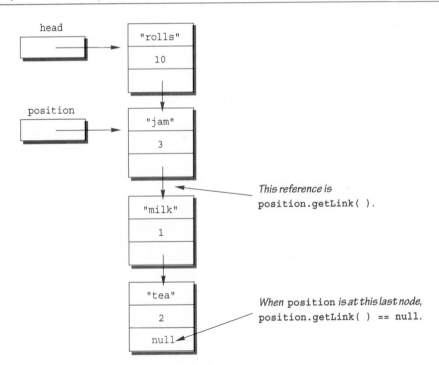

Indicating the End of a Linked List

The last node in a linked list should have its `link` instance variable set to `null`. That way, your code can check whether a node is the last node by checking whether its `link` instance variable is equal to `null`.

An Empty List Is Indicated by `null`

Suppose the variable head is supposed to contain a reference to the first node in a linked list. Linked lists usually start out empty. To indicate an empty linked list, give the variable head the value `null`. This is traditional and works out nicely for many linked list manipulation algorithms.

traversing a linked list

Before we go on to discuss how nodes are added and removed from a linked list, let us suppose that the linked list already has a few nodes and that you want to write out the contents of all the nodes to the screen. You can do this with the method outputList (Display 15.3), whose body is reproduced here:

```
Node1 position = head;
while (position != null)
{
    System.out.println(position.getItem( ) + " "
                        + position.getCount( ));
    position = position.getLink( );
}
```

The method uses a local variable named position that contains a reference to one node. The variable position starts out with the same reference as the head instance variable, so it starts out positioned at the first node. The position variable then has its position moved from one node to the next with the assignment

```
position = position.getLink( );
```

This is illustrated in Display 15.4. To see that this assignment "moves" the position variable to the next node, note that the position variable contains a reference to the node pointed to by the position arrow in Display 15.4. So, position is a name for that node, and position.link is a name for the link to the next node. The value of link is produced with the accessor method getLink. Thus, a reference to the next node in the linked list is position.getLink( ). You "move" the position variable by giving it the value of position.getLink( ).

The method `outputList` continues to move the `position` variable down the linked list and outputs the data in each node as it goes along. When `position` reaches the last node, it outputs the data in that node and then again executes

```
position = position.getLink( );
```

If you study Display 15.4, you will see that when `position` leaves the last node, its value is set to `null`. At this point, we want to stop the loop, so we iterate the loop

```
while (position != null)
```

A similar technique is used to traverse the linked list in the methods `size` and `find`.

adding a node

Next let us consider how the method `addToStart` adds a node to the start of the linked list so that the new node becomes the first node in the list. It does this with the single statement

```
head = new Node1(itemName, itemCount, head);
```

The new node is created with

```
new Node1(itemName, itemCount, head)
```

which returns a reference to this new node. The assignment statement sets the variable `head` equal to a reference to this new node, making the new node the first node in the linked list. To link this new node to the rest of the list, we need only set the `link` instance variable of the new node equal to a reference to the *old first node*. But we have already done that: `head` used to point to the old first node, so if we use the name `head` on *the right-hand side of the assignment operator*, `head` will denote a reference to the old first node. Therefore, the new node produced by

```
new Node1(itemName, itemCount, head)
```

points to the old first node, which is just what we wanted. This is illustrated in Display 15.5.

Later, we will discuss adding nodes at other places in a linked list, but the easiest place to add a node is at the start of the list. Similarly, the easiest place to delete a node is at the start of the linked list.

removing a node

The method `deleteHeadNode` removes the first node from the linked list and leaves the `head` variable pointing to (that is, containing a reference to) the old second node (which is now the first node) in the linked list. This is done with the following assignment:

```
head = head.getLink( );
```

Display 15.5   Adding a Node at the Start

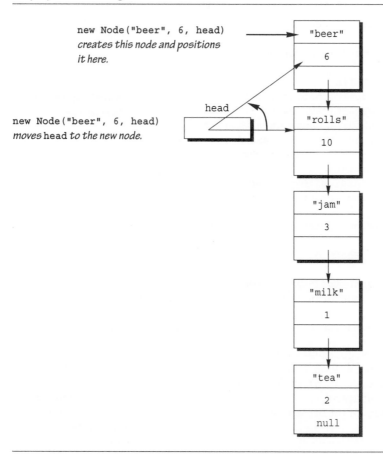

new Node("beer", 6, head)
creates this node and positions
it here.

new Node("beer", 6, head)
moves head to the new node.

head

"beer"

6

"rolls"

10

"jam"

3

"milk"

1

"tea"

2

null

This removes the first node from the linked list and leaves the linked list one node shorter. But what happens to the deleted node? At some point, Java will automatically collect it, along with any other nodes that are no longer accessible, and recycle the memory they occupy. This is known as **automatic garbage collection**.

automatic garbage collection

Display 15.6 contains a simple program that demonstrates how some of the methods in the class LinkedList1 behave.

Display 15.6   A Linked List Demonstration

```
1    public class LinkedList1Demo
2    {
3        public static void main(String[] args)
4        {
5            LinkedList1 list = new LinkedList1( );
6            list.addToStart("Apples", 1);
7            list.addToStart("Bananas", 2);
8            list.addToStart("Cantaloupe", 3);
9            System.out.println("List has " + list.size( )
10                               + " nodes.");
11           list.outputList( );
12           if (list.contains("Cantaloupe"))
13               System.out.println("Cantaloupe is on list.");
14           else
15               System.out.println("Cantaloupe is NOT on list.");

16           list.deleteHeadNode( );

17           if (list.contains("Cantaloupe"))
18               System.out.println("Cantaloupe is on list.");
19           else
20               System.out.println("Cantaloupe is NOT on list.");

21           while (list.deleteHeadNode( ))
22               ; //Empty loop body
23           System.out.println("Start of list:");
24           list.outputList( );
25           System.out.println("End of list.");
26       }
27   }
```

Cantaloupe is now in the head node. (arrow pointing to line 8)

Empties the list. There is no loop body because the method deleteHeadNode both performs an action on the list and returns a Boolean value. (arrow pointing to line 21)

Sample Dialogue

```
List has 3 entries.
Cantaloupe 3
Bananas 2
Apples 1
Cantaloupe is on list.
Cantaloupe is NOT on list.
Start of list:
End of list.
```

Self-Test Exercises

1. What output is produced by the following code?

```
LinkedList1 list = new LinkedList1( );
list.addToStart("apple pie", 1);

list.addToStart("hot dogs", 12);
list.addToStart("mustard", 1);
list.outputList( );
```

2. Define a `boolean` valued method named `is Empty` that can be added to the class `LinkedList1` (Display 15.3). The method returns `true` if the list is empty and `false` if the list has at least one node in it.

3. Define a `void` method named `clear` that can be added to the class `LinkedList1` (Display 15.3). The method has no parameters and it empties the list.

PITFALL: Privacy Leaks

It may help you to understand this section if you first review the Pitfall section of the same name in Chapter 5.

Consider the method `getLink` in the class `Node1` (Display 15.2). It returns a value of type `Node1`. That is, it returns a reference to a `Node1`. In Chapter 5, we said that if a method (such as `getLink`) returns a reference to an instance variable of a (mutable) class type, then the `private` restriction on the instance variable can easily be defeated because getting a reference to an object may allow a programmer to change the private instance variables of the object. There are a number of ways to fix this, the most straightforward of which is to make the class `Node1` a private inner class in the method `Node1`, as discussed in the next subsection.

There is no danger of a privacy leak with the class `Node1` when it is used in the class definition for `LinkedList1`. However, there is no way to guarantee that the class `Node1` will be used only in this way unless you take some precaution, such as making the class `Node1` a private inner class in the class `LinkedList1 Node1`.

An alternate solution is to place both of the classes `Node1` and `LinkedList1` into a package, and change the `private` instance variable restriction to the `package` restriction as discussed in Chapter 7.

Note that this privacy problem can arise in any situation in which a method returns a reference to a private instance variable of a class type. The method `getItem( )` of the class `Node1` comes very close to having this problem. In this case, the method `getItem` causes no privacy leak, but only because the class `String` is not a mutable class (that is, it has no methods that will allow the user to change the value of the string without changing the reference). If instead of storing data of type `String` in our list we had stored data of some mutable class type, then defining an accessor method similarly to `getItem` would produce a privacy leak. ■

Node Inner Classes

You can make a linked list, or any similar data structures, self-contained by making the node class an inner class. In particular, you can make the class `LinkedList1` more self-contained by making `Node1` an inner class, as follows:

```
public class LinkedList1
{
    private class Node1
    {
        <The rest of the definition of Node1 can be
          the same as in Display 15.2.>
    }

    private Node1 head;
    <The constructor and methods in Display 15.3 are inserted here.>
}
```

Note that we have made the class `Node1` a private inner class. If an inner class is not intended to be used elsewhere, it should be made private. Making `Node1` a private inner class hides all objects of the inner class and avoids a privacy leak.

If you are going to make the class `Node1` a private inner class in the definition of `LinkedList1`, then you can safely simplify the definition of `Node1` by eliminating the accessor and mutator methods (the `set` and `get` methods) and just allowing direct access to the instance variables (`item`, `count`, and `link`) from methods of the outer class. In Display 15.7, we have written a class similar to `LinkedList1` in this way. The rewritten version, named `LinkedList2`, is like the class `LinkedList1` in Display 15.3 in that it has the same methods that perform basically the same actions. To keep the discussion simple, `LinkedList2` has only one data field instead of two. We could easily have retained the two data fields, but we wanted a notationally simple example without any distracting details. (See Self-Test Exercise 8 for a version that has the same kind of data in each node as in the nodes of `LinkedList1`.)

Display 15.7   A Linked List Class with a Node Inner Class (part 1 of 3)

```
1   public class LinkedList2
2   {
3       private class Node
4       {
5           private String item;
6           private Node link;

7           public Node( )
8           {
9               item = null;
10              link = null;
11          }
```

Display 15.7   A Linked List Class with a Node Inner Class (part 2 of 3)

```
12          public Node(String newItem, Node linkValue)
13          {
14              item = newItem;
15              link = linkValue;
16          }
17      }//End of Node inner class

18      private Node head;

19      public LinkedList2( )
20      {
21          head = null;
22      }
23      /**
24       Adds a node at the start of the list with the specified data.
25       The added node will be the first node in the list.
26      */
27      public void addToStart(String itemName)
28      {
29          head = new Node(itemName, head);
30      }

31      /**
32       Removes the head node and returns true if the list contains at
33       least one node. Returns false if the list is empty.
34      */
35      public boolean deleteHeadNode( )
36      {
37          if (head != null)
38          {
39              head = head.link;
40              return true;
41          }
42          else
43              return false;
44      }

45      /**
46       Returns the number of nodes in the list.
47      */
48      public int size( )
49      {
50          int count = 0;
51          Node position = head;
52          while (position != null)
53          {
54              count++;
```

(continued)

Display 15.7 A Linked List Class with a Node Inner Class (part 3 of 3)

```
55              position = position.link;
56          }
57          return count;
58      }

59      public boolean contains(String item)
60      {
61          return (find(item) != null);
62      }

63      /**
64       Finds the first node containing the target item, and returns a
65       reference to that node. If target is not in the list, null is
         returned.
66      */
67      private Node find(String target)
68      {
69          Node position = head;
70          String itemAtPosition;
71          while (position != null)
72          {
73              itemAtPosition = position.item;
74              if (itemAtPosition.equals(target))
75                  return position;
76              position = position.link;
77          }
78          return null; //target was not found
79      }
80      public void outputList( )
81      {
82          Node position = head;
83          while (position != null)
84          {
85              System.out.println(position.item );
86              position = position.link;
87          }
88      }

89      public boolean isEmpty( )
90      {
91          return (head == null);
92      }

93      public void clear( )
94      {
95          head = null;
96      }
97  }
```

Note that the outer class has direct access to the inner class's instance variables, such as `link`.

Self-Test Exercises

4. Would it make any difference if we changed the Node inner class in Display 15.7 from a private inner class to a public inner class?

5. Keeping the inner class Node in Display 15.7 as private, what difference would it make if any of the instance variables or methods in the class Node had its access modifiers changed from private to public or package access?

6. Why does the definition of the inner class Node in Display 15.7 not have the accessor and mutator methods getLink, setLink, or other get and set methods for the link fields similar to those in the class definition of Node1 in Display 15.2?

7. Would it be legal to add the following method to the class LinkedList2 in Display 15.7?

```
public Node startNode( )
{
    return head;

}
```

8. Rewrite the definition of the class LinkedList2 in Display 15.7 so that it has data of a type named Entry, which is a public inner class. Objects of type Entry have two instance variables defined as follows:

```
private String item;
private int count;
```

This rewritten version of LinkedList2 will be equivalent to LinkedList1 in that it has the same methods doing the same things, and it will hold equivalent data in its nodes.

EXAMPLE: A Generic Linked List

Display 15.8 shows a generic linked list with a type parameter T for the type of data stored in a node. This generic linked list has the same methods, coded in basically the same way, as our previous linked list (Display 15.7), but we used a type parameter for the type of data in the nodes.

Display 15.10 contains a demonstration program for our generic linked list. The demonstration program uses the class Entry, defined in Display 15.9, as the type plugged in for the type parameter T. Note that if you want multiple pieces of data in each node, you simply use a class type that has multiple instance variables and plug in this class for the type parameter T.

Display 15.8   A Generic Linked List Class (part 1 of 3)

```
1   public class LinkedList3<T>
2   {
3       private class Node<T>
4       {
5           private T data;                         This linked list holds objects of type T.
6           private Node<T> link;                   The type T should have well-defined
7           public Node( )                          equals and toString methods.
8           {
9               data = null;
10              link = null;

11          }

12          public Node (T newData, Node<T> linkValue)
13          {
14              data = newData;
15              link = linkValue;
16          }
17      }//End of Node<T> inner class
18      private Node<T> head;

19      public LinkedList3( )
20      {
21          head = null;
22      }

23      /**
24       Adds a node at the start of the list with the specified data.
25       The added node will be the first node in the list.
26      */
27      public void addToStart(T itemData)
28      {
29          head = new Node<T> (itemData, head);
30      }
31      /**
32       Removes the head node and returns true if the list contains at
33       least one node. Returns false if the list is empty.
34      */
35      public boolean deleteHeadNode( )
36      {
37          if (head != null)
38          {
39              head = head.link;
40              return true;
41          }
42          else
43              return false;
44      }
45      /**
```

Display 15.8   A Generic Linked List Class (part 2 of 3)

```
46          Returns the number of nodes in the list.
47       */
48       public int size( )
49       {
50           int count = 0;
51           Node<T> position = head;
52           while (position != null)
53           {
54               count++;
55               position = position.link;
56           }
57           return count;
58       }

59       public boolean contains(T item)
60       {
61           return (find(item) != null);
62       }
63       /**
64        Finds the first node containing the target item, and returns a
65        reference to that node. If target is not in the list, null is
         returned.
66       */
67       private Node find(T target)
68       {
69           Node<T> position = head;
70           T itemAtPosition;
71           while (position != null)
72           {
73               itemAtPosition = position.data;
74               if (itemAtPosition.equals(target))
75                   return position;
76               position = position.link;
77           }
78           return null; //target was not found
79       }

80       /**
81        Finds the first node containing the target and returns a reference
82        to the data in that node. If target is not in the list, null is
         returned.
83       */
84       public T findData(T target)
85       {
86           Node<T> result = find(target);
87           if (result == null)
88               return null;
89           else
90               return result.data;
```

Type T must have a well-defined equals for this method to work.

(continued)

Display 15.8   A Generic Linked List Class (part 3 of 3)

```
 91        }
 92        public void outputList( )              Type T must have a well-defined toString
 93        {                                      methods for this to work.
 94            Node<T> position = head;
 95            while (position != null)
 96            {
 97                System.out.println(position.data);
 98                position = position.link;
 99            }
100        }

101        public boolean isEmpty( )
102        {
103            return (head == null);
104        }

105        public void clear( )
106        {
107            head = null;
108        }
109        /*
110         For two lists to be equal they must contain the same data items in
111         the same order. The equals method of T is used to compare data
            items.
112        */
113        public boolean equals(Object otherObject)
114        {
115            if (otherObject == null)
116                return false;
117            else if (getClass( ) != otherObject.getClass( ))
118                return false;
119            else
120            {
121                LinkedList3<T> otherList = (LinkedList3<T>)otherObject;
122                if (size( )!= otherList.size( ))
123                    return false;
124                Node<T> position = head;
125                Node<T> otherPosition = otherList.head;
126                while (position != null)
127                {
128                    if (!(position.data.equals(otherPosition.data)))
129                        return false;
130                    position = position.link;
131                    otherPosition = otherPosition.link;
132                }
133                return true; //no mismatch was not found
134            }
135        }
136 }
```

Display 15.9   A Sample Class for the Data in a Generic Linked List

```
1   public class Entry
2   {
3       private String item;
4       private int count;

5       public Entry(String itemData, int countData)
6       {
7           item = itemData;
8           count = countData;
9       }

10      public String toString( )
11      {
12          return (item + " " + count);
13      }

14      public boolean equals(Object otherObject)
15      {
16          if (otherObject == null)
17              return false;
18          else if (getClass( ) != otherObject.getClass( ))
19              return false;
20          else
21          {
22              Entry otherEntry = (Entry)otherObject;
23              return (item.equals(otherEntry.item)
24                          && (count == otherEntry.count));
25          }
26      }
```
<There should be other constructors and methods, including accessor
and mutator methods, but we do not use them in this demonstration.>
```
27  }
```

Display 15.10   A Generic Linked List Demonstration (part 1 of 2)

```
1   public class GenericLinkedListDemo
2   {
3       public static void main(String[] args)
4       {
5           LinkedList3<Entry> list = new LinkedList3<Entry>( );

6           Entry entry1 = new Entry("Apples", 1);
7           list.addToStart(entry1);
8           Entry entry2 = new Entry("Bananas", 2);
9           list.addToStart(entry2);
10          Entry entry3 = new Entry("Cantaloupe", 3);
11          list.addToStart(entry3);
12          System.out.println("List has " + list.size( )
13                              + " nodes.");
```

(continued)

Display 15.10   A Generic Linked List Demonstration (part 2 of 2)

```
14              list.outputList( );
15              System.out.println("End of list.");
16      }
17  }
```

Sample Dialogue

```
List has 3 nodes.
Cantaloupe 3
Bananas 2
Apples 1
End of list.
```

PITFALL: Using `Node` Instead of `Node<T>`

This pitfall is explained by example, using the `LinkedList3<T>` class in Display 15.8. However, the lesson applies to any generic linked structure with a node inner class. The type parameter need not be `T` and the node class name need not be `Node`, but for simplicity, we will use `T` and `Node`.

When defining the `LinkedList3<T>` class in Display 15.8, the type for a node is `Node<T>`; it is not `Node`. However, it is easy to forget the type specification `<T>` and write `Node` instead of `Node<T>`. If you omit the `<T>`, you may or may not get a compiler error message, depending on other details of your code. If you do get a compiler error message, it is likely to seem bewilderingly strange. The problem is that `Node` actually means something. (We do not have time to stop and explain what `Node` means, but it means something similar to a node with data type `Object`, rather than data type `T`.) Your only defense against this pitfall is to be very careful; if you do get a bewildering compiler error message, look for a missing `<T>`.

Sometimes a compiler warning message can be helpful when you make this mistake. If you get a warning that mentions a type cast from `Node` to `Node<T>`, look for an omitted `<T>`.

Finally, we should note that sometimes your code will compile and even run correctly if you omit the `<T>` from `Node<T>`. ■

The `equals` Method for Linked Lists

The linked lists we presented in Display 15.3 and 15.7 do not have an `equals` method. We did that to keep the examples simple and not detract from the main message. However, a linked list class should normally have an `equals` method.

`equals`

There is more than one approach to defining a reasonable `equals` method for a linked list. The two most obvious are the following:

1. Two linked lists are equal if they contain the same data entries (possibly ordered differently).

2. Two linked lists are equal if they contain the same data entries in the same order; that is, the data in the first node of the calling object equals the data in the first node of the other linked list, the data in the two second nodes are equal, and so forth.

It is not true that one of these is the correct approach to defining an equals method and the other is incorrect. In different situations, you might want different definitions of equals. However, the most common way to define equals for a linked list is approach 2. A definition of equals that follows approach 2 and that can be added to the class LinkedList2 in Display 15.7 is given in Display 15.11. The generic linked list in Display 15.8 also contains an equals method that follows approach 2.

Note that when we define equals for our linked list with type parameter T, we trust the programmer who wrote the definition for the type plugged in for T. We are assuming the programmer has redefined the equals method so that it provides a reasonable test for equality. Situations such as this are the reason it is so important to always include an equals method in the classes you define.

Display 15.11 An equals Method for the Linked List in Display 15.7

```
1    /*
2     For two lists to be equal they must contain the same data items in
3     the same order.
4    */
5    public boolean equals(Object otherObject)
6    {
7        if (otherObject == null)
8            return false;
9        else if (getClass( ) != otherObject.getClass( ))
10            return false;
11        else
12        {
13            LinkedList2 otherList = (LinkedList2)otherObject;
14            if (size( ) != otherList.size( ))
15                return false;
16            Node position = head;
17            Node otherPosition = otherList.head;
18            while (position != null)
19            {
20                if ( (!(position.item.equals(otherPosition.item))))
21                    return false;
22                position = position.link;
23                otherPosition = otherPosition.link;
24            }
25            return true; //A mismatch was not found
26        }
27    }
```

15.2   Copy Constructors and the `clone` Method ★

There are three ways to do anything:

The right way,

the wrong way,

and the army way.

Advice reputedly given to new army recruits

The way Java handles cloning, and object copying in general, is complicated and can be both subtle and difficult. Some authorities think that the `clone` method was done so poorly in Java that they prefer to ignore it completely and define their own methods for copying objects. I have some sympathy for that view, but before you dismiss Java's approach to cloning, it might be a good idea to see what the approach entails. Linked data structures, such as linked lists, are an excellent setting for discussing cloning because they are an excellent setting for discussing deep versus shallow copying.

This section first presents a relatively simple way to define copy constructors and the `clone` method, but this approach unfortunately produces only shallow copies. We then go on to present one way to produce a deep copy `clone` method and to do so within the official prescribed rules of the Java documentation.

Readers with very little programming experience may be better off skipping this entire section until they become more comfortable with Java. Other readers may prefer to read only the first subsection and possibly the Pitfall "The `clone` Method Is Protected in `Object` ★"

Simple Copy Constructors and `clone` Methods ★

Display 15.12 contains a copy constructor and `clone` method definitions that could be added to the definition of the generic linked list class in Display 15.8. The real work is done by the private helping method `copyOf`, so our discussion focuses on the method `copyOf`.

The private method `copyOf` takes an argument that is a reference to the head node of a linked list and returns a reference to the head node of a copy of that linked list. The easiest way to do this is to return the argument. This would, however, simply produce another name for the argument list. We do not want another name; we want another list. So, the method goes down the argument list one node at a time (with `position`) and makes a copy of each node. The linked list of the calling object is built up node by node by adding these new nodes to its linked list. However, there is a complication. We cannot simply add the new nodes at the head (start) end of the list being built. If we did, then the nodes would end up in the reverse of the desired order. So, the new nodes are added to the end of the linked list being built. The variable `end` of type `Node<T>` is kept positioned at the last node so that it is possible to add nodes at the end of the linked list being built. In this way, a copy of the list in the calling object is created so that the order of the nodes is preserved.

The copy constructor is defined by using the private helping method `copyOf` to create a copy of the list of nodes. Other details of the copy constructor and the `clone` method are done in the standard way.

Although the copy constructor and the `clone` method each produce a new linked list with all new nodes, the new list is not truly independent because the data objects are not cloned. See the Pitfall "The `clone` Method Is Protected in `Object` ★" for a discussion of this point. One way to fix this shortcoming is discussed later in the Programming Tip entitled "Use a Type Parameter Bound for a Better `clone`."

Exceptions ★

A generic data structure, such as the class `LinkedList` in Display 15.12, is likely to have methods that throw exceptions. Situations such as a `null` argument to the copy constructor might be handled differently in different situations, so it is best to throw a `NullPointerException` if this happens and let the programmer who is using the linked list handle the exception. This is what we did with the copy constructor in Display 15.12. A `NullPointerException` is an unchecked exception, which means that it need not be caught or declared in a `throws` clause. When thrown by a method of a linked list class, it can be treated simply as a run-time error message. The exception can instead be caught in a `catch` block if there is some suitable action that can be taken.

Display 15.12   A Copy Constructor and `clone` Method for a Generic Linked List (part 1 of 3)

```
1   public class LinkedList3<T> implements Cloneable
2   {
3       private class Node<T>
4       {                                     This copy constructor and this clone
5           private T data;                   method do not make deep copies. We
6           private Node<T> link;             discuss one way to make a deep copy in the
                                              Programming Tip "Use a Type Parameter
7           public Node( )                    Bound for a Better clone."
8           {
9               data = null;
10              link = null;
11          }

12          public Node(T newData, Node<T> linkValue)
13          {
14              data = newData;
15              link = linkValue;
16          }
17      }//End of Node<T> inner class
```

(continued)

Display 15.12   A Copy Constructor and `clone` Method for a Generic Linked List (part 2 of 3)

```
18          private Node<T> head;
            <All the methods from Display 15.8 are in the class definition,
                          but they are not repeated in this display.>

19          /**
20           Produces a new linked list, but it is not a true deep copy.
21           Throws a NullPointerException if other is null.
22          */
23          public LinkedList3(LinkedList3<T> otherList)
24          {
25              if (otherList == null)
26                  throw new NullPointerException( );
27              if (otherList.head == null)
28                  head = null;
29              else
30                  head = copyOf(otherList.head);
31          }
32
33
34          public LinkedList3<T> clone( )
35          {
36              try
37              {
38                  LinkedList3<T> copy =
39                                  (LinkedList3<T>)super.clone( );
40                  if (head == null)
41                      copy.head = null;
42                  else
43                      copy.head = copyOf(head);
44                  return copy;
45              }
46              catch(CloneNotSupportedException e)
47              {//This should not happen.
48                  return null; //To keep the compiler happy.
49              }
50          }

51          /*
52           Precondition: otherHead ! = null
53           Returns a reference to the head of a copy of the list
54           headed by otherHead. Does not return a true deep copy.
55          */
```

Display 15.12   A Copy Constructor and `clone` Method for a Generic Linked List (part 3 of 3)

```
56        private Node<T> copyOf(Node<T> otherHead)
57        {
58            Node<T> position = otherHead; //moves down other's list.
59            Node<T> newHead; //will point to head of the copy list.
60            Node<T> end = null; //positioned at end of new growing list.
```
Invoking `clone` *with* `position.data` *would be illegal.*
```
61            //Create first node:
62            newHead =
63                new Node<T>(position.data, null);
64            end = newHead;
65            position = position.link;

66            while (position != null)
67            {//copy node at position to end of new list.
68                end.link =
69                    new Node<T>(position.data, null);
70                end = end.link;
71                position = position.link;
72            }
```
Invoking `clone` *with* `position.data` *would be illegal.*
```
73            return newHead;
74        }
75    }
```

PITFALL: The `clone` Method Is Protected in `object` ★

When defining the copy constructor and `clone` method for our generic linked list (Display 15.12), we would have liked to have cloned the data in the list being copied. We would have liked to change the code in the helping method `copyOf` by adding invocations of the `clone` method as follows:

```
newHead =
    new Node((T)(position.data).clone( ), null);
end = newHead;
position = position.link;

while (position != null)
    {//copy node at position to end of new list.
        end.link =
            new Node((T)(position.data).clone( ), null);
        end = end.link;
        position = position.link;
    }
```

This code is identical to code in `copyOf` except for the addition of the invocations of `clone` and the type casts. (The type casts are needed because Java thinks `clone` returns a value of type `Object`.)

(continued)

PITFALL: (continued)

If this modified code (with the `clone` method) would compile (and if the type plugged in for T has a well-defined `clone` method that makes a deep copy), then this modified code would produce a truly independent linked list with no references in common with the list being copied. Unfortunately, this code will not compile.

If you try to compile this code, you will get an error message saying that the method `clone` is protected in the class `Object`. True, we used the type T, not the type `Object`, but any class can be plugged in for T. So when the generic linked list is compiled, all Java knows about the type T is that it is a descendent class of `Object`. Because the designers of the `Object` class chose to make the method `clone` protected, you simply cannot use the `clone` method in the definition of methods such as `copyOf`.

Why was the `clone` method labeled `protected` in `Object`? Apparently, this was done for security reasons. If a class could use the `clone` method unchanged from `Object`, then that would open the possibility of copying sections of memory unchanged and unchecked and so might give unauthorized memory access. The problem is made more serious by the fact that Java is used to run programs on other machines across the Internet.

The way Java defines the `clone` method in `Object` and the way it specifies how `clone` should be defined in other classes is controversial. Do not be surprised if some future version of Java handles the `clone` method differently. But for now, you are stuck with these `clone` problems.

In many situations, the version of `copyOf` in Display 15.12 (without the use of `clone`) is good enough, but there is a way to get a true deep copy. One way to get a deep copy is to somehow restrict the type T to classes that do have a public `clone` method that makes a deep copy. Something such as this can be done and is discussed in the Programming Tip "Use a Type Parameter Bound for a Better `clone`." ■

TIP: Use a Type Parameter Bound for a Better `clone` ★

One way to overcome the problem discussed in the previous Pitfall section is to place a bound on the type parameter T (in Display 15.12) so that it must satisfy some suitable interface. There is no standard interface that does the job, but it is very easy to define such an interface. The interface `PubliclyCloneable` given in Display 15.13 is just the interface we need. This short, simple interface guarantees all that we need to define generic linked lists whose clone method returns a deep copy.

Note that any class that implements the `PubliclyCloneable` interface has the following three properties:

1. The class implements the `Cloneable` interface. (This happens automatically because `PubliclyCloneable` extends `Cloneable`.)
2. The class has a public `clone` method.
3. The `clone` method for the class makes a deep copy (in the officially sanctioned way).

Condition 3 is not enforced by the Java compiler or run-time software, but like all interface semantics, it is the responsibility of the programmer defining the class to ensure that condition 3 is satisfied.

TIP: (continued)

It is now easy to define our generic linked list whose `clone` method produces a deep copy. The definition is given in Display 15.14. We have already discussed the main points involved in this definition. The Programming Example subsection, "A Linked List with a Deep Copy clone Method ★," discusses some of the minor, but possibly unclear, details of the definition.[1] ■

Display 15.13   The `PubliclyCloneable` Interface

```
1   /*
2    The programmer who defines a class implementing this interface
3    has the responsibility to define clone so it makes a deep copy
4    (in the officially sectioned way.)
5   */

6   public interface PubliclyCloneable extends Cloneable
7   {
8       public Object clone( );
9   }
```

Any class that implements `PubliclyCloneable` *must have a public* `clone` *method.*

Any class that implements `PubliclyCloneable` *automatically implements* `Cloneable`.

Display 15.14   A Generic Linked List with a Deep Copy `clone` Method (part 1 of 3)

```
1   public class LinkedList<T extends PubliclyCloneable>
2                                           implements PubliclyCloneable
3   {
4       private class Node<T>
5       {
6           private T data;
7           private Node<T> link;

8           public Node( )
9           {
10              data = null;
11              link = null;
12          }
```

(continued)

---

[1]You might wonder whether we could use a type parameter in the `PubliclyCloneable` interface and so avoid some type casts in the definition `copyOf`. We could do that, but that may be more trouble than it is worth and, at this introductory level of presentation, would be an unnecessary distraction.

Display 15.14   A Generic Linked List with a Deep Copy `clone` Method (part 2 of 3)

```java
13            public Node(T newData, Node<T> linkValue)
14            {
15                data = newData;
16                link = linkValue;
17            }
18        }//End of Node<T> inner class

19        private Node<T> head;

20        public LinkedList( )
21        {
22            head = null;
23        }
24        /**
25         Produces a new linked list, but it is not a true deep copy.
26         Throws a NullPointerException if other is null.
27        */
28        public LinkedList(LinkedList<T> otherList)
29        {
30            if (otherList == null)
31                throw new NullPointerException( );
32            if (otherList.head == null)
33                head = null;
34            else
35                head = copyOf(otherList.head);
36        }

37
38        public LinkedList<T> clone( )
39        {
40            try
41            {
42                LinkedList<T> copy =
43                            (LinkedList<T>)super.clone( );
44                if (head == null)
45                    copy.head = null;
46                else
47                    copy.head = copyOf(head);
48                return copy;
49            }
50            catch(CloneNotSupportedException e)
51            {//This should not happen.
52                return null; //To keep the compiler happy.
53            }
54        }

55        /*
56         Precondition: otherHead != null
57         Returns a reference to the head of a copy of the list
58         headed by otherHead. Returns a true deep copy.
59        */
60        private Node<T> copyOf(Node<T> otherHead)
```

Display 15.14   A Generic Linked List with a Deep Copy clone Method (part 3 of 3)

```
61          {
62              Node<T> position = otherHead; //moves down other's list.
63              Node<T> newHead; //will point to head of the copy list.
64              Node<T> end = null; //positioned at end of new growing list.
65              //Create first node:
66              newHead =
67                      new Node<T>((T)(position.data).clone( ), null);
68                      end = newHead;
69              position = position.link;
70              while (position != null)
71              {//copy node at position to end of new list.
72                      end.link =
73                          new Node<T>((T)(position.data).clone( ), null);
74                      end = end.link;
75                      position = position.link;
76              }

77              return newHead;
78          }

79
80          public boolean equals(Object otherObject)
81          {
82              if (otherObject == null)
83                  return false;
84              else if (getClass( ) != otherObject.getClass( ))
85                  return false;
86              else
87              {
88                      LinkedList<T> otherList = (LinkedList<T>)otherObject;
```

This definition of copyOf gives a deep copy of the linked list.

<The rest of the definition is the same as in Display 15.8. The only difference between this definition of equals and the one in Display 15.8 is that we have replaced the class name LinkedList3<T> with LinkedList<T>.>

```
89          }
```

<All the other methods from Display 15.8 are in the class definition, but are not repeated in this display.>

```
90          public String toString( )
91          {
92              Node<T> position = head;
93              String theString = "";
94              while (position != null)
95              {
96                      theString = theString + position.data + "\n";
97                      position = position.link;
98              }
99              return theString;
100         }
101     }
```

We added a toString method so LinkedList<T> would have all the properties we want T to have.

EXAMPLE: A Linked List with a Deep Copy `clone` Method ★

We have already discussed how and why the `clone` method of the generic linked list class in Display 15.14 returns a deep copy. Let us now look at some of the other details and see an example of using this linked list class.

Note the definition of the `clone` method. Why did we not simplify it to the following?

```
public LinkedList<T> clone( )
{
    return new LinkedList<T>(this);
}
```

This simple, alternative definition would still return a deep copy of the linked list and would work fine in most situations. It is likely that you would not notice any difference if you used this definition of `clone` in place of the one given in Display 15.14.

The only reason for all the other detail in the `clone` method definition given in Display 15.14 is to define the `clone` method as specified in the Java documentation. The reason that the Java documentation asks for those details has to do with security issues. (Some might say that there are three ways to define a `clone` method: the right way, the wrong way, and the Java way. This extra detail is the Java way.)

If you look only quickly at Display 15.14, you might think the following at the start of the definition is an unimportant detail:

```
implements PubliclyCloneable
```

However, it ensures that the linked list class implements the `Cloneable` interface. In order for a class to have a Java-approved `clone` method, it must implement the `Cloneable` interface. It also allows you to make linked lists of linked lists and have a deep copy `clone` method in the linked list of linked lists.

A sample class that implements the `PubliclyCloneable` interface is given in Display 15.15. Display 15.16 shows a demonstration program that makes a deep copy `clone` of a linked list of objects of this sample class.

Display 15.15   A `PubliclyCloneable` Class (part 1 of 2)

```
1   public class StockItem implements PubliclyCloneable
2   {
3       private String name;
4       private int number;

5       public StockItem( )
6       {
7           name = null;
8           number = 0;
9       }
```

Display 15.15   A `PubliclyCloneable` Class (part 2 of 2)

```
10        public StockItem(String nameData, int numberData)
11        {
12            name = nameData;
13            number = numberData;
14        }

15        public void setNumber(int newNumber)
16        {
17            number = newNumber;
18        }
19        public void setName(String newName)
20        {
21            name = newName;
22        }

23        public String toString( )
24        {
25            return (name + " " + number);
26        }

27        public Object clone( )
28        {
29           try
30           {
31              return super.clone( );
32           }
33           catch(CloneNotSupportedException e)
34           { //This should not happen.
35              return null; //To keep compiler happy.
36           }
37        }

39        public boolean equals(Object otherObject)
40        {
41            if (otherObject == null)
42                return false;
43            else if (getClass( ) != otherObject.getClass( ))
44                return false;
45            else
46            {
47                StockItem otherItem = (StockItem) otherObject;
48                return (name.equalsIgnoreCase(otherItem.name)
49                        && number == otherItem.number);
50            }
51        }
52    }
```

Display 15.16   Demonstration of Deep Copy `clone`

```
1   public class DeepDemo
2   {
3       public static void main(String[] args)
4       {
5           LinkedList<StockItem> originalList =
6                               new LinkedList<StockItem>( );
7           originalList.addToStart(new StockItem("red dress", 1));
8           originalList.addToStart(new StockItem("black shoe", 2));

9           LinkedList<StockItem> copyList = originalList.clone( );
10          if (originalList.equals(copyList))
11              System.out.println("OK, Lists are equal.");

12          System.out.println("Now we change copyList.");
13          StockItem dataEntry =
14                  copyList.findData(new StockItem("red dress", 1));
15          dataEntry.setName("orange pants");

16          System.out.println("originalList:");
17          originalList.outputList( );

18          System.out.println("copyList:");
19          copyList.outputList( );
20
21          System.out.println("Only one list is changed.");
22      }
23  }
```

Sample Dialogue

```
OK, Lists are equal.
Now we change copyList.
originalList:
black shoe 2
red dress 1
copyList:
black shoe 2
orange pants 1
Only one list is changed.
```

TIP: Cloning Is an "All or Nothing" Affair

If you define a `clone` method, then you should do so following the official Java guidelines, as we did in Display 15.14. In particular, you should always have the class implement the `Cloneable` interface. If you define a `clone` method in any other way, you may encounter problems in some situations. If you want to have a method for producing copies of objects but do not want to follow the official guidelines on how to define a `clone` method, then use some other name for your "clone-like" method, such as `copier`, or make do with just a copy constructor. ∎

Self-Test Exercises

9. In the definition of `copyOf` in Display 15.14, can we replace

```
newHead =
          new Node<T>((T)(position.data).clone( ), null);
```

with the following, which uses the copy constructor of `T` instead of the clone method of `T`?

```
newHead =
          new Node<T>(new T(position.data), null);
```

10. The definition of the `clone` method in Display 15.14 returns a value of type `LinkedList<T>`. But the class being defined implements the `PubliclyCloneable` interface, and that interface says the value returned must be of type `Object`. Is something wrong?

15.3 Iterators

Play it again, Sam.

Attributed (incorrectly) to the movie *Casablanca*, which contains similar lines.[2]

iterator   When you have a collection of objects, such as the nodes of a linked list, you often need to step through all the objects in the collection one at a time and perform some action on each object, such as writing it out to the screen or in some way editing the data in each object. An **iterator** is any object that allows you to step through the list in this way.

---

[2]There is a Woody Allen movie with this title, but it is based on the misquote from *Casablanca*, which was in common use before the movie came out.

Defining an Iterator Class

In Display 15.17, we have rewritten the class `LinkedList2` from Display 15.7 so that it has an inner class for iterators and a method `iterator( )` that returns an iterator for its calling object. We have made the inner class `List2Iterator` public so that we can have variables of type `List2Iterator` outside the class `LinkedList2`, but we do not otherwise plan to use the inner class `List2Iterator` outside of the outer class `LinkedList2`.

Use of iterators for the class `LinkedList2` is illustrated by the program in Display 15.18. Note that, given a linked list named `list`, an iterator for `list` is produced by the method `iterator` as follows:

```
LinkedList2.List2Iterator i = list.iterator( );
```

The iterator `i` produced in this way can only be used with the linked list named `list`. Be sure to notice that outside of the class, the type name for the inner class iterator must include the name of the outer class as well as the inner iterator class. The class name for one of these iterators is

```
LinkedList2.List2Iterator
```

Display 15.17   A Linked List with an Iterator (part 1 of 3)

```
1    import java.util.NoSuchElementException;

2    public class LinkedList2                    This is the same as the class in Display 15.7 and
3    {                                           15.11 except that the List2Iterator inner class
4        private class Node                      and the iterator() method have been added.
5        {
6            private String item;
7            private Node link;
```

<The rest of the definition of the Node inner class is given in Display 15.7.>

```
8        }//End of Node inner class

9        /**
10        If the list is altered any iterators should invoke restart or
11        the iterator's behavior may not be as desired.
12        */
13        public class List2Iterator  ←——————— An inner class for iterators for
14        {                                              LinkedList2.
15            private Node position;
16            private Node previous; //previous value of position
17            public List2Iterator( )
18            {
19                position = head; //Instance variable head of outer class.
20                previous = null;
21            }
```

Display 15.17   A Linked List with an Iterator (part 2 of 3)

```
22          public void restart( )
23          {
24              position = head; //Instance variable head of outer class.
25              previous = null;
26          }

27          public String next( )
28          {
29              if (!hasNext( ))
30                  throw new NoSuchElementException( );

31              String toReturn = position.item;
32              previous = position;
33              position = position.link;
34              return toReturn;
35          }

36          public boolean hasNext( )
37          {
38              return (position != null);
39          }
40          /**
41           Returns the next value to be returned by next( ).
42           Throws an IllegalStateExpression if hasNext( ) is false.
43          */
44          public String peek( )
45          {
46              if (!hasNext( ))
47                  throw new IllegalStateException( );
48              return position.item;
49          }

50          /**
51           Adds a node before the node at location position.
52           previous is placed at the new node. If hasNext( ) is
53           false, then the node is added to the end of the list.
54           If the list is empty, inserts node as the only node.
55          */
56          public void addHere(String newData)
57          {
58              if (position == null && previous != null)
59                  // at end of the list, add to end
60                  previous.link = new Node(newData, null);
61              else if (position == null || previous == null)
62                  // list is empty or position is head node
63                  LinkedList2.this.addtoStart(newData);
```

(continued)

Display 15.17   **A Linked List with an Iterator** (part 3 of 3)

```
64                   else
65                   { // previous and position are consecutive nodes
66                       Node temp = new Node(newData, position);
67                       previous.link = temp;
68                       previous = temp;
69                   }
70           }
71           /**
72            Changes the String in the node at location position.
73            Throws an IllegalStateException if position is not at a node,
74            */
75           public void changeHere(String newData)
```

< Self-Test Exercise 13 asks you to complete the rest of the method changeHere.>

```
76           /**
77            Deletes the node at location position and
78            moves position to the "next" node.
79            Throws an IllegalStateException if the list is empty.
80            */
81           public void delete( )
82           {
83               if (position == null)
84                   throw new IllegalStateException( );
85               else if (previous == null)
86               {    // remove node at head
87                   head = head.link;
88                   position = head;
89               }
90               else // previous and position are consecutive nodes
91               {
92                   previous.link = position.link;
93                   position = position.link;
94               }
95           }
96       private Node head;
97       public List2Iterator iterator( )
98       {
99           return new List2Iterator( );
100      }
```

If `list` *is an object of the class* LinkedList2, *then* `list.iterator()` *returns an iterator for list.*

<The other methods and constructors are identical to those in Display 15.7 and 15.11.>

```
101  }
```

Display 15.18   **Using an Iterator** (part 1 of 2)

```java
1   public class IteratorDemo
2   {
3       public static void main(String[] args)
4       {
5           LinkedList2 list = new LinkedList2( );
6           LinkedList2.List2Iterator i = list.iterator( );

7           list.addToStart("shoes");
8           list.addToStart("orange juice");
9           list.addToStart("coat");

10          System.out.println("List contains:");
11          i.restart( );
12          while(i.hasNext( ))
13              System.out.println(i.next( ));
14          System.out.println( );

15          i.restart( );
16          i.next( );
17          System.out.println("Will delete the node for " + i.peek( ));
18          i.delete( );

19          System.out.println("List now contains:");
20          i.restart( );
21          while(i.hasNext( ))
22              System.out.println(i.next( ));
23          System.out.println( );

24          i.restart( );
25          i.next( );
26          System.out.println("Will add one node before " + i.peek( ));
27          i.addHere("socks");
28          System.out.println("List now contains:");
29          i.restart( );
30          while(i.hasNext( ))
31              System.out.println(i.next( ));
32          System.out.println( );
33          System.out.println("Changing all items to credit card.");
34          i.restart( );
35          while(i.hasNext( ))
36          {
37              i.changeHere("credit card");
38              i.next( );
39          }
40          System.out.println( );
41          System.out.println("List now contains:");
```

(continued)

Display 15.18   **A Linked List with an Iterator** (part 2 of 2)

```
42              i.restart( );
43              while(i.hasNext( ))
44                  System.out.println(i.next( ));
45              System.out.println( );
46          }
47  }
```

Sample Dialogue

```
List contains:
coat
orange juice
shoes

Will delete the node for orange juice
List now contains:
coat
shoes

Will add one node before shoes
List now contains:
coat
socks
shoes

Changing all items to credit card.

List now contains:
credit card
credit card
credit card
```

The basic method for cycling through the elements in the linked list using an iterator is illustrated by the following code from the demonstration program:

```
System.out.println("List now contains:");
i.restart( );
while(i.hasNext( ))
    System.out.println(i.next( ));
```

The iterator is named i in this code. The iterator i is reset to the beginning of the list with the method invocation i.restart(), and each execution of i.next() produces the next data item in the linked list. After all the data items in all the nodes have been returned by i.next( ), the Boolean i.hasNext( ) becomes false and the while loop ends.

Internally, the local variable `position` references the current node in the linked list, whereas the local variable `previous` references the node linking to the current node. The purpose of the `previous` variable will be seen when adding and deleting nodes. In the constructor and the `restart( )` method, `position` is set to `head` and `previous` is set to `null`.

To determine if the end of the list has been reached, `hasNext( )` returns whether or not `position` is `null`:

```
return (position != null);
```

To step through the list, the `next( )` method first throws an exception if we have reached the end of the list:

```
if (!hasNext( ))
    throw new NoSuchElementException( );
```

Otherwise, the method retrieves the string value of the iterator referenced by `position` in the variable `toReturn`, advances `previous` to reference the current position, advances `position` to the next node in the list, and returns the string:

```
String toReturn = position.item;
previous = position;
position = position.link;
return toReturn;
```

The definition of the method `changeHere` is left to Self-Test Exercise 13. (If necessary, you can look up the definition in the answer to Self-Test Exercise 13.) The techniques for adding and deleting nodes are discussed in the next subsection.

The Java `Iterator` Interface

Java has an interface named `Iterator` that specifies how Java would like an iterator to behave. It is in the package `java.util` (and so requires that you import this package). Our iterators do not quite satisfy this interface, but they are in the same general spirit as that interface and could be easily redefined to satisfy the `Iterator` interface.

The `Iterator` interface is discussed in Chapter 16.

Adding and Deleting Nodes

To add or delete a node in a linked list, you normally use an iterator and add or delete a node at the (approximate) location of the iterator. Because deleting is a little easier than adding a node, we will discuss deleting first.

Display 15.19 shows the technique for deleting a node. The linked list is an object of the class `LinkedList2` (Display 15.17). The variables `position` and `previous` are the instance variables of an iterator for the linked list object. These variables each hold a reference to a node, indicated with an arrow. Each time `next( )` is invoked, `previous` and `position` reference subsequent nodes in the list. As indicated in Display 15.19, the node at location `position` is deleted by the following two lines of code:

```
previous.link = position.link;
position = position.link;
```

In Display 15.19, `next( )` has been invoked twice, so `position` is referencing the node with `"shoes"` and `previous` is referencing the node with `"socks"`.

To delete the node referenced by `position`, the link from the `previous` node is set to `positions` link. As shown in Display 15.19, this removes the linked list's reference to that node. The variable `position` is then set to the next node in the list to remove any references to the deleted node. As far as the linked list is concerned, the old node is no longer on the linked list. But the node is still in the computer's memory. If there are no longer any references to the deleted node, then the storage that it occupies should be made available for other uses. In many programming languages, you, the programmer, must keep track of items such as deleted nodes and must give explicit commands to return their memory for recycling. This is called **garbage collecting** or **explicit memory management**. In Java, this is done for you automatically, or, as it is ordinarily phrased, Java has automatic garbage collection.

garbage collecting

explicit memory management

Note that there are special cases that must be handled for deletion. First, if the list is empty, then nothing can be deleted and the `delete( )` method throws an exception. Second, if the node to delete is the head of the list, then there is no previous node to update. Instead, `head` is set to `head.link` to bypass the first node in the list and set a new head node.

Display 15.20 shows the technique for adding a node. We want to add a new node between the nodes named by `previous` and `position`. In Display 15.20, `previous` and `position` are variables of type `Node`, and each contains a reference to a node indicated with an arrow. Thus, the new node goes between the two nodes referenced by `previous` and `position`. In Display 15.20, the method `next( )` has been invoked twice to advance `previous` to `"orange juice"` and `position` to `"shoes"`.

A constructor for the class `Node` does a lot of the work for us: It creates the new node, adds the data, and sets the link field of the new node to reference the node named by `position`. All this is done with the following:

```
new Node(newData, position)
```

So that we can recognize the node with `newData` in it when we study Display 15.20, let us assume that `newData` holds the string `"socks"`. The following gets us from the first to the second picture:

```
temp = new Node(newData, position);
```

Display 15.19   Deleting a Node

1. Existing list with the iterator positioned at "shoes"

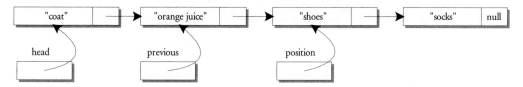

2. Bypass the node at `position` from `previous`

```
previous.link = position.link;
```

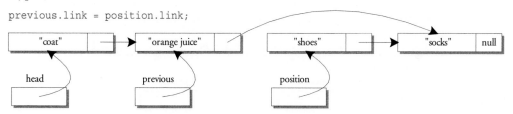

3. Update `position` to reference the next node

```
position = position.link;
```

Since no variable references the node "shoes" Java will automatically recycle the memory allocated for it.

4. Same picture with deleted node not shown

Display 15.20   Adding a Node between Two Nodes

1. Existing list with the iterator positioned at "shoes"

2. Create new Node with "socks" linked to "shoes"

```
temp = new Node(newData, position); // newData is "socks"
```

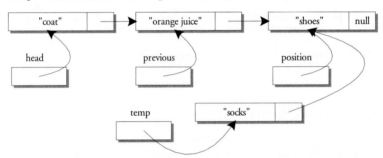

Local variable of type Node

3. Make `previous` link to the Node `temp`

```
previous.link = temp;
```

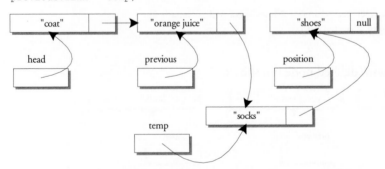

4. Picture redrawn for clarity, but structurally identical to picture 3

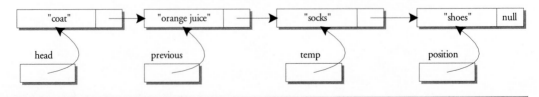

To finish the job, all we need to do is link the previous node to the new node. We want to move the arrow to the node named by `temp`. The following finishes our job:

```
previous.link = temp;
```

The new node is inserted in the desired place, but the picture is not too clear. The fourth picture is the same as the third one; we have simply redrawn it to make it neater.

To summarize, the following two lines insert a new node with `newData` as its data. The new node is inserted between the nodes named by `previous` and `position`.

```
temp = new Node(newData, position);
previous.link = temp;
```

`previous`, `position`, and `temp` are all variables of type `Node`. (When we use this code, `previous` and `position` will be instance variables of an iterator and `temp` will be a local variable.)

Just like deletion, special cases exist for insertion that must be handled. If the list is empty, then addition is done by adding to the front of the list. If the `position` variable is `null`, then the new node should be added to the end of the list.

Self-Test Exercises

11. Consider a variant of the class in Display 15.17 with no `previous` local variable. In other words, there is no reference kept to the node that links to the current node position. How could we modify the `delete` method to delete the `position` node and still maintain a correct list? The solution is less efficient than the version that uses `previous`.

12. Consider a variant of the class in Display 15.17 with no `previous` local variable. In other words, there is no reference kept to the node that links to the current node `position`. Write a method `addAfterHere(String newData)` that adds a new node after the node in `position`.

13. Complete the definition of the method `changeHere` in the inner class `List2Iterator` in Display 15.17.

14. Given an iterator pointing somewhere in a linked list, does `i.next( )` return the value that `i` is referencing prior to the invocation of `i.next( )` or does it return the value of the next node in the list?

15.4 Variations on a Linked List

I have called this principle, by which each slight variation, if useful, is preserved, by the term Natural Selection.

CHARLES DARWIN, *The Origin of Species*

In this section, we discuss some variations on linked lists, including the two data structures known as stacks and queues. Stacks and queues need not involve linked lists, but one common way to implement a stack or a queue is to use a linked list.

Doubly Linked List

doubly linked list

An ordinary linked list allows you to move down the list in one direction only (following the links). A **doubly linked list** has one link that has a reference to the next node and one that has a reference to the previous node. In some cases, the link to the previous node can simplify our code. For example, we will no longer need to have a `previous` instance variable to remember the node that links to the current position. Diagrammatically, a doubly linked list looks like the sample list in Display 15.21.

The node class for a doubly linked list can begin as follows:

```
private class TwoWayNode
{
    private String item;
    private TwoWayNode previous;
    private TwoWayNode next;

    . . .
```

The constructors and some of the methods in the doubly linked list class will require changes (from the singly linked case) in their definitions to accommodate the extra link. The major changes are to the methods that add and delete nodes. To make our code a little cleaner, we can add a new constructor that sets the previous and next nodes:

```
public TwoWayNode(String newItem, TwoWayNode previousNode,
                                       TwoWayNode nextNode)
{
    item = newItem;
    next = nextNode;
    previous = previousNode;
}
```

To add a new `TwoWayNode` to the front of the list requires setting links on two nodes instead of one. The general process is shown in Display 15.22. In the `addToStart` method, we first create a new `TwoWayNode`. Because the new node will go on the front of the list, we set the previous link to `null` and the next link to the current head:

```
TwoWayNode newHead = new TwoWayNode(itemName, null, head);
```

Display 15.21   A Doubly Linked List

Next, we must set the `previous` link on the old head node to reference the new head. We can do this by setting `head.previous = newHead`, but we must take care to ensure that `head` is not `null` (i.e., the list is not empty). Finally, we can set `head` to `newHead`.

```
if (head != null)
{
        head.previous = newHead;
}
head = newHead;
```

   To delete a node from the doubly linked list also requires updating the references on both sides of the node to delete. Thanks to the backward link, there is no need for an instance variable to keep track of the previous node in the list, as was required for the singly linked list. The general process of deleting a node referenced by `position` is shown in Display 15.23. Note that some cases must be handled separately, such as deleting a node from the beginning or the end of the list.

Display 15.22 Adding a Node to the Front of a Doubly Linked List

1. Existing list.

2. Create new TwoWayNode linked to "coat"

```
TwoWayNode newHead = new TwoWayNode(itemName, null, head) // itemName = "shirt"
```

3. Set backward link and set new head

```
head.previous = newHead;
head = newHead;
```

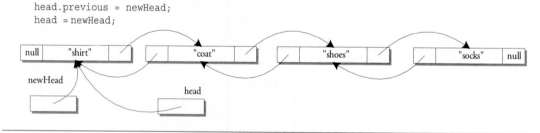

The process of inserting a new node into the doubly linked list is shown in Display 15.24. In this case, we will insert the new node in front of the iterator referenced by `position`. Note that there are also special cases for the insert routine when inserting to the front or adding to the end of the list. Only the general case of inserting between two existing nodes is shown in Display 15.24.

A complete example of a doubly linked list is shown in Display 15.25. The code in Display 15.25 is modified from the code in Display 15.17. Use of the doubly linked list is virtually identical to use of a singly linked list. Display 15.26 demonstrates addition, deletion, and insertion into the doubly linked list.

Display 15.23   Deleting a Node from a Doubly Linked List

1. Existing list with an iterator referencing "shoes"

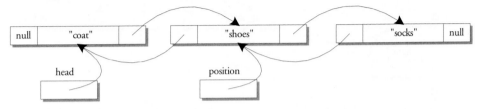

2. Bypass the "shoes" node from the next link of the previous node

```
position.previous.next = position.next;
```

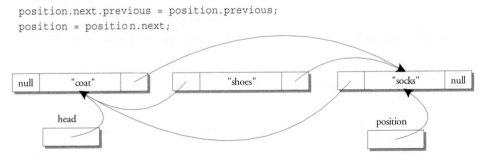

3. Bypass the "shoes" node from the previous link of the next node
    and move position off the deleted node

```
position.next.previous = position.previous;
position = position.next;
```

4. Picture redrawn for clarity with the "shoes" node removed since
    there are no longer references pointing to this node.

Display 15.24   Inserting a Node into a Doubly Linked List

1. Existing list with an iterator referencing "shoes"

2. Create new TwoWayNode with previous linked to "coat" and next to "shoes"

```
TwoWayNode temp = newTwoWayNode(newData, position.previous, position);
// newData = "shirt"
```

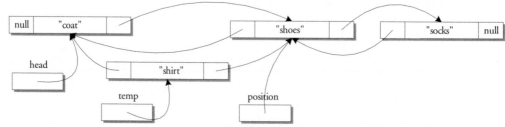

3. Set next link from "coat" to the new node of "shirt"

```
position.previous.next = temp;
```

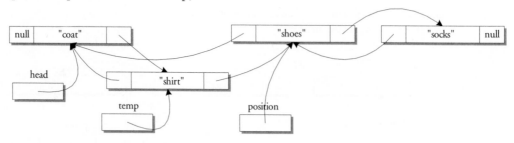

4. Set previous link from "shoes" to the new node of "shirt"

```
position.previous = temp;
```

Display 15.25   A Doubly Linked List with an Iterator (part 1 of 3)

```
1    import java.util.NoSuchElementException;

2    public class DoublyLinkedList
3    {
4        private class TwoWayNode
5        {
6            private String item;
7            private TwoWayNode previous;
8            private TwoWayNode next;

9            public TwoWayNode()
10           {
11               item = null;
12               next = null;
13               previous = null;
14           }
15           public TwoWayNode(String newItem, TwoWayNode previousNode,
                                                TwoWayNode nextNode)
16           {
17               item = newItem;
18               next = nextNode;
19               previous = previousNode;
20           }
21       } //End of TwoWayNode inner class

22       public class DoublyLinkedIterator
23       {
24           // We do not need a previous node when using a doubly linked
             // list
25           private TwoWayNode position = null;

26           public DoublyLinkedIterator( )
27           {
28               position = head;
29           }
30           public void restart( )
31           {
32               position = head;
33           }
34           public String next( )
35           {
36               if (!hasNext( ))
37                   throw new IllegalStateException( );
38               String toReturn = position.item;
39               position = position.next;
40               return toReturn;
41           }
```

(continued)

Display 15.25   **A Doubly Linked List with an Iterator** (part 2 of 3)

```
42          public void insertHere(String newData)
43          {
44                  if (position == null && head != null)
45                  {
46                          // Add to end. First move a temp
47                          // pointer to the end of the list
48                          TwoWayNode temp = head;
49                          while (temp.next != null)
50                                  temp = temp.next;
51                          temp.next = new TwoWayNode(newData, temp, null);
52                  }
53                  else if (head == null || position.previous == null)
54                          // at head of list
55                          DoublyLinkedList.this.addToStart (newData);
56                  else
57                  {
58                          // Insert before the current position
59                          TwoWayNode temp = new TwoWayNode(newData,
60                                  position. previous, position);
                           position.previous.next = temp;
61                          position.previous = temp;
62                  }
63          }

64          public void delete( )
65          {
66                  if (position == null)
67                          throw new IllegalStateException( );
68                  else if (position.previous == null)
69                  { // Deleting first node
70                          head = head.next;
71                          position = head;
72                  }
73                  else if (position.next == null)
74                  { // Deleting last node
75                          position.previous.next = null;
76                          position = null;
77                  }
78                  else
79                  {
80                          position.previous.next = position.next;
81                          position.next.previous = position.previous;
82                          position = position.next;
83                  }
84          }
85     }    // DoublyLinkedIterator
```

Display 15.25   **A Doubly Linked List with an Iterator** (part 3 of 3)

```
86          private TwoWayNode head;

87          public DoublyLinkedIterator iterator( )
88          {
89              return new DoublyLinkedIterator( );
90          }

91          public DoublyLinkedList( )
92          {
93              head = null;
94          }

95          /**
96           The added node will be the first node in the list.
97           */
98          public void addToStart(String itemName)
99          {
100             TwoWayNode newHead = new TwoWayNode(itemName, null, head);
101             if (head != null)
102             {
103                 head.previous = newHead;
104             }
105             head = newHead;
106         }
```

<The methods hasNext, peek, clear, and isEmpty are identical
to those in Display 15.17. Other methods would also normally
be defined here, such as deleteHeadNode, size, outputList,
equals, clone, find, or contains. They have been left off to
simplify the example.>

```
107 }            // DoublyLinkedList
```

Display 15.26   **Using a Doubly Linked List with an Iterator** (part 1 of 2)

```
1  public class DoublyLinkedListDemo
2  {
3          public static void main(String[] args)
4          {
5              DoublyLinkedList list = new DoublyLinkedList( );
6              DoublyLinkedList.DoublyLinkedIterator i = list.iterator( );

7              list.addToStart("shoes");
8              list.addToStart("orange juice");
9              list.addToStart("coat");
10             System.out.println("List contains:");
11             i.restart( );
```

(continued)

Display 15.26   Using a Doubly Linked List with an Iterator (part 2 of 2)

```
12              while (i.hasNext( ))
13                      System.out.println(i.next( ));
14              System.out.println( );

15              i.restart( );
16              i.next( );
17              i.next( );
18              System.out.println("Delete " + i.peek( ));
19              i.delete( );

20              System.out.println("List now contains:");
21              i.restart( );
22              while (i.hasNext( ))
23                      System.out.println(i.next( ));
24              System.out.println( );

25              i.restart( );
26              i.next( );
27              System.out.println("Inserting socks before " + i.peek( ));
28              i.insertHere("socks");

29              i.restart( );
30              System.out.println("List now contains:");
31              while (i.hasNext( ))
32                      System.out.println(i.next( ));
33              System.out.println( );
34      }
35  }
```

Sample Dialogue

```
List contains:
coat
orange juice
shoes

Delete shoes
List now contains:
Coat
Orange juice

Inserting socks before orange juice
List now contains:
coat
socks
orange juice
```

Self-Test Exercises

15. What operations are easier to implement with a doubly linked list compared with a singly linked list? What operations are more difficult?

16. If the `addToStart` method from Display 15.25 were removed, how could we still add a new node to the head of the list?

The Stack Data Structure

stack

A **stack** is not necessarily a linked data structure, but it can be implemented as a linked list. A stack is a data structure that removes items in the reverse of the order in which they were inserted. So if you insert "`one`", then "`two`", and then "`three`" into a stack and then remove them, they will come out in the order "`three`", then "`two`", and finally "`one`". Stacks are discussed in more detail in Chapter 11. A linked list that inserts and deletes only at the head of the list (such as those in Displays 15.3 or 15.8) is, in fact, a stack.

push and pop

You can imagine the stack data structure like a stack of trays in a cafeteria. You can **push** a new tray on top of the stack to make a taller stack. Alternately, you can **pop** the topmost tray off the stack until there are no more trays to remove. A definition of a `Stack` class is shown in Display 15.27 that is based on the linked list from Display 15.3. A short demonstration program is shown in Display 15.28. The `addToStart` method has been renamed to `push` to use stack terminology. Similarly, the `deleteHeadNode` method has been renamed to `pop` and returns the `String` from the top of the stack. Although not shown here to keep the definition simple, it would be appropriate to add other methods such as `peek`, `clone`, or `equals` or to convert the class to use a generic data type.

> ### Stacks
>
> A **stack** is a last-in/first-out data structure; that is, the data items are retrieved in the opposite order to which they were placed in the stack.

Display 15.27   **A Stack Class** (part 1 of 2)

```
1   import java.util.NoSuchElementException;

2   public class Stack
3   {
4       private class Node
5       {
6           private String item;
7           private Node link;
```

(continued)

Display 15.27   **A stack Class** (part 2 of 2)

```
 8              public Node( )
 9              {
10                   item = null;
11                   link = null;
12              }
13              public Node(String newItem, Node linkValue)
14              {
15                   item = newItem;
16                   link = linkValue;
17              }
18      }//End of Node inner class

19      private Node head;

20      public Stack( )
21      {
22           head = null;
23      }

24      /**
25           This method replaces addToStart
26      */
27      public void push(String itemName)
28      {
29           head = new Node(itemName, head);
30      }
31      /**
32           This method replaces deleteHeadNode and
33           also returns the value popped from the list
34      */
35      public String pop( )
36      {
37           if (head == null)
38                throw new IllegalStateException( );
39           else
40           {
41                String returnItem = head.item;
42                head = head.link;
43                return returnItem;
44           }
45      }
46      public boolean isEmpty( )
47      {
48           return (head == null);
49      }
50  }
```

Display 15.28   Stack Demonstration Program

```
1   public class StackExample
2   {
3       public static void main(String[] args)
4       {
5           Stack stack = new Stack( );
6           Stack.push("Billy Rubin");
7           Stack.push("Lou Pole");
8           Stack.push("Polly Ester");

9           while (!stack.isEmpty( ))
10          {
11              String s = stack.pop( );
12              System.out.println(s);
13          }
14      }
15  }
```

Items come out of the stack in the reverse order that they were added.

Sample Dialogue

```
Polly Ester
Lou Pole
Billy Rubin
```

MyProgrammingLab™

Self-Test Exercise

17. Display 15.27 does not contain a peek( ) method. Normally this method would return the data on the top of the stack without popping it off. How could a user of the Stack class get the same functionally as peek( ) even though it is not defined?

The Queue Data Structure

queue

A stack is a last-in/first-out data structure. Another common data structure is a **queue**, which handles data in a first-in/first-out fashion. A queue is like a line at the bank. Customers add themselves to the back of the line and are served from the front of the line. A queue can be implemented with a linked list. However, a queue needs a pointer

tail

at both the head of the list and at the **tail** (that is, the other end) of the linked list, because action takes place in both locations. It is easier to remove a node from the head of a linked list than from the tail of the linked list. So, a simple implementation will

front

remove nodes from the head of the list (which we will now call the **front** of the list) and we will add nodes to the tail end of the list, which we will now call the **back** of the

back

list (or the back of the queue).

The definition of a simple `Queue` class that is based on a linked list is given in Display 15.29. A short demonstration program is given in Display 15.30. We have not made our queue a generic queue to keep the definition simple, but it would be routine to replace the data type `String` with a type parameter.

> ### Queue
>
> A **queue** is a first-in/first-out data structure; that is, the data items are removed from the queue in the same order that they were added to the queue.

Display 15.29   A `Queue` Class (part 1 of 2)

```
1   public class Queue
2   {
3       private class Node
4       {
5           private String item;
6           private Node link;

7           public Node( )
8           {
9               item = null;
10              link = null;
11          }

12          public Node(String newItem, Node linkValue)
13          {
14              item = newItem;
15              link = linkValue;
16          }
17      }   //End of Node inner class

18      private Node front;
19      private Node back;

20      public Queue( )
21      {
22          front = null;
23          back = null;
24      }
```

Display 15.29   **A Queue Class** (part 2 of 2)

```
25        /**
26         Adds a String to the back of the queue.
27        */
28        public void addToBack(String itemName)
          <The definition of this method is defined in Self-Test Exercise 18.>

29        public boolean isEmpty( )
30        {
31            return (front == null);
32        }

33        public void clear( )
34        {
35            front = null;
36            back = null;
37        }
38        /**
39         Returns the String in the front of the queue.
40         Returns null if queue is empty.
41        */
42        public String whoIsNext( )
43        {
44            if (front == null)
45                return null;
46            else
47                return front.item;
48        }
49
50        /**
51         Removes a String from the front of the queue.
52         Returns false if the list is empty.
53        */
54        public boolean removeFront( )
55        {
56            if (front != null)
57            {
58                front = front.link;
59                return true;
60            }
61            else
62                return false;
63        }
64    }
```

Display 15.30   Demonstration of the `Queue` Class

```
1   public class QueueDemo
2   {
3       public static void main(String[] args)
4       {
5           Queue q = new Queue( );

6           q.addToBack("Tom");
7           q.addToBack("Dick");
8           q.addToBack("Harriet");
9           while(!q.isEmpty( ))
10          {
11              System.out.println(q.whoIsNext( ));
12              q.removeFront( );
13          }
14          System.out.println("The queue is empty.");
15      }
16  }
```

Items come out of the queue in the same order that they went into the queue.

Sample Dialogue

```
Tom
Dick
Harriet
The queue is empty.
```

Items come out of the queue in the same order that they went into the queue.

Self-Test Exercise

18. Complete the definition of the method `addToBack` in Display 15.29.

In order to have some terminology to discuss the efficiency of our `Queue` class and linked list algorithms, we first present some background on how the efficiency of algorithms is usually measured.

Running Times and Big-*O* Notation

If you ask a programmer how fast his or her program is, you might expect an answer such as "two seconds." However, the speed of a program cannot be given by a single number. A program will typically take a longer amount of time on larger inputs than it will on smaller inputs. You would expect that a program for sorting numbers would take less time to sort 10 numbers than it would to sort 1,000 numbers. Perhaps it takes 2 seconds to sort 10 numbers, but 10 seconds to sort 1,000 numbers. How, then, should the programmer answer the question "How fast is your program?" The programmer would have to give a table of values showing how long the program took

Display 15.31   Some Values of a Running-Time Function

Input Size	Running Time
10 numbers	2 seconds
100 numbers	2.1 seconds
1,000 numbers	10 seconds
10,000 numbers	2.5 minutes

for different sizes of input. For example, the table might be as shown in Display 15.31. This table does not give a single time, but instead gives different times for a variety of different input sizes.

function

The table is a description of what is called a **function** in mathematics. Just as a (non-void) Java method takes an argument and returns a value, so too does this function take an argument, which is an input size, and returns a number, which is the time the program takes on an input of that size. If we call this function T, then $T(10)$ is 2 seconds, $T(100)$ is 2.1 seconds, $T(1,000)$ is 10 seconds, and $T(10,000)$ is 2.5 minutes. The table is just a sample of some of the values of this function T. The program will take some amount of time on inputs of every size. So although they are not shown in the table, there are also values for $T(1)$, $T(2)$, ... , $T(101)$, $T(102)$, and so forth. For any positive integer N, $T(N)$ is the amount of time it takes for the

running time

program to sort N numbers. The function T is called the **running time** of the program.

So far we have been assuming that this sorting program will take the same amount of time on any list of N numbers. That need not be true. Perhaps it takes much less time if the list is already sorted or almost sorted. In this case, $T(N)$ is defined to be the time taken by the "hardest" list—that is, the time taken on that list of N numbers that

worst-case running time

makes the program run the longest. This is called the **worst-case running time**. In this chapter, we will always mean worst-case running time when we give a running time for an algorithm or for some code.

The time taken by a program or algorithm is often given by a formula, such as $4N + 3$, $5N + 4$, or N^2. If the running time $T(N)$ is $5N + 5$, then on inputs of size N, the program will run for $5N + 5$ time units.

Presented next is some code to search an array a with N elements to determine whether a particular value target is in the array:

```
int i = 0;
boolean found = false;
while (( i < N) && !(found))
{
    if (a[i] == target)
        found = true;
    else
        i++;
}
```

We want to compute some estimate of how long it will take a computer to execute this code. We would like an estimate that does not depend on which computer we use, either because we do not know which computer we will use or because we might use several different computers to run the program at different times.

One possibility is to count the number of "steps," but it is not easy to decide what a step is. In this situation, the normal thing to do is count the number of **operations**. The term *operations* is almost as vague as the term *step*, but there is at least some agreement in practice about what qualifies as an operation. Let us say that, for this Java code, each application of any of the following will count as an operation: =, <, &&, !, [], ==, and ++. The computer must do other things besides carry out these operations, but these seem to be the main things that it is doing, and we will assume that they account for the bulk of the time needed to run this code. In fact, our analysis of time will assume that everything else takes no time at all and that the total time for our program to run is equal to the time needed to perform these operations. Although this is an idealization that clearly is not completely true, it turns out that this simplifying assumption works well in practice, and so it is often made when analyzing a program or algorithm.

Even with our simplifying assumption, we still must consider two cases: Either the value target is in the array or it is not. Let us first consider the case when target is not in the array. The number of operations performed will depend on the number of array elements searched. The operation = is performed two times before the loop is executed. Because we are assuming that target is not in the array, the loop will be executed N times, one for each element of the array. Each time the loop is executed, the following operations are performed: <, &&, !, [], ==, and ++. This adds five operations for each of N loop iterations. Finally, after N iterations, the Boolean expression is again checked and found to be false. This adds a final three operations (<, &&, !).[3] If we tally all these operations, we get a total of $6N + 5$ operations when the target is not in the array. We will leave it as an exercise for the reader to confirm that if the target is in the array, then the number of operations will be $6N + 5$ *or less*. Thus, the worst-case running time is $T(N) = 6N + 5$ operations for any array of N elements and any value of target.

We just determined that the worst-case running time for our search code is $6N + 5$ operations. But an operation is not a traditional unit of time, such as a nanosecond, second, or minute. If we want to know how long the algorithm will take on some particular computer, we must know how long it takes that computer to perform one operation. If an operation can be performed in one nanosecond, then the time will be $6N + 5$ nanoseconds. If an operation can be performed in one second, the time will be $6N + 5$ seconds. If we use a slow computer that takes 10 seconds to perform an operation, the time will be $60N + 50$ seconds. In general, if it takes the computer c nanoseconds to perform one operation, then the actual running time will be approximately $c(6N + 5)$ nanoseconds. (We said *approximately* because we

---

[3]Because of short-circuit evaluation, !(found) is not evaluated, so we actually get two, not three, operations. However, the important thing is to obtain a good upper bound. If we add in one extra operation, that is not significant.

are making some simplifying assumptions and therefore the result may not be the absolutely exact running time.) This means that our running time of $6N + 5$ is a very crude estimate. To get the running time expressed in nanoseconds, you must multiply by some constant that depends on the particular computer you are using. Our estimate of $6N + 5$ is only accurate to within a constant multiple.

big-O notation

Estimates on running time, such as the one we just went through, are normally expressed in something called **big-O notation**. (The O is the letter "Oh," not the digit zero.) Suppose we estimate the running time to be, say, $6N + 5$ operations, and suppose we know that no matter what the exact running time of each different operation may turn out to be, there will always be some constant factor c such that the real running time is less than or equal to $c\,(6N + 5)$. Under these circumstances, we say that the code (or program or algorithm) runs in time $O(6N + 5)$. This is usually read as "big-O of $6N + 5$." We need not know what the constant c will be. In fact, it will undoubtedly be different for different computers, but we must know that there is one such c for any reasonable computer system. If the computer is very fast, the c might be less than 1—say, 0.001. If the computer is very slow, the c might be very large—say, 1,000. Moreover, because changing the units (say from nanosecond to second) involves only a constant multiple, there is no need to give any units of time.

Be sure to notice that a big-O estimate is an upper-bound estimate. We always approximate by taking numbers on the high side rather than the low side of the true count. Also notice that when performing a big-O estimate, we need not determine an exact count of the number of operations performed. We need only an estimate that is correct up to a constant multiple. If our estimate is twice as large as the true number, that is good enough.

An order-of-magnitude estimate, such as the previous $6N + 5$, contains a parameter for the size of the task solved by the algorithm (or program or piece of code). In our sample case, this parameter N was the number of array elements to be searched. Not surprisingly, it takes longer to search a larger number of array elements than it does to search a smaller number of array elements. Big-O running-time estimates are always expressed as a function of the size of the problem. In this chapter, all our algorithms will involve a range of values in some container. In all cases, N will be the number of elements in that range.

The following is an alternative, pragmatic way to think about big-O estimates:

> *Only look at the term with the highest exponent and*
> *do not pay attention to constant multiples.*

For example, all of the following are $O(N^2)$:

$$N^2 + 2N + 1, \quad 3N^2 + 7, \quad 100N^2 + N$$

All of the following are $O(N^3)$:

$$N^3 + 5N^2 + N + 1, \quad 8N^3 + 7, \quad 100N^3 + 4N + 1$$

These big-O running-time estimates are admittedly crude, but they do contain some information. They will not distinguish between a running time of $5N + 5$ and a running time of $100N$, but they do let us distinguish between some running times and so determine that some algorithms are faster than others. Look at the graphs in Display 15.32 and notice that all the graphs for functions that are $O(N)$ eventually fall below the graph for the function $0.5N^2$. The result is inevitable: An $O(N)$ algorithm will always run faster than any $O(N^2)$ algorithm, provided we use large enough values of N. Although an $O(N^2)$ algorithm could be faster than an $O(N)$ algorithm for the problem size you are handling, programmers have found that, in practice, $O(N)$ algorithms perform better than $O(N)$ algorithms for most practical applications that are intuitively "large." Similar remarks apply to any other two different big-O running times.

Display 15.32   Comparison of Running Times

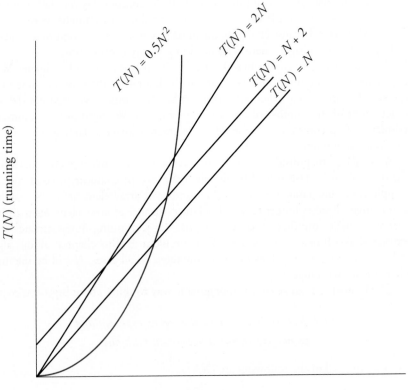

$T(N) = 0.5N^2$

$T(N) = 2N$

$T(N) = N + 2$

$T(N) = N$

$T(N)$ (running time)

N (problem size)

linear
running time

quadratic
running time

Some terminology will help with our descriptions of generic algorithm running times. **Linear running time** means a running time of $T(N) = aN + b$. A linear running time is always an $O(N)$ running time. **Quadratic running time** means a running time with a highest term of N^2. A quadratic running time is always an $O(N^2)$ running time. We will also occasionally have logarithms in running-time formulas. Those normally are given without any base, because changing the base is just a constant multiple. If you see log N, think log base 2 of N, but it would not be wrong to think log base 10 of N. Logarithms are very slow-growing functions. So, an $O(\log N)$ running time is very fast.

In many cases, our running-time estimates will be better than big-O estimates. In particular, when we specify a linear running time, that is a tight upper bound and you can think of the running time as being exactly $T(N) = cN$, although the c is still not specified.

Self-Test Exercises

19. Show that a running time $T(N) = aN + b$ is an $O(N)$ running time. (*Hint:* The only issue is the plus b. Assume N is always at least 1.)

20. Show that for any two bases a and b for logarithms, if a and b are both greater than 1, then there is a constant c such that $\log_a N \leq c \, (\log_b N)$. Thus, there is no need to specify a base in $O(\log N)$. That is, $O(\log_a N)$ and $O(\log_b N)$ mean the same thing.

Efficiency of Linked Lists

Now that we know about big-O notation, we can express the efficiency of various methods for our linked data structures. As an example of analyzing the run-time efficiency of an algorithm, consider the `find` method for the linked list class in Display 15.3. This method starts at the head of the list and sequentially iterates through each node to see whether it matches the target. If the linked list contains many nodes, then we might get lucky if the target is found at the head of the list. In this case, the computer had only to execute one step: Check the head of the list for the target. In the worst case, the computer might have to search through all n nodes before finding (or not finding) the target. In this case, the computer had to execute n steps. The worst case will obviously take longer to execute than the best case. On average, we might expect to search through about half of the list before finding the target. This would require $n/2$ steps. In our big-O notation, the find operation is $O(n)$. However, the `addToStart` method requires linking only a new node to the head of the list. This runs in $O(1)$ steps (that is, a constant upper bound on the running time that is independent of the size of the input).

Next we shall briefly examine more elaborate data structures that are capable of performing find operations in fewer steps. However, a detailed treatment of these more advanced data structures is beyond the scope of this chapter. The goal of this chapter is to teach you the basic techniques for constructing and manipulating data structures based on nodes and links (that is, nodes and references). The linked lists served as good examples for our discussion.

15.5 Hash Tables with Chaining

Seek, and ye shall find.

MATTHEW 7:7

hash table

hash map

A **hash table** or **hash map** is a data structure that efficiently stores and retrieves data from memory. There are many ways to construct a hash table; in this section, we will use an array in combination with singly linked lists. In the previous section, we saw that a linked list generally requires linear, or $O(n)$, steps to determine if a target is in the list. In contrast, a hash table has the potential to execute a fixed number of steps to look up a target, regardless of the size of n. We saw that a constant-time lookup is written $O(1)$. However, the hash table we will present may still require n steps, but such a case is unlikely.

An object is stored in a hash table by associating it with a *key*. Given the key, we can retrieve the object. Ideally, the key is unique to each object. If the object has no

hash function

intrinsically unique key, then we can use a **hash function** to compute one. In most cases, the hash function computes a number.

For example, let us use a hash table to store a dictionary of words. Such a hash table might be useful to make a spell-checker—words missing from the hash table might not be spelled correctly. We will construct the hash table with a fixed array in which each array element references a linked list. The key computed by the hash function will map to the index of the array. The actual data will be stored in a linked list at the hash value's index. Display 15.33 illustrates the idea with a fixed array of 10 entries. Initially, each entry of the array hashArray contains a reference to an empty singly linked list. First, we add the word "cat", which has been assigned the key or hash value of 2 (we will show how this was computed shortly). Next, we add "dog" and "bird", which are assigned hash values of 4 and 7, respectively. Each of these strings is inserted as the head of the linked list using the hash value as the index in the array. Finally, we add "turtle",

collision

which also has a hash of 2. Because "cat" is already stored at index 2, we now have a **collision**. Both "turtle" and "cat" map to the same index in the array. When this

chaining

occurs in a hash table with **chaining**, we simply insert the new node onto the existing linked list. In our example, there are now two nodes at index 2: "turtle" and "cat".

To retrieve a value from the hash table, we first compute the hash value of the target. Next we search the linked list that is stored at hashArray[hashValue] for the target, using an iterator to sequentially search the linked list. If the target is not found in this linked list, then the target is not stored in the hash table. If the size of the linked list is small, then the retrieval process will be quick.

Display 15.33   Constructing a Hash Table

1. Existing hash table initialized with 10 empty linked lists

    ```
    hashArray = new LinkedList 3[ SIZE]; // SIZE = 10
    ```

	0	1	2	3	4	5	6	7	8	9
hashArray	empty	empty	empty	empty	empty	empty	empty	empty	empty	empty

2. After adding "cat" with hash of 2

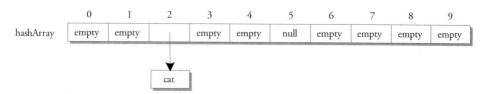

3. After adding "dog" with hash of 4 and "bird" with hash of 7

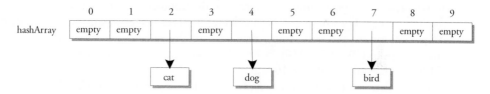

4. After adding "turtle" with hash of 2 – collision and chained to linked list with "cat"

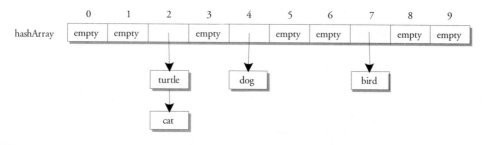

A Hash Function for Strings

A simple way to compute a numeric hash value for a string is to sum the ASCII value of
every character in the string and then compute the modulus of the sum using the size
of the fixed array. A subset of ASCII codes is given in Appendix 3. Code to compute
the hash value is shown next:

```
private int computeHash(String s)
{
    int hash = 0;
```

```
        for (int i = 0; i < s.length(); i++)
        {
            hash += s.charAt(i);
        }
        return hash % SIZE; // SIZE = 10 in example
    }
```

For example, the ASCII codes for the string "dog" are as follows:

```
    d -->100
    o -->111
    g -->103
```

The hash function is computed as follows:

```
    Sum                = 100 + 111 + 103 = 314
    Hash = Sum % 10 = 314 % 10 = 4
```

In this example, we first compute an unbounded value, the sum of the ASCII values in the string. However, the array was defined to only hold a finite number of elements. To scale the sum to the size of the array, we compute the modulus of the sum with respect to the size of the array, which is 10 in the example. In practice, the size of the array is generally a prime number larger than the number of items that will be put into the hash table.[4] The computed hash value of 4 serves like a fingerprint for the string "dog". However, different strings may map to the same value. We can verify that "cat" maps to $(99 + 97 + 116) \% 10 = 2$ and also that "turtle" maps to $(116 + 117 + 114 + 116 + 108 + 101) \% 10 = 2$.

A complete code listing for a hash table class is given in Display 15.34, and a demonstration is provided in Display 15.35. The hash table definition in Display 15.34 uses an array in which each element is a LinkedList2 class defined in Display 15.7.

VideoNote
Walkthrough of
the Hash Table
Class

Display 15.34   A Hash Table Class (part 1 of 2)

```
1  public class HashTable
2  {
3        // Uses the generic LinkedList2 class from Display 15.7
4        private LinkedList2[] hashArray;
5        private static final int SIZE = 10;

6        public HashTable( )
7        {
8              hashArray = new LinkedList2[SIZE];
9              for (int i=0; i < SIZE; i++)
10                   hashArray[i] = new LinkedList2( );
11       }
```

---

[4]A prime number avoids common divisors after modulus that can lead to collisions.

Display 15.34   **A Hash Table Class** (part 2 of 2)

```
12      private int computeHash(String s)
13      {
14              int hash = 0;
15              for (int i = 0; i < s.length( ); i++)
16              {
17                      hash += s.charAt(i);
18              }
19              return hash % SIZE;
20      }

21      /**
22       Returns true if the target is in the hash table,
23       false if it is not.
24      */
25      public boolean containsString(String target)
26      {
27              int hash = computeHash(target);
28              LinkedList2 list = hashArray[hash];
29              if (list.contains(target))
30                      return true;
31              return false;
32      }
33      /**
34      Stores or puts string s into the hash table
35      */
36      public void put(String s)
37      {
38              int hash = computeHash(s);// Get hash value
39              LinkedList2 list = hashArray[hash];
40              if (!list.contains(s))
41              {
42                      // Only add the target if it's not already
43                      // on the list.
44                      hashArray[hash].addToStart(s);
45              }
46      }
47 } // End HashTable class
```

Display 15.35 Hash Table Demonstration

```
1   public class HashTableDemo
2   {
3       public static void main(String[] args)
4       {
5           HashTable h = new HashTable( );

6           System.out.println("Adding dog, cat, turtle, bird");
7           h.put("dog");
8           h.put("cat");
9           h.put("turtle");
10          h.put("bird");
11          System.out.println("Contains dog? " +
12                  h.containsString("dog"));
13          System.out.println("Contains cat? " +
14                  h.containsString("cat"));
15          System.out.println("Contains turtle? " +
16                  h.containsString("turtle"));
17          System.out.println("Contains bird? " +
18                  h.containsString("bird"));

19          System.out.println("Contains fish? " +
20                  h.containsString("fish"));
21          System.out.println("Contains cow? " +
22                  h.containsString("cow"));
23      }
24  }
```

Sample Dialogue

```
Adding dog, cat, turtle, bird
Contains dog? true
Contains cat? true
Contains turtle? true
Contains bird? true
Contains fish? false
Contains cow? False
```

Efficiency of Hash Tables

The efficiency of our hash table depends on several factors. First, let us examine some extreme cases. The worst-case run-time performance occurs if every item inserted into the table has the same hash key. Everything will then be stored in a single linked list. With n items, the find operation will require $O(n)$ steps. Fortunately, if the items that we insert are somewhat random, the probability that all of them will hash to the same key is highly unlikely. In contrast, the best-case run-time performance occurs if every item inserted into the table has a different hash key. This means that there will be no collisions, so the find operation will require constant, or $O(1)$, steps because the target will always be the first node in the linked list.

We can decrease the chance of collisions by using a better hash function. For example, the simple hash function that sums each letter of a string ignores the ordering of the letters. The words `"rat"` and `"tar"` would hash to the same value. A better hash function for a string `s` is to multiply each letter by an increasing weight depending upon the position in the word. For example,

```
int hash = 0;
for (int i = 0; i < s.length( ); i++)
{
    hash = 31 * hash + s.charAt(i);
}
```

Another way to decrease the chance of collisions is by making the hash table bigger. For example, if the hash table array stored 10,000 entries but we are only inserting 1,000 items, then the probability of a collision is much smaller than if the hash table array stored only 1,000 entries. However, a drawback to creating an extremely large hash table array is wasted memory. If only 1,000 items are inserted into the 10,000-entry hash table, then at least 9,000 memory locations will go unused. This illustrates the **time-space** **tradeoff**. It is usually possible to increase run-time performance at the expense of memory space, and vice versa.

time-space tradeoff

Self-Test Exercises

21. Suppose that every student in your university is assigned a unique nine-digit ID number. You would like to create a hash table that indexes ID numbers to an object representing a student. The hash table has a size of N, where N has less than nine digits. Describe a simple hash function that you can use to map from a ID number to a hash index.

22. Write an `outputHashTable( )` method for the `HashTable` class that outputs every item stored in the hash table.

15.6 Sets

There are two classes in good society in England. The equestrian classes and the neurotic classes.

GEORGE BERNARD SHAW, *Heartbreak House*

A set is a collection of elements in which order and multiplicity are ignored. Many problems in computer science can be solved with the aid of a set data structure. A variation on linked lists is a straightforward way to implement a set. In this implementation, the items in each set are stored using a singly linked list. The `data` variable contains a reference to an object we wish to store in the set, whereas the `link` variable refers to the next `Node<T>` in the list (which in turn contains a reference to the next object to store in the set). The node class for a generic set of objects can begin as follows:

```
private class Node<T>
{
    private T data;
    private Node<T> link;

    . . .
```

A complete listing is provided in Display 15.37. The `Node` class is a private inner class, similar to how we constructed the generic `LinkedList3<T>` class in Display 15.8. In fact, the set operations of `add`, `contains`, `output`, `clear`, `size`, and `isEmpty` are virtually identical to those from Display 15.8. The `add` method (which was `addToStart`) has been slightly changed to prevent duplicate items from being added into the set. Display 15.36 illustrates two sample sets stored using this data structure. The set `round` contains `"peas"`, `"ball"`, and `"pie"`, whereas the set `green` contains `"peas"` and `"grass"`. Because the linked list is storing a reference to each object in the set, it is possible to place an item in multiple sets by referencing it from multiple linked lists. In Display 15.36, `"peas"` is in both sets because it is round and green.

Fundamental Set Operations

The fundamental operations that our set class should support are as follows:

- Add Element. Add a new item into a set.
- Contains. Determine if a target item is a member of the set.
- Union. Return a set that is the union of two sets.
- Intersection. Return a set that is the intersection of two sets.

Display 15.36 Sets Using Linked Lists

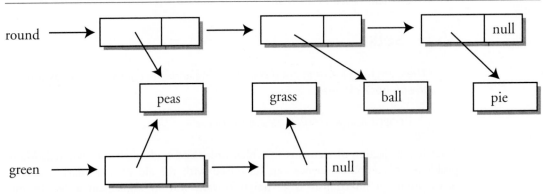

We should also make an iterator so that every element can be retrieved from a set. This is left as a programming project for the reader (Programming Project 15.7). Other useful set operations include methods to retrieve the cardinality of the set and to remove items from the set.

Code to implement sets is provided in Display 15.37. The add method is similar to adding a node to the front of a linked list. The head variable always references the first node in the list. The contains method is identical to the find method for a singly linked list. We simply loop through every item in the list looking for the target.

The union method combines the elements in the calling object's set with the elements from the set of the input argument, otherSet. To union these sets, we first create a new empty Set<T> object. Next, we iterate through both the calling object's set and otherSet's set. All elements are added (which creates new references to the items in the set) to the new set. The add method enforces uniqueness, so we do not have to check for duplicate elements in the union method.

The intersection method is similar to the union method in that it also creates a new empty Set<T> object. In this case, we populate the set with items that are common to both the calling object's set and otherSet's set. This is accomplished by iterating through every item in the calling object's set. For each item, we invoke the contains method for otherSet. If contains returns true, then the item is in both sets and can be added to the new set.

A short demonstration program is shown in Display 15.38.

Display 15.37   Set<T> Class (part 1 of 3)

```
1   // Uses a linked list as the internal data structure
2   // to store items in a set.
3   public class Set<T>
4   {
5       private class Node<T>
6       {
7           private T data;
8           private Node<T> link;
9           public Node( )
10          {
11              data = null;
12              link = null;
13          }
14          public Node(T newData, Node<T> linkValue)
15          {
16              data = newData;
17              link = linkValue;
18          }
19      }//End of Node<T> inner class
```

(continued)

Display 15.37 Set<T> Class (part 2 of 3)

```
20        private Node<T> head;

21        public Set( )
22        {
23              head = null;
24        }
25        /**
26         Add a new item to the set. If the item
27         is already in the set, false is returned;
28         otherwise, true is returned.
29        */
30        public boolean add(T newItem)
31        {
32              if (!contains(newItem))
33              {
34                    head = new Node<T>(newItem, head);
35                    return true;
36              }
37              return false;
38        }

39        public boolean contains(T item)
40        {
41            Node<T> position = head;
42            T itemAtPosition;
43            while (position != null)
44            {
45                itemAtPosition = position.data;
46                if (itemAtPosition.equals(item))
47                    return true;
48                position = position.link;
49            }
50            return false; //target was not found
51        }

52        public void output( )
53        {
54            Node position = head;
55            while (position != null)
56            {
57                System.out.print(position.data.toString( ) + " ");
58                position = position.link;
59            }
60            System.out.println( );
61        }
```

Display 15.37   `Set<T>` Class (part 3 of 3)

```
62      /**
63       Returns a new set that is the union
64       of this set and the input set.
65      */
66      public Set<T> union(Set<T> otherSet)
67      {
68              Set<T> unionSet = new Set<T>( );
69              // Copy this set to unionSet.
70              Node<T> position = head;
71              while (position != null)
72              {
73                      unionSet.add(position.data);
74                      position = position.link;
75              }
76              // Copy otherSet items to unionSet.
77              // The add method eliminates any duplicates.
78              position = otherSet.head;
79              while (position != null)
80              {
81                      unionSet.add(position.data);
82                      position = position.link;
83              }
84              return unionSet;
85      }

86      /**
87       Returns a new set that is the intersection
88       of this set and the input set.
89      */
90      public Set<T> intersection(Set<T> otherSet)
91      {
92              Set<T> interSet = new Set<T>( );
93              // Copy only items in both sets.
94              Node<T> position = head;
95              while (position != null)
96              {
97                      if (otherSet.contains(position.data))
98                          interSet.add(position.data);
99                      position = position.link;
100             }
101             return interSet;
102     }
103 }
```

The `clear`, `size`, and `isEmpty` methods are identical to those in Display 15.8 for the `LinkedList3` class.

Display 15.38   **Set Class Demo** (part 1 of 2)

```
1   public class SetDemo
2   {
3       public static void main(String[] args)
4       {
5           // Round things
6           Set round = new Set<String>( );
7           // Green things
8           Set green = new Set<String>( );

9           // Add some data to both sets
10          round.add("peas");
11          round.add("ball");
12          round.add("pie");
13          round.add("grapes");

14          green.add("peas");
15          green.add("grapes");
16          green.add("garden hose");
17          green.add("grass");

18          System.out.println("Contents of set round: ");
19          round.output( );
20          System.out.println("Contents of set green: ");
21          green.output( );
22          System.out.println( );

23          System.out.println("ball in set round? " +
24                  round.contains("ball"));
25          System.out.println("ball in set green? " +
26                  green.contains("ball"));
27          System.out.println("ball and peas in same set? " +
28                  ((round.contains("ball") &&
29                   (round.contains("peas"))) ||
30                  (green.contains("ball") &&
31                   (green.contains("peas")))));

32          System.out.println("pie and grass in same set? " +
33                  ((round.contains("pie") &&
34                   (round.contains("grass"))) ||
35                  (green.contains("pie") &&
36                   (green.contains("grass")))));

37          System.out.print("Union of green and round: ");
38          round.union(green).output( );
```

Display 15.38   **Set Class Demo** (part 2 of 2)

```
39              System.out.print("Intersection of green and round: ");
40              round.intersection(green).output( );
41      }
42  }
```

Sample Dialogue

```
Contents of set round:
grapes pie ball peas
Contents of set green:
Grass garden hose grapes peas

ball in set round? true
ball in set green? false
ball and peas in same set? true
pie and grass in same set? false
Union of green and round: garden hose grass peas ball pie grapes
Intersection of green and round: peas grapes
```

Efficiency of Sets Using Linked Lists

We can analyze the efficiency of our set data structure in terms of the fundamental set operations. Adding an item to the set always inserts a new node on the front of the list. This requires constant, or $O(1)$, steps. The contains method iterates through the entire set looking for the target, which requires $O(n)$ steps. When we invoke the union method for sets A and B, it iterates through both sets and adds each item into a new set. If there are n items in set A and m items in set B, then $n + m$ add methods are invoked. However, there is a hidden cost because the add method searches through its entire list for any duplicates before a new item is added. Although beyond the scope of this text, the additional cost results in $O(m + n)2$ steps. Finally, the intersection method applied to sets A and B invokes the contains method of set B for each item in set A. Because the contains method requires $O(m)$ steps for each item in set A, then this requires $O(m) \times O(n)$ steps, or $O(mn)$ steps. These are inefficient methods in our implementation of sets. A different approach to represent the set—for example, one that used hash tables instead of a linked list—could result in an intersection method that runs in $O(n + m)$ steps. Nevertheless, our linked list implementation would probably be fine for an application that uses small sets or for an application that does not frequently invoke the intersection method, and we have the benefit of relatively simple code that is easy to understand.

If we really need the efficiency, then we could maintain the same interface to the Set<T> class but replace our linked list implementation with something else. If we used the hash table implementation from Section 15.5, then the contains method could run in $O(1)$ steps instead of $O(n)$ steps. It might seem like the `intersection` method will now run in $O(n)$ steps, but by switching to a hash table, it becomes more difficult to iterate through the set of items. Instead of traversing a single linked list to retrieve every item in the set, the hash table version must now iterate through the hash table array and then for each index in the array iterate through the linked list at that index. If the array is size N and the number of items in the hash table is n, then the iteration time becomes $O(N + n)$. In practice, we would expect N to be larger than n. So although we have decreased the number of steps it takes to look up an item, we have increased the number of steps it takes to iterate over every item. If this is troublesome, you could overcome this problem with an implementation of `Set<T>` that uses both a linked list (to facilitate iteration) and a hash table (for fast lookup). However, the complexity of the code is significantly increased using such an approach. You are asked to explore the hash table implementation in Programming Project 15.10.

Self-Test Exercises

23. Write a method named `difference` that returns the difference between two sets. The method should return a new set that has items from the first set that are not in the second set. For example, if `setA` contains {1, 2, 3, 4} and `setB` contains {2, 4, 5}, then `setA.difference(setB)` should return the set {1, 3}.

24. What is the run time of the `difference` method for the previous question? Give your answer using big-O notation.

15.7 Trees

I think that I shall never see a data structure as useful as a tree.

ANONYMOUS

The tree data structure is an example of a more complicated data structure made with links. Moreover, trees are a very important and widely used data structure. So, we will briefly outline the general techniques used to construct and manipulate trees. This section is only a very brief introduction to trees to give you the flavor of the subject.

This section uses recursion, which is covered in Chapter 11.

Tree Properties

A tree is a data structure that is structured as shown in Display 15.39. In particular, in a tree you can reach any node from the top (root) node by some path that follows the links. Note that there are no cycles in a tree. If you follow the links, you eventually get to an "end." A definition for a tree class for this sort of tree of `ints` is outlined in Display 15.39. Note that each node has two references to other nodes (two links) coming from it. This sort of tree is called a **binary tree**, because each node has exactly

binary tree

two link instance variables. There are other kinds of trees with different numbers of link instance variables, but the binary tree is the most common case.

Display 15.39 **A Binary Tree**

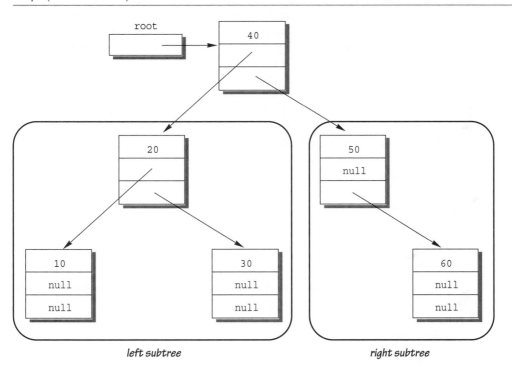

left subtree   right subtree

```
1   public class IntTree
2   {
3       public class IntTreeNode
4       {
5           private int data;
6           private IntTreeNode leftLink;
7           private IntTreeNode rightLink;
8       } //End of IntTreeNode inner class

9       private IntTreeNode root;
        <The methods and other inner classes are not shown.>

10  }
```

The instance variable named root serves a purpose similar to that of the instance variable head in a linked list (Display 15.3). The node whose reference is in the root instance variable is called the **root node**. Any node in the tree can be reached from the root node by following the links.

root node

The term *tree* may seem like a misnomer. The root is at the top of the tree, and the branching structure looks more like a root branching structure than a tree branching structure. The secret to the terminology is to turn the picture (Display 15.39) upside down. The picture then does resemble the branching structure of a tree, and the root node is where the tree's root would begin. The nodes at the ends of the branches with both link instance variables set to `null` are known as **leaf nodes**, a terminology that may now make some sense. By analogy to an empty linked list, an **empty tree** is denoted by setting the link variable `root` equal to `null`.

leaf node

empty tree

Note that a tree has a recursive structure. Each tree has, in effect, two subtrees whose root nodes are the nodes pointed to by the `leftLink` and `rightLink` of the root node. These two subtrees are circled in Display 15.39. This natural recursive structure makes trees particularly amenable to recursive algorithms. For example, consider the task of searching the tree in such a way that you visit each node and do something with the data in the node (such as writing it out to the screen). There is a general plan of attack that goes as follows:

Preorder Processing

1. Process the data in the root node.
2. Process the left subtree.
3. Process the right subtree.

Obtain a number of variants on this search process by varying the order of these three steps. Two more versions follow:

inorder

Inorder Processing

1. Process the left subtree.
2. Process the data in the root node.
3. Process the right subtree.

postorder

Postorder Processing

1. Process the left subtree.
2. Process the right subtree.
3. Process the data in the root node.

Binary Search
Tree Storage
Rule

The tree in Display 15.39 has numbers that were stored in the tree in a special way known as the **Binary Search Tree Storage Rule**. The rule is summarized in the following box.

Binary Search Tree Storage Rule

1. All the values in the left subtree are less than the value in the root node.
2. All the values in the right subtree are greater than or equal to the value in the root node.
3. This rule applies recursively to each of the two subtrees.

(The base case for the recursion is an empty tree, which is always considered to satisfy the rule.)

A tree that satisfies the Binary Search Tree Storage Rule is referred to as a **binary search tree**.

Note that if a tree satisfies the Binary Search Tree Storage Rule and you output the values using the Inorder Processing method, then the numbers will be output in order from smallest to largest.

For trees that follow the Binary Search Tree Storage Rule and that are short and fat rather than tall and thin, values can be very quickly retrieved from the tree using a binary search algorithm that is similar in spirit to the binary search algorithm we presented in Display 11.6. The topic of searching and maintaining a binary storage tree to realize this efficiency is a large topic that goes beyond what we have room for here. However, we give one example of a class for trees that satisfy the Binary Search Tree Storage Rule.

EXAMPLE: A Binary Search Tree Class ★

Display 15.40 contains the definition of a class for a binary search tree that satisfies the Binary Search Tree Storage Rule. For simplicity, this tree stores integers, but a routine modification can produce a similar tree class that stores objects of any class that implements the Comparable interface. Display 15.41 demonstrates the use of this tree class. Note that no matter in which order the integers are inserted into the tree, the output, which uses inorder traversal, outputs the integers in sorted order.

The methods in this class make extensive use of the recursive nature of binary trees. If aNode is a reference to any node in the tree (including possibly the root node), then the entire tree with root aNode can be decomposed into three parts:

1. The node aNode.
2. The left subtree with root node aNode.leftLink.
3. The right subtree with root node aNode.rightLink.

The left and right subtrees do themselves satisfy the Binary Search Tree Storage Rule, so it is natural to use recursion to process the entire tree by doing the following:

1. Processing the left subtree with root node aNode.leftLink
2. Processing the node aNode
3. Processing the right subtree with root node aNode.rightLink

Note that we processed the root node after the left subtree (inorder traversal). This guarantees that the numbers in the tree are output in the order smallest to largest. The method showElementsInSubtree uses a very straightforward implementation of this technique.

Other methods are a bit more subtle in that only one of the two subtrees needs to be processed. For example, consider the method isInSubtree, which returns true or false depending on whether or not the parameter item is in the tree with root node subTreeRoot. To see if the item is anyplace in the tree, set subTreeRoot equal

(continued)

EXAMPLE: (continued)

to the root of the entire tree, as we did in the method `contains`. However, to express our recursive algorithm for `isInSubtree`, we need to allow for the possibility of subtrees other than the entire tree.

The algorithm for `isInSubtree` expressed in pseudocode is as follows:

```
if (The root node subTreeRoot is empty.)
    return false;
else if (The node subTreeRoot contains item.)
  return true;
else if (item < subTreeRoot.data)
  return (The result of searching the tree
          with root node subTreeRoot.leftLink);
else
  //item > link.data
  return (The result of searching the tree
          with root node subTreeRoot.rightLink);
```

The reason this algorithm gives the correct result is that the tree satisfies the Binary Search Tree Storage Rule, so we know that if

```
item < subTreeRoot.data
```

then `item` is in the left subtree (if it is anywhere in the tree), and if

```
item > subTreeRoot.data
```

then `item` is in the right subtree (if it is anywhere in the tree).

The method with the following heading uses techniques very much like those used in `isInSubtree`:

```
private IntTreeNode insertInSubtree(
                int item, IntTreeNode subTreeRoot)
```

However, there is something new here. We want the method `insertInSubtree` to insert a new node with the data item into the tree with root node `subTreeRoot`. But in this case, we want to deal with `subTreeRoot` as a variable and not use it only as the value of the variable `subTreeRoot`. For example, if `subTreeRoot` contains `null`, then we want to change the value of `subTreeRoot` to a reference to a new node containing `item`. However, Java parameters cannot change the value of a variable given as an argument. (Review the discussion of parameters in Chapter 5 if this sounds unfamiliar.) So, we must do something a little different. To change the value of the variable `subTreeRoot`, we return a reference to what we want the new value to be, and we invoke the method `subTreeRoot` as follows:

```
subTreeRoot = insertInSubtree(item, subTreeRoot);
```

That explains why the method `insertInSubtree` returns a reference to a tree node, but we still have to explain why we know it returns a reference to the desired (modified) subtree.

EXAMPLE: (continued)

Note that the method `insertInSubtree` searches the tree just as the method `isInSubtree` does, but it does not stop if it finds `item`; instead, it searches until it reaches a leaf node—that is, a node containing `null`. This `null` is where the item belongs in the tree, so it replaces `null` with a new subtree containing a single node that contains `item`. You may need to think about the method `insertInSubtree` a bit to see that it works correctly; allow yourself some time to study the method `insertInSubtree` and be sure you are convinced that after the addition, like the following,

```
subTreeRoot = insertInSubtree(item, subTreeRoot);
```

the tree with root node `subTreeRoot` still satisfies the Binary Search Tree Storage Rule.

The rest of the definition of the class `IntTree` is routine.

Display 15.40 **A Binary Search Tree for Integers** (part 1 of 2)

```
1   /**
2    Class invariant: The tree satisfies the binary search tree storage rule.
3    */
4   public class IntTree
5   {
6       private static class IntTreeNode    ←————————
7       {
8           private int data;
9           private IntTreeNode leftLink;
10          private IntTreeNode rightLink;
11
12          public IntTreeNode(int newData, IntTreeNode newLeftLink,
13                                           IntTreeNode newRightLink)
14          {
15              data = newData;
16              leftLink = newLeftLink;
17              rightLink = newRightLink;
18          }
19      } //End of IntTreeNode inner class
20
21      private IntTreeNode root;
22
23      public IntTree( )
24      {
25          root = null;    ←
26      }
27
28      public void add(int item)
29      {
30          root = insertInSubtree(item, root);
31      }
```

The only reason this inner class is static is that it is used in the static methods insertInSubtree, isInSubtree, and showElementsInSubtree.

This class should have more methods. This is just a sample of possible methods.

(continued)

Display 15.40 **A Binary Search Tree for Integers** (part 2 of 2)

```java
29      public boolean contains(int item)
30      {
31          return isInSubtree(item, root);
32      }

33      public void showElements( )
34      {
35          showElementsInSubtree(root);
36      }
37      /**
38       Returns the root node of a tree that is the tree with root node
39       subTreeRoot, but with a new node added that contains item.
40       */
41      private static IntTreeNode insertInSubtree(int item,
42                                          IntTreeNode subTreeRoot)
43      {
44          if (subTreeRoot == null)
45              return new IntTreeNode(item, null, null);
46          else if (item < subTreeRoot.data)
47          {
48              subTreeRoot.leftLink = insertInSubtree(item, subTreeRoot.
                                                  leftLink);
49              return subTreeRoot;
50          }
51          else //item >= subTreeRoot.data
52          {
53              subTreeRoot.rightLink = insertInSubtree(item, subTreeRoot.
                                                  rightLink);
54              return subTreeRoot;
55          }
56      }

57      private static boolean isInSubtree(int item, IntTreeNode
                                                  subTreeRoot)
58      {
59          if (subTreeRoot == null)
60              return false;
61          else if (subTreeRoot.data == item)
62              return true;
63          else if (item < subTreeRoot.data)
64              return isInSubtree(item, subTreeRoot.leftLink);
65          else //item >= link.data
66              return isInSubtree(item, subTreeRoot.rightLink);
67      }

68      private static void showElementsInSubtree(IntTreeNode subTreeRoot)
69      { //Uses inorder traversal.
70          if (subTreeRoot != null)
71          {
72              showElementsInSubtree(subTreeRoot.leftLink);
73              System.out.print(subTreeRoot.data + " ");
74              showElementsInSubtree(subTreeRoot.rightLink);
75          } //else do nothing. Empty tree has nothing to display.
76      }
77  }
```

Display 15.41   Demonstration Program for the Binary Search Tree

```
1   import java.util.Scanner;

2   public class BinarySearchTreeDemo
3   {
4       public static void main(String[] args)
5       {
6           Scanner keyboard = new Scanner(System.in);
7           IntTree tree = new IntTree( );

8           System.out.println("Enter a list of nonnegative integers.");
9           System.out.println("Place a negative integer at the end.");
10          int next = keyboard.nextInt( );
11          while (next >= 0)
12          {
13              tree.add(next);
14              next = keyboard.nextInt( );
15          }

16          System.out.println("In sorted order:");
17          tree.showElements( );
18      }
19  }
```

Sample Dialogue

```
Enter a list of nonnegative integers.
Place a negative integer at the end.
40
30
20
10
11
22
33
44
-1
In sorted order:
10 11 20 22 30 33 40 44
```

Efficiency of Binary Search Trees ★

When searching a tree that is as short as possible (all paths from root to a leaf differ by at most one node), the search method isInSubtree, and hence also the method contains, is about as efficient as the binary search on a sorted array (Display 11.6). This should not be a surprise because the two algorithms are in fact very similar. In big-O notation, the worst-case running time is $O(\log n)$, where n is the number of nodes in the tree. This means that searching a short, fat binary tree is very efficient. To obtain this efficiency, the tree does not need to be as short as possible so long as it comes close to being as short as possible. As the tree becomes less short and fat and more tall and thin, the efficiency falls off until, in the extreme case, the efficiency is the same as that of searching a linked list with the same number of nodes.

Maintaining a tree so that it remains short and fat as nodes are added is a topic that is beyond the scope of what we have room for in this book. (The technical term for short and fat is *balanced*.) We will note only that if the numbers that are stored in the tree arrive in random order, then with very high probability the tree will be short and fat enough to realize the efficiency discussed in the previous paragraph.

Self-Test Exercises

25. Suppose that the code for the method showElementsInSubtree in Display 15.40 were changed so that

    ```
    showElementsInSubtree(subTreeRoot.leftLink);
    System.out.print(subTreeRoot.data + " ");
    showElementsInSubtree(subTreeRoot.rightLink);
    ```

    were changed to

    ```
    System.out.print(subTreeRoot.data + " ");
    showElementsInSubtree(subTreeRoot.leftLink);
    showElementsInSubtree(subTreeRoot.rightLink);
    ```

    Will the numbers still be output in ascending order?

26. How can you change the code for the method showElementsInSubtree in Display 15.40 so that the numbers are output from largest to smallest instead of from smallest to largest?

Chapter Summary

- A *linked list* is a data structure consisting of objects known as *nodes*, such that each node contains data and also a reference to one other node so that the nodes link together to form a list.

- Setting a link instance variable to `null` indicates the end of a linked list (or other linked data structure). `null` is also used to indicate an empty linked list (or other empty linked data structure).

- You can make a linked list (or other linked data structure) self-contained by making the node class an inner class of the linked list class.

- In many situations, a `clone` method or copy constructor is best defined so that it makes a deep copy.

- You can use an *iterator* to step through the elements of a collection, such as the elements in a linked list.

- Nodes in a *doubly linked list* have two links—one to the previous node in the list and one to the next node. This makes some operations, such as insertion and deletion, slightly easier.

- A *stack* is a data structure in which elements are removed in the reverse of the order they were added to the stack. A *queue* is a data structure in which elements are removed in the same order that they were added to the queue.

- *Big-O notation* specifies an upper bound for how many steps or how long a program will take to run based on the size of the input to the program. This can be used to analyze the efficiency of an algorithm.

- A *hash table* is a data structure that is used to store objects and retrieve them efficiently. A *hash function* is used to map an object to a value that can then be used to index the object.

- Linked lists can be used to implement sets, including common operations such as union, intersection, and set membership.

- A *binary tree* is a branching linked data structure consisting of nodes that each have two link instance variables. A tree has a special node called the *root node*. Every node in the tree can be reached from the root node by following links.

- If values are stored in a binary tree in such a way that the *Binary Search Tree Storage Rule* is followed, then there are efficient algorithms for reaching values stored in the tree.

Answers to Self-Test Exercises

1. ```
   mustard 1
   hot dogs 12
   apple pie 1
   ```

2. This method has been added to the class `LinkedList1` on the accompanying website.

   ```
   public boolean isEmpty( )
   {
       return (head == null);
   }
   ```

3. This method has been added to the class `LinkedList1` on the accompanying website.

   ```
   public void clear( )
   {
       head = null;
   }
   ```

   If you defined your method to remove all nodes using the `deleteHeadNode` method, your method is doing wasted work.

4. Yes. If we make the inner class `Node` a public inner class, it could be used outside the definition of `LinkedList2`, whereas leaving it as private means it cannot be used outside the definition of `LinkedList2`.

5. It would make no difference. Within the definition of an outer class, there is full access to the members of an inner class whatever the inner class member's access modifier is. To put it another way, inside the private inner class `Node`, the modifiers `private` and `package access` are equivalent to `public`.

6. Because the outer class has direct access to the instance variables of the inner class `Node`, no access or mutator methods are needed for `Node`.

7. It would be legal, but it would be pretty much a useless method, because you cannot use the type `Node` outside of the class `LinkedList2`. For example, outside of the class `LinkedList2`, the following is illegal (`listObject` is of type `LinkedList2`),

   ```
   Node v = listObject.startNode( ); //Illegal
   ```

   whereas the following would be legal outside of the class `LinkedList2` (although it is hard to think of anyplace you might use it):

   ```
   Object v = listObject.startNode( );
   ```

8. ```
   public class LinkedList2
   {
       public class Entry
       {
         private String item;
         private int count;

         public Entry( )
   ```

```java
        {
            item = null;
            count = 0;
        }

        public Entry(String itemData, int countData)
        {
            item = itemData;
            count = countData;
        }

        public void setItem(String itemData)
        {
            item = itemData;
        }

        public void setCount(int countData)
        {
            count = countData;
        }

        public String getItem( )
        {
            return item;
        }

        public int getCount( )
        {
            return count;
        }
    } // End of Entry inner class

    private class Node
    {
        private Entry item;
        private Node link;

        public Node( )
        {
            item = null;
            link = null;
        }
```

```
        public Node(Entry newItem, Node linkValue)
        {
            item = newItem;
            link = linkValue;
        }
    } //End of Node inner class

    private Node head;

    <Other definitions from LinkedList2 go here>

} //End of LinkedList2 class
```

The rest of the definition of LinkedList2 is essentially the same as in Display 15.7, but with the type String replaced by Entry. A complete definition is given in the subdirectory named "Exercise 8" on the website that accompanies this text.

9. No, T is not guaranteed to have a copy constructor. Even if T has a copy constructor, it is illegal to use T with new like this.

10. No, you can use any descendent class of Object (which means any class type) as the returned type, because the value returned will still be of type Object.

11. The delete method must now search through the list to find the previous node and then change the link to bypass the current position. This is less efficient than the code in Display 15.17 because the reference to the previous node is already set.

```
public void delete( )
{
    if (position == null)
    {
        throw new IllegalStateException( );
    }
    else
    {
        Node current = head;
        Node previous = null;
        while (current != null)
        {
            if (current == position)
            {
                // Found the node to delete
                // Check if we're at the head
                if (previous == null)
                {
                    head = head.link;
                    position = head;
                }
```

```
              else // Delete in middle of list
              {
                  previous.link = position.link;
                  position = position.link;
              }
              return;
          }
          previous = current;  // Advance references
          current = current.link;
      }
    }
}
```

12. One problem with adding after the iterator's position is that there is no way to add to the front of the list. It would be possible to make a special case in which the new node were added to the front (e.g., if position is null, add the new data to the head) if desired.

```
public void addAfterHere(String newData)
{
    if (position == null && head != null)
    {
        // At end of list; can't add here
        throw new IllegalStateException( );
    }
    else if (head == null)
        // at head of empty list, add to front
        LinkedList2Iter.this.addToStart(newData);
    else
    {
        // Add after current position
        Node temp = new Node(newData, position.link);
        position.link = temp;
    }
}
```

13.
```
public void changeHere(String newData)
{
    if (position == null)
        throw new IllegalStateException( );
    else
        position.item = newData;
}
```

14. When invoking i.next( ), the value of the node that i is referencing is copied to a local variable, the iterator moves to the next node in the link, and then the value of the local variable is returned. Therefore, the value that i is referencing prior to the invocation is returned.

15. Insertion and deletion is slightly easier with the doubly linked list because we no longer need a separate instance variable to keep track of the previous node due to the previous link. However, all operations require updating more links (e.g., both the next and previous instead of just the previous).

16. Use the iterator:

```
DoublyLinkedList.DoublyLinkedIterator i = list.iterator( );
i.restart( );
i.insertHere("Element At Front");
```

17. Pop the top of the stack and then push it back on:

```
String s = stack.pop( );
Stack.push(s);
// s contains the string on the top of the stack
```

18.
```
public void addToBack(String itemName)
{
    Node newEntry =
        new Node(itemName, null);
    if (front == null) //empty queue
    {
        back = newEntry;
        front = back;
    }
    else
    {
        back.link = newEntry;
        back = back.link;
    }
}
```

19. Just note that $aN + b \leq (a + b)N$, as long as $1 \leq N$.

20. This is mathematics, not Java. So, $=$ will mean *equals*, not assignment.

First note that $\log_a N = (\log_a b)(\log_b N)$.

To see this first identity, just note that if you raise a to the power $\log_a N$, you get N, and if you raise a to the power $(\log_a b)(\log_b N)$, you also get N.

If you set $c = (\log_a b)$, you get $\log_a N = c\,(\log_b N)$.

21. The simplest hash function is to map the ID number to the range of the hash table using the modulus operator:

```
hash = ID % N; // N is the hash table size
```

22.
```
public void outputHashTable( )
{
    for (int i=0; i< SIZE; i++)
    {
        if (hashArray[i].size( ) > 0)
            hashArray[i].outputList( );
    }
}
```

23. This code is similar to `intersection`, but adds elements if they are not in `otherSet`:

```
public Set<T> difference(Set<T> otherSet)
{
    Set<T> diffSet = new Set<T>( );
    // Copy only items in this set but not otherSet
    Node<T> position = head;
    while (position != null)
    {
        if (!otherSet.contains(position.data))
            diffSet.add(position.data);
        position = position.link;
    }
    return diffSet;
}
```

24. As implemented in Answer 23, the complexity is identical to the `intersection` method. For every element in the set, we invoke the `contains` method of `otherSet`. This requires $O(nm)$ steps, where n is the number of items in the calling object's set and m is the number of items in `otherSet`'s set.

25. No.

26. Change

```
showElementsInSubtree(subTreeRoot.leftLink);
System.out.print(subTreeRoot.data + " ");
showElementsInSubtree(subTreeRoot.rightLink);
```

to

```
showElementsInSubtree(subTreeRoot.rightLink);
System.out.print(subTreeRoot.data + " ");
showElementsInSubtree(subTreeRoot.leftLink);
```

MyProgrammingLab™ ## Programming Projects

Visit www.myprogramminglab.com to complete select exercises online and get instant feedback.

VideoNote
Solution to
Programming
Project 15.1

1. In an ancient land, the beautiful princess Eve had many suitors. She decided on the following procedure to determine which suitor she would marry. First, all of the suitors would be lined up one after the other and assigned numbers. The first suitor would be number 1, the second number 2, and so on up to the last suitor, number n. Starting at the suitor in the first position, she would then count three suitors down the line

(because of the three letters in her name), and the third suitor would be eliminated from winning her hand and removed from the line. Eve would then continue, counting three more suitors, and eliminate every third suitor. When she reached the end of the line, she would continue counting from the beginning.

For example, if there were six suitors, the elimination process would proceed as follows:

123456	Initial list of suitors; start counting from 1.
12456	Suitor 3 eliminated; continue counting from 4.
1245	Suitor 6 eliminated; continue counting from 1.
125	Suitor 4 eliminated; continue counting from 5.
15	Suitor 2 eliminated; continue counting from 5.
1	Suitor 5 eliminated; 1 is the lucky winner.

Write a program that creates a circular linked list of nodes to determine which position you should stand in to marry the princess if there are *n* suitors. Your program should simulate the elimination process by deleting the node that corresponds to the suitor that is eliminated for each step in the process.

2. Write a program that takes its input from a binary file of numbers of type `double`. The file contains statistical data from of type `double`. Your program should collect this data from the file and store it in the memory using an appropriate linked list class. The program outputs to the screen

- the highest number in the list
- the lowest number in the list
- the average and standard deviation of the numbers in the file.

The standard deviation of a list of numbers n1, n2, n3, and so forth is defined as the square root of the average of the following numbers:

$(n1 - a)^2$, $(n2 - a)^2$, $(n3 - a)^2$, and so forth.

The number a is the average of the numbers n1, n2, n3, and so forth.

3. Add a copy constructor to the `HugeNumber` class described in the previous problem that makes a deep copy of the input `HugeNumber`. Also create an `add` method that adds an input `HugeNumber` to the instance's `HugeNumber` value and returns a new `HugeNumber` that is set to the sum of the two values. Write code to test the additions to your class.

4. Give the definition of a generic class that uses a doubly linked list of data items. Include a copy constructor, an `equals` method, a `clone` method, a `toString` method, a method to produce an iterator, and any other methods that would normally be expected. Write a suitable test program.

5. Complete the definition of the binary search tree class `IntTree` in Display 15.39 by adding the following: Make `IntTree` implement the `Cloneable` interface, including the definition of a `clone` method; add a copy constructor; add an

equals method; add a method named sameContents as described later in this project; add a toString method; and add a method to produce an iterator. Define equals so that two trees are equal if (and only if) the two trees have the exact same shape and have the same numbers in corresponding nodes. The clone method and the copy constructor should each produce a deep copy that is equal to the original list according to the equals method. The boolean valued method sameContents has one parameter of type IntTree and returns true if the calling object and the argument tree contain exactly the same numbers, and returns false otherwise. Note that equals and sameContents are not the same. Also, write a suitable test program.

6. Write an addSorted method for the generic linked list from Display 15.8 such that the method adds a new node in the correct location so that the list remains in sorted order. Note that this will require that the type parameter T extend the Comparable interface. Write a suitable test program.

7. Add a remove method and an iterator for the Set class in Display 15.37. Write a suitable test program.

8. The hash table from Display 15.34 hashed a string to an integer and stored the same string in the hash table. Modify the program so that instead of storing strings, it stores Employee objects as defined in Display 7.2. Use the name instance variable as the input to the hash function. The modification will require changes to the linked list, because the LinkedList2 class created only linked lists of strings. For the most generality, modify the hash table so that it uses the generic LinkedList3 class defined in Display 15.8. You will also need to add a get method that returns the Employee object stored in the hash table that corresponds to the input name. Test your program by adding and retrieving several names, including names that hash to the same slot in the hash table.

9. Display 15.34 and 15.35 provide the beginnings of a spell-checker. Refine the program to make it more useful. The modified program should read in a text file, parse each word, see if it is in the hash table, and, if not, output the line number and word of the potentially misspelled word. Discard any punctuation in the original text file. Use the words.txt file as the basis for the hash table dictionary. This file can be found on the book's website. The file contains 87,314 words in the English language. Test your spell-checker on a short text document.

10. Write a class HighScores that keeps track of the high scores that could be used for a video game. Internally, the class should store the top scores in a linked list data structure. Each entry consists of a name and a score. The class should have methods to display the highest score in the list along with the player name, and to search for a player and return his/her score. Write a program to test the class Highscore.

11. The following figure is called a *graph*. The circles are called *nodes* and the lines are called *edges*. An edge connects two nodes. You can interpret the graph as a maze of rooms and passages. The nodes can be thought of as rooms, and an edge connects one room to another. Note that each node has at most four edges in the graph that follows.

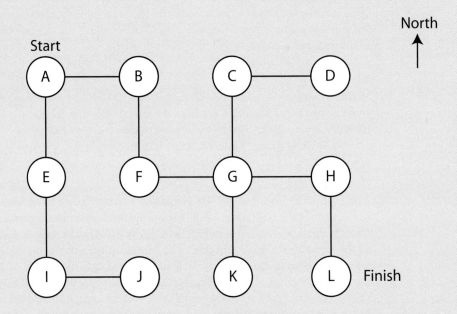

Write a program that implements the previous maze using references to instances of a Node class. Each node in the graph will correspond to an instance of Node. The edges correspond to links that connect one node to another and can be represented in Node as instance variables that reference another Node class. Start the user in node A. The user's goal is to reach the finish in node L. The program should output possible moves in the north, south, east, or west direction. Sample execution is shown next.

```
You are in room A of a maze of twisty little passages, all
alike. You can go east or south.
E
You are in room B of a maze of twisty little passages, all
alike. You can go west or south.
S
You are in room F of a maze of twisty little passages, all
alike. You can go north or east.
E
```

Collections, Maps and Iterators

16.1 COLLECTIONS   930
Wildcards   932
The Collection Framework   932
Concrete Collection Classes   940
Differences between `ArrayList<T>` and
   `Vector<T>`   950
Nonparameterized Version of the Collection
   Framework ★   950

16.2 MAPS   951
Concrete Map Classes   954

16.3 ITERATORS   958
The Iterator Concept   958
The `Iterator<T>` Interface   958
List Iterators   962

16 Collections, Maps and Iterators

Science is built up with facts, as a house is with stones. But a collection of facts is no more science than a heap of stones is a house.

Jules Henri Poincarè, Quoted by Bertrand Russell in the preface to
Science and Method

Introduction

collection

iterator

A **collection** is a data structure for holding elements. For example, an `ArrayList<T>` object is a collection. Java has a repertoire of interfaces and classes that give a uniform treatment of collections. An **iterator** is an object that cycles through all the elements in a collection. In this chapter, we discuss collections and iterators.

Prerequisites

Sections 16.1 to 16.3 can be considered one single large topic. These three sections require Chapters 1 through 9, Section 13.1 of Chapter 13, which covers interfaces, Chapter 14 on generics and the `ArrayList<T>` class, and Chapter 15 on linked data structures. The material on inner classes in Chapter 13 (Sections 13.2 and 13.3) is not needed except for a brief reference in the Programming Tip entitled "Defining Your Own Iterator Classes," which requires Section 13.2 (but not 13.3).

None of the material in this chapter is needed to understand Swing and GUIs. So, you may skip this and go directly to Chapter 17 if you prefer to cover Swing GUIs before considering the material of this chapter.

16.1 Collections

*Put all your eggs in one basket and
—WATCH THAT BASKET.*

MARK TWAIN, Pudd'nhead Wilson

A Java collection is a class that holds objects. This concept is made precise by the `Collection<T>` interface. A Java collection is any class that implements the `Collection<T>` interface. As we shall see, many of these classes can be used as predefined data structures similar to those we defined ourselves in Chapter 15. One example of a Java collection class, which you saw in Chapter 14, is the `ArrayList<T>` class. The `Collection<T>` interface allows you to write code that applies to all Java collections so that you do not have to rewrite the code for each specific collection type. There are other interfaces and abstract classes that are in some sense or another produced from the `Collection<T>` interface. Some of these are shown in Display 16.1. In this section, we give you an introduction to this Java collection framework. The topic is too large to treat exhaustively in this book, so this can only be an introductory treatment.

Display 16.1   The Collection Landscape

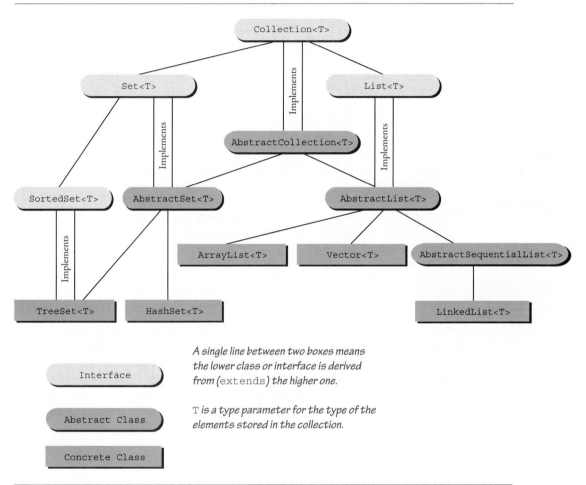

Collections are used along with *iterators*, which are discussed in Section 16.3. Separating collections and iterators into two sections turns out to be a handy way of organizing the material, but the two topics are intimately intertwined. In practice, you normally use them together.

Before we discuss the `Collection<T>` interface, we need a brief detour to learn a bit more about parameter type specifications.

Wildcards

Classes and interfaces in the collection framework use some parameter type specifications that we have not seen before. For example, they allow you to say things such as, "The argument must be a `ArrayList<T>` but it can have any base type." More generally these new parameter type specifications use generic classes but do not fully specify the type plugged in for the type parameter. Because they specify a wide range of argument types, they are known as **wildcards**.

wildcard<?>   The easiest wildcard to understand is `<?>`, which says that you can use any type in place of the type parameter. For example,

```
public void sampleMethod(String arg1, ArrayList<?> arg2)
```

is invoked with two arguments. The first argument must be of type `String`. The second argument can be a `ArrayList<T>` with any base type.

Note that `ArrayList<?>` is different from `ArrayList<Object>`. For example, if the type specification is `ArrayList<?>`, then you can plug in an argument of type `ArrayList<String>` (as well as other types); you cannot plug in an argument of type `ArrayList<String>` if the type specification is `ArrayList<Object>`.

You can place a bound on a wildcard saying the type used in place of the wildcard must be an ancestor type or a descendent type of some class or interface. For example,

extends   `<? extends String>` says that the argument plugged in can be an object of any descendent class of the class `String`. The notation, restrictions, and meaning are the same as what we described for type bounds such as `<T extends String>`, which we discussed in Chapter 14.

For example,

```
public void
    anotherMethod(String arg1, ArrayList<? extends String> arg2)
```

is invoked with two arguments. The first argument must be of type `String`, but the second argument can be of any `ArrayList<T>` object provided the base type of the `ArrayList<T>` is a descendent type of `String`.

super   To specify that the wildcard type be an ancestor type of some class or interface, use `super` rather than `extends`. For example, `ArrayList<? super String>` specifies an `ArrayList<T>` whose base type can be any ancestor class of the class `String`. As it turns out, we will have no occasion to use wildcard types involving `super`.

The Collection Framework

Collection<T>   The `Collection<T>` interface is the highest level of Java's framework for collection
interface   classes. This interface describes the basic operations that all collection classes should implement. A summary of these operations (method headings) for the `Collection<T>` interface are given in Display 16.2. A more complete description can be found in Appendix 5. Because an interface is a type, you can define methods with a parameter of type `Collection<T>`. That parameter can be filled in with an argument that is an object of any class in the collection framework (that is, any class that implements the

Collection<T> interface). This turns out to be a very powerful tool. Let us explore the possibilities. So far, we have seen one class that implements the Collection<T> interface, namely the class ArrayList<T>. In addition to the methods given in Chapter 14 for the ArrayList<T> class, the ArrayList<T> class also implements all the methods given in Display 16.2. There are a number of different predefined classes that implement the Collection<T> interface, and you can define your own classes to do this. If you write a method to manipulate a parameter of type Collection<T>, it will work for all of these classes. Also, the methods in the Collection<T> interface ensure that you can intermix the use of different collection classes. For example, consider the method

```
public boolean containsAll(Collection<?> collectionOfTargets)
```

You can use this with two ArrayList<T> objects (the calling object and the argument) to see if one contains all the elements of the other. The two ArrayList<T> objects do not even have to have the same base type. Moreover, you can also use it with an ArrayList<T> object and an object of any other class that implements the Collection<T> interface to compare the elements in these two different kinds of Collection<T> objects.

Display 16.2   Method Headings in the Collection<T> Interface (part 1 of 3)

The Collection<T> interface is in the java.util package.

CONSTRUCTORS

Although not officially required by the interface, any class that implements the Collection<T> interface should have at least two constructors: a no-argument constructor that creates an empty Collection<T> object, and a constructor with one parameter of type Collection<? extends T> that creates a Collection<T> object with the same elements as the constructor argument. The interface does not specify whether the copy produced by the one-argument constructor is a shallow copy or a deep copy of its argument.

METHODS

```
boolean isEmpty()
```
Returns true if the calling object is empty; otherwise returns false.

```
public boolean contains(Object target)
```
Returns true if the calling object contains at least one instance of target. Uses target.equals to determine if target is in the calling object.

```
public boolean containsAll(Collection<?> collectionOfTargets)
```
Returns true if the calling object contains all of the elements in collectionOfTargets. For an element in collectionOfTargets, this method uses element.equals to determine if element is in the calling object.

(continued)

`public boolean equals(Object other)`

This is the `equals` of the collection, not the `equals` of the elements in the collection. Overrides the inherited method `equals`. Although there are no official constraints on `equals` for a collection, it should be defined as we have described in Chapter 7 and also to satisfy the intuitive notion of collections being equal.

`public int size()`

Returns the number of elements in the calling object. If the calling object contains more than `Integer.MAX_VALUE` elements, returns `Integer.MAX_VALUE`.

`Iterator<T> iterator()`

Returns an iterator for the calling object. (Iterators are discussed in Section 16.3.)

`public Object[ ] toArray()`

Returns an array containing all of the elements in the calling object. If the calling object makes any guarantees as to what order its elements are returned by its iterator, this method must return the elements in the same order.

The array returned should be a new array so that the calling object has no references to the returned array. (You might also want the elements in the array to be clones of the elements in the collection. However, this is apparently not required by the interface, because library classes, such as `Vector<T>`, return arrays that contain references to the elements in the collection.)

`public <E> E[ ] toArray(E[ ] a)`

Note that the type parameter E is not the same as `T`. So, E can be any reference type; it need not be the type `T` in `Collection<T>`. For example, E might be an ancestor type of `T`.

Returns an array containing all of the elements in the calling object. The argument a is used primarily to specify the type of the array returned. The exact details are described next.

The type of the returned array is that of a. If the elements in the calling object fit in the array a, then a is used to hold the elements of the returned array; otherwise a new array is created with the same type as a.

If a has more elements than the calling object, the element in a immediately following the end of the copied elements is set to `null`.

If the calling object makes any guarantees as to what order its elements are returned by its iterator, this method must return the elements in the same order. (Iterators are discussed in Section 16.3.)

`public int hashCode()`

Returns the hash code value for the calling object. The hash code is a numeric key that is ideally a unique identifier for the calling object. (Hash codes are discussed in Section 15.5.)

Display 16.2   Method Headings in the `Collection<T>` Interface (part 3 of 3)

OPTIONAL METHODS

The following methods are optional, which means they still must be implemented, but the implementation can simply throw an `UnsupportedOperationException` if, for some reason, you do not want to give them a "real" implementation. An `UnsupportedOperationException` is a `RunTimeException` and so is not required to be caught or declared in a `throws` clause.

`public boolean` `add(T element)` *(Optional)*

Ensures that the calling object contains the specified `element`. Returns `true` if the calling object changes as a result of the call. Returns `false` if the calling object does not permit duplicates and already contains `element`; also returns `false` if the calling object does not change for any other reason.

`public boolean` `addAll(Collection<? extends T> collectionToAdd)` *(Optional)*

Ensures that the calling object contains all the elements in `collectionToAdd`. Returns `true` if the calling object changes as a result of the call; returns `false` otherwise.

`public boolean` `remove(Object element)` *(Optional)*

Removes a single instance of the element from the calling object, if it is present. Returns `true` if the calling object contained the element; returns `false` otherwise.

`public boolean` `removeAll(Collection<?> collectionToRemove)` *(Optional)*

Removes all the calling object's elements that are also contained in `collectionToRemove`. Returns `true` if the calling object is changed; otherwise returns `false`.

`public void` `clear()` *(Optional)*

Removes all the elements from the calling object.

`public boolean` `retainAll(Collection<?> saveElements)` *(Optional)*

Retains only the elements in the calling object that are also contained in the collection `saveElements`. In other words, removes from the calling object all of its elements that are not contained in the collection `saveElements`. Returns `true` if the calling object is changed; otherwise returns `false`.

> **Packages**
>
> All the collection classes and interfaces discussed in this chapter are in the `java.util` package.

Set<T> and List<T> interfaces

The relationships between some of the classes and interfaces that implement or extend the `Collection<T>` interface are given in Display 16.1. There are two main interfaces that extend the `Collection<T>` interface: the `Set<T>` interface and the `List<T>` interface. Classes that implement the `Set<T>` interface do not allow an element in the class to occur more than once. Classes that implement the `List<T>` interface have their elements ordered on a list, so there is a zeroth element, a first element, a second element, and so forth. A class that implements the `List<T>` interface allows elements to occur more than once. The `ArrayList<T>` class implements the `List<T>` interface.

The `Set<T>` interface has the same method headings as the `Collection<T>` interface, but in some cases the semantics (intended meanings) are different. For example, the semantics of adding new elements to the set do not allow duplicates. The add methods are described in Display 16.3. A complete list of the `Set<T>` interface is given in Appendix 5.

Display 16.3   Adding Elements in the `Set<T>` Interface

The `Set<T>` interface is in the `java.util` package.

The `Set<T>` interface extends the `Collection<T>` interface and has all the same method headings given in Display 16.2. However, the semantics of the add methods vary as described below.

```
public boolean add(T element) (Optional)
```

If `element` is not already in the calling object, `element` is added to the calling object and `true` is returned. If `element` is in the calling object, the calling object is unchanged and `false` is returned.

```
public boolean addAll(Collection<? extends > collectionToAdd) (Optional)
```

Ensures that the calling object contains all the elements in `collectionToAdd`. Returns `true` if the calling object changed as a result of the call; returns `false` otherwise. Thus, if `collectionToAdd` is a `Set<T>`, then the calling object is changed to the union of itself with `collectionToAdd`.

The `List<T>` interface has more method headings than the `Collection<T>` interface, and some of the methods inherited from the `Collection<T>` interface receive somewhat different semantics. For example, the semantics of adding new elements to the set allow duplicates, and rules must be made about which element should be removed when there are duplicates. These methods, along with new method definitions, are described in Display 16.4. A complete list of the `List<T>` interface is given in Appendix 5.

Display 16.4   Selected Methods in the `List<T>` Interface (part 1 of 3)

The `List<T>` interface is in the `java.util` package.

The `List<T>` interface extends the `Collection<T>` interface.

ADDING AND REMOVING ELEMENTS

```
public boolean add(T element) (Optional)
```

Adds element to the end of the calling object's list. Normally returns `true`. Returns `false` if the operation failed, but if the operation failed, something is seriously wrong and you will probably get a run-time error anyway.

```
public boolean addAll(Collection<? extends T> collectionToAdd) (Optional)
```

Adds all of the elements in `collectionToAdd` to the end of the calling object's list. The elements are added in the order they are produced by an iterator for `collectionToAdd`.

```
public boolean remove(Object element) (Optional)
```

Removes the first occurrence of element from the calling object's list, if it is present. Returns `true` if the calling object contained the element; returns `false` otherwise.

```
public boolean removeAll(Collection<?> collectionToRemove) (Optional)
```

Removes all the calling object's elements that are also in `collectionToRemove`. Returns `true` if the calling object was changed; otherwise returns `false`.

NEW METHOD HEADINGS

The following methods are in the `List<T>` interface but were not in the `Collection<T>` interface. Those that are optional are noted.

```
public void add(int index, T newElement) (Optional)
```

Inserts `newElement` in the calling object's list at location `index`. The old elements at location `index` and higher are moved to higher indices.

```
public boolean addAll(int index,
              Collection<? extends T> collectionToAdd) (Optional)
```

Inserts all of the elements in `collectionToAdd` to the calling object's list starting at location `index`. The old elements at location `index` and higher are moved to higher indices. The elements are added in the order they are produced by an iterator for `collectionToAdd`.

```
public T get(int index)
```
Returns the object at position `index`.

```
public T set(int index, T newElement) (Optional)
```

Sets the element at the specified index to `newElement`. The element previously at that position is returned.

```
public T remove(int index) (Optional)
```

Removes the element at position `index` in the calling object. Shifts any subsequent elements to the left (subtracts one from their indices). Returns the element that was removed from the calling object.

```
public int indexOf(Object target)
```
Returns the index of the first element that is equal to `target`. Uses the method `equals` of the object `target` to test for equality. Returns 1 if `target` is not found.

(continued)

Display 16.4   Selected Methods in the `List<T>` Interface (part 3 of 3)

`public int lastIndexOf(Object target)`

Returns the index of the last element that is equal to `target`. Uses the method `equals` of the object `target` to test for equality. Returns 1 if target is not found.

`public List<T> subList(int fromIndex, int toIndex)`

Returns a *view* of the elements at locations `fromIndex` to `toIndex` of the calling object; the object at `fromIndex` is included; the object, if any, at `toIndex` is not included. The *view* uses references into the calling object; so, changing the view can change the calling object. The returned object will be of type `List<T>` but need not be of the same type as the calling object. Returns an empty `List<T>` if fromIndex equals toIndex.

`ListIterator<T> listIterator()`

Returns a list iterator for the calling object. (Iterators are discussed in Section 16.3.)

`ListIterator<T> listIterator(int index)`

Returns a list iterator for the calling object starting at `index`. The first element to be returned by the iterator is the one at `index`. (Iterators are discussed in Section 16.3.)

Collection Interfaces

The primary interfaces for collection classes are the `Collection<T>`, `Set<T>`, and `List<T>` interfaces. Both the `Set<T>` and the `List<T>` interfaces are derived from the `Collection<T>` interface. The `Set<T>` interface is for collections that do not allow repetition of elements and do not impose an order on their elements. The `List<T>` interface is for collections that do allow repetition of elements and do impose an order on their elements.

For-Each Loops

You can use a for-each loop with any of the collections discussed in this chapter.

PITFALL: Optional Operations

What is the point of an optional method heading in an interface? The whole purpose of an interface is to specify what methods can be used with an object of the interface type so that you can write code for an arbitrary object of the interface type. The reasoning behind these optional methods is that they normally would be implemented, but in unusual situations a programmer may leave them "unsupported." (The alternative would be to have two interfaces, one with and one without the optional operations. Uncharacteristically, Java designers opted for a smaller number of interfaces.) But there is still more to the story.

PITFALL: (continued)

The optional methods are not, strictly speaking, optional. Like the other methods in an interface, the optional methods must have a method body so that the optional method heading is converted to a complete method definition. So, what is optional? The "optional" refers to the semantics of the method. If the method is optional, then you may give it a trivial implementation and you will not have shirked your responsibility to follow the (unenforced) semantics for the interface.

To keep these optional methods from producing unexplained failures, the interface semantics say that if you do not give an optional method a "real" implementation, then you should have the method body throw an UnsupportedOperationException. For example, the add method of the Collection<T> interface is optional and so can be implemented as follows (provided you have good reason for this):

```
public boolean add(T element)
{
    throw new UnsupportedOperationException();
}
```

The UnsupportedOperationException class is a derived class of the RunTimeException class, so an UnsupportedOperationException is an unchecked exception, meaning it need not be caught in a catch block or declared in a throws clause.

The intention is that the code for a class that implements an interface with optional methods would be written and used in such a way that this UnsupportedOperation Exception would only be thrown during debugging. These rules on optional methods are part of the semantics of the interface, and like all other parts of the semantics of an interface, they depend entirely on the good will and responsibility of the programmer defining the class that implements the interface. ■

Optional Methods

When an interface lists a method as "optional," you still need to implement it when defining a class that implements the interface. However, if you do not want to give it a "real" definition, you can simply have the method body throw an UnsupportedOperationException.

TIP: Dealing with All Those Exceptions

If you examine the Collection<T>, Set<T>, and List<T> interfaces in Appendix 5, you will see that many of the methods are liberally sprinkled with statements that certain exceptions are thrown. All these exception classes are unchecked exceptions, meaning that they need not be caught in a catch block and need not be declared in a throws clause. They are there primarily for debugging. If you are using an existing

(continued)

TIP: (continued)

collection class, you can view them as run-time error messages. If you are defining a class as a derived class of some other collection class, then most or all of the exception throwing will be inherited, so you need not worry too much about it. If you are defining a collection class from scratch and want your class to implement one of the collection interfaces, then you do need to throw suitable exceptions as specified for the interface.

With one exception (no pun intended), all the exception classes mentioned in this chapter are in the package `java.lang` and so do not require any import statement. The one exception is the `NoSuchElementException`, which is used with iterators in Section 16.3. The `NoSuchElementException` is in the `java.util` package, which requires an import statement if your code mentions the `NoSuchElementException` class. ∎

Self-Test Exercises

1. Give the definition of a `boolean` valued static generic method named `inSome`. The method `inSome` has two parameters of type `Collection<T>` and one parameter of type `T`. The method returns `true` if the parameter of type `T` is in either (or both) collections; it returns `false` otherwise.

2. Give the definition of a static generic method named `getFirst` that has one parameter of type `List<T>` and a return type of `T`. The method returns the first element in the list or `null` if the list is empty.

3. Give the definition of a static `boolean` valued method named `noNull`. The method `noNull` has one parameter of type `Set<?>` and removes `null` from the set if `null` is in the set; otherwise it leaves the set unchanged. The method returns `true` if the set is changed and `false` if it is not changed.

Concrete Collection Classes

Abstract
Set<T>

Abstract
List<T>

The abstract classes `AbstractSet<T>` and `AbstractList<T>` are there for convenience when implementing the `Set<T>` and `List<T>` interfaces, respectively. They have almost no methods beyond those in the interfaces they implement. Although these two abstract classes have only a few abstract methods, the other (nonabstract) methods have fairly useless implementations that must be overridden. When defining a derived class of either `AbstractSet<T>` or `AbstractList<T>`, you need to define not just the abstract methods but also all the methods you intend to use. It usually makes more sense to simply use (or define derived classes of) the `HashSet<T>`, `ArrayList<T>`, or `Vector<T>` classes, which are derived classes of `AbstractSet<T>` and `AbstractList<T>` and are full implementations of the `Set<T>` and `List<T>` interfaces.

Abstract
Collection<T>
The abstract class `AbstractCollection<T>` is a skeleton class for the `Collection<T>` interface. Although it is perfectly legal, you seldom, if ever, need to define a derived class of the `AbstractCollection<T>` class. Instead, you normally define a derived class of one of the descendent classes of the `AbstractCollection<T>` class.

HashSet<T>
If you want a class that implements the `Set<T>` interface and do not need any methods beyond those in the `Set<T>` interface, you can use the concrete class `HashSet<T>`. So, after all is said and done, if all you need is a collection class that does not allow elements to occur more than once, then you can use the `HashSet<T>` class and need not worry about all the other classes and interfaces in Display 16.1. The word *Hash* refers to the fact that the `HashSet<T>` class is implemented using a hash table, which was introduced in Section 15.5. The `HashSet<T>`, of course, implements all the methods in the `Set<T>` interface and adds no other methods beyond constructors. A summary of the `HashSet<T>` constructors and other methods is given in Display 16.5. If you want to define your own class that implements the `Set<T>` interface, you are probably better off using the `HashSet<T>` class rather than the `AbstractSet<T>` class as a base class.

Display 16.5   Methods in the `HashSet<T>` Class

The `HashSet<T>` class is in the `java.util` package.

The `HashSet<T>` class extends the `AbstractSet<T>` class and implements the `Set<T>` interface.

The `HashSet<T>` class implements all of the methods in the `Set<T>` interface (Display 16.3). The only other methods in the `HashSet<T>` class are the constructors. The three constructors that do not involve concepts beyond the scope of this book are given next.

All the exception classes mentioned are the kind that are not required to be caught in a `catch` block or declared in a `throws` clause.

All the exception classes mentioned are in the package `java.lang` and so do not require any import statement.

```
public HashSet()
```
Creates a new, empty set.

```
public HashSet(Collection<? extends T> c)
```
Creates a new set that contains all the elements of c. Throws a `NullPointerException` if c is null.

```
public HashSet(int initialCapacity)
```
Creates a new, empty set with the specified capacity.

Throws an `IllegalArgumentException` if initialCapacity is less than zero.

The methods are the same as those described for the `Set<T>` interface (Display 16.3).

It is important to note that if you intend to use the HashSet<T> class with your own class as the parameterized type T, then your class must override the following methods:

```
public int hashCode();
public boolean equals(Object obj);
```

The hashCode() method should return a numeric key that is ideally a unique identifier for an object in your class. See Section 15.5 for a discussion about hash codes. It is always a good idea to override the equals() method for any class you write, but you must override it in this scenario. Java will use the hash code to index the object and then use the equals() method to check if an object exists in the set. If the hash code for two different objects is identical, the objects will still be indexed correctly as long as equals() indicates they are unique. However, the identical hash codes will cause a collision that will decrease performance.

Display 16.6 shows a sample program that uses the HashSet<T> class. This program is conceptually similar to the program in Display 15.38, in which sets containing strings of round things and green things were manipulated in various

---

Display 16.6   **HashSet<T> Class Demo** (part 1 of 3)

```
1    import java.util.HashSet;
2    import java.util.Iterator;
3    public class HashSetDemo
4    {
5        private static void outputSet(HashSet<String> set)     The outputSet
6        {                                                      method uses an iterator
7            Iterator<String> i = set.iterator();               to print the contents of
8            while (i.hasNext())                                a HashSet<T> object.
9                System.out.print(i.next() + " ");              Iterators are described
10           System.out.println();                             in Section 16.3.
11       }

12       public static void main(String[] args)
13       {
14           HashSet<String> round = new HashSet<String>();
15           HashSet<String> green = new HashSet<String>();

16           // Add some data to each set
17           round.add("peas");
18           round.add("ball");
19           round.add("pie");
20           round.add("grapes");

21           green.add("peas");
22           green.add("grapes");
23           green.add("garden hose");
24           green.add("grass");
```

Display 16.6   **HashSet<T>** Class Demo (part 2 of 3)

```
25                  System.out.println("Contents of set round: ");
26                  outputSet(round);
27                  System.out.println("\nContents of set green: ");
28                  outputSet(green);

29                  System.out.println("\nball in set 'round'? " +
30                          round.contains("ball"));
31                  System.out.println("ball in set 'green'? " +
32                          green.contains("ball"));

33                  System.out.println("\nball and peas in same set? "+
34                          ((round.contains("ball") &&
35                           (round.contains("peas"))) ||
36                          (green.contains("ball") &&
37                           (green.contains("peas")))));
38                  System.out.println("pie and grass in same set? "+
39                          ((round.contains("pie") &&
40                           (round.contains("grass"))) ||
41                          (green.contains("pie") &&
42                           (green.contains("grass")))));

43                  // To union two sets we use the addAll method.
44                  HashSet<String>setUnion = new HashSet<String>(round);
45                  round.addAll(green);
46                  System.out.println("\nUnion of green and round:");
47                  outputSet(setUnion);

48                  // To intersect two sets we use the removeAll method.
49                  HashSet<String> setInter = new HashSet<String>(round);
50                  setInter.removeAll(green);
51                  System.out.println("\nIntersection of green and round:");
52                  outputSet(setInter);
53                  System.out.println();
54          }
55  }
```

Sample Dialogue

```
Contents of set round:
grapes pie ball peas

Contents of set green:
grass garden hose grapes peas
```

(continued)

Display 16.6 `HashSet<T>` Class Demo (part 3 of 3)

```
ball in set round? true
ball in set green? false

ball and peas in same set? True
pie and grass in same set? false

Union of green and round:
garden hose grass peas ball pie grapes

Intersection of green and round:
peas grapes
```

ways using our own `Set<T>` class implemented with linked lists. However, the code listing in Display 16.6 uses the `HashSet<T>` class in place of our custom `Set<T>` class. Nevertheless, most of the code is identical because the `Set<T>` class was designed to have an interface similar to the `HashSet<T>` class. Both have `add` and `contains` methods. Functionality similar to our `union` and `intersection` methods can be achieved by using the `HashSet<T>` `addAll` and `removeAll` methods. To output the items in a `HashSet<T>` object, we define an `outputSet` method. This method uses iterators, which are not discussed until Section 16.3, so for now you can ignore the details of how `outputSet` works.

In general, it is recommended that you use the collection classes unless they do not provide the functionality you need for your program. For example, say that you want every item added to the set to have a reference to the set that contains it. This could be useful if you want to determine whether two items are in the same set—you could just follow the reference to the containing set for each item and see whether they are the same. Without such a reference, you would have to invoke the `contains` method for every set to learn whether the items are in the same set. If this were an important feature for your program, you might want to develop your own class instead of using one of the collection classes. If the collection classes were sufficient, the result would be shorter code that is generally easier to develop and maintain. Moreover, the collection classes such as `HashSet<T>` have been designed with efficiency and scalability in mind.

`Vector<T>`   If you want a class that implements the `List<T>` interface and do not need any methods beyond those in this interface, you can use the `ArrayList<T>` or `Vector<T>` class. So, after all is said and done, if all you need is a collection class that allows elements to occur more than once, or you need a collection that orders its elements as on a list (that is, as in an array), or you need a class that has both of these properties, then you can use the `ArrayList<T>` or `Vector<T>` class and need not worry about all the other classes and interfaces in Display 16.1. The `ArrayList<T>` and `Vector<T>` classes implement all the methods in the `List<T>` interface. A table of methods for the `ArrayList<T>` class was given in Chapter 14 and a more complete table is given in

Display 16.7. A table of methods for the `Vector<T>` class is also given in Display 16.7. A more complete list of the methods in these classes is given in Appendix 5. If you want to define your own class that implements the `List<T>` interface, you would probably be better off using either the `ArrayList<T>` or the `Vector<T>` class rather than the `AbstractList<T>` class as a base class.

Abstract Sequential List<T>

The abstract class `AbstractSequentialList<T>` is derived from the `AbstractList<T>` class. Although it does override some methods inherited from the class `AbstractList<T>`, it adds no completely new methods. The point of the `AbstractSequentialList<T>` class is to provide for efficient implementation of sequentially moving through the list at the expense of having inefficient implementation of random access to elements (that is, inefficient implementation of the `get` method). The `LinkedList<T>` class is a concrete derived class of the abstract class `AbstractSequentialList<T>`. (The implementation of the `LinkedList<T>` class is similar to that of the linked list classes we discussed in Chapter 15.) If you need a `List<T>` with efficient random access to elements (that is, efficient implementation of

nkedList<T>

Display 16.7 Methods in the Classes `ArrayList<T>` and `Vector<T>` (part 1 of 4)

The `ArrayList<T>` and `Vector<T>` classes and the `Iterator<T>` and `ListIterator<T>` interfaces are in the `java.util` package.

All the exception classes mentioned are unchecked exceptions, which means they are not required to be caught in a `catch` block or declared in a `throws` clause. (If you have not yet studied exceptions, you can consider the exceptions to be run-time error messages.)

`NoSuchElementException` is in the `java.util` package, which requires an import statement if your code mentions the `NoSuchElementException` class. All the other exception classes mentioned are in the package `java.lang` and so do not require any import statement.

CONSTRUCTORS

```
public ArrayList(int initialCapacity)
```

Creates an empty `ArrayList<T>` with the specified initial capacity. When the `ArrayList<T>` needs to increase its capacity, the capacity doubles.

```
public ArrayList()
```

Creates an empty `ArrayList<T>` with an initial capacity of `10`. When the `ArrayList<T>` needs to increase its capacity, the capacity doubles.

```
public ArrayList(Collection<? extends T> c)
```

Creates an `ArrayList<T>` that contains all the elements of the collection c, in the same order. In other words, the elements have the same index in the `ArrayList<T>` created as they do in c. This is not quite a true copy constructor because it does not preserve capacity. The capacity of the created list will be `c.size()`, not `c.capacity`.

The `ArrayList<T>` created is only a shallow copy of the collection argument. The `ArrayList<T>` created contains references to the elements in c (not references to clones of the elements in c).

```
public Vector(int initialCapacity)
```

Creates an empty vector with the specified initial capacity. When the vector needs to increase its capacity, the capacity doubles.

(continued)

Display 16.7 Methods in the Classes `ArrayList<T>` and `Vector<T>` (part 2 of 4)

`public Vector()`

Creates an empty vector with an initial capacity of 10. When the vector needs to increase its capacity, the capacity doubles.

`public Vector(Collection<? extends T> c)`

Creates a vector that contains all the elements of the collection c, in the same order. In other words, the elements have the same index in the vector created as they do in c. This is not quite a `true` copy constructor because it does not preserve capacity. The capacity of the created vector will be `c.size()`, not `c.capacity`.

The vector created is only a shallow copy of the collection argument. The vector created contains references to the elements in c (not references to clones of the elements in c).

`public Vector(int initialCapacity, int capacityIncrement)`

Constructs an empty vector with the specified initial capacity and capacity increment. When the vector needs to grow, it will add room for `capacityIncrement` more items.

(`ArrayList<T>` does not have a corresponding constructor.)

ARRAYLIKE METHODS FOR BOTH `ArrayList<T>` AND `Vector<T>`

`public T set(int index, T newElement)`

Sets the element at the specified index to `newElement`. The element previously at that position is returned. If you draw an analogy to an array a, this is analogous to setting a`[index]` to the value `newElement`. The index must be a value greater than or equal to zero and strictly less than the current size of the list.

`public T get(int index)`

Returns the element at the specified index. This is analogous to returning a`[index]` for an array a. The index must be a value greater than or equal to 0 and less than the current size of the calling object.

METHODS TO ADD ELEMENTS FOR BOTH `ArrayList<T>` AND `Vector<T>`

`public boolean add(T newElement)`

Adds `newElement` to the end of the calling object's list and increases its size by one. The capacity of the calling object is increased if that is required. Returns `true` if the add was successful. This method is often used as if it were a `void` method.

`public void add(int index, T newElement)`

Inserts `newElement` as an element in the calling object at the specified index and increases the size of the calling object by one. Each element in the calling object with an index greater than or equal to `index` is shifted upward to have an index that is one greater than the value it had previously.

The index must be a value greater than or equal to zero and less than or equal to the size of the calling object (before this addition).

Note that you can use this method to add an element after the last current element. The capacity of the calling object is increased if that is required.

Display 16.7 Methods in the Classes `ArrayList<T>` and `Vector<T>` (part 3 of 4)

```
public boolean addAll(Collection<? extends T> c)
```
Appends all the elements in c to the end of the elements in the calling object in the order that they are enumerated by a c iterator. The behavior of this method is not guaranteed if the collection c is the calling object or any collection including the calling object either directly or indirectly.

```
public boolean addAll(int index, Collection<? extends T> c)
```
Inserts all the elements in c into the calling object starting at position index. Elements are inserted in the order that they are enumerated by a c iterator. Elements previously at positions index or higher are shifted to higher numbered positions.

METHODS TO REMOVE ELEMENTS FOR BOTH `ArrayList<T>` AND `Vector<T>`

```
public T remove(int index)
```
Deletes the element at the specified index and returns the element deleted. The size of the calling object is decreased by one. The capacity of the calling object is not changed. Each element in the calling object with an index greater than or equal to index is decreased to have an index that is one less than the value it had previously.

The index must be a value greater than or equal to zero and less than the size of the calling object (before this removal).

```
public boolean remove(Object theElement)
```
Removes the first occurrence of theElement from the calling object. If theElement is found in the calling object, then each element in the calling object with an index greater than or equal to theElement's index is decreased to have an index that is one less than the value it had previously. Returns true if theElement was found (and removed). Returns false if theElement is not found in the calling object. If the element was removed, the size is decreased by one. The capacity is not changed.

```
protected void removeRange(int fromIndex, int toIndex)
```
Removes all elements with index greater than or equal to fromIndex and strictly less than toIndex. Be sure to note that this method is protected, not public.

```
public void clear()
```
Removes all elements from the calling object and sets its size to zero.

SEARCH METHODS FOR BOTH `ArrayList<T>` AND `Vector<T>`

```
public boolean isEmpty()
```
Returns true if the calling object is empty (that is, has size 0); otherwise returns false.

```
public boolean contains(Object target)
```
Returns true if target is an element of the calling object; otherwise returns false. Uses the method equals of the object target to test for equality.

```
public int indexOf(Object target)
```
Returns the index of the first element that is equal to target. Uses the method equals of the object target to test for equality. Returns 1 if target is not found.

```
public int lastIndexOf(Object target)
```
Returns the index of the last element that is equal to target. Uses the method equals of the object target to test for equality. Returns 1 if target is not found.

(continued)

Display 16.7 Methods in the Classes `ArrayList<T>` and `Vector<T>` (part 4 of 4)

ITERATORS FOR BOTH `ArrayList<T>` AND `Vector<T>`

```
public Iterator<T> iterator()
```
Returns an iterator for the calling object. Iterators are discussed in Section 16.3.

```
public ListIterator<T> listIterator()
```
Returns a `ListIterator<T>` for the calling object. `ListIterator<T>` is discussed in Section 16.3.

```
ListIterator<T> listIterator(int index)
```
Returns a list iterator for the calling object starting at `index`. The first element to be returned by the iterator is the one at `index`. (Iterators are discussed in Section 16.3.)

CONVERTING TO AN ARRAY FOR BOTH `ArrayList<T>` AND `Vector<T>`

```
public Object[ ] toArray()
```
Returns an array containing all of the elements in the calling object. The elements of the array are indexed the same as in the calling object.

```
public <E> E[ ] toArray(E[ ] a)
```
Note that the type parameter E is not the same as T. So, E can be any reference type; it need not be the type T in `Collection<T>`. For example, E might be an ancestor type of T.

Returns an array containing all of the elements in the calling object. The elements of the array are indexed the same as in the calling object.

The argument a is used primarily to specify the type of the array returned. The exact details are described next.

The type of the returned array is that of a. If the collection fits in the array a, then a is used to hold the elements of the returned array; otherwise a new array is created with the same type as a.

If a has more elements than the calling object, then the element in a immediately following the end of the elements copied from the calling object is set to `null`.

MEMORY MANAGEMENT FOR BOTH `ArrayList<T>` AND `Vector<T>`

```
public int size()
```
Returns the number of elements in the calling object.

```
public int capacity()
```
Returns the current capacity of the calling object.

```
public void ensureCapacity(int newCapacity)
```
Increases the capacity of the calling object to ensure that it can hold at least `newCapacity` elements. Using `ensureCapacity` can sometimes increase efficiency, but it is not needed for any other reason.

```
public void trimToSize()
```
Trims the capacity of the calling object to be the calling object's current size. This is used to save storage.

MAKE A COPY FOR BOTH `ArrayList<T>` AND `Vector<T>`

```
public Object clone()
```
Returns a shallow copy of the calling object.

the get method), then use the `ArrayList<T>` or `Vector<T>` class or a class derived from one of these two classes. If you do not need efficient random access but need to efficiently move sequentially through the list, then use the `LinkedList<T>` class or a class derived from the `LinkedList<T>` class.

SortedSet<T>

TreeSet<T>

The interface `SortedSet<T>` and the concrete class `TreeSet<T>` are designed for implementations of the `Set<T>` interface that provide for rapid retrieval of elements (efficient implementation of the `contains` and similar methods). The implementation of the class is similar to the binary tree class discussed in Chapter 15 but with more sophisticated ways to do inserting that keep the tree balanced. We will not discuss the `SortedSet<T>` interface or the `TreeSet<T>` class in this text, but you should be aware of their existence so you know what to look for in the Java documentation should you need them.

MyProgrammingLab

Self-Test Exercises

4. Can an object that instantiates the `HashSet<T>` class contain multiple copies of some element?

5. Suppose you want to define a class that orders its elements like a `List<T>` but does not allow multiple occurrences of an element like a `Set<T>`. Would it be better to make it a derived class of the `ArrayList<T>` class or a derived class of the `HashSet<T>` class?

6. You would like to use the following class as the type in a `HashSet<T>` collection. What is missing and how would you fix it?

```java
public class Customer
{
    private String name;
    private String address;
    public Customer(String newName, String newAddress)
    {
        name = newName;
        address = newAddress;
    }
    public String toString()
    {
        return name + " : " + address;
    }
}
```

Differences between `ArrayList<T>` and `Vector<T>`

For most purposes, `ArrayList<T>` and `Vector<T>` are equivalent. There are only minor differences between the classes. The methods that are in both classes are given in Display 16.7. The class `Vector<T>` has more methods than `ArrayList<T>` does; these methods are not given in Display 16.7. However, most of the extra methods are little more than alternate names for methods that are in both `ArrayList<T>` and `Vector<T>`. None of the methods in `Vector<T>` do anything that cannot easily be done with an `ArrayList<T>`. The class `ArrayList<T>` is reputed to be more efficient than `Vector<T>`. The biggest difference between these two classes is that `ArrayList<T>` is newer than `Vector<T>` and was created as part of the Java collection framework, whereas `Vector<T>` is an older class that was retrofitted with extra method names to make it fit into the collection framework. You are encouraged to use `ArrayList<T>` rather than `Vector<T>`. However, a lot of existing code uses `Vector<T>`, so you should be familiar with it.[1]

Nonparameterized Version of the Collection Framework ★

Before version 5.0, Java did not have type parameters. So, the collection framework consisted of ordinary classes and interfaces, such as `Collection`, `List`, `ArrayList`, and so forth, all of which had no type parameters. Although this older collection framework has been supplanted by the new, generic version, the old version's classes and interfaces, without type parameters, are still in the standard libraries and in a lot of older code. There is no longer any need for the older classes and interfaces that do not have type parameters. They can sometimes be harder to use and are less versatile than the new, generic classes with type parameters. You should not use the older classes and interfaces without type parameters. However, you will often see them used in older code. When reading older code, you will not go too far wrong in thinking of `Collection` as meaning `Collection<Object>`, `ArrayList` as meaning `ArrayList<Object>`, and so forth. This is not, strictly speaking, correct. For example, the classes `ArrayList` and `ArrayList<Object>` are not the same, but they are very similar.

---

[1]The biggest difference between `Vector<T>` and `ArrayList<T>` classes is that `Vector<T>` objects are *synchronized* while `ArrayList<T>` objects are not. Synchronization is briefly discussed in Chapter 19.

PITFALL: Omitting the `<T>`

If you omit `<T>` or a corresponding class name, such as using `ArrayList` instead of `ArrayList<String>`, then you may get a compiler error message. If you do get a compiler error message, it is likely to seem bewilderingly strange. The problem is that `ArrayList` and other class and interface names with `<T>` omitted actually mean something. (We do not have time to stop and explain what they mean, but a hint is given in the starred subsection "Nonparameterized Version of the Collection Framework.") Your only defense against this pitfall is to be very careful; if you do get a bewildering compiler error message, look for a missing `<T>` or a missing `<Class_Name>`.

Sometimes a compiler warning message can be helpful when you make this mistake. If you get a warning that mentions a type case from a class name without a `<T>` to a class name with a `<T>` or with a `<Class_Name>`, look for an omitted `<T>` or an omitted `<Class_Name>`.

Finally, we should note that sometimes your code will compile and even run correctly if you omit the `<T>` from a class name in the collection framework. ■

16.2 Maps

A man has but one mother. But, a mother may have any number of sons.

Saying on a Wall Sampler

map

The Java **map** framework is similar in character to the collection framework, except that it deals with collections of ordered pairs. Objects in the map framework can implement mathematical functions and relations and so can be used to construct database classes. Think of the pair as consisting of a key `K` (to search for) and an associated value `V`. For example, the key might be a student ID number and the value might be an object storing information about the student (such as the name, major, address, or phone number) associated with that ID number. Commonly used interfaces and classes in this framework are shown in Display 16.8. In this chapter, we will focus on the `Map<K,V>` interface, the `AbstractMap<K,V>` class, and the `HashMap<K,V>` class.

Abstract
Map<K,V>

Hash
Map<K,V>

Map<K,V>
interface

Because the map interface will map a key to a value, we must now specify two types of parameters instead of one as we did with collections. The `Map<K,V>` interface specifies the basic operations that all map classes should implement. A summary of these operations is given in Display 16.9. A more detailed description is in Appendix 5. Note that there are many similarities to the `Collection<T>` interface.

Display 16.8 **The Map Landscape**

Interface

Abstract Class

Concrete Class

A single line between two boxes means the lower class or interface is derived from (extends) the higher one.

K and V are type parameters for the type of the keys and elements stored in the map.

Display 16.9 **Method Headings in the `Map<K,V>` Interface** (part 1 of 3)

The `Map<K,V>` interface is in the `java.util` package.

CONSTRUCTORS

Although not officially required by the interface, any class that implements the `Map<K,V>` interface should have at least two constructors: a no-argument constructor that creates an empty `Map<K,V>` object, and a constructor with one `Map<K,V>` parameter that creates a `Map<K,V>` object with the same elements as the constructor argument. The interface does not specify whether the copy produced by the one-argument constructor is a shallow copy or a deep copy of its argument.

Display 16.9   Method Headings in the `Map<K,V>` Interface (part 2 of 3)

METHODS

`boolean isEmpty()`

Returns `true` if the calling object is empty; otherwise returns `false`.

`public boolean containsValue(Object value)`

Returns `true` if the calling object contains at least one or more keys that map to an instance of `value`.

`public boolean containsKey(Object key)`

Returns `true` if the calling object contains `key` as one of its keys.

`public boolean equals(Object other)`

This is the `equals` of the map, not the `equals` of the elements in the map. Overrides the inherited method `equals`.

`public int size()`

Returns the number of (key, value) mappings in the calling object.

`public int hashCode()`

Returns the hash code value for the calling object.

`public Set<Map.Entry<K,V>> entrySet()`

Returns a set *view* consisting of (key, value) mappings for all entries in the map. Changes to the map are reflected in the set and vice versa.

`public Collection<V> values()`

Returns a collection *view* consisting of all values in the map. Changes to the map are reflected in the collection and vice versa.

`public V get(Object key)`

Returns the value to which the calling object maps `key`. If `key` is not in the map, then `null` is returned. Note that this does not always mean that the key is not in the map because it is possible to map a key to `null`. The `containsKey` method can be used to distinguish the two cases.

OPTIONAL METHODS

The following methods are optional, which means they still must be implemented, but the implementation can simply throw an `UnsupportedOperationException` if, for some reason, you do not want to give the methods a "real" implementation. An `UnsupportedOperationException` is a `RunTimeException` and so is not required to be caught or declared in a `throws` clause.

`public V put(K key, V value)` (*Optional*)

Associates `key` to `value` in the map. If `key` is associated with an existing value, then the old value is overwritten and returned. Otherwise `null` is returned.

(continued)

Display 16.9   Method Headings in the `Map<K,V>` Interface (part 3 of 3)

```
public void putAll(Map<? extends K,? extends V> mapToAdd)  (Optional)
```
Adds all mappings of `mapToAdd` into the calling object's map.

```
public V remove (Object key)  (Optional)
```
Removes the mapping for the specified key. If the key is not found in the map, then `null` is returned; otherwise the previous value for the key is returned.

Concrete Map Classes

The abstract class `AbstractMap<K,V>` is convenient for implementing the `Map<K,V>` interface, just as the `AbstractSet<T>` class served the same purpose for the `Set<T>` interface. When defining a derived class of `AbstractMap<K,V>`, you need to define not just the abstract methods but also all the methods you intend to use. It usually makes more sense to use (or define derived classes of) the `HashMap<K,V>` or `TreeMap<K,V>` classes, which are derived classes of `AbstractMap<K,V>` and are full implementations of the `Map<K,V>` interfaces. However, if you wish to implement your own map with your own data structures, then it would be appropriate to derive classes from `AbstractMap<K,V>`.

In this chapter, we will focus only on the `HashMap<K,V>` class, which is a concrete implementation of the `Map<K,V>` interface. Internally, the class uses a hash table similar to what we discussed in Chapter 15. Note that this class does not make any guarantee as to the order of elements placed in the map. If you require order, then you should use the `TreeMap<K,V>` class (which internally uses a tree to store its elements) or the `LinkedHashMap<K,V>` class, which uses a doubly linked list to maintain order inside a `HashMap<K,V>` object. The `LinkedHashMap<K,V>` class is derived from the `HashMap<K,V>` class.

Knowing how hash tables operate is helpful in optimizing a program that uses a `HashMap`. When we created a hash table in Chapter 15, we used a fixed-sized array where each array entry referenced a linked list. A hash function mapped an input value, such as a String, to an index in the array. If the size of the array is much smaller than the number of elements added, then there will be lots of collisions and execution performance will be low. On the other hand, if the size of the array is much larger than the number of elements added, then memory will be wasted. A similar trade-off exists with the `HashMap<K,V>` class. One of the constructors allows us to specify an **initial capacity** and a **load factor**. The initial capacity specifies how many "buckets" exist in the hash table. This would be analogous to the size of the array of the hash table. The load factor is a number between 0 and 1. This variable specifies a percentage such that if the number of elements added to the hash table exceeds the load factor, then the capacity of the hash table will automatically increase. The default load factor is 0.75 and the default initial capacity is 16. This means that the capacity will be increased (by roughly double) once 12 elements are added to the map. This process is called **rehashing**; it can be time consuming if you have a large number of elements in the map. Although the capacity will automatically increase when necessary, your program will run more efficiently if the capacity is initially set to the number of elements you expect will be added to the map.

initial capacity

load factor

rehashing

The HashMap<K,V>, of course, implements all the methods in the Map<K,V> interface and adds no other methods beyond constructors and an implementation of the clone() method. A summary of the HashMap<K,V> constructors and clone() is given in Display 16.10.

As with the HashSet<T> class, if you intend to use your own class as the parameterized type K in a HashMap<K,V> then your class must override the following methods:

```
public int hashCode();
public boolean equals(Object obj);
```

These methods are required for indexing and checking for uniqueness of the key. See the discussion in Section 16.1 about overriding these methods and Section 15.5 about hash functions.

Display 16.10   Methods in the **HashMap<K,V>** Class

The HashMap<K,V> class is in the java.util package.

The HashMap<K,V> class extends the AbstractMap<K,V> class and implements the Map<K,V> interface.

The HashMap<K,V> class implements all of the methods in the Map<K,V> interface (Display 16.9). The only other methods in the HashMap<K,V> class are the constructors.

All the exception classes mentioned are the kind that are not required to be caught in a catch block or declared in a throws clause.

All the exception classes mentioned are in the package java.lang and so do not require any import statement.

```
public HashMap()
```
Creates a new, empty map with a default initial capacity of 16 and load factor of 0.75.

```
public HashMap(int initialCapacity)
```
Creates a new, empty map with a default capacity of initialCapacity and load factor of 0.75.

Throws an IllegalArgumentException if initialCapacity is negative.

```
public HashMap(int initialCapacity, float loadFactor)
```
Creates a new, empty map with the specified capacity and load factor.

Throws an IllegalArgumentException if initialCapacity is negative or loadFactor is nonpositive.

```
public HashMap(Map<? extends K,? extends V> m)
```
Creates a new map with the same mappings as m. The initialCapacity is set to the same size as m and the loadFactor to 0.75.

Throws a NullPointerException if m is null.

```
public Object clone()
```
Creates a shallow copy of this instance and returns it. The keys and values are not cloned.

The remainder of the methods are the same as those described for the Map<K,V> interface (Display 16.9).

A program that demonstrates the HashMap<K,V> class is given in Display 16.11. This is a variant of Programming Project 15.8 from Chapter 15. In this example, the program uses the name instance variable as the key to map to an Employee object as defined in Display 7.2. Several sample Employee objects are created and added to the map using the first name as the key. The user is given the opportunity to type in names until enter is pressed on a blank line. Any name that exists in the map is retrieved and its information is output to the screen.

Display 16.11   **HashMap<K,V>** Class Demo (part 1 of 2)

```
1   // This class uses the Employee class defined in Chapter 7.
2   import java.util.HashMap;
3   import java.util.Scanner;
4   public class HashMapDemo
5   {
6       public static void main(String[] args)
7       {
8           // First create a hashmap with an initial size of 10 and
9           // the default load factor
10          HashMap<String,Employee> employees =
11                  new HashMap<String,Employee>(10);

12          // Add several employees objects to the map using
13          // their name as the key
14          employees.put("Joe",
15                  new Employee("Joe",new Date("September", 15, 1970)));
16          employees.put("Andy",
17                  new Employee("Andy",new Date("August", 22, 1971)));
18          employees.put("Greg",
19                  new Employee("Greg",new Date("March", 9, 1972)));
20          employees.put("Kiki",
21                  new Employee("Kiki",new Date("October", 8, 1970)));
22          employees.put("Antoinette",
23                  new Employee("Antoinette",new Date("May", 2, 1959)));
24          System.out.print("Added Joe, Andy, Greg, Kiki, ");
25          System.out.println("and Antoinette to the map.");

26          // Ask the user to type a name. If found in the map,
27          // print it out.
28          Scanner keyboard = new Scanner(System.in);
29          String name = "";
30          do
31          {
32              System.out.print("\nEnter a name to look up in the map. ");
33              System.out.println("Press enter to quit.");
```

Display 16.11   `HashMap<K,V>` Class Demo (part 2 of 2)

```
34                        name = keyboard.nextLine();
35                        if (employees.containsKey(name))
36                        {
37                            Employee e = employees.get(name);
38                            System.out.println("Name found: " + e.toString());
39                        }
40                        else if (!name.equals(""))
41                        {
42                            System.out.println("Name not found.");
43                        }
44                } while (!name.equals(""));
45        }
46  }
```

Sample Dialogue

```
Added Joe, Andy, Greg, Kiki, and Antoinette to the map.

Enter a name to look up in the map. Press enter to quit.
Joe
Name found: Joe September 15, 1970

Enter a name to look up in the map. Press enter to quit.
Andy
Name found: Andy August 22, 1971

Enter a name to look up in the map. Press enter to quit.
Kiki
Name found: Kiki October 8, 1970

Enter a name to look up in the map. Press enter to quit.
Myla
Name not found.
```

MyProgrammingLab™

Self-Test Exercises

7. Can an object that instantiates the `HashMap<K,V>` class contain multiple copies of some element as a key? How about multiple copies of some element as a value?

8. Suppose that you want a `HashMap<K,V>` that maps a unique employee ID number to an `Employee` object. Give the definition for a `HashMap<K,V>` variable that defines and allocates the `HashMap`. Expect to have 100 employees in your organization. If the employee ID number is an integer between 0 and 100, is a map a good choice for a data structure to store this information?

16.3 Iterators

The White Rabbit put on his spectacles. "Where shall I begin, please your Majesty?" he asked.
"Begin at the beginning," the King said, very gravely, "And go on till you come to the end: then stop."

LEWIS CARROLL, *Alice in Wonderland*

iterator An **iterator** is an object that is used with a collection to provide sequential access to the elements in the collection. In this section, we discuss iterators in general, and iterators in the Java collection framework in particular.

The Iterator Concept

In the next subsection, we will discuss the Java `Iterator` interface, but before that, let us consider the intuitive idea of an iterator. An iterator is something that allows you to examine and possibly modify the elements in a collection in some sequential order. So, an iterator imposes an order on the elements of a collection even if the collection, such as the class `HashSet<T>`, does not impose any order on the elements it contains.

Something that is not an object—and thus not, strictly speaking, a Java `Iterator`—but that satisfies the intuitive idea of an `iterator` is an `int` variable `i` used with an array `a`. This iterator `i` can be made to start out at the first array as follows:

```
i = 0;
```

The iterator can give you the current element; the current element is simply `a[i]`. The iterator can go to the next element and give you the next element as follows:

```
i++;
"Gives you a[i]"
```

The concept of an iterator is simple but powerful enough to be used frequently.

The `Iterator<T>` Interface

Iterator<T>
interface Java formalizes the concept of an iterator with the `Iterator<T>` generic interface. Any object of any class that satisfies the `Iterator<T>` interface is an `Iterator<T>`. So, an array index is not a Java `Iterator<T>`. However, the index could be an instance variable in an object of an `Iterator<T>` class.

An `Iterator<T>` object does not stand on its own. It must be associated with some collection object. How is the association accomplished? In Java, any class that satisfies the `Collection<T>` interface must have a method, named `iterator()`, that returns an `Iterator<T>`. For example, let us say `c` is an instance of the `HashSet<T>` collection class with some class plugged in for `T`. To make things concrete, let us plug in `String` for `T`; so `c` is an instance of the `HashSet<String>` collection class. You can obtain an iterator for `c` as follows:

```
Iterator<String> iteratorForC = c.iterator();
```

You may not know what class the `iteratorForC` is an instance of, but you do know it satisfies the `Iterator<String>` interface, so you know it has the methods in the `Iterator<T>` interface. These methods are given in Display 16.12.

Display 16.13 contains a simple demonstration of using an iterator with a `HashSet<T>` object. A `HashSet<T>` object imposes no order on the elements in the `HashSet<T>` object, but the iterator imposes an order on the elements—namely, the order in which they are produced by `next()`. There are no requirements on this ordering. If you run the program in Display 16.13 twice, the order of the elements' output will almost certainly be the same each time. However, it would not be an error if they are output in a different order each time the program runs.

If the collection used with an `Iterator<T>` imposes an order on its elements, such as an `ArrayList<T>` does, then the `Iterator<T>` will output the elements in that order. If you require an order with a `HashSet<T>` object, then you may use the `LinkedHashSet<T>` class, which uses an internal doubly linked list to store the items in the order that they are added.

Display 16.12   Methods in the `Iterator<T>` Interface

The `Iterator<T>` interface is in the `java.util` package.

All the exception classes mentioned are the kind that are not required to be caught in a `catch` block or declared in a `throws` clause.

`NoSuchElementException` is in the `java.util` package, which requires an import statement if your code mentions the `NoSuchElementException` class. All the other exception classes mentioned are in the package `java.lang` and so do not require any import statement.

`public T next()`

Returns the next element of the collection that produced the iterator.

Throws a `NoSuchElementException` if there is no next element.

`public boolean hasNext()`

Returns `true` if `next()` has not yet returned all the elements in the collection; returns `false` otherwise.

`public void remove()` *(Optional)*

Removes from the collection the last element returned by `next`.

This method can be called only once per call to `next`. If the collection is changed in any way, other than by using `remove`, the behavior of the iterator is not specified (and thus should be considered unpredictable).

Throws `IllegalStateException` if the next method has not yet been called, or if the remove method has already been called after the last call to the next method.

Throws an `UnsupportedOperationException` if the `remove` operation is not supported by this `Iterator<T>`.

Display 16.13 An Iterator

```
1    import java.util.HashSet;
2    import java.util.Iterator;

3    public class HashSetIteratorDemo
4    {
5        public static void main(String[] args)
6        {
7            HashSet<String> s = new HashSet<String>();

8            s.add("health");
9            s.add("love");
10           s.add("money");

11           System.out.println("The set contains:");

12           Iterator<String> i = s.iterator();
13           while (i.hasNext())
14               System.out.println(i.next());

15           i.remove();

16           System.out.println();
17           System.out.println("The set now contains:");

18           i = s.iterator();
19           while (i.hasNext())
20               System.out.println(i.next());

21           System.out.println("End of program.");
22       }
23   }
```

You cannot "reset" an iterator "to the beginning." To do a second iteration, you create another iterator.

Sample Dialogue

```
The set contains:
money
love
health

The set now contains:
money
love
End of program.
```

The HashSet<T> object does not order the elements it contains, but the iterator imposes an order on the elements.

> ## Iterators
>
> An iterator is something that allows you to examine and possibly modify the elements in a collection in some sequential order. Java formalizes this concept with the two interfaces `Iterator<T>` and `ListIterator<T>`.

TIP: For-Each Loops as Iterators

A for-each loop is not, strictly speaking, an iterator (because, among other things, it is not an object), but a for-each loop serves the same purpose as an iterator: It lets you cycle through the elements in a collection. When dealing with collections, you can often use a for-each loop in place of an iterator, and the for-each loop is usually simpler and easier to use than an iterator. For example, in Display 16.14, we have rewritten the program in Display 16.13 using for-each loops in place of iterators. Note that we needed to do some extra programming with the variable `last` in order to simulate `i.remove()`. Sometimes an iterator works best, and sometimes a for-each loop works best. Many authorities would say that our code would be better if we had not replaced the first iterator loop in Display 16.13 with a for-each loop. ∎

Display 16.14   **For-Each Loops as Iterators** (part 1 of 2)

```
1   import java.util.HashSet;
2   import java.util.Iterator;

3   public class ForEachDemo
4   {
5       public static void main(String[] args)
6       {
7           HashSet<String> s = new HashSet<String>();

8           s.add("health");
9           s.add("love");
10          s.add("money");

11          System.out.println("The set contains:");

12          String last = null;
13          for (String e : s)
14          {
15              last = e;
16              System.out.println(e);
17          }
```

(continued)

Display 16.14   For-Each Loops as Iterators (part 2 of 2)

```
18                    s.remove(last);

19                    System.out.println();
20                    System.out.println("The set now contains:");

21                    for (String e : s)
22                        System.out.println(e);

23                    System.out.println("End of program.");
24            }
25    }                              The output is the same as in Display 16.13.
```

List Iterators

The collection framework has two iterator interfaces: the Iterator<T> interface, which you have already seen and which works with any collection class that implements the Collection<T> interface; and the ListIterator<T> interface, which is designed to work with collections that implement the List<T> interface. The ListIterator<T> interface extends the Iterator<T> interface. A ListIterator<T> has all the methods that an Iterator<T> has, plus more methods that provide two new abilities: A ListIterator<T> can move in either direction along the list of elements in the collection, and a ListIterator<T> has methods, such as set and add, that can be used to change the elements in the collection. The methods for the ListIterator<T> interface are given in Display 16.15. See Appendix 5 for a more detailed description that includes all exceptions thrown.

List Iterator<T>

The map framework does not directly support the iterable interface, but you can use the map's keySet(), values(), or entrySet() methods, which return iterable sets containing the keys, values, or (key, value) mappings of the map.

Display 16.15   Methods in the **ListIterator<T>** Interface (part 1 of 2)

The ListIterator<T> interface is in the java.util package.

The *cursor position* is explained in the text and in Display 16.16.

All the exception classes mentioned are the kind that are not required to be caught in a catch block or declared in a throws clause.

NoSuchElementException is in the java.util package, which requires an import statement if your code mentions the NoSuchElementException class. All the other exception classes mentioned are in the package java.lang and so do not require any import statement.

```
public T next()
```
Returns the next element of the list that produced the iterator. More specifically, returns the element immediately after the cursor position.

Throws a NoSuchElementException if there is no next element.

Display 16.15   Methods in the `ListIterator<T>` Interface (part 2 of 2)

```
public T previous()
```
Returns the previous element of the list that produced the iterator. More specifically, returns the element immediately before the cursor position.

Throws a `NoSuchElementException` if there is no previous element.

```
public boolean hasNext( )
```
Returns `true` if there is a suitable element for `next()` to return; returns `false` otherwise.

```
public boolean hasPrevious( )
```
Returns `true` if there is a suitable element for `previous()` to return; returns `false` otherwise.

```
public int nextIndex( )
```
Returns the index of the element that would be returned by a call to `next()`. Returns the list size if the cursor position is at the end of the list.

```
public int previousIndex( )
```
Returns the index that would be returned by a call to `previous()`. Returns 1 if the cursor position is at the beginning of the list.

```
public void add(T newElement) (Optional)
```
Inserts `newElement` at the location of the iterator cursor (that is, before the value, if any, that would be returned by `next()` and after the value, if any, that would be returned by `previous()`).

Cannot be used if there has been a call to `add` or `remove` since the last call to `next()` or `previous()`.

Throws `IllegalStateException` if neither `next()` nor `previous()` has been called, or if the `add` or `remove` method has already been called after the last call to `next()` or `previous()`.

```
public void remove() (Optional)
```
Removes from the collection the last element returned by `next()` or `previous()`.

This method can be called only once per call to `next()` or `previous()`.

Cannot be used if there has been a call to `add` or `remove` since the last call to `next()` or `previous()`.

Throws `IllegalStateException` if neither `next()` nor `previous()` has been called, or if the `add` or `remove` method has already been called after the last call to `next()` or `previous()`.

```
public void set( T newElement) (Optional)
```
Replaces the last element returned by `next()` or `previous()` with `newElement`.

Cannot be used if there has been a call to `add` or `remove` since the last call to `next()` or `previous()`.

Throws `IllegalStateException` if neither `next()` nor `previous()` has been called, or if the `add` or `remove` method has been called since the last call to `next()` or `previous()`.

The general idea of *next* and *previous* is clear, but we need to make it precise if you are to understand the next() and previous() methods of the ListIterator<T> interface. Every ListIterator<T> has a position marker in the list known as the

cursor   **cursor**. If the list has *n* elements, they are numbered by indices 0 through *n*–1, but there are *n*+1 cursor positions, as indicated in Display 16.16. When next() is invoked, the element immediately following the cursor position is returned and the cursor is moved to the next cursor position. When previous() is invoked, the element immediately before the cursor position is returned, and the cursor is moved back to the preceding cursor position.

The ListIterator<T> Interface

The ListIterator<T> interface extends the Iterator<T> interface. The ListIterator<T> interface differs from the Iterator<T> interface by adding the following abilities: A ListIterator<T> can move in either direction along the list of elements in the collection, and a ListIterator<T> has methods, such as set and add, that can be used to change the elements in the collection.

Display 16.16   **ListIterator<T>** Cursor Positions

List

element 0   element 1   element 2   ...   element *n*-1

Cursor positions

The default initial cursor position is the leftmost one.

PITFALL: next Can Return a Reference

If i is an iterator, then i.next() returns an element of the collection that created i, but there are two meanings of "return an element."

1. The invocation i.next() could return a copy of the element in the collection (for example, using a copy constructor or a clone method).
2. Alternatively, i.next() could return a reference to the element in the collection.

In case (1), modifying i.next() *will not* change the element in the collection (provided the copy was a deep copy). In case (2), modifying i.next() *will* change the element in the collection. The APIs for both the Iterator<T> and ListIterator<T> interfaces are vague on whether you should follow policy (1) or (2), but the iterators for the standard predefined collection classes, such as `ArrayList<T>` and `HashSet<T>`, return references. So, you can modify the elements in the collection by using mutator methods on `i.next()`. This is illustrated in Display 16.17. The comments we made about `i.next()` also apply to `i.previous()`.

The fact that `next` and `previous` return references to elements in the collection is not necessarily bad news. It means you must be careful, but it also means you can cycle through all the elements in the collection and perform some processing that might modify the elements. For example, if the elements in the collection are records of some sort, you can use mutator methods to update the records.

If you read the APIs for the `Iterator<T>` and `ListIterator<T>` interfaces, they say that a `ListIterator<T>` can change the collection, but presumably, a plain old `Iterator<T>` cannot. These API comments do not refer to whether or not a reference is returned by `i.next()`. They simply refer to the fact that the `ListIterator<T>` interface has a set method, whereas the `Iterator<T>` interface does not. Do not confuse this with the point discussed in the previous paragraph. ∎

Display 16.17   An Iterator Returns a Reference (part 1 of 2)

```
1    import java.util.ArrayList;
2    import java.util.Iterator;

3    public class IteratorReferenceDemo
4    {
5        public static void main(String[] args)
6        {
7            ArrayList<Date> birthdays = new ArrayList<Date>();

8            birthdays.add(new Date(1, 1, 1990));
9            birthdays.add(new Date(2, 2, 1990));
10           birthdays.add(new Date(3, 3, 1990));

11           System.out.println("The list contains:");

12           Iterator<Date> i = birthdays.iterator();
13           while (i.hasNext())
14               System.out.println(i.next());

15           i = birthdays.iterator();
16           Date d = null; //To keep the compiler happy.
17           System.out.println("Changing the references.");
18           while (i.hasNext())
19           {
20               d = i.next();
21               d.setDate(4, 1, 1990);
22           }
```

The class Date is defined in Display 4.13, but you can easily guess all you need to know about Date for this example.

(continued)

Display 16.17   **An Iterator Returns a Reference** (part 2 of 2)

```
23              System.out.println("The list now contains:");

24              i = birthdays.iterator();
25              while (i.hasNext())
26                  System.out.println(i.next());

27              System.out.println("April fool!");
28          }
29      }
```

Sample Dialogue

```
The list contains:
January 1, 1990
February 2, 1990
March 3, 1990
Changing the references.
The list now contains:
April 1, 1990
April 1, 1990
April 1, 1990
April fool!
```

TIP: Defining Your Own Iterator Classes

There really is little need to define your own `Iterator<T>` or `ListIterator<T>` classes. The most common and easiest way to define a collection class is to make it a derived class of one of the library collection classes, such as `ArrayList<T>` or `HashSet<T>`. When you do this, you automatically get the method `iterator()`, and if need be, the method `listIterator()`, which takes care of iterators. However, if you should need to define a collection class in some other way, then the best way to define your iterator class or classes is to define them as inner classes of your collection class. ■

MyProgrammingLab™   **Self-Test Exercises**

9. Does a `HashSet<T>` object have a method to produce a `ListIterator<T>`? Does an `ArrayList<T>` object have a method to produce a `ListIterator<T>`?

10. Suppose `i` is a `ListIterator<T>`. Will an invocation of `i.next()` followed by `i.previous()` return the same element for each of the two invocations or might they return two different elements? What about `i.previous()` followed by `i.next()`?

Chapter Summary

- The main *collection* interfaces are Collection<T>, Set<T>, and List<T>. The Set<T> and List<T> interfaces extend the Collection<T> interface. The library classes that are standard to use and that implement these interfaces are HashSet<T>, which implements the Set<T> interface, and ArrayList<T>, which implements the List<T> interface.

- A Set<T> does not allow repeated elements and does not order its elements. A List<T> allows repeated elements and orders its elements.

- The Map<K, V> interface is used to store a mapping between a key K and a value V. It is commonly used to store databases in memory. The HashMap<K, V> class is a standard library class that implements a map.

- An *iterator* is something that allows you to examine and possibly modify the elements in a collection in some sequential order. Java formalizes this concept with the two interfaces Iterator<T> and ListIterator<T>.

- An Iterator<T> (with only the required methods implemented) goes through the elements of the collection in one direction only, from the beginning to the end. A ListIterator<T> can move through the collection list in both directions, forward and back. A ListIterator<T> has a set method; the Iterator<T> interface does not require a set method.

Answers to Self-Test Exercises

1.
```java
public static <T> boolean inSome(T target,
                        Collection<T> c1, Collection<T> c2)
{
        return (c1.contains(target) || c2.contains(target));
}
```
2.
```java
public static <T> T getFirst(List<T> aList)
{
    if (aList.isEmpty())
        return null;
    else
        return aList.get(0);
}
```
3.
```java
public static boolean noNull(Set<?> s)
{
    return (s.remove(null));
}
```
4. No.

5. It would make more sense to make it a derived class of the `ArrayList<T>` class. Then the elements are ordered. You can ensure against repeated elements by redefining all methods that add elements so that the methods check to see if the element is already in the class before entering it. A derived class of the `HashSet<T>` class would automatically ensure that no element is repeated, but it would seem to take a good deal of work to maintain the elements in order.

6. The `Customer` class must override `hashCode` and `equals`. A simple technique to implement `hashCode` when the class contains strings is to return the string's `hashCode` method. One possible implementation of these methods follows.

```
public int hashCode()
{
    return this.toString().hashCode();
}
public boolean equals(Object obj)
{
    Customer other = (Customer) obj;
    return (other.toString().equals(this.toString());
}
```

7. Multiple copies of some element are not allowed as a key, but are allowed as values.

8. The variable would be defined as

```
HashMap<Integer,Employee> employeeMap =
new HashMap<Integer,Employee>(100);
```

If the ID numbers are between 0 and 100, then the map will work, but a simple array or `ArrayList` might be a more appropriate data structure.

9. A `HashSet<T>` does not. An `ArrayList<T>` does.

10. The answer to both questions is the same: They will return the same element.

Programming Projects

Visit www.myprogramminglab.com to complete select exercises online and get instant feedback.

1. Redo Programming Project 6.8 in Chapter 6, but this time do it for a vector of strings to be sorted into lexicographic order.

2. The Sieve of Erastothenes is an ancient algorithm that generates prime numbers. Consider the list of numbers from 2 to 10 as follows:

        2   3   4   5   6   7   8   9   10

The algorithm starts with the first prime number in the list, which is 2, and then iterates through the remainder of the list, removing any number that is a multiple of 2 (in this case, 4, 6, 8, and 10), leaving

        2   3   5   7   9

We then repeat the process with the second prime number in the list, which is 3, and then iterate through the remainder of the list, removing any number that is a multiple of 3 (in this case 9), leaving

2   3   5   7

We then repeat starting with each successive prime number, but no elements are removed because there are no multiples of 5 or 7 (a more efficient implementation of the algorithm would stop without examining 5 or 7). The numbers that remain in the list are all prime numbers.

Implement this algorithm using an `ArrayList` of integers that is initialized to the values from 2 to 100. Your program can iterate numerically through the `ArrayList` from index 0 to index `size()-1` to get the current prime number, but should use an `Iterator` to scan through the remainder of the list to eliminate the multiples. You can use the `listIterator` method to retrieve the iterator starting at a specified index into the `ArrayList`. Output all remaining prime numbers to the console.

3. The birthday paradox is that there is a surprisingly high probability that two or more people in the same room happen to share the same birthday. By birthday, we mean the same day of the year (ignoring leap years), but not the exact birthday that includes the birth year or time of day. Write a program that approximates the probability that 2 or more people in the same room have the same birthday, for 2 to 50 people in the room.

The program should use simulation to approximate the answer. Over many trials (say, 5,000), randomly assign birthdays (i.e., a number from 1–365) to everyone in the room. Use a `HashSet` to store the birthdays. As the birthdays are randomly generated, use the `contains` method of a `HashSet` to see if someone with the same birthday is already in the room. If so, increment a counter that tracks how many times at least two people have the same birthday and then move on to the next trial. After the trials are over, divide the counter by the number of trials to get an estimated probability that two or more people share the same birthday for a given room size.

Your output should look something like the following. It will not be exactly the same due to the random numbers:

```
For 2 people, the probability of two birthdays is about 0.002

For 3 people, the probability of two birthdays is about 0.0082

For 4 people, the probability of two birthdays is about 0.0163

. . .

For 49 people, the probability of two birthdays is about 0.9654

For 50 people, the probability of two birthdays is about 0.969
```

4. The text files `boynames.txt` and `girlnames.txt`, which are included in the source code for this book, contain lists of the 1,000 most popular boy and girl names in the United States for the year 2005, as compiled by the Social Security Administration.

These are blank-delimited files where the most popular name is listed first, the second most popular name is listed second, and so on to the 1,000th most popular name, which is listed last. Each line consists of the first name followed by a blank

VideoNote
Solution to Programming Project 16.3

space followed by the number of registered births in the year using that name. For example, the `girlnames.txt` file begins with

```
Emily 25494
Emma 22532
```

This indicates that Emily is the most popular name with 25,494 registered namings, Emma is the second most popular with 22,532, and so on.

Write a program that determines how many names are on both the boys' and the girls' list. Use the following algorithm:

- Read each girl name as a String, ignoring the number of namings, and add it to a `HashSet` object.

- Read each boy name as a String, ignoring the number of namings, and add it to the same `HashSet` object. If the name is already in the `HashSet`, then the `add` method returns `false`. If you count the number of `false` returns, then this gives you the number of common namings.

- Add each common name to an `ArrayList` and output all of the common names from this list before the program exits.

VideoNote

Solution to Programming Project 16.5

5. Repeat the previous problem except create your own class, `Name`, that is added to a `HashMap` instead of a `HashSet`. The `Name` class should have three private variables, a String to store the name, an integer to store the number of namings for girls, and an integer to store the number of namings for boys. Use the first name as the key to the `HashMap`. The value to store is the `Name` object. Instead of ignoring the number of namings, as in the previous project, store the number in the `Name` class. Make the `ArrayList` a list of `Name` objects; each time you find a common name, add the entire `Name` object to the list. Your program should then iterate through the `ArrayList` and output each common name, along with the number of boy and girl namings.

6. In an ancient land, the beautiful princess Eve had many suitors. She decided on the following procedure to determine which suitor she would marry. First, all of the suitors would be lined up one after the other and assigned numbers. The first suitor would be number 1, the second number 2, and so on up to the last suitor, number n. Starting at the first suitor, she would then count three suitors down the line (because of the three letters in her name) and the third suitor would be eliminated from winning her hand and removed from the line. Eve would then continue, counting three more suitors, and eliminating every third suitor. When she reached the end of the line, she would reverse direction and work her way back to the beginning. Similarly, on reaching the first person in line, she would reverse direction and make her way to the end of the line.

For example, if there were five suitors, then the elimination process would proceed as follows:

12345   Initial list of suitors; start counting from 1.

1245   Suitor 3 eliminated; continue counting from 4 and bounce from end back to 4.

125   Suitor 4 eliminated; continue counting back from 2 and bounce from front back to 2.

15   Suitor 2 eliminated; continue counting forward from 5.

1   Suitor 5 eliminated; 1 is the lucky winner.

Write a program that uses an `ArrayList` or `Vector` to determine which position you should stand in to marry the princess if there are *n* suitors. Your program should use the `ListIterator` interface to traverse the list of suitors and remove a suitor. Be careful that your iterator references the proper object upon reversing direction at the beginning or end of the list. The suitor at the beginning or end of the list should only be counted once when the princess reverses the count.

7. In social networking websites, people link to their friends to form a social network. Write a program that uses `HashMaps` to store the data for such a network. Your program should read from a file that specifies the network connections for different usernames. The file should have the following format to specify a link:

```
source_usernamefriend_username
```

There should be an entry for each link, one per line. Here is a sample file for five usernames:

```
iba           java_guru
iba           crisha
iba           ducky
crisha        java_guru
crisha        iba
ducky         java_guru
ducky         iba
java_guru     iba
java_guru     crisha
java_guru     ducky
wittless      java_guru
```

In this network, everyone links to java_guru as a friend. iba is friends with java_guru, crisha, and ducky. Note that links are not bidirectional; wittless links with java_guru but java_guru does not link with wittless.

First, create a `User` class that has an instance variable to store the user's name and another instance variable that is of type `HashSet<User>`. The `HashSet<User>` variable should contain references to the `User` objects that the current user links to. For example, for the user iba there would be three entries, for java_guru, crisha, and ducky. Second, create a `HashMap<String,User>` instance variable in your main class that is used to map from a username to the corresponding `User` object. Your program should do the following:

- Upon startup, read the data file and populate the `HashMap` and `HashSet` data structures according to the links specified in the file.

- Allow the user to enter a name.
- If the name exists in the map, then output all usernames that are one link away from the user entered.
- If the name exists in the map, then output all usernames that are two links away from the user entered. To accomplish this in a general way, you might consider writing a recursive subroutine.

Do not forget that your User class must override the hashCode and equals methods.

8. You have collected a file of movie ratings where each movie is rated from 1 (bad) to 5 (excellent). The first line of the file is a number that identifies how many ratings are in the file. Each rating then consists of two lines: the name of the movie followed by the numeric rating from 1 to 5. Here is a sample rating file with four unique movies and seven ratings:

```
7
Harry Potter and the Half-Blood Prince
4
Harry Potter and the Half-Blood Prince
5
Army of the Dead
1
Harry Potter and the Half-Blood Prince
4
Army of the Dead
2
The Uninvited
4
Pandorium
3
```

Write a program that reads a file in this format, calculates the average rating for each movie, and outputs the average along with the number of reviews. Here is the desired output for the sample data:

```
Harry Potter and the Half-Blood Prince: 3 reviews, average of 4.3 / 5
Army of the Dead: 2 reviews, average of 1.5 / 5
The Uninvited: 1 review, average of 4 / 5
Pandorium: 1 review, average of 3 / 5
```

Use a HashMap or multiple HashMaps to calculate the output. Your map(s) should index from a string representing each movie's name to integers that store the number of reviews for the movie and the sum of the ratings for the movie.

9. The file words.txt included on the website contains a list of 87,314 English words. Write a program that uses this word list to implement a simple spell-checker. First, read all of the words into a HashSet<String> object. Then, allow the user to enter the name of a text file that contains written English. The program should output all of the words that are not in the set as potentially misspelled words.

Swing I 17

17.1 EVENT-DRIVEN PROGRAMMING   975
Events and Listeners   975

17.2 BUTTONS, EVENTS, AND OTHER SWING BASICS   976
Example: A Simple Window   977
Buttons   983
Action Listeners and Action Events   984
Example: A Better Version of Our First Swing GUI   987
Labels   990
Color   991
Example: A GUI with a Label and Color   992

17.3 CONTAINERS AND LAYOUT MANAGERS   994
Border Layout Managers   995
Flow Layout Managers   998
Grid Layout Managers   999
Panels   1003

Example: A Tricolor Built with Panels   1004
The `Container` Class   1008
The Model-View-Controller Pattern ★   1012

17.4 MENUS AND BUTTONS   1013
Example: A GUI with a Menu   1013
Menu Bars, Menus, and Menu Items   1013
Nested Menus ★   1018
The `AbstractButton` Class   1018
The `setActionCommand` Method   1021
Listeners as Inner Classes ★   1022

17.5 TEXT FIELDS AND TEXT AREAS   1025
Text Areas and Text Fields   1026
A Swing Calculator   1033

Chapter Summary   1038   Answers to Self-Test Exercises   1039   Programming Projects   1045

17 Swing I

"It Don't Mean a Thing If It Ain't Got That Swing"

SONG TITLE, *Duke Ellington*

Introduction

Swing

GUI

This is the first of three chapters that present the basic classes in the **Swing** package and teach the basic techniques for using these classes to define *GUIs*. **GUIs** are windowing interfaces that handle user input and output. *GUI* is pronounced "gooey" and stands for **graphical user interface**. Entire books have been written on Swing, so we will not be able to give you a complete description of Swing in just three chapters. However, we will teach you enough to allow you to write a variety of windowing interfaces.

GUI

Windowing systems that interact with the user are often called **GUIs**. *GUI* is pronounced "gooey" and stands for **graphical user interface**.

AWT

The **AWT (Abstract Window Toolkit)** package is an older package designed for doing windowing interfaces. Swing can be viewed as an improved version of the AWT. However, Swing did not completely replace the AWT package. Some AWT classes are replaced by Swing classes, but other AWT classes are needed when using Swing. We will use classes from both Swing and the AWT.

Swing GUIs are designed using a particular form of object-oriented programming that is known as *event-driven programming*. Our first section begins with a brief overview of event-driven programming.

Prerequisites

Before covering this chapter (and the two chapters on applets[1] and more Swing), you need to have read Chapters 1 through 5, Chapter 7 (inheritance), Chapter 13 (interfaces and inner classes), and Section 8.2 of Chapter 8 (abstract classes). (Section 8.2 of Chapter 8 does not require Section 8.1.) Except for one subsection at the end of this chapter, you need not have read any of the other chapters that precede this chapter.

To cover the last subsection of this chapter, entitled "A Swing Calculator," you need to first read Chapter 9, which covers exceptions. If you have not yet read Chapter 9, you can skip that last section.

---

[1] The chapter on applets is on the website that accompanies this book.

17.1   **Event-Driven Programming**

My duty is to obey orders.

THOMAS JONATHAN (STONEWALL) JACKSON

event-driven programming

Event-driven programming is a programming style that uses a signal-and-response approach to programming. Signals to objects are things called *events,* a concept we explain in this section.

Events and Listeners

event

listener

firing an event

Swing programs use events and event handlers. An **event** is an object that acts as a signal to another object known as a **listener**. The sending of the event is called **firing the event**. The object that fires the event is often a GUI component, such as a button. The button fires the event in response to being clicked. The listener object performs some action in response to the event. For example, the listener might place a message on the screen in response to a particular button being clicked. A given component may have any number of listeners, from zero to several listeners. Each listener might respond to a different kind of event, or multiple listeners might respond to the same events.

If you have read Chapter 9 on exception handling, then you have already seen one specialized example of event-driven programming.[2] An exception object is an event. The throwing of an exception is an example of firing an event (in this case, firing the exception event). The listener is the `catch` block that catches the event.

event handler

In Swing GUIs, an event often represents some action such as clicking a mouse, dragging the mouse, pressing a key on the keyboard, clicking the close-window button on a window, or any other action that is expected to elicit a response. A listener object has methods that specify what will happen when events of various kinds are received by the listener. These methods that handle events are called **event handlers**. You the programmer will define (or redefine) these event-handler methods. The relationship between an event-firing object, such as a button, and its event-handling listener is shown diagrammatically in Display 17.1.

Event-driven programming is very different from most programming you have seen before now. All our previous programs consisted of a list of statements executed in order. There were loops that repeat statements and branches that choose one of a list of statements to execute next. However, at some level, each run of a program consists of a list of statements performed by one agent (the computer) that executes the statements one after the other in order.

Event-driven programming is a very different game. In event-driven programming, you create objects that can fire events, and you create listener objects to react to the events. For the most part, your program does not determine the order in which things happen. The events determine that order. When an event-driven program is running,

---

[2]If you have not yet covered Chapter 9 on exceptions, you can safely ignore this paragraph.

Display 17.1   Event Firing and an Event Listener

The component (for example, a button) fires an event.

component → event → listener

This listener object invokes an event handler method with the event as an argument.

the next thing that happens depends on the next event. It is as though the listeners are robots that interact with other objects (possibly other robots) in response to events (signals) from these other objects. You program the robots, but the environment and other robots determine what any particular robot will actually end up doing.

If you have never done event-driven programming before, one aspect of it may seem strange to you: *You will be writing definitions for methods that you will never invoke in any program.* This will likely feel a bit strange at first, because a method is of no value unless it is invoked. So, somebody or something other than you, the programmer, must be invoking these methods. That is exactly what does happen. The Swing system automatically invokes certain methods when an event signals that the method needs to be called.

Event-driven programming with the Swing library makes extensive use of inheritance. The classes you define will be derived classes of some basic Swing library classes. These derived classes will inherit methods from their base class. For many of these inherited methods, library software will determine when these methods are invoked, but you will override the definition of the inherited method to determine what will happen when the method is invoked.

17.2   Buttons, Events, and Other Swing Basics

One button click is worth a thousand key strokes.

ANONYMOUS

In this section, we present enough about Swing to allow you to do some simple GUI programs.

EXAMPLE: A Simple Window

Display 17.2 contains a Swing program that produces a simple window. The window contains nothing but a button on which is written `"Click to end program."` If the user follows the instructions and clicks the button with his or her mouse, the program ends.

The `import` statements give the names of the classes used and which package they are in. What we and others call the *Swing library* is the package named `javax.swing`. The *AWT library* is the package `java.awt`. Note that one package name contains an `"x"` and one does not.

This program is a simple class definition with only a `main` method. The first line in the `main` method creates an object of the class `JFrame`. That line is reproduced as follows:

```
JFrame firstWindow = new JFrame();
```

This is an ordinary declaration of a variable named `firstWindow` and an invocation of the no-argument constructor for the class `JFrame`. A `JFrame` object is a basic window that includes a border and the usual three buttons for minimizing the window down to an icon, changing the size of the window, and closing the window. These buttons are shown in the upper-right corner of the window, which is typical, but if your operating system normally places these buttons someplace else, that is where they will likely be located in a `JFrame` on your computer.

The initial size of the `JFrame` window is set using the `JFrame` method `setSize`, as follows:

```
firstWindow.setSize(WIDTH, HEIGHT);
```

In this case, `WIDTH` and `HEIGHT` are defined `int` constants. The units of measure are pixels, so the window produced is 300 pixels by 200 pixels. (The term *pixel* is defined in the box entitled "Pixel.") As with other windows, you can change the size of a `JFrame` by using your mouse to drag a corner of the `JFrame` window.

The buttons for minimizing the window down to an icon and for changing the size of the window behave as they do in any of the other windows you have used. The minimization button shrinks the window down to an icon. (To restore the window, click the icon.) The second button changes the size of the window back and forth from full screen to a smaller size. The close-window button can behave in different ways depending on how it is set by your program.

The behavior of the close-window button is set with the `JFrame` method `setDefaultCloseOperation`. The line of the program that sets the behavior of the close-window button is reproduced next:

```
firstWindow.setDefaultCloseOperation(JFrame.DO_NOTHING_ON_CLOSE);
```

(continued)

EXAMPLE: (continued)

In this case, the argument `JFrame.DO_NOTHING_ON_CLOSE` is a defined constant named `DO_NOTHING_ON_CLOSE`, which is defined in the `JFrame` class. This sets the close-window button so that when it is clicked, nothing happens (unless we programmed something to happen, which we have not done). Other possible arguments are given in Display 17.3.

The method `setDefaultCloseOperation` takes a single `int` argument; each of the constants described in Display 17.3 is an `int` constant. However, do not think of them as `int` values. Think of them as policies for what happens when the user clicks the close-window button. It was convenient to name these policies by `int` values. However, they could just as well have been named by `char` values or `String` values or something else. The fact that they are `int` values is an incidental detail of no real importance.

Descriptions of some of the most important methods in the class `JFrame` are given in Display 17.3. Some of these methods will not be explained until later in this chapter. A more complete list of methods for the class `JFrame` is given in Appendix 5.

A `JFrame` can have components added, such as buttons, menus, and text labels. For example, the following line from Display 17.2 adds the `JButton` object named `endButton` to the `JFrame` named `firstWindow`:

```
firstWindow.add(endButton);
```

The description of how the `JButton` named `endButton` is created and programmed will be given in the two subsections entitled "Buttons" and "Action Listeners and Action Events" a little later in this section.

We end this subsection by jumping ahead to the last line of the program, which is

```
firstWindow.setVisible(true);
```

This makes the `JFrame` window visible on the screen. At first glance, this may seem strange. Why not have windows automatically become visible? Why would you create a window if you did not want it to be visible? The answer is that you may not want it to be visible at all times. You have certainly experienced windows that disappear and reappear. To hide the window, which is not desirable in this example, you would replace the argument `true` with `false`.

JFrame

An object of the class `JFrame` is what you think of as a window. It automatically has a border and some basic buttons for minimizing the window and similar actions. As you will see, a `JFrame` object can have buttons and many other components added to the window and programmed for action.

Display 17.2   **A First Swing Demonstration Program** (part 1 of 2)

```
1   import javax.swing.JFrame;
2   import javax.swing.JButton;              This program is not typical of
                                             the style we will use in Swing
3   public class FirstSwingDemo             programs.
4   {
5       public static final int WIDTH = 300;
6       public static final int HEIGHT = 200;

7       public static void main(String[] args)
8       {
9           JFrame firstWindow = new JFrame( );
10          firstWindow.setSize(WIDTH, HEIGHT);

11          firstWindow.setDefaultCloseOperation(
12                              JFrame.DO_NOTHING_ON_CLOSE);

13          JButton endButton = new JButton("Click to end program.");
14          EndingListener buttonEar = new EndingListener();
15          endButton.addActionListener(buttonEar);
16          firstWindow.add(endButton);

17          firstWindow.setVisible(true);
18      }
19  }                       This is the file FirstSwingDemo.java.
```

```
1   import java.awt.event.ActionListener;
2   import java.awt.event.ActionEvent;      This is the file EndingListener.java.

3   public class EndingListener implements ActionListener
4   {
5       public void actionPerformed(ActionEvent e)
6       {
7           System.exit(0);
8       }
9   }
```

(continued)

Display 17.2 **A First Swing Demonstration Program** (part 2 of 2)

Resulting GUI

Minimize (iconify)

Change window sixe to full screen

Close-window button

Click to end program.

Pixel

pixel

A **pixel** is the smallest unit of space on which your screen can write. With Swing, both the size and the position of objects on the screen are measured in pixels. The more pixels you have on a screen, the greater the screen resolution.

Resolution's Relationship to Object Size

The relationship between resolution and size can seem confusing at first. A high-resolution screen is a screen of better quality than a low-resolution screen, so why does an object look smaller on a high-resolution screen and larger on a low-resolution screen? Consider a very simple case—namely, a one-pixel "dot." For a screen of fixed size, if there are very many pixels (high resolution), then the one-pixel dot will be very small. If there are fewer pixels (low resolution) for the same size screen, then each pixel must be larger because the smaller number of pixels cover the same screen. So, if there are fewer pixels, the one-pixel dot will be larger. Similarly, a two-pixel figure or a figure of any number of pixels will look larger on a low-resolution (fewer pixels) screen.

Display 17.3 **Some Methods in the Class `JFrame`** (part 1 of 2)

The class `JFrame` is in the `javax.swing` package.

```
public JFrame()
```

Constructor that creates an object of the class `JFrame`.

Display 17.3   **Some Methods in the Class JFrame** (part 2 of 2)

```
public JFrame(String title)
```

Constructor that creates an object of the class JFrame with the title given as the argument.

```
public void setDefaultCloseOperation(int operation)
```

Sets the action that will happen by default when the user clicks the close-window button. The argument should be one of the following defined constants:

JFrame.DO_NOTHING_ON_CLOSE: Do nothing. The JFrame does nothing, but if there are any registered window listeners, they are invoked. (Window listeners are explained in Chapter 18.)

JFrame.HIDE_ON_CLOSE: Hide the frame after invoking any registered WindowListener objects.

JFrame.DISPOSE_ON_CLOSE: Hide and *dispose* the frame after invoking any registered window listeners. When a window is **disposed**, it is eliminated but the program does not end. To end the program, use the next constant as an argument to setDefaultCloseOperation.

JFrame.EXIT_ON_CLOSE: Exit the application using the System exit method. (Do not use this for frames in applets. Applets are discussed in Chapter 20 on the website.)

If no action is specified using the method setDefaultCloseOperation, then the default action taken is JFrame.HIDE_ON_CLOSE.

Throws an IllegalArgumentException if the argument is not one of the values listed above[3].

Throws a SecurityException if the argument is JFrame.EXIT_ON_CLOSE and the Security Manager will not allow the caller to invoke System.exit. (You are not likely to encounter this case.)

```
public void setSize(int width, int height)
```

Sets the size of the calling frame so that it has the width and height specified. Pixels are the units of length used.

```
public void setTitle(String title)
```

Sets the title for this frame to the argument string.

```
public void add(Component componentAdded)
```

Adds a component to the JFrame.

```
public void setLayout(LayoutManager manager)
```

Sets the layout manager. Layout managers are discussed later in this chapter in Section 17.3.

```
public void setJMenuBar(JMenuBar menubar)
```

Sets the menu bar for the calling frame. (Menus and menu bars are discussed later in this chapter in Section 17.4.)

```
public void dispose()
```

Eliminates the calling frame and all its subcomponents. Any memory they use is released for reuse. If there are items left (items other than the calling frame and its subcomponents), then this does not end the program. (The method dispose is discussed in Chapter 19.)

---

[3]If you have not yet covered Chapter 9 on exceptions, you can safely ignore all references to "throwing exceptions."

The `setVisible` Method

Many classes of Swing objects have a `setVisible` method. The `setVisible` method takes one argument of type `boolean`. If w is an object, such as a `JFrame` window, that can be displayed on the screen, then the call

```
w.setVisible(true);
```

will make w visible. The call

```
w.setVisible(false);
```

will hide w.

SYNTAX

```
Object_For_Screen.setVisible(Boolean_Expression);
```

EXAMPLE (FROM DISPLAY 17.2)

```
public static void main(String[] args)
{
    JFrame firstWindow = new JFrame();
       .
       .
       .
    firstWindow.setVisible(true);
}
```

PITFALL: Forgetting to Program the Close-Window Button

The following lines from Display 17.2 ensure that when the user clicks the close-window button, nothing happens:

```
firstWindow.setDefaultCloseOperation(
                    JFrame.DO_NOTHING_ON_CLOSE);
```

If you forget to program the close-window button, then the default action is as if you had set it the following way:

```
firstWindow.setDefaultCloseOperation(
                    JFrame.HIDE_ON_CLOSE);
```

In the program in Display 17.2, this would mean that if the user clicks the close-window button, the window will hide (become invisible and inaccessible), but the program will not end, which is a pretty bad situation. Because the window would be hidden, there would be no way to click the `"Click to end program."` button. You would need to use some operating system command that forces the program to end. That is an operating system topic, not a Java topic, and the exact command depends on which operating system you are using. ■

Self-Test Exercises

1. Which package provides the original foundation of graphics work in Java?

2. Identify the event and the event handler in the following code snippet:

```
int temp = 45;
try
{
        if (temp > 30)
        throw new Exception("Over 30.");
    else
        System.out.println("No exception.");
    }
catch(Exception thrownObject)
{
    System.out.println(thrownObject.getMessage());
}
```

3. Write a small code snippet that would create a simple window object `myWindow` with width 800 pixels and height 500 pixels.

4. Write a small code that would create a simple window object `myWindow` with a title `"Hello World"` with width 800 pixels and height 500 pixels.

5. What is the method call to set the close-window button of the `JFrame myWindow` so that the window is eliminated but the program does not end when the user clicks the close-window button in `myWindow`?

6. Suppose `someWindow` is a `JFrame` and n is an `int` variable with some value. Give a Java statement that will make `someWindow` visible if n is positive and hide `someWindow` otherwise.

Buttons

JButton

A button object is created in the same way that any other object is created, but you use the class `JButton`. For example, the following example from Display 17.2 creates a button:

```
JButton endButton = new JButton("Click to end program.");
```

The argument to the construct, in this case, `"Click to end program."`, is a string that will be written on the button when the button is displayed. If you look at the picture of the GUI in Display 17.2, you will see that the button is labeled `"Click to end program."`

adding a button

We have already discussed adding components, such as buttons, to a `JFrame`. The button is added to the `JFrame` by the following line from Display 17.2:

```
firstWindow.add(endButton);
```

In the next subsection, we explain the lines from Display 17.2 involving the method `addActionListener`.

The `JButton` Class

An object of the class `JButton` is displayed in a GUI as a component that looks like a button. Click the button with your mouse to simulate pushing it. When creating an object of the class `JButton` using `new`, you can give a string argument to the constructor and the string will be displayed on the button.

You can add a `JButton` object to a `JFrame` by using the method `add` with the `JFrame` as the calling object and the `JButton` object as the argument. You will later see that you can also add buttons to other GUI objects (known as "containers") in a similar way.

A button's action is programmed by registering a listener with the button using the method `addActionListener`.

EXAMPLE

```
JButton niceButton = new JButton("Click here");
niceButton.addActionListener(new SomeActionListenerClass());
someJFrame.add(niceButton);
```

The Close-Window Button Is Not in the Class `JButton`

The buttons that you add to a GUI are all objects of the class `JButton`. The close-window button and the other two accompanying buttons on a `JFrame` are not objects of the class `JButton`. They are part of the `JFrame` object.

Action Listeners and Action Events

Clicking a button with your mouse (or activating certain other items in a GUI) creates an object known as an event and sends the event object to another object (or objects) known as the listener(s). This is called **firing the event**. The listener then performs some action. When we say that the event is "sent" to the listener object, what we really mean is that some method in the listener object is invoked with the event object as the argument. This invocation happens automatically. Your Swing GUI class definition will not normally contain an invocation of this method. However, your Swing GUI class definition does need to do two things:

registering a listener

- First, for each button, it needs to specify what objects are listeners that will respond to events fired by that button; this is called **registering** the listener.

- Second, it must define the methods that will be invoked when the event is sent to the listener. Note that these methods will be defined by you, but in normal circumstances, you will never write an invocation of these methods. The invocations will take place automatically.

addAction Listener

The following lines from Display 17.2 create an `EndingListener` object named `buttonEar` and register `buttonEar` as a listener to receive events from the button named `endButton`:

```
EndingListener buttonEar = new EndingListener( );
endButton.addActionListener(buttonEar);
```

The second line says that `buttonEar` is registered as a listener to `endButton`, which means `buttonEar` will receive all events fired by `endButton`.

action event

`Action Listener`

Different kinds of components require different kinds of listener classes to handle the events they fire. A button fires events known as **action events**, which are handled by listeners known as **action listeners**.

An action listener is an object whose class implements the `ActionListener` interface. For example, the class `EndingListener` in Display 17.2 implements the `ActionListener` interface. The `ActionListener` interface has only one method heading that must be implemented, namely the following:

action Performed

```
public void actionPerformed(ActionEvent e)
```

In the class `EndingListener` in Display 17.2, the `actionPerformed` method is defined as follows:

```
public void actionPerformed(ActionEvent e)
{
    System.exit(0);
}
```

If the user clicks the button `endButton`, it sends an action event to the action listener for that button. But `buttonEar` is the action listener for the button `endButton`, so the action event goes to `buttonEar`. When an action listener receives an action event, the event is automatically passed as an argument to the method `actionPerformed` and the method `actionPerformed` is invoked. If the event is called `e`, then the following invocation takes place in response to `endButton` firing `e`:

```
buttonEar.actionPerformed(e);
```

In this case, the parameter `e` is ignored by the method `actionPerformed`. The method `actionPerformed` simply invokes `System.exit` and thereby ends the program. So, if the user clicks `endButton` (the one labeled `"Click to end program."`), the net effect is to end the program and so the window goes away.

Note that you never write any code that says

```
buttonEar.actionPerformed(e);
```

This action does happen, but the code for this is embedded in some class definition inside the Swing and/or AWT libraries. Somewhere the code says something like

```
bla.actionPerformed(e);
```

and somehow `buttonEar` gets plugged in for the parameter `bla` and this invocation of `actionPerformed` is executed. But, all this is done for you. All you do is define the method `actionPerformed` and register `buttonEar` as a listener for `endButton`.

Note that the method `actionPerformed` must have a parameter of type `ActionEvent`, even if your definition of `actionPerformed` does not use this parameter. This is because the invocations of `actionPerformed` were already programmed for you and so must allow the possibility of using the `ActionEvent` parameter `e`. As you will see, in other Swing GUIs the method `actionPerformed` does often use the event `e` to determine which button was clicked. This first example is a special, simple case because there is only one button. Later in this chapter, we will say more about defining the `actionPerformed` method in more complicated situations.

PITFALL: Changing the Heading for `actionPerformed`

When you define the method `actionPerformed` in an action listener, you are implementing the method heading for `actionPerformed` that is specified in the `ActionListener` interface. Thus, the header for the method `actionPerformed` is determined for you, and you cannot change the heading. It must have exactly one parameter, and that parameter must be of type `ActionEvent`, as in the following:

```
public void actionPerformed(ActionEvent e)
```

If you change the type of the parameter or if you add (or subtract) a parameter, you will not have given a correct definition of an action listener.[4] The only thing you can change is the name of the parameter e, because it is just a placeholder. So the following change is acceptable:

```
public void actionPerformed(ActionEvent theEvent)
```

Of course, if you make this change, then inside the body of the method `actionPerformed`, you will use the identifier `theEvent` in place of the identifier e.

You also cannot add a `throws` clause to the method `actionPerformed`.[5] If a checked exception is thrown in the definition of `actionPerformed`, then it must be caught in the method `actionPerformed`. (Recall that a checked exception is one that must be either caught in a `catch` block or declared in a `throws` clause.) ∎

TIP: Ending a Swing Program

A GUI program is normally based on a kind of infinite loop. There may not be a Java loop statement in a GUI program, but nonetheless the GUI program need not ever end. The windowing system normally stays on the screen until the user indicates that it should go away (for example, by clicking the `"Click to end program."` button in Display 17.2). If the user never asks the windowing system to go away, it will never go away. When you write a Swing GUI program, you need to use `System.exit` to end the program when the user (or something else) says it is time to do so. Unlike the kinds of programs we saw before this chapter, a Swing program will not end after it has executed all the code in the program. A Swing program does not end until it executes a `System.exit`. (In some cases, the `System.exit` may be in some library code and need not be explicitly given in your code.) ∎

`System.exit`

---

[4] Although it would be rather questionable style, you can overload the method named `actionPerformed` so that you have multiple versions of the method `actionPerformed`, each with a different parameter list. But only the version of `actionPerformed` shown here has anything to do with making a class into an action listener.

[5] If you have not yet covered exception handling (Chapter 9), you can safely ignore this paragraph.

Self-Test Exercises

7. Which interface is used for handling button events?

8. What method heading must be implemented in a class that implements the `ActionListener` interface?

9. Change the program in Display 17.2 so that the window displayed has the title `"My First Window"`. *Hint*: Consult the description of constructors in Display 17.3.

EXAMPLE: A Better Version of Our First Swing GUI

Display 17.4 is a rewriting of the demonstration program in Display 17.2 that includes a few added features. This new version produces a window that is similar to the one produced by the program in Display 17.2. However, this new version is done in the style you should follow in writing your own GUIs. Notice that the window is produced by defining a class (`FirstWindow`) whose objects are windows of the kind we want. The window is then displayed by a program (`DemoWindow`) that uses the class `FirstWindow`.

Observe that `FirstWindow` is a derived class of the class `JFrame`. This is the normal way to define a windowing interface. The base class `JFrame` gives some basic window facilities, and then the derived class adds whatever additional features you want in your window interface.

Note that the constructor in Display 17.4 starts by calling the constructor for the parent class `JFrame` with the line

```
super();
```

As we noted in Chapter 7, this ensures that any initialization that is normally done for all objects of type `JFrame` will in fact be done. If the base class constructor you call has no arguments, then it will be called automatically, so we could have omitted the invocation of `super()` in Display 17.4. However, if the base class constructor needs an argument, as it may in some other situations, then you must include a call to the base class constructor, `super`.

Note that almost all the initializing for the window `FirstWindow` in Display 17.4 is placed in the constructor for the class. That is as it should be. The initialization, such as setting the initial window size, should be part of the class definition and not actions performed by objects of the class (as they were in Display 17.2). All the initializing methods, such as `setSize` and `setDefaultCloseOperation`, are inherited from the class `JFrame`. Because they are invoked in the constructor for the window, the window itself is the calling object. In other words, a method invocation such as

```
setSize(WIDTH, HEIGHT);
```

is equivalent to

```
this.setSize(WIDTH, HEIGHT);
```

(continued)

EXAMPLE: (continued)

Similarly, the method invocations

```
setDefaultCloseOperation(
                JFrame.DO_NOTHING_ON_CLOSE);
```

and

```
add(endButton);
```

are equivalent to

```
this.setDefaultCloseOperation(
                JFrame.DO_NOTHING_ON_CLOSE);
```

and

```
this.add(endButton);
```

In the class `FirstWindow` (Display 17.4), we added the title `"First Window Class"` to the window as follows:

```
setTitle("First Window Class");
```

You can see where the title is displayed in a `JFrame` by looking at the picture of the GUI given in Display 17.4.

One thing we did differently in Display 17.4 than in Display 17.2 is to use an anonymous object in the following line:

```
endButton.addActionListener(new EndingListener());
```

The same action was performed by the following lines in Display 17.2:

```
EndingListener buttonEar = new EndingListener();
endButton.addActionListener(buttonEar);
```

In Display 17.2, we were trying to be extra clear and so we used these two steps. However, it makes more sense to use the anonymous object `new EndingListener()` because this listener object is never referenced again and so does not need a name.

The program `DemoWindow` in Display 17.4 simply displays an object of the class `FirstWindow` on the screen.

Almost all of the initialization details for the window in Display 17.4 have been moved to the constructor for the class `FirstWindow`. However, we have placed the invocations of the method `setVisible` in the application program that uses the window class `FirstWindow`. We could have placed an invocation of `setVisible` in the constructor for `FirstWindow` and omitted the invocation of `setVisible` from the application program `DemoWindow` (Display 17.4). If we had done so, we would have produced the same results when we ran the application program. However, in normal situations, the application program knows when the window should be displayed, so it is normal to put the invocation of the method `setVisible` in the application program. The programmer writing the class `FirstWindow` cannot anticipate when a programmer who uses the window will want to make it visible (or hide it).

Display 17.4   The Normal Way to Define a `JFrame`

```java
1   import javax.swing.JFrame;
2   import javax.swing.JButton;

3   public class FirstWindow extends JFrame
4   {
5       public static final int WIDTH = 300;
6       public static final int HEIGHT = 200;

7       public FirstWindow()
8       {
9          super();
10         setSize(WIDTH, HEIGHT);

11         setTitle("First Window Class");
12         setDefaultCloseOperation(
13                             JFrame.DO_NOTHING_ON_CLOSE);

14         JButton endButton = new JButton("Click to end program.");
15         endButton.addActionListener(new EndingListener());
16         add(endButton);
17      }
18  }
```

The class `EndingListener` *is defined in Display 17.2.*

This is the file `FirstWindow.java`.

```java
1   public class DemoWindow                  This is the file DemoWindow.java.
2   {
3       public static void main(String[] args)
4       {
5          FirstWindow w = new FirstWindow();
6          w.setVisible(true);
7       }
8   }
```

RESULTING GUI

JFrame Classes

When we say that a class is a **JFrame class**, we mean the class is a descendent class of the class JFrame. For example, the class FirstWindow in Display 17.4 is a JFrame class. When we say an object is a **JFrame**, we mean that it is an object of some JFrame class.

Self-Test Exercises

10. Change the program in Display 17.4 so that the title of the JFrame is not set by the method setTitle but is instead set by the call to the base class constructor. *Hint*: Recall Self-Test Exercise 9.

11. Change the program in Display 17.4 so that there are two ways to end the GUI program: The program can be ended by either clicking the "Click to end program." button or clicking the close-window button.

Labels

label

JLabel

We have seen how to add a button to a JFrame. If you want to add some text to your JFrame, use a label instead of a button. A **label** is an object of the class JLabel. A label is little more than a line of text. The text for the label is given as an argument to the JLabel constructor as follows:

```
JLabel greeting = new JLabel("Hello");
```

The label greeting can then be added to a JFrame just as a button is added. For example, the following might appear in a constructor for a derived class of JFrame:

```
JLabel greeting = new JLabel("Hello");
add(greeting);
```

The next Programming Example, includes a label in a JFrame GUI.

The JLabel Class

An object of the class JLabel is little more than one line of text that can be added to a JFrame (or, as we will see, added to certain other objects).

EXAMPLE (INSIDE A CONSTRUCTOR FOR A DERIVED CLASS OF JFRAME)

```
JLabel myLabel = new JLabel("Hi Mom!");
add(myLabel);
```

Color

You can set the color of a `JFrame` (or other GUI object). To set the background color of a `JFrame`, use

getContent
Pane

```
getContentPane().setBackground(Color);
```

For example, the following will set the color of the `JFrame` named `someFrame` to blue:

set
Background

```
someFrame.getContentPane().setBackground(Color.BLUE);
```

Color.BLUE

Alternatively, if you set the color in the constructor for the `JFrame`, the invocation takes the form

```
getContentPane().setBackground(Color.BLUE);
```

which is equivalent to

```
this.getContentPane().setBackground(Color.BLUE);
```

The next Programming Example, "A GUI with a Label and Color," shows a `JFrame` object (in fact, two of them) with color.

content pane

The method invocation `getContentPane()` returns something called the **content pane** of the `JFrame`. So,

```
getContentPane().setBackground(Color.BLUE);
```

actually sets the color of the content pane to blue. The content pane is the "inside" of the `JFrame`, so coloring the content pane has the effect of coloring the inside of the `JFrame`. However, you can think of

```
getContentPane().setBackground(Color);
```

as a peculiarly spelled method invocation that sets the color of the `JFrame`. (In this book, we will not be referring to the content pane of a `JFrame` except when we want to color the `JFrame`, so we will explain the content pane no further.)

get
Content
Pane

Use `getContentPane` only when you give color to a `JFrame`. As you will see, to set the color of some component in a `JFrame`, such as a button, simply use the method `setBackground` with the button or other component as the calling object. You will see examples of adding color to components in Section 17.3.

color

What kind of thing is a **color** when used in a Java Swing class? Like everything else in Java, a color is an object—in this case, an object that is an instance of the class `Color`. The class `Color` is in the `java.awt` package. (Note that the package name is `java.awt`, not `javax.awt`.)

Color

In a later chapter, you will see how you can define your own colors, but for now we will use the colors that are already defined for you, such as `Color.BLUE`, which is a constant named `BLUE` that is defined in the class `Color`. The constant, of course, represents the color blue. If you set the background of a `JFrame` to `Color.BLUE`, then the `JFrame` will have a blue background. The type of the constant `Color.BLUE` and other such constants is `Color`. The list of color constants that are defined for you are given in Display 17.5. The next Programming Example, "A GUI with a Label and Color," has an example of a constructor with one parameter of type `Color`.

Display 17.5 The Color Constants

```
Color.BLACK                    Color.MAGENTA
Color.BLUE                     Color.ORANGE
Color.CYAN                     Color.PINK
Color.DARK_GRAY                Color.RED
Color.GRAY                     Color.WHITE
Color.GREEN                    Color.YELLOW
Color.LIGHT_GRAY
```

The class `Color` is in the `java.awt` package.

EXAMPLE: A GUI with a Label and Color

Display 17.6 shows a class for GUIs with a label and a background color. We have already discussed the use of color for this window. The label is used to display the text string `"Close-window button works."` The label is created as follows:

```
JLabel aLabel = new JLabel("Close-window button works.");
```

The label is added to the `JFrame` with the method `add` as shown in the following line from Display 17.6:

```
add(aLabel);
```

The GUI class `ColoredWindow` in Display 17.6 programs the close-window button as follows:

```
setDefaultCloseOperation(JFrame.EXIT_ON_CLOSE);
```

This way, when the user clicks the close-window button, the program ends. Note that if the program has more than one window, as it does in Display 17.6, and the user clicks the close-window button in any one window of the class `ColoredWindow`, then the entire program ends and all windows go away.

Note that we set the title of the `JFrame` by making it an argument to `super` rather than an argument to `setTitle`. This is another common way to set the title of a `JFrame`.

If you run the program `DemoColoredWindow` in Display 17.6, then the two windows will be placed one on top of the other. To see both windows, you need to use your mouse to move the top window.

Setting the Title of a `JFrame`

The two most common ways to set the title of a `JFrame` are to use the method `setTitle`, as illustrated in Display 17.4, or to give the title as an argument to the base class constructor `super`, as illustrated in Display 17.6.

Self-Test Exercises

12. How would you modify the class definition in Display 17.6 so that the window produced by the no-argument constructor is magenta instead of pink?

13. Rewrite the following two lines from Display 17.6 so that the label does not have the name `aLabel` or any other name. *Hint:* Use an anonymous object.

```
JLabel aLabel = new JLabel("Close-window button works.");
add(aLabel);
```

Display 17.6   A `JFrame` with Color (part 1 of 2)

```
1   import javax.swing.JFrame;
2   import javax.swing.JLabel;
3   import java.awt.Color;

4   public class ColoredWindow extends JFrame
5   {
6       public static final int WIDTH = 300;
7       public static final int HEIGHT = 200;

8       public ColoredWindow(Color theColor)
9       {

10          super("No Charge for Color");
11          setSize(WIDTH, HEIGHT);
12          setDefaultCloseOperation(JFrame.EXIT_ON_CLOSE);

13          getContentPane().setBackground(theColor);

14          JLabel aLabel = new JLabel("Close-window button works.");
15          add(aLabel);
16      }
17      public ColoredWindow()                     This is an invocation of the
18      {                                          other constructor.
19          this(Color.BLUE);
20      }
21  }                                   This is the file ColoredWindow.java.
```

```
1   import java.awt.Color;                   This is the file ColoredWindow.java.

2   public class DemoColoredWindow
3   {
4       public static void main(String[] args)
5       {
6           ColoredWindow w1 = new ColoredWindow();
7           w1.setVisible(true);

8           ColoredWindow w2 = new ColoredWindow(Color.GRAY);
9           w2.setVisible(true);
10      }
11  }
```

(continued)

Display 17.6   A JFrame with Color (part 2 of 2)

RESULTING GUI

You will need to use your mouse to drag the top window or you will not see the bottom window.

17.3   Containers and Layout Managers

Don't put all your eggs in one basket.

PROVERB

There are two main ways to create new classes from old classes. One way is to use inheritance; this is known as the *Is-A relationship*. For example, an object of the class ColoredWindow in Display 17.6 *is a* JFrame because ColoredWindow is a derived class of the class JFrame. The second way to create a new class from an existing class (or classes) is to have instance variables of an already existing class type; this is known as *composition* or the *Has-A relationship*. The Swing library has already set things up so you can easily use composition. The actual code for declaring instance variables is in the Swing library classes, such as the class JFrame. Rather than declaring instance variables, add components to a JFrame using the add method. This does ultimately set some instance variables, but this is done automatically when you use the add method. In this section, we discuss adding and arranging components in a GUI or subpart of a GUI.

Thus far, we have only added one component, either a button or a label, to a JFrame. You can add more than one component to a JFrame. To do so, use the add method multiple times, but the add method simply tells which components are added to the JFrame; it does not say how they are arranged, such as side by side or one above the other. To describe how the components are arranged, you need to use a **layout manager**.

layout manager

In this section, we will see that there are other classes of objects besides JFrames that can have components added with the add method and arranged by a layout manager. All these classes are known as **container classes**.

container class

Border Layout Managers

If you do not specify a layout, then Java will use a `BorderLayout` by default. Display 17.7 contains an example of a GUI that uses a layout manager to arrange three labels in a `JFrame`. The labels are arranged one below the other on three lines.

A layout manager is added to the `JFrame` class in Display 17.7 with the following line:

`setLayout`

```
setLayout(new BorderLayout());
```

`Border Layout`

`BorderLayout` is a layout manager class, so `new BorderLayout()` produces a new anonymous object of the class `BorderLayout`. This `BorderLayout` object is given the task of arranging components (in this case, labels) that are added to the `JFrame`.

It may help to note that the previous invocation of `setLayout` is equivalent to the following:

```
BorderLayout manager = new BorderLayout();
setLayout(manager);
```

Display 17.7   The `BorderLayout` Manager (part 1 of 2)

```
1   import javax.swing.JFrame;
2   import javax.swing.JLabel;
3   import java.awt.BorderLayout;

4   public class BorderLayoutJFrame extends JFrame
5   {
6       public static final int WIDTH = 500;
7       public static final int HEIGHT = 400;

8       public BorderLayoutJFrame()
9       {
10          super("BorderLayout Demonstration");
11          setSize(WIDTH, HEIGHT);
12          setDefaultCloseOperation(JFrame.EXIT_ON_CLOSE);

13          setLayout(new BorderLayout( ));

14          JLabel label1 = new JLabel("First label");
15          add(label1, BorderLayout.NORTH);

16          JLabel label2 = new JLabel("Second label");
17          add(label2, BorderLayout.SOUTH);

18          JLabel label3 = new JLabel("Third label");
19          add(label3, BorderLayout.CENTER);
20      }
21  }
```
                    This is the file `BorderLayoutJFrame.java`*.*

(continued)

Display 17.7   The `BorderLayout` Manager (part 2 of 2)

This is the file BorderLayoutDemo java.

```
1   public class BorderLayoutDemo
2   {
3       public static void main(String[] args)
4       {
5           BorderLayoutJFrame gui = new BorderLayoutJFrame();
6           gui.setVisible(true);
7       }
8   }
```

RESULTING GUI

A `BorderLayout` manager places labels (or other components) into the five regions `BorderLayout.NORTH`, `BorderLayout.SOUTH`, `BorderLayout.EAST`, `BorderLayout.WEST`, and `BorderLayout.CENTER`. These five regions are arranged as shown in Display 17.8. The outside box represents the `JFrame` (or other container to which you will add things). None of the lines in the diagram will be visible unless you do something to make them visible. We drew them in to show you where each region is located.

Display 17.8 `BorderLayout` Regions

In Display 17.7, we added labels as follows:

```
JLabel label1 = new JLabel("First label");
add(label1, BorderLayout.NORTH);

JLabel label2 = new JLabel("Second label");
add(label2, BorderLayout.SOUTH);

JLabel label3 = new JLabel("Third label");
add(label3, BorderLayout.CENTER);
```

When you use a `BorderLayout` manager, you give the location of the component added as a second argument to the method `add`, as in the following:

```
add(label1, BorderLayout.NORTH);
```

The labels (or other components to be added) need not be added in any particular order, because the second argument completely specifies where the label is placed.

`BorderLayout.NORTH`, `BorderLayout.SOUTH`, `BorderLayout.EAST`, `Border Layout.WEST`, and `BorderLayout.CENTER` are five string constants defined in the class `BorderLayout`. The values of these constants are `"North"`, `"South"`, `"East"`, `"West"`, and `"Center"`. Although you can use a quoted string such as `"North"` as the second argument to `add`, it is more consistent with our general style rules to use a defined constant such as `BorderLayout.NORTH`.

You need not use all five regions. For example, in Display 17.7 we did not use the regions `BorderLayout.EAST` and `BorderLayout.WEST`. If some regions are not used, any extra space is given to the `BorderLayout.CENTER` region, which is the largest region.

(The space is divided between regions as follows: Regions are allocated space in the order first north and south, second east and west, and last center. So, in particular, if there is nothing in the north region, then the east and west regions will extend to the top of the space.)

From this discussion, it sounds as though you can place only one item in each region, but later in this chapter, when we discuss *panels*, you will see that there is a way to group items so that more than one item can (in effect) be placed in each region.

There are some standard layout managers defined for you in the `java.awt` package, and you can also define your own layout managers. However, for most purposes, the layout managers defined in the standard libraries are all that you need, and we will not discuss how you can create your own layout manager classes.

Flow Layout Managers

The `FlowLayout` **manager** is the simplest layout manager. It arranges components one after the other, going from left to right, in the order in which you add them to the `JFrame` (or other container class) using the method `add`. For example, if the class in Display 17.7 had used the `FlowLayout` manager instead of the `BorderLayout` manager, it would have used the following code:

```
setLayout(new FlowLayout());

JLabel label1 = new JLabel("First label");
add(label1);

JLabel label2 = new JLabel("Second label");
add(label2);

JLabel label3 = new JLabel("Third label");
add(label3);
```

Layout Managers

The components that you add to a container class are arranged by an object known as a **layout manager**. Add a layout manager with the method `setLayout`, which is a method of every container class, such as a `JFrame` or an object of any of the other container classes that we will introduce later in this chapter. If you do not add a layout manager, a default layout manager will be provided for you.

SYNTAX

Container_Object.`setLayout`(new *Layout_Manager_Class*());

EXAMPLE (WITHIN A CONSTRUCTOR FOR A CLASS CALLED `BorderLayoutJFrame`)

```
public BorderLayoutJFrame()
{
    ...
    setLayout(new BorderLayout());

    JLabel label1 = new JLabel("First label");
    add(label1, BorderLayout.NORTH);

    JLabel label2 = new JLabel("Second label");
    add(label2, BorderLayout.SOUTH);
    ...
}
```

Note that if we had used the `FlowLayout` manager, as in the preceding code, then the `add` method would have only one argument. With a `FlowLayout` manager, the items are displayed in the order they are added, so that the labels above would be displayed all on one line as follows:

```
First label Second label Third label
```

extra code on website

The full program is in the files `FlowLayoutJFrame.java` and `FlowLayoutDemo.java` on the accompanying website. You will see a number of examples of GUIs that use the `FlowLayout` manager class later in this chapter.

Grid Layout Managers

GridLayout

A **GridLayout manager** arranges components in a two-dimensional grid with some number of rows and columns. With a `GridLayout` manager, each entry is the same size. For example, the following says to use a `GridLayout` manager with `aContainer`, which can be a `JFrame` or other container:

```
aContainer.setLayout(new GridLayout(2, 3));
```

The two numbers given as arguments to the constructor `GridLayout` specify the number of rows and columns. This would produce the following sort of layout:

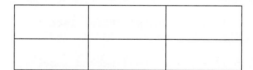

The lines will not be visible unless you do something special to make them so. They are just included here to show you the region boundaries.

When using a `GridLayout` manager, each component is stretched so that it completely fills its grid position.

Although you specify a number of rows and columns, the rules for the number of rows and columns is more complicated than what we have said so far. If the values for the number of rows and the number of columns are both nonzero, then the number of columns will be ignored. For example, if the specification is `new GridLayout(2, 3)`, then some sample sizes are as follows: If you add six items, the grid will be as shown. If you add seven or eight items, a fourth column is automatically added, and so forth. If you add fewer than six components, there will be two rows and a reduced number of columns.

There is another way to specify that the number of columns is to be ignored. You can do this by setting the number of columns to zero, which will allow any number of columns. So a specification of `(2, 0)` is equivalent to `(2, 3)`, and in fact is equivalent to `(2, n)` for any nonnegative value of n. Similarly, you can specify that the number of rows is to be ignored by setting the number of rows to zero, which will allow any number of rows.

When using the `GridLayout` class, the method `add` has only one argument. The items are placed in the grid from left to right, first filling the top row, then the second row, and so forth. You are not allowed to skip any grid position (although you will later see that you can add something that does not show and so gives the illusion of skipping a grid position).

A sample use of the `GridLayout` class is given in Display 17.9.

Display 17.9   The GridLayout Manager (part 1 of 2)

```
1   import javax.swing.JFrame;
2   import javax.swing.JLabel;
3   import java.awt.GridLayout;

4   public class GridLayoutJFrame extends JFrame
5   {
6       public static final int WIDTH = 500;
7       public static final int HEIGHT = 400;

8       public static void main(String[] args)
9       {
10          GridLayoutJFrame gui = new GridLayoutJFrame(2, 3);
11          gui.setVisible(true);
12      }

13      public GridLayoutJFrame(int rows, int columns )
14      {
15          super();
16          setSize(WIDTH, HEIGHT);
17          setTitle("GridLayout Demonstration");
18          setDefaultCloseOperation(JFrame.EXIT_ON_CLOSE);
19          setLayout(new GridLayout(rows, columns ));

20          JLabel label1 = new JLabel("First label");
21          add(label1);

22          JLabel label2 = new JLabel("Second label");
23          add(label2);

24          JLabel label3 = new JLabel("Third label");
25          add(label3);

26          JLabel label4 = new JLabel("Fourth label");
27          add(label4);

28          JLabel label5 = new JLabel("Fifth label");
29          add(label5);
30      }
31  }
```

Display 17.9   The GridLayout Manager (part 2 of 2)

Resulting GUI

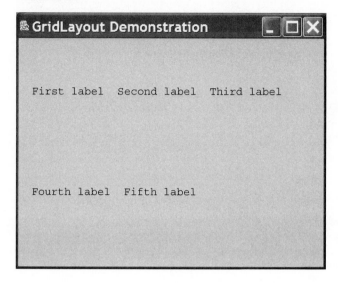

Note that we have placed a demonstration main method in the class definition in Display 17.9. This is handy, but is not typical. Normally, a Swing GUI is created and displayed in a main method (or other method) in some class other than the class that defines the GUI. However, it is perfectly legal and sometimes convenient to place a main method in the GUI class definition so that it is easy to display a sample of the GUI. Note that the main method that is given in the class itself is written in the same way as a main method that is in some other class. In particular, you need to construct an object of the class, as in the following line from the main method in Display 17.9:

```
GridLayoutJFrame gui = new GridLayoutJFrame(2, 3);
```

The three layout managers we have discussed are summarized in Display 17.10.

Next we will discuss *panels,* which will let you realize the full potential of layout managers.

VideoNote
**GUI Layout
using an IDE**

Display 17.10 Some Layout Managers

LAYOUT MANAGER	DESCRIPTION
These layout manager classes are in the `java.awt` package.	
FlowLayout	Displays components from left to right in the order in which they are added to the container.
BorderLayout	Displays the components in five areas: north, south, east, west, and center. You specify the area a component goes into in a second argument of the `add` method.
GridLayout	Lays out components in a grid, with each component stretched to fill its box in the grid.

Self-Test Exercises

14. In Display 17.7, would it be legal to replace

    ```
    JLabel label1 = new JLabel("First label");
    add(label1, BorderLayout.NORTH);
    JLabel label2 = new JLabel("Second label");
    add(label2, BorderLayout.SOUTH);
    JLabel label3 = new JLabel("Third label");
    add(label3, BorderLayout.CENTER);
    ```

    with the following?

    ```
    JLabel aLabel = new JLabel("First label");
    add(aLabel, BorderLayout.NORTH);
    aLabel = new JLabel("Second label");
    add(aLabel, BorderLayout.SOUTH);
    aLabel = new JLabel("Third label");
    add(aLabel, BorderLayout.CENTER);
    ```

    In other words, can we reuse the variable `aLabel` or must each label have its own variable name?

15. How would you modify the class definition in Display 17.7 so that the three labels are displayed as follows?

    ```
    First label
    Second label
    Third label
    ```

    (There may be space between each pair of lines.)

Self-Test Exercises (continued)

16. How would you modify the class definition in Display 17.7 so that the three labels are displayed as follows?

    ```
    First label
                            Second label
    Third label
    ```

    (There may be space between each pair of lines.)

17. Suppose you are defining a windowing GUI class in the usual way, as a derived class of the class `JFrame`, and suppose you want to specify a layout manager for the `JFrame` so as to produce the following sort of layout (five rows and three columns):

    What should the argument to `setLayout` be?

18. Suppose the situation is as described in Self-Test Exercise 17, except that you want the following sort of layout (that is, a one-column layout, typically having three rows):

    What should the argument to `setLayout` be?

Panels

panel

A GUI is often organized in a hierarchical fashion, with window-like containers, known as *panels*, inside of other window-like containers. A **panel** is an object of the class `JPanel`, which is a very simple container class that does little more than group objects. It is one of the simplest container classes, but an extremely useful one. A `JPanel` object is analogous to the braces used to combine a number of simpler Java statements into a single larger Java statement. It groups smaller objects, such as buttons and labels, into a larger component (the `JPanel`). You can then put the `JPanel` object in a JFrame. Thus, one of the main functions of JPanel objects is to subdivide a JFrame (or other container) into different areas.

For example, when you use a BorderLayout manager, you can place components in each of the five locations BorderLayout.NORTH, BorderLayout.SOUTH, BorderLayout.EAST, BorderLayout.WEST, and BorderLayout.CENTER. But what if you want to put two components at the bottom of the screen in the BorderLayout.SOUTH position? To do this, you would put the two components in a panel and then place the panel in the BorderLayout.SOUTH position.

You can give different layout managers to a JFrame and to each panel in the JFrame. Because you can add panels to other panels and each panel can have its own layout manager, this enables you to produce almost any kind of overall layout of the items in your GUI.

For example, if you want to place two buttons at the bottom of your JFrame GUI, you might add the following to the constructor of your JFrame GUI:

```
setLayout(new BorderLayout());

JPanel buttonPanel = new JPanel();
buttonPanel.setLayout(new FlowLayout());

JButton firstButton = new JButton("One");
buttonPanel.add(firstButton);

JButton secondButton = new JButton("Two");
buttonPanel.add(secondButton);

add(buttonPanel, BorderLayout.SOUTH);
```

The next Programming Example makes use of panels within panels.

EXAMPLE: A Tricolor Built with Panels

When first run, the GUI defined in Display 17.11 looks as shown in the first view. The entire background is light gray, and there are three buttons at the bottom of the GUI labeled "Green", "White", and "Gray". If you click any one of the buttons, a vertical stripe with the color written on the button appears. You can click the buttons in any order. In the last three views in Display 17.11, we show what happens if you click the buttons in left-to-right order.

The green, white, and gray stripes are the JPanes named greenPanel, whitePanel, and grayPanel. At first the panels are not visible because they are all light gray, so no borders are visible. When you click a button, the corresponding panel changes color and so is clearly visible.

Notice how the action listeners are set up. Each button registers the this parameter as a listener, as in the following line:

```
redButton.addActionListener(this);
```

Because this line appears inside of the constructor for the class PanelDemo, the this parameter refers to PanelDemo, which is the entire GUI. Thus, the entire JFrame

(continued)

EXAMPLE: (continued)

(the entire GUI) is the listener, not the `JPanel`. So when you click one of the buttons, it is the `actionPerformed` method in `PanelDemo` that is executed.

When a button is clicked, the `actionPerformed` method is invoked with the action event fired as the argument to `actionPerformed`. The method `actionPerformed` recovers the string written on the button with the following line:

```
String buttonString = e.getActionCommand();
```

The method `actionPerformed` then uses a multiway `if-else` statement to determine if `buttonString` is `"Blue"`, `"White"`, or `"Gray"` and changes the color of the corresponding panel accordingly. It is common for an `actionPerformed` method to be based on such a multiway `if-else` statement, although we will see another approach in the subsection entitled "Listeners as Inner Classes" later in this chapter.

Display 17.11 also introduces one other small but new technique. We gave each button a color. We did this with the method `setBackground`, using basically the same technique that we used in previous examples. You can give a button or almost any other item a color using `setBackground`. Note that you do not use `getContentPane` when adding color to any component other than a `JFrame`.

Display 17.11   **Using Panels** (part 1 of 4)

```
1   import javax.swing.JFrame;
2   import javax.swing.JPanel;
3   import java.awt.BorderLayout;
4   import java.awt.GridLayout;
5   import java.awt.FlowLayout;
6   import java.awt.Color;
7   import javax.swing.JButton;
8   import java.awt.event.ActionListener;
9   import java.awt.event.ActionEvent;

10  public class PanelDemo extends JFrame implements ActionListener
11  {
12      public static final int WIDTH = 300;
13      public static final int HEIGHT = 200;

14      private JPanel bluePanel;
15      private JPanel whitePanel;
16      private JPanel grayPanel;

17      public static void main(String[] args)
18      {
19          PanelDemo gui = new PanelDemo();
20          gui.setVisible(true);
21      }
```

In addition to being the GUI class, the class **PanelDemo** *is the action listener class. An object of the class* **PanelDemo** *is the action listener for the buttons in that object.*

We made these instance variables because we want to refer to them in both the constructor and the method **actionPerformed***.*

(continued)

Display 17.11   **Using Panels** (part 2 of 4)

```
22        public PanelDemo()
23        {
24            super("Panel Demonstration");
25            setSize(WIDTH, HEIGHT);
26            setDefaultCloseOperation(JFrame.EXIT_ON_CLOSE);
27            setLayout(new BorderLayout());

28            JPanel biggerPanel = new JPanel();
29            biggerPanel.setLayout(new GridLayout(1, 3));

30            bluePanel = new JPanel();
31            bluePanel.setBackground(Color.LIGHT_GRAY);
32            biggerPanel.add(bluePanel);

33            whitePanel = new JPanel();
34            whitePanel.setBackground(Color.LIGHT_GRAY);
35            biggerPanel.add(whitePanel);
36            grayPanel = new JPanel();
37            grayPanel.setBackground(Color.LIGHT_GRAY);
38            biggerPanel.add(grayPanel);

39            add(biggerPanel, BorderLayout.CENTER);

40            JPanel buttonPanel = new JPanel();
41            buttonPanel.setBackground(Color.LIGHT_GRAY);
42            buttonPanel.setLayout(new FlowLayout());

43            JButton blueButton = new JButton("Blue");
44            blueButton.setBackground(Color.BLUE);
45            blueButton.addActionListener(this);  ←────     An object of the class
46            buttonPanel.add(blueButton);                   PanelDemo is the
                                                             action listener for the
47            JButton whiteButton = new JButton("White");    buttons in that object.
48            whiteButton.setBackground(Color.WHITE);
49            whiteButton.addActionListener(this);
50            buttonPanel.add(whiteButton);

51            JButton grayButton = new JButton("Gray");
52            grayButton.setBackground(Color.GRAY);
53            grayButton.addActionListener(this);
54            buttonPanel.add(grayButton);

55            add(buttonPanel, BorderLayout.SOUTH);
56        }
57        public void actionPerformed(ActionEvent e)
58        {
59            String buttonString = e.getActionCommand();

60            if (buttonString.equals("Blue"))
61                bluePanel.setBackground(Color.BLUE);
```

Display 17.11   **Using Panels** (part 3 of 4)

```
62          else if (buttonString.equals("White"))
63              whitePanel.setBackground(Color.WHITE);
64          else if (buttonString.equals("Gray"))
65              grayPanel.setBackground(Color.GRAY);
66          else
67              System.out.println("Unexpected error.");
68      }
69  }
```

RESULTING GUI (When first run)

RESULTING GUI (After clicking Blue button)

RESULTING GUI (After clicking White button)

(continued)

Display 17.11 Using Panels (part 4 of 4)

RESULTING GUI (After clicking Gray button)

Adding Color

Color a JFrame as follows:

JFrame_Object.getContentPane().setBackground(*Color*);

If this is inside a constructor for the JFrame, then the expression simplifies to

getContentPane().setBackground(*Color*);

or the equivalent

this.getContentPane().setBackground(*Color*);

Color a button, label, or any other component (which is not a JFrame) as follows:

Component_Object.setBackground(*Color*);

Note that getContentPane() is only used with a JFrame.

EXAMPLE (INSIDE A CONSTRUCTOR FOR A DERIVED CLASS OF JFrame)

```
getContentPane().setBackground(Color.WHITE);
JButton redButton = new JButton("Red");
redButton.setBackground(Color.RED);
```

The Container Class

Container   The class called Container is in the java.awt package. Any descendent class of the class Container can have components added to it (or, more precisely, can have components added to objects of the class). The class JFrame is a descendent class of the class `Container`, so any descendent class of the class `JFrame` can serve as a container to hold labels, buttons, panels, or other components.

Similarly, the class `JPanel` is a descendent of the class `Container`, and any object of the class `JPanel` can serve as a container to hold labels, buttons, other panels, or other components. Display 17.12 shows a portion of the hierarchy of Swing and AWT classes. Note that the `Container` class is in the AWT library and not in the Swing library. This is not a major issue, but it does mean that the `import` statement for the `Container` class is

```
import java.awt.Container;
```

container
class

component

A **container class** is any descendent class of the class `Container`. The class `JComponent` serves a similar roll for components. Any descendent class of the class `JComponent` is called a `JComponent` or sometimes simply a **component**. You can add any `JComponent` object to any container class object.

The class `JComponent` is derived from the class `Container`, so you can add a `JComponent` to another `JComponent`. Often, this will turn out to be a viable option; occasionally it is something to avoid.[6]

The classes `Component`, `Frame`, and `Window` shown in Display 17.12 are AWT classes that some readers may have heard of. We include them for reference value, but we will have no need for these classes. We will eventually discuss all the other classes shown in Display 17.12.

When you are dealing with a Swing container class, you have three kinds of objects to deal with:

1. The container itself, probably some sort of panel or window-like object
2. The components you add to the container, such as labels, buttons, and panels
3. A layout manager, which positions the components inside the container

You have seen examples of these three kinds of objects in almost every `JFrame` class we have defined. Almost every complete GUI you build, and many subparts of the GUIs you build, will be made up of these three kinds of objects.

MyProgrammingLab™ **Self-Test Exercises**

19. What standard Java package contains the `Container` classes?

20. Is an object of the class `JPanel` a container class? Is it a component class?

21. With a `GridLayout` manager, you cannot leave any grid element empty, but you can do something that will make a grid element look empty to the user. What can you do?

(continued)

---

[6] In particular, it is legitimate and sometimes useful to add `JComponent`s to a `JButton`. We do not have space in this book to develop techniques for doing this effectively, but you may want to give it a try. You have covered enough material to do it.

Display 17.12 **Hierarchy of Swing and AWT Classes**

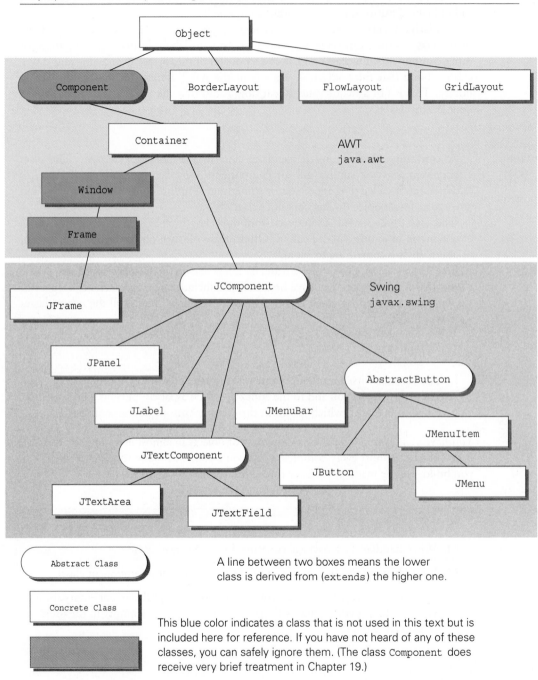

Self-Test Exercises (continued)

22. You are used to defining derived classes of the Swing class `JFrame`. You can also define derived classes of other Swing classes. Define a derived class of the class `JPanel` that is called `PinkJPanel`. An object of the class `PinkJPanel` can be used just as we used objects of the class `JPanel`, but an object of the class `PinkJPanel` is pink in color (unless you explicitly change its color). The class `PinkJPanel` will have only one constructor—namely, the no-argument constructor. (*Hint*: This is very easy.)

TIP: Code a GUI's Look and Actions Separately

You can divide the task of designing a Swing GUI into two main subtasks: (1) designing and coding the appearance of the GUI on the screen; (2) designing and coding the actions performed in response to button clicks and other user actions. This dividing of one big task into two simpler tasks makes the big task easier and less error prone.

For example, consider the program in Display 17.11. Your first version of this program might use the following definition of the method `actionPerformed`:

```
public void actionPerformed(ActionEvent e)
{}
```

This version of the method `actionPerformed` does nothing, but your program will run and will display a window on the screen, just as shown in Display 17.11. If you click any of the buttons, nothing will happen, but you can use this version of your GUI to adjust details, such as the order and location of buttons.

After you get the GUI to look the way you want it to look, you can define the action parts of the GUI, typically using the method `actionPerformed`.

If you include the phrase `implements ActionListener` at the start of your `JFrame` definition, then you must include some definition of the method `actionPerformed`. A method definition, such as

```
public void actionPerformed(ActionEvent e)
{}
```

stub   which does nothing (or does very little) is called a **stub**. Using stubs is a good programming technique in many contexts, not just in Swing programs.

Alternatively, when writing your first version of a Swing GUI like the one in Display 17.11, you could omit the definition of the method `actionPerformed` completely, *provided you also omit the phrase* `implements ActionListener` *and omit the invocations of* `addActionListener`. ■

The Model-View-Controller Pattern ★

Model-View-Controller

The technique we advocated in the previous Programming Tip is an example of a general technique known as the **Model-View-Controller** pattern. Display 17.13 gives a diagram of this pattern. The Model part of the pattern performs the heart of the application. The View part is the output part; it displays a picture of the Model's state. The Controller is the input part; it relays commands from the user to the Model. Each of the three interacting parts is realized as an object with responsibility for its own tasks. In a simple task such as the JFrame in Display 17.11, you can have a single object with different methods to realize each of the roles Model, View, and Controller.

To simplify the discussion, we have presented the Model-View-Controller pattern as if the user interacts directly with the Controller. The Controller need not be under the direct control of the user, but could be controlled by some other software or hardware component. In a Swing GUI, the View and Controller parts might be separate classes or separate methods combined into one larger class that displays a single window for all user interactions.

MyProgrammingLab™   **Self-Test Exercises**

23. Suppose you omit the method actionPerformed from the class in Display 17.11 and make no other changes. Would the class compile? If it compiles, will it run with no error messages?

24. Suppose you omit the method actionPerformed and the phrase implements ActionListener from the class in Display 17.11 and make no other changes. Would the class compile? If it compiles, will it run with no error messages?

Display 17.13   The Model-View-Controller Pattern

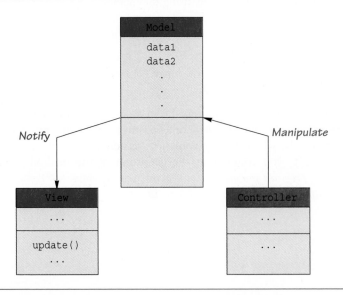

17.4 Menus and Buttons

For hours and location press 1.

For a recorded message describing services press 2.

For instructions on using our website press 3.

To use our automated information system press 4.

To speak to an operator between 8 am and noon Monday through

Thursdays press 7.

PHONE ANSWERING MACHINE

In this section, we describe the basics of Swing menus. Swing menu items (menu choices) behave essentially the same as Swing buttons. They generate action events that are handled by action listeners, just as buttons do.

EXAMPLE: A GUI with a Menu

Display 17.14 contains a program that is essentially the same as the GUI in Display 17.11 except that this GUI uses a menu instead of buttons. This GUI has a menu bar at the top of the window. The menu bar lists the names of all the pull-down menus. This GUI has only one pull-down menu, which is named "Add Colors". However, there could be more pull-down menus in the same menu bar.

The user can pull down a menu by clicking its name in the menu bar. Display 17.14 contains three pictures of the GUI. The first is what you see when the GUI originally appears. In that picture, the menu name "Add Colors" can be seen in the menu bar, but you cannot see the menu. If you click the words "Add Colors" with your mouse, the menu drops down, as shown in the second picture of the GUI. If you click "Green", "White", or "Gray" on the menu, then a vertical strip of the named color appears in the GUI.

In the next subsection, we go over the details of the program in Display 17.14.

Menu Bars, Menus, and Menu Items

When adding menus as we did in Display 17.14, use the three Swing classes JMenuItem, JMenu, and JMenuBar. Entries on a menu are objects of the class JMenuItem. These JMenuItems are placed in JMenus, and then the JMenus are typically placed in a JMenuBar. Let us look at the details.

menu   A **menu** is an object of the class JMenu. A choice on a menu is called a **menu item** and is an object of the class JMenuItem. A menu item is identified by the string that **menu item** labels it, such as "Blue", "White", or "Gray" in the menu in Display 17.14. You can add as many JMenuItems as you wish to a menu. The menu lists the items in the order

Display 17.14   A GUI with a Menu (part 1 of 3)

```
1    import javax.swing.JFrame;
2    import javax.swing.JPanel;
3    import java.awt.GridLayout;
4    Import java.awt.Color;
5    import javax.swing.JMenu;
6    import javax.swing.JMenuItem;
7    import javax.swing.JMenuBar;
8    import java.awt.event.ActionListener;
9    import java.awt.event.ActionEvent;

10   public class MenuDemo extends JFrame implements ActionListener
11   {
12       public static final int WIDTH = 300;
13       public static final int HEIGHT = 200;

14       private JPanel bluePanel;
15       private JPanel whitePanel;
16       private JPanel grayPanel;

17       public static void main(String[] args)
18       {
19           MenuDemo gui = new MenuDemo();
20           gui.setVisible(true);
21       }

22       public MenuDemo()
23       {
24           super ("Menu Demonstration");
25           setSize(WIDTH, HEIGHT);
26           setDefaultCloseOperation(JFrame.EXIT_ON_CLOSE);
27           setLayout(new GridLayout(1, 3));

28           bluePanel = new JPanel();
29           bluePanel.setBackground(Color.LIGHT_GRAY);
30           add(bluePanel);

31           whitePanel = new JPanel();
32           whitePanel.setBackground(Color.LIGHT_GRAY);
33           add(whitePanel);
34           grayPanel = new JPanel();
```

Display 17.14   A GUI with a Menu (part 2 of 3)

```
35          grayPanel.setBackground(Color.LIGHT_GRAY);
36          add(grayPanel);

37          JMenu colorMenu = new JMenu("Add Colors");

38          JMenuItem blueChoice = new JMenuItem("Blue");
39          blueChoice.addActionListener(this);
40          colorMenu.add(blueChoice);

41          JMenuItem whiteChoice = new JMenuItem("White");
42          whiteChoice.addActionListener(this);
43          colorMenu.add(whiteChoice);

44          JMenuItem grayChoice = new JMenuItem("Gray");
45          grayChoice.addActionListener(this);
46          colorMenu.add(grayChoice);

47          JMenuBar bar = new JMenuBar( );
48          bar.add(colorMenu);
49          setJMenuBar(bar);
50      }
```

The definition of `actionPerformed` *is identical to the
definition given in Display 17.11 for a similar GUI using buttons
instead of menu items.*

```
51      public void actionPerformed(ActionEvent e)
52      {
53          String buttonString = e.getActionCommand( );

54          if (buttonString.equals("Blue"))
55              bluePanel.setBackground(Color.BLUE);
56          else if (buttonString.equals("White"))
57              whitePanel.setBackground(Color.WHITE);
58          else if (buttonString.equals("Gray"))
59              grayPanel.setBackground(Color.GRAY);
60          else
61              System.out.println("Unexpected error.");
62      }
63  }
```

(continued)

Display 17.14 A GUI with a Menu (part 3 of 3)

RESULTING GUI

RESULTING GUI (after clicking Add Colors in the menu bar)

RESULTING GUI (after choosing Blue and White on the menu)

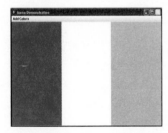

RESULTING GUI (after choosing all the colors on the menu)

in which they are added. The following code, taken from the constructor in Display 17.14, creates a new `JMenu` object named `colorMenu` and then adds a `JMenuItem` labeled `"Red"`. Other menu items are added in a similar way.

```
JMenu colorMenu = new JMenu("Add Colors");

JMenuItem blueChoice = new JMenuItem("Blue");
blueChoice.addActionListener(this);
colorMenu.add(blueChoice);
```

listeners   Note that, just as we did for buttons in Display 17.11, in Display 17.14 we registered the `this` parameter as an action listener for each menu item. Defining action listeners and registering listeners for menu items are done in the exact same way as for buttons. In fact, the syntax is even the same. If you compare Displays 17.14 and 17.11, you will see that the definition of the method `actionPerformed` is the same in both classes.

Add a `JMenuItem` to an object of the class `JMenu` using the method `add` in exactly the same way that you add a component, such as a button, to a container object. Moreover, if you look at the preceding code, you will see that you specify a string for a `JMenuItem` in the same way that you specify a string to appear on a button.

menu bar   A **menu bar** is a container for menus, typically placed near the top of a windowing interface. Add a menu to a menu bar using the method `add` in the same way that you add menu items to a menu. The following code from the constructor in Display 17.14 creates a new menu bar named `bar` and then adds the menu named `colorMenu` to this menu bar:

```
JMenuBar bar = new JMenuBar();
bar.add(colorMenu);
```

There are two different ways to add a menu bar to a `JFrame`. You can use the method `setJMenuBar`, as shown in the following code from the constructor in Display 17.14:

```
setJMenuBar(bar);
```

This sets an instance variable of type `JMenuBar` so that it names the menu bar named `bar`. Saying it less formally, this adds the menu bar named `bar` to the `JFrame` and places the menu bar at the top of the `JFrame`.

extra code   Alternatively, you can use the `add` method to add a menu bar to a `JFrame` (or to any
on website   other container). You do so in the same way that you add any other component, such as a label or a button. An example of using `add` to add a `JMenuBar` to a `JFrame` is given in the file `MenuAdd.java` on the accompanying website.

Menus

A **menu** is an object of the class `JMenu`. A choice on a menu is an object of the class `JMenuItem`. Menus are collected together in a **menu bar** (or menu bars). A menu bar is an object of the class `JMenuBar`.

Events and listeners for menu items are handled in exactly the same way as they are for buttons.

Nested Menus ★

As shown in Display 17.12, the class JMenu is a descendent of the JMenuItem class. So, every JMenu object is also a JMenuItem object. Thus, a JMenu can be a menu item in another menu. This means that you can nest menus. For example, the outer menu might give you a list of menus. You can display one of the menus on that list by clicking the name of the desired menu. You can then choose an item from that menu by using your mouse again. There is nothing new you need to know to create these nested menus. Simply add menus to menus just as you add other menu items. There is an example of nested menus in the file NestedMenus.java on the accompanying website.

extra code on website

The AbstractButton Class

As shown in Display 17.12, the classes JButton and JMenuItem are derived classes of the abstract class named AbstractButton. All of the basic properties and methods of the classes JButton and JMenuItem are inherited from the class AbstractButton. That is why objects of the class JButton and objects of the class JMenuItem are so similar. Some of the methods for the class AbstractButton are listed in Display 17.15. All these methods are inherited by both the class JButton and the class JMenuItem. (Some of these methods were inherited by the class AbstractButton from the class JComponent, so you may sometimes see some of the methods listed as "inherited from JComponent.")

Adding Menus to a JFrame

In the following, we assume that all code is inside a constructor for a (derived class of a) JFrame. To see the following examples put together to produce a complete GUI, see the constructor in Display 17.14.

Creating Menu Items

A menu item is an object of the class JMenuItem. Create a new menu item in the usual way, as illustrated by the following example. The string in the argument position is the displayed text for the menu item.

```java
JMenuItem redChoice = new JMenuItem("Red");
```

Adding Menu Item Listeners

Events and listeners for menu items are handled in the exact same way as they are for buttons: Menu items fire action events that are received by objects of the class ActionListener.

SYNTAX

JMenu_Item_Name.addActionListener(*Action_Listener*);

EXAMPLE
```
redChoice.addActionListener(this);
```

Creating a Menu

A menu is an object of the class `JMenu`. Create a new menu in the usual way, as illustrated by the following example. The string argument is the displayed text that identifies the menu.

```
JMenu colorMenu = new JMenu("Add Colors");
```

Adding Menu Items to a Menu

Use the method `add` to add menu items to a menu.

SYNTAX

JMenu_Name.`add`(*JMenu_Item*);

EXAMPLE(`colorMenu` IS AN OBJECT OF THE CLASS `JMenu`)
```
colorMenu.add(redChoice);
```

Creating a Menu Bar

A menu bar is an object of the class `JMenuBar`. Create a new menu bar in the usual way, as illustrated by the following example:

```
JMenuBar bar = new JMenuBar();
```

Adding a Menu to a Menu Bar

Add a menu to a menu bar using the method `add` as follows:

SYNTAX

JMenu_Bar_Name.`add`(*JMenu_Name*);

EXAMPLE (`bar` IS AN OBJECT OF THE CLASS `JMenubar`)
```
bar.add(colorMenu);
```

Adding a Menu Bar to a Frame

There are two different ways to add a menu bar to a `JFrame`. You can use the method `add` to add the menu bar to a `JFrame` (or to any other container). Another common way of adding a menu bar to a `JFrame` is to use the method `setJMenuBar` as follows:

SYNTAX

`setJMenuBar`(*JMenu_Bar_Name*);

EXAMPLE
```
setJMenuBar(bar);
```

Display 17.15 Some Methods in the Class `AbstractButton`

The abstract class `AbstractButton` is in the `javax.swing` package.

All of these methods are inherited by both of the classes `JButton` and `JMenuItem`.

```
public void setBackground(Color theColor)
```
Sets the background color of this component.

```
public void addActionListener(ActionListener listener)
```
Adds an `ActionListener`.

```
public void removeActionListener(ActionListener listener)
```
Removes an `ActionListener`.

```
public void setActionCommand(String actionCommand)
```
Sets the action command.

```
public String getActionCommand()
```
Returns the action command for this component.

```
public void setText(String text)
```
Makes text the only text on this component.

```
public String getText()
```
Returns the text written on the component, such as the text on a button or the string for a menu item.

```
public void setPreferredSize(Dimension preferredSize)
```
Sets the preferred size of the button or label. Note that this is only a suggestion to the layout manager. The layout manager is not required to use the preferred size. The following special case will work for most simple situations. The int values give the width and height in pixels.

```
public void setPreferredSize(
                new Dimension(int width, int height))
```

```
public void setMaximumSize(Dimension maximumSize)
```
Sets the maximum size of the button or label. Note that this is only a suggestion to the layout manager. The layout manager is not required to respect this maximum size. The following special case will work for most simple situations. The int values give the width and height in pixels.

```
public void setMaximumSize(
                new Dimension(int width, int height))
```

```
public void setMinimumSize(Dimension minimumSize)
```
Sets the minimum size of the button or label. Note that this is only a suggestion to the layout manager. The layout manager is not required to respect this minimum size.

Although we do not discuss the `Dimension` class, the following special case is intuitively clear and will work for most simple situations. The int values give the width and height in pixels.

```
public void setMinimumSize(
                new Dimension(int width, int height))
```

The `Dimension` Class

Objects of the class `Dimension` are used with buttons, menu items, and other objects to specify a size. The `Dimension` class is in the package `java.awt`. The parameters in the following constructor are pixels.

CONSTRUCTOR
```
Dimension(int width, int height)
```

EXAMPLE
```
aButton.setPreferredSize(new Dimension(30, 50));
```

The `setActionCommand` Method

action
command

When the user clicks a button or menu item, it fires an action event that normally goes to one or more action listeners where it becomes an argument to an `actionPerformed` method. This action event includes a `String` instance variable that is known as the **action command** for the button or menu item and that is retrieved with the accessor method `getActionCommand`. The action command in the event is copied from an instance variable in the button or menu item object. If you do nothing to change it, the action command is the string written on the button or the menu item. The method `setActionCommand` given in Display 17.15 for the class `AbstractButton` can be used with any `JButton` or `JMenuItem` to change the action command for that component. Among other things, this will allow you to have different action commands for two buttons, two menu items, or a button and menu item even though they have the same string written on them.

setAction
Command

The method `setActionCommand` takes a `String` argument that becomes the new action command for the calling button or menu item. For example, consider the following code:

```
JButton nextButton = new JButton("Next");
nextButton.setActionCommand("Next Button");
JMenuItem chooseNext = new JMenuItem("Next");
chooseNext.setActionCommand("Next Menu Item");
```

If we had not used `setActionCommand` in the preceding code, then the button `nextButton` and the menu item `chooseNext` would both have the action command `"Next"` and so we would have no way to tell which of the two components `nextButton` and `chooseNext` an action event `"Next"` came from. However, using the method `setActionCommand`, we can give them the different action commands `"Next Button"` and `"Next Menu Item"`.

The action command for a `JButton` or `JMenuItem` is kept as the value of a private instance variable for the `JButton` or `JMenuItem`. The method `setActionCommand` is simply an ordinary mutator method that changes the value of this instance variable.

---

setActionCommand and getActionCommand

Every button and every menu item has a string associated with it that is known as the **action command** for that button or menu item. When the button or menu item is clicked, it fires an action event e. The following invocation returns the action command for the button or menu item that fired e:

```
e.getActionCommand( )
```

The method `actionPerformed` typically uses this action command string to decide which button or menu item was clicked.

The default action command for a button or menu item is the string written on it, but if you want, you can change the action command with an invocation of the method `setActionCommand`. For example, the menu item `chooseNext` created by the following code will display the string "Next" when it is a menu choice, but will have the string "Next Menu Item" as its action command.

EXAMPLE

```
JMenuItem chooseNext = new JMenuItem("Next");
chooseNext.setActionCommand("Next Menu Item");
```

An alternate approach to defining action listeners is given in the next subsection. That technique is, among other things, another way to deal with multiple buttons or menu items that have the same thing written on them.

Listeners as Inner Classes ★

In all of our previous examples, our GUIs had only one action listener object to deal with all action events from all buttons and menus in the GUI. The opposite extreme also has much to recommend it. You can have a separate `ActionListener` class for each button or menu item, so that each button or menu item has its own unique action listener. There is then no need for a multiway `if-else` statement. The listener knows which button or menu item was clicked because it listens to only one button or menu item.

The approach outlined in the previous paragraph does have one down side: You typically need to give a lot of definitions of `ActionListener` classes. Rather than putting each of these classes in a separate file, it is much cleaner to make them private inner classes. This has the added advantage of allowing the `ActionListener` classes to have access to private instance variables and methods of the outer class.

In Display 17.16, we re-created the GUI in Display 17.14 using the techniques of this subsection.

Display 17.16   **Listeners as Inner Classes** (part 1 of 2)

<Import statements are the same as in Display 17.14.>

```
1    public class InnerListenersDemo extends JFrame
2    {
3        public static final int WIDTH = 300;
4        public static final int HEIGHT = 200;

5        private JPanel bluePanel;
6        private JPanel whitePanel;
7        private JPanel grayPanel;

8        private class blueListener implements ActionListener
9        {
10           public void actionPerformed(ActionEvent e)
11           {
12               bluePanel.setBackground(Color.BLUE);
13           }
14       } //End of greenListener inner class

15       private class WhiteListener implements ActionListener
16       {
17           public void actionPerformed(ActionEvent e)
18           {
19               whitePanel.setBackground(Color.WHITE);
20           }
21       } //End of WhiteListener inner class
22       private class grayListener implements ActionListener
23       {
24           public void actionPerformed(ActionEvent e)
25           {
26               grayPanel.setBackground(Color.GRAY);
27           }
28       } //End of grayListener inner class

29       public static void main(String[] args)
30       {
31           InnerListenersDemo gui = new InnerListenersDemo();
32           gui.setVisible(true);
33       }

34       public InnerListenersDemo()
35       {
36           super("Menu Demonstration");
37           setSize(WIDTH, HEIGHT);
38           setDefaultCloseOperation(JFrame.EXIT_ON_CLOSE);
39           setLayout(new GridLayout(1, 3));
```

The resulting GUI is the same as in Display 17.14

(continued)

Display 17.16   **Listeners as Inner Classes** (part 2 of 2)

```
40          bluePanel = new JPanel();
41          greenPanel.setBackground(Color.LIGHT_GRAY);
42          add(bluePanel);

43          whitePanel = new JPanel();
44          whitePanel.setBackground(Color.LIGHT_GRAY);
45          add(whitePanel);

46          grayPanel = new JPanel();
47          grayPanel.setBackground(Color.LIGHT_GRAY);
48          add(grayPanel);

49          JMenu colorMenu = new JMenu("Add Colors");

50          JMenuItem blueChoice = new JMenuItem("Blue");
51          blueChoice.addActionListener(new blueListener());
52          colorMenu.add(blueChoice);

53          JMenuItem whiteChoice = new JMenuItem("White");
54          whiteChoice.addActionListener(new WhiteListener());
55          colorMenu.add(whiteChoice);
56          JMenuItem grayChoice = new JMenuItem("Gray");
57          grayChoice.addActionListener(new grayListener());
58          colorMenu.add(grayChoice);

59          JMenuBar bar = new JMenuBar();
60          bar.add(colorMenu);
61          setJMenuBar(bar);
62      }

63  }
```

Self-Test Exercises

25. Which class or classes work as the action listener in Display 17.14?

26. Which class or classes work as the action listener in Display 17.16?

27. Write a code snippet that creates a menu bar named mbar, an object of the JMenuBar class and adds three menus m1, m2, and m3 with values "New", "Open", and "Save" respectively to the menu bar. The menus m1, m2, and m3 are of JMenu class.

Self-Test Exercises (continued)

28. If you want to change the action command for a `JButton`, use the method `setActionCommand`. What method do you use to change the action command for a `JMenuItem`?

29. Is the following legal in Java?

    ```java
    JMenu aMenu = new JMenu();
        . . .
    JMenu aSubMenu = new JMenu();
        . . .
    aMenu.add(aSubMenu);
    ```

30. How many `JMenuBar` objects can you have in a `JFrame`?

31. What would be the output of the following code?

    ```java
    JButton nextButton = new JButton("Click");
    System.out.println(nextButton.getActionCommand);
    ```

32. Write code to create a new menu item named `aChoice` that has the label `"Exit"`.

33. What would be the output of the following code?

    ```java
    JMenuItem save = new JMenuItem("Save");
    System.out.println(save.getActionCommand);
    ```

34. ★How can you modify the program in Display 17.16 so that when the `Blue` menu item is clicked, all three colors are shown? The `Red` and `White` choices remain the same. (Remember the menu items may be clicked in any order, so the `Blue` menu item can be the first or second item clicked.)

35. ★Rewrite the Swing GUI in Display 17.16 so that there is only one action listener inner class. The inner class constructor will have two parameters, one for a panel and one for a color.

17.5 Text Fields and Text Areas

Write your answers in the spaces provided.

COMMON INSTRUCTION FOR AN EXAMINATION

You have undoubtedly interacted with windowing systems that provide spaces for you to enter text information such as your name, address, and credit card number. In this section, we show you how to add these fields for text input and text output to your Swing GUIs.

Text Areas and Text Fields

A **text field** is an object of the class JTextField and is displayed as a field that allows the user to enter a single line of text. In Display 17.17, the following creates a text field named name in which the user will be asked to enter his or her name:

```
private JTextField name;
    . . .
name = new JTextField(NUMBER_OF_CHAR);
```

In Display 17.17, the variable name is a private instance variable. The creation of the JTextField in the last of the previous lines takes place inside the class constructor. The number NUMBER_OF_CHAR that is given as an argument to the JTextField constructor specifies that the text field will have room for at least NUMBER_OF_CHAR characters to be visible. The defined constant NUMBER_OF_CHAR is 30, so the text field is guaranteed to have room for at least 30 characters. You can type any number of characters into a text field but only a limited number will be visible; in this case, you know that at least 30 characters will be visible.

A Swing GUI can read the text in a text field and so receive text input; if this is desired, it can produce output by causing text to appear in the text field. The method getText returns the text written in the text field. For example, the following will set a variable named inputString to whatever string is in the text field name at the time that the getText method is invoked:

```
String inputString = name.getText();
```

The method getText is an input method, and the method setText is an output method. The method setText can be used to display a new text string in a text field. For example, the following will cause the text field name to change the text it displays to the string "This is some output":

```
name.setText("This is some output");
```

Display 17.17   A Text Field (part 1 of 3)

```
1    import javax.swing.JFrame;
2    import javax.swing.JTextField;
3    import javax.swing.JPanel;
4    import javax.swing.JLabel;
5    import javax.swing.JButton;
6    import java.awt.GridLayout;
7    import java.awt.BorderLayout;
8    import java.awt.FlowLayout;
9    import java.awt.Color;
10   import java.awt.event.ActionListener;
11   import java.awt.event.ActionEvent;

12   public class TextFieldDemo extends JFrame
13                             implements ActionListener
14   {
15       public static final int WIDTH = 400;
16       public static final int HEIGHT = 200;
```

Display 17.17   **A Text Field** (part 2 of 3)

```
17        public static final int NUMBER_OF_CHAR = 30;

18        private JTextField name;

19        public static void main(String[] args)
20        {
21            TextFieldDemo gui = new TextFieldDemo();
22            gui.setVisible(true);
23        }

24        public TextFieldDemo()
25        {
26            super("Text Field Demo");
27            setSize(WIDTH, HEIGHT);
28            setDefaultCloseOperation(JFrame.EXIT_ON_CLOSE);
29            setLayout(new GridLayout(2, 1));

30            JPanel namePanel = new JPanel();
31            namePanel.setLayout(new BorderLayout());
32            namePanel.setBackground(Color.WHITE);

33            name = new JTextField(NUMBER_OF_CHAR);
34            namePanel.add(name, BorderLayout.SOUTH);
35            JLabel nameLabel = new JLabel("Enter your name here:");
36            namePanel.add(nameLabel, BorderLayout.CENTER);

37            add(namePanel);
38            JPanel buttonPanel = new JPanel();
39            buttonPanel.setLayout(new FlowLayout());
40            buttonPanel.setBackground(Color.BLUE);
41            JButton actionButton = new JButton("Click me");
42            actionButton.addActionListener(this);
43            buttonPanel.add(actionButton);

44            JButton clearButton = new JButton("Clear");
45            clearButton.addActionListener(this);
46            buttonPanel.add(clearButton);

47            add(buttonPanel);
48        }

49        public void actionPerformed(ActionEvent e)
50        {
51            String actionCommand = e.getActionCommand();

52            if (actionCommand.equals("Click me"))
53                name.setText("Hello " + name.getText());
54            else if (actionCommand.equals("Clear"))
55                name.setText("");
56            else
57                name.setText("Unexpected error.");
58        }
59   }
```

This sets the text field equal to the empty string, which makes it blank.

(continued)

Display 17.17   **A Text Field** (part 3 of 3)

RESULTING GUI (When program is started and a name entered)

RESULTING GUI (After clicking the "Click me" button)

The following line from the method `actionPerformed` in Display 17.17 uses both `getText` and `setText`:

```
name.setText("Hello" + name.getText());
```

This line changes the string in the text field `name` to `"Hello"` followed by the old string value in the text field. The net effect is to insert the string `"Hello"` in front of the string displayed in the text field.

`getText` and `setText`

The classes `JTextField` and `JTextArea` both contain methods called `getText` and `setText`. The method `getText` can be used to retrieve the text written in the text field or text area. The method `setText` can be used to change the text written in the text field or text area.

SYNTAX

Name_of_Text_Component.`getText`() returns the text currently displayed in the text field or text area.

Name_of_Text_Component.`setText`(*New_String_To_Display*);

EXAMPLES
```
String inputString = ioComponent.getText();
ioComponent.setText("Hello out there!");
```

ioComponent may be an instance of either of the classes JTextField or JTextArea.

text area

JTextArea

A **text area** is an object of the class JTextArea. A text area is the same as a text field except that it allows multiple lines. Two parameters to the constructor for JTextArea specify the minimum number of lines and the minimum number of characters per line that are guaranteed to be visible. You can enter any amount of text in a text area, but only a limited number of lines and a limited number of characters per line will be visible. For example, the following creates a JTextArea named theText that will have at least 5 lines and at least 20 characters per line visible:

```
JTextArea theText = new JTextArea(5, 20);
```

There is also a constructor with one additional String parameter for the string initially displayed in the text area. For example,

```
JTextArea theText = new JTextArea("Enter\ntext here.", 5, 20);
```

Note that a string value can be multiple lines because it can contain the new-line character '\n'.

A JTextField has a similar constructor with a String parameter, as in the following example:

```
JTextField ioField =
            new JTextField("Enter numbers here.", 30);
```

If you look at Display 17.12, you will see that both JTextField and JTextArea are derived classes of the abstract class JTextComponent. Most of the methods for JTextField and JTextArea are inherited from JTextComponent and so JTextField and JTextArea have mostly the same methods with the same meanings except for minor redefinitions to account for having just one line or multiple lines. Display 17.18 describes some methods in the class JTextComponent. All of these methods are inherited and have the described meaning in both JTextField and JTextArea.

setLineWrap

You can set the line-wrapping policy for a JTextArea using the method setLineWrap. The method takes one argument of type boolean. If the argument is true, then at the end of a line, any additional characters for that line will appear on the following line of the text area. If the argument is false, the extra characters will be on the same line and will not be visible. For example, the following sets the line wrap policy for the JTextArea object named theText so that at the end of a line, any additional characters for that line will appear on the following line:

```
theText.setLineWrap(true);
```

output-only

setEditable

You can specify that a JTextField or JTextArea cannot be written in by the user. To do so, use the method setEditable, which is a method in both the JTextField and JTextArea classes. If theText names an object in either of the classes JTextField or JTextArea, then the following

```
theText.setEditable(false);
```

will set theText so that only your GUI program can change the text in the text component theText; the user cannot change the text. After this invocation of setEditable, if the user clicks the mouse in the text component named theText and then types at the keyboard, the text in the text component will not change.

To reverse things and make theText so that the user can change the text in the text component, use true in place of false, as follows:

```
theText.setEditable(true);
```

If no invocation of setEditable is made, then the default state allows the user to change the text in the text component.

Display 17.18   Some Methods in the Class JTextComponent

All these methods are inherited by the classes JTextField and JTextArea.

The abstract class JTextComponent is in the package javax.swing.text. The classes JTextField and JTextArea are in the package javax.swing.

```
public String getText()
```
Returns the text that is displayed by this text component.

```
public boolean isEditable()
```
Returns true if the user can write in this text component. Returns false if the user is not allowed to write in this text component.

```
public void setBackground(Color theColor)
```
Sets the background color of this text component.

```
public void setEditable(boolean argument)
```
If argument is true, then the user is allowed to write in the text component. If argument is false, then the user is not allowed to write in the text component.

```
public void setText(String text)
```
Sets the text that is displayed by this text component to be the specified text.

The Classes JTextField and JTextArea

The classes JTextField and JTextArea can be used to add areas for changeable text to a GUI. An object of the class JTextField has one line that displays some specified number of characters. An object of the class JTextArea has a size consisting of a specified number of lines and a specified number of characters per line. More text can be typed into a `JTextField` or `JTextArea` than is specified in its size, but the extra text may not be visible.

The number of characters per line and the number of lines are a guaranteed minimum. More lines and especially more characters per line may be visible. (The space per line is actually guaranteed to be *Characters_Per_Line* times the space for one uppercase letter M.)

SYNTAX

```
JTextField Name_of_Text_Field = new JTextField(Characters_Per_Line);
JTextArea Name_of_Text_Area =
            new JTextArea(Number_of_Lines, Characters_Per_Line);
```

EXAMPLES

```
JTextField name = new JTextField(30);
JTextArea someText = new JTextArea(10, 30);
```

There are also constructors that take an additional `String` argument that specifies an initial string to display in the text component.

SYNTAX

```
JTextField Name_of_Text_Field =
            new JTextField(Initial_String, Characters_Per_Line);
JTextArea Name_of_Text_Area =
    new JTextArea(Initial_String, Number_of_Lines, Characters_Per_Line);
```

EXAMPLES

```
JTextField name = new JTextField("Enter name here.", 30);
JTextArea someText =
    new JTextArea("Enter story here.\nClick button.", 10, 30);
```

Number of Characters per Line

The number of characters per line (given as an argument to constructors for `JTextField` or `JTextArea`) is not the number of just any characters. The number gives the number of em spaces in the line. An **em space** is the space needed to hold one uppercase letter M, which is the widest letter in the alphabet. So a line that is specified to hold 20 characters will always be able to hold at least 20 characters and will almost always hold more than 20 characters.

Scroll Bars

Scroll bars for text areas and text fields are discussed in Chapter 18. They are a nice touch, but until you reach Chapter 18, your GUI programs will work fine without them.

TIP: Labeling a Text Field

Sometimes you want to label a text field. For example, suppose the GUI asks for a name and a credit card number and expects the user to enter these in two text fields. In this case, the GUI needs to label the two text fields so that the user knows in which field to type the name and in which field to type the credit card number. You can use an object of the class JLabel to label a text field or any other component in a Swing GUI. Simply place the label and text field in a JPanel and treat the JPanel as a single component. For example, we did this with the text field name in Display 17.17. ■

Self-Test Exercises

36. What is the difference between an object of the class JTextArea and an object of the class JTextField?

37. What would happen if when running the GUI in Display 17.17 you do not enter your name and click the "Click me" button three times?

38. Rewrite the program in Display 17.17 so that it uses a text area in place of a text field. Change the label "Enter your name here:" to "Enter your story here:". When the user clicks the "Click me" button, your GUI should change the string displayed in the text area to "Your story is " + lineCount + "lines long.". The variable lineCount is a variable of type int that your program sets equal to the number of lines currently displayed in the text area. Use a BorderLayout manager and place your text area in the region BorderLayout.CENTER so that there is room for it. You can assume the user enters at least one line before clicking the "Click me" button. The last line in the text area will have no '\n' so you may need to add one if you are counting the number of occurrences of '\n'. Blank lines are counted.

TIP: Inputting and Outputting Numbers

When you want to input numbers using a Swing GUI, your GUI must convert input text to numbers. For example, when you input the number 42 in a JTextField, your program will receive the string "42", not the number 42. Your program must convert the input string value "42" to the integer value 42. When you want to output numbers using a GUI constructed with Swing, you must convert the numbers to a string and then output that string. For example, if you want to output the number 40, your program would convert the integer value 40 to the string value "40". With Swing, all input typed by the user is string input and all displayed output is string output. The techniques for converting back and forth between strings and numbers were given in Chapter 5 in the subsection titled "Static Methods in Wrapper Classes" and the Programming Example entitled "Another Approach to Keyboard Input." A simple example of a Swing GUI with numeric input and output is given in the next subsection. ■

A Swing Calculator

Designing a realistic Swing calculator is the subject of Programming Project 17.3. In this programming example, we will develop a simplified calculator to get you started on that Programming Project. Display 17.19 contains a GUI for a calculator that keeps a running total of numbers. The user enters a number in the text field and then clicks either the + or − button. The number in the text field is then added into or subtracted from a running total that is kept in the instance variable `result`, and then the new total (the new value of `result`) is given in the text field. If the user clicks the `"Reset"` button, then the running total—that is, the value of `result`—is set to zero. When the GUI is first run, the running total, that is, the value of `result`, is set to zero.

Most of the details are similar to things you have already seen, but one new element is the use of exception handling. If the user enters a number in an incorrect format, such as placing a comma in a number, then one of the methods throws a `NumberFormatException`. If the user enters a number in an incorrect format, such as `2,000` with a comma instead of `2000`, the method `assumingCorrectNumberFormats` invokes the method `stringToDouble` with the alleged number string `"2,000"` as an argument. Then `stringToDouble` calls `Double.parseDouble`, but `Double.parseDouble` throws a `NumberFormatException` because no Java number string can contain a comma. Because the invocation of `Double.parseDouble` takes place within an invocation of the method `stringToDouble`, `stringToDouble` in turn throws a `NumberFormatException`. The invocation of `stringToDouble` takes place inside the invocation of `assumingCorrectNumberFormats`, so `assumingCorrectNumberFormats` throws the `NumberFormatException` that it received from the invocation of `stringToDouble`. However, the invocation of `assumingCorrectNumberFormats` is inside a `try` block. The exception is caught in the following `catch` block. At this point, the `JTextField` (named `ioField`) is set to the error message `"Error: Reenter Number."`.

Notice that if a `NumberFormatException` is thrown, the value of the instance variable `result` is not changed. A `NumberFormatException` can be thrown by an invocation of `stringToDouble` in either of the following lines of code from the method `assumingCorrectNumberFormats`:

```
result = result + stringToDouble(ioField.getText());
```

or

```
result = result - stringToDouble(ioField.getText());
```

If the exception is thrown, execution of the method `stringToDouble` ends immediately and control passes to the `catch` block. Thus, control passes to the `catch` block before the previous addition or subtraction is performed. So `result` is unchanged, and the user can reenter the last number and proceed with the GUI as if that incorrect number were never entered.

Uncaught Exceptions

In a Swing program, throwing an uncaught exception does not end the GUI, but it may leave it in an unpredictable state. It is best to always catch any exception that is thrown even if all that the `catch` block does is output an instruction to redo something, such as reentering some input or just outputting an error message.

Display 17.19   **A Simple Calculator** (part 1 of 4)

```
1   import javax.swing.JFrame;
2   import javax.swing.JTextField;
3   import javax.swing.JPanel;
4   import javax.swing.JLabel;
5   import javax.swing.JButton;
6   import java.awt.BorderLayout;
7   import java.awt.FlowLayout;
8   import java.awt.Color;
9   import java.awt.event.ActionListener;
10  import java.awt.event.ActionEvent;

11  /**
12   A simplified calculator.
13   The only operations are addition and subtraction.
14  */
15  public class Calculator extends JFrame
16                          implements ActionListener
17  {
18      public static final int WIDTH = 400;
19      public static final int HEIGHT = 200;
20      public static final int NUMBER_OF_DIGITS = 30;

21      private JTextField ioField;
22      private double result = 0.0;

23      public static void main(String[] args)
24      {
25          Calculator aCalculator = new Calculator();
26          aCalculator.setVisible(true);
27      }

28      public Calculator()
29      {
30          setTitle("Simplified Calculator");
31          setDefaultCloseOperation(JFrame.EXIT_ON_CLOSE);
32          setSize(WIDTH, HEIGHT);
33          setLayout(new BorderLayout());

34          JPanel textPanel = new JPanel();
35          textPanel.setLayout(new FlowLayout());
36          ioField =
37              new JTextField("Enter numbers here.",NUMBER_OF_DIGITS);
38          ioField.setBackground(Color.WHITE);
39          textPanel.add(ioField);
40          add(textPanel, BorderLayout.NORTH);
41          JPanel buttonPanel = new JPanel();
42          buttonPanel.setBackground(Color.BLUE);
43          buttonPanel.setLayout(new FlowLayout());
```

Display 17.19   A Simple Calculator (part 2 of 4)

```
44          JButton addButton = new JButton("+");
45          addButton.addActionListener(this);
46          buttonPanel.add(addButton);
47          JButton subtractButton = new JButton("−");
48          subtractButton.addActionListener(this);
49          buttonPanel.add(subtractButton);
50          JButton resetButton = new JButton("Reset");
51          resetButton.addActionListener(this);
52          buttonPanel.add(resetButton);

53          add(buttonPanel, BorderLayout.CENTER);
54      }

55      public void actionPerformed(ActionEvent e)
56      {
57          try
58          {
59              assumingCorrectNumberFormats(e);
60          }
61          catch (NumberFormatException e2)
62          {
63              ioField.setText("Error: Reenter Number.");
64          }
65      }
```

A `NumberFormatException` *does not need to be declared or caught in a catch block.*

```
66      //Throws NumberFormatException.
67      public void assumingCorrectNumberFormats(ActionEvent e)
68      {
69          String actionCommand = e.getActionCommand();

70          if (actionCommand.equals("+"))
71          {
72              result = result + stringToDouble(ioField.getText());
73              ioField.setText(Double.toString(result));
74          }
75          else if (actionCommand.equals("−"))
76          {
77              result = result - stringToDouble(ioField.getText());
78              ioField.setText(Double.toString(result));
79          }
80          else if (actionCommand.equals("Reset"))
81          {
82              result = 0.0;
83              ioField.setText("0.0");
84          }
85          else
86              ioField.setText("Unexpected error.");
87      }
```

(continued)

Display 17.19   **A Simple Calculator** (part 3 of 4)

```
88        //Throws NumberFormatException.
89        private static double stringToDouble(String stringObject)
90        {
91            return Double.parseDouble(stringObject.trim());
92        }
93    }
```

RESULTING GUI (When started)

RESULTING GUI (After entering 2,000)

RESULTING GUI (After clicking +)

Display 17.19   **A Simple Calculator** (part 4 of 4)

RESULTING GUI (After entering 2000.0 and clicking +)

RESULTING GUI (After entering 42)

RESULTING GUI (After clicking +)

MyProgrammingLab™   ## Self-Test Exercises

39. In the GUI in Display 17.19, why did we make the text field `ioField` an instance variable but did not make instance variables of any of the buttons `addButton`, `subtractButton`, or `resetButton`?

40. What would happen if the user running the GUI in Display 17.19 were to run the GUI and simply click the addition button without typing anything into the text field?

(continued)

Self-Test Exercises (continued)

41. What would happen if the user running the GUI in Display 17.19 were to type the number `10` into the text field and then click the addition button three times? Explain your answer.

42. Suppose you change the `main` method in Display 17.19 to the following:

```
public static void main(String[] args)
{
    Calculator calculator1 = new Calculator();
    calculator1.setVisible(true);
    Calculator calculator2 = new Calculator();
    calculator2.setVisible(true);
}
```

This will cause two calculator windows to be displayed. (If one is on top of the other, you can use your mouse to move the top one.) If you add numbers in one of these calculators, will anything change in the other calculator?

43. Suppose you change the `main` method in Display 17.19 as we described in Self-Test Exercise 42. This will cause two calculator windows to be displayed. If you click the close-window button in one of the windows, will one window go away or will both windows go away?

Chapter Summary

- Swing GUIs (graphical user interfaces) are programmed using event-driven programming. In event-driven programming, a user action, such as a button click, generates an event, which is automatically passed to an event-handling method that performs the appropriate action.

- There are two main techniques for designing a Swing GUI class. You can use inheritance to create a derived class of one of the library classes such as `JFrame` or you can build a GUI by adding components to a container class. You normally use both of these techniques when defining a Swing GUI class.

- A *windowing GUI* is usually defined as a derived class of the class `JFrame`.

- A *button* is an object of the class `JButton`. Clicking a button fires an action event that is handled by an action listener. An *action listener* is any class that implements the `ActionListener` interface.

- A *label* is an object of the class `JLabel`. You can use a label to add text to a GUI.

- When adding components to an object of a container class, such as adding a button to a panel or `JFrame`, use the method `add`. The components in a container are arranged by an object called a *layout manager*.

- A *panel* is a container object that is used to group components inside of a larger container. Panels are objects in the class JPanel.

- A *menu item* is a choice on a menu. A menu item is realized in your code as an object of the class JMenuItem. A *menu* is an object of the class JMenu. A menu item is added to a JMenu with the method add. A *menu bar* is an object of the class JMenuBar. A menu is added to a JMenuBar with the method add.

- A JMenuBar can be added to a JFrame with the method setJMenuBar. It can also be added using the method add, just as any other component can be added.

- Both buttons and menu items fire action events and so normally have one or more action listeners registered with them to respond to the events.

Answers to Self-Test Exercises

1. The AWT package. The Swing package is an improved version of AWT.

2. The exception object thrownObject is the event and the catch block is the event handler.

3. ```
JFrame myWindow = new JFrame();
myWindow.setSize(800, 500);
```

4. ```
JFrame myWindow = new JFrame("Hello World!");
myWindow.setSize(800, 500);
```

5. `myWindow.setDefaultCloseOperation(JFrame.DISPOSE_ON_CLOSE);`

6. `someWindow.setVisible(n > 0);`

   The following also works but is not good style:

   ```
   if (n > 0)
       someWindow.setVisible(true);
   else
       someWindow.setVisible(false);
   ```

7. ActionListener interface.

8. `public void actionPerformed(ActionEvent e)`

9. Change
   ```
   JFrame firstWindow = new JFrame();
   ```
   to
   ```
   JFrame firstWindow = new JFrame("My First Window");
   ```
   Alternatively, you can add the following:
   ```
   firstWindow.setTitle("My First Window");
   ```

10. Delete

```
setTitle("First Window Class");
```

and replace

```
super();
```

with

```
super("First Window Class");
```

11. Change

```
setDefaultCloseOperation(
                JFrame.DO_NOTHING_ON_CLOSE);
```

to

```
setDefaultCloseOperation(
                JFrame.EXIT_ON_CLOSE);
```

12. Change the following line in the no-argument constructor in Display 17.6 from

```
this(Color.PINK);
```

to

```
this(Color.MAGENTA);
```

13. `add(new JLabel("Close-window button works."));`

14. Yes, it is legal. It is OK to reuse a variable name such as `aLabel`.

15. You need to change the `add` statements, as in the following rewritten section of code:

```
JLabel label1 = new JLabel("First label");
add(label1, BorderLayout.NORTH);

JLabel label2 = new JLabel("Second label");
add(label2, BorderLayout.CENTER);

JLabel label3 = new JLabel("Third label");
add(label3, BorderLayout.SOUTH);
```

16. You need to change the `add` statements, as in the following rewritten section of code:

```
JLabel label1 = new JLabel("First label");
add(label1, BorderLayout.NORTH);

JLabel label2 = new JLabel("Second label");
add(label2, BorderLayout.EAST);

JLabel label3 = new JLabel("Third label");
add(label3, BorderLayout.SOUTH);
```

17. `setLayout(new GridLayout(5, 3));`

18. The argument should be `new GridLayout(0, 1)`. So, the entire method invocation is

```
setLayout(new GridLayout(0, 1));
```

Alternatively, you could use `new GridLayout(3, 1)`, if you know there will be at most three components added, but if more than three components are added, then a second column will be added. It is also possible to do something similar with a `BorderLayout` manager, but a `GridLayout` manager will work nicer here.

19. `java.awt` package.

20. An object of the class `JPanel` is both a container class and a component class.

21. To make it look as though you have an empty grid element, add an empty panel to the grid element.

22.
```java
import javax.swing.JPanel;
import java.awt.Color;

public class PinkJPanel extends JPanel
{
    public PinkJPanel()
    {
        setBackground(Color.PINK);
    }
}
```

extra code on website

The class `PinkJPanel` is on the website that accompanies this text.

23. It will not compile, but will give a compiler error message saying that `actionPerformed` is not defined (because it claims to implement the `ActionListener` interface).

24. It will not compile, but will give compiler error messages saying that, in effect, the invocations of `addActionListener` such as

`redButton.addActionListener(this);`

have arguments of an incorrect type.

25. the `MenuDemo` class.

26. There are three inner action listener classes – `blueListener, WhiteListener` and `grayListener` – for each menu item.

27.
```java
JMenu m1 = new JMenu("New");
JMenu m2 = new JMenu("Open");
JMenu m3 = new JMenu("Save");
JMenuBar mbar = new JMenuBar( );
mbar.add(m1); mbar.add(m2); mbar.add(m3);
setJMenuBar(bar);
```

28. To change the action command for a `JMenuItem`, use the method `setActionCommand`, just as you would for a `JButton`.

29. Yes, it is legal.

30. As many as you want. Only one can be added with the method `setJMenuBar`, but any number of others can be added to using the `add` method.

31. `Click`

32. `JMenuItem aChoice = new`
    `JMenuItem("Exit");`

33. `Save`

34. Register all three types of listeners with `blueChoice`, as follows:

    ```
    blueChoice.addActionListener(new RedListener());
    blueChoice.addActionListener(new WhiteListener());
    blueChoice.addActionListener(new BlueListener());
    ```

35. Replace the three inner classes with the following inner class:

    ```
    private class ColorListener implements ActionListener
    {
        private JPanel thePanel;
        private Color theColor;

        public ColorListener(Color c, JPanel p)
        {
            theColor = c;
            thePanel = p;
        }

        public void actionPerformed(ActionEvent e)
        {
            thePanel.setBackground(theColor);
        }
    } //End of ColorListener inner class
    ```

    Replace

    `redChoice.addActionListener(new RedListener());`

    with

    ```
    redChoice.addActionListener(
                    new ColorListener(Color.RED, redPanel));
    ```

    Also make similar changes to the menu items `whiteChoice` and `blueChoice`, with the obvious changes to colors and panels.

    This is not really preferable to what we did in Display 17.16, but it is a good exercise. The complete program done this way is on the accompanying website in the file named `InnerListenersDemo2.java`.

**extra code
on website**

36. A `JTextField` object displays only a single line. A `JTextArea` object can display more than one line of text.

37. The contents of the text field would change to `"Hello Hello Hello"`.

38. This program is on the website that accompanies this text.

extra code
on website

```java
import javax.swing.JFrame;
import javax.swing.JTextArea;
import javax.swing.JPanel;
import javax.swing.JLabel;
import javax.swing.JButton;
import java.awt.GridLayout;
import java.awt.BorderLayout;
import java.awt.FlowLayout;
import java.awt.Color;
import java.awt.event.ActionListener;
import java.awt.event.ActionEvent;

public class TextAreaDemo extends JFrame
                         implements ActionListener
{
    public static final int WIDTH = 400;
    public static final int HEIGHT = 200;
    public static final int NUMBER_OF_LINES = 10;
    public static final int NUMBER_OF_CHAR = 30;

    private JTextArea story;

    public static void main(String[] args)
    {
        TextAreaDemo gui = new TextAreaDemo();
        gui.setVisible(true);
    }

    public TextAreaDemo()
    {
        setTitle("Text Area Demo");
        setSize(WIDTH, HEIGHT);
        setDefaultCloseOperation(JFrame.EXIT_ON_CLOSE);
        setLayout(new GridLayout(2, 1));
        JPanel storyPanel = new JPanel();
        storyPanel.setLayout(new BorderLayout());
        storyPanel.setBackground(Color.WHITE);

        story = new JTextArea(NUMBER_OF_LINES, NUMBER_OF_CHAR);
```

```
            storyPanel.add(story, BorderLayout.CENTER);
            JLabel storyLabel = new JLabel("Enter your story here:");
            storyPanel.add(storyLabel, BorderLayout.NORTH);

            add(storyPanel);

            JPanel buttonPanel = new JPanel( );
            buttonPanel.setLayout(new FlowLayout( ));
            buttonPanel.setBackground(Color.PINK);
            JButton actionButton = new JButton("Click me");
            actionButton.addActionListener(this);
            buttonPanel.add(actionButton);

            JButton clearButton = new JButton("Clear");
            clearButton.addActionListener(this);
            buttonPanel.add(clearButton);

            add(buttonPanel);
        }

        public void actionPerformed(ActionEvent e)
        {
            String actionCommand = e.getActionCommand( );

          if (actionCommand.equals("Click me"))
          {
                int lineCount = getLineCount();
                story.setText("Your story is "
                                    + lineCount + " lines long.");
          }
          else if (actionCommand.equals("Clear"))
             story.setText("");
          else
             story.setText("Unexpected error.");
        }
        private int getLineCount()
        {
            String storyString = story.getText();
            int count = 0;

            for (int i = 0; i < storyString.length(); i++)
              if (storyString.charAt(i) == '\n')
                  count++;

            return count + 1;//The last line has no '\n'.
        }
    }
```

39. We made the text field an instance variable because we needed to refer to it in the definition of the method `actionPerformed`. On the other hand, the only direct reference we had to the buttons was in the constructor. So, we need names for the buttons only in the constructor definition.

40. The GUI would try to add the string `"Enter numbers here."` as if it were a string for a number. This will cause a `NumberFormatException` to be thrown and the string `"Error: Reenter Number."` would be displayed in the text field.

41. Every time the user clicks the addition button, the following assignment is executed:

```
result = result + stringToDouble(ioField.getText());
```

So, the number in the text field is added to the total as many times as the user clicks the addition button. But, the value in the text field is the running total, so the running total is added to itself. Thus, the running total is added to the total as many times as the user clicks the addition button.

Let us say that the user starts the GUI, types in 10, and clicks the addition button. That adds 10 to `result`, so the value of `result` is then 0 plus 10, which is 10, and 10 is displayed. Now the user clicks the addition button a second time. That adds 10 to result again, so the value of result is 10 plus 10, which is 20, and 20 is displayed. Next the user clicks the addition button a third time. This time, 20 is in the text field, and so it is added to result, which is also 20. Thus, the value of `result` is now 40, and 40 is displayed. Note that it is always the number in the text field that is added in.

42. The two calculator windows are completely independent. Each has its own instance variable `result`, which has no effect on the other's instance variable `result`.

43. If you click the close-window button in either calculator window, the entire program ends because that causes an invocation of `System.exit`. There is no invocation of `System.exit` in Display 17.19, but the following ensures that a `System.exit` that is in some library class will be invoked:

```
setDefaultCloseOperation(JFrame.EXIT_ON_CLOSE);
```

MyProgrammingLab™ ## Programming Projects

Visit www.myprogramminglab.com to complete select exercises online and get instant feedback.

VideoNote
Solution to
Programming
Project 17.1

1. Design and code a Swing GUI to translate text that is input in English into Pig Latin. You can assume that the sentence contains no punctuation. The rules for Pig Latin are as follows:

   a. For words that begin with consonants, move the leading consonant to the end of the word and add "ay." Thus, "ball" becomes "allbay"; "button" becomes "uttonbay"; and so forth.

   b. For words that begin with vowels, add "way" to the end of the word. Thus, "all" becomes "allway"; "one" becomes "oneway"; and so forth.

Use a `FlowLayout` with a `JTextArea` for the source text and a separate `JTextArea` for the translated text. Add a `JButton` with an event to perform the translation. A sample application is shown next with the text translated to Pig Latin.

To parse the source text, note that you can use the `Scanner` class on a `String`. For example the following code

```
Scanner scan = new Scanner("foo bar zot");
while (scan.hasNext())
{
  System.out.println(scan.next());
}
```

will output

```
foo
bar
zot
```

2. Design and code a Swing GUI for a two-player tic-tac-toe (noughts and crosses) game on a 3×3 game board. The `JFrame` should use a `BorderLayout` with a `JLabel` in the NORTH region to display messages (e.g., who won the game), and a `JPanel` in the CENTER region to display the game board. For the game board in the `JPanel`, use a `GridLayout` manager with a 3×3 layout of `JButton`'s in each cell to display the game board. The button labels should initially be blank. When a player clicks on an empty button, an appropriate "X" or "O" should be placed in the label field of the button. If there is a winner (three in a row), then the program should display the winner in the `JLabel` located at the top of the window. If all nine cells have been filled without a winner, the program should indicate that there is a tie.

3. Design and code a Swing GUI calculator. You can use Display 17.19 as a starting point, but your calculator will be more sophisticated. Your calculator will have two text fields that the user cannot change: One labeled `"Result"` will contain the result of performing the operation, and the other labeled `"Operand"` will be for the user to enter a number to be added, subtracted, and so forth from the result. The user enters the number for the `"Operand"` text field by clicking buttons labeled with the digits `0` through `9` and a decimal point, just as in a real calculator. Allow the operations of addition, subtraction, multiplication, and division. Use a `GridLayout` manager to produce a button pad that looks similar to the keyboard on a real calculator.

When the user clicks a button for an operation, the following occurs: the operation is performed, the `"Result"` text field is updated, and the `"Operand"` text field is cleared. Include a button labeled `"Reset"` that resets the `"Result"` to `0.0`. Also include a button labeled `"Clear"` that resets the `"Operand"` text field so it is blank.

Hint: Define an exception class named `DivisonByZeroException`. Have your code throw and catch a `DivisonByZeroException` if the user attempts to "divide by zero." Your code will catch the `DivisonByZeroException` and output a suitable message to the `"Operand"` text field. The user may then enter a new substitute number in the `"Operand"` text field. Because values of type `double` are, in effect, approximate values, it makes no sense to test for equality with `0.0`. Consider an operand to be "equal to zero" if it is in the range `-1.0e-10` to `+1.0e-10`.

4. (The Swing part of this project is pretty easy, but to do this programming project you need to know how to convert numbers from one base to another.) Write a program that converts integers from base ten (ordinary decimal) notation to base two notation. Use Swing to perform input and output via a window interface. The user enters a base ten numeral in one text field and clicks a button with `"Convert"` written on it; the equivalent base two numeral then appears in another text field. Be sure to label the two text fields. Include a `"Clear"` button that clears both text fields when clicked. (*Hint:* Include a private method that converts the string for a base ten numeral to the string for the equivalent base two numeral.)

5. Re-do or do for the first time the trivia game described in Programming Projects 6.12 and 6.13, except create a GUI for the game interface. Use a layout of your choice with the appropriate text fields, labels, and buttons to implement your design. The game should ask only one question at a time and output the correct answer if the player answers a question incorrectly. When all questions have been answered, show the final score and exit the program.

6. Write a program that implements a simple text editor. Use a `JTextArea` for the area that the user can enter text. Add a button that allows the user to save the text to a file and a button that allows the user to load the text from a file.

Swing II 18

18.1 WINDOW LISTENERS 1050

Example: A Window Listener Inner Class 1052

The `dispose` Method 1055

The `WindowAdapter` Class 1056

18.2 ICONS AND SCROLL BARS 1058

Icons 1058

Scroll Bars 1064

Example: Components with Changing Visibility 1069

18.3 THE `Graphics` CLASS 1073

Coordinate System for Graphics Objects 1073

The Method `paint` and the Class `Graphics` 1074

Drawing Ovals 1079

Drawing Arcs 1079

Rounded Rectangles ★ 1083

`paintComponent` for Panels 1084

Action Drawings and `repaint` 1084

Some More Details on Updating a GUI ★ 1090

18.4 COLORS 1090

Specifying a Drawing Color 1091

Defining Colors 1092

The `JColorChooser` Dialog Window 1094

18.5 FONTS AND THE `drawString` METHOD 1097

The `drawString` Method 1097

Fonts 1100

Chapter Summary 1103   **Answers to Self-Test Exercises** 1103   **Programming Projects** 1107

18 Swing II

Window listeners?
I thought windows were for looking not for listening.

Student answer on an exam

Introduction

This chapter is a continuation of Chapter 17, presenting more details about designing regular Swing GUIs. Chapter 20 on applets is a side issue that may be read after this chapter if you prefer.

Prerequisites

This chapter uses material from Chapter 17 (and its prerequisites).

Section 18.2 on icons and scroll bars is not used in subsequent sections and so may be skipped or postponed.

18.1 Window Listeners

A man may see how this world goes with no eyes.
Look with thine ears... .

WILLIAM SHAKESPEARE, *King Lear*

In Chapter 17, we used the method `setDefaultCloseOperation` to program the close-window button in a `JFrame`. This allows for only a limited number of possibilities for what happens when the close-window button is clicked. When the user clicks the close-window button (or either of the two accompanying buttons), the `JFrame` fires an event known as a **window event**. A `JFrame` can use the method `setWindowListener` to register a **window listener** to respond to such window events. A window listener can be programmed to respond to a window event in any way you wish. Window events are objects of the class `WindowEvent`. A window listener is any class that satisfies the `WindowListener` interface.

The method headings in the `WindowListener` interface are given in Display 18.1. If a class implements the `WindowListener` interface, it must have definitions for all seven of these method headings. If you do not need all of these methods, then you can define the ones you do not need to have empty bodies, like this:

```
public void windowDeiconified(WindowEvent e)

{}
```

window event

window listener

`WindowEvent`

`Window Listener`

Display 18.1   Methods in the `WindowListener` Interface

The `WindowListener` interface and the `WindowEvent` class are in the package `java.awt.event`.

`public void windowOpened(WindowEvent e)`

Invoked when a window is opened.

`public void windowClosing(WindowEvent e)`

Invoked when a window is in the process of being closed. Clicking the close-window button causes an invocation of this method.

`public void windowClosed(WindowEvent e)`

Invoked when a window has been closed.

`public void windowIconified(WindowEvent e)`

Invoked when a window is iconified. When you click the minimize button in a `JFrame`, it is iconified.

`public void windowDeiconified(WindowEvent e)`

Invoked when a window is deiconified. When you activate a minimized window, it is deiconified.

`public void windowActivated(WindowEvent e)`

Invoked when a window is activated. When you click in a window, it becomes the activated window. Other actions can also activate a window.

`public void windowDeactivated(WindowEvent e)`

Invoked when a window is deactivated. When a window is activated, all other windows are deactivated. Other actions can also deactivate a window.

The `WindowListener` Interface

When the user clicks any of the three standard `JFrame` buttons (for closing the window, minimizing the window, and resizing the window), it generates a window event. Window events are sent to window listeners. In order to be a window listener, a class must implement the `WindowListener` interface. The method headings for the `WindowListener` interface are given in Display 18.1.

EXAMPLE: A Window Listener Inner Class

Display 18.2 gives an example of a JFrame class with a window listener class that is an inner class. The window listener inner class is named CheckOnExit. A window listener class need not be an inner class, but it is frequently convenient to make a window listener class (or other kind of listener class) an inner class.

The main JFrame in Display 18.2 simply displays a message. What is interesting is how the window listener programs the close-window button. You can apply the window listener used in this JFrame to any JFrame. When the close-window button is clicked, a second, smaller window appears and asks "Are you sure you want to exit?" If the user clicks the "Yes" button, the entire program ends and so both windows go away. If the user clicks the "No" button, only the smaller window disappears; the program and the main window continue. Let us look at the programming details.

When the close-window button in the main window is clicked, this fires a window event. The only registered window listener is the anonymous object that is the argument to addWindowListener. Next we repeat the relevant line of code, which is in the constructor for WindowListenerDemo:

```
addWindowListener(new CheckOnExit());
```

This anonymous window listener object receives the window event fired when the close-window button is clicked and then invokes the method windowClosing. The method windowClosing creates and displays a window object of the class ConfirmWindow, which contains the message "Are you sure you want to exit?" as well as the two buttons labeled "Yes" and "No".

If the user clicks the "Yes" button, the action event fired by that button goes to the actionPerformed method, which ends the program with a call to System. exit. If the user clicks the "No" button, then the actionPerformed method invokes the method dispose. The method dispose, discussed in the next subsection, makes its calling object go away but does not end the program. The calling object for dispose is the smaller window (which is an object of the class ConfirmWindow), so this smaller window goes away but the main window remains.

Notice that even though we have registered a window listener, which says what should happen when the close-window button is clicked, we still need to invoke the method setDefaultCloseOperation. When the close-window button is clicked, the policy set by setDefaultCloseOperation is always carried out in addition to any action by window listeners. If we do not include any invocation of setDefaultCloseOperation, then the default action is to make the window go away (but not to end the program). We do not want our main window to go away, so we set the policy as follows:

```
setDefaultCloseOperation(JFrame.DO_NOTHING_ON_CLOSE);
```

This means that clicking the close-window button causes no action other than the actions of any window listeners. If you are using a window listener to set the action of the close-window button, you invariably want an invocation of setDefaultCloseOperation with the argument JFrame.DO_NOTHING_ON_CLOSE.

Display 18.2   **A Window Listener** (part 1 of 3)

```
1    import javax.swing.JFrame;
2    import javax.swing.JPanel;
3    import java.awt.BorderLayout;
4    import java.awt.FlowLayout;
5    import java.awt.Color;
6    import javax.swing.JLabel;
7    import javax.swing.JButton;
8    import java.awt.event.ActionListener;
9    import java.awt.event.ActionEvent;
10   import java.awt.event.WindowListener;
11   import java.awt.event.WindowEvent;

12   public class WindowListenerDemo extends JFrame
13   {
14       public static final int WIDTH = 300; //for main window
15       public static final int HEIGHT = 200; //for main window
16       public static final int SMALL_WIDTH = 200; //for confirm window
17       public static final int SMALL_HEIGHT = 100; //for confirm window

18       private class CheckOnExit implements WindowListener
19       {
20           public void windowOpened(WindowEvent e)
21           {}
```

This WindowListener class is an inner class.

```
22           public void windowClosing(WindowEvent e)
23           {
24               ConfirmWindow checkers = new ConfirmWindow();
25               checkers.setVisible(true);
26           }

27           public void windowClosed(WindowEvent e)
28           {}

29           public void windowIconified(WindowEvent e)
30           {}

31           public void windowDeiconified(WindowEvent e)
32           {}
```

A window listener must define all the method headings in the `WindowListener` interface, even if some are trivial implementations.

```
33           public void windowActivated(WindowEvent e)
34           {}

35           public void windowDeactivated(WindowEvent e)
36           {}
37       }//End of inner class CheckOnExit

38       private class ConfirmWindow extends JFrame implements
                         ActionListener
```

Another

```
39       {
40           public ConfirmWindow()
41           {
42               setSize(SMALL_WIDTH, SMALL_HEIGHT);
43               getContentPane().setBackground(Color.YELLOW);
```

(continued)

Display 18.2   **A Window Listener** (part 2 of 3)

```
44              setLayout(new BorderLayout());
45              JLabel confirmLabel = new JLabel(
46                          "Are you sure you want to exit?");
47              add(confirmLabel, BorderLayout.CENTER);

48              JPanel buttonPanel = new JPanel();
49              buttonPanel.setBackground(Color.ORANGE);
50              buttonPanel.setLayout(new FlowLayout());

51              JButton exitButton = new JButton("Yes");
52              exitButton.addActionListener(this);
53              buttonPanel.add(exitButton);

54              JButton cancelButton = new JButton("No");
55              cancelButton.addActionListener(this);
56              buttonPanel.add(cancelButton);

57              add(buttonPanel, BorderLayout.SOUTH);
58          }
59      public void actionPerformed(ActionEvent e)
60      {
61          String actionCommand = e.getActionCommand();

62          if (actionCommand.equals("Yes"))
63              System.exit(0);
64          else if (actionCommand.equals("No"))
65              dispose(); //Destroys only the ConfirmWindow.
66          else
67              System.out.println(
                   "Unexpected Error in Confirm Window.");
68      }
69  } //End of inner class ConfirmWindow
70
71  public static void main(String[] args)
72  {
73      WindowListenerDemo demoWindow = new WindowListenerDemo();
74      demoWindow.setVisible(true);
75  }
76
77  public WindowListenerDemo()
78  {
79      setSize(WIDTH, HEIGHT);
80      setTitle("Window Listener Demonstration");
81
82      setDefaultCloseOperation(JFrame.DO_NOTHING_ON_CLOSE);
83      addWindowListener(new CheckOnExit());
84
85      getContentPane().setBackground(Color.LIGHT_GRAY);
86      JLabel aLabel = new JLabel(
            "I like to be sure you are sincere.");
87      add(aLabel);
88  }
89 }
```

Even if you have a window listener, you normally must still invoke `setDefaultCloseOperation`.

Display 18.2　**A Window Listener** (part 3 of 3)

RESULTING GUI

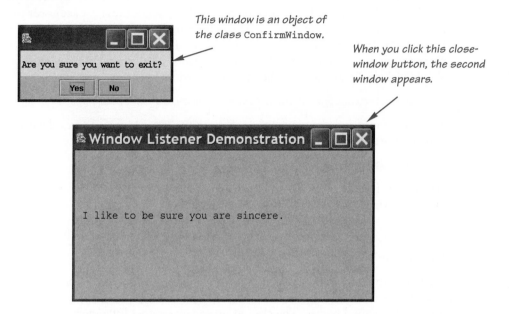

This window is an object of the class ConfirmWindow.

When you click this close-window button, the second window appears.

The dispose Method

dispose　The method dispose is a method in the class JFrame that releases any resources used by the JFrame or any of its components. So, a call to dispose eliminates the JFrame and its components, but if the program has items that are not components of the JFrame, then the program does not end. For example, in Display 18.2, the smaller window of the class ConfirmWindow invokes dispose (if the user clicks the "No" button). That causes that smaller window to go away, but the larger window remains.

The dispose Method

The class JFrame has a method named dispose that will eliminate the invoking JFrame without ending the program. When dispose is invoked, the resources consumed by the JFrame and its components are returned for reuse, so the JFrame is gone, but the program does not end (unless dispose eliminates all elements in the program, as in a one-window program). The method dispose is often used in a program with multiple windows to eliminate one window without ending the program.

SYNTAX

JFrame_Object.dispose();

The *JFrame_Object* is often an implicit this. A complete example of using dispose can be seen in Display 18.2.

PITFALL: Forgetting to Invoke `setDefaultCloseOperation`

If you register a window listener to respond to window events from a `JFrame`, you should also include an invocation of the method `setDefaultCloseOperation`, typically in the `JFrame` constructor. This is because the default or other behavior set by `setDefaultCloseOperation` takes place even if there is a window listener. If you do not want any actions other than those provided by the window listener(s), you should include the following in the `JFrame` constructor:

```
setDefaultCloseOperation(JFrame.DO_NOTHING_ON_CLOSE);
```

If you do not include any invocation of `setDefaultCloseOperation`, the default action is the same as if you had included the invocation

```
setDefaultCloseOperation(JFrame.HIDE_ON_CLOSE);
```

which hides the `JFrame` when the close-window button is clicked. (The actions of any registered window listener are also performed.) ∎

The `WindowAdapter` Class

In Display 18.2, we gave empty bodies to most of the method headings in the `WindowListener` interface. The abstract class `WindowAdapter` is a way to avoid all those empty method bodies. The class `WindowAdapter` does little more than provide trivial implementations of the method headings in the `WindowListener` interface. So, if you make a window listener a derived class of the class `WindowAdapter`, then you have only to define the method headings in the `WindowListener` interface that you need. The other method headings inherit trivial implementations from `WindowAdapter`. (`WindowAdapter` is unusual in that it is an abstract class with no abstract methods.)

For example, in Display 18.3 we have rewritten the inner class `CheckOnExit` from Display 18.2, but this time we made it a derived class of the `WindowAdapter` class. This definition of `CheckOnExit` is much shorter and cleaner than the one in Display 18.2, but the two implementations of `CheckOnExit` are equivalent. Thus, you can replace the definition of `CheckOnExit` in Display 18.2 with the shorter one in Display 18.3. The file `WindowListenerDemo2` on the accompanying website contains a version of Display 18.2 with this shorter definition of `CheckOnExit`.

extra code on website

The class `WindowAdapter` is in the `java.awt.event` package and so requires an `import` statement such as the following:

```
import java.awt.event.WindowAdapter;
```

You cannot always define your window listeners as derived classes of `WindowAdapter`. For example, suppose you want a `JFrame` class to be its own window listener. To accomplish this, the class must be a derived class of `JFrame` and so cannot be a derived class of any other class such as WindowAdapter. In such cases, you make the class a derived class of JFrame and have it implement the WindowListener interface. See Self-Test Exercise 4 for an example.

Display 18.3   Using WindowAdapter

This requires the following import

```
        import java.awt.event.WindowAdapter;
        import java.awt.event.WindowEvent;
```

```
1    private class CheckOnExit extends WindowAdapter
2    {
3        public void windowClosing(WindowEvent e)
4        {
5            ConfirmWindow checkers = new ConfirmWindow();
6            checkers.setVisible(true);
7        }
8    } //End of inner class CheckOnExit
```

If the definition of the inner class CheckOnExit *in Display 18.2 were replaced with this definition of* CheckOnExit, *there would be no difference in how the outer class or any class behaves.*

Self-Test Exercises

1. When using a window frame, if your program needs to remove that window from the screen when it is closed, how it could be achieved?

2. The GUI in Display 18.2 has a main window. When the user clicks the close-window button in the main window, a smaller window appears that says "Are you sure you want to exit?" What happens if the user clicks the close-window button in this smaller window? Explain your answer.

3. If you want a Swing program to end completely, you can invoke the method System.exit. What if you want a JFrame window to go away, but you do not want the program to end? What method can you have the JFrame invoke?

4. Rewrite the class in Display 18.2 so that the class is its own window listener. *Hint*: The constructor will contain

```
addWindowListener(this);
```

18.2 **Icons and Scroll Bars**

I ♥ ICONS.

Bumper sticker

Icons

icon   JLabels, JButtons, and JMenuItems can have icons. An **icon** is simply a small picture, although it is not required to be small. The label, button, or menu item may have just a string displayed on it, just an icon, or both (or nothing at all). An icon is an

ImageIcon   instance of the ImageIcon class and is based on a digital picture file. The picture file can be in almost any standard format, such as .gif, .jpg, or .tiff.

The class ImageIcon is used to convert a picture file to a Swing icon. For example, if you have a picture in a file named duke_waving.gif, the following will produce an icon named dukeWavingIcon for the picture duke_waving.gif:

```
ImageIcon dukeIcon = new ImageIcon("duke_waving.gif");
```

The file duke_waving.gif should be in the same directory as the class in which this code appears. Alternatively, you can use a complete or relative pathname to specify the picture file. Note that the picture file is given as a value of type String that names the picture file. The file duke_waving.gif and other picture files we will use in this chapter are all provided on the website that accompanies this text.

setIcon   You can add an icon to a label with the method setIcon, as follows:

```
JLabel dukeLabel = new JLabel("Mood check");
dukeLabel.setIcon(dukeIcon);
```

Alternatively, you give the icon as an argument to the JLabel constructor, as follows:

```
JLabel dukeLabel = new JLabel(dukeIcon);
```

You can leave the label as created and it will have an icon but no text, or you can add
setText   text with the method setText, as follows:

```
dukeLabel.setText("Mood check");
```

Icons and text may be added to JButtons and JMenuItems in the same way as they are added to a JLabel. For example, the following is taken from Display 18.4, which is a demonstration of the use of icons:

```
JButton happyButton = new JButton("Happy");
ImageIcon happyIcon = new ImageIcon("smiley.gif");
happyButton.setIcon(happyIcon);
```

Display 18.4   **Using Icons** (part 1 of 2)

```
 1   import javax.swing.JFrame;
 2   import javax.swing.JPanel;
 3   import javax.swing.JTextField;
 4   import javax.swing.ImageIcon;
 5   import java.awt.BorderLayout;
 6   import java.awt.FlowLayout;
 7   import java.awt.Color;
 8   import javax.swing.JLabel;
 9   import javax.swing.JButton;
10   import java.awt.event.ActionListener;
11   import java.awt.event.ActionEvent;

12   public class IconDemo extends JFrame implements ActionListener
13   {
14       public static final int WIDTH = 500;
15       public static final int HEIGHT = 200;
16       public static final int TEXT_FIELD_SIZE = 30;

17       private JTextField message;
18       public static void main(String[] args)
19       {
20           IconDemo iconGui = new IconDemo();
21           iconGui.setVisible(true);
22       }


23       public IconDemo()
24       {
25           super("Icon Demonstration");
26           setSize(WIDTH, HEIGHT);
27           setDefaultCloseOperation(JFrame.EXIT_ON_CLOSE);

28           setBackground(Color.WHITE);
29           setLayout(new BorderLayout());

30           JLabel dukeLabel = new JLabel("Mood check");
31           ImageIcon dukeIcon = new ImageIcon("duke_waving.gif");
32           dukeLabel.setIcon(dukeIcon);
33           add(dukeLabel, BorderLayout.NORTH);

34           JPanel buttonPanel = new JPanel();
35           buttonPanel.setLayout(new FlowLayout());
36           JButton happyButton = new JButton("Happy");
37           ImageIcon happyIcon = new ImageIcon("smiley.gif");
38           happyButton.setIcon(happyIcon);
39           happyButton.addActionListener(this);
40           buttonPanel.add(happyButton);
41           JButton sadButton = new JButton("Sad");
42           ImageIcon sadIcon = new ImageIcon("sad.gif");
43           sadButton.setIcon(sadIcon);
44           sadButton.addActionListener(this);
```

(continued)

Display 18.4   Using Icons (part 2 of 2)

```
45              buttonPanel.add(sadButton);
46              add(buttonPanel, BorderLayout.SOUTH);

47              message = new JTextField(TEXT_FIELD_SIZE);
48              add(message, BorderLayout.CENTER);
49          }

50      public void actionPerformed(ActionEvent e)
51      {
52          String actionCommand = e.getActionCommand();
53          if (actionCommand.equals("Happy"))
54              message.setText(
55                      "Smile and the world smiles with you!");
56          else if (actionCommand.equals("Sad"))
57              message.setText(
58                      "Cheer up. It can't be that bad.");
59          else
60              message.setText("Unexpected Error.");
61      }
62  }
```

RESULTING GUI[1]

View after clicking the "Sad" button.

---

button with only an icon   You can produce a button or menu item with (just) an icon on it by giving the ImageIcon object as an argument to the JButton or JMenuItem constructor. For example,

```
ImageIcon happyIcon = new ImageIcon("smiley.gif");
JButton smileButton = new JButton(happyIcon);
JMenuItem happyChoice = new JMenuItem(happyIcon);
```

If you create a button or menu item in this way and do not add text with the method setText, you should use setActionCommand to explicitly give the button or menu item an action command, because there is no string on the button or menu item.

---

[1]Java, Duke, and all Java-based trademarks and logos are trademarks or registered trademarks of Oracle, Inc. in the United States and other countries.

All of the classes `JButton`, `JMenuItem`, and `JLabel` have constructors that let you specify text and an icon to appear on the button, menu item, or label. The constructor can specify no text or icon, text only, an icon only, or both text and an icon. When you specify both text and an icon, the text is the first argument and the icon is the second argument; also, the constructor for a `JLabel` requires a third argument, as described in Display 18.5. If you omit either text or an icon (or both) from the constructor, you can add them later with the methods `setText` and `setIcon`. Some of these methods for the classes `JButton`, `JMenuItem`, and `Jlabel` are given in Display 18.5.

Icons and the Class `ImageIcon`

An **icon** is simply a small picture, although it is not really required to be small. The class `ImageIcon` is used to convert a picture file to a Swing icon.

SYNTAX

```
ImageIcon Name_Of_ImageIcon =
        new ImageIcon(Picture_File_Name);
```

The *Picture_File_Name* is a string giving either a relative or absolute path name to the picture file. (So if the picture file is in the same directory as your program, you need give only the name of the picture file.)

EXAMPLE

```
ImageIcon happyIcon =
        new ImageIcon("smiley.gif");
```

Display 18.5   Some Methods in the Classes `JButton`, `JMenuItem`, and `JLabel` (part 1 of 2)

```
public JButton()
public JMenuItem()
public JLabel()
```

Creates a button, menu item, or label with no text or icon on it. (Typically, you will later use `setText` and/or `setIcon` with the button, menu item, or label.)

```
public JButton(String text)
public JMenuItem(String text)
public JLabel(String text)
```

Creates a button, menu item, or label with the text on it.

```
public JButton(ImageIcon picture)
public JMenuItem(ImageIcon picture)
public JLabel(ImageIcon picture)
```

Creates a button, menu item, or label with the icon `picture` on it and no text.

(continued)

Display 18.5 **Some Methods in the Classes `JButton`, `JMenuItem`, and `JLabel`** (part 2 of 2)

```
public JButton(String text, ImageIcon picture)
public JMenuItem(String text, ImageIcon picture)
public JLabel(
        String text, ImageIcon picture, int horizontalAlignment)
```

Creates a button, menu item, or label with both the text and the icon picture on it. horizontalAlignment is one of the constants SwingConstants.LEFT, SwingConstants.CENTER, SwingConstants.RIGHT, SwingConstants.LEADING, or SwingConstants.TRAILING.

The interface SwingConstants is in the javax.swing package.

```
public void setText(String text)
```

Makes text the only text on the button, menu item, or label.

```
public void setIcon(ImageIcon picture)
```

Makes picture the only icon on the button, menu item, or label.

```
public void setMargin(Insets margin)
```

JButton and JMenuItem have the method setMargin, but JLabel does not.

The method setMargin sets the size of the margin around the text and icon in the button or menu item. The following special case will work for most simple situations. The int values give the number of pixels from the edge of the button or menu item to the text and/or icon.

```
public void setMargin(new Insets(
            int top, int left, int bottom, int right))
```

The class Insets is in the java.awt package. (We will not be discussing any other uses for the class Insets.)

```
public void setVerticalTextPosition(int textPosition)
```

Sets the vertical position of the text relative to the icon. The textPosition should be one of the constants SwingConstants.TOP, SwingConstants.CENTER (the default position), or SwingConstants.BOTTOM.

The interface SwingConstants is in the javax.swing package.

```
public void setHorizontalTextPosition(int textPosition)
```

Sets the horizontal position of the text relative to the icon. The textPosition should be one of the constants SwingConstants.RIGHT, SwingConstants.LEFT, SwingConstants. CENTER, SwingConstants.LEADING, or SwingConstants.TRAILING.

The interface SwingConstants is in the javax.swing package.

The `Insets` Class

Objects of the class `Insets` are used to specify the size of the margin in a button or menu item. The `Insets` class is in the package `java.awt`. The parameters in the following constructors are in pixels.

CONSTRUCTOR

```
public Insets(int top, int left, int bottom, int right)
```

EXAMPLES

```
aButton.setMargin(new Insets(10, 20, 10, 20));
```

`setIcon` and `setText`

The method `setIcon` can be used to add an icon to a `JButton`, `JMenuItem`, or `JLabel`. The argument to `setIcon` must be an `ImageIcon` object.

SYNTAX

Component.`setIcon`(*ImageIcon_Object*) ;

The *Component* can be a `JButton`, `JMenuItem`, or `JLabel`.

EXAMPLE

```
JLabel helloLabel = new JLabel("Hello");
ImageIcon dukeIcon = new ImageIcon("duke_waving.gif");
helloLabel.setIcon(dukeIcon);
```

The method `setText` can be used to add text to a `JButton`, `JMenuItem`, or `JLabel`.

SYNTAX

Component.`setText`(*Text_String*) ;

The *Component* can be a `JButton`, `JMenuItem`, or `JLabel`.

EXAMPLE

```
ImageIcon dukeIcon = new ImageIcon("duke_waving.gif");
JLabel helloLabel = new JLabel(dukeIcon);
helloLabel.setText("Hello");
```

The two examples are equivalent.

Self-Test Exercises

5. Write code to create a button that has on it both the text `"Magic Button"` and the picture in the file `wizard.gif`.

6. Write code to add the picture in the file `wizard.gif` to the `JPanel` named `picturePanel`. Assume that `picturePanel` has a `FlowLayout` manager.

7. Write code to create a small picture frame of 4 pictures and add these pictures to the `JPanel` named `picturePanel`. The pictures are named `img1.gif`, `img2.gif`, `img3.gif`, and `img4.gif`. Assume that `picturePanel` has a `GridLayout` manager.

Scroll Bars

When you create a text area, you specify the number of lines that are visible and the number of characters per line, as in the following example:

```
JTextArea memoDisplay = new JTextArea(15, 30);
```

The text area `memoDisplay` will have room for 15 lines of text, and each line will have room for at least 30 characters. The user can enter more text, but only a limited amount of text will be visible. It would be better not to have a firm limit on the number of lines or the number of characters per line that the user can see in some convenient way. The way to accomplish this is to add scroll bars to the text area, although, as you will see, the Java code looks more like adding the text area to the scroll bars rather than the other way around.

view port   When using scroll bars, the text is viewed through a **view port** that shows only part of the text at a time. You can view a different part of the text by using the scroll bars that are placed along the side and bottom of the view port. It is as if the text were written on an unbounded sheet of paper, but the paper is covered by another piece of paper with a rectangular cutout that lets you see only a portion of the text. The cutout is the view port. This is illustrated in Display 18.6. You use the scroll bars to move the view port so that different portions of the text can be seen through the cutout view port. (You may prefer to think of the view port as fixed and the text as moving. These two ways of thinking are equivalent.) Swing allows you to add scroll bars to your text areas by using the class `JScrollPane`.

JScrollPane   An object of the class `JScrollPane` is essentially a view port with scroll bars. When you create a `JScrollPane`, you give the text area as an argument to the `JScrollPane` constructor. For example, if `memoDisplay` is an object of the class `JTextArea` (as created in the line of code at the start of this subsection), you can place `memoDisplay` in a `JScrollPane` as follows:

```
JScrollPane scrolledText = new JScrollPane(memoDisplay);
```

Display 18.6   View Port for a Text Area

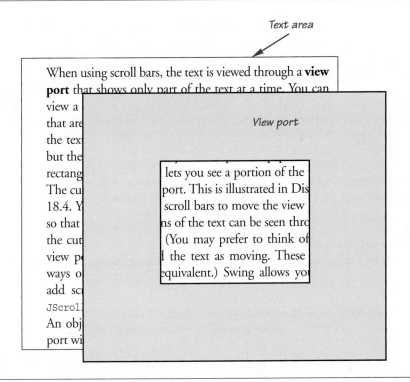

Display 18.7   Some Methods in the Class `JScrollPane` (part 1 of 2)

The `JScrollPane` class is in the `javax.swing` package.

    public JScrollPane(Component objectToBeScrolled)

Creates a new `JScrollPane` for the `objectToBeScrolled`. Note that the `objectToBeScrolled` need not be a `JTextArea`, although that is the only type of argument considered in this book.

    public void setHorizontalScrollBarPolicy(int policy)

Sets the policy for showing the horizontal scroll bar. The `policy` should be one of the following:

    JScrollPane.HORIZONTAL_SCROLLBAR_ALWAYS
    JScrollPane.HORIZONTAL_SCROLLBAR_NEVER
    JScrollPane.HORIZONTAL_SCROLLBAR_AS_NEEDED

The phrase AS_NEEDED means the scroll bar is shown only when it is needed. This is explained more fully in the text. The meanings of the other policy constants are obvious from their names.

(As indicated, these constants are defined in the class `JScrollPane`. You should not need to even be aware of the fact that they have `int` values. Think of them as policies, not as `int` values.)

    public void setVerticalScrollBarPolicy(int policy)

(continued)

Display 18.7   Some Methods in the Class `JScrollPane` (part 2 of 2)

Sets the policy for showing the vertical scroll bar. The `policy` should be one of the following:

```
JScrollPane.VERTICAL_SCROLLBAR_ALWAYS
JScrollPane.VERTICAL_SCROLLBAR_NEVER
JScrollPane.VERTICAL_SCROLLBAR_AS_NEEDED
```

The phrase AS_NEEDED means the scroll bar is shown only when it is needed. This is explained more fully in the text. The meanings of the other policy constants are obvious from their names. (As indicated, these constants are defined in the class `JScrollPane`. You should not need to even be aware of the fact that they have `int` values. Think of them as policies, not as `int` values.)

The `JScrollPane` can then be added to a container, such as a `JPanel` or `JFrame`, as follows:

```
textPanel.add(scrolledText);
```

This is illustrated by the program in Display 18.8.

Note the following two lines in the constructor definition in Display 18.8:

setting scroll
bar policies
```
scrolledText.setHorizontalScrollBarPolicy(
            JScrollPane.HORIZONTAL_SCROLLBAR_ALWAYS);
scrolledText.setVerticalScrollBarPolicy(
            JScrollPane.VERTICAL_SCROLLBAR_ALWAYS);
```

Despite the imposing length of these two method invocations, they perform a very simple task. The first merely specifies that the horizontal scroll bar will always be present. The second specifies that the vertical scroll bar will always be present.

If you omit the invocation of the two methods `setHorizontalScrollBarPolicy` and `setVerticalScrollBarPolicy`, the scroll bars will be visible only when you need them. In other words, if you omit these two method invocations and all the text fits in the view port, then no scroll bars will be visible. When you add enough text to need scroll bars, the needed scroll bars will appear automatically.

Display 18.7 summarizes what we have said about the class `JScrollPane`. We are interested in using `JScrollPane` only with text areas. However, as we note in Display 18.7, `JScrollPane` can be used with almost any sort of component.

Display 18.8   A Text Area with Scroll Bars (part 1 of 3)

```
1   import javax.swing.JFrame;
2   import javax.swing.JTextArea;
3   import javax.swing.JPanel;
4   import javax.swing.JLabel;
5   import javax.swing.JButton;
6   import javax.swing.JScrollPane;
7   import java.awt.BorderLayout;
8   import java.awt.FlowLayout;
9   import java.awt.Color;
10  import java.awt.event.ActionListener;
11  import java.awt.event.ActionEvent;
```

Display 18.8   A Text Area with Scroll Bars (part 2 of 3)

```
12    public class ScrollBarDemo extends JFrame
13                               implements ActionListener
14    {
15        public static final int WIDTH = 600;
16        public static final int HEIGHT = 400;
17        public static final int LINES = 15;
18        public static final int CHAR_PER_LINE = 30;


19        private JTextArea memoDisplay;
20        private String memo1;
21        private String memo2;


22        public static void main(String[] args)
23        {
24            ScrollBarDemo gui = new ScrollBarDemo();
25            gui.setVisible(true);
26        }


27        public ScrollBarDemo()
28        {
29            super("Scroll Bars Demo");
30            setSize(WIDTH, HEIGHT);
31            setDefaultCloseOperation(JFrame.EXIT_ON_CLOSE);
32            JPanel buttonPanel = new JPanel();
33            buttonPanel.setBackground(Color.LIGHT_GRAY);
34            buttonPanel.setLayout(new FlowLayout());
35            JButton memo1Button = new JButton("Save Memo 1");
36            memo1Button.addActionListener(this);
37            buttonPanel.add(memo1Button);

38            JButton memo2Button = new JButton("Save Memo 2");
39            memo2Button.addActionListener(this);
40            buttonPanel.add(memo2Button);

41            JButton clearButton = new JButton("Clear");
42            clearButton.addActionListener(this);
43            buttonPanel.add(clearButton);

44            JButton get1Button = new JButton("Get Memo 1");
45            get1Button.addActionListener(this);
46            buttonPanel.add(get1Button);

47            JButton get2Button = new JButton("Get Memo 2");
48            get2Button.addActionListener(this);
49            buttonPanel.add(get2Button);

50            add(buttonPanel, BorderLayout.SOUTH);

51            JPanel textPanel = new JPanel();
52            textPanel.setBackground(Color.BLUE);
```

(continued)

Display 18.8 A Text Area with Scroll Bars (part 3 of 3)

```
53          memoDisplay = new JTextArea(LINES, CHAR_PER_LINE);
54          memoDisplay.setBackground(Color.WHITE);

55          JScrollPane scrolledText = new JScrollPane(memoDisplay);
56          scrolledText.setHorizontalScrollBarPolicy(
57                      JScrollPane.HORIZONTAL_SCROLLBAR_ALWAYS);
58          scrolledText.setVerticalScrollBarPolicy(
59                      JScrollPane.VERTICAL_SCROLLBAR_ALWAYS);

60          textPanel.add(scrolledText);

61          add(textPanel, BorderLayout.CENTER);
62      }
63      public void actionPerformed(ActionEvent e)
64      {
65          String actionCommand = e.getActionCommand();

66          if (actionCommand.equals("Save Memo 1"))
67              memo1 = memoDisplay.getText();
68          else if (actionCommand.equals("Save Memo 2"))
69              memo2 = memoDisplay.getText();
70          else if (actionCommand.equals("Clear"))
71              memoDisplay.setText("");
72          else if (actionCommand.equals("Get Memo 1"))
73              memoDisplay.setText(memo1);
74          else if (actionCommand.equals("Get Memo 2"))
75              memoDisplay.setText(memo2);
76          else
77              memoDisplay.setText("Error in memo interface");
78      }
79  }
```

RESULTING GUI

Scroll Bars

The class `JScrollPane` is used to add scroll bars to a `JTextArea` (and certain other components). The `JTextArea` object is given as an argument to the constructor that creates the `JScrollPane`. The `JScrollPane` class is in the `javax.swing` package.

SYNTAX

```
JScrollPane Identifier = new JScrollPane(Text_Area_Object);
```

EXAMPLES

```
JTextArea memoDisplay = new JTextArea(LINES, CHAR_PER_LINE);
JScrollPane scrolledText = new JScrollPane(memoDisplay);
textPanel.add(scrolledText);
```

Self-Test Exercises

8. When setting up a `JScrollPane`, do you have to invoke both of the methods `setHorizontalScrollBarPolicy` and `setVerticalScrollBarPolicy`?

9. In Display 18.7, we listed the constructor for `JScrollPane` as follows:

```
public JScrollPane(Component objectToBeScrolled)
```

This indicates that the argument to the constructor must be of type `Component`. But we used the constructor with an argument of type `JTextArea`. Isn't this some sort of type violation?

EXAMPLE: Components with Changing Visibility

The GUI in Display 18.9 has labels that change from visible to invisible and back again. Because the labels contain nothing but an icon each, it appears as if the icons also change roles from visible to invisible and back again. When the GUI is first run, the label with Duke not waving is shown. When the `"Wave"` button is clicked, the label with Duke not waving disappears and the label with Duke waving appears. When the button labeled `"Stop"` is clicked, the label with Duke waving disappears and the label with Duke not waving returns. Note that you can make a component invisible without making the entire GUI invisible.

(continued)

EXAMPLE: (continued)

In this GUI, a label becomes visible or invisible when a button is clicked. For example, the following code from the method `actionPerformed` in Display 18.9 determines what happens when the button with the text `"Wave"` on it is clicked:

```
if (actionCommand.equals("Wave"))
{

    wavingLabel.setVisible(true);
    standingLabel.setVisible(false);

}
```

We used the `setVisible` method on the labels containing the icons rather than directly on the icons because the class `ImageIcon` does not have the `setVisible` method.

The two statements

```
wavingLabel.setVisible(true);
standingLabel.setVisible(false);
```

make `wavingLabel` visible and `standingLabel` invisible.

Display 18.9   Labels with Changing Visibility (part 1 of 3)

```
1    import javax.swing.JFrame;
2    import javax.swing.ImageIcon;
3    import javax.swing.JPanel;
4    import javax.swing.JLabel;
5    import javax.swing.JButton;
6    import java.awt.BorderLayout;
7    import java.awt.FlowLayout;
8    import java.awt.Color;
9    import java.awt.event.ActionListener;
10   import java.awt.event.ActionEvent;

11   public class VisibilityDemo extends JFrame
12                               implements ActionListener
13   {
14       public static final int WIDTH = 300;
15       public static final int HEIGHT = 200;
16       private JLabel wavingLabel;
17       private JLabel standingLabel;
```

Display 18.9   Labels with Changing Visibility (part 2 of 3)

```
18        public static void main(String[] args)
19        {
20            VisibilityDemo demoGui = new VisibilityDemo();
21            demoGui.setVisible(true);
22        }

23        public VisibilityDemo()
24        {
25            setSize(WIDTH, HEIGHT);
26            setDefaultCloseOperation(JFrame.EXIT_ON_CLOSE);
27            setTitle("Visibility Demonstration");

28            setLayout(new BorderLayout());

29            JPanel picturePanel = new JPanel();
30            picturePanel.setBackground(Color.WHITE);
31            picturePanel.setLayout(new FlowLayout());

32            ImageIcon dukeStandingIcon =
33                    new ImageIcon("duke_standing.gif");
34            standingLabel = new JLabel(dukeStandingIcon);
35            standingLabel.setVisible(true);
36            picturePanel.add(standingLabel);

37            ImageIcon dukeWavingIcon = new ImageIcon("duke_waving.gif");
38            wavingLabel = new JLabel(dukeWavingIcon);
39            wavingLabel.setVisible(false);
40            picturePanel.add(wavingLabel);

41            add(picturePanel, BorderLayout.CENTER);

42            JPanel buttonPanel = new JPanel();
43            buttonPanel.setBackground(Color.LIGHT_GRAY);
44            buttonPanel.setLayout(new FlowLayout());

45            JButton waveButton = new JButton("Wave");
46            waveButton.addActionListener(this);
47            buttonPanel.add(waveButton);

48            JButton stopButton = new JButton("Stop");
49            stopButton.addActionListener(this);
50            buttonPanel.add(stopButton);
51            add(buttonPanel, BorderLayout.SOUTH);
52        }
53        public void actionPerformed(ActionEvent e)
```

(continued)

Display 18.9   Labels with Changing Visibility (part 3 of 3)

```
54        {
55            String actionCommand = e.getActionCommand();
56            if (actionCommand.equals("Wave"))
57            {
58                wavingLabel.setVisible(true);
59                standingLabel.setVisible(false);
60            }
61            else if (actionCommand.equals("Stop"))
62            {
63                standingLabel.setVisible(true);
64                wavingLabel.setVisible(false);
65            }
66            else
67                System.out.println("Unanticipated error.");
68        }
69   }
```

Resulting GUI (After clicking Stop button)

Resulting GUI (After clicking Wave button)

18.3 The Graphics Class

Drawing is my life!

THE GRAPHICS CLASS

In this section, we show you how to produce drawing for your GUIs using the Graphics class.

Coordinate System for Graphics Objects

origin

(x, y)

bounding box

When drawing objects on the screen, Java uses the coordinate system shown in Display 18.10. The **origin** point (0, 0) is the upper-left corner of the screen area used for drawing (usually a JFrame or JPanel). The *x*-coordinate, or horizontal coordinate, is positive and increasing to the right. The *y*-coordinate, or vertical coordinate, is positive and increasing in the downward direction. The point (*x*, *y*) is located *x* pixels in from the left edge of the screen and down *y* pixels from the top of the screen. All coordinates are normally positive. Units as well as sizes of figures are in pixels. When placing a rectangle on the screen, Java often uses a coordinate such as (200, 150) to specify where the rectangle is located.

Note that, when specifying the location of a rectangle or other figure, the coordinates do not indicate the center of the rectangle, but instead indicate the location of the upper-left corner of the rectangle. In Display 18.10, the X marks the location of the point (200, 150) and the rectangle shown is at location (200, 150).

When placing a figure other than a rectangle on the screen, Java encloses the figure in an imaginary tightly fitting rectangle, sometimes called a **bounding box**, and positions the upper-left corner of the imaginary rectangle. For example, in Display 18.10, the oval displayed is located at point (200, 150).

Display 18.10   Screen Coordinate System

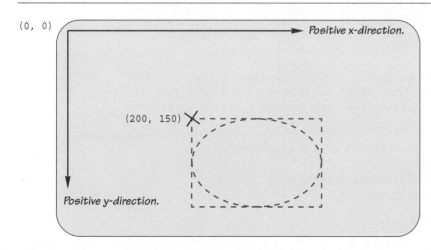

The Method `paint` and the Class `Graphics`

Almost all Swing and Swing-related components and containers have a method named `paint`. The method `paint` draws the component or container on the screen. Up until now, we have had no need to redefine this method or to even mention it. It is defined for you and is called automatically when the figure is displayed on the screen. However, to draw geometric figures, such as circles and boxes, you need to redefine the method `paint`. It is this method that draws the figures.

Display 18.11 shows a GUI program that displays a `JFrame` with a rather primitive face drawn inside of it. The mouth and eyes are just straight line segments. We will soon see how to get round eyes and a smile (and more), but the basic technique can be seen more clearly in this simple figure. The code for drawing the face is given in the method `paint`.

VideoNote

Walkthrough of a Simple Drawing Program

Display 18.11   Drawing a Very Simple Face (part 1 of 2)

```
1   import javax.swing.JFrame;
2   import java.awt.Graphics;
3   import java.awt.Color;
4   public class Face extends JFrame
5   {
6       public static final int WINDOW_WIDTH = 400;
7       public static final int WINDOW_HEIGHT = 400;

8       public static final int FACE_DIAMETER = 200;
9       public static final int X_FACE = 100;
10      public static final int Y_FACE = 100;

11      public static final int EYE_WIDTH = 20;
12      public static final int X_RIGHT_EYE = X_FACE + 55;
13      public static final int Y_RIGHT_EYE = Y_FACE + 60;
14      public static final int X_LEFT_EYE = X_FACE + 130;
15      public static final int Y_LEFT_EYE = Y_FACE + 60;

16      public static final int MOUTH_WIDTH = 100;
17      public static final int X_MOUTH = X_FACE + 50;
18      public static final int Y_MOUTH = Y_FACE + 150;

19      public static void main(String[] args)
20      {
21          Face drawing = new Face();
22          drawing.setVisible(true);
23      }
24      public Face()
25      {
```

Display 18.11   **Drawing a Very Simple Face** (part 2 of 2)

```
26              super("First Graphics Demo");
27              setSize(WINDOW_WIDTH, WINDOW_HEIGHT);
28              setDefaultCloseOperation(JFrame.EXIT_ON_CLOSE);
29              getContentPane().setBackground(Color.white);
30          }
31      public void paint(Graphics g)
32      {
33          super.paint(g);
34          g.drawOval(X_FACE, Y_FACE, FACE_DIAMETER, FACE_DIAMETER);
35          //Draw Eyes:
36          g.drawLine(X_RIGHT_EYE, Y_RIGHT_EYE,
37                              X_RIGHT_EYE + EYE_WIDTH,Y_RIGHT_EYE);
38          g.drawLine(X_LEFT_EYE, Y_LEFT_EYE,
39                              X_LEFT_EYE + EYE_WIDTH, Y_LEFT_EYE);
40          //Draw Mouth:
41          g.drawLine(X_MOUTH, Y_MOUTH, X_MOUTH + MOUTH_WIDTH, Y_MOUTH);
42      }
43  }
```

Resulting GUI

(X_FACE, Y_FACE)

(X_MOUTH,Y_MOUTH)

FACE_DIAMETER

The dashed box is not shown on the screen. It is there to help you understand the relationship between the paint method code and the resulting drawing.

The method paint is called automatically, and you normally should not invoke it in your code. If you do not redefine it, the method paint for a JFrame object simply draws a frame border, title, and other standard features, and then asks the components to all invoke their paint methods. If we do not redefine the method paint, then the

JFrame would have a border and title but would contain nothing. The code in the redefinition of paint explains how to draw the face. Let us look at the details.

Graphics

Notice that the method paint has a parameter g of type Graphics. Graphics is an abstract class in the java.awt package. Every container and component that can be drawn on the screen has an associated Graphics object. (To be precise, every JComponent has an associated Graphics object.) This associated Graphics object has data specifying what area of the screen the component or container covers. In particular, the Graphics object for a JFrame specifies that the drawing takes place inside the borders of the JFrame object. (Because Graphics is an abstract class, every Graphics object is an instance of some concrete descendent class of the Graphics class, but we usually do not care about which descendent class. All we normally need to know is that it is of type Graphics.)

The Graphics class, and so any Graphics object g, has all the methods that we will use to draw figures, such as circles, lines, and boxes, on the screen. Almost the entire definition of the paint method in Display 18.11 consists of invocations of various drawing methods with the parameter g as the calling object.

When the paint method in Display 18.11 is (automatically) invoked, the parameter g will be replaced by the Graphics object associated with the JFrame, so the figures drawn will be inside the JFrame. Let us look at the code in this method paint.

Notice the first line in the definition of paint in Display 18.11:

```
super.paint(g);
```

Recall that super is a name for the parent class of a derived class. The class in Display 18.11 is derived from the class JFrame, so super.paint is the paint method for the class JFrame. Whenever you redefine the method paint, you should start with this invocation of super.paint. This ensures that your definition of paint will do all the things the standard paint method does, such as draw the title and border for the JFrame. (This lesson applies even if the class is derived from some class other than JFrame.)

drawOval

The following invocation from the method paint draws the circle forming the head:

```
g.drawOval(X_FACE, Y_FACE, FACE_DIAMETER, FACE_DIAMETER);
```

The last two arguments give the width and height of the enclosing rectangle, shown in red. The fact that these two arguments are equal is what makes it a circle instead of a typical oval. The first two arguments give x- and y-coordinates for the position of the circle. Note that a figure is positioned by giving the position of the upper-left corner of an enclosing rectangle.

drawLine

The only other drawing statements in the method paint are invocations of g.drawLine. The method g.drawLine draws a straight line between two points with x- and y-coordinates (x_1, y_1) and (x_2, y_2), where the argument positions for the four coordinate numbers are indicated as follows:

```
g.drawLine(x₁, y₁, x₂, y₂)
```

For example, the invocation that draws the mouth is as follows:

```
g.drawLine(X_MOUTH, Y_MOUTH, X_MOUTH + MOUTH_WIDTH, Y_MOUTH);
```

Because both *y*-coordinates (Y_MOUTH) are the same, the line is horizontal. The line for the mouth begins at coordinates (X_MOUTH, Y_MOUTH) and extends to the right for MOUTH_WIDTH pixels.

The Graphics Class

Every container and component that can be drawn on the screen has an associated Graphics object. This associated Graphics object has data specifying what area of the screen the component or container covers. In particular, the Graphics object for a JFrame specifies that the drawing takes place inside the borders of the JFrame object.

When an object g of the class Graphics is used as the calling object for a drawing method, the drawing takes place inside the area of the screen specified by g. For example, if g is the Graphics object for a JFrame, the drawing takes place inside the borders of the JFrame object.

Some of the commonly used methods of the class Graphics are given in Display 18.12.

Graphics is an abstract class in the java.awt package.

Some of the commonly used methods of the class Graphics are given in Display 18.12. Note that most methods come in pairs, one whose name starts with draw and one whose name starts with fill, such as drawOval and fillOval. The one that starts with draw will draw the outline of the specified figure. The one that starts with fill will draw a solid figure obtained by filling the inside of the specified figure. In the next few subsections, we discuss some of these methods.

Display 18.12   Some Methods in the Class Graphics (part 1 of 3)

Graphics is an abstract class in the java.awt package.

Although many of these methods are abstract, we always use them with objects of a concrete descendent class of Graphics, even though we usually do not know the name of that concrete class.

```
public abstract void drawLine(int x1, int y1, int x2, int y2)
```

Draws a line between points (x1, y1) and (x2, y2).

```
public abstract void drawRect(int x, int y,
                                    int width, int height)
```

Draws the outline of the specified rectangle. (x, y) is the location of the upper-left corner of the rectangle.

```
public abstract void fillRect(int x, int y,
                                   int width, int height)
```

Fills the specified rectangle. (x, y) is the location of the upper-left corner of the rectangle.

(continued)

Display 18.12 **Some Methods in the Class `Graphics`** (part 2 of 3)

```
public void draw3DRect(int x, int y, int width,
                                int height, boolean raised)
```

Draws the outline of the specified rectangle. (x, y) is the location of the upper-left corner. The rectangle is highlighted to look like it has thickness. If `raised` is `true`, the highlight makes the rectangle appear to stand out from the background. If `raised` is `false`, the highlight makes the rectangle appear to be sunken into the background.

```
public void fill3DRect(int x, int y, int width,
                                int height, boolean raised)
```

Fills the rectangle specified by

```
draw3DRec(x, y, width, height, raised)
```

```
public abstract void drawRoundRect (int x, int y,
           int width, int height, int arcWidth, int arcHeight)
```

Draws the outline of the specified round-cornered rectangle. (x, y) is the location of the upper-left corner of the enclosing regular rectangle. `arcWidth` and `arcHeight` specify the shape of the round corners. See the text for details.

```
public abstract void fillRoundRect(int x, int y,
           int width, int height, int arcWidth, int arcHeight)
```

Fills the rounded rectangle specified by

```
drawRoundRec(x, y, width, height, arcWidth, arcHeight)
```

```
public abstract void drawOval(int x, int y,
                                int width, int height)
```

Draws the outline of the oval with the smallest enclosing rectangle that has the specified width and height. The (imagined) rectangle has its upper-left corner located at (x, y).

```
public abstract void fillOval (int x, int y,
                                int width, int height)
```

Fills the oval specified by

```
drawOval(x, y, width, height)
```

```
public abstract void drawArc(int x, int y,
                                int width, int height,
                                int startAngle, int arcSweep)
```

Draws part of an oval that just fits into an invisible rectangle described by the first four arguments. The portion of the oval drawn is given by the last two arguments. See the text for details.

```
public abstract void fillArc(int x, int y,
                             int width, int height,
                             int startAngle, int arcSweep)
```

Fills the partial oval specified by

```
drawArc(x, y, width, height, startAngle, arcSweep)
```

Drawing Ovals

An oval is drawn by the method drawOval. The arguments specify the location, width, and height of the smallest rectangle that encloses the oval. For example, the following line draws an oval:

drawOval

```
g.drawOval(100, 50, 300, 200);
```

This draws an oval that just fits into an invisible rectangle whose upper-left corner is at coordinates (100, 50) and that has a width of 300 pixels and a height of 200 pixels. Note that the point that is used to place the oval on the screen is not the center of the oval or anything like the center, but is something like the upper-left corner of the oval.

Note that a circle is a special case of an oval in which the width and height of the rectangle are equal. For example, the following line from the definition of paint in Display 18.11 draws a circle for the outline of the face:

```
g.drawOval(X_FACE, Y_FACE, FACE_DIAMETER, FACE_DIAMETER);
```

Because the enclosing rectangle has the same width and height, this produces a circle.

Some of the methods you can use to draw simple figures are shown in Display 18.12. A similar table is given in Appendix 5.

Drawing Arcs

Arcs, such as the smile on the happy face in Display 18.13, are described by giving an oval and then specifying what portion of the oval will be used for the arc. For example, the following statement from Display 18.13 draws the smile on the happy face:

drawArc

```
g.drawArc(X_MOUTH, Y_MOUTH, MOUTH_WIDTH, MOUTH_HEIGHT,
          MOUTH_START_ANGLE, MOUTH_ARC_SWEEP);
```

which is equivalent to

```
g.drawArc(X_MOUTH, Y_MOUTH, MOUTH_WIDTH, MOUTH_HEIGHT, 180, 180);
```

The arguments MOUTH_WIDTH and MOUTH_HEIGHT determine the size of an invisible rectangle. The arguments X_MOUTH and Y_MOUTH determine the location of the rectangle. The upper-left corner of the rectangle is located at the point (X_MOUTH, Y_MOUTH) . Inside this invisible rectangle, envision an invisible oval that just fits inside the invisible rectangle. The last two arguments specify the portion of this invisible oval that is made visible.

Display 18.14 illustrates how these last two arguments specify an arc of the invisible oval to be made visible. The next-to-last argument specifies a start angle in degrees. The last argument specifies how many degrees of the oval's arc will be made visible. If the last argument is 360 (degrees), then the full oval is made visible.

Display 18.13   Drawing a Happy Face (part 1 of 2)

```
 1  import javax.swing.JFrame;
 2  import java.awt.Graphics;
 3  import java.awt.Color;

 4  public class HappyFace extends JFrame
 5  {
 6      public static final int WINDOW_WIDTH = 400;
 7      public static final int WINDOW_HEIGHT = 400;


 8      public static final int FACE_DIAMETER = 200;
 9      public static final int X_FACE = 100;
10      public static final int Y_FACE = 100;

11      public static final int EYE_WIDTH = 20;
12      public static final int EYE_HEIGHT = 10;
13      public static final int X_RIGHT_EYE = X_FACE + 55;
14      public static final int Y_RIGHT_EYE = Y_FACE + 60;
15      public static final int X_LEFT_EYE = X_FACE + 130;
16      public static final int Y_LEFT_EYE = Y_FACE + 60;

17      public static final int MOUTH_WIDTH = 100;
18      public static final int MOUTH_HEIGHT = 50;
19      public static final int X_MOUTH = X_FACE + 50;
20      public static final int Y_MOUTH = Y_FACE + 100;
21      public static final int MOUTH_START_ANGLE = 180;
22      public static final int MOUTH_ARC_SWEEP = 180;
23      public static void main(String[] args)
24      {
25        HappyFace drawing = new HappyFace();
26        drawing.setVisible(true);
27      }
```

Display 18.13   **Drawing a Happy Face (part 2 of 2)**

```
28        public HappyFace()
29        {
30            super("Graphics Demonstration 2");
31            setSize(WINDOW_WIDTH, WINDOW_HEIGHT);
32            setDefaultCloseOperation(JFrame.EXIT_ON_CLOSE);
33            getContentPane().setBackground(Color.white);
34        }
35    public void paint(Graphics g)
36        {
37            super.paint(g);
38            g.drawOval(X_FACE, Y_FACE, FACE_DIAMETER, FACE_DIAMETER);
39            //Draw Eyes:
40            g.fillOval(X_RIGHT_EYE, Y_RIGHT_EYE, EYE_WIDTH, EYE_HEIGHT);
41            g.fillOval(X_LEFT_EYE, Y_LEFT_EYE, EYE_WIDTH, EYE_HEIGHT);
42            //Draw Mouth:
43            g.drawArc(X_MOUTH, Y_MOUTH, MOUTH_WIDTH, MOUTH_HEIGHT,
44                      MOUTH_START_ANGLE, MOUTH_ARC_SWEEP);
45        }
46    }
```

Resulting GUI

Display 18.14 Specifying an Arc

```
g.drawArc(x, y, width, height, 0, 90);
```

```
g.drawArc(x, y, width, height, 0, -90);
```

```
g.drawArc(x, y, width, height, 0, 360);
```

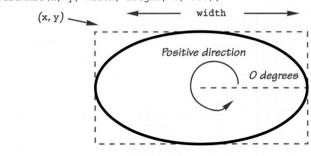

```
g.drawArc(x, y, width, height, 180, 90);
```

The angles are numbered with zero degrees, as shown in Display 18.14. In the first figure, the start angle is zero degrees. The counterclockwise direction is positive. So a start angle of 90 degrees would start at the top of the oval. A start angle of –90 degrees would start at the bottom of the oval. For example, the smile on the happy face in Display 18.13 has a start angle of 180 degrees, so it starts on the left end of the invisible oval. The last argument is also 180, so the arc is made visible through a counterclockwise direction of 180 degrees, or halfway around the oval in the counterclockwise direction.

MyProgrammingLab™

Self-Test Exercises

10. Give an invocation of a method to draw a rectangle from point (20, 30) to point (120, 130). The calling object of type `Graphics` is named g.

11. Give an invocation of a method to draw a horizontal line of length 100 starting at position (30, 40) and extending to the right. The calling object of type `Graphics` is named g.

12. What would be the output of the following code? Assume that the window height and width are both 100 pixels.

    ```
    g.drawOval(25, 25, 50, 50);
    ```

13. Give an invocation of a method to draw a horizontal line along the right border of a window keeping a margin of 30 pixels. Assume the window height is 200 pixels and the calling object of type `Graphics` is named g.

14. Give an invocation of a method to draw a vertical line along the top border of a window keeping a margin of 30 pixels. Assume the window width is 300 pixels and the calling object of type `Graphics` is named g.

15. Give an invocation of a method to draw a circle of diameter 100 with the center at position (300, 400). The calling object of type `Graphics` is named g.

16. Replace the rectangular border of the previous example with a rounded rectangle. The arc height and arc width both are of 15 pixels.

Rounded Rectangles ★

rounded rectangle

A **rounded rectangle** is a rectangle whose corners have been replaced by arcs so that the corners are rounded. For example, suppose g is of type `Graphics` and consider what would be drawn by the following:

```
g.drawRoundRect(x, y, width, height, arcWidth, arcHeight)
```

The arguments x, y, `width`, and `height` determine a regular rectangle in the usual way. The upper-left corner is at the point (x, y). The rectangle has the specified `width` and height. The last two arguments, `arcWidth` and `arcHeight`, specify the arcs that will be used for the corners so as to produce a rounded rectangle. Each corner is replaced with a quarter of an oval that is `arcWidth` pixels wide and `arcHeight` pixels high. This is illustrated in Display 18.15. To obtain corners that are arcs of circles, just make `arcWidth` and `arcHeight` equal.

`paintComponent` for Panels

You can draw figures on a `JPanel` and place the `JPanel` in a `JFrame`. When defining a `JPanel` class that contains a graphics drawing, use the method `paintComponent` instead of the method `paint`, but otherwise the details are similar to what we have seen for `JFrame`s. `JFrame`s use the method `paint`. However, `JPanel`s—and in fact all `JComponent`s—use the method `paintComponent`. A very simple example of using `paintComponent` with a `JPanel` is given in Display 18.16.

If you look back at Display 17.12 in Chapter 17, you will see that a `JPanel` is a `JComponent`, but a `JFrame` is not a `JComponent`. A `JFrame` is only a `Component`. This is why they use different methods to paint the screen.

Action Drawings and `repaint`

The program in Display 18.17 is similar to the program in Display 18.13. It draws a happy face similar to the happy face given in Display 18.13, but with one difference: There is a button at the bottom of the GUI that says `Click for a Wink`. When you click that button, the left eye winks. (Remember the left eye is on your right.) Let us see the details.

Display 18.15   A Rounded Rectangle

`g.drawRoundRect(x, y, width, height, arcWidth, arcHeight);`
produces:

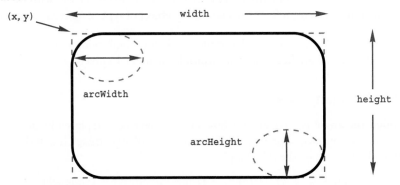

Display 18.16 `paintComponent` Demonstration (part 1 of 2)

```
1    import javax.swing.JFrame;
2    import javax.swing.JPanel;
3    import java.awt.GridLayout;
4    import java.awt.Graphics;
5    import java.awt.Color;

6    public class PaintComponentDemo extends JFrame
7    {
8        public static final int FRAME_WIDTH = 400;
9        public static final int FRAME_HEIGHT = 400;

10       private class FancyPanel extends JPanel
11       {
12           public void paintComponent(Graphics g)
13           {
14               super.paintComponent(g);
15               setBackground(Color.YELLOW);
16               g.drawOval(FRAME_WIDTH/4, FRAME_HEIGHT/8,
17                       FRAME_WIDTH/2, FRAME_HEIGHT/6);
18           }
19       }

20       public static void main(String[] args)
21       {
22           PaintComponentDemo w = new PaintComponentDemo();
23           w.setVisible(true);
24       }
25       public PaintComponentDemo()
26       {
27           setSize(FRAME_WIDTH, FRAME_HEIGHT);
28           setDefaultCloseOperation(JFrame.EXIT_ON_CLOSE);
29           setTitle("The Oval Is in a Panel");
30           setLayout(new GridLayout(2, 1));
31           FancyPanel p = new FancyPanel();
32           add(p);
33           JPanel whitePanel = new JPanel();
34           whitePanel.setBackground(Color.WHITE);
35           add(whitePanel);
36       }
37   }
```

(continued)

Display 18.16 `paintComponent` Demonstration (part 2 of 2)

RESULTING GUI

The program in Display 18.17 has a private instance variable `wink` of type `boolean`. When the value of `wink` is `false`, the `paint` method draws an ordinary happy face. When the value of `wink` is `true`, the `paint` method draws the face the same except that the left eye is just a straight line, which looks like the eye is closed. The variable `wink` is initialized to `false`.

When the button labeled `Click for a Wink` is clicked, this sends an action event to the method `actionPerformed`. The method `actionPerformed` then changes the value of the variable `wink` to `true` and invokes the method `repaint`. This use of the method `repaint` is new, so let us discuss it a bit.

Every `JFrame` (in fact, every `Component` and every `Container`) has a method named `repaint`. The method `repaint` will repaint the screen so that any changes to the graphics being displayed will show on the screen. If you omit the invocation of `repaint` from the method `actionPerformed`, then the variable `wink` will change to `true`, but the screen will not change. Without an invocation of `repaint`, the face will not change, because the method `paint` must be called again with the new value of `wink` before the change takes effect. The method `repaint` does a few standard things and, most importantly, will also invoke the method `paint`, which redraws the screen. Be sure to note that you should invoke `repaint` and not `paint`.

Now we explain why, when `wink` has the value `true`, the method `paint` draws the face with the left eye changed. The relevant part of the code is the following, which draws the left eye:

```
if (wink)

    g.drawLine(X_LEFT_EYE, Y_LEFT_EYE,
                        X_LEFT_EYE + EYE_WIDTH, Y_LEFT_EYE);
else
    g.fillOval(X_LEFT_EYE, Y_LEFT_EYE, EYE_WIDTH, EYE_HEIGHT);
```

repaint

Display 18.17   **An Action Drawing** (part 1 of 3)

```
1    import javax.swing.JFrame;
2    import javax.swing.JButton;
3    import java.awt.event.ActionListener;
4    import java.awt.event.ActionEvent;
5    import java.awt.BorderLayout;
6    import java.awt.Graphics;
7    import java.awt.Color;

8    public class ActionFace extends JFrame
9    {
10       public static final int WINDOW_WIDTH = 400;
11       public static final int WINDOW_HEIGHT = 400;

12       public static final int FACE_DIAMETER = 200;
13       public static final int X_FACE = 100;
14       public static final int Y_FACE = 100;

15       public static final int EYE_WIDTH = 20;
16       public static final int EYE_HEIGHT = 10;
17       public static final int X_RIGHT_EYE = X_FACE + 55;
18       public static final int Y_RIGHT_EYE = Y_FACE + 60;
19       public static final int X_LEFT_EYE = X_FACE + 130;
20       public static final int Y_LEFT_EYE = Y_FACE + 60;

21       public static final int MOUTH_WIDTH = 100;
22       public static final int MOUTH_HEIGHT = 50;
23       public static final int X_MOUTH = X_FACE + 50;
24       public static final int Y_MOUTH = Y_FACE + 100;
25       public static final int MOUTH_START_ANGLE = 180;
26       public static final int MOUTH_ARC_SWEEP = 180;

27       private boolean wink;

28       private class WinkAction implements ActionListener
29       {
30           public void actionPerformed(ActionEvent e)
31           {
32               wink = true;
33               repaint();
34           }
35       } // End of WinkAction inner class
```

(continued)

Display 18.17 **An Action Drawing** (part 2 of 3)

```
36      public static void main(String[] args)
37      {
38          ActionFace drawing = new ActionFace();
39          drawing.setVisible(true);
40      }

41      public ActionFace()
42      {
43          setSize(WINDOW_WIDTH, WINDOW_HEIGHT);
44          setDefaultCloseOperation(JFrame.EXIT_ON_CLOSE);
45          setTitle("Hello There!");
46          setLayout(new BorderLayout());
47          getContentPane().setBackground(Color.white);

48          JButton winkButton = new JButton("Click for a Wink.");
49          winkButton.addActionListener(new WinkAction());
50          add(winkButton, BorderLayout.SOUTH);
51          wink = false;
52      }

53      public void paint(Graphics g)
54      {
55          super.paint(g);
56          g.drawOval(X_FACE, Y_FACE, FACE_DIAMETER, FACE_DIAMETER);
57          //Draw Right Eye:
58          g.fillOval(X_RIGHT_EYE, Y_RIGHT_EYE, EYE_WIDTH, EYE_HEIGHT);
59          //Draw Left Eye:
60          if (wink)
61              g.drawLine(X_LEFT_EYE, Y_LEFT_EYE,
62                          X_LEFT_EYE + EYE_WIDTH, Y_LEFT_EYE);
63          else
64              g.fillOval(X_LEFT_EYE, Y_LEFT_EYE, EYE_WIDTH, EYE_HEIGHT);
65          //Draw Mouth:
66          g.drawArc(X_MOUTH, Y_MOUTH, MOUTH_WIDTH, MOUTH_HEIGHT,
67                      MOUTH_START_ANGLE, MOUTH_ARC_SWEEP);
68      }

69  }
```

Display 18.17   **An Action Drawing** (part 3 of 3)

Resulting GUI (When started)

Resulting GUI (After clicking the button)

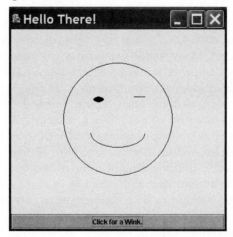

If wink has the value true, then the eye is drawn as a line, which looks like a closed eye. If wink has the value false, then the eye is drawn as an oval, which looks like an open eye.

The `repaint` and `paint` Methods

When you change the graphic's contents in a window and want to update the window so that the new contents show on the screen, do not call `paint`; call `repaint`. The `repaint` method takes care of some overhead and then calls the `paint` method. Normally, you do not define `repaint`. As long as you define the `paint` method correctly, the `repaint` method should work correctly. Note that you often define `paint`, but you normally do not call it. On the other hand, normally you do not define `repaint`, but you do sometimes call it.

Some More Details on Updating a GUI ★

Most of the changes to a GUI windowing system that we have seen are updated automatically so that they are visible on the screen. This is done by an object known as the **repaint manager**. The repaint manager works automatically, and you need not even be aware of its presence. However, there are a few updates that the repaint manager will not do for you. You have already learned that you need an invocation of `repaint` when your GUI changes the figure drawn in the `JFrame` as in Display 18.17.

Two other updating methods that you will often see when looking at Swing code are `validate` and `pack`.

Every container class has the method `validate`, which has no arguments. An invocation of `validate` causes the container to lay out its components again. An invocation of `validate` is a kind of "update" action that makes changes in the components actually happen on the screen. Many simple changes that are made to a Swing GUI, such as changing color or changing the text in a text field, happen automatically. Other changes, such as some kinds of addition of components or changes in visibility, may require an invocation of `validate` or some other "update" method. Sometimes it is difficult to decide whether an invocation of `validate` is necessary. When in doubt, include an invocation of `validate`. Although invoking `validate` when it is not needed can make your program a little less efficient, it will have no other ill effects on your GUI.

The method `pack` causes the window to be resized, usually to a smaller size, but more precisely to an approximation of a size known as the *preferred size*. (Yes, you can change the preferred size, but we do not have room to cover all of the Swing library in these few chapters.)

We do not have enough space in this book to go into all the details of how a GUI is updated on the screen, but these few remarks may make some code you find in more advanced books a little less puzzling.

(margin notes: repaint manager, validate, pack)

18.4 Colors

One colored picture is worth a thousand black and white pictures.

VARIATION ON A CHINESE PROVERB

In this section, we tell you how to specify colors for the figures you draw with the graphics methods. We also show you how to define your own colors using the class `Color`.

Specifying a Drawing Color

setColor

When drawing figures with methods such as drawLine inside of the definition of the paint method, you can think of your drawing as being done with a pen that can change colors. The method setColor will change the color of the pen.

extra
code on
website

For example, consider the happy face that is drawn by the GUI in Display 18.13. If you change the definition of the paint method to the version shown in Display 18.18, the eyes will be blue and the mouth will be red. (The file HappyFaceColor.java on the accompanying website contains a version of the changed program. It consists of the program in Display 18.13 with the definition of the paint method replaced by the one in Display 18.18 and with the class name changed from HappyFace to HappyFaceColor.)

The setColor Method

When you are doing drawings with an object of the class Graphics, you can set the color of the drawing with an invocation of setColor. The color specified can later be changed with another invocation of setColor, so a single drawing can have multiple colors.

SYNTAX

Graphics_Object.setColor(*Color_Object*);

EXAMPLE

g.setColor(Color.BLUE);

Display 18.18   Adding Color

```
1    public void paint(Graphics g)
2    {
3        super.paint(g);
4        //Default is equivalent to: g.setColor(Color.black);
5        g.drawOval(X_FACE, Y_FACE, FACE_DIAMETER, FACE_DIAMETER);
6        //Draw Eyes:
7        g.setColor(Color.BLUE);
8        g.fillOval(X_RIGHT_EYE, Y_RIGHT_EYE, EYE_WIDTH, EYE_HEIGHT);
9        g.fillOval(X_LEFT_EYE, Y_LEFT_EYE, EYE_WIDTH, EYE_HEIGHT);
10       //Draw Mouth:
11       g.setColor(Color.RED);
12       g.drawArc(X_MOUTH, Y_MOUTH, MOUTH_WIDTH, MOUTH_HEIGHT,
13                 MOUTH_START_ANGLE, MOUTH_ARC_SWEEP);
14   }
```

If you replace the method paint *in Display 18.13 with this version of* paint, *then the happy face will have blue eyes and red lips.*

Defining Colors

Display 17.5 in Chapter 17 lists the standard colors in the class `Color`, which are defined for you. If that table does not have the colors you want, you can use the class `Color` to define your own colors. To understand how this is done, you need to first know a few basic facts about colors. By mixing red, green, and blue light in varying amounts, the human eye can be given the sensation of viewing any color the eye is capable of seeing. This is what an ordinary television set does to produce all the colors it displays. The television mixes red, green, and blue light and shines these lights on the screen in differing amounts. This is often called the **RGB color system**, for obvious reasons. Because a computer monitor is basically the same thing as a television set, colors for computer monitors can be produced in the same way. The Java `Color` class mixes amounts of red, green, and blue to produce any new color you might want.

RGB color system

When specifying the amount of each of the colors red, green, and blue, you can use either integers in the range 0 to 255 (inclusive) or `float` values in the range 0.0 to 1.0 (inclusive). For example, brown is formed by mixing red and green. So, the following defines a color called `brown` that will look like a shade of brown:

Color constructors

```
Color brown = new Color(200, 150, 0);
```

This color `brown` will have a 200.0/255 fraction of the maximum amount of red possible, a 150.0/255 fraction of the maximum amount of green possible, and no blue. If you want to use fractions to express the color, you can. The following is an equivalent way of defining the same color `brown`:

```
Color brown =
new Color((float)(200.0/255), (float)(150.0/255), (float)0.0);
```

You need the type casts `(float)` because the constructors for the class `Color` accept only arguments of type `int` or `float`, and numbers such as 200.0/255 and 0.0 are considered to be of type `double`, not of type `float`.

Some constructors for the class `Color` and some of the commonly used methods for the class `Color` are summarized in Display 18.19.

RGB Colors

The class `Color` uses the RGB method of creating colors. That means that every color is a combination of the three colors red, green, and blue.

Display 18.19 Some Methods in the Class `Color` (part 1 of 2)

The class `Color` is in the `java.awt` package.

```
public Color(int r, int g, int b)
```

Constructor that creates a new `Color` with the specified RGB values. The parameters `r`, `g`, and `b` must each be in the range 0 to 255 (inclusive).

Display 18.19   Some Methods in the Class `Color` (part 2 of 2)

```
public Color(float r, float g, float b)
```

Constructor that creates a new `Color` with the specified RGB values. The parameters `r`, `g`, and `b` must each be in the range `0.0` to `1.0` (inclusive).

```
public int getRed()
```

Returns the red component of the calling object. The returned value is in the range `0` to `255` (inclusive).

```
public int getGreen()
```

Returns the green component of the calling object. The returned value is in the range `0` to `255` (inclusive).

```
public int getBlue()
```

Returns the blue component of the calling object. The returned value is in the range `0` to `255` (inclusive).

```
public Color brighter()
```

Returns a brighter version of the calling object color.

```
public Color darker()
```

Returns a darker version of the calling object color.

```
public boolean equals(Object c)
```

Returns `true` if c is equal to the calling object color; otherwise, returns `false`.

PITFALL: Using `doubles` to Define a Color

Suppose you want to make a color that is made of half the possible amount of red, half the possible amount of blue, and no green. The following seems reasonable:

```
Color purple = new Color(0.5, 0.0, 0.5);
```

However, this will produce a compiler error. The numbers `0.5` and `0.0` are considered to be of type `double`, and this constructor requires arguments of type `float` (or of type `int`). So, an explicit type cast is required, as follows:

```
Color purple = new Color((float)0.5, (float)0.0, (float)0.5);
```

Java does allow the following method of specifying that a number is of type `float`, which can be simpler than the previous line of code:

```
Color purple = new Color(0.5f, 0.0f, 0.5f);
```

(continued)

An even easier way to avoid these problems is to simply use `int` arguments, as in the following:

```
purple = new Color(127, 0, 127);
```

(You may feel that the values of `127` should be replaced by `128`, but that is a minor point. You are not likely to even notice the difference in color between, say, `127` red and `128` red.)

In any final code produced, these `float` numbers should normally be replaced by defined constants, such as

```
public static final float RED_VALUE = (float)0.5;
public static final float GREEN_VALUE = (float)0.0;
public static final float BLUE_VALUE = (float)0.5;
```

Note that even though the defined constants are specified to be of type `float`, you still need a type cast. ■

The `JColorChooser` Dialog Window

The class `JColorChooser` can be used to produce a dialog window that allows you to choose a color by looking at color samples or by choosing RGB values. The static method `showDialog` in the class `JColorChooser` produces a window that allows the user to choose a color. A sample program using this method is given in Display 18.20. The statement that launches the `JColorChooser` dialog window is the following:

```
sampleColor =
    JColorChooser.showDialog(this, "JColorChooser", sampleColor);
```

When this statement is executed, the window shown in the second GUI picture in Display 18.20 is displayed for the user to choose a color. Once the user has chosen a color and clicked the `OK` button, the window goes away and the chosen color is returned as the value of the `JColorChooser.showDialog` method invocation. So, in this example, the `Color` object returned is assigned to the variable `sampleColor`. If the user clicks the `Cancel` button, then the method invocation returns `null` rather than a color.

The method `JColorChooser.showDialog` takes three arguments. The first argument is the parent component, which is the component from which it was launched. In most simple cases, it is likely to be `this`, as it is in our example. The second argument is a title for the color chooser window. The third argument is the initial color for the color chooser window. The window shows the user samples of what the color he or she chooses will look like. The user can choose colors repeatedly, and each will be displayed in turn until the user clicks the `OK` button. The color displayed when the color chooser window first appears is that third argument.

The color chooser window has three tabs at the top labeled `Swatches`, `HSB`, and `RGB`. This gives the user three different ways to choose colors. If the `Swatches` tab is clicked, the window displays color samples for the user to choose from. This is the

Display 18.20   `JColorChooser` Dialog (part 1 of 2)

```
1    import javax.swing.JFrame;
2    import javax.swing.JPanel;
3    import javax.swing.JButton;
4    import javax.swing.JColorChooser;
5    import java.awt.event.ActionListener;
6    import java.awt.event.ActionEvent;
7    import java.awt.BorderLayout;
8    import java.awt.FlowLayout;
9    import java.awt.Color;

10   public class JColorChooserDemo extends JFrame
11                                  implements ActionListener
12   {
13       public static final int WIDTH = 400;
14       public static final int HEIGHT = 200;

15       private Color sampleColor = Color.LIGHT_GRAY;


16       public static void main(String[] args)
17       {
18           JColorChooserDemo gui = new JColorChooserDemo();
19           gui.setVisible(true);
20       }

21       public JColorChooserDemo()
22       {
23           setDefaultCloseOperation(JFrame.EXIT_ON_CLOSE);
24           getContentPane().setBackground(sampleColor);
25           setLayout(new BorderLayout());
26           setTitle("JColorChooser Demo");
27           setSize(WIDTH, HEIGHT);
28           JPanel buttonPanel = new JPanel();
29           buttonPanel.setBackground(Color.WHITE);
30           buttonPanel.setLayout(new FlowLayout());
31           JButton chooseButton = new JButton("Choose a Color");
32           chooseButton.addActionListener(this);
33           buttonPanel.add(chooseButton);
34           add(buttonPanel, BorderLayout.SOUTH);
35       }
```

(continued)

Display 18.20 **JColorChooser** Dialog (part 2 of 2)

```
36        public void actionPerformed(ActionEvent e)
37        {
38            if (e.getActionCommand().equals("Choose a Color"))
39            {
40                sampleColor =
41                    JColorChooser.showDialog(this,
                         "JColorChooser", sampleColor);
42                if (sampleColor != null)//If a color was chosen
43                    getContentPane().setBackground(sampleColor);
44            }
45            else
46                System.out.println("Unanticipated Error");
47        }
48 }
```

Resulting GUI (Three views of one GUI)

way the window first comes up. So, if the user clicks no tab, it is the same as clicking the Swatches tab. The RGB tab allows the user to choose a color by specifying the red, green, and blue values. The HSB tab gives the user a chance to choose colors in a way we will not discuss. To really understand the JColorChooser dialog window, you need to run the program in Display 18.20 to see it in action.

Self-Test Exercises

17. How would you change the method paint in Display 18.18 so that the happy face has one blue eye (the right eye) and one green eye (the left eye)?

18. How would you change the method paint in Display 18.18 so that the happy face not only has blue eyes and a red mouth, but also has brown skin?

18.5 Fonts and the drawString Method

It is not of so much consequence what you say,
as how you say it.

ALEXANDER SMITH, *Dreamthorp. On the Writing of Essays*

Java has facilities to add text to drawings and to modify the font of the text. We will show you enough to allow you to do most things you might want to do with text and fonts.

The drawString Method

Display 18.21 contains a demonstration program for the method drawString. When the program is run, the GUI displays the text "Push the button." When the user clicks the button, the string is changed to "Thank you. I needed that." The text is written with the method drawString.

The method drawString is similar to the drawing methods in the class Graphics, but it displays text rather than a drawing. For example, the following line from Display 18.21 writes the string stored in the variable theText starting at the *x*- and *y*-coordinates X_START and Y_START:

```
g.drawString(theText, X_START, Y_START);
```

The string is written in the current font. A default font is used if no font is specified. The details about fonts are discussed in the next subsection.

Display 18.21 Using `drawString` (part 1 of 2)

```
1   import javax.swing.JFrame;
2   import javax.swing.JPanel;
3   import javax.swing.JButton;
4   import java.awt.event.ActionListener;
5   import java.awt.event.ActionEvent;
6   import java.awt.BorderLayout;
7   import java.awt.Graphics;
8   import java.awt.Color;
9   import java.awt.Font;

10  public class DrawStringDemo extends JFrame
11                               implements ActionListener
12  {
13      public static final int WIDTH = 350;
14      public static final int HEIGHT = 200;
15      public static final int X_START = 20;
16      public static final int Y_START = 100;
17      public static final int POINT_SIZE = 24;

18      private String theText = "Push the button.";
19      private Color penColor = Color.BLACK;
20      private Font fontObject =
21                      new Font("SansSerif", Font.PLAIN, POINT_SIZE);

22      public static void main(String[] args)
23      {
24          DrawStringDemo gui = new DrawStringDemo();
25          gui.setVisible(true);
26      }


27      public DrawStringDemo()
28      {
29          setSize(WIDTH, HEIGHT);
30          setDefaultCloseOperation(JFrame.EXIT_ON_CLOSE);
31          setTitle("drawString Demonstration");

32          getContentPane().setBackground(Color.WHITE);
33          setLayout(new BorderLayout());

34          JPanel buttonPanel = new JPanel();
35          buttonPanel.setBackground(Color.GRAY);
36          buttonPanel.setLayout(new BorderLayout());
37          JButton theButton = new JButton("The Button");
38          theButton.addActionListener(this);


39          buttonPanel.add(theButton, BorderLayout.CENTER);


40          add(buttonPanel, BorderLayout.SOUTH);
41      }
```

Display 18.21   **Using drawString** (part 2 of 2)

```
42        public void paint(Graphics g)
43        {
44            super.paint(g);
45            g.setFont(fontObject);
46            g.setColor(penColor);
47            g.drawString(theText, X_START, Y_START);
48        }

49        public void actionPerformed(ActionEvent e)
50        {
51            penColor = Color.RED;
52            fontObject =
53                    new Font("Serif", Font.BOLD|Font.ITALIC, POINT_SIZE);
54            theText = "Thank you.  I needed that.";

55            repaint();
56        }
57  }
```

RESULTING GUI (Start view)

RESULTING GUI (After clicking the button)

Fonts

The program in Display 18.21 illustrates how the font for the method `drawString` is set. That program sets the font with the following line in the definition of the method `paint`:

setFont

```
g.setFont(fontObject);
```

In this program, `fontObject` is a private instance variable of type `Font`. `Font` is a class in the `java.awt` package. Objects of the class `Font` represent fonts.

In Display 18.21, the variable `fontObject` is set using a constructor for the class `Font`. The initial font is set as part of the instance variable declaration in the following lines taken from Display 18.21:

```
private Font fontObject =
              new Font("SansSerif", Font.PLAIN, POINT_SIZE);
```

Font

The constructor for the class `Font` creates a font in a given style and size. The first argument, in this case `"SansSerif"`, is a string that gives the name of the font (that is, the basic style). Some typical font names are `"Times"`, `"Courier"`, and `"Helvetica"`. You may use any font currently available on your system. Java guarantees that you will have at least the three fonts `"Monospaced"`, `"SansSerif"`, and `"Serif"`. To see what these fonts look like on your system, run the program `FontDisplay.java` on the accompanying website. It will produce the window shown in Display 18.22.

extra code
on website

Most font names have no real meaning. The names just sounded right to the creator. However, the terms "Serif," "Sans Serif," and "Monospaced" do mean something,

---

Display 18.22   Result of Running `FontDisplay.java`

Fonts may look somewhat different on your system.

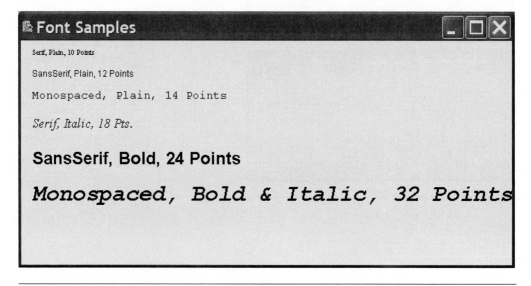

which may help you keep the names of the three guaranteed fonts clear in your mind. **Serifs** are those small lines that sometimes finish off the ends of the lines in letters. For example, **S** has serifs (at the two ends of the curved line), but s does not have serifs. The `"Serif"` font will always have these decorative little lines. *Sans* means without, so the `"SansSerif"` font will not have these decorative little lines. As you might guess, `"Monospaced"` means that all the characters have equal width.

Fonts can be given style modifiers, such as bold or italic, and they can come in different sizes. The second and third arguments to the constructor for `Font` specify the style modifications and size for the font, as in the following, which occurs in the `actionPerformed` method in Display 18.21:

```
new Font("Serif", Font.BOLD|Font.ITALIC, POINT_SIZE);
```

The second argument specifies style modifications. Note that you can specify multiple style modifications by connecting them with the symbol | as in `Font.BOLD|Font.ITALIC`.[2] The last argument specifies the size of the letters in the version of the font created.

point size Character sizes are specified in units known as *points*, so the size of a particular version of a font is called a **point size**. One **point** is 1/72 of an inch, but measurements of font sizes are not as precise as might be ideal; two different fonts of the same point size may be slightly different in size.

The method `setFont` sets the font for the `Graphics` object, which is named g in Display 18.21. The font remains in effect until it is changed. If you do not specify any font, then a default font is used.

There is no simple way to change the properties of the current font, such as making it italic. Every change in a font normally requires that you define a new `Font` object and use it as an argument to `setFont`.

Display 18.23 gives some useful details about constructors, methods, and constants that are members of, or are related to, the class `Font`.

The `drawString` Method

The `drawString` method writes the text given by the *String* at the point (*X, Y*) of the *Graphics_Object*. The text is written in the current font, color, and font size.

SYNTAX

Graphics_Object.`drawString(`*String, X, Y*`)`;

EXAMPLE

```
g.drawString("I love you madly.", X_START, Y_START);
```

---

[2]The symbol | produces a "bitwise or of the numbers," but that detail need not concern you. You need not even know what is meant by a "bitwise or of the numbers." Just think of | as a special way to connect style specifications.

Display 18.23   Some Methods and Constants for the Class `Font`

The class `Font` is in the `java.awt` package.

CONSTRUCTOR FOR THE CLASS `Font`

```
public Font(String fontName, int styleModifications, int size)
```

Constructor that creates a version of the font named by `fontName` with the specified `styleModifications` and `size`.

CONSTANTS IN THE CLASS `Font`

```
Font.BOLD
```

Specifies bold style.

```
Font.ITALIC
```

Specifies italic style.

```
Font.PLAIN
```

Specifies plain style—that is, not bold and not italic.

NAMES OF FONTS (These three are guaranteed by Java. Your system will probably have others as well as these.)

```
"Monospaced"
```

See Display 18.22 for a sample.

```
"SansSerif"
```

See Display 18.22 for a sample.

```
"Serif"
```

See Display 18.22 for a sample.

METHOD THAT USES `Font`

```
public abstract void setFont(Font fontObject)
```

This method is in the class `Graphics`. Sets the current font of the calling `Graphics` object to `fontObject`.

Self-Test Exercises

19. Suppose g is an object of type `Graphics`. Write a line of code that will set the font for g to Sans Serif bold of size 14 points.

20. Suppose g is an object of type `Graphics`. Write a line of code that will set the font for g to Sans Serif bold and italic of size 14 points.

Chapter Summary

- You can define a *window listener* class by having it implement the `WindowListener` interface.

- An *icon* is an object of the class `ImageIcon` and is created from a digital picture. You can add icons to `JButtons`, `JLabels`, and `JMenuItems`.

- You can use the class `JScrollPane` to add scroll bars to a text area.

- You can draw figures such as lines, ovals, and rectangles using methods in the class `Graphics`.

- You can use the method `setColor` to specify the color of each figure or text drawn with the method of the class `Graphics`.

- You can define your own colors using the class `Color`.

- Colors are defined using the *RGB* (red/green/blue) system.

- You can use the method `drawString` of the class `Graphics` to add text to a `JFrame` or `JPanel`.

- You can use the method `setFont` to set the font, style modifiers, and point size for text written with the `drawString` method of the `Graphics` class.

Answers to Self-Test Exercises

1. You can make the main window disappears but not disposed by adding `setVisible(false)` in the `windowClosing()` method of the `WindowListener` interface.

2. The smaller window goes away but the larger window stays. This is the default action for the close-window button and we did not change it for the smaller window.

3. `dispose`

4. The import statements are the same as in Display 18.2. The rest of the definition follows. This definition is in the file `WindowListenerDemo3` on the accompanying website.

extra code on website

```
public class WindowListenerDemo3 extends JFrame
                              implements WindowListener
{
    public static final int WIDTH = 300; //for main window
    public static final int HEIGHT = 200; //for main window
    public static final int SMALL_WIDTH = 200;
                            //for confirm window
    public static final int SMALL_HEIGHT = 100;
                            //for confirm window

    private class ConfirmWindow extends JFrame
                            implements ActionListener
```

```java
{
    public ConfirmWindow()
    {
        setSize(SMALL_WIDTH, SMALL_HEIGHT);
        getContentPane().setBackground(Color.YELLOW);
        setLayout(new BorderLayout());

        JLabel confirmLabel = new JLabel(
                    "Are you sure you want to exit?");
        add(confirmLabel, BorderLayout.CENTER);

        JPanel buttonPanel = new JPanel();
        buttonPanel.setBackground(Color.ORANGE);
        buttonPanel.setLayout(new FlowLayout());

        JButton exitButton = new JButton("Yes");
        exitButton.addActionListener(this);
        buttonPanel.add(exitButton);

        JButton cancelButton = new JButton("No");
        cancelButton.addActionListener(this);
        buttonPanel.add(cancelButton);

        add(buttonPanel, BorderLayout.SOUTH);
    }

    public void actionPerformed(ActionEvent e)
    {
        String actionCommand = e.getActionCommand();

        if (actionCommand.equals("Yes"))
            System.exit(0);
        else if (actionCommand.equals("No"))
            dispose();//Destroys only the ConfirmWindow.
        else
            System.out.println(
                    "Unexpected Error in Confirm Window.");
    }
} //End of inner class ConfirmWindow

public static void main(String[] args)
{
    WindowListenerDemo3 demoWindow =
                        new WindowListenerDemo3();
    demoWindow.setVisible(true);
}
```

```java
        public WindowListenerDemo3()
        {
            setSize(WIDTH, HEIGHT);
            setTitle("Window Listener Demonstration");

            setDefaultCloseOperation(
                        JFrame.DO_NOTHING_ON_CLOSE);
            addWindowListener(this);

            getContentPane().setBackground(Color.LIGHT_GRAY);
            JLabel aLabel =
                    new JLabel("I like to be sure you are sincere.");
            add(aLabel);
        }


        //The following are now methods of the class
        //WindowListenerDemo3:
        public void windowOpened(WindowEvent e)
        {}

        public void windowClosing(WindowEvent e)
        {
            ConfirmWindow checkers = new ConfirmWindow();
        checkers.setVisible(true);
        }

        public void windowClosed(WindowEvent e)
        {}

        public void windowIconified(WindowEvent e)
        {}

        public void windowDeiconified(WindowEvent e)
        {}

        public void windowActivated(WindowEvent e)
        {}

        public void windowDeactivated(WindowEvent e)
        {}
    }
```

5.
```java
JButton magicButton = new JButton("Magic Button");
ImageIcon wizardIcon = new ImageIcon("wizard.gif");
magicButton.setIcon(wizardIcon);
```

There are a number of other ways to accomplish the same thing. Here are two of a number of valid alternatives:

```
JButton magicButton = new JButton("Magic Button");
magicButton.setIcon(new ImageIcon("wizard.gif"));

ImageIcon wizardIcon = new ImageIcon("wizard.gif");
JButton magicButton =
                new JButton("Magic Button", wizardIcon);
```

6. ```
ImageIcon wizardIcon = new ImageIcon("wizard.gif");
JLabel wizardPicture = new JLabel(wizardIcon);
picturePanel.add(wizardPicture);
```

There are a number of other ways to accomplish the same thing. Here is one valid alternative:

```
picturePanel.add(new JLabel(
                new ImageIcon("wizard.gif")));
```

7. ```
picturePanel.setLayout(new GridLayout(2,2);
    for(int x =1, x <=4; x++)
    {
        ImageIcon img = new ImageIcon("img" + x + ".gif");
        picturePanel.add(img);
    }
```

8. No. You can invoke none, one, or both methods.

9. No. The class JTextArea is a descendent class of the class Component. So, every JTextArea is also a Component.

10. `g.drawRect(20, 30, 120, 130);`

11. `g.drawLine(30, 40, 130, 40);`

12. It would draw a circle of diameter 50 with the center at the intersection of the diagonals of the window.

13. `g.drawLine(30, 0, 30, 200);`

14. `g.drawLine(0, 30, 300, 30);`

15. `g.drawOval(250, 350, 100, 100);`

16. `g. drawRoundRec(30, 20, 240, 160, 15, 15);`

17. Insert `g.setColor(Color.GREEN)` as indicated next:
```
//Draw Eyes:
g.setColor(Color.BLUE);
g.fillOval(X_RIGHT_EYE, Y_RIGHT_EYE, EYE_WIDTH, EYE_HEIGHT);
g.setColor(Color.GREEN);
g.fillOval(X_LEFT_EYE, Y_LEFT_EYE, EYE_WIDTH, EYE_HEIGHT);
```

18. Replace the following line in the `paint` method

```
g.drawOval(X_FACE, Y_FACE, FACE_DIAMETER, FACE_DIAMETER);
```

with

```
Color brown =
        new Color(200, 150, 0);
g.setColor(brown);
g.fillOval(X_FACE, Y_FACE, FACE_DIAMETER, FACE_DIAMETER);
```

Note that there is no predefined color constant `Color.BROWN`, so you need to define a color for brown. You may prefer some other arguments instead of `(200, 150, 0)` so that you get a shade of brown that is more to your liking.

19. `g.setFont(new Font("SansSerif", Font.BOLD, 14));`

20. `g.setFont(new Font("SansSerif", Font.BOLD|Font.ITALIC, 14));`

MyProgrammingLab™ ## Programming Projects

Visit www.myprogramminglab.com to complete select exercises online and get instant feedback.

1. A Sierpinski Gasket or Triangle is a type of fractal named after the Polish mathematician Waclaw Sierpinski who described some of its interesting properties in 1916. It is a nice example of how an orderly structure can be created as a result of random, chaotic behavior.

   One way to create the fractal is to start with an equilateral triangle. Let us say that the corners are labeled `X`, `Y`, and `Z`.

   1. Set `current` equal to point `X`.

   2. Repeat many times (you can try 10000).

      a. Randomly pick `target` as one of the three `X`, `Y`, or `Z`.

      b. Calculate the point halfway between `current` and `target`.

      c. Set `current` to this halfway point.

      d. Draw a pixel at location `current`. One way to do this is to fill or draw a tiny rectangle at this coordinate.

   Write a program that draws a Sierpinski Gasket. You can pick the coordinates for the corners of the triangle. It may seem like you should get a random mess of dots but instead you get a very orderly picture!

   To draw a single pixel at coordinate (X,Y), use the `drawLine` method where the start and endpoints are both (X,Y).

2. The file named `humphrey-img.txt` contained with the website for this book holds raw image data[3] of a Martian rock called "Humphrey" that was taken by the Mars Exploration Rover Spirit. The format of this text file is as follows:

   First line: single number indicating the height and width of the image (in this case, 461).

   Lines 2–462: A row of 461 numbers each separated by a space. Each number represents a pixel in grayscale and ranges from 0 to 255 where 0 is black and 255 is white.

   For example, the following data describes a 3×3 square where every pixel is white except for a black line along the diagonal from the upper-left corner to the bottom-right corner:

   ```
   3
   0 255 255
   255 0 255
   255 255 0
   ```

   a) Write a program to read in the data from the file and display it in a `JFrame` window. To draw a single pixel at coordinate (X,Y), use the `drawLine` method where the start and endpoints are both (X,Y). For speed, the contents of the file should be read into an array once and the array data used in the `paint()` method to draw the image.

   b) In this particular image, only about 2/3 of the shades of gray are used. For example, if the image consists entirely of shades in the range from 150–160, then the entire image would appear to be almost the same shade of gray. One method to enhance such an image is to scale the shade of each pixel to the entire range from 0 to 255. Pixels that were originally at value 150 would be drawn with the value 0, pixels that were originally 151 would be drawn with the value 25, and so on up to pixels of the shade 160, which would be drawn with the value 255. This technique spaces out the shading so the details are easier to see.

   To compute the new shade for a pixel at coordinate (i, j), do the following:

   $$\text{NewShade}(i, j) = \frac{255 \times (\text{OriginalShade}(i, j) - \text{MinOriginalShade})}{(\text{MaxOriginalShade} - \text{MinOriginalShade})}$$

   `MinOriginalShade` is the smallest scale of gray in the original image and `MaxOriginalShade` is the largest scale of gray in the original image.

   Modify your program so that the image is drawn using the scaling technique described above. The brightness and details in the resulting image should be a little bit easier to distinguish.

3. Write a GUI program that uses the methods in the `Graphics` class to draw a smiley face when the window is activated, and a frowny face when the window is deactivated. This will require use of a `WindowListener` to detect the activation or deactivation events.

---

[3]The original raw image data has been cropped and converted to a textual format for purposes of this project.

4. Write a "skeleton" GUI program that implements the `WindowListener` interface. Write code for each of the methods in Display 18.1 that simply prints out a message identifying which event occurred. Print the message out in a text field. Note that your program will not end when the close-window button is clicked (but will instead simply send a message to the text field saying that the `windowClosing` method has been invoked). Include a button labeled `Exit` that the user can click to end the program.

5. Enhance the face drawing in Display 18.17 in the following ways: Add color so the eyes are blue and the mouth is red. When the face winks, the line that represents a closed eye is black not blue. Add a nose and a brown handlebar mustache. Add buttons labeled "`Smile`" and "`Frown`". When the "`Frown`" button is clicked, the face shows a frown (upside down smile); when the "Smile" button is clicked, the face shows a smile. When the user clicks the close-window button, a window pops up to ask if the user is sure he or she wants to exit, as in Display 18.2.

6. Write a GUI program to sample different fonts. The user enters a line of text in a text field. The user then selects a font from a font menu. Offer the three guaranteed fonts and at least two other fonts. The user also selects any desired style modifiers (bold and/or italic) from a style menu, and selects point size from a point size menu that offers the following choices: 9, 10, 12, 14, 16, 24, and 32. There is also a "`Display`" button. When the "`Display`" button is clicked, the text is displayed in the font, style, and point size chosen.

VideoNote

Solution to Programming Project 18.7

7. The `MouseListener` interface allows you to retrieve mouse events. A program implements this interface in a manner similar to the `WindowListener` interface. For example, the following program creates a `JFrame` and outputs the X and Y coordinates of any mouse clicks within the `JFrame`. The `MouseListener` interface requires the implementing class to define the `mouseClicked`, `mouseEntered`, `mousePressed`, `mouseReleased`, and `mouseExited` methods. In the example, only the `mouseClicked` method has been completed.

```
import javax.swing.JFrame;
import java.awt.event.MouseListener;
import java.awt.event.MouseEvent;

public class MouseDemo extends JFrame implements MouseListener
{
    public void mouseClicked (MouseEvent e)
    {
        System.out.println(e.getX() + " " + e.getY());
    }
    public void mouseEntered (MouseEvent e) {}
    public void mousePressed (MouseEvent e) {}
    public void mouseReleased (MouseEvent e) {}
    public void mouseExited (MouseEvent e) {}
```

```
        public MouseDemo()
        {
            super();
            setSize(600,400);
            setTitle("Mouse Demo");
            setDefaultCloseOperation(JFrame.EXIT_ON_CLOSE);
            addMouseListener(this); // Add listener for this object
        }

        public static void main(String[] args)
        {
            MouseDemo m = new MouseDemo();
            m.setVisible(true);
        }
    }
```

Modify this program to create a simple drawing program. When the mouse button is clicked, a solid circle with a radius of three pixels should be drawn in the JFrame centered at the mouse coordinates. Draw the circle in the color of your choice. Make sure that the drawing is correctly redrawn if the JFrame is minimized and then displayed again.

8. Write a program that graphically displays a vertical bar chart. The input is an array of integers. Use the index of an array entry as the label on the X axis. The height of the bar should correspond to the value of the array entry. Scale the height proportionally so the bar chart fits on the screen. For example, if the array values are {3000, 4000, 5000}, then the bars should not be drawn 3,000; 4,000; and 5,000 pixels tall. Instead they should fit on the screen but remain in the correct proportion to the original values (e.g., perhaps 300, 400, and 500 pixels tall, but the actual values will depend upon the size of your window).

Java Never Ends

19.1 MULTITHREADING 1112
Example: A Nonresponsive GUI   1113
`Thread.sleep`   1113
The `getGraphics` Method   1117
Fixing a Nonresponsive Program Using Threads   1118
Example: A Multithreaded Program   1118
The Class `Thread`   1119
The `Runnable` Interface ★   1122
Race Conditions and Thread Synchronization ★   1125

**19.2 NETWORKING WITH STREAM
     SOCKETS**   1130
Sockets   1130
Sockets and Threading   1134

19.3 JAVABEANS   1135
The Component Model   1135
The JavaBeans Model   1136

**19.4 JAVA AND DATABASE
     CONNECTIONS**   1137
Relational Databases   1137
Java DB and JDBC   1137
SQL   1139

**19.5 WEB PROGRAMMING WITH JAVA
     SERVER PAGES**   1150
Applets, Servlets, and Java Server Pages   1150
Oracle GlassFish Enterprise Server   1152
HTML Forms—the Common Gateway Interface   1153
JSP Declarations, Expressions, Scriptlets,
     and Directives   1155

Chapter Summary   1132   **Answers to Self-Test Exercises**   1133   **Programming Projects**   1134

And thick and fast they came at last,
And more, and more, and more—

LEWIS CARROLL, *Through the Looking-Glass*

Introduction

Of course there is only a finite amount of Java, but when you consider all the standard libraries and other accompanying software, the amount of power and the amount to learn seem to be endless. In this chapter, we give you a brief introduction to five topics to give you a flavor of some of the directions you can take in extending your knowledge of Java. The five topics are multithreading, networking with stream sockets, JavaBeans, the interaction of Java with database systems, and Web programming with Java Server Pages.

Prerequisites

You really should cover most of the book before covering this chapter. However, Section 19.1 requires only Chapters 17 and 18 and their prerequisites. Section 19.2 requires Chapters 1 through 5, 9, and 10. Sections 19.3 and 19.4 require only Chapters 1 through 6. Section 19.5 requires an understanding of HTML, which is given in Chapter 20. Chapter 20 is distributed as a file on the website included in this book. Aside from references to Section 19.1 in Section 19.2, all sections are independent of each other and may be read in any order.

19.1 Multithreading

"Can you do two things at once?"
"I have trouble doing one thing at once."

Part of a job interview

thread   A **thread** is a separate computation process. In Java, you can have programs with multiple threads. You can think of the threads as computations that execute in parallel. On a computer with enough processors, the threads might indeed execute in parallel. However, in most normal computing situations, the threads do not really do this. Instead, the computer switches resources between threads so that each thread in turn does a little bit of computing. To the user, this looks like the processes are executing in parallel.

You have already experienced threads. Modern operating systems allow you to run more than one program at the same time. For example, rather than waiting for your virus scanning program to finish its computation, you can go on to, say, read your e-mail while the virus scanning program is still executing. The operating system is using threads to make this happen. There may or may not be some work being done in parallel depending on your computer and operating system. Most likely, the two computation threads are simply sharing computer resources so that they take turns using the computer's resources. When reading your e-mail, you may or may not notice that response is slower because resources are being shared with the virus scanning program. Your e-mail reading program is indeed slowed down, but because humans are so much slower than computers, any apparent slowdown is likely to be unnoticed.

EXAMPLE: A Nonresponsive GUI

Display 19.1 contains a very simple action GUI. When the `"Start"` button is clicked, the GUI draws circles one after the other until a large portion of the window is filled with circles. There is 1/10 of a second pause between the drawing of each circle. So, you can see the circles appear one after the other. If you are interested in Java programming, this can be pretty exciting for the first few circles, but it quickly becomes boring. You are likely to want to end the program early, but if you click the close-window button, nothing will happen until the program is finished drawing all its little circles. We will use threads to fix this problem, but first let us understand this program, which does not really use threads in any essential way, despite the occurrence of the word `Thread` in the program. We explain this Swing program in the next few subsections.

Thread.sleep

In Display 19.1, the following method invocation produces a 1/10 of a second pause after drawing each of the circles:

```
doNothing(PAUSE);
```

which is equivalent to

```
doNothing(100);
```

The method `doNothing` is a private helping method that does nothing except call the method `Thread.sleep` and take care of catching any thrown exception. So, the pause is really created by the method invocation

Thread.sleep
```
Thread.sleep(100);
```

This is a static method in the class `Thread` that pauses whatever thread includes the invocation. It pauses for the number of milliseconds (thousandths of a second) given as an argument. So, this pauses the computation of the program in Display 19.1 for 100 milliseconds or 1/10 of a second.

"Wait a minute," you may think, "the program in Display 19.1 was not supposed to use threads in any essential way." That is basically true, but every Java program uses threads in some way. If there is only one stream of computation, as in Display 19.1, then that is treated as a single thread by Java. So, threads are always used by Java, but not in an interesting way until more than one thread is used.

You can safely think of the invocation of

```
Thread.sleep(milliseconds);
```

as a pause in the computation that lasts (approximately) the number of milliseconds given as the argument. (If this invocation is in a thread of a multithreaded program, then the pause, like anything else in the thread, applies only to the thread in which it occurs.)

The method `Thread.sleep` can sometimes be handy even if you do not do any multithreaded programming. The class `Thread` is in the package `java.lang` and so requires no import statement.

Display 19.1   Nonresponsive GUI (part 1 of 3)

```
1    import javax.swing.JFrame;
2    import javax.swing.JPanel;
3    import javax.swing.JButton;
4    import java.awt.BorderLayout;
5    import java.awt.FlowLayout;
6    import java.awt.Graphics;
7    import java.awt.event.ActionListener;
8    import java.awt.event.ActionEvent;

9    /**
10    Packs a section of the frame window with circles, one at a time.
11    */
12   public class FillDemo extends JFrame implements ActionListener
13   {
14       public static final int WIDTH = 300;
15       public static final int HEIGHT = 200;
16       public static final int FILL_WIDTH = 300;
17       public static final int FILL_HEIGHT = 100;
18       public static final int CIRCLE_SIZE = 10;
19       public static final int PAUSE = 100; //milliseconds

20       private JPanel box;

21       public static void main(String[] args)
22       {
23           FillDemo gui = new FillDemo();
24           gui.setVisible(true);
25       }
```

Display 19.1   **Nonresponsive GUI** (part 2 of 3)

```
26        public FillDemo()
27        {
28            setSize(WIDTH, HEIGHT);
29            setTitle("FillDemo");
30            setDefaultCloseOperation(JFrame.EXIT_ON_CLOSE);
31            setLayout(new BorderLayout());
32            box = new JPanel();
33            add(box, "Center");

34            JPanel buttonPanel = new JPanel();
35            buttonPanel.setLayout(new FlowLayout());
36            JButton startButton = new JButton("Start");
37            startButton.addActionListener(this);
38            buttonPanel.add(startButton);
39            add(buttonPanel, "South");
40        }

41        public void actionPerformed(ActionEvent e)
42        {
43            fill( );
44        }
```

Nothing else can happen until `actionPerformed` *returns, which does not happen until* `fill` *returns.*

```
45        public void fill()
46        {
47            Graphics g = box.getGraphics();

48            for (int y = 0; y < FILL_HEIGHT; y = y + CIRCLE_SIZE)
49                for (int x = 0; x < FILL_WIDTH; x = x + CIRCLE_SIZE)
50                {
51                    g.fillOval(x, y, CIRCLE_SIZE, CIRCLE_SIZE);
52                    doNothing(PAUSE);
53                }
54        }
```

Everything stops for 100 milliseconds (1/10 of a second).

```
55        public void doNothing(int milliseconds)
56        {
57            try
58            {
59                Thread.sleep(milliseconds);
60            }
61            catch(InterruptedException e)
62            {
63                System.out.println("Unexpected interrupt");
64                System.exit(0);
65            }
66        }
67    }
```

(continued)

Display 19.1 Nonresponsive GUI (part 3 of 3)

RESULTING GUI (When started)

RESULTING GUI (While drawing circles)

If you click the close-window button while the circles are being drawn, the window will not close until all the circles are drawn.

RESULTING GUI (After all circles are drawn)

The method `Thread.sleep` can throw an `InterruptedException`, which is a checked exception—that is, it must be either caught in a `catch` block or declared in a `throws` clause. We do not discuss `InterruptedException` in this book, leaving it for more advanced books on multithreaded programming, but it has to do with one thread interrupting another thread. We will simply note that an `InterruptedException` may be thrown by `Thread.sleep` and so must be accounted for—in our case, by a simple `catch` block. The class `InterruptedException` is in the `java.lang` package and so requires no import statement.

> ### `Thread.sleep`
>
> `Thread.sleep` is a static method in the class `Thread` that pauses the thread that includes the invocation. It pauses for the number of milliseconds (thousandths of a second) given as an argument.
>
> The method `Thread.sleep` may throw an `InterruptedException`, which is a checked exception and so must be either caught in a `catch` block or declared in a `throws` clause.
>
> The classes `Thread` and `InterruptedException` are both in the package `java.lang`, so neither requires any import statement.
>
> Note that `Thread.sleep` can be invoked in an ordinary (single thread) program of the kind we have seen before this chapter. It will insert a pause in the single thread of that program.
>
> **SYNTAX**
>
> `Thread.sleep(`*Number_Of_Milliseconds*`);`
>
> **EXAMPLE**
>
> ```
> try
> {
>     Thread.sleep(100); //Pause of 1/10 of a second
> }
> catch(InterruptedException e)
> {
>     System.out.println("Unexpected interrupt");
> }
> ```

The `getGraphics` Method

The other new method in Display 19.1 is the `getGraphics` method, which is used in the following line from the method `fill`:

`getGraphics`

```
Graphics g = box.getGraphics();
```

The `getGraphics` method is almost self-explanatory. As we already noted in Chapter 18, almost every item displayed on the screen (more precisely, every `JComponent`) has an associated `Graphics` object. The method `getGraphics` is an accessor method that returns the associated `Graphics` object (of the calling object for `getGraphics`)—in this case, the `Graphics` object associated with the panel `box`. This gives us a `Graphics` object that can draw circles (or anything else) in the panel `box`.

We still need to say a bit more about why the program in Display 19.1 makes you wait before it will respond to the close-window button, but otherwise this concludes our explanation of Display 19.1. The rest of the code consists of standard things we have seen before.

---

getGraphics

Every JComponent has an associated Graphics object. The method getGraphics is an accessor method that returns the associated Graphics object of its calling object.

SYNTAX

Component.getGraphics( );

EXAMPLE (see Display 19.1 for context)

Graphics g = box.getGraphics( );

Fixing a Nonresponsive Program Using Threads

Now that we have discussed the new items in the program in Display 19.1, we are ready to explain why it is nonresponsive and to show you how to use threads to write a responsive version of that program.

Recall that when you run the program in Display 19.1, it draws circles one after the other to fill a portion of the frame. Although there is only a 1/10 of a second pause between drawing each circle, it can still seem like it takes a long time to finish. So, you are likely to want to abort the program and close the window early. But, if you click the close-window button, the window will not close until the GUI is finished drawing all the circles.

Here is why the close-window button is nonresponsive: The method fill, which draws the circles, is invoked in the body of the method actionPerformed. So, the method actionPerformed does not end until after the method fill ends. And, until the method actionPerformed ends, the GUI cannot go on to do the next thing, which is probably to respond to the close-window button.

Here is how we fixed the problem: We have the method actionPerformed create a new (independent) thread to draw the circles. Once actionPerformed does this, the new thread is an independent process that proceeds on its own. The method actionPerformed has nothing more to do with this new thread; the work of actionPerformed is ended. So, the main thread (the one with actionPerformed) is ready to move on to the next thing, which will probably be to respond promptly to a click of the close-window button. At the same time, the new thread draws the circles. So, the circles are drawn, but at the same time a click of the close-window button will end the program. The program that implements this multithreaded solution is given in the next Programming Example.

EXAMPLE: A Multithreaded Program

Display 19.2 contains a program that uses a main thread and a second thread to implement the technique discussed in the previous subsection. The general approach was outlined in the previous subsection, but we need to explain the Java code details. We do that in the next few subsections.

The Class `Thread`

In Java, a thread is an object of the class `Thread`. The normal way to program a thread is to define a class that is a derived class of the class `Thread`. An object of this derived class will be a thread that follows the programming given in the definition of the derived (thread) class.

Where do you do the programming of a thread? The class `Thread` has a method named `run`. The definition of the method `run` is the code for the thread. When the thread is executed, the method `run` is executed. Of course, the method defined in the class `Thread` and inherited by any derived class of `Thread` does not do what you want your thread to do. So, when you define a derived class of `Thread`, you override the definition of the method `run` to do what you want the thread to do.

In Display 19.2, the inner class `Packer` is a derived class of the class `Thread`. The method `run` for the class `Packer` is defined to be exactly the same as the method `fill` in our previous, unresponsive GUI (Display 19.1). So, an object of the class `Packer` is a thread that will do what `fill` does, namely draw the circles to fill up a portion of the window.

The method `actionPerformed` in Display 19.2 differs from the method `actionPerformed` in our older, nonresponsive program (Display 19.1) in that the

invocation of the method `fill` is replaced with the following:

```
Packer packerThread = new Packer( );
packerThread.start( );
```

This creates a new, independent thread named `packerThread` and starts it processing. Whatever `packerThread` does, it does as an independent thread. The main thread can then allow `actionPerformed` to end and the main thread will be ready to respond to any click of the close-window button.

Display 19.2   Threaded Version of `FillDemo` (part 1 of 3)

```
1   import javax.swing.JFrame;
2   import javax.swing.JPanel;
3   import javax.swing.JButton;
4   import java.awt.BorderLayout;
5   import java.awt.FlowLayout;
6   import java.awt.Graphics;
7   import java.awt.event.ActionListener;
8   import java.awt.event.ActionEvent;

9   public class ThreadedFillDemo extends JFrame implements ActionListener
10  {
11      public static final int WIDTH = 300;
12      public static final int HEIGHT = 200;
13      public static final int FILL_WIDTH = 300;
14      public static final int FILL_HEIGHT = 100;
15      public static final int CIRCLE_SIZE = 10;
16      public static final int PAUSE = 100; //milliseconds
```

The GUI produced is identical to the GUI produced by Display 19.1 except that in this version the close-window button works even while the circles are being drawn, so you can end the GUI early if you get bored.

(continued)

Display 19.2   **Threaded Version of `FillDemo`** (part 2 of 3)

```
17        private JPanel box;

18        public static void main(String[] args)
19        {
20            ThreadedFillDemo gui = new ThreadedFillDemo();
21            gui.setVisible(true);
22        }

23        public ThreadedFillDemo()
24        {
25            setSize(WIDTH, HEIGHT);
26            setTitle("Threaded Fill Demo");
27            setDefaultCloseOperation(JFrame.EXIT_ON_CLOSE);

28            setLayout(new BorderLayout());

29            box = new JPanel();
30            add(box, "Center");

31            JPanel buttonPanel = new JPanel();
32            buttonPanel.setLayout(new FlowLayout());
33            JButton startButton = new JButton("Start");
34            startButton.addActionListener(this);
35            buttonPanel.add(startButton);
36            add(buttonPanel, "South");
37        }

38        public void actionPerformed(ActionEvent e)
39        {
40            Packer packerThread = new Packer();
41            packerThread.start();
42        }

43        private class Packer extends Thread
44        {
45            public void run()
46            {
47                Graphics g = box.getGraphics();
48                for (int y = 0; y < FILL_HEIGHT; y = y + CIRCLE_SIZE)
49                    for (int x = 0; x < FILL_WIDTH; x = x + CIRCLE_SIZE)
50                    {
51                        g.fillOval(x, y, CIRCLE_SIZE, CIRCLE_SIZE);
52                        doNothing(PAUSE);
53                    }
54            }
```

You need a thread object, even if there are no instance variables in the class definition of `Packer`.

`start` *"starts" the thread and calls* `run`.

`run` *is inherited from* `Thread` *but needs to be overridden. This definition of* `run` *is identical to that of* `fill` *in Display 19.1.*

Display 19.2 **Threaded Version of `FillDemo`** (part 3 of 3)

```
55              public void doNothing(int milliseconds)
56              {
57                  try
58                  {
59                      Thread.sleep(milliseconds);
60                  }
61                  catch(InterruptedException e)
62                  {
63                      System.out.println("Unexpected interrupt");
64                      System.exit(0);
65                  }
66              }
67          } //End Packer inner class

68  }
```

We need only to discuss the method `start` and we will be through with our explanation. The method `start` initiates the computation (process) of the calling thread. It performs some overhead associated with starting a thread and then it invokes the `run` method for the thread. As we have already seen, the `run` method of the class `Packer` in Display 19.2 draws the circles we want, so the invocation

`run()`

```
packerThread.start( );
```

does this as well, because it calls `run`. Note that you do not invoke `run` directly. Instead, you invoke `start`, which does some other needed things and then invokes `run`.

This ends our explanation of the multithreaded program in Display 19.2, but there is still one, perhaps puzzling, thing about the class `Packer` that we should explain. The definition of the class `Packer` includes no instance variables. So, why do we need to bother with an object of the class `Packer`? Why not simply make all the methods static and call them with the class name `Packer`? The answer is that the only way to get a new thread is to create a new `Thread` object. The things inherited from the class `Thread` are what the object needs to be a thread. Static methods do not a thread make. In fact, not only will static methods not work, the compiler will not even allow you to define `run` to be static. This is because `run` is inherited from `Thread` as a nonstatic method; this cannot be changed to static when overriding a method definition. The compiler will not let you even try to do this without creating an object of the class `Packer`.

> ### The `Thread` Class
>
> A thread is an object of the class `Thread`. The normal way to program a thread is to define a class that is a derived class of the class `Thread`. An object of this derived class will be a thread that follows the programming given in the definition of the derived (thread) class's method named `run`.
>
> Any thread class inherits the method start from the class `Thread`. An invocation of start by an object of a thread class will start the thread and invoke the method run for that thread.
>
> See Display 19.2 for an example.

The `Runnable` Interface ★

There are times when you would rather not make a thread class a derived class of the class `Thread`. The alternative to making your class a derived class of the class `Thread` is to have your class instead implement the `Runnable` interface. The `Runnable` interface has only one method heading:

```
public void run()
```

A class that implements the `Runnable` interface must still be run from an instance of the class `Thread`. This is usually done by passing the `Runnable` object as an argument to the thread constructor. The following is an outline of one way to do this:

```
public class ClassToRun extends SomeClass implements Runnable
{
    . . . .
    public void run()
    {
        //Fill this just as you would if ClassToRun
        //were derived from Thread.
    }
    . . . .
    public void startThread()
    {
        Thread theThread = new Thread(this);
        theThread.run();
    }
    . . . .
}
```

The previous method `startThread` is not compulsory, but it is one way to produce a thread that will in turn run the `run` method of an object of the class `ClassToRun`. In Display 19.3, we have rewritten the program in Display 19.2 using the `Runnable` interface. The program behaves exactly the same as the one in Display 19.2.

Display 19.3   The `Runnable` Interface (part 1 of 2)

```
1    import javax.swing.JFrame;
2    import javax.swing.JPanel;
3    import javax.swing.JButton;
4    import java.awt.BorderLayout;
5    import java.awt.FlowLayout;
6    import java.awt.Graphics;
7    import java.awt.event.ActionListener;
8    import java.awt.event.ActionEvent;

9    public class ThreadedFillDemo2 extends JFrame
10                                    implements ActionListener, Runnable
11   {
12       public static final int WIDTH = 300;
13       public static final int HEIGHT = 200;
14       public static final int FILL_WIDTH = 300;
15       public static final int FILL_HEIGHT = 100;
16       public static final int CIRCLE_SIZE = 10;
17       public static final int PAUSE = 100; //milliseconds
18       private JPanel box;

19       public static void main(String[] args)
20       {
21           ThreadedFillDemo2 gui = new ThreadedFillDemo2();
22           gui.setVisible(true);
23       }

24       public ThreadedFillDemo2()
25       {
26           setSize(WIDTH, HEIGHT);
27           setTitle("Threaded Fill Demo");
28           setDefaultCloseOperation(JFrame.EXIT_ON_CLOSE);

29           setLayout(new BorderLayout());

30           box = new JPanel();
31           add(box, "Center");

32           JPanel buttonPanel = new JPanel();
33           buttonPanel.setLayout(new FlowLayout());

34           JButton startButton = new JButton("Start");
35           startButton.addActionListener(this);
36           buttonPanel.add(startButton);
37           add(buttonPanel, "South");
38       }
```

(continued)

Display 19.3   The `Runnable` Interface (part 2 of 2)

```
39        public void actionPerformed(ActionEvent e)
40        {
41            startThread();
42        }

43        public void run()
44        {
45            Graphics g = box.getGraphics();
46            for (int y = 0; y < FILL_HEIGHT; y = y + CIRCLE_SIZE)
47              for (int x = 0; x < FILL_WIDTH; x = x + CIRCLE_SIZE)
48              {
49                  g.fillOval(x, y, CIRCLE_SIZE, CIRCLE_SIZE);
50                  doNothing(PAUSE);
51              }
52        }

53        public void startThread()
54        {
55            Thread theThread = new Thread(this);
56            theThread.start();
57        }

58        public void doNothing(int milliseconds)
59        {
60            try
61            {
62                Thread.sleep(milliseconds);
63            }
64            catch (InterruptedException e)
65            {
66                System.out.println("Unexpected interrupt");
67                System.exit(0);
68            }
69        }
70    }
```

MyProgrammingLab™

Self-Test Exercises

1. Because `sleep` is a static method, how can it possibly know what thread it needs to pause?

2. Where was polymorphism used in the program in Display 19.2? (*Hint*: We are looking for an answer involving the class `Packer`.)

Race Conditions and Thread Synchronization ★

When multiple threads change a shared variable, it is sometimes possible that the variable will end up with the wrong (and often unpredictable) value. This is called a **race condition** because the final value depends on the sequence in which the threads access the shared value.

For example, consider two threads where each thread runs the following code:

```
int local;
local = sharedVariable;
local++;
sharedVariable = local;
```

The intent is for each thread to increment `sharedVariable` by one so if there are two threads, then `sharedVariable` should be incremented by two. However, consider the case where `sharedVariable` is 0. The first thread runs and executes the first two statements, so its variable `local` is set to 0. Now there is a context switch to the second thread. The second thread executes all four statements, so its variable `local` is set to 0 and incremented, and `sharedVariable` is set to 1. Now we return to the first thread and it continues where it left off, which is the third statement. The variable `local` is 0 so it is incremented to 1 and then the value 1 is copied into `sharedVariable`. The end result after both threads are done is that `sharedVariable` has the value 1, and we lost the value written by thread two!

You might think that this problem could be avoided by replacing our code with a single statement such as

```
sharedVariable++;
```

Unfortunately, this will not solve our problem because the statement is not guaranteed to be an "atomic" action and there could still be a context switch to another thread "in the middle" of executing the statement.

To demonstrate this problem, consider the `Counter` class shown in Display 19.4. This simple class merely stores a variable that increments a counter. It uses the somewhat roundabout way to increment the counter on purpose to increase the likelihood of a race condition.

The way we will demonstrate the race condition is to do the following:

1. Create a single instance of the `Counter` class.
2. Create an array of many threads (30,000 in the example) where each thread references the single instance of the `Counter` class.
3. Each thread runs and invokes the `increment()` method.
4. Wait for each thread to finish and then output the value of the counter. If there are no race conditions, then its value should be 30,000. If there are race conditions, then the value will be less than 30,000.

We create many threads to increase the likelihood that the race condition occurs. With only a few threads, it is not likely that there will be a switch to another thread inside the `increment()` method at the right point to cause a problem.

ace condition

Display 19.4 The `Counter` Class

```
1   public class Counter
2   {
3     private int counter;
4     public Counter()
5     {
6         counter = 0;
7     }
8     public int value()
9     {
10        return counter;
11    }
12    public void increment()
13    {
14        int local;
15        local = counter;
16        local++;
17        counter = local;
18    }
19  }
```

The only new tool that we need for our demonstration program is a way to wait for all the threads to finish. If we do not wait, then our program might output the counter before all the threads have had a chance to increment the value. We can wait by invoking the `join()` method for every thread we create. This method waits for the thread to complete. The `join()` method throws `InterruptedException`. This is a checked exception so we must use the try/catch mechanism.

VideoNote
Walkthrough
of a Program
with Race
Conditions

The class `RaceConditionTest` in Display 19.5 illustrates the race condition. You may have to run the program several times before you get a value less than 30,000. Problems as a result of race conditions are often rare occurrences. This makes them extremely hard to find and debug!

Display 19.5 The `RaceConditionTest` Class (part 1 of 2)

```
1   public class RaceConditionTest extends Thread
2   {
3     private Counter countObject;             ←——— Stores a reference to a
                                                     single Counter object.
4     public RaceConditionTest(Counter ctr)
5     {
6         countObject = ctr;
7     }
```

Display 19.5   The `RaceConditionTest` Class (part 2 of 2)

```
 8      public void run()                          Invokes the code in Display 19.4
 9      {                                          where the race condition occurs.
10          countObject.increment();
11      }

12      public static void main(String[] args)
13      {                                          The single instance of the Counter object.
14          int i;                                 Array of 30,000 threads.
15          Counter masterCounter = new Counter();
16          RaceConditionTest[] threads = new RaceConditionTest[30000];

17          System.out.println("The counter is " + masterCounter.value());
18          for (i = 0; i < threads.length; i++)
19          {
20              threads[i] = new RaceConditionTest(masterCounter);
21              threads[i].start();
22          }                                      Give each thread a reference to
                                                   the single Counter object and
23          // Wait for the threads to finish      start each thread.
24          for (i = 0; i < threads.length; i++)
25          {
26              try
27              {
28                  threads[i].join();             Waits for the thread to complete.
29              }
30              catch (InterruptedException e)
31              {
32                  System.out.println(e.getMessage());
33              }
34          }
35          System.out.println("The counter is " + masterCounter.value());
37      }
38  }
```

Sample Dialogue (output will vary)

```
The counter is 0
The counter is 29998
```

So how do we fix this problem? The solution is to make each thread wait so only one thread can run the code in `increment()` at a time. This section of code is called **critical region** a **critical region**. Java allows you to add the keyword **synchronized** around a critical **synchronized** region to enforce the requirement that only one thread is allowed to execute in this region at a time. All other threads will wait until the thread inside the region is finished.

In this particular case, we can add the keyword `synchronized` to either the method or around the specific code. If we add `synchronized` to the `increment()` method in the `Counter` class, then it looks like this:

```
public synchronized void increment()
{
  int local;
  local = counter;
  local++;
  counter = local;
}
```

If we add `synchronized` inside the code, then we can write

```
public void increment()
{
  int local;
  synchronized (this)
  {
  local = counter;
  local++;
  counter = local;
  }
}
```

Either version will result in a counter whose final value is always 30,000. There are many other issues involved in thread management, concurrency, and synchronization. These concepts are often covered in more detail in an operating systems or parallel programming course.

MyProgrammingLab

Self-Test Exercises

3. You can pause a thread's execution using the `sleep` method. What is the argument you pass to the `sleep()` method? Write a small code snippet to display the numbers 1 to 10 on the screen; however, the thread should be stopped for 100 milliseconds after displaying each number.

4. Here is some code that synchronizes thread access to a shared variable. How come it is not guaranteed to output 30,000 every time it is run?

```
public class Counter
{
  private int counter;
  public Counter()
  {
      counter = 0;
  }
```

Self-Test Exercises (continued)

```java
    public int value()
    {
      return counter;
    }
    public synchronized void increment()
    {
      counter++;
    }
}
public class RaceConditionTest extends Thread
{
  private Counter countObject;
  public RaceConditionTest(Counter ctr)
  {
      countObject = ctr;
  }
  public void run()
  {
    countObject.increment();
  }
  public static void main(String[] args)
  {
    int i;
    Counter masterCounter = new Counter();
    RaceConditionTest[] threads = new RaceConditionTest[30000];
    System.out.println("The counter is " + masterCounter.
    value());
    for (i = 0; i < threads.length; i++)
    {
        threads[i] = new RaceConditionTest(masterCounter);
        threads[i].start();
    }
    System.out.println("The counter is " + masterCounter.
    value());
  }
}
```

19.2 Networking with Stream Sockets

Since in order to speak, one must first listen, learn to speak by listening.

MEVLANA RUMI

When computers want to communicate with each other over a network, each computer must speak the same "language." In other words, the computers need to communicate using the same *protocol*. One of the most common protocols today is **TCP**, or the **Transmission Control Protocol**. For example, the HTTP protocol used to transmit Web pages is based on TCP. TCP is a stream-based protocol in which a stream of data is transmitted from the sender to the receiver. TCP is considered a reliable protocol because it guarantees that data from the sender is received in the same order in which it was sent. An analogy to TCP is the telephone system. A connection is made when the phone is dialed and the participants communicate by speaking back and forth. In TCP, the receiver must first be listening for a connection, the sender initiates the connection, and then the sender and receiver can transmit data. The program that is waiting for a connection is called the **server** and the program that initiates the connection is called the **client**.

> **Transmission Control Protocol (TCP)**
>
> **server**
>
> **client**
>
> **User Datagram Protocol (UDP)**

An alternate protocol is **UDP**, or the **User Datagram Protocol**. In UDP, packets of data are transmitted but no guarantee is made regarding the order in which the packets are received. An analogy to UDP is the postal system. Letters that are sent might be received in an unpredictable order, or lost entirely with no notification. Although Java provides support for UDP, we will only introduce TCP in this section.

Sockets

> **sockets**
>
> **port**

Network programming is implemented in Java using **sockets**. A socket describes one end of the connection between two programs over the network. A socket consists of an address that identifies the remote computer and a **port** for both the local and remote computer. The port is assigned an integer value between 0 and 65,535 that is used to identify which program should handle data received from the network. Two applications may not bind to the same port. Typically, ports 0 to 1,024 are reserved for use by well-known services implemented by your operating system.

The process of client/server communication is shown in Display 19.6. First, the server waits for a connection by listening on a specific port. When a client connects to this port, a new socket is created that identifies the remote computer, the remote port, and the local port. A similar socket is created on the client. Once the sockets are created on both the client and the server, data can be transmitted using streams in a manner very similar to the way we implemented file I/O in Chapter 10.

Display 19.7 shows how to create a simple server that listens on port 7654 for a connection. Once it receives a connection, a new socket is returned by the accept( ) method. From this socket, we create a `BufferedReader`, just as if we were reading from a text file described in Chapter 10. Data is transmitted to the socket using a `DataOutputStream`, which is similar to a `FileOutputStream`. The `ServerSocket`

Display 19.6   Client/Server Network Communication through Sockets

1. The server listens and waits for a connection on port 7654.

2. The client connects to the server on port 7654. It uses a local port that is assigned automatically, in this case, port 20314.

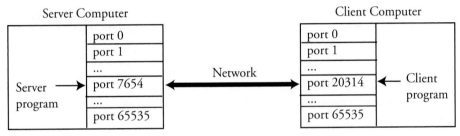

The server program can now communicate over a socket bound locally to port 7654 and remotely to the client's address at port 20314.

The client program can now communicate over a socket bound locally to port 20314 and remotely to the server's address at port 7654.

and `Socket` classes are in the `java.net` package, while the `BufferedReader` and `DataOutputStream` classes are in the `java.io` package. Once the streams are created, the server expects the client to send a name. The server waits for the name with a call to `readLine( )` on the `BufferedReader` object and then sends back the name concatenated with the current date and time. Finally, the server closes the streams and sockets.

Display 19.6 shows how to create a client that connects to our date and time server. First, we create a socket with the name of the computer running the server along with the corresponding port of 7654. If the server program and client program are running **localhost** on the same computer, then you can use **localhost** as the name of the machine. Your computer understands that any attempt to connect across a network to the machine named `localhost` really corresponds to a connection with itself. Otherwise, the hostname should be set to the name of the computer (e.g., my.server.com). After a connection is made, the client creates stream objects, sends its name, waits for a reply, and prints the reply.

Display 19.7   **Date and Time Server** (part 1 of 2)

```
1   import java.util.Date;
2   import java.net.ServerSocket;
3   import java.net.Socket;
4   import java.io.DataOutputStream;
5   import java.io.BufferedReader;
6   import java.io.InputStreamReader;
7   import java.io.IOException;

8   public class DateServer
9   {
10    public static void main(String[] args)
11    {
12          Date now = new Date();

13          try
14          {
15              System.out.println("Waiting for a connection on port 7654.");
16              ServerSocket serverSock = new ServerSocket(7654);
17              Socket connectionSock = serverSock.accept();

18              BufferedReader clientInput = new BufferedReader(
19                  new InputStreamReader(connectionSock.getInputStream()));
20              DataOutputStream clientOutput = new DataOutputStream(
21                  connectionSock.getOutputStream());

22              System.out.println("Connection made, waiting for client " +
23                  "to send their name.");
24              String clientText = clientInput.readLine();
25              String replyText = "Welcome, " + clientText +
26                  ", Today is " + now.toString() + "\n";
27              clientOutput.writeBytes(replyText);
28              System.out.println("Sent: " + replyText);

29              clientOutput.close();
30              clientInput.close();
31              connectionSock.close();
32              serverSock.close();
33          }
34          catch (IOException e)
35          {
36              System.out.println(e.getMessage());
37          }
38      }
39  }
```

Display 19.7   **Date and Time Server** (part 2 of 2)

Sample Dialogue   *Output when the client program in Display 19.8 connects to the server program.*

```
Waiting for a connection on port 7654.
Connection made, waiting for client to send their name.
Sent: Welcome, Dusty Rhodes, Today is Sun Nov 20 12:18:21 AKDT 2011
```

Display 19.8   **Date and Time Client** (part 1 of 2)

```
1   import java.net.Socket;
2   import java.io.DataOutputStream;
3   import java.io.BufferedReader;
4   import java.io.InputStreamReader;
5   import java.io.IOException;

6   public class DateClient
7   {
8     public static void main(String[] args)
9     {
10        try
11        {
12          String hostname = "localhost";
13          int port = 7654;

14          System.out.println("Connecting to server on port " + port);
15          Socket connectionSock = new Socket(hostname, port);

16          BufferedReader serverInput = new BufferedReader(
17              new InputStreamReader(connectionSock.getInputStream()));
18          DataOutputStream serverOutput = new DataOutputStream(
19              connectionSock.getOutputStream());

20          System.out.println("Connection made, sending name.");
21          serverOutput.writeBytes("Dusty Rhodes\n");

22          System.out.println("Waiting for reply.");
23          String serverData = serverInput.readLine();
24          System.out.println("Received: " + serverData);

25          serverOutput.close();
26          serverInput.close();
27          connectionSock.close();
28        }
```

localhost refers to the same, or local, machine that the client is running on. Change this string to the appropriate hostname (e.g., my.server.com) if the server is running on a remote machine.

(continued)

Display 19.8 Date and Time Client (part 2 of 2)

```
29              catch (IOException e)
30              {
31                  System.out.println(e.getMessage());
32              }
33          }
34      }
```

Sample Dialogue   *Output when client program connects to the server program in Display 19.7.*

```
Connecting to server on port 7654
Connection made, sending name.
Waiting for reply.
Received: Welcome, Dusty Rhodes, Today is Fri Oct 13 03:03:21 AKDT 2011
```

Note that the socket and stream objects throw checked exceptions. This means that their exceptions must be caught or declared in a `throws` block.

Sockets and Threading

blocking

If you run the program in Display 19.7, then you will notice that the server waits, or **blocks**, at the `serverSock.accept( )` call until a client connects to it. Both the client and server also block at the `readLine( )` call if data from the socket is not yet available. In a client with a GUI, you would notice this as a nonresponsive program while it is waiting for data. For the server, this behavior makes it difficult to handle connections with more than one client. After a connection is made with the first client, the server will become nonresponsive to the client's requests while it waits for a second client.

The solution to this problem is to use threads. One thread will listen for new connections while another thread handles an existing connection. Section 19.1 describes how to create threads and make a GUI program responsive. On the server, the `accept( )` call is typically placed in a loop and a new thread is created to handle each client connection:

```
while (true)
{
    Socket connectionSock = serverSock.accept( );
    ClientHandler handler = new ClientHandler(connectionSock);
    Thread theThread = new Thread(handler);
    theThread.start( );
}
```

In this code, `ClientHandler` is a class that implements `Runnable`. The constructor keeps a reference to the socket in an instance variable, and the `run( )` method would handle all communications. A complete implementation of a threaded server is left as Programming Projects 19.7 and 19.8.

Self-Test Exercises

5. What is the basic difference between the TCP and the UDP protocol?

6. Is the following code legal? What does it indicate?

```
Socket connectionSock = new Socket("127.0.0.1", 7654);
```

19.3   JavaBeans

Insert tab A into slot B.

Common assembly instruction

JavaBeans   **JavaBeans** refers to a framework that facilitates software building by connecting software components from diverse sources. Some of the components might be standard existing pieces of software. Some might be designed for the particular application. Typically, the various components were designed and coded by different teams. If the components are all designed within the JavaBeans framework, it simplifies the process of integrating the components and means that the components produced can more easily be reused for future software projects. JavaBeans have been widely used. For example, the AWT and Swing packages were built within the JavaBeans framework.

The Component Model

You are most likely to have heard the word *component* when shopping for a home entertainment system. The individual pieces, such as a receiver/amplifier, DVD player, speakers, and so forth, are called *components*. Connect the components to produce a working system, but do not connect them in just any way. You must connect them following the interface rules for each component. The speaker wire must connect to the correct plug, and there better be a plug for it to connect to. You may think it is obvious that a receiver/amplifier needs to have connections for speakers; it is obvious if the receiver/amplifier design is going to be used to make many identical units for use by many different people. However, if you are only making one receiver/amplifier for one home entertainment system, you might just "open the box" and connect the wire inside. Software systems, unfortunately, are often constructed using the "open the box" approach. The component model says that components should always have well-defined connections for other components—which in our case will be other software components, not speakers—but the idea is the same.

The JavaBeans Model

A component model specifies how components interact with one another. In the case of JavaBeans, the software components (classes) are required to provide at least the following interface services or abilities:

1. **Rules to Ensure Consistency in Writing Interfaces:**
   For example, the rules say, among other things, that the name of an accessor method must begin with `get` and that the name of a mutator method must start with `set`. This same rule has always been a style rule for us in this book, but it was a "should do." In the JavaBeans framework, it becomes a "must do." Of course, there are other rules as well. This is just a sample rule.

event handling

2. **An Event Handling Model:**
   This is essentially the event-handling model we presented for the AWT and Swing. (Remember the AWT and Swing were done within the JavaBeans framework.)

persistence

3. **Persistence:**
   This means that an object has an identity that extends beyond one session. For example, a `JFrame` of the kind we have seen so far may be used; when you are finished using it, it goes away. The next time you use it, it starts out completely new, born again just as it started before. Persistence means the `JFrame` or other component can retain information about its former use; its state is saved, for example, in a database someplace.

introspection

4. **Introspection:**
   This is an enhancement of simple accessor and mutator methods. It includes facilities to find out what access to a component is available as well as providing access.

5. **Builder Support:**
   These are primarily IDEs (Integrated Development Environments) designed to connect JavaBean components to produce a final application. Some examples are the open source NetBeans, the Eclipse Foundation's Eclipse, and JetBrain's IntelliJ IDEA.

What Is a JavaBean?

A **JavaBean** (often called a *JavaBean* component or simply a *Bean*) is a reusable software component (Java class or classes) that satisfies the requirements of the JavaBeans framework and that can be manipulated in an IDE designed for building applications out of Beans.

What Are Enterprise JavaBeans?

The **Enterprise JavaBean** framework extends the `JavaBeans` framework to more readily accommodate business applications.

Self-Test Exercises

7. What is meant by *persistence*?

8. What event-handling model is used with JavaBeans?

19.4 Java and Database Connections

It is a capital mistake to theorize before one has data.

Sir Arthur Conan Doyle *(Sherlock Holmes), Scandal in Bohemia*

As an example of how Java has been extended to interact with other software systems, in this section, we will briefly describe how Java interacts with database management systems. This introduction is just enough for you to construct and manipulate databases at a fairly basic level. The intent of this section is to introduce some common database manipulations to let you know what kinds of things are available to you for database programming in Java.

Relational Databases

database management system (DBMS)

A **database** is a structured collection of data, and the software that manages a database is known as a **database management system (DBMS)**. A DBMS is especially useful when dealing with a large amount of data, because it simplifies the data creation, storage, and retrieval from the perspective of an application. Consequently, a database system is almost universally employed with any large-scale application that requires the storage of information. For example, applications that manage financial transactions, employee records, products, or customer data will typically use a database.

relational database

The most common database model used today is the **relational database**, which was defined by Edgar Codd at the IBM Almaden Research Center in 1970. A relational database refers to a collection of relations, which are more commonly referred to as **tables**. A table consists of records that comprise the rows of the table. The fields for each record comprise the columns of the table. Tables may be related to one another through their fields, hence the term *relational database*.

Java DB and JDBC

Java DB

Apache Derby

In this section, we will give examples based on Oracle's relational database management system called **Java DB**. Java DB is a version of the open source database known as **Apache Derby**. It is packaged with version 6 or higher of the Java Software Development Kit (SDK). Depending on what version of the Java SDK that is installed on your system, you may not have the complete Derby package (e.g., one that includes documentation and source code examples) so you may wish to download it from

Oracle's Web page. Alternately, other database systems (such as Oracle, SQL Server, or MySQL) will also work with Java, but they will require appropriate drivers and minor changes to the source code. These changes are primarily in the specification of the connection string.

Installing Derby may require some additional configuration of your system. It will require setting several environment variables in your operating system. The DERBY_INSTALL variable should be set to the pathname of the folder that contains the installed Derby files, the CLASSPATH variable should include derby.jar, which is in the lib folder of the main Derby folder, and your PATH variable should contain the bin folder of the main Derby folder. See the documentation that comes with the Derby software for more detailed instructions.

Derby runs in one of two modes: network server mode or embedded mode. In network server mode, the Derby server program stores and processes the data while a client program connects to the server using sockets. Queries, commands, and results are transmitted between the client and server over sockets. This mode allows the database server to run on one machine, while database clients run on separate machines. In embedded mode, the classes for the Derby engine are embedded in your program and executed in the same thread as your application. In this section, we will only use embedded mode, but only minor changes are required to create a program that runs under server mode.

Application programs typically access databases through several layers of abstraction. The lowest level is the database engine, which handles tasks such as indexing, storing, and retrieving data from the disk drive. In our case, these tasks are performed by the Derby engine. A set of higher-level classes provides a connection to Derby along with a consistent interface so that few code changes are necessary at higher levels if the underlying database provider is changed. **Java Database Connectivity (JDBC)** is a common API used to access databases. JDBC is included in version 5 or higher of the Java SDK. Various Microsoft and Oracle database systems are among the many commercially available database systems that are compatible with JDBC, along with Derby. Typically, you need to download and install a JDBC driver for your database system. Conceptually, JDBC is simple: Establish a connection to a database system (either on your computer or over the Internet) and execute database commands, and do this all within your Java code.

SQL

Finally, applications send commands and queries to JDBC using strings formatted in **SQL**. SQL is a standard for database access that has been adopted by virtually all relational database vendors. The initials *SQL* stand for *Structured Query Language*. Display 19.9 illustrates the relationships among these components for an embedded Derby database.

Display 19.9   Relationships between JDBC, Embedded Derby, and SQL

SQL

SQL is pronounced either by saying the letters or by saying the word "sequel." SQL is a language for formulating queries for a relational database. SQL is not part of Java, but JDBC allows you to embed SQL commands in your Java code.

SQL works with relational databases. As an example, suppose we were organizing a catalog of books and authors. A relational database can be thought of as a collection of named tables with rows and columns, such as those shown in Display 19.10. In this case, we have created a table with author information (author name, unique author ID, and URL), a table with book information (title and ISBN), and a table that identifies which author has written which book (unique author ID and ISBN).

In this brief introduction, we will not go into the details of the constraints on tables. However, to see that there are some constraints, note that in the three tables in Display 19.10, no relationship is repeated. If we had one entry for each book with all the information—title, author, ISBN number,[1] and author's URL—then there would be two entries giving Dan Simmons' URL, because he has two books in our database.

To manipulate the database, we issue SQL commands, also known as SQL queries, to the database. The following is a sample SQL command:

```
SELECT Titles.Title, Titles.ISBN, BooksAuthors.Author_ID
FROM Titles, BooksAuthors
WHERE Titles.ISBN = BooksAuthors.ISBN
```

---

[1]The ISBN number is a unique identification number assigned to (almost) every book published.

Display 19.10 Relational Database Tables

Names

AUTHOR	AUTHOR_ID	URL
Adams, Douglas	1	http:// ...
Simmons, Dan	2	http:// ...
Stephenson, Neal	3	http:// ...

Titles

TITLE	ISBN
Snow Crash	0-553-38095-8
Endymion	0-553-57294-6
The Hitchhikers Guide to the Galaxy	0-671-46149-4
The Rise of Endymion	0-553-57298-9

BooksAuthors

ISBN	AUTHOR_ID
0-553-38095-8	3
0-553-57294-6	2
0-671-46149-4	1
0-553-57298-9	2

Display 19.11 Result of SQL Command in Text

Result

TITLE	ISBN	AUTHOR_ID
Snow Crash	0-553-38095-8	3
Endymion	0-553-57294-6	2
The Hitchhikers Guide to the Galaxy	0-671-46149-4	1
The Rise of Endymion	0-553-57298-9	2

This will produce the table shown in Display 19.11. That table contains all titles with matching ISBN number and author ID. The ISBN number is the bridge that connects the tables Titles and BooksAuthors.

As a more detailed example, let us connect to an embedded Derby database and issue the SQL commands to create a new table, insert a new row (record) into the table, select rows, and modify rows. Note that this is not a comprehensive list of commands but rather a small subset of SQL.

First, our Java program must import the SQL libraries java.sql.Connection, java.sql.DriverManager, java.sql.SQLException, and java.sql.Statement. When processing results, we will also need to import java.sql.ResultSet. Next we must load the database drivers:

```
String driver = "org.apache.derby.jdbc.EmbeddedDriver";
Class.forName(driver).newInstance( );
```

This code throws three checked exceptions that must be caught: `ClassNotFound Exception`, `InstantiationException`, and `IllegalAccessException`. For simplicity, we catch only the superclass `Exception` in the code shown in Display 19.12.

Once the database drivers are loaded, we can connect to the database. This is done by passing a **connection string** to the `DriverManager.getConnection` method. The connection string specifies the protocol, database name, and other parameters, such as whether or not a new database should be created. For example, to connect to and create a database named `BookDatabase` using Derby, we would use

connection string

```
Connection conn = null;
conn = DriverManager.getConnection(
        "jdbc:derby:BookDatabase; create = true");
```

This creates a subdirectory named `BookDatabase` in the active working directory that will contain the database, files. You could specify a pathname in front of `BookDatabase` if you want to create the database somewhere else on the file system. If you ever wish to delete the database, then simply delete the `BookDatabase` directory. Note that if the database already exists, then the attribute `create=true` will not delete the existing database but will instead connect to the existing database.

Additional parameters are specified in the command string by separating them with semicolons. For example, if the database requires a username and password, then the connection string would look like this:

```
conn = DriverManager.getConnection
        ("jdbc:derby:BookDatabase;create=true;user=username;" +
        "password = pass");
```

When we are finished accessing the database, invoke the `close( )` method to close the connection. The `DriverManager.getConnection( )` method requires that `SQLException` be caught, so this code should be placed inside an appropriate try/catch block.

SQL commands or queries can be issued to JDBC once the database connection is established. First, a `Statement` object must be constructed and then invoked by calling the `execute` or `executeQuery` method with a SQL string as its argument. The `execute` method can be used to execute any SQL statement, but it is generally used for SQL commands where return values are not needed or ignored (e.g., creating a new table or deleting a row). It returns `true` if the command results in a set of data and `false` if there is no result or an update count. The `executeQuery` method is used with a SQL query that is expected to return some rows from the database. It returns a `ResultSet` object that contains the data produced by the query. These methods throw `SQLException` if there is a database error. Display 19.12 illustrates how to create a new table and insert three rows using the `CREATE TABLE` and `INSERT` commands. The result is identical to the `names` table in Display 19.10. Note that the program should only be run once. If you attempt to run it a second time, the program will throw an exception when executing the `CREATE TABLE` command, because it is invalid to create a new table that matches an existing name.

Common SQL Statements

SQL Statements are constructed as strings and passed to JDBC. The syntax and examples for the `CREATE TABLE`, `INSERT`, `UPDATE`, and `SELECT` statements follow.

SYNTAX

`CREATE TABLE`	Create a new table named newtable with fields `field1`, `field2`, etc. Data types are similar to Java and include: `int`, `bigint`, `float`, `double`, and `var(size)` which is equivalent to a `String` of maximum length `size`.	`CREATE TABLE newtable (field1 datatype, field2 datatype, ...)`
`INSERT`	Insert a new row into the table tableName where `field1` has the value `field1Value`, `field2` has the value `field2Value`, etc. The data types for the values must match those for the corresponding fields when the table was created. String values should be enclosed in single quotes.	`INSERT INTO tableName VALUES (field1Value, field2Value, ...)`
`UPDATE`	Change the specified fields to the new values for any rows that match the `WHERE` clause. Op is a comparison operator such as `=`, `<>` (not equal to), `<`, `>`, etc.	`UPDATE tableNameSET field1 = newValue, field2 = newValue, ...WHERE fieldName Op someValue`
`SELECT`	Retrieve the specified fields for the rows that match the `WHERE` clause. The `*` may be used to retrieve all fields. Omit the `WHERE` clause to retrieve all rows from the table.	`SELECT field1, field2 FROM tableName WHERE fieldname Op someValue`

EXAMPLE

```
CREATE TABLE names(author varchar(50), author_id int, url
     varchar(80))
INSERT INTO names VALUES ('Adams, Douglas', 1, 'http://
     www.douglasadams.com')
UPDATE names SET url = 'http://www.douglasadams.com/dna/bio.html'
     WHERE author_id = 1
SELECT author, author_id, url FROM names
SELECT author, author_id, url FROM names WHERE author_id > 1
```

Display 19.12   **Creating a Derby Embedded Database and Table** (part 1 of 2)

```
1   import java.sql.Connection;
2   import java.sql.DriverManager;
3   import java.sql.SQLException;
4   import java.sql.Statement;

5   public class CreateDB
6   {
7       private static final String driver =
            "org.apache.derby.jdbc.EmbeddedDriver";
8       private static final String protocol = "jdbc:derby:";
9       public static void main(String[] args)
10      {
11          try                         Load the embedded Derby driver.

12          {
13              Class.forName(driver).newInstance();
14              System.out.println("Loaded the embedded driver.");
15          }
16          catch (Exception err)        Must catch ClassNotFoundException,
                                         InstantiationException, Illegal
                                         AccessException.
17          {
18              System.err.println("Unable to load the embedded driver.");
19              err.printStackTrace(System.err);
20              System.exit(0);
21          }

22          String dbName = "BookDatabase";
23          Connection conn = null;
24          try
25          {
26              System.out.println(
                  "Connecting to and creating the database...");
27              conn = DriverManager.getConnection(protocol + dbName +
                  ";create=true");
28              System.out.println("Database created.");
                                                         Create a statement object
                                                         to run SQL statements.
29              Statement s = conn.createStatement();
                                                     Create a table called
                                                     "names" with three
30              s.execute("CREATE TABLE names" +      fields, 50 characters
31                  "(author varchar(50), author_id " +  for an author and an
                    "int, url varchar(80))");         integer author ID,
32              System.out.println("Created 'names' table.");  and 80 characters
                                                         for a URL, then insert
33              System.out.println("Inserting authors.");  sample data.
34              s.execute("INSERT INTO names " +
35                  "VALUES ('Adams, Douglas', 1," +
                    "'http://www.douglasadams.com')");
```

(continued)

Display 19.12 **Creating a Derby Embedded Database and Table** (part 2 of 2)

```
36              s.execute("INSERT INTO names " +
37                "VALUES ('Simmons, Dan', 2, 'http://www.dansimmons.com')");
38              s.execute("INSERT INTO names " +
39                "VALUES ('Stephenson, Neal', 3, " +
                        "'http://www.nealstephenson.com')");
40              System.out.println("Authors inserted.");
41               conn.close();
42          }
43      catch (SQLException err)
44      {
45              System.err.println("SQL error.");
46              err.printStackTrace(System.err);
47              System.exit(0);
48          }
49        }
50    }
```

Sample Dialogue

```
Loaded the embedded driver.
Connecting to and creating the database.
Database created.
Created 'names' table.
Inserting authors.
Authors inserted.
```

Display 19.13 shows how to retrieve rows from an existing database and table using the SELECT statement. The syntax of the SELECT statement is given in the box "Common SQL Statements." The desired fields must be specified or an * placed after the SELECT statement to retrieve all fields. After specifying the name of the table, an optional WHERE clause may be inserted that contains conditions that must be met, much like the Boolean condition you might place after an if statement. If the WHERE clause is left off, then all rows from the table will be retrieved. Otherwise, only those rows that match the conditions of the WHERE clause are returned.

A SELECT statement can be executed by invoking the executeQuery( ) method of a Statement object. The return value is an object of type ResultSet. The ResultSet object maintains a cursor to each matching row in the database. Initially, the cursor is positioned before the first row. The next( ) method is used to advance the cursor to the next row. If there is no next row, then false is returned. Otherwise, true is returned. Typically, a while loop is used to iterate over all rows in the set by looping until the next( ) method returns false. Note that iteration is forward only, similar to reading data from an input stream. Once the cursor is positioned over a row, we can use one of following methods to retrieve data from a specific column in the current row:

```
intVal = resultSet.getInt("name of int field");
lngVal = resultSet.getLong("name of bigint field");
strVal = resultSet.getString("name of varchar field");
dblVal = resultSet.getDouble("name of double field");
fltVal = resultSet.getFloat("name of float field");
```

The program in Display 19.13 can run once the database is created with the program given in Display 19.12. It retrieves and outputs all rows in the table by executing a SELECT query with no WHERE clause and then retrieves and outputs only those rows with any author_id greater than 1. Invoke the close( ) method to free resources when finished using a ResultSet object.

Finally, we can change the contents of an existing row using the SQL UPDATE command. In the UPDATE command, we specify the table, field(s) to change, new value(s), and a WHERE clause to indicate which rows should be changed. If the WHERE clause is omitted, then every row in the table is updated. The syntax is described in the box "Common SQL Statements." Display 19.14 shows an example where the URL field is changed to a new value entered by the user. The URL field is only changed for the row that matches the author_id entered by the user.

Display 19.13   Retrieving Rows with the SELECT Statement (part 1 of 3)

```
1   import java.sql.Connection;            The database must be created (Display 19.12)
2   import java.sql.DriverManager;         before running the program.
3   import java.sql.ResultSet;
4   import java.sql.SQLException;
5   import java.sql.Statement;

6   public class ReadDB
7   {
8       private static final String driver =
            "org.apache.derby.jdbc.EmbeddedDriver";
9       private static final String protocol = "jdbc:derby:";

10      /*
11      Outputs the author, ID, and URL of the current
12      author in the ResultSet
13      */
14      public static void displayNameRow(ResultSet rs) throws SQLException

15      {
16          int id = rs.getInt("author_id");        The accessor methods
17          String author = rs.getString("author"); throw the checked exception
18          String url = rs.getString("url");       SQLException.
```

(continued)

Display 19.13 **Retrieving Rows with the SELECT Statement** (part 2 of 3)

```
19              System.out.println("ID = " + id + ", Author = "
20                          + author + ", URL = " + url);
21          }

22      public static void main(String[] args)
23      {
24      try
25      {
26              Class.forName(driver).newInstance();
27              System.out.println("Loaded the embedded driver.");
28      }
29      catch (Exception err)
30      {
31              System.err.println("Unable to load the embedded driver.");
32              err.printStackTrace(System.err);
33              System.exit(0);
34      }

35      String dbName = "BookDatabase";
36      Connection conn = null;
37      try
38      {
39              System.out.println("Connecting to the database...");
40              conn = DriverManager.getConnection(protocol + dbName);

41      System.out.println("Connected.");

42      Statement s = conn.createStatement();

43      ResultSet rs = null;
44      System.out.println("All rows:");
45      rs = s.executeQuery("SELECT author, author_id, url FROM names");
46      while( rs.next() )
47      {
48              displayNameRow(rs);
49      }
50      rs.close();

51      System.out.println();
52      System.out.println("All rows with an ID > 1:");
53      rs = s.executeQuery("SELECT author, author_id, url " +
54          "FROM names WHERE author_id > 1");
55      while( rs.next() )
56      {
57              displayNameRow(rs);
58      }
```

The text `create=true;` *has been left off the connection string to connect to an existing database.*

Display 19.13   **Retrieving Rows with the SELECT Statement** (part 3 of 3)

```
59        rs.close();
60        Conn.close();
61        }
62        catch (SQLException err)
63        {
64                System.err.println("SQL error.");
65                err.printStackTrace(System.err);
66                System.exit(0);
67                }
68        }
69   }
```

Sample Dialogue

```
Loaded the embedded driver.
Connecting to the database.
Connected.
All rows:
ID = 1, Author = Adams, Douglas, URL = http://www.douglasadams.com
ID = 2, Author = Simmons, Dan, URL = http://www.dansimmons.com
ID = 3, Author = Stephenson, Neal, URL = http://www.nealstephenson.com

All rows with an ID > 1:
ID = 2, Author = Simmons, Dan, URL = http://www.dansimmons.com
ID = 3, Author = Stephenson, Neal, URL = http://www.nealstephenson.com
```

Display 19.14   **Updating Rows with the UPDATE Statement** (part 1 of 3)

```
1    import java.sql.Connection;
2    import java.sql.DriverManager;
3    import java.sql.ResultSet;
4    import java.sql.SQLException;
5    import java.sql.Statement;
6    import java.util.Scanner;

7    public class UpdateDB
8    {
9         private static final String driver =
               "org.apache.derby.jdbc.EmbeddedDriver";
10        private static final String protocol = "jdbc:derby:";
```

The database must be created (Display 19.12) before running this program. Use the program in Display 19.13 to view the changes made by this program.

(continued)

Display 19.14   Updating Rows with the **UPDATE** Statement (part 2 of 3)

```
11        public static void main(String[] args)
12        {
13            try
14            {
15                    Class.forName(driver).newInstance();
16                    System.out.println("Loaded the embedded driver.");
17            }
18            catch (Exception err)
19            {
20                    System.err.println("Unable to load the embedded
                        driver.");
21                err.printStackTrace(System.err);
22                System.exit(0);
23            }
24            String dbName = "BookDatabase";
25            Connection conn = null;
26            try
27            {
28                System.out.println("Connecting to the database...");
29                conn = DriverManager.getConnection(protocol + dbName);
30                System.out.println("Connected.");

31                System.out.println(
                        "Enter the ID number of the author to change:");
32                Scanner scan = new Scanner(System.in);
33                int id = scan.nextInt();          kips the newline left after nextInt().
34                scan.nextLine();
35                System.out.println("Enter the new URL for this author.");
36                String newURL = scan.nextLine();

37                Statement s = conn.createStatement();
38                s.execute("UPDATE names " +
39                        "SET URL = '" + newURL + "' WHERE author_id = "
                        + id);
40                System.out.println("URL changed to " + newURL);
41                conn.close();
42            }
43            catch (SQLException err)
44            {
45                System.err.println("SQL error.");
46                err.printStackTrace(System.err);
47                System.exit(0);
48            }
49        }
50    }
```

Display 19.14   Updating Rows with the UPDATE Statement (part 3 of 3)

Sample Dialogue

```
Loaded the embedded driver.
Connecting to the database...
Connected.
Enter the ID number of the author to change:
2
Enter the new URL for this author:
http://www.dansimmons.com/about/bio.htm
URL changed to http://www.dansimmons.com/about/bio.htm
```

There is much more to SQL and JDBC than what we have discussed here. However, this section should give you a good idea about how to integrate SQL into a Java application and provide a starting point to learn more.

Self-Test Exercises

9. Give the SQL SELECT command to produce a table of book titles with corresponding author and author ID from the table Result in Display 19.11 and one of the tables in Display 19.10. Follow the example of the SQL command in the text used to produce the Result table.

10. What is a connection string?

11. What is the difference between the execute( ) and executeQuery( ) methods of the JDBC Statement class?

12. Give the SQL statement to create the BooksAuthors table shown in Display 19.10.

13. Give the SQL statement to insert the four entries shown in Display 19.10 into the BooksAuthors table.

19.5 **Web Programming with Java Server Pages**

Everything is connected... no one thing can change by itself.

PAUL HAWKEN

Up to this point, we have used Java to create stand-alone applications. However, Java is also used to create interactive websites. In this section, we briefly introduce ways that Java can be used on the Web with an emphasis on Java Server Pages. This section requires a basic understanding of HTML. An introduction to HTML is given in Chapter 20, which is included on the website with this book. This section is not a complete enough introduction to allow you to immediately start writing Java Web applications. The intent is to introduce the major concepts behind Java Server Pages so you can learn what kinds of things are possible should you wish to learn more with a book or other resource dedicated to the topic.

Applets, Servlets, and Java Server Pages

When you instruct your Web browser to view a page from a Web server on the Internet, your Web browser requests the page from the Web server, the Web server processes the request (which may involve reading the requested page from a file on the hard drive), and then the Web server sends the requested page to your Web browser. Your Web browser formats, or renders, the received data to fit on your computer screen. This interaction is a specific case of the client/server model described in Section 19.2. Your Web browser is the client program, your computer is the client computer, the remote website is the server computer (e.g., http://www.remotesite.com), and the Web server software running on the remote website is the server program.

In the context of a Web application, the client/server model is important because Java code can run in two places: on the client or on the server. There are trade-offs to both approaches. Server-based programs have easy access to information that resides on the server, such as customer orders or inventory data. Because all of the computation is done on the server and results are transmitted to the client as HTML, a client does not need a powerful computer to run a server-based program. On the other hand, a client-based program may require a more powerful client computer, because all computation is performed locally. However, richer interaction is possible, because the client program has access to local resources, such as the graphics display (e.g., perhaps using Swing) or the operating system. Many systems today are constructed using code that runs on both the client and the server to reap the benefit of both approaches.

Web applications built with Java include **Java applets**, **Java servlets**, and **Java Server Pages (JSP)**. Java applets run on the client computer and are discussed in Chapter 20. JavaScript, which is a different language than Java despite its similar name, also runs on the client computer as part of the Web browser. Java servlets and Java Server Pages run on the server. In this chapter, we focus primarily on Java Server Pages, which are a dynamic version of Java servlets. Servlets must be compiled before they can run, just like a normal Java program. In contrast, JSP code is embedded with the corresponding HTML and is compiled "on the fly" into a servlet when the page

Java applet

Java servlet

Java Server Pages

Display 19.15   **Running a Java Applet**

(1) The client's Web browser sends a request to the server for a Web page with a Java applet.

(2) The server sends the HTML for the Web page and applet class files to the client.

(3) The client runs the applet using the Java Virtual Machine and displays its output in the Web browser.

Display 19.16   **Running a Java Servlet**

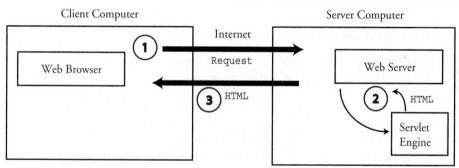

(1) The client's Web browser sends a request to the server for a Web page that runs a Java servlet.

(2) The Web server instructs the servlet engine to execute the requested servlet, which consists of running precompiled Java code. The servlet outputs HTML that is returned to the Web server.

(3) The Web server sends the servlet's HTML to the client's Web browser to be displayed.

is requested. This flexibility can make it easier to develop Web applications using JSP than with Java servlets. Displays 19.15, 19.16, and 19.17 illustrate the differences for a website that runs an applet, servlet, or JSP.

Display 19.17   **Running a Java Server Page (JSP) Program**

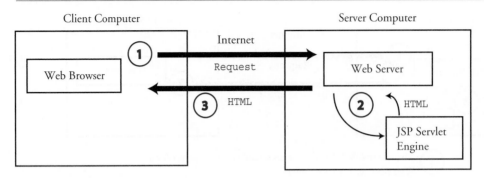

The client's Web browser sends a request to the server for a Web page that contains JSP code.

The JSP servlet engine dynamically compiles the JSP source code into a Java servlet if a current, compiled servlet doesn't exist.
The servlet runs and outputs HTML that is returned to the Web server.

The Web server sends the servlet's HTML to the client's Web browser to be displayed.

Oracle GlassFish Enterprise Server

JSP requires a Web server with a JSP servlet engine. In this section, we will use the Oracle GlassFish Enterprise Server, previously known as the Sun Java System Application Server. It is distributed by Oracle as part of the Java Enterprise Edition SDK. However, you may use any Web server that supports Java servlets and JSP. Another popular choice is the open source Apache Tomcat server. Follow the installation instructions that come with the server that you select.

The GlassFish server will ask you to select an administrator username and password during the installation procedure. It will also ask you for a location on the hard drive to place the server files. We will refer to the pathname you select as <glassfish_home>. On a Windows machine, this may default to C:\Sun\SDK. After the installation is complete, start the GlassFish Web service. If the installation is successful, then you should be able to see the administrator's page by opening http://localhost:4848 in your Web browser. The default URL for accessing applications is http://localhost:8080. Substitute localhost with the name of the machine if you are using a remote server.

At this point, you can test your server by creating or copying an HTML file into <glassfish_home>\domains\domain1\docroot and opening it with your Web browser. For example, if you create an HTML file named test.html in this directory, then you should be able to access it with your Web browser by navigating to http://localhost:8080/test.html. If you cannot read the page, check your configuration settings. To run JSP programs, your Web browser must open the page through the GlassFish Web server and not directly load the page from the HTML file on the disk drive.

HTML Forms—the Common Gateway Interface

HTML Form

The HTML form is a common mechanism for users to input data to Web applications. If you have ever visited a Web page in which you enter data using textboxes and buttons, then you have used an HTML form. In this section, we introduce just a handful of tags that can be used in an HTML form and then show how submitted data can be processed by a JSP program. The information you enter into an HTML form is transmitted to the Web server using a protocol called the **Common Gateway Interface (CGI)**. The server processes the information using a program such as a Java servlet and then returns the results back to the user.

Common Gateway Interface

An HTML form is created with the `<form>`tag. The syntax is as follows:

```
<FORM ACTION="Path_To_CGI_Program" METHOD="GET or POST">
     Form_Elements
</FORM>
```

The ACTION string identifies the program that will process the form input. In our case, this will consist of a JSP program. The METHOD string specifies how data will be sent to the server and is either GET or POST. GET means that the data will be sent as part of the URL while POST means that the data will be sent as part of the data and will not be visible in the URL.

Elements that can be inserted inside the form include selection lists, textboxes, checkboxes, radio buttons, and several other common GUI widgets. In this section, we will only introduce textboxes and submission buttons. A textbox has the following syntax:

```
<INPUT TYPE="TEXT" NAME="Textbox_Name" VALUE="Default_Text"
SIZE="Length_In._Characters"
MAXLENGTH="Maximum_Number_Of_Allowable_Characters">
```

All of the attributes are optional except for the input type. However, the name of the textbox will be required to retrieve the textbox's value from JSP. If you would like a default value to be entered in the textbox, you can put it in the VALUE field or leave it blank for no text. The SIZE field controls the length of the textbox while MAXLENGTH limits the number of characters that may be entered.

The submission button has the following syntax:

```
<INPUT TYPE="SUBMIT" NAME="Name" VALUE="Button_Text">
```

The NAME field can be used to identify the submission button in case there are multiple submission buttons and you wish to identify which one was clicked. VALUE determines what text is placed in the button's label.

A sample form with two text fields and a submission button is shown in Display 19.18. The form, when opened in a Web browser, is shown in Display 19.19. It asks the user to enter an Author ID and a new URL with the intent of changing the URL to the submitted value for the specified Author ID. Because we have not created a JSP program that processes the form, the Web browser will display an error message if the Submit button is clicked. We will write the JSP program in the next subsection.

Display 19.18 An HTML Form Document

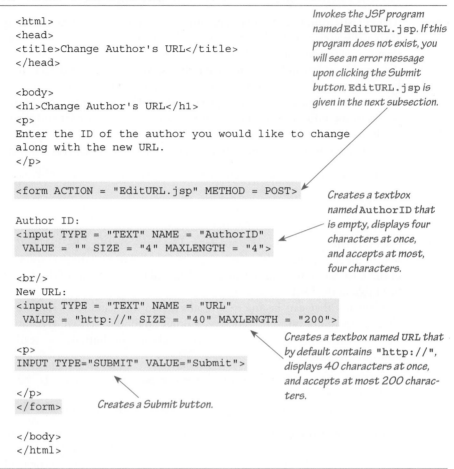

```
<html>
<head>
<title>Change Author's URL</title>
</head>

<body>
<h1>Change Author's URL</h1>
<p>
Enter the ID of the author you would like to change
along with the new URL.
</p>

<form ACTION = "EditURL.jsp" METHOD = POST>

Author ID:
<input TYPE = "TEXT" NAME = "AuthorID"
  VALUE = "" SIZE = "4" MAXLENGTH = "4">

<br/>
New URL:
<input TYPE = "TEXT" NAME = "URL"
  VALUE = "http://" SIZE = "40" MAXLENGTH = "200">

<p>
INPUT TYPE="SUBMIT" VALUE="Submit">

</p>
</form>

</body>
</html>
```

Invokes the JSP program named EditURL.jsp. If this program does not exist, you will see an error message upon clicking the Submit button. EditURL.jsp is given in the next subsection.

Creates a textbox named AuthorID that is empty, displays four characters at once, and accepts at most, four characters.

Creates a textbox named URL that by default contains "http://", displays 40 characters at once, and accepts at most 200 characters.

Creates a Submit button.

Display 19.19 Browser View of Display 19.18

Change Author's URL

Enter the ID of the author you would like to change along with the new URL.

Author ID: [   ]
New URL: [http://   ]

[Submit]

JSP Declarations, Expressions, Scriptlets, and Directives

A JSP Web page is created the same way you make an HTML file, except JSP code is added along with the HTML code. Additionally, instead of naming the file with an extension of `.HTM` or `.HTML`, the extension is `.JSP`. The file should be placed in the root folder of your Web server so it can be accessed by and processed through the Web server.

JSP elements

declaration

The JSP elements we will briefly discuss are **declarations**, **expressions**, **scriptlets**, and **directives**. All of these elements are identified by their own tags. The **declarations** tag allows us to define variables and methods. The variables and methods are accessible from any scriptlets and expressions on the same page. Variable declarations are compiled as instance variables for a class that corresponds to the JSP page. Declarations are defined with the syntax

```
<%!
    Declarations
%>
```

For example, the following defines an instance variable named `count` and a method named `incrementCount` that increments the `count` variable:

```
<%!
    private int count = 0;

    private void incrementCount()
    {
        count++;
    }
%>
```

expression

We can access variables defined in declarations with **expression**. The syntax to embed an expression is as follows:

```
<%=
    Expression
%>
```

Expressions are embedded directly into the HTML. The Web browser will display the value of the expression in place of the tag. For example, we can output the value of the `count` variable in bold type with the following piece of HTML:

```
The value of count is <b> <%= count %> </b>
```

scriptlet

Blocks of Java code can be embedded in a **scriptlet**. The syntax for a scriptlet is as follows:

```
<%
    Java code
%>
```

If you wish to output HTML within a scriptlet, then this is done using `out.println()`, which is used in the same manner as `System.out.println( )`. The variable `out` is already defined for us and is of type `javax.servlet.jsp.JspWriter`. Also note that

`System.out.println( )` will output to the console, which is useful for debugging purposes, while `out.println( )` will output to the browser. The following scriptlet invokes the `incrementCount( )` method and then outputs the value in `count`:

```
<%
    out.println("The counter's value is " + count + "<br />");
    incrementCount();
%>
```

Display 19.20 is a JSP page with a declaration, expression, and scriptlet that outputs text inside a header tag from levels 1 to 6. The identifier LASTLEVEL is declared as the last heading level that is to be displayed. LASTLEVEL is modified by `static final`, because it is intended as a constant. A loop inside the scriptlet outputs sample text for each level. The HTML that is generated by the JSP page is shown in Display 19.21, and the browser view is shown in Display 19.22.

Display 19.20   JSP Code to Display Heading Levels

```
1    <html>
2    <title>
3    Displaying Heading Tags with JSP
4    </title>

5    <body>
6    <%!
7        private static final int LASTLEVEL = 6;          ← JSP declaration.
8    %>

9    <p>
10   This page uses JSP to display Heading Tags from
11   Level 1 to Level <%= LASTLEVEL %>  ← JSP expression that evaluates
12   </p>                                   to the value 6.

13   <%                                     JSP scriptlet that contains
14       int i;                             a block of Java code.
15       for (i = 1; i <= LASTLEVEL; i++)  ←
16       {
17           out.println("<H" + i + ">" +
18              "This text is in Heading Level " + i +
19              "</H" + i + ">");
20       }
21   %>

22   </body>
23   </html>
```

Display 19.21   HTML Generated by JSP in Display 19.20

```
<html>
<title>
Displaying Heading Tags with JSP
</title>

<body>

<p>
This page uses JSP to display Heading Tags from
Level 1 to Level 6
</p>

<H1>This text is in Heading Level 1</H1>
<H2>This text is in Heading Level 2</H2>
<H3>This text is in Heading Level 3</H3>
<H4>This text is in Heading Level 4</H4>
<H5>This text is in Heading Level 5</H5>
<H6>This text is in Heading Level 6</H6>

</body>
</html>
```

Display 19.22   Browser View of Display 19.21

This page uses JSP to display Heading Tags from Level 1 to Level 6

This text is in Heading Level 1

This text is in Heading Level 2

This text is in Heading Level 3

This text is in Heading Level 4

This text is in Heading Level 5

This text is in Heading Level 6

To make a JSP page more interactive, we can read and process the data entered in an HTML form. One way to read these values is to call the `request.getParameter` method. This method takes a `String` parameter as input that identifies the name of an HTML form element and returns the value entered by the user for that element on the form. For example, if there is a textbox named `AuthorID`, then we can retrieve the value entered in that textbox with the following scriptlet code:

```
String value = request.getParameter("AuthorID");
```

If the user leaves the field blank, then `getParameter` returns an empty string. A simple example is given in Display 19.23. This JSP program echoes back the data entered by the user in Display 19.18. The name of the JSP file must match the value supplied for the `ACTION` tag of the form. In this case, the name is `EditURL.jsp`.

Display 19.23   Echoing Values Submitted by a Browser Viewing Display 19.18

```
<html>
<title>Edit URL: Echo submitted values</title>
<body>
<h2>Edit URL>/h2>
```

This program should be saved as `EditURL.jsp` and must match the value in the `ACTION` field of the HTML form tag.

```
<p>
This version of EditURL.jsp simply echoes back to the
user the values that were entered in the textboxes.
</p>
```

The `getParameter` method calls return as Strings the values entered by the user in the URL and `AuthorID` textboxes from Display 19.18.

```
<%
    String url = request.getParameter("URL");
    String stringID = request.getParameter("AuthorID");
    int author_id = Integer.parseInt(stringID);
    out.println("The submitted author ID is: " + author_id);
    out.println("<br/>");
    out.println("The submitted URL is: " + url);
%>
</body>
</html>
```

Sample Dialogue   *Submitted on the Web browser when viewing Display 19.18.*

```
Author ID:
2
New URL:
http://www.dansimmons.com/about/bio.htm

Edit URL        Web browser display after clicking Submit.

This version of EditURL.jsp simply echoes back to the user the
values that were entered in the textboxes.

The submitted author ID is: 2
The submitted URL is:
http://www.dansimmons.com/about/bio.htm
```

directive

Finally, let us introduce one more JSP tag, the **directive**. In general terms, directives instruct the compiler how to process a JSP program. Examples include the definition of our own tags, including the source code of other files, and importing packages. The syntax for directives is as follows:

```
<%@
    Directives
%>
```

page import

In this introduction, we will cover only the **page import** directive. The purpose of this directive is the same as the normal Java `import` statement, but the syntax is slightly different. First, we identify the directive and then specify the packages to import inside a string. Multiple packages are separated by a comma, e.g.,

```
<%@
    page import="java.util.*,java.sql.*"
%>
```

A JSP program that uses Derby to create an embedded database is shown in Display 19.24. The page import directive is used to import the necessary SQL packages. The program in Display 19.24 is almost identical to the stand-alone program in Display 19.12, except all of the code has been moved into a scriptlet. If the JSP program is in a file named `CreateDB.jsp`, then it would be invoked by navigating to `http://localhost:8080/CreateDB.jsp`. The database files on a GlassFish server will be created in `<glassfish_home>\domains\domain1\config` if you do not specify a pathname. If you run the program more than once, then it will throw an exception the second time, because the database table `names` already exists and cannot be created again. If you wish to start over with a new database, then you can delete the `BookDatabase` directory in the `<glassfish_home>\domains\domain1\config` directory.

Display 19.24   JSP Program to Create a Derby Database and Table (part 1 of 3)

```
1   <%@ page import="java.sql.*" %>          Directive to import the Java
2   <html>                                   SQL packages.
3   <title>Create New Database</title>
4   <body>
5   <H2>Create New Database</h2>

6   <p>
7   This program creates a new Derby database named 'BookDatabase'
8   and puts sample data into the 'person' table.
9   </p>

10  <%
11      String driver = "org.apache.derby.jdbc.EmbeddedDriver";
12      String protocol = "jdbc:derby:";
```

Refer to Display 19.12 for an explanation of the database code in this scriptlet.

(continued)

Display 19.24 JSP Program to Create a Derby Database and Table (part 2 of 3)

```
13        try
14        {
15              Class.forName(driver).newInstance();
16              out.println("Loaded the embedded driver.<br>");
17        }
18        catch (Exception err)
19        {
20              out.println(
                    "Unable to load the embedded driver.</body></html>");
21              return;          A return statement will
22        }                       terminate the JSP program.

23   String dbName = "BookDatabase";
24   Connection conn = null;
25   try
26   {
27              out.println(
                    "Connecting to and creating the database...<br />");
28              conn = DriverManager.getConnection(protocol + dbName +
                                                        ";create=true");
29              out.println("Connected.<br />");

30        Statement s = conn.createStatement();

31        s.execute("CREATE TABLE names" +
32              "(author varchar(50), author_id int, url varchar(80))");
33        out.println("Created 'names' table.<br />");

34        out.println("Inserting authors.<br />");
35        s.execute("INSERT INTO names " +
36              "VALUES ('Adams, Douglas', 1, 'http://www.douglasadams.com')");
37        s.execute("INSERT INTO names " +
38              "VALUES ('Simmons, Dan', 2, 'http://www.dansimmons.com')");
39        s.execute("INSERT INTO names " +
40              "VALUES ('Stephenson, Neal', 3," +
                    "'http://www.nealstephenson.com')");
41        out.println("Authors inserted.<br />");

42        conn.close();
43        }
44        catch (Exception err)
45        {
46          out.println("SQL error.<br />");
47        }
48   %>
49   </body>
50   </html>
```

Display 19.24 JSP Program to Create a Derby Database and Table (part 3 of 3)

Sample Dialogue

Create New Database

This program creates a new Derby database named 'BookDatabase'
and puts sample data into the 'names' table.

Loaded the embedded driver.

Connecting to and creating the database...

Connected.

Created 'names' table.

Inserting authors.

Authors inserted.

In this second part, to complete our example, let us modify the EditURL.jsp program from Display 19.23 to make it change the contents of the database instead of echoing back values submitted by the HTML form. Our new program will require running the program in Display 19.24 once in order to create and initialize the database. Once this is done, you can open the HTML form in Display 19.18 in a Web browser, which prompts the user to submit a new URL for an author ID, and then the new URL will be updated in the database by the program in Display 19.25. The program in Display 19.25 is a combination of Display 19.14 (updating a Derby database) and Display 19.23 (echoing values submitted by a Web browser). Instead of prompting the user to input an author ID and new URL from the console as in Display 19.14, these values are submitted to the JSP program by the HTML form in Display 19.18. The JSP program then updates the database to the submitted values in the same manner as the program in Display 19.14.

Display 19.25 JSP Program to Update Database Entries Submitted by a Browser Viewing
Display 19.18 (part 1 of 3)

```
1   <%@ page import="java.sql.*" %>
2   <html>
3   <title>Edit URL: Update new URL in a database</title>
4   <body>
5   <h2>Edit URL</h2>

6   <p>
7   This version of EditURL.jsp updates the URL field
8   of a Derby database to the submitted value for the
9   row with a matching Author ID.
10  </p>

11  <%
12  String newURL = request.getParameter("URL");
13  String stringID = request.getParameter("AuthorID");
14  int author_id = Integer.parseInt(stringID);
```

This program should be saved as EditURL.jsp and must match the value in the ACTION field of the HTML form tag.

The getParameter method calls return as Strings the values entered by the user in the URL and AuthorID textboxes from Display 19.18.

(continued)

Display 19.25   JSP Program to Update Database Entries Submitted by a Browser Viewing
Display 19.18 (part 2 of 3)

```
15  String driver = "org.apache.derby.jdbc.EmbeddedDriver";
16  String protocol = "jdbc:derby:";          Refer to Displays 19.13 and 19.14 for
17  try                                        an explanation of the database code in
18  {                                          this scriptlet.
19    Class.forName(driver).newInstance();
20      out.println("Loaded the embedded driver.<br>");
21  }
22  catch (Exception err)
23  {
24    out.println("Unable to load the embedded driver.</body></html>");
25    return;
26  }

27  String dbName = "BookDatabase";
28  Connection conn = null;
29  try
30  {
31    out.println("Connecting to and creating the database...<br />");
32        conn = DriverManager.getConnection(protocol + dbName +
                                                   ";create=true");
33    out.println("Connected.<br />");

34    Statement s = conn.createStatement();     The URL in the database is changed to the
35    s.execute("UPDATE names " +               submitted value if the Author IDs match.
36      "SET URL = '" + newURL + "' WHERE author_id = " + author_id);
37    out.println("<br/><b>URL changed to " + newURL +
38      "for Author ID = " + author_id + "</b><br />");

39    out.println("<br />Displaying all rows:<br />");
40    ResultSet rs = null;
41    rs = s.executeQuery("SELECT author, author_id, url FROM names");
42    out.println("<ol>");                This loop outputs all rows in the database
43    while( rs.next() )                  inside a numbered list.
44    {
45        int id = rs.getInt("author_id");
46        String author = rs.getString("author");
47        String url = rs.getString("url");
48        out.println("<li>ID = " + id + ", Author = "
49        + author + ", URL = " + url + "</li>");
50    }
51    out.println("</ol>");
52    rs.close();

53        conn.close();
54  }
55    catch (Exception err)
56    {
57        out.println("SQL error.<br />");
58    }
```

Display 19.25   JSP Program to Update Database Entries Submitted by a Browser Viewing
Display 19.18 (part 3 of 3)

```
59  %>
60  </body>
61  </html>
```

Sample Dialogue   *Submitted on the Web browser when viewing Display 19.18.*

Author ID:

2

New URL:

http://www.dansimmons.com/about/bio.htm

Web browser display after clicking Submit.
Edit URL

This version of EditURL.jsp updates the URL field of a Derby database to
the submitted value for the row with a matching Author ID.

Loaded the embedded driver.
Connecting to and creating the database...
Connected.

URL changed to http://www.dansimmons.com/about/bio.htm for Author ID = 2

Displaying all rows:

1. ID = 1, Author = Adams, Douglas, URL = http://www.douglasadams.com

2. ID = 2, Author = Simmons, Dan, URL = http://www.dansimmons.com/about/
   bio.htm

3. ID = 3, Author = Stephenson, Neal, URL = http://www.nealstephenson.com

Although we have covered enough JSP to write fairly sophisticated programs, there is much more that we have not discussed. For example, beans can be used as a convenient way to encapsulate data submitted from a HTML form. Additionally, we have not covered sessions, tag libraries, security, and numerous other topics that are important in the construction of JSP pages. In particular, the technique of generating SQL read and write queries based on user-entered values is not secure—a malicious user could enter values that potentially run arbitrary SQL Statements. A more secure solution is to use a precompiled SQL statement that is supported by the java.sql.PreparedStatement class. Refer to a textbook dedicated to JSP or database programming to learn more.

Self-Test Exercises

14. What is a major difference between a website implemented with a Java applet and a website implemented with Java Server Pages?

15. Give the HTML to create a form with two elements: a textbox named `FirstName` that holds a maximum of 50 characters, and a Submit button. The form should submit its data to a JSP program called `ProcessName.jsp` using the `POST` method.

16. Identify the following JSP tags: `<% %>`, `<%@ %>`, `<%! %>`, `<%= %>`

17. Write a JSP scriptlet that handles the form created in Self-Test Exercise 13 and outputs the name in a bold heading font.

Chapter Summary

- A *thread* is a separate computation process. A Java program can have multiple threads.

- Use the class `Thread` to produce multiple threads.

- The static method `Thread.sleep` inserts a pause into the thread in which it is invoked.

- A thread's `join()` method is used to wait for threads to finish. The `synchronized` keyword restricts a critical region of code to a single thread only.

- A *socket* refers to an endpoint that connects two programs over a network.

- *TCP* refers to a reliable, streaming protocol for network communication. It ensures that data is received in the same order it was sent.

- *JavaBeans* refers to a framework for producing Java components that are easy to combine with other JavaBean components to produce new applications.

- A *relational database* organizes data in related tables. Records are stored as rows in a table. The fields for each record are stored as columns in a table.

- *Java DB* or *Derby* is a database that runs in client/server or embedded mode.

- JDBC allows you to insert SQL commands into your Java code to access and manipulate databases.

- The SQL `SELECT`, `UPDATE`, `CREATE TABLE`, and `INSERT` commands allow data to be retrieved, modified, created, or inserted into a database.

- *Java Server Pages (JSP)* refers to a framework that allows a programmer to create Web-based Java applications that run on the server. JSP requires a Web server capable of compiling and running Java servlets and JSP.

- HTML forms are a common mechanism to input user-specified data into a JSP application.

- Java code is added to a JSP page through *directive*, *expression*, *declaration*, and *scriptlet* tags.

Answers to Self-Test Exercises

1. The invocation of `Thread.sleep` takes place inside a thread. Every action in Java takes place inside some thread. Any action performed by a method invocation in a specific thread takes place in that thread. Even if it does not know where it is, a method's action takes place where the method invocation is; if you are lost and yell out, you might not know where you are but the yell would still be wherever it is you are.

2. The class `Packer` inherits the method `start` from the base class `Thread` and is not overridden. The method `start` invokes the method `run`, but when `start` is invoked by an object of the class `Packer`, it is the definition of `run` that is given in the class `Packer` that is used, not the definition of `run` given in the definition of `Thread`. That is exactly what is meant by *late binding* or *polymorphism*.

3. The argument passed to the sleep method is the amount of time to pause, in milliseconds.

```
for(int i =1; i <= 10; i++)
    {
        System.out.println(i);
        Thread.sleep(100);
            }
```

4. The code synchronizes access to the shared variable but the `main` method does not wait for all threads to finish before printing out the value of the shared variable. Thus, it is possible that `main` will output a premature value of `counter` if `main` completes before any one of the threads that it creates. To correct this problem, invoke the `join()` method on each thread before outputting counter as illustrated in Display 19.5.

5. TCP is a connection oriented protocol that guarantees that data sent from one end reaches the other end in the same order it was sent. It is therefore considered a reliable protocol. On the other hand, UDP sends independent packets of data, called datagrams that does not maintain the order of delivery.

6. Yes it is legal. It creates a socket using the IP 127.0.0.1, which is equivalent to localhost and a port number 7654.

7. *Persistence* means that a component's state can be saved so that the next time it is used it remembers what state it was in.

8. The same one that is used for Swing and AWT.

9.
```
SELECT Result.Title, Names.Author, Result.Author_ID
FROM Result, Names
WHERE Result.Author_ID = Names.Author_ID
```

10. A connection string is used to connect to (and possibly create) a database via JDBC. The protocol, database name, and other parameters (such as the username, password, or flag to create a new database) are specified in the connection string.

11. The `execute` method can be used to execute any SQL statement, but it is generally used for SQL commands where return values are not needed. It returns a Boolean value. The `executeQuery` method returns a `ResultSet` object that contains the rows matching a query.

12. `CREATE TABLE BooksAuthors (ISBN varchar(15), author_id int)`

13.
```
INSERT INTO BooksAuthors VALUES('0-553-38095-8',3)
INSERT INTO BooksAuthors VALUES('0-553-57294-6',2)
INSERT INTO BooksAuthors VALUES('0-671-46149-4',1)
INSERT INTO BooksAuthors VALUES('0-553-57928-9',2)
```

14. A java applet is downloaded and executed on the client, while a JSP program is written alongside HTML and runs on the server.

15.
```
<html>
<head>
<title>Submit Firstname</title>
</head>

<body>
<form ACTION = "ProcessName.jsp" METHOD = POST>
First Name:
<input TYPE = "TEXT" NAME = "FirstName" VALUE = "" MAXLENGTH = "50">
<input TYPE="SUBMIT" VALUE="Submit">
</form>
</body>
</html>
```

16. `<% %>` is a scriptlet, `<%@ %>` is a directive, `<%! %>` is a declaration, `<%= %>` is an expression.

17.
```
<%
String firstName = request.getParameter("FirstName");
out.println("<h1><b>" + firstName + "</b></h1>");
%>
```

MyProgrammingLab **Programming Projects**

Visit www.myprogramminglab.com to complete select exercises online and get instant feedback.

1. Write a GUI program that uses the methods in the `Graphics` class together with threads to draw a smiley face, wait two seconds, draw a frowny face, wait two seconds, and repeat starting with the smiley face. A separate thread should be started to implement the two-second timer. The application should be responsive and exit immediately if the user decides to close the window.

2. Create a class named `TimerAlarm` that extends `Thread` and implements a timer. Do not use the built-in Timer class for this exercise. Your class constructor should

take as input an integer named t representing time in milliseconds and an interface object named obj that defines a method named alarmAction( ). You will need to define this interface. Every t milliseconds the class should invoke method obj. alarmAction( ). Add pause( ) and play( ) methods that disable and enable the invocation of alarmAction( ). Test your class with code that increments and prints out a counter.

VideoNote

**Solution to
Programming
Project 19.3**

3. Write a GUI program that animates a four-colored "beach ball" in place by rotating the colors. The beach ball can be drawn as a solid circle with four different colors in each of the four quadrants of the circle. Use a thread to rotate the colors every quarter second.

4. Modify the GUI in Display 19.2 so that the circles are alternately red, white, and blue, and so that they fill the area from bottom to top instead of top to bottom.

5. Produce a GUI similar to the one in Display 19.2 except that instead of filling an area with circles, it launches a ball (which is just a circle) and the ball bounces around inside a rectangle. You can create the illusion of a moving ball by repeatedly erasing the ball and redrawing it at a location a little farther along its path. Look up the method setXORMode in the class Graphics. It will take care of the erasing.

6. This project shows how to create a simple Web server. Create a server program that listens on port 8000. When a client connects to the server, the program should send the following data to the client,

```
"HTTP/1.0 200 OK\n\n" + body
```

where body is the String "<HTML><TITLE>Java Server</TITLE>This web page was sent by our simple <B>Java Server</B></HTML>". If you know HTML, feel free to insert your own content. The header line identifies the message as part of the HTTP protocol that is used to transmit Web pages.

When the server is running, you should be able to start a Web browser and navigate to your machine on port 8000 and view the message. For example, if the server is running on your local machine, you could point your Web browser to http://localhost:8000 and the message in body should be displayed.

7. Modify the server from Programming Project 19.6 so that the content for body is read from a file on the local hard drive instead of hard-coded into the program. This file should contain the HTML string from Programming Project 19.6. In addition, modify the server so that a new thread is created for each connection. Test the server by starting up two or more Web browsers and navigate to your site. Each browser should display the message.

8. Create a threaded chat server and a corresponding chat client. Using the port of your choice, create a server that starts a new thread for every client that connects to it. Every message that the server receives from a client should be broadcast back to all other clients. The chat client should allow the user to type in a string of text and have it sent to the server upon pressing enter. Use threads on the client so messages can be retrieved from the server and displayed even while the user is typing. Test your server by connecting to it with multiple clients and verifying that messages are transmitted back and forth.

9. The program in Display 19.12 creates a database with the `Names` table from Display 19.10. Modify this program so it also creates the `Titles` and `BooksAuthors` tables with identical data entries as shown in Display 19.10. Next, create a separate program that prompts the user to input the name of an author and then outputs all book titles written by that author.

10. Create an HTML form that prompts the user to enter a temperature in Fahrenheit. When the form is submitted, a JSP Web page should run that displays the temperature converted to Celsius. The temperature in Celsius is 5 * (Fahrenheit − 32) / 9.

VideoNote

Solution to Programming Project 19.11

11. Create an HTML form that serves as a random baby name generator. The form should prompt the user to enter a last name. When the form is submitted, a JSP Web page should run that randomly picks the first name of a boy and the first name of a girl and then outputs the random first names coupled with the entered last name. For example, if the last name entered is "Savitch" and if the JSP program randomly selects "Emma" as the girl name and "Homer" as the boy name, then the output would be

```
If your baby is a boy, consider the name Homer Savitch.
If your baby is a girl, consider the name Emma Savitch.
```

The boy and girl names should be randomly selected from the files `boynames.txt` and `girlnames.txt` that are included in the source code on the website for this book.

These files contain the 1,000 most popular boy and girl names in the United States for the year 2003 as compiled by the Social Security Administration.

12. Recreate Programming Project 19.9 as JSP pages instead of as a stand-alone application. One JSP page should create the database, tables, and populate the tables with data. Create an HTML form that allows the user to enter the name of an author. The form should invoke another JSP page that displays all titles written by the specified author that are stored in the database.

13. This program simulates what might happen if two people who share the same bank account happen to make a simultaneous deposit or withdrawal and the bank does not account for race conditions by recreating the situation described in Displays 19.4 and 19.5 with a simple `BankAccount` class. The `BankAccount` class should store an account balance and have methods to retrieve the balance, make a deposit, and make a withdrawal. Do not worry about negative balances.

Next, create an array of thousands of threads where each thread has a reference to the same `BankAccount` object. In the `run()` method, even numbered threads deposit one dollar and odd numbered threads withdraw one dollar. If you create an even number of threads, then after all threads are done the account balance should be zero. See if you can find a number of threads so that you consistently end up with a balance that is not zero. If you want to increase the likelihood of a race condition, then make each thread sleep a short random number of milliseconds in the `run()` method.

Add the `synchronized` keyword to fix the problem and ensure a balance of zero after all the threads are done.

Applets and HTML 20

20.1 A BRIEF INTRODUCTION TO HTML 1171

HTML Formatting Commands 1171
Outline of an HTML Document 1173
Hyperlinks 1176
Inserting a Picture 1177

20.2 PROGRAMMING APPLETS 1182

Defining an Applet 1182
Running an Applet 1183
Menus in a JApplet 1185
Adding Icons to an Applet ★ 1189

20.3 APPLETS IN HTML DOCUMENTS 1192

Inserting an Applet in an HTML Document 1192
Running an Applet over the Internet ★ 1195
Applets and Security ★ 1196

This chapter is available on the book's website.

abstract	final	public
assert*	finally	return
boolean	float	short
break	for	static
byte	goto	strictfp
case	if	super
catch	implements	switch
char	import	synchronized
class	instanceof	this
const	int	throw
continue	interface	throws
default	long	transient
do	native	true*
double	new	try
else	null*	void
enum	package	volatile
extends	private	while
false*	protected	

* These are not listed as keywords in the Oracle documentation. However, some authorities list them as keywords. Preferring to err on the side of more safety, this book treats them as keywords.

PRECEDENCE	ASSOCIATIVITY
From highest at top to lowest at bottom. Operators in the same group have equal precedence.	
Dot operator, array indexing, and method invocation: `.`, `[ ]`, `( )`	Left to right
`++` (postfix, as in `x++`), `--` (postfix)	Right to left
The unary operators: `+`, `-`, `++` (prefix, as in `++x`), `--` (prefix), `!`, `~` (bitwise complement)[1]	Right to left
`new` and type casts (`Type`)	Right to left
The binary operators `*`, `/`, `%`	Left to right
The binary operators `+`, `-`	Left to right
The binary operators `<<`, `>>`, `>>>` (shift operators)[1]	Left to right
The binary operators `<`, `>`, `<=`, `>=`, `instanceof`	Left to right
The binary operators `==`, `!=`	Left to right
The binary operator `&`	Left to right
The binary operator `^` (exclusive or)[1]	Left to right
The binary operator `|`	Left to right
The binary operator `&&`	Left to right
The binary operator `||`	Left to right
The ternary operator (conditional operator) `? :`	Right to left
The assignment operators `=`, `*=`, `/=`, `%=`, `+=`, `-=`, `&=`, `|=`, `^=`, `<<=`, `>>=`, `>>>=`	Right to left

---

[1] Not discussed in this book.

The characters shown here form the ASCII character set, which is the subset of the Unicode character set that is commonly used by English speakers. The numbering is the same whether the characters are considered to be members of the Unicode character set or of the ASCII character set. Character number 32 is the blank. Printable characters only are shown.

32		56	8	80	P	104	h
33	!	57	9	81	Q	105	i
34	"	58	:	82	R	106	j
35	#	59	;	83	S	107	k
36	$	60	<	84	T	108	l
37	%	61	=	85	U	109	m
38	&	62	>	86	V	110	n
39	'	63	?	87	W	111	o
40	(	64	@	88	X	112	p
41	)	65	A	89	Y	113	q
42	*	66	B	90	Z	114	r
43	+	67	C	91	[	115	s
44	,	68	D	92	\	116	t
45	-	69	E	93	]	117	u
46	.	70	F	94	^	118	v
47	/	71	G	95	_	119	w
48	0	72	H	96	`	120	x
49	1	73	I	97	a	121	y
50	2	74	J	98	b	122	z
51	3	75	K	99	c	123	{
52	4	76	L	100	d	124		
53	5	77	M	101	e	125	}
54	6	78	N	102	f	126	~
55	7	79	O	103	g		

SYNTAX

System.out.printf(*Format_String, Output_1, Output_2, ..., Output_Last*);

Format_String is a string including one format specifier for each *Output* argument. *Format_String* is output with each format specifier replaced by its corresponding *Output* argument in the format given by the *Output* argument's format specifier.

Display A4.1   Format Specifiers for `System.out.printf`

CONVERSION CHARACTER	TYPE OF OUTPUT	EXAMPLES
d	Decimal (ordinary) integer.	`%5d` `%d`
f	Fixed-point (everyday notation) floating-point.	`%6.2f` `%f`
e	E-notation floating point.	`%8.3e` `%e`
g	General floating point. (Java decides whether to use E-notation or not.)	`%8.3g` `%g`
s	String.	`%12s` `%s`
c	Character.	`%2c` `%c`
b	Boolean. The corresponding *Output* argument is a Boolean expression. Outputs `true` or `false`.	`%6b` `%b`
n	Denotes a line break. This does not correspond to an *Output* argument. It is approximately equivalent to `\n`.	`%n`

A number of the form $N.M$ in a format specifier specifies a field width of N spaces with M digits after the decimal point. If one number N is given only, it specifies a field width; if there is a decimal point in the output, then the number of digits after the decimal point is determined by Java.

When the value output does not fill the field width specified, then blanks are added in front of the value output. The output is then said to be *right justified*. If you add a hyphen (-) after the `%`, then any extra blank space is placed after the value output and the output is said to be *left justified*. For example, `%8.2f` is right justified and `%-8.2f` is left justified.

This appendix summarizes most of the library classes used in this book. This appendix includes some methods, and even some classes, that are not discussed in the text. The lists of class methods and other class members contain the most commonly used members and the members used in this book, but they are not complete lists of methods for the classes given here.

If a class or interface is derived from another class or interface, respectively, then in some cases, the table for the derived class or interface lists only new methods and does not list all the inherited methods.

Abstract Button

Package: `javax.swing`
The classes `JButton` and `JMenuItem` are also in this package.
All these methods are inherited by the classes `JButton` and `JMenuItem`.
`AbstractButton` is an abstract class.
Ancestor classes:

```
        Object
          |
          +--Component
              |
              +--Container
                  |
                  +--JComponent
                      |
                      +AbstractButton
                          |           \
                          +--JButton   +--JMenuItem
```

public void addActionListener(ActionListener listener)

Adds an `ActionListener`.

public String getActionCommand()

Returns the action command for this component.

public String getText()

Returns the text written on the component, such as the text on a button or the string for a menu item.

public void removeActionListener(ActionListener listener)

Removes an `ActionListener`.

public void setActionCommand(String actionCommand)

Sets the action command.

```
public void setBackground(Color theColor)
```

Sets the background color of this component.

```
public void setMaximumSize(Dimension maximumSize)
```

Sets the maximum size of the button or label. Note that this is only a suggestion to the layout manager. The layout manager is not required to respect this maximum size. The following special case will work for most simple situations. The int values give the width and height in pixels.

```
public void setMaximumSize(
                new Dimension(int width, int height))
```

```
public void setMinimumSize(Dimension minimumSize)
```

Sets the minimum size of the button or label. Note that this is only a suggestion to the layout manager. The layout manager is not required to respect this minimum size.
Although we do not discuss the Dimension class, the following special case is intuitively clear and will work for most simple situations. The int values give the width and height in pixels.

```
public void setMinimumSize(
                new Dimension(int width, int height))
```

```
public void setPreferredSize(Dimension preferredSize)
```

Sets the preferred size of the button or label. Note that this is only a suggestion to the layout manager. The layout manager is not required to use the preferred size. The following special case will work for most simple situations. The int values give the width and height in pixels.

```
public void setPreferredSize(
                new Dimension(int width, int height))
```

```
public void setText(String text)
```

Makes text the only text on this component.

ArrayList<T>

Package: java.util

Ancestor classes:

```
        Object
          |
        +--AbstractCollection<T>
             |
             +--AbstractList<T>
                  |
                  +--ArrayList<T>
```

All the exception classes mentioned are unchecked exceptions, which means they are not required to be caught in a catch block or declared in a throws clause.
NoSuchElementException is in the java.util package, which requires an import statement if your code mentions the NoSuchElementException class. All the other exception classes mentioned are in the package java.lang and so do not require any import statement.

CONSTRUCTORS

`public ArrayList(int initialCapacity)`

Creates an empty `ArrayList<T>` with the specified initial capacity. When the `ArrayList<T>` needs to increase its capacity, the capacity doubles.
Throws an `IllegalArgumentException` if `initialCapacity` is negative.

`public ArrayList()`

Creates an empty `ArrayList<T>` with an initial capacity of `10`. When the `ArrayList<T>` needs to increase its capacity, the capacity doubles.

`public ArrayList(Collection<? extends <T> c)`

Creates an `ArrayList<T>` that contains all the elements of the collection `c` in the same order as they have in `c`. In other words, the elements have the same index in the `ArrayList<T>` created as they do in `c`. This is not quite a true copy constructor because it does not preserve capacity. The capacity of the created `ArrayList<T>` will be `c.size()`, not `c.capacity`. The `ArrayList<T>` created is only a shallow copy of the collection argument. The `ArrayList<T>` created contains references to the elements in `c` (not references to clones of the elements in `c`).

Throws:

`NullPointerException` if `c` is `null`.

ARRAYLIKE METHODS

`public T set(int index, T newElement)`

Sets the element at the specified `index` to `newElement`. The element previously at that position is returned. If you draw an analogy to an array `a`, this is analogous to setting `a [index]` to the value `newElement`. The `index` must be a value greater than or equal to `0` and strictly less than the current size of the list.

Throws:

`IndexOutOfBoundsException` if the `index` is not in this range.

`public T get(int index)`

Returns the element at the specified index. This is analogous to returning `a [index]` for an array `a`. The `index` must be a value greater than or equal to `0` and less than the current size of the calling object.

Throws:

`IndexOutOfBoundsException` if the `index` is not in the required range.

METHODS TO ADD ELEMENTS

```
public boolean add(T newElement)
```

Adds `newElement` to the end of the calling object's list and increases its size by one. The capacity of the calling object is increased if that is required. Returns `true` if the add was successful. This method is often used as if it were a `void` method.

```
public void add(int index, T newElement)
```

Inserts `newElement` as an element in the calling object at the specified index and increases the size of the calling object by one. Each element in the calling object with an index greater than or equal to `index` is shifted upward to have an index that is one greater than it had previously. The `index` must be a value greater than or equal to 0 and less than *or equal to* the size of the calling object (before this addition).
Note that you can use this method to add an element after the last current element. The capacity of the calling object is increased if that is required.

Throws:

`IndexOutOfBoundsException` if the index is not in the prescribed range.

```
public boolean addAll(Collection<? extends T> c)
```

Appends all the elements in `c` to the end of the elements in the calling object in the order that they are enumerated by a `c` iterator. The behavior of this method is not guaranteed if the collection `c` is the calling object or any collection including the calling object either directly or indirectly.

Throws:

`NullPointerException` if c is null.

```
public boolean addAll(int index, Collection<? extends T> c)
```

Inserts all the elements in `c` into the calling object starting at position `index`. Elements are inserted in the order that they are enumerated by a `c` iterator. Elements previously at positions `index` or higher are shifted to higher numbered positions.

Throws:

`IndexOutOfBoundsException` if index is not both greater than or equal to zero and less than `size()`.
`NullPointerException` if c is null.

METHODS TO REMOVE ELEMENTS

```
public T remove(int index)
```

Deletes the element at the specified index and returns the element deleted. The size of the calling object is decreased by one. The capacity of the calling object is not changed. Each element in the calling object with an index greater than or equal to `index` is decreased to have an index that is one less than the value it had previously.
The `index` must be a value greater than or equal to 0 and less than the size of the calling object (before this removal).

Throws:

`IndexOutOfBoundsException` if the `index` is not in the prescribed range.

```
public boolean remove(Object theElement)
```

Removes the first occurrence of theElement from the calling object. If theElement is found in the calling object, then each element in the calling object with an index greater than or equal to theElement's index is decreased to have an index that is one less than the value it had previously. Returns true if theElement was found (and removed). Returns false if theElement was not found in the calling object. If the element was removed, the size is decreased by one. The capacity is not changed.

```
protected void removeRange(int fromIndex, int toIndex)
```

Removes all elements with index greater than or equal to fromIndex and strictly less than toIndex. Be sure to note that this method is protected, not public.

```
public void clear()
```

Removes all elements from the calling object and sets its size to zero.

SEARCH METHODS

```
public boolean isEmpty()
```

Returns true if the calling object is empty (that is, has size 0); otherwise returns false.

```
public boolean contains(Object target)
```

Returns true if target is an element of the calling object; otherwise returns false. Uses the method equals of the object target to test for equality.

```
public int indexOf(Object target)
```

Returns the index of the first element that is equal to target. Uses the method equals of the object target to test for equality. Returns −1 if target is not found.

```
public int lastIndexOf(Object target)
```

Returns the index of the last element that is equal to target. Uses the method equals of the object target to test for equality. Returns −1 if target is not found.

ITERATORS

```
public Iterator<T> iterator()
```

Returns an iterator for the calling object. Iterators are discussed in Section 16.3.

```
public ListIterator<T> listIterator()
```

Returns a ListIterator<T> for the calling object. ListIterator<T> is discussed in Section 16.3.

```
ListIterator<T> listIterator(int index)
```

Returns a list iterator for the calling object starting at `index`. The first element to be returned by the iterator is the one at `index`. (Iterators are discussed in Section 16.3.)

Throws:

`IndexOutOfBoundsException` if index does not satisfy:
`0 <= index <= size()`

CONVERTING TO AN ARRAY

```
public Object[] toArray()
```

Returns an array containing all of the elements in the calling object. The elements of the array are indexed the same as in the calling object.

```
public <E> E[] toArray(E[] a)
```

Note that the type parameter `E` is not the same as `T`. So, `E` can be any reference type; it need not be the type `T` in `Collection<T>`. For example, `E` might be an ancestor type of `T`.
Returns an array containing all of the elements in the calling object. The elements of the array are indexed the same as in the calling object.
The argument a is used primarily to specify the type of the array returned. The exact details are as follows:
The type of the returned array is that of a. If the collection fits in the array a, then a is used to hold the elements of the returned array; otherwise a new array is created with the same type as a.
If a has more elements than the calling object, then the element in a immediately following the end of the elements copied from the calling object are set to `null`.

Throws:

`ArrayStoreException` if the type of a is not an ancestor type of the type of every element in the calling object.
`NullPointerException` if a is `null`.

MEMORY MANAGEMENT

```
public int size()
```

Returns the number of elements in the calling object.

```
public int capacity()
```

Returns the current capacity of the calling object.

```
public void ensureCapacity(int newCapacity)
```

Increases the capacity of the calling object to ensure that it can hold at least `newCapacity` elements. Using `ensureCapacity` can sometimes increase efficiency, but its use is not needed for any other reason.

```
public void trimToSize()
```

Trims the capacity of the calling object to be the calling object's current size. This is used to save storage.

MAKE A COPY

```
public Object clone()
```

Returns a shallow copy of the calling object.

Boolean

This is a wrapper class for `boolean`. See Section 5.1 in Chapter 5.

BufferedReader

Package: `java.io`
The `FileReader` class is also in this package.
Ancestor classes:

```
Object
   |
   +--Reader
         |
         +--BufferedReader
```

```
public BufferedReader(Reader readerObject)
```

This is the only constructor you are likely to need. There is no constructor that accepts a file name as an argument. If you want to create a stream using a file name, use

```
new BufferedReader(new FileReader(File_Name))
```

When used in this way, the `FileReader` constructor, and thus the `BufferedReader` constructor invocation, can throw a `FileNotFoundException`, which is a kind of `IOException`.
If you want to create a stream using an object of the class `File`, use

```
new BufferedReader(new FileReader(File_Object))
```

When used in this way, the `FileReader` constructor, and thus the `BufferedReader` constructor invocation, can throw a `FileNotFoundException`, which is a kind of `IOException`.

```
public void close() throws IOException
```

Closes the stream's connection to a file.

```
public int read() throws IOException
```

Reads a single character from the input stream and returns that character as an `int` value. If the read goes beyond the end of the file, then –1 is returned. Note that the value is returned as an `int`. To obtain a `char`, you must perform a type cast on the value returned. The end of a file is signaled by returning –1. (All of the "real" characters return a positive integer.)

```
public String readLine() throws IOException
```

Reads a line of input from the input stream and returns that line. If the read goes beyond the end of the file, `null` is returned. (Note that an `EOFException` is not thrown at the end of a file. The end of a file is signaled by returning `null`.)

```
public long skip(long n) throws IOException
```

Skips n characters.

Byte

This is a wrapper class for `byte`. See Section 5.1 in Chapter 5.

Character

Package: `java.lang`
Ancestor classes:

```
        Object
          |
        +--Character
```

Implemented interfaces: `Comparable, Serializable`
The `Character` class is marked `final`, which means it cannot be used as a base class to derive other classes.

```
public static boolean isDigit(char argument)
```

Returns `true` if its argument is a digit; otherwise returns `false`.

EXAMPLES

`Character.isDigit('5')` returns `true`. `Character.isDigit('A')` and `Character.isDigit('%')` both return `false`.

```
public static boolean isLetter(char argument)
```

Returns `true` if its argument is a letter; otherwise returns `false`.

EXAMPLES

`Character.isLetter('A')` returns `true`. `Character.isLetter('%')` and `Character.isLetter('5')` both return `false`.

```
public static boolean isLetterOrDigit(char argument)
```

Returns `true` if its argument is a letter or a digit; otherwise returns `false`.

EXAMPLES

`Character.isLetterOrDigit('A')` and `Character.isLetterOrDigit('5')` both return `true`. `Character.isLetterOrDigit('&')` returns `false`.

```
public static boolean isLowerCase(char argument)
```

Returns `true` if its argument is a lowercase letter; otherwise returns `false`.

EXAMPLES

`Character.isLowerCase('a')` returns `true`. `Character.isLowerCase('A')` and `Character.isLowerCase('%')` both return `false`.

```
public static boolean isUpperCase(char argument)
```

Returns `true` if its argument is an uppercase letter; otherwise returns `false`.

EXAMPLES

`Character.isUpperCase('A')` returns `true`. `Character.isUpperCase('a')` and `Character.isUpperCase('%')` both return `false`.

```
public static boolean isWhitespace(char argument)
```

Returns `true` if its argument is a whitespace character; otherwise returns `false`. Whitespace characters are those that print as whitespace, such as the space character (blank character), the tab character (`'\t'`), and the new-line character (`'\n'`).

EXAMPLES

`Character.isWhitespace(' ')` returns `true`. `Character.isWhitespace('A')` returns `false`.

```
public static char toLowerCase(char argument)
```

Returns the lowercase version of its argument. If the argument is not a letter, it is returned unchanged.

EXAMPLE

`Character.toLowerCase('a')` and `Character.toLowerCase('A')` both return `'a'`.

```
public static char toUpperCase(char argument)
```

Returns the uppercase version of its argument. If the argument is not a letter, it is returned unchanged.

EXAMPLE

`Character.toUpperCase('a')` and `Character.toUpperCase('A')` both return `'A'`.

`Collection<T>` **Interface**

Package: `java.util`
Ancestor interfaces: none
All the exception classes mentioned are unchecked exceptions, which means they are not required to be caught in a `catch` block or declared in a `throws` clause.
All the exception classes mentioned are in the package `java.lang` and so do not require any `import` statement.

CONSTRUCTORS

Although not officially required by the interface, any class that implements the `Collection<T>` interface should have at least two constructors: a no-argument constructor that creates an empty `Collection<T>` object, and a constructor with one parameter of type `Collection<? extends T>` that creates a `Collection<T>` object with the same elements as the constructor argument. The interface does not specify whether the copy produced by the one-argument constructor is a shallow copy or a deep copy of its argument.

```
public boolean contains(Object target)
```

Returns `true` if the calling object contains at least one instance of `target`. Uses `target.equals` to determine if `target` is in the calling object.

Throws:

`ClassCastException` if the type of `target` is incompatible with the calling object (optional).
`NullPointerException` if `target` is `null` and the calling object does not support `null` elements (optional).

```
public boolean containsAll(Collection<?> collectionOfTargets)
```

Returns `true` if the calling object contains all of the elements in `collectionOfTargets`. For `element` in `collectionOfTargets`, this method uses `element.equals` to determine if `element` is in the calling object.

Throws:

`ClassCastException` if the types of one or more elements in `collectionOfTargets` are incompatible with the calling object (optional).
`NullPointerException` if `collectionOfTargets` contains one or more `null` elements and the calling object does not support `null` elements (optional).
`NullPointerException` if `collectionOfTargets` is `null`.

```
public boolean equals(Object other)
```

This is the `equals` of the collection, not the `equals` of the elements in the collection. Overrides the inherited method `equals`. Although there are no official constraints on `equals` for a collection, it should be defined as we have described in Chapter 7 and also satisfy the intuitive notion of collections being equal.

```
    public int hashCode()
```

Returns the hash code value for the calling object. Neither hash codes nor this method are discussed in this book. This entry is only here to make the definition of the `Collection<T>` interface complete. You can safely ignore this entry until you go on to study hash codes in a more advanced book. In the meantime, if you need to implement this method, have the method throw an `UnsupportedOperationException`.

```
    public boolean isEmpty()
```

Returns `true` if the calling object is empty; otherwise returns `false`.

```
    Iterator<T> iterator()
```

Returns an iterator for the calling object. (Iterators are discussed in Section 16.3.)

```
    public Object[] toArray()
```

Returns an array containing all of the elements in the calling object. If the calling object makes any guarantees as to what order its elements are returned by its iterator, this method must return the elements in the same order.
The array returned should be a new array so that the calling object has no references to the returned array. (You might also want the elements in the array to be clones of the elements in the collection. However, this is apparently not required by the interface, because library classes, such as `Vector<T>`, return arrays that contain references to the elements in the collection.)

```
    public <E> E[] toArray(E[] a)
```

Note that the type parameter `E` is not the same as `T`. So, `E` can be any reference type; it need not be the type `T` in `Collection<T>`. For example, `E` might be an ancestor type of `T`.
Returns an array containing all of the elements in the calling object. The argument `a` is used primarily to specify the type of the array returned. The exact details are as follows:
The type of the returned array is that of `a`. If the elements in the calling object fit in the array `a`, then `a` is used to hold the elements of the returned array; otherwise a new array is created with the same type as `a`.
If `a` has more elements than the calling object, the element in `a` immediately following the end of the copied elements is set to `null`.
If the calling object makes any guarantees as to what order its elements are returned by its iterator, this method must return the elements in the same order. (Iterators are discussed in Section 16.3.)

Throws:

`ArrayStoreException` if the type of `a` is not an ancestor type of the type of every element in the calling object.
`NullPointerException` if `a` is null.

```
    public int size()
```

Returns the number of elements in the calling object. If the calling object contains more than `Integer.MAX_VALUE` elements, returns `Integer.MAX_VALUE`.

OPTIONAL METHODS

The following methods are optional, which means they still must be implemented, but the implementation can simply throw an `UnsupportedOperationException` if for some reason you do not want to give them a "real" implementation. An `UnsupportedOperationException` is a `RunTimeException` and so is not required to be caught or declared in a `throws` clause.

```
public boolean add(T element) (Optional)
```

Ensures that the calling object contains the specified `element`. Returns `true` if the calling object changed as a result of the call. Returns `false` if the calling object does not permit duplicates and already contains `element`; also returns `false` if the calling object does not change for any other reason.

Throws:

`UnsupportedOperationException` if this method is not supported by the class that implements this interface.
`ClassCastException` if the class of `element` prevents it from being added to the calling object.
`NullPointerException` if element is `null` and the calling object does not support `null` elements. `IllegalArgumentException` if some other aspect of `element` prevents it from being added to the calling object.

```
public boolean addAll(Collection<? extends T> collectionToAdd) (Optional)
```

Ensures that the calling object contains all the elements in `collectionToAdd`. Returns `true` if the calling object changed as a result of the call; returns `false` otherwise. If the calling object changes during this operation, its behavior is unspecified; in particular, it behavior is unspecified if `collectionToAdd` is the calling object.

Throws:

`UnsupportedOperationException` if this method is not supported by the class that implements this interface.
`ClassCastException` if the class of an element of `collectionToAdd` prevents it from being added to the calling object.
`NullPointerException` if `collectionToAdd` contains one or more `null` elements and the calling object does not support `null` elements, or if `collectionToAdd` is `null`.
`IllegalArgumentException` if some aspect of an element of `collectionToAdd` prevents it from being added to the calling object.

```
public void clear() (Optional)
```

Removes all the elements from the calling object.

Throws:

`UnsupportedOperationException` if this method is not supported by the class that implements this interface.

```
public boolean remove(Object element) (Optional)
```

Removes a single instance of `element` from the calling object, if it is present. Returns `true` if the calling object contained `element`; returns `false` otherwise.

Throws:

`UnsupportedOperationException` if this method is not supported by the class that implements this interface.
`ClassCastException` if the type of `element` is incompatible with the calling object (optional).
`NullPointerException` if element is `null` and the calling object does not support `null` elements (optional).

```
    public boolean removeAll(Collection<?> collectionToRemove)  (Optional)
```

Removes all the calling object's elements that are also contained in `collectionToRemove`. Returns `true` if the calling object was changed; otherwise returns `false`.

Throws:

`UnsupportedOperationException` if this method is not supported by the class that implements this interface.
`ClassCastException` if the types of one or more elements in `collectionToRemove` are incompatible with the calling collection (optional).
`NullPointerException` if `collectionToRemove` contains one or more `null` elements and the calling object does not support `null` elements (optional).
`NullPointerException` if `collectionToRemove` is `null`.

```
    public boolean retainAll(Collection<?> saveElements)  (Optional)
```

Retains only the elements in the calling object that are also contained in the collection `saveElements`. In other words, removes from the calling object all of its elements that are not contained in the collection `saveElements`. Returns `true` if the calling object was changed; otherwise returns `false`.

Throws:

`ClassCastException` if the types of one or more elements in `saveElements` are incompatible with the calling object (optional).
`NullPointerException` if `saveElements` contains one or more `null` elements and the calling object does not support `null` elements (optional).
`NullPointerException` if `saveElements` is `null`.

```
Color
```

Package: `java.awt`
Ancestor classes:

```
        Object
          |
        +--Color
```

CONSTRUCTORS

```
    public Color(float r, float g, float b)
```

Constructor that creates a new `Color` with the specified RGB values. The parameters `r`, `g`, and `b` must each be in the range `0.0` to `1.0` (inclusive).

```
    public Color(int r, int g, int b)
```

Constructor that creates a new `Color` with the specified RGB values. The parameters `r`, `g`, and `b` must each be in the range 0 to 255 (inclusive).

METHODS

```
public Color brighter()
```
Returns a brighter version of the calling object color.

```
public Color darker()
```
Returns a darker version of the calling object color.

```
public boolean equals(Object c)
```
Returns `true` if c is equal to the calling object color; otherwise returns `false`.

```
public int getBlue()
```
Returns the blue component of the calling object. The returned value is in the range 0 to 255 (inclusive).

```
public int getGreen()
```
Returns the green component of the calling object. The returned value is in the range 0 to 255 (inclusive).

```
public int getRed()
```
Returns the red component of the calling object. The returned value is in the range 0 to 255 (inclusive).

CONSTANTS

Color.BLACK	Color.MAGENTA
Color.BLUE	Color.ORANGE
Color.CYAN	Color.PINK
Color.DARK_GRAY	Color.RED
Color.GRAY	Color.WHITE
Color.GREEN	Color.YELLOW
Color.LIGHT_GRAY	

`Comparable` Interface

Package: `java.lang`
Ancestor interfaces: none
The `Comparable` interface has only one method heading that must be implemented.

```
public int compareTo(Object other)
```
The method `compareTo` should return
a negative number if the calling object "comes before" the parameter `other`,
a zero if the calling object "equals" the parameter `other`,
and a positive number if the calling object "comes after" the parameter `other`.
The "comes before" ordering that underlies `compareTo` should be a total ordering. Most normal ordering, such as less-than on numbers and lexicographic ordering on strings, are total orderings.

Double

This is a wrapper class for `double`. See Section 5.1 in Chapter 5.

File

Package: `java.io`
Ancestor classes:

```
        Object
          |
        +--File
```

Many of these methods throw a `SecurityException` if a security manager exists and is unhappy with the method invocation. This is not likely to be a concern for readers of this book, and we have not noted this in the method descriptions.
The class `SecurityException` is an unchecked exception class, which means you need not catch it or declare it in a `throws` clause.

`public File(String fileName)`

Constructor. `fileName` can be either a full or a relative pathname (which includes the case of a simple file name). `fileName` is referred to as the **abstract pathname**.

Throws:

`NullPointerException` if the pathname `fileName` is `null`.

`public boolean canRead()`

Tests whether the program can read from the file. Returns `true` if the file named by the abstract pathname exists and is readable by the program; otherwise returns `false`.

`public boolean canWrite()`

Tests whether the program can write to the file. Returns `true` if the file named by the abstract pathname exists and is writable by the program; otherwise returns `false`.

`public boolean createNewFile()`

Creates a new empty file named by the abstract pathname, provided that a file of that name does not already exist. Returns `true` if successful; returns `false` otherwise.

Throws:

`IOException` if an I/O error occurs.

`public boolean delete( )`

Tries to delete the file or directory named by the abstract pathname. A directory must be empty to be removed. Returns `true` if it was able to delete the file or directory. Returns `false` if it was unable to delete the file or directory.

`public boolean exists()`

Tests whether there is a file with the abstract pathname.

```
public String getName()
```

Returns the last name in the abstract pathname (that is, the simple file name). Returns the empty string if the abstract pathname is the empty string.

```
public String getPath()
```

Returns the abstract pathname as a `String` value.

```
public boolean isDirectory()
```

Returns `true` if a directory (folder) exists that is named by the abstract pathname; otherwise returns `false`.

```
public boolean isFile()
```

Returns `true` if a file exists that is named by the abstract pathname and the file is a normal file; otherwise returns `false`. The meaning of *normal* is system dependent. Any file created by a Java program is guaranteed to be normal.

```
public long length()
```

Returns the length in bytes of the file named by the abstract pathname. If the file does not exist or the abstract pathname names a directory, then the value returned is not specified and may be anything.

```
public boolean mkdir()
```

Makes a directory named by the abstract pathname. Will not create parent directories. See `mkdirs`. Returns `true` if successful; otherwise returns `false`.

```
public boolean mkdirs()
```

Makes a directory named by the abstract pathname. Will create any necessary but nonexistent parent directories. Returns `true` if successful; otherwise returns `false`. Note that if it fails, then some of the parent directories may have been created.

```
public boolean renameTo(File newName)
```

Renames the file represented by the abstract pathname to `newName`. Returns `true` if successful; otherwise returns `false`. `newName` can be a relative or absolute pathname. This may require moving the file. Whether or not the file can be moved is system dependent.

Throws:

`NullPointerException` if parameter `newName` is `null`.

```
public boolean setReadOnly()
```

Sets the file represented by the abstract pathname to be read only. Returns `true` if successful; otherwise returns `false`.

`Float`

This is a wrapper class for `float`. See Section 5.1 in Chapter 5.

`Font`

Package: `java.awt`
Ancestor classes:

```
        Object
          |
          +--Font
```

CONSTRUCTOR

    `public Font(String fontName, int styleModifications, int size)`

Constructor that creates a version of the font named by `fontName` with the specified `styleModifications` and `size`.

CONSTANTS

    `Font.BOLD`

Specifies bold style.

    `Font.ITALIC`

Specifies italic style.

    `Font.PLAIN`

Specifies plain style—that is, not bold and not italic.

NAMES OF Fonts
(These three are guaranteed by Java. Your system will probably have others as well as these.)

    `"Monospaced"`

See Chapter 18 for a sample.

    `"SansSerif"`

See Chapter 18 for a sample.

    `"Serif"`

See Chapter 18 for a sample.

METHOD THAT USES Font

    `public abstract void setFont(Font fontObject)`

This method is in the class `Graphics`. Sets the current font of the calling `Graphics` object to `fontObject`.

Graphics

Package: `java.awt`
Ancestor classes:

```
        Object
          |
        +--Graphics
```

`Graphics` is an abstract class.
Although many of these methods are abstract, we always use them with objects of a concrete descendent class of `Graphics`, even though we usually do not know the name of that concrete class.

```
public abstract void drawRect(int x, int y,
                                   int width, int height)
```

Draws the outline of the specified rectangle. (x, y) is the location of the upper-left corner of the rectangle.

```
public abstract void fillRect(int x, int y,
                                   int width, int height)
```

Fills the specified rectangle. (x, y) is the location of the upper-left corner of the rectangle.

```
public void draw3DRect(int x, int y, int width,
                                   int height, boolean raised)
```

Draws the outline of the specified rectangle. (x, y) is the location of the upper-left corner. The rectangle is highlighted to look like it has thickness. If `raised` is `true`, the highlight makes the rectangle appear to stand out from the background. If `raised` is `false`, the highlight makes the rectangle appear to be sunken into the background.

```
public void fill3DRect(int x, int y, int width,
                                   int height, boolean raised)
```

Fills the rectangle specified by

```
draw3DRec(x, y, width, height, raised)
```

```
public abstract void drawArc(int x, int y,
                              int width, int height,
                              int startAngle, int arcSweep)
```

Draws part of an oval that just fits into an invisible rectangle described by the first four arguments. The portion of the oval drawn is given by the last two arguments. See Chapter 18 for details.

```
public abstract void drawLine(int x1, int y1, int x2, int y2)
```

Draws a line between points (x1, y1) and (x2, y2).

```
public abstract void drawOval(int x, int y,
                                   int width, int height)
```

Draws the outline of the oval with the smallest enclosing rectangle that has the specified width and height. The (imagined) rectangle has its upper-left corner located at (x, y).

`HashSet<T>`

Package: `java.util`
Ancestor classes:

```
        Object
          |
      +--AbstractCollection<T>
              |
          +--AbstractSet<T>
                  |
              +--HashSet<T>
```

Implements interfaces: `Cloneable`, `Collection<T>`, `Serializable`, `Set<T>`
The `HashSet<T>` class implements all of the methods in the `Set<T>` interface. The only other methods in the `HashSet<T>` class are the constructors. The class `T` must implement the `equals` and `hashCode` methods. The two constructors that do not involve concepts beyond the scope of this book are given as follows.
All the exception classes mentioned are the kind that are not required to be caught in a `catch` block or declared in a `throws` clause.
All the exception classes mentioned are in the package `java.lang` and so do not require any import statement.

`public HashSet()`

Creates a new, empty set.

`public HashSet(Collection<? extends T> c )`

Creates a new set that contains all the elements of c.

Throws:

`NullPointerException` if c is null.

`public HashSet(int initialCapacity)`

Creates a new, empty set with the specified capacity.

Throws:

`IllegalArgumentException` if `initialCapacity` is less than zero.

The methods are the same as those described for the `Set<T>` interface.

`Integer`

This is a wrapper class for `int`. See Section 5.1 in Chapter 5.

Iterator<T> Interface

Package: `java.util`
Ancestor interfaces: none
All the exception classes mentioned are the kind that are not required to be caught in a `catch` block or declared in a `throws` clause.
`NoSuchElementException` is in the `java.util` package, which requires an `import` statement if your code mentions the `NoSuchElementException` class. All the other exception classes mentioned are in the package `java.lang` and so do not require any `import` statements.

`public boolean hasNext()`

Returns `true` if `next()` has not yet returned all the elements in the collection; returns `false` otherwise.

`public T next()`

Returns the next element of the collection that produced the iterator.

Throws:

`NoSuchElementException` if there is no next element.

`public void remove()` *(Optional)*

Removes from the collection the last element returned by `next`.
This method can be called only once per call to `next`.

Throws:

`IllegalStateException` if the next method has not yet been called, or the `remove` method has already been called after the last call to the `next` method.
`UnsupportedOperationException` if the `remove` operation is not supported by this `Iterator`.

JButton

See `AbstractButton`.

JFrame

Package: `javax.swing`
Ancestor classes:

```
        Object
           |
        +--Component
              |
           +--Container
                 |
              +--Window
                    |
                 +--Frame
                       |
                    +--JFrame
```

```
public JFrame()
```
Constructor that creates an object of the class JFrame.

```
public JFrame(String title)
```
Constructor that creates an object of the class JFrame with the title given as the argument.

```
public Component add(Component componentAdded)
```
Adds componentAdded to the JFrame. Typically used as a void method.

```
public Container getContentPane()
```
Returns the content pane of the calling JFrame object. Container is a class in the package java.awt.

To set the color of a JFrame, use

```
getContentPane().setBackground(Color c)
```
If you use setBackground without the getContentPane(), you will not get any error messages, but you will probably not see the color.

```
public void setDefaultCloseOperation(int operation)
```
Sets the action that will happen by default when the user clicks the close-window button. The argument should be one of the following defined constants:

JFrame.DO_NOTHING_ON_CLOSE: Do nothing. The JFrame does nothing, but if there are any registered window listeners, they are invoked. (Window listeners are explained in Chapter 18.)
JFrame.HIDE_ON_CLOSE: Hide the frame after invoking any registered WindowListener objects.
JFrame.DISPOSE_ON_CLOSE: Hide and *dispose* the frame after invoking any registered window listeners. When a window is **disposed**, it is eliminated but the program does not end. To end the programs, use the next constant as an argument to setDefaultCloseOperation.
JFrame.EXIT_ON_CLOSE: Exit the application using the System exit method. (Do not use this for frames in applets. Applets are discussed on the accompanying CD.)

If no action is specified using the method setDefaultCloseOperation, then the default action taken is JFrame.HIDE_ON_CLOSE.

Throws:

IllegalArgumentException if the argument is not one of the values listed previously. SecurityException if the argument is JFrame.EXIT_ON_CLOSE and the Security Manager will not allow the caller to invoke System.exit. (You are not likely to encounter this case.)

```
public void setLayout(LayoutManager manager)
```
Makes manager the layout manager for the JFrame.

```
public void setSize(int width, int height)
```
Sets the size of the calling frame so that it has the width and height specified. Pixels are the units of length used.

```
public void setTitle(String title)
```
Sets the title for this frame to the argument string.

```
public void dispose()
```
Eliminates the calling frame and all its subcomponents. Any memory they use is released for reuse. If there are items left (items other than the calling frame and its subcomponents), then this does not end the program. (The method dispose is discussed in Chapter 18.)

```
public void setJMenuBar(JMenuBar menubar)
```
Sets the menu bar for the calling frame.

JMenuItem

See AbstractButton.

JPanel

Package: javax.swing
Ancestor classes:

```
        Object
          |
        +--Component
            |
            +--Container
                |
                +--JComponent
                    |
                    +--JPanel
```

```
public JPanel()
```
Constructor that creates an object of the class JPanel.

```
public JPanel(LayoutManager manager)
```
Constructor that creates an object of the class JPanel with the given layout manager.

```
public Component add(Component componentAdded)
```
Adds componentAdded to the JPanel. Typically used as a void method.

```
public void setBackground(Color c)
```
Sets the color of the JPanel.

```
public void setLayout(LayoutManager manager)
```
Makes manager the layout manager for the JPanel.

JScrollPane

Package: `javax.swing`
Ancestor classes:

```
Object
   |
   +--Component
         |
         +--Container
               |
               +--JComponent
                     |
                     +--JScrollPane
```

public JScrollPane(Component objectToBeScrolled)

Creates a new `JScrollPane` for the `objectToBeScrolled`. Note that the `objectToBeScrolled` need not be a `JTextArea`, although that is the only type of argument considered in this book.

public void setHorizontalScrollBarPolicy(int policy)

Sets the policy for showing the horizontal scroll bar. The `policy` should be one of
```
JScrollPane.HORIZONTAL_SCROLLBAR_ALWAYS
JScrollPane.HORIZONTAL_SCROLLBAR_NEVER
JScrollPane.HORIZONTAL_SCROLLBAR_AS_NEEDED
```
The phrase `AS_NEEDED` means the scroll bar is shown only when it is needed. This is explained more fully in Chapter 17. The meanings of the other policy constants are obvious from their names.
(As indicated, these constants are defined in the class `JScrollPane`. You should not need to even be aware of the fact that they have `int` values. Think of them as policies, not as `int` values.)

public void setVerticalScrollBarPolicy(int policy)

Sets the policy for showing the vertical scroll bar. The `policy` should be one of
```
JScrollPane.VERTICAL_SCROLLBAR_ALWAYS
JScrollPane.VERTICAL_SCROLLBAR_NEVER
JScrollPane.VERTICAL_SCROLLBAR_AS_NEEDED
```
The phrase `AS_NEEDED` means the scroll bar is shown only when it is needed. This is explained more fully in Chapter 18. The meanings of the other policy constants are obvious from their names.
(As indicated, these constants are defined in the class `JScrollPane`. You should not need to even be aware of the fact that they have `int` values. Think of them as policies, not as `int` values.)

JTextArea

See JTextComponent.

JTextComponent

Package: javax.swing.text
The classes JTextField and JTextArea are in the package javax.swing.
All these methods are inherited by the classes JTextField and JTextArea.
Ancestor classes:

```
Object
   |
   +--Component
         |
         +--Container
               |
               +--JComponent
                     |
                     +--JTextComponent
                     |                 \
                     +--JTextField   +--JTextArea
```

public String getText()

Returns the text that is displayed by this text component.

public boolean isEditable()

Returns true if the user can write in this text component. Returns false if the user is not allowed to write in this text component.

public void setBackground(Color theColor)

Sets the background color of this text component.

public void setEditable(boolean argument)

If argument is true, then the user is allowed to write in the text component. If argument is false, then the user is not allowed to write in the text component.

public void setText(String text)

Sets the text that is displayed by this text component to be the specified text.

JTextField

See JTextComponent.

List<T> Interface

Package: `java.util`
Ancestor interfaces: `Collection<T>`, `Iterable<T>`
All the exception classes mentioned are the kind that are not required to be caught in a `catch` block or declared in a `throws` clause.
All the exception classes mentioned are in the package `java.lang` and so do not require any `import` statement.

CONSTRUCTORS

Although not officially required by the interface, any class that implements the `List<T>` interface should have at least two constructors: a no-argument constructor that creates an empty `List<T>` object, and a constructor with one parameter of type `Collection<? extends T>` that creates a `List<T>` object with the same elements as the constructor argument. If the argument imposes an ordering on its elements, then the `List<T>` created should preserve this ordering.

```
public boolean contains(Object target)
```

Returns `true` if the calling object contains at least one instance of `target`. Uses `target.equals` to determine if `target` is in the calling object.

Throws:

`ClassCastException` if the type of `target` is incompatible with the calling object (optional). `NullPointerException` if `target` is `null` and the calling object does not support `null` elements (optional).

```
public boolean containsAll(Collection<?> collectionOfTargets)
```

Returns `true` if the calling object contains all of the elements in `collectionOfTargets`. For `element` in `collectionOfTargets`, uses `element.equals` to determine if `element` is in the calling object. The elements need not be in the same order or have the same multiplicity in `collectionOfTargets` and in the calling object.

```
public boolean equals(Object other)
```

If the argument is a `List`, returns `true` if the calling object and the argument contain exactly the same elements in exactly the same order; otherwise returns `false`. If the argument is not a `List`, `false` is returned.

```
public int hashCode()
```

Returns the hash code value for the calling object. Neither hash codes nor this method is discussed in this book. This entry is only here to make the definition of the `List` interface complete. You can safely ignore this entry until you go on to study hash codes in a more advanced book. In the meantime, if you need to implement this method, have it throw an `UnsupportedOperationException`.

```
boolean isEmpty()
```

Returns `true` if the calling object is empty; otherwise returns `false`.

```
Iterator<T> iterator()
```

Returns an iterator for the calling object. (Iterators are discussed in Section 16.3.)

```
public Object[] toArray()
```

Returns an array containing all of the elements in the calling object. The elements in the returned array are in the same order as in the calling object. A new array must be returned so that the calling object has no references to the returned array.

```
public <E> E[] toArray(E[] a)
```

Note that the type parameter E is not the same as T. So, E can be any reference type; it need not be the type T in Collection<T>. For example, E might be an ancestor type of T. Returns an array containing all of the elements in the calling object. The elements in the returned array are in the same order as in the calling object. The argument a is used primarily to specify the type of the array returned. The exact details are described in the table for the Collection<T> interface.

Throws:

ArrayStoreException if the type of a is not an ancestor type of the type of every element in the calling object.
NullPointerException if a is null.

```
public int size()
```

Returns the number of elements in the calling object. If the calling object contains more than Integer.MAX_VALUE elements, returns Integer.MAX_VALUE.

OPTIONAL METHODS

As with the Collection<T> interface, the following methods are optional, which means they still must be implemented, but the implementation can simply throw an UnsupportedOperationException if for some reason you do not want to give them a "real" implementation. An UnsupportedOperationException is a RunTimeException and so is not required to be caught or declared in a throws clause.

```
public boolean add(T element) (Optional)
```

Adds element to the end of the calling object's list. Normally returns true. Returns false if the operation failed, but if the operation failed, something is seriously wrong and you will probably get a run-time error anyway.

Throws:

UnsupportedOperationException if the add method is not supported by the calling object.
ClassCastException if the class of element prevents it from being added to the calling object.
NullPointerException if element is null and the calling object does not support null elements.
IllegalArgumentException if some aspect of element prevents it from being added to the calling object.

`public boolean addAll(Collection<? extends T> collectionToAdd)` *(Optional)*

Adds all of the elements in `collectionToAdd` to the end of the calling object's list. The elements are added in the order they are produced by an iterator for `collectionToAdd`.

Throws:

`UnsupportedOperationException` if the `addAll` method is not supported by the calling object.
`ClassCastException` if the class of an element in `collectionToAdd` prevents it from being added to the calling object.
`NullPointerException` if `collectionToAdd` contains one or more `null` elements and the calling object does not support `null` elements, or if `collectionToAdd` is null.
`IllegalArgumentException` if some aspect of an element in `collectionToAdd` prevents it from being added to the calling object.

`public void clear()` *(Optional)*

Removes all the elements from the calling object.

Throws:

`UnsupportedOperationException` if the `clear` method is not supported by the calling object.

`public boolean remove(Object element)` *(Optional)*

Removes the first occurrence of `element` from the calling object's list, if it is present. Returns `true` if the calling object contained the `element`; returns `false` otherwise.

Throws:

`ClassCastException` if the type of `element` is incompatible with the calling object *(optional)*.
`NullPointerException` if `element` is `null` and the calling object does not support `null` elements (optional).
`UnsupportedOperationException` if the `remove` method is not supported by the calling object.

`public boolean removeAll(Collection<?> collectionToRemove)` *(Optional)*

Removes all the calling object's elements that are also in `collectionToRemove`. Returns `true` if the calling object was changed; otherwise returns `false`.

Throws:

`UnsupportedOperationException` if the `removeAll` method is not supported by the calling object.
`ClassCastException` if the types of one or more elements in the calling object are incompatible with `collectionToRemove` (optional).
`NullPointerException` if the calling object contains one or more `null` elements and `collectionToRemove` does not support `null` elements (optional).
`NullPointerException` if `collectionToRemove` is null.

```
public boolean retainAll(Collection<?> saveElements) (Optional)
```

Retains only the elements in the calling object that are also in the collection `saveElements`. In other words, removes from the calling object all of its elements that are not contained in the collection `saveElements`. Returns `true` if the calling object was changed; otherwise returns `false`.

Throws:

`UnsupportedOperationException` if the `retainAll` method is not supported by the calling object.
`ClassCastException` if the types of one or more elements in the calling object are incompatible with `saveElements` (optional).
`NullPointerException` if the calling object contains one or more `null` elements and `saveElements` does not support `null` elements (optional).
`NullPointerException` if the collection `saveElements` is `null`.

NEW METHOD HEADINGS

The following methods are in the `List<T>` interface but were not in the `Collection<T>` interface. Those that are optional are noted.

```
public void add(int index, T newElement) (Optional)
```

Inserts `newElement` in the calling object's list at location `index`. The old elements at location `index` and higher are moved to higher indices.

Throws:

`IndexOutOfBoundsException` if the index is not in the range:
`0 <= index <= size()`.
`UnsupportedOperationException` if this add method is not supported by the calling object.
`ClassCastException` if the class of `newElement` prevents it from being added to the calling object.
`NullPointerException` if `newElement` is `null` and the calling object does not support `null` elements.
`IllegalArgumentException` if some aspect of `newElement` prevents it from being added to the calling object.

```
public boolean addAll(int index,
             Collection<? extends T> collectionToAdd) (Optional)
```

Inserts all of the elements in `collectionToAdd` to the calling object's list starting at location `index`. The old elements at location `index` and higher are moved to higher indices. The elements are added in the order they are produced by an iterator for `collectionToAdd`. Returns `true` if successful; otherwise returns `false`.

Throws:

`IndexOutOfBoundsException` if the index is not in the range:
`0 <= index <= size()`.
`UnsupportedOperationException` if the `addAll` method is not supported by the calling object.
`ClassCastException` if the class of one of the elements of `collectionToAdd` prevents it from being added to the calling object.
`NullPointerException` if `collectionToAdd` contains one or more `null` elements and the calling object does not support `null` elements, or if `collectionToAdd` is `null`.
`IllegalArgumentException` if some aspect of one of the elements of `collectionToAdd` prevents it from being added to the calling object.

```
public int indexOf(Object target)
```

Returns the index of the first element that is equal to `target`. Uses the method `equals` of the object `target` to test for equality. Returns –1 if `target` is not found.

Throws:

`ClassCastException` if the type of `target` is incompatible with the calling object (optional). `NullPointerException` if `target` is `null` and the calling object does not support `null` elements (optional).

```
public int lastIndexOf(Object target)
```

Returns the index of the last element that is equal to `target`. Uses the method `equals` of the object `target` to test for equality. Returns –1 if `target` is not found.

Throws:

`ClassCastException` if the type of `target` is incompatible with the calling object (optional). `NullPointerException` if `target` is `null` and the calling object does not support `null` elements (optional).

```
public List<T> subList(int fromIndex, int toIndex)
```

Returns a *view* of the elements at locations `fromIndex` to `toIndex` of the calling object; the object at `fromIndex` is included; the object, if any, at `toIndex` is not included. The *view* uses references into the calling object; so, changing the *view* can change the calling object. The returned object will be of type `List<T>` but need not be of the same type as the calling object. Returns an empty `List<T>` if `fromIndex` equals `toIndex`.

Throws:

`IndexOutOfBoundsException` if `fromIndex` and `toIndex` do not satisfy:
`0 <= fromIndex <= toIndex <= size()`.

```
ListIterator<T> listIterator()
```

Returns a list iterator for the calling object. (Iterators are discussed in Section 16.3.)

```
ListIterator<T> listIterator(int index)
```

Returns a list iterator for the calling object starting at `index`. The first element to be returned by the iterator is the one at `index`. (Iterators are discussed in Section 16.3.)

Throws:

`IndexOutOfBoundsException` if `index` does not satisfy:
`0 <= index <= size()`

```
public T get(int index)
```

Returns the object at position `index`.
Throws an `IndexOutOfBoundsException` if the `index` is not in the range:
`0 <= index < size()`.

`public T remove(int index)` *(Optional)*

Removes the element at position `index` in the calling object. Shifts any subsequent elements to the left (subtracts one from their indices). Returns the element that was removed from the calling object.

Throws:

`UnsupportedOperationException` if the `remove` method is not supported by the calling object.
`IndexOutOfBoundsException` if `index` does not satisfy:
`0 <= index < size()`

`public T set(int index, T newElement)` *(Optional)*

Sets the element at the specified `index` to `newElement`. The element previously at that position is returned.

Throws:

`IndexOutOfBoundsException` if the `index` is not in the range:
`0 <= index < size()`.
`UnsupportedOperationException` if the `set` method is not supported by the calling object.
`ClassCastException` if the class of `newElement` prevents it from being added to the calling object.
`NullPointerException` if `newElement` is `null` and the calling object does not support null elements.
`IllegalArgumentException` if some aspect of `newElement` prevents it from being added to the calling object.

`ListIterator<T>` Interface

Package: `java.util`
Ancestor interfaces: `Iterator<T>`
The *cursor position* is explained in Chapter 16.
All the exception classes mentioned are the kind that are not required to be caught in a `catch` block or declared in a `throws` clause.
`NoSuchElementException` is in the `java.util` package, which requires an `import` statement if your code mentions the `NoSuchElementException` class. All the other exception classes mentioned are in the package `java.lang` and so do not require any `import` statements.

`public void add(T newElement)` *(Optional)*

Inserts `newElement` at the location of the iterator cursor (that is, before the value, if any, that would be returned by `next()` and after the value, if any, that would be returned by `previous()`). Cannot be used if there has been a call to `add` or `remove` since the last call to `next()` or `previous()`.

Throws:

`IllegalStateException` if neither `next()` nor `previous()` has been called, or the `add` or `remove` method has already been called after the last call to `next()` or `previous()`.
`UnsupportedOperationException` if the `remove` operation is not supported by this `Iterator`.
`ClassCastException` if the class of `newElement` prevents it from being added.
`IllegalArgumentException` if some property other than the class of `newElement` prevents it from being added.

`public boolean hasNext()`

Returns `true` if there is a suitable element for `next()` to return; returns `false` otherwise.

`public boolean hasPrevious()`

Returns `true` if there is a suitable element for `previous()` to return; returns `false` otherwise.

`public int nextIndex()`

Returns the index of the element that would be returned by a call to `next()`. Returns the list size if the cursor position is at the end of the list.

`public T next()`

Returns the next element of the list that produced the iterator. More specifically, returns the element immediately after the cursor position.

Throws:

`NoSuchElementException` if there is no next element.

`public T previous()`

Returns the previous element of the list that produced the iterator. More specifically, returns the element immediately before the cursor position.

Throws:

`NoSuchElementException` if there is no previous element.

`public int previousIndex()`

Returns the index that would be returned by a call to `previous()`. Returns -1 if the cursor position is at the beginning of the list.

`public void remove()` (*Optional*)

Removes from the collection the last element returned by `next()` or `previous()`.
This method can be called only once per call to `next()` or `previous()`.
Cannot be used if there has been a call to `add` or `remove` since the last call to `next()` or `previous()`.

Throws:

`IllegalStateException` if neither `next()` nor `previous()` has been called, or the `add` or `remove` method has already been called after the last call to `next()` or `previous()`.
`UnsupportedOperationException` if the `remove` operation is not supported by this `Iterator`.

```
public void set(T newElement) (Optional)
```

Replaces the last element returned by next() or previous() with newElement. Cannot be used if there has been a call to add or remove since the last call to next() or previous().

Throws:

UnsupportedOperationException if the set operation is not supported by this Iterator. IllegalStateException if neither next() nor previous() has been called, or the add or remove method has been called since the last call to next() or previous(). ClassCastException if the class of newElement prevents it from being added. IllegalArgumentException if some property other than the class of newElement prevents it from being added.

Long

This is a wrapper class for long. See Section 5.1 in Chapter 5.

Math

Package: java.lang

```
        Object
          |
        +--Math
```

The Math class is marked final, which means it cannot be used as a base class to derive other classes.

```
public static double abs(double argument)

public static float abs(float argument)

public static long abs(long argument)

public static int abs(int argument)
```

Returns the absolute value of the argument. (The method name abs is overloaded to produce four similar methods.)

EXAMPLES

Math.abs(-6) and Math.abs(6) both return 6. Math.abs(-5.5) and Math.abs(5.5) both return 5.5.

```
public static double ceil(double argument)
```

Returns the smallest whole number greater than or equal to the argument.

EXAMPLE

Math.ceil(3.2) and Math.ceil(3.9) both return 4.0.

```
public static double floor(double argument)
```

Returns the largest whole number less than or equal to the argument.

EXAMPLE

Math.floor(3.2) and Math.floor(3.9) both return 3.0.

```
public static double max(double n1, double n2)

public static float max(float n1, float n2)

public static long max(long n1, long n2)

public static int max(int n1, int n2)
```

Returns the maximum of the arguments n1 and n2. (The method name max is overloaded to produce four similar methods.)

EXAMPLE

Math.max(3, 2) returns 3.

```
public static double min(double n1, double n2)

public static float min(float n1, float n2)

public static long min(long n1, long n2)

public static int min(int n1, int n2)
```

Returns the minimum of the arguments n1 and n2. (The method name min is overloaded to produce four similar methods.)

EXAMPLE

Math.min(3, 2) returns 2.

```
public static double pow(double base, double exponent)
```

Returns base to the power exponent.

EXAMPLE

Math.pow(2.0,3.0) returns 8.0.

```
public static double random()
```

Returns a random number greater than or equal to 0.0 and less than 1.0.

EXAMPLE

Math.random() returns 0.5505562535943004 (example value only; will return a pseudo-random number that is less than 1 and greater than or equal to 0 the next time the statement is executed)

```
public static long round(double argument)

public static int round(float argument)
```

Rounds its argument.

EXAMPLES

Math.round(3.2) returns 3. Math.round(3.6) returns 4.

```
public static double sqrt(double argument)
```

Returns the square root of its argument.

EXAMPLE

Math.sqrt(4) returns 2.0.

`Map<K,V>` Interface

Package: `java.util`
Ancestor interfaces: none
All the exception classes mentioned are unchecked exceptions, which means they are not required to be caught in a `catch` block or declared in a `throws` clause. No `import` statement is required because these exception classes are in the package `java.lang`.

CONSTRUCTORS

Although not officially required by the interface, any class that implements the `Map<K,V>` interface should have at least two constructors: a no-argument constructor that creates an empty `Map<K,V>` object, and a constructor with one `Map<K,V>` parameter that creates a `Map<K,V>` object with the same elements as the constructor argument. The interface does not specify whether the copy produced by the one-argument constructor is a shallow copy or a deep copy of its argument.

METHODS

```
public boolean containsKey(Object key)
```

Returns `true` if the calling object contains `key` as one of its keys.

Throws:

`ClassCastException` if the type of `key` is incompatible with the type for this map (optional).
`NullPointerException` if the key is `null` and this map does not permit `null` keys (optional).

```
public boolean containsValue(Object value)
```

Returns `true` if the calling object contains one or more keys that map to an instance of `value`.

Throws:

`ClassCastException` if the type of `value` is incompatible with the type for this map (optional).
`NullPointerException` if the value is `null` and this map does not permit `null` values (optional).

```
public Set<Map.Entry<K,V>> entrySet()
```

Returns a set view consisting of (key, value) mappings for all entries in the map. Changes to the map are reflected in the set and vice-versa.

```
public boolean equals(Object other)
```

This is the `equals` of the map, not the `equals` of the elements in the map. Overrides the inherited method `equals`.

```
public V get(Object key)
```

Returns the value onto which the calling object maps `key`. If `key` is not in the map, then `null` is returned. Note that this does not always mean that the key is not in the map, because it is possible to map a key to `null`. The `containsKey` method can be used to distinguish the two cases.

Throws:

`ClassCastException` if the type of `key` is incompatible with the type for this map (optional).
`NullPointerException` if the `key` is `null` and this map does not permit `null` keys (optional).

```
public int hashCode()
```

Returns the hash code value for the calling object. The hash code of a map is defined to be the sum of the `hashCodes` of each entry in the map's `entrySet` view.

```
public boolean isEmpty()
```

Returns `true` if the calling object is empty; otherwise returns `false`.

```
public int size()
```

Returns the number of (key, value) mappings in the calling object.

```
public Collection<V> values()
```

Returns a collection view consisting of all values in the map. Changes to the map are reflected in the collection and vice-versa.

OPTIONAL METHODS

The following methods are optional, which means they still must be implemented, but the implementation can simply throw an `UnsupportedOperationException` if, for some reason, you do not want to give them a "real" implementation. An `UnsupportedOperationException` is a `RunTimeException` and so is not required to be caught or declared in a `throws` clause.

```
public V put(K key, V value) (Optional)
```

Associates `key` to `value` in the map. If `key` was associated with an existing value, then the old value is overwritten and returned. Otherwise `null` is returned.

Throws:

`ClassCastException` if the type of `key` or `value` is incompatible with the type for this map (optional).
`NullPointerException` if the key or value is `null` and this map does not permit `null` keys or values (optional).
`IllegalArgumentException` if some aspect of the key or value prevents it from being stored in this map (optional).
`UnsupportedOperationException` if the put operation is not supported by this map (optional).

```
public void putAll(Map<? extends K,? extends V> mapToAdd) (Optional)
```

Adds all mappings of `mapToAdd` into the calling object's map.

Throws:

`ClassCastException` if any type of `key` or `value` of `mapToAdd` is incompatible with the type for this map (optional).
`NullPointerException` if `mapToAdd` is `null` or any key or value of `mapToAdd` is null and this map does not permit null keys or values (optional).
`IllegalArgumentException` if some aspect of the key or value from `mapToAdd` prevents it from being stored in this map (optional).
`UnsupportedOperationException` if the `putAll` operation is not supported by this map (optional).

public V remove(Object key) *(Optional)*

Removes the mapping for the specified key. If the key is not found in the map, then null is returned, otherwise the previous value for the key is returned.

Throws:

ClassCastException if the type of key is incompatible with the type for this map (optional). NullPointerException if the key is null and this map does not permit null keys (optional). UnsupportedOperationException if the remove operation is not supported by this map (optional).

ObjectInputStream

Package: java.io
The FileInputStream class is also in this package.
Ancestor classes:

```
Object
  |
  +--InputStream
        |
        +--ObjectInputStream
```

public ObjectInputStream(InputStream streamObject)

There is no constructor that takes a file name as an argument. If you want to create a stream using a file name, use

new ObjectInputStream(new FileInputStream(*File_Name*))

Alternatively, you can use an object of the class File in place of the *File_Name*, as follows:

new ObjectInputStream(new FileInputStream(*File_Object*))

The constructor for FileInputStream may throw a FileNotFoundException, which is a kind of IOException. If the FileInputStream constructor succeeds, then the constructor for ObjectInputStream may throw a different IOException.

public void close()throws IOException

Closes the stream's connection to a file.

public boolean readBoolean()throws IOException

Reads a boolean value from the input stream and returns that boolean value. If readBoolean tries to read a value from the file and that value was not written using the method writeBoolean of the class ObjectOutputStream (or written in some equivalent way), then problems will occur.

If an attempt is made to read beyond the end of the file, an EOFException is thrown.

`public char readChar()throws IOException`

Reads a char value from the input stream and returns that char value. If readChar tries to read a value from the file and that value was not written using the method writeChar of the class ObjectOutputStream (or written in some equivalent way), then problems will occur.

If an attempt is made to read beyond the end of the file, an EOFException is thrown.

`public double readDouble()throws IOException`

Reads a double value from the input stream and returns that double value. If readDouble tries to read a value from the file and that value was not written using the method writeDouble of the class ObjectOutputStream (or written in some equivalent way), then problems will occur.

If an attempt is made to read beyond the end of the file, an EOFException is thrown.

`public float readFloat()throws IOException`

Reads a float value from the input stream and returns that float value. If readFloat tries to read a value from the file and that value was not written using the method writeFloat of the class ObjectOutputStream (or written in some equivalent way), then problems will occur.

If an attempt is made to read beyond the end of the file, an EOFException is thrown.

`public int readInt()throws IOException`

Reads an int value from the input stream and returns that int value. If readInt tries to read a value from the file and that value was not written using the method writeInt of the class ObjectOutputStream (or written in some equivalent way), then problems will occur.

If an attempt is made to read beyond the end of the file, an EOFException is thrown.

`public long readLong()throws IOException`

Reads a long value from the input stream and returns that long value. If readLong tries to read a value from the file and that value was not written using the method writeLong of the class ObjectOutputStream (or written in some equivalent way), then problems will occur.

If an attempt is made to read beyond the end of the file, an EOFException is thrown.

`Object readObject()throws ClassNotFoundException, IOException`

Reads an object from the input stream. The object read should have been written using writeObject of the class ObjectOutputStream.

Throws:

ClassNotFoundException if the class of a serialized object cannot be found.
If an attempt is made to read beyond the end of the file, an EOFException is thrown.
May throw various other IOExceptions.

```
public int readShort()throws IOException
```

Reads a short value from the input stream and returns that short value. If readInt tries to read a value from the file and that value was not written using the method writeShort of the class ObjectOutputStream (or written in some equivalent way), then problems will occur.

If an attempt is made to read beyond the end of the file, an EOFException is thrown.

```
public String readUTF()throws IOException
```

Reads a String value from the input stream and returns that String value. If readUTF tries to read a value from the file and that value was not written using the method writeUTF of the class ObjectOutputStream (or written in some equivalent way), then problems will occur.

If an attempt is made to read beyond the end of the file, an EOFException is thrown.

```
public int skipBytes(int n) throws IOException
```

Skips n bytes.

ObjectOutputStream

Package: java.io
The FileOutputStream class is also in this package.
Ancestor classes:

```
        Object
          |
          +--OutputStream
                 |
                 +--ObjectOutputStream
```

```
public ObjectOutputStream(OutputStream streamObject)
```

There is no constructor that takes a file name as an argument. If you want to create a stream using a file name, use

```
new ObjectOutputStream(new FileOutputStream(File_Name))
```

This creates a blank file. If there already is a file named *File_Name*, then the old contents of the file are lost.
If you want to create a stream using an object of the class File, use

```
new ObjectOutputStream(new FileOutputStream(File_Object))
```

The constructor for FileOutputStream may throw a FileNotFoundException, which is a kind of IOException. If the FileOutputStream constructor succeeds, then the constructor for ObjectOutputStream may throw a different IOException.

```
public void close()throws IOException
```

Closes the stream's connection to a file. This method calls flush before closing the file.

```
public void flush()throws IOException
```

Flushes the output stream. This forces an actual physical write to the file of any data that has been buffered and not yet physically written to the file. Normally, you should not need to invoke `flush`.

```
public void writeBoolean(boolean b) throws IOException
```

Writes the `boolean` value b to the output stream.

```
public void writeChar(int n) throws IOException
```

Writes the `char` value n to the output stream. Note that it expects its argument to be an `int` value. However, if you simply use the `char` value, then Java will automatically type cast it to an `int` value. The following are equivalent:

```
outputStream.writeChar((int)'A');
```

and

```
outputStream.writeChar('A');
```

```
public void writeDouble(double x) throws IOException
```

Writes the `double` value x to the output stream.

```
public void writeFloat(float x) throws IOException
```

Writes the `float` value x to the output stream.

```
public void writeInt(int n) throws IOException
```

Writes the `int` value n to the output stream.

```
public void writeLong(long n) throws IOException
```

Writes the `long` value n to the output stream.

```
public void writeObject(Object anObject) throws IOException
```

Writes its argument to the output stream. The object argument should be an object of a serializable class, a concept discussed in Chapter 10.

Throws:

Various `IOExceptions`.

```
public void writeShort(short n) throws IOException
```

Writes the `short` value n to the output stream.

```
public void writeUTF(String aString) throws IOException
```

Writes the `String` value aString to the output stream. UTF refers to a particular method of encoding the string. To read the string back from the file, you should use the method `readUTF` of the class `ObjectInputStream`.

PrintWriter

Package: `java.io`
The `FileOutputStream` class is also in this package.
Ancestor classes:

```
Object
  |
  +--Writer
        |
        +--PrintWriter
```

public PrintWriter(OutputStream streamObject)

This is the only constructor you are likely to need. There is no constructor that accepts a file name as an argument. If you want to create a stream using a file name, use

```
new PrintWriter (new FileOutputStream(File_Name))
```

When the constructor is used in this way, a blank file is created. If there already was a file named *File_Name*, then the old contents of the file are lost. If you want instead to append new text to the end of the old file contents, use

```
new PrintWriter(new FileOutputStream (File_Name, true))
```

(For an explanation of the argument `true`, see Chapter 10.)
When used in either of these ways, the `FileOutputStream` constructor, and so the `PrintWriter` constructor invocation, can throw a `FileNotFoundException`, which is a kind of `IOException`. If you want to create a stream using an object of the class `File`, you can use a `File` object in place of the *File_Name*.

public void close()

Closes the stream's connection to a file. This method calls `flush` before closing the file.

public void flush()

Flushes the output stream. This forces an actual physical write to the file of any data that has been buffered and not yet physically written to the file. Normally, you should not need to invoke `flush`.

public final void print(*Argument*)

Same as `println`, except that this method does not end the line, and so the next output will be on the same line.

public final void println(*Argument*)

The *Argument* can be a string, character, integer, floating-point number, boolean value, or any combination of these, connected with + signs. The *Argument* can also be any object, although it will not work as desired unless the object has a properly defined `toString()` method. The *Argument* is output to the file connected to the stream. After the *Argument* has been output, the line ends, and so the next output is sent to the next line.

Random

Package: `java.util`
Ancestor classes:

```
        Object
          |
        +--Random
```

public Random()

Creates a new random number generator.

public Random(long seed)

Creates a new random number generator with the specified seed value.

public int nextInt(int n)

Returns a pseudo-random, uniformly distributed `int` value between 0 (inclusive) and the value n (exclusive).

public double nextDouble(double n)

Returns a pseudo-random, uniformly distributed `double` value between 0 (inclusive) and 1 (exclusive).

RandomAccessFile

Package: `java.io`

```
        Object
          |
        +--RandomAccessFile
```

public RandomAccessFile(String fileName, String mode)

public RandomAccessFile(File fileObject, String mode)

Opens the file, does not delete data already in the file, but does position the file pointer at the first (zeroth) location.
The mode must be one of the following:
`"r"` Open for reading only.
`"rw"` Open for reading and writing.
`"rws"` Same as `"rw"`, and also requires that every update to the file's content or metadata be written synchronously to the underlying storage device.
`"rwd"` Same as `"rw"`, and also requires that every update to the file's content be written synchronously to the underlying storage device.
`"rws"` and `"rwd"` are not covered in this book text.

public void close()throws IOException

Closes the stream's connection to a file.

```
public void setLength(long newLength) throws IOException
```

Sets the length of this file.

If the present length of the file as returned by the `length` method is greater than the `newLength` argument, then the file will be truncated. In this case, if the file pointer location as returned by the `getFilePointer` method is greater than `newLength`, then after this method returns, the file pointer location will be equal to `newLength`.

If the present length of the file as returned by the `length` method is smaller than `newLength`, then the file will be extended. In this case, the contents of the extended portion of the file are not defined.

```
public long getFilePointer() throws IOException
```

Returns the current location of the file pointer. Locations are numbered starting with 0.

```
public long length() throws IOException
```

Returns the length of the file.

```
public int read() throws IOException
```

Reads a byte of data from the file and returns it as an integer in the range 0 to 255.

```
public int read(byte[] a) throws IOException
```

Reads up to a.length bytes of data from the file into the array of bytes. Returns the total number of bytes read or -1 if the end of the file is reached.

```
public final boolean readBoolean() throws IOException
```

Reads a `boolean` value from the file and returns that value.

If an attempt is made to read beyond the end of the file, an `EOFException` is thrown.

```
public final byte readByte() throws IOException
```

Reads a `byte` value from the file and returns that value.

If an attempt is made to read beyond the end of the file, an `EOFException` is thrown.

```
public final char readChar() throws IOException
```

Reads a `char` value from the file and returns that value.

If an attempt is made to read beyond the end of the file, an `EOFException` is thrown.

```
public final double readDouble() throws IOException
```

Reads a `double` value from the file and returns that value.

If an attempt is made to read beyond the end of the file, an `EOFException` is thrown.

```
public final float readFloat() throws IOException
```

Reads a `float` value from the file and returns that value.

If an attempt is made to read beyond the end of the file, an `EOFException` is thrown.

```
public final int readInt() throws IOException
```
Reads an int value from the file and returns that value.

If an attempt is made to read beyond the end of the file, an EOFException is thrown.

```
public final long readLong() throws IOException
```
Reads a long value from the file and returns that value.

If an attempt is made to read beyond the end of the file, an EOFException is thrown.

```
public final short readShort() throws IOException
```
Reads a short value from the file and returns that value.

If an attempt is made to read beyond the end of the file, an EOFException is thrown.

```
public final String readUTF() throws IOException
```
Reads a String value from the file and returns that value.

If an attempt is made to read beyond the end of the file, an EOFException is thrown.

```
public void seek(long location) throws IOException
```
Moves the file pointer to the specified location.

```
public void write(byte[] a) throws IOException
```
Writes a.length bytes from the specified byte array to the file.

```
public void write(int b) throws IOException
```
Writes the specified byte to the file.

```
public final void writeBoolean(boolean b ) throws IOException
```
Writes the boolean b to the file.

```
public final void writeByte(byte b ) throws IOException
```
Writes the byte b to the file.

```
public final void writeChar(char c ) throws IOException
```
Writes the char c to the file.

```
public final void writeDouble(double d ) throws IOException
```
Writes the double d to the file.

```
public final void writeFloat(float f ) throws IOException
```
Writes the float f to the file.

```
public final void writeInt(int n ) throws IOException
```
Writes the int n to the file.

```
public final void writeLong(long n ) throws IOException
```
Writes the long n to the file.

```
public final void writeShort(short n ) throws IOException
```
Writes the short n to the file.

```
public final void writeUTF(String s ) throws IOException
```
Writes the String s to the file.

Scanner

Package: java.util
Ancestor classes:

```
        Object
          |
        +--Scanner
```

The Scanner class can be used to obtain input from files as well as from the keyboard. Values to be read should be separated by whitespace characters, such as blanks and/or new lines. When reading values, these whitespace characters are skipped. (It is possible to change the separators from whitespace to something else, but whitespace is the default.)

```
public Scanner(InputStream streamObject)
```
There is no constructor that accepts a file name as an argument. If you want to create a stream using a file name, you can use

```
new Scanner(new FileInputStream(File_Name))
```
When used in this way, the FileInputStream constructor, and thus the Scanner constructor invocation, can throw a FileNotFoundException, which is a kind of IOException.
To create a stream connected to the keyboard, use

```
new Scanner(System.in)
```

```
public Scanner(File fileObject)
```
If you want to create a stream using a file name, you can use

```
new Scanner(new File(File_Name))
```

```
public int nextInt()
```
Returns the next token as an int, provided the next token is a well-formed string representation of an int.

Throws:

NoSuchElementException if there are no more tokens.
InputMismatchException if the next token is not a well-formed string representation of an int.
IllegalStateException if the Scanner stream is closed.

```
public boolean hasNextInt()
```

Returns `true` if the next token is a well-formed string representation of an `int`; otherwise returns `false`.

Throws:

`IllegalStateException` if the `Scanner` stream is closed.

```
public long nextLong()
```

Returns the next token as a `long`, provided the next token is a well-formed string representation of a `long`.

Throws:

`NoSuchElementException` if there are no more tokens.
`InputMismatchException` if the next token is not a well-formed string representation of a `long`.
`IllegalStateException` if the `Scanner` stream is closed.

```
public boolean hasNextLong()
```

Returns `true` if the next token is a well-formed string representation of a `long`; otherwise returns `false`.

Throws:

`IllegalStateException` if the `Scanner` stream is closed.

```
public byte nextByte()
```

Returns the next token as a `byte`, provided the next token is a well-formed string representation of a `byte`.

Throws:

`NoSuchElementException` if there are no more tokens.
`InputMismatchException` if the next token is not a well-formed string representation of a `byte`.
`IllegalStateException` if the `Scanner` stream is closed.

```
public boolean hasNextByte()
```

Returns `true` if the next token is a well-formed string representation of a `byte`; otherwise returns `false`.

Throws:

`IllegalStateException` if the `Scanner` stream is closed.

```
public short nextShort()
```

Returns the next token as a `short`, provided the next token is a well-formed string representation of a `short`.

Throws:

`NoSuchElementException` if there are no more tokens.
`InputMismatchException` if the next token is not a well-formed string representation of a `short`.
`IllegalStateException` if the `Scanner` stream is closed.

```
public boolean hasNextShort()
```

Returns `true` if the next token is a well-formed string representation of a `short`; otherwise returns `false`.

Throws:

`IllegalStateException` if the `Scanner` stream is closed.

```
public double nextDouble()
```

Returns the next token as a `double`, provided the next token is a well-formed string representation of a `double`.

Throws:

`NoSuchElementException` if there are no more tokens.
`InputMismatchException` if the next token is not a well-formed string representation of a `double`.
`IllegalStateException` if the `Scanner` stream is closed.

```
public boolean hasNextDouble()
```

Returns `true` if the next token is a well-formed string representation of a `double`; otherwise returns `false`.

Throws:

`IllegalStateException` if the `Scanner` stream is closed.

```
public float nextFloat()
```

Returns the next token as a `float`, provided the next token is a well-formed string representation of a `float`.

Throws:

`NoSuchElementException` if there are no more tokens.
`InputMismatchException` if the next token is not a well-formed string representation of a `float`.
`IllegalStateException` if the `Scanner` stream is closed.

```
public boolean hasNextFloat()
```

Returns `true` if the next token is a well-formed string representation of a `float`; otherwise returns `false`.

Throws:

`IllegalStateException` if the `Scanner` stream is closed.

```
public String next()
```

Returns the next token.

Throws:

`NoSuchElementException` if there are no more tokens.
`IllegalStateException` if the `Scanner` stream is closed.

```
public boolean hasNext()
```

Returns `true` if there is another token. May wait for a next token to enter the stream.

Throws:

`IllegalStateException` if the `Scanner` stream is closed.

```
public boolean nextBoolean()
```

Returns the next token as a `boolean` value, provided the next token is a well-formed string representation of a `boolean`.

Throws:

`NoSuchElementException` if there are no more tokens.
`InputMismatchException` if the next token is not a well-formed string representation of a `boolean` value.
`IllegalStateException` if the `Scanner` stream is closed.

```
public boolean hasNextBoolean()
```

Returns `true` if the next token is a well-formed string representation of a `boolean` value; otherwise returns `false`.

Throws:

`IllegalStateException` if the `Scanner` stream is closed.

```
public String nextLine()
```

Returns the rest of the current input line. Note that the line terminator `'\n'` is read and discarded; it is not included in the string returned.

Throws:

`NoSuchElementException` if there are no more lines.
`IllegalStateException` if the `Scanner` stream is closed.

```
public boolean hasNextLine()
```

Returns `true` if there is a next line. May wait for a next line to enter the stream.

Throws:

`IllegalStateException` if the `Scanner` stream is closed.

```
public Scanner useDelimiter(String newDelimiter);
```

Changes the delimiter for input so that `newDelimiter` will be the only delimiter that separates words or numbers. See the subsection "Other Input Delimiters" in Chapter 2 for the details. (You can use this method to set the delimiters to a more complex pattern than just a single string, but we are not covering that.)

Returns the calling object, but we have always used it as a `void` method.

`Serializable` Interface

See Section 10.4 in Chapter 10.

`Set<T>` Interface

Package: `java.util`
Ancestor interfaces: `Collection <T>`
All the exception classes mentioned are the kind that are not required to be caught in a `catch` block or declared in a `throws` clause.
All the exception classes mentioned are in the package `java.lang` and so do not require any `import` statement.

CONSTRUCTORS

`public boolean contains(Object target)`

Returns `true` if the calling object contains at least one instance of `target`. Uses `target.equals` to determine if `target` is in the calling object.

Throws:

`ClassCastException` if the type of `target` is incompatible with the calling object (optional).
`NullPointerException` if `target` is `null` and the calling object does not support `null` elements (optional).

`public boolean containsAll(Collection<?> collectionOfTargets)`

Returns `true` if the calling object contains all of the elements in `collectionOfTargets`. For element in `collectionOfTargets`, this method uses `element.equals` to determine if element is in the calling object. If `collectionOfTargets` is itself a `Set <T>`, this is a test to see if `collectionOfTargets` is a subset of the calling object.

Throws:

`ClassCastException` if the types of one or more elements in `collectionOfTargets` are incompatible with the calling object (optional).
`NullPointerException` if `collectionOfTargets` contains one or more `null` elements and the calling object does not support null elements (optional).
`NullPointerException` if `collectionOfTargets` is `null`.

`public boolean equals(Object other)`

If the argument is a `Set <T>`, returns `true` if the calling object and the argument contain exactly the same elements; otherwise returns `false`. If the argument is not a `Set <T>`, `false` is returned.

`public int hashCode()`

Returns the hash code value for the calling object. Neither hash codes nor this method are discussed in this book. This entry is only here to make the definition of the `Set <T>` interface complete. You can safely ignore this entry until you go on to study hash codes in a more advanced book. In the meantime, if you need to implement this method, have it throw an `UnsupportedOperationException`.

`public boolean isEmpty()`

Returns `true` if the calling object is empty; otherwise returns `false`.

```
Iterator <T> iterator()
```

Returns an iterator for the calling object. (Iterators are discussed in Section 16.3.)

```
public Object[] toArray()
```

Returns an array containing all of the elements in the calling object. A new array should be returned so that the calling object has no references to the returned array.

```
public <E> E[] toArray(E[] a)
```

Note that the type parameter E is not the same as T. So, E can be any reference type; it need not be the type T in Collection <T>. For example, E might be an ancestor type of T. Returns an array containing all of the elements in the calling object. The argument a is used primarily to specify the type of the array returned. The exact details are described in the table for the Collection <T> interface.

Throws:

ArrayStoreException if the type of a is not an ancestor type of the type of every element in the calling object.
NullPointerException if a is null.

```
public int size()
```

Returns the number of elements in the calling object. If the calling object contains more than Integer.MAX_VALUE elements, returns Integer.MAX_VALUE.

ADDING AND REMOVING ELEMENTS

Although many are optional, the following methods are almost always implemented for classes that implement the Set <T> interface.

```
public boolean add(T element)  (Optional)
```

If element is not already in the calling object, element is added to the calling object and true is returned. If element is in the calling object, the calling object is unchanged and false is returned.

Throws:

UnsupportedOperationException if the add method is not supported by the set.
ClassCastException if the class of element prevents it from being added to the set.
NullPointerException if element is null and the set does not support null elements.
IllegalArgumentException if some other aspect of element prevents it from being added to this set.

```
public boolean addAll(Collection<? extends T> collectionToAdd)  (Optional)
```

Ensures that the calling object contains all the elements in collectionToAdd. Returns true if the calling object changed as a result of the call; returns false otherwise. Thus, if collectionToAdd is a Set <T>, then the calling object is changed to the union of itself with collectionToAdd.

Throws:

UnsupportedOperationException if the addAll method is not supported by the set.
ClassCastException if the class of some element of collectionToAdd prevents it from being added to the calling object.
NullPointerException if collectionToAdd contains one or more null elements and the calling object does not support null elements, or if collectionToAdd is null.
IllegalArgumentException if some aspect of some element of collectionToAdd prevents it from being added to the calling object.

```
public void clear()
```

Removes all the elements from the calling object.

Throws:

UnsupportedOperationException if the clear method is not supported by the calling object.

```
public boolean remove(Object element)
```

Removes the element from the calling object, if it is present. Returns true if the calling object contained the element; returns false otherwise.

Throws:

ClassCastException if the type of element is incompatible with the calling object (optional).
NullPointerException if element is null and the calling object does not support null elements (optional).
UnsupportedOperationException if the remove method is not supported by the calling object.

```
public boolean removeAll(Collection<?> collectionToRemove)   (Optional)
```

Removes all the calling object's elements that are also contained in collectionToRemove. Returns true if the calling object was changed; otherwise returns false.

Throws:

UnsupportedOperationException if the removeAll method is not supported by the calling object.
ClassCastException if the types of one or more elements in collectionToRemove are incompatible with the calling object (optional).
NullPointerException if the calling object contains a null element and collectionToRemove does not support null elements (optional).
NullPointerException if collectionToRemove is null.

```
public boolean retainAll(Collection<?> saveElements)   (Optional)
```

Retains only the elements in the calling object that are also contained in the collection saveElements. In other words, removes from the calling object all of its elements that are not contained in the collection saveElements. Returns true if the calling object was changed; otherwise returns false. If the argument is itself a Set <T>, this changes the calling object to the intersection of itself with the argument.

Throws:

UnsupportedOperationException if the retainAll method is not supported by the calling object.
ClassCastException if the types of one or more elements in the calling object are incompatible with saveElements (optional).
NullPointerException if saveElements contains a null element and the calling object does not support null elements (optional).
NullPointerException if saveElements is null.

Short

Wrapper class for `short`. See Section 5.1 in Chapter 5.

String

Package: `java.lang`
`String` is marked `final` and so you cannot use it as a base class to derive another class.
Implements interfaces: `CharSequence`, `Comparable`, `Serializable`
Ancestor classes:

```
Object
  |
  +--String
```

CONSTRUCTORS

```
public String()
```

Creates a `String` object that represents an empty character sequence. Note that this is a pretty useless constructor because `String` objects are immutable.

```
public String(BufferedString buffer)
```

Creates a new `String` object that contains the same sequence of characters that is currently contained in the `BufferedString` argument. This is a deep copy; subsequent modification of the `BufferedString` object does not affect the newly created string.

Throws:

`NullPointerException` if buffer is `null`.

```
public String(char[] value, int offset, int count)
```

Creates a new `String` that contains characters from a subarray of the character array argument. The `offset` argument is the index of the first character of the subarray, and the `count` argument specifies the length of the subarray. The contents of the subarray are copied. This is a deep copy; subsequent modifications of the character array do not affect the newly created string.

Throws:

`IndexOutOfBoundsException` if the elements specified by `offset` and `count` are not all within the bounds of the `value` array.
`NullPointerException` if value is `null`.

```
public String(String original)
```

Creates a new `String` object so that it represents the same sequence of characters as the argument. Unless an explicit copy of `original` is needed, use of this constructor is unnecessary because `String` objects are immutable.

Throws:

`NullPointerException` if original is `null`.

METHODS

```
public char charAt(int position)
```

Returns the character in the calling object string at the position. Positions are counted 0, 1, 2, etc.

EXAMPLE

After program executes String greeting = "Hello!";
greeting.charAt(0) returns 'H', and
greeting.charAt(1) returns 'e'.

Throws:

IndexOutOfBoundsException if position is negative or not less than the length of the calling object string.

```
public int compareTo(String aString)
```

Compares the calling object string and the string argument to see which comes first in the lexicographic ordering. Lexicographic order is the same as alphabetical order but with the characters ordered as in Appendix 3. Note that in Appendix 3 all the uppercase letters are in regular alphabetical order and all the lowercase letters are in alphabetical order, but all the uppercase letters precede all the lowercase letters. So, lexicographic ordering is the same as alphabetical ordering when either both strings are all uppercase letters or both strings are all lowercase letters. If the calling string is first, it returns a negative value. If the two strings are equal, it returns zero. If the argument is first, it returns a positive number.

EXAMPLE

After program executes String entry = "adventure";
entry.compareTo("zoo") returns a negative number,
entry.compareTo("adventure") returns 0, and
entry.compareTo("above") returns a positive number.

Throws:

NullPointerException if aString is null.

```
public int compareToIgnoreCase(String aString)
```

Compares the calling object string and the string argument to see which comes first in the lexicographic ordering, treating upper- and lowercase letters as being the same. (To be precise, all uppercase letters are treated as if they were their lowercase versions in doing the comparison.) Thus, if both strings consist entirely of letters, the comparison is for ordinary alphabetical order. If the calling string is first, it returns a negative value. If the two strings are equal, ignoring cases, it returns zero. If the argument is first, it returns a positive number.

EXAMPLE

After program executes String entry = "adventure";
entry.compareToIgnoreCase("Zoo") returns a negative number,
entry.compareToIgnoreCase("Adventure") returns 0, and
"Zoo".compareToIgnoreCase(entry) returns a positive number.

Throws:

NullPointerException if aString is null.

```
public boolean contentEquals(StringBuffer stringBufferObject)
```

Returns `true` if and only if this `String` represents the same sequence of characters as the `StringBuffer` argument.

Throws:

`NullPointerException` if `stringBufferObject` is null.

```
public boolean equals(String otherString)
```

Returns `true` if the calling object string and the `otherString` are equal. Otherwise returns `false`.

EXAMPLE

After program executes `String greeting = "Hello";`
`greeting.equals("Hello")` returns `true`
`greeting.equals("Good-Bye")` returns `false`
`greeting.equals("hello")` returns `false`
Note that case matters: `"Hello"` and `"hello"` are not equal because one starts with an uppercase letter and the other starts with a lowercase letter.

```
public boolean equalsIgnoreCase(String otherString)
```

Returns `true` if the calling object string and the `otherString` are equal, considering upper- and lowercase versions of a letter to be the same. Otherwise returns `false`.

EXAMPLE

After program executes `String name = "mary";`
`name.equalsIgnoreCase("Mary")` returns `true`.

```
public int indexOf(String aString)
```

Returns the index (position) of the first occurrence of the string `aString` in the calling object string. Positions are counted 0, 1, 2, etc. Returns –1 if `aString` is not found.

EXAMPLE

After program executes `String greeting = "Hi Mary!";`
`greeting.indexOf("Mary")` returns 3, and
`greeting.indexOf("Sally")` returns –1.

Throws:

`NullPointerException` if `aString` is null.

```
public int indexOf(String aString, int start)
```

Returns the index (position) of the first occurrence of the string `aString` in the calling object string that occurs at or after position `start`. Positions are counted 0, 1, 2, etc. Returns –1 if `aString` is not found.

EXAMPLE

After program executes `String name = "Mary, Mary quite contrary";`
`name.indexOf("Mary", 1)` returns 6.
The same value is returned if 1 is replaced by any number up to and including 6.
`name.indexOf("Mary", 0)` returns 0.
`name.indexOf("Mary", 8)` returns –1.

Throws:

`NullPointerException` if `aString` is null.

```
public int lastIndexOf(String aString)
```

Returns the index (position) of the last occurrence of the string `aString` in the calling object string. Positions are counted 0, 1, 2, etc. Returns –1 if `aString` is not found.

EXAMPLE

After program executes `String name = "Mary, Mary, Mary quite so";`
`greeting.indexOf("Mary")` returns 0, and
`name.lastIndexOf("Mary")` returns 12.

Throws:

`NullPointerException` if `aString` is null.

```
public int length()
```

Returns the length of the calling object (which is a string) as a value of type `int`.

EXAMPLE

After program executes `String greeting = "Hello!";`
`greeting.length()` returns 6.

```
public String substring(int start)
```

Returns the substring of the calling object string starting from `start` through to the end of the calling object. Positions are counted 0, 1, 2, etc. Be sure to notice that the character at position `start` is included in the value returned.

EXAMPLE

After program executes `String sample = "AbcdefG";`
`sample.substring(2)` returns `"cdefG"`.

Throws:

`IndexOutOfBoundsException` if `start` is negative or larger than the length of the calling object.

```
public String substring(int start, int end)
```

Returns the substring of the calling object string starting from position `start` through, but not including, position end of the calling object. Positions are counted 0, 1, 2, etc. Be sure to notice that the character at position `start` is included in the value returned, but the character at position end is not included.

EXAMPLE

After program executes `String sample = "AbcdefG";`
`sample.substring(2, 5)` returns `"cde"`.

Throws:

`IndexOutOfBoundsException` if the `start` is negative, or end is larger than the length of this `String` object, or start is larger than end.

```
public String toLowerCase()
```

Returns a string with the same characters as the calling object string, but with all letter characters converted to lowercase.

EXAMPLE

After program executes `String greeting = "Hi Mary!";`
`greeting.toLowerCase()` returns `"hi mary!"`.

```
public String toUpperCase()
```

Returns a string with the same characters as the calling object string, but with all letter characters converted to uppercase.

EXAMPLE

After program executes `String greeting = "Hi Mary!";`
`greeting.toUpperCase()` returns `"HI MARY!"`.

```
public String trim()
```

Returns a string with the same characters as the calling object string, but with leading and trailing whitespace removed. Whitespace characters are the characters that print as whitespace on paper, such as the blank (space) character, the tab character, and the new-line character `'\n'`.

EXAMPLE

After program executes `String pause = " Hmm ";`
`pause.trim()` returns `"Hmm"`.

StringBuffer

Package: `java.lang`
`StringBuffer` is marked `final` and so you cannot use it as a base class to derive another class.
Ancestor classes:

```
        Object
            |
          +--StringBuffer
```

CONSTRUCTORS

```
public StringBuffer()
```

Creates a `StringBuffer` object with no characters in it and an initial capacity of 16 characters.

```
public StringBuffer(int capacity)
```

Constructs a `StringBuffer` object with no characters in it and an initial capacity specified by the argument.

Throws:

`NegativeArraySizeException` if `length` is less than 0. `NegativeArraySizeException` is a derived class of `RuntimeException`, and so is an unchecked exception, which means it is not required to be caught or declared in a `throws` clause.

```
public StringBuffer(String ordinaryString)
```

Constructs a string buffer so that it represents the same sequence of characters as the `ordinaryString` argument; in other words, the initial content of the string buffer is a copy of `ordinaryString`. The initial capacity of the string buffer is 16 plus the length of `ordinaryString`.

Throws:

`NullPointerException` if `ordinaryString` is `null`.

METHODS

```
public StringBuffer append(char[] charArray, int offset, int length)
```

Appends the string representation of the characters in `charArray` starting at `charArray[offset]` and extending for a total of `length` characters. Note that the calling object is changed and a reference to the changed calling object is returned.

Throws:

`ArrayIndexOutOfBoundsException` if `offset` and `length` are not consistent with the range of `charArray`.

```
public StringBuffer append(char c)
```

Appends the character argument to the `StringBuffer` calling object and returns this longer string.

```
public StringBuffer append(char[] charArray)
```

Appends the string representation of the `char` array argument to this string buffer. Note that the calling object is changed and a reference to the changed calling object is returned.

```
public StringBuffer append(double d)
```

Appends the string representation of the `double` argument to the `StringBuffer` calling object and returns this longer string.

```
public StringBuffer append(float d)
```

Appends the string representation of the `float` argument to the `StringBuffer` calling object and returns this longer string.

    public StringBuffer append(int n)

Appends the string representation of the int argument to the StringBuffer calling object and returns this longer string.

    public StringBuffer append(long n)

Appends the string representation of the long argument to the StringBuffer calling object and returns this longer string.

    public StringBuffer append(String ordinaryString)

Appends the String argument to the StringBuffer calling object and returns this longer string. If ordinaryString is null, then the four characters "null" are appended to this string buffer. Note that the calling object is hanged and a reference to the changed calling object is returned.

    public StringBuffer append(StringBuffer bufferedString)

Appends the StringBuffer argument to the StringBuffer calling object and returns this longer string. If bufferedString is null, then the four characters "null" are appended to this string buffer. Note that the calling object is changed and a reference to the changed calling object is returned.

    public int capacity()

Returns the current capacity of the calling object. The capacity is the amount of storage currently available for characters. The capacity will automatically be increased if necessary.

    public char charAt(int position)

Returns the character in the calling object string at position. Positions are counted 0, 1, 2, etc.

Throws:

IndexOutOfBoundsException if position is negative or not less than the length of the calling object.

    contentEquals

There is no such method for the class StringBuffer, but see the method contentEquals for the class String.

    public StringBuffer delete(int start, int end)

Removes the characters in a substring of the calling object. The substring to remove begins at the specified start and extends to the character at index end − 1 or to the end of the calling object if no such character exists. If start is equal to end, no changes are made. Note that the calling object is changed and a reference to the changed calling object is returned.

Throws:

StringIndexOutOfBoundsException if start is negative, greater than length(), or greater than end. StringIndexOutOfBoundsException is a derived class of RuntimeException, and so is an unchecked exception, which means it is not required to be caught or declared in a throws clause.

    public void ensureCapacity(int minimumCapacity)

Ensures that the capacity of the calling object is at least equal to minimumCapacity. If the current capacity of the calling object is less than minimumCapacity, then the capacity is increased. The new capacity is the larger of: minimumCapacity and twice the old capacity, plus 2. If the minimumCapacity is nonpositive, this method takes no action and simply returns.

Start public boolean `equals(Object otherObject)`

Warning: This is the method inherited from `Object`. It is not overridden for the class `StringBuffer` and does not work as you might expect. Normally, it should not be used.

public int `indexOf(String aString)`

Returns the index (position) of the first occurrence of the string `aString` in the calling object. Positions are counted 0, 1, 2, etc. Returns −1 if `aString` is not found. Note that the argument is of type `String`, not `StringBuffer`.

Throws:

`NullPointerException` if `aString` is null.

public int `indexOf(String aString, int start)`

Returns the index (position) of the first occurrence of the string `aString` in the calling object that occurs at or after position `start`. Positions are counted 0, 1, 2, etc. Returns −1 if `aString` is not found. Note that the argument is of type `String`, not `StringBuffer`.

Throws:

`NullPointerException` if `aString` is null.

public int `lastIndexOf(String aString)`

Returns the index (position) of the last occurrence of the string `aString` in the calling object string. Positions are counted 0, 1, 2, etc. Returns −1 if `aString` is not found. Note that the argument is of type `String`, not `StringBuffer`.

Throws:

`NullPointerException` if `aString` is null.

public int `length()`

Returns the length of the calling object as a value of type `int`.

public StringBuffer `replace(int start, int end, String ordinaryString)`

Replaces the characters in a substring of the calling object with characters in the `ordinaryString`. The substring begins at the specified `start` and extends to the character at index end −1 or to the end of the calling object if no such character exists. First the characters in the substring are removed and then the specified `ordinaryString` is inserted at `start`. (The calling object will be lengthened to accommodate the `ordinaryString` if necessary.) Note that the calling object is changed and a reference to the changed calling object is returned.

Throws:

`StringIndexOutOfBoundsException` if `start` is negative, greater than `length()`, or greater than end. `StringIndexOutOfBoundsException` is a derived class of `RuntimeException`, and so is an unchecked exception, which means it is not required to be caught or declared in a throws clause.

```
public void setLength(int newLength)
```

Sets the length of the calling object. The calling object is altered to represent a new character sequence whose length is specified by the argument. For every nonnegative index *k* less than newLength, the character at index *k* in the new character sequence is the same as the character at index *k* in the old sequence. If the newLength argument is less than the current length of the string buffer, the string buffer is truncated to contain exactly the number of characters given by the newLength argument.
If the newLength argument is greater than the current length, sufficient null characters ('\u0000') are appended to the string buffer so that length becomes the newLength argument.

Throws:

IndexOutOfBoundsException if newLength is negative.

```
public String substring(int start)
```

Returns the substring of the calling object starting from start through to the end of the calling object. Positions are counted 0, 1, 2, etc. Be sure to notice that the character at position start is included in the value returned. Note that the substring is returned as a value of type String, not StringBuffer.

Throws:

StringIndexOutOfBoundsException if start is negative or larger than the length of the calling object. StringIndexOutOfBoundsException is a derived class of RuntimeException, and so is an unchecked exception, which means it is not required to be caught or declared in a throws clause.

```
public String substring(int start, int end)
```

Returns the substring of the calling object starting from position start through, but not including, position end of the calling object. Positions are counted 0, 1, 2, etc. Be sure to notice that the character at position start is included in the value returned, but the character at position end is not included. Also note that the substring is returned as a value of type String, not StringBuffer.

Throws:

StringIndexOutOfBoundsException if start is negative, or end is larger than the length of this calling object, or start is larger than end. StringIndexOutOfBoundsException is a derived class of RuntimeException, and so is an unchecked exception, which means it is not required to be caught or declared in a throws clause.

```
public String toString()
```

Creates a new String object that contains the same character sequence calling object and returns that String object. Subsequent changes to the calling object do not affect the contents of the String returned.

StringTokenizer

Package: java.util.
Ancestor classes:

```
        Object
          |
        +--StringTokenizer
```

```
public StringTokenizer(String theString)
```
Constructor for a tokenizer that will use whitespace characters as separators when finding tokens in `theString`.

```
public StringTokenizer(String theString, String delimiters)
```
Constructor for a tokenizer that will use the characters in the string `delimiters` as separators when finding tokens in `theString`.

```
public StringTokenizer(String theString, String delimiters,
                       boolean returnDelimiters)
```
Creates a tokenizer similar to `StringTokenizer(String theString, String delimiters)`, but with the following differences: If `returnDelimiters` is true, the delimiters are also returned by `nextToken`; each delimiter is returned as a one-character `String`. If `returnDelimiters` is `false`, the deliminters are not returned by `nextToken`. Thus, if `returnDelimiters` is `false`, the tokenizer created is the same as with `StringTokenizer(String theString, String delimiters)`.

```
public int countTokens()
```
Returns the number of tokens remaining to be returned by `nextToken`.

```
public boolean hasMoreElements()
```
Same as `hasMoreTokens`.

```
public boolean hasMoreTokens()
```
Tests whether there are more tokens available from this tokenizer's string. When used in conjunction with `nextToken`, it returns `true` as long as `nextToken` has not yet returned all the tokens in the string; returns `false` otherwise.

```
public String nextToken()
```
Returns the next token from this tokenizer's string.

Throws:

`NoSuchElementException` if there are no more tokens to return. `NoSuchElementException` is one of the exceptions that need not be declared in a `throws` clause or caught in a `catch` block.

`Vector<T>`

Package: `java.util`
Ancestor classes:

```
        Object
          |
        +--AbstractCollection<T>
               |
             +--AbstractList<T>
                    |
                  +--Vector<T>
```

```
public Vector()
```

Creates an empty vector with an initial capacity of 10. When the vector needs to increase its capacity, the capacity doubles.

```
public Vector(Collection<? extends T> c)
```

Creates a vector that contains all the elements of the collection c in the same order as they have in c. If c is a vector, the capacity of the created vector will be c.size(), not c.capacity.

Throws:

NullPointerException if c is null.

```
public Vector(int initialCapacity)
```

Creates an empty vector with the specified initial capacity. When the vector needs to increase its capacity, the capacity doubles.

```
public Vector(int initialCapacity, int capacityIncrement)
```

Constructs an empty vector with the specified initial capacity and capacity increment. When the vector needs to grow, it will add room for capacityIncrement more items.

```
public T get(int index)
```

Returns the element at the specified index. This is analogous to returning a[index] for an array a.

Throws:

ArrayIndexOutOfBoundsException if the index is not greater than or equal to 0 and less than the current size of the vector.

```
public T set(int index, T newElement)
```

Sets the element at the specified index to newElement. The element previously at that position is returned. If you draw an analogy between the vector and an array a, this is analogous to setting a[index] to the value newElement.

Throws:

ArrayIndexOutOfBoundsException if the index is not greater than or equal to 0 and strictly less than the current size of the vector.

```
public void add(int index, T newElement)
```

Inserts newElement as an element in the calling vector at the specified index. Each element in the vector with an index greater or equal to index is shifted upward to have an index that is one greater than the value it had previously.
Note that you can use this method to add an element after the last current element. The capacity of the vector is increased if this is required.

Throws:

ArrayIndexOutOfBoundsException if the index is not greater than or equal to 0 and less than *or equal to* the current size of the vector.

```
public boolean add(T newElement)
```

Adds newElement to the end of the calling vector and increases its size by one. The capacity of the vector is increased if this is required. Returns true if successful. Normally used as a void method.

METHODS TO REMOVE ELEMENTS

```
public void clear()
```

Removes all elements from the calling vector and sets its size to zero.

```
public T remove(int index)
```

Deletes the element at the specified index and returns the element deleted. Each element in the vector with an index greater than or equal to index is decreased to have an index that is one less than the value it had previously.

Throws:

ArrayIndexOutOfBoundsException if the index is not greater than or equal to 0 and less than the current size of the vector.

```
public boolean remove(Object theElement)
```

Removes the first occurrence of theElement from the calling vector. If theElement is found in the vector, then each element in the vector with an index greater than or equal to theElement's index is decreased to have an index that is 1 less than the value it had previously. Returns true if theElement was found (and removed). Returns false if theElement was not found in the calling vector.

SEARCH METHODS

```
public boolean contains(Object target)
```

Returns true if target is an element of the calling vector; otherwise returns false.

```
public int indexOf(Object target)
```

Returns the index of the first element that is equal to target. Uses the method equals of the object target to test for equality. Returns −1 if target is not found.

```
public int indexOf(Object target, int startIndex)
```

Returns the index of the first element that is equal to target, but considers only indices that are greater than or equal to startIndex. Uses the method equals of the object target to test for equality. Returns − 1 if target is not found.

```
public boolean isEmpty()
```

Returns true if the calling vector is empty (that is, has size 0); otherwise returns false.

```
public int lastIndexOf(Object target)
```

Returns the index of the last element that is equal to target. Uses the method equals of the object target to test for equality. Returns −1 if target is not found.

```
public T firstElement()
```

Returns the first element of the calling vector.

Throws:

NoSuchElementException if the vector is empty.

```
public T lastElement()
```

Returns the last element of the calling vector.

Throws:

NoSuchElementException if the vector is empty.

ITERATORS

```
public Iterator <T> iterator()
```

Returns an iterator for the calling vector. (Iterators are discussed in Chapter 16.)

```
ListIterator <T> listIterator()
```

Returns a list iterator for the calling vector. (Iterators are discussed in Chapter 16.)

```
ListIterator <T> listIterator(int index)
```

Returns a list iterator for the calling vector starting at index. The first element to be returned by the iterator is the one at index. (Iterators are discussed in Chapter 16.)

CONVERTING TO AN ARRAY

```
public Object[] toArray()
```

Returns an array containing all of the elements in the vector. The elements of the array are indexed the same as in the vector.

```
public <E> E[] toArray(E[] a)
```

Note that the type parameter E is not the same as T. So, E can be any reference type; it need not be the type T in Collection <T>. For example, E might be an ancestor type of T. Returns an array containing all of the elements in the calling object. The elements in the returned array are in the same order as in the calling object. The argument a is used primarily to specify the type of the array returned. The exact details are described in the table for the Collection <T>.

Throws:

ArrayStoreException if the base type of a is not an ancestor class of all the elements in the vector.
NullPointerException if a is null.

MEMORY MANAGEMENT

```
public int capacity()
```

Returns the current capacity of the calling vector.

```
public void ensureCapacity(int newCapacity)
```

Increases the capacity of the calling vector to ensure that it can hold at least `newCapacity` elements. Using `ensureCapacity` can sometimes increase efficiency, but its use is not needed for any other reason.

```
public void setSize(int newSize)
```

Sets the size of the calling vector to `newSize`. If `newSize` is greater than the current size, the new elements receive the value `null`. If `newSize` is less than the current size, all elements at index `newSize` and greater are discarded.

Throws:

`ArrayIndexOutOfBoundsException` if `newSize` is negative.

```
public int size()
```

Returns the number of elements in the calling vector.

```
public void trimToSize()
```

Trims the capacity of the calling vector to be the vector's current size. This is used to save storage.

MAKE A COPY

```
public Object clone()
```

Returns a clone of the calling vector. The clone is an identical copy of the calling vector.

OLDER METHODS

These are methods that are not part of the newer collection framework, but are retained for backward compatibility. You should use the previously described newer methods instead. But, you may find these used in older code.

```
public void addElement(T newElement)
```

Same as add.

```
public void insertElementAt(T newElement, int index)
```

Same as add.

```
public T elementAt(int index)
```

Same as get.

```
public void removeAllElements()
```

Same as clear.

```
public boolean removeElement(Object theElement)
```

Same as remove.

```
public void removeElementAt(int index)
```
Same as `remove` but does not return the element removed.

```
public void setElementAt(T newElement, int index)
```
Same as `set` with the arguments reversed but does not return the element replaced.

`WindowListener` **Interface**

Package: `java.awt.event`
The `WindowEvent` class is also in this package.
Extends the `EventListener` interface.

```
public void windowActivated(WindowEvent e)
```
Invoked when a window is activated. When you click in a window, it becomes the activated window. Other actions can also activate a window.

```
public void windowClosed(WindowEvent e)
```
Invoked when a window has been closed.

```
public void windowClosing(WindowEvent e)
```
Invoked when a window is in the process of being closed. Clicking the close-window button causes an invocation of this method.

```
public void windowDeactivated(WindowEvent e)
```
Invoked when a window is deactivated. When a window is activated, all other windows are deactivated. Other actions can also deactivate a window.

```
public void windowDeiconified(WindowEvent e)
```
Invoked when a window is deiconified. When you activate a minimized window, it is deiconified.

```
public void windowIconified(WindowEvent e)
```
Invoked when a window is iconified. When you click the minimize button in a `JFrame`, it is iconified.

```
public void windowOpened(WindowEvent e)
```
Invoked when a window has been opened.

Symbols

\# (sharp), 723

% (modulo, remainder) operator, 55, 58–59

%n (line break), 97

&& (and) operator, 151, 156

' (quote), 55

() (parentheses), 56–58, 133, 157–163

-- **(decrement) operator**, 62–64

$ (dollar sign), 45, 46

* (asterisk), 49

* (conditional) operator, 144–145

* (multiplication), 55

/* symbol, 81–82

*/ symbol, 81–82

... (ellipsis), 414, 723

@ **tags**, 363–364

[] (square brackets), 380, 382

{} (braces), 37, 134, 135, 219

|| (or) operator, 151–152, 156

~ (tilde), 723

+ (concatenation) operator, 66–67

+ (plus) operator, 55, 237

++ **(increment) operator**, 62–64

= (assignment operator), 39, 48–50, 146, 159

  with arrays, 392–394

  with class type variables, 323

= (equal sign), 39, 48

== (equality) operator, 146–148, 182, 236

  with arrays, 392–394

  with enumerated types, 427

  with variables of class type, 327–328

/ (division) operator, 55, 58, 60

. (dot), 39

/ (forward slash), 638

; (semicolons), in for statements, 175–176

- (subtraction), 55

, (commas), in for statements, 173–174

A

abbreviations, 81

abs method, 305

AbstractButton class, 1018, 1020, 1179–1180

abstract classes, 516, 541–548

  interfaces, implementing, 747, 748

AbstractCollection<T> class, 941

abstraction, 239. *See also* information hiding

AbstractList<T> class, 940

AbstractMap<K,V> class, 951–952, 954

abstract methods, 542, 544–545

abstract names, 641

abstract path names, 643

AbstractSequential-List<T> class, 945

AbstractSet<T> class, 940

Abstract Window Toolkit (AWT), 974, 1009–1010

accept method, 1130

access

  ArrayList class, 795–796

  arrays, 379–382

  default, 488, 489

  friendly, 488, 489

  inner/outer classes, 767

  packages, 487–492

  permissions, overriding, 472–473

  private members, 247–248

  random access to binary files, 664–670

  to redefined base method, 493–495

  static variables, 300

access modifiers, 487–492

accessor methods, 242–248, 347–349, 408

  for array instance variable, 416–419

  with exception classes, 578–580

action command, 1021–1022

action drawings, 1084, 1086–1090

action events, 984–990

ActionListener interface, 985, 986, 1022–1024

action listeners, 984–990, 1017

actionPerformed method, 985–986, 1005, 1011, 1028, 1119

activation records, 691–692

actual parameters, 227. *See also* arguments

Adaptor (Adapter) pattern, 727–728

addActionListener method, 984, 1020

addAll method, 935, 936, 937, 947

adding

  to ArrayList class, 796–798

  colors, 1008, 1091

  menus, to JFrame, 1018–1019

  nodes, 842–843, 873–877, 879–882

add method, 796–797, 800, 905, 935, 936, 937, 946, 963, 994

addresses, 317

  memory, 323, 389, 392–393

addToStart method, 842
ADT (abstract data type), 239
algorithms, 166–169
  binary search, 700–711
  selection sort, 420–423
  sorting, 729–736
Allman style, 135
alphabetical order, 148–149
ancestor classes, 470
and (&&) operator, 151, 156
anonymous classes, 778–780
anonymous objects, 330–331
Apache Derby, 1137–1139,
    1143–1144, 1159–1161
Apache Tomcat, 1152
API (application programming
    interface), 239, 362
appending, to a file, 619–621
applets, 36–37, 1150–1151
applet viewer, 36–37
applications, 36. *See also*
    programs
  sample, 37–40
arcs, drawing, 1079–1083
areas (text), 1025–1038
  scroll bars, 1031, 1064–1069
  view port, 1064, 1065
arg array, 413
`args` identifier, 397–398
arguments, 39, 68, 69, 221,
    223–225, 227
  array, 390–392, 395–396
  automatic type conversion,
    254–256
  constructor, 264
  copy constructors, 345–351
  correspondence, 223
  indexed variables as, 390
  length of arrays, 379, 385
  no-argument constructors,
    267–268, 270, 315, 336
  null as, 341
  wrapper classes, 315
arithmetic expressions, 55–56
  evaluating, 153
arithmetic if, 144–145

arithmetic if operators. *See*
    conditional operators
arithmetic operators, 55–56
`ArrayIndexOutOf`
    `BoundsException`,
    384, 601
`ArrayList<T>` class, 933,
    944–950, 1180–1185
`ArrayList` class, 792–810
  accessing, 795–796
  adding to, 796–798
  base type, 794
  capacity, 794, 808
  creating and naming objects,
    795
  example, 805–808
  `for-each` loop, 802–805
  methods, 799–802, 808–809
  nonparameterized, 810
  using, 794–799
arrays
  accessing, 379–382
  arguments, 390–392,
    395–396
  base type, 379, 390
  in binary files, 662–664
  creating, 379–382, 432
  declaring, 380, 431, 432
  enumerated types, 424–431
  equality testing, 394, 396–397
  `for-each` loops with,
    408–412
  indexed variables, 432
  indices, 384, 432
  initializing, 385
  instance variables, 416–419,
    434
  introduction to, 378–387
  length (size), 379, 385
  `length` instance variable,
    382–383
  `for` loops with, 384, 434
  for `main` method, 397–398
  methods that return,
    399–400, 435–441
  multidimensional, 431–442

as objects, 388–389
  out of bounds, 384
  parameters, 390–392, 395,
    398
  partially filled, 401–410
  privacy leaks with, 416–418
  programming with,
    400–431
  ragged, 435
  references and, 388–400
  sorting, 420–423
  vs. strings, 387
  two-dimensional, 432–434
  use of = and == with,
    392–394
array type, 389
  indexed variables, 392
  names, 400
arrows, in inheritance
    diagrams, 724–725
ASCII
  character set, 53, 75–76, 650,
    899–900, 1175
  files, 611. *See also* text files
assertion checks, 189–191
`AssertionError` class,
    600–601
assertions, 189
assert statement, 189
assignment operator (=), 39,
    48–50, 146, 159
  with arrays, 392–394
  with class type variables, 323
assignment statements,
    48–52
  Boolean expressions, 154
  compatibility, 52–54
  with primitive types, 49
associativity rules, 57,
    157–163, 1173
@author, 363
-author option, 365
automatic boxing, 310–312,
    818–819
automatic garbage collection,
    843

automatic type conversion, 254–256
automatic unboxing, 311
AWT (Abstract Window Toolkit), 974, 1009
classes, 1010

B
back, of list, 889
background color, 991
backslash (\), 74–75, 638
BadNumberException, 578–580
BankAccount class, 767–770
bars
  menu, 1017, 1019
  scroll, 1031, 1064–1069
base cases, 688, 694
base classes, 460, 464, 467, 470, 480
  instance variables, 468, 476, 485–486
  private methods, 486–487
  super constructor, 474–476
base types, 379, 794, 802
Big-*O* notation, 895–897
binary files, 611–612, 645–670
  array objects in, 662–664
  binary I/O of objects, 658–662
  checking for end of, 656–658
  closing, 650, 654
  opening, 648–649, 652
  random access to, 664–670
  reading from, 651–655
  UTF and, 650–651
  writing to, 646–650
binary operators, 159
binary search, 700–711
binary search tree, 913–918
Binary Search Tree Storage Rule, 912–913
binary trees, 910–911
binding, 160, 517–518

bits, 318
block comments, 81–82
blocks, 219–220, 557, 559, 562–563, 569–570, 598–599, 618, 1134
  catch, 557–559, 569–570
  multiple catch, 583–587
  nested, 598
  try-catch, 65, 557–559, 598
body
  of loops, 164
  of method, 213
Boolean class, 313, 1185–1186
Boolean expressions, 132, 145–164
  associatively rules, 157–163
  building, 151–152
  evaluating, 152–164
  if-else statements, 132–139
  lexicographic and alphabetical order, 148–149
  loops and, 164–166
  precedence rules, 157–163
  simple, 145–148
boolean types, 48, 53, 55, 132, 154–155, 231–234
  methods that return, 231–234
  returned by mutator methods, 248
boolean variables, 154–155
BorderLayout class, 995–998, 1002, 1004
border layout managers, 995–998
bottom-up testing, 237
bounding boxes, 1073
bounds
  multiple, 823
  type parameter, 821–824, 860–861
boxing, 309, 310–312, 818–819

braces {}, 37, 134, 135, 219
branching mechanisms, 132–145
  compound statements, 134–135
  conditional operator, 144–145
  if-else statements, 132–136
  if statements, 133, 134, 136
  multiway if-else statements, 136–139
  nested statements, 136
  switch statement, 139–144
break statement, 140, 143, 180–181
brighter method, 1093
BufferedReader class, 621, 1130–1131
  methods, 633–634
  reading numbers with, 635
  reading text file using, 631–635
  testing for end of file with, 635–637
buffers, 617
bug, 44
buttons, 983–984
  AbstractButton class, 1018, 1020
  close-window, 982, 984
  with icons, 1060
  setActionCommand method, 1021–1022
Byte class, 1186–1187
byte-code, 35, 41–42
bytes, 317, 318
byte type, 48, 53, 56

C
calculator, Swing, 1033–1038
call-by-reference parameter mechanism, 324
call-by-value parameter mechanism, 224, 225

calling, 39
  methods, 39, 68
  objects, 68
  recursive methods, 684–687
canRead method, 644
canWrite method, 644
capacity, 794, 808
capacity method, 948
case labels, 140
case reserved word, 140
case-sensitivity, 46
Catch_Block_Parameter,
  570
catch blocks, 557–559,
  569–570
  multiple, 583–587
  nested, 598
  parameters, 558–559
Catch or Declare Rule, 591,
  592, 594
  exception to, 593–594
ceil method, 306, 307
censor method, 415–416
c format specifier, 95, 96
chaining, hash tables with,
  898–910
Character class, 313–316,
  334
character sets
  ASCII, 75–76
  Unicode, 75–77
characters per line, 1031
charAt method, 71
char type, 48, 53, 54
checked exceptions, 594
child classes, 470. *See also*
  derived classes
class diagrams, 723–724
classes, 35–36, 42, 67–69
  abstract, 516, 541–548, 747
  AbstractButton, 1018,
    1020, 1179–1180
  AbstractCollection<T>,
    941
  AbstractList<T>, 940

AbstractMap<K,V>,
  951–952, 954
AbstractSequential
  List<T>, 945
AbstractSet<T>, 940
accessor methods, 242–248
ancestor, 470
anonymous, 778–780
ArrayList, 792–810
ArrayList<T>, 933,
  944–950, 1180–1185
AssertionError, 600–601
BankAccount, 767–770
base, 460, 464, 467, 470,
  480
Boolean, 313, 1185–1186
BorderLayout, 995–998,
  1002, 1004
BufferedReader, 621
Byte, 1186–1187
Character, 313, 334
child, 470
collection, 408–411, 802,
  930–951
Color, 1092–1093,
  1191–1192
commenting, 362–364
compiling, 42–43, 360–361
concrete, 545, 940–949,
  954–957
constructors, 258–279,
  474–477
container, 994, 1009
Container, 1008–1009
Counter, 1126
creating, 994
DataOutputStream, 646
Date, 342–343
DateClient, 1133–1134
DateServer, 1132–1133
definitions, 206–238, 270
derived, 460–473, 477–480,
  594–595
descendent, 470
Dimension, 1021

DivisionByZero
  Exception, 572–576,
  591
Double, 1193
encapsulation, 239–250
EndingListener, 985
Error, 593
errors, 594
Exception, 564–565,
  570–571, 820–821
exceptions, 569–583
File, 627, 641–645,
  1193–1194
FileInputStream, 121
FileNotFoundException,
  121
FileOutputStream, 613
FileReader, 633
final modifier, 519
Float, 1195
FlowLayout, 998–999, 1002
Font, 1100, 1101, 1102,
  1195
generic, 810–828. *See also*
  generics
Graphics, 1073–1090,
  1196–1197
GridLayout, 999–1002
HashMap<K,V>, 951–952,
  954–957, 1198
HashSet<T>, 941–944, 1199
HashTable, 900–901
helping, 766–771
hierarchy, 461
ImageIcon, 1058, 1061
immutable, 351–354
implementation, 362
importing, 102–104
information hiding, 239–250
inner, 744
  anonymous, 778–780
  .class file, 771
  inheritance and, 777
  listeners ad, 1022–1024
  nested, 777

node, 846–849
public, 773–777
static, 772–773
uses of, 766–772
window listener, 1052
Insets, 1063
instance of, 206, 207
instance variables, 209–212
Integer, 309, 310, 1199
interactions, 724
interface, 362
IOException, 615
iterators, 868–873. *See also*
    iterators
JButton, 983–984,
    1061–1062
JColorChooser,
    1094–1097
JFrame, 978, 980–982,
    987–990, 1008–1009,
    1200–1202
JLabel, 990, 997,
    1061–1062
JMenu, 1013, 1017
JMenuBar, 1013, 1017
JMenuItem, 1013, 1017,
    1061–1062, 1202
JPanel, 1003–1008, 1009,
    1084
JScrollPanel, 1064–1069,
    1203
JTextArea, 1029–1031
JTextComponent, 1030,
    1204
JTextField, 1026–1029,
    1030–1031
LinkedHashMap<K,V>,
    954
LinkedList, 834
LinkedList<T>, 945, 949
Locale, 102, 103
Long, 1212
Math, 305–309, 356,
    1212–1213
MergeSort, 733

methods. *See* methods
mutable, 351–354
mutator methods, 242–248
name clashes, 361
naming conventions, 46, 68
NumberFormat, 99–102, 103
Object, 496–497
ObjectInputStream,
    645–646, 651–655,
    1216–1218
ObjectOutputStream,
    645–650, 1218–1219
objects, 68, 206–209
outer, 766, 767, 775–776
overloading, 250–258
packages, 354–366
Packer, 1119, 1121
parameterized, 810
parameters. *See* parameters
parent, 470
Person, 336–341, 344,
    345–347
vs. primitive types, 68
PrintWriter, 611–619,
    1220
Queue, 890–892
RaceConditionTest,
    1126–1127
Random, 192–193, 1221
RandomAccessFile,
    664–670, 1221–1224
RuntimeException, 593
Scanner, 108–120, 621–
    626, 1224–1227
SelectionSort, 422–423
serializable, 659–662
ServerSocket,
    1130–1131
Set<T>, 944
Short, 1231
Stack, 887–889
String, 65–77, 356,
    1231–1235
StringBuffer, 75,
    1235–1239

StringTokenizer,
    274–279, 331–332,
    481–484, 1239–1240
subclasses, 464, 467, 480
superclasses, 464, 467, 480
System, 181
Thread, 1119–1122
Throwable, 593
TreeSet<T>, 949
UML, 723–726
Vector, 809–810
Vector<T>, 944–950,
    1240–1245
WindowAdapter,
    1056–1057
WindowEvent, 1050
wrapper, 309–316, 356
classes, loaders, 42
.class files, 43
    for inner class, 771
class instance variables, 661
class invariant, 336–341
ClassNotFoundException,
    1141
class path
    not including current
        directory in, 360
    specifying, when compiling,
        360–361
-classpath option, 365
CLASSPATH variable,
    356–361
class types
    arrays with, 390
    mixing, in same file, 662
    parameters of, 225, 229,
        323–329
    variables of, 316–317,
        318–323, 327–328
clause (throws), 589–592,
    594–595
clear method, 800, 935, 947
clients, 1130
client/server model,
    1130–1131, 1150

`Cloneable` interface,
761–765, 864, 867

`clone` method, 347, 350, 497,
536–541, 761–764, 801,
948

copy constructors, 538–541,
856–867

`HashMap<K,V>` class, 955

shallow copies, 808–809

`close` method, 617–618,
648, 665

close-window button, 982, 984

closing
binary files, 650, 654
text files, 617–618

code, 35, 42
incremental development,
188–189
legacy, 98
review, 188–189

`Collection<T>` interface,
930–935, 941,
1188–1191

collections, 408–411, 802,
930–951
concrete classes, 940–949
exceptions, 939–940
`for-each` loops, 938
framework, 932–940
interfaces, 938
iterators and, 931
nonparameterized, 950
optional operations, 938–939
overview of, 930–931
wildcards, 932

collisions, 898

`Color` class, 1092–1093,
1191–1192

color constructors, 1092

colors
adding, 1008, 1091
constants, 992
defining, 1092–1094
`JColorChooser` dialog
window, 1094–1097

RGB color system, 1092
setting, 991–994
specifying, 1091
Swing, 1090–1097

commands
action, 1021–1022
run, 42
SQL, 1138–1149

commas, in for statements,
173–174

comments, 79, 81–82
block, 81–82
for `javadoc`, 362–364
line, 81, 82
when to add, 82

**Common Gateway Interface
(CGI)**, 1153–1154

`Comparable` interface, 735,
751–757, 822, 1192

compare method, 735

`compareToIgnoreCase`
method, 73, 149

`compareTo` method, 73, 148,
427, 735, 751, 822

comparing, strings, 150, 193

comparison operators, 146

compiler, 35, 40
Just-In-Time (JIT), 41

compiler errors, 146, 240, 951

compiling, 40–42
classes, 42–43, 360–361
-Xlint option, 813

complete evaluation, 156

component model, 1135–1136

components, 1009
with changing visibility,
1069–1072

composition, 493

compound statements,
134–135, 219–220

concatenation (+) operator,
66–67

concatenation, of strings,
66–67

concrete classes, 545

collections, 940–949
maps, 954–957

conditional (*) operator,
144–145

connections
databases, 1137–1149
networks. *See* networking

connection strings, 1141

console I/O, 90
file input, 121–124
screen output, 90–108
using `Scanner` class,
108–120

constants, 53–55
color, 992
defined, in interfaces, 757–761
inconsistent, 758–759
location, 102
`Math` class, 307
naming, 78–80
null, 329–330, 341
static import of, 335
`String`, 65–66

constructors, 258–279
arguments, 264
color, 1092
copy, 345–351, 856–867
default, 268
definitions, 258–266
exception classes, 572–573
nested, 638–639
no-argument, 267–268, 270,
315, 336
`StringTokenizer` class,
274–279
`super`, 474–476, 495, 577
`this`, 266–267, 476–477
use of, 265–266
using, 273–274
variable initialization, 269
wrapper classes, 315

Container class, 1008–1009

container classes, 994, 1009

Container-Iterator pattern,
727

containers, 727

`containsAll` method, 933

`containsKey` method, 953

`contains` method, 800, 905, 909–910, 933, 947

`containsValue` method, 953

content pane, 991

`continue` statement, 180–181

controlling expressions, 140

conversion characters, 95

coordinate system, for graphics objects, 1073

copy constructors, 345–351, 536, 538–541

`clone` method, 856–867

`copyOf` method, 856, 859

`Counter` class, 1126

`countTokens` method, 277

covariant return types, 471–472

`createNewFile` method, 644

CREATE TABLE statements, 1141, 1142

critical region, 1127

currency format, 99–102

current directory, 360, 361

cursor, 964

D

database management system (DBMS), 1137

databases

Apache Derby, 1137–1138, 1143–1144, 1159–1161

connections, 1137–1149

Java DB, 1137–1138

JDBC, 1138

relational, 1137, 1140

tables, 1137, 1140

updating, 1161–1163

`DataClass`, 763–764

`DataOutputStream` class, 646, 1130

data structures. *See* linked data structures

data types, 317

`Date` class, 342–343

date classes, 232–234, 241, 243–246

`DateClient` class, 1133–1134

`DateServer` class, 1132–1133

debugging, 44, 182–191

assertion checks, 189–191

collections, 939–940

examples, 184–188

general techniques, 183–184

loop bugs, 182

preventive coding, 188–189

tracing variables, 182–183

`DecimalFormat` class, 104–108

decimal points, 54

decimals, formatting, 104–108

declarations, 1155

declaring, 47, 590–592

arrays, 380, 431, 432

variables, 47, 220

decrement operator (--), 62–64

deep copy, 353, 416, 536

`clone` method, 861–866

default access, 488, 489

default constructors, 268

default package, 359–360, 490

default section, 140

defined constants, in interfaces, 757–761

defining

classes, 206–238, 270

equals method, 497–503

exception classes, 572–578

iterators, 868–873, 966

`JFrame` class, 987–990

methods, 210, 212–218

`deleteHeadNode` method, 842–843

`delete` method, 644

deletion, of nodes, 873–877, 879–882

delimiters

choosing, 276

input, 119–120

@deprecated, 363, 364

deprecated methods, 364

derived classes, 460–470, 480

constructors, 474–476

generic, 826–828

instance variables, 476, 485–486

objects, 477–479

overriding methods, 471–473

package access, 487–492

protected access, 487–492

redefined methods, 493–494

`throws` clause in, 594–595

derived interfaces, 747–748

descendent classes, 470

`d` format specifier, 95

diagrams

class, UML, 723–724

inheritance, 724–726

`Dimension` class, 1021

directives, 1155, 1159

directories, 43

current, 360, 361

package, 356–359

`dispose` method, 981, 1055

division

floating-point numbers, 59

integer, 58–60

whole numbers, 60

`DivisionByZeroException` class, 572–576, 591

`doNothing` method, 1113

-d option, 365

dot (.), 39

`Double` class, 1193

`Double.parseDouble` method, 331–333

double quotes, 55

`double` type, 48, 54, 55, 56

doubly linked lists, 878–887

`do-while` statements, 164–166, 167

downcasting, 529–535

`draw3DRect` method, 1078

drawArc method, 1078, 1079–1083
drawing
  action, 1084, 1086–1090
  arcs, 1079–1083
  in JPanel, 1084
  objects, 1073–1090
  ovals, 1079
  paint method, 1074–1077
drawLine method, 1076–1077
drawOval method, 1076, 1078, 1079
drawRect method, 1077
drawRoundRect method, 1078
drawString method, 1097–1099, 1101
driver programs, 237
dynamic binding. *See also* late binding
dynamic binding, 517–518

E
early binding, 517
echo input, 116
E constant, 307
e format specifier, 95
elements, of array, 379
ellipsis (...), 414, 723
empty lists, 840, 841
empty statements, 175–176
empty strings, 116
empty trees, 912
em spaces, 1031
encapsulation, 239–250, 362, 484–492
endButton, 984–985
EndingListener class, 985
end-of-line character, 112, 115–116
enhanced for loops, 411. *See also* for-each loops
EnhancedStringTokenizer class, 481–484

e notation, 54, 106
ensureCapacity method, 801, 948
Enterprise JavaBeans, 1136
entrySet method, 953
enumerated types, 424–431
  methods, 426–429
  in switch statements, 429–431
environment variable, 356–357
EOFException, 656–658
equalArrays method, 394
equality (==) operator, 146–148, 182, 236
  with arrays, 392–394
  with class type variables, 327–328
  with enumerated types, 427
equality testing, 182, 327–328
  arrays, 394, 396–397
equal sign (=), 39, 48
equalsIgnoreCase method, 70, 146, 147
equals method, 70, 146–148, 233–237, 247, 328, 341, 426–427, 496, 801, 953
  Collection<T> interface, 934
  Color class, 1093
  defining, 497–503
  linked lists, 854–855
  overriding, 942
error classes, 593, 594
error messages, redirecting, 640–641
errors
  compiler, 146, 240, 951
  debugging, 182–191
  logic, 44
  loop, 182
  null pointer exception, 330, 390
  off-by-one, 182

out of bounds, 384
round-off, 59
run-time, 44
stack overflow, 692
syntax, 44
escape character, 74–75, 638
escape sequences, 74–75, 112
evaluating
  arithmetic expressions, 153
  Boolean expressions, 152–164
evaluation
  complete, 156
  short-circuit, 156
event-driven programming, 596, 974–976
event handlers, 975
event handling model, 1136
events, 975–976
  action, 984–990
  firing, 596, 975, 976, 984
  window, 1050
Exception class, 564–565, 570–571, 820–821
exception classes, 569–583
  accessor methods, 578–580
  constructors, 572–573
  defining, 572–578
  from standard packages, 570–572
exception handlers, 558
exception handling
  basics of, 556–587
  as event-driven programming, 596
  example, 564–569
  exception classes, 569–583
  loops, 560–561
  in methods, 588–597
  programming techniques for, 598–601
  with Scanner class, 559–560
  try-catch mechanism, 557–559
exception objects, 577

exceptions
ArrayIndexOutOfBounds
    Exception, 601
BadNumberException,
    578–580
checked, 594
ClassNotFoundException,
    1141
collections, 939–940
copy constructors and, 857
declaring, 590–592
EOFException, 656–658
as events, 975
FileNotFoundException,
    613, 615, 622, 634
IllegalAccessException,
    1141
IllegalArgument
    Exception, 429, 981
IllegalStateException,
    959, 963
InstantiationException,
    1141
InterruptedException,
    1116
IOException, 615, 634
in methods, 588–597
multiple, 583–587
NegativeNumber
    Exception, 586
NoSuchElementException,
    940, 962
NullPointerException,
    857
predefined, 570–572
rethrowing, 600
SecurityException, 981
SQLException, 1141
throwing, 556, 557, 562–565
uncaught, 594, 1033
unchecked, 594, 630
UnsupportedOperation
    Exception class, 939,
    959
when to use, 595–596

execute method, 1141
executeQuery method, 1141,
    1144
exists method, 643
exit statement, 181
**explicit memory
    management**, 874
exponents, 54
expressions
    arithmetic, 55–58
    Boolean, 132, 145–164
    JSP, 1155
    precedence rules with, 56–58
extends phrase, 464, 932

F
false value, 48, 53, 55, 132,
    152–155
f format specifier, 95
fields, 207
field width, 94
File class, 627, 641–645,
    1193–1194
    methods, 643–645
    programming with, 641–643
FileInputStream class, 121
file I/O
    of array object, 662–664
    binary, of objects, 658–662
    binary files, 645–670
    File class, 641–645
    introduction to, 121–124,
    610–612
    nested constructors, 638–639
    random access to binary files,
    664–670
    text files, 121–124, 611–641
FileNotFoundException
    class, 121, 613, 615, 622,
    634
FileOutputStream class, 613
file pointer, 664
FileReader class, 633
files
    ASCII, 611

binary, 611–612, 645–670
    array objects in, 662–664
    binary I/O of objects,
    658–662
    checking for end of,
    656–658
    closing, 650, 654
    opening, 648–649, 652
    random access to, 664–670
    reading from, 651–655
    UTF and, 650–651
    writing to, 646–650
locations, 211
names, 211, 613, 615,
    637–638
opening, 612–613
output, 618–619
text, 611–612
    appending, 619–621
    closing, 617–618
    opening, 614
    path names, 637–638
    reading, 621–624, 631–635
    testing for end of, 624–626,
    635–637
    writing to, 611–619
fill3DRect method, 1078
fillArc method, 1079
fillOval method, 1078
fillRect method, 1077
fillRoundRect method,
    1078
finally block, 598–599
final modifier, 300, 471, 519
firing the event, 596, 975,
    976, 984
Float class, 1195
floating-point notation, 54
floating-point numbers, 47,
    48, 54, 55, 56
    comparing, 182
    division of, 59
    round-off errors in, 59
float type, 48, 55
floor method, 306, 307

FlowLayout manager,
  998–999, 1002
flow of control
  Boolean expressions, 145–164
  branching mechanism,
    132–145
  debugging, 182–191
  loops, 164–181
  random number generation,
    191–194
flush method, 617
folders, 43
follows method, 746, 750
Font class, 1100, 1101, 1102,
  1195
fonts
  point size, 1101
  serifs, 1101
  Swing, 1097–1102
for-each loops, 408–412,
  428, 802–805, 938
  as iterators, 961–962
formal parameters. *See*
  parameters
format method, 100–101,
  104–106
format specifiers, 94–95
format strings, 96
formatting
  decimals, 104–108
  money, 97, 99–102, 103
  output, 93–99
forms, HTML, 1153–1154,
  1158
for statements, 170–176
  with arrays, 384, 434
  comma in, 173–174
  declaring variables in, 220
  extra semicolon in, 175–176
friendly access, 488, 489
front, of list, 889
full path names, 637–638
fully qualified class names, 361
functions, 893
  hash, 898

G
garbage collection, 874
  automatic, 843
generics, 792, 810
  basics of, 77989
  bounds for type parameters,
    821–824
  class definition, 819
  Exception class, 820–821
  inheritance with, 826–828
  instantiation, 811, 818
  interfaces, 824
  linked lists, 849–854,
    861–866
  methods, 824–825
  ordered pairs, 813–816,
    818–819
getActionCommand method,
  1020, 1022
getBlue method, 1093
getClass method, 499–502
getContentPane method, 991
getFilePointer method, 665
getGraphics method,
  1117–1118
getInsideArray method,
  418
getMessage method, 563,
  576–578
get method, 800, 946, 953
getName method, 644
getPath method, 644
getRed method, 1093
getText method, 1020, 1026,
  1028–1029, 1030
g format specifier, 95
GlassFish Enterprise Server,
  1152
global variables, 219
Golsing, James, 34
**graphical user interfaces
  (GUIs)**, 974
  adding and arranging
    components in,
    994–1011

calculator, 1033–1038
components with changing
  visibility, 1069–1072
designing, 1011
ending, 986
with labels and color,
  992–994
with menu, 1013–1017
nonresponsive, 1113–1116,
  1118
panels, 1003–1008
programs, 594, 728
updating, 1090
Graphics class, 1073–1090,
  1196–1197
  arcs, drawing, 1079–1083
  coordinate system, 1073
  methods, 1074–1079
  ovals, drawing, 1079
  repaint method,
    1086–1090
  rounded rectangles,
    1083–1084
Graphics object, 1076
greater than (>), 146
greater than or equal to, 146
GridLayout managers,
  999–1002

H
handlers
  event, 975
  exception, 558
handling
  events, 1136
  exceptions. *See* exception
    handling
"has a" relationship, 493, 994
hashCode method, 934, 942,
  953
hash functions, 898
  for strings, 899–902
HashMap<K, V> class,
  951–952, 954–957, 1198
hash maps. *See* hash tables

HashSet<T> class, 941–944, 1199
HashSet method, 941
HashTable class, 900–901
hash tables
    constructing, 898–899
    efficiency of, 902–903
    HashMap<K,V> class, 954–955
    linked data structures, 898–910
hasMoreTokens method, 276, 277
hasNextBoolean method, 629
hasNextByte method, 628
hasNextDouble method, 629
hasNextFloat method, 629
hasNextInt method, 624, 626, 627
hasNextLine method, 624–626, 630
hasNextLong method, 628
hasNext method, 629, 873, 959, 963
hasNextShort method, 628
hasPrevious method, 963
heading levels, 1156–1157
headings, 210
head nodes, 834
head variable, 905
helping classes, 766–771
higher precedence, 57, 157
high-level languages, 40
HotJava, 35
HTML, 362, 1150
HTML forms, 1153–1154, 1158

I

icons
    button, 1060
    changing visibility, 1069–1072

Swing, 1058–1064
    using, 1059–1060
identifiers, 45–46
    naming conventions, 80–81
if-else statements, 132–133
    compound, 134–135
    multiple alternatives, 135
    multiway, 136–139
    nested, 136
    placement of braces in, 135
if statements, 133, 134, 136
IllegalAccessException, 1141
IllegalArgument Exception, 429, 981
IllegalStateException, 959, 963
ImageIcon class, 1058, 1061
immutable classes, 351–354
immutable objects, 75, 352
implementation, 362
importing
    classes, 102–104
    packages, 102–104
import method, 104, 108
import statements, 90, 103–104, 794
    packages and, 355–356
    static, 333–335
inconsistent interfaces, 758–759
incremental development, 188–189
increment method, 1125, 1128
increment operator (++), 62–64
indentation, 82–83
    nested statements, 136
indexed variables, 379, 380, 389, 390, 432
    as arguments, 390–391
indexes, 73–74
    array, 384, 432
indexOf method, 72, 801, 937, 947

inequalities, strings of, 152
i.next method, 964–965
infinite loops, 176–177, 182, 656
infinite recursion, 689
information hiding, 239–250, 362
inheritance, 994
    derived classes, 461–470
    encapsulation, 484–492
    with generic classes, 826–828
    inner classes and, 777
    instance variables, 485–486
    overriding method definition, 471
    overview of, 460–484
    private methods, 486–487
    programming with, 493–503
    static variables, 493
    in Swing, 976
inheritance diagrams, 724–726
initial capacity, 954
initialization
    arrays, 385
    automatic, 385
    default, 300
    instance variables, 258, 264, 336
    variables, 50–51, 269–274, 300
inner classes, 744
    access privileges, 767
    anonymous, 778–780
    .class file, 771
    helping classes, 766–771
    inheritance and, 777
    listeners as, 1022–1024
    nested, 777
    node, 846–849
    public, 773–777
    reasons to use, 780
    static, 772–773
    uses of, 766–772
    window listener, 1052

inorder processing, 912
input. *See also* file I/O
   delimiters, 119–120
   echo, 116
   file, 121–124
   numbers, 1032
   prompt, 116
   text file, 121–124
   using Scanner class,
      108–120
   using StringTokenizer
      class, 274–279, 331–332
InputMismatchException,
   559–561
input streams, 610–611
INSERT statements, 1142
Insets class, 1063
instanceof operator,
   499–501, 533
instances, 206, 207
instance variables, 50, 207,
   209–212, 219, 269–274
   accessor methods for,
      416–419
   base class, 468, 476, 485–486
   class, 661
   initializing, 258, 264, 336
   interfaces and, 758
   length, 382–383, 389, 434
   privacy leaks with, 416–418
   private, 240, 416–418,
      485–486
   protected and package access,
      487–492
   resetting values, 265
instantiation, generic classes,
   811, 818
InstantiationException,
   1141
int, 39
Integer class, 309, 310, 1199
integers, 53
   binary search tree for, 915–916
   division of, 58–60

Integrated Development
   Environment (IDE),
   42, 182
interfaces, 362
   abstract classes, 747, 748
   ActionListener, 985, 986,
      1022–1024
   Cloneable, 761–765
   Collection<T>, 930–931,
      941, 1188–1191
   Comparable, 751–757,
      822, 1192
   defined constants in,
      757–761
   derived, 747–748
   extending, 747–748
   generic, 824
   implementing, 745–747
   inconsistent, 758–759
   introduction to, 744–747
   Iterator, 873
   Iterator<T>, 958–961,
      1200
   List<T>, 935–938, 944,
      1205–1210
   ListIterator<T>,
      962–964, 1210–1212
   Map<K,V>, 1214–1216
   NumberCarrier, 779–780
   Ordered, 745, 750
   Runnable, 1122–1124
   semantics, 749–750
   Serializable, 761, 1228
   Set<T>, 935–936, 938, 941,
      944, 1228–1230
   SortedSet<T>, 949
   WindowListener, 1245
intermediate language, 35
interpreters, 41
InterruptedException,
   1116
intersection method, 905
introspection, 1136
int type, 48, 53, 54, 55–56

intValue method, 310
invocation, 39
   constructors, 264
   methods, 68, 69, 70,
      210–211, 213, 266,
      295–296
IOException class, 615, 634
"is a" relationship, 478, 493,
   994
isDigit method, 314
isDirectory method, 644
isEditable method, 1030
isEmpty method, 933, 947,
   953
isFile method, 644
isLetter method, 314
isLetterOrDigit method,
   314
isLowerCase method, 314
isUpperCase method, 314
isWhitespace method, 314
iteration, 164
   vs. recursion, 692–693
   iterative version, 692–693,
      706–707
Iterator<T> interface,
   958–961, 1200
Iterator interface, 873
iterator method, 934, 948
iterators, 410, 727, 867–877,
   930
   collections and, 931
   defining, 868–873, 966
   doubly linked list with,
      883–886
   for-each loops as,
      961–962
   Iterator<T> interface,
      958–961
   list, 962–964
   nodes, adding and deleting,
      873–877
   overview of, 958
   references, returning,
      964–966

J

Java
  introduction to, 34–45
  naming of, 36
  origins of, 34–35
Java applets, 1150–1151
Java application programs
  compiling, 42–43
  running, 43
  sample, 37–40
  styles, 78–83
`java.awt` class, 1076
JavaBeans, 1135–1137
Java byte-code, 35
`javac` command, 42–43
`java` command, 43
Java Database Connectivity
  (JDBC), 1138, 1139
Java DB, 1137–1138
`javadoc` program, 81–82,
  354
  commenting classes for,
    362–364
  introduction to, 362
  options, 365
  running, 364–366
.java files, 42
`java.io` package, 612
`java.lang` package, 104,
  334, 356
Java Server Pages (JSP),
  1150–1164
  applets, 1150–1151
  declarations, 1155
  directives, 1155, 1159
  expressions, 1155
  HTML forms, 1153–1154,
    1158
  Oracle GlassFish Enterprise
    Server, 1152
  scriptlets, 1155–1156
  servlets, 1150–1151
Java servlets, 1150–1151
Java Software Development
  Kit (SDK), 1137–1138

`java.text`, 102–103
`java.util` package, 102,
  103, 108–109, 277, 935
Java Virtual Machine (JVM),
  41–42
`JButton` class, 983–984,
  1061–1062
`JColorChooser` class,
  1094–1097
JDBC (Java Database
  Connectivity), 1138, 1139
JDK, 42
`JFrame` class, 978, 1008–
  1009, 1200–1202
  color, adding, 1008
  color, setting, 991–994
  content pane, 991
  defining, 987–990
  `dispose` method, 1055
  menus, adding, 1018–1019
  methods, 980–982
  title, setting, 992
`JLabel` class, 990, 997,
  1061–1062
`JMenuBar` class, 1013, 1017
`JMenu` class, 1013, 1017
`JMenuItem` class, 1013, 1017,
  1061–1062, 1202
`join` method, 729, 1126
`JPanel` class, 1003–1008,
  1009, 1084
`JScrollPane` class,
  1064–1069, 1203
`JTextArea` class, 1029–1031
`JTextComponent` class, 1030,
  1204
`JTextField` class, 1026–
  1029, 1030–1031
Just-In-Time (JIT), 41
JVM (Java Virtual Machine),
  41–42

K

Kernighan & Ritchie (K&R)
  style, 135

keyboard input. *See also* file
  I/O; input
  using `Scanner` class, 108–120
  using `StringTokenizer`
    class, 274–279, 331–332
keys, hash table, 898
keywords, 46, 1171

L

labels
  with changing visibility,
    1069–1072
  icon, 1058
  statement, 180–181
  Swing, 990, 992–994, 997
  text field, 1032
largest and smallest values,
  312
`lastIndexOf` method, 72,
  801, 938, 947
last-in/first-out (LIFO), 691,
  889
late binding, 517–518, 531
  example, 520–527
  final modifier and, 519
  static methods and, 528–529,
    530
  with `toString`, 527–528
layout managers, 994–1003
  border, 995–998, 1004
  flow, 998–999
  grid, 999–1002
lazy evaluation, 156
leaf nodes, 912
leaks. *See* privacy leaks
left justified output, 96
legacy code, 98
length, of array, 379, 385
`length` instance variable,
  382–383, 389, 434
`length` method, 70, 665
less than (<), 146
less than or equal to, 146
lexicographic ordering,
  148–149

LIFO. *See* last-in/first-out
(LIFO)
line, characters per, 1031
linear running time, 897
line breaks, 96–97
line comments, 81, 82
line terminator
'BACKSLASHn', 112,
115–116
linked data structures
Big-*O* notation, 895–897
copy constructors and clone
method, 856–867
doubly linked lists, 878–887
hash tables, 898–910
introduction to, 834–835
iterators, 867–877
linked lists, 834, 836–855,
897–898
queues, 889–892
running times, 892–897
sets, 903–910
stacks, 887–889
trees, 910–918
LinkedHashMap<K,V> class,
954
LinkedList<T> class, 945,
949
LinkedList class, 834
linked lists, 780, 834–855
copy constructor and clone
method for, 857–859
with deep copy clone
method, 861–866
doubly, 878–887
efficiency of, 897–898
empty, 840, 841
end of, 841
equals method, 854–855
example, 836, 844
generic, 849–854
inner classes, 846–849
with iterator, 868–873
nodes, adding and deleting,
873–877, 879–882

nodes, adding and removing,
842–843
privacy leaks, 845
sets using, 904–905,
909–910
traversing, 840–842
variations on, 878–898
working with, 840–845
-link option, 365
links, 834, 835
List<T> interface, 935–938,
944, 1205–1210
listeners, 975–976
action, 984–990, 1017
as inner classes, 1022–1024
menu item, 1018–1019
registering, 984
window, 1050–1057
ListIterator<T> interface,
962–964, 1210–1212
listIterator method, 938,
948
lists
empty, 840, 841
iterators, 962–964
linked. *See* linked lists
literals, 53–55. *See also*
constants
loaders, classes, 42
load factor, 954
Locale class, 102, 103
localhost method, 1131
local variables, 50, 218–219
initializing, 269
parameters as, 225–227
location constants, 102
logic errors, 44
Long class, 1212
long type, 48
loops, 164–181
with arrays, 384
body of, 164
break statement, 180–181
continue statement, 180–181
debugging, 182

do-while statement,
164–166, 167
for exception handling,
560–561
exit statement, 181
for-each, 408–412, 428,
938, 961–962
infinite, 176–177, 182, 656
iteration, 164
nested, 177
repeating, 175
sentinel values, 169
for statement, 170–176,
220, 384
while statement, 164–166,
167, 176
low-level languages, 40

M
machine language, 40
main memory, 317
main method, 36, 37, 43,
218–219, 225, 296–299
arguments for, 397–398
GUI programs, 1001
mantissa, 106
Map<K,V> interface, 951–954,
1214–1216
maps, 951–957
concrete classes, 954–957
masks, 230
Math class, 305–309, 356,
1212–1213
Math.random method, 193
max method, 305, 412–413
members, 207
memory
address, 323, 389, 392–393
explicit management, 874
location, 317
main, 317
secondary, 317
variables and, 317–320
menu bars, 1017, 1019
menu items, 1013, 1017–1019

menus
  adding, to `JFrame`, 1018–
    1019
  menu bars, 1017, 1019
  menu items, 1013, 1017–
    1019
  nested, 1018
  `setActionCommand`
    method, 1021–1022
  Swing, 1013–1025
merge sort, 730, 731–732, 733
MergeSort class, 733
messages, sending, 39, 68
method calls, 68
  recursive, 684–687
method headings, inconsistent,
  759
methods, 35–36, 39, 69,
  206–207, 529
  `abs`, 305
  abstract, 542, 544–545
  `accept`, 1130
  accessor, 242–248, 347–349,
    408
  `actionPerformed`,
    985–986, 1005, 1011,
    1028, 1119
  `add`, 796–797, 800, 905,
    935, 936, 937, 946,
    963, 994
  `addActionListener`, 1020
  `addAll`, 935, 936, 937, 947
  `addToStart`, 842
  arguments, 341
  `ArrayList` class, 799–802
  body, 210, 213
  `brighter`, 1093
  `canRead`, 644
  `canWrite`, 644
  `capacity`, 948
  `ceil`, 306, 307
  `censor`, 415–416
  `charAt`, 71
  `clear`, 800, 935, 947
  `clone`, 350, 497, 536–541,
    801, 808–809, 955

`close`, 617–618, 648, 665
`Collection<T>` interface,
  933–935
`compare`, 735
`compareTo`, 73, 148, 427,
  735, 751, 822
`compareToIgnoreCase`,
  73, 149
constructors, 258–279
`contains`, 800, 905,
  909–910, 933, 947
`containsAll`, 933
`containsKey`, 953
`containsValue`, 953
`copyOf`, 856, 859
`countTokens`, 277
`createNewFile`, 644
defining, 210, 212–218
`delete`, 644
`deleteHeadNode`, 842–843
deprecated, 364
`dispose`, 981, 1055
`doNothing`, 1113
`Double.parseDouble`,
  331–333
`draw3DRect`, 1078
`drawArc`, 1078, 1079–1083
`drawLine`, 1076–1077
`drawOval`, 1076, 1078,
  1079
`drawRect`, 1077
`drawRoundRect`, 1078
`drawString`, 1097–1099,
  1101
`ensureCapacity`, 801, 948
`entrySet`, 953
with enumerated types,
  426–429
`equalArrays`, 394
`equals`, 70, 146–148,
  233–237, 247, 328, 341,
  426, 427, 496–503, 801,
  934, 942, 953, 1093
`equalsIgnoreCase`, 70,
  146, 147
`execute`, 1141

`executeQuery`, 1141, 1144
`exists`, 643
`File` class, 643–645
`fill3DRect`, 1078
`fillArc`, 1079
`fillOval`, 1078
`fillRect`, 1077
`fillRoundRect`, 1078
`floor`, 306, 307
`flush`, 617
`follows`, 750
`format`, 100–101, 104–106
generic, 824–825
`get`, 800, 946, 953
`getActionCommand`,
  1020, 1022
`getBlue`, 1093
`getClass`, 499–502
`getContentPane`, 991
`getFilePointer`, 665
`getGraphics`, 1117–1118
`getInsideArray`, 418
`getMessage`, 563, 576–577,
  578
`getName`, 644
`getPath`, 644
`getRed`, 1093
`getText`, 1020, 1026,
  1028–1029, 1030
`hashCode`, 934, 942, 953
`HashSet`, 941
`hasMoreTokens`, 276, 277
`hasNext`, 629, 873,
  959, 963
`hasNextBoolean`, 629
`hasNextByte`, 628
`hasNextDouble`, 629
`hasNextFloat`, 629
`hasNextInt`, 627
`hasNextLine`, 630
`hasNextLong`, 628
`hasNextShort`, 628
`hasPrevious`, 963
`import`, 104, 108
`increment`, 1125, 1128
`indexOf`, 72, 801, 937, 947

methods *(continued)*
  inherited, 468, 471
  intersection, 905
  intValue, 310
  invoking, 39, 68, 69, 70,
      210–211, 213, 266,
      295–296
  isDigit, 314
  isDirectory, 644
  isEditable, 1030
  isEmpty, 933, 947, 953
  isFile, 644
  isLetter, 314
  isLetterOrDigit, 314
  isLowerCase, 314
  isUpperCase, 314
  isWhitespace, 314
  iterator, 948
  join, 729, 1126
  lastIndexOf, 72, 801,
      938, 947
  late binding, 517–518
  length, 70, 665
  listIterator, 938, 948
  local variables, 218–219
  main, 218–219, 225,
      296–299
  Math, 305–309
  Math.random, 193
  max, 305, 412–413
  min, 305
  mkdir, 644
  mkdirs, 645
  multidimensional arrays,
      435–441
  mutator, 242–248, 349–350,
      352
  next, 112, 113, 629, 959,
      962, 964, 965
  nextBoolean, 114, 629
  nextByte, 113, 628
  nextDouble, 110–112, 113,
      628
  nextFloat, 113, 629
  nextIndex, 963

  nextInt, 110, 113, 212, 627
  nextLine, 112, 114,
      115–116, 630
  nextLong, 113
  nextShort, 113, 628
  nextToken, 276, 277
  optional, 938–939
  ordinal, 427
  out.println, 1155
  overloading, 250–258
  overriding, 471
    changing access permission,
        472–473
    changing return type,
        471–472
    invoking old version, 494
    vs. overloading, 473–474
  pack, 1090
  paint, 1074–1077, 1090
  paintComponent, 1084,
      1085–1086
  parameters, 220–228
  parseDouble, 312–313
  parseInt, 313
  postconditions, 249–250
  pow, 305
  power, 694–697, 699
  precedes, 248, 747, 750
  preconditions, 249–250
  previous, 963, 964, 965
  previousIndex, 963
  print, 91–92, 612,
      615–616
  printf, 93–99, 616, 1177
  println, 90–92, 212, 236,
      425, 527–528, 612, 615
  private, 486–487, 544
  protected, 487
  public, 240
  put, 953
  putAll, 954
  random, 306
  read, 634, 666
  readBoolean, 653, 667
  readByte, 666

  readChar, 653, 667
  readDouble, 653, 667
  readFloat, 653, 667
  readInt, 653, 667
  readLine, 631, 633, 635
  readLong, 653, 667
  readObject, 654, 662
  readShort, 653, 666
  readUTF, 654, 667
  recursive, 237, 680, 693–698
  redefined, 493–494
  remove, 800, 935, 937, 947,
      954, 959, 963
  removeActionListener,
      1020
  removeAll, 935
  removeRange, 800, 947
  renameTo, 644
  repaint, 1084, 1086–1090
  retainAll, 935
  returned values, 69
  round, 306
  run, 1119, 1121
  Scanner class, 113–114,
      627–630
  search, 704–706
  set, 270, 273–274, 799,
      946, 963
  setActionCommand, 1020,
      1021–1022, 1060
  setBackground, 1030
  setColor, 1091
  setDate, 265
  setDefaultClose
      Operation, 981, 1056
  setEditable, 1029–1030
  setFont, 1100, 1101, 1102
  setHorizontal
      ScrollBarPolicy,
      1065
  setIcon, 1058, 1062, 1063
  setJMenuBar, 981
  setLayout, 981, 995, 998
  setLength, 665, 667
  setLineWrap, 1029

setMargin, 1062
setMaximumSize, 1020
setMinimumSize, 1020
setPreferredSize, 1020
setSize, 981
setText, 1020, 1026,
    1028–1029, 1058,
    1060, 1062, 1063
setTitle, 981
setVertical
    ScrollBarPolicy,
    1065–1066
setVertical
    TextPosition, 1062
setVisible, 982, 1070
setWindowListener, 1050
size, 797–798, 801, 934,
    948, 953
skipBytes, 654
sort, 420–421
split, 729, 735–736
sqrt, 306
start, 1121
startThread, 1122
static, 293–299, 312–316,
    528–529, 530
String class, 68–74
stringToDouble, 1033
sublist, 938
substring, 71–72
System.out.println,
    1155–1156
testing, 237–238
that return arrays, 399–400,
    435–441
that return a value,
    212–215
that return Boolean values,
    231–234
Thread.sleep, 1113–1114,
    1116–1117
throwing exceptions in,
    588–597
toArray, 801, 934, 948
toLowerCase, 71, 313

toString, 233–237, 330,
    426, 493, 496,
    527–528, 531
toUpperCase, 71, 313
trim, 71, 313
trimToSize, 801, 948
useDelimiter, 114, 630
validate, 1090
valueOf, 427, 429
values, 427, 428–429,
    953
with variable number of
    parameters, 412–418
void, 212–216, 225,
    681–693, 700
windowActivated, 1051
windowClosed, 1051
windowClosing, 1051
windowDeconified, 1051
windowIconified, 1051
windowOpened, 1051
write, 665
writeBoolean, 666
writeByte, 666
writeChar, 650, 666
writeDouble, 647, 666
writeFloat, 648, 666
writeInt, 647, 649, 666
writeLong, 647, 666
writeObject, 648, 662
writeOutput, 229, 236
writeShort, 647, 666
writeUTF, 648, 650–651,
    666
method signature, 250, 253,
    256
min method, 305
mixing types, 55–56
mkdir method, 644
mkdirs method, 645
Model-View-Controller
    pattern, 728–729, 1012
modifiers
    final, 519
    protected, 488

public/private, 240–241,
    418, 488
modifying, access permissions,
    472–473
modulo (%) operator, 55,
    58–59
money
    formatting, 97, 99–102
    outputting, 103
moneyFormatter object,
    99–102
multidimensional arrays,
    431–442
    parameters and returned
        values, 435–441
multithreading, 1112–1129
    getGraphics method,
        1117–1118
    race conditions, 1125–1129
    Runnable interface,
        1122–1124
    Thread class, 1119–1122
    Thread.sleep method,
        1113–1114, 1116–1117
    thread synchronization,
        1125–1129
multiway if-else statements,
    136–139
mutable classes, 351–354
mutable objects, 352, 353
mutator methods, 242–248,
    349–350, 352

N

names. *See also* identifiers
    abstract, 641
    array type, 400
    clashes, 361
    package, 356–359
    path, 637–638
naming conventions, 46, 68
    constants, 78–80
    files, 211, 615
    spelling conventions, 80–81
Naughton, Patrick, 35

NegativeNumberException, 586
nested constructors, 638–639
nested inner classes, 777
nested loops, 177
nested menus, 1018
nested statements, 136
Netscape, 35
networking, with stream sockets, 1130–1135
\n (new line) character, 74
new operator, 207–209, 264–265, 330–331
nextBoolean method, 114, 629
nextByte method, 113, 628
nextDouble method, 110–112, 113, 628
nextFloat method, 113, 629
nextIndex method, 963
nextInt method, 110, 113, 212, 627
nextLine method, 112, 114, 115–116, 630
nextLong method, 113
next method, 112, 113, 629, 959, 962, 964, 965
nextShort method, 113, 628
nextToken method, 276, 277
no-argument (no-arg) constructor, 267–268, 270, 315, 336, 577, 578
Node<T> class, 854
Node class, 837, 854
nodes, 834, 835
adding and deleting, 842–843, 873–877, 879–882
head node, 834
inner classes, 846–849
leaf, 912
root node, 911
tree, 911–912
nonstatic methods, invoking, with static method, 295–296

NoSuchElementException, 940, 962
notation
Big-O, 895–897
e, 54, 106
not equal to, 146
null constant, 329–330, 341, 841
NullPointerException, 330, 390, 857
null statements, 175–176
NumberCarrier interface, 779–780
NumberFormat class, 99–102, 103
numbers. *See also* integers
E-notation, 106
floating-point. *See* floating-point numbers
inputting and outputting, 1032
naming, 78–80
percentages, 106
pseudorandom, 191
random, 191–194, 309
reading, 635
vertical, 681–684
whole, 60
numerical analysis, 59

O
Object class, 496–497
clone method, 536–541, 859–860
object code, 42
ObjectInputStream class, 645–646, 651–655, 1216–1218
object-oriented programming (OOP), 35–36, 206, 460, 516, 722
ObjectOutputStream class, 645–646, 647–648, 649–650, 1218–1219
object program, 42

objects, 35–36, 39, 68, 69, 206–207
anonymous, 330–331
ArrayList, 795
binary I/O of, 658–662
calling, 68
copying, 345–351, 353
creating, 207–209, 264–265
derived classes, 477–479
drawing, 1073–1090
exception, 577
graphics, 1073–1090
Graphics, 1076
immutable, 75, 352
members of, 207
method definitions and, 531
mutable, 352, 353
private members of, 247–248
resetting values, 265
sending messages to, 39
String, 65–66
objects, arrays as, 388–389
off-by-one errors, 182
OOP. *See* object-oriented programming (OOP)
opening files, 614, 648–649, 652
operations, 894
optional, 938–939
sets, 904–905
operators
and, 151, 156
arithmetic, 55–56
assignment, 39, 48–50, 323, 392–394
binary, 159
binding, 160
comparison, 146
concatenation, 66–67
conditional, 144–145
decrement, 62–64
equality, 146–148, 182, 236, 392–394, 427
increment, 62–64
instanceof, 499–501, 533

new, 207–209, 264–265, 330–331
or, 151–152, 156
overloading, 257
plus, 237
precedence, 157–163
remainder, 58–59
options
 javadoc, 365
 -Xlint, 813
or (||) operator, 151–152, 156
Oracle Corporation, 35
Oracle GlassFish Enterpise Server, 1152
Ordered interface, 745, 750
ordered pairs, 813–816, 818–819
ordinal method, 427
origin, 1073
outer classes, 766, 767, 775–776
out of bounds, 384
out.println method, 1155
output. *See also* file I/O
 buffered, 617–618
 formatting, 93–99
 money formats, 99–102, 103
 numbers, 1032
 redirecting, 639–641
 screen, 90–108
output files, overwriting, 618–619
outputList method, 842
output streams, 610–611, 639–641
outputStream variable, 612–613
ovals, drawing, 1079
overloading, 250–258, 412
 automatic type conversion and, 254–256
 constructors, 264
 operators, 257
 vs. overriding, 473–474
 rules for, 250–253
overriding
 access permission, 472–473

equals method, 942
 invoking old version, 494
 method definition, 471
 vs. overloading, 473–474
 return type, 471–472

P
packages, 90, 102, 108, 354–366
 access, 487–492
 default, 359–360, 490
 directories, 356–359
 importing, 102–104
 import statements, 355–356
 java.lang, 356
 name clashes, 361
 names, 356–359
Packer class, 1119, 1121
pack method, 1090
page import directive, 1159
paintComponent method, 1084, 1085–1086
paint method, 1074–1077, 1090
pair programming, 189
panels, 1003–1008
 paintComponent method, 1084
@param, 363, 364
parameterized classes, 810. *See also* generics
parameter lists, 213
parameters, 220–231
 arguments, 221, 223–225, 227
 array, 390–392, 395–396, 398
 catch block, 558–559
 of class type, 225, 229, 323–329
 as local variables, 225–227
 methods with variable number of, 412–416, 417–418
 multidimensional arrays, 435–441
 of a primitive type, 220–228, 325, 326–327

terminology, 227
 this, 229–231, 266–267
 type, 811–812, 816–817, 819–820
parent classes, 470. *See also* base classes
parentheses (), 56–58, 133
 precedence rules and, 157–163
parseDouble method, 312–313
parseInt method, 313
partially filled arrays, 401–410
path names, 356–357, 637–638
PATH variable, 292, 354–355, 357
patterns, 104–106
 Adaptor (Adapter), 727–728
 Container-Iterator, 727
 formalism, 736
 introduction to, 722, 727
 Model-View-Controller, 728–729, 1012
 sorting, 729–736
Payne, Jonathan, 35
percentages, 106
persistence, 1136
Person class, 336–341, 344, 345–347
PI constant, 307–308
pixels, 980
point, 1101
pointers, 320
point size, 1101
polymorphism
 clone method, 536–541
 downcasting and upcasting, 529–535
 final modifier, 519
 introduction to, 516
 late binding, 517–518, 520–528
pop, 887
ports, 1130

positions, 73
position variable, 841–842, 873, 874
postconditions, 249–250
postorder processing, 912
power method, 694–697, 699
pow method, 305
precedence rules, 1173
    arithmetic expressions, 56–58
    Boolean expressions, 157–163
precedes method, 248, 746, 747, 750
preconditions, 249–250
predefined words, 46
preorder processing, 912
preventive coding, 188–189
previousIndex method, 963
previous method, 963, 964, 965
previous variable, 873
primitive types, 48, 68
    assignment compatibility, 52–53, 54
    assignment statements with, 49
    largest and smallest values of, 312
    mixing, 55–56
    parameters of, 220–228, 325, 326–327
    type parameters and, 817
    variables of, 316–317, 318, 320
printf method, 93–99, 616, 1177
println method, 38, 39, 90, 212, 236, 387, 425, 527–528, 612, 615
    vs. print, 91–92
print method, 91–92, 612, 615–616
PrintWriter class, 611–619, 1220

privacy leaks, 347–350, 354, 761–762
    arrays, 416–418
    linked lists, 845
private instance variables, 416–418
private members, access to, 247–248
private methods, 486–487, 544
private modifier, 239, 240–241, 418, 488
-private option, 365
programming
    with arrays, 400–431
    event-driven, 596, 974, 975–976
    with File class, 641–643
    with inheritance, 493–503
    object-oriented, 35–36, 206, 460, 516, 722
    pair, 189
    web, 1150–1164
programming languages
    high-level languages, 40
    intermediate language, 35
    low-level languages, 40
    machine language, 40
    object-oriented, 35–36
    semantics, 44
    syntax, 44
programs
    comments, 81–82
    compiling, 42–43
    driver, 237
    indenting, 82–83
    javadoc, 81–82, 354, 362–366
    running, 43
    running times, 892–897
    styles, 78–83
    Swing. See Swing
protected access, 487–492
protected method, 487
protected modifier, 488

protocols, 1130
pseudocode, 166–169, 722–723
pseudorandom numbers, 191
public, 207, 212
public inner classes, 773–777
PubliclyCloneable interface, 860, 864–865
public modifier, 240–241, 488
public static final, 80
push, 887
putAll method, 954
put method, 953

Q
quadratic running time, 897
Queue class, 890–892
queues, 878, 889–892
quick sorts, 730, 732–735
quoted strings, 65
quotes, 55

R
race conditions, 1125–1129
RaceConditionTest class, 1126–1127
ragged arrays, 435
random access, to binary files, 664–670
RandomAccessFile class, 664–670, 1221–1224
Random class, 192–193, 1221
random method, 306
random numbers, generating, 191–194, 309
Random object, 192–193
readBoolean method, 653, 667
readByte method, 666
readChar method, 653, 667
readDouble method, 653, 667
readFloat method, 653, 667

reading
  files, 621–624, 631–635,
      651–655
  numbers, 635
  text files, 121–124
readInt method, 653, 667
readLine method, 631, 633,
      635
readLong method, 653, 667
read method, 634, 666
readObject.readShort
      method, 653, 666
readUTF method, 654, 667
rectangles, rounded, 1083–
      1084
recursion
  binary search, 700–711
  calls, tracing, 684–687
  design techniques, 699–711
  infinite, 689
  introduction to, 680–681
  vs. iteration, 692–693
  methods, returning values,
      693–698
  stacks, 690–692
  tail, 708
  void method, 681–693, 700
recursive methods, 237, 680
redefined methods, base, access
      to, 493–495
references, 318–323
  arrays and, 388–400
  holding, 320
  iterators returning, 964–966
  to mutable objects, 353
  use of, 335–354
reference types, 320
registering, listeners, 984
rehashing, 954
relational databases, 1137,
      1140
relative path names, 637–638
removeActionListener
      method, 1020

removeAll method, 935
remove method, 800, 935,
      937, 947, 954, 959, 963
removeRange method, 800,
      947
renameTo method, 644
repaint manager, 1090
repaint method, 1084,
      1086–1090
reserved words, 46
resolution, 980
retainAll method, 935
rethrowing exceptions, 600
@return, 363
returned values, 69
  multidimensional arrays,
      435–441
return statements, 213–214,
      215, 234
return type
  changing, of overridden
      method, 471–472
  covariant, 471–472
**RGB (red, green, blue) color
      system**, 1092
right justified output, 96
root nodes, 911
rounded rectangles,
      1083–1084
round method, 306
rules
  associatively, 57, 157–163,
      173
  Boolean expressions, 157–163
  Catch or Declare, 591, 592,
      594
  expressions, 56–58
  overloading, 250–253
  precedence, 56–58, 157–163
  spelling conventions, 80–81
run command, 42
run method, 1119, 1121
Runnable interface,
      1122–1124

running, Java programs, 43
running times, 892–897
run-time errors, 44
RuntimeException class, 593

S
Scanner class, 559–560,
      1224–1227
  console input, 108–120
  keyboard input, 114–115
  methods, 113–114, 627–630
  reading text file using,
      621–624
  testing for end of file with,
      624–626
  text file input, 121–124
scientific notation, 54
screen coordinate system,
      1073
screen output, 90–108
scriptlets, 1155–1156
scroll bars, 1031, 1064–1069
SDK, 42
search method, 704–706
secondary memory, 317
SecurityException, 981
@see, 363
SelectionSort class,
      422–423
selection sorts, 420–423, 736
SELECT statements, 1142,
      1144–1147
self-documenting, 82
semantics, 44
  interface, 749–750
semicolons (;), in for
      statements, 175–176
sending a message, 39, 68
sentinel values, 169
separator characters, 276–277
Serializable interface,
      658–662, 761, 1228
serifs, 1101
server, 1130

`ServerSocket` class, 1130–1131

servlets, 1150–1151

`Set<T>` interface, 905–907, 909–910, 935–936, 938, 941, 944, 1228–1230

`setActionCommand` method, 1020, 1021–1022, 1060

`setBackground` method, 1030

`setColor` method, 1091

`setDate` method, 265

`setDefaultClose Operation` method, 977, 981, 978, 1056

`setEditable` method, 1029–1030

`setFont` method, 1100, 1101, 1102

`setHorizontal ScrollBarPolicy` method, 1065

`setIcon` method, 1058, 1062, 1063

`setJMenuBar` method, 981

`setLayout` method, 981, 995, 998

`setLength` method, 665, 667

`setLineWrap` method, 1029

`setMargin` method, 1062

`setMaximumSize` method, 1020

`set` method, 270, 273–274, 799, 946, 963

`setMinimumSize` method, 1020

`setPreferredSize` method, 1020

sets, 903–910
  efficiency of, 909–910
  fundamental operations, 904–905
  linked lists, 904–905

`setSize` method, 981

`setText` method, 1020, 1026, 1028–1029, 1058, 1060, 1062, 1063

`setTitle` method, 981

`setVertical ScrollBarPolicy` method, 1065–1066

`setVerticalTextPosition` method, 1062

`setVisible` method, 982, 1070

`setWindowListener` method, 1050

s format specifier, 95, 96

shallow copy, 353, 808–809

short-circuit evaluation, 156

`Short` class, 1231

`short` type, 48, 53, 56

side effects, 161–163

signature, method, 250, 253, 256

single quotes, 55

size
  of array, 379, 385
  resolution and, 980

size method, 797–798, 801, 934, 948, 953

`skipBytes` method, 654

`Socket` class, 1131

sockets, 1130–1135
  threading and, 1134

`SortedSet<T>` interface, 949

sorting
  arrays, 420–423
  quick sort, 730, 732–735

sorting pattern, 729–736
  efficiency of, 735–736
  restrictions on, 735

sort method, 420–421

source code, 42

source program, 42

spelling conventions, 80–81

split method, 729, 735–736

splitting value, 730

splitting value, 732

SQL (Structured Query Language), 1138–1149

`SQLException`, 1141

sqrt method, 306

square brackets [], 380, 382

`Stack` class, 887–889

stack frames, 691–692

stack overflow, 692

stacks, 690–692, 878, 887–889

start method, 1121

`startThread` method, 1122

statements
  assignment, 48–54, 154
  break, 140, 143, 180–181
  compound, 134–135, 219–220
  continue, 180–181
  CREATE TABLE, 1141, 1142
  do-while, 164–167
  empty, 175–176
  exit, 181
  for, 170–176, 220, 384, 434
  if, 133, 134, 136
  if-else, 132–139
  import, 90, 103–104, 333–335, 355–366, 794
  INSERT, 1142
  multiway, 136–139
  nested, 136
  null, 175–176
  return, 213–215, 234
  SELECT, 1142, 1144–1147
  SQL, 1142
  static import, 333–335
  switch, 139–144, 180, 429–431
  throw, 562–563, 569–570, 572
  UPDATE, 1142, 1145, 1147–1149
  while, 164–167, 176

static import statements, 333–335

static inner classes, 772–773

static keyword, 293

static methods, 293–299
  late binding and, 528–529, 530
  in wrapper classes, 312–316

static variables, 50, 219, 300–304, 493

stopping cases, 688, 694, 701–702
streams, 610–611, 621
  sockets, networking with, 1130–1135
`StringBuffer` class, 75, 1235–1239
`String` class, 48, 65–77, 356, 1231–1235
  classes, 67–69
  concatenation, 66–67
  constants and variables, 65–66
  escape sequences, 74–75
  indexes, 73–74
  methods, 68–74, 313
  processing, 75, 76
  Unicode character set, 75–77
strings
  vs. arrays, 387
  comparing, 150, 193
  decomposing, 274–279
  empty, 116
  format, 96
  hash functions for, 899–902
  patterns, 104–106
  processing, 312–316, 415–416, 417–418
  using == with, 147–148, 236
strings, of inequalities, 152
`stringToDouble` method, 1033
`StringTokenizer` class, 274–279, 331–332, 481–484, 1239–1240
`String` variables, 426, 613
Structured Query Language. *See* SQL (Structured Query Language)
stubs, 238, 1011
subclasses, 464, 467, 480. *See also* derived classes
subdirectories, 359
`sublist` method, 938
subscripted variables, 379
`substring` method, 71–72

Sun Microsystems, 34, 35
superclasses, 464, 467, 480
super constructor, 474–476, 495, 577, 932
super.paint, 1076
super relationships, 493–494
Swing, 974
  action events, 984–990
  action listeners, 984–990, 1017
  buttons, 983–984, 1018
  calculator, 1033–1038
  class hierarchy, 1010
  close-window button, 982, 984
  colors, 991–994, 1008, 1090–1097
  `Container` class, 1008–1009
  `drawString` method, 1097–1099, 1101
  ending, 986
  event-driven programming, 975–976
  fonts, 1097–1102
  `Graphics` class, 1073–1090
  icons, 1058–1064
  labels, 990, 992–994, 997
  layout managers, 994–1003
  menus, 1013–1025
  Model-View-Controller pattern, 1012
  numbers, 1032
  overview of, 976–994
  panels, 1003–1008
  scroll bars, 1064–1069
  text fields and areas, 1025–1038
  updating, 1090
  window listeners, 1050–1057
  windows, 977–978
switch statements, 139–144, 180
  enumerated types in, 429–431
// symbol, 81

synchronized keyword, 1127–1128
syntactic variables, 47
syntax, 44
syntax errors, 44
`System` class, 181
`System.err`, 639–640
`System.exit`, 986
`System.in`, 611, 639–640
`System.out`, 90, 611, 639–640
`System.out.print`, 92, 612
`System.out.printf`, 93–99, 414
`System.out.println`, 38–39, 236, 612, 1155–1156
  screen output, 90–93

T
<T>, omitting, 951
tables, 1137, 1140
  hash. *See* hash tables
  truth, 153–154
tail recursion, 708
tails, 889
ternary operator, 144–145
testing
  bottom-up, 237
  methods, 237–238
text
  areas, 1025–1038
    scroll bars, 1031, 1064–1069
    view port, 1064, 1065
  fields, 1032
  files, 611–612, 1025–1038
    appending, 619–621
    vs. binary files, 611–612
    closing, 617–618
    input, 121–124
    opening, 614, 622
    path names, 637–638
    reading, 121–124, 621–624, 631–635
    testing for end of, 624–626, 635–637
    writing to, 611–619

this constructor, 476–477
this parameter, 229–231,
    266–267, 1017
Thread class, 1119–1122
threads, 1112–1113, 1118,
    1122. *See also*
    multithreading
sockets and, 1134
Thread.sleep method,
    1113–1114, 1116–1117
thread synchronization,
    1125–1129
Throwable class, 593
throwing an exception, 556
@throws, 363
throws clause, 589–592, 594
    in derived classes, 594–595
throw statements, 562–563,
    569–570, 572
tilde (~), 723
time-space tradeoff, 903
toArray method, 801, 934,
    948
tokens, 275–277
toLowerCase method, 71, 313
toString method, 233–237,
    330, 426, 493, 496, 529,
    531
    late binding with, 527–528
    text file output and, 620
toUpperCase method, 71,
    313
tracing variables, 182–183
Transmission Control Protocol
    (TCP), 1130
TreeMap<K, V> class, 954
trees, 910–918
    binary, 910–911
    binary search, 913–918
    empty, 912
    properties, 910–913
TreeSet<T> class, 949
trim method, 71, 313
trimToSize method, 801,
    808, 948

true, 48, 53, 55, 132, 152–155
truth tables, 153–154
try blocks, 557, 559,
    562–563, 569–570, 618
try-catch-finally
    mechanism, 598–599
try-catch mechanism,
    557–559
    nested, 598
try-throw-catch
    mechanism, 569–570
two-dimensional arrays,
    432–434
type casting, 53, 61–62, 223
type coercion, 62
type inference, 794, 812
type mismatch, 52–53
type parameters, 811–812,
    816–817, 819–820
    bound, 821–824, 860–861
    bounds for, 821–824
    collections, 950
    multiple, 819–820

U
UML. *See* Unified Modeling
    Language (UML)
unboxing, 310–312
uncaught exceptions, 594, 1033
unchecked exceptions, 594,
    630
Unicode, 53, 75–77, 650
**Unified Modeling Language
    (UML)**
    class diagrams, 723–724
    class hierarchy, 726
    class interactions, 724
    history of, 723
    inheritance diagrams,
        724–726
    introduction to, 722–723
uninitialized variables, 50
UNIX, 358, 638
UnorderedPair class,
    826–827

Unsupported
    OperationException
    class, 939, 959
upcasting, 529–535
UPDATE statements, 1142,
    1145, 1147–1149
useDelimiter method,
    114, 630
User Datagram Protocol
    (UDP), 1130
UTF coding, 650–651

V
v++ versus ++v, 63
validate method, 1090
valueOf method, 427, 429
values method, 427,
    428–429, 953
vararg specification, 414, 415
variables, 47–48
    of array type, 388
    assignment compatibility,
        52–53, 54
    within blocks, 219–220
    boolean, 154–155
    CLASSPATH, 356–359,
        360–361
    of class type, 316–323,
        327–328
    declaring, 47, 220
    environment, 356–357
    global, 219
    indexed, 379, 380, 389, 390,
        432
    initializing, 50–51, 269–274,
        300
    instance. *See* instance
        variables
    int, 39
    local, 50, 218–219,
        225–227, 269
    masks, 230
    memory and, 317–320
    naming conventions, 46
    PATH, 354–355, 357

primitive types, 48, 316–318, 320

static, 50, 219, 300–304, 493

String, 65–66, 426

subscripted, 379

syntactic, 47

tracing, 182–183

uninitialized, 50

Vector<T> class, 944–950, 1240–1245

Vector class, 809–810

@version, 363

-version option, 365

vertical numbers, 681–684

view ports, 1064, 1065

visibility, components with changing, 1069–1072

void method, 212, 213, 214, 215, 216, 225, 700

recursive, 681–693

W

web programming, with Java Server Pages, 1150–1164

while statements, 164–167, 176

whitespace, 110, 113, 119, 276

whole numbers, 60

wildcards, 932

windowActivated method, 1051

WindowAdapter class, 1056–1057

windowClosed method, 1051

windowClosing method, 1051

windowDeconified method, 1051

WindowEvent class, 1050

window events, 1050

windowIconified method, 1051

Windowing interface, 36–37

WindowListener interface, 1050–1051, 1245

window listeners, 1050–1057

dispose method, 1055

inner class, 1052

WindowAdapter class, 1056–1057

windowOpened method, 1051

windows

close-window button, 982, 984

disposed, 981

Swing, 977–978

words, 112

worst-case running time, 893–895

wrapper classes, 309–312, 356

no-argument constructors and, 315

static methods in, 312–316

writeBoolean method, 666

writeByte method, 666

writeChar method, 650, 666

writeDouble method, 647, 666

writeFloat method, 648, 666

writeInt method, 647, 649, 666

writeLong method, 647, 666

write method, 665

writeObject method, 648, 662

writeOutput method, 229, 236

writeShort method, 647, 666

writeUTF method, 648, 650–651, 666

X

x-coordinate, 1073

-Xlint option, 813

Y

y-coordinate, 1073